# Lecture Notes in Computer Science 12666

More information about this subseries at http://www.springer.com/series/7412

Alberto Del Bimbo · Rita Cucchiara ·
Stan Sclaroff · Giovanni Maria Farinella ·
Tao Mei · Marco Bertini ·
Hugo Jair Escalante · Roberto Vezzani (Eds.)

# Pattern Recognition

## ICPR International Workshops and Challenges

Virtual Event, January 10–15, 2021
Proceedings, Part VI

 Springer

*Editors*
Alberto Del Bimbo ⓘ
Dipartimento di Ingegneria
dell'Informazione
University of Firenze
Firenze, Italy

Stan Sclaroff ⓘ
Department of Computer Science
Boston University
Boston, MA, USA

Tao Mei
Cloud & AI, JD.COM
Beijing, China

Hugo Jair Escalante ⓘ
Computational Sciences Department
National Institute of Astrophysics,
Optics and Electronics (INAOE)
Tonantzintla, Puebla, Mexico

Rita Cucchiara ⓘ
Dipartimento di Ingegneria "Enzo Ferrari"
Università di Modena e Reggio Emilia
Modena, Italy

Giovanni Maria Farinella ⓘ
Dipartimento di Matematica e Informatica
University of Catania
Catania, Italy

Marco Bertini ⓘ
Dipartimento di Ingegneria
dell'Informazione
University of Firenze
Firenze, Italy

Roberto Vezzani ⓘ
Dipartimento di Ingegneria "Enzo Ferrari"
Università di Modena e Reggio Emilia
Modena, Italy

ISSN 0302-9743        ISSN 1611-3349  (electronic)
Lecture Notes in Computer Science
ISBN 978-3-030-68779-3        ISBN 978-3-030-68780-9  (eBook)
https://doi.org/10.1007/978-3-030-68780-9

LNCS Sublibrary: SL6 – Image Processing, Computer Vision, Pattern Recognition, and Graphics

This Springer imprint is published by the registered company Springer Nature Switzerland AG
The registered company address is: Gewerbestrasse 11, 6330 Cham, Switzerland

# Foreword by General Chairs

It is with great pleasure that we welcome you to the post-proceedings of the 25th International Conference on Pattern Recognition, ICPR2020 Virtual-Milano. ICPR2020 stands on the shoulders of generations of pioneering pattern recognition researchers. The first ICPR (then called IJCPR) convened in 1973 in Washington, DC, USA, under the leadership of Dr. King-Sun Fu as the General Chair. Since that time, the global community of pattern recognition researchers has continued to expand and thrive, growing evermore vibrant and vital. The motto of this year's conference was *Putting Artificial Intelligence to work on patterns*. Indeed, the deep learning revolution has its origins in the pattern recognition community – and the next generations of revolutionary insights and ideas continue with those presented at this 25th ICPR. Thus, it was our honor to help perpetuate this longstanding ICPR tradition to provide a lively meeting place and open exchange for the latest pathbreaking work in pattern recognition.

For the first time, the ICPR main conference employed a two-round review process similar to journal submissions, with new papers allowed to be submitted in either the first or the second round and papers submitted in the first round and not accepted allowed to be revised and re-submitted for second round review. In the first round, 1554 new submissions were received, out of which 554 (35.6%) were accepted and 579 (37.2%) were encouraged to be revised and resubmitted. In the second round, 1696 submissions were received (496 revised and 1200 new), out of which 305 (61.4%) of the revised submissions and 552 (46%) of the new submissions were accepted. Overall, there were 3250 submissions in total, and 1411 were accepted, out of which 144 (4.4%) were included in the main conference program as orals and 1263 (38.8%) as posters (4 papers were withdrawn after acceptance). We had the largest ICPR conference ever, with the most submitted papers and the most selective acceptance rates ever for ICPR, attesting both the increased interest in presenting research results at ICPR and the high scientific quality of work accepted for presentation at the conference.

We were honored to feature seven exceptional Keynotes in the program of the ICPR2020 main conference: David Doermann (Professor at the University at Buffalo), Pietro Perona (Professor at the California Institute of Technology and Amazon Fellow at Amazon Web Services), Mihaela van der Schaar (Professor at the University of Cambridge and a Turing Fellow at The Alan Turing Institute in London), Max Welling (Professor at the University of Amsterdam and VP of Technologies at Qualcomm), Ching Yee Suen (Professor at Concordia University) who was presented with the IAPR 2020 King-Sun Fu Prize, Maja Pantic (Professor at Imperial College UK and AI Scientific Research Lead at Facebook Research) who was presented with the IAPR 2020 Maria Petrou Prize, and Abhinav Gupta (Professor at Carnegie Mellon University and Research Manager at Facebook AI Research) who was presented with the IAPR 2020 J.K. Aggarwal Prize. Several best paper prizes were also announced and awarded, including the Piero Zamperoni Award for the best paper authored by a student, the BIRPA Best Industry Related Paper Award, and Best Paper Awards for each of the five tracks of the ICPR2020 main conference.

The five tracks of the ICPR2020 main conference were: (1) Artificial Intelligence, Machine Learning for Pattern Analysis, (2) Biometrics, Human Analysis and Behavior Understanding, (3) Computer Vision, Robotics and Intelligent Systems, (4) Document and Media Analysis, and (5) Image and Signal Processing. The best papers presented at the main conference had the opportunity for publication in expanded format in journal special issues of *IET Biometrics* (tracks 2 and 3), *Computer Vision and Image Understanding* (tracks 1 and 2), *Machine Vision and Applications* (tracks 2 and 3), *Multimedia Tools and Applications* (tracks 4 and 5), *Pattern Recognition Letters* (tracks 1, 2, 3 and 4), or *IEEE Trans. on Biometrics, Behavior, and Identity Science* (tracks 2 and 3).

In addition to the main conference, the ICPR2020 program offered workshops and tutorials, along with a broad range of cutting-edge industrial demos, challenge sessions, and panels. The virtual ICPR2020 conference was interactive, with real-time live-streamed sessions, including live talks, poster presentations, exhibitions, demos, Q&A, panels, meetups, and discussions – all hosted on the Underline virtual conference platform.

The ICPR2020 conference was originally scheduled to convene in Milano, which is one of the most beautiful cities of Italy for art, culture, lifestyle – and more. The city has so much to offer! With the need to go virtual, ICPR2020 included interactive **virtual tours** of Milano during the conference coffee breaks, which we hoped would introduce attendees to this wonderful city, and perhaps even entice them to visit Milano once international travel becomes possible again.

The success of such a large conference would not have been possible without the help of many people. We deeply appreciate the vision, commitment, and leadership of the ICPR2020 Program Chairs: Kim Boyer, Brian C. Lovell, Marcello Pelillo, Nicu Sebe, René Vidal, and Jingyi Yu. Our heartfelt gratitude also goes to the rest of the main conference organizing team, including the Track and Area Chairs, who all generously devoted their precious time in conducting the review process and in preparing the program, and the reviewers, who carefully evaluated the submitted papers and provided invaluable feedback to the authors. This time their effort was considerably higher given that many of them reviewed for both reviewing rounds. We also want to acknowledge the efforts of the conference committee, including the Challenge Chairs, Demo and Exhibit Chairs, Local Chairs, Financial Chairs, Publication Chair, Tutorial Chairs, Web Chairs, Women in ICPR Chairs, and Workshop Chairs. Many thanks, also, for the efforts of the dedicated staff who performed the crucially important work behind the scenes, including the members of the ICPR2020 Organizing Secretariat. Finally, we are grateful to the conference sponsors for their generous support of the ICPR2020 conference.

We hope everyone had an enjoyable and productive ICPR2020 conference.

Rita Cucchiara
Alberto Del Bimbo
Stan Sclaroff

# Preface

The 25th International Conference on Pattern Recognition Workshops (ICPRW 2020) were held virtually in Milan, Italy and rescheduled to January 10 and January 11 of 2021 due to the Covid-19 pandemic. ICPRW 2020 included timely topics and applications of Computer Vision, Image and Sound Analysis, Pattern Recognition and Artificial Intelligence. We received 49 workshop proposals and 46 of them have been accepted, which is three times more than at ICPRW 2018. The workshop proceedings cover a wide range of areas including Machine Learning (8), Pattern Analysis (5), Healthcare (6), Human Behavior (5), Environment (5), Surveillance, Forensics and Biometrics (6), Robotics and Egovision (4), Cultural Heritage and Document Analysis (4), Retrieval (2), and Women at ICPR 2020 (1). Among them, 33 workshops are new to ICPRW. Specifically, the ICPRW 2020 volumes contain the following workshops (please refer to the corresponding workshop proceeding for details):

- CADL2020 – Workshop on Computational Aspects of Deep Learning.
- DLPR – Deep Learning for Pattern Recognition.
- EDL/AI – Explainable Deep Learning/AI.
- (Merged) IADS – Integrated Artificial Intelligence in Data Science, IWCR – IAPR workshop on Cognitive Robotics.
- ManifLearn – Manifold Learning in Machine Learning, From Euclid to Riemann.
- MOI2QDN – Metrification & Optimization of Input Image Quality in Deep Networks.
- IML – International Workshop on Industrial Machine Learning.
- MMDLCA – Multi-Modal Deep Learning: Challenges and Applications.
- IUC 2020 – Human and Vehicle Analysis for Intelligent Urban Computing.
- PATCAST – International Workshop on Pattern Forecasting.
- RRPR – Reproducible Research in Pattern Recognition.
- VAIB 2020 – Visual Observation and Analysis of Vertebrate and Insect Behavior.
- IMTA VII – Image Mining Theory & Applications.
- AIHA 2020 – Artificial Intelligence for Healthcare Applications.
- AIDP – Artificial Intelligence for Digital Pathology.
- (Merged) GOOD – Designing AI in support of Good Mental Health, CAIHA – Computational and Affective Intelligence in Healthcare Applications for Vulnerable Populations.
- CARE2020 – pattern recognition for positive teChnology And eldeRly wEllbeing.
- MADiMa 2020 – Multimedia Assisted Dietary Management.
- 3DHU 2020 – 3D Human Understanding.
- FBE2020 – Facial and Body Expressions, micro-expressions and behavior recognition.
- HCAU 2020 – Deep Learning for Human-Centric Activity Understanding.
- MPRSS - 6th IAPR Workshop on Multimodal Pattern Recognition for Social Signal Processing in Human Computer Interaction.

- CVAUI 2020 – Computer Vision for Analysis of Underwater Imagery.
- MAES – Machine Learning Advances Environmental Science.
- PRAConBE - Pattern Recognition and Automation in Construction & the Built Environment.
- PRRS 2020 – Pattern Recognition in Remote Sensing.
- WAAMI - Workshop on Analysis of Aerial Motion Imagery.
- DEEPRETAIL 2020 - Workshop on Deep Understanding Shopper Behaviours and Interactions in Intelligent Retail Environments 2020.
- MMForWild2020 – MultiMedia FORensics in the WILD 2020.
- FGVRID – Fine-Grained Visual Recognition and re-Identification.
- IWBDAF – Biometric Data Analysis and Forensics.
- RISS – Research & Innovation for Secure Societies.
- WMWB – TC4 Workshop on Mobile and Wearable Biometrics.
- EgoApp – Applications of Egocentric Vision.
- ETTAC 2020 – Eye Tracking Techniques, Applications and Challenges.
- PaMMO – Perception and Modelling for Manipulation of Objects.
- FAPER – Fine Art Pattern Extraction and Recognition.
- MANPU – coMics ANalysis, Processing and Understanding.
- PATRECH2020 – Pattern Recognition for Cultural Heritage.
- (Merged) CBIR – Content-Based Image Retrieval: where have we been, and where are we going, TAILOR – Texture AnalysIs, cLassificatiOn and Retrieval, VIQA – Video and Image Question Answering: building a bridge between visual content analysis and reasoning on textual data.
- W4PR - Women at ICPR.

We would like to thank all members of the workshops' Organizing Committee, the reviewers, and the authors for making this event successful. We also appreciate the support from all the invited speakers and participants. We wish to offer thanks in particular to the ICPR main conference general chairs: Rita Cucchiara, Alberto Del Bimbo, and Stan Sclaroff, and program chairs: Kim Boyer, Brian C. Lovell, Marcello Pelillo, Nicu Sebe, Rene Vidal, and Jingyi Yu. Finally, we are grateful to the publisher, Springer, for their cooperation in publishing the workshop proceedings in the series of Lecture Notes in Computer Science.

December 2020                                      Giovanni Maria Farinella
                                                              Tao Mei

# Challenges

Competitions are effective means for rapidly solving problems and advancing the state of the art. Organizers identify a problem of practical or scientific relevance and release it to the community. In this way the whole community can contribute to the solution of high-impact problems while having fun. This part of the proceedings compiles the best of the competitions track of the *25th International Conference on Pattern Recognition (ICPR)*.

Eight challenges were part of the track, covering a wide variety of fields and applications, all of this within the scope of ICPR. In every challenge organizers released data, and provided a platform for evaluation. The top-ranked participants were invited to submit papers for this volume. Likewise, organizers themselves wrote articles summarizing the design, organization and results of competitions. Submissions were subject to a standard review process carried out by the organizers of each competition. Papers associated with seven out the eight competitions are included in this volume, thus making it a representative compilation of what happened in the ICPR challenges.

We are immensely grateful to the organizers and participants of the ICPR 2020 challenges for their efforts and dedication to make the competition track a success. We hope the readers of this volume enjoy it as much as we have.

November 2020

Marco Bertini
Hugo Jair Escalante

# ICPR Organization

## General Chairs

| | |
|---|---|
| Rita Cucchiara | Univ. of Modena and Reggio Emilia, Italy |
| Alberto Del Bimbo | Univ. of Florence, Italy |
| Stan Sclaroff | Boston Univ., USA |

## Program Chairs

| | |
|---|---|
| Kim Boyer | Univ. at Albany, USA |
| Brian C. Lovell | Univ. of Queensland, Australia |
| Marcello Pelillo | Univ. Ca' Foscari Venezia, Italy |
| Nicu Sebe | Univ. of Trento, Italy |
| René Vidal | Johns Hopkins Univ., USA |
| Jingyi Yu | ShanghaiTech Univ., China |

## Workshop Chairs

| | |
|---|---|
| Giovanni Maria Farinella | Univ. of Catania, Italy |
| Tao Mei | JD.COM, China |

## Challenge Chairs

| | |
|---|---|
| Marco Bertini | Univ. of Florence, Italy |
| Hugo Jair Escalante | INAOE and CINVESTAV National Polytechnic Institute of Mexico, Mexico |

## Publication Chair

| | |
|---|---|
| Roberto Vezzani | Univ. of Modena and Reggio Emilia, Italy |

## Tutorial Chairs

| | |
|---|---|
| Vittorio Murino | Univ. of Verona, Italy |
| Sudeep Sarkar | Univ. of South Florida, USA |

## Women in ICPR Chairs

| | |
|---|---|
| Alexandra Branzan Albu | Univ. of Victoria, Canada |
| Maria De Marsico | Univ. Roma La Sapienza, Italy |

## Demo and Exhibit Chairs

Lorenzo Baraldi                  Univ. Modena Reggio Emilia, Italy
Bruce A. Maxwell                 Colby College, USA
Lorenzo Seidenari                Univ. of Florence, Italy

## Special Issue Initiative Chair

Michele Nappi                    Univ. of Salerno, Italy

## Web Chair

Andrea Ferracani                 Univ. of Florence, Italy

## Corporate Relations Chairs

Fabio Galasso                    Univ. Roma La Sapienza, Italy
Matt Leotta                      Kitware, Inc., USA
Zhongchao Shi                    Lenovo Group Ltd., China

## Local Chairs

Matteo Matteucci                 Politecnico di Milano, Italy
Paolo Napoletano                 Univ. of Milano-Bicocca, Italy

## Financial Chairs

Cristiana Fiandra                The Office srl, Italy
Vittorio Murino                  Univ. of Verona, Italy

# Contents – Part VI

## ManifLearn - Manifold Learning in Machine Learning, from Euclid to Riemann

## MANPU - The 4th International Workshop on coMics ANalysis, Processing and Understanding

## MMDLCA - Multi-modal Deep Learning: Challenges and Applications

## MOI2QDN - Workshop on Metrification and Optimization of Input Image Quality in Deep Networks

**MPRSS - 6th IAPR Workshop on Multimodal Pattern Recognition
for Social Signal Processing in Human Computer Interaction**

# MAES - Machine Learning Advances Environmental Science

# Workshop on Machine Learning Advances Environmental Science (MAES)

Dates back to 2007 the Jim Gray's pioneering vision of "The Fourth Paradigm" of science that of data-intensive scientific discovery, where technological developments made it possible the harvesting of a heterogeneous information deluge, ready to be managed and then analyzed. Since then, all fields of science have experienced an impressive increase in available data, not only in terms of quantity but also in terms of quality and sharing, thus calling for new theories, techniques, and tools to enable scientists and information stakeholders to properly exploit the oceans of distributed and diverse data in knowledge extraction. Environmental sciences are no exception, natural and environmental data are growing steadily in volume, complexity, and diversity to Big Data mainly driven by advanced sensor technology. By now, it's ordinary for scientists to cope with complex decision-making processes for assessing potential impacts or risks associated with a given specific threaten and for understanding behaviors and dynamics of natural phenomena, e.g., when simulating the export of nutrients from river basins to forecast salinity, to forecast ozone levels, to predict air pollution and the functional characteristics of ecosystems, to model algal growth and transport in rivers, to assess the risk of mortality of sensible species associated with the deliberate release of genetically modified organisms or plants in the environment, and to analyze the degradation of pesticides in soils used in agriculture through the analysis of physical and chemical parameters, just to name a few. Machine Learning (ML) can offer superior techniques for unraveling complexity, knowledge discovery, and predictability of Big Data environmental science.

In this context, the aim of the workshop was to provide a state-of-the-art survey of environmental research topics that can benefit from ML methods and techniques, and also a forum for researchers and practitioners working on both fields, on successful environmental applications of ML and pattern recognition techniques to diverse domains of Environmental Research. This first edition of the International Workshop on Machine Learning Advances Environmental Science(MAES) was held on-line, due to the Covid-19 pandemic, within the 25th International Conference on Pattern Recognition (ICPR 2020), originally planned to be held in Milan, Italy. The format of the workshop included two keynotes followed by technical presentations. We received 21 submissions for reviews, from authors belonging to 18 distinct countries. After an accurate and thorough peer-review process, we selected 15 papers for presentation at the workshop. The review process focused on the quality of the papers, their scientific novelty, and their applicability to real-world environmental domains. The acceptance of the papers was the result of the reviewers' discussion and agreement. All the high-quality papers were accepted, and the acceptance rate was 71%. The accepted articles represent an interesting repertoire of Machine and Deep learning techniques to solve a heterogeneous collection of applications from environmental and natural sciences. The workshop program was completed by two invited talks titled "Harnessing big environmental data by Machine Learning" given by Friedrich Recknagel from the University of Adelaide, Australia, and "25 years of Machine Learning applications in marine ecology: a personal perspective", given by Michele Scardi, from the University of Rome "Tor Vergata".

Eventually, we hope that the workshop has represented a stimulating place for presenting and discussing new or little-explored case studies to encourage more and more interdisciplinary collaborations in a so fascinating and essential application domain.

Last but not least, we would like to thank the MAES Program Committee, whose members made the workshop possible with their rigorous and timely review process, and Fabio Bellavia for his precious disseminating activity as a workshop publicity chair.

# Organization

## MAES Chairs

Francesco Camastra      University of Naples Parthenope, Italy
Friedrich Recknagel      University of Adelaide, Australia
Antonino Staiano      University of Naples Parthenope, Italy

## Publicity Chair

Fabio Bellavia      University of Palermo, Italy

## Program Committee

Ioannis Athanasiadis      Wageningen University and Research,
     The Netherlands

Thierry Bouwmans      University of La Rochelle, France
Alexander Brenning      Friedrich-Schiller University, Jena, Germany
Simon C. Brewer      The University of Utah, USA
Giovanni Burgio      University of Bologna, Italy
Francesco Camastra      University of Naples Parthenope, Italy
Hong Fu      The Education University of Hong Kong,
     Hong Kong

Mikhail Kanevski      University of Lausanne, Switzerland
Ludovic Journaux      University of Burgundy, France
Henry Joutsijoki      Tampere University, Finland
Giosuè Lo Bosco      University of Palermo, Italy
Engelbert M. Nguifo      Blaise Pascal University, Clermont-Ferrand,
     France

Friedrich Recknagel      University of Adelaide, Australia
Antonino Staiano      University of Naples Parthenope, Italy

## Additional Reviewers

Fabio Bellavia      Masoomeh Mirrashid
Cesario Di Sarno      Riccardo Rizzo
Alessio Ferone      Daniele Schicchi
Antonio Maratea      Blake Vernon
Ben Marconi

# Finding Relevant Flood Images
# on Twitter Using Content-Based Filters

Björn Barz[1](✉) ⓘ, Kai Schröter[2]ⓘ, Ann-Christin Kra[2],
and Joachim Denzler[1]ⓘ

[1] Computer Vision Group, Friedrich Schiller University Jena, Jena, Germany
{bjoern.barz,joachim.denzler}@uni-jena.de
[2] Section of Hydrology, Deutsches GeoForschungsZentrum, Potsdam, Germany
{kai.schroeter,annkra}@gfz-potsdam.de

**Abstract.** The analysis of natural disasters such as floods in a timely manner often suffers from limited data due to coarsely distributed sensors or sensor failures. At the same time, a plethora of information is buried in an abundance of images of the event posted on social media platforms such as Twitter. These images could be used to document and rapidly assess the situation and derive proxy-data not available from sensors, e.g., the degree of water pollution. However, not all images posted online are suitable or informative enough for this purpose.

Therefore, we propose an automatic filtering approach using machine learning techniques for finding Twitter images that are relevant for one of the following information objectives: assessing the flooded area, the inundation depth, and the degree of water pollution. Instead of relying on textual information present in the tweet, the filter analyzes the image contents directly. We evaluate the performance of two different approaches and various features on a case-study of two major flooding events. Our image-based filter is able to enhance the quality of the results substantially compared with a keyword-based filter, improving the mean average precision from 23% to 53% on average.

**Keywords:** Flood impact analysis · Natural hazards analysis · Content-based image retrieval · Computer vision

## 1 Introduction

Floods cause severe damages in urban areas every year. Up-to-date information about the flood is crucial for reacting quickly and appropriately by providing assistance and coordinating disaster recovery [2]. However, traditional sensors such as water level gauges often fail to provide the required information [12], either because of failures, a too coarse spatio-temporal resolution, or even the absence of sensors, e.g., in the case of surface water flooding, which can occur far off the next stream.

For a rapid flood impact analysis and documentation, more versatile sources of information are hence desirable for augmenting the data obtained from sensors. One such source of information, which is available in abundance nowadays,

A. Del Bimbo et al. (Eds.): ICPR 2020 Workshops, LNCS 12666, pp. 5–14, 2021.
https://doi.org/10.1007/978-3-030-68780-9_1

consists in images of the flood posted by citizens on social media platforms. Thanks to the widespread adoption of smartphones, this information is usually available rapidly during the flood event and covers populated areas with a better resolution than traditional sensors. Though images do not provide accurate measurements, as opposed to sensors, they are in many cases still useful to estimate important information. For example, the boundaries of the flooded area can easily be identified in an image. The grade of water pollution can also be assessed visually for certain types of pollution such as, e.g., oil spills. It can even be possible to estimate the inundation depth if the image shows objects of known height in the flooded area, such as traffic signs, cars, or people.

Fohringer et al. [5] made use of this information by manually inspecting the images of all tweets that contained a flood-related keyword and were posted in the area and timeframe of interest. Beyond simple keyword matching, sophisticated machine learning techniques have recently been applied to filter event-related tweets based on their text [8]. These text-based approaches have two major drawbacks when it comes to finding images of the event: First and foremost, a text-based filter captures far too many images for manual inspection in the context of rapid flood impact assessment. Secondly, users may not always mention the flood directly in the text of the tweet, since the topic is already recognizable from the image. A text-based filter would miss these images and, therefore, ignore potentially useful information.

To overcome these issues, Barz et al. [1] recently proposed a filtering technique based solely on the content of the images using an interactive image retrieval approach. In their framework, the user initiates the process by providing an example image illustrating what they are looking for. The system then retrieves a first set of similar images in which the user flags a handful of images as relevant or irrelevant to subsequently refine the search results over several feedback rounds. Such an interactive approach is suitable in face of an open set of possible search objectives, since the system adapts to the user's needs from scratch during each session. While this seems useful for a detailed post factum analysis of the event, the interactive feedback process is too time-consuming for rapid flood impact analysis during the flood. Moreover, the set of important search objectives is usually more limited during this phase of analysis and focuses on a few key metrics such as the spread and depth of the flood. In such a scenario, it is redundant to refine the system from scratch several times. Instead, a classifier trained in advance on an annotated dataset can be used to filter the social media images of the event quickly without user interaction.

Therefore, this work focuses on developing a pre-trained non-interactive filter for relevant flood images. We use the annotated European Flood 2013 dataset from Barz et al. [1] as training data and demonstrate that the filters learned on those images collected from Wikimedia Commons also perform well in practice on Twitter images. To this end, we evaluate their performance on images we collected from Twitter regarding two real flooding events, which occurred in 2017 and 2018 in Germany. We find that such pre-trained filters clearly outperform a purely keyword-based approach, which ignores the image content.

**Fig. 1.** Comparison of naïve flood image retrieval based on textual keywords and the time of the tweet (top row) and three classification-based filters optimized for different information objectives (last three rows). Each row shows six top-scoring images from the Harz17 dataset.

Figure 1 shows an example illustrating the value of task-aware image-based filtering. The results in the top row have been retrieved based on textual keywords and their temporal proximity to the peak of the event. Besides flood images, they also contain irrelevant images without flooding, memes, and still images from news shows. The following three rows, in contrast, show the top-scoring results obtained from three different filters: The results of the *flooding* filter mainly contain images depicting the boundary between flooded and non-flooded areas. The *inundation depth* filter focuses on visual clues that are helpful for determining the approximate depth of the flood such as traffic signs and people standing in the water. Finally, the *pollution* filter searches for images of heavily polluted water.

We describe these tasks and the datasets used in this study in more detail in the following Sect. 2 and then explain the different filtering approaches developed and tested in this work in Sect. 3. Experimental results on the European Flood 2013 dataset and our two novel twitter datasets are shown in Sect. 4 and Sect. 5 concludes this work.

Our two Twitter datasets and the best filter models are publicly available at https://github.com/cvjena/twitter-flood-dataset.

## 2 Datasets and Search Objectives

We use an existing annotated dataset of flood images for training our filters and evaluate them on two novel flood datasets collected from Twitter.

## 2.1  The European Flood 2013 Dataset

The European Flood 2013 dataset [1] is a multi-label dataset comprising 3,710 images collected from the Wikimedia Commons category "Central Europe floods, May/June 2013". Each image has been annotated by experts from hydrology regarding its relevance with respect to the following three search objectives:

*Flooding* Does the image help to determine whether a certain area is flooded or not? An image considered as relevant would show the boundary between flooded and dry areas. Images that do not show any inundation at all are considered not relevant.

*Inundation depth* Is it possible to derive an estimate of the inundation depth from the image due to visual clues such as, for example, traffic signs or other structures with known height? If there is no flooding at all, the image is considered as not relevant for inundation depth.

*Water pollution* Does the image show any pollution substances? The focus is on heavy contamination by chemical substances such as oil, for example.

For each of these objectives, between 100 and 250 images have additionally been selected as "ideal queries", which are considered to represent the information objective particularly well. We will use these queries later to compare our pre-trained filters with a retrieval-based method (see Sect. 3).

The dataset is typically augmented with 97,085 distractor images from the Flickr100k dataset [9] (excluding images with the tags "water" and "river"), which are not considered as relevant for any of the aforementioned tasks. We use the combined dataset of almost 100,800 images for our experiments and split it randomly into 75% for training and 25% for testing.

## 2.2  Real-World Twitter Data

To evaluate the performance of the methods investigated in this work in a realistic scenario, we collected images posted on Twitter during two major flood events in Germany: The flood of July 2017 in the *Harz* region caused severe damages to buildings, public infrastructure, and dikes in many cities in the center of Germany. In January 2018, a flood of the river *Rhine* in western Germany affected one of the largest German cities, Cologne, so that we can expect a high number of tweets relating to this flood. We denote these two events as *Harz17* and *Rhine18* in the following.

We extracted potentially flood-related tweets during these two months from a database that we constructed using the Twitter Streaming API over the course of several years. While our method is, in principle, purely image-based and does not rely on textual cues, the limitations of the API enforced us to pre-filter tweets based on the appearance of flood-related keywords[1]. However, the results still contain numerous unrelated tweets, as can be seen in the top row of Fig. 1.

---

[1] The German keywords were: Hochwasser, Flut, Überschwemmung, Überschwemmungen, überschwemmt, überflutet, Sturmflut, Pegel.

At the time of writing, 3,314 out of the 3,765 images posted on Twitter during these months were still accessible. After a near-duplicate removal step using feature similarity and manual inspection of suspect duplicates, 704 images remain for the Harz17 dataset and 1,848 for the Rhine18 dataset.

We asked two experts from hydrology to annotate these datasets according to the same criteria as the European Flood 2013 dataset. Due to the high number of images and limited resources, each image was annotated by a single expert.

## 3 Methods

We compare three methods for filtering relevant tweets: an objective-agnostic baseline relying on textual keywords and the date of the tweet, a retrieval approach, and a classification-based method.

*Text-Time-Based Baseline:* As a naïve baseline ignoring the image contents, we rank all tweets containing a flood-related keyword by the proximity of their time of posting to the hour of maximum tweet frequency during the flood event.

*Filtering by Retrieval:* In a general content-based image retrieval (CBIR) scenario, the user initially provides a set of query images represented by feature vectors $Q = \{q_1, \ldots, q_m\} \subset \mathbb{R}^D$ and the system then ranks the images in the database by decreasing similarity of their feature vectors $X = \{x_1, \ldots, x_n\} \subset \mathbb{R}^D$ to the queries. Since we are not focusing on interactivity in this work but on a fixed set of search objectives, we relieve the user from the burden of specifying query images and fix $Q$ to the set of "ideal queries" for the respective task from the European Flood 2013 dataset.

For computing the similarity between an image feature vector $x \in X$ from the database and all queries, we use kernel density estimation (KDE), inspired by Deselaers et al. [4]:

$$\text{sim}(x, Q) = \frac{1}{|Q|} \sum_{q \in Q} \exp\left(-\gamma \cdot \|x - q\|^2\right) . \tag{1}$$

The hyper-parameter $\gamma \in \mathbb{R}^+$ is tuned on the training set of the European Flood 2013 dataset. The exact value can be found in Table 1.

To compute feature vectors describing the images, we employ convolutional neural networks (CNNs), which learned important image features such as, e.g., the appearance of certain shapes or textures, from large amounts of data. First, we use features extracted from the last convolutional layer of a VGG16 architecture [11] and a ResNet-50 architecture [7], both pre-trained on 1.2 million images from ImageNet [10]. These regional features are averaged and finally $L^2$-normalized, resulting in a 512-dimensional feature space for VGG16 and 2048 features for ResNet-50. The images are initially resized and cropped to $768 \times 512$ or $512 \times 768$ pixels, depending on their orientation. This resolution corresponds to the median aspect ratio (3:2) in the Twitter datasets.

**Table 1.** Values of the hyper-parameters $\gamma$ for retrieval and $C$ for classification.

|          | VGG16 | ResNet-50 | Deep R-MAC |
|----------|-------|-----------|------------|
| $\gamma$ | 10.0  | 5.0       | 5.0        |
| $C$      | 2.5   | 0.5       | 0.005      |

Secondly, we examine the use of features optimized for instance retrieval: The Deep R-MAC architecture [6] is based on ResNet-101 and aggregates 2048-dimensional image features across several regions of interest and image resolutions, decorrelates them using PCA, and finally applies $L^2$-normalization. It has been pre-trained on a landmark dataset using a metric learning objective that forces similar images to be closer than dissimilar images by a pre-defined margin. This representation has been identified by Barz et al. [1] to be more powerful than VGG16 features for interactive flood image retrieval, but they did not compare it with other ResNets trained on different datasets (e.g., ImageNet).

*Filtering by Classification:* For each of the search objectives defined in Sect. 2.1, we train a binary linear support vector machine (SVM) [3] using all images from the European Flood 2013 dataset annotated as relevant for that task as positive example and all remaining images as well as the images from the Flickr100k dataset as negative examples. We examine the same image features used for the retrieval technique (see above) and optimize the regularization hyper-parameter $C \in \mathbb{R}^+$ of the SVMs using 5-fold cross-validation on the training set. The resulting value for all network architectures can be found in Table 1.

## 4    Experiments

We evaluate the performance of the different approaches and feature representations in two scenarios: First, we investigate a ranking task, where all images in a given dataset should be ranked according to their relevance, from the most to the least relevant. This corresponds to a post-hoc analysis of the event, where all potentially useful images have already been collected from the web and an analyst will go through the ordered list. This approach avoids hard decisions, which are prone to erroneously excluding relevant images, but instead allows the analysts to decide when to stop, while they go through the ranked list.

Second, we turn our attention to an on-line filtering task, which is more suitable for a *rapid* flood impact analysis scenario. In this setting, the event is still ongoing, and we need to decide for every newly posted image immediately whether it is worth looking at or irrelevant.

### 4.1    Ranking Images by Relevance

The ranking scenario reflects a classical retrieval task, and we hence use established retrieval metrics for our experimental evaluation: *average precision (AP)*

**Table 2.** AP for all tested methods on all datasets. Numbers are in %. The best value per column is set in bold. Cls. = Classification, Ret. = Retrieval.

| | European Flood 2013 | | | | Harz17 | | | | Rhine18 | | | |
|---|---|---|---|---|---|---|---|---|---|---|---|---|
| Method | Flood | Depth | Poll. | mAP | Flood | Depth | Poll. | mAP | Flood | Depth | Poll. | mAP |
| Text-Time-based | — | — | — | — | 45.6 | 30.5 | 0.6 | 25.6 | 41.7 | 21.4 | 0.3 | 21.1 |
| Cls. (VGG16) | 80.7 | 65.2 | 56.0 | 67.3 | 84.1 | 66.8 | 3.4 | 51.4 | 82.5 | 66.4 | **2.4** | **50.4** |
| Cls. (ResNet-50) | **92.1** | **77.8** | **90.4** | **86.8** | 86.4 | **71.1** | 9.6 | **55.7** | **83.1** | 65.2 | 1.0 | 49.8 |
| Cls. (Deep R-MAC) | 92.0 | 77.1 | 70.9 | 80.0 | **86.9** | 70.8 | 3.1 | 53.6 | 81.5 | 59.5 | 1.0 | 47.3 |
| Ret. (VGG16) | 62.0 | 53.2 | 14.0 | 43.1 | 71.2 | 58.4 | 0.5 | 43.4 | 76.2 | 63.4 | 0.7 | 46.7 |
| Ret. (ResNet-50) | 69.6 | 54.2 | 37.5 | 53.8 | 64.7 | 53.7 | 1.0 | 39.8 | 75.2 | 61.0 | 1.1 | 45.8 |
| Ret. (Deep R-MAC) | 62.8 | 46.4 | 28.4 | 45.9 | 83.3 | 64.6 | 2.9 | 50.3 | 80.1 | 60.0 | 1.3 | 47.1 |

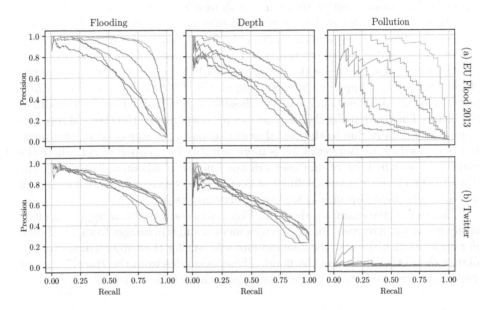

**Fig. 2.** Precision-recall curves for the European Flood 2013 test set (top row) and the combined Twitter datasets (bottom row).

and its mean (mAP) over the three search objectives. AP assesses the quality of the entire ranking of all images by computing the area under the *precision-recall curve*. *Recall* is the fraction of all relevant images found up to a certain position in the ranking and *precision* is the fraction of images among those found up to this position that are relevant.

The results for both the European Flood 2013 dataset and our two novel Twitter datasets are given in Table 2. In addition, the precision-recall curves in Fig. 2 provide detailed insights into the performance for different recall-precision trade-offs on the European Flood 2013 test set and a combination of the two Twitter datasets.

On the European Flood 2013 dataset, the classification-based approach outperforms retrieval by a large margin. ResNet-50 features work best for both approaches across all tasks. This is an interesting finding because Barz et al. [1]

identified Deep R-MAC as the best representation on this dataset, but only compared it with VGG16 and not with ResNet-50.

These findings transfer well to the Harz17 dataset, where classification with ResNet-50 features performs best as well on average. It also performs quite well on the Rhine18 dataset but is slightly outperformed there by VGG16 features, which provide surprisingly good results on that dataset only.

On both Twitter datasets, our approach efficiently filters images relevant for the flooding and depth task, but performs much worse for the pollution task than on the European Flood 2013 data. First, there are very few relevant pollution images on Twitter (0.5% in our dataset). Secondly, we observed that reflections on the water surface were often mistaken for oil films. This difficult category certainly requires more work in the future, parts of which should focus on collecting dedicated pollution image data for a more robust evaluation.

The discrepancy between the performance of the retrieval approach and the classification-based approach is not as big on the Twitter data as on the European Flood 2013 dataset, because the classifiers were trained on the domain of the latter. That ranking by classification scores outperforms the classical retrieval approach is simply due to the closed-world scenario we employed in this work: Retrieval as done by Barz et al. [1] is more suitable for an open world, where the categories searched for by the user are not known in advance. Restricting the filter to the three categories defined in Sect. 2.1, however, gives classification an advantage by being optimized for these particular tasks.

The qualitative examples shown in Fig. 1 illustrate that our approach effectively filters out irrelevant images such as memes and still images from TV shows. For each search objective, the images more relevant for that objective are ranked higher than other images of the flood. These examples from the Harz17 dataset were generated using the classification approach with ResNet-50 features.

## 4.2   On-Line Filter with Hard Decisions

In the scenario of filtering a stream of incoming images, a hard decision about the relevance of individual images must be enforced. This can be done by thresholding the scores predicted by the SVMs in case of the classification-based approach or thresholding the distance to the query images in case of retrieval. Due to this hard decision, we only obtain one pair of recall and precision values on each of our Twitter datasets, in contrast to the retrieval setting. We combine these by computing the so-called F1-score, which is the harmonic mean of recall and precision. The maximum F1-scores over all possible thresholds are shown in Table 3. This means, we assume that an optimal threshold has already been found, which usually needs to be done using held-out training data or cross-validation.

In this scenario, the superiority of the classification-based approach is more pronounced as in the retrieval setting. Again, we can observe that VGG16 features only perform well on the Rhine18 data, while ResNet-50 features provide best or competitive performance for both datasets. Averaged over both datasets, classification with ResNet-50 features achieves a precision of 73% and a 89% recall for the flooding task and a precision of 65% with a recall of 67% for the

**Table 3.** Best possible F1-score (in %) that can be obtained with each method.

| Method | Harz17 | | | | Rhine18 | | | |
| --- | --- | --- | --- | --- | --- | --- | --- | --- |
| | Flood | Depth | Poll. | Avg | Flood | Depth | Poll. | Avg |
| Text-Time-based | 59.5 | 43.7 | 3.4 | 35.5 | 59.9 | 38.6 | 0.9 | 33.1 |
| — Classification (VGG16) | 78.6 | 64.6 | 20.0 | 54.4 | 78.8 | **62.4** | **16.7** | **52.6** |
| — Classification (ResNet-50) | 81.1 | **68.7** | **33.3** | **61.0** | **79.1** | 61.8 | 8.7 | 49.9 |
| — Classification (Deep R-MAC) | **81.2** | 66.5 | 12.5 | 53.4 | 76.5 | 61.1 | 5.0 | 47.5 |
| — Retrieval (VGG16) | 65.0 | 55.1 | 1.6 | 40.6 | 70.6 | 60.0 | 4.1 | 44.9 |
| — Retrieval (ResNet-50) | 58.4 | 52.0 | 5.4 | 38.6 | 69.5 | 58.1 | 7.1 | 44.9 |
| — Retrieval (Deep R-MAC) | 77.3 | 64.9 | 9.3 | 50.5 | 76.3 | 57.8 | 5.6 | 46.6 |

depth task. This illustrates the benefit of using machine learning for filtering relevant social media images, since only every fourth image passing the filter will not show flooding, while still 89% of all relevant images are found. If one would aim for 99% recall, the precision on the flooding task would still be 54%.

## 5 Conclusions

We presented an automatic filter for images posted on Twitter with respect to their relevance for obtaining various information about floodings and rapidly assessing flood impacts, so that response and recovery can be coordinated quickly and adequately. To this end, we have shown that classifiers trained on data from Wikimedia Commons can be applied successfully to real Twitter data. While retrieval-based approaches used in the past are flexible and enable the user to refine the results easily by giving feedback, classification is faster, does not require interactivity, and provides better filtering performance, which makes it more suitable for gaining insights rapidly during the event from streaming data. Thus, we recommend our classification model based on ResNet-50 features for use in practice, since it provides best or at least competitive performance across tasks and datasets. A realistic application scenario, however, poses further challenges: Since many images posted on Twitter lack accurate geodata, a technique for automatic geolocalization of tweets or images is crucial. In this work, we focused on finding relevant images, and leave the geolocalization to future work.

**Acknowledgements.** This work was supported by the German Research Foundation as part of the programme "Volunteered Geographic Information: Interpretation, Visualisation and Social Computing" (SPP 1894, contract DE 735/11-1).

## References

1. Barz, B., et al.: Enhancing flood impact analysis using interactive retrieval of social media images. Arch. Data Sci. Ser. A A06, 21 S. (2018). https://doi.org/10.5445/KSP/1000087327/06

2. Comfort, L.K., Ko, K., Zagorecki, A.: Coordination in rapidly evolving disaster response systems: the role of information. Am. Behav. Sci. **48**(3), 295–313 (2004). https://doi.org/10.1177/0002764204268987
3. Cortes, C., Vapnik, V.: Support-vector networks. Mach. Learn. **20**(3), 273–297 (1995). https://doi.org/10.1007/BF00994018
4. Deselaers, T., Paredes, R., Vidal, E., Ney, H.: Learning weighted distances for relevance feedback in image retrieval. In: International Conference on Pattern Recognition (ICPR), pp. 1–4. IEEE (2008). https://doi.org/10.1109/ICPR.2008.4761730
5. Fohringer, J., Dransch, D., Kreibich, H., Schröter, K.: Social media as an information source for rapid flood inundation mapping. Nat. Hazards Earth Syst. Sci. **15**(12), 2725–2738 (2015). https://doi.org/10.5194/nhess-15-2725-2015
6. Gordo, A., Almazán, J., Revaud, J., Larlus, D.: End-to-end learning of deep visual representations for image retrieval. Int. J. Comput. Vis. **124**(2), 237–254 (2017). https://doi.org/10.1007/s11263-017-1016-8
7. He, K., Zhang, X., Ren, S., Sun, J.: Deep residual learning for image recognition. In: 2016 IEEE Conference on Computer Vision and Pattern Recognition (CVPR), pp. 770–778, June 2016. https://doi.org/10.1109/CVPR.2016.90
8. Kruspe, A., Kersten, J., Klan, F.: Detecting event-related tweets by example using few-shot models. In: Conference on Information Systems for Crisis Response and Management (ISCRAM), pp. 825–835, May 2019
9. Philbin, J., Chum, O., Isard, M., Sivic, J., Zisserman, A.: Object retrieval with large vocabularies and fast spatial matching. In: Proceedings of the IEEE Conference on Computer Vision and Pattern Recognition (2007). https://doi.org/10.1109/CVPR.2007.383172. http://www.robots.ox.ac.uk/~vgg/data/oxbuildings/flickr100k.html
10. Russakovsky, O., et al.: ImageNet large scale visual recognition challenge. Int. J. Comput. Vis. **115**(3), 211–252 (2015). https://doi.org/10.1007/s11263-015-0816-y
11. Simonyan, K., Zisserman, A.: Very deep convolutional networks for large-scale image recognition. arXiv:1409.1556 (2014)
12. Thieken, A.H., et al.: The flood of June 2013 in Germany: how much do we know about its impacts? Nat. Hazards Earth Syst. Sci. **16**(6), 1519–1540 (2016). https://doi.org/10.5194/nhess-16-1519-2016

# Natural Disaster Classification Using Aerial Photography Explainable for Typhoon Damaged Feature

Takato Yasuno(✉), Masazumi Amakata, and Masahiro Okano

Research Institute for Infrastructure Paradigm Shift, Yachiyo Engineering Co., Ltd.,
Asakusabashi 5-20-8, Taito-ku, Tokyo, Japan
{tk-yasuno,amakata,ms-okano}@yachiyo-eng.co.jp

**Abstract.** Recent years, typhoon damages has become social problem owing to climate change. In 9 September 2019, Typhoon Faxai passed on the Chiba in Japan, whose damages included with electric provision stop because of strong wind recorded on the maximum 45 m/s. A large amount of tree fell down, and the neighbour electric poles also fell down at the same time. These disaster features have caused that it took 18 days for recovery longer than past ones. Immediate responses are important for faster recovery. As long as we can, aerial survey for global screening of devastated region would be required for decision support to respond where to recover ahead. This paper proposes a practical method to visualize the damaged areas focused on the typhoon disaster features using aerial photography. This method can classify eight classes which contains land covers without damages and areas with disaster. Using target feature class probabilities, we can visualize disaster feature map to scale a colour range. Furthermore, we can realize explainable map on each unit grid images to compute the convolutional activation map using Grad-CAM. We demonstrate case studies applied to aerial photographs recorded at the Chiba region after typhoon.

**Keywords:** Typhoon disaster response · Aerial survey · Tree-fallen · Classification · Grad-CAM · Damaged feature mapping

## 1 Introduction

### 1.1 Typhoon Damage Prediction for Immediate Response and Recovery

This paper highlights the typhoon disaster feature extracted by the aero-photographs because it is reasonable cost more than satellite imagery and it has advantage of global sky view more than drone images. As shown these related works at next Sect. 1.2, one of typhoon disaster features, whose complex features contains the tree-fallen, is not clearly explored. First, the tree-fallen feature has green-colour of leafs and blown-colour of blanches, so this region of interest is completely colour segmented using the straight forward colour slicing and the standard image processing. Second, it seems that the shape is various owing to the damage intensity of tree-fallen range from light level to extremely

© Springer Nature Switzerland AG 2021
A. Del Bimbo et al. (Eds.): ICPR 2020 Workshops, LNCS 12666, pp. 15–25, 2021.
https://doi.org/10.1007/978-3-030-68780-9_2

one. More flexible learning methods are required for disaster features extraction using deep neural networks.

Figure 1 shows our proposed workflow to classify disaster damages and to visualize a target classified feature. Immediate responses towards typhoon damages are important for faster recovery which consists with electric stop caused by tree-fallen. Therefore, more reasonable sky view screening of devastated region is required for decision support to respond where to prioritize recovery actions. An advantage of aerial photograph is higher resolution that is 0.2 m, than satellite imagery and it also enables to wider search efficiently than drone flight. This paper proposes a method to predict the damaged area focused on the typhoon disaster features using aero-photograph images.

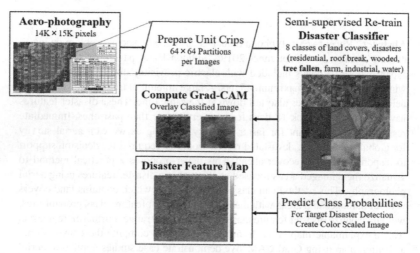

**Fig. 1.** A proposed workflow to classify disaster damages and to visualize a target feature

## 1.2 Related Works and Papers

**Aerial Survey for Natural Disaster Monitoring.** In order to recognize a status after natural disaster, several aerial surveys are available from various height overview such as satellite imagery, aircraft, helicopter, and drone. There are many related works around the devastated area where some disaster occurred at each phase of preparedness, urgent response, and recovery. For example, Chou et al. [1] proposed the drone-based photographing workflow for disaster monitoring and management operation to get real-time aerial photos. The pro of drone use is to overcome transport barriers to quickly acquire all the major affected area of the real-time disaster information. But, the con is that drone is not able to keep a long flight more than 30 min. Kentosch et al. [2] studied UAV based tree species classification task in Japanese mixed forests for deep learning in two different mixed forest types. This research has tended to focus on the identification tree species rather than the natural disaster feature such as tree fallen. Next, the JICA survey team [3] used a helicopter owned by the air force of Sri Lanka to investigate the flood and sediment disaster damages caused by the strong winds and the heavy rain-falls during 15 to 18 May 2016, named as Cyclone Roanu. They also collected the Light Detection and Ranging (LiDAR) data to compare between before normal status and after landslide. The aerial photograph could visualize the damages where roads are flooded, river water exceeded a dike in residential areas, landslide or collapse, debris flow on the top of mountain. The advantage of LiDAR is that beside rain and clouds, no other weather conditions limit their use [4]. As an active sensor, missions in the night-time are possible. In Japan, there is a Bosai platform [5] for disaster preparedness, response and recovery. Several private company have investigated after natural disaster using aerial survey and made a disaster mapping for emergency use. However, it takes high cost of satellite image over global viewpoint and it needs longer time to get a target image of fully covered region. On the other hand, drone surveillance takes lowest cost though the flight time is twenty or thirty minutes, and the scope is narrow due to the constraint of height available flight.

## 1.3   Feature Extraction for Natural Disaster Damage Assessment

There are a lot of earthquake disaster detection especially building damage using satellite imagery, LiDAR point clouds, and drone images. For example, He et al. [6] presented 3D shape descriptor of individual roofs for detecting surface damage and roof exhibiting structural damage. However, it is not always possible to acquire an airborne LiDAR data of devastated region to be full-covered after each disaster. This approach would take too high cost to prepare the input data source for damage assessment. In addition, Nex et al. [7] presented a method to autonomously map building damages with a drone in near real-time. Unfortunately, this study is too narrow experience to explore the practical use for disaster response. The limitation of method based on drone is also the short flight time less than 30 min to search the devastated region. Regarding typhoon damage assessment, Liu et al. [8] reported the Landsat-8 automatic image processing system (L-8 AIPS) which enables to the most up-to-date scenes of Taiwan to be browsed, and in only one hour's time after receiving the raw data from United States Geological Survey (USGS) level-1 product. However, this application depended on the specific satellite imagery and each country must customize such an application, the limitation is the 15 m resolution for monitoring disaster damages. Furthermore, Gupta et al. [9] proposed to identify impacted areas and accessible roads and buildings in post-disaster scenarios. However, this research has been tended to focus on the grasp of post-disaster recovery scenario rather than the immediate respond of early restoration. On the other hand, Rahnemoonfar et al. [10] studied a hurricane Michael dataset HRUD for visual perception in disaster scenarios using semantic segmentation including with the class of building destruction. But, one of the major drawbacks to use the semantic segmentation is the scarcity of natural disaster feature, the difficulty of data mining for high accuracy, and much workforce of annotation for accurate damage region of interest. Furthermore, Sheykhmousa et al. [11] focused on the post-disaster recovery process before typhoon and after four years, and they classified the five classes of land cover and land use changes to visualize the recovery map which enables to signal positive recovery, neutral, and negative recovery, etc. Natural forces are heavy winds, storm surges, and destroyed existing urban facilities. Their damage classes contained with inundated land and flattened trees. They demonstrated a land cover and land use recovery map that quantify the post-disaster recovery process at the pixel level. However, this study is not immediate recovery but four years long recovery process. The classified recovery map is too far view based on satellite imagery at the 2 m resolution to extract the damage feature in more detail.

## 2  Modelling

### 2.1  Partition Clips and Learning Disaster Features

**Prepare 64 by 64 Partitioned Clips Divided 14 K by 15 K Pixels into 221 by 243**
Figure 2 shows a proposed machine learning workflow that consist of the former part of disaster damaged annotation and the later part of classification modelling. First, the size of aero-photographs is 14 thousands by 15 thousands pixels, so the original size is too large and it is not fitted as the input of deep neural networks whose size is frequently 224 by 224 and 229 by 229. High quality learning requires to keep the original RGB data per pixel without resize as far as we can. Therefore, this method make a set of base partitions 64 by 64 into each unit grid image clips with 221 by 243 pixel size. This aerial photograph has the 0.196 m resolution so that the real size of unit grid square stands for 44 by 48 m distance.

**Efficient Annotation via Semi-supervised Prediction using Pre-trained Classifier**
This paper highlights on the typhoon disaster feature such as tree-fallen and normal land covers without damages. Table 1 shows a proposed hierarchical eight classes which contains seven land covers and the tree-fallen features. We could use 26 images of aerial photograph. Total amount of clip images is almost always very large more than hundred thousands, so human annotation by hands is difficult to divide subgroup of land cover and disaster feature classes. Owing to the hurdle of efficient learning, firstly, we propose to train a base classifier using twenty percent of clip images with the order of twenty thousand images. Secondly, using remained clips with order of eighty thousands as the added input for semi-supervised learning, we can predict the label per clip and it takes less works of annotation because almost labels are correct and error corrections are less than the case without pre-trained model. And then using the classified labels, we can almost automate to divide their clips into eight subfolders efficiently. Thirdly, human check is possible whether each subfolder contains errors or not, and can correct their miss-classification of clips less works than fully human works.

**Accuracy Comparison with Deep Neural Networks**
We can train classification models based on ten candidates of deep neural networks with advantage of the whole accuracy and two disaster classes of accuracies, that is house roof break and tree fallen. We propose and compare usable deep neural networks such as AlexNet [12, 13], VGG16 [14], GoogleNet, Inception-v3 [15], ResNet50, ResNet101 [16], Inception-ResNet-v2 [17], DenseNet-201 [18]. Furthermore, MobileNet-v2 [19] and ShuffleNet [20, 21] has less parameters and fitted to mobile devices, where the later network uses special techniques such as channel shuffle and group convolution. We

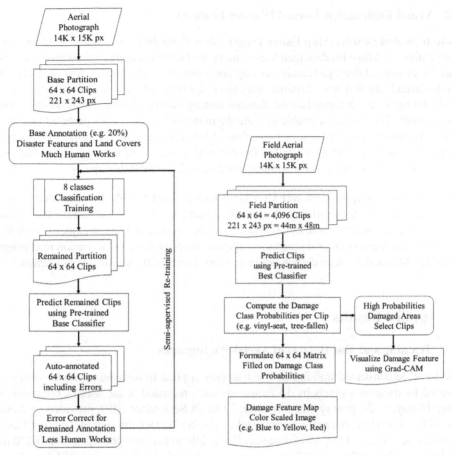

**Fig. 2.** (Left) A machine learning workflow of disaster damaged annotation and classification, (Right) An application workflow for damaged feature mapping filled on class probabilities and for visualized damage feature per clip area computing the Grad-CAM

**Table 1.** Hierarchical classes setting including land covers and typhoon disaster features

| | |
|---|---|
| 1 residential area (without damage) | 5 farm field (rice, crop) |
| 2 **house roof break** (remained vinyl seat) | 6 industrial area (manufacturing) |
| 3 wooded field (without damage) | 7 water cover (sea, river, lake) |
| 4 **tree fallen field** (caused by strong wind) | 8 cloudy cover (partial or full) |

can evaluate their accuracy with both recall and precision to compute their confusion matrix. Here, the recall is more important than precision because we should avoid miss-classification in spite of that it contains disaster features.

## 2.2   Visual Explanation Toward Disaster Features

**Colour Scaled Feature Map Using Target Class Probabilities.** Figure 2 shows an application workflow for damaged feature mapping filled on damaged class probabilities and for visualized damage feature per clip area computing the Grad-CAM [22]. Based on the already trained best classifier, we can compute target class probabilities per unit grid, and then we can formulate the damage feature matrix which consists 64 rows and 64 columns. Therefore, we enable to scale the matrix of specific class probabilities into colour feature map ranged among two colours [23]. This paper realize a damage feature map. We can formulate a tree fallen feature map to scale colour range from blue to yellow. The yellow side is huge damage, the blue side is small damage.

**Visual Disaster Explanation per Unit Grid Using Grad-CAM.** In case that some grid area has a high probability at a specific damage class, we can create the micro damage feature map for more detailed scale per unit grid area. We can explain the damage features on each unit grid images to compute the convolutional activation map using Grad-CAM based on deep classification network layers with optimized parameters.

# 3   Applied Results

## 3.1   Training and Test Dataset of Aerial-Photographs

We have demonstrated training and test studies applied to aero-photographs with the size of 14 thousands pixels by 15 thousands ones recorded at the south Chiba region after 18 days at the post typhoon disaster, 27 to 28 September 2019, provided by Aero Asahi Co. Ltd. Here, the real size per pixel on the land is 19.6 cm so that the size of unit grid square contains 44 by 48 m distance. The height to get aero-photographs is 3,270 m and the number of them is 452 images. The number of clip images is 5,954 for a base classifier training at the region of Kimitsu city on the Chiba prefecture. Here, we set the division of train and test is 7:3. Several test aero-photographs are located at the region of Kyonan town and Tateyama city on the south Chiba prefecture.

## 3.2   Damage Feature Classifier Trained Results

The author applied to ten classification deep neural networks as base model towards the number of 5,954 of unit grid clips, which are randomly divided into rates with training 70 and 30 test. The training images are pre-processed by three specific augmentation operations such as randomly flip the training images along the vertical axis, and randomly translate them up to 30 pixels, and scale them up to 10% horizontally and vertically. Then transfer learning is useful for faster training and disaster response. Here, the author make freeze the round 70 to 80% of deep network layers at the concatenation point combined with convolutional layers and skip connections. Table 2 indicates the accuracy comparison between ten deep neural networks, which has each number of whole layers setting with the frozen layer point. In this study, the mini-batch size is 32, and the maximum epoch is 30 with shuffle every epoch. One epoch has 130 iterations, the total batch learning results in 3,900 iterations. Further, the initial learning rate is 0.0005, and learning rate schedule is every 5 epoch with drop factor 0.75. From computing results, the ShuffleNet has the most accurate for 30% test clips validation. Also the damage class accuracy of both recall and precision has higher score than other nine deep neural networks. Table 3 shows the confusion matrix of the most promising ShuffleNet as far as we implemented our comparison.

**Table 2.** Accuracy comparison between various models.

| CNN models | Total validation accuracy | house roof break (covered vinyl-seat) accuracy | | tree-fallen accuracy | | Frozen layer /Whole layer | Runing time (minutes) |
|---|---|---|---|---|---|---|---|
| | | recall | precision | recall | precision | | |
| AlexNet | 89.59 | 67.9 | 97.6 | 95.8 | 68.8 | 16/25 | 20 |
| VGG16 | 88.07 | 66.3 | 89.9 | 87.8 | 71.2 | 32/41 | 50 |
| GoogleNet | 89.75 | **78.6** | 92.7 | 93.1 | 69.5 | 110/144 | 27 |
| Inception-v3 | 90.26 | 70.1 | 97.7 | **99.9** | 66.1 | 249/315 | 79 |
| MobileNet-v2 | 88.63 | 64.6 | 98.1 | **99.6** | 65.6 | 104/154 | 38 |
| **ResNet50** | **90.48** | **74.5** | 96.8 | **99.6** | **74.1** | 120/177 | 46 |
| ResNet101 | 88.02 | 63.8 | **98.7** | **99.6** | 69.1 | 290/347 | 70 |
| **DenseNet-201** | **92.16** | 75.3 | 96.3 | 97.7 | **77.1** | 647/708 | 193 |
| Inception-ResNet-v2 | 88.52 | 69.5 | **98.3** | 95.1 | **74.3** | 766/824 | 175 |
| **ShuffleNet** | **93.39** | **82.3** | **98.1** | 98.9 | **79.7** | 137/172 | 33 |

**Table 3.** Confusion matrix of the ShuffleNet best classifier (row: truth, column: prediction).

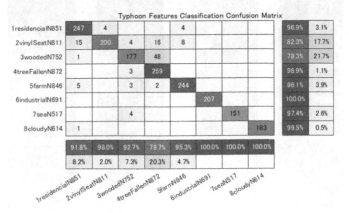

## 3.3   Damage Feature Map and Unit Grid Visualization Results

**Tree-Fallen Feature Mapping Results.** Figure 3 shows the tree-fallen damage feature map based on the class probabilities per clip. The colour is scaled between the blue and yellow. The yellow side is positive tree-fallen caused by strong wind. Here, we can understand that a lot of tree-fallen areas are located besides river and around mountain.

**Fig. 3.** Tree fallen feature map using damage class probabilities (Color figure online)

Figure 4 shows the visual explanation of tree-fallen more detail scale per unit grid with the size of 221 × 243 using Grad-CAM, where each pair of original clip and activation map are overlaid. The heat map with colour range is scaled between the blue and yellow. The yellow side is positive tree-fallen feature caused by strong wind of typhoon.

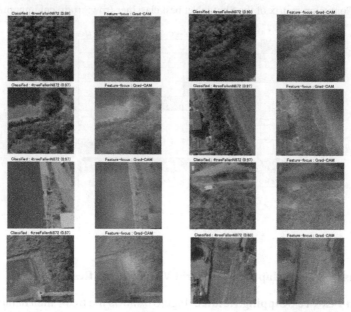

**Fig. 4.** Visual explanation of tree-fallen (yellow-blue range) using Grad-CAM, each pair of original clip and activation map. The yellow side is positive tree-fallen caused by strong wind. (Color figure online)

# 4   Concluding Remarks

## 4.1   Disaster Features Visualization for Immediate Response Support

This paper proposed a method to predict the damaged area highlighted on the typhoon disaster feature such as tree-fallen using aero-photographs images. This method was able to classify land covers without damages and with ones. We trained the preferable deep network classifier with advantage of disaster class accuracy, the ShuffleNet compared with ten practical candidates of usable deep neural networks. Using target class probabilities per unit grid, we were able to visualize disaster features map to scale the colour range from blue to yellow. Furthermore, we were able to explain the disaster features on each unit grid images to compute the convolutional activation map using Grad-CAM. We demonstrated training and test studies applied to aero-photographs with the size of 14 thousands pixels by 15 thousands ones recorded at the south Chiba region after eighteen days at the post Typhoon Faxai, 27 to 28 September 2019.

We aware that our method may have two primary limitations. The first is a supervised learning approach based on the past experienced data. Natural disaster are rare events, so the data mining opportunity is limited, and results in the scarcity of disaster region of interest images. The second is based on the input images from a point of sky-view using an aero-photography. We should incorporate the ground-view data to be more useful for immediate disaster response. We should be comprehensive learning using another resources such as public surveillance camera, private mobile contents.

## 4.2   Future Works for Disaster Visual Mining and Learning Variations

This paper studied the one of disaster features of strong wind due to typhoon. We also focused on the damaged class of house roof break, and computed the feature map and explain the vinyl seat on the roof using Grad-CAM. These results have been shown as Fig. 5 in Appendix because of limited space. Further, we try to carry out data mining towards another supervised sky view images though disaster event is rare, so we need to continue to collect aerial photographs at next coming typhoon with different damage features, for example flooded area and levee break point. Though it needs many annotation works to divide subgroup of clips, we can build a prototype of classifier and using the base model we can almost automate to classify subgroup of clips. Furthermore, we can try to learn and represent various disaster features and so it could be possible to make the visual explanation for immediate response support to faster recovery.

**Acknowledgements.** We gratefully acknowledge the constructive comments of the anonymous referees. Support was given by the Aero Asahi Co. of Jun Miura, who provided us the aerial photographs recorded at the Chiba after the Typhoon Faxai. We thank Takuji Fukumoto and Shinichi Kuramoto for supporting us MATLAB resources.

# Appendix

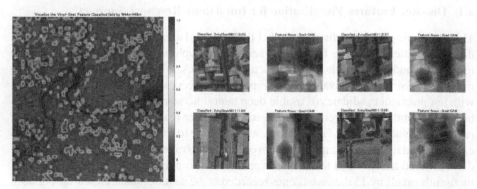

**Fig. 5.** (Left) House roof break feature map, (Right) Visual explanation of roof break (red-blue range) using Grad-CAM, each pair of original clip and activation map, roof break covered with vinyl seat. The red is positive roof break affected by strong wind (Color figure online)

# References

1. Chou, T.-Y., Yeh, M.-L., et al.: Disaster monitoring and management by the unmanned aerial vehicle technology. In: Wanger, W., Szekely, B. (eds.) ISPRS TC VII Symposium, Austria, vol. XXXVIII, Part 7B (2010)
2. Kentsche, S., Karatsiolis, S., Kamilaris, A., et al.: Identification of tree species in Japanese forests based on aerial photography and deep learning, arXiv:2007.08907 (2020)
3. JICA Survey Team: Aerial Survey Report on Inundation Damages and Sediment Disasters, 15th June 2016
4. Altan, M.O., Kemper, G.: Innovative airborne sensors for disaster management. The International Archives of Photogrammetry, Remote Sensing and Spatial Information Sciences, vol. XLI-B8, XXIII ISPRS Congress, Czech Republic, July 2016
5. Japan Bosai Platform. https://www.bosai-jp.org/en. Accessed 10 Oct 2020
6. He, M., et al.: A 3D shape descriptor based on contour clusters for damaged roof detection using airborne LiDAR point clouds. MDPI **8**, 189 (2016)
7. Nex, F., et al.: Towards real-time building damage mapping with low-cost UAV solutions. MDPI Remote Sens. **11**, 287 (2019)
8. Liu, C.-C., Nakamura, R., et al.: Near real-time browable landsat-8 imagery. MDPI Remote Sens. **9**, 79 (2017)
9. Gupta, A., Watson, S., Yin, H.: Deep learning-based aerial image segmentation with open data for disaster impact assessment, arXiv:2006.05575v1 (2020)
10. Rahnemoonfar, M., Murphy, R.: Comprehensive semantic segmentation on high resolution UAV imagery for natural disaster damage assessment, arXiv:2009.01193v2 (2020)
11. Sheykhmousa, M., et al.: Post-disaster recovery assessment with machine learning-derived land cover and land use information. MDPI Remote Sens. **11**, 1174 (2019)
12. Krizhevsky, A., Ilya, S., Hinton, G.E.: ImageNet classification with deep convolutional neural networks. In: Advances in Neural Information Processing Systems (2012)
13. Szegedy, C., Wei, L., Yangqing, J., et al.: Going deeper with convolutions. In: Proceedings of the IEEE Conference on Computer Vision and Pattern Recognition, pp. 1–9 (2015)

14. Simoniyan, K. et al.: Very deep convolutional networks for large-scale image recognition. In: ICLR, VGG model, the Visual Geometry Group at University of Oxford (2015)
15. Szegedy, C., Vincent, V., Sergey, I., et al.: Rethinking the inception architecture for computer vision. In: CVPR, Inception v3 Model, pp. 2818–2826 (2015)
16. Kaiming, H., Xiangyu, Z., Shaoqing, R., et al.: Deep residual learning for image recognition, ResNet Model, arXiv:1512.03385v1 (2015)
17. Szegedy, C., Sergey, I., Vincent, V., et al.: Inception-v4, Inception-ResNet and Impact of Residual Connections on Learning, Inception-ResNet-v2 Model (2016)
18. Huang, H., Liu, Z., Maaten, L., et al.: Densely connected convolutional networks. In: CVPR, DenseNet Model (2017)
19. Sandler, M., Howard, A., et al.: MobileNetV2: inverted residuals and linear bottlenecks, arXiv: 1801.04381v4, 21 March 2019
20. Zhang, X., Zhou, X., et al.: ShuffleNet: an extremely efficient convolutional neural network for mobile devices, arXiv:1707.01083v2, 7 December 2017
21. Ma, N., Zhang, X., et al.: ShuffleNet V2: practical guidelines for efficient CNN architecture design, arXiv:1807.11164v1, 30 July 2018
22. Selvaraju, R., Cogswell, M., et al.: Grad-CAM: visual explanations from deep networks via gradient-based localization, arXiv:1610.02391v3, 21 March 2017
23. Gonzalez, R., Woods, R., Eddins, S.: Digital Image Processing Using MATLAB, 2nd edn. McGrawHill Education, New York (2015)

# Environmental Time Series Prediction with Missing Data by Machine Learning and Dynamics Recostruction

Francesco Camastra[1]($\boxtimes$), Vincenzo Capone[1], Angelo Ciaramella[1],
Tony Christian Landi[2], Angelo Riccio[1], and Antonino Staiano[1]

[1] Department of Science and Technology, University of Naples Parthenope,
Centro Direzionale Isola C4, 80143 Naples, Italy
camastra@ieee.org, vincenzo.capone9@gmail.com,
{angelo.ciaramella,angelo.riccio,
antonino.staiano}@uniparthenope.it
[2] Istituto di Scienze dell' Atmosfera e del Clima (ISAC), CNR,
Via Gobetti 101, 40129 Bologna, Italy
t.landi@isac.cnr.it

**Abstract.** Environmental time series are often affected by missing data, namely data unavailability at certain time points. In this paper, it is presented an *Iterated Prediction and Imputation* algorithm, that makes possible time series prediction in presence of missing data. The algorithm uses Dynamics Reconstruction and Machine Learning methods for estimating the model order and the skeleton of time series, respectively. Experimental validation of the algorithm on an environmental time series with missing data, expressing the concentration of Ozone in a European site, shows an average percentage prediction error of 0.45% on the test set.

**Keywords:** Missing data · Model order · Grassberger-Procaccia · Hough transform · Support vector machine regression

## 1 Introduction

A time series is a data series listed in time order. In Environmental Sciences, time series are quite useful for studying how a given variable evolves in time, e.g., air pollution data [1], ozone concentration, population of a given animal (or plant) species. Environmental time series are often affected by missing data namely, there are data of time series whose value is unknown due, e.g., to temporary failure or maintenance of a measurement device feeding the time series, or, in general, to data unavailiability at certain points in time. The prediction of an Environmental Time Series has a twofold relevance, the former is to obtain, even in presence of missing data, reliable future predictions; the latter is to obtain reliable estimation of missing data of the time series.

In this paper, it is presented an *Iterated Prediction and Imputation* algorithm, that allows making time series prediction in presence of missing data.

© Springer Nature Switzerland AG 2021
A. Del Bimbo et al. (Eds.): ICPR 2020 Workshops, LNCS 12666, pp. 26–33, 2021.
https://doi.org/10.1007/978-3-030-68780-9_3

The algorithm uses Dynamics Reconstruction and Machine Learning methods for computing the model order of time series (i.e., how many past data are required to adequately model the time series), and for time series skeleton estimation, respectively.

The paper is organized as follows. Section 2 describes how the model order of a time series can be estimated by using Grassberger-Procaccia algorithm; In Sect. 3, Support Vector Machine for Regression is briefly reviewed; Section 4 describes the proposed *Iterated Prediction and Imputation Algorithm* that makes prediction in time series with missing data; Section 5 presents some experimental results; finally, In Sect. 6, some conclusions are drawn and future possible developments are provided.

## 2    Model Order Estimation by Grassberger-Procaccia Algorithm

A deterministic time series $x(t)$, with $t = 1, \dots, \ell$, can be described effectively, by an autoregressive model as follows: $x(t) = F(x(t-1), \dots, x(t-p+1))$, where $F(\cdot)$ and $p - 1$ are the so-called skeleton and model order of time series, respectively. The model order, i.e., the number of past samples required to correctly model the time series, can be estimated through several methods [2]. Although *Cross-validation* [3,4] could be the simplest solution, just picking the model order which gives the lowest prediction error, it is often unfeasible by its computational cost. An alternative and effective way for estimating the model order in time series is provided by Nonlinear Dynamics methods with the *model reconstruction* of time series [5]. Using this approach, the time series can be represented as a set of points $\Omega = \{\boldsymbol{X}(t) : \boldsymbol{X}(t) = [x(t), x(t-1), \dots, x(t-p+1)], \ t = p, \dots, \ell\}$ in a $p$-dimensional space. If $p$ is large enough, there is a diffeomorphism between the manifold $\mathcal{M}$, so-generated by $\Omega$, and the attractor $\mathcal{U}$ of the underlying dynamic system that generated the time series $x(t)$, namely $\mathcal{M}$ and $\mathcal{U}$ shares the same physical properties. The *Takens Embedding Theorem* [6,7] asserts that to construct a diffeomorphism between $\mathcal{M}$ and $\mathcal{U}$, it must be fulfilled the inequality:

$$2D_{\mathcal{U}} + 1 \leq p \tag{1}$$

where $D_{\mathcal{U}}$ denotes the dimension of the attractor $\mathcal{U}$, and $p$ is called the *embedding dimension* of the system.

Among several *dimension* definitions that are available (see [8] for a review), the *Correlation Dimension* [9] is the simplest to compute.

The Correlation Dimension of a set $\Omega$ is defined as follows. If the Correlation Integral $C(r)$ is defined as:

$$C(r) = \lim_{\ell \to \infty} \frac{2}{\ell(\ell-1)} \sum_{i=1}^{\ell} \sum_{j=i+1}^{\ell} \mathcal{I}(\|\boldsymbol{x}_j - \boldsymbol{x}_i\| \leq r), \tag{2}$$

where $\mathcal{I}(\cdot)$ is an indicator function[1], then the *Correlation Dimension* $D_\Omega$ is given by:

$$D_\Omega = \lim_{r \to 0} \frac{\ln(C(r))}{\ln(r)}. \tag{3}$$

The Grassberger–Procaccia algorithm consists in plotting $\ln C(r)$ versus $ln(r)$. The Correlation Dimension is given by the slope of the linear portion of the curve, manually detected [10]. In this paper, the computation of the Correlation Dimension is performed by a slightly modified version of *Hough transform* [11] that takes, as input, the log-log plot and returns the slope of the line that receives the maximum of votes in the accumulation matrix of the Hough Transform.

## 3   Support Vector Machine for Regression

The skeleton $F(\cdot)$ of time series can be estimated by *Support Vector Machine (SVM) for Regression* [12]. We briefly describe support vector machines for regression in the case of *quadratic-$\epsilon$-insensitive loss* [13].

Given a data set $\mathcal{D} = \{(\boldsymbol{x}_1, y_1), \ldots, (\boldsymbol{x}_\ell, y_\ell)\}$, the task is to estimate the function $f : \mathbb{R} \to \mathbb{R}$, that receives $\boldsymbol{x}$ as input, and gives $y$ as output. If it assumed that $f(\cdot)$ is an hyperplane, it can be described by $f(\boldsymbol{x}) = \boldsymbol{w} \cdot \boldsymbol{x} + b$. To solve this problem, it is used the same approach of computing the optimal hyperplane in SVM for Classification. Therefore the following functional is minimized:

$$\tau(\boldsymbol{w}) = \frac{1}{2}\|w\|^2 + C \sum_{i=1}^{\ell} |y - f(\boldsymbol{x})|_\epsilon^2, \tag{4}$$

where $|\cdot|_\epsilon^2$ is the quadratic-$\epsilon$-insensitive loss[2] and $C$ is the regularization constant that manages the trade-off between the first term, i.e., the margin, and the second term, i.e., a quadratic-$\epsilon$-insensitive loss. It is worth to remark that both the presence of the $\epsilon$-insensitive loss and the regularization constant makes Support Vector Machines for Regression quite robust w.r.t. overfitting. The minimization problem of the Eq. (4) can be solved with Lagrange Multipliers by Kuhn-Tucker Theorem, obtaining, after some mathematical steps, the following formulation:

$$\max_\beta \sum_{i=1}^{\ell} y_i\beta_i - \epsilon \sum_{i=1}^{\ell} |\beta_i| - \frac{1}{2}\sum_{i=1}^{\ell}\sum_{j=1}^{\ell} \beta_i\beta_j(\boldsymbol{x}_i \cdot \boldsymbol{x}_j + \frac{1}{C}\delta_{ij}) \qquad subject\ to\ \sum_{i=1}^{\ell} \beta_i = 0. \tag{5}$$

The algorithm can be empowered using the *kernel trick* [14] namely, replacing the dot product $(\boldsymbol{x}_i \cdot \boldsymbol{x}_j)$ in Eq. (5) with $K(x_i, \boldsymbol{x}_j)$, where $K(\cdot)$ is a proper Mercer Kernel [12], yielding in this way the final form:

$$\max_\beta \sum_{i=1}^{\ell} y_i\beta_i - \epsilon \sum_{i=1}^{\ell} |\beta_i| - \frac{1}{2}\sum_{i=1}^{\ell}\sum_{j=1}^{\ell} \beta_i\beta_j(K(\boldsymbol{x}_i, \boldsymbol{x}_j) + \frac{1}{C}\delta_{ij}) \qquad subject\ to\ \sum_{i=1}^{\ell} \beta_i = 0. \tag{6}$$

---

[1] $\mathcal{I}(u)$ is 1 if the condition $u$ is fulfilled, 0 otherwise.
[2] $|u|_\epsilon^2$ is $u$ if $u \geq \epsilon$, 0 otherwise.

The vectors, whose respective multipliers $\beta_i$ are non-null, are called *support vectors*, justifying the name of the regression algorithm. SVM for Regression implements the following regressor $F(\boldsymbol{x}) = \sum_{i=1}^{\ell} \beta_i K(x_i, \boldsymbol{x}) + b$ .

Examples of Mercer kernels, used in SVM for Regression, are the so-called *Linear* $K(x_i, \boldsymbol{x}_j) = (\boldsymbol{x}_i \cdot \boldsymbol{x}_j)$, and *Gaussian* $G(x_i, \boldsymbol{x}_j) = \exp(-\frac{\|\boldsymbol{x}-\boldsymbol{y}\|^2}{\sigma^2})$, with $\sigma \in \mathbb{R}$.

In this work, SVM for Regression trials have been performed using SVMLight [15] software package.

# 4  Iterated Prediction and Imputation Algorithm

Both algorithms for model order and skeleton estimation of time series require that in time series there are no missing data. Methods that deal with missing data can be divided in two big families [16]: Methods ignoring missing data and methods with imputation. The former deletes the missing data, and this cannot be applied to a time series since, so doing it would be destroyed the temporal dependence among data in the time series. The latter consists in making a data imputation namely, in making the replacement of each missing data with a known data (*imputed data*), fixed by any method. The strategy mentioned above seems to be the only strategy that can be applied to a time series with missing data, without breaking up the dependence among data themselves.

Having said that, we pass to describe the *Iterated Prediction and Imputation* (IPI) algorithm that allows making a prediction in a time series with missing data. IPI algorithm uses an *EM*-like strategy. In the initialization step, a first imputation of missing data is carried out. Then, at each iteration, the following actions are performed:

1. The model order of the time series is computed, by Grassberger-Procaccia (GP) algorithm.
2. The prediction by SVM for Regression (SVMR) is performed.
3. If the Test Error decreases w.r.t. the one measured in the previous iteration, missing data imputations are updated using the prediction by SVMR and a further iteration restarts, otherwise the loop terminates, returning the predicted time series and the Test Error computed in the previous stage.

The pseudocode of the IPI algorithm is reported below.

**INPUT:** The time series with missing data $x(t)$ with $t = 1, \ldots, \ell$.
**OUTPUT:** The predicted time series $x^P(t)$ with $t = 1, \ldots, \ell$.
1. Divide Time Series in Training and Test Sets paying attention that all missing data are in Training Set.
2. Initialize Missing Data in Training Set.
3. *iteration* $\leftarrow 0$
4. *TestSet_Error*[*iteration*] $\leftarrow +\infty$
5. **Do**
6.      *iteration* $\leftarrow$ *iteration* $+ 1$
7.      Compute *Model_Order*[*iteration*] by GP algorithm

8.      Train SVMR on Training Set and Compute $TestSet\_Error[iteration]$
9.      Impute Missing Data by Training SVMR on Training Set
10. **While** $TestSet\_Error[iteration] < TestSet\_Error[iteration - 1]$
11. **Return** the predicted time series $x^P(t)$ at $iteration - 1$.

It has been underlined that, unlike EM algorithm [17], IPI algorithm does not guarantee that a local minimum of the test error is reached.

## 5    Experimental Results

The proposed algorithm has been validated on the environmental time series M356 that hourly measures the concentration of Ozone, expressed in $\mu g/m^3$, in an European atmospheric station, for one year. The time series has about 10% missing data. The time series was divided in training and test sets. The former formed by 28 weeks, the latter formed by 24 weeks. All of the missing data were concentrated in the training set. The skeleton of the time series was estimated by SVM for Regression (SVMR), using a Linear Kernel. The SVMR parameters, i.e. $\epsilon, C$, were estimated by cross-validation [3,4]. The results, each for a single week, are shown in Table 1. In Fig. 1, it is reported the prediction for a full week.

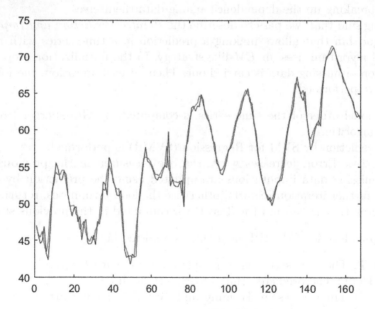

**Fig. 1.** Prediction of M356 Time Series in $29^{th}$ week. The predicted and the target values are in blue and in red, respectively. (Color figure online)

Finally, in order to prove the determinism of the time series, a *Scheinkman-Le Baron test* [18] was applied to the predicted time series. All the sample of time series were permuted randomly, destroying, in this way, any time dependencies

**Table 1.** Results on test set of M356 time series.

| Week | Average absolute error in $\mu g/m^3$ | Average percentage error |
|------|------|------|
| $2^{nd}$ | 0.273 | 0.47% |
| $4^{th}$ | 0.240 | 0.39% |
| $5^{th}$ | 0.278 | 0.50% |
| $7^{th}$ | 0.367 | 0.47% |
| $9^{th}$ | 0.295 | 0.48% |
| $11^{th}$ | 0.358 | 0.47% |
| $14^{th}$ | 0.350 | 0.44% |
| $17^{th}$ | 0.382 | 0.41% |
| $18^{th}$ | 0.491 | 0.45% |
| $20^{th}$ | 0.452 | 0.43% |
| $22^{nd}$ | 0.461 | 0.30% |
| $23^{rd}$ | 0.367 | 0.51% |
| $26^{th}$ | 0.376 | 0.44% |
| $27^{th}$ | 0.677 | 0.44% |
| $29^{th}$ | 0.780 | 0.50% |
| $34^{th}$ | 0.370 | 0.44% |
| $35^{th}$ | 0.335 | 0.41% |
| $37^{th}$ | 0.315 | 0.42% |
| $38^{th}$ | 0.419 | 0.45% |
| $40^{th}$ | 0.288 | 0.49% |
| $44^{th}$ | 0.275 | 0.50% |
| $45^{th}$ | 0.294 | 0.45% |
| $47^{th}$ | 0.300 | 0.40% |
| $48^{th}$ | 0.269 | 0.42% |
| All weeks | 0.375 | 0.45% |

in the time series. After that, the Correlation Dimension was measured again and, as shown in Table 2, a much higher value was obtained, thus confirming what expected by the Scheinkman-Le Baron test.

**Table 2.** Results of Scheinkman-Le Baron test.

|  | Correlation dimension |
|------|------|
| M356 | 3.60 |
| M356 permuted randomly | 24.5 |

# 6    Conclusions

In this paper, it is presented the IPI algorithm that makes prediction in time series affected by missing data. The algorithm uses Dynamics Reconstruction methods and regression SVM for computing the model order and estimating the skeleton of time series, respectively. Tests of the algorithm on a time series with missing data, expressing the concentration of Ozone in a European site, shows an average percentage prediction error of 0.45% on the test set.

In the next future, we plan to strengthen the experimental validation of IPI algorithm. Then, regarding the estimation of the skeleton of time series, we will investigate the possible replacement of SVM for Regression with *Gaussian Processes* [19] or *HMMs* [20].

**Acknowledgements.** Vincenzo Capone developed part of the work as final dissertation for B. Sc. in Computer Science, under supervision of F. Camastra, at University Parthenope of Naples.

# References

1. Chianese, E., Camastra, F., Ciaramella, A., Landi, T., Staiano, A., Riccio, A.: Spatio-temporal learning in predicting ambient particulate matter concentration by multi-layer perceptron. Ecol. Inf. **49**, 54–61 (2019)
2. Hirshberg, D., Merhav, N.: Robust methods for model order estimation. IEEE Trans. Signal Process. **44**, 620–628 (1996)
3. Duda, R., Hart, P., Stork, D.: Pattern Classification. Wiley, New York (2001)
4. The Elements of Statistical Learning. SSS. Springer, New York (2009). https://doi.org/10.1007/978-0-387-84858-7_9
5. Camastra, F., Filippone, M.: A comparative evaluation of nonlinear dynamics methods for time series prediction. Neural Comput. Appl. **18**, 1021–1029 (2009)
6. Mañé, R.: On the dimension of the compact invariant sets of certain non-linear maps. In: Rand, D., Young, L.-S. (eds.) Dynamical Systems and Turbulence, Warwick 1980. LNM, vol. 898, pp. 230–242. Springer, Heidelberg (1981). https://doi.org/10.1007/BFb0091916
7. Takens, F.: Detecting strange attractor in turbolence. In: Dynamical Systems and Turbolence, Warwick, pp. 366–381. MIT Press (1981)
8. Camastra, F., Staiano, A.: Intrinsic dimension estimation: advances and open problems. Inf. Sci. **328**, 26–41 (2016)
9. Grassberger, P., Procaccia, I.: Measuring the strangeness of strange attractors. Physica D **9**, 189–208 (1983)
10. Camastra, F., Esposito, F., Staiano, A.: Linear SVM-based recognition of elementary juggling movements using correlation dimension of Euler angles of a single arm. Neural Comput. Appl. **26**, 1005–1013 (2018)
11. Trucco, E., Verri, A.: Introductory Techniques for 3-D Computer Vision. Prentice Hall, Englewood Cliffs (1998)
12. Vapnik, V.: Statistical Learning Theory. Wiley, New York (1998)
13. Cristianini, N., Shawe-Taylor, J.: An Introduction to Support Vector Machines. Cambridge University Press, Cambridge (2000)
14. Schölkopf, B., Smola, A.: Learning with Kernels. MIT Press, Cambridge (2002)

15. Joachim, T.: Making large-scale SVM learning practical. In: Advances in Kernel Methods-Support Vector Learning, pp. 169–184. MIT Press (1999)
16. Allison, P.: Missing Data. Sage Publications, Thousand Oaks (2002)
17. Dempster, A., Laird, N., Rubin, D.: Maximum likelihood from incomplete data via the EM algorithm. J. R. Stat. Soc. **39**(1), 1–38 (1977)
18. Scheinkman, J., Le Baron, B.: Nonlinear dynamics and stock returns. J. Bus. **62**, 311–337 (1989)
19. Williams, C., Rasmussen, C.: Gaussian Processes for Machine Learning. MIT Press, Cambridge (2006)
20. Camastra, F., Vinciarelli, A.: Markovian models for sequential data. In: Advanced Information and Knowledge Processing, pp. 294–340. MIT Press (2015)

# Semi-Supervised Learning for Grain Size Distribution Interpolation

Konstantin Kobs$^{(\boxtimes)}$, Christian Schäfer, Michael Steininger, Anna Krause,
Roland Baumhauer, Heiko Paeth, and Andreas Hotho

University of Würzburg, Würzburg, Germany
{kobs,steininger,anna.krause,hotho}@informatik.uni-wuerzburg.de,
{christian.d.schaefer,baumhauer,heiko.paeth}@uni-wuerzburg.de

**Abstract.** High-resolution grain size distribution maps for geographical
regions are used to model soil-hydrological processes that can be used
in climate models. However, measurements are expensive or impossible,
which is why interpolation methods are used to fill the gaps between
known samples. Common interpolation methods can handle such tasks
with few data points since they make strong modeling assumptions
regarding soil properties and environmental factors. Neural networks
potentially achieve better results as they do not rely on these assumptions and approximate non-linear relationships from data. However, their
performance is often severely limited for tasks like grain size distribution
interpolation due to their requirement for many training examples. Semi-
supervised learning may improve their performance on this task by taking
widely available unlabeled auxiliary data (e.g. altitude) into account.

We propose a novel semi-supervised training strategy for spatial interpolation tasks that pre-trains a neural network on weak labels obtained
by methods with stronger assumptions and then fine-tunes the network
on the small labeled dataset. In our research area, our proposed strategy
improves the performance of a supervised neural network and outperforms other commonly used interpolation methods.

**Keywords:** Spatial interpolation · Semi-supervised learning · Neural
networks

## 1 Introduction

The composition of different grain sizes in the soil affects many hydrological
processes such as groundwater recharge, infiltration rates or surface flow. For
example, soils with dominating clay fractions (grain size $\leq 0.002\,\mathrm{mm}$) retain
water better than sandy soils ($0.063\,\mathrm{mm} <$ grain size $\leq 2.0\,\mathrm{mm}$). Given accurate
grain size distribution maps, it is possible to estimate hydrological parameters for
environmental modelling purposes, e.g. regional climate models. Since sampling
is expensive or even impossible due to inaccessible terrain, spatial interpolation
methods are used to estimate grain size distributions for unknown locations.

© Springer Nature Switzerland AG 2021
A. Del Bimbo et al. (Eds.): ICPR 2020 Workshops, LNCS 12666, pp. 34–44, 2021.
https://doi.org/10.1007/978-3-030-68780-9_4

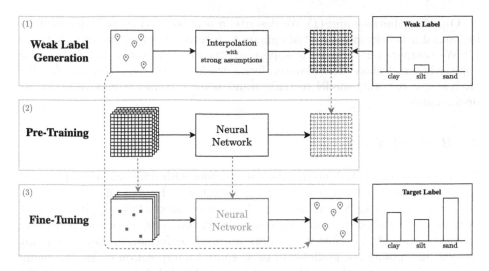

**Fig. 1.** In our proposed semi-supervised training method, (1) a spatial interpolation method with strong assumptions is trained on the labeled dataset. (2) The neural network is pre-trained on weak labels obtained by applying the interpolation method to the unlabeled data. The network gets locations and auxiliary data as inputs. (3) It is then fine-tuned on the labeled dataset.

A model for grain size distribution interpolation has the following requirements: (1) The model input is a location with (potentially) additional auxiliary data (e.g. altitude). (2) The model outputs distributions across the grain size classes (clay, silt, sand) for each unknown location. (3) The model works with few labeled data points, since soil samples are rare.

Distance based interpolation methods such as k Nearest Neighbors or Inverse Distance Weighting can output distributions and are applicable to small labeled datasets due to their strong assumptions. However, they do not take auxiliary data into account which can benefit performance [11,17]. Neural networks can learn non-linear relationships from data, are able to incorporate additional auxiliary inputs, and are able to output distributions across grain size classes. However, they usually need many labeled training data points [15]. The idea of semi-supervised learning utilizes large unlabeled datasets to support network training [8]. In recent years, most methods for semi-supervised learning were designed for image classification, which are not applicable to our setting.

Therefore, in this paper, we bring semi-supervised learning specifically to the task of grain size distribution interpolation for spatial inputs. We propose a training strategy that makes use of weak labels produced by an interpolation method with stronger modeling assumptions. Figure 1 gives a schematic overview of our proposed three-step process. In our experiments for the region of Lower Franconia, we show that our approach improves the performance of a supervised neural network and outperforms other common interpolation methods. Furthermore, we analyze the effects of the proposed training strategy on model performance.

Our contributions are: (1) We describe a semi-supervised training strategy for neural networks in the spatial domain to interpolate grain size distributions. (2) We compare our strategy to supervised training and common interpolation approaches and show that it outperforms them in our research area. (3) We analyze the resulting model to understand what factors are important for its performance.

## 2   Related Work

There are various spatial interpolation techniques with different properties used in environmental sciences, e.g. k Nearest Neighbors, Inverse Distance Weighting, or Kriging [16]. Neural networks have been successfully applied in such tasks since they allow auxiliary data as input features and can model non-linear relationships [5,20,23]. However, to obtain robust performance, they need many labeled data points not available in most spatial interpolation tasks [15]. Semi-supervised training promotes the use of large unlabeled datasets to support the training of neural networks with few labeled data points [8]. For image classification, which is the most popular semi-supervised learning task, domain-specific strategies such as image augmentation have been proposed, which are not trivial to apply in our setting. Classification specific approaches such as using the softmax output of the network as confidence for a weak label [26] are not directly applicable to our task, since our desired output is a distribution and not a class.

For our semi-supervised training strategy, we adapt so-called "distant supervision" from other domains [10,14] by training the network on weak labels. Obtaining weak labels from more traditional interpolation methods and fine-tuning the network on labeled data afterwards is a new approach in this area.

## 3   Research Area and Dataset

In this section, we describe the research area and the dataset we use for the interpolation task. Inputs to the interpolation models are the *latitude*, *longitude*, and multiple features from different auxiliary data sources that we suspect to have an influence on or are influenced by the grain size distribution. While only 315 locations have a target grain size distribution, the auxiliary data is widely available in a fine grid of 25 m × 25 m cells (overall 11 952 963 grid cells).

The research area is Lower Franconia, northern Bavaria, Germany. It covers 8530 km and falls within 49.482°N to 50.566°N and 8.978°E to 10.881°E. The topography of this region is characterized by alluvial zones with surrounding low mountain ranging from 96 m to 927 m in altitude.

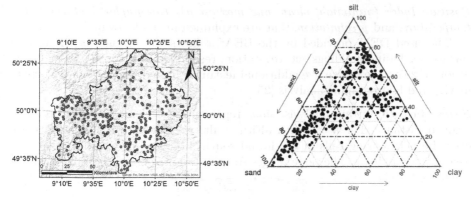

(a) Labeled data point locations. Map tiles by ESRI, USGS, NOAA, data by BEA.

(b) Distribution of target grain size distributions.

**Fig. 2.** Map showing labeled locations and distribution of the labels.

## 3.1   Target Variable: Grain Size Distribution

Soils are compositions of grain sizes. To get soil conditions for the research area, we use a soil profile database of the Bavarian Environment Agency (BEA)[1]. The database covers detailed information on in-depth grain size distribution on 431 sites in Lower Franconia. The sampling took place in-between 1989 and 2017 and exposes grain size distributions of the fine earth fraction per soil-horizon through combined sieve and pipette analysis [12]. The method of sampling varies between drill cores and complete profile excavations.

While each observed location lists multiple layers, we limit the interpolation task to two dimensions by only using soil information from 14 cm–15 cm as most recorded layers span across this range. This common approach [6] results in 315 labeled locations, shown in Fig. 2a.

Given the detailed grain sizes, we represent each location as a composition of three grain size classes [1]: **clay** (grain size $\leq 0.002\,\mathrm{mm}$), **silt** ($0.002\,\mathrm{mm} <$ grain size $\leq 0.063\,\mathrm{mm}$), and **sand** ($0.063\,\mathrm{mm} <$ grain size $\leq 2.0\,\mathrm{mm}$). Each label is a three dimensional distribution vector, e.g. 20 % clay, 50 % silt, and 30 % sand. The label distribution is shown in Fig. 2b. The task is to estimate this distribution for a location given other locations and auxiliary data.

## 3.2   Auxiliary Data

While there are only 315 labeled data points, auxiliary data is available for all locations in Lower Franconia (11 952 963 grid cells). For this work, we use a Digital Elevation Model (DEM) and meteorological data to generate ten features for each grid cell: *latitude*, *longitude*, *altitude*, *slope*, *Multi-Scale Topographic*

---

[1] Unpublished data; reference: https://www.lfu.bayern.de/umweltdaten/.

*Position Index (minimum, mean, and maximum)*, *Topographic Wetness Index*, *temperature*, and *precipitation*, that are explained in the following.

The used DEM provided by the BEA[2] reflects the *altitude* of the terrain surface, excluding buildings and vegetation, resampled to our grid's spatial resolution of 25 m. We derive five additional features through topographic, morphometric and hydrographic analysis [25].

**Slope.** In basic terrain analysis, *slope* represents the change in elevation over a given distance. For a cell with altitude alt, we calculate the mean altitude over the neighboring cells in north and south direction $\overline{\mathrm{alt}}_{\mathrm{NS}}$ and in west and east direction $\overline{\mathrm{alt}}_{\mathrm{WE}}$. The slope ranges from 0° (a horizontal plane) to 90° and is calculated using $\mathrm{slope} = \dfrac{180}{\pi \cdot \sqrt{\left(\overline{\mathrm{alt}}_{\mathrm{NS}} - \mathrm{alt}\right)^2 + \left(\overline{\mathrm{alt}}_{\mathrm{WE}} - \mathrm{alt}\right)^2}}$.

**Multi-scale Topographic Position Index.** The Topographic Position Index (TPI) [24] is defined as the altitude difference between a location of interest and the mean altitude of a square area around it, giving values that indicate local ridges and valleys. We obtain TPIs on multiple scales by altering the side length of the square from 3 grid cells (75 m) to 41 grid cells (1025 m) in steps of two cells, having the current location in the square's center. From the resulting 19 TPIs, we take the *minimum*, *mean*, and *maximum* as features. They describe the morphology of our study area at different scales as numeric factors.

**Topographic Wetness Index.** To represent spatial variations of soil moisture content and soil water drainage, a *terrain-based wetness index (TWI)* is computed [4]. The index is high for locations where water normally collects due to the topographic setting. It is calculated as a tangent function of the cell's slope angle w.r.t. the cell's area (625 m$^2$): $\mathrm{TWI} = \ln\left(\dfrac{625}{\tan(\mathrm{slope})}\right)$.

**Meteorological Data.** In addition to terrain based features described above, we also obtain meteorological data provided by the German Meteorological Service (DWD). The data reflects the 30-year (1971–2000) means of the monthly averaged mean daily air *temperature* 2 m above the ground and *precipitation*.[3] The grid-based data was obtained by accurate interpolation methods for temperature and precipitation at a resolution of 1 km$^2$ [19] and resampled to the target grid size of 25 m using nearest neighbor interpolation.

## 4 Methodology

Given the data described above, we now have a large dataset of unlabeled data as well as a small labeled dataset. A neural network should now learn to estimate the grain size distribution of a location based on the ten input features. To make use of the large unlabeled dataset, we propose a three step semi-supervised training strategy that pre-trains the neural network on weak labels created by an interpolation method with stronger assumptions:

---

[2] https://geodatenonline.bayern.de/geodatenonline/seiten/dgm_info.

[3] https://opendata.dwd.de/climate_environment/CDC/grids_germany/multi_annual/ *air_temperature_mean* and *precipitation*.

**1. Weak Label Generation.** We apply a common interpolation method such as Inverse Distance Weighting (IDW) on the small labeled dataset. Note that these methods usually do not take auxiliary data into account. Due to the strong modeling assumptions of such algorithms, they are able to work with small datasets. The trained model then estimates the target labels for the large unlabeled dataset, which are used as weak labels in the next step.

**2. Pre-training.** The neural network is pre-trained using the large amount of available weakly labeled data, thus being exposed to the property assumptions of the weak label generator. This way, the network learns representations from all input features, including the auxiliary data, and is guided to create more realistic outputs. Since interpolation methods such as IDW represent the location information as distances, the network has to learn from different features, as we will show in Sect. 6.1. Calculating the euclidean distance from locations is hard for the network, therefore it tries to find other correlations as well.

**3. Fine-tuning.** The pre-trained network is fine-tuned on the labeled dataset. This reinforces or weakens some correlations the network has found. For fine-tuning, a smaller learning rate is used in order to keep the previously trained weights intact. The resulting model can then be used on all locations.

## 5   Experiments

Now, we compare our self-supervised training strategy to the traditional supervised method and other common interpolation methods on the grain size distribution task. Note that not all methods can output distributions, so we will only apply methods that are able to handle this task-specific output type.

### 5.1   Methods

**Mean.** Always predicts the mean of all training examples. As the average of multiple distributions is also a distribution, the prediction is valid.

**k Nearest Neighbors (kNN).** Calculates the average label of the nearest $k$ training locations [2]. We set $k = 3$ based on a parameter search on validation data for $k \in \{1, \ldots, 10\}$.

**Inverse Distance Weighting (IDW).** Same as kNN, but the average is inversely weighted based on the distance to a labeled location [22]. A parameter search for $k \in \{1, \ldots, 10\}$ results in $k = 7$.

**Multilayer Perceptron (MLP).** Trains a Multilayer Perceptron on the labeled dataset in a supervised learning setting. The ten-dimensional input is normalized to zero mean and unit variance. It is then fed through three hidden layers with 256 neurons each with ReLU activation functions [9] in a batch of size 1024. The three-dimensional output is then converted to a probability distribution by applying the softmax activation function. These hyperparameters have been

**Table 1.** Test results (mean ± standard deviation) for each model. Best values are written in bold.

|  | MAE | MSE | JSD |
|---|---|---|---|
| **Mean** | 0.5210 ± 0:0384 | 0.1337 ± 0.0183 | 0.0549 ± 0.0076 |
| **kNN** | 0.4267 ± 0.0412 | 0.1011 ± 0.0223 | 0.0398 ± 0.0090 |
| **IDW** | 0.4188 ± 0.0417 | 0.0954 ± 0.0225 | 0.0381 ± 0.0090 |
| **MLP** | 0.4361 ± 0.0552 | 0.1068 ± 0.0251 | 0.0426 ± 0.0088 |
| **SemiMLP** (after pre-training) | 0.4781 ± 0.0577 | 0.1296 ± 0.0283 | 0.0497 ± 0.0099 |
| **SemiMLP** (after fine-tuning) | **0.4078 ± 0.0445** | **0.0952 ± 0.0195** | **0.0377 ± 0.0077** |

found on validation data. The standard cross entropy loss function is used that allows distributions as targets. The network is optimized with Adam [13] and a learning rate of $10^{-1}$ for at most 1000 epochs. Early stopping [18] stops the training if the validation loss does not improve at least $10^{-5}$ for ten epochs.

*Semi-supervised MLP (SemiMLP).* We apply our semi-supervised training strategy to the same MLP architecture as above. We generate weak labels using the IDW baseline with $k = 7$ as it achieved the best baseline validation results. We train the network with learning rates $10^{-1}$ and $10^{-3}$ for pre-training and fine-tuning, respectively.

### 5.2 Evaluation

To evaluate the methods described above, we perform a ten-fold cross-validation (i.e. 31 or 32 examples per fold) using the labeled dataset. We average over 50 repetitions to account for the random initialization of the neural networks. Three metrics are used for evaluation: **Mean Absolute Error (MAE)**, **Mean Squared Error (MSE)**, and **Jensen-Shannon Divergence (JSD)**. While MAE and MSE compute the mean (absolute and squared) deviation from the correct values, JSD is specifically designed to measure the difference between two distributions [7]. Note that MAE and MSE sum the errors up for an example before averaging over all examples.

## 6    Results

Table 1 shows the test results for all models. The model with our training strategy (SemiMLP) yields the best test results. While the supervised MLP performs worse than kNN, the fine-tuned SemiMLP even improves the performance of the IDW baseline. In fact, a Wilcoxon signed rank test ($\alpha = 0.01$) on the MSE indicates that the improvement w.r.t. IDW is significant. We suspect that the network's improvement comes from having direct access to locations as well as auxiliary data that it uses during training, while IDW only relies on distances between locations as inputs.

## 6.1   Analysis

***Pre-training Matters***. For our experiments, we altered the MLP baseline by adding the pre-training step to obtain SemiMLP, while the architecture and preprocessing were fixed. Thus, SemiMLP's better performance compared to MLP (cf. Table 1) shows that pre-training has a positive effect on SemiMLP. Pre-training the network seems to build better representations for the downstream task than random initialization.

***Fine-tuning Matters***. While it helps, pre-training alone does not give superior performance. Table 1 shows that only pre-training on weak labels gives worse performance than most baselines and the supervised MLP. This indicates that the network is not able to imitate the IDW baseline, which generated the weak labels. This may be due to IDW using distances between new and labeled locations to assess its predictions. SemiMLP does not get distance information as input and is not able to directly access the labeled dataset. Thus, it learns a surrogate function that fits the training data but will not exactly match IDW's output for new data points. Also, SemiMLP gets more features than IDW, increasing the chance that the network exploits other correlations to predict the output. After the fine-tuning step, the method is superior to all baselines.

***Auxiliary Data Matters***. The features that may be influenced by or influence the target variable also have an effect on the performance. To investigate this, we apply the permutation importance for feature evaluation method [3] that permutes the values of a feature to see how much the predictive quality of the trained model changes. The more important a feature is, the higher the drop in performance if its input is altered. We average the features' importances for each test fold over ten different permutations to get more robust results.

Figure 3 shows the resulting feature importances. Besides location, the features temperature, precipitation, and altitude have the largest influence. According to previous research, soil is formed by the alteration of present bedrock under the influence of *climate, relief, organisms,* and *human activity* over time [21]. Since we do not provide features describing organisms and human activity, the model focuses on climatic (30-year means of temperature and precipitation) and relief-based (altitude) influences. While we expected other relief-based features such as TPI or TWI to be more important for the model, altitude and location seem to be descriptive enough.

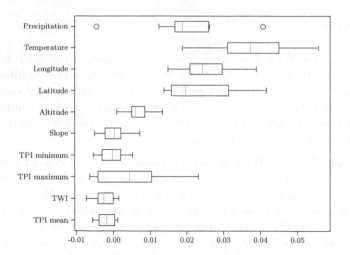

**Fig. 3.** Drop in MAE performance when the feature column was permuted.

# 7 Discussion

Neural networks make no modeling assumptions for the interpolation task. Compared to common interpolation methods, the network can model non-linear relationships in the data and can utilize any kind of auxiliary data. Our method circumvents the necessity of large training datasets by guiding the network towards more realistic outputs using weak labels before fine-tuning on few real labels. It is very easy to replace the weak label generator with a potentially better interpolation method. The required pre-training of the network on weakly labeled data takes extensively longer. However, depending on the neural network architecture, input data, and size of the research area, inference can be faster than other approaches, as we can compute outputs in batches on specialized hardware without any distance calculations.

As stated in Sect. 3, we restrict this work to the two-dimensional case of grain size distribution interpolation. While depth information is expected to increase performance, it is not trivial to use it in the weak label generation methods. Labeled locations usually have large distances (hundreds to thousands of meters), while labeled soil layers have very small distances (millimeters to few centimeters). Distance based approaches such as IDW will only take the nearest labeled location into account and average its soil layers as these are overall the closest to the desired location. While this is not resolved, building a model for each depth layer is the simplest approach that we can apply in practice.

# 8 Conclusion

In this paper we have proposed a semi-supervised training method for spatial interpolation tasks. For our grain size distribution task, additional pre-training on weak labels improved the network's performance compared to supervised learning and common interpolation methods. Testing other weak label generators and sampling strategies to optimize pre-training remains future work. Mixing weak labels from methods with different modeling assumptions might enrich the learned representations of the network. Future challenges include adding the depth dimension, allowing the exploitation of soil layer relations. Further, we will evaluate the interpolated map in a soil-hydrological simulation model.

**Acknowledgements.** This research was conducted in the BigData@Geo project supported by the European Regional Development Fund (ERDF).

# References

1. Ad-hoc-AG Boden: Bodenkundliche Kartieranleitung. Schweizerbart, 5 edn. (2005)
2. Altman, N.S.: An Introduction to kernel and nearest-neighbor nonparametric regression. Am. Stat. **46**(3) (1992)
3. Breiman, L.: Random forests. Mach. Learn. **45**(1) (2001)
4. Böhner, J., Selige, T.: Spatial prediction of soil attributes using terrain analysis and climate regionalization. Gottinger Geographische Abhandlungen **115** (2002)
5. Dai, F., Zhou, Q., Lv, Z., Wang, X., Liu, G.: Spatial prediction of soil organic matter content integrating artificial neural network and ordinary kriging in Tibetan Plateau. Ecol. Indicators **45** (2014)
6. Deshmukh, K.K., Aher, S.P.: Particle Size Analysis of Soils and Its Interpolation using GIS Technique from Sangamner Area, vol. 3. Maharashtra, India (2014)
7. Endres, D.M., Schindelin, J.E.: A new metric for probability distributions. IEEE Trans-IT **49**(7) (2003)
8. van Engelen, J.E., Hoos, H.H.: A survey on semi-supervised learning. Mach. Learn. **109**(2), 373–440 (2019). https://doi.org/10.1007/s10994-019-05855-6
9. Glorot, X., Bordes, A., Bengio, Y.: Deep Sparse rectifier neural networks. In: 14th AISTATS (2011)
10. Go, A., Bhayani, R., Huang, L.: Twitter sentiment classification using distant supervision. CS224N project report, Stanford, vol. 1(12) (2009)
11. Hengl, T.: A Practical Guide to Geostatistical Mapping. 2. extended edn. (2009)
12. ISO Central Secretary: Soil quality - determination of particle size distribution in mineral soil material - method by sieving and sedimentation. Technical Report (2009)
13. Kingma, D.P., Ba, J.: Adam: A Method for Stochastic Optimization. arXiv:1412.6980 (2017)
14. Kobs, K., et al.: Emote-controlled: obtaining implicit viewer feedback through emote-based sentiment analysis on comments of popular twitch.tv channels. TSC **3**(2) (2020)
15. LeCun, Y., Bengio, Y., Hinton, G.: Deep learning. Nature **521**(7553) (2015)
16. Li, J., Heap, A.D.: Spatial interpolation methods applied in the environmental sciences: a review. Environ. Model. Softw. **53** (2014)

17. Meyer, S.: Climate change impact assessment under data scarcity. Dissertation, LMU München (2016)
18. Orr, G.B., Müller, K.-R. (eds.): Neural Networks: Tricks of the Trade. LNCS, vol. 1524. Springer, Heidelberg (1998). https://doi.org/10.1007/3-540-49430-8
19. Rauthe, M., Steiner, H., Riediger, U., Mazurkiewicz, A., Gratzki, A.: A central European precipitation climatology part i: Generation and validation of a high-resolution gridded daily data set (hyras). Meteorologische Zeitschrift **22**(3) (2013)
20. Rezaei, K., et al.: Feed forward neural network and interpolation function models to predict the soil and subsurface sediments distribution in Bam. Iran. Acta Geophysica **57**(2) (2009)
21. Semmel, A.: Relief, Gestein. Boden. Wiss, Buchges (1991)
22. Shepard, D.: A two-dimensional interpolation function for irregularly-spaced data. In: 23rd ACM National Conference (1968)
23. Tarasov, D., Buevich, A., Sergeev, A., Shichkin, A.: High variation topsoil pollution forecasting in the Russian Subarctic: Using artificial neural networks combined with residual kriging. Appl. Geochem. **88** (2018)
24. Weiss, A.: Topographic position and landforms analysis. In: Poster presentation, ESRI user Conference, vol. 200, San Diego, CA
25. Wilson, J.P.: Terrain analysis. Wiley (2000)
26. Xie, Q., Luong, M.T., Hovy, E., Le, Q.V.: Self-training with noisy student improves imagenet classification. In: IEEE/CVF CVPR (2020)

# Location-Specific vs Location-Agnostic Machine Learning Metamodels for Predicting Pasture Nitrogen Response Rate

Christos Pylianidis[1]([⊠]) (iD), Val Snow[2] (iD), Dean Holzworth[2,3], Jeremy Bryant[2] (iD),
and Ioannis N. Athanasiadis[1] (iD)

[1] Wageningen University, Wageningen, Netherlands
{christos.pylianidis,ioannis.athanasiadis}@wur.nl
[2] AgResearch, Christchurch, New Zealand
{Val.Snow,Dean.Holzworth,Jeremy.Bryant}@agresearch.co.nz
[3] CSIRO, Brisbane, Australia

**Abstract.** In this work we compare the performance of a location-specific and a location-agnostic machine learning metamodel for crop nitrogen response rate prediction. We conduct a case study for grass-only pasture in several locations in New Zealand. We generate a large dataset of APSIM simulation outputs and train machine learning models based on that data. Initially, we examine how the models perform at the location where the location-specific model was trained. We then perform the *Mann–Whitney U test* to see if the difference in the predictions of the two models (i.e. location-specific and location-agnostic) is significant. We expand this procedure to other locations to investigate the generalization capability of the models. We find that there is no statistically significant difference in the predictions of the two models. This is both interesting and useful because the location-agnostic model generalizes better than the location-specific model which means that it can be applied to virgin sites with similar confidence to experienced sites.

**Keywords:** Machine learning · Process-based simulation · APSIM · Metamodels

## 1 Introduction

Environmental data are growing in an unprecedented way [8]. Many domains of Environmental Research utilize those data and combine them with Machine Learning (ML) techniques [7] to enable understanding. However, there are domains like grassland-based primary production systems where certain areas (e.g. pasture production, nitrogen leaching) have limited, low quality data, making them poor candidates for ML applications. In such areas, dynamic models are deployed to seek causality and make predictions based on first principles but sometimes they need data that is not available.

© Springer Nature Switzerland AG 2021
A. Del Bimbo et al. (Eds.): ICPR 2020 Workshops, LNCS 12666, pp. 45–54, 2021.
https://doi.org/10.1007/978-3-030-68780-9_5

ML has been used in a complementary way with dynamic models to summarize them and capture their embedded knowledge. The resulting ML models are also known as metamodels, surrogate models or emulators. The knowledge summarization is achieved by training ML models using the output of dynamic model simulations. Advantages of this technique include the reduction in need of observation data [1], the use of fewer inputs [10] and faster computation times [13] for large scale systems than the dynamic models. The paradigm of summarizing dynamic models is applied in several disciplines from physics [2] to hydrology [14].

Dynamic model summarization has also been studied in agriculture [11]. Several studies have examined the application of ML surrogate models for sensitivity analysis [4], the performance of different ML algorithms for crop model summarization [12] and the amount of data needed for accurate predictions [12]. In these works, the authors trained ML models in generated datasets to examine how well the models can generalize, using either one or all the available locations, and not testing in other locations. However, the generalization capability of a model over multiple locations does not mean that it performs better than a model specifically trained for that location. Since there are cases where the interest lies in absolute performance or generalizability of the summarization model it would be compelling to investigate how location-specific and location-agnostic models compare in those aspects.

The purpose of this work is to investigate the performance difference of location-specific and location-agnostic ML metamodels using a case study approach. To achieve this goal, we first generate a large dataset across several locations using a crop simulation framework. Second, we aggregate the generated data and train a ML model using all the available locations, and a second ML model using only one location. Next, we test the ML models on a dataset comprised of samples of the latter location. We compare the results using statistical metrics, and examine if they are statistically different using the *Mann–Whitney U test* [9] which has been used for comparing ML models in other works [5]. Finally, we investigate the trade-off between model performance and generalizability by testing the models in the rest of the locations of our dataset.

## 2    Materials and Methods

### 2.1    Case Study, Data Description

A case study was performed to predict the grass-only pasture nitrogen response rate in different locations in New Zealand. The application of nitrogen along with environmental factors such as temperature and time of year greatly affects pasture growth [3] so it is important to know the nitrogen response rate. Our dataset consisted of grass pasture growth simulations performed with the APSIM modeling and simulation framework [6]. A hyperspace of parameters was created and put to the simulator. The simulation parameters for APSIM included daily historical weather data from eight locations in New Zealand and management treatment options which can be seen in Table 1. The cross-product of those parameters was used to create a hyperspace of input combinations for APSIM. The total number of simulations was 1,658,880 which should have yielded 1,382,400 nitrogen response rates. However, the input combinations included application of fertilizer at times when pasture growth was near zero because of dry soil conditions or cold temperatures. These were excluded from the analysis as the calculated N response rate was known to be unreliable. In total there were 1,036,800 response rates available for further analysis. Our target was to predict the 3-month nitrogen response rate – the additional pasture dry matter grown in the three months after fertilizer application over that from a non-fertilizer control divided by the kg of nitrogen in the fertilizer applied. The outputs of APSIM consisted of the nitrogen response rate, biophysical variables related to fertilizer concentration in grass and moisture in soil.

**Table 1.** The simulation parameters of APSIM. The cross-product of those parameters was used to create a hyperspace of input combinations.

|  | Simulation parameters |
|---|---|
| Location | Weather from eight sites spanning the country |
| Soil water | 42 or 77 mm of plant-available water stored to 600 mm deep |
| Soil fertility | Carbon concentration in the top 75 mm of 2, 4, or 6% |
| Irrigation | Irrigated with a centre-pivot or dryland |
| Fertilizer year | All years from 1979 to 2018 |
| Fertilizer month | All months of the year |
| Fertilizer day | 5th, 15th and 25th of the month |
| Fertilizer rate | 0 (control), 20, 40, 60, 80 and 100 kg N /ha |

## 2.2 Data Preprocessing

The generated data were preprocessed to formulate a regression problem where the target variable was the nitrogen response rate and the inputs were the weather, some treatment options regarding the fertilizer and irrigation, and some biophysical variables. The generated data were aggregated from a daily to a simulation basis, to imbue memory to the data. First, the data were split into training and test sets to avoid information leakage during the latter stages of processing. The split happened based on the year, taking one year to the test set every five years and the rest to the training set. The resulting percentage of training and test samples was 80/20%. Second, from the generated daily data only the samples in a window of 28 days before fertilization were kept. This range was selected because grass pasture is known to not be affected by past conditions further than this window provided it is not under- or over-grazed. Also, weather data after the first fertilization was not considered because preliminary work has shown that it is not needed to achieve meaningful results. Third, only the variables related to the weather, simulation parameters, nitrogen response rate and to some of the biophysical variables were preserved which were considered to be likely drivers, based on expert knowledge of the nitrogen response rate. Fourth, the weather and biophysical variables were aggregated using their weekly mean values. Finally, the aforementioned steps were repeated once to form an aggregated dataset containing all the locations, and once for each of the eight locations contained in our dataset. The output of those steps was an aggregated dataset (training set) for the location-specific model, an aggregated dataset (training set) for the location-agnostic model, and an aggregated dataset (test set) for each location.

## 2.3   Machine Learning Pipeline

The aggregated datasets were then passed to the ML stage. In this stage, the training and test data were standardized using the same data transformer to keep the same mean for both transformations. To clarify further, each test set was using the scaler of the location-agnostic model and the location-specific model so that each model can have a version of the test set according to the mean of its training set. Categorical variables were converted to ordinal by substituting them with numbers. Then, hyperparameter optimization was performed to the Random Forest algorithm using gridsearch with 5-fold cross-validation. The gridsearch parameters were $n\_estimators$ {200, 300, 400, 500}, $max\_depth$ {3, 5, 7, 11}, $min\_samples\_split$ {2, 3, 4, 8, 16}, $min\_samples\_leaf$ {1, 2, 4, 8, 16} and $max\_features$ {0.33, sqrt, None}. The out-of-bag score was used for the building of the Random Forest trees. No feature selection was performed because the number of features was small (64) compared to the size of the training datasets (1,044,060 and 130,095 samples for the multiple and single locations correspondingly). After training, the optimized models of the location-agnostic and location-specific models were tested using the test set of location *Waiotu* where the location-specific model was trained. The pipeline of the ML stage is shown in Fig. 1.

## 2.4   Evaluation

The performance of the location-specific and location-agnostic models was first evaluated by comparing error metrics (MAE, RMSE, $R^2$) of their results on the test set. Then, the *Mann–Whitney U test* was performed on the models' results on the test set to see if the differences were significant. The *Mann–Whitney U test* examines if the distributions of the populations of two groups are equal and it was preferred among other statistical tests because first it is non-parametric, second it assumes that the pairs in the samples do not come from the same populations and third that the observations are ordinal, all of which fit our problem. Consequently, error metrics and the *Mann–Whitney U test* were calculated for the rest of the locations to test the models' generalizability.

## 2.5   Implementation

The data preprocessing stage was developed utilizing the Apache Spark framework. The ML models were developed using the *scikit-learn* library in Python. The experiments took place in a Databricks node consisting of 96 cores and 384 GB of RAM to speed up procedures through parallelization.

# 3   Results

The hyperparameter tuning procedure selected the following parameters for both models: *n_estimators* 400, *max_depth* 11, *min_samples_split* 2, *min_samples_leaf* 1, *max_features* 0.33. The results of the ML models on the training and test sets are shown in Fig. 2, along with the distributions of the simulation and the model predictions. We observe that the angle between the identity and regression lines on the test set is smaller for the location-specific model which means that it fits better the location-specific test data. The data points on the test set of the location-agnostic model are more dispersed. Also, we notice that the distributions of the location-specific and location-agnostic model predictions on the test set appear to be similar. The mean and variance of the distributions appear to be close as it can be seen in Table 2.

Regarding the error metrics, in Table 3 we observe the Mean Average Error, Root Mean Square Error and coefficient of determination ($R^2$) for both models on the test set of each location. For the location where the location-specific model was trained (Waiotu), we observe that the location-specific model performs better than the location-agnostic model. For the rest of the locations, the location-agnostic model outperforms the location-specific one.

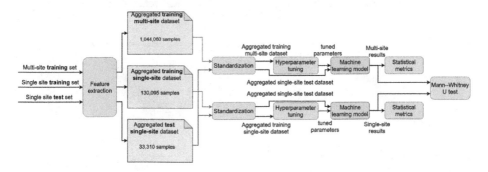

**Fig. 1.** The pipeline for the training and testing of the models on the location where the location-specific model was trained. At the end there is also the evaluation stage. The process starts by taking the training and test datasets from the preprocessing stage. It has to be explicitly noted that hyperparameter tuning was performed only on the training set. More specifically the test set was the same for both models but it was standardized for each model individually to preserve the same mean which was used for each training set.

**Table 2.** The distribution characteristics of the two models for the test set predictions on the location where the location-specific model was trained.

|  | Location-specific | Location-agnostic |
|---|---|---|
| Mean | 18.47 | 18.44 |
| Variance | 44.73 | 40.99 |
| Skewness | 0.11 | 0.18 |
| Kurtosis | −0.90 | −0.82 |

In Table 3 we also observe the results of the *Mann–Whitney U test* for each location. For the location where the location-specific model was trained (*Waiotu*) we see that there is no statistically significant difference between the models. The same applies to the location *Ruakura*.

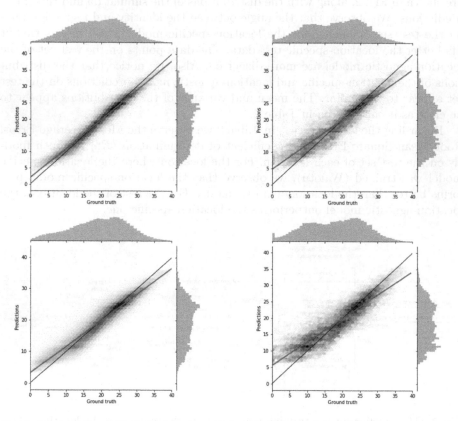

**Fig. 2.** The results of the **location-specific model (top row)** and **location-agnostic model (bottom row)** for the **training (left)** and **test (right)** sets. The test set is common for both models and contains data from the location where the location-specific model was trained (*Waiotu*). On the vertical axes are the predictions of the model and on the horizontal axes the simulated values. On top and right of the plots are the distributions of the simulated and predicted values correspondingly. The black lines are the identity lines. The red lines are the regression of Prediction on Ground truth. Darker spots indicate that more predictions fall on the same area. (Color figure online)

**Table 3.** The error metrics of the location-specific and site agnostic models on the different locations. On the first row are the locations existing in our dataset. *Waiotu* is the location where the site specific model was trained. On the second row are the mean absolute error (MAE), root mean squared error (RMSE) and coefficient of determination ($R^2$), for each model and location. The blue and red colors indicate the models with the highest and lowest performance correspondingly, for each location and error metric. On the third row, statistically significant difference on *Mann–Whitney U test* between the predictions of the two models is denoted with as asterisk.

| | | Waiotu | Ruakura | Wairoa | Marton | Mahana | Kokatahi | Lincoln | Wyndham |
|---|---|---|---|---|---|---|---|---|---|
| Location-specific | MAE | 2.37 | 2.72 | 2.92 | 3.27 | 3.44 | 4.36 | 4.96 | 5.62 |
| | RMSE | 3.19 | 3.62 | 4.03 | 4.41 | 4.2 | 5.81 | 6.63 | 7.29 |
| | $R^2$ | 0.85 | 0.78 | 0.68 | 0.66 | 0.66 | 0.5 | 0.41 | 0.38 |
| Location-agnostic | MAE | 2.71 | 2.13 | 2.71 | 2.06 | 2.29 | 2.56 | 2.88 | 2.31 |
| | RMSE | 3.55 | 2.95 | 3.91 | 2.83 | 3.04 | 3.33 | 4.08 | 3.06 |
| | $R^2$ | 0.81 | 0.85 | 0.7 | 0.86 | 0.82 | 0.83 | 0.78 | 0.89 |
| MannWhitney U test | | | | * | * | * | * | * | * |

# 4  Discussion

The results showed slightly better error metrics for the location-specific model over the location-agnostic model for *Waiotu*. The reason may be that the location-specific model learns the local conditions better since they are only from this location and fewer than those included in the training of the site-agnostic model. For the rest of the locations, the location-agnostic model performs better because it was trained with more data, which also included these locations and as a result, it can generalize better. An interesting finding is that the errors of the location-specific model increase as we move further away from *Waiotu*, as shown in Fig. 3. The locations can be seen in Fig. 4. This finding indicates that the further away a prediction is made from the training location, the higher the error will be for a location-specific model. On the other hand, the location-agnostic model is not affected since it was trained in a larger dataset which included data from those locations.

Another finding was that there was no statistical difference between the predictions of the two models for *Waiotu*. The location-specific model may perform better but it seems that the gain is marginal and is lost when moving to other locations. The second location with no statistical difference between the models' predictions is *Ruakura*. We assume that this happens because *Ruakura* and *Waiotu* are close to each other and as a result, environmental factors do not vary substantially between those locations.

We deduct that there seems to be a trade-off between accuracy and generalization performance. The location-specific model is trained on a smaller dataset and overfits the data. As a result it performs better for *Waiotu* but the location-agnostic model generalizes better. In our opinion, the decision for which model to deploy depends on the use. We emphasize though that the performance difference in this case study is not dramatic for *Waiotu*. On the other hand, the generalization performance is evident especially as we move further away from the location where the location-specific model was trained.

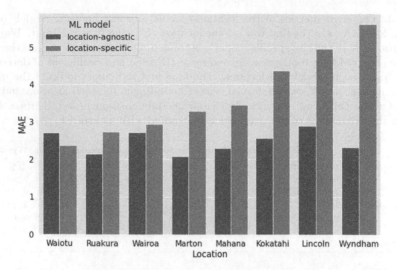

**Fig. 3.** The mean absolute error (MAE) of the location-specific and agnostic models for all the locations in our dataset. On the vertical axis is the error and on the horizontal the locations. The orange and blue colors indicate the results of the location-specific and agnostic models respectively. (Color figure online)

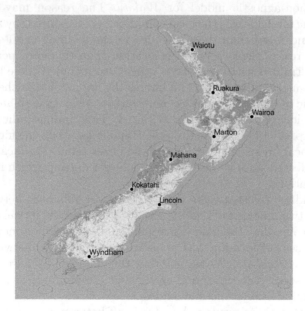

**Fig. 4.** The locations in New Zealand which were included in our dataset. On the top right is *Waiotu* which was used to train the location-specific model. Right next to *Waiotu* is *Ruakura*. The rest of the locations are further away.

## 5    Limitations

A limitation of our study regarding the performance comparison of the ML models is that the location-agnostic model was trained using data from all the locations. As a result we did not test how the models would perform in a location that would be new to both of them.

Another limitation is that the performance of both models was affected by the way we partitioned years into the training/test split. That is due to seasonality in the generated data, which was not taken into account when performing the split.

## 6    Conclusion and Future Work

In this work, we examined the performance difference between a location-specific and a location-agnostic metamodel using error metrics and the *Mann–Whitney U test*. We tested the models in different locations including the location where the location-specific model was trained. We found that the location-specific model performs better for the location where it was trained, although not in a statistically significant way. Also, the error metrics in other locations showed that the location-agnostic model generalizes better.

Future work could include the setup of the methodology in a way to test location-specific models for all the available locations to examine if the results will be the same. Also, a location could be left out of both training sets to allow testing in a new location for both models. Besides, different machine learning algorithms could be deployed and tuned even further. The performance of the models could also be improved by adding complex features and features based on agronomic knowledge.

**Acknowledgements.** This work has been partially supported by the European Union Horizon 2020 Research and Innovation programme (Grant #810775, Dragon); the Wageningen University and Research Investment Programme "Digital Twins" and AgResearch Strategic Science Investment Fund (SSIF) under "Emulation of pasture growth response to nitrogen application".

## References

1. Albert, A.T., Rhoades, A., Ganguly, S., Feldman, D., Jones, A.D., Prabhat, M.: Towards generative deep learning emulators for fast hydroclimate simulations. In: AGU Fall Meeting Abstracts, vol. 2018, pp. IN21C-0723, December 2018
2. Garrido Torres, J.A., Jennings, P.C., Hansen, M.H., Boes, J.R., Bligaard, T.: Low-Scaling algorithm for nudged elastic band calculations using a surrogate machine learning model. Phys. Rev. Lett. **122**(15), 156001 (2019). https://doi.org/10.1103/PhysRevLett.122.156001
3. Gillingham, A.G., Morton, J.D., Gray, M.H.: Pasture responses to phosphorus and nitrogen fertilisers on east coast hill country: 2. Clover and grass production from easy slopes. N. Z. J. Agric. Res. **51**(2), 85–97 (2008). https://doi.org/10.1080/00288230809510438

4. Gladish, D.W., Darnell, R., Thorburn, P.J., Haldankar, B.: Emulated multivariate global sensitivity analysis for complex computer models applied to agricultural simulators. J. Agric. Biol. Environ. Stat. **24**(1), 130–153 (2018). https://doi.org/10.1007/s13253-018-00346-y

5. Goetz, J.N., Brenning, A., Petschko, H., Leopold, P.: Evaluating machine learning and statistical prediction techniques for landslide susceptibility modeling. Comput. Geosci. **81**, 1–11 (2015). https://doi.org/10.1016/j.cageo.2015.04.007

6. Holzworth, D.P., et al.: APSIM - evolution towards a new generation of agricultural systems simulation. Environ. Model. Softw. **62**, 327–350 (2014). https://doi.org/10.1016/j.envsoft.2014.07.009

7. Lima, A.R., Cannon, A.J., Hsieh, W.W.: Nonlinear regression in environmental sciences using extreme learning machines: a comparative evaluation. Environ. Model. Softw. **73**, 175–188 (2015). https://doi.org/10.1016/j.envsoft.2015.08.002

8. Lokers, R., Knapen, R., Janssen, S., van Randen, Y., Jansen, J.: Analysis of big data technologies for use in agro-environmental science. Environ. Model. Softw. **84**, 494–504 (2016). https://doi.org/10.1016/j.envsoft.2016.07.017

9. Mann, H.B., Whitney, D.R.: On a test of whether one of two random variables is stochastically larger than the other. Ann. Math. Stat. **18**(1), 50–60 (1947). https://doi.org/10.1214/aoms/1177730491

10. Ramanantenasoa, M.M.J., Génermont, S., Gilliot, J.M., Bedos, C., Makowski, D.: Meta-modeling methods for estimating ammonia volatilization from nitrogen fertilizer and manure applications. J. Environ. Manage. **236**, 195–205 (2019). https://doi.org/10.1016/j.jenvman.2019.01.066

11. Ramankutty, P., Ryan, M., Lawes, R., Speijers, J., Renton, M.: Statistical emulators of a plant growth simulation model. Clim. Res. **55**(3), 253–265 (2013). https://doi.org/10.3354/cr01138

12. Shahhosseini, M., Martinez-Feria, R.A., Hu, G., Archontoulis, S.V.: Maize yield and nitrate loss prediction with machine learning algorithms. Environ. Res. Lett. **14**(12), p. 124026, December 2019. https://doi.org/10.1088/1748-9326/ab5268

13. Weber, T., Corotan, A., Hutchinson, B., Kravitz, B., Link, R.: Technical note: deep learning for creating surrogate models of precipitation in earth system models. Atmos. Chem. Phys. **20**(4), 2303–2317 (2020). https://doi.org/10.5194/acp-20-2303-2020

14. Zhang, R., Zen, R., Xing, J., Arsa, D.M.S., Saha, A., Bressan, S.: Hydrological process surrogate modelling and simulation with neural networks. In: Lauw, H.W., Wong, R.C.-W., Ntoulas, A., Lim, E.-P., Ng, S.-K., Pan, S.J. (eds.) PAKDD 2020. LNCS (LNAI), vol. 12085, pp. 449–461. Springer, Cham (2020). https://doi.org/10.1007/978-3-030-47436-2_34

# Pattern Classification from Multi-beam Acoustic Data Acquired in Kongsfjorden

Giovanni Giacalone[1], Giosué Lo Bosco[2], Marco Barra[3], Angelo Bonanno[1],
Giuseppa Buscaino[1], Riko Noormets[4], Christopher Nuth[5], Monica Calabrò[1],
Gualtiero Basilone[1], Simona Genovese[1], Ignazio Fontana[1], Salvatore Mazzola[1],
Riccardo Rizzo[6]([✉]) [iD], and Salvatore Aronica[1]

[1] IAS-CNR - National Research Council, Campobello di Mazara, TP, Italy
[2] DMI, University of Palermo, Palermo, Italy
[3] ISMAR-CNR - National Research Council, Napoli, Italy
[4] Department of Arctic Geology, The University Centre in Svalbard (UNIS),
Longyearbyen, Norway
[5] Department of Geosciences, University of Oslo, Oslo, Norway
[6] ICAR-CNR - National Research Council, Palermo, Italy
riccardo.rizzo@icar.cnr.it

**Abstract.** Climate change is causing a structural change in Arctic
ecosystems, decreasing the effectiveness that the polar regions have in
cooling water masses, with inevitable repercussions on the climate and
with an impact on marine biodiversity. The Svalbard islands under study
are an area greatly influenced by Atlantic waters. This area is undergo-
ing changes that are modifying the composition and distribution of the
species present. The aim of this work is to provide a method for the
classification of acoustic patterns acquired in the Kongsfjorden, Svalbard, Arctic Circle using multibeam technology. Therefore the general
objective is the implementation of a methodology useful for identifying the acoustically reflective 3D patterns in the water column near the
Kronebreen glacier. For each pattern identified, characteristic morphological and energetic quantities were extracted. All the information that
describes each of the patterns has been divided into more or less homogeneous groupings by means of a K-means partitioning algorithm. The
results obtained from clustering suggest that the most correct interpretation is that which divides the data set into 3 distinct clusters, relating
to schools of fish. The presence of 3 different schools of fish does not
allow us to state that they are 3 different species. The method developed
and implemented in this work is a good method for discriminating the
patterns present in the water column, obtained from multibeam data, in
restricted contexts similar to those of the study area.

**Keywords:** Echo-survey · Multibeam · k-means

## 1 Introduction

In recent years, sea temperatures have risen with consequences on habitats and
ecosystems. In fact, global climate change affects all levels of the ecological

© Springer Nature Switzerland AG 2021
A. Del Bimbo et al. (Eds.): ICPR 2020 Workshops, LNCS 12666, pp. 55–64, 2021.
https://doi.org/10.1007/978-3-030-68780-9_6

organization. The most visible and worrying climate changes occur at the poles. Especially in the Arctic area, the effects of global warming are more evident, the increase in temperatures has in fact accelerated the phenomenon of melting glaciers, with visible consequences globally. The polar regions play a fundamental role in the evolution of the circulation of ocean currents (the so-called thermohaline circulation) [1] and if these regions will continue to lose ice, the effectiveness of their cooling function of water masses it will decrease with consequences on the climate and on the biodiversity. For these reasons, the world scientific community is collaborating to understand the effects of these changes on the Earth, through the collection of data and the study of changes in the Arctic system. The invasion of alien species in the areas surrounding the Arctic is also an expanding phenomenon and this causes a reduction in the living space of endemic species. The case of Atlantic cod (*Gadus morhua*) competing with the Arctic cod (Polar cod, *Boreogadus saida*) [2] is one such example.

This work is the result of the analysis of the data collected as part of the CalvingSEIS international project (Glacier dynamic ice loss quantified through seismic eyes). A group of researchers belonging to different European institutions are part of this interdisciplinary project (University of Oslo, Norway, National Research Council (CNR), Italy, University in Kiel, Germany, GAMMA Remote Sensing Ag, Switzerland and NORSAR, Norway) in order to study the melting of glaciers, their dynamics and the influence of these phenomena on terrestrial and marine ecosystems within the Arctic circle. The project consists of simultaneous and continuous observation through a network of sensors for monitoring the dynamics of the glaciers of the Kongsfjord, in Svalbard, and in particular of the Kronebreen glacier. One of the instruments used within this project is a multi-beam scientific echosounder by Kongsberg for the reconstruction of the bathymetry of the fjord bottom (Kongsfjorden) never investigated until its first known melting. Along with the data relating to the seabed, during the survey the multi-beam also acquired data from the water column; and the present work focused on this part of the acoustic data. The use of these acoustic instruments allows to estimate the biomass and the spatial distribution of stocks of fish species of commercial or ecological interest, thus representing increasingly tools important for marine resource management [3]. The contribution of this work is the implementation of a methodology useful for identifying any acoustic patterns (or reflective objects) present in the water column, by analyzing the geometries and Energetic values of the various patterns in the three dimensions obtained with ad-hoc programmed algorithms and applying an unsupervised clustering method on the resulting data.

## 2    Background

Svalbard is a group of islands between the parallels 74° N e 81° N and cover an area of 63,000 km². This is a highly frozen Arctic archipelago (57%) with a mix of land and sea glaciers and ice caps [4]. The Kongsfjorden area of is of Svalbard highly scientific interest due to its biodiversity [5]. In the innermost part of the fjord there is one of the largest glaciers of Svalbard which is called Kronebreen. Its front ends directly on the sea, generates an interface from which icebergs are generated in the Kongsfjord and is greatly influenced by Atlantic waters [5]. These complex environmental interactions result in a species composition that includes Atlantic and Arctic species in close association [6]. In the area, besides several species of marine mammals, there are mainly three species of fish found along the water column. The one with the greatest distribution is the species *Boreogadus saida* (polar cod), a fish with an average length between 25 and 40 cm [7]. Among the North Atlantic species in the area, a clear predominance in the shallow waters of the *Gadus morhua* species (Atlantic cod) was highlighted [6]. This species has demersal characteristics with an average length of 100 cm [7]. Finally, another species is very abundant in the area. This is the demersal species *Melanogramus aeglefinus* (haddock) [8]. This species have an average length of 35 cm, but can 112 cm in length [9].

## 3    Materials and Methods

The study for the identification of patterns present in the water column is commonly carried out using acoustic techniques that allow, with a non-invasive methodology, to investigate large portions of the sea in a relatively short time. This methodology exploits the propagation of acoustic waves in the water, obtaining a synoptic display in real time of what is present vertically below the instrument. The data used in this work were acquired from 23 to 26 August 2016 on board the VIKING EXPLORER. The data was acquired using MBES Kongsberg EM2040 instrumentation mounted on a pole on the side of the boat, with an operating frequency of 300 kHz [10]. The sampling plan provided for a coverage of the area under study corresponding to the interface with the glacier front inside the fjord. All the recordings in the survey along the water column were stored on the data server, for post-processing, on binary files.

**Table 1.** Energetic and Morphological characteristics extracted.

| Characteristics of the extracted patterns | | | |
|---|---|---|---|
| Energetic | SV Mean | Morphological | Height |
| | Std Sv | | Width |
| | Sv Max | | Length |
| | Sv Min | | Volume |
| | | | Surface area |
| | | | Roughness |

These files are subsequently converted and ad-hoc algorithms are applied on the data obtained, to identify the patterns present along the water column. For each obtained pattern, Morphological and Energetic characteristics are extracted. Specifically, the characteristics extracted are those presented in the table (see Table 1) divided by category into: Energetic and Morphological characteristics.

It was also necessary to further process the data in order to obtain meaningful clusters. For this purpose, frequency histograms were carried out to determine the distribution of the variables, thus highlighting those characterized by long tails of poorly represented values that could affect the final result (see Fig. 1).

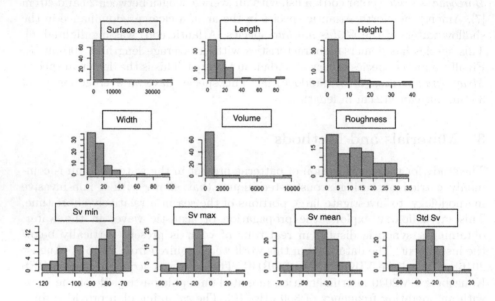

**Fig. 1.** Frequency distribution of the 10 input variables.

To support these graphs, some statistical parameters have been calculated for each of the variables considered. This allowed us to verify which of the variables had an unbalanced frequency distribution to the right or to the left. The parameter to be taken into greater consideration for evaluating the asymmetry of the distributions is the Skewness parameter (or asymmetry index). Another useful index in determining the variables most characterized by unbalanced frequency distributions is the difference between the mean value and the median value, which coincide when the frequency distribution is of the Gaussian type. From the combined analysis of the frequency histograms, the skewness index and the deviation between the mean and median value, it was possible to determine for which variables it was appropriate to adopt a transformation. In the following Table 2 the variables whose distributions strongly deviate from the symmetry are highlighted in bold, showing an unbalance on the left, as also visible in Fig. 1 and a deviation between the average value and median. To reduce the influence of the extreme values due to the long tails of the frequency distributions, a logarithmic transformation was performed on these five variables. This transformation also tends to reduce the effects of outliers.

**Table 2.** Basic statistical parameters.

|  | Min | Q2.5 | Q25 | Median | Q75 | Q97.5 | Max | Mean | Sk |
|---|---|---|---|---|---|---|---|---|---|
| **Surface area** | 15.20 | 33.57 | 120.67 | 336.67 | 1240.61 | 11047.24 | 38150.85 | 1622.19 | **6.17** |
| **Length** | 1.59 | 2.53 | 5.76 | 9.37 | 16.22 | 45.92 | 83.85 | 13.28 | **3.52** |
| **Width** | 1.91 | 2.85 | 6.56 | 10.50 | 18.87 | 41.77 | 90.26 | 14.47 | **3.19** |
| **Height** | 0.81 | 1.01 | 2.68 | 4.55 | 7.09 | 20.08 | 36.44 | 6.20 | **2.47** |
| **Volume** | 0.60 | 1.19 | 8.10 | 39.83 | 180.62 | 2764.08 | 9227.65 | 338.57 | **6.32** |
| Roughness | 3.02 | 3.35 | 4.86 | 12.12 | 17.01 | 28.89 | 32.28 | 12.44 | 0.59 |
| Sv mean | −65.91 | −64.29 | −41.10 | −33.26 | −25.68 | −17.06 | −3.99 | −34.79 | −0.52 |
| Std Sv | −66.02 | −64.53 | −34.64 | −26.66 | −18.26 | −8.44 | 13.60 | −28.18 | −0.54 |
| Sv max | −59.27 | −56.08 | −23.94 | −15.56 | −6.14 | 7.68 | 33.44 | −16.25 | −0.41 |
| Sv min | −117.12 | −114.92 | −97.08 | −83.92 | −75.33 | −67.12 | −65.56 | −86.34 | −0.46 |

Finally, a standardization was applied to make the variables expressed with different units of measurement easily comparable.

## 3.1 Clustering Method

In order to understand the meaning of the data signals a simple clustering method was used. The K-means method is simple enough to obtain a fast result with a little knowledge on the data structure.

Not knowing the actual number of clusters in which to divide the data set, it was decided to carry out various analyses, using a different number of clusters each time. The analyses were carried out considering a number of clusters between 2 10. A number of 10 iterations were performed and the average values obtained were then taken into consideration.

In order to verify the validity of this result, and therefore to evaluate how many clusters to consider to determine the optimal clustering solution, internal validity indices have been applied.

The choice of these indices, among those present within the NClust statistical analysis program, was performed by taking into consideration all the indices used for partition clustering Table 3. The result of this evaluation gave an equal probability for clustering with 2, 3 and 4 clusters. In fact, out of a number of 15 indexes used, 4 of them suggest that the data set can be divided into 2, 3 or 4 clusters, while only one suggests the presence of 7, 8 or 10 clusters Table 4.

In order to further investigate the suitable number of clusters a direct analysis of the variable values in each clustering result was carried on. The box-plots for each of the variables obtained from a clustering with cluster numbers equal to 2, 3 and 4 were examined. From the analysis of the box plots obtained with k = 4 Fig. 2, it is not possible to highlight a clear separation between the variables in the 4 clusters. In most of the box plots there is a pairwise similarity between the various clusters for the Morphological characteristics while there is no clear separation for the Energetic characteristics. Therefore, taking into account these considerations and on the basis of the first analyses carried out

**Table 3.** Indexes used to evaluate the clusters number (Charrad et al.2014).

| | Index name | Optimal cluster value |
|---|---|---|
| 1 | "ch" (Calinski and Harabasz 1974) | Maximum value of the index |
| 2 | "duda" (Duda and Hart 1973) | Smallest number of clusters such that index > criticalValue |
| 3 | "cindex" (Hubert and Levin 1976) | Minimum value of the index |
| 4 | "beale" (Beale 1969) | Number of clusters such that critical value >= alpha |
| 5 | "ptbiserial" (Milligan 1980 1981) | Maximum value of the index |
| 6 | "db" (Davies and Bouldin 1979) | Minimum value of the index |
| 7 | "hartigan" (Hartigan 1975) | Maximum difference between hierarchy levels of the index |
| 8 | "ratkowsky" (Ratkowsky and Lance 1978) | Maximum value of the index |
| 9 | "ball" (Ball and Hall 1965) | Maximum difference between hierarchy levels of the index |
| 10 | "mcclain" (McClain and Rao 1975) | Minimum value of the index |
| 11 | "kl" (Krzanowski and Lai 1988) | Maximum value of the index |
| 12 | "silhouette" (Rousseeuw 1987) | Maximum value of the index |
| 13 | "gap" (Tibshirani et al. 2001) | Smallest number of clusters such that $criticalValue >= 0$ |
| 14 | "sdindex" (Halkidi et al. 2000) | Minimum value of the index |
| 15 | "sdbw" (Halkidi and Vazirgiannis 2001) | Minimum value of the index |

**Table 4.** Determination of number of clusters through statistical indices.

| Cluster | 2 | 3 | 4 | 7 | 8 | 10 |
|---|---|---|---|---|---|---|
| Index numbers | 4 | 4 | 4 | 1 | 1 | 1 |

with a variable number of K between 2 and 10, which highlighted the presence of three main modes, the existence of 4 clusters can be excluded with certainty. From the analysis of the box plots obtained from clustering with k-means equal to 3 Fig. 3, a greater separation of the variables in the 3 classes emerges. However, it can be noted that in terms of Morphological variables, classes 2 and 3 have similarities, while a slight separation is evident for the same classes in the Energetic characteristics. The same procedure was performed with k-means equal to 2 Fig. 4. In this case, there is a clear separation between the classes in all Morphological variables considered and in relation to the minimum Sv variable.

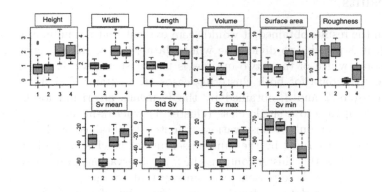

**Fig. 2.** Box-plots obtained from a clustering by k-means equal to 4.

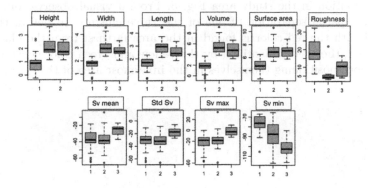

**Fig. 3.** Box-plot obtained from a clustering by k-means equal to 3.

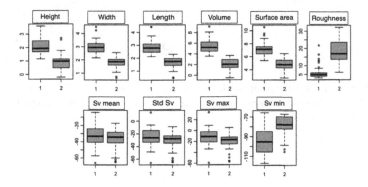

**Fig. 4.** Box-plot obtained from a clustering by k-means equal to 2.

## 4   Results

Based on the results obtained, it would seem evident that the number of clusters in which it is possible to divide the whole data-set is certainly between 2 and 3. To choose which of these two options is the most correct, it was decided to verify how the data for both clustering cases (K = 2 and K = 3). The result is that clusters 2 and 3, obtained by the K-means algorithm for k = 3, are actually grouped into a single class (cluster 1) when k-means is applied with k = 2, except for only 4 observations Cluster 1, obtained with k-means for k = 3, is instead formed by the same observations as cluster 2, obtained from k-means for k = 2; this cluster contains the four observations previously excluded from cluster 1. For these reasons, we can say that the number of clusters that best represents the data-set from a numerical point of view is 3, but from a biological point of view the division into three cluster may not identify three distinct species. To highlight any differences/similarities between the clusters, a spatial representation of the various patterns was prepared, in order to highlight their distribution in the study area Fig. 5. From a visual observation, we can see a clear spatial separation of one of the three clusters. In detail, the class identified with the red color is found in the area farthest from the glacier. On the contrary, the classes identified by the yellow and green color show a spatial overlap, both positioning themselves in the innermost area of the fjord.

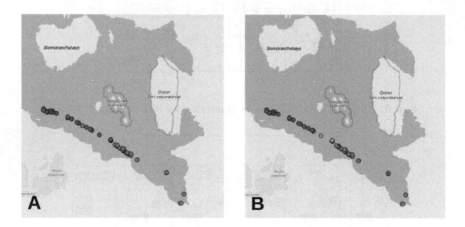

**Fig. 5.** Clusters spatial distribution: figure A shows the position of the patterns divided in K = 2 clusters, figure B shows the position of the patterns for K = 3 clusters. (Color figure online)

# 5    Discussion

This work represents the first attempt to use the multibeam data acquired in the water column in the Svalbard Islands. For this area there is no previous knowledge relating to the acoustic patterns identified. The use of the Morphological and Energetic characteristics of the patterns identified, together with the results of the algorithms used, made it possible to hypothesize that the most correct interpretation of the results obtained from the clustering carried out by k-means is to divide the data set into 3 distinct clusters of schools of fish. In reality, the presence of a third cluster, which differs from the other two only for some characteristics, suggests that this may refer to one of the species associated with one of the other two clusters. Specifically, it is possible to hypothesize that in the three-cluster classification, cluster 2 and cluster 3 correspond to the same species, since the only variables that distinguish these clusters from each other are attributable only to the Energetic characteristics. This can be justified by the fact that some species of pelagic and demersal fish show different behaviors in relation to the life stage. In order to arrive at a more precise classification of the species present in the area, it would be appropriate to implement the study with further characteristics for each of the patterns identified. Characteristics that could help us to arrive at a classification of the species are, for example, the characteristics of a bathymetric positional type. These characteristics will allow us to distinguish species on the basis of their biological behavior.

# 6    Conclusions

The results of this work show that, if from a numerical point of view the data set appears to be composed of three clusters, from a biological point of view the species associated with the identified patterns are probably 2 of which one has different life stages and different Energetic characteristics. An in - deep analysis with a more sophisticate clustering algorithm is left to a future work.

In the light of the results obtained, we can affirm that it is possible, starting from raw data and without onerous operations, to distinguish fish schools in relation to some Morphological and Energetic parameters of the aggregations, in particular study areas such as the one analyzed in this context. This work opens up different scenarios on the possibility of identifying fish species and therefore represents a starting point for possible future works in this area.

# References

1. Stouffer, R.J., et al.: Investigating the causes of the response of the thermohaline circulation to past and future climate changes. J. Clim. **19**, 1365–1387 (2006). University of Technology, Australia, p. 208
2. Fey, D.P., Weslawski, J.M.: Age, growth rate, and otolith growth of polar cod (Boreogadus saida) in two fjords of Svalbard, Kongsfjorden and Rijpfjorden. Oceanologia **59**(2017), 576–584 (2017)

3. Simmonds, E.J., MacLennan, D.N.: Fisheries Acoustics: Theory and Practice,2nd edn. Blackwell Publishing, Oxford (2005)

4. Nuth, C., et al.: Decadal changes from a multi-temporal glacier inventory of Svalbard. Cryosphere **7**(5), 1603–1621 (2013)

5. Hop, H., et al.: The marine ecosystem of Kongsfjorden, Svalbard. Polar Res. **21**, 167–208 (2002)

6. Brand, M., Fischer, P.: Species composition and abundance of the shallow water fish community of Kongsfjorden, Svalbard. Polar Biol. **39**(11), 2155–2167 (2016). https://doi.org/10.1007/s00300-016-2022-y

7. Cohen, D.M., Inada, T., Iwamoto, T., Scialabba, N.: FAO species catalogue. Vol. 10. Gadiform fishes of the world (Order Gadiformes). An annotated and illustrated catalogue of cods, hakes, grenadiers and other gadiform fishes known to date. FAO Fish. Synop. 125(10). FAO, Rome (1990). 442 p

8. Mark, F.C.: Physical oceanography during HEINCKE cruise HE408. AlfredWegener Institute, Helmholtz Center for Polar and Marine Research, Bremerhaven (2013). https://doi.org/10.1594/PANGAEA.824703

9. Scott, W.B., Scott, M.G.: Atlantic fishes of Canada. Can. Bull. Fish. Aquat. Sci. **219**, 731 (1988). https://fishbase.org

10. Kongsberg, E.M.: Series multibeam echo sounder EM datagram formats (2016).    https://www.km.kongsberg.com/ks/web/nokbg0397.nsf/AllWeb/ 253E4C58DB98DDA4C1256D790048373B/$file/160692_em_datagram_formats. pdf

# Unsupervised Classification of Acoustic Echoes from Two Krill Species in the Southern Ocean (Ross Sea)

Ignazio Fontana[1], Giovanni Giacalone[1], Riccardo Rizzo[2], Marco Barra[3(✉)], Olga Mangoni[4], Angelo Bonanno[1], Gualtiero Basilone[1], Simona Genovese[1], Salvatore Mazzola[1], Giosuè Lo Bosco[5,6], and Salvatore Aronica[1]

[1] IAS-CNR, National Research Council, Campobello di Mazara, TP, Italy
[2] ICAR-CNR, National Research Council, Palermo, Italy
[3] ISMAR-CNR, National Research Council, Napoli, Italy
marco.barra@cnr.it
[4] Department of Biology, University of Napoles Federico II, Napoli, Italy
[5] DMI, University of Palermo, Via Archirafi, Palermo, Italy
[6] IEMEST, Via Miraglia 20, Palermo, Italy

**Abstract.** This work presents a computational methodology able to automatically classify the echoes of two krill species recorded in the Ross sea employing scientific echo-sounder at three different frequencies (38, 120 and 200 kHz). The goal of classifying the gregarious species represents a time-consuming task and is accomplished by using differences and/or thresholds estimated on the energy features of the insonified targets. Conversely, our methodology takes into account energy, morphological and depth features of echo data, acquired at different frequencies. Internal validation indices of clustering were used to verify the ability of the clustering in recognizing the correct number of species. The proposed approach leads to the characterization of the two krill species (*Euphausia superba* and *Euphausia crystallorophias*), providing reliable indications about the species spatial distribution and relative abundance.

**Keywords:** Krill identification · Ross Sea · Acoustic data · Machine learning for pelagic species classification

## 1  Introduction

In the last decades, fishery science widely used acoustic-based technique to obtain information about the spatial distribution and abundance of economically and ecologically important pelagic organisms characterized by aggregative behaviour. Such organisms usually live in groups, often referred to as school or shoals, and thus are easily detected by using acoustic methods. The use of scientific echo-sounder allowed to investigate large sea sectors in a relatively

---

L. B. Giosuè and A. Salvatore—Equal contribution.

A. Del Bimbo et al. (Eds.): ICPR 2020 Workshops, LNCS 12666, pp. 65–74, 2021.
https://doi.org/10.1007/978-3-030-68780-9_7

small amount of time, leading to a synoptic and spatially detailed view of the status of aquatic resources. Usually, acoustic data are recorded along specific routes following a parallel-transects survey design. Biological sampling is performed to identify the species inhabiting the water column thus partitioning the recorded echoes among the observed species. Even if the acquisition of acoustic data is a non-invasive procedure, the biological sampling is not, and the sampling effort strongly depends on several factors such as the number of species characterizing the considered ecosystem, the spatial overlap among species, and the possibility to discriminate among different species based on specific acoustic characteristics and/or the shape and structure of observed aggregations. In some complex operative scenarios or particularly vulnerable ecosystems, the possibility to discriminate among species utilizing semi-automatic classification procedures, thus avoiding or reducing the biological sampling effort, represents an important aspect. Recently, a number of scientific papers focused the attention on this topic [1–4]. Anyway, in mixed-species ecosystems, due to a number factors affecting the characteristics of observed echoes, it is difficult to develop a fully-automatic procedure matching echoes and species [5], and it is necessary to contextualize and validate the procedure according to a deep knowledge of the biology and behaviour of the target species. In this work, we tested the use of an unsupervised clustering algorithm (k-means), to partition the echoes recorded during a multi-purpose survey carried out in the Ross Sea (Southern Ocean) during 2016/2017 austral summer under the umbrella of the Italian National Antarctic Research Program. Acoustic data collected during the survey and relative to the upper water column stratum showed mainly the presence of two krill species, namely *Euphausia superba* (Dana, 1850) and *Euphausia crystallorophias* (Holt & Tattersall, 1906). In this context, it was evaluated if the performed classification confirmed some general features (related to the spatial distribution, relative biomass and energetic differences) reported in the literature, providing a way to obtain information about population status even in the case the biological sampling was missing or non-representative.

## 2 Materials and Methods

### 2.1 Acoustic Data: Acquisition and Processing

Acoustic data were collected in the period 05/01/2017–11/02/2017 during the XXXII Antarctic expedition on board of the R/V Italica under the Italian National Antarctic Research Program and in the framework of P-ROSE project (Plankton biodiversity and functioning of the Ross Sea ecosystems in a changing southern ocean). In particular, acoustic data were collected through EK60 scientific echo-sounder at three different frequencies (38 kHz, 120 kHz and 200 kHz) and calibrated following standard techniques [6]. Acoustic sampling followed an opportunistic strategy (Fig. 1), recording data among the sampling stations. A total of 2200 nmi were recorded. Acoustic row data were then processed through Echoview© software [7] to extract all the echoes related to aggregations of pelagic organisms. In the first step, the depth range for the analysis was defined. In particular, the region between 0 and 8.5 m depth was excluded, avoiding artefacts due to beam formation distance and noise due to cavitation and waves. Similarly, the echogram region related to depths higher than 350 m was removed due to the strong attenuation of signals at 120 kHz and 200 kHz. In a second step, background noise was removed by applying the algorithm proposed by De Robertis and Higginbottom [8]; all the echogram regions affected by another noise type (i.e. instrumental, waves, ice etc.) were identified and removed manually. Finally, working on the 120 kHz frequency, all the aggregations (schools) were identified using school detection module in Echoview©. The school detection was applied on the 120 kHz as it was the reference frequency for krill species [9].

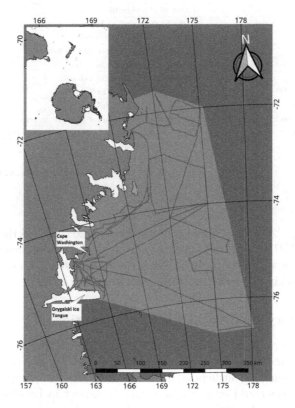

**Fig. 1.** Study area and acoustic tracks.

Once the school were identified, for each aggregation several parameters related to the energetic, geometric and positioning characteristics were extracted (Table 1).

In addition to the parameters computed by means of Echoview© software, four more parameters were computed, namely: the frequency response at 120 and 200 kHz (respectively computed as $FR_{120\_38} = Nasc_{120}/Nasc_{38}$ and $FR_{200\_38} =$

**Table 1.** Energetic and geometric parameters extracted for each aggregation identified by means of school detection module. The * symbol indicate that the variable was extracted for each of the frequencies. The variables that were log-transformed (see Sect. 2.2) are indicated by using the # symbol (in the case of Sv min, the log transformation was applied only on the 120 kHz)

| Parameter | Units | Description |
|---|---|---|
| Lat | | Average latitude |
| Lon | | Average longitude |
| Height mean# | $m$ | Average school height |
| Depth mean | $m$ | Average school depth |
| Length# | $m$ | Length of the identified school |
| Thickness# | $m$ | Thickness of the identified school |
| Perimeter# | $m$ | Perimeter of the identified school |
| Area# | $m^2$ | Area of the identified school |
| Beam volume sum# | $m^3$ | Sum of the beam volumes |
| Sv mean* | dB re 1 m$^{-1}$ | Average recorded Sv value |
| NASC*# | $m^2/nmi^2$ | Nautical Area Scattering Coefficient |
| Sv max* | dB re 1 m$^{-1}$ | Maximum recorded Sv value |
| Sv min* | dB re 1 m$^{-1}$ | Minimum recorded Sv value |
| Standard deviation*# | | Standard deviation of Sv values |
| Skewness*# | dB re 1 m$^{-1}$ | Skewness of Sv values |
| Horizontal roughness*# | dB re 1 m$^2$/m$^3$ | Horizontal dispersion of acoustic energy within the school |
| Vertical roughness*# | dB re 1 m$^2$/m$^3$ | Vertical dispersion of acoustic energy within the school |
| FR_120_38# | | Frequency ratio |
| FR_200_38# | | Frequency ratio |
| $\Delta MVBS$ | dB re 1 m$^{-1}$ | Difference of average Sv 120 kHz minus 38 kHz of the school |
| AP.ratio# | | Ratio between perimeter and area |

$Nasc_{200}/Nasc_{38}$ [2]), the difference of MVBS at 120 and 38 kHz ($\Delta MVBS = MVBS_{120} - MVBS_{38}$) [10], and the ratio between the school area and perimeter as an index of shape compactness ($AP.ratio = Perimeter^2/Area$). The resulting data matrix was characterized by 4482 rows and 35 columns.

## 2.2 Exploratory Analysis and Data Preparation

A preliminary data analysis was carried out to evaluate the presence of outliers and multicollinearity, as they can negatively impact on the clustering performance. The presence of outliers could lead to a bad clustering, while strongly correlated variables could over-weight a specific aspect in building the clusters. To reduce the effect of multicollinearity and to highlight the presence of multivariate outlier Principal Component Analysis (PCA) was carried out. In applying PCA it is important to scale the variable if they are expressed in different units, to avoid that a specific set of variables gain much importance only due to a scale problem. Furthermore, the presence of highly skewed distribution and/or non-linear relationships among variables could introduce distortion in the axes rotation thus leading to incorrect ordination. Before applying PCA all the variables characterized by highly skewed probability distribution were natural log-transformed (Table 2, variables marked by using the # symbol). The performance of transformation was checked both using a statistical test (Shapiro-Wilks) and by inspecting the qq-plot. Small deviations from normality were considered not impacting PCA results and were ignored. Subsequently, all the variables were scaled and centred. Based on the PCA results, only the principal components (PC) accounting for more than 80% of the total variance was retained and used for clustering.

## 2.3   Clustering

Let $X = \{x_1, .., x_n\}$ a dataset, $d$ a distance measure between element of $X$, and $C_1, ..C_k$ the $k$ clusters found by a generic clustering algorithm. K-means clustering algorithm is one of the most used among the unsupervised clustering methods. The clustering procedure identify the clusters by minimizing the following function:

$$J = \sum_{i=1}^{k} \sum_{x \in C_i} d^2(x, c_i) \tag{1}$$

where $c_i$ is the mean (centroid) of elements belonging to cluster $C_i$.

In this context, standardization is an important preprocessing step to avoid scale problems. Besides, the number of clusters must be defined a priori. In the present study, the correct $k$ value is 2, as only two species were found in the echogram. Anyway, to test if the number of groups was an intrinsic property of the data matrix, or if sub-group could be found in terms of specific acoustic and morphological features, the number of clusters was validated employing validation indices. In particular, due to the lack of the *true* schools classification, internal indices were used. Internal validation indices are based on the concept of "good" cluster structure [11,12]. In particular, in the present study, four validation indices were used, to verify if the number of clusters was correctly identified. All of them are based on the *compactness* and *separation* measures, i.e. the average distance between elements inside the same clusters and the average distance of elements belonging to different clusters. In the following, the used indices are formally defined.

The Silhouette index [13] combines the compactness and separation according to the following formula:

$$S(k) = \frac{1}{k} \sum_{i=1}^{k} \frac{1}{n_i} \sum_{x \in C_i} \frac{b(x) - a(x)}{max\{b(x), a(x)\}} \tag{2}$$

Assuming $C_i$ as the cluster of $n_i$ elements where $x$ belongs, $a(x)$ is the average distance between $x$ and all other elements in $C_i$ while $b(x)$ is the average distance between $x$ and all the elements belonging to all the clusters $C_j$ with $j \neq i$.

The Calinski-Harabasz index [14] evaluate the number of cluster according to the following:

$$CH(k) = \frac{\sum_{i=1}^{k} n_i \sum_{x \in C_i} \frac{d^2(c_i,g)}{(k-1)}}{\sum_{i=1}^{k} \sum_{x \in C_i} \frac{d^2(x,c_i)}{(n-k)}} \tag{3}$$

In the case of the Dunn index [15] the clustering is evaluated based on the ratio between the separation and compactness:

$$D(k) = \frac{\min_{i \neq j.i,j \leq k} d(c_i, c_j)}{\max_{i \leq k} \max_{x,y \in C_i, x \neq y} d(x, y)} \tag{4}$$

Finally, the Hartigan index [16] takes into consideration the ratio between the compactness of two clustering solutions relative to $k - 1$ and $k$, in the following way:

$$H(k) = \left( \frac{\sum_{i=1}^{k-1} \sum_{x \in C_i} d^2(x, c_i)}{\sum_{i=1}^{k} \sum_{x \in C_i} d^2(x, c_i)} - 1 \right) (n - k - 1) \tag{5}$$

For all the above-mentioned indices, the optimal number of clusters is the one maximizing the index value.

## 3  Results

The skewness index computed for each considered variables showed the presence of highly positive skewed variables. In order to reduce the degree of skewness, all the variables characterized by a skewness index higher than 2 were log-transformed. PCA highlighted the presence of strong patterns (Table 2); the first 5 PC's accounted for about 83% of the total variance and were selected to be subjected to k-means clustering. In particular, the first and second PCs accounted for more than 50% of the total variance and the first PC was strongly related to energetic-related variables (Table 2), while the second one to geometric ones (Perimeter, Area, Length and AP.ratio). The remaining PCs were correlated to a lower number of variables all related to energetic aspects except the $5^{th}$ PC that was found significantly correlated to the Height_mean only. In terms of outliers, plotting the observation in the PC spaces does not evidence the presence of erratic data points. Internal validation indices (Table 2) were computed on the first 5 PCs (accounting for most of the variance), by testing a vector of cluster numbers from 2 to 10 using the k-means algorithm with $d$ corresponding to Euclidean distance. All considered validation indices highlighted $k = 2$ as the best solution (Table 3).

K-means partitioning was then applied considering the first 5 PCs and $k = 2$. Partitioning results identified 2367 observations as belonging to the cluster 1 and 2217 belonging to cluster 2. Plotting observations (categorized by cluster id) in the PCs space, highlighted that the clustering was mainly driven by the $1^{th}$ PC (Fig. 2).

In particular, looking at variables correlation values of the $1^{th}$ PC, the first cluster was characterized by lower energetic values and a more homogeneous internal structure than the second one. Finally, to evidence possible differences in the spatial distribution, the two clusters were plotted in the geographical space (Fig. 3).

**Table 2.** PC variables correlation. Only variables characterized by a correlation value higher than 0.6 (absolute value) are reported.

| | PC1 | | PC2 | | PC3 | | PC4 | | PC5 | |
|---|---|---|---|---|---|---|---|---|---|---|
| | cor | $cos^2$ | cor | $cos^2$ | cor | $cos^2$ | cor | $cos^2$ | cor | $cos^2$ |
| Sv_mean_38 | 0.82 | 0.68 | | | | | | | | |
| Sv_mean_120 | 0.74 | 0.55 | | | | | | | | |
| Sv_mean_200 | 0.71 | 0.5 | | | | | | | | |
| Sv_max_38 | 0.88 | 0.78 | | | | | | | | |
| Sv_max_120 | 0.81 | 0.65 | | | | | | | | |
| Sv_max_200 | 0.78 | 0.61 | | | | | | | | |
| NASC_38 | 0.88 | 0.77 | | | | | | | | |
| Sv_max_120 | 0.79 | 0.62 | | | | | | | | |
| Sv_max_200 | 0.77 | 0.6 | | | | | | | | |
| Horizontal_roughness_38 | 0.84 | 0.7 | | | | | | | | |
| Horizontal_roughness_120 | 0.71 | 0.5 | | | | | | | | |
| Horizontal_roughness_200 | 0.67 | 0.45 | | | | | | | | |
| Vertical_roughness_38 | 0.81 | 0.65 | | | | | | | | |
| Vertical_roughness_120 | 0.72 | 0.51 | | | | | | | | |
| Vertical_roughness_200 | 0.73 | 0.53 | | | | | | | | |
| Standard_deviation_38 | 0.86 | 0.75 | | | | | | | | |
| Standard_deviation_120 | 0.77 | 0.6 | | | | | | | | |
| Standard_deviation_200 | 0.75 | 0.57 | | | | | | | | |
| Perimeter | | | 0.83 | 0.69 | | | | | | |
| Length | | | 0.77 | 0.59 | | | | | | |
| Area | | | 0.73 | 0.53 | | | | | | |
| AP.ratio | | | 0.72 | 0.52 | | | | | | |
| RF_200_38 | | | | | 0.82 | 0.68 | | | | |
| Sv_min_200 | | | | | 0.67 | 0.45 | | | | |
| $\Delta MVBS$ | | | | | | | 0.82 | 0.66 | | |
| RF_120_38 | | | | | | | 0.82 | 0.66 | | |
| Height_mean | | | | | | | | | -0.72 | 0.52 |

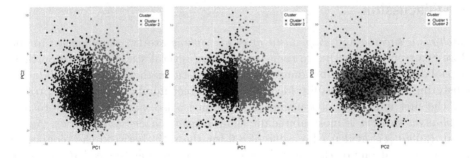

**Fig. 2.** PCA biplot for the first three components.

**Table 3.** Validation values of internal indices as the parameter k varies for the "k-means" clustering algorithm and Euclidean distance.

| Index | k = 2 | k = 3 | k = 4 | k = 5 | k = 6 | k = 7 | k = 8 | k = 9 | k = 10 |
|-------|-------|-------|-------|-------|-------|-------|-------|-------|--------|
| S | **0.2644** | 0.1809 | 0.1857 | 0.1919 | 0.1764 | 0.1679 | 0.1622 | 0.1685 | 0.1677 |
| CH | **1910.46** | 1391.28 | 1192.81 | 1095.63 | 1024.38 | 957.06 | 894.72 | 849.85 | 812.33 |
| D | **1.4078** | 1.0655 | 1.1846 | 1.1246 | 1.1636 | 1.0462 | 0.8965 | 0.8449 | 0.8605 |
| H | **1910.46** | 611.68 | 491.29 | 447.37 | 374.14 | 289.89 | 228.59 | 223.85 | 203.83 |

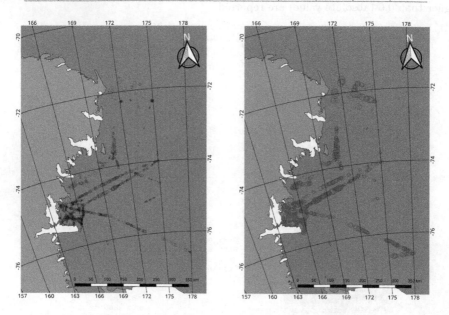

**Fig. 3.** Spatial distribution of the two identified cluster (*Euphausia crystallorophias* cluster 1, left panel; *Euphausia superba*, cluster 2, right panel). Circle size are proportional to the natural logarithm of $NASC_{120}$ values.

## 4   Discussion

*Euphausia superba* and *Euphausia crystallorophias* are two key species in the Ross Sea trophic web. Due to their importance, several studies focused on their spatial distribution and abundance through acoustic methods [17–19]. Validation clustering indices successfully identified the correct number of clusters, providing the first indication of k-means performance. Also, according to literature, *Euphausia superba* is most abundant than *Euphausia crystallorophias*; Azzali et al. (2006) [17] evidenced a value of 8.6 for the ratio between the biomass of the former and one of the latter species. By considering the $NASC_{120}$ as an abundance index, the above-mentioned ratio according to the obtained classification is 7.9 thus comparable to the one reported in the literature. Looking at spatial distribution, according to literature [18], obtained classification also evidenced the dominance of *Euphausia superba* in the northern sector of the study area (Fig. 3). Finally, it must be considered that in terms of acoustic properties the two species evidenced a clear separation when comparing, using a scatterplot, the $Sv_{38}$ vs $Sv_{120}$ [19]. This separation was also confirmed by the k-means classification results (Fig. 4).

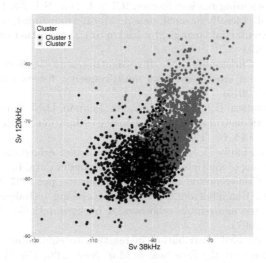

**Fig. 4.** Scatter plot of Sv_mean_38 vs Sv_mean_120 values, categorized according to clustering results (cluster 1 is black).

Due to the agreement between the information reported in the literature and the ones obtained from the classification results, the application of the k-means algorithm could be considered as a stable, fast and reliable solution to extract the main features of the two population from acoustic data, allowing the extraction of summary indices about the population status despite the lack of biological sampling.

## 5   Conclusions

Unsupervised classification of aggregations detected during acoustic surveys represents a useful tool in the post-processing of large acoustic dataset. In the present work, k-means clustering was able to distinguish between the two considered krill species, recognizing the correct number of clusters and providing indications about the species spatial distribution and relative abundance coherent to the ones reported in the literature. We plan to use the same methodology by employing other clustering algorithms, such as the hierarchical ones, and other cluster validation indices, to improve the consensus about the clustering solution.

## References

1. Fernandes, P.G.: Classification trees for species identification of fish-school echotraces. ICES J. Mar. Sci. **66**, 1073–1080 (2009)

2. D'Elia, M., et al.: Analysis of backscatter properties and application of classification procedures for the identification of small pelagic fish species in the central Mediterranean. Fish. Res. **149**, 33–42 (2014)
3. Fallon, N.G., Fielding, S., Fernandes, P.G.: Classification of Southern Ocean krill and icefish echoes using random forests. ICES J. Mar. Sci. **73**, 1998–2008 (2016)
4. Aronica, S., et al.: Identifying small pelagic Mediterranean fish schools from acoustic and environmental data using optimized artificial neural networks. Ecol. Inform. **50**, 149–161 (2019)
5. Campanella, F., Christopher, T.J.: Investigating acoustic diversity of fish aggregations in coral reef ecosystems from multifrequency fishery sonar surveys. Fish. Res. **181**, 63–76 (2016)
6. Foote, K.G., Knudsen, H.P., Vestnes, G., MacLennan, D.N., Simmonds, E.J.: Calibration of acoustic instruments for fish density estimation: a practical guide. ICES Coop. Res. Rep. **144**, 69 (1987)
7. Higginbottom, I., Pauly, T.J., Heatley, D.C.: Virtual echograms for visualization and post-processing of multiple-frequency echosounder data. In: Proceedings of the Fifth European Conference on Underwater Acoustics, pp. 1497–1502. Ecua (2000)
8. De Robertis, A., Higginbottom, I.: A post-processing technique to estimate the signal-to-noise ratio and remove echosounder background noise. ICES J. Mar. Sci. **64**, 1282–1291 (2007)
9. Leonori, I., et al.: Krill distribution in relation to environmental parameters in mesoscale structures in the Ross Sea. J. Mar. Syst. **166**, 159–171 (2017)
10. Watkins, J.L., Brierley, A.S.: Verification of the acoustic techniques used to identify Antarctic krill. ICES J. Mar. Sci. **59**, 1326–1336 (2002)
11. Hassani, M., Seidl, T.: Using internal evaluation measures to validate the quality of diverse stream clustering algorithms. Vietnam J. Comput. Sci. **4**(3), 171–183 (2016). https://doi.org/10.1007/s40595-016-0086-9
12. Charrad, M., Ghazzali, N., Boiteau, V., Niknafs, A.: NbClust: an R package for determining the relevant number of clusters in a data set. J. Stat. Softw. **61**, 1–36 (2014)
13. Rousseeuw, P.: Silhouettes: a graphical aid to the interpretation and validation of cluster analysis. J. Comput. Appl. Math. **20**, 53–65 (1987)
14. Calinski, T., Harabasz, J.: A dendrite method for cluster analysis. Comm. Stat. **3**, 1–27 (1974)
15. Dunn, J.C.: Well-separated clusters and optimal fuzzy partitions. J. Cybern. **4**, 95–104 (1974)
16. Hartigan, J.A.: Clustering Algorithms. Wiley, New York (1975). ISBN 047135645X
17. Azzali, M., Leonori, I., De Felice, A., Russo, A.: Spatial-temporal relationships between two euphausiid species in the Ross Sea. Chem. Ecol. **22**, 219–233 (2006)
18. Davis, L.B., Hofmann, E.E., Klinck, J.M., Pinones, A., Dinniman, M.S.: Distributions of krill and Antarctic silverfish and correlations with environmental variables in the western Ross Sea, Antarctica. Mar. Ecol. Progress Ser. **584**, 45–65 (2017)
19. La, H.S., et al.: High density of ice krill (Euphausia crystallorophias) in the Amundsen sea coastal polynya, Antarctica. Deep Sea Res. **95**, 75–84 (2015)

# Multi-Input ConvLSTM for Flood Extent Prediction

Leo Muckley[✉] and James Garforth

University of Edinburgh, Edinburgh, UK
{l.j.muckley,james.garforth}@ed.ac.uk

**Abstract.** Flooding is among the most destructive natural disasters in
the world. The destruction that floods cause has led to an urgency in
developing accurate prediction models. One aspect of flood prediction
which has yet to benefit from machine learning techniques is in the prediction of flood extent. However, due to the many factors that can cause
flooding, developing predictive models that can generalise to other potential flooding locations has proven to be a difficult task. This paper shows
that a Multi-Input ConvLSTM can exploit several flood conditioning
factors to effectively model flood extent while generalising well to other
flood locations under certain conditions. Furthermore, this study compares the sub-components of the system to demonstrate their efficacy
when applied to various flood types.

**Keywords:** Flood prediction · Remote sensing · Deep learning

## 1 Introduction

Floods are among Earth's most common and most destructive natural disasters.
According to the Organisation for Economic Cooperation and Development,
floods cause more than \$40 billion in damage worldwide annually [10]. There
has been a lot of effort put into detecting floods ahead of time using machine
learning techniques with varying success, however one common shortcoming is
the inability of models to generalise well to other flood events [9]. This can be
attributed to the various types of flooding that exist and the various factors
which determine the location and extent of these events. For example, countries can be prone to fluvial flooding (i.e. river flooding), pluvial flooding (i.e.
flash floods) and coastal flooding due to storm surges. As a consequence of this,
developing a general model that can incorporate all the underpinning features
of every variant of flooding to accurately detect a specific flood event ahead of
time is difficult.

In this study, we propose an approach to predicting flood extent by using
a novel deep learning technique, namely a Multi-Input ConvLSTM. This approach is developed to model both the spatial and temporal elements of flooding,
where a limited quantity of training data is available while utilising the spatial autocorrelation in the dataset. Furthermore, the results show the ability of
the Multi-Input ConvLSTM technique to generalise to a variety of flood events
across several countries in Africa, under certain conditions.

© Springer Nature Switzerland AG 2021
A. Del Bimbo et al. (Eds.): ICPR 2020 Workshops, LNCS 12666, pp. 75–85, 2021.
https://doi.org/10.1007/978-3-030-68780-9_8

## 2   Related Work

Flood extent prediction is the task of predicting the level of inundation for a specific location based on a set of flood conditioning factors. In flood extent prediction, the goal is to determine *where* flooding is going to happen and to what extent. This contrasts with flood forecasting where the main goal is to determine *when* a flood is going to happen, to aid flood warning systems. The task of flood forecasting is a widely studied area and various type of statistical and machine learning models have been developed.

**Flood Forecasting** techniques mostly utilise precipitation and hydrological data to forecast water levels in river basins to aid flood warning systems. Generally, these predictive models are specifically tuned for one area or for a specific type of flood (i.e. pluvial, fluvial flooding etc.) resulting in the inability of the model to generalise well to other flood events. Nevertheless, machine learning techniques have shown some success in flood forecasting tasks [9].

Early applications of feed-forward neural networks have been applied to modelling river water level to effectively forecast riverine flooding [1] in Tagliamento, Italy. In this scenario, the neural network used information from various rain gauges along the river as the features for the model. The results of this model were quite accurate with a mean square error less than 4% when used within a 1-h time window. However, when the time window is increased, the prediction accuracy decreases as the feed-forward neural network is not able to model the time lag between the water level and the rainfall, which is an important aspect of flood forecasting.

More recent developments in flood forecasting utilise recurrent neural networks to model the temporal element of flooding. An example of this showed the efficacy of LSTM networks when utilised with discharge and rainfall information in the Da River basin in Vietnam [7]. The LSTM network modelled one-day, two-day and three-day flow rate forecasting with Nash–Sutcliffe efficiency (NSE), a metric used to assess the efficacy of hydrological models, reaching 99%, 95%, and 87% respectively. These results demonstrate how well-suited LSTM networks are for flood forecasting due to their ability to effectively deal with time lags and exploit the temporal dependencies in the data. However, the LSTM network does not consider the spatial relationships between the different hydrological stations.

**Flood Extent Prediction** is one area of environmental research that has yet to benefit from machine learning techniques. However, a similar problem to flood extent prediction is the modelling of flood susceptibility. This modelling is closely related as factors that determine flood susceptibility are likely to have predictive power in modelling flood extent. A GIS-based spatial prediction approach which modelled flood prone areas in the Xing Guo region of China was proposed using an ensemble of techniques [12]. The goal was to accurately classify the flood prone areas using a test set of ground truth levels of flood susceptibility. The ensemble of Logistic Regression and Weight of Evidence models achieved the highest performance of accuracy 90.36% when modelled on the following conditioning factors: (1) altitude, (2) slope, (3) aspect, (4) geology, (5) distance from river, (6) distance from road, (7) distance from fault, (8) soil type, (9) LULC, (10) rainfall, (11) Normalized Difference Vegetation Index (NDVI), (12) Stream Power Index (SPI), (13) Topographic Wetness Index (TWI), (14) Sediment Transport Index (STI) and (15) curvature. The result of this report supports the prior expectation that less vegetated areas at low altitude with high levels of rainfall are more susceptible to flooding. Flood susceptibility is not equivalent to flood extent, however, for an area with a high susceptibility of flooding it would be expected that there would be a positive correlation between the two values. As a result of this, the features used to model susceptibility can be expected to be useful for modelling flood extent.

One example of machine learning for predicting flood extent in an urban context uses both an LSTM and a Logistic Regression model [5]. This methodology first utilises the LSTM to predict the overflow of the storm water management system. The output of the total overflow is then used as a feature for the Logistic Regression model which determines the presence of flooding in each grid of the urban map. The results of this study show the potential for improving urban flood extent prediction using machine learning techniques. However, the methodology developed was specifically for the purpose of urban mapping and is not suitable for generalising to various types of flood events.

**Deep Learning** architectures that incorporate both recurrent and convolutional structures have been developed for the purpose of spatio-temporal modelling. The ConvLSTM has shown success in precipitation forecasting by utilising sequence of satellite imagery [6,15]. Deep learning models that incorporate a ConvLSTM architecture have the ability to predict the future state of a cell based on previous states of that cell and the states of the neighbours of that cell. As a result of this, the ConvLSTM is particularly useful for spatio-temporal modelling when adequate training data is available so that the spatial dependencies in the data can be modelled over time.

The effectiveness of the ConvLSTM has been shown in other problems beyond precipitation forecasting, such as traffic accident prediction, where heterogeneous urban data is utilised for training [16]. The main challenges highlighted was the rarity of traffic accidents and the spatial heterogeneity of the data. Spatial graph features were developed with an adjacency matrix to overcome the challenge of spatial heterogeneity. This allowed the ConvLSTM to handle the spatial heterogeneity and temporality at the same time while incorporating all the most important features for predicting traffic accidents. Therefore, this study showed that the ConvLSTM is suitable to problems where a trade-off between spatial heterogeneity and rarity of events exists, if the unique data properties are handled properly.

In computer vision, one method for handling unique data properties is to adopt a multi-input approach which is used for deep learning models that receives input of different data types [11,13]. These models adopt a multi-input CNN architecture to make use of a variety of different images or viewing planes as more than one data input is necessary to fully represent the target feature. A similar multi-input approach is utilised in the derivation of soil clay content from

a synergy of multi-temporal optical and radar imagery data [14]. The results of
this research demonstrated the applicability of multi-input architectures when
utilising a variety of satellite imagery for the training of deep learning models.

## 3   Method

The prediction of flood extent and location is a task of trying to predict the level
of inundation $y$, where $0 \leq y \leq 1$, at time $t$ based on $M$ features for the previous
$k$ points in time. In this problem, the level of inundation is the fraction of a
region (i.e. over a $1\,\mathrm{km}^2$ distance) that is covered in flood water at time $t$ and
each feature $m \in M$, is a sequence of $k$ timesteps (e.g. sequence of daily total
precipitation). It is these $M$ sequences that are then utilised for the prediction
of flood extent.

The flood conditioning factors utilised for modelling are the following: (a)
constant features, consisting of *distance to water, elevation, slope, clay content*
and *soil organic carbon*; (b) temporal features, consisting of *max precipitation,
total precipitation, std precipitation, normalised difference vegetation index* and
*soil moisture*. When utilising satellite imagery for machine learning tasks, it is
often the case that the features extracted have a mix of data types. In addition, these images are generally not available for every time step due to satellite
repetition rates. For this problem, each input to the network is either temporal,
and therefore a sequence of the previous $t - 1$ timesteps, or constant, therefore
the input is a single timestep. To summarise, an effective flood extent prediction
model needs to be able to deal with the following two cases: (1) data that is temporal by nature but the measurements may not be available for every timestep
(e.g. soil moisture); (2) data measurements that have a very long repetition rate
(e.g. 365 days) and can be thus considered a constant feature (e.g. elevation). So
a model that is robust to different data types is desirable.

**Multi-input** architecture is a type of network where the network receives input
of different data types. Inspired by [13] which adopts a multi-input architecture
for the purpose of flower grading using computer vision. In this context, each
sample contains three images which is fed into a CNN model. Here the multi-
input type architecture is favoured as one image cannot fully represent the flower
for grading as one image equates to only a partial region of the flower. The motivation for using multi-input architecture on flood extent prediction is similar:
the problem cannot be sufficiently modelled based on one type of data input.

In flood extent prediction, input features are generally a mixture of both
constant features and temporal features, extracted from satellite imagery. The
architecture of the Multi-Input network allows the model to effectively exploit
the specific characteristics of each data type and thus, eradicating the need
to model non-temporal or constant features in a temporal model. Introducing
constant features, that do not vary over time, into a recurrent layer will not
correlate with the output and over many timesteps the weights will converge to
zero [8]. Therefore, adding constant features to a LSTM would add redundant
information or noise at the potentially at the cost of greater model performance.

Considering this, the design consists of a recurrent neural network for the temporal input and a feed-forward network for constant input before being concatenated at an intermediate step. Separating the two models based on input and then combining at a subsequent layer has the benefit of learning from each set of input most effectively and then learning interactions between features at the subsequent layer.

**ConvLSTM** is a type of architecture that was devised for the purpose of modelling spatio-temporal relationships in the short-term prediction of precipitation [15]. This method was shown to surpass state-of-the-art predictions by utilising satellite imagery. In order to achieve this, lots of data was available because rainfall is not a rare weather event, unlike flood prediction where a training set may consist of only a single image. As a consequence of not having sufficient image data for training, it is not feasible to train a conventional ConvLSTM on full image data as this type of architecture generally uses a two-dimensional filter to extract spatial features from the data.

A ConvLSTM layer is similar to an LSTM layer as both are recurrent except that in the ConvLSTM architecture the internal operations now utilise convolutions. This would generally mean that the internal matrix operations of the LSTM are now replaced with convolutional operations, with the input dimension, $d$, a three-dimensional tensor instead of a one-dimensional tensor that is seen in the LSTM. Generally, for convolutions the filter size is $n \times n$, which effectively extracts spatial dependencies with a sufficient amount of training. However, for the purpose of flood extent prediction, a filter size of $1 \times n$ is proposed. The benefits of this is that the modelling can still exploit local spatial dependencies across multiple features while still being modelled in a sequence. Therefore, the ConvLSTM method utilises a one-dimensional filter to learn high-level local spatial features in the data.

**Multi-Input ConvLSTM** is now proposed to effectively model both the temporal and spatial dependencies in the data for the purpose of flood extent prediction[1]. This novel approach solves some of the issues involving modelling extreme weather events using satellite imagery, such as: the ability to model sequential problems with a mixture of data types without redundant information being included in the modelling; the ability to exploit local spatial dependencies in the absence of large high-dimensional training sets. Figure 1 outlines the flow of operations for the Multi-Input ConvLSTM. This architecture is also divided into two components: (1) for modelling the temporal features, the ConvLSTM model will be utilised; (2) for modelling the constant features a feed-forward network (MLP) will be used. These two components will be combined at a subsequent layer for before being propagated to the output layer.

For the temporal modelling, 3 hidden layers were chosen: a ConvLSTM layer, an LSTM layer and an LSTM layer with dropout. For the ConvLSTM layer, the number of filters and the size of the kernel are to be considered. For the filter size, 64 was chosen and considering the ConvLSTM layer will be used for sequential

---

[1] https://github.com/leomuckley/malawi-flood-prediction.

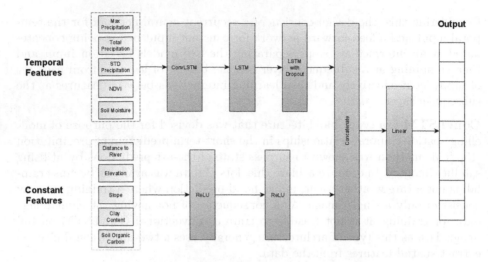

**Fig. 1.** Multi-Input ConvLSTM.

data the kernel size must be one-dimensional. For this a kernel size $1 \times 5$ was chosen as the model could capture a greater amount of the spatial dependencies in the data. For the LSTM layers 2 hidden layers with 64 hidden units was chosen for the first layer and 32 hidden units for the second was chosen. To reduce chances of overfitting, the second layer applied a dropout rate of 0.10 was used. For the constant features, the feed-forward network with two hidden layers, containing 32 and 16 hidden units with a ReLU activation functions, respectively.

For the modelling, choice of loss function used for training the models was the Huber loss is robust to outliers and in the context of flood extent prediction as it would better handle the infrequent cases of high-valued flood extent.

$$
L_\delta(y, f(x)) = \begin{cases} \frac{1}{2}(y - f(x))^2 & \text{for } |y - f(x)| \leq \delta \\ \delta|y - f(x)| - \frac{1}{2}\delta^2 & \text{otherwise} \end{cases} \tag{1}
$$

The Adam optimiser [4] was chosen for the learning process as it has an adaptive learning rate which reduces the need to optimise the learning rate hyperparameter. In addition, the models in this study all used mini-batching which updates the error gradient after seeing a only a subset of the data.

## 4    Experiments

The data collection process used for creating the training and test sets involves extracting the relevant features from raster images, downloaded from Google Earth Engine [2]. For a given flood event, the flood extent target feature can be calculated through a change detection algorithm, where the resulting raster layer highlights the pixels flagged as flooding [3]. The fraction of flooding can then be extracted from this layer to be utilised for experimentation.

To determine the accuracy of the models developed, each model was cross-validated (K-Fold = 3) with the results of the experiments reporting the Root Mean Squared Error (RMSE) and the standard deviation to allow for a measure of confidence. The data sets used for training and testing were carefully selected. The reason for careful selection was to test if the models could generalise to various flood events. To test this the following data sets were used:

1. Malawi used for training and testing
2. Mozambique used for training and Malawi used for testing
3. Mozambique used for training and Kenya used for testing

First, the models were trained and tested on homogeneous data to better understand the ability of the models to perform on data of a similar nature. This is a similar to the setup for a Zindi competition[2], as both the training and test set were extracted from identical coordinates in Malawi. Thus, the majority of the underlying features in both training and test sets being similar (e.g. elevation; distance to water).

Second, the models were trained and tested on heterogeneous data, which was comprised of two different datasets. These datasets were selected due to their different geographic features (e.g. land cover type; elevation etc.) but also due to the varying types of flood events. For instance, if a model was trained using pluvial flood data and the target flood event was due to fluvial flooding, this would make the prediction problem a much more difficult task. Therefore, this would test the ability of the models to generalise well to other flood events.

For validation, each dataset was further split into a training set and a validation set. This consisted of the following split: 80% for training the model and 20% for validation. The purpose of this split is to test the performance of a model in parallel allowing for a predefined stopping condition for the training process to be set. Furthermore, each model that was trained, a specific validation strategy was used. Each model was trained using a max epoch value of 1000 and early-stopping applied.

The benchmark to be utilised in this study is based a Light Gradient Boosting Model (LGBM) with model averaging to allow for appropriate comparison in the experiments[3]. This is based on the winning solution for a Zindi competition where the goal was to predict the flood extent in Malawi.

### 4.1  Homogeneous Data

Table 1 exhibits the results for the models utilised in this study. These models have been trained and tested on homogeneous data, where the training and testing data are sourced from the same flood event and type. In this case, the models were trained and tested on Malawi flood data. The results report the RMSE for each model and standard deviation.

---

[2] https://zindi.africa/competitions/2030-vision-flood-prediction-in-malawi.

[3] https://github.com/belkhir-aziz/Flood-Prediction-in-Malawi-winning-solution-.

**Table 1.** Results of training on Malawi flood data and testing on Malawi flood data using RMSE.

| Model | Dataset |
|---|---|
| | Malawi |
| LSTM | 0.0525 ± 0.0004 |
| LSTM-Autoencoder | 0.0542 ± 0.01 |
| Multi-Input LSTM | 0.0532 ± 0.001 |
| ConvLSTM | **0.0519 ± 0.0002** |
| Multi-Input ConvLSTM | 0.0572 ± 0.001 |
| LGBM | 0.1021 ± 0.0001 |

In the scenario of homogeneous data, the ConvLSTM surpasses the other models. It achieves the lowest RMSE of 0.0519 with the second lowest RMSE coming from the LSTM model achieving 0.0525. The LSTM-Autoencoder and Multi-Input LSTM report slightly higher RMSE than these models, with 0.0542 and 0.0532 respectively. The Multi-Input ConvLSTM is the worst performing deep learning technique with an RMSE of 0.0572. However, the deep learning techniques developed for this study all surpass the LGBM model as that model reports an RMSE of 0.1021. From Table 1 we see for all the deep learning techniques developed for this study had a RMSE range of between 0.0519 and 0.0572.

The results for the homogeneous dataset demonstrate the ability of each variant of LSTM network to predict flood extent as each model outperforms the LGBM model. This evidence suggests that the LSTM network is well-suited to the problem of flood extent prediction due to the ability of the recurrent layers to model the temporal features. This contrasts with the LGBM model where all the features utilised in the model were considered constant.

### 4.2 Heterogeneous Data

Table 2 presents the results for testing the ability of the models developed to generalise to other flood events. These models have been trained and tested on heterogeneous data, where the training and testing data are sourced from the different flood events with different flood types. In this case, the models were trained on Mozambique data and tested on both Malawi and Kenya flood data. The results in the table report the RMSE for each model with standard deviation.

For the Malawi data, the Multi-Input LSTM achieves the lowest RMSE. This model has a RMSE of 0.0803 and the second lowest RMSE coming from the Multi-Input LSTM model achieving 0.0890. The LSTM-Autoencoder reports a slightly higher RMSE of 0.1117. The LSTM and ConvLSTM report the worst RMSE results with 0.1471 and 0.1350, respectively. However, the deep learning techniques developed for this study all surpass the LGBM model as that model reports an RMSE of 0.2815.

**Table 2.** Results of training on Mozambique flood data and testing on Malawi and Kenya flood data.

| Model | Dataset | |
|---|---|---|
| | Malawi | Kenya |
| LSTM | $0.1471 \pm 0.03$ | $0.2270 \pm 0.01$ |
| LSTM-Autoencoder | $0.1117 \pm 0.02$ | $0.2333 \pm 0.01$ |
| Multi-Input LSTM | $\mathbf{0.0803 \pm 0.01}$ | $\mathbf{0.2120 \pm 0.01}$ |
| ConvLSTM | $0.1350 \pm 0.02$ | $0.2180 \pm 0.01$ |
| Multi-Input ConvLSTM | $0.0890 \pm 0.01$ | $0.2169 \pm 0.02$ |
| LGBM | $0.2815 \pm 0.002$ | $0.2554 \pm 0.01$ |

For the Kenya data, the Multi-Input LSTM again achieves the lowest RMSE. This model has a RMSE of 0.2120 and the second lowest RMSE coming from the Multi-Input ConvLSTM model with a RMSE of 0.2169. The ConvLSTM reports a slightly higher RMSE of 0.2180. The LSTM and LSTM-Autoencoder report the worst RMSE results with 0.2270 and 0.2333, respectively. However, the deep learning techniques developed for this study all surpass the LGBM model as that model reports an RMSE of 0.2554.

One reason why the models that utilise convolutions do not perform any better here is due to Malawi having less spatial autocorrelation. The Moran's I statistic was computed for each dataset used in the study and the results of these statistical tests showed that Malawi dataset has a lower amount of spatial autocorrelation (0.68), leading to less spatial dependencies in the data to exploit.

The ability of each model to generalise to different types of floods is assessed. The general trend here is that both the Multi-Input LSTM and Multi-Input ConvLSTM outperform the other models for both the Malawi and Kenya datasets. When comparing the performance across datasets, we see the stronger performance on the Malawi dataset in comparison to the Kenya dataset.

## 5   Conclusion

In this paper, we develop a novel solution for the flood extent prediction problem by proposing a Multi-Input ConvLSTM network which can exploit the spatio-temporal aspect of flooding. In the proposed solution, we split and separate the input features based on their temporality. This solves some issues related to the modelling of extreme weather events using satellite imagery, such as handling conditioning factors consisting of mixed data types, the varying repetition rates of the satellite imagery and the ability to exploit local spatial dependencies in the absence of large training sets.

The results of the experiments show that converting the original flood extent prediction problem into a temporal problem outperforms the current state-of-the-art model in generalising to various types of flood events. Furthermore, we compare the sub-components of the Multi-Input ConvLSTM model to demonstrate their efficacy separately. These comparisons show that the ConvLSTM is particularly effective when the data has high spatial autocorrelation and that the Multi-Input architecture is more effective when the data has higher levels of spatial heterogeneity.

The work presented in this study showed the ability of deep learning techniques when applied to flood extent prediction. Not only has this work provided a useful resource to help mitigate the damage inflicted by flooding, but also provides a foundation for future research in the area of deep learning for flood extent prediction.

# References

1. Campolo, M., Andreussi, P., Soldati, A.: River flood forecasting with a neural network model. Water Resour. Res. **35**(4), 1191–1197 (1999). https://doi.org/10.1029/1998WR900086. https://agupubs.onlinelibrary.wiley.com/doi/abs/10.1029/1998WR900086
2. Gorelick, N., Hancher, M., Dixon, M., Ilyushchenko, S., Thau, D., Moore, R.: Google earth engine: planetary-scale geospatial analysis for everyone. Remote Sens. Environ. (2017). https://doi.org/10.1016/j.rse.2017.06.031
3. Huang, M., Jin, S.: Rapid flood mapping and evaluation with a supervised classifier and change detection in Shouguang using Sentinel-1 SAR and Sentinel-2 optical data. Remote Sens. **12**(13), 2073 (2020)
4. Jais, I.K.M., Ismail, A.R., Nisa, S.Q.: Adam optimization algorithm for wide and deep neural network. Knowl. Eng. Data Sci. **2**(1), 41–46 (2019)
5. Kim, H.I., Han, K.Y., Lee, J.Y.: Prediction of urban flood extent by LSTM model and logistic regression. J. Korean Soc. Civ. Eng. **40**(3), 273–283 (2020)
6. Kim, S., Hong, S., Joh, M., Song, S.k.: DeepRain: ConvLSTM network for precipitation prediction using multichannel radar data. arXiv preprint arXiv:1711.02316 (2017)
7. Le, X.H., Ho, H.V., Lee, G., Jung, S.: Application of long short-term memory (LSTM) neural network for flood forecasting. Water **11**(7), 1387 (2019)
8. Ma, K., Leung, H.: A novel LSTM approach for asynchronous multivariate time series prediction. In: 2019 International Joint Conference on Neural Networks (IJCNN), pp. 1–7 (2019). https://doi.org/10.1109/IJCNN.2019.8851792
9. Mosavi, A., Ozturk, P., Chau, K.w.: Flood prediction using machine learning models: literature review. Water **10**(11), 1536 (2018)
10. OECD: Financial Management of Flood Risk (2016). https://doi.org/10.1787/9789264257689-en, https://www.oecd-ilibrary.org/content/publication/9789264257689-en
11. Oktay, O., et al.: Multi-input cardiac image super-resolution using convolutional neural networks. In: Ourselin, S., Joskowicz, L., Sabuncu, M.R., Unal, G., Wells, W. (eds.) MICCAI 2016. LNCS, vol. 9902, pp. 246–254. Springer, Cham (2016). https://doi.org/10.1007/978-3-319-46726-9_29
12. Shafapour Tehrany, M., Shabani, F., Neamah Jebur, M., Hong, H., Chen, W., Xie, X.: GIS-based spatial prediction of flood prone areas using standalone frequency ratio, logistic regression, weight of evidence and their ensemble techniques. Geomatics Nat. Hazards Risk **8**(2), 1538–1561 (2017)

13. Sun, Y., Zhu, L., Wang, G., Zhao, F.: Multi-input convolutional neural network for flower grading. J. Electr. Comput. Eng. **2017** (2017)
14. Tziolas, N., Tsakiridis, N., Ben-Dor, E., Theocharis, J., Zalidis, G.: Employing a multi-input deep convolutional neural network to derive soil clay content from a synergy of multi-temporal optical and radar imagery data. Remote Sens. **12**(9), 1389 (2020)
15. Xingjian, S., Chen, Z., Wang, H., Yeung, D.Y., Wong, W.K., Woo, W.c.: Convolutional LSTM network: a machine learning approach for precipitation nowcasting. In: Advances in Neural Information Processing Systems, pp. 802–810 (2015)
16. Yuan, Z., Zhou, X., Yang, T.: Hetero-convLSTM: a deep learning approach to traffic accident prediction on heterogeneous spatio-temporal data. In: Proceedings of the 24th ACM SIGKDD International Conference on Knowledge Discovery & Data Mining, pp. 984–992 (2018)

# Developing a Segmentation Model for Microscopic Images of Microplastics Isolated from Clams

Ji Yeon Baek[1] , Maria Krishna de Guzman[2,3] , Ho-min Park[1,6(✉)] ,
Sanghyeon Park[1] , Boyeon Shin[2], Tanja Cirkovic Velickovic[2,3,4,5], Arnout Van
Messem[1,7] , and Wesley De Neve[1,6]

[1] Center for Biotech Data Science, Ghent University Global Campus,
Incheon, South Korea
{jiyeon.baek,homin.park,sanghyeon.park,arnout.vanmessem,
wesley.deneve}@ghent.ac.kr
[2] Center for Food Chemistry and Technology, Ghent University Global Campus,
Incheon, South Korea
{mariakrishna.deguzman,boyeon.shin,tanja.velickovic}@ghent.ac.kr
[3] Department of Food Technology, Safety and Health, Ghent University,
Ghent, Belgium
[4] University of Belgrade - Faculty of Chemistry, Belgrade, Serbia
[5] Serbian Academy of Sciences and Arts, Belgrade, Serbia
[6] IDLab, Department of Electronics and Information Systems, Ghent University,
Ghent, Belgium
[7] Department of Applied Mathematics, Computer Science and Statistics,
Ghent University, Ghent, Belgium

**Abstract.** Microplastics (MP) have become a major concern, given the
threat they pose to marine-derived food and human health. One way to
investigate this threat is to quantify MP found in marine organisms, for
instance making use of image analysis to identify ingested MP in fluorescent microscopic images. In this study, we propose a deep learning-based
segmentation model to generate binarized images (masks) that make it
possible to clearly separate MP from other background elements in the
aforementioned type of images. Specifically, we created three variants
of the U-Net model with a ResNet-101 encoder, training these variants
with 99 high-resolution fluorescent images containing MP, each having a
mask that was generated by experts using manual color threshold adjustments in ImageJ. To that end, we leveraged a sliding window and random
selection to extract patches from the high-resolution images, making it
possible to adhere to input constraints and to increase the number of
labeled examples. When measuring effectiveness in terms of accuracy,
recall, and $F_2$-score, all segmentation models exhibited low scores. However, compared to two ImageJ baseline methods, the effectiveness of
our segmentation models was better in terms of precision, $F_{0.5}$-score,
$F_1$-score, and mIoU: U-Net (1) obtained the highest mIoU of 0.559,
U-Net (2) achieved the highest $F_1$-score of 0.682, and U-Net (3) had the
highest precision and $F_{0.5}$-score of 0.594 and 0.626, respectively, with

J. Y. Baek, M. K. de Guzman, H. Park, and S. Park—Contributed equally.

© Springer Nature Switzerland AG 2021
A. Del Bimbo et al. (Eds.): ICPR 2020 Workshops, LNCS 12666, pp. 86–97, 2021.
https://doi.org/10.1007/978-3-030-68780-9_9

our segmentation models, in general, detecting less false positives in the predicted masks. In addition, U-Net (1), which used binary cross-entropy loss and stochastic gradient descent, and U-Net (2), which used dice loss and Adam, were most effective in discriminating MP from other background elements. Overall, our experimental results suggest that U-Net (1) and U-Net (2) allow for more effective MP identification and measurement than the macros currently available in ImageJ.

**Keywords:** Deep learning · Environmental monitoring · Image segmentation · Microplastics

# 1 Introduction

The production of plastics has increased rapidly since the 1940s, mainly due to the attractive properties of plastic goods (durable, lightweight, corrosion resistant) and inexpensive methods of manufacturing. At present, however, plastics have become a major environmental concern [4]. Specifically, in the marine environment, microplastics or MP (<5 mm) are currently the most dominant form of aquatic plastic litter [5], originating from synthetic polymers that are primarily manufactured in small sizes (primary source) or from the degradation of large plastic fragments (secondary source) [25].

Due to their small size, MP can be ingested by marine organisms during feeding, which raises significant concerns regarding the safety of seafood [27]. As such, MP consumption by marine biota is typically investigated by extracting and isolating MP through filtration. Using a microscope, particles are then manually sorted and counted, often requiring the involvement of more than one researcher to avoid bias in the measurements. Since this method is labor intensive and time consuming, the MP-VAT (microplastics visual analysis tool) macro in ImageJ [24] was developed in 2019. With MP-VAT, the quantity, size, and shape of MP can be automatically and rapidly measured [18,19].

Despite the increased throughput enabled by MP-VAT, this macro is prone to errors caused by background fluorescence and fluorescence halos from very bright particles [19]. In this context, additional corrections have to be made to the image beforehand (i.e., adjustment of the color threshold). This introduces an extra manual step in the process that is subjective and also time consuming. Hence, there is a need for a solution that performs better in terms of MP recognition and measurement.

In this study, we propose a deep learning-based approach that embeds the calibration criteria used by researchers, facilitating the automatic measurement of MP in terms of quantity, size, and shape. Specifically, we created an image segmentation model using deep neural networks, obtaining training data from high-resolution microscopic images of fluorescently-dyed MP isolated from clams.

## 2   Background

### 2.1   Measurement of Microplastics in Seafood Using MP-VAT

Plastic litter has been transferred, directly or indirectly, to the marine environment due to poor waste disposal and management. Because of this, plastic debris is now ubiquitous in all areas of the ocean [1]. As such, MP could be ingested intentionally by marine biota when they are mistakenly seen as plankton or other prey, or accidentally by filter feeding [27]. Bivalves (mussels, clams, and oysters) are commonly used subjects for MP ingestion research since they are non-selective feeders, abundant worldwide, and easy to handle [27]. Aside from these observations, bivalves are usually eaten whole, making them suitable for the assessment of health risks associated with human consumption of food contaminated with MP [9].

Through visual sorting and counting using a microscope, MP measurement was initially performed manually. By making use of fluorescent staining and subsequent image processing in ImageJ, the throughput of MP measurement could be greatly improved, hereby also reducing bias [11]. Nonetheless, until 2019, image analysis still had to be mainly done manually [8]. With the introduction of the MP-VAT macro in ImageJ, the size, shape, and quantity of MP could also be measured automatically [19]. However, a major drawback is the presence of bright image areas, significantly hampering the effectiveness of MP-VAT. This issue is aggravated when images are taken under a microscope, which is the case in most laboratories. Indeed, as a result of high magnification, fluorescence halos and bright areas in the background become more prominent, leading to MP-VAT producing compromised results. Because of this, additional image editing is needed and optimal photography settings have to be determined.

To improve MP-VAT, MP-VAT 2.0 [18] was developed. This second macro eliminates white reflections by subtracting the green from the red channel, which improves the detection of red fluorescent particles. In addition, the color threshold method changed from maximum entropy to Renyi entropy [23]. However, as in the previous case, photographic conditions greatly affect the results, making it necessary to exactly replicate the conditions used by the developers to maximize the effectiveness of both MP-VAT and MP-VAT 2.0. Since there is limited flexibility in this aspect, there is room for an improved automated MP measurement approach based on images.

### 2.2   Image Segmentation and Deep Learning

Image segmentation refers to the process of dividing an image into several meaningful sets of pixels. For example, in everyday life, segmentation is used to divide the pixels in a personal photograph into human and background pixels, and in the medical field, segmentation can be used to make a distinction between cancerous and non-cancerous pixels in magnetic resonance imaging (MRI) slice. In general, this is done by finding a threshold that can distinguish between the region of interest and the background. However, for images containing noise and occlusion, various conditions may have to be considered simultaneously. To solve this problem, many machine learning models have been developed [17]. Given the recent success of deep neural networks, several deep learning-based models have been proposed as well [3, 16, 20].

# 3 Dataset Acquisition

## 3.1 Wet-Lab Phase

**Sampling.** Manila clam samples (*Ruditapes philippinarum*) were bought at the Incheon Complex Fish Market (Incheon, Korea) in May 2019. Immediately after the purchase, the samples were kept on ice. After transport to the laboratory, the clams were wrapped in aluminum foil and stored in a $-20\,^{\circ}C$ freezer.

**Extraction (Digestion) and Purification.** All steps were performed inside a clean bench to avoid contamination. Frozen whole clam tissue was separated from the shell and organic matter was dissolved by incubation $250\,\mathrm{mL}$ 10% KOH at $60\,^{\circ}C$, applying stirring for $24\,\mathrm{h}$ [6]. Through this digestion step, the microplastics that were inside the organism were obtained. Once digestion was completed, samples were vacuum filtered and MP were collected on GF/A (glass microfiber) filters. To separate MP from marine contaminants (sand and silt), filter papers were resuspended in $1.37\,\mathrm{g/ml}$ Zinc Chloride with sonication. After three repetitions, the solutions were centrifuged and the supernatant was filtered to recover MP [14].

**Staining.** Nile Red ($1\,\mathrm{mg/mL}$ in acetone) was added to the purified sample solution at a final concentration of $10\,\mathrm{\mu g/ml}$. The dye was incubated with the sample at $50\,^{\circ}C$ for $30\,\mathrm{min}$ with constant mixing. Solutions were vacuum filtered using a GF/A filter and excess dye was washed with absolute ethanol until minimal background fluorescence was achieved [14].

## 3.2 Dry-Lab Phase

**Capturing and Stitching.** Stained microplastics on filter paper were viewed under a stereomicroscope (Olympus SZX10) equipped with a fluorescence filter unit (RFP filter Ex 545–580 nm, Em 610 nm). Because the filter paper was too large to be captured as a single image, photos were taken by sections (Fig. 1(a)). These sections were combined using Microsoft Image Composite Editor to create a complete image of the sample.

**Binarization.** Each composite image was loaded in ImageJ. First, the scale was set (Analyze > Set Scale) and a representative fluorescent particle was selected to determine the optimal RGB threshold (Image > Adjust > Color threshold) for the automated selection of microplastics. When necessary, RGB values were adjusted manually to ensure the selection of all MP. Afterward, a "mask" image was generated (Edit > Selection > Create mask).

**Counting and Measuring.** The MP-ACT macro [19] was used to automatically measure the size, shape, and quantity of MP in each mask (Plugins > Macros > MP-ACT). MP-ACT is an ImageJ macro that functions similar to MP-VAT, but that allows for manual color thresholding by the user, as opposed to the maximum entropy thresholding technique of MP-VAT.

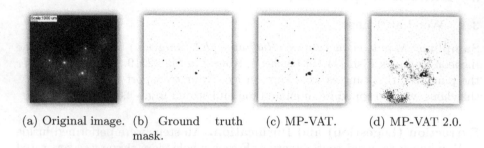

(a) Original image.    (b) Ground    truth    (c) MP-VAT.    (d) MP-VAT 2.0.
                           mask.

**Fig. 1.** (a) A section of the filter paper image with stained MP. In this section, only the very bright particles are MP and the rest is background. (b) The corresponding mask image generated by color threshold adjustments and binarization in ImageJ. In this image, the background noise is removed and only MP are present. (c) The output of MP-VAT [19]. (d) The output of MP-VAT 2.0 [18].

## 4    Methods

As shown in Fig. 1(c) and Fig. 1(d), a major drawback of using the MP-VAT macro is the overestimation of MP. To prevent this from happening, researchers resort to manual color thresholding, as described in Sect. 3.2, which is time consuming, subjective, and prone to error. To solve this problem, we propose a deep learning-based approach that can generate a binarized image (mask) in a few seconds. This approach automatically learns the expert criteria for identifying MP using the 99 original images and their corresponding masks.

### 4.1    Problem Definition

Given an image dataset $\mathcal{D} = (x_i, y_i)_{i=1}^{n}$, where $x_i \in \mathbb{R}^{l \times l}$ is a patch extracted from an original image and where $y_i \in \mathbb{R}^{l \times l}$ is its corresponding mask, let $\mathcal{M}$ be a segmentation model that takes $x_i$ as input and that predicts $\hat{y}_i \in \mathbb{R}^{l \times l}$ as an approximation of the true mask $y_i$:

$$\mathcal{M}(x_i; \theta) = \hat{y}_i \approx y_i, \tag{1}$$

where $\theta$ are the model parameters. The difference between the predicted mask $\hat{y}_i$ and the ground truth mask $y_i$ is quantified by a loss function $L$. Given a segmentation model $\mathcal{M}$ and a loss function $L$, we want to find the values for $\theta$ that minimize the total loss based on the dataset $\mathcal{D}$. Ideally, when a new patch $x_j$ comes in, the trained model $\mathcal{M}$ makes a prediction $\hat{y}_j$ that is close to $y_j$.

## 4.2    Dataset Characteristics

The dataset is composed of 99 original microscopic images, varying in size from $1,280 \times 960$ to $7,140 \times 5,424$ pixels, annotated with corresponding labels (masks). Considering the total number of pixels over all masks, 99.985% of these pixels are background pixels, whereas 0.015% of these pixels are MP pixels, pointing to a substantial imbalance in the type of pixels available. Hence, the original microscopic images and their corresponding masks were divided into five datasets in such a way that each dataset comes with a similar total number of MP pixels. As a result, 19 images were placed in Dataset 1, which was used as the test set, and 20 images were placed in each of the Datasets 2, 3, 4, and 5, and where the latter were used as training and validation sets.

Since each input image should come with a fixed size of $l \times l$ (see Sect. 4.1), which is a common requirement for machine learning methods, the 99 high-resolution images were cropped into patches with a fixed size of $256 \times 256$ pixels, coming with corresponding masks of the same size. Note that, before calculating any performance metrics, the original images (each with a predicted mask) need to be reconstructed from the patches in order to be able to correctly determine the MP quantity, size, and shape per filter paper image.

Patches are extracted by leveraging a sliding window method, using a step size of 30 pixels for both the $x$ and $y$ coordinates. A patch is saved if at least one of its pixels represents MP (as indicated in the corresponding mask). Denoting the number of patches with MP as $N$, then $\lceil N \times 0.05 \rceil$ additional patches without MP are saved, selecting the coordinates for cropping in a random way. A total of 157,474 patches were generated after cropping, with each dataset receiving on average $31,494.8$ ($\pm 5,303.6$) patches, of which, on average, $30,003.8$ ($\pm 5,051.8$) contain MP and $1,491.0$ ($\pm 251.8$) do not contain MP. The number of patches per dataset ranged from $21,645$ to $36,508$.

Given that the number of patches differed from dataset to dataset, the different datasets were adjusted in order to each have a number of patches equal to 20,000. This adjustment was carried out by random deletion of patches, hereby keeping the number of patches without MP at approximately 5% of the number of patches with MP. Thus, each dataset now consists of 20,000 patches, where, on average, $19,084.2$ ($\pm 13.3$) patches contain MP, and $915.8$ ($\pm 13.3$) patches do not contain MP. Overall, 95.4% of the 100,000 patches contain MP, while the remaining 4.6% does not contain MP.

## 4.3    Model Training

We used U-Net [20], a popular convolutional neural network, as our segmentation model $\mathcal{M}$. In particular, U-Net is an encoder-decoder model that was initially developed for medical image segmentation. For our experiments, we chose a U-Net model with a ResNet-101 [10] encoder, pre-trained on ImageNet [22]. A high-level Application Programming Interface (API) [28] has been utilized to build our segmentation model.

**Optimization Methods.** Gradient descent was used to update the parameters $\theta$ of our segmentation model in the negative direction of the gradient of the objective function $\nabla_\theta J(\theta)$, with the goal of minimizing the objective function $J(\theta)$, where $J(\theta)$ corresponds to the average loss. Two different optimization methods were used: (1) Stochastic Gradient Descent (SGD) and (2) Adaptive Moment Estimation (Adam). For both methods, the model parameters are optimized by using the objective function obtained over mini batches consisting of 10 patches.

*Stochastic Gradient Descent.* The mathematical form of SGD is, for instance, described in the technical documentation of PyTorch[1]. Two hyperparameters of SGD need to be determined, namely the momentum $\lambda$ and the learning rate $\alpha$. $\lambda$ allows accelerating the optimization performed by SGD with less fluctuation, whereas $\alpha$ determines the step size made when updating the parameters in each iteration [21]. These hyperparameters were set to 0.9 and 0.003, respectively.

*Adaptive Moment Estimation.* When making use of Adam, the learning rate is computed individually for each parameter. Unlike SGD, which uses gradients directly, Adam utilizes exponentially moving averages of the gradient and the squared gradient [13]. The four hyperparameters of Adam, which are the exponential decay rates $\beta_1$ and $\beta_2$, the learning rate $\alpha$, and the constant for numerical stability $\epsilon$, were set to their default values: $\beta_1 = 0.9$, $\beta_2 = 0.999$, $\alpha = 0.001$, and $\epsilon = 10^{-8}$.

**Loss Functions.** Our experiments used the three loss functions discussed below.

*Binary Cross-Entropy (BCE) with Logits Loss.* BCE with logits loss is a modification of the regular BCE loss function [12], combining the sigmoid activation function and the BCE loss function into a single layer. The use of BCE with logits loss is numerically more stable than the use of the sigmoid activation function and the BCE loss function independently. To mitigate severe class imbalance, the hyperparameter $p$ can be used to weigh the positive samples. In our experiments, $p$ was set to 9.

*Dice Loss.* The dice coefficient, which is widely used for evaluating the effectiveness of segmentation models [26], is a measure for the overlap between a predicted and a ground truth segmentation map. This measure can be used as a loss function which is insensitive to data imbalance [15]. The hyperparameter $\epsilon$, which avoids numerical issues when both the prediction and the ground truth are 0, was set to 1.

*BCE with Dice Loss.* As discussed in [7], BCE and dice loss can be combined. The dice loss focuses on the similarity between the prediction and the ground truth at the image level, whereas the BCE loss focuses on the pixel-wise differences between the prediction and the ground truth.

---

[1] https://pytorch.org/docs/stable/optim.html.

**Model Definition.** We created three different segmentation models, with all three models using a ResNet-101 encoder pre-trained on ImageNet: U-Net (1) uses BCE with logits loss and SGD; U-Net (2) uses dice loss and Adam; and U-Net (3) uses BCE with dice loss and Adam. The effectiveness of the three afore-mentioned segmentation models is compared to the effectiveness of the ImageJ macros MP-VAT and MP-VAT 2.0, with the latter two macros acting as our baselines.

**Cross-Validation.** Among the five available datasets, Dataset 1 was set aside as our test set. Four-fold cross-validation was performed using Datasets 2, 3, 4, and 5, meaning that in each round, one of the four available datasets was used as a validation set and the other three formed the training set. For each of the three segmentation models, four parameter sets were thus obtained. For each segmentation model, the parameter set that gave the lowest validation loss was selected as the optimal parameter set, leading to optimal models for U-Net (1), U-Net (2), and U-Net (3). Using different performance metrics, the effectiveness of these optimal models was then evaluated and compared to the effectiveness of the baselines MP-VAT and MP-VAT 2.0.

## 4.4   Performance Metrics

To evaluate the effectiveness of our segmentation models, we used seven metrics: balanced accuracy, precision, recall, intersection over union (IoU), and three variations of the $F_\beta$-score ($F_{0.5}$-, $F_1$-, and $F_2$-score) (Fig. 2).

$$\text{Precision} = \frac{TP}{TP + FP} \qquad \text{Balanced Accuracy} = \frac{1}{2} \times \left( \frac{TP}{TP + FN} + \frac{TN}{FP + TN} \right)$$

$$\text{Recall} = \frac{TP}{TP + FN} \qquad \text{IoU} = \frac{|A \cap B|}{|A \cup B|} \qquad F_\beta\text{-score} = \frac{(1 + \beta^2) \times (\text{precision} \times \text{recall})}{\beta^2 \times \text{precision} + \text{recall}}$$

**Fig. 2.** The performance metrics used. $TP$ denotes the number of true positives, $TN$ the number of true negatives, $FP$ the number of false positives, and $FN$ the number of false negatives. For IoU, $A$ denotes the number of MP pixels in the ground truth mask, whereas $B$ denotes the number of MP pixels in the predicted mask. In case of the $F_\beta$-score, $\beta$ values of 0.5, 1, and 2 were used to calculate the $F_{0.5}$-, $F_1$-, and $F_2$-score, respectively.

Note that all metrics, with the exception of IoU, are calculated using the average $TP$, $TN$, $FP$, and $FN$ values, as obtained from four-fold cross valida-tion. In this context, the obtained balanced accuracy value is referred to as the mean balanced accuracy (mAcc). On a similar note, the average IoU value, as obtained for the 19 images in the test set, is denoted as mean IoU (mIoU).

## 5   Results and Discussion

Our experimental results are summarized in Table 1. Overall, the effectiveness of MP-VAT 2.0 was found to be low for all performance metrics used. As can be seen in Fig. 1(d), holes are prominently present in the center of several MP elements. Indeed, MP-VAT 2.0 seems to have removed the highest values in the image when subtracting both the green and blue channels. As a result, the center of several MP elements is missing in a mask, making it difficult for these MP elements to be properly identified.

**Table 1.** Performance evaluation.

| Model | mAcc | Precision | Recall | mIoU | $F_{0.5}$-score | $F_1$-score | $F_2$-score |
|---|---|---|---|---|---|---|---|
| MP-VAT | 0.986 | 0.431 | 0.971 | 0.392 | 0.485 | 0.597 | 0.777 |
| MP-VAT 2.0 | 0.719 | 0.002 | 0.455 | 0.139 | 0.003 | 0.005 | 0.012 |
| U-Net (1) | 0.934 | 0.505 | 0.868 | 0.559 | 0.551 | 0.638 | 0.759 |
| U-Net (2) | 0.906 | 0.587 | 0.812 | 0.557 | 0.622 | 0.682 | 0.755 |
| U-Net (3) | 0.899 | 0.594 | 0.799 | 0.519 | 0.626 | 0.681 | 0.747 |

MP-VAT, on the other hand, comes with higher effectiveness, achieving an mAcc of 0.986, a recall of 0.971, and an $F_2$-score of 0.777. As shown in Fig. 1(c), highly fluorescent MP are intact and visible in the mask. However, similar to MP-VAT 2.0, some areas of the background are also mistaken to be MP. Because of this, MP-VAT scores are low in terms of mIoU, $F_{0.5}$-score, $F_1$-score, and precision. In comparison, all U-Net-based models score higher with respect to these four metrics. U-Net (1) and U-Net (2) have the best scores for mIoU and $F_1$-score, respectively. U-Net (3) obtains the best scores for $F_{0.5}$-score and precision. The increase in precision using the U-Net-based models greatly reduces the number of $FPs$, thereby improving the discrimination between MP and background. This fact is also observed through the $F_{0.5}$-score, since all U-Net-based models obtain higher values than MP-VAT. Within the U-Net-based models, both U-Net (2) and U-Net (3) show better handling of FPs than U-Net (1). As illustrated in Fig. 3(c), Fig. 3(d), and Fig. 3(e), the predicted masks are closer to the ground truth mask. Moreover, the impact of background fluorescence and fluorescence halos was considerably reduced, as compared to Fig. 3(a) and Fig. 3(b).

Based on the values obtained for the different metrics, it is not straightforward to select which U-Net-based model is most effective. However, U-Net (3) seems to be the least effective among the different models used, coming with the lowest mAcc, recall, $F_2$-score, and mIoU. In spite of these low scores, the generated masks, with an example shown in Fig. 3(e), still demonstrate considerable improvement in discriminating MP from other elements in a fluorescent image.

In summary, our results show that the U-Net-based models are more effective at predicting MP, compared to MP-VAT and MP-VAT 2.0. Specifically, despite

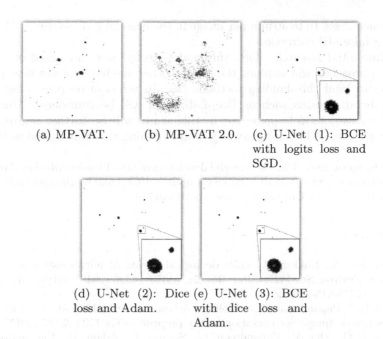

(a) MP-VAT.    (b) MP-VAT 2.0.    (c) U-Net (1): BCE with logits loss and SGD.

(d) U-Net (2): Dice loss and Adam.    (e) U-Net (3): BCE with dice loss and Adam.

**Fig. 3.** Visual comparison of the segmentation quality obtained for each segmentation model: black denotes MP that has been correctly predicted ($TP$), red denotes predicted MP that is not MP ($FP$), and green denotes MP that has not been predicted ($FN$). (Color figure online)

a lower balanced accuracy and recall, U-Net (1), U-Net (2), and U-Net (3) introduce significant gains in terms of mIoU, $F_{0.5}$-score, $F_1$-score, and precision.

## 6    Conclusions and Future Work

Effective and efficient MP identification and measurement in biological samples remain a challenge. Currently available methods that rely on image processing, such as MP-VAT and MP-VAT 2.0, come with limited flexibility and are prone to errors. In this study, we present a deep learning-based segmentation approach for MP measurement, serving as an alternative to MP-VAT and MP-VAT 2.0. Three variations of U-Net, all using a pre-trained ResNet-101 encoder, were tested in terms of generating masks that depict true MP.

Compared to the MP-VAT macros, all U-Net-based models exhibited better mIoU, $F_{0.5}$-score, $F_1$-score, and precision values, with the masks generated by these U-Net-based models containing less false positives. In this context, the effectiveness of U-Net (1) and U-Net (2) was found to be slightly better than the effectiveness of U-Net (3). Furthermore, since the U-Net-based models have a response time of less than two seconds after input of the original image, their usage is expected to significantly reduce the time and effort required to produce a mask, which takes 10 to 30 min per image in the original process using MP-VAT, including false MP correction.

In this initial research effort, the models tested were all based on U-Net. Future approaches will explore the use of other models, for instance paying attention to local thresholding methods [29]. In terms of deep learning, other state-of-the-art models such as DeepLabV3 [2] will be considered. Moreover, the U-Net-based models presented in this study will be further improved by modifying the model training strategy and enriching the training dataset used.

**Acknowledgements.** The research and development activities described in this paper were funded by Ghent University Global Campus (GUGC) and by the Special Research Fund (BOF) of Ghent University (grant no. 01N01718).

# References

1. Anbumani, S., Kakkar, P.: Ecotoxicological effects of microplastics on biota: a review. Environ. Sci. Pollut. Res. **25**(15), 14373–14396 (2018). https://doi.org/10.1007/s11356-018-1999-x
2. Chen, L.C., Papandreou, G., Schroff, F., Adam, H.: Rethinking Atrous Convolution for Semantic Image Segmentation. arXiv preprint arXiv:1706.05587 (2017)
3. Chen, L.-C., Zhu, Y., Papandreou, G., Schroff, F., Adam, H.: Encoder-decoder with atrous separable convolution for semantic image segmentation. In: Ferrari, V., Hebert, M., Sminchisescu, C., Weiss, Y. (eds.) ECCV 2018. LNCS, vol. 11211, pp. 833–851. Springer, Cham (2018). https://doi.org/10.1007/978-3-030-01234-2_49
4. Cole, M., Lindeque, P., Halsband, C., Galloway, T.S.: Microplastics as contaminants in the marine environment: a review. Mar. Pollut. Bull. **62**(12), 2588–2597 (2011)
5. Cressey, D.: The plastic ocean. Nature **536**(7616), 263–265 (2016)
6. Dehaut, A., et al.: Microplastics in seafood: benchmark protocol for their extraction and characterization. Environ. Pollut. **215**, 223–233 (2016)
7. Deng, R., Shen, C., Liu, S., Wang, H., Liu, X.: Learning to predict crisp boundaries. In: Ferrari, V., Hebert, M., Sminchisescu, C., Weiss, Y. (eds.) ECCV 2018. LNCS, vol. 11210, pp. 570–586. Springer, Cham (2018). https://doi.org/10.1007/978-3-030-01231-1_35
8. Erni-Cassola, G., Gibson, M.I., Thompson, R.C., Christie-Oleza, J.A.: Lost, but found with nile red: a novel method for detecting and quantifying small microplastics (1 mm to 20 μm) in environmental samples. Environ. Sci. Technol **51**(23), 13641–13648 (2017)
9. Galloway, T.S.: Micro- and nano-plastics and human health. In: Bergmann, M., Gutow, L., Klages, M. (eds.) Mar. Anthropogenic Litter, pp. 343–366. Springer, Cham (2015). https://doi.org/10.1007/978-3-319-16510-3_13
10. He, K., Zhang, X., Ren, S., Sun, J.: Deep residual learning for image recognition. In: Proceedings of the IEEE Conference on Computer Vision and Pattern Recognition (CVPR) (2016)
11. Isobe, A., Kubo, K., Tamura, Y., Nakashima, E., Fujii, N., et al.: Selective transport of microplastics and mesoplastics by drifting in coastal waters. Mar. Pollut. Bull. **89**(1–2), 324–330 (2014)
12. Jadon, S.: A survey of loss functions for semantic segmentation. arXiv preprint arXiv:2006.14822 (2020)

13. Kingma, D.P., Ba, J.: Adam: A Method for Stochastic Optimization. arXiv preprint arXiv:1412.6980 (2014)
14. Maes, T., Jessop, R., Wellner, N., Haupt, K., Mayes, A.G.: A rapid-screening approach to detect and quantify microplastics based on fluorescent tagging with Nile Red. Sci. Rep. **7**(1), 1–10 (2017)
15. Milletari, F., Navab, N., Ahmadi, S.A.: V-Net: fully convolutional neural networks for volumetric medical image segmentation. In: 2016 Fourth International Conference on 3D Vision (3DV), pp. 565–571. IEEE (2016)
16. Minaee, S., Boykov, Y., Porikli, F., Plaza, A., Kehtarnavaz, N., Terzopoulos, D.: Image Segmentation Using Deep Learning: A Survey. arXiv preprint arXiv:2001.05566 (2020)
17. Murphy, K.P.: Machine Learning: A Probabilistic Perspective. MIT press, Cambridge (2012)
18. Prata, J.C., Alves, J.R., da Costa, J.P., Duarte, A.C., Rocha-Santos, T.: Major factors influencing the quantification of Nile Red stained microplastics and improved automatic quantification (MP-VAT 2.0). Sci. Total Environ. **719**, 137498 (2020)
19. Prata, J.C., Reis, V., Matos, J.T., da Costa, J.P., Duarte, A.C., Rocha-Santos, T.: A new approach for routine quantification of microplastics using Nile Red and automated software (MP-VAT). Sci. Total Environ. **690**, 1277–1283 (2019)
20. Ronneberger, O., Fischer, P., Brox, T.: U-Net: convolutional networks for biomedical image segmentation. In: Navab, N., Hornegger, J., Wells, W.M., Frangi, A.F. (eds.) MICCAI 2015. LNCS, vol. 9351, pp. 234–241. Springer, Cham (2015). https://doi.org/10.1007/978-3-319-24574-4_28
21. Ruder, S.: An overview of gradient descent optimization algorithms. arXiv preprint arXiv:1609.04747 (2016)
22. Russakovsky, O., et al.: ImageNet large scale visual recognition challenge. Int. J. Comput. Vis. **115**(3), 211–252 (2015). https://doi.org/10.1007/s11263-015-0816-y
23. Rényi, A.: On measures of entropy and information. In: Proceedings of the Fourth Berkeley Symposium on Mathematical Statistics and Probability: Contributions to the Theory of Statistics, vol. 1, pp. 547–561. The Regents of the University of California, University of California Press (1961)
24. Schneider, C.A., Rasband, W.S., Eliceiri, K.W.: NIH Image to ImageJ: 25 years of image analysis. Nat. Methods **9**(7), 671–675 (2012)
25. Silva, A.B., Bastos, A.S., Justino, C.I., da Costa, J.P., Duarte, A.C., Rocha-Santos, T.A.: Microplastics in the environment: challenges in analytical chemistry - a review. Analytica Chimica Acta **1017**, 1–19 (2018)
26. Sudre, C.H., Li, W., Vercauteren, T., Ourselin, S., Jorge Cardoso, M.: Generalised dice overlap as a deep learning loss function for highly unbalanced segmentations. In: Cardoso, M.J., et al. (eds.) DLMIA/ML-CDS -2017. LNCS, vol. 10553, pp. 240–248. Springer, Cham (2017). https://doi.org/10.1007/978-3-319-67558-9_28
27. Wesch, C., Bredimus, K., Paulus, M., Klein, R.: Towards the suitable monitoring of ingestion of microplastics by marine biota: A review. Environ. Pollut. **218**, 1200–1208 (2016)
28. Yakubovskiy, P.: Segmentation Models (2019). https://github.com/qubvel/segmentation_models
29. Yan, F., Zhang, H., Kube, C.R.: A multistage adaptive thresholding method. Pattern Recogn. Lett **26**(8), 1183–1191 (2005).https://doi.org/10.1016/j.patrec.2004.11.003, http://www.sciencedirect.com/science/article/pii/S0167865504003290

# A Machine Learning Approach to Chlorophyll *a* Time Series Analysis in the Mediterranean Sea

F. Mattei[1,2](✉) and M. Scardi[1,2]

[1] Experimental Ecology and Aquaculture Laboratory, Department of Biology,
University of Rome "Tor Vergata", Rome, Italy
francesco.mattei90@yahoo.it
[2] CoNISMa, Piazzale Flaminio, 9, 00196 Rome, Italy

**Abstract.** Understanding the dynamics of natural system is a crucial task in ecology especially when climate change is taken into account. In this context, assessing the evolution of marine ecosystems is pivotal since they cover a large portion of the biosphere.

For these reasons, we decided to develop an approach aimed at evaluating temporal and spatial dynamics of remotely-sensed chlorophyll *a* concentration. The concentrations of this pigment are linked with phytoplankton biomass and production, which in turn play a central role in marine environment.

Machine learning techniques proved to be valuable tools in dealing with satellite data since they need neither assumptions on data distribution nor explicit mathematical formulations. Accordingly, we exploited the Self Organizing Map (SOM) algorithm firstly to reconstruct missing data from satellite time series of chlorophyll *a* and secondly to classify them. The missing data reconstruction task was performed using a large SOM and allowed to enhance the available information filling the gaps caused by cloud coverage. The second part of the procedure involved a much smaller SOM used as a classification tool. This dimensionality reduction enabled the analysis and visualization of over 37 000 chlorophyll *a* time series. The proposed approach provided insights into both temporal and spatial chlorophyll *a* dynamics in the Mediterranean Basin.

**Keywords:** Chlorophyll *a* · Time series analysis · Self organizing maps

## 1 Introduction

Natural systems are inherently complex and dynamic. The understanding of this complexity is one of the most fascinating and challenging tasks in the ecological field. This is especially true in a climate change context in which the anthropogenic influences exert a major role in driving the ecosystems evolution and interactions [1, 2]. In this framework, it is important to study the temporal variability of biotic and abiotic processes taking place in natural systems.

Marine ecosystems cover roughly 70% of the Earth's surface and they are intimately linked with the climate of our planet through a series of complex interactions with terrestrial and atmospheric systems [3, 4]. Chlorophyll *a* concentration is one of the most

© Springer Nature Switzerland AG 2021
A. Del Bimbo et al. (Eds.): ICPR 2020 Workshops, LNCS 12666, pp. 98–109, 2021.
https://doi.org/10.1007/978-3-030-68780-9_10

important parameters in the study of aquatic environment. In fact, the concentration of this pigment is a proxy for phytoplankton biomass and an indicator of its physiological state [5]. In turn, phytoplankton accounts for the bulk of marine primary production, thus providing the main source of energy for structuring the marine food webs [6]. As autotrophs organisms, their $CO_2$ sequestration from the aquatic environment plays a central role in the air-sea interaction [7]. Furthermore, the sinking of organic matter is one of the process that determines the oceans ability to buffer the anthropogenic $CO_2$ emission [8].

For these reasons, we believe that the chlorophyll *a* dynamics are a crucial topic in modern oceanography and we decided to develop a methodology to investigate their evolution through time. Satellite platforms provide synoptic measurements of chlorophyll *a* surface concentration repeated through time at regular intervals, i.e. daily or monthly. Each satellite chlorophyll *a* measurement for a given point repeated trough time can be seen as a time series. This remotely-sensed information represents a valuable source of data for oceanographers and can be exploited to enhance our understanding of the marine environment. Dealing with big data is a challenging task but computer science could provide game changing approaches, such as machine learning techniques [9]. If properly employed and their results accurately interpreted, these techniques can help extracting patterns from the data as well as classifying available records and forecasting new values [10–12].

In this work we developed an approach to pre-process and analysed remotely-sensed chlorophyll *a* time. We retrieved all the chlorophyll *a* data from the SeaWiFS and the MODIS-aqua satellites. We chose the 9 km monthly mean data since they represented the longest available series, i.e. from 1998 to present. We merged all the data in single dataset in which each row represented a scanned pixel in the Mediterranean while the 264 columns corresponded to the monthly surface chlorophyll *a* concentration from 1998 to 2019.

We aimed at developing an approach that would provide insights on the studied system evolving dynamics in a climate change context. To reach our goal, we exploited the Self Organizing Map (SOM) algorithm [13]. We utilized the SOM technique to both fill the gap in the data and classify the Mediterranean chlorophyll *a* time series [14, 15]. We wanted to find the balance between the ordination and classification behaviours of this versatile technique to fulfil our scopes. We built a large map which helped us reconstructing missing data due to cloud coverage, while a smaller one allowed to classify and extract patterns from the chlorophyll *a* time series. We analysed for each class whether a trend was present or not and the characteristics of the series in relation to both geographical area and eventual trends. To the best of our knowledge, this type of approach has never been used to analyse remotely-sensed oceanographical data in which each pixel of the study area was associated with an independent time series. Therefore, in this work we took into account both temporal and spatial dynamics of chlorophyll *a* and analysed them from an ecological perspective.

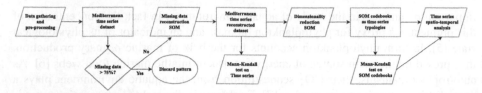

**Fig. 1.** Chlorophyll *a* time series analysis flowchart

## 2  Materials and Methods

### 2.1  Data Collection and Pre-processing

The chlorophyll *a* data for this work were downloaded from the NASA ocean color website (https://oceancolor.gsfc.nasa.gov/). We chose the 9 km monthly mean data for their span time. In fact, these data were collected during both the SeaWiFS mission (September 1997–December 2010) and the MODIS-aqua one (July 2003–Present), thus representing the longest series available. We used the SeaWiFS data from 1998 to 2003 and the MODIS-aqua ones from 2004 to 2019 for a total of 22 years (264 months). Each monthly grid comprised $2160 \times 4320$ (latitude $\times$ longitude) data points including missing data and land points (Fig. 1).

We decided to limit the study area to the Mediterranean Basin for the development of a new approach to chlorophyll *a* spatial time series analysis. This allowed to test several SOM architectures and to exploit ecological knowledge to find the best solution for the data analysis. Therefore, we extracted only the Mediterranean related data for each month creating 264 grids with a dimension of $188 \times 509$ (latitude $\times$ longitude). The latitude of each grid ranged from 45.79 to 30.20°, while the longitude ranged from $-6.04$ to 36.29°. Afterwards, we merged the 264 grids into a single dataset. The new dataset comprised 39412 rows, one for each pixel in the Mediterranean, and 264 columns, one for each monthly chlorophyll *a* value from 1998 to 2019.

We decided to apply a logarithmic transformation to our series before performing any further analysis. This transformation minimized the effect of large values which could have skewed the whole work.

### 2.2  SOM as a Missing Data Reconstruction Technique

We analysed the missing data in our dataset. The series with no missing values were 80.07% of the total while only 5.06% lacked more than 25% of the data. We decided to exclude from our analysis only the latter group of series and to fill the gaps in the ones which presented at maximum 25% of missing values. The lack of information for certain pixels was due to cloud coverage which impeded the satellite to receive information from the ocean surface. This is an important limiting factor in the application of satellite-based measures and being able to reconstruct missing values from available ones could be extremely valuable [16, 17].

We decided to use a SOM algorithm to assess the missing values. This machine learning technique is able to transform a high dimensional input space into a simpler low-dimensional one while preserving the topology of the data. Moreover, no assumption regarding the distribution of the variables or their independence is needed. These features could be crucial in analysing time series. Finally, this algorithm can easily deal with missing and noisy data, which is particularly valuable when working with environmental variables [14, 15]. Accordingly, when a training pattern shows missing data, the distance between the pattern and the SOM units is computed using only the available data. For this work we used the R package Kohonen (3.0.1) [18], which provides a user-friendly implementation of the SOM algorithm.

To evaluate the ability of the SOM algorithm to reconstruct missing data in our dataset, we divided the data in a training set (35843 series) and a test set (1575 series). The test patterns were extracted only among the series which did not present missing values. Firstly, we used a k-means algorithm to divide the complete series in five groups. We arbitrarily set k equal to five since this step aimed only at stratify our data. Secondly, we randomly sampled 5% of the data from each of the five groups. This procedure allowed to build a randomly sampled test set which was representative of the whole dataset variability. Finally, we randomly eliminated 25% of the data from each test set series. The latter procedure created a collection of artificially missing data. After training the SOM, we assessed its accuracy in filling the data gaps by mapping the test set on the trained map and comparing the artificially removed data with the BMU ones. We used the Mean Square Error (MSE) as error metric. The test subset was used to evaluate the trained SOMs ability to reconstruct time series missing values on the basis of existing ones.

We trained ten SOMs with 96, 150, 300, 408, 500, 600, 750, 875, 1050 and 1200 nodes respectively. According to Vesanto and Alhoniemi (2000) [19] as rule of thumb the optimal number of nodes should be $5 \times \sqrt{(N\_samples)}$ so we did not largely exceed this number in our tests. We used the Euclidean distance as distance measure and a gaussian neighbourhood function. The neighbourhood radius was set to 2/3 of all unit-to-unit distance and decreased linearly to 0 during the epochs. We opted for a hexagonal non toroidal topology for our maps and we performed an online training with 500 epochs. The learning rate value was set to 0.05 and it decreased linearly to 0.01 over the number of epochs.

Subsequently, we mapped the test set series on the trained SOMs, we reconstructed the missing values using those in the Best Matching Unit (BMU) of the map and computed the error comparing the reconstructed value with the real one. We performed this procedure filling five different percentages of missing values for each series, i.e. 5%, 10%, 15%, 20% and 25%, and evaluated the SOMs ability to assess the missing information.

After the data recovery phase, the new dataset comprised 37418 chlorophyll *a* series without any missing value. By exploiting the new information, we tested the significance of a monotonic trend for each Mediterranean pixel series using the seasonal version of the Mann-Kendall test ($\alpha = 0.05$) [20, 21].

### 2.3 SOM as a Classifier for Pattern Extraction

Due to the large numerosity, we could not investigate the behaviour of all the time series. We decided to reduce the dimensionality of our dataset exploiting the SOM algorithm again. We opted for a small dimensional map to constrain the Mediterranean series into classes represented by the SOM codebooks and analysed these vectors to extract patterns from our dataset [15, 19, 22].

We trained ten SOMs with 12, 15, 18, 20, 24, 30, 35, 40, 48 and 54 nodes respectively to find the best number of nodes to represent the chlorophyll $a$ data. We joined two different criteria to find the best solution. As previously done for the Mediterranean pixels, we tested the significance of a monotonic trend for each codebook using the seasonal version of the Mann-Kendall test ($\alpha = 0.05$). We compared the trend direction and significance of the pixel series with the ones of their BMU. The number of matching trends over the total number of patterns was used as accuracy measure for the SOMs. In this way, we evaluated if the dataset series and their BMUs presented the same monotonic trend features. The second criterion was the proportion of codebooks that showed a significant trend. This measure helped us evaluate if the increased number of nodes was followed by an increase in the dataset features representation.

Once selected the optimal SOM for extracting pattern from our dataset, we analysed the position of the codebooks on the SOM map in relation to both their trends and the differences between the series contained in them. Finally, we analysed the characteristics of the SOM from a geographical perspective. Accordingly, we mapped the chlorophyll $a$ series associated with codebooks that showed a significant trend.

The use of the SOM algorithm as a classifier for pattern extraction was performed in a dual mode. In the first one we trained the SOMs with unscaled data to keep the magnitude signal of the series into account. The alternative modality of SOMs training was carried out after scaling each series in the 0–1 range. In this way each series was reduced to a temporal shape, thus excluding the series magnitude information.

We compared the results of the two approaches to evaluate whether or not they led to the same conclusions.

# 3 Results and Discussion

## 3.1 Missing Data Reconstruction

To assess the ability of the SOM algorithm to reconstruct the missing chlorophyll $a$ information from the available one, we divided our dataset into a training (35843 series) and a test set (1575 series). The latter patterns were selected only among complete series, i.e. no missing values. Afterwards, we randomly removed 25% of each test set series and evaluated the accuracy of 10 different SOMs in reconstructing these data points computing the MSE between the real and the estimated values. The larger the number of nodes the lower the MSE. Moreover, the MSE oscillations related to the different percentage of missing data tend to level out for number of nodes greater than 750. We also computed the quantization error which showed a linearly decreasing pattern as expected. Since the only scope in this phase was to exploit the SOM algorithm to reconstruct missing data, we opted for the SOM with 1200 nodes. This solution showed the lowest error for each percentage of missing data and the lowest quantization error.

Subsequently, we applied the Mann-Kendall seasonal tests to our chlorophyll $a$ series in order to check the sign and the significance of a monotonic trend. Since we used monthly data for our work, we set the period parameter of the test to 12. We set $\alpha$ equal to 0.05 to determine whether the test was significant or not and we used the $\tau$ value to

**Fig. 2.** Mann-Kendal τ. Blue pixels showed a decreasing trend, while the red ones presented an increasing trend. The white pixel did not show a significant monotonic trend with an α = 0.05. (Color figure online)

check the direction of significant trends. The larger the absolute value of τ the stronger is the trend intensity, while the sign of this parameter indicates the direction of the trend. The map of the Mann-Kendall τ for the Mediterranean basin is showed in Fig. 2.

The number of time series that showed no trend, increasing and decreasing trend were 26198, 5604, 5616 respectively.

From Fig. 2 we can notice that the eastern portion of the basin showed little to no trend, with the exception of the area around the Strait of Gibraltar, the Balearic Islands and the area south of Ibiza. The Tyrrhenian Sea showed a significant increasing trend in coastal areas and in a large southern portion, i.e. off the coast of Campania, Calabria and Sicilia. The Adriatic and the Ionian Sea showed a prevalence of increasing trend in chlorophyll *a* surface concentration. On the other hand, the South-central portion of the basin was characterized by a predominant decreasing trend with the exception of the coastal areas which showed the presence of an increasing one. The western Mediterranean presented both increasing and decreasing coastal trends and an increasing trend south of Kriti Island. Finally, the Aegean Sea showed an increasing trend off the coast of Turkey and a decreasing trend in the northern zone off the coast of Greece.

The above described map was the representation of a large number of series. This large amount of data complicated any further analysis. We decided to reduce the dataset dimensionality by classifying our series to get a deeper insight into the evolution of the phytoplankton biomass time series in the Med bas during the two last decades.

### 3.2 Classification of Chlorophyll *a* Time Series

We used the SOM algorithm as a classifier to reduce the dataset dimensionality and further investigate the remotely-sensed chlorophyll *a* time series [15, 19, 22, 23].

We trained 10 relatively small SOMs, i.e. from 12 to 54 nodes, and used the nodes codebooks as representative series for all the data that fell into them.

This classification caused a loss of details with respect to the whole collection of data but it allowed extracting general patterns from the dataset.

We merged two different criteria in order to select the optimal classifier. The first one was the agreement between the chlorophyll *a* time series monotonic trend and the trend of their BMU codebook. The larger the accuracy value, the larger the agreement between the SOM classification and the satellite data. The second element taken into account was the proportion of nodes showing a significant trend. This index helped us in determining whether or not the augmented complexity in the SOM structure was justified by an enhanced representation of the dataset characteristics. Following these criteria, we selected the SOM with 35 nodes as the optimal solution. This SOM configuration showed the highest level of accuracy and the second largest proportion of significant nodes over the total number of units. After the classification SOM choice, we investigated both the codebooks characteristics and their distribution on the SOM (Fig. 3). Figure 3 shows that the nodes with an increasing trend were characterized by a large level of variability.

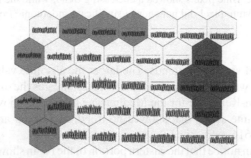

**Fig. 3.** Optimal classification SOM (35 nodes). Each codebook was plotted inside its unit. The red nodes presented a codebook with a significant increasing trend, the blue ones showed a decreasing trend, while the Mann-Kendall test was not significant for the white unit codebooks. (Color figure online)

In fact, we can highlight three typologies of codebooks. The ones in the lower left corner of the map presented a high magnitude of chlorophyll *a* concentration, especially the first node of the second row. On the other hand, the red nodes in the top row showed the lowest values among the increasing trend codebooks. In between these two groups we had the first node of the fourth row which showed an intermediate biomass level coupled with an increasing trend.

Conversely, the codebooks characterized by a decreasing trend formed a single group in the middle right portion of the map. The principal feature shared by these nodes was the low chlorophyll *a* value.

**Fig. 4.** Series trend derived by the classification SOM with 35 nodes. Red areas represent the series which fell into codebooks with increasing trend while the blue areas showed the decreasing trend ones. (Color figure online)

The majority of the codebooks did not show any significant monotonic trend in accordance with the real data. This group was the most heterogeneous one encompassing time series with different features. From a general perspective, the codebooks clearly showed that the biomass signal deeply influenced the SOM training. We can notice a clear magnitude drop from the bottom left corner towards the top right one.

Figure 4 shows the pattern of increasing and decreasing trends reconstructed by the classification SOM with 35 nodes. Regardless the inevitable loss of information with respect to the real series, we can see that the main signal has been captured (Fig. 4 vs Fig. 2) with the exception of the increasing trend in the Tyrrhenian Sea and the decreasing one in the northern Aegean Sea. Moreover, this simplification allowed to extract temporal and spatial patterns from over 37 000 time series.

In order to evaluate the relation between the nodes in Fig. 3 and the trend map (Fig. 4), we produced a second map in which the codebooks with significant trend were represented with different colours (Fig. 5).

**Fig. 5.** Geographical position of Fig. 3 nodes that showed a codebook with significant trend. In the map each node is represented by a different colour. (Color figure online)

This allowed to analyse the geographical distribution of these codebooks. We noted an increase in biomass from the coast towards the open sea in the series with an increasing trend. The orange series BMU was first node of the second row which showed the largest chlorophyll *a* values.

Accordingly, the orange points were close to the coastline. The areas mainly characterized by these series were a north-western portion of the basin, the north Adriatic Sea, the Gulf of Manfredonia in the south Adriatic Sea, the Gulf of Gabes in Tunisia, the coast of Egypt and Israel. The next series in term of magnitude was the yellow one which corresponded to the first node of the first row. This cluster was present in the same zones of the orange one plus an area around the Strait of Gibraltar. Figure 4 shows that the orange and the yellow clusters are the ones associated with the largest values of Mann-Kendall $\tau$, thus showing a stronger increasing trend. The last node of the increasing trend group with largest biomass was the second node of the second row which was represented in red in Fig. 5. This series were mainly distributed along the western Mediterranean coastlines, the Tyrrhenian Sea coastal areas, the southern portion of the Adriatic Sea and the north-eastern Aegean Sea. The dark-red points referred to the first node of the fourth row, which was the one with intermediate level of biomass among the increasing trend codebooks. This cluster characterized mainly the Adriatic Sea, the Strait of Gibraltar and the area off the coast of Tunisia. The increasing trend group with lower biomass referred to the second, third and fourth nodes of the last row represented by the colour pink, fuchsia and violet-red respectively. These groups were mainly localized in the central Adriatic, Ionian and Aegean Sea plus the area off shore of the Tunisia, the coastlines of Libya, Lebanon, Syria and Turkey.

As to the decreasing group of codebooks, they interested the South portion of the Mediterranean Basin between Sicily Island and north Africa. These series showed a clear trend of decreasing biomass from East to West.

Since the chlorophyll *a* magnitude played an important role in the SOMs training, we decided to repeat the classification procedure scaling each series in the 0–1 range. Performing this operation allowed to remove the amplitude signal from the time series. We trained the same number of SOMs with the same configuration and we chose the best one using the previously described criteria. In this case we chose the SOM with 20 nodes (Fig. 6).

When the SOMs were trained with the scaled series, it seems that the trend in both its direction and magnitude guided the classification (Fig. 6). In fact, we had two macro groups characterized by the direction of the trend and a pattern of decreasing intensity from lower left nodes to the upper right ones.

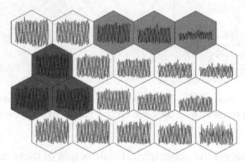

**Fig. 6.** Optimal classification SOM with scaled time series (20 nodes). Each codebook was plotted inside its unit. The red nodes presented a codebook with a significant increasing trend, the blue ones showed a decreasing trend, while the Mann-Kendall test was not significant for the white unit codebooks. (Color figure online)

The latter feature can be evinced comparing Fig. 7 and 8. As to the increasing trend codebooks, they showed an increase in the Mann-Kendall τ (Fig. 7) from the third to the last unit of the last row which corresponded to yellow, red and orange points respectively (Fig. 8).

The same observation can be applied to the decreasing trend codebook, which showed a decrease in the trend magnitude from west to east.

From a general perspective, the analysis of scaled series highlighted the same features showed by the non-scaled one. This result was not surprising but provided additional information. In fact, the presence of a trend should be deeply influence by this type o data manipulation. The agreement proved that the trend was not determined by variation in chlorophyll *a* magnitude as expected in a climate change scenario.

**Fig. 7.** Scaled series trend derived by the classification SOM with 20 nodes. Red areas represent the series which fell into codebooks with increasing trend while the blue areas showed the decreasing trend ones. (Color figure online)

**Fig. 8.** Geographical position of Fig. 6 nodes that showed a codebook with significant trend. In the map each node is represented by a different colour. (Color figure online)

The concordance between the two analysis suggests that the chlorophyll *a* dynamics in the Mediterranean Basin are changing. Moreover, from this work emerged that the direction and intensity of this change depends on both the geographic area and the chlorophyll *a* concentration magnitude.

The cons of the analysis proposed in this work are related to the nature of the satellite data. In fact, these data are gathered only from the surface layers of the water column. On the other hand, satellite platforms provide free information on a synoptic scale, which could be crucial for several oceanographical studies. Moreover, the proposed approach is not a turnkey method since several tests are needed to find the optimal solution. The pros of our approach are twofold. Firstly, reconstructing the time series missing data using the SOM algorithm mimed a k-nearest neighbors approach with the advantage of a variable k instead of a fixed one. In fact, the larger the data density of a SOM area the larger the value of k-neighbors from which the codebook is derived. Moreover, the alternative method for this task would have been an interpolation technique which has its own pro and cons. Finally, the dimensionality reduction allowed to assign several geographical areas to a single time series typology. This complexity reduction enabled an easier analysis and presentation of both spatial and temporal chlorophyll *a* dynamics.

# 4    Conclusions

In this work we aimed at exploiting the valuable information provided by satellite platforms to perform an analysis of the chlorophyll *a* concentration dynamics. Firstly, we used the SOM algorithm to fill the gaps in the dataset caused by cloud coverage. Subsequently, we exploited the classification behaviour of this technique to reduce the dimensionality of our data and extract both temporal and spatial patterns from them. This approach allowed to investigate a big dataset of remotely-sensed time series which were structured in time and space. We believe that the assessment of natural system dynamics should be a key topic in modern ecology, especially in a climate change context, and that machine learning approaches could be valuable tools to fit this scope.

# References

1. Barange, M., et al.: Impacts of climate change on marine ecosystem production in societies dependent on fisheries. Nat. Clim. Change. **4**, 211–216 (2014). https://doi.org/10.1038/ncl imate2119
2. Grimm, N.B., et al.: The impacts of climate change on ecosystem structure and function. Front. Ecol. Environ. **11**, 474–482 (2013). https://doi.org/10.1890/120282
3. Costanza, R.: The ecological, economic, and social importance of the oceans. Ecol. Econ. **31**, 199–213 (1999). https://doi.org/10.1016/S0921-8009(99)00079-8
4. Kildow, J.T., McIlgorm, A.: The importance of estimating the contribution of the oceans to national economies. Mar Policy **34**, 367–374 (2010). https://doi.org/10.1016/j.marpol.2009. 08.006
5. Behrenfeld, M.J., Falkowski, P.G.: Photosynthetic rates derived from satellite-based chlorophyll concentration. Limnol. Oceanogr. **42**, 1–20 (1997). https://doi.org/10.4319/lo.1997.42. 1.0001
6. Duarte, C.M., Cebrián, J.: The fate of marine autotrophic production. Limnol. Oceanogr. **41**, 1758–1766 (1996). https://doi.org/10.4319/lo.1996.41.8.1758
7. Longhurst, A.R., Glen Harrison, W.: The biological pump: profiles of plankton production and consumption in the upper ocean. Prog. Oceanogr. **22**, 47–123 (1989). https://doi.org/10. 1016/0079-6611(89)90010-4
8. Falkowski, P.G., Wilson, C.: Phytoplankton productivity in the North Pacific ocean since 1900 and implications for absorption of anthropogenic $CO_2$. Nature **358**, 741–743 (1992). https:// doi.org/10.1038/358741a0
9. Peters, D.P.C., Havstad, K.M., Cushing, J., Tweedie, C., Fuentes, O., Villanueva-Rosales, N.: Harnessing the power of big data: infusing the scientific method with machine learning to transform ecology. Ecosphere **5**, art67 (2014). https://doi.org/10.1890/ES13-00359.1.
10. Recknagel, F.: Applications of machine learning to ecological modelling. Ecol. Model. **146**, 303–310 (2001). https://doi.org/10.1016/S0304-3800(01)00316-7
11. Olden, J.D., Lawler, J.J., Poff, N.L.: Machine learning methods without tears: a primer for ecologists. Q. Rev. Biol. **83**, 171–193 (2008). https://doi.org/10.1086/587826
12. Lek, S., Delacoste, M., Baran, P., Dimopoulos, I., Lauga, J., Aulagnier, S.: Application of neural networks to modelling nonlinear relationships in ecology. Ecol. Model. **90**, 39–52 (1996). https://doi.org/10.1016/0304-3800(95)00142-5
13. Kohonen, T.: Self-organized formation of topologically correct feature maps. Biol. Cybern. **43**, 59–69 (1982). https://doi.org/10.1007/BF00337288

14. Céréghino, R., Park, Y.-S.: Review of the Self-Organizing Map (SOM) approach in water resources: commentary. Environ. Model. Softw. **24**, 945–947 (2009). https://doi.org/10.1016/j.envsoft.2009.01.008

15. Kohonen, T.: Essentials of the self-organizing map. Neural Netw. **37**, 52–65 (2013). https://doi.org/10.1016/j.neunet.2012.09.018

16. Jouini, M., Lévy, M., Crépon, M., Thiria, S.: Reconstruction of satellite chlorophyll images under heavy cloud coverage using a neural classification method. Remote Sens. Environ. **131**, 232–246 (2013). https://doi.org/10.1016/j.rse.2012.11.025

17. Nkiaka, E., Nawaz, N.R., Lovett, J.C.: Using self-organizing maps to infill missing data in hydro-meteorological time series from the Logone catchment, Lake Chad basin. Environ. Monit. Assess. **188**(7), 1–2 (2016). https://doi.org/10.1007/s10661-016-5385-1

18. Wehrens, R., Kruisselbrink, J.: Flexible self-organizing maps in kohonen 3.0. J. Stat. Softw. **87**, 1–18 (2018). https://doi.org/10.18637/jss.v087.i07

19. Vesanto, J., Alhoniemi, E.: Clustering of the self-organizing map. IEEE Trans. Neural Netw. **11**, 586–600 (2000). https://doi.org/10.1109/72.846731

20. Kendall, M.G.: Rank Correlation Methods. Griffin, London (1975)

21. Mann, H.B.: Nonparametric tests against trend. Econometrica. **13**, 245–259 (1945). https://doi.org/10.2307/1907187

22. Barbariol, F., Falcieri, F.M., Scotton, C., Benetazzo, A., Carniel, S., Sclavo, M.: Wave extreme characterization using self-organizing maps. Ocean Sci. **12**, 403–415 (2016). https://doi.org/10.5194/os-12-403-2016

23. Matić, F., et al.: Oscillating adriatic temperature and salinity regimes mapped using the self-organizing maps method. Cont. Shelf Res. **132**, 11–18 (2017). https://doi.org/10.1016/j.csr.2016.11.006

# Plankton Recognition in Images with Varying Size

Jaroslav Bureš[1,2], Tuomas Eerola[1]($\boxtimes$) (iD), Lasse Lensu[1] (iD), Heikki Kälviäinen[1] (iD), and Pavel Zemčík[2] (iD)

[1] Computer Vision and Pattern Recognition Laboratory, LUT University, Lappeenranta, Finland
{tuomas.eerola,lasse.lensu,heikki.kalviainen}@lut.fi
[2] Faculty of Information Technology, Brno University of Technology, Brno, Czech Republic
zemcik@fit.vutbr.cz

**Abstract.** Monitoring plankton is important as they are an essential part of the aquatic food web as well as producers of oxygen. Modern imaging devices produce a massive amount of plankton image data which calls for automatic solutions. These images are characterized by a very large variation in both the size and the aspect ratio. Convolutional neural network (CNN) based classification methods, on the other hand, typically require a fixed size input. Simple scaling of the images into a common size contains several drawbacks. First, the information about the size of the plankton is lost. For human experts, the size information is one of the most important cues for identifying the species. Second, downscaling the images leads to the loss of fine details such as flagella essential for species recognition. Third, upscaling the images increases the size of the network. In this work, extensive experiments on various approaches to address the varying image dimensions are carried out on a challenging phytoplankton image dataset. A novel combination of methods is proposed, showing improvement over the baseline CNN.

**Keywords:** Plankton recognition · Convolutional neural networks · Varying input size

## 1 Introduction

Plankton are a diverse collection of organisms living in large bodies of water that are drifted by the current. They are an important part of the ecosystem as they provide the basis for the aquatic food web. Apart from this, the plankton are also the top producers of oxygen on the Earth and can be used as a good indicator of the ocean health. Therefore, monitoring plankton populations is essential. Modern imaging devices are able to produce a massive amount of plankton image data which calls for automatic solutions to analyze the data. In practice, this means recognizing the species of plankton using computer vision techniques.

© Springer Nature Switzerland AG 2021
A. Del Bimbo et al. (Eds.): ICPR 2020 Workshops, LNCS 12666, pp. 110–120, 2021.
https://doi.org/10.1007/978-3-030-68780-9_11

A large amount of works on plankton recognition already exists. Recently, the majority of efforts has been put on the development of convolutional neural networks (CNN) based recognition methods that have shown to outperform traditional hand-engineering based methods with a large margin [4]. For example, in [1] a CNN architecture for plankton recognition was proposed based on the well-known VGG architecture. In [11], various CNN architectures were compared with different plankton image datasets. Moreover, different transfer learning strategies were evaluated. In [12], machine performance was compared to that of humans, and the CNN-based methods were shown to outperform the humans on the data consisting of planktic foraminifera.

The CNN based image recognition methods typically require a fixed size input. Therefore, the vast majority of existing plankton recognition methods start by rescaling the images. This, however, is not an ideal approach for typical plankton image data that are characterized with an extreme variation in both the image size and the aspect ratio (see Fig. 1). When the image is rescaled the information about the size of the plankton is lost. For human experts, the size information is one of the most important cues for identifying the species suggesting its usefulness also in automatic recognition. Downscaling images leads to the loss of fine details, such as flagella essential for species recognition. On the other hand, upscaling images increases the size of the network, resulting as longer training times and higher requirements for the amount of training data.

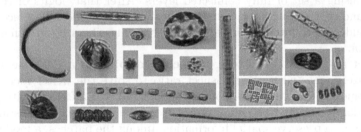

**Fig. 1.** Examples of plankton images with different sizes and aspect ratios.

In this paper, the problem of extreme variations in plankton image size is considered. First, existing approaches to address the varying input size on CNN-based image classification are reviewed. Then, extensive experiments on challenging plankton image data are carried out to compare the existing approaches. Finally, based on the experiments a multi-stream network utilizing a novel combination of different models is proposed.

## 2  CNNs with Varying Image Size

Typical CNN architecture requires a fixed size input. In this section, existing approaches to bypass this limitation are presented.

**Spatial Pyramid Pooling** (SPP) [6] allows training of a single CNN with multiple image sizes in order to obtain higher scale-invariance and reduction of over-fitting. The convolutional and pooling layers accept feature maps of any size as they work in a sliding window manner. Limitation for input size lies in the fully connected layers, as they need an input of a fixed size. SPP accepts an input of any size and aspect ratio and produces an output of a fixed size. SPP uses a defined number of bins where each one performs pooling from one fraction of the image. For example, one bin performs pooling with the whole image (also known as global pooling), next 4 bins execute pooling with one quarter and finally 9 bins pool one ninth of the image each.

A straightforward approach to utilize the image size in the recognition is to include **the size as metadata**. This does not directly provide a solution to the need to rescale the original images but allows the recognition model to use the size information in the prediction. Various approaches to utilize the metadata in CNN-based classification models can be found in literature. Ellen et al. [5] compared several approaches for plankton recognition. Experiments on plankton images and different metadata (e.g., geometric and geotemporal data) showed that the best accuracy is achieved with the architecture with several fully connected layers after metadata concatenation. In [3], two approaches to combine image data with metadata (GPS coordinates were used in the study) were proposed. The first approach takes advantage of post-processing of an image classifier by embedding its output together with the metadata. Metadata was processed using a set of fully connected layers. After that, logits of the image classifier and metadata classifier are simply merged together. The second approach includes more interaction between the two classifiers by utilizing feature modulation.

Xing et al. [17] proposed to use **patch cropping** in a CNN-based model to recognize images with a high aspect ratio to solve the writer identification task for handwritten text. The proposed model, called Half DeepWriter takes a set of randomly selected patches cropped from the original image as an input. Furthermore, to preserve spatial information among the patches, a model, called DeepWriter was presented. This DeepWriter consisted of two Half DeepWriters. Two patches next to each other were cropped. Each patch was then supplied to one of the Half DeepWriters. These CNNs share their parameters. $N$ pairs of patches are cropped from an input image and are fed to the model. For each pair a score vector $f_i$ is computed and by averaging the values. The final score vector is constructed as $f_j = \frac{1}{N} \sum_{i=1}^{N} f_{ij}$.

In [13], **multi-stream CNNs** were proposed as a solution to deal with both scale-variant and scale-invariant features with CNNs. The core idea is to combine multiple CNNs and to train each one with a different input image size. The method was shown to outperform the traditional single CNN trained with images resized to a common size on the task of artwork classification. The architecture of the network was based on the ImageNet model [15] where the final average pooling layer is replaced with a global average pooling layer. Therefore, the output feature map contain the fixed size for all image scales. When applying to a new image, all softmax class posteriors from each CNN are averaged into a single prediction. With this approach the total number of parameters is increased as the networks do not share parameters. However, the networks can be trained individually in parallel.

## 3   Experiments

Addressing size variation has proved to increase the accuracy of CNNs. This section provides the comparative experiments on the suitability of these approaches on plankton recognition. Four approaches are considered: SPP, metadata inclusion, patch cropping, and multi-stream networks.

### 3.1   Data

The data consists of phytoplankton images (see Fig. 1) and it was collected from the Baltic Sea using Imaging FlowCytobot (IFCB) [14]. The dataset contains about 33000 images labeled by a taxonomist expert into 32 different classes. The number of samples varies from 100 to 4606 per class. The images consist of one channel and their sizes are in ranges of 64 to 1276 pixels for the width and 26 to 394 pixels for the height. This variation can be considered extreme. A more detailed description of the data can be found in [2].

The data was split into 20% testing and 80% training partitions using stratified sampling. The training data was balanced so that each class contained exactly 1000 samples. If a class contained more samples, only the first 1000 images were used. If there were fewer samples then new realistic images were created through data augmentation. The following data augmentations were used: horizontal and vertical flipping, rotation of 90°, scaling with the factor of 0.9 to 1.1, blurring, adjusting brightness, and adding Gaussian noise with a variance of 0.001.

### 3.2   CNN Architectures and Implementation Details

To provide the baseline and to select CNN architectures for further experiments, a number of architectures were compared. For this experiment, all the images were scaled to the common size (the input size of a CNN architecture) using bicubic interpolation. To maintain the aspect ratio padding using the mean color computed from the image boundaries was used. Gaussian noise was used to reduce any artificial edges caused by homogeneous regions. Each image was normalized by subtracting the mean value from every pixel of the image and dividing the result by a standard deviation. These values were computed from the whole training set.

The following architectures were compared: *AlexNet* [10], *DenseNet121* [9], *ResNet50* [7], *MobileNet* [8], and *InceptionV3* [16], as well as, *VGG16* based models called *Al-Barazanchi* [1] and *Ellen* [5] developed especially for plankton recognition. All models were trained with the cross-validation of 10 folds with a stratified selection. The stochastic gradient descent optimizer was used, together with the Nesterov momentum, the initial learning rate set to 0.01, the weight decay of $10^{-6}$ and the momentum of 0.9. For *AlexNet*, *Al-Barazanchi*, and *Ellen*, the batch size of 256 was chosen as well as training with 60 epochs. For the rest of these architectures, the batch size was set to 64 due to memory limitations and the number of epochs to 80.

**Table 1.** The baseline plankton recognition accuracy for the different architectures.

| Architecture | Input size | Parameters | Accuracy |
|---|---|---|---|
| Al-Barazanchi | 224 × 224 | 2 993 655 | 0.9341 ± 0.0025 |
| Al-Barazanchi$_{2:1}$ | 316 × 158 | | 0.9204 ± 0.0136 |
| Al-Barazanchi$_{4:1}$ | 448 × 112 | | 0.8909 ± 0.0079 |
| AlexNet | 224 × 224 | 46 854 880 | 0.9274 ± 0.0053 |
| DenseNet121 | 224 × 224 | 7 087 607 | 0.9441 ± 0.0065 |
| Ellen | 128 × 128 | 885 143 | 0.9110 ± 0.0084 |
| InceptionV3 | 299 × 299 | 21 914 903 | **0.9520 ± 0.0013** |
| InceptionV3$_{2:1}$ | 420 × 210 | | **0.9525 ± 0.0033** |
| InceptionV3$_{4:1}$ | 600 × 150 | | 0.9463 ± 0.0031 |
| MobileNet | 224 × 224 | 3 284 663 | 0.9420 ± 0.0045 |
| ResNet50 | 224 × 224 | 23 694 135 | 0.9201 ± 0.0244 |

The results are shown in Table 1. The deeper networks provide higher accuracy. However, this comes with the cost of longer training time. The highest accuracy of 95.20% was achieved with the *InceptionV3*. *Al-Barazanchi* obtained comparable accuracy of 93.41% with a one-third of the training time. Therefore, these two architectures were selected for further experiments.

The two architectures were further examined by training them with images of different aspect ratios to better preserve the details for images containing long plankton samples. First, the *Al-Barazanchi*$_{2:1}$ architecture was constructed for images with an aspect ratio of 2:1 where the stride of the second pooling layer was changed to (2,1). This architecture accepts images with the size of 316 × 158 pixels. Similarly, the *Al-Barazanchi*$_{4:1}$ architecture was constructed for images with an aspect ratio of 4:1 (448 × 112 pixels) where the stride of the second convolutional layer was adjusted to (4,1). Furthermore, the convolutional kernel size for the same layer was changed from (3,3) to (6,3). The same modifications were done for the *InceptionV3* architecture. To evaluate the networks, all images were flipped in such a way that the horizontal dimension was larger than the vertical dimension. The results are shown in Table 1. The architectures with the modified aspect ratio for input did not improve the results. This is as expected since the majority of the images contain the aspect ratio closer to 1:1. However, it was noticed that the modified architectures were able to correctly classify several test images for which the baseline model failed.

## 3.3  Spatial Pyramid Pooling

The spatial pyramid pooling layer was leveraged to enable training with images of varying resolution. This layer replaces the last pooling layer of the architecture and has a shape of $\{6 \times 6, 3 \times 3, 2 \times 2, 1 \times 1\}$ with a bin count of 50. The network was then trained with predefined image sizes (see Table 2). In one epoch both images for training and validation were resized to one of the sizes so that the whole batch consists of images with a single fixed size. After the epoch was finished, the size is switched to the next one and the process is repeated.

The *Al-Barazanchi* architecture was used for the initial experiments due to its fast training. The number of epochs was 90. The experiments with multiple different image sizes were evaluated. First, the network was evaluated with one size only ($224 \times 224$) to see how the SPP layer affects the accuracy. Next, the combinations of multiple sizes ($224 \times 224$, $180 \times 180$, and $256 \times 256$) were evaluated. The results are shown in Table 2. It can be seen that the SPP layer had only a minor positive effect on the recognition accuracy on its own. The same experiment was also repeated with *Inception V3*. However, the accuracy with SPP layer (86.93%–87.61%) was considerably lower than with the baseline model (95.20%). Therefore, the search for other size combinations was not continued.

**Table 2.** Accuracy for the *Al-Barazanchi* architecture using the SPP layer.

| Image sizes | Accuracy |
|---|---|
| $(224 \times 224)$ | $0.9058 \pm 0.0105$ |
| $(224 \times 224)$, $(180 \times 180)$ | $0.9205 \pm 0.0111$ |
| $(224 \times 224)$, $(256 \times 256)$ | $0.9327 \pm 0.0060$ |
| $(224 \times 224)$, $(180 \times 180)$, $(256 \times 256)$ | **$0.9387 \pm 0.0052$** |

## 3.4  Metadata

The next experiment was to evaluate the effect of utilizing the size (the width and the height in pixels) of the original image as metadata. In addition, two time related features (the season and the hour) were utilized as metadata. The time metadata are motivated by the facts that there is a high seasonal variation in the plankton communities and their activity varies between the part of the day. All metadata values were normalized to $[-1; 1]$. Three architectures to include metadata proposed in [5] and [3] were examined. These are visualized in Fig. 2.

Two different approaches of training were examined. The first approach trains the whole architecture together with an embedded image model initialized with random weights. The second approach uses an image classifier that is initialized with weights loaded from a trained model and its weights are kept fixed for the time of training. Therefore, only the metadata part and the common part of the network are trained. The results for the *Al-Barazanchi* architecture as an

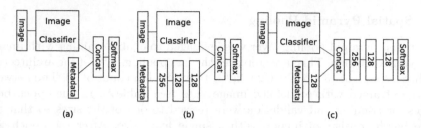

**Fig. 2.** Different architectures to include metadata: (a) Simple concatenation [3]; (b) Metadata interaction [5]; (c) More interaction [5].

image model are shown in Table 3. The best results were obtained using the pretrained image model and the Metadata interaction architecture. The effect of different types of metadata was further evaluated with the best model. While including only size information improved the accuracy over the baseline, the best accuracy was obtained using all metadata (time and size). Finally, the architecture with more interaction among metadata with both *time* and *shape* included was applied with the *InceptionV3* as the image model. The inclusion of metadata provided insignificant improvement over baseline with the accuracy of 95.22% and 95.20%, respectively.

**Table 3.** Accuracy for the *Al-Barazanchi* architecture with metadata.

| Model | Architecture | Accuracy |
|---|---|---|
|  | No metadata | $0.9341 \pm 0.0022$ |
| Blank image model | Simple concatenation | $0.9392 \pm 0.0037$ |
|  | Metadata interaction | $0.9418 \pm 0.0041$ |
|  | More interaction | $0.9378 \pm 0.0061$ |
| Pretrained image model | Simple concatenation | $0.9391 \pm 0.0034$ |
|  | Metadata interaction (all metadata) | $\mathbf{0.9432 \pm 0.0021}$ |
|  | Metadata interaction (size) | $0.9414 \pm 0.0036$ |
|  | Metadata interaction (time) | $0.9433 \pm 0.0025$ |
|  | More interaction | $0.9424 \pm 0.0024$ |

### 3.5 Patch Cropping

Multiple different methods of an image patch cropping were examined. The first method uses a single patch which is randomly cropped alongside of the image. The second method uses a pair of patches to preserve spatial information between them as described in [17]. The images are padded in their width to guarantee enough space for two consecutive patches to be cropped. This pair is then supplied to the *DeepWriter* model [17]. Note that any backbone CNN architecture can be used. The third method was to utilize the *DeepWriter* model without padding resulting in overlapping image patches for images with close to square shape. All the three methods of patch cropping are depicted in Fig. 3.

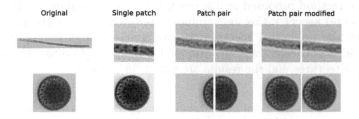

**Fig. 3.** Different patch cropping methods.

The first set of the experiments was carried out using *Al-Barazanchi* as the backbone architecture. Each image was first rotated into the horizontal position so that its width is greater than its height. After that, the image was resized in a way that the height of the image was the same as the height of the patch to be cropped while keeping the original aspect ratio. The model was trained for 90 epochs with a batch size of 64. The evaluation was performed through a sliding window where $N$ patches or pairs of patches were subsequently selected from the image. Each of these patches was then evaluated by the network resulting in $N$ prediction vectors. These vectors were finally combined by averaging them into a single prediction as described in Sect. 2. The results are shown in Table 4.

**Table 4.** Accuracy for the patch cropping with the *Al-Barazanchi* architecture.

| Patches | Single patch | Patch pair | Patch pair mod |
|---------|-------------|------------|----------------|
| 2 | 0.8987 ± 0.0045 | **0.9298 ± 0.0030** | 0.9219 ± 0.0057 |
| 4 | 0.9285 ± 0.0052 | **0.9370 ± 0.0025** | 0.9257 ± 0.0062 |
| 8 | 0.9301 ± 0.0050 | **0.9392 ± 0.0017** | 0.9276 ± 0.0063 |
| 16 | 0.9299 ± 0.0042 | **0.9420 ± 0.0021** | 0.9289 ± 0.0059 |

With enlarging the number of iterations, the accuracy increases. However, the time for evaluation is gradually increasing as well. While switching from 8 to 16 patches there was no significant improvement. The methods utilizing the patch pairs outperformed the single patch method which suggests that the DeepWriter architecture indeed benefits from having extra spatial information preserved by selecting two consecutive patches. The DeepWriter model outperformed the baseline model. This suggests that this method leverages small details that are being lost due to resizing. Finally, the experiment was repeated by using *Inception V3* as the backbone architecture. This model was trained for 90 epochs with a batch size of 32. The non-modified patch pair approach was utilized for cropping and the number of patches was set to 4. The accuracy of 95.28% was achieved which is only slightly better than the baseline.

## 3.6  Multi-stream CNN

To experiment with the multi-stream CNN, i.e., combining multiple CNN based models, the method proposed in [13] was utilized. Various models with different input sizes and aspect ratios were trained separately, and for the final recognition model, the prediction vectors were combined through averaging similarly to [13]. The experiment was repeated for both the *Al-Barazanchi* and *InceptionV3* architectures and the results are shown in Table 5.

**Table 5.** Accuracy for different model combinations. $Model_{x:1}$ stands for modification of the baseline model with the input aspect ratio of $x{:}1$.

| Model combination | Al-Barazanchi | InceptionV3 |
|---|---|---|
| Baseline ($Model_{1:1}$) | $0.9341 \pm 0.0022$ | $0.9577 \pm 0.0011$ |
| $Model_{1:1}$ + $Model_{2:1}$ | $0.9439 \pm 0.0024$ | $0.9577 \pm 0.0011$ |
| $Model_{1:1}$ + $Model_{4:1}$ | $0.9383 \pm 0.0031$ | $0.9562 \pm 0.0020$ |
| $Model_{1:1}$ + $Model_{2:1}$ + $Model_{4:1}$ | $0.9444 \pm 0.0022$ | $0.9596 \pm 0.0005$ |
| $Model_{1:1}$ + patch cropping | $0.9488 \pm 0.0015$ | $0.9580 \pm 0.0023$ |
| $Model_{1:1}$ + $Model_{2:1}$ + patch cropping | $\mathbf{0.9499 \pm 0.0018}$ | $\mathbf{0.9616 \pm 0.0008}$ |
| $Model_{1:1}$ + $Model_{4:1}$ + patch cropping | $0.9466 \pm 0.0024$ | $0.9606 \pm 0.0002$ |

The best improvement for *Al-Barazanchi* was found in combining it together with *Al-Barazanchi$_{2:1}$* and *DeepWriter*. This suggests that combining CNNs where each one is targeted on images with different aspect ratios can result in significant boost in accuracy. Using a method that leverages patch cropping proved to be more effective than CNNs that are fed with whole images of larger aspect ratios. The similar results were obtained also for the *InceptionV3* architecture.

## 3.7  Comparison of the Approaches

The summary of the results for the different approaches can be seen in Table 6. For the *Al-Barazanchi* architecture every approach improved the accuracy, while the multi-stream approach provided the best accuracy. In the case of *InceptionV3* only using the multi-stream method affected significantly. This is possibly due to the already high accuracy of *InceptionV3* as well as its high complexity. It is also worth noting that while baseline accuracy is noticeably higher for *InceptionV3* compared to *Al-Barazanchi* with the multi-stream version *Al-Barazanchi* provides comparable performance. In the plankton research, image datasets are typically obtained with different imaging devices and contain different species compositions, making it necessary to retrain the model for each dataset separately often with a limited amount of training data. Therefore, shallower models are preferred. More detailed experiments can be found in [2].

**Table 6.** Comparison of the accuracy for the different approaches.

| Approach | Al-Barazanchi | InceptionV3 |
|---|---|---|
| Baseline | 0.9341 ± 0.0022 | 0.9520 ± 0.0014 |
| SPP | 0.9387 ± 0.0052 | 0.8761 ± 0.0153 |
| Metadata | 0.9432 ± 0.0021 | 0.9522 ± 0.0021 |
| Patch cropping | 0.9392 ± 0.0017 | 0.9528 ± 0.0009 |
| Multi-stream | **0.9499 ± 0.0018** | **0.9616 ± 0.0008** |

## 4   Conclusions

In this paper, various approaches to address the extreme variation in both the image size and the aspect ratio were studied for the task of plankton recognition. First, a comparison of CNN architectures was carried out. Based on the results, two architectures, *Al-Barazanchi* developed specifically for plankton recognition and considerably deeper *InceptionV3*, were selected for further experiments. Four modifications to the baseline architectures were evaluated: 1) spatial pyramid pooling, 2) metadata inclusion, 3) patch cropping, and 4) multi-stream networks. The multi-stream network combining the patch cropping model with the full image models for various aspect ratios was shown to outperform the baseline and to produce the highest accuracy for both backbone architectures. With this approach, the considerably shallower *Al-Barazanchi* architecture (3M parameters) provided comparable performance to the *InceptionV3* architecture (22M parameters), making it an attractive choice for wider use in the plankton research, characterized by a large pool of datasets with different imaging device and species compositions.

**Acknowledgements.** The research was carried out in the FASTVISION project (No. 321991) funded by the Academy of Finland. The authors would also like to thank Kaisa Kraft, Dr. Sanna Suikkanen, Prof. Timo Tamminen, and Prof. Jukka Seppälä from Finnish Environment Institute (SYKE) for providing the data for the experiments.

## References

1. Al-Barazanchi, H.A., Verma, A., Wang, X.S.: Intelligent plankton image classification with deep learning. Int. J. Comput. Vision Robot. **8**, 561–571 (2018)
2. Bureš, J.: Classification of varying-size plankton images with convolutional neural network. Master's thesis, Brno University of Technology, Czech Republic (2020)
3. Chu, G., et al.: Geo-aware networks for fine-grained recognition. In: ICCV Workshops (2019)
4. Eerola, T., et al.: Towards operational phytoplankton recognition with automated high-throughput imaging and compact convolutional neural networks. Ocean Science Discussions (2020)
5. Ellen, J.S., Graff, C.A., Ohman, M.D.: Improving plankton image classification using context metadata. Limnol. Oceanogr. Methods **17**, 439–461 (2019)

6. He, K., Zhang, X., Ren, S., Sun, J.: Spatial pyramid pooling in deep convolutional networks for visual recognition. IEEE Trans. Pattern Anal. Mach. Intell. **37**(9), 1904–1916 (2015)
7. He, K., Zhang, X., Ren, S., Sun, J.: Deep residual learning for image recognition. In: CVPR (2016)
8. Howard, A.G., et al.: Mobilenets: efficient convolutional neural networks for mobile vision applications. arXiv preprint arXiv:1704.04861 (2017)
9. Huang, G., Liu, Z., Van Der Maaten, L., Weinberger, K.Q.: Densely connected convolutional networks. In: CVPR (2017)
10. Krizhevsky, A., Sutskever, I., Hinton, G.E.: Imagenet classification with deep convolutional neural networks. In: NIPS (2012)
11. Lumini, A., Nanni, L.: Deep learning and transfer learning features for plankton classification. Ecol. Inform. **51**, 33–43 (2019)
12. Mitra, R., et al.: Automated species-level identification of planktic foraminifera using convolutional neural networks, with comparison to human performance. Mar. Micropaleontol. **147**, 16–24 (2019)
13. Noord, N., Postma, E.: Learning scale-variant and scale-invariant features for deep image classification. Pattern Recogn. **61**, 583–592 (2016)
14. Olson, R.J., Sosik, H.M.: A submersible imaging-in-flow instrument to analyze nano-and microplankton: imaging flowcytobot. Limnol. Oceanogr. Methods **5**, 195–203 (2007)
15. Springenberg, J.T., Dosovitskiy, A., Brox, T., Riedmiller, M.: Striving for simplicity: The all convolutional net. arXiv preprint arXiv:1412.6806 (2014)
16. Szegedy, C., et al.: Going deeper with convolutions. In: CVPR (2015)
17. Xing, L., Qiao, Y.: Deepwriter: a multi-stream deep CNN for text-independent writer identification. In: ICFHR (2016)

# Environment Object Detection
# for Marine ARGO Drone
# by Deep Learning

Angelo Ciaramella$^{(\boxtimes)}$ (ORCID), Francesco Perrotta, Gerardo Pappone, Pietro Aucelli,
Francesco Peluso, and Gaia Mattei

Department of Science and Technology, University of Naples "Parthenope",
Centro Direzionale, Isola C4, 80143 Naples, Italy
{angelo.ciaramella,gerardo.pappone,pietro.aucelli,
francesco.peluso,gaia.mattei}@uniparthenope.it,
francescoperrotta988@gmail.com

**Abstract.** Aim of this work is to implement an environment object detection system for a marine drone. A Deep Learning based model for object detection is embedded on ARGO drone equipped with geophysical sensors and several on-board cameras. The marine drone, developed at iMTG laboratory in partnership with NEPTUN-IA laboratory, was designed to obtain high-resolution mapping of nearshore-to-foreshore sectors and equipped with a system able to detect and identify Ground Control Point (GCP) in real time. A Deep Neural Network is embedded on a Raspberry PI platform and it is adopted for developing the object detection module. Real experiments and comparisons are conducted for identifying GCP among the roughness and vegetation present in the seabed.

**Keywords:** Marine drone · Ground Control Point · Landscape reconstuction · Deep learning · Embedded systems

## 1 Introduction

Sea Science is a field where applications of Artificial Intelligence are continuously increasing, due to the programming of autonomous procedure tools capable of processing large amounts of data with good reliability in order to reconstruct models and trends. Moreover, the underwater sectors, especially in nearshore zones, are by nature dynamic environments, strongly modified by waves action, longshore currents, sedimentary processes, and human activity. In particular along the Mediterranean coasts, these environments often host underwater archaeological sites, representing significant evidence of past coastal settlements, nowadays submerged due to an historical relative sea level rise related to the interplay of glacio-isostatic and tectonic processes [1 8,13–17]. Documenting and reconstructing this cultural seascapes is a goal of great scientific interest in order to understand the responses of natural and anthropic environments to the present accelerated trend in sea level rise due to the ongoing

© Springer Nature Switzerland AG 2021
A. Del Bimbo et al. (Eds.): ICPR 2020 Workshops, LNCS 12666, pp. 121–129, 2021.
https://doi.org/10.1007/978-3-030-68780-9_12

climate changes. Typical geophysical instruments used to reconstruct the under-water landscape are the single beam SBES (Single Beam Echosounder), MBES (Multi Beam Echosounder), and Side Scan Sonar SSS (Side Scan Sonar). How-ever, many operational problems need be addressed during these surveys, taking into account that the instruments are installed on the hull of a boat or towed with a cable several meters long. The main obstacle for coastal researches is to sail with a traditional boat in very shallow water sectors (<5 m), often in the presence of submerged and emerged obstacles as archaeological remains. In the last years, thanks to the technological innovation applied to the miniatur-ization of geophysical instruments, the use of robots, such as UVS (Unmanned Surface Vehicles), allowed carrying out measurements in the above-mentioned sectors, where a traditional boat is poorly manoeuvrable. For this kind of sur-veys, the research group headed by the iMTG (Innovation Marine Technology for Geology and Archaeology) laboratory of the Department of Science and Tech-nology of the University of Naples Parthenope has successfully designed and engineered robotic technologies such as MicroVega (Micro Vessel for Geo Appli-cation) and ARGO (Archaeological and GeO Application) drones. This marine system provide high-resolution data for mapping underwater morphologies form the nearshore up to the shoreline.

However, in order to make the acquired data compliant with international standards and valid for a subsequent phase of study and analysis, it is important to carry out a metric reconstruction of submerged targets, also useful to create 3D models of the underwater landscape. In addition, for performing a detailed survey using a UVS surface drone, equipped with geophysical and photogram-metric instrumentations, is therefore necessary plan a grid of navigation lines (Fig. 1) with suitable spatial distance to provide high resolution data.

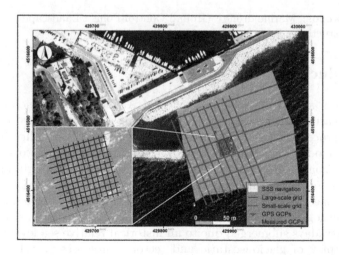

**Fig. 1.** Survey Area of Nisida, Naples with the navigation grid performed by the drone and the positions of the Ground Control Points (GCP) (GEAC Laboratory iMTG).

Finally, for using the acquired images for a 3D reconstruction we should "hook" each image to the actual size and orientation. Only in this way, the topographic survey is measurable and comparable. To carry out this "hooking" operation, Ground Control Points (GCP) (or targets) of various sizes and shapes are adopted. The aim of the work is to create an application for the automatic detection and identification of different kinds of GCPs present in the seabed. In addition, the application can associate the geographic position to each frame containing one ore more targets.

The paper is organised as follows. In Sect. 2, we introduce the ARGO drone. In Sect. 3 we describe the object detection models and Sect. 4 some experimental results. Finally, in Sect. 5, some conclusions and future remarks are reported.

## 2  ARGO Drone

The ARGO drone is the latest prototype developed by the iMTG of the Department of Science and Technology at the Parthenope University of Naples, upgraded during the PAUN project[1]. This USV is able to operate in nearshore-to-foreshore areas and in presence of semi-submerged obstacles, with a minimal impact on the sea environment due to the presence of electric motors powered by 12V DC [12, 15].

ARGO drone is equipped with geophysical and optical sensors optimized to carry out geomorphological and geoarchaeological surveys of submerged coastal environments, and in particular: a 200 Khz digital sounder; a 450 MHz Tritech Starfish side scan sonar; a photogrammetric system with 3 high definition video cameras; different positioning sensors (GPS, IMU, RC). An additional video camera RaspiCam is perpendicularly positioned with respect to the GPS antenna for images and video acquisitions. The PMS (Platform Management System) of Argo is based on a VB7008 x86 low power Mini IT single board computer with VIA C7-D 1.6 GHz processor, two Arduino MEGA 10 bit microcontrollers and a Raspberry Pi 4 B, connected via communication ports with on-board systems. The data transmission module is based on a local Wi-Fi network at 5 GHz that allows transmitting all data in real time on multiple devices such as PC, tablet and smartphone. Finally, the hull of the USV was designed and built as part of a scientific collaboration with Galleno Plastica Srl (an Italian company leader since 1981 in the vacuum thermoforming sector), by using ASA MIC, based on styrene, a polymeric resistant, non-deformable, scratchproof, anti-corrosion, brilliant and easy to customize plastic.

## 3  Object Detection Models

Object detection is a Computer Vision technique for identifying and locate objects in images or videos. Nowadays, Deep learning approaches, based on

---

[1] DIST_POFESR_PAUN_Ricerca Progetto "Rete Intelligente dei Parchi Archeologici" (RIPA -PAUN).

**Fig. 2.** Argo drone (GEAC Laboratory iMTG).

Neural Networks (RNNs) and in particular Convolutional NNs (CNNs), are successful adopted for object detection. A Region-based Convolutional Network (R-CNN) [21] is a special type of CNN that is able to locate and detect objects in images. In R-CNN the output are a set of bounding boxes that closely match each of the detected objects and the class output for each detected object. A Fast R-CNN network [18] is an enhanced R-CNN model:

- The network processes the whole image with several convolutional (conv) and max pooling layers to produce a conv feature map;
- For each object proposal a region of interest pooling layer extracts a fixed-length feature vector from the feature map;
- Each vector feature is fed into a sequence of fully connected layers that finally branch into two sibling output layers: $K$ object classes and another layer that outputs four real-valued numbers for each of the $K$ object classes. Each set of 4 values encodes refined bounding-box positions for one of the $K$ classes.

While accurate, these approaches have been too computationally intensive for embedded systems and, even with high-end hardware, too slow for real-time applications (Faster R-CNN, operates at only 7 frames per second). On the other hand, the Single Shot MultiBox Detector (SSD) model [20] is able to detect objects in images by a single deep NN achieving a significant improvement in speed and high-accuracy detection. The SSD approach is based on a feed-forward CNN that produces a fixed-size collection of bounding boxes and scores for the presence of object class instances in those boxes, and on a non-maximum suppression for producing the final detections. The early network layers are based on a standard architecture used for high quality image classification, VGG-16 network (see Fig. 3 for the overall architecture). The key difference between training SSD and training a typical detector that uses region proposals, is that ground truth information needs to be assigned to specific outputs in the fixed set of detector outputs. On the other hand, the Inception Deep Convolutional Architecture was designed in [22] to perform under strict constraints on memory and computational time. Moreover, the MobileNet [19] has been developed for mobile and embedded vision applications. The network architecture is a special class of CNNs that uses depth-wise separable convolutions resulting more lightweight in terms of their parameter count and computational complexity. The integration of Fast R-CNN and Inception Resnet (FRCNN-IR) and MobileNet into the SSD (SSD-MN) framework is one main aspect of this work. The learned models are successively embedded on a single board Raspberry Pi 4, with Linux environment, installed on the ARGO marine drone equipped by on-board camera.

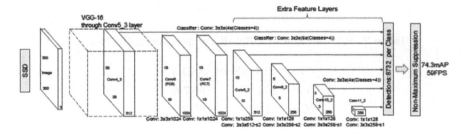

**Fig. 3.** Single shot MultiBox detector architecture [20].

## 4    Experimental Results

In this Section we describe some experimental results and comparisons obtained by using the object detection models, FRCNN-IR and SSD-MN, embedded on the ARGO drone that operate in a real environment. Both models are pre-trained on the COCOCO images dataset (300 × 300 pixels). Successively, a transfer learning technique is applied. The new dataset is obtained through the use of images collected from videos and images captured during recent geological, geomorphological and geoarchaeological surveys by using the MicroVEGA and ARGO drones. The targets to be identified were of two types named $GCP_A$ and $GCP_B$ (Fig. 4) and the dataset was composed by 772 images. An image augmentation technique is also applied (vertical and horizontal flips, rotation and random noise) obtaining 3000 images. A cross-validation approach is adopted by considering 70% for training set, 15% for validation and 15% for the test sets. We stress that, Faster R-CNN uses selective search to find out the region proposals. Selective search is a slow and time-consuming process affecting the performance of the network. SSD combines region proposal and region classification in a single step, simultaneously providing the boundary boxes and the classes, when examining the image. In Table 1 we report the results of classification obtained by models on the training set and in Table 2 on the test set. In Fig. 5 we show some examples of classification of the target $GCP_A$ and $GCP_B$, also in hard situations as that in Fig. 5b, by using SSD-MN. We observed from the several experiments we conducted in real environments that FRCNN-IR and SSD-MN achieve comparable results but SSD-MN performs better under strict constraints on memory and computational time.

**Table 1.** SSD-MN and FRCNN-IR comparison on the training set.

|         | FRCNN-IR | SSD-MN |
|---------|----------|--------|
| $GCP_A$ | 92.94%   | 91.56% |
| $GCP_B$ | 98.02%   | 97.34% |

**Table 2.** SSD-MN and FRCNN-IR comparison on the test set.

|         | FRCNN-IR | SSD-MN |
|---------|----------|--------|
| $GCP_A$ | 91.23%   | 90.78% |
| $GCP_B$ | 97.12%   | 96.39% |

a)                                                                b)

**Fig. 4.** GCP targets: a) $GCP_A$; b) $GCP_B$.

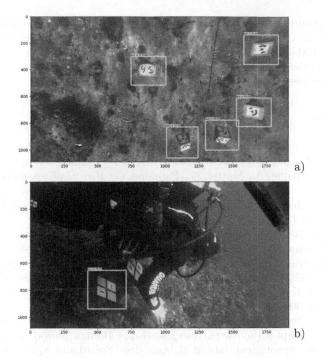

**Fig. 5.** GCP identification results by SSD-MN.

## 5 Conclusions

In this work, we introduced an object detection system installed on-board of ARGO drone, built in the Innovative Marine Technology for Geology and Geoarchaeology laboratory, in partnership with the NEPTUN-IA laboratory. This technological project aims to integrate well-consolidated methods with innovative techniques in order to obtain an efficient approach to the high-resolution reconstruction of natural and anthropic submerged landscapes. The GCP object detection module is embedded by a Raspberry PI device. We considered two Deep Neural Network models, Fast R-CNN with Inception Resnet and SSD with MobileNet. From the comparisons in real environments, we observed that the model have a comparable performance but SSD with MobileNet satisfies our strict constraints on memory and computational time. In the next future, the authors focus on georeferencing in real time the detected GCPs. This step is fundamental to quickly build high-resolution photogrammetric models of underwater environments of high value from natural and anthropic points of views. Following steps, also, concern classifying different kinds of objects (e.g., rocks, sand, plastic), also on the basis of pre-processing [10,11] and data integration methodologies [9], and the use of the ARGO drone for discovering marine litter.

128    A. Ciaramella et al.

**Acknowledgments.** ARGO drone was funded by Distretto ad alta tecnologia per i beni culturali DATABENC, PON 03PE_00164 "Rete Intelligente dei Parchi Archeologici (RIPA - PAUN)". The authors sincerely thanks Gallenoplastica Srl for the active collaboration in the hull construction. This paper also benefited from the discussion(s) at the Neptune meeting (INQUA CMP project 2003P).

# References

1. Ascione, A., et al.: Geomorphology of Naples and the Campi Flegrei: human and natural landscapes in a restless land. J. Maps, 1–11 (2020)
2. Aucelli, P., Cinque, A., Mattei, G., Pappone, G.: Historical sea level changes and effects on the coasts of Sorrento Peninsula (Gulf of Naples): New constrains from recent geoarchaeological investigations. Palaeogeogr. Palaeoclimatol. Palaeoecol. **463**, 112–125 (2016a)
3. Aucelli, P., Cinque, A., Giordano, F., Mattei, G.: A geoarchaeological survey of the marine extension of the Roman archaeological site Villa del Pezzolo, Vico Equense, on the Sorrento Peninsula. Italy. Geoarchaeology **31**(3), 244–252 (2016b)
4. Aucelli, P.P.C., Cinque, A., Mattei, G., Pappone, G.: Late Holocene landscape evolution of the gulf of Naples (Italy) inferred from geoarchaeological data. J. Maps **13**(2), 300–310 (2017)
5. Aucelli, P., Cinque, A., Mattei, G., Pappone, G., Stefanile, M.: Coastal landscape evolution of Naples (Southern Italy) since the Roman period from archaeological and geomorphological data at Palazzo degli Spiriti site. Qua. Int. **483**, 23–38 (2018a). https://doi.org/10.1016/j.quaint.2017.12.040
6. Aucelli, P.P., Cinque, A., Mattei, G., Pappone, G., Stefanile, M.: First results on the coastal changes related to local sea level variations along the Puteoli sector (Campi Flegrei, Italy) during the historical times. Alp. Mediterr. Quat. **31**, 13–16 (2018b)
7. Aucelli, P., Cinque, A., Mattei, G., Pappone, G., Rizzo, A.: Studying relative sea level change and correlative adaptation of coastal structures on submerged Roman time ruins nearby Naples (southern Italy). Quat. Int. **501**, 328–348 (2019). https://doi.org/10.1016/j.quaint.2017.10.011
8. Aucelli, P.P.C., et al.: Ancient Coastal Changes Due to Ground Movements and Human Interventions in the Roman Portus Julius (Pozzuoli Gulf, Italy): Results from Photogrammetric and Direct Surveys. Water **12**(3), 658 (2020). https://doi.org/10.3390/w12030658
9. Ciaramella, A., Nardone, D., Staiano, A.: Data integration by fuzzy similarity-based hierarchical clustering. BMC Bioinform. **21**, 350 (2020)
10. Ciaramella, A., Gianfico, M., Giunta, G.: Compressive sampling and adaptive dictionary learning for the packet loss recovery in audio multimedia streaming. Multimed. Tools Appl. **75**(24), 17375–17392 (2016)
11. Ciaramella, A., De Lauro, E., De Martino, S., Di Lieto, B., Falanga, M., Tagliaferri, R.: Characterization of Strombolian events by using independent component analysis. Nonlin. Process. Geophys. **11**(4), 453–461 (2004)
12. Giordano, F., Mattei, G., Parente, C., Peluso, F., Santamaria, R.: Integrating sensors into a marine drone for bathymetric 3D surveys in shallow waters. Sensors (MDPI) **16**(1), 41 (2016). https://doi.org/10.3390/s16010041
13. Mattei, G., Troisi, S., Aucelli, P., Pappone, G., Peluso, F., Stefanile, M.: Sensing the Submerged Landscape of Nisida Roman Harbour in the Gulf of Naples from Integrated Measurements on a USV. Water **10**(11), 1686 (2018a)

14. Mattei, G., Troisi, S., Aucelli, P.P., Pappone, G., Peluso, F., Stefanile, M.: Multi-scale reconstruction of natural and archaeological underwater landscape by optical and acoustic sensors. In: 2018 IEEE International Workshop on Metrology for the Sea; Learning to Measure Sea Health Parameters (MetroSea), pp. 46–49. IEEE (2018b)

15. Mattei, G., Rizzo, A., Anfuso, G., Aucelli, P.P.C., Gracia, F.J.: A tool for evaluating the archaeological heritage vulnerability to coastal processes: the case study of Naples Gulf (southern Italy). Ocean Coastal Manage. **179**, 104876 (2019)

16. Mattei, G., Aucelli, P.P., Caporizzo, C., Rizzo, A., Pappone, G.: New geomorphological and historical elements on morpho-evolutive trends and relative sea-level changes of Naples coast in the last 6000 years. Water **12**(9), 2651 (2020)

17. Pappone, G., Aucelli, P.P., Mattei, G., Peluso, F., Stefanile, M., Carola, A.: A detailed reconstruction of the roman Landscape and the submerged archaeological structure at "Castel dell'Ovo islet" (Naples, Southern Italy). Geosciences **9**(4), 170 (2019)

18. Girshick, R.: Fast R-CNN. In: 2015 IEEE International Conference on Computer Vision (ICCV), Santiago, pp. 1440–1448 (2015). https://doi.org/10.1109/ICCV.2015.169

19. Howard, A.G.: MobileNets: efficient convolutional neural networks for mobile vision applications. CoRR abs/1704.04861 (2017)

20. Liu, W., Anguelov, D., Erhan, D., Szegedy, C., Reed, S., Fu, C.-Y., Berg, A.C.: SSD: single shot MultiBox detector. In: Leibe, B., Matas, J., Sebe, N., Welling, M. (eds.) ECCV 2016. LNCS, vol. 9905, pp. 21–37. Springer, Cham (2016). https://doi.org/10.1007/978-3-319-46448-0_2

21. Ren, S., He, K., Girshick, R.: Sun. Towards real-time object detection with region proposal networks, NIPS, Faster R-CNN (2015)

22. Szegedy, C.: Going deeper with convolutions. In: Proceedings of the IEEE Conference on Computer Vision and Pattern Recognition, pp. 1–9 (2015)

# Unsupervised Learning of High Dimensional Environmental Data Using Local Fractality Concept

Mikhail Kanevski[1]([⊠]) [iD] and Mohamed Laib[2] [iD]

[1] University of Lausanne, 1015 Lausanne, Switzerland
Mikhail.Kanevski@unil.ch
http://www.unil.ch/idyst
[2] Luxembourg Institute of Science and Technology, Esch-sur-Alzette, Luxembourg
Mohamed.Laib@list.lu

**Abstract.** The research deals with an exploration of high dimensional environmental data using unsupervised learning algorithms and the concept of local fractality. The proposed methodology is applied to geospatial data used for the wind speed prediction in a complex mountainous region. It is shown, that the approach provides important additional information on data manifold useful in data analysis, data visualisation and predictive modelling.

**Keywords:** Unsupervised learning · Environmental data · Fractals

## 1 Introduction

Many real cases of complex phenomena, like environmental risks, natural hazards, and renewable resources assessments, have to be considered in high dimensional input feature spaces (IFS). This input space is usually constructed using available information, expert knowledge and objectives of the study [1]. The challenging part of constructing an IFS for environmental studies relies on capturing all necessary information. Thus, it is difficult to find out if the IFS under study is redundant or even incomplete.

The quality and relevancy of IFS is of great importance in data analysis and in development of predictive models. For instance, construction of the input space can be considered as an embedding in time series analysis and forecasting. In many geo-environmental studies, the input space is not sufficiently explored. A comprehensive analysis of IFS helps in the understanding of data, phenomena, and in deeper interpretability of the results.

In the present paper, two fundamental concepts are applied in order to study the high dimensional environmental data:

- Fractal concepts (sandbox counting method)

A. Del Bimbo et al. (Eds.): ICPR 2020 Workshops, LNCS 12666, pp. 130–138, 2021.
https://doi.org/10.1007/978-3-030-68780-9_13

- Unsupervised learning (dimension reduction and clustering)

These topics have a huge literature, see, for example, references in some selected books and reviews relevant to the present study: on fractals [2–7]; and on clustering [8–10].

Fractal concepts are widely used in different contexts: exploratory analysis of data and their scaling properties, long memory/dependencies in data, clustering, etc. In most cases the global fractal dimension is estimated, sometimes completed with a Lacunarity measure. In machine learning fractal dimensions are used as well, e.g. in the estimation of intrinsic dimension (ID) and feature engineering. Applications of ID and fractals in unsupervised and supervised feature selection algorithms are discussed in [11,12], where relevant review of the literature is given.

In the present research, the so called sandbox counting approach often used to estimate fractal dimension of data is applied to study an IFS in order to characterize data local density and clustering. This method of calculation is known under different names in different scientific disciplines and with different interpretations: Ripley's k-function in analysis of point processes and clustering in spatial statistics and geography [13], in time series as a correlation dimension used to quantify the dimensionality of strange attractors and to find relevant embedding [14], mass fractals/multifractals in theoretical physics [15], in environmental data studies to quantify the dimensional and spatial resolutions of monitoring networks and their capability to detect phenomena [1,16], etc. In the present paper we use the sandbox terminology.

A complementary approach can be based on considering the number of neighbours instead of distances. Such approach can be very efficient and interesting in case of very clustered data. One of such implementations with theoretical considerations was proposed in [17]. Another kind of local ID estimator was proposed in [18,19] where many potential applications of local ID are discussed as well. Based on local ID, Allegra et al. proposed a data segmentation method using a Bayesian approach [20].

In this work, we study a challenging dataset, containing geomorphological information, using local fractality and clustering. Besides the proposed methodology, one of the main output of this work is also the investigation of spatial variability with regard to the local ID, which can be very useful in supervised learning part (spatial prediction of environmental phenomena).

The remainder of the paper is organized as follows. Section 2 discusses briefly the sandbox method and how it was applied in the research. Section 3 presents the real data case study, with some exploratory data analysis and redundancy minimisation. Section 4 presents the results on the local fractality and its impact on clustering analysis.

## 2    Method

The main method is based on a local, even point-wise, study of Local Growth Curves (LGC) usually used to estimate a fractal dimension [21]. In this paper we will use complete curve and not only the fractal dimension which is a slope of the curve in the log-log presentation.

The computation of LGC is very simple. *Every* data point $X_i$ is considered as a center and the number of points $N(X_i, R)$ falling into the hyper-sphere of radius $R$ is counted (therefore, "sand box counting"). Then, the radius is changed and a set of $LGC_i = N(X_i, R_{k=1,...M})$ is produced. The number of LGC curves equals to the number of data points [22] and each curve at point $X_i$ is characterized my $M$-points. In a general setting it is not necessary to use all points, and there could be many variants of how to select a data subset.

These curves characterize changes of local density and local fractal dimension in space. In general, LGC form a set of functional data (curves), which can be studied using different advanced techniques as well [23].

In summary, in the present research, we use both LGC and local fractal dimension in order to study local intrinsic properties of the input feature space and (2) machine learning clustering algorithms to reveal characteristic groups in LGC.

The calculation of LGC and an estimation of the local dimension are performed using the *FractalTools* R library which is available on GitHub [24].

## 3   Cases Study

The real case study consists of original 13-dimensional input space used for the prediction of monthly wind speed. The digital elevation model (DEM), see Fig. 1 was a basis to develop additional to the geographical coordinates features. Therefore, there could be a redundancy in the engineered feature space. The original resolution of DEM was $[250 \times 250]$ m$^2$. More details on the preparation of feature space can be found in [25].

The raw IFS used in this study was composed of twelve variables which were transformed to Z-score values to have the same range of variability. The altitude, being a basis for the generation of additional input features, was not used. It means, that the IFS was composed from the geographical coordinates and features produced from the altitude without using altitude itself ($13d - altitude = 12d$). Other feature spaces configuration can be studied as well, for example, by removing geographical coordinates. Of course, even in this space the redundancy is present: there are some complex dependencies between features, see below. Therefore, a redundancy reduction method based on Morisita index, also connected to fractal concepts, was applied [11].

From the original data set, 30000 points were randomly selected for the computational and visualisation purposes.

The main steps of the analysis include: exploratory data analysis and data pre-processing; estimation of the global fractal dimension of raw and reduced input feature spaces ($RIFS$); estimation and mapping of the local fractality of the $RIFS$; clustering of the growth curves and mapping of the clusters detected, understanding of the results.

The global analysis of fractal dimension estimated via sandbox counting method ($Fdim$) and ID by Morisita index [26] ($IDMI$) gave the dimensionality of the manifold between 3 and 4 which is much smaller than the dimension of the Euclidean space ($DEucl = 12$). It was expected, taking into account the redundancy in raw data.

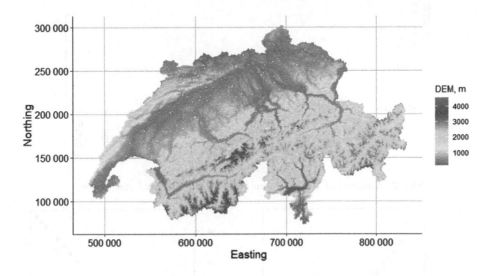

**Fig. 1.** Swiss digital elevation model.

Therefore, the next step was to remove the redundant features from the 12-dimensional space. The application of the method proposed in [11] gives rise to the following result, presented in Fig. 2. The original variables are ranking from left to right according to their contribution to the increase of ID. After reaching the level of global ID, variables are considered as redundant.

From the analysis performed, it follows that only five variables are non-redundant: geographical coordinates (X, Y), derivatives at different scales (sslope, mslope) and variability at small scale (difference between two Gaussian smoothings). This reduced space ($RIFS$) is used in the following studies.

Re-estimated Morisita ID and global sandbox fractal dimension in the $RIFS$ are presented as log–log curves in Fig. 3. They are much closer to the dimensionality of the embedding Euclidean space (=5).

As mentioned above, instead of computing the global fractal estimation, we consider each point separately, in order to study the $RIFS$ locally. Thus, for each data point, a local fractal dimension is computed.

Local growth curves were calibrated (number of radii and scaling parameters) using the results from the global analysis. In the present paper the LGC are characterised by 18 different radii. The map of local fractal dimension is shown in Fig. 4. It is interesting to observe high variability of the local ID changing in space

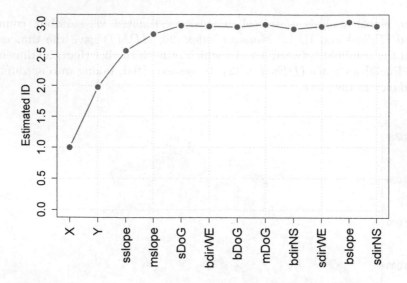

**Fig. 2.** Analysis of the redundancy in 12-dimensional raw space.

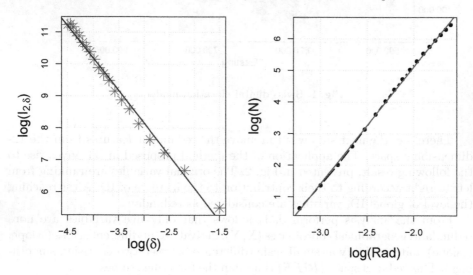

**Fig. 3.** Morisita index $(ID)$ estimation (left, $ID = 3.0$). Sand box fractal dimension $(Fdim)$ estimation (right, $Fdim = 3.7$) in reduced input feature space

related to geomorphology. This information is important both to understand the feature space and to construct predictive models according to the revealed clusters.

In order to decide about the number of clusters, thirty validation indexes characterizing clustering quality and using a particular algorithm were applied [27]. According to the majority votes, when using k-means clustering with a

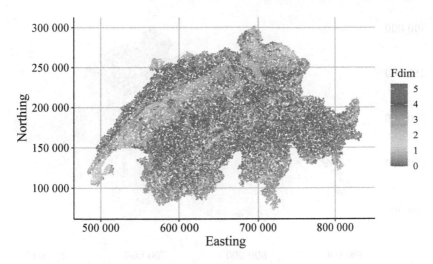

**Fig. 4.** Local fractal dimension estimated in $RIFS$.

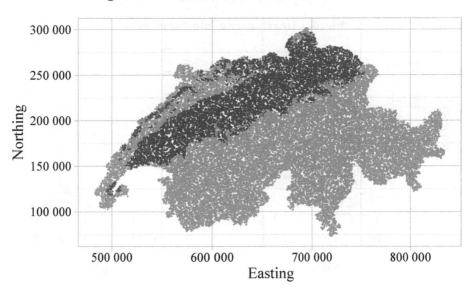

**Fig. 5.** Clara clustering into 2 clusters

selected subset of data (8000 data points) in the 5-dimensional $RIFS$, the optimal number of clusters proposed is three.

Next step is to consider clustering in this 18-dimensional feature space constructed from local growth curves. In the research several algorithms were applied, studied and compared. The main results of the clara algorithm [10], which is a good and robust choice for large data sets, are presented below, see Fig. 5 and Fig. 6.

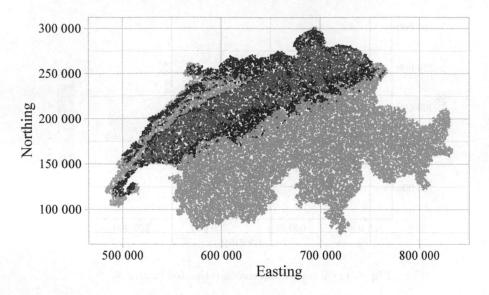

**Fig. 6.** Clara clustering into 3 clusters

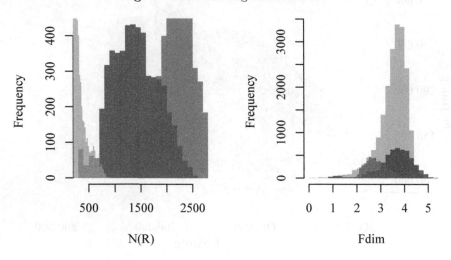

**Fig. 7.** Histograms of the estimated local densities and local fractal dimensions for three clusters

## 4   Discussion and Conclusions

The paper offers insights on the IFS advanced analysis to reveal existing clusters in high dimensional environmental data. The first results are quite promising and help in understanding of high dimensional modelling space. In order to better interpret the result of clustering, the histograms of the estimated fractal dimensions and local densities for the case of three clusters are presented in

Fig. 7. The density is estimated as a number of data points within a fixed radius. It is evident, that both density and dimension are important in curves separation.

Another interesting observation is that local fractal dimension (ID) depends on the geomorphological unit. This information is important in feature selection and model development when supervised problem of wind speed prediction will be considered.

In the present research the whole LGC were analysed. In fact, local fractal dimension and/or local density can be used independently as complementary features in other kinds of data analysis.

There are many possibilities to extend and advance the research: from experimenting with input feature spaces and applying the proposed approach in feature engineering to the application of advanced clustering algorithms.

The main objective of the present study was rather methodological, i.e. to demonstrate the possibility of mixing different scientific concepts in order to extract interesting patterns useful in data understanding, visualisation and modelling. The exploration of new challenging case studies from environmental risks and natural hazards assessments are in progress.

**Acknowledgements.** The research was partly supported by the Swiss National Research Program "Big Data" (PNR75), project "Hybrid Renewable Energy Potential for the Built Environment using Big Data: Forecasting and Uncertainty Estimation" (no. 4075-40_167285).

# References

1. Kanevski, M., Pozdnoukhov, A., Timonin, V.: Machine Learning of Spatial Environmental Data. Theory, Applications and Software. EPFL Press, Lausanne (2009)
2. Mandelbrot, B.: The Fractal Geometry of Nature. W. H. Freeman, San Francisco (1982)
3. Theiler, J.: Estimating fractal dimension. JOSA A Opt. Soc. Am. **7**, 1055–1073 (1990)
4. Turcotte, D.L.: Fractals and Chaos in Geology and Geophysics. Cambridge University Press, Cambridge (1997)
5. Camastra, F.: Intrinsic dimension estimation: advances and open problems. Inf. Sci. **328**, 26–41 (2015)
6. Seuront, L.: Fractals and Multifractals in Ecology and Aquatic Science. CRC Press, Boca Raton (2009)
7. Ghanbarian, B., Hunt, A.: Fractals: Concepts and Applications in Geosciences. CRC Press, Boca Raton (2017)
8. Hastie, T., Tibshirani, R., Friedman, J.: The Elements of Statistical Learning. Springer, New York (2009). https://doi.org/10.1007/978-0-387-84858-7
9. Hennig, Ch., Meila, M., Murtagh, F., Rocci, R.: Handbook of Cluster Analysis. CRC, Boca Raton, Florida (2015)
10. Kaufman, L., Rousseeuw, P.: Finding Groups in Data: An Introduction to Cluster Analysis. Wiley, Hoboken (2009)
11. Golay, J., Kanevski, M.: Unsupervised feature selection based on the Morisita estimator of intrinsic dimension. Knowl.-Based Syst. **135**, 125–134 (2017)

12. Golay, J., Leuenberger, M., Kanevski, M.: Feature selection for regression problems based on the Morisita estimator of intrinsic dimension. Pattern Recogn. **70**, 126–138 (2017)
13. Ripley, B.: Spatial Statistics. Wiley, Hoboken (1981)
14. Kantz, H., Schreiber, Th.: Nonlinear time Series Analysis. Cambridge University Press, Cambridge (2004)
15. Vicsek, T.: Mass multifractals. Physica A **168**(1), 490–497 (1990)
16. Kanevski, M. (ed.): Advanced Mapping of Environmental Data. iSTE & Wiley, London (2008)
17. Facco, E., d'Errico, M., Rodriguez, A., Laio, A.: Estimating the intrinsic dimension of datasets by a minimal neighborhood information. Sci. Rep. **7**, 1–8 (2017)
18. Carter, K., Raich, R., Hero III, A.: On local intrinsic dimension estimation and its applications. IEEE Trans. Signal Process. **58**, 650–663 (2009)
19. Houle, M.: Local intrinsic dimensionality I: an extreme-value-theoretic foundation for similarity applications, In: Beecks, C., Borutta, F., Kröger, P., Seidl, T. (eds.) Similarity Search and Applications. International Conference on Similarity Search and Applications, pp. 64–79. Springer, Cham (2017). https://doi.org/10.1007/978-3-319-68474-1_5
20. Allegra, M., Facco, E., Denti, F., et al.: Data segmentation based on the local intrinsic dimension. Sci. Rep. **10**, 16449 (2020)
21. Gionis, A., Hinneburg, A., Papadimitriou, S., Tsaparas, P.: Dimension induced clustering. In: Eleventh ACM SIGKDD International Conference on Knowledge Discovery in Data Mining, pp. 51–60 (2005)
22. Kanevski, M., Pereira, M.: Local fractality: the case of forest fires in Portugal. Physica A **479**(5), 400–410 (2017)
23. Ramsay, J., Silverman, B.: Functional Data Analysis, 2nd edn. Springer, New York (2009). https://doi.org/10.1007/b98888
24. Laib, M., Kanevski, M., FractalTools: R library for estimating fractal dimension. https://github.com/mlaib/FractalTools. Accessed 20 Oct 2020
25. Robert, S., Foresti, L., Kanevski, M.: Spatial prediction of monthly wind speeds in complex terrain with adaptive general regression neural networks. Int. J. Climatol. **33**(7), 1793–1804 (2013)
26. Golay, J., Kanevski, M.: A new estimator of intrinsic dimension based on the multipoint Morisita index. Pattern Recogn. **48**, 4070–4081 (2015)
27. Charrad, M., Ghazzali, N., Boiteau, V., Niknafs, A.: NbClust: an R package for determining the relevant number of clusters in a data set. J. Stat. Softw. **61**(6), 1–36 (2014)

# Spatiotemporal Air Quality Inference of Low-Cost Sensor Data; Application on a Cycling Monitoring Network

Jelle Hofman[1]([✉]) [iD], Tien Huu Do[2,4], Xuening Qin[3,4], Esther Rodrigo[2,4],
Martha E. Nikolaou[1], Wilfried Philips[3,4], Nikos Deligiannis[2,4],
and Valerio Panzica La Manna[1]

[1] imec The Netherlands, High Tech Campus 31, 5656 Eindhoven, The Netherlands
Jelle.Hofman@imec.nl
[2] Department of Electronics and Informatics, Vrije Universiteit Brussel, Pleinlaan 2,
1050 Brussels, Belgium
[3] imec-TELIN-IPI, Department of Telecommunications and Information Processing,
Ghent University, Sint-Pietersnieuwstraat 25, 9000 Ghent, Belgium
[4] imec, Kapeldreef 75, 3001 Leuven, Belgium

**Abstract.** Air quality monitoring in heterogeneous cities is challenging as a high resolution in both space and time is required to accurately assess population exposure. As regulatory monitoring networks are sparse due to high investment and maintenance costs, recent advances in sensor and IoT technologies have resulted in innovative sensing approaches like mobile sensing to increase the spatial monitoring resolution. An example of such an opportunistic mobile monitoring network is "Snuffelfiets", a project where air quality data is collected from mobile sensors attached to bicycles in Utrecht (NL). The collected data results in a sparse spatiotemporal matrix of measurements which can be completed using data-driven techniques. This work reports on the potential of two machine learning approaches to infer the collected air quality measurements in both space and time; a deep learning model based on Variational Graph Autoencoders (AVGAE) and a Geographical Random Forest model (GRF). A temporal validation exercise is performed at two regulatory monitoring stations following the FAIRMODE modelling quality objectives protocol. This work demonstrates the potential of data-driven techniques for spatiotemporal air quality inference of sensor data as the considered models performed well in terms of accuracy and correlation. The model observed performance metrics approach current state-of-the-art physical models in terms of performance while needing much lower resources, computational power, infrastructure and processing time.

**Keywords:** IoT · Urban · Air quality · Mobile · Sensors · Machine learning

## 1 Introduction

### 1.1 Urban Air Quality

Air Pollution is Regarded as the Biggest Environmental Health Risk in Europe, Affecting people's Health and the Environment [1]. According to the European Environmental

© Springer Nature Switzerland AG 2021
A. Del Bimbo et al. (Eds.): ICPR 2020 Workshops, LNCS 12666, pp. 139–147, 2021.
https://doi.org/10.1007/978-3-030-68780-9_14

Agency (EEA), 77% of the European Urban Population is Exposed to Fine Particulate Matter ($PM_{2.5}$) Concentrations Exceeding the WHO Guideline Values [1, 2]. Especially in Urban Environments, Where Both Pollution Sources and People Affected by Pollution Are Concentrated, Air Pollution Tends to Peak. As Pollution Levels Can Vary Dramatically Over Short Distances or Time Instances [3–8], a High Monitoring Resolution in Both Space and Time Should Be Pursued to Accurately Estimate Population Exposure. Since Traditional Air Quality Monitoring Stations Are Rather Costly and Cumbersome, Cities Typically Only Deploy Few at Representative Locations (E.G. Roadside, Urban Background,…). In Order to Properly Assess people's Exposure to Air Pollution, There is an Urgent Need for Higher Monitoring Granularity.

Thanks to rapid advances in sensor and 'Internet Of Things' (IoT) technologies, cities can now collect data from a wide range of static and mobile sensors. In response to the need for higher monitoring granularity, recent mobile sensing networks have been collecting data on routine service fleets, like postal vans in Antwerp (BE) [9], garbage trucks in Cambridge, Massachusetts (US) [10] or trams and buses in Lausanne and Zurich (CH) [11], but also by personal monitors on bicycles [5, 6, 12–14] and city wardens [15]. These networks provide valuable *in situ* data on experienced exposure levels throughout the city. Nevertheless, the collected datapoints are confined in time and space and need interpolation in order to be effective for air quality mapping and fine-grained exposure assessments.

This work demonstrates the potential of data-driven techniques for air quality data inference in space and time by feeding two machine learning approaches with mobile data collected by a cycling sensor network and temporally validate predicted $PM_{2.5}$ data at two regulatory monitoring locations. Inferring spatiotemporal point measurements to derive highly granular air quality based on real-time sensor measurements is vital for policy makers and researchers to detect pollution events, evaluate local vs regional source contributions, evaluate policy measures *in situ* and improve existing air quality models with experimental data.

## 2    Material and Methods

### 2.1    Snuffelfiets

The "Snuffelfiets" project aims at mobile data gathering on bicycles in Utrecht, the Netherlands (https://snuffelfiets.nl/). Utrecht is a medium-sized (99 km², 3.812 inhabitants/km²) city with a temperate climate located along the Rijn river, in the centre of the Netherlands. Mobile data includes ambient particulate matter (PM), GPS, road surface quality, temperature, relative humidity and Volatile Organic Compounds (VOCs) and is collected opportunistically at a 10 s resolution in Utrecht, the Netherlands, using mobile sensors developed by SODAQ (https://sodaq.com/sodaq-snifferbike/). Data are transmitted using LTE-M and collected in a cloud-based data platform developed by Civity (https://civity.nl/en/). Our study focused on the particulate matter measurements ($PM_1$, $PM_{2.5}$ and $PM_{10}$) quantified by an onboard SPS30 (Sensirion) sensor. The National Institute for Public Health and the Environment (RIVM) tested the performance of four sensors next to three reference stations (Utrecht Kardinaal de Jongweg, Cabauw, Breuke-len) and observed good agreement for $PM_{2.5}$ with uncertainties of ~ 5–10 $\mu g\, m^{-3}$ while a much lower performance is observed for $PM_{10}$ [16].

RIVM cleaned $PM_{2.5}$ outliers with unrealistic cycling speeds (>45 km $h^{-1}$) and calibrated the $PM_{2.5}$ data based on a mass factor, derived from the sensor-reference comparison (average reference/average sensor) at three regulatory stations. This calibrated $PM_{2.5}$ data was subsequently used to feed our air quality inference models (§2.2). Snuffelfiets data for June, 2020, was downloaded from https://dataplatform.nl/#/data/ 3660d2e1-84ee-46bf-a7b6-7e9ac1fcaf3a, while the regulatory data of monitoring stations NL10636 and 10643 was collected via an open API https://api-docs.luchtmeet net.nl/.

## 2.2 Data Inference in Space and Time

Mounting air quality sensors on mobile platforms – in this case bicycles – enables *in situ* opportunistic collection of highly granular measurements. The collected data is valuable, as it is collected dynamically at the roadside, reflecting the actual cyclist exposure. Mobile monitoring studies have revealed large spatiotemporal variability in pollutant exposure before, impacted by various factors, i.e., road traffic, meteorology, street topology and background emission dynamics, not represented by measurements derived from nearest regulatory monitoring stations [5, 6, 13, 17]. Nevertheless, these data points are still sparse and require spatiotemporal interpolation in order to generalize air quality assessments; e.g. to disentangle impacts of location and time and for air quality mapping purposes (Fig. 1).

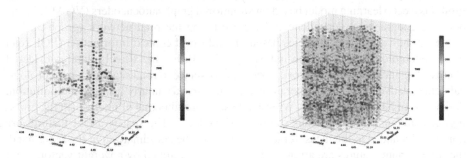

**Fig. 1.** Concept visualization of matrix completion on air quality data. Left: Combination of fixed and mobile sensor measurements represented as a sparse data matrix in space (x-y plane) and time (z plane). Right: Inferred air quality predictions by the ML model.

Focusing on available regulatory air quality data from Antwerp, Belgium, it can be observed that pollutant concentrations tend to temporally covary at different monitoring locations (Fig. 2). Due to the observed associations in both space and time, data matrices of air quality data can be considered low rank and thus explainable by statistical/numerical techniques [18, 19]. The underlying low rank and slowly time-varying structure of the air quality data can be leveraged to create numerical models that facilitate an effective spatiotemporal extrapolation [20]. Machine learning (ML) approaches allow for training of underlying dependencies based on large air quality datasets and supplied context information (traffic, meteorology, street type, speed limit), hereby enabling data inference or matrix completion in both space and time (Fig. 1).

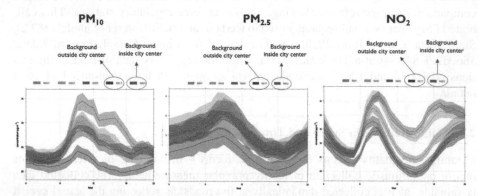

**Fig. 2.** Experienced diurnal variability for $PM_{10}$, $PM_{2.5}$ and $NO_2$ at different urban regulatory monitoring locations (R801, R802, R805, R817, R803) in Antwerp, Belgium. Hourly-averages are calculated based on >1 year hourly timeseries (April, 2018–July, 2019).

Two ML models have recently been developed by the Interuniversity Microelectronics Centre (IMEC), trained on mobile air quality sensors mounted on postal vans in Antwerp, Belgium, and evaluated against regulatory data at four different monitoring stations [21]. The same models are now applied on the Snuffelfiets data. The **AVGAE model** is a deep learning model based on variational graph autoencoders (VGAE), incorporating geographical dependencies by considering the road network (graph), while training time-variant dependencies based on additional context information (POI, road type, meteorology, street canyon index,…) [22, 23]. For the Utrecht data, considered context data included road network (road type, distance to road segment), meteorological data (relative humidity, temperature and wind speed), hourly background pollution, derived from NL10644 Cabauw-Wielsekade station and points of interest (POIs; crossing, gas station, traffic light, bus station, taxi rank,…). The space-variant features are horizontally added to the measurement matrix, like the coordinates. On the other hand, the time-variant features are arranged in a matrix, multiplied by a weight vector. After applying a tiling operation, we obtain an adjustment matrix from the time-variant features. This adjustment matrix is added to output of the AVGAE model. The measurement aspect refers to the spatiotemporal correlation that exists internally in the measurements. The internal spatial correlation in this case is incorporated via graph convolutional layers leveraging the road network (the graph). The internal temporal correlation is considered by adding an extra term in the loss function [22].

The **Geographical Random Forest (GRF) model** allows for spatial non-stationarity in the relationship between a dependent and a set of independent variables. This technique adopts the idea of Geographically Weighted Regression (GWR), moving a spatially weighted window over the observations, while being coupled with a flexible non-linear model which is very hard to overfit due to its bootstrapping nature. While a global model (weight 0.8) is trained on random sensor and context data subsets, a local model (weight 0.2, 200 trees) was trained on subsets from nearest neighbors (20; geographical + context features). The GRF model included context information, namely road network (road type, distance to road segment), meteorological data (relative humidity, temperature and wind speed) and hourly background pollution, derived from NL10644 Cabauw-Wielsekade station.

### 2.3 Model Performance

Following an earlier model validation exercise on one month of mobile nitrogen dioxide ($NO_2$) measurements collected by postal vans in Antwerp, Belgium [21], this study differentiates by testing the generalizability of our approach on existing datasets (Snuffelfiets). Moreover, we focus on another pollutant ($PM_{2.5}$) and on mobile collection platform (bicycles instead of postal vans).Model performances are evaluated from one month (June, 2020) of mobile PM data in Utrecht, the Netherlands.

Both ML models are trained on the bicycle-collected PM data during June 2020 in Utrecht (NL), together with available context information on road type, meteorology and background pollution, and subsequently applied to infer air quality measurements in space and time (Fig. 3). The inherent model performance was evaluated using 5-fold cross validation.

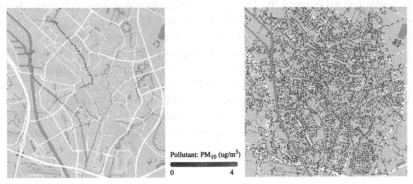

**Fig. 3.** Measured mobile $PM_{10}$ concentrations (left) and inferred AVGAE model predictions (right) in Utrecht (June 2nd, 2020, 11h).

Temporal model validation of both ML models (AVGAE, GRF) was performed following the FAIRMODE 'Guidance document on Modelling Quality Objectives and Benchmarking' [24, 25], developed under Air Quality Directive 2008/50/EC. The performance metrics are calculated based on hourly model predictions for June, 2020, and associated reference data at two different regulatory monitoring locations in Utrecht; a roadside (NL10636 Kardinaal de Jongweg) and urban background (NL10643 Griftpark) station. Performance metrics included Mean Absolute Error (MAE), Root mean Squared Error (RMSE), Index of Agreement (IA), Accuracy, Pearson correlation, Normalized Mean Bias (NMB), Normalized Mean Squared Deviation (NMSD) and the

Model Quality Indicator (MQI) and Model Performance Criteria for bias (MPC$_{bias}$), correlation (MPC$_{corr}$) and standard deviation (MPC$_{stdev}$) as defined by the FAIRMODE Guidance Document [24, 25].

## 3 Results

The Snuffelfiets dataset of PM$_{2.5}$ for June, 2020, consisted of 928047 measurements, was clipped to the Utrecht area [(5.0596, 52.0568) (5.1636, 52.1242)], temporally aggregated to hourly values at 8262 locations (road network) and resulted in a known entry rate of 0.95% of the spatiotemporal matrix for June, 2020. The measured PM$_{2.5}$ concentration range was 1.0/4.07/3.0/11.0 $\mu$g m$^{-3}$ (min/mean/median/max).

From the AVGAE and GRF hourly predicted PM$_{2.5}$ concentrations at each of the regulatory monitoring stations and the associated regulatory data, we calculated the resulting performance metrics shown in Table 1. Both models perform well in terms of accuracy (MAE = 2.83–3.14 (AVGAE) and 2.74–2.88 (GRF)) and correlation (r = 0.63–0.72 (AVGAE) and 0.73–0.77 (GRF)) with GRF slightly outperforming AVGAE. Associated model performance criteria (MPC) for bias, correlation and standard deviation are all within the bounds set by the FAIRMODE protocol (not shown). Residuals of hourly modelled concentrations showed normal distributions. Comparing our observations to reported performance metrics (r = 0.73–0.9, RMSE 8.29–18.93 and MBE: −5.61–0.94 (NO$_2$)) of the current physical model applied for policy making in Flanders, Belgium (ATMOStreet [26, 27]), the considered data-driven techniques seem to approach the state-of-the-art in terms of performance. Moreover, as the Model Quality Indicator (MQI) defined by FAIRMODE is <1 (Table 1), the considered air quality models can be considered as suitable for policy purposes [25]. The physical ATMOStreet model which is currently used for policy purposes in Belgium integrates multiple spatial scales (regional-local) using a RIO-IFDM-OSPM modelling chain, with the RIO module spatially interpolating regulatory measurements, IFDM (bi-gaussian dispersion model) simulating emission plumes from known point and line emission sources and OSPM being a street canyon module implementing the effect of urban topology ("street canyon effect") on the resulting pollutant dispersion [26, 27].

**Table 1.** Temporal validation statistics for the AVGAE and GRF model at two different regulatory stations in Utrecht (NL10636 Kardinaal de Jongweg, NL10643 Griftpark).

| Model | Station | MAE | MBE | RMSE | IA | Acc | Corr | NMB | NMSD | MQI |
|-------|---------|-----|-----|------|-----|-----|------|------|-------|-----|
| AVGAE | NL10636 | 3.14 | 1.79 | 3.99 | 0.82 | 0.64 | 0.72 | −0.21 | −0.07 | 0.20 |
| AVGAE | NL10643 | 2.83 | 0.15 | 3.73 | 0.75 | 0.58 | 0.63 | −0.02 | −0.35 | 0.19 |
| GRF | NL10636 | 2.88 | 1.99 | 3.8 | 0.79 | 0.67 | 0.77 | −0.23 | −0.34 | 0.43 |
| GRF | NL10643 | 2.74 | −1.05 | 3.49 | 0.79 | 0.6 | 0.73 | 0.15 | −0.37 | 0.44 |
| **AVGAE** | **Avg** | **2.99** | **0.97** | **3.86** | **0.79** | **0.61** | **0.68** | **−0.12** | **−0.21** | **0.20** |
| **GRF** | **Avg** | **2.81** | **0.47** | **3.65** | **0.79** | **0.64** | **0.75** | **−0.04** | **−0.36** | **0.44** |

Time series graphs of the AVGAE and GRF predicted PM$_{2.5}$ concentrations are provided in Fig. 4 and illustrate that predicted PM$_{2.5}$ concentrations (M$_i$) agree reasonably well with the reported reference data (O$_i$) for each of the considered models at each location, mostly falling within the uncertainty bounds of the reference equipment (RMSU; provided by FAIRMODE) and the MQI limits defined by FAIRMODE as twice (k = 2) the reference measurement uncertainty [25].

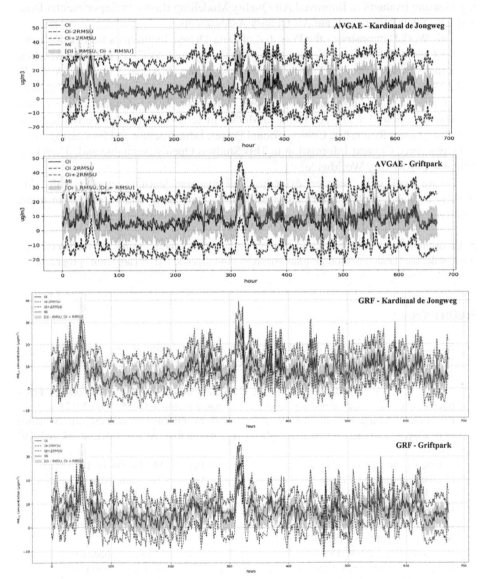

**Fig. 4.** Time series graphs of AVGAE (15 days; upper 2 panels) and GRF (full month, lower 2 panels) predicted (M$_i$) and RIVM reported (O$_i$) PM2.5 concentrations with associated uncertainty bounds of the reference equipment (RMSU; purple) and model quality limits (2 x RMSU; dashed lines) defined by FAIRMODE.

## 4 Conclusions

Inferring Spatiotemporal Point Measurements to Derive Highly Granular Air Quality Maps Based on Real-Time Sensor Data is Vital for Citizens, Policy Makers and Researchers as It Opens up a Range of Potential Applications Including Real-Time Hotspot Detection, Evaluation of Local vs Regional Source Contributions, in Situ Policy Measure Evaluation, Improved Air Quality Modelling Based on Experimental Data, and Ultimately More Accurate Air Quality Assessments.

This Work Demonstrates the Potential of Data-Driven Techniques for Spatiotemporal Air Quality Inference of Sensor Data. The Considered AVGAE and GRF Machine Learning Models Performed Well in Terms of Accuracy (MAE = 2.83–3.14 (AVGAE) and 2.74–2.88 (GRF)) and Correlation (R = 0.63–0.72 (AVGAE) and 0.73–0.77 (GRF)) with GRF Slightly Outperforming AVGAE. Moreover, This Validation Shows They Approach the State-Of-The-Art Physical Models in Terms of Performance While Needing Much Lower Resources, Computational Power, Infrastructure and Processing Time. All Considered Context Information in This Study is Openly Available and, Therefore, Scalable to Any City Worldwide.

Future work will focus on extending our machine learning models with additionally available context information, and on its application and validation in future deployments, as an additional air quality mapping tool for policy making.

**Acknowledgement.** This research was supported in part by funding from the Flemish Government under the "Onderzoeksprogramma Artificiële Intelligentie (AI) Vlaanderen" programme.

## References

1. EEA: Air quality in Europe 2019. European Environment Agency, Luxembourg (2019)
2. WHO: Air pollution. https://www.who.int/health-topics/air-pollution#tab=tab_1. Accessed 16 Jul 2020
3. Pirjola, L., et al.: Spatial and temporal characterization of traffic emissions in urban microenvironments with a mobile laboratory. Atmos. Environ. **63**, 156–167 (2012)
4. Pattinson, W., Longley, I., Kingham, S.: Using mobile monitoring to visualise diurnal variation of traffic pollutants across two near-highway neighbourhoods. Atmos. Environ. **94**, 782–792 (2014)
5. Peters, J., Van den Bossche, J., Reggente, M., Van Poppel, M., De Baets, B., Theunis, J.: Cyclist exposure to UFP and BC on urban routes in Antwerp, Belgium. Atmos. Environ. **92**, 31–43 (2014)
6. Hofman, J., Samson, R., Joosen, S., Blust, R., Lenaerts, S.: Cyclist exposure to black carbon, ultrafine particles and heavy metals: an experimental study along two commuting routes near Antwerp, Belgium. Environ. Res. **164**, 530–538 (2018)
7. Kumar, P., Patton, A.P., Durant, J.L., Frey, H.C.: A review of factors impacting exposure to PM 2.5, ultrafine particles and black carbon in Asian transport microenvironments. Atmos. Environ. **187**, 301–316 (2018)
8. Int Panis, L., et al.: Exposure to particulate matter in traffic: a comparison of cyclists and car passengers. Atmos. Environ. 44(19), 2263–2270 (2010)

9. Qin, X., et al.: Context-based analysis of urban air quality using an opportunistic mobile sensor network. In: Santos, H., Pereira, G.V., Budde, M., Lopes, S.F., Nikolic, P. (eds.) SmartCity 360 2019. LNICSSITE, vol. 323, pp. 285–300. Springer, Cham (2020). https://doi.org/10. 1007/978-3-030-51005-3_24

10. deSouza, P., Anjomshoaa, A., Duarte, F., Kahn, R., Kumar, P., Ratti, C.: Air quality monitoring using mobile low-cost sensors mounted on trash-trucks: Methods development and lessons learned. Sustain. Cities Soc. **60**, 102239 (2020)

11. Mueller, M.D., Hasenfratz, D., Saukh, O., Fierz, M., Hueglin, C.: Statistical modelling of particle number concentration in Zurich at high spatio-temporal resolution utilizing data from a mobile sensor network. Atmos. Environ. **126**, 171–181 (2016)

12. Franco, J.F., Segura, J.F., Mura, I.: Air pollution alongside bike-paths in Bogotá-Colombia. Front. Environ. Sci. **4**, 77 (2016)

13. Qiu, Z., Wang, W., Zheng, J., Lv, H.: Exposure assessment of cyclists to UFP and PM on urban routes in Xi'an China. Environ. Pollut. **250**, 241–250 (2019)

14. Genikomsakis, K.N., et al.: Development and on-field testing of low-cost portable system for monitoring PM2.5 concentrations. Sensors (Basel) **18**(4), 1056 (2018)

15. van den Bossche, J., Theunis, J., Elen, B., Peters, J., Botteldooren, D., de Baets, B.: Opportunistic mobile air pollution monitoring: a case study with city wardens in Antwerp. Atmos. Environ. **141**, 408–421 (2016)

16. Wesseling, J.: Verzamelde data stofmetingen op de fiets. In: Presented at the Presentation First Results of Snifferbike Project, Utrecht, January 2020

17. Gelb, J., Apparicio, P.: Modelling cyclists' multi-exposure to air and noise pollution with low-cost sensors—the case of Paris. Atmosphere **11**(4), 422 (2020)

18. Udell, M., Townsend, A.: Why are big data matrices approximately low rank? SIAM J. Math. Data Sci. **1**(1), 144–160 (2019)

19. Asif, M.T., Mitrovic, N., Dauwels, J., Jaillet, P.: Matrix and tensor based methods for missing data estimation in large traffic networks. IEEE Trans. Intell. Transp. Syst. **17**(7), 1816–1825 (2016)

20. Paliwal, C., Biyani, P., Rajawat, K., Sutaria, R.: Scalable spatio-temporal measurements and analysis of air pollution data using vehicle mounted sensors. In: Presented at the Air Sensors International Conference - Virtual Fall Series (2020)

21. Hofman, J., et al.: Mapping air quality in IoT cities: cloud calibration and air quality inference of sensor data. In: IEEE SENSORS 2020 Conference Proceedings (2020)

22. Do, T., et al.: Matrix completion with variational graph autoencoders: application in hyperlocal air quality inference. In: Presented at the IEEE International Conference on Acoustics, Speech, and Signal Processing (ICASSP) (2019)

23. Do, T.H., et al.: Graph-deep-learning-based inference of fine-grained air quality from mobile IoT sensors. IEEE Internet Things J. **7**, 8943–8955 (2020)

24. Kushta, J., et al.: Evaluation of EU air quality standards through modeling and the FAIRMODE benchmarking methodology. Air Qual. Atmos. Health **12**(1), 73–86 (2019). https://doi.org/ 10.1007/s11869-018-0631-z

25. Janssen, S., Guerreiro, C., Viaene, P., Georgieva, E., Thunis, P.: Guidance document on modelling quality objectives and benchmarking (2016)

26. Irceline: Validatie luchtkwaliteitsmodel. ATMO - Street (Vlaanderen)voor NO$_2$ in 2017, Irceline (2017)

27. Lefebvre, W., Van Poppel, M., Maiheu, B., Janssen, S., Dons, E.: Evaluation of the RIO-IFDM-street canyon model chain. Atmos. Environ. **77**, 325–337 (2013)

# How Do Deep Convolutional SDM Trained on Satellite Images Unravel Vegetation Ecology?

Benjamin Deneu[1,2](✉) ⓘ, Alexis Joly[1] ⓘ, Pierre Bonnet[2,3] ⓘ,
Maximilien Servajean[4] ⓘ, and François Munoz[5] ⓘ

[1] INRIA, UMR LIRMM, Univ Montpellier, Montpellier, France
[2] AMAP, Univ Montpellier, CIRAD, CNRS, INRAE, IRD, Montpellier, France
`benjamin.deneu@inria.fr`
[3] CIRAD, UMR AMAP, 34398 Montpellier, France
[4] LIRMM, Université Paul Valéry, University of Montpellier, CNRS, Montpellier, France
[5] CNRS, LECA, Grenoble, France

**Abstract.** Species distribution models (SDM) assess and predict how species spatial distributions depend on the environment, due to species ecological preferences. These models are used in many different scenarios such as conservation plans or monitoring of invasive species. The choice of a model and of environmental data have strong impact on the model's ability to capture important ecological information. Specifically, state-of-the-art models generally rely on local, punctual environmental information, and do not take into account environmental variation in surrounding landscape. Here we use a convolutional neural network model to analyze and predict species distributions depending on high resolution data including remote sensing images, land cover and altitude. We show that the model unravel the functional response of vegetation to both local and large-scale environmental variation. To demonstrate the ecological significance of the results, we propose an original statistical analysis of t-SNE nonlinear dimension reduction. We illustrate and test the traits-species-environment relationships learned by the model and expressed in t-SNE dimensions.

**Keywords:** Species distribution model · Convolutional neural network · Ecological interpretation · Plant functional traits · Trait–environment relationships · t-SNE

## 1 Introduction

Understanding and predicting the geographic distribution of species is a key objective in ecology and conservation. Species Distribution Models (SDM) aim at characterizing the relationship between the environment and species occurrences, depending on species ecological niches [14]. The ecological niche is multidimensional, and involves factors playing in a complex fashion (*i.e.* non linear system) and at multiple spatial scales. Most SDMs are correlative methods

© Springer Nature Switzerland AG 2021
A. Del Bimbo et al. (Eds.): ICPR 2020 Workshops, LNCS 12666, pp. 148–158, 2021.
https://doi.org/10.1007/978-3-030-68780-9_15

relating known species occurrence data to potential environmental predictors [1,17,25]. Popular examples of such methods include MAXENT [26,27], random forest [9] and boosted regression trees [10,15]. Earlier works devised SDMs based on single-layer neural networks [2,22], and recently deep neural networks have proved relevant to better address the complexity of ecological niches, allowing to recognized a larger complexity in the way environment shapes ecological niches [4,6]. Key advantages of deep learning are that (i) it allows characterizing complex structuring of ecological niche depending on multiple environmental factors, (ii) it can learn ecological features common to a large number of species, and thus grasp the signatures of common ecological processes and improve SDM predictions across species [5,7].

A specific class of neural networks initially proposed in [21], named Convolutional Neural Networks (CNN), has very recently been proposed for SDM [5,13]. A property of CNN is that they rely on spatial environmental tensors rather than on local values of environmental factors. These tensors represent the spatial realization of environmental factors around each point. Unlike other SDM approaches, CNN-based SDMs (CNN-SDMs) can use this very large input data and therefore potentially capture richer information than in punctual vectors. CNNs were originally designed for image classification [21] and proved to outperform any other statistical or machine learning methods in the task of learning complex visual patterns. This largely explains why CNN-based architectures are the most popular deep learning implementations in ecological studies since few years [7].

In this paper, we use a deep species distribution model based on a convolutional neural network applied to high resolution remote sensing images as one of the input covariables. This model has already been evaluated and compared to other more classical methods revealing superior performance to state of the art models. In this paper we are interested in the interpretation of these performances. The major contribution of the paper is to provide an ecological interpretation of the model. Therefore, we propose to rely on t-SNE [23], a nonlinear dimension reduction technique widely used in data science to visualize high-dimensional feature spaces. More precisely, we use it to build a low-dimensional embedding of the 2028-dimensional representation space learned by the convolutional neural network (*i.e.* the 2028 neurons used as input of the species prediction layer of the model). The resulting low-dimensional embedding is then used in two ways: (i) to visualize the relationships between the learned features, the species traits and the environment, and (ii) to quantify these relationships using statistical tests. The main outcome of our study is that the statistical tests clearly demonstrate that the model was able to capture meaningful relationships between the species traits and the environment. This is particularly remarkable in the sense that none of these information were used as input covariables during the training of the model. The model was actually capable of inferring them directly from the high-resolution spatialized images used as input and the species occurrences.

# 2    Materials and Methods

## 2.1    CNN-SDM Model Training and Validation

**Training Dataset.** A detailed description of the dataset (named GeoLife-CLEF 2020) is provided in [8]. It consists of 1,921,123 observations from the US (1,097,640) and France (823,483) covering $31,435$ plant and animal species (Table 1). Each species observation is paired with high-resolution covariates (RGB-IR imagery, land cover and altitude), see Fig. 1. We used RGB-IR imagery from the 2009–2011 cycle of the National Agriculture Imagery Program (NAIP) in the U.S.[1], and from the BD-ORTHO® 2.0 and ORTHO-HR® 1.0 databases from IGN in France[2]. Land cover data originates from the National Land Cover Database (NLCD) [20] for the U.S. and from CESBIO[3] for France. All elevation data comes from the NASA Shuttle Radar Topography Mission (SRTM)[4]. All of these high-resolution covariates were homogenized at a spatial resolution of 1 m per pixel and provided as $256 \times 256$ images covering a $256\,\text{m} \times 256\,\text{m}$ square centered on each observation (some were oversampled and some where downsampled).

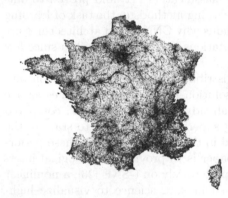

(b) Example of high-resolution covariates patch (respectively: RGB imagery, IR imagery, altitude, land cover).

(a) Occurrences

**Fig. 1.** Occurrences distribution (training data in blue, test data in red) in France (a), and an example high-resolution tensor (b). RGB patch is displayed with native colors, IR imagery, altitude and land cover are in artificial colors from purple (lowest values) to yellow (highest values). (Color figure online)

---

[1]  National Agriculture Image Program, https://www.fsa.usda.gov.
[2]  https://geoservices.ign.fr.
[3]  http://osr-cesbio.ups-tlse.fr/~oso/posts/2017-03-30-carte-s2-2016/.
[4]  https://lpdaac.usgs.gov/products/srtmgl1v003/.

**Table 1.** Number of occurrences, of species and of occurrences per species grouped for plants and animals, and per region (for the training set).

| Kingdom | Nb. of occurrences | | Nb. of species | | Nb. of occ. per sp. | |
|---|---|---|---|---|---|---|
| | US | France | US | France | US | France |
| Plants | 524,280 | 741,010 | 11,369 | 3,114 | 46.1 | 238.0 |
| Animals | 551,563 | 61,865 | 13,882 | 4,899 | 39.7 | 12.6 |
| All | 1,622,120 | 802,875 | 25,251 | 8,013 | 42.6 | 100.2 |

**Deep Convolutional SDM Architecture.** Our deep convolutional neural network is the composition of non linear transformations of the input space $z = \phi(x)$ with a linear classifier $\psi(z)$. The vector $z$ is called the representation vector, or feature vector of the input tensor $x$. The architecture used is based on the Inception V3 [28] model adapted in the same way introduced in [11]. The representation layer has size 2048 and the loss is the cross-entropy. The output of the model can be interpreted as the probability for each species.

**Predictive Performance.** We evaluated the model and compared it to other more classical approaches, such as a random forest learned on environmental data (RF), using a spatial block holdout procedure[5]. On a top-30 score, the CNN obtained 23.5% success compared to the 20.4% success of the random forest environmental model. This evaluation allowed us to validate the performance of the model (CNN-SDM) that we will study later in this report.

## 2.2 Ecological Interpretation of the Learned Features

We considered environmental and species trait data not used during model training. We assess the extent to which the model could capture ecological information such as the functional response of plant species to environmental constraints (specifically, climatic and pedological factors). In the following subsections, we first describe the environmental and species traits data used (Sect. 2.3). In Subsect. 2.4, we then describe the non linear dimension reduction technique that we used to embed the 2048-dimensional feature vectors $z$ into a low-dimensional space of 2 or 3 dimensions aimed at conserving only the most structuring information. In Subsect. 2.5, we describe the statistical tests that were performed on top of the resulting low-dimensional embedding for the ecological interpretation. Finally, in Subsect. 2.6, we describe some additional methodological details that were used for visualization purposes.

---

[5] Test occurrences are contained in $5 \times 5$ km quadrats with no train occurrences and represent 2.5% of the overall set.

## 2.3  Environmental and Trait Data

We used 19 bio-climatic rasters ($30\text{arcsec}^2$/pixel (above $1\,\text{km}^2$/pixel) from WorldClim [19]) and 8 pedologic rasters ($250\,\text{m}^2$/pixel, from SoilGrids [18]), for more details refer to the supplementary material Table A1[12].

We used ecological information available for more than 1,400 plant species, in terms of Ellenberg's indicator values (EIVs) [16] (for more details refer to the supplementary material Table A2 [12]). These variables represent an ordinal classification of ecological strategies for major environmental constraints and the use of essential resources [3].

## 2.4  Dimension Reduction

CNNs train a representation space in which species occurrences projections $\mathbf{z} = \phi(\mathbf{x})$ tend to be linearly separable (thanks to the multinomial logistic regression $\psi$ trained on top of $\mathbf{z}$). We analyzed how the structure of the learned space could grasp major ecological and environmental information unused during learning. We identified major dimensions of the learned space by projecting the feature vectors $\mathbf{z}$ into a very low-dimensional space of 2 or 3 dimensions. For this purpose, we used the t-SNE dimension reduction method [23]. Our procedure is composed of two steps. First a PCA is applied followed by a t-SNE. More details are available in the supplementary material Sect. 2 (Dimension reduction) [12]. In the following, we denote as $\tilde{\mathbf{z}} = g(\mathbf{z})$ the resulting 2-dimensional feature vectors where the function $g$ denotes the complete dimension reduction function (PCA+t-SNE).

## 2.5  Ecological Interpretation of T-SNE Dimensions

**Relationship of T-SNE Dimensions to Ecological Traits and Environmental Factors.** For each of the two variables $\tilde{\mathbf{z}}_1$ and $\tilde{\mathbf{z}}_2$, corresponding in the two axis of the t-SNE, we fitted a linear model using either the environmental variables or the species trait variables as input covariates (lm function in R environment).

The link between the representation space learned by the model (condensed in the t-SNE space) and these data (not used during the learning process) offers a way to interpret the ecological significance of patterns learned by the CNN-SDM models.

**Traits-Environment Relationships.** Trait-environment relationship represent essential functional responses of plants to changing environmental conditions. Characterizing these relationships is an essential goal in functional biogeography [29]. We tested whether t-SNE axes unravel such relationships by mean of weighted correlation analysis. We calculated the correlation between species trait and environmental value for each training occurrence, weighted by the score of the occurrence along each t-SNE axis. Under the null hypothesis, the t-SNE axis does not reflect any linkage between trait and environment, under the alternative hypothesis, increasing score is associated to joint variation of trait and environment. We measured the weighted correlation [24] for each t-SNE variable $\tilde{z}_k$ and for each pair of ecological trait and environmental variable. We used the function wtd.cor package weights in R. Furthermore, because we computed many tests for all pairs of trait and environmental variables, we corrected the p-value of the tests by the method false discovery rate (p.adjust function in R).

## 2.6   Visualization

We used different types of visualisations to illustrate the main sources of ecological variation expressed in the two-dimensional t-SNE space. We discretized the space of the t-SNE by applying an $n \times n$-sized grid mesh. For each cell of this grid we retrieved the m-coordinate vector of the center of the cell and we search for the nearest neighbor among the set of vectors $\tilde{z}$ using scikitlearn's nearest neigbhor function. Once the closest point to the center of each cell is retrieved, only those that are actually inside the respective cell are kept by a filter on these coordinates. This results in associating for each cell the occurrence closest to the center if there is one. The different figures of this visualization consist in the display, for each cell, of a data relative to the associated occurrence. For the first Fig. 3a, we displayed the RGB patch of the remote sensing imagery corresponding to this occurrence. For the other Figs. (2a and b) we displayed the value of an ecological trait of the corresponding species or the realization of one of the environmental variables at the point of occurrence.

The second representation is based on the 3-dimensional t-SNE space and, conversely, represents the realization of this space on the geographical space. This 3-dimensional t-SNE space was obtained by the same process as the 2-dimensional space described in detail in Sect. 2.4 but with one difference, the dimension reduction was not performed with the same set of occurrences. As this representation is geographical, it requires a better coverage of the territory than the simple random selection of a certain number of occurrences. We selected occurrences with a method of nearest neighbor. For a grid of points with a resolution of 1 km over the whole territory, we associated each point to the nearest occurrence. The selected occurrences are those used for dimension reduction. Then to plot the 3-dimensional t-SNE on the map, we re-scale each axis such as the values are included in 0–255. Each point can then be associated to a RGB color by its coordinates. The resulting map is the plot of each point as a color pixel at its geographical position.

## 3   Results and Discussion

The statistical analysis of the learned t-SNE space reveals that the CNN-based SDM could grasp important ecological processes shaping the large scale distributions of plants. Indeed, almost all linear models linking scores along t-SNE to

**Table 2.** Ellenberg linear models

|  | tsne_1 | tsne_2 |
|---|---|---|
|  | Estimate (Std. Error) | Estimate (Std. Error) |
| EIV L | −1.562*** (0.236) | 2.630*** (0.214) |
| EIV T | −5.035*** (0.260) | 9.478*** (0.235) |
| EIV K | 2.523*** (0.389) | 0.150 (0.352) |
| EIV AirH | 0.732* (0.378) | −0.869** (0.341) |
| EIV F | 1.461*** (0.409) | 2.328*** (0.370) |
| EIV R | 0.461** (0.213) | −0.686*** (0.192) |
| EIV TroL | 2.902*** (0.181) | 3.851*** (0.163) |
| EIV S | −2.714*** (0.366) | −0.981*** (0.331) |
| EIV SoiT | 1.649*** (0.252) | 2.848*** (0.228) |
| EIV N | 0.211 (0.212) | −0.598*** (0.192) |
| Constant | −5.951 (3.947) | −113.831*** (3.569) |
| $R^2$ | 0.111 | 0.232 |
| Adjusted $R^2$ | 0.111 | 0.231 |

*Note:* *p<0.1; **p<0.05; ***p<0.01

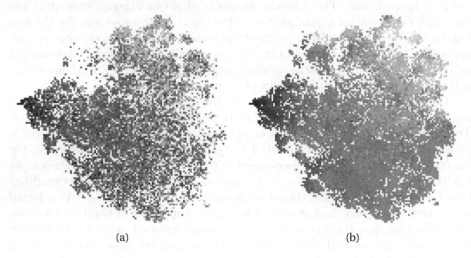

(a)                                    (b)

**Fig. 2.** Visualization of the occurrences' species preferences in temperature (EIV T) (a) and the annual mean temperature (bio_1) at occurrences location (b) on the t-SNE space. Artificial colors from purple (lowest values) to yellow (highest values). (Color figure online)

species traits provided highly significant relationships (Table 2). We can in particular note a strong coefficient on EIV T (species preferences in Temperature) on both axes. The plant Ellenberg indicator values could alone explain a large part of the variation of species scores along t-SNE axes (Adjusted $R^2$ of 0.111

and 0.231). These results show that the model is able to capture information related to the ecology of the species in the patches.

(a)                                    (b)

**Fig. 3.** (a) Visualization of the remote sensing imagery patch (RGB) of occurrences on the t-SNE space. (b) Geographical projection of the 3-dimensional t-SNE space on the territory.

Figure 2a represent the species preferences in temperature and Fig. 2b represent Annual mean temperature of occurrences data on the t-SNE. We found a clear gradient of mean annual temperature on the t-SNE. The fact that this gradient is particularly sharp on t-SNE, which is the result of a dimension reduction, indicates that information strongly correlated with annual temperature is captured and important in the model. It is quite logical that the figure on the associated ecological trait (EIV T) is similar confirming that the plants with the coolest temperature preferences are found in the coldest areas and vice versa. These results highlight that the information captured by the model is strongly related to the environment and ecology of the species, even though this data was not used directly. Figure 3a represent RGB patches from the model training data on the t-SNE space and Fig. 3b represents the geographical projection of the 3-dimensional t-SNE space on the territory with the colors defined by the position in the t-SNE space.

These two figures highlight two complementary pieces of information. On the one hand, the display of the patches on the t-SNE highlights the landscape factors that the CNN is able to identify and differentiate in its representation space. Indeed the Fig. 3a highlights different areas of the t-SNE corresponding to several major types of distinct landscapes. We can note for example the mountain areas on the left next to which we find the forests a little lower down. The more agricultural areas also stand out while the lower and right part of the t-SNE is dominated by urban type landscapes. On the other hand, Fig. 3b shows learning on a larger scale. This map shows how the CNN has learned to distinguish large eco-geographic regions. Of particular note is the Mediterranean region (on southern part of the map), and the mountainous areas (*i.e.* the Pyrenees on the south-western part, and the Alps on the south-eastern part), which seem to be well identified. More generally the map allows to show coherence on a large scale, between typical vegetation zones well identified by ecologists, and bio-geographic zones well characterized on the field in previous studies. The confrontation of these two results shows that the model is capable of discerning both large regions and different habitats within the same large geographical area (such as urban-rural). The ability to identify factors at different scales based on fine scale imaging training data is an important result that highlights one of the advantage of the CNN models. Concerning the species trait-environment relationships, the detailed results matrix of each pair for each axis is given in supplementary materials Tables C1 and C2 [12]. A general finding is that most of the species trait-environment correlations weighted by the t-SNE axes are highly significant. This shows that the CNN is capable of learning a relationship between environment and species ecology through the use of high-resolution covariate patches. All these results highlight a strong point of the CNN model which is capable of capturing information related to the environment and the ecology of species through the use of data accessible at large scale and fine resolution, but also to highlight links between the environment and the ecology of species. This model could therefore be useful in many ecological scenarios where the objective would be to study this link. All these points are also insights for interpreting the performance of the CNN models. By learning a representation space common to all the studied species, the model is able to extract common information between species that are directly correlated to environmental factors or related to the ecology of the species.

## 4  Conclusion

Our study shows the interest of using convolutional neural networks for species distribution modelling (CNN-SDM), at high spatial resolution over large geographical areas. The use of the t-SNE technique made it possible for the first time to visualise and test the learning capacities of this type of model to capture relationships between ecological strategies of plants and environmental conditions at their occurrence locations. The methodological framework established here offers a new way of statistically assessing the extent to which the relationships between the plant traits and their environments are correlated, inspired by the conceptual and methodological framework of functional biogeography [29]. It also allows visualizing through t-SNE the clusters of visual information (from satellite images) deemed most relevant during the learning phase of the CNN-SDMs. This work shows that the approach captures richer information on the landscape context than the specific ponctual data related to the environment for predicting the presence of species, and will undoubtedly open up new perspectives in the analysis of plant-environment trait relationships.

**Acknowledgement.** This project has received funding from the French National Research Agency under the Investments for the Future Program, referred as ANR-16-CONV-0004 and from the European Union's Horizon 2020 research and innovation program under grant agreement No 863463 (Cos4Cloud project).

# References

1. Antoine, G., Wilfried, T.: Predicting species distribution: offering more than simple habitat models. Ecol. Lett. **8**(9), 993–1009 (2005). https://doi.org/10.1111/j.1461-0248.2005.00792.x
2. Baran, P., Lek, S., Delacoste, M., Belaud, A.: Stochastic models that predict trout population density or biomass on a mesohabitat scale. Hydrobiologia **337**(1), 1–9 (1996). https://doi.org/10.1007/BF00028502
3. Bartelheimer, M., Poschlod, P.: Functional characterizations of Ellenberg indicator values-a review on ecophysiological determinants. Funct. Ecol. **30**(4), 506–516 (2016)
4. Benkendorf, D.J., Hawkins, C.P.: Effects of sample size and network depth on a deep learning approach to species distribution modeling. Ecol. Inform. **60**, 101137 (2020)
5. Botella, C., Joly, A., Bonnet, P., Monestiez, P., Munoz, F.: A deep learning approach to species distribution modelling. In: Joly, A., Vrochidis, S., Karatzas, K., Karppinen, A., Bonnet, P. (eds.) Multimedia Tools and Applications for Environmental & Biodiversity Informatics. MSA, pp. 169–199. Springer, Cham (2018). https://doi.org/10.1007/978-3-319-76445-0_10
6. Chen, D., Xue, Y., Chen, S., Fink, D., Gomes, C.P.: Deep multi-species embedding. CoRR abs/1609.09353 (2016). http://arxiv.org/abs/1609.09353
7. Christin, S., Hervet, É., Lecomte, N.: Applications for deep learning in ecology. Methods Ecol. Evol. **10**(10), 1632–1644 (2019)
8. Cole, E., et al.: The GeoLifeCLEF 2020 dataset. arXiv preprint arXiv:2004.04192 (2020)
9. Cutler, D.R., et al.: Random forests for classification in ecology. Ecology **88**(11), 2783–2792 (2007). https://doi.org/10.1890/07-0539.1
10. De'ath, G.: Boosted trees for ecological modeling and prediction. Ecology **88**(1), 243–251 (2007). https://doi.org/10.1890/0012-9658(2007)88[243:BTFEMA]2.0.CO;2
11. Deneu, B., Servajean, M., Joly, A.: Participation of LIRMM/Inria to the geo-lifeclef 2020 challenge. CLEF working notes (2020)
12. Deneu, B., Joly, A., Bonnet, P., Servajean, M., Munoz, F.: Supplementary materials: How do deep convolutional SDM trained on satellite images unravel vegetation ecology? https://gitlab.inria.fr/bdeneu/supplementary-materials-maes2020-paper-19
13. Deneu, B., Servajean, M., Botella, C., Joly, A.: Location-based species recommendation using co-occurrences and environment- GeoLifeCLEF 2018 challenge. In: CLEF Working Notes 2018 (2018)
14. Elith, J., Leathwick, J.R.: Species distribution models: ecological explanation and prediction across space and time. Annu. Rev. Ecol. Evol. Syst. **40**, 677–697 (2009)
15. Elith, J., Leathwick, J.R., Hastie, T.: A working guide to boosted regression trees. J. Anim. Ecol. **77**(4), 802–813 (2008). https://doi.org/10.1111/j.1365-2656.2008.01390.x

16. Ellenberg, H.H.: Vegetation Ecology of Central Europe. Cambridge University Press, Cambridge (1988)
17. Guisan, A., Zimmermann, N.E.: Predictive habitat distribution models in ecology. Ecol. Model. **135**(2), 147–186 (2000). https://doi.org/10.1016/S0304-3800(00)00354-9
18. Hengl, T., et al.: SoilGrids250m: global gridded soil information based on machine learning. PLoS One **12**(2), e0169748 (2017)
19. Hijmans, R.J., Cameron, S.E., Parra, J.L., Jones, P.G., Jarvis, A.: Very high resolution interpolated climate surfaces for global land areas. Int. J. Climatol. J. R. Meteorol. Soc. **25**(15), 1965–1978 (2005)
20. Homer, C., et al.: Completion of the 2011 national land cover database for the conterminous united states-representing a decade of land cover change information. Photogram. Eng. Remote Sens. **81**(5), 345–354 (2015)
21. LeCun, Y., et al.: Backpropagation applied to handwritten zip code recognition. Neural Comput. **1**(4), 541–551 (1989)
22. Lek, S., Delacoste, M., Baran, P., Dimopoulos, I., Lauga, J., Aulagnier, S.: Application of neural networks to modelling nonlinear relationships in ecology. Ecol. Model. **90**(1), 39–52 (1996). https://doi.org/10.1016/0304-3800(95)00142-5
23. Maaten, L., Hinton, G.: Visualizing data using t-SNE. J. Mach. Learn. Res. **9**, 2579–2605 (2008)
24. Miller, J.E., Damschen, E.I., Ives, A.R.: Functional traits and community composition: a comparison among community-weighted means, weighted correlations, and multilevel models. Methods Ecol. Evol. **10**(3), 415–425 (2019)
25. Peterson, A.T.: Ecological Niches and Geographic Distributions. Princeton University Press, Princeton (2011)
26. Phillips, S.J., Anderson, R.P., Schapire, R.E.: Maximum entropy modeling of species geographic distributions. Ecol. Model. **190**(3–4), 231–259 (2006)
27. Phillips, S.J., Dudík, M.: Modeling of species distributions with maxent: new extensions and a comprehensive evaluation. Ecography **31**(2), 161–175 (2008). https://doi.org/10.1111/j.0906-7590.2008.5203.x
28. Szegedy, C., Vanhoucke, V., Ioffe, S., Shlens, J., Wojna, Z.: Rethinking the inception architecture for computer vision. In: Proceedings of the IEEE Conference on Computer Vision and Pattern Recognition, pp. 2818–2826 (2016)
29. Violle, C., Reich, P.B., Pacala, S.W., Enquist, B.J., Kattge, J.: The emergence and promise of functional biogeography. Proc. Natl. Acad. Sci. **111**(38), 13690–13696 (2014)

# ManifLearn - Manifold Learning
# in Machine Learning, from Euclid
# to Riemann

# Preface

Manifold Learning - from Euclid to Riemann - workshop is a forum for researchers and practitioners working on machine learning on non-linear manifold. ML has been the subject of intensive study over the past two decades in the computer vision and machine learning communities. Originally, manifold learning techniques aim to identify the underlying structure (usually low-dimensional) of data from a set of observations (in the form of high-dimensional vectors). The recent advances in deep learning make one wonder whether data-driven learning techniques can benefit from the theoretical findings from ML studies. This innocent looking question becomes more important if we note that deep learning techniques are notorious for being data-hungry and (mostly) supervised. On the contrary, many ML techniques unravel data structures without much supervision. This workshop considers itself as the frontier to raise the question of how classical ML techniques can help deep learning and vice versa, and targets studies and discussions that bridge this gap. Besides, the use of Riemannian geometry in tackling/modelling various problems in computer vision has seen a surge of interest recently. In this workshop, we will explore the latest development in machine learning techniques developed to work on, as well as benefit from, the non-linear manifolds. We will also target challenges and future directions related to the application of non-linear geometry and Riemannian manifolds in computer vision and machine learning. This workshop also acts as an opportunity for cross-disciplinary discussions and collaborations.

The second edition of the International Workshop on Manifold Learning from Euclid to Riemann was held virtually. After a per review process by at least 2 reviews, this edition of the workshop includes three contributions.

We would like to thank the reviewers for their invaluable time and effort. We also thank our outstanding colleagues Shantanu H. Joshi, Hà Quang Minh, Xavier Pennec and Nicolas Boumal for their invaluable contribution as keynote speakers.

# Organization

## General Chairs

Mohamed Daoudi      IMT Lille Douai, France
Mehrtash Harandi      Monash University, Australia
Vittorio Murino      University of Verona, Italy, Huawei
                 Technologies Ltd., Ireland, and Istituto
                 Italiano di Tecnologia, Italy

## Program Committee

Pierre-Antoine Absil      Université Catholoque de Louvain
Stefano Berretti      Florence University
Rudrasis Chakraborty      University of California, Berkeley
Samitha Herath      Monash University
Zhiwu Huang      ETHZ, Switzerland.
Estelle Massart      Oxford
Pietro Pala      Florence University
Anis Kacem      Université du Luxembourg
Xavier Pennec      Inria Sophia-Antipolis
Soumava Kumar Roy      Australian National University
TongZhang      Australian National University
Florian Yger      Université Paris-Dauphine
Sylvain Chevallier      Université de Versailles Saint-Quentin
Ujjal Dutta      Myntra Designs
Tong Zhang      École polytechnique fédérale de Lausanne
Naima Otberdout      Mohammed V University in Rabat, Morocco

# Latent Space Geometric Statistics

Line Kühnel[1], Tom Fletcher[2], Sarang Joshi[3], and Stefan Sommer[1(✉)]

[1] University of Copenhagen, Copenhagen, Denmark
`kuhnel@math.ku.dk`, `sommer@di.ku.dk`
[2] University of Virginia, Charlottesville, VA, USA
`ptf8v@virginia.edu`
[3] University of Utah, Salt Lake City, UT, USA
`sjoshi@sci.utah.edu`

**Abstract.** Deep generative models, e.g., variational autoencoders and generative adversarial networks, result in latent representation of observed data. The low dimensionality of the latent space provides an ideal setting for analysing high-dimensional data that would otherwise often be infeasible to handle statistically. The linear Euclidean geometry of the high-dimensional data space pulls back to a nonlinear Riemannian geometry on latent space where classical linear statistical techniques are no longer applicable. We show how analysis of data in their latent space representation can be performed using techniques from the field of geometric statistics. Geometric statistics provide generalisations of Euclidean statistical notions including means, principal component analysis, and maximum likelihood estimation of parametric distributions. Introduction to estimation procedures on latent space are considered, and the computational complexity of using geometric algorithms with high-dimensional data addressed by training a separate neural network to approximate the Riemannian metric and cometric tensor capturing the shape of the learned data manifold.

## 1 Introduction

The mapping $f : Z \to X$ from a latent space $Z$ to a data space $X$ defined by a deep generative model constitutes an embedding of $Z$ into $X$ under mild assumptions on the network architecture. The embedding allows the image $f(Z)$ to inherit the Riemannian metric and hence the geometry from the Euclidean ambient space $X$. Equivalently, the metric structure of $X$ pulls back via $f$ to a nonlinear Riemannian structure on $Z$. Starting with the papers [1–3], various aspects of the geometry of latent spaces have been explored including numerical schemes for geodesic integration, parallel transport, mean estimation, simulation of Brownian motion, and interpolation. Recent works continuing this exploration includes [4–11]. With this paper, we focus on performing subsequent statistical analysis after learning the latent representation of the data defined by the embedding $f$.

Variational autoencoders learn a latent space $Z$ in which training data follows a normal distribution. Performing statistical analysis on the data used for

A. Del Bimbo et al. (Eds.): ICPR 2020 Workshops, LNCS 12666, pp. 163–178, 2021.
https://doi.org/10.1007/978-3-030-68780-9_16

training the latent space $Z$ is hence unnatural. On the contrary, we aim at learning the latent space representation $Z$ given a training dataset and then use constructions, tools, and methods from geometric statistics [12] to perform statistical analysis on newly observed data in the latent representation.

Deep generative models are excellent tools for learning the intrinsic geometry of a low-dimensional data manifold $f(Z)$, subspace of the data space $X$. When the highest modes of data variation can be expressed in a few intrinsic dimensions, statistical analyses exploiting the lower dimensionality can be more efficient than conducting analyses directly in the high-dimensional data space. Performing statistical analysis in lower-dimensional manifolds learned with deep generative models, we simultaneously adapt the statistics to the intrinsic geometry of the data manifold, exploit the compact representation, and avoid unnecessary dimensions in the high-dimensional space $X$ affecting the statistical analysis. As an example, we compare two-sample test in the full data space with a generalised two-sample test in the non-linear latent space. The presented example shows that the test in the latent space results in a more significant test of the two generated populations than the test in the high-dimensional data space.

Exemplified on three datasets, synthetic data on the sphere $\mathbb{S}^2$ for visualization, the MNIST digits dataset, and landmark representation of diatoms, we show how statistical procedures such as principal component analysis can be performed on the latent space. We will subsequently define and infer parameters of geometric distributions allowing the definition and inference of maximum likelihood estimates via simulation of diffusion processes. Both VAEs and GANs themselves learn distributions representing the input training data. The aim is to perform geometric statistical analyses for data independent of the training data and with a different distribution, but which are elements of the same low-dimensional manifold of the data space. The latent representation can in this way be learned unsupervised from large numbers of unlabeled training samples where subsequently the low-dimensional space can be used to perform statistical analysis on datasets of a small sample size. This setting occurs for example in medical imaging where brain MR scans are abundant while controlled disease progression studies are of a much smaller sample size. The approach resembles the common task of using principal component analysis to represent data in the span of fewer principal eigenvectors, with the critical difference that in the present case a nonlinear manifold is learned using deep generative models instead of standard linear subspace approximation.

The field of geometric statistics provide generalizations of statistical constructions and tools from linear Euclidean vector spaces to Riemannian manifolds. Such constructs, e.g.., the mean value, often have many equivalent definitions in Euclidean space. However, nonlinearity and curvature generally break this equivalence leading to a plethora of different generalizations. For this reason, we here focus on a subset of selected methods to exemplify the use of geometric statistical tools in the latent space setting: Principal component analysis on manifolds with the principal geodesic analysis (PGA, [13]), inference of maximum likelihood means from intrinsic diffusion processes [14] and a generalisation of Hotelling two-sample test [15].

The learned manifold defines a Riemannian metric on the latent representation. The often high dimensionality of the data manifold makes it computationally costly to evaluate the metric. The computational cost is severely amplified when calculating higher-order derivatives needed for geometric concepts such as the curvature tensor and the Christoffel symbols that are crucial for numerical integration of geodesics and simulation of sample paths for Brownian motions. We present a new method for handling the computational complexity of evaluating the metric by training a second neural network to approximate the local metric tensor of the latent space thereby achieving a massive speed up in the implementation of the geometric and geometric statistical algorithms.

The paper thus presents the following contributions:

1. we couple tools from geometric statistics with deep end-to-end differentiable generative models for analyzing data using a pre-trained low-dimensional latent representation,
2. we show how an additional neural network can be trained to learn the metric tensor and thereby greatly speed up the computations needed for the geometric statistics algorithms,
3. we develop a method for maximum likelihood estimation of diffusion processes in the latent geometry and use this to estimate ML means from Riemannian Brownian motions.
4. we give an example of two-sample test for which the latent space representation results in a more significant test than the two-sample test in the high-dimensional data space.

We show examples of the presented methods on latent geometries learned from synthetic data in $\mathbb{R}^3$, on the MNIST dataset and on data of diatoms. The statistical computations are implemented in the Theano Geometry package [16] that using the automatic differentiation features of the Theano framework allows for easy and concise expression of differential geometry concepts.

The paper starts with a brief description on latent space geometry based on the papers [1–3]. We then discuss the definition of mean values in the nonlinear latent geometry, the use of the principal geodesic analysis (PGA) procedure, and make a description of a generalised two-sample test on nonlinear spaces. We end the paper with developing a scheme for maximum likelihood estimation of parameters with Riemannian Brownian motion using a diffusion bridge sampling scheme before performing experiments on the described datasets.

## 2   Latent Space Geometry

Deep generative models such as generative adversarial networks (GANs, [17]) and autoencoders/variational autoencoders (VAEs, [18]) learn mappings from a latent space $Z$ to the data space $X$. In the VAE case, the decoder mapping $f : Z \to X$ describes the mean of the data distribution, $P(X|z) = \mathcal{N}(X \mid f(z), \sigma(z)^2 I)$, and is complemented by an encoder $h : X \to Z$. Both $Z$ and $X$ are Euclidean spaces, with dimension $d$ and $n$ respectively and generally $d \ll n$.

When the push forward $f_*$, and the differential $df$ of $f$, is of rank $d$ for any point $z$, the image $f(Z)$ in $X$ is an embedded differentiable manifold of dimension $d$. We denote this manifold by $M$. Generally, for deep models, $f$ is nonlinear making $M$ a nonlinear manifold. An example of a trained manifold with a VAE is shown in Fig. 1. Here we simulate synthetic data on the sphere $\mathbb{S}^2$ by the transition distribution of a Riemannian Brownian motion starting at the north pole. The learned submanifold approximates $\mathbb{S}^2$ on the northern hemisphere containing the greatest concentration of samples.

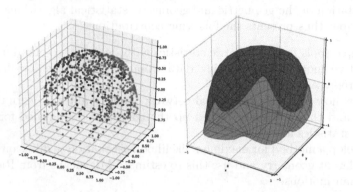

**Fig. 1.** (left) Samples from the data distribution (blue) with corresponding predictions from the VAE (red). (right) The trained manifold. (Color figure online)

The learned manifold $M$ inherits differential and geometric structure from $X$. In particular, the standard Euclidean inner product restricts to tangent spaces $T_x M$ for $x \in M$ to give a Riemannian metric $g$ on $M$, i.e. for $v, w \in T_x M$, $g(v, w) = \langle v, w \rangle = v^T w$. Locally, we invert $f$ to obtain charts on $M$, and get the standard expression $g_{ij}(z) = \langle \partial_{z_i} f, \partial_{z_j} f \rangle$ for the metric tensor in $Z$ coordinates. Using Jacobian matrix $Jf = (\partial_{z_i} f^j)^i_j$, the matrix expression of $g(z)$ is $g(z) = (Jf(z))^T Jf(z)$. The metric tensor on $Z$ can be seen as the pullback $f^*g$ of the Riemannian metric on $X$.

The geometry of latent spaces was explored in [1,2]. In addition to setting up the geometric foundation, efficient algorithms for geodesic integration, parallel transport, and Fréchet mean estimation on the latent space were developed. The algorithms make particular use of the encoder function $h\colon X \to Z$ trained as part of the VAEs. Instead of explicitly computing Christoffel symbols for geodesic integration, the presence of $h$ allows steps of the integration algorithm to be taken in $X$ and then subsequently mapped back to $Z$. Execution speed increases significantly when avoiding computation of Christoffel symbols, a critical improvement for the heavy computations involved with the typically high dimensions of $X$. If the $z$-variability of the variance $\sigma(z)$ of VAEs is taking into account, the Jacobian of $\sigma$ appears in the expected metric as shown in [3].

## 2.1   Latent Data Representations

Given sampled data $y_1, \ldots, y_N$ in $X$, the aim is here to perform statistical analysis on the data after mapping to the low-dimensional latent space $Z$. Note that the mapping $f$ can thus be trained unsupervised and afterwards used to perform statistics on new data in the low-dimensional representation. Therefore, the data $y_1, \ldots, y_N$ are generally different from the training data used to train $f$. In particular, $N$ can be much lower than the size of the training set.

For VAEs, the mapping of $y_i$ to corresponding points in the latter representation $z_i$ is directly available from the encoder function $h$, i.e. $z_i = h(y_i)$. In more general settings where $h$ is not present, we need to construct $z_i$ from $y_i$. A natural approach is to define $z_i$ from the optimization problem

$$z_i = \arg\min_{z \in Z} \| f(z) - y_i \|^2 . \tag{1}$$

This can be seen as a projection from $X$ to $M$ using the Euclidean distance in $X$.

## 2.2   Geodesics and Brownian Motions

The pullback metric $f^*g$ on $Z$ defines geometric concepts such as geodesics, exponential and logarithm map, and Riemannian Brownian motions on $Z$. Using $f$, each of these definitions is equivalently expressed on $M$ viewing it as a submanifold of $X$ with inherited metric. Given $z \in Z$ and $v \in T_z Z$, the exponential map $\mathrm{Exp}_z \colon T_z Z \to Z$ is defined as the geodesic $\gamma_t^v$ at time $t = 1$ with starting point $z$ and initial velocity $v$, i.e. $\mathrm{Exp}_z(v) = \gamma_1^v$. The logarithm map $\mathrm{Log} \colon Z \times Z \to TZ$ is the local inverse of $\mathrm{Exp}$: Given two points $z_1, z_2 \in Z$, $\mathrm{Log}_{z_1}(z_2)$, returns the tangent vector $v \in T_{z_1} Z$ defining the minimizing geodesic between $z_1$ and $z_2$. The Riemannian metric defines the geodesic distance expressed from the logarithm map by $d(z_1, z_2) = \| \mathrm{Log}_{z_1}(z_2) \|_g$. Using $Z$ as coordinates for $M$ by local inverses of $f$, the Riemannian Brownian motions on $Z$, and equivalently on $M$, is defined by the coordinate expression

$$dz_t^j = -\frac{1}{2} g(z)^{kl} \Gamma_{kl}^j dt + \sqrt{(g(z))^{-1}}^j dB_{t,j}, \tag{2}$$

where $\Gamma_{kl}^j$ denotes Christoffel symbols, $g^{-1}$ the cometric, i.e. the inverse of the metric tensor $g$, and $B_t$ a standard Brownian motion in $\mathbb{R}^d$. Notice that Einstein notation is used for index summation.

## 3   Computational Representation

While metric computation is easily expressed using automatic differentiation to compute the Jacobian $Jf$ of the embedding map $f$, the high dimensionality of the data space has a computational cost when evaluating the metric. The computational cost is particularly emphasised when computing higher-order differential concepts such as Christoffel symbols, used for geodesic integration, curvature, and Brownian motion simulation. The reason being the multiple derivatives and metric inverse computations involved. For integration of geodesics and Brownian motion, one elegant way to avoid the computation of Christoffel symbols is to take each step of the integration in the ambient data space of $M$ and map the result back to the latent space using the encoder mapping $h$ [1]. This procedure requires $h$ to be close to the inverse of $f$ restricted to $M$ and limits the method to VAEs where $h$ is trained along with the decoder, $f$.

We here propose an additional way to allow efficient computations without using the encoder map $h$. The approach, therefore, works for both GANs and VAEs. The latent space $Z$ is of low dimension, and the only entity needed for encoding the geometry is the metric $g : Z \to \mathrm{Sym}_+(d)$ which to each $z$ assigns a positive symmetric $d \times d$ matrix. $\mathrm{Sym}_+(d)$ has dimension $d(d+1)/2$. Hence, the high dimensionality of the data space does not appear directly when defining the geometry, and $X$ is only used for the actual computation of $g(z)$. We therefore train a second neural network $\tilde{g}$ to act as a function approximator for $g$, i.e. we train $\tilde{g}$ to produce an element of $\mathrm{Sym}_+(d)$ that is close to $g(z)$ for each $z$. Notice that this network does not evaluate a Jacobian matrix when computing $g(z)$, and no derivatives are hence needed for evaluating the metric. The lack of complexity and due to both input and output space of the network being of low dimensions, $d$ and $d(d+1)/2$ respectively, makes the computational effort of evaluating $\tilde{g}$ and Christoffel symbols, computed from $\tilde{g}$, orders of magnitude faster than evaluating $g$ directly. The speedup is especially present when the dimensionality $n$ of $X$ is high compared to $d$: Integration of the geodesic equation with 100 time steps in the MNIST case presented later takes $\approx 30$ s., when computing the metric from $Jf$, compared to $\approx 30$ ms., when using the second neural network to predict $g$.

Inverting $\tilde{g}(z)$ is sensitive to the approximation of $g$ provided by $\tilde{g}$. The cometric tensor $g^{-1}$ is therefore more sensitive to the approximation when computed from $\tilde{g}$ than from $g$ itself. This is emphasized when $g(z)$ has small eigenvalues. As a solution, we let the second neural network predict both the metric $g(z)$ and cometric $g(z)^{-1}$. Defining the loss function for training the network, we balance the norm between predicted matrices $\tilde{g}$ and $\tilde{g}^{-1}$. In addition, we ensure that the predicted $\tilde{g}$ and $\tilde{g}^{-1}$ are close to being actual inverses. These observations are expressed in the loss function

$$\mathrm{loss}_{g,g^{-1}\text{-approximator}}(g_{\text{true}}, g_{\text{true}}^{-1}, g_{\text{predicted}}, g_{\text{predicted}}^{-1})$$
$$= \|g_{\text{true}} - g_{\text{predicted}}\|^2 / \|g_{\text{true}}\|^2$$
$$+ \|g_{\text{true}}^{-1} - g_{\text{predicted}}^{-1}\|^2 / \|g_{\text{true}}^{-1}\|^2$$
$$+ \|g_{\text{predicted}}^{-1} g_{\text{predicted}} - \mathrm{Id}_d\|^2, \tag{3}$$

using Frobenius matrix norms. We train a neural network with two dense hidden layers to minimize (3), and use this network for the geometry calculations. The network predicts the upper triangular part of each matrix, and this part is symmetrized to produce $g_{\text{predicted}}$ and $g_{\text{predicted}}^{-1}$. Note that additional methods could be employed to ensure the predicted metric being positive definite, see e.g.

[19]. For the presented examples, it is our observations that the loss (3) ensures positive definiteness without further measures.

# 4    Nonlinear Latent Space Statistics

We now discuss aspects of geometric statistics applicable to the latent geometry setting. We start by focusing on means, particularly Fréchet and maximum likelihood (ML) means, before modeling variation around the mean with the principal geodesic analysis procedure and ending the section with a description of a generalised two-sample test.

## 4.1    Fréchet and ML Means

Fréchet mean [20] of a distribution on $M$, and its sample equivalent, minimise the expected squared Riemannian distance: $\hat{x} = \arg\min_{x \in M} \mathbb{E}[d(x, y)^2]$ and $\hat{x} = \arg\min_{x \in M} \frac{1}{N} \sum_{i=1}^{N} d(x, y_i)^2$.

The standard way to estimate a sample Frechet mean is to employ an iterative optimisation to minimise the sum of squared Riemannian distances. The Riemannian gradient of the squared distance can be expressed using the Riemannian Log map [12] by $\nabla_x d(x, y)^2 = 2\operatorname{Log}_x(y)$.

The Fréchet mean generalises the Euclidean concept of a mean value as a distance minimiser. In Euclidean space, this is equivalent to the standard Euclidean estimator $\hat{x} = \frac{1}{N} \sum_i y_i$. From a probabilistic viewpoint, the equivalence between the log-density function of a Euclidean normal distribution and the squared distance results in $\hat{x}$ as an ML fit of a normal distribution to data:

$$\hat{x} = \arg\min_x \operatorname{Log} p_{\mathcal{N},x}(y), \tag{4}$$

with $p_{\mathcal{N},x}(y) \propto \exp(-\frac{1}{2}\|x - y\|^2)$ being the density of a normal distribution with mean $x$. While the normal distribution does not have a canonical equivalent on Riemannian manifolds, an intrinsic generalisation comes from the transition density of a Riemannian Brownian motion. This density on $M$ arise as the solution to the heat PDE, $\frac{\partial}{\partial t} p_{x,t} = \frac{1}{2}\Delta_g p_{x,t}$, using the Laplace-Beltrami operator $\Delta_g$, or, equivalently, from the law of the Brownian motion started at $M$. In [14,21,22], this density is used to generalise the ML definition of the Euclidean mean,

$$\hat{x} = \arg\min_x \operatorname{Log} p_{x,T}(y). \tag{5}$$

for at fixed $T > 0$. We will develop approximation schemes for evaluating the log-density and for solving the optimisation problem (5) in Sect. 5.

## 4.2  Principal Component Analysis

Euclidean principal component analysis (PCA) estimates subspaces of the data space that explain the majority of variation in the data, either by maximising variance or minimising residuals. PCA builds around the linear vector space structure and the Euclidean inner product. Defining procedures that resemble PCA for manifold-valued data hence become challenging, as neither inner products between arbitrary vectors nor the concept of linear subspaces are defined on manifolds.

[13] presented a generalised version of Euclidean PCA denoted principal geodesic analysis (PGA). PGA estimates nested geodesic submanifolds of $M$ that capture the most variation of the data projected to each submanifold. The geodesic subspaces hence take the place of the linear subspaces found with the Euclidean PCA.

Let $z_1, \ldots, z_N \in Z$ be latent space representations of the data $y_1, \ldots, y_N$ in $M$, and let $\mu$ be a Fréchet mean of the samples $z_1, \ldots, z_N$. We assume the observations are located in a neighbourhood $U$ of $\mu$ where $\mathrm{Exp}_\mu$ is invertible and the logarithm map, $\mathrm{Log}_\mu$, thus well-defined. We search for an orthonormal basis of tangent vectors in $T_\mu Z$ such that for each nested submanifold, $H_k = \mathrm{Exp}_\mu(\mathrm{span}\{v_1, \ldots, v_k\})$, the variance of the data projected on $H_k$ is maximised. The projection map used is based on the geodesic distance, $d$, and is defined by, $\pi_H(z) = \arg\min_{z_1 \in H} d(z, z_1)^2$.

The tangent vectors $v_1, \ldots, v_k$ in the orthonormal basis of $T_\mu Z$ are found by optimising the Fréchet variance of the projected data on the submanifold $H$, i.e.

$$v_k = \arg\max_{\|v\|=1} \sum_{i=1}^n d(\mu, \pi_H(z_i))^2, \tag{6}$$

where $H = \mathrm{Exp}_\mu(\mathrm{span}\{v_1, \ldots, v_{k-1}, v\})$. For a more detailed description of the PGA procedure, including computational approximations of the projection map in the tangent space of $\mu$, see [13]. In the experiment section, we perform PGA on the manifold defined by the latent space of a deep generative model for the MNIST dataset.

## 4.3  Generalised Two-Sample Test

This section describes another example of the usage of the latent space representation to perform statistical analyses on high-dimensional data. More specifically, we apply a permutation test based on the test statistic from the generalised Hotelling two-sample test presented in [15].

Given two populations, $X = (x_1, \ldots, x_n)$ and $Y = (y_1, \ldots, y_m)$, in the latent space $Z$, we test the null hypothesis $H_0 : \mu_1 = \mu_2$ of equal Fréchet mean against the alternative hypothesis, $H_1 : \mu_1 \neq \mu_2$. The test relies on several assumptions including the existence of an element $p \in \mathcal{M}$ such that the exponential chart

$\phi^{-1} = \text{Exp}_p$ contains both populations, $X$ and $Y$, i.e. $Y, X \subset \text{Exp}_p(V)$ for $V \subset \mathbb{R}^d$. The test statistic for the generalised Hotelling two-sample test is given as

$$T_{mn} = (n + m)(\hat{\mu}_1 - \hat{\mu}_2)^T \hat{\Sigma}^{-1}(\hat{\mu}_1 - \hat{\mu}_2) \tag{7}$$

where $\hat{\mu}_i$ is the Fréchet sample mean for the $i$'th population and $\hat{\Sigma}$ denotes the pooled sample covariance,

$$\hat{\Sigma} = (m + n)\left(\frac{1}{n}\hat{\Lambda}_1^{-1}\hat{\Sigma}_1\hat{\Lambda}_1^{-1} + \frac{1}{m}\hat{\Lambda}_2^{-1}\hat{\Sigma}_2\hat{\Lambda}_2^{-1}\right). \tag{8}$$

The pooled covariance matrix is based on $\hat{\Lambda}_1 = \frac{1}{n}\sum_{i=1}^n D_y^2(\|\text{Log}(\phi^{-1}x_i, \phi^{-1}y)\|^2)|_{y=\phi\hat{\mu}_1}$ and $\Sigma_1 = \text{Cov}\left(D_y(\|\text{Log}(\phi^{-1}x_i, \phi^{-1}y)\|^2)|_{y=\phi\mu_1}\right)$ such that $\hat{\Sigma}_1$ denotes the sample covariance of $\Sigma_1$. Calculations of the derivatives of the geodesic distance can be found in [23,24].

Based on the test statistic $T_{mn}$ the significance of the test is determined based on a permutation test. The permutation test uses the assumption of equal means under the null-hypothesis, i.e. if the null-hypothesis is true permuting the samples between populations would not change the population means. Running several permutations under the null-hypothesis creates a distribution of the test statistic under the null for which it is possible to obtain a p-value.

## 5     Maximum Likelihood Inference of Diffusions

As in Euclidean statistics, parameters of distributions on manifolds can be inferred from data by maximum likelihood or, from a Bayesian viewpoint, maximum a posteriori. These methods can even be used to define statistical notions as exemplified by the ML mean in Sect. 4. The probabilistic viewpoint relies on the existence of parametric families of distributions in the geometric spaces, and the ability to evaluate likelihoods. One example of such a distribution is the transition distribution of the Riemannian Brownian motion, see, e.g. [25]. In this section, we show how likelihoods of data in the latent space $Z$ under the transition distribution can be evaluated by Monte Carlo sampling of conditioned diffusion bridges. As previous, assume that a separate training dataset has been used to train the geometry of $Z$. We wish to perform statistical analysis on newly observed data represented by $z_i$. To determine the transition distribution of a Brownian motion on the data manifold, we apply a conditional diffusion bridge simulation procedure defined in [26]. The following section makes a description of this procedure. The sampling scheme has previously been used for geometric spaces in [22,27].

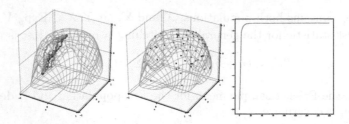

**Fig. 2.** (left) Brownian bridge sample paths on the trained data manifold. (middle) The estimated ML mean (blue) from the data (black points). (right) The likelihood values from the MLE procedure. (Color figure online)

## 5.1 Bridge Simulation and Parameter Inference

Let $z_1, \ldots, z_N \in Z$ be $N$ observations in $Z$. We assume $z_i$ are time $T$ observations from a Brownian motion, $z_t$ defined by (2), on $Z$ started at $x \in Z$. The aim is to optimise for the initial point $x$ by maximising the likelihood of the observed data and thereby find the ML mean (5). The mean value of the data distribution is thus defined as the starting point of the process maximising the data likelihood, $L_\theta(z_1, \ldots, z_N) = \prod_{i=1}^{N} p_{T,\theta}(z_i)$, where $p_{T,\theta}(z_i)$ is the time $T$ transition density of $z_t$ evaluated at $z_i$. The difficulty is to determine the transition density $p_{T,\theta}(z_i)$, i.e. the time $T$ density conditional on $z_T = z_i$. In [26] it was shown that this conditional probability can be calculated based on the notion of a guided process

$$d\tilde{z}_t^j = -\frac{1}{2}g(z)^{kl}\Gamma_{kl}^j dt - \frac{\tilde{z}_t^j - z_i^j}{T-t}dt + \sqrt{(g(z))^{-1}}^j dB_t, \qquad (9)$$

which, without conditioning, almost surely hits the observation $z_i$ at time $t = T$. In fact, the conditional process $z_t|z_T = z_i$ is absolutely continuous with respect to the guided process with Radon-Nikodym derivative, $dP_{z|z_i}/dP_{\tilde{z}} = \varphi(\tilde{z})/E_{\tilde{z}}[\varphi(\tilde{z}_t)]$. Based on the above arguments, an expression of the transition density is

$$p_{T,\theta}(z_i) = \sqrt{\frac{|g(z_i)|}{(2\pi T)^d}} e^{-\frac{\|(x-z_i)^T g(x)(x-z_i)\|^2}{2T}} E_{\tilde{z}_t}[\varphi(\tilde{z}_t)], \qquad (10)$$

see [26], and [22] for more details. We use Monte Carlo sampling of $\tilde{z}_t$ to approximate $E_{\tilde{z}_t}[\varphi(\tilde{z}_t)]$ and hence determine $p_{T,\theta}(z_i)$ by (10). The likelihood can then be iteratively optimised to find the ML mean by computing gradients with respect to $x$.

Figure 2 shows sample paths of a Brownian bridge on the trained manifold for the synthetic data on $\mathbb{S}^2$ in addition to the ML estimated mean (middle). The likelihood values at each iteration are plotted in the same figure and illustrates convergence for the MLE procedure.

# 6    Experiments

We give examples of the analyses described above for the MNIST dataset and a dataset of landmark representations of diatoms [28]. The computations are performed with the Theano Geometry package http://bitbucket.com/stefansommer/theanogeometry/ described in [16]. The package contains implementations of differential geometry concepts and corresponding statistical algorithms.

## 6.1    MNIST

The MNIST dataset consists of images of handwritten digits from 0 to 9 with each observation of dimension $28 \times 28$. A VAE is trained on the full dataset providing a 2-dimensional latent space representation. The VAE [29] has one hidden dense layer for both encoder and decoder, each layer containing 256 neurons, and results in a 2d latent space $Z$.

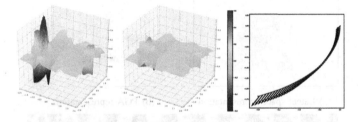

**Fig. 3.** (left) Scalar curvature of space $Z$. (middle) Min. eigenvalue of the Ricci curvature tensor. (right) Parallel transport of a tangent vector in $Z$. The transported vectors have constant length measured by the Riemannian metric.

Figure 3 shows the scalar (left) and minimum Ricci curvature (middle) in a neighbourhood of the origin of $Z$. Moreover, an example of parallel transport of a tangent vector along a curve in the latent space is presented in the same figure (right). Note that the transported vector has a constant length as measured by the metric $g$ which is not the case for the Euclidean $\mathbb{R}^2$ norm.

The top row of Fig. 4 shows samples of Brownian motions and Brownian bridges in the latent space $Z$. Each of these Brownian bridges corresponds to a bridge in the data manifold of the MNIST data. Examples of bridges in the high dimensional space $X$ are shown in the bottom row of Fig. 4.

We now perform PGA on the latent space representation of the subset of the MNIST data consisting of even digits. PGA is a nonlinear coordinate change of the latent space around the Fréchet mean. PGA is applied to the data in Fig. 5(a) where the resulting data represented in the PGA basis is shown in Fig. 5(b). The variation along the two principal component directions are visualised in the full dimensional data space in the bottom row of Fig. 5.

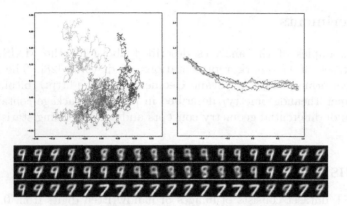

**Fig. 4.** (top left) Samples from a Riemannian Brownian motion in latent space. (top right) Samples from a Brownian bridge simulated by (9). (bottom) Examples of Brownian bridges of MNIST data between two fixed 9s (left-/rightmost). The variance of the Brownian motion has been increased to visually emphasize the image variation.

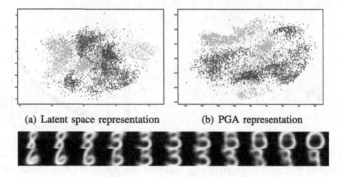

(a) Latent space representation          (b) PGA representation

**Fig. 5.** (top left) Latent space representation of data. (top right) PGA analysis on the sub-space of even digits. (bottom) Variation along first (1. row) and second (2. row) principal components.

Figure 6 (bottom left) shows the maximum likelihood mean image for a subset of 256 even digits estimated by the ML procedure described in Sect. 5. Figure 6 (bottom right) shows the corresponding Fréchet mean. The iterations, for both ML and Fréchet mean in latent space, are presented in Fig. 6 (upper left), with the upper right plot showing the likelihood values for each step of the ML optimisation.

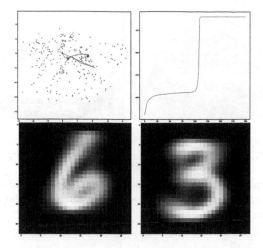

**Fig. 6.** From top left row-wise: (1.) Iterations of ML (green) and Fréchet mean (red) for subset of even MNIST digits. (2.) Likelihood evolution during the MLE. Estimated ML mean (3.) and Fréchet mean (4.).

## 6.2  Diatoms

As a final experiment we compare two-sample tests for equal mean for two populations of diatoms in the full data space against a nonlinear two-sample test in the latent space. The diatom dataset consists of 780 observations each a landmark representation of a diatom with 45 landmark points. A VAE has been trained on the diatom data with one hidden layer in both encoder and decoder. The hidden layer consists of 20 neurons and the dimension of the latent space is again set to 2. In Fig. 7 is shown examples of data observations. The goal is to test the hypothesis of equal mean for two populations of diatoms shown in Fig. 7. The two populations have been generated such that the populations overlap, but are not drawn from the same distribution. We compare a normal Hotelling test in the full data space with a generalised Hotelling two-sample test in the latent space using the non-linear geometry induced by the decoder mapping. The generalised Hotelling test was presented in Sect. 4.3.

For the diatom example, we investigate whether the test using the dimensionality reduction is better at separating the two populations compared to the two-sample test in the full data space. Performing statistical analysis of high-dimensional data often leads to difficulties if the sample size is too small. Similar to the dimensionality reduction based on principal component analysis, we use the low-dimensional latent representation to resolve the curse of dimensionality. On the contrary, when considering the low-dimensional representation of data, important information might have been excluded resulting in no difference between the two populations in latent space. The presented test with the diatom data shows an example where performing two-sample test in the latent space results in a more significant test of the null-hypothesis of equal mean than conducting the analysis in the high-dimensional data space.

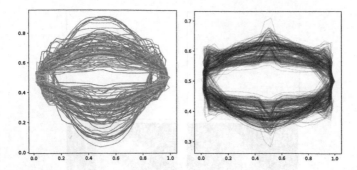

**Fig. 7.** (left) Examples of data observations. (right) The two populations tested for equal mean. The populations have been generated such that they overlap but still differ in distribution.

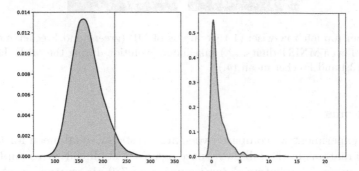

**Fig. 8.** (left) Estimated density plot of the test statistic for the two-sample test in high-dimensional data space. The data statistic is shown as the red line. (right) Density plot for the test in latent space with the red line defining the data statistic.

Figure 8 shows the test statistic for the sample data and a histogram for the permutation based statistics. We notice that the normal Hotelling two-sample test in the full data space (left of Fig. 8) results in a p-value of approximately 0.042, compared to the generalised Hotelling test in the latent space which significantly rejects the hypothesis of equal Fréchet mean for the two populations with a p-value of approximately 0.0025.

## 7   Conclusion

Deep generative models define an embedding of a low dimensional latent space $Z$ to a high dimensional data space $X$. The embedding can be used to reduce data dimensionality and move statistical analysis from $X$ to the low-dimensional latent representation in $Z$. This method can be seen as a nonlinear equivalent to the dimensionality reduction commonly performed by PCA. Some versions of generative models project data used for training the low dimensional structure to a specific distribution on the latent space. Performing statistical analysis on the training data is hence unnatural. We proposed to learn the low dimensional structure of the latent space as a predefined step and subsequently perform statistical analysis on newly observed data. The nonlinear structure of data can be represented compactly, and the induced geometry necessitates the use of non-linear statistical tools. We considered principal geodesic analysis on the latent space, maximum likelihood estimation of the mean using simulations of conditioned diffusion processes and performed a generalised Hotelling two-sample test. The test resulted in a more significant rejection of the null hypothesis for the test in the latent space compared to the two-sample test in the high-dimensional data space. To enable fast computation of the geometric algorithms that involve high-order derivatives of the metric, we fit a second neural network, to predict the metric $g$ and its inverse, which vastly speeds up computations. We visualised examples on 3D synthetic data simulated on $\mathbb{S}^2$ and performed analyses on the MNIST dataset and shape contours of diatoms based on a trained VAE with a 2D latent space.

**Acknowledgment.** The work presented in this paper was supported by the CSGB Centre for Stochastic Geometry and Advanced Bioimaging funded by a grant from the Villum foundation, the Villum Foundation grant 00022924, the Novo Nordisk Foundation grant NNF18OC0052000, and the NSF DMS grant number 1912030.

# References

1. Shao, H., Kumar, A., Thomas Fletcher, P.: The Riemannian geometry of deep generative models. In: Proceedings of the IEEE Conference on Computer Vision and Pattern Recognition Workshops, pp. 315–323 (2018)
2. Chen, N., Klushyn, A., Kurle, R., Jiang, X., Bayer, J., van der Smagt, P.: Metrics for deep generative models. In: AISTAT 2018, November 2017
3. Arvanitidis, G., Hansen, L.K., Hauberg, S.: Latent space oddity: on the curvature of deep generative models. In: ICLR 2018. arXiv:1710.11379, October 2017
4. Yang, T., Arvanitidis, G., Fu, D., Li, X., Hauberg, S.: Geodesic clustering in deep generative models. arXiv:1809.04747, September 2018
5. Shukla, A., Uppal, S., Bhagat, S., Anand, S., Turaga, P.: Geometry of deep generative models for disentangled representations. In: Proceedings of the 11th Indian Conference on Computer Vision, Graphics and Image Processing, ser. ICVGIP 2018. New York, NY, USA. Association for Computing Machinery, pp. 1–8, December 2018
6. Grattarola, D., Livi, L., Alippi, C.: Adversarial autoencoders with constant-curvature latent manifolds. Appl. Soft Comput. **81**, 105511 (2019)
7. Chen, N., Ferroni, F., Klushyn, A., Paraschos, A., Bayer, J., van der Smagt, P.: Fast approximate geodesics for deep generative models. In: Tetko, I.V., Kůrková, V., Karpov, P., Theis, F. (eds.) ICANN 2019. LNCS, vol. 11728, pp. 554–566. Springer, Cham (2019). https://doi.org/10.1007/978-3-030-30484-3_45
8. Rey, L.A.P., Portegies, J., Menkovski, V.: Diffusion variational autoencoders. In: Twenty-Ninth International Joint Conference on Artificial Intelligence, vol. 3, pp. 2704–2710, July 2020
9. Arvanitidis, G., Hauberg, S., Schölkopf, B.: Geometrically enriched latent spaces. arXiv:2008.00565, August 2020

10. Skopek, O., Ganea, O.-E., Bécigneul, G.: Mixed-curvature variational autoencoders. arXiv:1911.08411, February 2020
11. Connor, M.C., Canal, G.H., Rozell, C.J.: Variational Autoencoder with Learned Latent Structure. arXiv:2006.10597, June 2020
12. Pennec, X.: Intrinsic statistics on Riemannian manifolds: basic tools for geometric measurements. J. Math. Imaging Vis. **25**(1), 127–154 (2006)
13. Fletcher, P., Lu, C., Pizer, S., Joshi, S.: Principal geodesic analysis for the study of nonlinear statistics of shape. IEEE Trans. Med. Imaging **23**(8), 995–1005 (2004)
14. Sommer, S., Svane, A.M.: Modelling anisotropic covariance using stochastic development and sub-Riemannian frame bundle geometry. J. Geom. Mech. **9**(3), 391–410 (2017)
15. Bhattacharya, A., Bhattacharya, R.: Nonparametric statistics on manifolds with applications to shape spaces, 0805.3282, May 2008
16. Kühnel, L., Sommer, S., Arnaudon, A.: Differential geometry and stochastic dynamics with deep learning numerics. Appl. Math. Comput. **356**, 411–437 (2019)
17. Goodfellow, I., et al.: Generative adversarial nets. In: Advances in Neural Information Processing Systems 27. Curran Associates Inc., pp. 2672–2680 (2014)
18. Bengio, Y.: "Learning Deep Architectures for AI," foundations and trends®. Mach. Learn. **2**(1), 1–127 (2009)
19. Huang, Z., Van Gool, L.: A Riemannian network for SPD matrix learning. In: AAAI-17. arXiv:1608.04233, August 2016
20. Frechet, M.: Les éléments aléatoires de nature quelconque dans un espace distancie. Ann. Inst. H. Poincaré **10**, 215–310 (1948)
21. Nye, T.: Construction of distributions on tree-space via diffusion processes. Mini-Workshop: Asymptotic Statistics on Stratified Spaces, Mathematisches Forschungsinstitut Oberwolfach (2014)
22. Sommer, S., Arnaudon, A., Kuhnel, L., Joshi, S.: Bridge simulation and metric estimation on landmark manifolds. In: Cardoso, M.J., et al. (eds.) GRAIL/MFCA/MICGen -2017. LNCS, vol. 10551, pp. 79–91. Springer, Cham (2017). https://doi.org/10.1007/978-3-319-67675-3_8
23. Pennec, X.: Barycentric subspace analysis on manifolds. arXiv:1607.02833, July 2016
24. Sommer, S., Lauze, F., Nielsen, M.: Optimization over geodesics for exact principal geodesic analysis. Adv. Comput. Math. **40**(2), 283–313 (2013). https://doi.org/10.1007/s10444-013-9308-1
25. Hsu, E.P.: Stochastic Analysis on Manifolds. American Mathematical Soc. (2002)
26. Delyon, B., Hu, Y.: Simulation of conditioned diffusion and application to parameter estimation. Stochastic Process. Appl. **116**(11), 1660–1675 (2006)
27. Arnaudon, A., Holm, D.D., Sommer, S.: A geometric framework for stochastic shape analysis. Found. Computat. Math. **19**(3), 653–701 (2018). https://doi.org/10.1007/s10208-018-9394-z
28. Jalba, A., Wilkinson, M., Roerdink, J.: Shape representation and recognition through morphological curvature scale spaces. IEEE Trans. Image Process. **15**(2), 331–341 (2006)
29. Kingma, D.P., Welling, M.: Auto-encoding variational bayes. arXiv:1312.6114, December 2013

# Improving Neural Network Robustness Through Neighborhood Preserving Layers

Bingyuan Liu[1], Christopher Malon[2], Lingzhou Xue[1], and Erik Kruus[2(✉)]

[1] Department of Statistics, Penn State University, University Park, PA, USA
[2] NEC Labs America, Princeton, NJ, USA
`kruus@nec-labs.com`

**Abstract.** One major source of vulnerability of neural nets in classification tasks is from overparameterized fully connected layers near the end of the network. In this paper, we propose a new neighborhood preserving layer which can replace these fully connected layers to improve the network robustness. Networks including these neighborhood preserving layers can be trained efficiently. We theoretically prove that our proposed layers are more robust against distortion because they effectively control the magnitude of gradients. Finally, we empirically show that networks with our proposed layers are more robust against state-of-the-art gradient descent based attacks, such as a PGD attack on the benchmark image classification datasets MNIST and CIFAR10.

## 1 Introduction

In the past decade, significant research in machine learning has focused on designing deep neural network architectures for superior prediction performance, especially in visual and natural language processing problems. In a deep neural net, a small perturbation of original data can have a significant effect on the prediction result because of the accumulation effect through overparameterized layers. This fact makes neural network models not robust against adversarial attack. If we carefully design some 'adversarial examples' that are slightly modified from the original sample, the network is likely to misclassify these examples [1,2]. Many works have been established to design algorithms to find imperceptible perturbations to fool the neural networks [3–5]. It is a major topic in machine learning and computer vision to study how to design networks to be robust against such adversarial attacks.

Adversarial attack methods can be mainly divided into black-box attacks and white-box attacks, based on whether the attack approach has access to the model and model parameters [6]. White-box attacks are known to be stronger since the attacker gets access to the gradients and model parameters [3–5,7]. Most white-box attacks generate adversarial examples based on the gradient of the loss function with respect to the input. Some representative white-box attacks are the C&W attack [8] and the projected gradient descent (PGD) attack [5]. In the C&W attack, the proposed objective function aims at decreasing

A. Del Bimbo et al. (Eds.): ICPR 2020 Workshops, LNCS 12666, pp. 179–195, 2021.
https://doi.org/10.1007/978-3-030-68780-9_17

the probability of the correct class and minimizing the distance between the adversarial example and the original input image. They calculate the gradients with respect to data, and update the data towards the direction of decreasing the probability of correct classification. The PGD attack directly controls the distortion level by imposing an $\ell_\infty$ norm bound $\epsilon$ on the possible change for each input. Because the distortion level can be controlled, the PGD attack is a fair attack method to evaluate the robustness of models against adversarial attack. We will apply this attack approach in this paper to evaluate the performance of different models.

Many theoretical and empirical studies investigate the reason of networks' vulnerability to adversarial attack [5, 9, 10]. These works indicate the large scales of gradients are the major source of vulnerability of networks. By the effect of large scales of gradients, a tiny perturbation in the original data can have a huge effect on the final prediction layer [1]. Especially when the dimensionality of network weights is high, such large scales of gradients are significant. These large gradients usually appear in fully connected layers near the final prediction, serving as dimension reduction layers. For example, in the state-of-art Resnet [11] or VGG [12] models, we usually encode the image into a 1000 or so dimensional embedding through convolutional layers, and then need several fully connected layers to reduce the dimension of the embedding from $\sim$1000 to $\sim$10 (the number of classes) for final prediction. These fully connected layers have a huge number of weight parameters, and are one major source of the large scale of gradients. For example, in a standard 2-layer CNN network for MNIST dataset, convolutional layers only have less than 20000 parameters, but fully-connected dimension reduction layers have more than 1 million parameters. Such overparameterization is the major source of scales of gradients. If we can control the scale of gradients in such dimension reduction layers, the robustness of neural nets can be significantly improved.

Based on this observation, we introduce a new neighborhood preserving layer that can replace these fully connected layers, achieving dimension reduction and maintaining all other parts of the neural nets. It has comparable prediction performance but a much smaller scale of gradients. Our proposed neighbor preserving layers share the same input and output dimension as the fully connected layers they replace, thus serving as dimension reduction layers toward the final output. Their property of neighborhood preservation is the key to improving robustness. The neighborhood preservation property guarantees that a small perturbation in any direction will not dramatically change the neighborhood structure, thus will not change the prediction dramatically. More specifically, with same level of attack, our layer has smaller expectation of distortions on the output than fully-connected layers. We verify this property of our layer theoretically and empirically.

To construct a neighborhood preserving layer, we need to evaluate the quality of neighborhood preservation between inputs and outputs. In literature, many neighbor preserving based dimension reduction methods are related to this topic. Local Linear Embedding(LLE) [13] learns the weights of local neighbors for each point, and then find the optimal low-dimensional embedding in aspect of reconstruction. Neighborhood Preserving Embedding(NPE) [14] learns linear projections of original data such that the neighborhood structure are most maintained. Isomap [15] learns the geodesic distance between data points, and construct embeddings such that reconstruct the distance best. In recent years, UMAP [16] and t-SNE [17] are the two most popular ones. Both methods have high-dimensional data input, and output a corresponding low-dimensional embedding that can largely maintain the neighborhood structure. These two algorithms have similar ideas. They optimize the low-dimensional embedding such that it minimizes the discrepancy between the neighborhood graphs of the high- and low-dimensional embeddings. The main difference of the two methods is their loss function. The loss function of t-SNE is motivated from a likelihood function, while UMAP is motivated from a uniform manifold assumption, constructing a fuzzy set of the neighborhood graph and then evaluating the discrepancy between the high- and low-dimensional fuzzy sets as the loss function. In this paper, we build our model based on the UMAP loss function, because UMAP is faster and performs better when the dimension of the generated embedding is higher than 2. In Sect. 3, we will explicitly explain how we incorporate this UMAP loss function into our neighborhood preserving layer.

This paper is organized as follows. Section 2 introduces the details of the model setup, the adversarial attack setup, and background knowledge of neighborhood preserving methods. Section 3 introduces a novel neighborhood preserving layer. The proposed layer can replace fully connected layers in a general classification network, and improve the robustness of a network. We also introduce how to effectively train this network, and combine it with other adversarial training methods. Section 4 theoretically proves why our proposed method is more robust against adversarial attack. Section 5 empirically evaluates the performance of our model on two benchmark datasets: MNIST and CIFAR10. Section 6 concludes our paper.

## 2   Model Setup and Background

In this section, we introduce the general neural nets and adversarial attack setup, and also relevant dimension reduction methods. In this paper, we will focus on a general setup of neural nets, which is generally applied to most of the state of the art neural network models for prediction. It is worth mentioning that our proposal is also flexible to be applied to other models with internal bottleneck layers under the same philosophy.

### 2.1   Model Setup

We consider a general network which can be divided into three parts as follows. **(1) Encoder:** First the original data is fed into an encoder network, and the output of the encoder is a high-dimensional embedding. The encoder network is usually a multi-layer CNN network for vision tasks with a flattening layer, such as Resnet or VGG. **(2): Dimension reduction**: Then we pass the data to a dimension reduction layer, where the input dimension is high and output dimension is low; we refer to it as the low dimensional embedding in this paper. It is usually one or multiple fully connected layers. **(3): Classifier**: Finally, the low-dimensional embedding is a good representation of the data, and can be fed to a small MLP network to determine the final prediction. The final output $\mathbf{y}$ is a vector, whose $c^{th}$ component represents the probability of taking the $c^{th}$ class, and all components sum up to 1.

This network setup fits general classification neural network models, especially for vision tasks. After the encoder, the dimension is usually high. Dimension reduction layers are necessary to map this high-dimensional embedding to a final low-dimensional prediction. For these three steps, we denote the encoder, dimension reduction and classifier functions as $g_1(\cdot)$, $g_2(\cdot)$ and $g_3(\cdot)$ separately; denote input data as $\mathbf{x}_i, i = 1, \ldots, n$; let corresponding final prediction vectors $\mathbf{y}_i$ represent the probability that data belongs to each class; and let the correct class label of $\mathbf{x}_i$ be $c(i)$. Then our model can be represented as

$$\mathbf{y}_i = f(\mathbf{x}_i) = g_3(g_2(g_1(\mathbf{x}_i))),$$

and we aim at minimizing the classification log likelihood loss(or cross entropy) $loss = -\sum_{i=1}^n log(y_{ic(i)})$, where $y_{ic(i)}$ is the probability that point $\mathbf{x}_i$ is correctly classified.

In a typical network, $g_2(\cdot)$ is identified as the first one of several fully connected layers [11,12]. Because a high-dimensional fully connected layer has a large number of parameters, these layers are very vulnerable to adversarial attack, especially to gradient-based adversarial attacks, such as the state of the art PGD attack.

## 2.2    Adversarial Attack

Adversarial attacks aim to perturb natural samples without being discovered by humans, but causing a neural net to misclassify the resulting samples. In this paper, we will mainly consider the PGD attack, which is a state of the art white-box adversarial attack model. PGD attacks work as follows. For each data sample, the attack updates the perturbation direction over a certain number of iterations. In each iteration, the PGD attack finds the direction that decreases the probability of the original class most, and then projects the result back to the $\epsilon$-ball of the input in $\ell_\infty$ norm. Specifically, for data point $\mathbf{x}$ in the $t+1^{st}$ iteration, the PGD attack considers moving the original data towards the direction with largest gradient:

$$\mathbf{x}^{t+1} = \Pi_{\mathbf{x}+\epsilon}\{\mathbf{x}^t + \alpha sign(\nabla_{\mathbf{x}}\ell(f(\mathbf{x}^t), y_0))\}$$

where $\Pi_{\mathbf{x}+\epsilon}\{\cdot\}$ represents the projection (clipping) into an $\epsilon$ ball in $\ell_\infty$ norm, centered at point $\mathbf{x}$. It makes perturbations with magnitude $\epsilon$.

## 2.3   Dimension Reduction with Neighborhood Preservation

Here we briefly introduce dimension reduction algorithms which aim at preserving neighborhood structure, such as UMAP and t-SNE, which are closely related to our model.

UMAP and t-SNE are two state-of-the-art unsupervised dimension reduction methods, which can effectively preserve the neighborhood structure of a set of points. The two methods share lots of similarity, and their key idea can be summarized as the following two steps: (1) Construct a neighborhood graph to quantify the membership strength between different points in the input (high dimensional embedding). (2) Find a low dimensional embedding of these points such that its neighborhood graph is most similar to that of the input.

Both methods provide a way to evaluate the similarity of neighborhood graphs. Here we consider UMAP. In step one, we compute the strength between points based on whether they are each others' nearest neighbors and their distances. Doing this for high- and low-dimensional representations of points yields membership strengths $\mu$ and $\nu$ respectively. Denote by A the set of all unordered pairs of points. For each pair, their membership strength is a value between 0 and 1, representing how close are they in distance. Then in step two, we evaluate the cross entropy C of two fuzzy sets $(A, \mu)$ and $(A, \nu)$:

$$C((A,\mu),(A,\nu)) = \sum_{a \in A} (\mu(a) \log(\frac{\mu(a)}{\nu(a)}) + (1 - \mu(a)) \log(\frac{1 - \mu(a)}{1 - \nu(a)}))$$

The low dimensional embedding which minimizes this cross entropy is found using stochastic gradient descent.

The two methods provide effective ways to evaluate the similarity between neighborhood structure in high- and low-dimensional embeddings. Typical usage involves a fixed set of input points. In Sect. 3, we describe how we extend UMAP to work as a *trainable* neighborhood-preserving dimension reduction layer, $g_2(\cdot)$. In Sect. 4 we consider the properties of such a mapping from a theoretical perspective, followed by empirical demonstrations in Sect. 5.

# 3   A Novel Neighborhood Preserving Layer

## 3.1   Network Structure

In this section, we propose a novel neighborhood preserving layer that can replace fully connected layers in dimension reduction, which can significantly improve network robustness.

As we discuss, the dimension reduction part $(g_2(\cdot))$ is a major source of vulnerability. If we can bridge the high-dim embedding and low-dim embedding without introducing a dimension reduction layer with large scale gradients, the robustness can be significantly improved. The proposed layer serves as a new $g_2(\cdot)$, and replaces one or many fully-connected layers for dimension reduction in a general classification neural network introduced in Sect. 2.

To achieve neighborhood preservation in dimension reduction layer, the key is to find a nice representation of low-dimensional embedding $g_2(g_1(\mathbf{x}))$ satisfying the following conditions: (1) **Neighbor Preservation**: It preserves the neighborhood structure of the high-dimensional embedding $g_1(\mathbf{x})$. (2) **Precise Prediction**: It achieves a good prediction performance after the classifier $g_3(\cdot)$, i.e. $g_3(g_2(g_1(\mathbf{x})))$ is a good prediction. Therefore it is important to establish criteria to evaluate both neighborhood preservation and prediction error.

For condition (2) on prediction, it can be evaluated by the standard log likelihood loss function as introduced in Sect.2.1. For condition (1) on neighborhood preservation, we need to introduce a metric to evaluate the discrepancy between the neighborhood structure of the high dimensional embedding and low dimensional one. This type of metric already is used in UMAP and t-SNE algorithms. Here we follow the spirit of dimension reduction methods, and propose a metric to evaluate neighborhood preservation through the similarity between two neighborhood graphs. We introduce explicit steps to compute this similarity metric, following the loss function of the UMAP algorithm in [16]. We denote $A$ as the set of all pairs between $1, \ldots, n$, who are neighbors of each other. For any unordered pair $(i, j) \in A$, $\mu(i, j)$ represents the membership strength of the pair $(\mathbf{x}_i, \mathbf{x}_j)$. Membership strengths $\mu(i, j)$ are computed in the following steps:

- For each point $x_i$, we search its $k$ nearest neighbors, and denote the distance to these neighbors as $d_{i1}, \ldots, d_{ik}$. Then we normalize these distances as: $d'_{ij} = d_{ij} - \min_{t=1,\ldots,k}\{d_{it}\}$.
- Compute the ordered membership strength between $x_i$ and its neighbor $x_j$ as: $z_{ij} = e^{-d'_{ij}}$.
- For each pair $(i, j) \in A$, the unordered membership strength is computed as the average of two ordered ones $z_{ij}$ and $z_{ji}$: $\mu(i, j) = \frac{z_{ij} + z_{ji}}{2}$.

For the ease of notation, the previous procedure of computing membership strengths is denoted by the function $\mathcal{M}(\cdot)$, i.e. $(A, \mu) = \mathcal{M}(g_1(\mathbf{x}))$. [16] provides complete theoretical justification for this procedure of computing membership strength.

Equipped with these metrics, we propose a novel neighborhood preserving layer in a general classification network. Instead of using a fully connected layer as $g_2(\cdot)$, we don't assume a one-to-one continuous parameterized function as $g_2(\cdot)$ here. Instead, we store a table that maps a reference set of high dimensional points to their low dimensional embeddings. We consider this reference set to be obtained from training data, so their high dimensional point is $\mathbf{u}^i_{high} = g_1(\mathbf{x}_i)$ for a set of data point indices $\{i\}$. Their corresponding low-dimensional embeddings $\mathbf{u}_{low}$ are stored and learned. We store a mapping $G_2 : i \mapsto \mathbf{u}^i_{low}$, over the fixed set of inputs $\{i\}$. In this aspect, $\mathbf{u}^i_{low}$ can be treated as the parameters of our layer, and we update them through back propagation, with respect to the full loss function. In the back propagation, we back propagate the derivative with respect to parameters in encoder(CNN) and classifier(purple arrows in Fig. 1), and also the low dimensional embeddings $\mathbf{u}_{low}$.

We visualize the pipeline of our proposed training network in Fig. 1. The explicit procedure of all steps are summarized as follows.

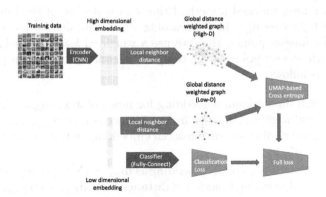

**Fig. 1.** Training network architecture (Color figure online)

- **Encoder(CNN)**: $\mathbf{u}_{high} = g_1(\mathbf{x})$
- **Local neighbor distance(High-D)**:$(A, \mu) = \mathcal{M}(\mathbf{u}_{high})$
- **Local neighbor distance(Low-D)**:$(A, \nu) = \mathcal{M}(\mathbf{u}_{low})$
- **Cross entropy loss**: $L_G = \sum_{a \in A}(\mu(a) \log(\frac{\mu(a)}{\nu(a)}) + (1 - \mu(a) \log(\frac{1-\mu(a)}{1-\nu(a)}))$
- **Classification loss**: $L_C = -\sum_{i=1}^{n} log(y_{ic(i)})$
- **Full loss**: $L_{full} = L_C + \alpha L_G$

In Fig. 1, the blue and purple arrows show the data flow for forward propagation. The key difference between a general classification network and our proposed network is that, during the back-propagation, our low-dimensional embedding is *not* viewed as a parameterized function $g_2(\cdot)$ of the high-dimensional embedding. There is no data flow arrow directly from the high-dimensional to low-dimensional embedding $\mathbf{u}_{high} \mapsto \mathbf{u}_{low}$. Instead, each embedding is independently updated through back-propagation to maintain the neighborhood structure of the high-dimensional embedding as much as possible, and also achieve good classifier predictions.

By combining the classification loss and neighborhood preserving loss, we update the parameters to achieve a good classification result and maintain the consistency between neighborhood graphs of the high-dimensional and low-dimensional embeddings at the same time. The proposed algorithm also needs an initialization of the low-dimensional embedding for each data point to start training. A reliable initialization can be obtained by performing the UMAP algorithm on the high-dimensional embedding. We stop the back propagation when the loss function converges in the training procedure.

After training, we obtained trained weights of the encoder and classifier, and also the low-dimensional embedding for all points in the training data. Here we call the low dimensional embedding for all training data as 'reference points', because they can be the reference for us to predict unseen data. Then we discuss how we can predict unseen new points. They cannot be fed into the training network directly, because these unseen points don't have a low dimensional embedding yet. Therefore, we need a method that can make use of the information of the mapping $G_2 : i \mapsto \mathbf{u}_{low}^i$ in the training set, to obtain the low dimensional embedding for unseen points. Here we use a weighted k-nearest neighbors approach. For each unseen point $\mathbf{x}$, the complete forward propagation procedure is summarized as follows:

- Compute high dimensional embedding for new point $\mathbf{x}$: $\mathbf{u}_{high} = g_1(\mathbf{x})$
- Find k-nearest neighbors of $\mathbf{u}_{high}$ from reference points: $\mathbf{u}_{high}^1, \ldots, \mathbf{u}_{high}^k$. Suppose the corresponding low-dimensional embedding of these $k$ reference points are $\mathbf{u}_{low}^1, \ldots, \mathbf{u}_{low}^k$.
- Compute the low dimensional embedding as $\mathbf{u}_{low} = (\sum_{i=1}^k w_i \mathbf{u}_{low}^i)/(\sum_{i=1}^k w_i)$. Weight $w_i$ is a decreasing function of distance from $\mathbf{u}_{high}$ to $\mathbf{u}_{high}^i$.
- Feed this low-dimensional embedding to the classifier to obtain the final prediction.

The complete prediction pipeline is displayed in Fig. 2. Our weights computation in prediction is consistent with training framework, thus provide us an accurate prediction on whether the point would be if it is in the training data. Comparing with the out-of-sample prediction for LLE and ISOmap [18], we emphasize the pair-wise distance thus further guarantee the robustness against perturbations.

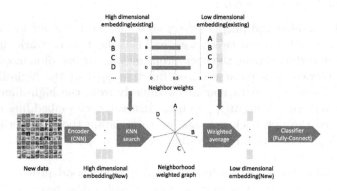

**Fig. 2.** Prediction network architecture. Here A,B,C,D are neighboring *reference points* that establish an interpolated mapping of $\mathbf{u}_{high} \mapsto \mathbf{u}_{low}$.

Instead of imposing regularizations [19] or dropout [20] on fully-connected layers, Our proposed layer fundamentally reduce the number of parameters in our network, such that it boosts the robustness of our models.

## 3.2    Adversarial Training

Our framework can also adapt standard adversarial training approaches, to further improve the robustness against adversarial attack. In adversarial training, for each batch of training data, we generate an 'adversarial batch' through the attack method, such as PGD attack. Then we assume the labels of adversarial batch are the same as in the training batch, and we train the model weights on both the original batch and the adversarial batch. In this way, the network will be less sensitive to the attack.

This procedure also works for our network. With each training batch, the adversarial batch can also be generated using the PGD attack algorithm. The prediction of an adversarial batch is forward propagated using the prediction procedure as introduced in Sect. 2.1. Because the prediction procedure is completely differentiable, the adversarial batch can be generated and forward propagated smoothly. Finally, we evaluate the loss function on both the true data and a generated 'adversarial batch'. The pipeline of the adversarial training procedure is shown in Fig. 3.

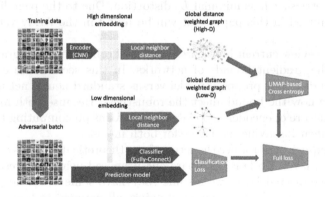

**Fig. 3.** Adversarial training network architecture.

## 3.3    Using Representative Points

In a more general case, $G_2 : \mathbf{u}^r_{high} \mapsto \mathbf{u}^r_{low}$ for $r = 1 \ldots R$. This might happen when input data includes a potentially infinite stream of input points (like data augmentation). We store this and learn a more general table, but it might cost a lot of memory to store the domain $\{\mathbf{u}^r_{high}\}$. We might save storage by using *representative points* that have occurred as actual inputs $\{\mathbf{x}_r\}$ and recalculating $\mathbf{u}^r_{high} = g_1(\mathbf{x}_r)$ as needed. In this case, we need to construct the set of representative points.

We introduce a heuristic approach to construct a smaller set of representative points. First, we train the network as same as proposed in Sect. 3.1. Using all high-dimensional embeddings, we use the K-means clustering algorithm with 100 clusters inside each class. For the 10-class MNIST dataset, we then have 1000 clusters with cluster centers $\mathbf{x}_i$ and $\mathbf{z}_i$ in high and low dimensions. The center of high/low dimensional embedding of these 1000 clusters are the 'representative points'. Each cluster has weight $v_i$, which is the size of the cluster. This reference point set with size 1000 is a good representation of all points. By such properly selected representative points, we can largely reduce the computational burden and maintain a good prediction performance.

The size of representative points can be further reduced if proper points can be selected. For example, [21,22] propose a way to choose representative points based on the exterior of well-separated clusters.

## 4   Theoretical Analysis

In this section, we illustrate the theoretical advantage of our proposed network structure. We prove that our proposed dimension reduction layer has a smaller gradient upper bound compared with the general neural network structure with fully-connected layers. We show that the decreasing of the gradient bound leads to significant improvement of network robustness, as measured by acknowledged robustness metrics such as minimal $L_p$ distortion. Due to the page limit, all the proofs are omitted in this paper, but will be found in the Arxiv version of our paper.

First let's review current literature. Studies of robustness of neural nets heavily rely on the gradient bounds of networks. In this section, we compare the gradient bounds of our proposed model versus standard neural net models, and then examine how the bound affect the robustness. Because both models share the same structure of encoder and classifier, we focus on computing the gradient bounds of dimension reduction layers for both models.

Here we explicitly introduce the setup of our theoretical analysis of the dimension reduction layer. To fairly compare our proposed neighbor preserving layer with a fully connected layer, we assume they have same scale, i.e. both layers map $\mathbf{x} \in \mathbb{R}^p \mapsto \mathbf{y} \in \mathbb{R}^d$, with boundary points all mapped to boundary points. Without loss of generality, we assume inputs and outputs are bounded by $\ell_2$ bounds around origin with fixed radius. Fixing the scale will not affect the prediction ability of the network, since the network between layers can be adjusted by a multiplier correspondingly.

Our proposed layer is based on a mapping of representatives $G_2 : \mathbf{x}_r \in \mathbb{R}^p \mapsto \mathbf{y}_r \in \mathbb{R}^d$ for $r = 1 \ldots N$. Mapping a generic input $\mathbf{x}_0$ follows the same neighborhood weighted average approach we used in the prediction network:

$$f(\mathbf{x}_0) = \frac{\sum_{i=1}^{k} w_i \mathbf{y}_i}{\sum_{i=1}^{k} w_i},$$

for neighbor representatives $\{\mathbf{x}_1, \ldots, \mathbf{x}_k\}$ of $\mathbf{x}_0 \in \mathbb{R}^p$. It is worth mentioning that, in our analysis, instead of fixing the number of nearest neighbors $k$, we fix the maximum distance between neighbors and point $\mathbf{x}_0$. We choose all points which are inside $\mathbb{B}_r(\mathbf{x}_0)$ as the neighbors. We denote the number of points inside

$\mathbb{B}_r(\mathbf{x}_0)$ as $n$ in this section. Choosing the radius of ball $r$ is equivalent to choosing a specific number of neighbors $k$.

We introduce another assumption to bound the neighborhood update frequency. It represents the ratio of points changed as an $\mathbb{B}_r$-ball moves by a small $\epsilon$.

**Assumption 1.** $\mathbf{x}$ *follows a distribution* $\mathbb{P}$ *with* $\|\mathbf{x}\|_{max} \leq C_0$ *for some constant* $C_0$. *We assume* $\mathbb{P}$ *is uniformly bounded in density almost everywhere.*

Furthermore, we introduce a class of distribution beforehand. We say a distribution is an $\alpha$-even distribution if for any two regions with same volume A, B in feasible region $S$, and any point $x \in P$:

$$\max_{vol(A)=vol(B)} \frac{p(x \in A)}{p(x \in B)} \leq \alpha$$

All uniformly bounded distributions with density almost everywhere can be represented as an $\alpha$-even distribution since their density is both upper and lower bounded.

**Lemma 1.** *If* $\mathbf{x}$ *follows an* $\alpha$-even *distribution, then for any fixed point* $\mathbf{x}_0$, *then as the sample size* $N \to \infty$, *with probability going to 1:*

$$\lim_{N \to \infty} \lim_{\|\epsilon\|_2 \to 0} \frac{Card(Old) + Card(New)}{N\epsilon} = 0$$

*where* $Card(Old) = Card_x(x \in \mathbb{B}_r(\mathbf{x}_0), x \notin \mathbb{B}_r(\mathbf{x}_0 + \epsilon))$, *and* $Card(New) = Card_x(x \in \mathbb{B}_r(\mathbf{x}_0 + \epsilon), x \notin \mathbb{B}_r(\mathbf{x}_0))$.

Another assumption is that all the points in $\mathbb{B}_r(\mathbf{x}_0)$ and $\mathbb{B}_r(\mathbf{x}_0 + \epsilon)$ are uniformly bounded in $\ell_2$ norm.

**Assumption 2.** *For point* $\mathbf{x}_0$, *we assume for any point* $\mathbf{x}_i \in \mathbb{B}_r(\mathbf{x}_0)$, *its embedding* $\mathbf{y}_i$ *satisfies* $\|\mathbf{y}_i\|_2 \leq C_4$.

Since our goal is to obtain a well-behaved low-dimensional embedding, such a bound is reasonable in our setting.

We also introduce necessary notation. We introduce a scalar distance-weighting function $h$ with derivative $h'$, which can be applied element-wise to vectors as $h(\mathbf{z})$. We use $cov_{\mathbf{z} \in S}(\mathbf{z}, h(\mathbf{z}))$ to represent the element-wise population covariance between each element in random vector $\mathbf{z}$ and a random scalar $h(\mathbf{z})$, restricting $\mathbf{z}$ inside set $S$. This covariance has the same dimension as $\mathbf{z}$. Further, for a data point $\mathbf{x}_0$, we assume its neighbors in $\mathbb{B}_r(\mathbf{x}_0)$ are $\mathbf{x}_1, \ldots, \mathbf{x}_n$ and their embeddings are $\mathbf{y}_1, \ldots, \mathbf{y}_n$. Their distances to $\mathbf{x}_0$ are denoted as $d(\mathbf{x}_0, \mathbf{x}_i)$ for $i = 1, \ldots, n$. In practice, we use $w_i = h(d(\mathbf{x}_0, \mathbf{x}_i)) = \exp(-d(\mathbf{x}_0, \mathbf{x}_i))$ as our weight function.

**Theorem 1.** *Suppose data follows distribution* $\mathbb{P}$ *in space* $\mathbb{R}^p$, *and we uniformly sample* $N$ *points from* $\mathbb{P}$. *Take all points inside* $\mathbb{B}_r(\mathbf{x}_0)$ *as the reference points of* $\mathbf{x}_0$. *Take* $C_1$ *and* $C_2$ *such that* $E_{\mathbf{z} \in \mathbb{B}_r(\mathbf{x}_0)} h(d(\mathbf{x}_0, \mathbf{z})) \geq C_1$ *and*

$E_{\mathbf{z} \in \mathbb{B}_r(\mathbf{x}_0)}|h'(d(\mathbf{x}_0, \mathbf{z}))| \leq C_2$. *Assume assumption 1 and 2 apply with constant* $C_4$. *Given* $\delta > 0$, *for all direction vector* $\mathbf{u}$ *normalized so that* $\|u\| = 1$, *we have for* $N$ *sufficiently large:*

$$\lim_{c \to 0} \|\frac{f(\mathbf{x}_0 + c\hat{\mathbf{u}}) - f(\mathbf{x}_0)}{c}\|_2 \leq 2C_4(\frac{C_2}{C_1}) + \delta$$

*with probability going to 1.*

**Remark 1.** *From the theorem, we see that the Lipschitz bound of neighborhood weighted embedding is determined by* $(C_1, C_2, C_4, \alpha)$. *By the definition, we know* $C_1 \leq 1$ *by our choice of radius* $r$; $C_2$ *is lower bounded as long as we choose a function decay sufficiently fast. For example, if we choose* $h(x) = exp(-x)$, *we have* $C_2 \leq 1$; $C_4$ *is also a small constant independent of* $p$.

*Therefore the Lipschitz bound of our neighborhood embedding layer is smaller and will not diverge with* $p$, *and is free from the scale of* $\mathbf{x}$.

**Remark 2.** *Connection with intrinsic dimension: The theorem results also implicitly connect with the intrinsic dimension of* $\mathbf{x}$. *Here we take a sufficient large* $N$, *but actually this* $N$ *is connected with the intrinsic dimensionality of* $\mathbf{x}$. *From (Levina and Bickel 2005), we know if the intrinsic dimension of* $\mathbf{x}$ *is* $m$, *then the Euclidean distance from a fixed point* $\mathbf{x}$ *to its* $k$-*th nearest neighbor* $T_k(\mathbf{x})$ *approximately satisfies:* $\frac{k}{N} \approx f(\mathbf{x})(T_k(\mathbf{x}))^m V(m)$, *where* $V(m) = \frac{\pi^{m/2}}{\Gamma(m/2+1)}$, *is the volume of the unit sphere in* $\mathbb{R}^m$.

*Here for our neighbor search procedure in Theorem 1, we have* $T_k(\mathbf{x}) = r$ *fixed. Therefore for any fixed* $N$, *the number of neighbors* $k$ *can be approximated as:*

$$k \approx Nf(\mathbf{x})(r)^m V(m) \approx \frac{N}{\sqrt{\pi m}}f(\mathbf{x})(2e\frac{\pi r^2}{m})^{m/2}$$

*This is an increasing function of* $m$ *roughly when* $m < 2e\pi r^2$. *Therefore we know the sample size we need is small when* $m$ *is not large. It explains why we can achieve a much smaller gradient upper bound with relatively small sample sizes, when the intrinsic dimension is not large. It also suggests that we should choose* $r$ *according to the true intrinsic dimensionality. The larger the intrinsic dimension, the larger the* $r$ *should be.*

After deriving the Lipschitz upper bound of neighborhood preserving layer, we compare it with the Lipschitz bound of a fully-connected layer. We know when only one layer is considered, given $\mathbf{X} \in \mathbb{R}^{n*p}$ and $\mathbf{y} \in \mathbb{R}^{n*d}$, the best fully-connected layer is equivalent to a multi-response regression problem. Denoting $\mathbf{W} = (\mathbf{w}^{(1)}, \ldots, \mathbf{w}^{(d)})$, we have: $\mathbf{w}^{(i)} = (\mathbf{X}^T\mathbf{X})^{-1}\mathbf{X}^T\mathbf{y}_i$. This choice of weights can minimize the $\ell_2$ loss in this specific layer, and is the best unbiased linear weight. When a single layer is considered, this is the target weight we should use. The corresponding feed forward function is defined as $f(\mathbf{x}) = \mathbf{W}\mathbf{x}$. To proceed with the analysis, we introduce a set of regularity conditions for $\mathbf{x}$ and $\mathbf{y}$.

**Assumption 3.** *We assume* $\mathbf{x}_i$'s *are independently distributed from* $\mathbb{P}$ *such that* $E(\mathbf{x}) = \mathbf{0}$ *and* $cov(\mathbf{x}) \lesssim C_5 \mathbf{I}_p$.

$A \lesssim B$ means that $B - A$ is a positive definite matrix. The assumption requires that the distribution of the low dimensional embedding $\mathbf{y}$ is well behaved, and the covariance matrix has eigenvalue upper bound. It holds naturally as long as $\mathbf{x}$ is bounded. Further we assume each $\mathbf{x}^{(i)}$ and $\mathbf{y}_j$ have correlation $r_{ij}$. All these assumptions can also be easily achieved by our neighborhood preserving layer.

**Theorem 2.** *When Assumption 3 holds, given $\delta > 0$, if $n$ is sufficiently large then $\mathbf{W}$ satisfies:*

$$\|\mathbf{w}^{(j)}\|_2 \geq \frac{1}{C_5 + \delta} \sqrt{\sum_{i=1}^{p} D_i^2 r_i^2 - \delta}$$

*Furthermore, there exists a direction of $\epsilon$ such that:*

$$\lim_{c \to 0} \left\| \frac{f(\mathbf{x}_0 + c\epsilon) - f(\mathbf{x}_0)}{c} \right\|_2 \geq \frac{1}{C_5 + \delta} \sqrt{\sum_{i=1}^{p} D_i^2 r_i^2 - \delta}$$

*where $D_i = sd(\mathbf{x}^{(i)})sd(y_i)$, is the product of two standard deviations, providing a lower bound on the Lipschitz constant of this fully connected layer.*

So far we have derived the Lipschitz upper bound of our neighborhood preserving layer: $T_1 = 2C_4(\frac{C_2}{C_1}) + \delta$, and the lower bound of the fully connected regression layer: $T_2 = \frac{1}{C_5+\delta}\sqrt{\sum_{i=1}^{p} C_i^2 r_i^2} - \delta$. We see $\frac{T_1}{T_2} = o(1/\sqrt{p})$ when all $r_i$ are O(1). It means in general our neighborhood layer is on the $o(1/\sqrt{p})$ order of the Lipschitz bound of the fully connected layer.

The derived Lipschitz bound is closely related to the robustness of the network, and also the gradient descent based attack method. If the Lipschitz constant is small overall, then perturbations from all directions cannot significantly change the loss function, and the gradient descent based attack will be ineffective.

To illustrate this effect, first we need to introduce 'minimal $L_p$ distortion', which is a well acknowledged metric for robustness evaluation (Hein and Andriushchenko 2017).

**Definition 1.** *Let $C$ be the set of samples with label $c$, $l$ be a class, and $f_c(x)$ be the predicted probability that a point $x$ belongs to class $c$. Then we say a network has minimal $L_p$ distortion $\delta_p$ at point $x$, if $\delta_p$ is defined as:*

$$\min_{\delta \in \mathbb{R}^d} \|\delta\|_p \quad s.t. \quad \max_{l \neq c} f_l(x + \delta) \geq f_c(x + \delta) \quad and \quad x \in C$$

$\delta_p$ is the maximal distortion $L_p$ norm allowed such that all distortions smaller than this magnitude will not change the classification label. This metric is closely related to the performance of a network against a C&W attack [8]. In a C&W attack, we exactly look for a $L_2$ distortion in $S$ that maximizes the difference in loss function.

**Corollary 1.** *If the conditions in Theorem 1 and 2 hold, then the upper bound of minimal $L_2$ distortion bound introduced in Hein and Andriushchenko (2017) will be improved by $\frac{T_2}{T_1}$ times by replacing a fully-connected layer with our proposed neighborhood preserving layer.*

So far, we have analyzed how our neighborhood preserving layer helps shrink the Lipschitz constant and thus helps improve the minimal distortion bound. [5] propose the saddle point problem, which is well recognized as a good measure of the robustness of a network:

$$\rho = \mathbb{E}_{x,y}[\max_{\delta \in S} L(\theta, x + \delta, y)]$$

where $S$ is the feasible region of a small distortion with radius $\epsilon$, and $y$ is the class associated to input point $x$.

An alternate measure of distortion is:

$$g_\delta = \mathbb{E}_{x,y}[\max_{\delta \in S} L(\theta, x + \delta, y)] - \mathbb{E}_{x,y}[L(\theta, x, y)]$$

Here we show that taking advantage of the result from Theorem 1, our robustness will also be significantly improved under this metric.

**Theorem 3.** *Suppose all conditions in Theorem 1 are satisfied, and the loss function for classification is chosen as negative log likelihood loss. Then the network with bottleneck $f(\cdot)$ (a neighborhood preserving layer or a fully-connected layer) has distortion expectation upper bound:*

$$g_\delta \leq L_a L_b \epsilon \int_{\mathbb{R}^p} \max_{\delta \in S} Lip(f(z + L_a \delta)) dz$$

*where $Lip(\cdot)$ is the Lipschitz constant at a specific point, and $L_a$ is the Lipschitz constant prior to the bottleneck layer, and $L_b$ is the Lipschitz constant after the bottleneck layer. Under Assumptions 1-3, the distortion bound of fully-connected layer is $\frac{T_2}{T_1}$ times of our neighborhood preserving layer.*

From Theorem 3, we see that the distortion bound is proportion to its Lipschitz constant bound. The ratio of bounds between the neighborhood preserving and fully connected bottleneck layers is $\frac{T_1}{T_2}$. Considering $\frac{T_1}{T_2} = o(\frac{1}{\sqrt{p}})$, the distortion expectation of our algorithm has much smaller bounds, making our algorithm more robust against adversarial attack.

## 5  Experiments

In this section, we demonstrate the practical superiority of our proposed layer on benchmark datasets. Explicitly, we compare the performance of our proposed algorithm (neighbor preserving layer) with benchmark CNN models against a PGD attack. The experiments are conducted on two benchmark datasets:

- **MNIST**: handwritten digit dataset, which consists of 60,000 training images and 10,000 testing images. Theses are $28 \times 28$ black and white images in ten different classes.
- **CIFAR10**: natural image dataset, which contains 50,000 training images and 10,000 testing images in ten different classes. These are low resolution three-channel $32 \times 32$ color images.

For the MNIST dataset, the encoder is setup as a two-layer CNN with kernel size $5 \times 5$ and $5/20$ output channels in the first and second layer, and a $2 \times 2$ pooling following each convolutional layer. The encoder leads to a 800-dimensional high-dimensional embedding. For CIFAR10 dataset, we employ VGG16 architecture as the encoder, and it leads to a 512-dimensional high-dimensional embedding. For the classifier, we employ two fully-connected layers with ReLU activation, and then a softmax function to obtain the final 10-dimensional prediction probability for 10 classes. For dimension reduction layers, two type of dimension reduction layers are employed: (1) Fully-connected layers with ReLU activation. (2) Our proposed neighborhood preserving layer.

We consider the strongest white-box PGD attack over two datasets. Explicitly in our experiment, the $\Pi_\epsilon$ is considered as $\ell_\infty$ projection over the data. We normalize the data to the ranges from 0 to 1. Therefore $\epsilon = 0.01$ represents changes up to about 3 pixels, and $\epsilon = 0.05$ represents changes up to about 15 pixels, and so forth. In the table, 'FC' represents fully-connected dimension reduction layers, 'NP' represents proposed neighborhood preserving dimension reduction layers, and 'Ref' represents proposed neighborhood preserving layers with only 1000 reference point instead of full datasets. The subscript indicates the output dimension of the layer. We provide a table with $\ell_\infty$ projection attack under different bottleneck layers for MNIST (Table 1) and CIFAR (Table 2).

**Table 1.** MNIST data set: Accuracy result under $\ell_\infty$ projection PGD attack

| Perturbation | $FC_8$ | $FC_{16}$ | $NP_8$ | $NP_{16}$ | $Ref_8$ | $Ref_{16}$ |
|---|---|---|---|---|---|---|
| $\epsilon = 0.01$ | 98.56 | **98.98** | 96.85 | 96.95 | 94.42 | 94.52 |
| $\epsilon = 0.05$ | 84.78 | 88.46 | **94.82** | 94.26 | 90.40 | 90.95 |
| $\epsilon = 0.1$ | 37.82 | 46.13 | **91.67** | 90.72 | 81.76 | 82.69 |
| $\epsilon = 0.2$ | 9.67 | 11.30 | **89.73** | 89.04 | 73.89 | 74.92 |

From these two tables, we draw several conclusions: (1) Coinciding with our theoretical results, our proposed layer is much more robust against a PGD attack compared with fully-connected layers, especially when $\epsilon$ is large. (2) Comparing the two tables, we can see the true intrinsic dimension of a dataset is important to the performance of networks. The MNIST dataset is known to be a simpler dataset and has smaller intrinsic dimension than CIFAR10. It helps explain why $NP_8$ outperforms $NP_{16}$ in MNIST, while $NP_{16}$ outperforms $NP_8$ in CIFAR10. Our results coincide with both our findings about intrinsic dimension of the

**Table 2.** CIFAR10 data set: Accuracy result under $\ell_\infty$ projection PGD attack

| Perturbation | $FC_8$ | $FC_{16}$ | $NP_8$ | $NP_{16}$ |
|---|---|---|---|---|
| $\epsilon = 0.01$ | 66.66 | 68.43 | 76.17 | **77.76** |
| $\epsilon = 0.05$ | 19.29 | 20.50 | 65.40 | **66.10** |
| $\epsilon = 0.1$ | 7.38 | 8.06 | 61.33 | **62.04** |
| $\epsilon = 0.2$ | 5.46 | 5.57 | 58.84 | **59.91** |

two datasets. (3) In the MNIST dataset, we also consider different choices of reference points. We consider using all training data as reference points, versus using 1000 points as reference points. We see that using 1000 reference points sacrifices a bit of prediction performance, while it can significantly reduce the computational burden, reducing 98.3% of reference points. (4) For MNIST data, $\epsilon = 0.01$ is a weak attack, and we see that our model maintain high accuracy under these settings. It demonstrates the general interest of our layer.

Overall in this section, we illustrate that our algorithm can replace dimension reduction layers and effectively improve the robustness of models. It is also compatible with other state-of-art adversarial training methods.

## 6   Conclusion

In this paper, we propose a novel dimension reduction layer through neighborhood preservation. The proposed layer can replace fully connected layers in general neural nets to improve robustness against adversarial attack. We provide theoretical analysis and empirical experiments to show that the proposed layer enjoys a smaller gradient upper bound, and is more robust against gradient-based adversarial attack. Neural networks with our proposed layers can be efficiently trained, and are also flexible in adapting other adversarial training procedures.

## References

1. Goodfellow, I.J., Shlens, J., Szegedy, C.: Explaining and harnessing adversarial examples, arXiv preprint arXiv:1412.6572 (2014)
2. Szegedy, C., et al.: Intriguing properties of neural networks, arXiv preprint arXiv:1312.6199 (2013)
3. Moosavi-Dezfooli, S.-M., Fawzi, A., Frossard, P.: Deepfool: a simple and accurate method to fool deep neural networks. In: Proceedings of the IEEE Conference on Computer Vision and Pattern Recognition, pp. 2574–2582 (2016)
4. Dong, Y., et al.:Boosting adversarial attacks with momentum. In: Proceedings of the IEEE Conference on Computer Vision and Pattern Recognition, pp. 9185–9193 (2018)
5. Madry, A., Makelov, A., Schmidt, L., Tsipras, D., Vladu, a.: Towards deep learning models resistant to adversarial attacks" arXiv preprint arXiv:1706.06083 (2017)
6. Chakraborty, A., Alam, M., Dey, V., Chattopadhyay, A., Mukhopadhyay, D.: Adversarial attacks and defences: a survey, arXiv preprint arXiv:1810.00069 (2018)

7. Chen, P.-Y., Sharma, Y., Zhang, H., Yi, J., Hsieh, C.-J..: Ead: elastic-net attacks to deep neural networks via adversarial examples. In: 32nd AAAI Conference on Artificial Intelligence (2018)
8. Carlini, N., Wagner, D.: Towards evaluating the robustness of neural networks. In: 2017 IEEE Symposium on Security and Privacy (sp), pp. 39–57. IEEE (2017)
9. Hein, M., Andriushchenko, M.:Formal guarantees on the robustness of a classifier against adversarial manipulation. In: Advances in Neural Information Processing Systems, pp. 2266–2276 (2017)
10. Weng, T.-W., et al.: Evaluating the robustness of neural networks: An extreme value theory approach, arXiv preprint arXiv:1801.10578 (2018)
11. Szegedy, C., Ioffe, S., Vanhoucke, V., Alemi, A.: Inception-v4, inception-resnet and the impact of residual connections on learning. In: 31st AAAI Conference on Artificial Intelligence (2017)
12. Simonyan, K., Zisserman, A.: Very deep convolutional networks for large-scale image recognition, arXiv preprint arXiv:1409.1556 (2014)
13. Roweis, S.T., Saul, L.K.: Nonlinear dimensionality reduction by locally linear embedding. Science **290**(5500), 2323–2326 (2000)
14. He, X., Cai, D., Yan, S., Zhang, H.-J.: Neighborhood preserving embedding. In: 10th IEEE International Conference on Computer Vision (ICCV 2005) Volume 1, vol. 2, pp. 1208–1213. IEEE (2005)
15. Tenenbaum, J.B., De Silva, V., Langford, J.C.: A global geometric framework for nonlinear dimensionality reduction. Science **290**(5500), 2319–2323 (2000)
16. McInnes, L., Healy, J., Melville, J.: Umap: uniform manifold approximation and projection for dimension reduction, arXiv preprint arXiv:1802.03426 (2018)
17. Maaten, L.V.D., Hinton, G.: Visualizing data using t-sne. J. Mach. Learn. Res. **9**(11), 2579–2605 (2008)
18. Bengio, Y., Paiement, J.-F., Vincent, P., Delalleau, O., Roux, N. L. Ouimet, M.: Out-of-sample extensions for lle, isomap, mds, eigenmaps, and spectral clustering. In: Advances in Neural Information Processing Systems, pp. 177–184 (2004)
19. Ross, A. S., Doshi-Velez, F.: Improving the adversarial robustness and interpretability of deep neural networks by regularizing their input gradients, arXiv preprint arXiv:1711.09404 (2017)
20. Srivastava, N., Hinton, G., Krizhevsky, A., Sutskever, I., Salakhutdinov, R.: Dropout: a simple way to prevent neural networks from overfitting. J. Mach. Learn. Res. **15**(1), 1929–1958 (2014)
21. Afsar, F. A., Akram, A., Arif, M., Khurshid, J.: A pruned fuzzy k-nearest neighbor classifier with application to electrocardiogram based cardiac arrhytmia recognition. In: 2008 IEEE International Multitopic Conference, pp. 143–148. IEEE (2008)
22. Arif, M., Akram, M.U., et al.: Pruned fuzzy k-nearest neighbor classifier for beat classification. J. Biomed. Sci. Eng. **3**(04), 380 (2010)

# Metric Learning on the Manifold of Oriented Ellipses: Application to Facial Expression Recognition

Mohamed Daoudi[1], Naima Otberdout[2(✉)], and Juan-Carlos Álvarez Paiva[3]

[1] IMT Lille Douai, Univ. Lille, CNRS, UMR 9189 CRIStAL, 59000 Lille, France
[2] Univ. Lille, CNRS, Centrale Lille, UMR 9189 CRIStAL, 59000 Lille, France
naimaotberd@gmail.com
[3] Univ. Lille, CNRS, UMR 8524 - Laboratoire Paul Painlevé, 59000 Lille, France

**Abstract.** In this paper we propose a new family of metrics on the manifold of oriented ellipses centered at the origin in Euclidean n-space, the double cover of the manifold of positive semi-definite matrices of rank two, in order to measure similarities between landmark representations. The metrics, whose distance functions are remarkably simple, are parametrized by the choice of a n-by-n positive semi-definite matrix P. This allows us to learn the parameter P from the training data and increase the efficiency of the metric. We evaluate the proposed metric on facial expression recognition from 2D facial landmarks. The conducted experiments demonstrate the effectiveness of the learned metric to classify facial shapes under different expressions.

## 1 Introduction

Positive-semidefinite (PSD) matrices appear in many domains ranging from action recognition [1,2], facial expression recognition [3,4], EEG emotion recognition [5] to medical applications [22], [6]. In this paper, we consider the applications where the rank of the matrices is assumed to be fixed. This is for example the case when the data points are low-rank representatives of large PSD matrices. The data belong then to the set $\mathcal{S}^+(d, n)$ of fixed-rank PSD matrices of size $n$ and rank $d$, which can also be identified as the space of ellipsoids of dimension $d$ and centered at the origin in Euclidean $n$-space. Many state-of-the-art works have adopted such representation to model and analyse data for different applications. In [2], Kacem et al. use PSD matrices to model facial expression and human action in videos. They model the temporal evolution of face and body landmarks as parametrized trajectories on the Riemannian manifold of PSD matrices of fixed-rank. Accordingly, they exploit a metric defined on the underlying manifold to classify their data. However, their metric involves a parameter to be set empirically, while this parameter greatly affects the discriminating power of the used metric. To overcome this drawback, Szczapa et al. [1] exploit

---

M. Daoudi, N. Otberdout and J.-C.Á. Paiva—Equal contribution.

© Springer Nature Switzerland AG 2021
A. Del Bimbo et al. (Eds.): ICPR 2020 Workshops, LNCS 12666, pp. 196–206, 2021.
https://doi.org/10.1007/978-3-030-68780-9_18

the same data representation but with a novel metric. Their framework was applied to the problem of human action recognition. In the context of medical applications, Daoudi et al. [6] adopt a representation of the body shape on a PSD manifold with a Riemannian metric to assess the depression severity of a patient, while Szczapa et al. [22], exploit facial landmarks to model the face motion as trajectories on PSD manifold that were used for pain intensity estimation.

The discussed approaches above exploit different metrics in the space of PSD matrices of fixed rank according to their data structure and the task at hand. Indeed, many metrics can be defined on the $\mathcal{S}^+(d, n)$ and this begs the question, can we automatically learn the suitable metric that is discriminative enough for our task in this space?

To answer this question, a potential solution is to incorporate the metric learning to learn the best metric appropriate for a given data. Metric learning algorithms are used to learn distance function suitable for specific data that can faithfully measure their similarities. Various methods have been proposed to learn the metric, with different objective functions designed for specific tasks (e.g., clustering and classification). While the majority of these approaches learn metrics in Euclidean space, some non-linear methods [7,8] are proposed to learn the metric on a manifold instead of the Euclidean space. In this work, we aim to learn a metric on $\mathcal{S}_c^+(2, n)$, the space of oriented ellipses centered at the origin in Euclidean $n$-space and the double cover of the manifold of $n \times n$ PSD matrices of rank two. We identify this covering space as the quotient of the set of $n \times 2$ real matrices of rank two by the right action of the group of $2 \times 2$ rotation matrices. This identification leads to a privileged family of metrics on the nonlinear manifold $\mathcal{S}_c^+(2, n)$ whose distance functions are remarkably easy to compute.

Furthermore, we propose to exploit Average neighborhood margin maximization which is a metric learning algorithm to enhance the discriminative power of the proposed metric by exploiting the data at hand. This is achieved, by parametrizing the proposed metric with a $n \times n$ PSD matrix $P$, which is automatically learned from the data.

In summary, the main contributions of this paper are:

- We identify the manifold $\mathcal{S}_c^+(2, n)$ with the quotient manifold $\mathbb{R}_*^{n \times 2}/SO_2$.
- We exploit this identification to propose a family of metrics on $\mathcal{S}_c^+(2, n)$ depending on the choice of an $n \times n$ PSD matrix $P$ and investigate the dependence of the metric on this parameter.
- We adopt a metric learning algorithm to enhance the discriminating power of the proposed metric.
- We evaluate our proposed metric on facial expression recognition task. According to this evaluation, our learned metric achieves good performance and comparative results with the literature.

The remaining of this paper is organized as follows: In Sect. 2 we provide the required background regarding the identification of the manifold $\mathcal{S}_c^+(2, n)$ with the quotient manifold $\mathbb{R}_*^{n \times 2}/SO_2$ before presenting our proposed metric. The metric learning algorithm exploited to learn the metric will be explained in

Sect. 3, while we evaluate our proposed metric on the task of facial expression recognition in Sect. 4. Finally, Sect. 5 is dedicated to conclusion and future directions.

## 2   A Class of Metrics on the Shape Space $\mathcal{S}_c^+(2, n)$

In this paper we consider the quotient manifold $\mathcal{S}_c^+(2, n) := \mathbb{R}_*^{n \times 2}/SO_2$ whose elements are the equivalence classes

$$[Z] = ZSO_2 := \{ZR | R \in SO_2\}.$$

Here $Z$ is an $n \times 2$ real matrix of rank 2 and $SO_2$ denotes the group of $2 \times 2$ rotation matrices. Although we are unaware of any previous use of this shape space in the computer science literature, it is closely related to the manifold $\mathcal{S}^+(2, n)$ of rank-two PSD $n \times n$ matrices that were studied in [9–11]. Indeed, just as the orthogonal group $O_2$ is a double cover of $SO_2$, the manifold $\mathcal{S}_c^+(2, n)$ is a double cover of $\mathcal{S}^+(2, n) = \mathbb{R}_*^{n \times 2}/O_2$ with covering map $\pi([Z]) := ZZ^T$. Geometrically speaking, the manifold $\mathcal{S}^+(2, n)$ is the space of ellipses centered at the origin in $\mathbb{R}^n$ while its chiral version $\mathcal{S}_c^+(2, n)$ is the space of *oriented* ellipses centered at the origin in $\mathbb{R}^n$.

Trivially adapting an idea of [12], we can use the standard Riemannian metric in $\mathbb{R}^{n \times 2}$ to endow $\mathcal{S}_c^+(2, n)$ with a quotient Riemannian metric. In fact, we will endow $\mathcal{S}_c^+(2, n)$ with the *family* of metrics and, more generally, pseudometrics induced from the family of Euclidean and degenerate Euclidean metrics in $\mathbb{R}^{n \times 2}$ that are invariant under the right action of $SO_2$.

For any $n \times n$ PSD matrix $P$, the expression

$$\langle Z_1, Z_2 \rangle_P = \text{tr}(Z_2^t P Z_1)$$

defines a possibly degenerate (i.e., $\langle Z, Z \rangle_P$ could be zero for a nonzero $Z$) inner product in $\mathbb{R}^{n \times 2}$ that is invariant under the right action of $SO_2$. By definition of a quotient metric and using the previous expression for the inner product $\langle Z_1, Z_2 \rangle_P$, the square of the distance in $\mathcal{S}_c^+(2, n)$ between two equivalence classes $[Z_1]$ and $[Z_2]$ is given by the formula

$$\tilde{\Delta}_P^2([Z_1], [Z_2]) = \min_{R \in SO_2} \text{tr}((Z_1 R - Z_2)^t P (Z_1 R - Z_2)).$$

This quantity admits a simple expression: if $J$ denotes the matrix

$$\begin{pmatrix} 0 & -1 \\ 1 & 0 \end{pmatrix},$$

then

$$\tilde{\Delta}_P^2([Z_1], [Z_2]) = \text{tr}(Z_1^t P Z_1) + \text{tr}(Z_2^t P Z_2) \\ - 2\sqrt{(\text{tr}(Z_2^t P Z_1))^2 + (\text{tr}(J Z_2^t P Z_1))^2}. \tag{1}$$

Such simplification is an immediate consequence of the following

**Lemma 1.** *Given a $2 \times 2$ real matrix $A$, the maximum value of the quantity* $\mathrm{tr}(AR)$ *as $R$ ranges over the group of rotation matrices $SO_2$ equals*

$$\sqrt{(\mathrm{tr}(A)^2 + (\mathrm{tr}(JA))^2}.$$

*Proof.*

$$\mathrm{tr}\left(\begin{pmatrix} a\ b \\ c\ d \end{pmatrix}\begin{pmatrix} \cos(\theta)\ -\sin(\theta) \\ \sin(\theta)\ \ \cos(\theta) \end{pmatrix}\right) = (a+d)\cos(\theta) + (b-c)\sin(\theta).$$

Regarding this quantity as an inner product in $\mathbb{R}^2$, the Cauchy-Schwarz inequality tells us that its maximum value is

$$\sqrt{(a+d)^2 + (b-c)^2} = \sqrt{(\mathrm{tr}(A)^2 + (\mathrm{tr}(JA))^2}.$$

## 2.1 Gradient

The simple formula for $\tilde{\Delta}_P^2([Z_1], [Z_2])$ makes it evident that this quantity is smooth in all variables away from set of triples $(Z_1, Z_2, P)$ satisfying $\mathrm{tr}(Z_1^t P Z_1) = 0$ and $\mathrm{tr}(J Z_2^t P Z_1) = 0$. We are particularly interested on the dependency of the positive semi-definite matrix $P$.

Replacing $P$ for $P + tX$ in Formula 1, where $X$ is any symmetric $n \times n$ matrix, and differentiating with respect to $t$, we easily compute the directional derivative:

$$\nabla_P \tilde{\Delta}_P^2([Z_1], [Z_2]) \cdot X = \mathrm{tr}(Z_1^t X Z_1) + \mathrm{tr}(Z_2^t X Z_2)$$
$$- 2\frac{\mathrm{tr}(Z_2^t P Z_1)\mathrm{tr}(Z_2^t X Z_1) + \mathrm{tr}(J Z_2^t P Z_1)\mathrm{tr}(J Z_2^t X Z_1)}{\sqrt{(\mathrm{tr}(Z_2^t P Z_1))^2 + (\mathrm{tr}(J Z_2^t P Z_1))^2}}. \tag{2}$$

If we consider the set of positive semidefinite matrices as a subset of the space of all $n \times n$ symmetric matrices provided with the Euclidean structure

$$\langle A, B \rangle := \mathrm{tr}(AB),$$

we can define and compute the gradient of $\nabla_P \tilde{\Delta}_P^2([Z_1], [Z_2])$ as a function of $P$: we use the definition of the gradient through its relation to the directional derivative,

$$\nabla_P \tilde{\Delta}_P^2([Z_1], [Z_2]) \cdot X = \mathrm{tr}(\nabla_P \tilde{\Delta}_P^2([Z_1], [Z_2])X),$$

and the fact that the trace of the product of a symmetric and an anti-symmetric matrix is always zero, to write the gradient $\nabla_P \tilde{\Delta}_P^2([Z_1], [Z_2])$ as the symmetric $n \times n$ matrix

$$\nabla_P \tilde{\Delta}_P^2([Z_1], [Z_2]) = Z_1 Z_1^t + Z_2 Z_2^t$$
$$- \frac{\mathrm{tr}(Z_2^t P Z_1)(Z_1 Z_2^t + Z_2 Z_1^t) + \mathrm{tr}(J Z_2^t P Z_1)(Z_1 J Z_2^t - Z_2 J Z_1^t)}{\sqrt{(\mathrm{tr}(Z_2^t P Z_1))^2 + (\mathrm{tr}(J Z_2^t P Z_1))^2}}. \tag{3}$$

## 3  Metric Learning

Our metric learning algorithm is based on the *Average neighborhood margin maximization* (ANMM) [13]. Given data belonging to different classes, this algorithm aims to maximize the within-class similarity and the inter-class separability. This objective is achieved through exploiting two sets of neighbors; homogeneous neighborhood $\mathcal{N}_s^P(i)$ and heterogeneous neighborhood $\mathcal{N}_o^P(i)$.

Let $\mathcal{Z} := \{Z_1, \ldots, Z_N\}$ be the set of all training points. For each point $(Z_i, y_i)$, with $y_i$ the label of the class of $Z_i$, and for $K_s$ and $K_o$ two parameters, we define two sets of neighbors:

- Homogeneous neighborhood $\mathcal{N}_s^P(i)$ is the set of the $K_s$ nearest neighbors of $Z_i$ (excluding $Z_i$ itself), that belong to the same class as $Z_i$, for the distance (1).
- Heterogeneous neighborhood $\mathcal{N}_o^P(i)$ is the set of the $K_o$ nearest neighbors of $Z_i$, that belong to other classes than $Z_i$, for the distance (1).

Accordingly, the cost function for our metric learning is given by the average neighborhood margin:

$$cost(P) = \sum_{i \in \mathcal{N}} \frac{1}{K_{Cl(i)}} (C_s(i) - C_o(i)), \tag{4}$$

where,

$$C_s(i) = \frac{1}{K_s} \sum_{j \in \mathcal{N}_s^P(i)} \tilde{\Delta}_P^2([Z_i], [Z_j]),$$

and,

$$C_o(i) = \frac{1}{K_o} \sum_{j \in \mathcal{N}_o^P(i)} \tilde{\Delta}_P^2([Z_i], [Z_j]).$$

$K_{Cl(i)}$ is the number of points of the training set associated to the class of the training point $Z_i$. This helps in the situation of unbalanced classes.

Due to the dependence of the sets $\mathcal{N}_s^P(i)$ and $\mathcal{N}_o^P(i)$ on the variable $P$, the cost function is nonsmooth. However, at each iteration (for fixed sets $\mathcal{N}_s^P(i)$ and $\mathcal{N}_o^P(i)$), we can compute the gradient:

$$\nabla_P(cost(P)) = \sum_{i \in \mathcal{N}} \frac{1}{K_{Cl(i)}} (\nabla_P(C_s(i)) - \nabla_P(C_o(i))), \tag{5}$$

where,

$$\nabla_P(C_s(i)) = \frac{1}{K_s} \sum_{j \in \mathcal{N}_s^P(i)} \nabla_P \tilde{\Delta}_P^2([Z_i], [Z_j]),$$

and,

$$\nabla_P(C_o(i)) = \frac{1}{K_o} \sum_{j \in \mathcal{N}_o^P(i)} \nabla_P \tilde{\Delta}_P^2([Z_i], [Z_j]).$$

There are many possible neighbors for each sample, However, randomly choosing these neighbors can greatly slow the convergence. Therefore, It is crucial to carefully chose the neighbors that will contribute effectively to the optimization. To tackle this problem, we select for each sample $Z_i$ its hard neighbors $Z_s$ and $Z_o$. These neighbors are defined by, $\arg\max_{\mathcal{N}_s^P(i)} \Delta_P^2([Z_s], [Z_i])$ for hard homogeneous neighbors, and $\arg\max_{\mathcal{N}_o^P(i)} \Delta_P^2([Z^o], [Z_i])$ for hard heterogeneous ones.

## 4  Experiments

In order to evaluate the discriminative ability of our proposed metric, we conducted experiments on facial expressions recognition based on this metric. In what follows, we introduce the representation adopted to model 2D facial expressions, the manner in which we classify these representations in $\mathcal{S}_c^+(2, n)$ based on our learned metric. Finally, we report the experimental setting and discuss our results.

### 4.1  Formulation of Facial Expression Recognition in $\mathcal{S}^+(d, n)$

Let us consider the configurations $Z = [p_1, p_2, ..., p_n]$ of facial landmark points in two dimensional space given by, $p_1 = (x_1, y_1), ..., p_n = (x_n, y_n)$. A robust facial shape representation that is invariant up to rotation and translation was proposed in [4]. This representation is constructed by firstly centring the landmarks configurations, by subtracting the center of mass from their coordinates. Then, computing their associated Gram matrix $G$, defined by, $G = ZZ^T$, where the entries of $G$ are the pairwise inner products of the points $p_1, ..., p_n$. This representation is a positive semi-definite matrix belonging to the positive semi-definite cone $\mathcal{S}^+(d, n)$. In our experiments, we exploit this representation to model facial expression in $\mathcal{S}^+(d, n)$. This allows us to use our metric defined in $\mathcal{S}_c^+(2, n)$ to measure similarities between different facial expressions and classify them.

Regarding the classification, we adopted a multi-class SVM with a Gaussian kernel. For more clarity, we provide in Algorithm 1 a summary of steps needed to classify a test expression sample using our metric.

### 4.2  Experimental Setting

The proposed metric was evaluated on facial expression recognition using a publicly available dataset commonly used in the state of the art. To extract facial landmarks, we have used the method proposed in [14] that provides 68 facial landmarks. As a pre-processing, all landmarks were normalized by subtracting

---

**Algorithm 1:** Metric learning in $\mathcal{S}^+(d, n)$ and classification of test sample with the learned metric.

---

**Data**: $N_{tr}$ training samples $\mathcal{Z} = \{(Z^i, y^i)\}_1^{N_{tr}}$ with their associated labels, testing sample $Z_{test}$, $K_o$, $K_s$ numbers of s/o neighbors.

**Result**: $Y_{test}$ Predicted label of $Z_{test}$

/* Optimization                                                          */
1  $P \leftarrow I(n)$, identity matrix of dimension $n$. ;
2  **for** $i = 1 \ldots N_{tr}$ **do**
3  | Define $\mathcal{N}_s^P(i)$ and $\mathcal{N}_o^P(i)$ for each sample $Z^i$ using the metric in Eq. 1 ;
   **end**
4  $Cost \leftarrow cost(P, \mathcal{N}_s^P, \mathcal{N}_o^P)$, $cost(.)$ is given by Eq.4;
5  $Grad \leftarrow grad(P, \mathcal{N}_s^P, \mathcal{N}_o^P)$, $grad(.)$ is given by Equ.5;
6  $P_{op} \leftarrow SteepestDescent(P, Cost, Grad)$, $SteepestDescent(.)$ is the steepest descent optimization algorithm in $\mathcal{S}^+(2, n)$;
   /* Classification                                                      */
7  **for** $j = 1 \ldots N_{tr}$ **do**
8  | **for** $k = 1 \ldots N_{tr}$ **do**
9  | | $K_{tr}(j, k) = distance(P_{op}, Z^j, Z^k)$, $distance(.)$ is given by Eq. 1;
   | **end**
10 | $K_{tst}(k) = distance(P_{op}, Z^j, Z_{test})$, $distance(.)$ is given by Eq. 1;
   **end**
11 Train SVM using kernel $K_{tr}$;
12 $Y_{test} \leftarrow$ SVM using vector $K_{tst}$;

---

the center of mass from the coordinates and then dividing into the standard deviation. The parameters involved by SVM and the Gaussian kernel were set using cross validation with grid search. The number of neighbors used by average neighborhood margin maximization (ANMM) algorithm was set empirically. In Fig. 2, we present the effect of neighbors number used by ANMM on the facial expression recognition accuracy. Based on this experiment, the number of neighbors was set to $K_s = K_o = 5$. The optimization was performed using the framework proposed in [15] with the classical first-order steepest descent algorithm using the cost function and the gradient given by Eq. 1 and 3, respectively.

### 4.3 Datasets

**Cohn-Kanade Extended (CK+) Dataset** [16]. This dataset, is one of the mostly used facial expressions databases. It contains 123 subjects and 593 frontal image sequences of posed expressions. Among them, 118 subjects are annotated with the seven facial expression labels – *anger, contempt, disgust, fear, happy, sad* and *surprise*. Note that each sequence starts with a neutral expression, and reaches the peak expression in the last frame. Following the state-of-the-art experimental setting [2,17], all our reported results on this dataset were obtained with ten-fold subjects-independent cross validation after ordering subjects by their ID in ascending order.

**Table 1.** Overall accuracy (Acc %) on CK+ dataset of our optimal solution compared to the Identity matrix using different number of peak frames.

| # peak frames | Acc (%) Id. matrix | Acc (%) learned metric |
|---|---|---|
| 1 | 85.53 | **90.53** |
| 3 | 83.05 | **88.24** |
| 5 | 84.80 | **87.43** |

From each sequence, we exploit only the peak frames where the expression attains its peak. We tried different numbers of peak frames (for 1 to 5 peak frames) and their labels were assigned according to the label of the sequence.

## 4.4   Results and Discussion

As first analysis, we investigate the performance of using the metric learning to learn the optimal metric. To this end, we compare results obtained with the learned metric and the metric with the parameter $P = I$, where I is the identity matrix of size $n$. In Table 1, we provide the obtained accuracies with the optimal solution and the identity matrix when using one, three and five last peak frames from each sequence. According to these results, the metric learned achieves significant improvement over the identity matrix, with a gain of around 5%, which demonstrates the effectiveness of the proposed representation and the importance of the metric learning step in our method.

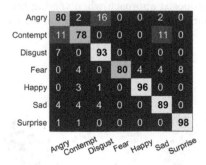

**Fig. 1.** Confusion Matrix of CK+ dataset.

We report in Fig. 1 the confusion matrix obtained for CK+ dataset. The confusion matrix reported here is obtained with the best results in Table 2. Our approach is able to recognize the majority of the emotions with an accuracy that surpasses 90% except contempt (78%), sadness (80%) and fear (80%). This is explained by the relatively small number of samples corresponding to these emotions with respect to the other classes in CK+ dataset.

In Fig. 3, we show a 2D visualization of the CK+ data using t-SNE algorithm [18] based on our proposed metric with the optimal solution. This visualization shows that the metric proposed can differentiate different classes, while keeping close the emotions that share some interclass similarities. Surprise, happiness and disgust are easily distinguished, while contempt, sadness and fear are close and interfere between each other. These results are consistent with the reported confusion matrix in Fig. 1.

In Table 2 we provide a comparison of our proposed approach with the state-of-the-art facial expression recognition. In order to provide a fair comparison, we exclude the recent works based on appearance features and we compare our work here only with geometric methods that perform facial expression from facial landmarks. Overall, our approach achieves competitive performance with respect to the most compared approaches. On CK+ we obtained the third highest accuracy 90.53%. The best accuracy was obtained by Kacem et al. [2]. However, their metric involves a parameter $k$ to carefully be chosen for each dataset (For more details, we refer the reader to Fig. 3 in [4]).

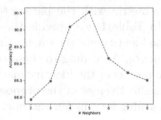

**Fig. 2.** Accuracy of the proposed approach when varying the number of neighbors for Average neighborhood margin maximization algorithm for CK+ dataset.

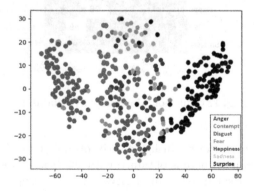

**Fig. 3.** 2D visualization of CK+ data using t-SNE using our proposed metric.

**Table 2.** Comparison with State-of-the-art solutions on CK+ dataset.

| Method | CK+ |
|---|---|
| Taheri et al. [19] | 82.80 |
| Jain et al. [20] | 85.84 |
| Wang et al. [21] | 86.30 |
| Tanfous et al. [17] *Intrinsic SCDL* | 89.43 |
| Tanfous et al. [17] *Extrinsic SCDL* | 95.73 |
| Kacem et al. [2] | **96.87** |
| Identity Matrix (ours) | 85.53 |
| Optimal solution (ours) | **90.53** |

# 5   Conclusion

We have shown in this paper that the manifold of oriented ellipses centered at the origin in Euclidean n-space is equivalent to the quotient manifold $\mathbb{R}_*^{n\times 2}/SO_2$. Taking advantage of this equivalence we learn with a metric learning algorithm a new metric on this manifold which is discriminative enough to classify landmarks representations. Our experiments on facial expression recognition from 2D facial landmarks showed that the proposed approach gives comparative results to those of the literature. In Future work, we aim to explore how to generalize our proposed metric in $\mathcal{S}_c^+(2,n)$ to $\mathcal{S}_c^+(d,n)$. Moreover, we can target new applications such as action recognition from temporal 3D skeletons.

**Acknowledgment.** The proposed work was partially supported by the French State, managed by the National Agency for Research (ANR) under the Investments for the future program with reference ANR-16-IDEX-0004 ULNE.

# References

1. Szczapa, B., Daoudi, M., Berretti, S., Bimbo, A.D., Pala, P., Massart, E.M.: Fitting, comparison, and alignment of trajectories on positive semi-definite matrices with application to action recognition. In: 2019 IEEE/CVF International Conference on Computer Vision Workshops, ICCV Workshops 2019, Seoul, Korea (South), 27–28 October 2019, pp. 1241–1250 (2019)
2. Kacem, A., Daoudi, M., Ben Amor, B., Berretti, S., Alvarez-Paiva, J.C.: A novel geometric framework on Gram matrix trajectories for human behavior understanding. IEEE Trans. Pattern Anal. Mach. Intell. **42**(1), 1–14 (2020)
3. NOtberdout, N., Kacem, A., Daoudi, M., Ballihi, L., Berretti, S.: Automatic analysis of facial expressions based on deep covariance trajectories. IEEE Trans. Neural Netw. Learn. Syst. **31**, 3892–3905 (2019)
4. Kacem, A., Daoudi, M., Ben Amor, B., Alvarez-Paiva, J.C.: A novel space-time representation on the positive semidefinite cone for facial expression recognition. In: IEEE International Conference on Computer Vision, ICCV 2017, Venice, Italy, 22–29 October 2017, pp. 3199–3208 (2017)
5. Abdel-Ghaffar, E.A., Daoudi, M.: Emotion recognition from multidimensional electroencephalographic signals on the manifold of symmetric positive definite matrices. In: IEEE Conference on Multimedia Information Processing and Retrieval (MIPR) 2020, pp. 354–359 (2020)

6. Daoudi, M., Hammal, Z., Kacem, A., Cohn, J.F.: Gram matrices formulation of body shape motion: an application for depression severity assessment. In: 2019 8th International Conference on Affective Computing and Intelligent Interaction Workshops and Demos (ACIIW), pp. 258–263 (2019)
7. Huang, Z., Wang, R., Shan, S., Chen, X.: Projection metric learning on Grassmann manifold with application to video based face recognition. In: Proceedings of the IEEE Conference on Computer Vision and Pattern Recognition, pp. 140–149 (2015)
8. Zadeh, P., Hosseini, R., Sra, S.: Geometric mean metric learning. In: International Conference on Machine Learning, pp. 2464–2471 (2016)
9. Bonnabel, S., Sepulchre, R.: Riemannian metric and geometric mean for positive semidefinite matrices of fixed rank. SIAM J. Matrix Anal. Appl. **31**(3), 1055–1070 (2010)
10. Massart, E.M., Hendrickx, J.M., Absil, P.-A.: Matrix geometric means based on shuffled inductive sequences. Linear Algebra Appl. **542**, 334–359 (2018)
11. Massart, E., Hendrickx, J.M., Absil, P.-A.: Curvature of the manifold of fixed-rank positive-semidefinite matrices endowed with the Bures–Wasserstein metric. In: Nielsen, F., Barbaresco, F. (eds.) GSI 2019. LNCS, vol. 11712, pp. 739–748. Springer, Cham (2019). https://doi.org/10.1007/978-3-030-26980-7_77
12. Massart, E., Absil, P.-A.: Quotient geometry with simple geodesics for the manifold of fixed-rank positive-semidefinite matrices. SIAM J. Matrix Anal. Appl. **41**(1), 171–198 (2020)
13. Wang, F., Zhang, C.: Feature extraction by maximizing the average neighborhood margin. In: IEEE Conference on Computer Vision and Pattern Recognition, pp. 1–8 (2007)
14. Baltrusaitis, T., Zadeh, A., Lim, Y.C., Morency, L.-P.: OpenFace 2.0: facial behavior analysis toolkit. In: 13th IEEE International Conference on Automatic Face & Gesture Recognition, pp. 59–66 (2018)
15. Townsend, J., Koep, N., Weichwald, S.: Pymanopt: a python toolbox for optimization on manifolds using automatic differentiation. J. Mach. Learn. Res. **17**(137), 1–5 (2016)
16. Lucey, P., Cohn, J.F., Kanade, T., Saragih, J.M., Ambadar, Z., Matthews, I.A.: The extended Cohn-Kanade dataset (CK+): a complete dataset for action unit and emotion-specified expression. In: IEEE Conference on Computer Vision and Pattern Recognition Workshop (CVPRW), pp. 94–101 (2010)
17. Tanfous, A.B., Drira, H., Amor, B.B.: Sparse coding of shape trajectories for facial expression and action recognition. IEEE Trans. Pattern Anal. Mach. Intell. **42**(10), 2594–2607 (2019)
18. Van der Maaten, L., Hinton, G.: Visualizing data using t-SNE. J. Mach. Learn. Res. **9**, 2579–2605 (2008)
19. Taheri, S., Turaga, P., Chellappa, R.: Towards view-invariant expression analysis using analytic shape manifolds. IEEE Face Gesture **2011**, 306–313 (2011)
20. Jain, S., Hu, C., Aggarwal, J.K.: Facial expression recognition with temporal modeling of shapes. In: IEEE International Conference on Computer Vision Workshops (ICCV Workshops) 2011, pp. 1642–1649 (2011)
21. Wang, Z., Wang, S., Ji, Q.: Capturing complex spatio-temporal relations among facial muscles for facial expression recognition. In: Proceedings of the IEEE Conference on Computer Vision and Pattern Recognition, pp. 3422–3429 (2013)
22. Szczapa, B., Daoudi, M., Berretti, S., Pala, P., Del Bimbo, A., Hammal Z.: Automatic estimation of self-reported pain by interpretable representations of motion dynamics (2020). arXiv preprint arXiv:2006.13882

# MANPU - The 4th International Workshop on coMics ANalysis, Processing and Understanding

# The 4th International Workshop on coMics ANalysis, Processing and Understanding (MANPU2020)

## Workshop Description

MANPU is the main workshop related to comics. It gathers mainly researchers in the field of computer science, but also some researchers in the field of human sciences. Comics is a medium constituted of images combined with text and graphic information in order to narrate a story. Nowadays, comic books are a widespread cultural expression all over the world. The market of comics, and especially the market of digital comics continues to grow. For example, the market in Japan is about 5.5 billion USD, 1.2 million USD in the US and 500 million € in France. The part of the digital market has reached respectively 2 billion USD, 200 million USD and 7 million € in these countries. From a research point of view, comics images are attractive targets because the structure of a comics page includes various elements (such as panels, speech balloons, captions, leading characters, and so on), the drawing of which depends on the style of the author and presents a large variability. Therefore comics image analysis is not a trivial problem and is still immature compared with other kinds of image analysis. Moreover, digital comics such as webtoons introduce new challenges in terms of analysis and indexing.

In 2016, we held the 1st MANPU in Cancun, Mexico in conjunction with ICPR 2016. We received 17 submissions and accepted 12 papers (acceptance rate: 70%). MANPU 2016 consisted of one invited talk, two oral sessions (6 presentations), one poster session (6 posters), and one panel discussion. MANPU 2016 involved researchers from seven countries. In 2017, we held the 2nd MANPU in Kyoto, Japan in conjunction with ICDAR 2017.We received 18 submissions and accepted 12 papers (acceptance rate: 70%). MANPU 2017 consisted of two oral sessions (6 presentations), two invited talks, and one poster session (6 posters). As a characteristic point, the latter part of MANPU 2017 was held in Kyoto International Manga Museum near to conference place. Moreover, one invited speaker was the person of digital manga publishing company. MANPU 2017 involved researchers from nine countries. In 2019, we held the 3rd MANPU in Thessaloniki, Greece in conjunction with MMM 2019. We received 8 submissions and accepted 6 papers (acceptance rate: 75%). MANPU 2019 consisted of two oral sessions (6 presentations) and one invited talk. The invited speaker was the Director of the Cultural Programmation of "Cité de l'Image et de la Bandes Dessinés" including a museum, a heritage library, a specialized public library, a documentation center, an international artists' residence, and so on. The invited talk was quite unique and fruitful. MANPU 2019 involved researchers from seven countries.

This year we received 5 submissions for reviews, from authors belonging to 4 distinct countries. After an accurate and thorough peer-review process, we selected 4 papers for presentation at the workshop. MANPU 2020 involved researchers from eight countries.

Last but not least, we would like to thank the MANPU 2020 Program Committee, whose members made the workshop possible with their precise and prompt review process. We would also like to thank ICPR 2020 staffs for hosting the workshop, and the ICPR workshop/publication chairs for the valuable help and support.

January 2021

Jean-Christophe Burie
Motoi Iwata
Miki Ueno
Rita Hartel
Yusuke Matsui
Tien-Tsin Wong

# Organization

## General Co-chairs

Jean-Christophe Burie      University of La Rochelle, France
Motoi Iwata      Osaka Prefecture University, Japan
Miki Ueno      Osaka Institute of Technology, Japan

## Program Co-chairs

Rita Hartel      Paderborn University, Germany
Yusuke Matsui      National Institute of Informatics, Japan
Tien-Tsin Wong      The Chinese University of Hong Kong,
     Hong Kong

## Advisory Board

Kiyoharu Aizawa      The University of Tokyo, Japan
Koichi Kise      Osaka Prefecture University, Japan
Jean-Marc Ogier      University of La Rochelle, France
Toshihiko Yamasaki      The University of Tokyo, Japan

## Program Committee

John Bateman      University of Bremen, Germany
Ying Cao      City University of Hong Kong, Hong Kong
Wei-Ta Chu      National Chung Cheng University, Taiwan
Mathieu Delalandre      Tours University, France
Alexander Dunst      Paderborn University, Germany
Seiji Hotta      Tokyo University of Agriculture and
     Technology, Japan
Rynson W. H. Lau      City University of Hong Kong, Hong Kong
Jochen Laubrock      University of Potsdam, Germany
Tong-Yee Lee      National Cheng-Kung University, Taiwan
Mitsunori Matsushita      Kansai University, Japan
Tetsuya Mihara      University of Tsukuba, Japan
Muhammad Muzzamil Luqman      University of La Rochelle, France
Mitsuharu Nagamori      University of Tsukuba, Japan

# An OCR Pipeline and Semantic Text Analysis for Comics

Rita Hartel[(✉)] and Alexander Dunst

Paderborn University, Warburger Straße 100, 33098 Paderborn, Germany
rst@upb.de, dunst@mail.upb.de

**Abstract.** Optical character recognition has remained a challenge for comics, given the high variability of placement of text on the page, the wide variety of frequently handwritten fonts, and the limited availability and small size of datasets. This paper reports on currently on-going work on an OCR pipeline that includes text spotting with the help of a U-Net based fully convolutional neural network and OCR training with the open-source software Calamari, which was performed on the "Graphic Narrative Corpus" of book-length graphic novels written in English. Based on the results of the OCR training, we then present an analysis of the textual properties of 129 graphic novels correlated with page length, historical development, and genre affiliation.

**Keywords:** Comics · Graphic novels · OCR · Text spotting · Semantic analysis

## 1 Introduction: Context & Previous Work

Computational comics analysis has made significant strides in recent years (for a recent overview see [1]), both in document analysis and content generation. While automated text recognition has become routine for many types of documents, however, it represents an on-going challenge for comics and its subtypes, from comic strips and Japanese manga to French bande dessinée and graphic novels. Figure 1 shows some examples of texts within captions or balloons of a graphic novel that are difficult to detect automatically. There are several reasons for this status quo: Both visually and textually, comics are characterized by the high variability typical of artistic production. Text fonts, the types of texts used, and their placement on the page may differ from one strip or book to another, or even within a single work. Traditionally, text was handwritten by authors or, in the case of more industrially-produced comics, by specialized letterers. Today, they are as likely to be digitized by using samples of such handwriting, or produced from existing fonts that aim to give the impression of being handwritten, particularly in translation or in serial comics.

The variability of text fonts extends to text types. Speech and thought representation are usually placed inside balloons that indicate their source via a tail. In addition, onomatopoeia, or sequences of letters that imitate sounds, and diegetic text—from street signs to characters reading newspapers—may be found anywhere on the comics page. Graphic novels further include a substantial amount of narrative text, commonly placed

A. Del Bimbo et al. (Eds.): ICPR 2020 Workshops, LNCS 12666, pp. 213–222, 2021.
https://doi.org/10.1007/978-3-030-68780-9_19

in captions. As indicated, there are graphic conventions for these different types, but authors may choose to disregard them to make stylistic statements or pursue narrative goals. Because some of these conventions and their application differ significantly between subtypes, the transfer of heuristics presents significant difficulties. Similarly, pretrained OCR engines based on neural network architectures lead to relatively high error rates [2]. As a direct consequence, semantic and syntactic text analysis has remained unusually limited for these documents, drawing on small sets of manually annotated texts or so-called paratexts, such as letters to the editor [3, 4]. Based on a preliminary version of the OCR pipeline presented below, Hartel & Dunst presented an exploratory bag-of-words based analysis of a small number of graphic novels written in English [5].

**Fig. 1.** Examples for texts in graphic novels that are hard to detect automatically

To the best of our knowledge, no information on even the basic textual properties of comics text is currently available. Among other potential uses, such data would allow for a comparison with other textual or multimodal media, from films and television to novels and dramatic plays, or within the aforementioned subtypes of comics. This information can also be used to compare visual and textual features, the two semiotic modes present in most comics. In a step towards the further document analysis of this medium, the paper details the construction of an OCR pipeline via a U-Net based page segmentation recently developed by Dubray & Laubrock [6] and the open-source OCR software Calamari [7], trained on the Graphic Narrative Corpus," which currently consists of 255 book-length graphic novels [8]. Some of the visual properties of this copyright-protected corpus had been analyzed in an earlier paper [9], but automatic text recognition and analysis had heretofore eluded us. We then report on the methodology and results of the OCR training for a sample of 131 graphic novels from the GNC. Finally, we include an overview of basic textual properties and an analysis of the textual complexity of different genres contained in the GNC.

## 2 Methodology and Dataset

Two basic avenues exist for optical character recognition. Bottom-up approaches aim at separating text from graphic elements without prior page segmentation. This has the advantage that text types such onomatopoeia or diegetic text that do not follow established graphic conventions in their placement may more easily be included in recognition tasks. However, this approach has led to high error rates in the past [2]. Here we follow the opposite path, that is to say, we begin with page segmentation but exclude onomatopoeia and diegetic text. This decision is motivated by the expectation that prior segmentation will lead to better recognition results but also accords with the specific properties of the documents under discussion. Graphic novels are book-length comics, often running to a length of several hundred pages. As their name implies, they share some properties of other print literature, including a large amount of narrative text. Onomatopoeia plays a much smaller role than in manga and related traditions. While diegetic text helps create atmosphere and may contain clues for detailed interpretation, it is usually of little importance for an understanding of the story.

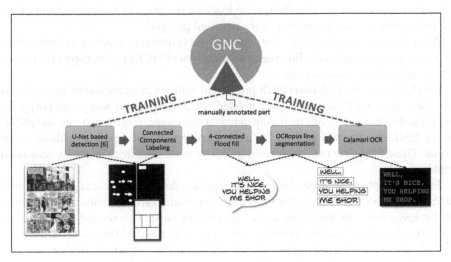

**Fig. 2.** Pipeline for automated GNML annotation

For page segmentation, Dubray & Laubrock employed a U-Net-based fully neural network model that distinguishes between speech balloons, captions, and panels. This architecture was trained on 3,430 manually annotated pages taken from 200 graphic novels in the GNC [8]. The F1 scores were 95% for speech balloons, 91.8% for captions, and 98.6% for panels, significantly above the results reported by Nguyen et al. [10].

In a first phase, we then train Calamari OCR [7] on a training set consisting of 12,838 lines of text extracted from the manually annotated pages. We chose Calamari over the LSTM-based Tesseract, as in our preliminary tests Calamari achieved better results. We evaluated the training with a test set consisting of 4,726 lines of text (i.e., 80% training data and 20% test data).

Figure 2 shows how the pipeline automatically generates GNML annotations for scans of graphic images. Input to the pipeline is a scan in form of a PNG image. The **U-NET based detection** uses Dubray & Laubrock's model that classifies which pixels in the scanned graphic novels are part of a panel, a caption, a balloon, or belong to other components of the comics image. In more precise terms, the output of the trained system are three bitmaps: one for panels, one for captions, and one for speech balloons. Each pixel has a (grayscale) value between 0 and 255, where the higher the value, the higher the probability that the pixel belongs to the specified class (panel, caption, balloon).

These bitmaps are analyzed in a post-processing step. We first perform **Connected Component Labeling**, i.e., we search for connected components within the bitmaps. Looking specifically at the background of the black-and-white version of the original scan, we then perform a **4-connected flood-fill** approach on each connected component within the bitmap. This process leads to more precise shapes than if we based our analysis only on the machine learning approach. In order to produce input for the next step in the pipeline—OCR with the help of the trained Calamari model—we removed noise that is likely to belong to the border of the speech balloon or the caption. For this step, we once again employed the 4-connected flood-fill approach to remove all areas that consist of border pixels (in most cases these were black in the black-and-white version of the original scan) that touch the border of the detected polygon.

After extracting the polygons that included the text objects (caption or balloon) as binary images, we applied the **line segmentation tool of OCRopus/ocropy** [12] to split these images into separate text lines.

Finally, the trained **Calamari OCR** proceeded with detecting the text within each text line image. After OCR processing is completed, all of the retrieved data (panel polygons, caption and balloon polygons including detected text) were transformed into an GNML file, an XML dialect developed for the analysis of the graphic novels contained in our corpus. These files were then analyzed together with the data from manually annotated graphic novels.

In a second phase, we extended the OCR pipeline described above to graphic novels that had not yet been annotated. Automated analyses were corrected manually, which was still far less effort than annotating text completely by hand. This second phase resulted in an extended training set of 58,608 lines and a test set of 14,597 lines of texts. Training yielded an average character error rate of 3,47% on the test set. In further semantic analyses for a digital humanities project, we focus on methods that are performed not on the texts themselves but on the bag-of-words for individual graphic novels, meaning that word order does not matter. As a consequence, we measure the overall quality of the OCR system in terms of what we call the Bag Error Rate (BER) instead of the more character or word error rates [5]. The BER is computed by comparing the bag-of-words of the original text and of the recognized text, calculating the number of different entries, and dividing it by the total number of words contained in the original text. Figure 3 shows a histogram of the BER for phases 1 and 2. As can be seen from the leftward movement on the X-axis of the histogram, the BER decreased significantly as we moved from phase 1 to phase 2 in the OCR pipeline, with the vast majority of texts now showing an error rate between 0–20% and occurrences of very high error rates much lower than was the case after phase 1. In our pipeline, text lines are often read in the wrong sequence due to the shape of individual balloons. Therefore, one frequent error concerns incorrect word order. Consequently, the CER is a bit worse than the BER. Yet, the overall trend in phase 2 is similar, as evidenced by the significant leftward movement after phase 2 that results in an average CER of 28%.

# 3   OCR Pipeline: Results and Discussion

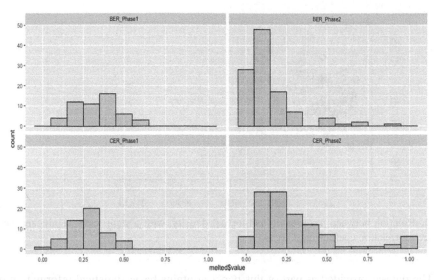

**Fig. 3.** Comparison of BER (Bag Error Rate, top) and CER (Character Error Rate, bottom) after phase 1 (left) and after phase 2 (right)

Of the 255 full-length graphic novels currently available as retro-digitized book scans in the GNC, we have manual annotations of the entire text in captions and balloons for 15 graphic novels, plus further annotations of roughly 10% of the pages of 106 graphic novels. After the first phase of the pipeline, we semi-automatically annotated 10% of the pages of 25 additional graphic novels. That is to say, we ran our trained system to produce automatic text annotations and checked them for accuracy manually. Automatic annotations that had few errors were then corrected by hand to add to the training set.

We used the partial annotations of these 131 graphic novels to evaluate the quality of our automatic annotations and computed that 70 of these met our conditions for further semantic text analysis. In addition to publication in North America, either in translation or in the original English, these requirements include that at least 80% of the objects (panels, caption, balloons) were recognized correctly and that the BER amounted to less than 20%. While earlier tests [5] showed that bag-of-words analyses can produce meaningful results starting at a BER of up to 50%, the higher threshold was chosen to meet recognition rates comparable to those used in research on major text formats, from historical newspapers to other print literature. Furthermore, we computed automated annotations for the remaining graphic novels for which no ground truth existed. 10% of the pages were manually checked by trained research assistants to see whether most of the objects (once again around 80%) were detected correctly and whether the OCR confidence for these texts reached a minimum of 80%. In total, 114 automated annotations fulfilled our quality requirements. To these were added 15 manually annotated graphic novels. Taken together, then, 129 texts were used for the analysis of textual properties described below.

## 4   Some Textual Properties of 129 Graphic Novels

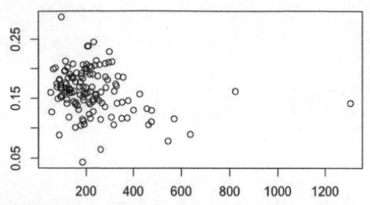

**Fig. 4.** Relation between page length and textual density, with a statistically significant weak negative correlation coefficient of –0.244

The dataset provided as part of this paper contains basic statistical information on the textual properties of 129 graphic novels. This information is given for each page of these book-length graphic novels (29,926 pages in total), with the exception of pages that only contain bibliographical or additional texts such as forewords and do not contribute to the overall narrative. Pages are numbered starting with the cover page of each graphic novel. Bibliographic information, including the ISBN numbers that enable identification of the editions used for digitization, are available in a separate database. The linguistic measurements include: syllable and sentence length, the number of unique words, normalized type-token ratio (cttr), and the number of words per page. While the first are standard measurements in computational linguistics, the last makes use of the single comics page as a stable, functional and semantic, unit. The data was extracted from the full text using the text analysis package KoRpus [11] and can be downloaded from our homepage.[1]

For our text analyses, we further calculated a complexity score for each graphic novel, consisting of the averages of syllable and sentence length, cttr, and words per page. The first two are widely used to calculate the readability of written text, for instance in the Gunning Fog index and Flesh reading ease test. Sentence length and variants of normalized type-token ratio have also become standard measures in the digital humanities, specifically in digital literary studies [13, 14]. Finally, the number of words per page was added because cognitive studies of comics have shown that text consumes the vast majority of a reader's attention, with the time spent looking at panels increasing with the amount of text [15]. The complexity scores were then correlated with information about page length, year of publication, and genre affiliation, which can be found in the aforementioned GNC database. Figure 4 shows a weak inverse relationship between page length and textual density. In other words, the more page numbers a title has, the

---

[1] https://groups.uni-paderborn.de/graphic-literature/gncorpus/TextFeaturesGNC.csv.zip.

lower its textual density will be. This accords with recent studies that have found a similarly negative correlation between the complexity of novels and the productivity of their authors [16].

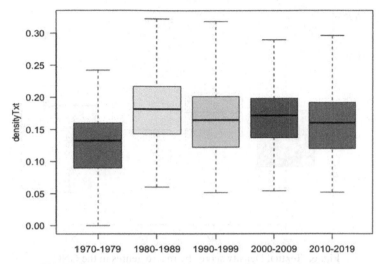

**Fig. 5.** Textual Density scores of 129 graphic novels by decade

Graphic novels have steadily increased their page length over the last two decades, a development that has come at a time when they are dominantly sold through general market bookstores rather than specialized comic shops. As the combination of Fig. 4 and Fig. 5 indicates, this has led to lower textual complexity, both in relation to page length and during the last decade. A possible reason could lie in the attempt to appeal to readers that are not used to the complex text-image combinations found in comics and might struggle with the cognitive demands placed on them as a consequence. However, more detailed study will be needed to support this or other potential explanations.

Genre affiliation has been shown to constitute an influential determinant for the visual style of comics [9]. The analysis of textual complexity shows this to be the case for its linguistic components as well. Figure 6 compares four large groups represented in the GNC: graphic fantasy, an umbrella term for the genres of superhero, science fiction, fantasy, and horror narratives; graphic memoirs; graphic novels in the narrow sense of literary fiction in the comics medium; and other non-fiction, specifically graphic journalism, travel narratives, and historical non-fiction. It is this last group which records the highest textual complexity. Graphic non-fiction is followed by graphic memoirs. Somewhat surprisingly, the fictional genre of the graphic novel features the second-lowest textual complexity, a result that goes against common assumptions about the particular complexity of more prestigious texts. However, Jannidis, Konle, and Leinen had already found that literary novels are not necessarily more complex linguistically than dime novels [13]. Our results support this view and extend it to book-length comics. Less surprising, perhaps, is the complexity score of the popular genres classed as graphic fantasy: These are narratives of visual spectacle and show a significantly lower investment in complex texts.

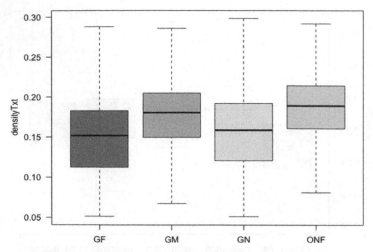

**Fig. 6.** Textual Density scores by macro genres in the GNC

## 5   Conclusion and Future Work

In this paper, we presented an OCR pipeline that builds on prior work on text spotting for comics and the open-source OCR software Calamari, which was then trained on the GNC. The results show that optical character recognition for comics and graphic novels has now reached a point where it can lead to meaningful analysis of comics text beyond manually-annotated datasets. Given the specific challenges of comics as a document type, this pipeline involves significant post-processing steps and currently excludes onomatopoeia and diegetic background text. The significant error rates and the exclusion of almost half of the corpus even with the comparatively low threshold chosen for this paper also indicate that much work remains to be done. This future research includes training the neural network architecture employed for text spotting in this paper to recognize onomatopoeia and diegetic text as additional classes. Further training with larger training sets, time-intensive manual correction of OCR results, and the refinement of available OCR software are likely to form part of future improvements in text recognition for comics as well. Beyond these immediate steps, the production of synthetic training data may offer a way to overcome copyright restrictions and the limited representativeness of existing but small data sets.

As this discussion indicates, a significant factor in these on-going challenges continues to be the limited availability of publicly accessible datasets. Unfortunately, the GNC is no exception in this regard, given that all included works are protected by copyright. In addition to prohibiting the dissemination of the retro-digitized scans, these restrictions also mean that we currently cannot share the OCR model developed for this paper. However, variants of semantic text analysis may proceed without full texts of copyrighted works becoming available if detailed statistical information is provided on a page-by-page level instead. Such text segments are usually chosen on the basis of word length for print literature such as novels or plays. The fact that individual pages represent a stable, basic unit for comics makes identification of text segments, and comparison with the visual components of specific pages, far easier. Such data is not subject to copyright restrictions because the original works cannot be reconstructed on this basis and therefore represents one avenue of sharing research results. The data provided as part of this paper makes a first step in this direction. Given the needs of different communities within computer science and related disciplines, for instance in graphic document analysis, machine learning, and the digital humanities, this can only be a partial solution. Others will have to be found for research on copyrighted comics to advance further in the coming years.

# References

1. Laubrock, J., Dunst, A.: Computational approaches to comics analysis. Top. Cogn. Sci. **12**(1), 1–37 (2020). https://doi.org/10.1111/tops.12476
2. Rigaud, C., Burie, J., Ogier, J.: Segmentation-free speech text recognition for comic books. In: 14th IAPR International Conference on Document Analysis and Recognition, vol. 3, pp. 29–34. IEEE, Los Alamitos, CA (2017). https://doi.org/10.1109/ICDAR.2017.288
3. Unser-Schutz, G.: Influential or influenced? the relationship between genre, gender and language in manga. Gend. Lang. **9**, 223–254 (2015). https://doi.org/10.1558/genl.v9i2.17331
4. Walsh, J.A., Martin, S., St. Germain, J.: The spider's web: an analysis of fan mail from amazing spider-man, 1963–1995. In: Dunst, A., Laubrock, J., Wildfeuer, J. (eds.) Empirical Comics Research: Digital, Cognitive, and Multimodal Methods, pp. 62–84. Routledge, New York (2018)
5. Hartel, R., Dunst, A.: How good is good enough? establishing quality thresholds for the automatic text analysis of retro-digitized comics. In: Kompatsiaris, I., Huet, B., Mezaris, V., Gurrin, C., Cheng, W.-H., Vrochidis, S. (eds.) MMM 2019. LNCS, vol. 11296, pp. 662–671. Springer, Cham (2019). https://doi.org/10.1007/978-3-030-05716-9_59
6. Dubray, D., Laubrock J.: Multi-class semantic segmentation of comics: a U-Net based approach. In: Graphics Recognition (GREC) Workshop, International Conference on Document Analysis and Recognition (ICDAR), Sydney, pp. 5–6 (2019)
7. Wick, C., Reul C., Puppe F.: Calamari—A High Performance Tensorflow-based Deep Learning Package for Optical Character Recognition. https://arxiv.org/ftp/arxiv/papers/1807/1807.02004.pdf
8. Dunst, A., Hartel, R., Laubrock, J.: The graphic narrative corpus (GNC): design, annotation, and analysis for the digital humanities. In: 2nd International Workshop on coMics Analysis, Processing, and Understanding, 14th IAPR International Conference on Document Analysis and Recognition, Kyoto, Japan (2017). https://doi.org/10.1109/ICDAR.2017.286
9. Dunst, A., Hartel, R.: The quantitative analysis of comics: towards a visual stylometry of graphic narrative. In: Dunst, A., Laubrock, J., Wildfeuer, J. (eds.) Empirical Comics Research: Digital, Multimodal, and Cognitive Methods, Chap. 12, pp. 239–263. Routledge, New York (2018)

10. Nguyen, N.-V., Rigaud, C., Burie, J.-C.: Multi-task model for comic book image analysis. In: Kompatsiaris, I., Huet, B., Mezaris, V., Gurrin, C., Cheng, W.-H., Vrochidis, S. (eds.) MMM 2019. LNCS, vol. 11296, pp. 637–649. Springer, Cham (2019). https://doi.org/10.1007/978-3-030-05716-9_57

11. Michalke, M.: koRpus. An R package for text analysis. https://reaktanz.de/?c=hacking&s=koRpus (2020)

12. Breuel, T.M.: The OCRopus open source OCR system. DRR (2008). https://doi.org/10.1117/12.783598

13. Jannidis, F., Konle, L, Leinen, P.: Makroanalytische Untersuchung von Heftromanen. In: Sahle, P. (ed.) DHd 2019 Book of Abstracts, pp. 167–173 (2019). https://zenodo.org/record/2596095

14. Jones, E., Nulty, P.: Quantitative measures of lexical complexity in modern prose fiction. Digit. Scholarsh. Hum. **34**, 914–937 (2019). https://doi.org/10.1093/llc/fqz020

15. Kirtley, C., Murray, C., Vaughan, P.B., Tatler, B.W.: Reading words and images: factors influencing eye movements in comics reading. In: Empirical Comics Research [9], pp. 264–283, Routledge, New York (2018)

16. Liddle, D.: Could fiction have an information history? statistical probability and the rise of the novel. J. Cult. Anal. (2019). https://doi.org/10.22148/16.033

# Manga Vocabulometer, A New Support System for Extensive Reading with Japanese Manga Translated into English

Jin Kato$^{(\boxtimes)}$, Motoi Iwata$^{(\boxtimes)}$, and Koichi Kise$^{(\boxtimes)}$

Graduate School of Engineering, Osaka, Osaka Prefecture, Japan
kato@m.cs.osakafu-u.ac.jp, {iwata,kise}@cs.osakafu-u.ac.jp
http://imlab.jp/

**Abstract.** Extensive Reading, called "Tadoku" in Japan, is a method of learning a second language to improve reading speed and fluency. Japanese comics translated into English is used as one of the materials for extensive reading, where Japanese comics are called manga. Using manga to learn English is considered to be a good way to learn English because the content can be inferred from the pictures. However, some learners cannot memorize and learn all the words when they read many books. Therefore, if there is a function to automatically save unknown words in the books they read or to create flashcards, they can learn English more efficiently.

In this paper, we introduce Manga Vocabulometer, the support system for extensive reading. It is a web-based system that allows students to choose their favorite manga to read. It is also able to check for unknown words, so the system can present flashcards to learners. To confirm the advantage of the proposed system, we compare two memorization methods: one is the memorization method using Manga Vocabulometer and the other is the traditional simple memorization method.

**Keywords:** Education · Learning system · Web application · Extensive reading · Comic computing

## 1 Introduction

Japanese comics called manga has been translated into a variety of languages and is widely read around the world. The manga translated into English are not only read by foreign people but also by Japanese people for learning English. The merits of using manga to learn English are that they are familiar to Japanese people and that they are easy to read in English because they provide the situation of a scene as pictures. This paper focuses on extensive reading with manga translated into English. Extensive reading is the method of learning foreign languages by enjoying reading books that are easy to understand. In this manner, the improve reading speed and the difficulty of books are gradually improved. As a general rule in extensive reading, learners should not refer to a dictionary, but

© Springer Nature Switzerland AG 2021
A. Del Bimbo et al. (Eds.): ICPR 2020 Workshops, LNCS 12666, pp. 223–235, 2021.
https://doi.org/10.1007/978-3-030-68780-9_20

skip over the unfamiliar parts of the book, and stop reading if it is not attractive. In learning to read a lot of books within these rules, learners will be more efficient if they are able to store the words of the books they read. If learners can save the words in the book, learners can pick up the unknown words to make flashcards and recommend books based on the learner's vocabulary. So if we can create a system that can do this, we can make learning more efficient.

As a tool to support extensive reading of text-based documents, Augereau [1] developed Vocabulometer, which analyzes the difficulty level of a document and the vocabulary read by learners using their eye gaze information during reading. It is a web-platform application that aims to contribute to the development of learning system. Using an eye tracker that tracks the user's eye gaze position on the screen, the system can detect which words in a document the user is reading in real-time and store them by the paragraph in the database. It also has a function to recommend suitable documents for a learner's English skills based on the accumulated vocabulary. Yamaguchi et al. proposed Mobile Vocabulometer which is implemented as the app on smartphones [2]. Their experimental results found that Mobile Vocabulometer was more effective in memorization than standard flashcards for many participants. However, Mobile Vocabulometer was not effective for some participants. We assume that some participants cannot concentrate to read English texts because they are not familiar to English texts.

In this paper, we propose Manga Vocabulometer, a new support system for extensive reading to learn English with manga translated into English. By changing the learning materials from text to manga, it is expected that learners can easily grasp the content through pictures and do not get bored. The system extracts and presents English words in the manga according to the learner's English level. In this way, the system can be adapted to the learner's English level. We conducted an experiment to compare memorization learning using Manga Vocabulometer with flashcards at a similar level of unknown words.

The rest of this paper is organized as follows: Sect. 2 describes the related work of learning English. Section 3 describes the structure of Manga Vocabulometer and how to learn with it. Section 4 describes our experiments and evaluation of learning English with Manga Vocabulometer. Section 5 presents our result and discussion of experiments. Section 6 presents our conclusions.

## 2   Related Work

Yamaguchi et al. developed the text-based Vocabulometer on smartphones [2]. The application had the advantage of allowing users to learn English anytime, anywhere. The experimental results confirmed that it is more useful than flashcards. However, their research is text-based, which makes it difficult to maintain motivation. Hosler et al. compared scores for learning with and without manga in the sciences [9]. This experiment found that manga as learning materials can help learners learn in science. This predicts that the use of cartoons in learning will increase the effectiveness of learning. Researchers have debated the effectiveness of context in helping learners acquire vocabulary, but the results have been mixed [5,6]. For example, Webb et al. [7]. Found that there was no significant difference between the scores of subjects who encountered the target word in a single sentence and those who learned a pair of words. This suggests that the context of a single glossy sentence may have little effect on vocabulary knowledge. However, Hidi et al. [8]. Showed that learners' interest and comprehension were correlated.

## 3   Application Architecture

In this section, we describe each component of Manga Vocabulometer and the application-based learning in detail.

### 3.1   Each Component of Manga Vocabulometer

Figure 1 shows the learning flow using Manga Vocabulometer. It is composed of the initial setup and the learning cycle including select, read, and feedback, followed by the review with flashcards. The detail of each component is described at the following paragraphs:

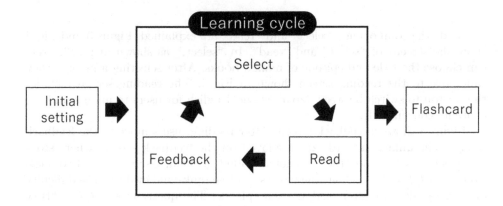

**Fig. 1.** Learning flow

First of all, we explain how to log in. Figure 2 shows login screen. In order to log in, we ask the user to fill out the data required to create his or her account. The user's information is managed on firebase [4]. When users are logged in, users can set up own initial setting. The user registers some topics of their interest and answer the vocabulary questions defined by San Diego Quick Assessment [3] to estimate their English level. Then, the component "initial setting" generates the users' word list based on their estimated vocabulary and the word frequency list. The word frequency list is the list of levels or ranked lists by frequency of occurrence in a particular text. By setting the user's English level, Manga

Vocabulometer can suggest the list of unknown words that match the user's level in the component "feedback".

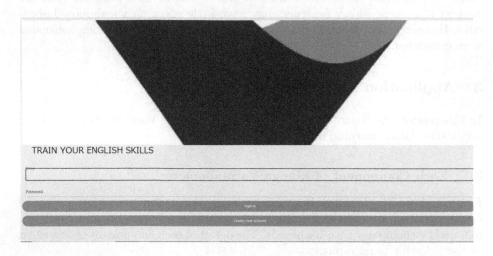

**Fig. 2.** Login screen

Next, the components "select" and "read" are explained. Figure 3 and Fig. 4 show the screens of "select" and "read". In "select," as shown in Fig. 3, users can choose the title and episode of manga books. After selecting a manga, they can move to the reading screen shown in Fig. 4. The reading screen includes the button to switch between Japanese and English for users to understand the contents conveniently.

Figure 5 shows a feedback screen. After reading, users move to the feedback screen. The unknown words are displayed on the feedback screen, where stopwords such as "a" and "the" are not included in them. Users answer two questionnaires $Q1$ and $Q2$ about the interest on five ranks and evaluate the difficulty on three ranks just after reading each episode. The questionnaire $Q1$ is "How interesting is the episode?" and $Q2$ is "How long would you like to read more episodes?". The choices of the highest rank (r5) of $Q1$ and $Q2$ are "very interesting" and "I want to read now", respectively, while r1 is the lowest rank. In $Q1$ and $Q2$, the middle rank response (r3) is "No strong opinion." Manga Difficulty is evaluated on three ranks: easy, balance, and hard. The above questionnaires will be used for future research in this system. The screen of "feedback" also presents a list of potential unknown words in the manga that are matched to the user's English level and asks the user to select a word they don't know. The selected words are then stored in the database and can be used for learning unknown words with flashcards. The user's unknown word list is updated every time the user answers the questionnaire form. In other words, the system will improve the user's unknown word list every time user reads manga.

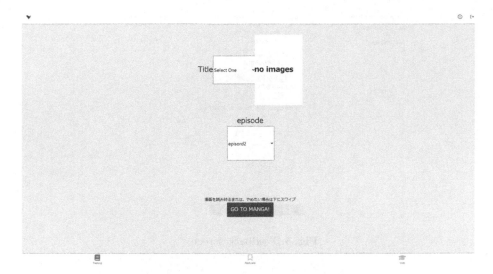

**Fig. 3.** Manga book selection screen

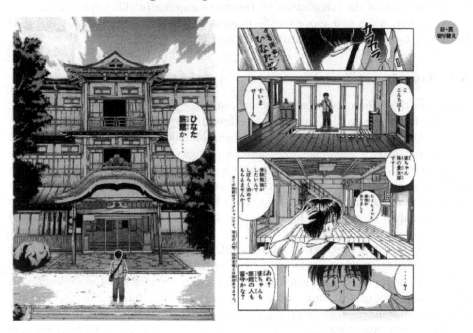

**Fig. 4.** Manga display screen (LoveHina©Ken Akamatsu)

Next, the component "flashcard" is explained. Figure 6 shows flashcard screen. The flashcard screen displays one of the unknown words in user's word list. There is a function to display the Japanese translation of the word, where it is generated by Google Translate. We used Google Translate for automatic

**Fig. 5.** Feedback screen

translation instead of manual translation which takes time and effort. We checked the correctness of the translation by random sampling in this experiment.

Moreover, users can move to the manga screen where the word is included for understanding how the word is used in practice.

### 3.2  Learning Material

Users use the pairs of a Japanese manga and the English translated one. Also, to store the words in the database, we should know what words are written in manga. Unfortunately, We cannot use data in Manga109 [12] for this experiment, where Manga109 is one of the most famous manga datasets with the annotations of the positions and text information. It is because there is no English manga in Manga109. We prepared the text information in English translated manga in the following manner: Firstly, the regions of English words are detected from English manga page images based on the character detection method proposed by Beak et al. [10].

We applied the method of Smith et al. [11] to obtain text information by cropping images from a single word-by-word region acquired by text detection. We use 22 manga titles in English and Japanese versions for the experiments, where the genres of the manga are various, for example, Fantasy, Sports, Comedy, Suspense, Romance, and so on.

The reason why there are some different genres of manga is to help learners choose manga that match their interests and help them learn.

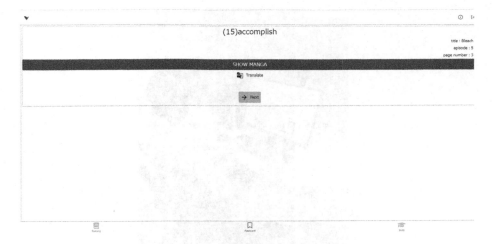

**Fig. 6.** Flashcard screen

# 4   Experiment

In this section, we describe our experiments with Manga Vocabulometer. In this experiment, we tested the degree of memorization retention to compare using Manga Vocabulometer with using just flashcard.

## 4.1   Experimental Condition

We conducted an experiment to evaluate the effectiveness of our method. In the experiment, 20 participants learn unknown words with both just memorization and our Manga Vocabulometer. The participants were all Japanese including 9 males and 11 females. They used Manga Vocabulometer as the app working on a desktop PC with a high-speed camera and an eye tracker. The high-speed camera and eye tracker is Blackfly S USB3 and Tobii Eye tracker 4C pro upgrade version, respectively. Figure 7 shows the setup of the experiment. As shown in Fig. 7, the eye gaze information, and the video of the participant's face were recorded while the participants read the manga. This data was not used in this evaluation although they will be used for analysing users' reading behaviors.

## 4.2   Details of Experiment

In this subsection, we describe the details and procedures of the experiment. In this experiment, we compared English word memorization using Manga Vocabulometer with simple one just looking at the text. In this experiment, there are two phases: the reading phase and the memorization phase. The reading phase is conducted using the functions in the learning cycle in Fig. 3, and the memorization phase is conducted using the flashcard in Fig. 3.

**Fig. 7.** Setup of experiment

Firstly, participants freely selected and read English translated manga. After that, they answered questionnaires related to interest and labeled the subjective difficulty and unknown words in each episode. The participants repeated this task until 20 unknown words are collected or one hour. We call these unknown words Wordset A. Then, we selected another 20 words called Wordset B with similar word frequency to the words in Wordset A. The average word-rank is 7430 in Wordset A and 7420 in Wordset B. The smaller this rank, the greater the frequency of the word in the general document. Therefore, Wordset A and B have the similar difficulty each other based on the word frequency. The participants memorized the words in Wordset A using Manga Vocabulometer. They also memorized the words in Wordset B by simply looking at them.

The time for the memorization was fixed for 2 h so that the participants can learn the total 40 words by heart. We conducted four confirmation tests at the intervals of 1, 2, 4, and 8 days after they had memorized all the words. The confirmation test consists of 5 words in Wordset A and 5 words in Wordset B, for a total of 10 words. For the 17th participant (P17), the experiment was conducted with 12 words both in Wordset A and B because P17 collected only 12 unknown words in Wordset A. Then, we selected another 12 words called Wordset B with similar word frequency to the words in Wordset A for P17. The confirmation test for P17 consists of 3 words in Wordset A and 3 words in Wordset B, for a total of 12 words.

# 5    Result and Discussion

Figure 8 shows the results of the confirmation test. The horizontal axis in Fig. 8 represents the difference of scores for Wordset A and B, where a score means the number of correct answers. Therefore, positive values in the horizontal axis means that Manga Vocabulometer is effective in the memorization of words. The vertical axis in Fig. 8 represents the number of participants which is corresponding to each score. As shown in Fig. 8, 17 out of 20 users scored better on the confirmation test of Wordset A than Wordset B. Due to the small memorized words, the statistical comparison of the test per user is limited and the order of the tests is not taken into account, so it is difficult to infer much from the sum of the differences.

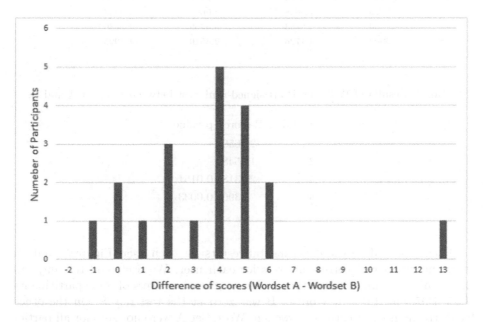

**Fig. 8.** Results of confirmation tests based on the difference between the numbers of correct answers for Wordset A and B.

To confirm the performance, we introduced a two-tailed Wicoxon-Pratt Signed-Rank test [13] which is a non-parametric statistical hypothesis test. This test uses the pairs of dependent data for a non-parametric distribution. For using the test, we calculated the mean and standard deviation of the percentages of participants' correct answers for Wordset A and Wordset B. Table 1 shows the calculated mean and standard deviation for Wordset A and B. As shown in Table 1, we can find that the means in Wordset A are greater than those in Wordset B for all test days. The difference in Wordset's performance appears to be greater the more remote the day of the test, suggesting that the proposed method has better long-term retention. Table 2 shows the results of the Wicoxon-Pratt signed-rank test. The reason why p-values in "Test Day 1" and "Test Day 2" are undefined is because there is not much difference between the results of the tests which means that many of them are tied. In general, if p-value is less than 0.05, the result of the test is effective. The results in Table 2 indicate that Manga Vocabulometer is effective for inducing better English vocabulary retention.

**Table 1.** Mean and standard deviation of the percentages of correct answers for Wordset A and B.

| Test day | Wordset A Mean | Wordset A STDEV | Wordset B Mean | Wordset B STDEV |
|---|---|---|---|---|
| 1 | 4.8125 | 0.5266 | 4.1176 | 0.8455 |
| 2 | 4.5625 | 0.8638 | 4.0657 | 1.3448 |
| 4 | 4.1250 | 1.2183 | 3.6769 | 1.2686 |
| 8 | 4.0000 | 1.1726 | 2.3610 | 1.5995 |

**Table 2.** Results of Wilcoxon-Pratt signed-rank test between Wordset A and B.

| Test day | Z-score | p-value |
|---|---|---|
| 1 | −2.6656 | − |
| 2 | −1.9548 | − |
| 4 | −2.4318 | 0.0151 |
| 8 | −2.9396 | 0.0033 |

Then, we analyse the experimental results for each user. Figure 9a and 9b show the number of correct answers for each user, Wordset, and test day. As shown in Fig. 9a and Fig. 9b, the number of correct answers of some participants (P05, P07, and P08) in Wordset B was zero at the test day 8. On the other hand, the number of correct answers in Word Set A were not zero for all participants at the test day 8. Moreover, the numbers of correct answers in Wordset A were higher than or equal to those in Wordset B except for P03. Therefore, the experimental results confirmed that the memorization method using Manga Vocabulometer was effective for retention in some results. Here we describe the considerations from the results we obtained with the component "feedback". We also found in this experiment that there was no correlation between the difficulty of the manga perceived by the reader and memory retention. In other words, the memorization method using Manga Vocabulometer does not correlate well with the difficulty of the manga when reading, since the reader associates the picture with the content. Furthermore, the results of the questionnaire on interest level revealed that extensive reading using Manga Vocabulometer was easy to maintain motivation.

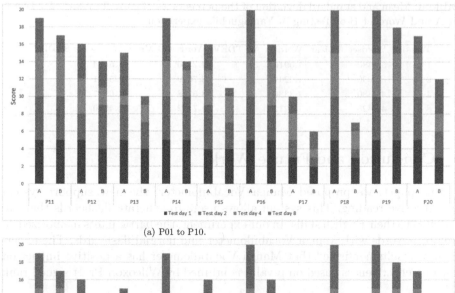

(a) P01 to P10.

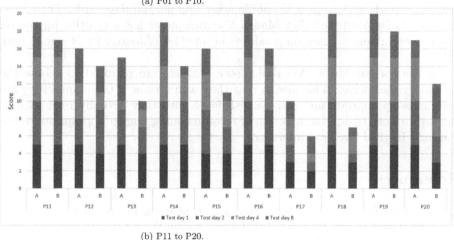

(b) P11 to P20.

**Fig. 9.** Number of correct answers for each user, Wordset, and interval

We compare Manga Vocabulometer with Mobile Vocabulometer proposed by Yamaguchi et al. which is a smartphone app for learning English with texts. In the experiment for Mobile Vocabulometer, they compared memorization using the Mobile Vocabulometer with flashcard memorization. It is similar to our experiment, however, they used 32 words while we used 20 words. Table 3 shows the mean and standard deviation of the percentages of correct answers for Wordset A and B in their experiments cited from their paper [2], where the setting of Wordset A and B is same as our setting except for the replacement of Manga Vocabulometer with Mobile Vocabulometer. As shown in Table 3, it is shown that learning with Mobile Vocabulometer is effective. Therefore, it was found that manga and text-based learning materials were more effective than flashcards, depending on the participant.

**Table 3.** Mean and standard deviation of the percentages of correct answers for Wordset A and Wordset B of Testing in Yamaguchi's experiment

| Test day | Wordset A Mean | Wordset A STDEV | Wordset B Mean | Wordset B STDEV |
|---|---|---|---|---|
| 1 | 5.2380 | 1.0910 | 4.2380 | 1.5134 |
| 2 | 5.0000 | 1.2247 | 3.7619 | 1.5461 |
| 4 | 4.2380 | 1.3380 | 3.5238 | 1.6917 |
| 8 | 4.1428 | 1.6212 | 2.7142 | 1.4540 |

## 6    Conclusion and Future Work

In this paper, we proposed Manga Vocabulometer, the new support system for extensive reading. This system allows users to generate flashcards that are matched to their English skills. In our experiment, the participants memorized 40 unknown words with Manga Vocabulometer and normal flashcards. The experimental results confirmed that Manga Vocabulometer has a positive impact on learning effectiveness based on p-values obtained by Wilcoxon-Pratt signed-rank test.

In the current Manga Vocabulometer, learners are required to choose the manga by themselves. This means that they won't know if the manga they are reading is appropriate for their English level until they actually read it. It is the future work to add the function of recommending manga appropriate to the learner's English level and interests.

## References

1. Augereau, O., et al.: Vocabulometer: a web platform for document and reader mutual analysis. In: 2018 13th IAPR International Workshop on Document Analysis Systems (DAS). IEEE (2018)
2. Yamaguchi, K., Iwata, M., Vargo, A., Kise, K.: Mobile vocabulometer: a context-based learning mobile application to enhance English vocabulary acquisition. In: Adjunct Proceedings of the 2020 ACM International Joint Conference on Pervasive and Ubiquitous Computing and Proceedings of the 2020 ACM International Symposium on Wearable Computers (UbiComp-ISWC '20). Association for Computing Machinery, New York, NY, USA, pp. 156–159 (2020)
3. La Pray, M., Ross, R.: The graded word list: quick gauge of reading ability. J. Read. **12**(4), 305–307 (1969)
4. https://firebase.google.com/
5. Israel, S.E., Duffy, G.G.: Handbook of Research on Reading Comprehension, 2nd edn. Guilford Publications, New York (2017). https://books.google.co.jp/books?id=xeK0DAAAQBAJ
6. Shintani, N.: A comparative study of the effects of input-based and production-based instruction on vocabulary acquisition by young EFL learners. Lang. Teach. Res. **15**(2), 137–158 (2011)
7. Webb, S.: Learning word pairs and glossed sentences: the effects of a single context on vocabulary knowledge. Lang. Teach. Res. **11**(1), 63–81 (2007)

8. Hidi, S.: Interest, reading, and learning: theoretical and practical considerations. Educ. Psychol. Rev. **13**(3), 191–209 (2001). https://doi.org/10.1023/A: 1016667621114

9. Hosler, J., Boomer, K.B.: Are comic books an effective way to engage nonmajors in learning and appreciating science? CBE-Life Sci. Educ. **10**(3), 309–317 (2011)

10. Baek, Y., Lee, B., Han, D., Yun, S., Lee, H.: Character region awareness for text detection. In: Proceedings of the IEEE Conference on Computer Vision and Pattern Recognition, pp. 9365–9374 (2019)

11. Smith, R.: An overview of the tesseract OCR engine. In: Ninth International Conference on Document Analysis and Recognition (ICDAR 2007), vol. 2, pp. 629–633. IEEE (2007)

12. Matsui, Y., et al.: Sketch-based manga retrieval using manga109 dataset. Multimedia Tools Appl. **76**(20), 21811–21838 (2016). https://doi.org/10.1007/s11042-016-4020-z

13. Pratt, J.W.: Remarks on zeros and ties in the Wilcoxon signed rank procedures. J. Amer. Statist. Assoc. **54**(287), 655–667 (1959)

# Automatic Landmark-Guided Face Image Generation for Anime Characters Using C²GAN

Junki Oshiba$^{(\boxtimes)}$, Motoi Iwata$^{(\boxtimes)}$, and Koichi Kise$^{(\boxtimes)}$ (iD)

Graduate School of Engineering, Osaka Prefecture University,
1-1 Gakuen-cho, Naka, Sakai, Osaka, Japan
oshiba@m.cs.osakafu-u.ac.jp, {iwata,kise}@cs.osakafu-u.ac.jp

**Abstract.** Recently, comics with animations, called motion comics, has appeared. However, due to the time and effort required to create the animations, only a few famous comics have been converted to motion comics. In this study, we propose a method for generating landmark-based face images of anime characters using C²GAN with the aim of automatically generating animation of facial expressions, where C²GAN proposed by Hao et al. is a framework for generating keypoint-guided image. In addition, this paper explains how to create datasets almost automatically from anime videos. In the experiment, we firstly trained C²GAN with dataset created from anime videos, and then we tried to improve the performance by changing the representation of facial landmarks.

**Keywords:** Comic Computing · Image generation · Facial landmark · GAN

## 1 Introduction

In recent years, with the spread of electronic devices such as smartphones and tablets, we have more and more opportunities to read comics on them. In addition, motion comics, comics with animation, have appeared, taking the advantages of electronic devices that can play music and movies. However, the number of comics that can be enjoyed as motion comics is limited due to the time and effort required to create them. The ultimate goal of this study is to automatically generate motion comics from existing comics so that many comics can be enjoyed as motion comics.

In the motion comics, the animations of characters' facial expressions appear frequently. Furthermore, it is more difficult to create facial expression change animations than other types of animations, such as parallel shifts of characters, scaling of speech balloons, and swinging onomatopoeia. Therefore, we focus on the automatic generation of the animation of an character's facial expression.

Pramook proposed a method to generate a face image based on a face pose vector with six parameters [2]. However, the only parameters related to facial

© Springer Nature Switzerland AG 2021
A. Del Bimbo et al. (Eds.): ICPR 2020 Workshops, LNCS 12666, pp. 236–249, 2021.
https://doi.org/10.1007/978-3-030-68780-9_21

expressions are the opening of the eyes and mouth. Moreover, the animations of facial changes are limited to blinking and lip-sync.

Choi et al. proposed StarGAN [1], which takes a human face image and an emotion label (Happy, Angry, etc.) as input and generates a face image based on that emotion label. However, emotion labels cannot represent fine expressions, and this method cannot generate face images with arbitrary expressions.

To solve the problem, several works introduce keypoints to generate face images. Keypoints are the collection of dots and contain the object information of shape and position. The keypoints allow for more arbitrary image generation. Hao et al. proposed a $C^2GAN$, which is keypoint-guided image generation method that is not limited to a single target.

In this paper, we propose a new method to generate animations of various facial expressions of an anime character automatically by referring to the existing method $C^2GAN$ for real-world human face images. In addition, a large amount of data is needed to use $C^2GAN$, and it is difficult to prepare a dataset from comic images alone. Therefore, we focus on the anime characters and prepare a dataset from the anime videos. The reason why we do not use comics characters is because the Japanese comics characters are usually drawn with monochrome and more difficult to be used for automatic image generation.

## 2 Related Works

### 2.1 Face Image Generation for Anime Characters

Pramook's method [2] generates a face image of an anime character with six parameters for facial movement. However, the only parameters related to facial expressions are the opening of the eyes and mouth. Therefore, the types of generated expressions are limited, and the generated animations are also limited to blinking and lip-sync. In addition, it is assumed that the input is an image with the eyes and mouth open. Therefore, it is not possible to generate open eyes from closed eyes.

### 2.2 Face Image Generation Based on Landmarks

Hao et al. proposed $C^2GAN$ [5], the network for the task of keypoint-guided image generation. The keypoint is the set of points which represent the characteristics of the target object. Hao et al. showed that $C^2GAN$ is effective for generating real-world human face images using facial landmark as keypoints. In this paper, we refer to the network itself as $C^2GAN$, and the method for automatic generation of real-world human face images based on landmarks using $C^2GAN$ as Hao et al.'s method.

## 3 Proposed Method

In this section, We describe the outline of the proposed method in Sect. 3.1, the keypoint for the face of anime characters in Sect. 3.2, the network structure in

**Fig. 1.** Example of a facial landmark for comics character which consists of 60 dots.

Sect. 3.3, and the generation of the anime character dataset from anime videos in Sect. 3.4.

### 3.1 Outline of Proposed Method

The proposed method uses the facial landmarks as keypoints. Also C²GAN is used to generate the face image of an anime character based on the facial landmark. In Hao et al.'s method, C²GAN is trained with the Radboud Faces Dataset (RaFD) [3], which is a dataset of real-world human faces. However, in the proposed method, C²GAN is adapted to the face images of anime characters by training the network with a dataset generated from anime videos.

### 3.2 Facial Landmarks of Anime Characters as Keypoints

We introduce the definition of the facial landmark of comics characters proposed by Stricker et al. [4]. Figure 1[1] shows an example of a facial landmark of comics characters. As shown in Fig. 1, it consists of 60 dots.

### 3.3 Network Structure

Figure 2 shows the flow of training C²GAN with the face images of anime characters. Four images $x$, $y$, $L_x$, and $L_y$ are used for the training. The input face images $x$ and $y$ are two face images of the same anime character with different expressions. The input landmark images $L_x$ and $L_y$ are the landmarks corresponding to the face images $x$ and $y$, respectively, where the landmarks are

---

[1] ©Takuji.

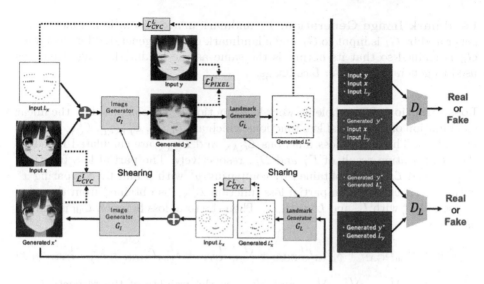

**Fig. 2.** Flow of training $C^2GAN$ with anime character face images

plotted as black dots on the white background. $C^2GAN$ consists of four sub networks: Image Generator $G_I$, Image Discriminator $D_I$, Landmark Generator $G_L$, and Landmark Discriminator $D_L$.

The image generator $G_I$ generates a face image from the input face image and the landmark image. The image discriminator $D_I$ identifies whether the input triplet is the triplet of $x$, $L_y$, and $y$ (Real) or the triplet of $x$, $L_y$, and the generated face image $y^*$ (Fake). The right side of Fig. 2 is the training flow of the discriminators, where the green and red rectangles indicate the Real pair and the Fake pair, respectively. The image discriminator $D_I$ learns to discriminate between Real and Fake correctly, while the image generator $G_I$ learns to generate images so that $D_I$ misidentifies them as Real. This architecture improves the quality of the generated images. Also, the landmark generator $G_L$ generates a landmark image for the input face image. The landmark discriminator $D_L$ identifies whether the input duplex is the duplex of $y^*$ and $L_y$ (Real), or the duplex of $y^*$ and the generated landmark image $L_y^*$ (Fake). The relationship between $G_L$ and $D_L$ is the same as that between $G_I$ and $D_I$.

The sub networks are trained by three main tasks: image generation, image regeneration, and landmark image generation. The details are as follows.

**Image Generation.** In the image generation task, a face image $y^*$ is generated by inputting $x$ and $L_y$ to $G_I$. $G_I$ is trained so that $y^*$ and $y$ are the same.

**Image Regeneration.** In the image regeneration task, the original face image $x^*$ is generated again by $G_I$ from the $y^*$ and $L_x$. The $x^*$ is generated to be the same as the $x$.

**Landmark Image Generation.** In landmark image generation, a face image generated by $G_I$ is input to $G_L$ and a landmark image is generated for the input. $G_L$ is trained so that its output is the same as the landmark image that was used to generate the input face image.

**Loss Function.** The whole network loss function $\mathcal{L}_{\text{all}}$ is composed by the linear combination of five partial loss functions which are $\mathcal{L}_{\text{GAN}}^I$, $\mathcal{L}_{\text{PIXEL}}^I$, $\mathcal{L}_{\text{CYC}}^I$, $\mathcal{L}_{\text{GAN}}^L$, and $\mathcal{L}_{\text{CYC}}^L$. The partial loss functions $\mathcal{L}_{\text{GAN}}^I$ and $\mathcal{L}_{\text{GAN}}^L$ are calculated based on the identification result of $D_I$ and $D_L$, respectively. The partial loss functions $\mathcal{L}_{\text{PIXEL}}^I$ and $\mathcal{L}_{\text{CYC}}^I$ are obtained by comparing $y^*$ with $y$ and by comparing $x^*$ with $x$, respectively. The partial loss function $\mathcal{L}_{\text{CYC}}^L$ is obtained from the comparison of $L_y^*$ with $L_y$ and $L_x^*$ with $L_x$. Then the total loss function $\mathcal{L}_{\text{all}}$ is defined as follows:

$$\mathcal{L}_{\text{all}} = \lambda_{\text{gan}}^I \mathcal{L}_{\text{GAN}}^I + \lambda_{\text{pixel}}^I \mathcal{L}_{\text{PIXEL}}^I + \lambda_{\text{cyc}}^I \mathcal{L}_{\text{CYC}}^I + \lambda_{\text{gan}}^L \mathcal{L}_{\text{GAN}}^L + \lambda_{\text{cyc}}^L \mathcal{L}_{\text{CYC}}^L \quad (1)$$

where $\lambda_{\text{gan}}^I$, $\lambda_{\text{pixel}}^I$, $\lambda_{\text{cyc}}^I$, $\lambda_{\text{gan}}^L$, and $\lambda_{\text{cyc}}^L$ are the weights of the respective loss functions.

### 3.4   Anime Character Dataset Generation

In this section, we explain the procedure for generating datasets using anime videos. As described in Sect. 3.3, training of $C^2$GAN requires four images: two face images of the same character with different expressions and their corresponding landmark images. In this paper, we call the set of those four images an input set. The dataset for training $C^2$GAN consists of the input set. Hao et al.'s method used RaFD, which is a dataset of real-world human faces, to train $C^2$GAN. They also used OpenFace for landmark detection. Our proposed method requires two face images and their landmarks that satisfy the condition that the expressions of the same anime character are different (condition A). In addition, it is difficult for the proposed method to respond to changes in the outside of the face (background, clothing, hairstyle, etc.) because the facial landmarks only have information about the inside of the face. Therefore, it is desirable for the two face images with different expressions to satisfy the condition that there are no changes in the outside of the face (condition B) in addition to condition A. In the Radboud Faces Dataset, the background is unified with a white wall, all the people photographed are wearing T-shirts of the same design, and the change in hairstyle between the same person, so the condition B is satisfied in advance. On the other hand, it is difficult to generate a dataset from anime videos, even if the frame images depict the same character, the background, clothes and hairstyle are not always the same. Then, we generate input sets satisfying conditions A and B by shot division.

In the following, we explain the detailed procedure for generating datasets using anime videos.

**Shot Division.** Firstly, the anime videos are divided into shots. A shot is one of the units of a video and is a sequence of motion pictures taken by a single camera. Two images obtained from the same shot satisfy condition A because they depict the same character with different expressions. Sometimes the same shot contains an image of a face with exactly the same expression, but only one such image is kept and the rest are deleted. We will explain how to do this later. The background, clothing, and hairstyle tend not to change significantly in the same shot. Therefore, two images extracted from the same shot are stored as the same group, assuming that they satisfy the conditions A and B.

Shot division is automatically done based on the similarity between the $N$-th frame image and the $(N+1)$-th frame image of the anime video. The boundary of shots is detected if the similarity of them is under the threshold. As the similarity, we use the correlation of the histogram of the density of each channel (R, G, and B channels in the anime videos, the density is 0–255 with 256 levels) for two frame images. That is, to compute the similarity between two images $X$, $Y$, the histograms $H_{XR}$, $H_{XG}$, $H_{XB}$ and $H_{YR}$, $H_{YG}$, $H_{YB}$ are firstly obtained from two images $X$ and $Y$. Next, we compute the correlation of the two histograms for each channel. Finally, the average of these values is the similarity. The similarity between the same images is 1.

**Face Detection.** The face regions are detected and cropped from the shots to obtain face images with OpenCV[2]. Then, the shots without face regions are deleted. The obtained face images are stored as a separate group for each shot.

**Landmark Detection.** Facial landmarks are detected from the face images using the method of Stricker et al. [4]. Although the method of Stricker et al. is applied to monochrome comic images, the method can also detect landmarks for colored anime images.

**Normalization.** Figure 4 shows the normalization procedure for aligning the position, size and orientation of a character face in all face images. Firstly, a face image is rotated so that the lines passing through the center of gravity of each eye are horizontal. In this case, the area outside the image is padded by black pixels. Next, the square face area is calculated based on the left-most, right-most and bottom-most points in the contours landmark. The normalized image is cropped by extending the 10% face area of one side of the square. Also, the landmarks are normalized to correspond to the normalized images.

**Removal of Exact Same Facial Images.** The exact same images may be used several times in the same shot for anime videos. For example, the animation of a speaking character is often composed of the repetition of three face images (opened mouth, half-opened mouth, and closed mouth). The exact same images

---

[2] https://github.com/nagadomi/lbpcascade_animeface

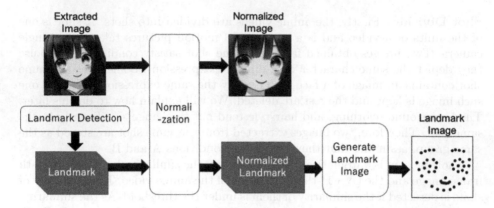

**Fig. 3.** Flow of obtaining the normalized face and landmark images from extracted face images

in the same shot should be removed because the input set which the input image and the target image are the same may adversely affect the learning of $C^2GAN$. For detecting exact same images, the difference of landmarks is employed. We computed the sum of the distances of each dot of the two landmarks obtained from input and target images. Then one of the two landmarks are removed if the sum of the distances is less than the threshold (Fig. 3).

**Landmark Image Generation.** The normalized landmark is put on a white image as black dots to generate a landmark image.

**Input Sets Generation.** After completing the above procedures, the normalized face images are grouped. Images in the same group satisfy the conditions A and B, and in each group, input sets are generated for all pairs of images in the group.

## 4　Experiment

In Sect. 4.1, we investigated the image quality of generated face images of anime characters with $C^2GAN$. Then in Sect. 4.2, we investigated the effect of the styles of landmarks to the performance of the proposed method.

### 4.1　Anime Character Face Image Generation Using $C^2GAN$

In this section, we train $C^2GAN$ using the dataset generated from anime videos. We evaluate the effectiveness of $C^2GAN$ for generating face images of anime characters through quantitative evaluations and qualitative assessments.

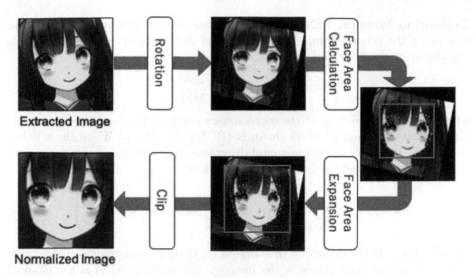

**Fig. 4.** Normalization procedure

**Table 1.** Number of data created from each episode

| Episode | 2 | 3 | 4 | 5 | 6 |
|---|---|---|---|---|---|
| Shots in which a face was detected | 60 | 58 | 57 | 65 | 52 |
| Face images | 351 | 357 | 343 | 416 | 339 |
| Input sets | 1,243 | 1,291 | 1,277 | 1,822 | 1,202 |

**Dataset.** In this experiment, we prepared a dataset using five episodes of anime videos with the same title in the manner described in Sect. 3.4. The threshold for shot division was set to 0.7 based on preliminary experiments. The generated dataset did not contain any pairs of different characters. Therefore, the shot division using the correlation of the histogram of the density worked well in the generation of the dataset in our study.

We employed the five-fold cross-validation in which one episode was used for testing and the rest four episodes are used for training. Here, if the same shots exist in different episodes, same data will exist both in the training and test data. Such situation is not suitable for valid evaluation. Therefore, we remove such shots in advance. In practice, the opening and ending animations were the same for the five episodes, so they had been removed. Furthermore, images with incorrect face regions and images with incorrectly extracted facial landmarks were manually deleted. Finally, the images and the landmark images were resized to 256×256 pixels to prepare input sets. Table 1 shows the number of shots, the number of face images, and the number of input sets generated from each episode. The number of face images is the number of images after removing non-face images and images with incorrectly extracted landmarks.

**Evaluation Metrics.** PSNR and SSIM [6] are used to quantitatively evaluate how much the generated image $y^*$ is the same as the correct image $y$. PSNR is calculated by the following equation:

$$\text{PSNR} = 10\log_{10}\frac{255^2}{\text{MSE}}, \tag{2}$$

where MSE is the average of the mean square errors of pixels at the same coordinate between $y$ and $y^*$ in all channels (RGB). Let $H$ and $W$ be the number of pixels in the vertical and horizontal directions, respectively, of the image, and the MSE is calculated by the following equation:

$$\text{MSE} = \frac{1}{3}\sum_{c\in\{R,G,B\}}\left(\frac{1}{HW}\sum_{i=0}^{H-1}\sum_{j=0}^{W-1}[y_c(i)(j) - y_c^*(i)(j)]^2\right) \tag{3}$$

where $y_c(i)(j)$ is the channel $c$ ($c$ is one of R, G or B) component of the $i$ row and $j$ column of pixel values in the image $y$. Similarly, $y_c^*(i)(j)$ is the channel $c$ component of the $i$ row and $j$ column of pixel values in the image $y^*$. The SSIM was calculated using the compare_ssim function, which is included in the measure module of skimage, a Python image library.

The facial landmarks used in the proposed method do not contain the information out of the face region. Therefore, it is difficult to generate the background and hair regions appropriately. In consideration of it, we define PSNRmask and SSIMmask, which are not affected by the generation results outside the face region based on the mask only on face regions. The mask is the interior of the contour and the landmarks of both eyebrows connected together. The PSNR-mask and SSIMmask have different image areas to be compared.

The PSNRmask is calculated by comparing only the regions in the mask based on Eq. (4).

$$\text{PSNRmask} = 10\log_{10}\frac{255^2}{\text{MSEmask}} \tag{4}$$

The MSEmask is calculated by the Eq. (5), where the mask region is $\mathbf{M}$ and the number of pixels in the mask region is $N$.

$$\text{MSEmask} = \frac{1}{3}\sum_{c\in\{R,G,B\}}\left(\frac{1}{N}\sum_{(i,j)\in\mathbf{M}}[y_c(i)(j) - y_c^*(i)(j)]^2\right) \tag{5}$$

On the other hand, The SSIMmask is calculated by filling the area outside the mask with white pixels and then comparing the rectangular area inscribed in the mask.

**Parameter Settings.** The parameters for training C$^2$GAN are batch size, the number of epochs, and weights for each loss function. In this experiment, the batch size was set to 8, the number of epochs was set to 200, and the weights of each loss function were trained for C$^2$GAN with $\lambda_{\text{gan}}^I, \lambda_{\text{pixel}}^I, \lambda_{\text{cyc}}^I, \lambda_{\text{gan}}^L$ and $\lambda_{\text{cyc}}^L$ as 1, 10, 10, 1, and 10, respectively, similar to Hao et al.'s method.

**Table 2.** Quantitative evaluation of this experiment and the quantitative evaluation of the experiment in the paper by Hao et al.[5]

| Method | Network | Test data | Evaluation area | PSNR | SSIM |
|---|---|---|---|---|---|
| Ours | $C^2$GAN trained with anime characters | Anime character face images | All | 15.0044 | 0.4808 |
| | | | Mask | 15.7184 | 0.6763 |
| Hao et al. | $C^2$GAN trained with real-world human | real-world human face images | All | 21.9192 | 0.8618 |

**Quantitative Evaluation.** Table 2 shows the quantitative results of the proposed method and the quantitative results of Hao et al.'s method [5]. The results of the proposed method and Hao et al.'s method are not directly comparable due to the difference in test data, but they are listed together in order to make the relationship between PSNR and SSIM values and image quality easier to understand. In addition, it is considered that the proposed method is more difficult because the expressions of anime characters vary widely compared to real-world human, and the differences in appearance between different individuals are large. PSNR and SSIM are both indicators that the higher the value, the closer to the correct image is generated. In Hao et al.'s paper, the averages of PSNR and SSIM were evaluated to be 21.9192 dB and 0.8618, respectively, where the images generated by Hao et al.'s method were indistinguishable from the correct images. The averages of PSNR and SSIM of the proposed method were 15.0044 dB and 0.4048, respectively. The averages of PSNRmask and SSIMmask of the proposed method were 15.7184 dB and 0.6763, respectively. In both PSNR and SSIM metrics, the mask region has higher evaluation value, indicating that the generation of the face region performs better than the generation outside of it.

**Qualitative Assessment.** Figure 5 shows an example of the generated images. To avoid copyright trouble, we use the examples based on Tohoku Zunko which can be used for non-commercial purpose without an application although it is not used in the experiments.

In the generation examples, the images whose PSNRmask and SSIMmask values are close to the PSNEmask and SSIMmask values shown in Table 2 are selected. Although the contours are generally fuzzy, face images based on landmarks have been generated.

**Problem with Landmark Images Generated by $C^2$GAN.** As explained in Sect. 3.1, $C^2$GAN includes the landmark generator which generates the landmark image from the image generated by the image generator. The landmark images generated by the landmark generator are shown in Fig. 6. As shown in Fig. 6, almost the same landmark images are generated regardless of the character and the clarity of the generated image. We consider to improve the face image generation by improving the performance of landmark image generation.

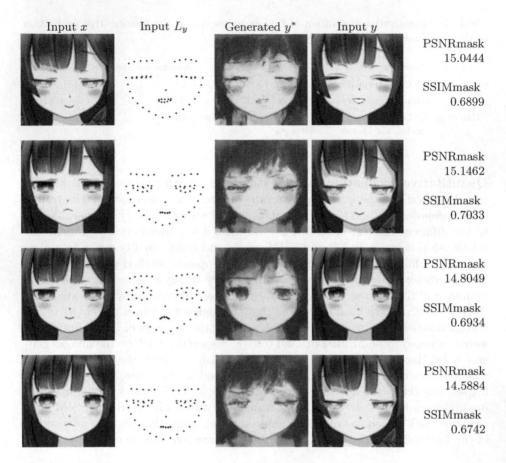

**Fig. 5.** Examples of the qualitative results of C²GAN on Tohoku Zunko test data (The numbers on the right are the PSNRmask and SSIMask values for Generated $y$ versus Input $y^*$.)

## 4.2 Effect of Styles of Landmarks to Performance

In this section, we discuss what styles of landmarks are suitable for generating face images of anime characters.

**Styles of Landmark.** Based on the three ideas, we propose four new styles of the landmark in addition to the default style. The first idea is to draw a landmark with lines, the second idea is to color-code each part of the face, and the third idea is to make the lines thicker. Each point in a landmark extracted by the method of Marco et al. has information about which part of the landmark is which point. Therefore, it is easy to represent landmarks with lines and to color-code them by parts. Figure 7 shows examples of landmark images drawn by different styles. The detail of five styles of facial landmark are as follows:

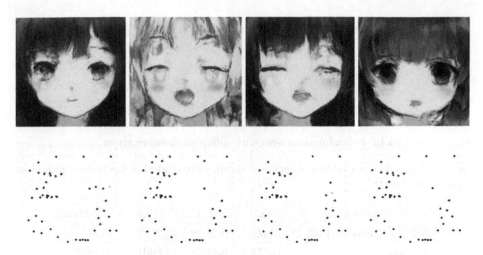

**Fig. 6.** Examples of landmark images generated by landmark generator in $C^2$GAN. The upper row is the generated face images that are inputs to the landmark generator, and the lower row are the outputs of the landmark generator for each face image.

Black Dot (default)
- The default style used in the experiments in Sect. 4.1
- Each point of facial landmarks is drawn in black (0, 0, 0) with a 2-pixel radius

Black Line
- Draw a series of landmark points as a straight line with a thickness of 1 pixel

Color Dot
- Green (0, 255, 0) for the contour landmark, blue (255, 0, 0) for the eyes, red (0, 0, 255) for the mouth
- The radius of points are the same as black point

Color Line
- Color scheme same as Color Dot
- Line thickness same as Black Line

Bold Color Line
- Drawing with double the thickness of the Color Line

**Dataset.** We prepared four new datasets with different landmark images using the face images and landmarks obtained in Sect. 4.1. Four episodes were used to train $C^2$GAN under the same conditions as the experiment described in Sect. 4.1.

**Quantitative Evaluation of Generated Face Images.** The results of the quantitative evaluation are shown in Table 3. Comparing Black Dot with other styles, we found that the Black Line and Color Line improved the evaluation metrics. In particular, the Color Line has the highest value in all four evaluation metrics.

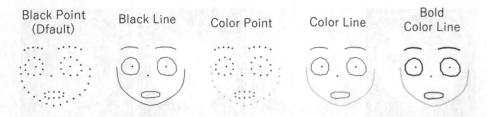

**Fig. 7.** landmark images with different drawing styles

**Table 3.** Quantitative evaluation results of varying the rendering method of landmarks on the input image

| Drawing style of landmark | PSNR | SSIM | PSNRmask | SSIMmask |
|---|---|---|---|---|
| Black Dot (same as Table 2) | 15.0044 | 0.4808 | 15.7187 | 0.6763 |
| Black Line | 15.0983 | 0.4873 | 15.8001 | 0.6802 |
| Color Dot | 15.0265 | 0.4806 | 15.7286 | 0.6750 |
| Color Line | **15.1738** | **0.4902** | **15.8517** | **0.6845** |
| Bold Color Line | 15.0662 | 0.4802 | 15.7672 | 0.6771 |

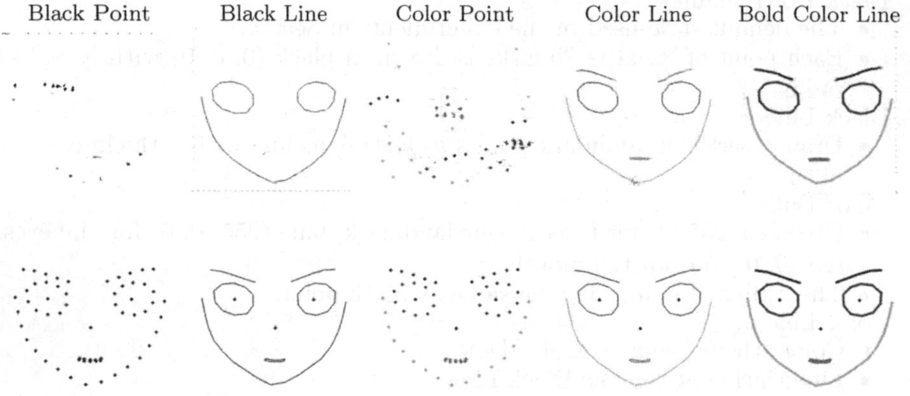

**Fig. 8.** Examples of the qualitative comparison of the facial landmark drawing styles. The upper row is the landmark images generated by the facial landmark generator and the lower row is the target landmark images.

**Qualitative Assessment of Generated Landmark Images.** Figure 8 shows some examples of landmark images generated by the $C^2$GAN landmark generator. The top row is the generated landmark images and the bottom row is the correct landmark images. In the case of Color Dot, the generated landmark images were almost the same for all the test data as in the case of Black Dot, but in the case of Black Line, Color Line, and Bold Color Line, the landmark images corresponding to the input images were generated. In particular, some models were able to generate the landmarks of the eyebrows, eyes, mouth, and facial contours correctly in Color Line and Bold Color Line, which improved the problems described in Sect. 4.1.

## 5    Conclusion

In this paper, we prepared datasets of face images of anime characters and generated face images of anime characters based on landmarks by using $C^2GAN$. We were able to generate face images corresponding to input landmarks although their outlines were not so clear. The quantitative evaluation metrics PSNR, SSIM, PSNRmask, and SSIMmask were improved by 0.1694, 0.0094, 0.133, and 0.0082, respectively, by dividing the landmarks into different colors for each face part and representing them as lines. Future work is to propose a model that can generate images with more characters and clearer outlines.

## References

1. Choi, Y., Choi, M., Kim, M., Ha, J.W., Kim, S., Choo, J.: StarGAN: unified generative adversarial networks for multi-domain image-to-image translation. In: Proceedings of the IEEE Conference on Computer Vision and Pattern Recognition, pp. 8789–8797 (2018)
2. Khungurn, P.: Talking head anime from a single image (2019). https://pkhungurn. github.io/talking-head-anime/2020212
3. Langner, O., Dotsch, R., Bijlstra, G., Wigboldus, D.J.H., Hawk, S.T., Van Knippenberg, A.D.: Presentation and validation of the radboud faces database. Cogn. Emot. **24**(8), 1377–1388 (2010)
4. Stricker, M., Augereau, O., Kise, K., Iwata, M.: Facial landmark detection for manga images. arXiv preprint arXiv:1811.03214 (2018)
5. Tang, H., Xu, D., Liu, G., Wang, W., Sebe, N., Yan, Y.: Cycle in cycle generative adversarial networks for keypoint-guided image generation. In: ACM Multi Media (2019)
6. Wang, Z., Bovik, A.C., Sheikh, H.R., Simoncelli, E.P.: Image quality assessment from error visibility to structural similarity. IEEE Trans. Image Process. **13**(4), 600–612 (2004)

# Text Block Segmentation in Comic Speech Bubbles

Christophe Rigaud$^{(\boxtimes)}$ ⓘ, Nhu-Van Nguyen, and Jean-Christophe Burie ⓘ

Laboratoire L3i, SAIL Joint Laboratory, Université de La Rochelle,
17042 La Rochelle CEDEX 1, France
{christophe.rigaud,nhu-van.nguyen,jean-christophe.burie}@univ-lr.fr

**Abstract.** Comics and manga text recognition are attracting an increasing research and industrial interest. Also, the state of the art text detection and OCR performances is starting to be mature enough to provide automatic text recognition for a variety of comics and manga writing styles. However, comics text layout sometimes prevents usual text line detection to be applied successfully, even within speech bubbles. In this paper, we propose a domain specific text block detection method able to detect single and multiple text block regions inside speech bubbles, in order to enhance OCR transcription and further post-processing. This approach presents very satisfactory results on all tested bubble styles from Latin and non-Latin scripts.

**Keywords:** Text block detection · Layout analysis · Comics analysis

## 1 Introduction

Comics around the world are following some commonly accepted rules and a lot of particularities [14]. In this paper we are tackling one of them related to speech bubble content layout. Speech bubbles (or speech balloons) are specific "easy to read" regions were most of the text of the story is encapsulated. Most of the time there is a single block of text within each speech bubble but sometimes there are several blocks. For instance, when one character has multiple balloons within a panel, often only the balloon nearest to the speaker's head has a tail, and the others are connected to it in sequence, sometimes using narrow bands (Fig. 1). In the first case, a classical OCR (Optical Recognition System) system is able to recognize characters, words and text lines if appropriately trained. However, in the case of sequential text block contained by several inter-connected speech bubbles, text lines can get mixed up between text block and the corresponding output transcription not following the natural reading order anymore (Fig. 2).

Multiple text blocks within speech bubble might be absent, rare or frequent depending on the album. For instance, in the eBDtheque dataset [8], even if there are not annotated they can be considered as rare because we counted only 21 over 1081 total speech balloon occurrences over its hundred images. In Manga109 dataset [2], there seems to be more frequent but as there are not

© Springer Nature Switzerland AG 2021
A. Del Bimbo et al. (Eds.): ICPR 2020 Workshops, LNCS 12666, pp. 250–261, 2021.
https://doi.org/10.1007/978-3-030-68780-9_22

**Fig. 1.** Examples of connected bubbles. Image credits from eBDtheque [8]: *Cyb - Bubblegom p. 36, Inoue Kyoumen pp. 6–13, Lubbin - Les bulles du labo p. 1, Zig et Puce - Millionaire p. 15 and Lamisseb - Et Pis Taf p. 13.* (Color figure online)

annotated neither. Unfortunately, we couldn't count them all manually in this dataset because they are too many annotated text boxes (147,918). On another hand, in some volumes of Belgian comics like XIII[1] or Thorgal[2], private albums shared by a partner from our SAIL joint laboratory, we visually counted 1 to 3 inter-connected bubble per page.

When such bubble configuration appears on almost every page, it becomes essential to correctly detect the blocks of text, without mixing up text lines of nearby blocks. Especially, when one is interested in the automatic text recognition (OCR), translation or speech synthesis (with coherent reading order). This process is part of a global understanding process consisting of segmenting regions like panel, bubble, text, comic character and "connecting" them all together. For instance, after a complete understanding, it would be possible to retrieve that "Hello Bob" is written in bubble $A$ which should be read before the connected bubble $B$ containing text "How are you?", both said by the comic character $C$ to the comic character $D$ and all these four elements are contained by panel $E$ in page $F$ of album $G$.

In order to contribute on this specific issue, we review the related literature in Sect. 2, propose a first approach in Sect. 3, present our results in Sect. 4 and conclude this work in Sect. 5.

---

[1] https://en.wikipedia.org/wiki/XIII_(comics).

[2] https://en.wikipedia.org/wiki/Thorgal.

**Fig. 2.** Example of mixed up text line detection (left) and the corrected detection using the proposed text block segmentation (right). Image credits: *XIII (Mystery) - vol. 11, Dargaud, p. 19.* (Color figure online)

## 2   Related Works

Text block segmentation has been largely studied in the literature and seems to be considered as solved for many types of documents. The most used technique for segmenting words, text lines and text blocks from letters (connected components) is Run Length Smoothing Algorithm (RLSA) [21]. This algorithm has been originally designed for Manhattan document layout analysis and rely on horizontal/vertical thresholds. Indeed, too high thresholds could erroneously merge different blocks in the document, while too low ones could return an excessively fragmented layout. Later approaches have attempted to set these thresholds automatically for Manhattan and non-Manhattan layout (RLSO) [7,20]. This approach has been applied to newspaper, scientific article, trademarks and administrative documents sometimes handwritten [4,22].

Another algorithm called Docstrum [16] consist in a bottom-up approach based on the nearest neighborhood clustering of connected components extracted from the document image.

Almost a decade later, Delaunay triangulation and its dual graph the Voronoi diagram have started to be applied to document segmentation [10,11]. The general problem they are trying to solve using Voronoi method is the following: given a set of element centers in the plane (center of letters, words or text lines), they associate with each element a region consisting of all points in the plane closer to that element than any other element. Then, a threshold is applied to segment blocks far enough away. It relates to inter-character spacing and inter-word/line spacing thresholds. These can be determined statistically from the document page and their effects is well described in [1].

A comparison of the above-mentioned methods is compiled in the following paper comparing performance of six-page segmentation algorithms [19].

Since the Convolutional Neural Network (CNN) era, researchers have used the RLSA method to build text blocks from scientific papers and classify them using bi-dimensional CNN [3]. Also, a recent work applied an on-the-shelf fully convolutional neural network (EAST) [24] to detect text in comic books but without considering text block regions [17].

Most of the works presented in the above literature are highly application-related which makes them hardly applicable to comic books because they often have a specific and variable layout. Moreover, the reviewed methods have been tested on Latin script and their effectiveness on non-Latin (complex) scripts like Japanese, Arabic, Indian and Korean is not obvious [12]. Most of them require application-related thresholds that can difficultly be learned from comic book image or speech bubble themselves because they contain very few words compared to other documents. We remarked that comics share some characteristics with free style documents such as posters, business card, envelope etc. [23]. For instance, isolated text and complex background.

Another related study proposed a method for computing speech bubble reading order but did not consider the underlying text block separation/ordering within speech bubbles [9].

From our knowledge, there isn't any method from the literature presenting results about text blocks segmentation within speech bubbles. Therefore, in the next section we present a first adaptive and parameter-free method able to separate text blocks in speech bubbles with horizontal or vertical text.

## 3   Proposed Approach

The proposed approach focuses on segmenting text blocks from speech bubbles more precisely than previous methods in order to be able to also segment multiple text blocks within the same bubble (when existing). This precise segmentation can enhance, for example, the straightforward text recognition step by avoiding text line mixing and also accurate reading order computing.

Most of the text being located in the speech bubble, we propose to rely on this domain-specific feature because it has been demonstrated that domain knowledge can boost text segmentation performances [6].

The specific multiple text block layout of these speech balloons makes previous method not straightforward applicable. Moreover, it currently prevents from using any training-based method because of the lack of training data. From our knowledge, publicly available datasets provide multiple text line (eBDtheque) or single text block (Manga109) location annotations within speech bubbles but none of them provide multiple text block annotation (in connected balloons).

Even though there are not as frequent as single text block speech bubbles, they may be a key issue for some specific albums as previously mentioned in the introduction. Note that the proposed approach is designed to be independent from text language and script, and assumes that speech bubble has been previously segmented. One interested by segmenting speech bubbles can use any methods from the literature such as [5, 13, 15, 18].

Regarding the literature, the Voronoi approaches seems to be the most appropriate for separating text blocks but it requires several parameters such as interletter space. On another hand, speech bubble segmentation methods from the literature do not guarantee to detect multi text block bubble as separated bubbles so text line lines may be confused in the subsequent text recognition step. To tackle this challenge, we preferred to propose a new adaptive approach based on each speech bubble content (robust to script and letter size changes).

The proposed method is best when applied within previously segmented speech bubbles. However, it can also be applied on the full image with some extra processing depending on the comics layout. The method consists in three steps:

1. Content detection
2. Bounding box enlarging
3. Text block detection

The proposed process is illustrated in Fig. 4 from top to bottom, we detail it in the next three paragraphs.

**Content Detection.** The first step consists in detecting all connected components contained inside bubble region using for instance connected components labelling (also called blob extraction). Then we compute their bounding boxes to be used in next step (see red boxes and corresponding masks in the Fig. 4).

**Box Enlarging.** The objective it to merge these bounding boxes in order to form a single region surrounding all letters from the same text block and not overlapping other text blocks. To do so, we magnify the width and the height of previously computed bounding boxes pixel by pixel and centered on the original box. Then, we analyse the evolution on the number of contours in the corresponding mask and stop the enlargement just at the beginning of the period when the number of components remains stable the longest before getting down to zero. In Fig. 4, its start with 38 contours and the longest period before zero is the one with 2 contours where the process automatically stops (see bar graph in the Fig. 3).

The growing region is limited to balloon contour, this means the set of enlarged boxes is cropped afterward if getting out. At that end, this should form a homogeneous region surrounding contained text blocks without touching any other.

**Text Block Detection.** We detect the external contours within the corresponding mask and label them as text block regions. Once the text blocks are extracted, they can be sent to an OCR system in place of the speech balloon. By sending properly segmented text blocks instead of speech bubbles to the OCR system, we avoid text line confusions.

After these three steps, the text blocks can be analysed independently by, for instance, an OCR system and text line detection and reading order should no longer get mixed up. Note that in this very simple example, other trivial methods could have been effective, such as horizontal/vertical histogram projection, but this last can not be generalised to more complex examples that will be presented in the next section.

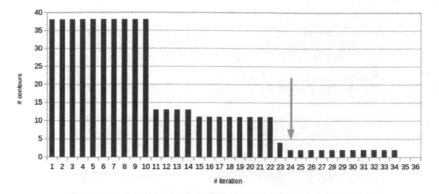

**Fig. 3.** Number of detected contours according to the number of iterations of bounding box enlarging and stop point (red arrow). (Color figure online)

## 4    Results

We evaluated the proposed method for text block segmentation on several albums of Latin and Japanese scripts. Despite the ground truth, we performed only a qualitative evaluation on comics images from three datasets: eBDtheque (Fig. 5), Manga109 (Fig. 6) and other private albums (Fig. 7). (Color figure online) In these three illustrations, the speech bubble segmentation shown with green line is used as prerequisite of the proposed method (text block segmentation). The detected text line bounding boxes are represented with a red line and are results from Tesseract OCR text line segmentation module (not part of the proposed method). There are shown only to visually measure the impact of one of the most frequent post-processing. Only the text block segmentation shown with a blue line are results from the proposed method.

### 4.1    eBDtheque Dataset

Qualitative results on some images from the eBDtheque dataset are presented in Fig. 5. They consist in different speech bubbles from a French webcomic on the left, a Japanese manga in the center and two printed French comics on the right-hand side. Unfortunately, we did not find any connected balloon of American comics style in image from this dataset. We consider the results on the webcomic as perfect because the three computed text block polygons are surrounding each of the three text blocks contained in the connected bubble, without touching any of the text letter (which is a common source of error for OCR system). The center manga bubble is also considered as a perfect result for the same reasons, even if the script is totally different from Latin. The third column bubbles shows some errors. Two of them are due to a missed character from the bubble segmentation algorithm (green line) which had difficulties to process these border-free bubbles in this low definition image. Another cause of error due to very close character from different lines of text is visible in the bottom-right image where there are no extra spaces between the second and the third text line.

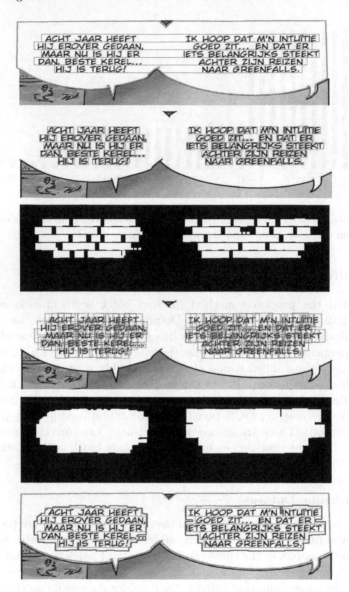

**Fig. 4.** Text block segmentation steps: from top to bottom, original erroneous text line detection (red) inside their properly segmented balloon (green); connected component (CC) bounding box detection (red) and corresponding mask; final enlarged CC and mask; text block detection (blue) and text line detection within text block. Image credits: *XIII (Mystery) - vol. 11, Dargaud, p. 19.* (Color figure online)

**Fig. 5.** Correct (left and center columns) and wrong (right column) results on eBDtheque dataset in French and Japanese (digitized images). Image credits from eBDtheque: *Lamisseb - Et Pis Taf p. 5, Inoue Kyoumen p. 6, Lubbin - Les bulles du labo p. 1 and Zig et Puce - Millionaire p. 15.* (Color figure online)

### 4.2 Manga109 Dataset

Qualitative results on some images from the Manga109 dataset are presented in Fig. 6. They are selected from two random titles from Manga109 dataset: Seishinki Vulnus 2 and Platinum Jungle 1. Even if the Japanese script is more complex than Latin script, the proposed method still performs well for text block detection. Vertical text lines are well grouped into text blocks will juxtaposed Furigana character as well (which sometime appear no detected by the text line detection algorithm used has illustrative post-processing here). In the bottom-right corner, we added an interesting single block speech bubble where spaced dots have been segmented as separated text blocks by mistake. This is due to their successive small size that did not successfully merge with other surrounding components during the enlargement step.

### 4.3 Private Dataset

We evaluated our method on other images from private albums in Dutch and French (non-shareable due to copyright). These images are from recent digital born Franco-Belgium comics and therefore has the advantage to be very clean and avoids any error due to image degradation. On the left half of Fig. 7, all text blocks have been well detected, even the "..." at the end of some sentences. However, on the two top bubbles, there are an exaggerated extension on the left side of the text block. This is due to the touching letters of the word "MAAR" which produces an extension equivalent to half of the word size instead of half of the letter size, as on the remaining of the text block outline.

The two connected balloons in the right column have not been well separated which makes mixed line detection (same as without text block detection). In each block, there are some letters or punctuation symbols from the two connected bubbles that are very close, relatively to their size, and the proposed method did not succeed in separating them.

**Fig. 6.** Vertical text line detection before (left) and after (right) text block detection in Manga109 dataset in Japanese (digitized images). Image credits from Manga109: *Seishinki Vulnus 2 (Yuzuru Shimazaki) and Platinum Jungle 1 (Masami Shinohara).* (Color figure online)

**Fig. 7.** Correct (left columns) and wrong (right column) results on private albums in Dutch and French (digital-born images). Image credits: *XIII (Mystery) - vol. 12, Dargaud, p. 30, 44 and Le Feu de Thesee (Survivre) - Les Humanoïdes Associés, p. 5, 18.* (Color figure online)

### 4.4 Synthesis

We qualitatively evaluated the proposed method over few images from diverse datasets in order to demonstrate its robustness. All the reported errors have different importance depending on the bubble layout. For instance, in vertical Japanese script, if a text block is at the right or on the left of another text block it will probably not have any impact on the post-processing step because the text line detection will not get mixed anyway. However, if it is located above or below another text block within the same bubble, the text lines from the two blocks have more chances to be merged by text line detection algorithms writing (see Fig. 8). Note that in all the experiments we performed, we observed that the enlargement step mainly stops between 2 and 4 times the original bounding box width and height (inter-dependent) e.g. $width * 2$ and $height * 2$.

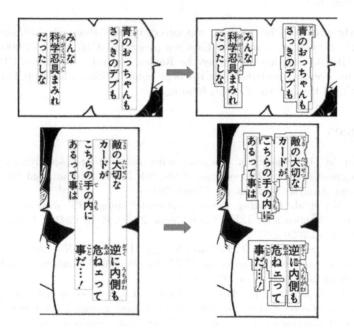

**Fig. 8.** Examples of vertical text line detection before (left) and after (right) text block detection for vertically and horizontally connected bubbles in Japanese manga. Image credits: *Boruto - vol. 7, Kana, p. 82, 103.* (Color figure online)

## 5   Conclusion

In this paper we proposed a simple, fast, parameter-free and efficient domain-specific method for segmenting single and multiple text blocks from single and connected speech bubbles. Even if connected speech bubbles are not so frequent, this method requiring little processing can easily complement other techniques such as speech balloon segmentation, comics OCR system and speech synthesis, to boost their results when connected speech bubble appear. We tested it only within pre-processed speech bubbles but we believe that it is not mandatory and will do more experiments in this direction. The proposed method turned out to be more suitable for detached writing (non-cursive) because it is based on connected component analysis and word size is much more variable than character size which alters the precision of the boundary of the computed blocks. Also, it works very well in the great majority of tested bubbles but sometimes fails when text blocks are very close (spaced by less than a letter/symbol size).

In the future, we plan to carry out experiments on other scripts like Arabic, Indian, Korean, etc. Also, we would like to remove the width and height inter-dependence to better fit text blocks, especially for non-Latin scripts. The annotation of existing comic book image datasets with precise text block positions and corresponding text line transcriptions would allow quantitative results and comparisons.

**Acknowledgements.** This work is supported by the Research National Agency (ANR) in the framework of the 2017 LabCom program (ANR 17-LCV2-0006-01), the CPER NUMERIC program funded by the Region Nouvelle Aquitaine, CDA, Charente Maritime French Department, La Rochelle conurbation authority (CDA) and the European Union through the FEDER funding.

# References

1. Agrawal, M., Doermann, D.: Context-aware and content-based dynamic Voronoi page segmentation. In: Proceedings of the 9th IAPR International Workshop on Document Analysis Systems, pp. 73–80 (2010)
2. Aizawa, K., et al.: Building a manga dataset "Manga109" with annotations for multimedia applications. IEEE MultiMedia **27**(2), 8–18 (2020). https://doi.org/10.1109/mmul.2020.2987895
3. Augusto Borges Oliveira, D., Palhares Viana, M.: Fast CNN-based document layout analysis. In: Proceedings of the IEEE International Conference on Computer Vision Workshops, pp. 1173–1180 (2017)
4. Barlas, P., Adam, S., Chatelain, C., Paquet, T.: A typed and handwritten text block segmentation system for heterogeneous and complex documents. In: 2014 11th IAPR International Workshop on Document Analysis Systems, pp. 46–50. IEEE (2014)
5. Dubray, D., Laubrock, J.: Deep CNN-based speech balloon detection and segmentation for comic books. In: 2019 International Conference on Document Analysis and Recognition (ICDAR), pp. 1237–1243. IEEE (2019)
6. Fan, K.C., Liu, C.H., Wang, Y.K.: Segmentation and classification of mixed text/graphics/image documents. Pattern Recogn. Lett. **15**(12), 1201–1209 (1994). https://doi.org/10.1016/0167-8655(94)90110-4
7. Ferilli, S., Leuzzi, F., Rotella, F., Esposito, F.: A run length smoothing-based algorithm for non-Manhattan document segmentation. Convegno del Gruppo Italiano Ricercatori in Pattern Recognition (2012)
8. Guérin, C., et al.: eBDtheque: a representative database of comics. In: 2013 12th International Conference on Document Analysis and Recognition, pp. 1145–1149 (Aug 2013)

9. Guérin, C., Rigaud, C., Bertet, K., Revel, A.: An ontology-based framework for the automated analysis and interpretation of comic books' images. Inf. Sci. **378**, 109–130 (2017). https://doi.org/10.1016/j.ins.2016.10.032
10. Kise, K., Sato, A., Iwata, M.: Segmentation of page images using the area Voronoi diagram. Comput. Vis. Image Underst. **70**(3), 370–382 (1998)
11. Koo, H.I., Cho, N.I.: State estimation in a document image and its application in text block identification and text line extraction. In: Daniilidis, K., Maragos, P., Paragios, N. (eds.) ECCV 2010, Part II. LNCS, vol. 6312, pp. 421–434. Springer, Heidelberg (2010). https://doi.org/10.1007/978-3-642-15552-9_31
12. Kumar, K.S., Kumar, S., Jawahar, C.: On segmentation of documents in complex scripts. In: Ninth International Conference on Document Analysis and Recognition (ICDAR 2007), vol. 2, pp. 1243–1247. IEEE (2007)
13. Liu, X., Li, C., Zhu, H., Wong, T.-T., Xu, X.: Text-aware balloon extraction from manga. Vis. Comput. **32**(4), 501–511 (2015). https://doi.org/10.1007/s00371-015-1084-0
14. McCloud, S.: Understanding Comics: The Invisible Art. Harper Perennial, Northampton (1993)
15. Nguyen, N.-V., Rigaud, C., Burie, J.-C.: Multi-task model for comic book image analysis. In: Kompatsiaris, I., Huet, B., Mezaris, V., Gurrin, C., Cheng, W.-H., Vrochidis, S. (eds.) MMM 2019, Part II. LNCS, vol. 11296, pp. 637–649. Springer, Cham (2019). https://doi.org/10.1007/978-3-030-05716-9_57
16. O'Gorman, L.: The document spectrum for page layout analysis. IEEE Trans. Pattern Anal. Mach. Intell. **15**(11), 1162–1173 (1993). https://doi.org/10.1109/34.244677
17. Rayar, F., Uchida, S.: Comic text detection using neural network approach. In: Kompatsiaris, I., Huet, B., Mezaris, V., Gurrin, C., Cheng, W.-H., Vrochidis, S. (eds.) MMM 2019, Part II. LNCS, vol. 11296, pp. 672–683. Springer, Cham (2019). https://doi.org/10.1007/978-3-030-05716-9_60
18. Rigaud, C., Burie, J.-C., Ogier, J.-M.: Text-independent speech balloon segmentation for comics and manga. In: Lamiroy, B., Dueire Lins, R. (eds.) GREC 2015. LNCS, vol. 9657, pp. 133–147. Springer, Cham (2017). https://doi.org/10.1007/978-3-319-52159-6_10
19. Shafait, F., Keysers, D., Breuel, T.: Performance evaluation and benchmarking of six-page segmentation algorithms. IEEE Trans. Pattern Anal. Mach. Intell. **30**, 941–54 (2008). https://doi.org/10.1109/TPAMI.2007.70837
20. Sun, H.M.: Page segmentation for Manhattan and non-Manhattan layout documents via selective CRLA. In: Eighth International Conference on Document Analysis and Recognition (ICDAR'05), pp. 116–120. IEEE (2005)
21. Wahl, F.M., Wong, K.Y., Casey, R.G.: Block segmentation and text extraction in mixed text/image documents. Comput. Graph. Image Process. **20**(4), 375–390 (1982). https://doi.org/10.1016/0146-664X(82)90059-4
22. Wang, D., Srihari, S.N.: Classification of newspaper image blocks using texture analysis. Comput. Vis. Graph. Image Process. **47**(3), 327–352 (1989). https://doi.org/10.1016/0734-189X(89)90116-3
23. Xiaolu, S., Changsong, L., Xiaoqing, D., Yanming, Z.: Text line extraction in free style document. In: Document Recognition and Retrieval XVI, vol. 7247, pp. 72470L1 72470L12 (2009). https://doi.org/10.1117/12.805695. International Society for Optics and Photonics
24. Zhou, X., et al.: EAST: an efficient and accurate scene text detector. CoRR abs/1704.03155 (2017). http://arxiv.org/abs/1704.03155

# MMDLCA - Multi-modal Deep Learning: Challenges and Applications

# Workshop on Multi-modal Deep Learning: Challenges and Applications (MMDLCA)

## Workshop Description

Deep learning is now recognized as one of the key software engines that drives the new industrial revolution. The majority of current deep learning research efforts have been dedicated to single-modal data processing. Pronounced manifestations are deep learning based visual recognition and speech recognition. Although significant progress made, single-modal data is often insufficient to derive accurate and robust deep models in many applications. Our digital world is by nature multi-modal, that combines different modalities of data such as text, audio, images, animations, videos and interactive content. Multi-modal is the most popular form for information representation and delivery. For example, posts for hot social events are typically composed of textual descriptions, images and videos. For medical diagnosis, the joint use of medical imaging and textual reports is also essential. Multi-modal data is common for human to make accurate perceptions and decisions. Multi-modal deep learning that is capable of learning from information presented in multiple modalities and consequently making predictions based on multi-modal input is much in demand.

MMDLCA workshop calls for scientific works that illustrate the most recent progress on multi-modal deep learning, e.g., multi-modal data capture, integration, modelling, understanding and analysis, and how to leverage them to derive accurate and robust AI models in many applications. It is a timely topic following the rapid development of deep learning technologies and their remarkable applications to many fields. It serves as a forum to bring together active researchers and practitioners to share their recent advances in this exciting area.

MMDLCA workshop 2020 was organized in conjunction with the 25th International Conference on Pattern Recognition. The format of the workshop included invited keynotes and technical presentations. The workshop is hold online and is expected to be attended by around 20 people on average. This year we received 19 submissions for reviews, from authors belonging to 9 distinct countries. After an accurate and thorough peer-review process, we selected 11 papers for presentation at the workshop. The review process focused on the quality of the papers, their scientific novelty and applicability to existing multi-modal deep learning techniques. The acceptance of the papers was the result of the reviewers' discussion and agreement. All the high quality papers were accepted, and the acceptance rate was 58%.The accepted articles represent an interesting mix of techniques to solve recurrent as well as theories and novel application scenarios related to multi-modal deep learning, as well as surveying the recent progress in this area.

Last but not least, we would like to thank the MMDLCA 2020 Program Committee, whose members made the workshop possible with their rigorous and timely review process. We would also like to thank ICPR for hosting the workshop and our emerging community, and the ICPR workshop chairs for the valuable help and support.

# Organization

## MMDLCA Chairs

Zhineng Chen      Chinese Academy of Sciences, China
Xirong Li      Renmin University of China, China
Efstratios Gavves      University of Amsterdam, Netherlands
Mei Chen      Microsoft Cloud & AI, USA
Ioannis Kompatsiaris      CERTH-ITI, Greece

## Program Committee

Marco Bertini      University of Florence, Italy
Juan Cao      Chinese Academy of Sciences, China
Jingjing Chen      Fudan University, China
Wen-Huang Cheng      National Chiao Tung University, Taiwan
Huazhu Fu      Inception Institute of Artificial Intelligence, UAE
Chuang Gan      MIT, USA
Bogdan Ionescu      University Politehnica of Bucharest, Romania
Anan Liu      Tianjin University, China
Symeon Papadopoulos      CERTH-ITI, Greece
Tiberio Uricchio      University of Florence, Italy
Nikolaos V. Boulgouris      Brunel University London, UK
Wei Zhang      JD AI Research, China
Kai Hu      Xiangtan University, China
Hongtao Xie      University of Science and Technology of China, China
Lei Huang      Ocean University of China, China
Zheng Lin      Chinese Academy of Sciences, China
Jiaming Xu      Chinese Academy of Sciences, China
Shuai Zhao      Chinese Academy of Sciences, China

## Additional Reviewers

Shuyan Liu
Zheng Wang
Yuqian Fu
Jinyi Long

# Organization

# Hierarchical Consistency and Refinement for Semi-supervised Medical Segmentation

Zixiao Wang[1,2], Hai Xu[2], Youliang Tian[1(✉)], and Hongtao Xie[1,2]

[1] Guizhou Provincial Key Laboratory of Public Big Data, Guizhou University,
Guiyang 550025, China
yltian@gzu.edu.cn
[2] School of Information Science and Technology, University of Science
and Technology of China, Hefei 230026, China

**Abstract.** Semi-supervised learning exploits unlabeled data to improve generalization ability with insufficient annotations. In recent years, Mean Teacher method (MT) obtained impressive performance using prediction consistency as regularization. However, severe ambiguity in medical images makes the targets in the teacher model highly unreliable in obscure regions, thereby limits the model capability. To address this problem, we propose a novel multi-task learning semi-supervised framework to gain hierarchical consistency through training process. Specifically, we introduce region and shape predictions as subtasks to obtain the coarse-grained location and fine-grained boundary information. Then we predict pixel-level segmentation by fusing the hierarchical feature. Since calculating consistency loss in more loose regions typically alleviates the degradation caused by learning from unreliable targets, our teacher model generate guidance from each of the subtasks. Moreover, we focus on the geometrical correlations in different tasks and proposed the constraint method to refine the segmentation for accurate guidance. Experiments on the left atrium segmentation dataset show our algorithm achieves state-of-the-art performance comparing with other semi-supervised methods.

**Keywords:** Semi-supervised learning · Mean-teacher · Multi-task · Medical image segmentation

## 1 Introduction

Segmentation is an important part of medical images analysis that contains valuable information for medical diagnosis and treatment. Recently, convolutional neural networks (CNNs) have achieved tremendous success and been widely applied in medical segmentation tasks. However annotating medical images is expensive and time-consuming. Therefore, semi-supervised learning which

© Springer Nature Switzerland AG 2021
A. Del Bimbo et al. (Eds.): ICPR 2020 Workshops, LNCS 12666, pp. 267–276, 2021.
https://doi.org/10.1007/978-3-030-68780-9_23

exploits unannotated data to improve the capability of models is a necessary and effective way for medical image segmentation task.

The main challenge of semi-supervised learning lies in how to exploit underlying knowledge of unlabeled data to improve the segmentation performance. Quite a few approaches [3,5] simultaneously optimize both supervised and unsupervised objectives with multi-task learning to utilize unlabeled data. For example, [3] uses an attention mechanism to separate brain MR images into different class regions and train a semi-supervised network with corresponding reconstruction loss. Besides, predicting in edge-level as a auxiliary task has been widely used in supervised learning recently [9,15]. Similarly, [8] introduces a pre-trained edge detection model to convert the boundary details to segmentation knowledge with transfer learning on unlabeled dataset. However, existing methods employ boundary segmentation by introduced complex sub-network which makes it difficult to optimise on limited labeled dataset. Consistency regularization, which encourages consistent predictions for unlabeled input under different perturbations, is also widely employed to enable the model to learn intrinsic invariances. Bortsova et al. [2] propose a Siamese architecture with two identical branches to learn transformation equivalence for semi-supervised chest X-ray segmentation. $\Pi$-model [6] presents the peer-consistency where predictions are inferred by the same model with random augmentation and dropout. Self-ensembling strategy [12], which integrates information of intermediate training steps, can help improve the quality of targets. Cui et al. [4] extends the Teacher-student model to extract segmentation consistency for semi-supervised brain lesion segmentation. To strengthen the reliability of the targets, Yu et al. [13] propose an uncertainty-aware framework which selects more reliable targets based on model uncertainty estimation. However, image obscurity and ambiguity notably increase the prediction uncertainty. Therefore, some hard but informative areas (e.g., boundaries) may be ignored consistently during training, which limits the potential of model capability.

In this paper, we propose a multi-task learning framework based on MT method [12] (ML-MT) to obtain more reliable guidance. We design a multi-task segmentation architecture to build the student and teacher model. The teacher model is updated by the exponential moving average (EMA) of the student weights while the student is optimized with the auxiliary of the teacher's prediction. To overcome the drawback of teacher model's single high-unreliable prediction and diminish the influence of the noisy guidance, we utilize two subtasks to generate hierarchical segmentations and optimise ensemble consistency loss which combines multi-level predictions. Specifically, a region-level detection task is introduced since predictions in more loose regions typically alleviates the unreliability of targets. Then we define a shape-level detection task relatively to gain the boundary map and provide the fine-grained information. As a consequence, the pixel-level segmentation is predicted by fusing the multi-level feature above and the hierarchical consistency loss can be calculated from different views of the object. In consider of the spatial correlations in multi tasks, we further propose a constraint method to refine the segmentation for more reliable guidance.

Experiments on the Atrial Segmentation Challenge dataset show that our method has remarkable improvements and outperforms other semi-supervised segmentation methods.

## 2    Method

In this section, we first introduce the details of our multi-task segmentation architecture for hierarchical objective prediction. Then we adjust mean teacher method and present our ML-MT framework to get better performance with hierarchical consistency and refinement method.

### 2.1    Hierarchical Task Decompose

Due to the severe noise and ambiguities in medical images, segmentation networks encounter difficulties in extracting the valuable feature and thereby influence the label reliability from teacher model. To capture more useful information and enhance model capability, we propose a multi-task model to decompose the original segmentation task into three hierarchical tasks: region-level, shape-level, and object-level segmentation.

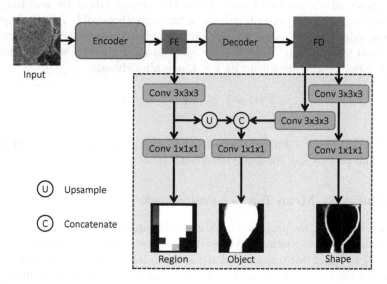

**Fig. 1.** The structure of our multi-task segmentation model. FE and FD stand for the output features from the encoder and decoder respectively. Conv3 × 3 × 3 denotes a convolution layer that combined 3 × 3 × 3 convolution - batch normalization – ReLU together. Conv1 × 1 × 1 means the 1 × 1 × 1 convolution layer, applied to generate segmentation maps to predict the region, shape and object.

**Multi-task Segmentation Architecture.** As illustrated in Fig. 1, our multi-task segmentation model is based on the general encoder-decoder structure (e.g., V-Net [10]). We utilize feature maps from both the encoder and decoder (FE & FD) to capture multi-level information. Then some light-weight layers is introduced to generate hierarchical predictions using features in the relevant level. Region segmentation is a fundamental task which aims to get the coarse segmentation and doesn't need rich local information. Hence we take advantages of the high-level semantic feature FE from encoder to detect the region-level map. As shown in Fig. 1, we employ a $3 \times 3 \times 3$ convolution block and a $1 \times 1 \times 1$ convolutional layer for transformation and prediction. Relatively, shape segmentation is presented to segment edge-around regions. We choose The feature map FD (output by the decoder) to capture the geometric information and employ the same structure as the region segmentation. With the discriminative capability of intermediate features enhanced by auxiliary tasks, we finally fuse the upsampled FE and FD to generate object segmentation through a convolutional layer.

**Label Formulation.** To supervise the training process with hierarchy segmentation, we introduce an implement-friendly algorithm to generate labels for subtasks. For region-level detection, our goal is to segment foreground in loose regions. So we divide the input into cubes by a $s \times s \times s$ grid ($s$ stands for the output stride of the encoder) and obtain the region labels by selecting cubes with foreground pixel percentage over a manual threshold. As to shape-level detection, edge-around pixels should be predicted to describe the geometrical fine-grained information. We define the edge-around pixel by whether there is a different label neighbour within its $k \times k$ neighbourhood:

$$F(i) = 1 - \prod_{j \in Nb(i)} \mathbb{1}[l_j = l_i] \tag{1}$$

where $Nb(i)$ is the $k \times k$ neighbour of $i$; $\mathbb{1}[l_j = l_i]$ is a binary indicator denotes whether the pixel $j$ has the same label with pixel $i$.

## 2.2 Multi-task Mean Teacher Framework

As shown in Fig. 2, we proposed a multi-task semi-supervised framework based on the mean teacher method. We use the segmentation architecture described in Sect. 2.1 to build our teacher and student model. During the training process, the teacher model generates multi target predictions to guide the optimization of the student model.

For the 3D MR image dataset $X = (x_i)_{i \in [N+M]}$, let $X_l = (x_l)_{l \in [N]}$ indicate the annotated samples with labels $Y_l = (y_l)_{l \in [N]}$, and $X_u = (x_u)_{u \in [N+1,M]}$ denotes the unlabeled samples. Following the label generation algorithm in Sect. 2.1, we can get $Y_{r_l} = (y_{r_l})_{l \in [N]}$ as the region label and $Y_{s_l} = (y_{s_l})_{l \in [N]}$ as the shape label. Then for labeled data $X_l$, the student model is optimized by minimizing supervised loss:

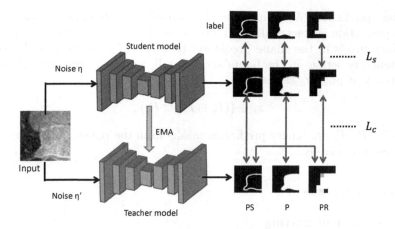

**Fig. 2.** The pipeline of our MT method. $L_s$ means the supervised loss with labeled data. $L_c$ means the consistency loss between the student model and teacher model.

$$L_S = \sum_{l=1}^{N} \{L(f_o(x_l, \theta), y_l) + L(f_r(x_l, \theta), y_{r_l}) + L(f_s(x_l, \theta), y_{s_l})\} \quad (2)$$

Where $f_o(\cdot)$ denotes the object segmentation branch of the network, $f_r(\cdot)$ denotes the region segmentation branch, $f_s(\cdot)$ denotes the shape segmentation branch and $L(\cdot)$ denotes the supervised loss (e.g., cross-entropy loss and dice loss).

**Hierarchical Consistency Loss.** Based on the multi-task segmentation model, we replace the single consistency guidance with hierarchical consistency loss to takes advantages of teacher model's multiple predictions. Specifically, three consistency losses (i.e., $L_{c_r}$, $L_{c_b}$, and $L_{c_o}$) between the student model and teacher model are defined with respect to each target. Empirically, we adopt the mean square error (MSE) to measure the consistency loss. The total consistency loss becomes,

$$L_c = \sum_{i=1}^{N+M} \sum_{f \in \{f_o, f_r, f_s\}} L_{MSE}(f(x_i, \theta, \eta), f(x_i, \theta', \eta')), \quad (3)$$

Where $\theta, \theta'$ denotes parameters of the student model and teacher model; $\eta$ and $\eta'$ represent corresponding input perturbations. To filter the highly unreliable areas, when calculating the consistency loss $L_c$, we only select heigh score areas with a manual threshold.

**Refinement Consistency Guidance.** As assembling the consistency loss in each tasks directly does not take into account the spatial correlations between them, to make full use of the subtasks, we further propose a refinement strategy on object prediction. We assume the object prediction should be included in the region prediction geometrically and filter inconsistent areas. Besides, we exploit boundary pixels in the shape prediction to ensure the object branch also has consistent prediction on the boundary. Overall, we finally calculate the object consistency at pixel $x_i$ subject to,

$$x_i \in \{(P_r \cap P_o) \cup P_s\}, \tag{4}$$

where $P_r$, $P_o$, $P_s$ are binary prediction masks from the region, object and shape branches, respectively.

## 3   Experiments

### 3.1   Experiment Setting

**Data Description.** We evaluate our method on the Atrial Segmentation Challenge dataset, including 100 annotated 3D MR images with isotropic resolution of $0.625 \times 0.625 \times 0.625 \, \mathrm{mm}^3$. To ensure comparison fairness, we perform data pre-processing and split the data as referred to settings in [13]. Overall, we have 80 cases for training and 20 cases for evaluation. All input patches are cropped around the heart region and normalized the data to zero mean and unit variance.

**Implement Details.** We use V-Net [10] without residual connections as our backbone. A joint loss (i.e., cross-entropy loss and dice loss) is used to supervise the object segmentation and shape segmentation for labeled data and only the cross-entropy loss is used for the region prediction. Emprically, the threshold in selecting region label is set to 0.2 and the neighbour to determine edge-pixel is 4. The threshold we set to gain heigh score areas is 0.8. During training process, the ratio of the consistency loss is controlled by a time-dependent Gaussian warming up weight $w(t) = 1 * e^{-5(1-t/t_{max})^2}$, where $t$ is the current iteration number and $t_{max}$ is the total iteration number in training. Student parameters are optimized by SGD with a $l_2$ weight decay of 0.0001 and momentum of 0.9. The base learning rate is 0.01 and divided by 10 after 4000 iterations. The EMA decay to update teacher parameters is 0.99 in the first 4000 Iterations and changes it to 0.999 in the rest iterations. After training process, we choose teacher model's object segmentation as the final result. All networks are implemented in Pytorch with a gtx1080ti GPU and the batch size is set to 4. We train a total of 6000 iterations to get the best results.

### 3.2   Evaluation of Our Method

We first conduct a series of experiments to test the validity of our method. We use four metrics to evaluate the segmentation performances, including Dice, Jaccard, ASD (average surface distance) and 95HD (95% Hausdorff Distance). As referred to [13], we split the training data into two subsets, i.e., 16 cases (twenty percent) as labeled data and 64 cases as unlabeled data for semi-supervised learning.

**Table 1.** Quantitative performances of our multi-task network

| Method | Labeled | Unlabeled | Dice [%] | Jaccard [%] | ASD [voxel] | 95HD [voxel] |
|---|---|---|---|---|---|---|
| Vanilla V-Net | 16 | 0 | 84.13 | 73.26 | 4.75 | 17.93 |
| Multi-task V-Net | 16 | 0 | 86.71 | 77.08 | 2.16 | 9.01 |
| Vanilla V-Net | 80 | 0 | 90.25 | 82.40 | 1.91 | 8.29 |
| Multi-task V-Net | 80 | 0 | 91.45 | 84.33 | 1.52 | 5.78 |
| V-Net MT | 16 | 64 | 88.23 | 79.29 | 2.73 | 10.64 |
| Multi-task MT | 16 | 64 | 89.27 | 80.85 | 2.29 | 8.41 |

**Evaluation of Multi-task Network.** As shown in Table 1, compared with the Vanilla V-Net, our multi-task segmentation network improves the performance in both supervised task and semi-supervised task. When using 16 cases for supervised segmentation, the Multi-task V-Net achieving 2.6% improvements of Dice. The promotion is still over 1% when training with 80 cases, with a quite convincing segmentation Dice of 91.45%. As for 95HD the multi-task model also obtained impressive performance with a reduce of 9 and 3 voxels which means our model predicts more accurately in the edge-around regions. Moreover, results in Table 1 of semi-supervised experiments (the last two rows) also indicate the effectiveness of Multi-task learning in semi-supervised segmentation with a 1% improvement. Overall, from the experiments on multi-task segmentation architecture, we can see our model gains an obvious improvement especially using less labeled data though only some light-weight layers is employed.

**Table 2.** Quantitative performances of our semi-supervised framework

| Method | Labeled | Unlabeled | Dice [%] | Jaccard [%] | ASD [voxel] | 95HD [voxel] |
|---|---|---|---|---|---|---|
| ML-MT-OC | 16 | 64 | 89.27 | 80.85 | 2.29 | 8.41 |
| ML-MT-NR | 16 | 64 | 90.09 | 82.10 | 1.91 | 6.83 |
| ML-MT | 16 | 64 | 90.57 | 82.86 | 1.76 | 6.28 |

**Evaluation of Semi-supervised Framework.** To evaluate the effectiveness of our semi-supervised framework, we carry out some ablation studies on ML-MT with the same set of hyperparameters. We first evaluate ML-MT optimizing with only object consistency loss as ML-MT-OC. Then the hierarchical consistency loss without refinement strategy is introduced in ML-MT-NR. As illustrated in Table 2, with hierarchical consistency on multiple targets, ML-MT-NR gains an improvement of 0.8% Dice. With the refinement consistency guidance, ML-MT achieves 90.57% Dice and further improves the performance by 0.5%. The comparison results above demonstrate the hierarchical consistency is validity for strengthening the robustness using unlabeled data set. Moreover, combining with geometrical priori works better than simply fusing the multiple tasks together.

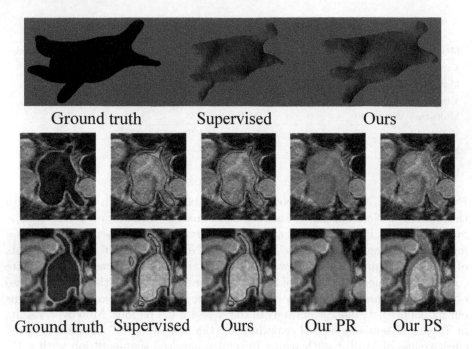

Ground truth          Supervised          Ours

Ground truth   Supervised      Ours        Our PR       Our PS

**Fig. 3.** Examples of segmentation results of supervised learning and ML-MT. Blue shows the ground truth and red shows the prediction of models. PR and PS denote region prediction and shape prediction. (Color figure online)

### 3.3 Comparison with the State-of-the-Art

We further compare the Multi-task Learning Mean teacher (ML-MT) network with several existing state-of-the-art semi-supervised methods. These methods explore underlying knowledge of unlabeled data from different perspectives: self-training [1], deep adversarial network [14], adversarial learning [11] and transformation consistency [7]. The results and comparison are illustrated in Table 3. As listed, ML-MT, which employs hierarchical consistencies of multiple targets, outperforms previous state-of-the-art methods with a Dice of 90.57%. We also employ experiment ML-MT-UN which calculates consistency loss only on unlabeled data and the result performs closely to ML-MT, which demonstrates the main contribution comes from taking advantage of unlabeled data. To intuitively understand the validity of ML-MT, we propose 2D/3D qualitative segmentation results shown in Fig. 3. Blue and red regions denote the ground truth and model's predictions, respectively. In order to better compare the foreground regions, we only display their contours on the second and third rows. As can be seen, our results are close to the ground truth. When compared with supervised results training without unlabeled data, our results contain less false positives and behave much better in the edge regions.

**Table 3.** Quantitative semi-supervised performances compared with state-of-the-art methods

| Method | Labeled | Unlabeled | Dice [%] | Jaccard [%] | ASD [voxel] | 95HD [voxel] |
|---|---|---|---|---|---|---|
| Self-training [1] | 16 | 64 | 86.92 | 77.28 | 2.21 | 9.19 |
| DAN [14] | 16 | 64 | 87.52 | 78.29 | 2.42 | 9.01 |
| ASDNet [11] | 16 | 64 | 87.90 | 78.85 | 2.08 | 9.24 |
| TCSE [7] | 16 | 64 | 88.15 | 79.20 | 2.44 | 9.57 |
| UA-MT [13] | 16 | 64 | 88.88 | 80.21 | 2.26 | 7.32 |
| **ML-MT-UN** | 16 | 64 | 90.37 | 82.54 | 1.96 | 6.91 |
| **ML-MT** | 16 | 64 | **90.57** | **82.86** | **1.76** | **6.28** |

# 4 Conclusion

In this paper, we propose a novel Multi-task Learning Mean Teacher framework (ML-MT) for semi-supervised medical image segmentation. We combine multi-task learning with mean teacher method by introducing region-level and shape-level predictions. To generate reliability guidance, our network calculates hierarchical consistency loss using multi-scale predictions. Instead of learning segmentation in isolation, we present a geometrical refinement to capture the correlations between hierarchical targets. Extensive experiments on the 3D left atrium segmentation MR dataset demonstrate the superior performance of our method.

**Acknowledgment.** This work is supported by the Major Scientific and Technological Special Project of Guizhou Province (20183001), the National Nature Science Foundation of China (61976008).

# References

1. Bai, W., et al.: Semi-supervised learning for network-based cardiac MR image segmentation. In: Descoteaux, M., Maier-Hein, L., Franz, A., Jannin, P., Collins, D.L., Duchesne, S. (eds.) MICCAI 2017, Part II. LNCS, vol. 10434, pp. 253–260. Springer, Cham (2017). https://doi.org/10.1007/978-3-319-66185-8_29

2. Bortsova, G., Dubost, F., Hogeweg, L., Katramados, I., de Bruijne, M.: Semi-supervised medical image segmentation via learning consistency under transformations. In: Shen, D., et al. (eds.) MICCAI 2019, Part VI. LNCS, vol. 11769, pp. 810–818. Springer, Cham (2019). https://doi.org/10.1007/978-3-030-32226-7_90

3. Chen, S., Bortsova, G., García-Uceda Juárez, A., van Tulder, G., de Bruijne, M.: Multi-task attention-based semi-supervised learning for medical image segmentation. In: Shen, D., et al. (eds.) MICCAI 2019, Part III. LNCS, vol. 11766, pp. 457–465. Springer, Cham (2019). https://doi.org/10.1007/978-3-030-32248-9_51

4. Cui, W., et al.: Semi-supervised brain lesion segmentation with an adapted mean teacher model. In: Chung, A.C.S., Gee, J.C., Yushkevich, P.A., Bao, S. (eds.) IPMI 2019. LNCS, vol. 11492, pp. 554–565. Springer, Cham (2019). https://doi.org/10.1007/978-3-030-20351-1_43

5. Feng, Z., Nie, D., Wang, L., Shen, D.: Semi-supervised learning for pelvic MR image segmentation based on multi-task residual fully convolutional networks. In: 2018 IEEE 15th International Symposium on Biomedical Imaging (ISBI 2018), pp. 885–888. IEEE (2018)

6. Laine, S.M., Aila, T.O.: Temporal ensembling for semi-supervised learning. US Patent App. 15/721,433, 12 Apr 2018

7. Li, X., Yu, L., Chen, H., Fu, C., Heng, P.: Semi-supervised skin lesion segmentation via transformation consistent self-ensembling model. In: British Machine Vision Conference 2018, BMVC 2018, Northumbria University, Newcastle, UK, 3–6 Sept 2018, p. 63. BMVA Press (2018)

8. Li, X., Yang, F., Cheng, H., Liu, W., Shen, D.: Contour knowledge transfer for salient object detection. In: Ferrari, V., Hebert, M., Sminchisescu, C., Weiss, Y. (eds.) ECCV 2018, Part XV. LNCS, vol. 11219, pp. 370–385. Springer, Cham (2018). https://doi.org/10.1007/978-3-030-01267-0_22

9. Liu, S., Shi, J., Liang, J., Yang, M.H.: Face parsing via recurrent propagation. arXiv preprint arXiv:1708.01936 (2017)

10. Milletari, F., Navab, N., Ahmadi, S.: V-net: fully convolutional neural networks for volumetric medical image segmentation. In: Fourth International Conference on 3D Vision, 3DV 2016, Stanford, CA, USA, 25–28 Oct 2016, pp. 565–571. IEEE Computer Society (2016)

11. Nie, D., Gao, Y., Wang, L., Shen, D.: ASDNet: attention based semi-supervised deep networks for medical image segmentation. In: Frangi, A.F., Schnabel, J.A., Davatzikos, C., Alberola-López, C., Fichtinger, G. (eds.) MICCAI 2018, Part IV. LNCS, vol. 11073, pp. 370–378. Springer, Cham (2018). https://doi.org/10.1007/978-3-030-00937-3_43

12. Tarvainen, A., Valpola, H.: Mean teachers are better role models: weight-averaged consistency targets improve semi-supervised deep learning results. In: Advances in Neural Information Processing Systems, pp. 1195–1204 (2017)

13. Yu, L., Wang, S., Li, X., Fu, C.-W., Heng, P.-A.: Uncertainty-aware self-ensembling model for semi-supervised 3D left atrium segmentation. In: Shen, D., et al. (eds.) MICCAI 2019, Part II. LNCS, vol. 11765, pp. 605–613. Springer, Cham (2019). https://doi.org/10.1007/978-3-030-32245-8_67

14. Zhang, Y., Yang, L., Chen, J., Fredericksen, M., Hughes, D.P., Chen, D.Z.: Deep adversarial networks for biomedical image segmentation utilizing unannotated images. In: Descoteaux, M., Maier-Hein, L., Franz, A., Jannin, P., Collins, D.L., Duchesne, S. (eds.) MICCAI 2017, Part III. LNCS, vol. 10435, pp. 408–416. Springer, Cham (2017). https://doi.org/10.1007/978-3-319-66179-7_47

15. Zhang, Z., Fu, H., Dai, H., Shen, J., Pang, Y., Shao, L.: Et-net: a generic edge-attention guidance network for medical image segmentation. In: International Conference on Medical Image Computing and Computer-Assisted Intervention, pp. 442–450 (2019)

# BVTNet: Multi-label Multi-class Fusion of Visible and Thermal Camera for Free Space and Pedestrian Segmentation

Vijay John[1(✉)], Ali Boyali[2], Simon Thompson[2], and Seiichi Mita[1]

[1] Toyota Technological Institute, Nagoya, Japan
{vijayjohn,smita}@toyota-ti.ac.jp
[2] Tier IV, Tokyo, Japan
{ali.boyali,simon.thompson}@tier4.jp

**Abstract.** Deep learning-based visible camera semantic segmentation report state-of-the-art segmentation accuracy. However, this approach is limited by the visible camera's susceptibility to varying illumination and environmental conditions. One approach to address this limitation is visible and thermal camera-based sensor fusion. Existing literature utilizes this sensor fusion approach for object segmentation, but the approach's application to free space segmentation has not been reported. Here, a multi-label multi-class visible-thermal camera learning framework, termed as the BVTNet, is proposed for the semantic segmentation of pedestrians and the free space. The BVTNet estimates the pedestrians and free space in an individual multi-class output branch. Additionally, the network also separately estimates the free space and pedestrian boundaries in another multi-class output branch. The boundary semantic segmentation is integrated within the full semantic segmentation framework in a post-processing step. The proposed framework is validated on the public MFNet dataset. A comparative analysis with baseline algorithms and ablation studies with BVTNet variants show that the proposed framework report state-of-the-art segmentation accuracy in real-time in challenging environmental conditions.

**Keywords:** Sensor fusion · Semantic segmentation · Thermal camera · Autonomous driving

## 1 Introduction

Visible camera-based semantic segmentation is an important perception problem for autonomous driving [1,6,13]. Traditional and machine learning approaches segment and assign pixel labels to the image. With the advent of deep learning, significant advances have been made in this problem. However, the problem has not been completely solved owing to the visible camera's susceptibility to variations in illumination and environmental conditions. One approach to address these challenges is the effective sensor fusion of the visible camera with complementary sensors [7,9]. The thermal camera is one such complementary sensor,

© Springer Nature Switzerland AG 2021
A. Del Bimbo et al. (Eds.): ICPR 2020 Workshops, LNCS 12666, pp. 277–288, 2021.
https://doi.org/10.1007/978-3-030-68780-9_24

which can be fused with the visible camera for semantic segmentation [8,11]. Many researchers have adopted the visible-thermal camera fusion framework for the semantic segmentation of objects in the image [3,16], reporting state-of-the-art accuracy. However, the existing literature does not apply the visible-thermal fusion framework to the free space semantic segmentation. In this work, a novel multi-label multi-class framework termed as the BVTNet (Boundary-Visible-Thermal Network) is proposed for the free space and pedestrian semantic segmentation. The BVTNet, a multi-label visible-thermal fusion framework, contains two separate multi-class output branches. The first branch performs the multi-class semantic segmentation of free space and pedestrians. The second branch performs the multi-class semantic segmentation of their boundaries. The outputs of the two branches are combined in a post-processing step, which increases the overall semantic segmentation accuracy (Sect. 5).

Apart from the output branches, the network also contains three input encoder branches and one decoder branch. The three input encoder branches contain the following: a visible camera feature extraction branch; a thermal camera feature extraction branch; and a feature fusion branch. The feature maps extracted in the encoder branches are transferred to the decoder branch using the skip connection [15]. The visible-thermal feature fusion occurs in the feature fusion branch (encoder) as well as the decoder branch. The proposed network is validated on the MFNet public dataset [3], and the results are compared with baseline algorithms. Additionally, a detailed ablation study is also performed with BVTNet variants. The results show that the proposed framework reports better segmentation accuracy than the baseline algorithms while reporting real-time computational complexity. To the best of our knowledge, the main contribution of this work is as follows:

- A novel visible-thermal sensor fusion which performs multi-label and multi-class semantic segmentation.
- Free space segmentation using thermal-visible camera fusion.
- Separate semantic segmentation of the object boundaries, and their subsequent integration with the "full" semantic segmentation.

The remainder of the paper is structured as follows. In Sect. 2, we review the literature. The proposed framework is presented in Sect. 3. The variants of the proposed network used in the ablation study are presented in Sect. 4. The experimental results are shown in Sect. 5, and the summary is presented in Sect. 6.

## 2    Literature Review

Recently, deep learning-based semantic segmentation for the visible camera have achieved state-of-the-art results in this task [1,12–15,17]. The visible camera-based semantic segmentation are susceptible to limited segmentation accuracy in varying illumination and environmental conditions, due to the visible camera's limitations. This limitation is addressed by sensor fusion of the visible camera

**Fig. 1.** Sample images from the MFNet dataset. The limitations of the visible camera and the advantages of the thermal camera are highlighted.

with complementary sensors such as the depth camera [5,9], thermal camera [3,16] and the milliwave radar [10] (Fig. 1).

John et al. [9] proposed the ChiNet to fuse the depth image and the visible image for free space and obstacle detection. The ChiNet, based on the encoder-decoder architecture, contained two encoder branches and two decoder branches for the feature extraction and segmentation, respectively. Similar work was proposed by Hazirbas et al. [5] in the FuseNet, where the depth image features are fused with the visible image features using an element-wise summation in the encoder branch, and indoor object segmentation is performed.

Recently, Ha et al. [3] proposed the MFNet for the semantic segmentation using the visible and thermal cameras. The MFNet performs semantic segmentation of objects in the driving environment. The MFNet, similar to the ChiNet, contains two encoder branches for the visible image and thermal image feature extractions. The extracted features are then concatenated and added to the single decoder branch. A similar work is reported by Sun et al. [16] in the RTFNet, where the objects in the driving environment are segmented using the visible and thermal camera. The RTFNet, based on the encoder-decoder, contains two encoder branches for the visible and thermal camera feature extraction. The decoder branch is not a mirrored version of the encoder, and is designed to be smaller.

Compared to the existing literature, in this work, a novel sensor fusion framework for the visible and thermal camera fusion is proposed for free space and pedestrian semantic segmentation. Moreover, a multi-label multi-class framework is proposed to separately estimate the objects and their boundaries, which are then combined in a post-processing step.

## 3   Algorithm

BVTNet is a multi-label multi-class semantic segmentation network which performs visible-thermal fusion to estimate the pedestrian and free space. The network contains three encoder branches, one decoder branch and two output branches. The first two encoder branches extract the thermal and visible camera features, which are then fused in the third encoder branch. The fused feature maps are then transferred to the decoder branch using skip connections. The two

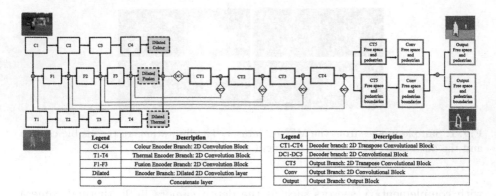

**Fig. 2.** A detailed overview of the BVTNet.

| | | | | |
|---|---|---|---|---|
| **C1:** C (64, 3, 1) P (2) | **C2:** C (128, 3,1) P (2) | **C3:** C (256, 3, 1) P (2) | **C4:** C (256, 3, 1) P (2) | **Dil. C:** C(256, 3) D(2) |
| **T1:** C (64, 3, 1) P (2) | **T2:** C (128, 3,1) P (2) | **T3:** C (256, 3, 1) P (2) | **T4:** C (256, 3, 1) P (2) | **Dil. Th:** C(256, 3) D(2) |
| **F1:** C (256, 3, 1) P (2) | **F2:** C (256, 3, 1) P (2) | **F3:** C (256, 3, 1) P (2) | **Dil. Fu:** C(256, 3) D(2) | |
| **DC1:** C (256, 3, 1) Pad (S) | **DC2:** C (256, 3, 1) Pad (S) | **DC3:** C (256, 3, 1) Pad (S) | **DC4:** C (256, 3, 1) Pad (S) | **DC5:** C (256, 3, 1) Pad (S) |
| **CT1:** TC (256, 5, 1) | **CT2:** TC (256, 4, 2) | **CT3:** TC (256, 4, 2) | **CT4:** TC (256, 5, 2) | |
| **CT5:** TC (256, 4, 2) | **Conv:** C (64, 1, 1) | **Output:** C(3, 1, 1) | | |

**Fig. 3.** The parameters of the different blocks. C (filters, kernel size, stride) denotes 2D convolutional layer. P (kernel size) is the max-pooling layer. D (dilation rate). Pad (S) denotes the "same" padding. TC (filters, kernel size, stride) denotes 2D transpose convolutional layer.

**Table 1.** Different variants of the BVTNet

| **BVTNet** | Proposed architecture | **BVTNet-A** | Four independent binary output branches for free space, pedestrian, and their boundaries |
|---|---|---|---|
| **BVTNet-B** | No concatenation before the output layer | **BVTNet-C** | No skip connections from encoder branch |
| **BVTNet-D** | No decoder convol. block for the skip connections | **BVTNet-Vis** | Only color input |
| **BVTNet-Th** | Only thermal input | **BVTNet-E** | Only two inputs without fusion branch |
| **BVTNet-F** | Individual binary branches for pedestrians and freespace. No boundaries segmented | **BVTNet-G** | One multiclass branch for free space and pedestrians. No boundaries segmented |

output branches individually estimate the "full" semantic segments (free space, pedestrians) and their boundaries (free space and pedestrian boundaries), respectively. The "full" segmentation and the boundary segmentation are combined in a post-processing step. An overview of the proposed architecture is shown in Fig. 2. We next present the details of the encoder, decoder and output branches.

## 3.1   Encoder Branches

The first two encoder branches extract and sub-sample the visible and thermal features using 5 convolutional blocks. The first four convolutional blocks ($C$ and $T$) contains a $2D$ convolutional layer with batch-normalization and leaky-relu activation function. This is followed by a max-pooling layer. The final convolutional block contains a 2-dilated convolutional layer with batch-normalization and leaky-relu activation function.

The fusion encoder branch has 4 convolutional blocks ($FC$) for the fusion of the thermal and visible features. The first 3 block contains a $2D$ convolutional layer with batch-normalization and leaky-relu activation function, followed by a max-pooling layer. The final block is a 2-dilated convolutional layer with batch-normalization and leaky-relu activation function. The concatenation of the thermal and visible features, and the inputs to the different blocks are illustrated in Fig. 2. The parameter details of the individual blocks are given in Fig. 3.

## 3.2   Decoder Branch

The decoder branch uses 4 transpose convolutional blocks and 5 convolutional blocks. This branch up-samples the encoded feature maps to their original resolution. Each transpose convolutional block contains a $2D$ transpose convolutional layer with batch-normalization and leaky-relu activation function.

The fused feature maps from the fusion encoder branch are transferred to the convolutional blocks using the skip connection. Each convolutional block contains a $2D$ convolutional layer with batch-normalization and *leaky-relu* activation function.

The outputs of the transpose convolutional block and the convolutional block are concatenated before given as input to the subsequent transpose convolutional block. The detailed concatenation and layout of the decoder branch are illustrated in Fig. 2. The parameter details of the individual blocks are given in Fig. 3.

## 3.3   Output Branches

Formulated as a multi-label framework, the two output branches estimate the "full" free-space and pedestrian segments and their boundaries in a multi-class framework. Each output branch contains a transpose convolutional block, a convolutional block and an output block. The transpose convolutional block contains a $2D$ transpose convolutional layer with batch-normalization and leaky-relu activation function. The convolutional block contains a $2D$ convolutional layer with batch-normalization and leaky-relu activation function. The final output block is a $1 \times 1$ convolutional layer with a softmax activation function.

As shown in Fig. 2, there is a concatenation layer in between the two convolutional blocks and the two output blocks. This concatenation layer backpropagates the training loss from the two output blocks to the entire BVTNet. This can be viewed as a formulation where the loss from the complete segments and boundaries influence each other. The layout and the parameter details of the output branches are shown in Fig. 2 and Fig. 3.

### 3.4   Training

The BVTNet is trained with input images from the thermal and visible camera and output semantic segmentation of the "full" objects and their corresponding boundaries.

The ground truth semantic segmentation of the "full" objects are obtained through manual annotation. The manual annotations are then used to generate the boundary ground truths by boundary detection and image dilation. The boundary detection is done using the Moore-Neighbor tracing algorithm [2]. The boundary is then dilated [4] to aid the boundary semantic segmentation.

BVTNet was trained with a Adam optimizer with learning rate of 0.001 with two sparse categorical cross entropy loss functions.

### 3.5   Post-processing

Following its training, the BVTNet performs the semantic segmentation of the "full" objects and their boundaries. However, since the estimated boundaries are dilated, a skeletonize operation is performed. The skeletonized boundaries with their multiclass labels are then added to the "full" segmentation output to obtain the final semantic segmentation. Our experimental results show that the post-processing step improves the segmentation accuracy. An illustration of the post-processing is shown in Fig. 4.

## 4   Algorithm Variants: Ablation Study

An ablation study is done by varying different components of the proposed architecture. Within the proposed architecture, the encoder branches, the decoder branch, the output branches and the semantic segmentation problem are varied. The different variants considered are presented in Table 1.

## 5   Experimental Results

The proposed algorithm was validated on the MFNet dataset [3]. Since the MFNet dataset does not contain the free space annotation, we manually annotated the free space for this study. Apart from the different network variants

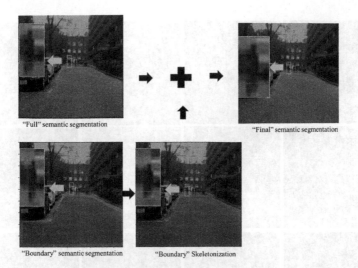

"Full" semantic segmentation

"Final" semantic segmentation

"Boundary" semantic segmentation    "Boundary" Skeletonization

**Fig. 4.** An illustration of the post processing step. Green box shows the improvement with the post-processing step (Color figure online)

presented in the ablation study, we also evaluate our algorithm with baseline algorithms.

The baseline algorithms include the MFNet [3], the ChiNet [9] and the FuseNet [5]. The proposed network, the variants and the baseline algorithms were trained with batch size 4 for 100 epochs. The performance is measured using the pixel segmentation accuracy and the intersection-over-union (IOU) measure. The IoU measure is the calculated from the overlap between the prediction and segmentation divided by the area of their union. The networks were implemented on a dual Nvidia Geforce 1080 Ubuntu 18.04 machine using Tensorflow 2.

## 5.1   Comparative Analysis

A brief introduction to the baseline networks are presented in Sect. 2. While the MFNet was designed for visible-thermal fusion, the ChiNet and Fusenet were designed for visible-depth fusion. Thus, for the comparative analysis, the ChiNet and FuseNet input layers were modified for visible-thermal fusion.

The performance of the different networks are tabulated in Table 2, Table 3 and Table 4. The different tables show the results on the complete samples, the day samples and the night samples of the MFNet dataset. The results show that the BVTNet is shown to be better than the baseline networks (Figs. 5 and 6).

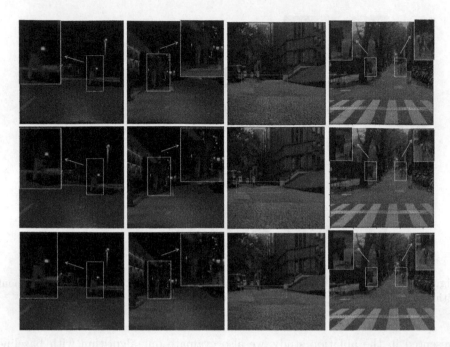

**Fig. 5.** Sample results of the BVTNet (First row), the ChiNet (second row) and the MFNet (Third row). The highlighted regions show the BVTNet's improved performance.

**Table 2.** Comparative analysis of the BVTNet with baseline algorithms for the full dataset.

| Proposed Algo. | Pixel Acc. % | | IOU. % | | Time (ms) |
|---|---|---|---|---|---|
| | Free space | Ped. | Free space | Ped. | |
| Proposed | **96.21** | **69.02** | **0.91** | **0.53** | 52 |
| MFNet [3] | 94.64 | 65.36 | 0.90 | 0.53 | 28 |
| ChiNet [9] | 95.00 | 62.89 | 0.90 | 0.51 | 41 |
| FuseNet [5] | 94.72 | 42.11 | 0.89 | 0.35 | 22 |

**Table 3.** Comparative analysis of the BVTNet with baseline algorithms for the day samples.

| Proposed Algo. | Pixel Acc. % | | IOU. % | |
|---|---|---|---|---|
| | Free space | Ped. | Free space | Ped. |
| Proposed | **96.46** | **73.12** | **0.91** | 0.54 |
| MFNet [3] | 95.26 | 70.97 | 0.90 | **0.55** |
| ChiNet [9] | 95.51 | 69.90 | 0.90 | 0.53 |
| FuseNet [5] | 95.36 | 48.85 | 0.90 | 0.38 |

**Table 4.** Comparative analysis of the BVTNet with baseline algorithms for the night samples.

| Proposed Algo. | Pixel Acc. % | | IOU. % | |
|---|---|---|---|---|
| | Free space | Ped. | Free space | Ped. |
| Proposed | **95.95** | **64.61** | **0.91** | **0.52** |
| MFNet [3] | 93.98 | 59.45 | 0.90 | 0.51 |
| ChiNet [9] | 94.46 | 55.45 | 0.90 | 0.49 |
| FuseNet [5] | 94.02 | 34.96 | 0.89 | 0.31 |

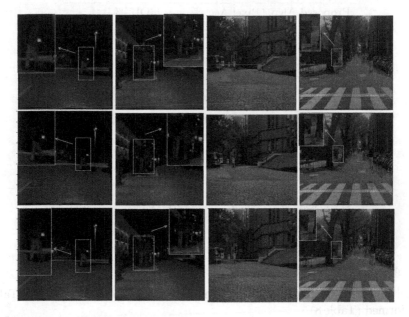

**Fig. 6.** Sample results of the BVTNet (First row), the BVTNet-Vis (second row) and the BVTNet-Th (Third row). The highlighted regions show the BVTNet's improved performance.

## 5.2   Ablation Study

**Sensor Fusion.** Here, we validate sensor fusion, by comparing the BVTNet with the visible-only network and the thermal-only network. The advantages of the sensor fusion is shown in Table 5, Table 5 and Table 7. The performance of the visible-alone is degraded with environment and illumination changes. Comparatively, the performance of the thermal-alone network is better. However, the results show that the sensor fusion approach reports the best results.

**Table 5.** Sensor fusion analysis of the BVTNet on the full dataset.

| Proposed Algo. | Pixel Acc. % | | IOU. % | | Time (ms) |
| --- | --- | --- | --- | --- | --- |
| | Free space | Ped. | Free space | Ped. | |
| Proposed | **96.21** | **69.02** | **0.91** | **0.53** | 52 |
| BVTNet-Vis | 95.33 | 25.71 | 0.89 | 0.18 | 45 |
| BVTNet-Th | 94.83 | 61.01 | 0.89 | 0.48 | 44 |

**Table 6.** Sensor fusion analysis of the BVTNet on the day samples.

| Proposed Algo. | Pixel Acc. % | | IOU. % | |
| --- | --- | --- | --- | --- |
| | Free space | Ped. | Free space | Ped. |
| Proposed | **96.46** | **73.12** | **0.91** | **0.54** |
| BVTNet-Vis | 95.39 | 33.18 | 0.90 | 0.25 |
| BVTNet-Th | 93.57 | 64.69 | 0.88 | 0.48 |

**Table 7.** Sensor fusion analysis of the BVTNet on the night samples.

| Proposed Algo. | Pixel Acc. % | | IOU. % | |
| --- | --- | --- | --- | --- |
| | Free space | Ped. | Free space | Ped. |
| Proposed | 95.95 | **64.61** | **0.91** | **0.52** |
| BVTNet-Vis | 95.29 | 17.61 | 0.88 | 0.11 |
| BVTNet-Th | **96.19** | 57.18 | 0.90 | 0.47 |

## 5.3   Architecture Variations

Here, a validation of the BVTNet with the different network variations in Table 1 is performed (Table 8).

**Table 8.** Architecture variations of the BVTNet on the full dataset.

| Proposed Algo. | Pixel Acc. % | | IOU. % | | Time (ms) |
| --- | --- | --- | --- | --- | --- |
| | Free space | Ped. | Free space | Ped. | |
| Proposed | 96.21 | **69.02** | **0.91** | **0.53** | 52 |
| BVTNet-B | 96.26 | 65.06 | 0.90 | 0.50 | 52 |
| BVTNet-C | 95.02 | 52.46 | 0.90 | 0.40 | 36 |
| BVTNet-D | **96.31** | 66.51 | 0.90 | 0.52 | 48 |
| BVTNet-E | 94.45 | 57.16 | 0.89 | 0.46 | 44 |

## 5.4   Semantic Segmentation Formulation

Here, varying semantic segmentation formulation are considered. The multi-label multi-class formulation of the BVTNet is compared with multi-label four binary

(BVTNet-A), multi-label two binary (BVTNet-F) and multi-class alone formulations (BVTNet-G). The results tabulated in Table 9 show that the multi-label multi-class formulation is better than the other formulations.

**Table 9.** Semantic segmentation formulation of the BVTNet on the full dataset.

| Proposed Algo. | Pixel Acc. % | | IOU. % | | Time (ms) |
|---|---|---|---|---|---|
| | Free space | Ped. | Free space | Ped. | |
| Proposed | **96.21** | **69.02** | **0.91** | **0.53** | 52 |
| BVTNet-A | 95.90 | 67.22 | 0.90 | 0.52 | 87 |
| BVTNet-F | 92.85 | 62.95 | 0.89 | 0.49 | 55 |
| BVTNet-G | 95.81 | 56.09 | 0.90 | 0.49 | 39 |

### 5.5 Boundary Estimation and Integration

Here, we validate the boundary estimation and integration proposal of the BVT-Net. Network variants without the boundary estimation are considered and their performance tabulated in Table 10. The results show that the boundary estimation and subsequent skeletonization and integration within the "full" semantic segments increases the accuracy.

**Table 10.** Boundary estimation and integration formulation of the BVTNet on the full dataset.

| Proposed Algo. | Pixel Acc. % | | IOU. % | | Time (ms) |
|---|---|---|---|---|---|
| | Free space | Ped. | Free space | Ped. | |
| Proposed | **96.21** | **69.02** | **0.91** | **0.53** | 52 |
| BVTNet-F | 92.85 | 62.95 | 0.89 | 0.49 | 55 |
| BVTNet-G | 95.81 | 56.09 | 0.90 | 0.49 | 39 |

## 6   Conclusion

In this work, a novel deep learning-based thermal and visible camera semantic segmentation approach termed as the BVTNet is proposed. The BVTNet is a multi-label multi-class network which estimates the pedestrians, free space and their boundaries. The boundaries are estimated and subsequently integrated within the "full" semantic segmentation. The proposed network is validated on the MFNet dataset. The performance of the BVTNet is compared with baseline algorithms. Additionally, a detailed ablation study of the BVTNet is also performed. The results show that the BVTNet robustly segments the free space and pedestrians in real-time and is shown to be better than the baseline algorithms.

# References

1. Badrinarayanan, V., Kendall, A., Cipolla, R.: SegNet: a deep convolutional encoder-decoder architecture for image segmentation. In: CVPR (2015)
2. Gonzalez, R.C., Woods, R.E., Eddins, S.L.: Digital Image Processing Using MAT-LAB. Prentice-Hall Inc., USA (2003)
3. Ha, Q., Watanabe, K., Karasawa, T., Ushiku, Y., Harada, T.: MFNet: towards real-time semantic segmentation for autonomous vehicles with multi-spectral scenes. In: 2017 IEEE/RSJ International Conference on Intelligent Robots and Systems (IROS), pp. 5108–5115 (2017)
4. Haralick, R.M., Shapiro, L.G.: Computer and Robot Vision, 1st edn. Addison-Wesley Longman Publishing Co. Inc, Boston (1992)
5. Hazirbas, C., Ma, L., Domokos, C., Cremers, D.: FuseNet: incorporating depth into semantic segmentation via fusion-based CNN architecture. In: Lai, S.-H., Lepetit, V., Nishino, K., Sato, Y. (eds.) ACCV 2016. LNCS, vol. 10111, pp. 213–228. Springer, Cham (2017). https://doi.org/10.1007/978-3-319-54181-5_14
6. John, V., Guo, C., Mita, S., Kidono, K., Guo, C., Ishimaru, K.: Fast road scene segmentation using deep learning and scene-based models. In: ICPR (2016)
7. John, V., Mita, S.: RVNet: deep sensor fusion of monocular camera and radar for image-based obstacle detection in challenging Environments. In: Lee, C., Su, Z., Sugimoto, A. (eds.) PSIVT 2019. LNCS, vol. 11854, pp. 351–364. Springer, Cham (2019). https://doi.org/10.1007/978-3-030-34879-3_27
8. John, V., Mita, S., Liu, Z., Qi, B.: Pedestrian detection in thermal images using adaptive fuzzy c-means clustering and convolutional neural networks. In: 14th IAPR International Conference on Machine Vision Applications, pp. 246–249 (2015)
9. John, V., et al.: Sensor fusion of intensity and depth cues using the ChiNet for semantic segmentation of road scenes. In: IEEE Intelligent Vehicles Symposium, pp. 585–590 (2018)
10. John, V., Nithilan, M.K., Mita, S., Tehrani, H., Sudheesh, R.S., Lalu, P.P.: SO-Net: joint semantic segmentation and obstacle detection using deep fusion of monocular camera and radar. In: Dabrowski, J.J., Rahman, A., Paul, M. (eds.) PSIVT 2019. LNCS, vol. 11994, pp. 138–148. Springer, Cham (2020). https://doi.org/10.1007/978-3-030-39770-8_11
11. Liu, Q., Zhuang, J., Ma, J.: Robust and fast pedestrian detection method for far-infrared automotive driving assistance systems. Infrared Phys. Technol. **60**, 288–299 (2013)
12. Long, J., Shelhamer, E., Darrell, T.: Fully convolutional networks for semantic segmentation. In: CVPR, November 2015
13. Noh, H., Hong, S., Han, B.: Learning deconvolution network for semantic segmentation. CoRR abs/1505.04366 (2015)
14. Paszke, A., Chaurasia, A., Kim, S., Culurciello, E.: ENet: a deep neural network architecture for real-time semantic segmentation. CoRR abs/1606.02147 (2016)
15. Ronneberger, O., Fischer, P., Brox, T.: U-Net: convolutional networks for biomedical image segmentation. In: Navab, N., Hornegger, J., Wells, W.M., Frangi, A.F. (eds.) MICCAI 2015. LNCS, vol. 9351, pp. 234–241. Springer, Cham (2015). https://doi.org/10.1007/978-3-319-24574-4_28
16. Sun, Y., Zuo, W., Liu, M.: RTFNet: RGB-thermal fusion network for semantic segmentation of urban scenes. IEEE Robotics Autom. Lett. **4**(3), 2576–2583 (2019)
17. Zhao, H., Shi, J., Qi, X., Wang, X., Jia, J.: Pyramid scene parsing network. CoRR abs/1612.01105 (2016)

# Multimodal Emotion Recognition Based on Speech and Physiological Signals Using Deep Neural Networks

Ali Bakhshi$^{(\boxtimes)}$ ⓘ and Stephan Chalup ⓘ

The University of Newcastle, Callaghan 2308, Australia
ali.bakhshi@uon.edu.au, stephan.chalup@newcastle.edu.au

**Abstract.** A suitable combination of data in a multimodal emotion recognition model allows conveying and combining each channel's information to achieve a better recognition of the encoded emotion than would be possible using only a single modality and channel. In this paper, we focus on combining speech and physiological signals to predict the arousal and valence levels of the emotional states of a person. We designed a neural network that can use the information from raw audio signals, electrocardiograms, heart rate variability, electro-dermal activity, and skin conductance levels, to predict emotional states. The proposed deep neural network architecture works as an end-to-end process, which means, neither any pre-processing of the input data nor post-processing of the prediction of the network was applied. Using the data of the modalities available in the publicly accessible part of the RECOLA database, we achieved results comparable to other state-of-the-art approaches.

**Keywords:** Multimodal data · Emotion recognition · Deep neural network

## 1 Introduction

Emotions play a key role in personal and social life, allowing people to communicate by expressing themselves through different channels. Emotion recognition is essential for complete interaction between humans and machines, just as affective information is inevitable for human interactions [23]. In recent years, methods of combining different modalities such as physiological signals, audio, video, hand gestures, and body movements contributed to progress in the field of emotion recognition. The automated perception of emotions provides a natural interface between humans and machines, whereby the system can understand and interpret emotions and respond accordingly. The emotion recognition systems primarily were focused on audio signals and facial expressions. However, recent research utilizing other modalities has tried to understand emotional states through a wider lens. Emotion recognition technologies become more and more important in the context of various emerging human-machine interaction applications such

A. Del Bimbo et al. (Eds.): ICPR 2020 Workshops, LNCS 12666, pp. 289–300, 2021.
https://doi.org/10.1007/978-3-030-68780-9_25

as human-like robots, babysitter robots, and call centers, where machines have to be able to interpret perceived human emotional states and respond accordingly.

Speech, as one of the fastest and simplest communication channels between humans, conveys beneficial information about the emotional states of a person. On the other hand, physiological signals are also changing in response to the variation of emotional states. Using physiological signals with other verbal or non-verbal modalities has two significant advantages in emotion recognition. First, some physical modalities such as facial expression and speech, can be controlled intentionally by a person, and almost everyone can conceal real emotions. Second, in some cases, such as people with a facial or verbal disability, using physical modalities is not possible. Hence, it seems considering speech data and physiological signals can lead to a better prediction of arousal and valence states.

Traditional machine learning algorithms have been used for many years at different levels for classifying or predicting emotions. In the context of emotion recognition tasks it is important to specify the emotion model that was used to label the data. Feature extraction, feature selection, and feature classification are the three steps used by traditional machine learning methods in classification tasks. With the emergence of DNNs and considering the breakthroughs that were achieved by applying DNNs in many disciplines, more and more researchers started using DNNs to solve queries previously addressed by traditional machine learning algorithms. Certain DNN models have become standard tools and can be applied to a wide range of problems. Among the most notable of these tools are Convolutional Neural Networks (CNNs) [13], Deep Belief Networks (DBNs) [6], autoencoder (AE) or auto associator [7], Recurrent Neural Networks (RNNs) [1,8], and Generative Adversarial Networks (GANs) [4]. DNNs can be used both in an end-to-end process or in conjunction with other algorithms as feature extractor or classifier.

Inspired by new advancements in various research fields, and considering the importance of speech and physiological signals in emotion recognition, we proposed an automatic multimodal emotion recognition model based on DNNs for predicting arousal and valence states using various modalities. These modalities included speech signals, electrocardiogram (ECG), heart rate variability (HRV), electrodermal activity (EDA), and skin conductance levels (SCL). The contributions to this work can be listed as follows:

- We used speech and physiological signals in a multimodal system. Since both are 1D signals, the computational cost is lower than other multimodal systems that used audio-visual data.
- The proposed model predicts the arousal and valence states in an end-to-end process, which means there is no pre-processing on inputs or any post-processing on the predictions of the model.
- Only half of the RECOLA database is publicly available. We used this part of the data to obtain a small training set for which we designed a deep model.

The rest of the paper is organized as follows: In Sect. 2, recent works in the field of emotion recognition are reviewed. The proposed model is described in Sect. 3. Section 4 presents the experimental results, and the conclusions are discussed in Sect. 5.

## 2   Related Work

In this section, we review recent work in the field of emotion recognition. Since we present a multimodal emotion recognition using speech and physiological signals, the related efforts on both unimodal models and multimodal models are addressed.

The human voice is one of the most important channels for emotion recognition as it contains useful information about the affective states of the person. There are many efforts in the literature on Speech Emotion Recognition (SER) using both traditional machine learning methods and DNNs. Since there is already a comprehensive review of traditional approaches for SER available in literature [3], we only focused on those works that applied DNNs to SER. Lalitha et al. [11] used the three layers of DNN as a classifier for SER using perception-based speech features. These perceptual speech features which involving Mel frequency cepstral coefficients (MFCCs), perceptual linear predictive cepstrum (PLPC), Mel frequency perceptual linear prediction cepstrum (MFPLPC), bark frequency cepstral coefficient (BFCC), revised perceptual linear prediction coefficient's (RPLP), and inverted Mel frequency cepstral coefficients (IMFCC) has used to identify the predominant features. Another study conducted by Zhao et al. [28] proposed 1D and 2D CNN LSTM network with similar architecture to learn local and global features from speech and log-Mel spectrogram, respectively. The proposed architectures were consisting of four local feature learning blocks (LFLBs) and one long short-term memory (LSTM) layer, where each LFLB contained one convolutional layer and one max-pooling layer. Using 2D CNN LSTM, they achieved 95.33% and 95.89% recognition accuracies on Berlin EmoDB for speaker-dependent and speaker-independent experiments, respectively. Besides, they reached 89.16% and 52.14% classification accuracies on the IEMOCAP database for speaker-dependent and speaker-independent experiments, respectively. In [27], the authors utilized a Deep CNN (DCNN) to bridge the affective gap in subjective emotions and low-level features of the speech signals. They extracted three channels of Mel-spectrograms involving static, delta, and delta-delta. These three channels were represented by red, green, and blue (RGB)in the DCNN input images. Then, using a pre-trained AlexNet, high-level feature representations of each segment have been learned. Besides, they used the discriminant temporal pyramid matching (DTPM) strategy to aggregate the learned segment-level features. They evaluated the performance of their model on four popular benchmarks consisting of EMO-DB, RML, eNTERFACE05, and BAUM-1s. Yang et al. [25] proposed an end-to-end CNN-BLSTM model that used both 1D speech waveforms and spectrograms of the signal as the input to predict the arousal and valence states in the SEMAINE and the RECOLA databases. They used two convolutional layers that each were followed by a max-pooling layer for both, the 1D waveform and spectrogram. Considering the

6-sec time-sequence of the input, they extracted the features from the 1D and 2D inputs. Then, the outputs of the last pooling layers were applied to a two-layer BLSTM with 256 hidden layers, where the last BLSTM was followed by a linear fully connected layer with two outputs corresponding to the arousal and valence states. They evaluated the performance of their model using four different inputs consisting of the hand-crafted features in the baseline model, the raw waveforms, the spectrograms, and the combination of raw waveforms and spectrograms. Trigeorgis et al. [22] proposed an end-to-end speech emotion recognition approach based on Bidirectional LSTM (BiLSTM) CNNs. They extracted the features using two consecutive convolutional layers, which each were followed by a max-pooling layer. Then, to keep the temporal dependencies between the sequence of data, the authors used two layers of BiLSTM stacked on top of the convolutional layers. They used a chain of post-processing steps such as median filtering, centering, time-shifting, and scaling on the prediction of the network to improve the prediction rate of the model, especially during the validation phase. The performance of their proposed model was evaluated on the whole RECOLA dataset using arousal and valence states. The other study carried out by Tzirakis et al. [24] introduced an end-to-end SER model based on a CNN-LSTM architecture. They used three convolutional layers followed by two LSTM layers, to extract the emotion-related features and to consider the temporal dependencies between the sequence of raw speech data, respectively. In their proposed architecture, each convolutional layer was followed by a max-pooling layer where the pooling size was determined according to a ratio called the rate of overlap. All three pooling layers were applied across time to reduce the frame rate of the signal. They demonstrated the performance of their model on the full RECOLA database for the prediction of arousal and valence states. They used a chain of post-processing steps like those used in [22] to improve the prediction of the network.

Physiological signals contain beneficial information about emotional states and can be used individually or in combination with other modalities for emotion recognition. There exist a few reviews for emotion recognition using physiological signals in [2,20]. In [2], Egger et al. have reviewed the most commonly used physiological signals for emotion recognition. Moreover, they summarized the benefits and limitations of each modality as well as the application area and the statistical method used for extracting relevant features from each one. In another study, Yin et al. [26] proposed an ensemble deep learning model for emotion recognition from multimodal physiological signals. They utilized a multiple-fusion-layer based ensemble classifier of stacked autoencoders (SAE) to discriminate between emotion classes. In their proposed SAE, three hidden layers are used to filter unwanted noise, as well as drive the stable feature representation. Next, they used an additional deep model to achieve SAE ensembles. Another study, conducted by Li et al. [14], introduced an attention-based BiLSTM-RNNs model to classify arousal and valence states using three physiological signals, including electroencephalogram (EEG), galvanic skin response (GSR), and ECG. They used spectrogram images of the physiological signals as the inputs of the model so that the model learned the temporal features of the data. Then, after feeding a DNN to predict the probability of emotional outputs, a decision level fusion strategy was applied to predict final emotions.

The combination of speech and physiological signals in a multimodel system has not been considered much in previous studies. There is little work that used speech and physiological modalities in a multimodal model. In one study, Matsuda et al. [15] proposed a multimodal emotion recognition framework using audio-visual features and physiological signals. They used these modalities in designing a context-aware tourist guidance system that recognizes the emotional states of tourists during sightseeing. In another study, Ranganathan et al. [16] introduced four DBN models for generating robust multimodal features for unsupervised emotion recognition. In their model, after extracting the corresponding components of speech, facial expressions, body gestures, and physiological signals, they used a convolutional DBN (CDBN) for learning striking multimodal features and classifying the features in proper emotion classes. In the present paper, we proposed an efficient architecture for the recognition of emotion, utilizing the information acquired from raw speech signals and physiological signals, including ECG, EDA, HRV, and SCL.

## 3  Proposed Method

To design the overall multimodal architecture, we propose to fuse two different DNN models, one for speech signals and the other for the physiological signals. These two sub-models are shown in Fig. 1 and Fig. 2, respectively. The final multimodal model is formed by combining the two sub-models, where a small change to the last fully connected layer of each of the two sub-models is introduced, and then a sequence of fully connected layers is added on top as a fusion block. As shown in Fig. 3, the last fully connected layer of each of the two sub-models is expanded so that it generates 50 outputs instead of 2. Then, these outputs are concatenated to form the final feature vector. Finally, the last fully connected

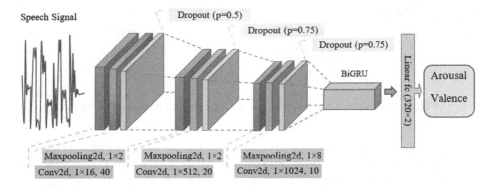

**Fig. 1.** Unimodal DNN model for emotion recognition using speech signals

layer of the fusion model generates two outputs that correspond to the arousal and valence states.

Our unimodal DNN model for emotion recognition using speech signals is shown in Fig. 1. In this model the raw speech signal is fed to a convolutional layer followed by the ReLU activation function, and after extracting the long-term characteristics of the signal, the generated features are down-sampled by a max-pooling layer with a stride of 2. The finer-scale components of the signal are extracted by the second convolutional layer and then the second max-pooling layer decreases the frame rate by a factor of two. Next, the third convolution layer extracts the lower-scale properties of the signal in this resolution, then, to reduce the dimensionality of the features, the last max-pooling layer with a stride of 8 is added along the channel. It should be noted that all three layers are followed by a batch-normalization layer and the dropout regularization term. Finally, the resulting features of the convolutional layers are fed into a BiGRU, which can extract the contextual information of the sequence of the speech data. Moreover, a linear fully connected layer has been used as the last layer of the model, which generates two outputs corresponding to arousal and valence states.

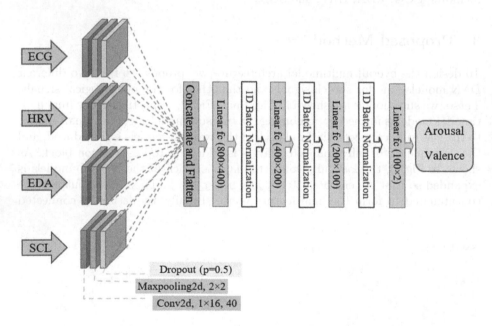

**Fig. 2.** DNN model for emotion recognition using physiological signals

In the physiological DNN model, as indicated in Fig. 2, four different physiological features are fed into a convolutional block separately. Each convolutional layer in each block is followed by a ReLU activation function, dropout regularization term, batch normalization, and also a max-pooling layer with a stride of 2. Then, the extracted features resulting from each input block are concatenated and to form a joint feature vector. As can be seen from Fig. 2, this feature vector is fed into a sequence of four fully connected layers, where each of the first three layers is followed by a batch-normalization layer. It seemed, as the structure of the physiological data is not as complicated as the speech signal, using further convolutional layers would degrade the performance of the model by unwanted manipulation of the useful information.

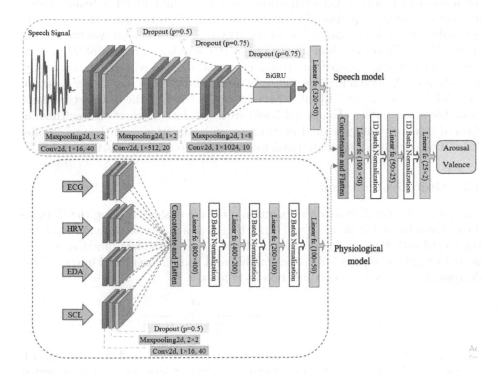

**Fig. 3.** Multimodal model for emotion recognition using speech and physiological signals

The overall multimodal model is shown in Fig. 3. It fuses the two above described sub-models by introducing a small change that expands the last linear fully connected layer of each sub-model to 50 outputs. The extended output features of each sub-model are concatenated, and after flattening, the resulting feature vector is fed into a sequence of three linear fully connected layers so that the last fully connected layer generates 2 values that represent the desired final prediction of arousal and valence.

## 4 Experiments and Results

### 4.1 Dataset

In this paper, we used the Remote Collaborative and Affective (RECOLA) dataset introduced by Ringeval et al. [19] for prediction of emotion through speech signals. This dataset includes the socio-affective data of 46 French-speaking participants in 9.5 h. The collected data consists of the audio, video, and physiological (ECG and EDA) recordings of online dyadic interaction between the participants. The first five minutes of interaction were annotated by six French speaking assistants every 40 ms using labels for the arousal and valence states. Considering the labeling time interval of the dataset, there are 7500 values for arousal and valence per each 5 min recording. The RECOLA team policies and consent matters permit the collected data of 23 participants to be publicly accessible. There is another subset of the RECOLA dataset that was used in the Audio-Visual Emotion Challenge (AVEC). It comprises the data of 27 participants and is equally divided into training, validation, and test sets. In our study, we only used the training (9 participants) and validation (9 participants) sets of the AVEC subset of the RECOLA dataset, as the labels of the test part were not available to the public. We applied 5-fold cross-validation, where the multimodal data of 9 participants was used for training and validation, and the multimodal data of the another 9 separate participants was employed for testing.

## 4.2  Objective Function

The proposed speech emotion recognition model is evaluated using the Concordance Correlation Coefficient ($\rho_c$) [12,17,18]. In this paper, to train and evaluate the model with the same metric, we used the $1 - \rho_c$ as the loss function, as suggested by [23]. The $\rho_c$ is fully differentiable and can be integrated into gradient descent. $L_c$ is defined as cost function as follows:

$$L_c = 1 - \rho_c = 1 - \frac{2\sigma_{xy}^2}{\sigma_x^2 + \sigma_y^2 + (\mu_x - \mu_y)^2} \tag{1}$$

where $\mu_x = E(x)$, $\mu_y = E(y)$, $\sigma_x^2 = var(x)$, $\sigma_y^2 = var(y)$, and $\sigma_{xy}^2 = cov(x,y)$. To minimize $L_c$, the gradient of the weights of the last layer are back-propagated using

$$\frac{\partial L_c}{\partial x} \propto 2\frac{\sigma_{xy}^2(x - \mu_y)}{\psi^2} + \frac{\mu_y - y}{\psi}, \tag{2}$$

where $\psi = \sigma_x^2 + \sigma_y^2 + (\mu_x - \mu_y)^2$ and all vector operations are made element-wise in the above equation.

## 4.3  Experimental Setup

In this paper, we used various time sequences as inputs representing each modality to evaluate the performance of the DNN model. During training of all three proposed DNN architectures, we employed the Adam optimizer [10] where the initial learning rate ($LR_{init}$) and the weight decay factor, were selected as $10^{-4}$ and $10^{-6}$, respectively. Mini-batch sizes of 10, 25, and 50 were used in all experiments. Moreover, a dropout regularization term [21] with different options was used to avoid overfitting, as shown in the Figs. 1, 2 and 3. All experiments employed implementations in the Pytorch framework of the Python programming language. The models were training using two 32 GB V100 GPUs on our school's Nvidia DGX Station.

## 4.4    Experimental Results

In this section, the prediction results of the proposed two sub-models and the multimodal model for arousal and valence states are summarized. As stated previously, considering the sequential nature of the emotional states, we fed a sequence of frames as input to the network. The period of annotation of arousal and valence states in the RECOLA data is 40 ms at a sampling frequency of 16 kHz. For input time sequences of 4 and 8 s the audio signal will result in the feature vectors of 64000 and 128000 samples, respectively. The physiological signals were sampled at a frequency of 1 kHz. Hence the feature vectors of the physiological signals comprise 4000 and 8000 samples for the input time sequence length of 4 and 8 s, correspondingly. The prediction results of the speech model, the physiological model, and the multimodal model are summarized in Table 1.

**Table 1.** The prediction results of proposed models for arousal and valence states in terms of $\rho_c$

| Model Name | Seq_Length | Batch Size 25 | | Batch Size 50 | |
|---|---|---|---|---|---|
| | | Ar | Val | Ar | Val |
| Speech | 4 | 0.613 | 0.103 | 0.592 | 0.128 |
| Speech | 8 | 0.628 | 0.109 | 0.608 | 0.119 |
| Physiological | 4 | 0.190 | 0.335 | 0.184 | 0.367 |
| Physiological | 8 | 0.181 | 0.353 | 0.179 | 0.396 |
| Multimodal | 4 | 0.586 | 0.316 | 0.566 | 0.363 |
| Multimodal | 8 | 0.640 | 0.378 | 0.626 | 0.337 |

Seq_Length: Sequence Length  Ar: Arousal  Val: Valence

As demonstrated in the table, the speech network showed better prediction for the arousal dimension while it didn't predict the valence state very well. On the other hand, the physiological model showed a more satisfying performance in the prediction of valence state. Finally, the proposed multimodal emotion recognition model has reasonable performance for the prediction of arousal and valence states. Besides, according to our experiments on the influence of each physiological data on the prediction of the model, we found that the ECG and EDA data have more impact on the prediction of the model. However, adding the HRV and SCL data improves the prediction of the model.

A direct comparison between our prediction results and the previously published state-of-the-art results was not possible because the full RECOLA dataset was not made available. In addition there are a few points that should be noted:

First, there is no multimodal model that used the speech and physiological signals of the RECOLA dataset. Second, all previous multimodal models used the audio-visual data and utilized the whole dataset, which involved the data of 46 people. We used only the publicly available subset which included the labeled data for 18 of the participants. Third, the data divisions in the current paper and the previous papers are different.

Considering all these criteria, we still compared the prediction results of our proposed model and other multimodal approaches on this dataset to show the effectiveness of our proposed multimodal model. Table 2 summarized the comparison results.

As shown in Table 2, using half of the dataset, the proposed model achieved predictions that are comparable to state-of-the-art results, especially in terms of arousal state.

**Table 2.** Prediction performance of the proposed model and related work on the RECOLA dataset in terms of $\rho_c$

| Method | Arousal | Valence |
| --- | --- | --- |
| Han et al. [5] | 0.610 | 0.463 |
| OA RVM-SR [9] | 0.770 | 0.545 |
| Tzirakis (raw) [23] | 0.789 | 0.691 |
| Proposed | 0.640 | 0.378 |

## 5   Conclusion

In this paper, we presented a DNN model for multimodal emotion recognition using speech and physiological signals. We proposed one model for the speech signals, a second model for the physiological signals and a fusion model that combined the first two models into one. Our experimental results showed that the speech model performed better when predicting the arousal dimension, while the physiological model performed better when predicting the valence dimension. Hence we fused the speech model and the physiological models into one multimodal model. The experiments with the multimodal model resulted in better prediction outcomes when compared to the two individual sub-models. An approximate comparison of the prediction results of our multimodal model with previous results of other state-of-the-art multimodal architectures that used versions of the RECOLA dataset indicated comparable performance.

## References

1. Cho, K., et al.: Learning phrase representations using RNN encoder-decoder for statistical machine translation. In: EMNLP 2014: Conference on Emprical Methods in Natural Language Processing (2014)

2. Egger, M., Ley, M., Hanke, S.: Emotion recognition from physiological signal analysis: a review. Electron. Notes Theoret. Comput. Sci. **343**, 35–55 (2019)
3. El Ayadi, M., Kamel, M.S., Karray, F.: Survey on speech emotion recognition: features, classification schemes, and databases. Pattern Recogn. **44**(3), 572–587 (2011)
4. Goodfellow, I., et al.: Generative adversarial nets. In: Advances in Neural Information Processing Systems, pp. 2672–2680 (2014)
5. Han, J., Zhang, Z., Cummins, N., Ringeval, F., Schuller, B.: Strength modelling for real-world automatic continuous affect recognition from audiovisual signals. Image Vis. Comput. **65**, 76–86 (2017)
6. Hinton, G.E., Osindero, S., Teh, Y.W.: A fast learning algorithm for deep belief nets. Neural Comput. **18**(7), 1527–1554 (2006)
7. Hinton, G.E., Zemel, R.S.: Autoencoders, minimum description length and Helmholtz free energy. In: Advances in Neural Information Processing Systems, pp. 3–10 (1994)
8. Hochreiter, S., Schmidhuber, J.: Long short-term memory. Neural Comput. **9**(8), 1735–1780 (1997)
9. Huang, Z., et al.: Staircase regression in OA RVM, data selection and gender dependency in AVEC 2016. In: Proceedings of the 6th International Workshop on Audio/Visual Emotion Challenge, pp. 19–26 (2016)
10. Kingma, D.P., Ba, J.: Adam: a method for stochastic optimization. arXiv preprint arXiv:1412.6980 (2014)
11. Lalitha, S., Tripathi, S., Gupta, D.: Enhanced speech emotion detection using deep neural networks. Int. J. Speech Technol. **22**(3), 497–510 (2018). https://doi.org/10.1007/s10772-018-09572-8
12. Lawrence, I., Lin, K.: A concordance correlation coefficient to evaluate reproducibility. Biometrics **45**, 255–268 (1989)
13. LeCun, Y.: Generalization and network design strategies. Connect. Pers. **19**, 143–155 (1989)
14. Li, C., Bao, Z., Li, L., Zhao, Z.: Exploring temporal representations by leveraging attention-based bidirectional LSTM-RNNs for multi-modal emotion recognition. Inf. Process. Manage. **57**(3), 102185 (2020)
15. Matsuda, Y., Fedotov, D., Takahashi, Y., Arakawa, Y., Yasumoto, K., Minker, W.: EmoTour: multimodal emotion recognition using physiological and audio-visual features. In: Proceedings of the 2018 ACM International Joint Conference and 2018 International Symposium on Pervasive and Ubiquitous Computing and Wearable Computers, pp. 946–951 (2018)
16. Ranganathan, H., Chakraborty, S., Panchanathan, S.: Multimodal emotion recognition using deep learning architectures. In: 2016 IEEE Winter Conference on Applications of Computer Vision (WACV), pp. 1–9. IEEE (2016)
17. Ringeval, F., et al.: Prediction of asynchronous dimensional emotion ratings from audiovisual and physiological data. Pattern Recogn. Lett. **66**, 22–30 (2015)
18. Ringeval, F., et al.: Av+ EC 2015: the first affect recognition challenge bridging across audio, video, and physiological data. In: Proceedings of the 5th International Workshop on Audio/Visual Emotion Challenge, pp. 3–8. ACM (2015)
19. Ringeval, F., Sonderegger, A., Sauer, J., Lalanne, D.: Introducing the RECOLA multimodal corpus of remote collaborative and affective interactions. In: 2013 10th IEEE International Conference and Workshops on Automatic Face and Gesture Recognition (FG), pp. 1–8. IEEE (2013)
20. Shu, L., et al.: A review of emotion recognition using physiological signals. Sensors **18**(7), 2074 (2018)

21. Srivastava, N., Hinton, G., Krizhevsky, A., Sutskever, I., Salakhutdinov, R.: Dropout: a simple way to prevent neural networks from overfitting. J. Machine Learn. Res. **15**(1), 1929–1958 (2014)
22. Trigeorgis, G., et al.: Adieu features? End-to-end speech emotion recognition using a deep convolutional recurrent network. In: 2016 IEEE International Conference on Acoustics, Speech and Signal Processing (ICASSP), pp. 5200–5204. IEEE (2016)
23. Tzirakis, P., Trigeorgis, G., Nicolaou, M.A., Schuller, B.W., Zafeiriou, S.: End-to-end multimodal emotion recognition using deep neural networks. IEEE J. Sel. Top. Sig. Process. **11**(8), 1301–1309 (2017)
24. Tzirakis, P., Zhang, J., Schuller, B.W.: End-to-end speech emotion recognition using deep neural networks. In: 2018 IEEE International Conference on Acoustics, Speech and Signal Processing (ICASSP), pp. 5089–5093. IEEE (2018)
25. Yang, Z., Hirschberg, J.: Predicting arousal and valence from waveforms and spectrograms using deep neural networks. In: INTERSPEECH, pp. 3092–3096 (2018)
26. Yin, Z., Zhao, M., Wang, Y., Yang, J., Zhang, J.: Recognition of emotions using multimodal physiological signals and an ensemble deep learning model. Comput. Methods Programs Biomed. **140**, 93–110 (2017)
27. Zhang, S., Zhang, S., Huang, T., Gao, W.: Speech emotion recognition using deep convolutional neural network and discriminant temporal pyramid matching. IEEE Trans. Multimedia **20**(6), 1576–1590 (2017)
28. Zhao, J., Mao, X., Chen, L.: Speech emotion recognition using deep 1D & 2D CNN LSTM networks. Biomed. Signal Process. Control **47**, 312–323 (2019)

# Cross-modal Deep Learning Applications: Audio-Visual Retrieval

Cong Jin[1(✉)], Tian Zhang[1,2], Shouxun Liu[3], Yun Tie[2(✉)], Xin Lv[4(✉)],
Jianguang Li[1], Wencai Yan[2], Ming Yan[1], Qian Xu[4], Yicong Guan[4],
and Zhenggougou Yang[5]

[1] School of Information and Communication Engineering,
Key Laboratory of Convergent Media and Intelligent Technology,
Ministry of Education, Communication University of China, Beijing 100024, China
jincong0623@cuc.edu.cn
[2] School of Information and Engineering, Zhengzhou University,
Zhengzhou 450001, China
ieytie@zzu.edu.cn
[3] Communication University of China, Beijing 100024, China
[4] School of Animation and Digital Arts, Communication University of China,
Beijing 100024, China
Lvxincuc@163.com
[5] Broadcasting and Anchoring School, Communication University of China,
Beijing 100024, China

**Abstract.** Recently, deep neural networks have exhibited as a powerful architecture to well capture the nonlinear distribution of high-dimensional multimedia data such as image, video, text and audio, so naturally does for multi-modal data. How to make full use of multimedia data? This leads to an important research direction: cross-modal learning. In this paper, we introduce a method based on the content of audio and video data modalities implemented with a novel two-branch neural network is to learn the joint embeddings from a shared subspace for computing the similarity between the two modalities. In particular, the contribution of proposed method is mainly manifested in the three aspects: i) Using feature selection model for choosing top-k audio and visual feature representation; ii) A novel combination of training loss function concerning inter-modal similarity and intra-modal invariance is used; iii) Due to the lack of video-music paired dataset, we construct dataset of video-music pairs from YouTube 8M and MER31K datasets. The experiments have proved that our proposed model has a better performance compared with other methods.

**Keywords:** Cross-modal learning · Audio-visual retrieval · Common subspace · Attention network

## 1  Introduction

"Big data" is always collected from different resources that have different data structures. With the rapid development of information technologies, current

A. Del Bimbo et al. (Eds.): ICPR 2020 Workshops, LNCS 12666, pp. 301–313, 2021.
https://doi.org/10.1007/978-3-030-68780-9_26

precious data resources are characteristic of multi-modes. As a result, based on classical machine learning strategies, cross-modal learning has become a valuable research topic, enabling computers to process and understand "big data". The cognitive process of human beings is multi-modal. When individuals perceive scenes, they can quickly receive visual, auditory, even touch and smell signals, and then carry out fusion processing and semantic understanding. Cross-modal learning method is closer to the form of human understanding of the world. "Modality" is a more fine-grained concept compared with multimedia data partition forms such as image, video, audio and text, and different modes can exist in the same medium [1].

From the perspective of semantic perception, multimodal data involves the information received by different perception channels such as vision, hearing, touch and smell; At the data level, multimodal data can be regarded as a combination of various types, such as images, numerical values, texts, symbols, audio and time series, or composite data forms composed of different data structures such as collections, trees and graphs, or even the combination of various information resources from different databases and different knowledge bases. The mining analysis of multi-source heterogeneous data can be understood as "Multimodal learning". Data from different sources or composed of different feature subsets are called multi-view data, and from each source or type can be regarded as a view. A modality can be regarded as a view, and a large number of multi-view learning methods are classified as multi-modal learning algorithms [2]. Concretely, the contributions of this study are shown as below:

1) Feature selection. Propose the feature selection model to score the extracted feature data of music and video segments, then select representative audio and visual data chunks for subsequent training process to reduce redundant data and improve efficiency [3]. 2) Sample mining. Before training, optimize the structure of the corresponding sample pairs so that the training efficiency will be improved. 3) Utilization of Novel loss function. Instead of the traditional triplet loss function, utilize a novel loss function combination for similarity learning.

## 2    Related Work

In recent years, many cross-modal related tasks have begun to use neural networks [4–9]. From the point of view of model structure, our method is similar to the double-branch neural network commonly used in graphic retrieval. Early researches on cross-modal matching of images and texts were carried out on MSCOCO [10] and Flickr30K [11] databases, and each image in the data set has five independent descriptions. They use the corresponding loss function to learn the linear relationship of modal data in the common embedding space. In order to better understand the relationship between visual and text modes [12], neural network-related methods have become popular. Because neural network can learn the nonlinear relationship between modes, the model effect has been improved. Among them, the model of Acar et al. [13] is related to the method in this paper. They put forward a framework based on emotional tags of music and videos, and used convolutional neural networks to learn more advanced non-linear feature expressions from low-level audio-visual features. However, unlike our proposed model, only the deep network structure is used as the intermediate feature extractor of music and images, instead of learning the relationship between cross-modal data.

In this paper, a content-based audio-visual cross-modal retrieval method is proposed, which only uses the content-based information derived from music or video data to achieve the task of matching appropriate music for a given video. The key of the research is to design a cross-modal retrieval model without metadata and hard-coded mapping functions first. Secondly, it is very important to obtain a database containing couples of matched video and music, which needs to learn a large number of neural network models. Thirdly, the matching criteria between video and music are more blurred than those of other cross-modal tasks (such as image-to-text retrieval). Large-scale video-music data set must be obtained so that the data can be feed into the deep neural network to learn the corresponding relationship between video and music.

## 3   Proposed Models

Our proposed model in this paper makes use of deep neural network to learn the potential correspondence between video and music, thus realizing the task of matching the corresponding music for a specific video by means of audio-visual cross-modal retrieval. The framework's structure is shown in Fig. 1. According to the functions of each part, the whole system is divided into three parts: feature extraction, embedding network and training loss function.

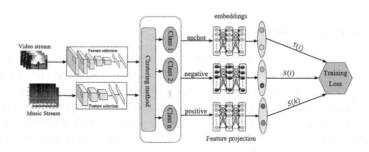

**Fig. 1.** The framework of audio-visual retrieval

### 3.1   Feature Extraction

In this part, we combine with attention mechanism [14] based on the VGGish and inception [15] model respectively, to form music and video feature selection model. At the preprocessing stage, two kinds of data are divided into chunks of fixed length. The model is used to evaluate the sentiment information contained in each chunk, to retain the characteristic ones with top strong sentiment attributes for the following experiments. The basic music or video feature extraction model is normally used to acquire semantic features of data, where the convolutional layer extracts data features, the maximum pooling layer aggregates the feature temporally, and the fully connected layer learns the relationship between features and sentiment tags. Rectified linear unit is used as activation function of each layer. The differences are that, firstly, the model we proposed divides the data by a fixed length, and secondly, the attention calculation network layer is added to the output of the max pooling layer, for weighting sentiment distribution of each segmented data. The first layer is the attention scoring, and the function is defined as follows:

$$U_{g(i)} = W^T \tanh(W_{v(x)} V_{g(i)} + \theta) \tag{1}$$

where $V_g$ and $V_i$ represent the output of the basic VGGish and inception model, $W_v, W_x$ and $\theta$ are learnable parameters. The second layer uses the softmax function as the activation function to normalize the scoring results:

$$a = soft \max(U_{g(i)}) \tag{2}$$

The final representation is generated by the weighted pooling layer which fuses the output of FC ($O_c$) and attention calculation layer ($a_c$):

$$\tilde{y} = \sum_{c=1}^{n} a_c O_c \tag{3}$$

$\tilde{y}$ represents the final sentiment evaluation coefficient of the data blocks, and we select the ones with top-k performance to improve accuracy and reduce redundant data.

### 3.2 Embedding Network

After extracting the respective feature data of music and video through the above feature selection model, in order to compare and learn the data of two different modes, an embedding network is designed, whose purpose is to calculate and map the feature vectors of music and video into the same common feature space through neural network, which can also be called embedding space. Thus, cross-modal data can be compared in the same feature space. This part is mainly composed of label prediction classifier, sample mining network and feature mapping network.

1. Label Prediction Classifier

In order to ensure that the data of two modes can be mapped into the common subspace for comparison as far as possible, that is, the similar data of two modes have similar distances in the subspace [16], but different distances are far away, a label prediction network similar to a classifier is considered when designing the embedded network, with the aim of enabling each modal data to still have its own semantic information in the common space and maintaining semantic discrimination. The cross-modal data in subspace can be matched with each other within the same class, and the differences between different classes can be compared, which ensures the matching accuracy and makes the matching results more flexible and diverse.

A classifier network is added to the subspace embedding network, and its structure is essentially a feedforward network with *softmax* as the activation function. The classifier takes the extracted music and video features as input training data, and generates the probability distribution of the semantic category of each item of data as output. The following formula is the loss function of intra-modal semantic discrimination used for training classifiers:

$$L_{lp} = -\frac{1}{n} \sum_{i=1}^{n} (y_i(\log \hat{p}_i(v_i) + \log \hat{p}_i(m_i))) \tag{4}$$

$L_{lp}$ represents the multi-classification cross entropy of this semantic classification model, $n$ represents the number of samples trained in each batch, $y_i$ refers to the label information of samples, and $\hat{p}_i$ represents the probability of model output, that is the probability of $i$.

2. Sample Mining Network

Metric learning [17] loss function inevitably generates many sample pairs, but plenty of them are redundant, and uninformative, thus it will slow the training effect and degrade model performance. Therefore, this paper proposes the corresponding sample mining strategy. The inspiration for this solution comes from the LMNN [18] method. Specifically, we compare the negative sample pair to the positive pair with the least similarity, and compare the positive pair to negative pair with highest similarity, which can be defined as follows:

$$\begin{aligned} d(i,j) > \max d(i,k) + margin \text{ if } y_i = y_k \\ d(i,j) < \max d(i,k) + margin \text{ if } y_i \neq y_k \end{aligned} \tag{5}$$

where $d(i,j)$ denotes the distance between anchor and negative (positive) when $y_i = y_k$ ($y_i \neq y_k$). Other similar sampling schemes always focus on the mining of hard negative samples, but this often leads to overfitting. The mining method proposed in this paper made some adjustments to transform the sampling problem into the weighting of pairs.

## 3.3 Training Loss Function

Then the next step is to design the corresponding measurement learning loss function to train the data in subspace. The first is the similarity between modes, and the second is the invariance within modes. Similarity between modes is the theoretical basis for us to achieve cross-modal matching, and modal invariance needs to ensure that the feature data in subspaces remain unchanged in their original feature spaces. Next, the loss function will be introduced from two aspects of inter-modal and intra-modal.

1. Inter-modal ranking loss

In order to improve the performance of model, the loss function we used in this work is multi-similarity loss function [19], which focuses on the modeling of similarity in multi aspects, and performs better than the traditional ones only considering single similarity. The loss function is defined as follows:

$$L_{MS} = \frac{1}{m} \sum_{i=1}^{m} \left\{ \frac{1}{a} \log \left[ 1 + \sum_{k \in p_i} e^{-\alpha(S_{ik}-\lambda)} \right] \right.$$
$$\left. + \frac{1}{\beta} \log \left[ 1 + \sum_{k \in N_i} e^{\beta(S_{ik}-\lambda)} \right] \right\} \quad (6)$$

where $\alpha$, $\beta$, $\lambda$ are hyper-parameters. Specifically, the expression of MS loss combines the self-similarity of sample pair and the relative similarity, which takes all neighborhood negative and positive pairs into consideration.

2. Intra-modal structure preservation

In order not to lose these structural characteristics during the training process, and to result in reducing model accuracy, the intra-modal preservation loss function is added to the inter-modal loss. The combination of them two is the multi-modal subspace training function used in this work. Specifically, taking the modality of music as an instance, since we try to maintain the internal structure of the modality, the vectors should satisfy the following relationship:

$$d(m_i, m_j) < d(m_i, m_k) \text{ if } d(\tilde{m}_i, \tilde{m}_j) < d(\tilde{m}_i, \tilde{m}_k) \quad (7)$$

where $m_i$, $m_j$, $m_k$ respectively represent the music features in subspace. $m_i$, $m_j$, $m_k$ denote the music features in original space. However, after considering that the matching relationship between video and music is more flexible, we defines the loss function expression as follows instead of using margin-based distance loss function [20]:

$$L_{intra} = \lambda_1 \sum_{i \neq k \neq j} c_{ijk}(v)(v_i^T v_j - v_i^T v_k)$$
$$+ \lambda_2 \sum_{i \neq k \neq j} c_{ijk}(m)(m_i^T m_j - m_i^T m_k) \quad (8)$$

$$c_{ijk}(x) = sign(x_i^T x_j - x_i^T x_k) - sign(\tilde{x}_i^T \tilde{x}_j - \tilde{x}_i^T \tilde{x}_k) \quad (9)$$

In order to make the constraint of the loss function more flexible, a symbolic function is introduced to the work. $x_i$, $x_j$, $x_k$ are the representation in the common subspace, respectively. $\tilde{x}_i$, $\tilde{x}_j$, $\tilde{x}_k$ represent the original feature data. The purpose of using symbolic function is to avoid the problem of rigidity of the matching result caused by using the Euclidean distance loss function. After the feature projection through the embedding network, the samples are combined with each other in the form of triples for training. In this process, four types of triples are constructed: $(v_i, m_i, m_j)$, $(m_i, v_i, v_j)$, $(v_i, v_j, v_k)$, $(m_i, m_j, m_k)$. Then we define the total multi-modal embedding training loss as:

$$L_{multi-modal} = \lambda_1 L_{inter} + \lambda_2 L_{intra} \quad (10)$$

# 4    Experiment

## 4.1    Datasets and Evaluation Metrics

Among the data sets related to tasks of cross-modal retrieval, many of them are formed for graphic retrieval, however, few are about video-to-music cross-modal retrieval. At present, the data set that can be found and tested on it is VEGAS [21], which contains 28,103 video-music pairs. But the disadvantage is that only one piece of music matches each video, which makes neural network unable to fully learn the corresponding relationship between video and music. Therefore, drawing lessons from the construction experience of VEGAS data set, this paper establishes a new music video cross-modal matching data set containing 7353 video-music pairs. Referring to the structure of Flickr30K [11], we choose five pieces of music as ground truth of each video clip, and every matching pair shares a common category label. According to the matching degree between video and music, the corresponding weights p (0:45; 0:25; 0:15; 0:1; 0:05) are assigned to each piece of music in turn. AS for evaluation, we decide to adopt the evaluation metrics of Recall and Mean Average Precision.

- **Recall** It is a commonly-used evaluation in image-text retrieval tasks. It means the percentage of the top k results obtained by using each video query include at least one pair of ground truth pair when we input all the test set.
- **Mean Average Precision (MAP)** It is different from the Recall k, is also standard protocol takes all the retrieval results into consideration, and its calculation formula is as follows:

$$Map = \frac{1}{N} \sum_{j=1}^{k} p_j * rel(j) \tag{11}$$

where $p_j$ is a weight value considering music quality, $N$ represents the number of similar music related to the retrieved video, $rel(j)$ represents a binary function, and it is 1 when the $j$th music falls within the marked range, otherwise it is 0.

## 4.2    Experiment Setting

The following parameters are used in our experiments:

- **Network Parameters** After extracting the advanced features from the feature selection model, a two-layer fully connected network is set up at the video end of the dual-stream processing network, including 2048 and 512 nodes respectively. A three-layer fully connected network with 2048, 1024 and 512 nodes is set up at the audio end, and the activation functions used are *sigmoid* and *tanh*. *L*2 normalization method is adopted before the input loss function network layer of video and audio data, so as to solve the problem of the balance of the number ratio between music and video features and alleviate over-fitting.

- **Experimental Parameters** After debugging in the training stage, in order to balance the training efficiency and the accuracy of the results, the optimal batch is 550 and epoch is 40.
- **Learning Rate** ADAM optimizer with learning rate of 0.001 is applied in this method, and the probability of deactivation is 0.2.

### 4.3   Experiment Result and Analysis

1. Key Factors

In order to explore the influence of some key parameters on the results of the model, relevant experiments were carried out while training the model, and the results are shown in Table 1. In the experiment, three variables are set: the weight of loss function, the number of layers of full connection and the $s/t$ value of feature selection model ($s$ represents the number of selected feature data and $t$ represents the total number of feature segmentation), and each variable is adjusted while the other two variables remain unchanged. Firstly, keep the number of fully connected layers $(1, 1)$ and $s/t$ as $1/3$ (which means dividing modal feature data into three segments, selecting one of them) unchanged, adjusting the weight parameters of loss function and recording the performance of the model, it is found that if the value of $\lambda_1$ is larger than $\lambda_2$, the accuracy of the model will be higher, but the value of $\lambda_1$ cannot be greater than 5, otherwise the performance of the model will be worse.

Then, the number of layers of all connections in the embedding network is changed with the weight of loss function $(1, 1)$ and $s/t$ at $1/3$ unchanged, and the experimental results are observed. If only one layer of fully connected network is set up, the effect of the model will become worse, which also proves that a deeper network structure is helpful to improve the experimental accuracy. And with the deepening of the network layer, the performance of the model is getting better and better. However, it can be known from experiments that when the video processing end of the model has more than three layers of full connection, the training will not converge, which is also the case that the performance of the model is degraded easily due to the deep network.

Finally, in order to explore the influence of the relationship between the total amount of divided data $t$ and the selected amount of data $s$ in the feature selection model, we set related experiment parameters unchanged as following: the weight $(1, 1)$ and the total number of fully connected layers $(2, 2)$. We keep $s/t$ as constant and increase the number of $s$ and $t$, which can improve the performance of the model in a certain range, but when $s$ increases to 12, the experimental results are not improved. The optimal parameters obtained by the experiment are: the weight of loss function $(1, 1)$, the number of fully connected layers $(3, 2)$, and the $s/t$ value $3/9$.

In addition, batch size and the margin we used in sample mining also play roles in performance and time consumption of the system. We also do some experiments to explore the impact of them both.

**Table 1.** Retrieval results with respect to the key factors

| Parameters | | Visual-to-audio | | | |
|---|---|---|---|---|---|
| | | Recall 5 | Recall 10 | Recall 15 | Recall 20 |
| Weight of loss $(\lambda_1, \lambda_2)$ | (1,3) | 9.6 | 17.3 | 23.5 | 29.8 |
| | (1,5) | 9.2 | 15 | 19.9 | 22.7 |
| | (1,1) | 10.4 | 13.2 | 18.1 | 23.1 |
| | (3,1) | 12.5 | 19.3 | 24.1 | 31.4 |
| | (5,1) | 9.0 | 17.8 | 21.6 | 25.2 |
| Number of layers $(N_{music}, N_{video})$ | (1,1) | 4.3 | 16.1 | 24.9 | 25.6 |
| | (2,2) | 7.5 | 16.5 | 26.4 | 27.3 |
| | (2,3) | 7.4 | 16.8 | 25.9 | 26.4 |
| | (3,2) | 8.5 | 19.2 | 27.5 | 29.1 |
| | (4,2) | 8.2 | 18.5 | 25.5 | 27.3 |
| $s/t$ ($s$: selected, $t$: total) | 1/3 | 17.0 | 16.3 | 16.4 | 16.7 |
| | 2/6 | 18.5 | 18.2 | 17.5 | 18.1 |
| | 3/9 | 18.4 | 19.2 | 18.8 | 18.7 |
| | 4/12 | 16.1 | 16.5 | 16.8 | 17.6 |

Batch size is a hyper-parameter which represents the number of samples trained by model during an iteration. Specifically, we set different batch sizes by changing batch number. We record the MAP value and time consumption of the system as shown in Table 2. Notice that when batch number reaches 400, we can get the best MAP value of 75.31%. But considering the efficiency of the system, we choose 550 as our batch number.

**Table 2.** MAP under different batch sizes when margin is 0.5

| Batches | 300 | 350 | 400 | 450 | 500 | 550 | 600 | 650 | 700 | 800 | 900 |
|---|---|---|---|---|---|---|---|---|---|---|---|
| Video-music | 74.49 | 73.63 | **75.31** | 74.50 | 74.51 | 74.99 | 74.87 | 74.58 | 74.12 | 62.96 | 61.28 |
| Time(h) | 32 | 27 | 21 | 16 | 12 | 9 | 6 | 4 | 3 | 2 | 2 |

The Table 3 shows the MAP value of video-music retrieval based on the margin ranges from 0.1 to 1.0 and set the number of batches to 500. When the margin is 0.5 the MAP gets the highest value.

**Table 3.** MAP with respect to different margins

| Margin | 0.1 | 0.2 | 0.3 | 0.4 | 0.5 | 0.6 | 0.7 | 0.8 | 0.9 | 1.0 |
|---|---|---|---|---|---|---|---|---|---|---|
| Video-music | 64.73 | 68.82 | 74.30 | 74.59 | **75.31** | 74.17 | 74.15 | 73.80 | 74.68 | 65.30 |

## 2. Method Comparison

We have done comparisons of our model with the previous commonly used models applied to video-music cross-modal retrieval task, and experiments have been done on both VEGAS [21] and self-established databases. Table 4 shows the Recall rate and MAP of different models on self-built database. These models can be roughly divided into two types: linear and non-linear. Among them, linear methods include PCA [22], PLSCA [23], and CCA [24], they can learn linear relationships between modalities. Non-linear methods include VMNET [25], DCCA [26] and DANN [27]. Especially, the architecture of DCCA model is similar to this work, with dual-stream neural network structure, which is used for image-text retrieval originally. We use this model to achieve video-music cross-modal matching task, and it has still achieved excellent results.

**Table 4.** Comparison of results using different methods

| Method | Recall@5 | Recall@10 | Recall@15 | MAP |
|---|---|---|---|---|
| CCA | 52.3 | 54.0 | 61.7 | 59.8 |
| PCA | 50.9 | 51.3 | 51.1 | 55.6 |
| PLSVVD | 53.7 | 53.9 | 52.8 | 57.4 |
| PLSCA | 56.0 | 55.2 | 56.4 | 59.3 |
| VMNET | 68.6 | 71.2 | 74.9 | 76.1 |
| DCCA | 72.5 | 74.8 | 77.3 | 78.2 |
| DANN | 73.1 | 74.5 | 76.2 | 75.8 |
| Proposed (triplet loss+intra-modal loss) | 75.0 | 74.3 | 75.5 | **76.7** |
| Proposed (MS loss+intra-modal loss) | 81.5 | 76.4 | 78.6 | **83.5** |

By comparing the performance of different models on the same data set, it can be found that the traditional linear model does not perform well in cross-modal retrieval, while the nonlinear model based on neural networks has excellent performance. Besides, the training loss function in this work performs better than the traditional triplet loss function, the multi-similarity loss function is easier to converge in the training stage. The PR curves shown in Fig. 2 and Fig. 3 depict the performance of the eight models on the two datasets, intuitively showing the performance of different methods. The model we proposed outperforms on the self-built data set and the standard dataset VEGAS.

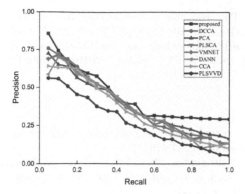

**Fig. 2.** Precision-recall curves of different models on VEGAS dataset

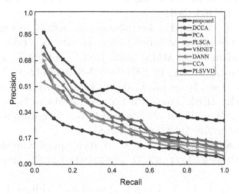

**Fig. 3.** Precision-recall curves of different models on self-established dataset

## 5    Conclusion

In this paper, a framework of cross-modal music video retrieval based on dual-stream neural network is proposed to achieve the task of matching corresponding music for a given video. This paper improves the dual-stream network from two aspects. The first is the feature extraction stage. In this section, we propose two different feature selection networks for music and video feature respectively based on CNN. Through deep model, the feature representation is projected in common space and compared each other for similarity calculation, and the selected features are used to replace the overall for training, which can suppress redundant data and improve training efficiency. Furthermore, according to the properties cross and within the modalities, we utilize a better loss function combo and get high performance. However, at present, the video and music used in the experiment are very short in length, and in the future research, we will continue to explore the cross-modal retrieval of long video and music.

**Acknowledgment.** This research was supported by the National Natural Science Foundation of China (Grant No. 61631016 and 61901421), National Key R &D Program of China (Grant No. 2018YFB1403903) and the Fundamental Research Funds for the Central Universities (Grant No. CUC200B017, 2019E002 and CUC19ZD003).

# References

1. O'Halloran, K.L.: Interdependence, interaction and metaphor in multi-semiotic texts. Soc. Semiotics **9**(3), 317 (1999)
2. Morency, L.P., Baltrusaitis, T.: Tutorial on multimodal machine learning, Language Technologies Institute (2019). https://www.cs.cmu.edu/morency/MMMLTutorial-ACL2017.pdf
3. Yan, M., Chan, C.A., Li, W., Lei, L., Gygax, A.F., Chih-Lin, I.: Assessing the energy consumption of proactive mobile edge caching in wireless networks. IEEE Access **7**, 104394–104404 (2019)
4. Sasaki, S., Hirai, T., Ohya, H., Morishima, S.: Affective music recommendation system based on the mood of input video. In: He, X., Luo, S., Tao, D., Xu, C., Yang, J., Hasan, M.A. (eds.) MMM 2015. LNCS, vol. 8936, pp. 299–302. Springer, Cham (2015). https://doi.org/10.1007/978-3-319-14442-9_33
5. Liwei, W., Yin, L., Jing, H., et al.: Learning two branch neural networks for image-text matching tasks. IEEE Trans. Pattern Anal. Mach. Intell. **41**, 210–223 (2018)
6. Lee, K.-H., Xi, C., Gang, H., et al.: Stacked Cross Attention for Image-Text Matching, arXiv preprint arXiv:1803.08024 (2018)
7. Jin, C., Tie, Y., Bai, Y., Lv, X., Liu, S.: A style-specific music composition neural network. Neural Process. Lett. **52**(3), 1893–1912 (2020). https://doi.org/10.1007/s11063-020-10241-8
8. Andrej, K., Armand, J., Li, F.: Deep fragment embeddings for bidirectional image sentence mapping. In: NeurIPS, pp. 1889–1897 (2014)
9. Peng, Z., Li, Z., Zhang, J., Li, Y., Qi, G.J., Tang, J.: Few-shot image recognition with knowledge transfer. In: Proceedings of ICCV, pp. 441–449 (2019)
10. Lin, T.-Y., et al.: Microsoft COCO: common objects in context. In: Fleet, D., Pajdla, T., Schiele, B., Tuytelaars, T. (eds.) ECCV 2014. LNCS, vol. 8693, pp. 740–755. Springer, Cham (2014). https://doi.org/10.1007/978-3-319-10602-1_48
11. Young, P., Lai, A., Hodosh, M., et al.: From image descriptions to visual denotations: new similarity metrics for semantic inference over event descriptions. Trans. Assoc. Comput. Linguist. **2**, 67–78 (2014)
12. Li, Z., Tang, J.: Weakly supervised deep matrix factorization for social image understanding. IEEE Trans. Image Process. **26**(1), 276–288 (2016)
13. Acar, E., Hopfgartner, F., Albayrak, S.: Understanding affective content of music videos through learned representations. In: Gurrin, C., Hopfgartner, F., Hurst, W., Johansen, H., Lee, H., O'Connor, N. (eds.) MMM 2014. LNCS, vol. 8325, pp. 303–314. Springer, Cham (2014). https://doi.org/10.1007/978-3-319-04114-8_26
14. Xu, Y., Kong, Q., Huang, Q., Wang, W., Plumbley, M.D.: Attention and localization based on a deep convolutional recurrent model for weakly supervised audio tagging, arXiv preprint arXiv:1703.06052 (2017)
15. Szegedy, C., Liu, W., Jia, Y., et al.: Going deeper with convolutions. In: Proceedings of CVPR, pp. 1–9 (2015)
16. Li, Z., Liu, J., Tang, J., Lu, H.: Robust structured subspace learning for data representation. IEEE Trans. Pattern Anal. Mach. Intell. **37**(10), 2085–2098 (2015)

17. Li, Z., Tang, J.: Weakly supervised deep metric learning for community-contributed image retrieval. IEEE Trans. Multimedia **17**(11), 1989–1999 (2015)
18. Song, K., Nie, F., Han, J., Li, X.: Parameter free large margin nearest neighbor for distance metric learning. In: AAAI (2017)
19. Wang, X., Han, X., Huang, W., Dong, D., Scott, M.R.: Multi-similarity loss with general pair weighting for deep metric learning. In: Proceedings of CVPR, pp. 5022–5030 (2019)
20. Ge, W., Huang, W., Dong, D., Scott, M.R.: Deep metric learning with hierarchical triplet loss. In: Ferrari, V., Hebert, M., Sminchisescu, C., Weiss, Y. (eds.) ECCV 2018. LNCS, vol. 11210, pp. 272–288. Springer, Cham (2018). https://doi.org/10.1007/978-3-030-01231-1_17
21. Zhou, Y., Wang, Z., Fang, C., et al.: Visual to sound: generating natural sound for videos in the wild. In: Proceedings of the CVPR, pp. 3550–3558 (2018)
22. Canyi, L., Jiashi, F., Yudong, C., et al.: Tensor robust principal component analysis with a new tensor nuclear norm. IEEE Trans. Pattern Anal. Mach. Intell. **42**(4), 925–938 (2019)
23. Wegelin, J.A., et al.: A survey of Partial Least Squares (PLS) methods, with emphasis on the two-block case. University of Washington, Technical report (2000)
24. Hardoon, D.R., Szedmak, S., Shawe-Taylor, J.: Canonical correlation analysis: an overview with application to learning methods. Neural comput. **16**(12), 2639–2664 (2004)
25. Surís, D., Duarte, A., Salvador, A., Torres, J., Giró-i-Nieto, X.: Cross-modal embeddings for video and audio retrieval. In: Leal-Taixé, L., Roth, S. (eds.) ECCV 2018. LNCS, vol. 11132, pp. 711–716. Springer, Cham (2019). https://doi.org/10.1007/978-3-030-11018-5_62
26. Andrew, G., Arora, R., Bilmes, J., Livescu, K.: Deep canonical correlation analysis. In: Proceedings of ICML, pp. 1247–1255 (2013)
27. Ganin, Y., et al.: Domain-adversarial training of neural networks. J. Mach. Learn. Res. **17**(1), 2030–2096 (2016)

# Exploiting Word Embeddings for Recognition of Previously Unseen Objects

Karan Sharma[1]($\boxtimes$), Hemanth Dandu[2], Arun C. S. Kumar[2], Vinay Kumar[2], and Suchendra M. Bhandarkar[2]

[1] Keysight Technologies, Atlanta, GA 30308, USA
karan1234@gmail.com
[2] Department of Computer Science, University of Georgia, Athens, GA 30602-7404, USA
hemanth.dandu@uga.edu, arunkarthikcs@gmail.com, vinay453@gmail.com, suchi@uga.edu

**Abstract.** A notable characteristic of human cognition is its ability to derive reliable hypotheses in situations characterized by extreme uncertainty. Even in the absence of relevant knowledge to make a correct inference, humans are able to draw upon related knowledge to make an approximate inference that is semantically close to the correct inference. In the context of object recognition, this ability amounts to being able to hypothesize the identity of an object in an image without previously having ever seen any visual training examples of that object. The paradigm of low-shot (i.e., zero-shot and few-shot) classification has been traditionally used to address these situations. However, traditional zero-shot and few-shot approaches entail the training of classifiers in situations where a majority of classes are previously *seen* or visually observed whereas a minority of classes are previously *unseen*, in which case the classifiers for the *unseen* classes are learned by expressing them in terms of the classifiers for the *seen* classes. In this paper, we address the *related but different* problem of object recognition in situations where only a few object classes are visually observed whereas a majority of the object classes are previously unseen. Specifically, we pose the following questions: (a) Is it possible to hypothesize the identity of an object in an image without previously having seen any visual training examples for that object? and (b) Could the visual training examples of a few *seen* object classes provide reliable priors for hypothesizing the identities of objects in an image that belong to the majority *unseen* object classes? We propose a model for recognition of objects in an image in situations where visual classifiers are available for only a limited number of object classes. To this end, we leverage word embeddings trained on publicly available text corpora and use them as natural language priors for hypothesizing the identities of objects that belong to the *unseen* classes. Experimental results on the *Microsoft Common Objects in Context* (MS-COCO) data set show that it is possible to come up with reliable hypotheses with regard to object identities by exploiting word embeddings trained on the *Wikipedia* text corpus even in the absence of explicit visual classifiers for those object

A. Del Bimbo et al. (Eds.): ICPR 2020 Workshops, LNCS 12666, pp. 314–329, 2021.
https://doi.org/10.1007/978-3-030-68780-9_27

classes. To bolster our hypothesis, we conduct additional experiments on larger dataset of concepts (themes) that we created from the *Conceptual Captions* dataset. Even on this extremely challenging dataset, our results, though not entirely impressive, serve to provide an important proof-of-concept for the proposed model.

# 1  Introduction

One of the characteristics of human intelligence is its ability to generate plausible hypotheses about unknown situations in the face of extreme uncertainty. Even in cases where relevant knowledge to draw an inference about a situation is lacking, humans can still retrieve related knowledge to draw a meaningful inference about the underlying situation. In the context of object recognition, this ability is tantamount to being able to hypothesize the identity of an object in an image without previously ever having visually observed any training examples of that specific object. The low-shot (i.e., zero-shot and few-shot) classification paradigm has been traditionally used to address such situations [1]. However, conventional approaches to low-shot classification entail the training of visual classifiers for situations where a *large majority* of the object classes are visually observed whereas only a *small minority* of object classes are unseen. Additionally, these approaches learn a classifier for an unseen object class by expressing it in terms of classifiers for seen object classes. However, consider a situation where we have very few *seen* object classes and a vast majority of object classes are *unseen*. Could we hypothesize the identities of the objects in an image in such situations? Could a very few previously seen object classes provide reliable priors for drawing reliable hypotheses regarding the presence of the many previously unseen object classes in an image? We seek to address these questions in this paper. It should be noted that the problem we address in this paper is substantively different from most existing published work in zero-shot or few-shot object recognition and localization where the goal is to recognize and/or localize a few unseen object categories after having trained the system on a large number of seen object categories. In contrast, in this paper we address the problem of inferring *several* previously unseen object categories from *very few* previously seen categories which is substantively different from that addressed by conventional zero-shot or few-shot approaches. Hence, drawing a direct comparison between the experimental results of our approach with those of conventional zero-shot or few-shot approaches is not instructive.

In this paper, we propose a model that aims to correctly identify the objects in an image using a limited number of visual classifiers. The proposed model is capable of formulating hypotheses regarding the class of an object in an image even when the object class that the visual classifier is trained to detect is not present in the image. For instance, if the visual classifier indicates that a *car* is the most likely object in an image even when the image does not contain a car, then using a natural language (NL) model that exploits word embeddings obtained via training on a publicly available NL corpus, alternative hypotheses based on other vehicles and/or transport-related entities, such as *train*, *bus*, or even *road* or *pedestrian*, are proposed. Likewise, if the visual classifier indicates that the image contains a *bird*, then NL-based priors allow the system to propose an *airplane* as an alternate hypothesis. In summary, the proposed model is based on the premise that nonspecific visual classifiers could still prove useful in accurately identifying an actual object in an image, as the most likely object deduced by the visual classifier could belong to the same general category as the actual object in the image. Alternatively, the overall context of the most likely object deduced by the visual classifier could be similar to that of the actual object in an image, or the most likely object deduced by the visual classifier and actual object in an image could coexist or co-occur in the real world with high probability.

In the proposed approach (Fig. 1), as a first step, $k$-means clustering is performed on NL word embeddings obtained via training on a publicly available NL text corpus. This results in the formation of object clusters such that entities within a cluster share some degree of semantic similarity. From each object cluster, a representative object is selected to train the corresponding visual classifier. Typically, the object within the cluster with the greatest number of available training instances is deemed to be the representative object for that cluster. After the visual classifiers for all of the representative objects have been trained, they are employed on real test images. The visual classifiers for all the representative objects are executed on the test image to determine the object(s) in the test image. Using the most probable object hypothesis and NL word embeddings obtained via training on a public text corpus, it is possible to refine the initial object hypothesis to propose alternative object hypotheses for the test image. Previously, Sharma et al. [2] presented a preliminary object detection and classification model based on the above approach with encouraging results. In their approach, Sharma et al. [2] used word embeddings trained on the NL captions that accompanied the test images to aid low-shot context-aware object recognition. In this paper, we extend the previous approach by exploiting pretrained NL word embeddings (such as FastText) obtained via training on a general text corpus (such as Wikipedia) and perform a more comprehensive analysis of the results.

## 2   Motivation

To generate a plausible hypothesis about the identity of an object in an image, the proposed approach embodies the following observations about the real world:

**Observation 1:** The first observation is that similarity in the deep-learned visual feature space for object categories that belong to a more general category often translates to proximity of the corresponding NL word embeddings in the hypothetical space (Fig. 2). For instance, since the object categories *orange* and *apple* belong to the more general *fruit* category, their corresponding word embeddings would be expected to lie in close proximity in the hypothetical space, as would the word embeddings of the objects *car*, *truck* and *train* since they belong to the more general *vehicle* category. Conversely, in the visual world,

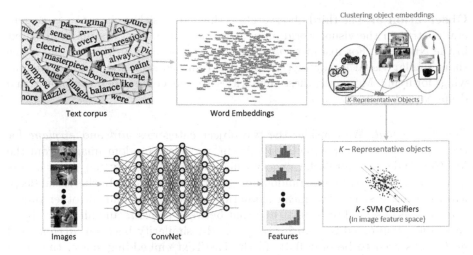

**Fig. 1.** Overview of the proposed approach.

many object categories that belong to a single general category tend to share the same (or similar) deep-learned visual features.

*Toy Experiment:* We conduct a toy experiment on the category *car* in the *Microsoft Common Objects in Context* (MS-COCO) data set. We select a random *car* image as well as one random image of each annotated object in the MS-COCO data set [3], ensuring that each image has only one annotated object. Using these images, we compute the similarity between the *car* image and all the other objects in the visual deep learned feature space. For NL-based textual similarity, we consider the vectors of the pretrained FastText embeddings of the entity *car* and all the other annotated entities in the MS-COCO data set. Using these embedding vectors, we compare the similarity between the entity *car* and the other entities. Next, we compute the correlation coefficient between the similarity measures in the visual deep-learned feature space and the word embedding space. The correlation coefficient was observed to be ≈ 0.4, which can be considered moderate, thus suggesting a moderate correlation between the visual features and the NL-derived textual features.

**Observation 2:** The second observation is that the general semantic context in the form of object co-occurrences in NL is effectively captured by the word embeddings in the hypothetical space. Moreover, object co-occurrences in NL often correspond to object co-occurrences in the visual world.

To revisit the previous example, a local search in the hypothetical space will yield alternative object hypotheses for *car*, such as *truck* along with other vehicle categories that are in semantic proximity to the word embedding of the object *car*. Conversely, the entities *car*, *truck* and other vehicle categories that are in semantic proximity in the hypothetical space will share similar visual features.

**Observation 3:** The third observation is that objects that share the same general context in the visual world often share the same general semantic context in the NL world. For instance, *bird* and *airplane* both fly in the sky and hence share similar visual features because of their shared semantic context, such as wings for flying. Moreover, these similarities are reflected in their common visual deep-learned features.

*Toy Experiment:* We consider the two object categories *bird* and *airplane* for the purpose of this toy experiment. Again, we select random images from the MS-COCO data set for each category while ensuring that only one object occurs in an image. We extract one random image for each category. In the visual deep-learned feature space, the mean similarity between *bird* and all other object categories is observed to be 0.22, and that between *airplane* and all other object categories is observed to be 0.26. However, the similarity between *airplane* and *bird* is observed to be only 0.31. In the FastText embedding space, the mean similarity between *bird* and all other object categories is observed to be 0.13, and that between *airplane* and all other object categories is observed to be 0.16. However, the similarity between *bird* and *airplane* is observed to be 0.19. Thus, in both the visual deep-learned feature space and textual word embedding space, the computed similarity between the object categories *airplane* and *bird* is observed to be greater than the mean similarities between *bird* and other object categories and between *airplane* and other object categories. This suggests that the detection of *bird* could aid in the detection of *airplane* and vice versa. Although the difference in the computed similarity values is not particularly strong, we contend that it is sufficiently substantial to matter in many real-world situations.

## 3   Related Work

In recent years, a wide variety of models for context-based object recognition have been proposed in the research literature. Divvala et al. [4] have identified and categorized various sources of contextual information: pixel-level interactions, semantic context, GIST, geographic context, illumination and weather, cultural context, and photogrammetric context, among others. Divvala et al. [4] further demonstrated that incorporation of each type of contextual information leads to moderate improvements in the recognition accuracy. However, two classes of contextual models have gained prominence in recent years, i.e., scene-based contextual models and object-based contextual models [5]. In a scene-based contextual model, the statistics pertaining to the entire scene are used to detect and locate the scene objects, whereas in an object-based contextual model, objects in the spatial vicinity of the target object are used to recognize the target object.

In one of the early influential models, object-based *Co-occurrence Location and Appearance* (CoLA) contextual model [6], bottom-up image segmentation is followed by a bag-of-words-based object recognition system. Additionally, a conditional random field (CRF) is used to capture the inter-object interactions in the data set. Although capable of capturing obvious reoccurring patterns in the real world, the CRF-based contextual model cannot identify certain subtle patterns that may characterize similar objects. For example, a rear view of car is often encountered in the spatial vicinity of an oblique view of a building, yet this subtlety not captured by a CRF-based contextual model [7]. The *visual memex* model, which is based on the premise *"ask not what this is, but what this is like"*, addresses these shortcomings [7]. The visual memex model uses a graph-theoretic approach to model real-world images, where similar objects are connected by similarity edges while objects that are contextually related are connected by context edges. Consequently, using the earlier example, different types of buildings are connected by similarity edges, whereas a building and a car are linked via a context edge [7]. The graph-theoretic model automatically learns the visual memex graph from the input images and is shown to successfully outperform the CoLA model [5] on Torralba's context challenge data set [8].

Heitz and Koller [9] have introduced the *Things-and-Stuff* (TAS) model, a category-free model that relies on unsupervised learning. In the TAS model, a *thing* is an object that has a concrete shape and size, whereas *stuff* is malleable but has a repetitive pattern and typically contains *things*. For instance, a *car* (thing) is most likely to be found on a *road* (stuff), and likewise a *cow* (thing) on *grass* (stuff). The TAS model is shown to capture regularities not inherent in other contextual models. Another category of contextual models that has gained prominence in recent times is scene-based models. Choi et al. [10] proposed a scene-based contextual model developed using pre-labeled images by optimizing information derived from GIST features, the relative locations of objects, and a co-occurrence tree. The co-occurrence tree is generated using a hierarchical CRF, where a positive edge denotes object co-occurrence, and a negative edge indicates that the corresponding objects do not occur together. Choi et al. [10] used a deformable parts model as their baseline detector on the SUN data set introduced by Xiao et al. [11]. They showed that application of the scene-based contextual model to the output of the baseline detector outperformed the baseline detector by itself when deformable object parts are present in the input image.

More recently, with the advent of deep learning, several effective attempts have been made to incorporate contextual information within deep learning methods [12]. For instance, Sun and Jacobs [13] proposed a deep learning architecture that can be employed to predict a missing object in an image by exploiting contextual information. Similarly, Zhang et al. [14] integrated 3D context into deep learning for 3D holistic scene understanding, whereas Gonzalez et al. [15] employed a deep learning model to detect object parts by using object context. One disadvantage of all of the aforementioned contextual models is that a very constrained environment is assumed in the model learning phase, i.e., that pre-labeled images are readily available and that the labeled images reliably capture the co-occurrence patterns. The approach proposed in this work is unique in that, instead of using context to improve object recognition performance the context itself is implicitly deduced based on the output from a small number of visual object classifiers.

Several recent papers have addressed the problem of zero-shot and few-shot object identification and object detection, where the goal is to identify and localize an object in the input image, with the system having been exposed to very few or no visual training examples of the object [16–20]. In our approach, we attempt to hypothesize the most probable identity of an object in the input image, without having to localize it, thus making our approach closer to zero-shot or few-shot object recognition. However, our approach is fundamentally different from existing zero-shot and few-shot object detection and recognition approaches in that we hypothesize the probable identities of objects in an input image after having been exposed to visual examples of very few object categories during training. In particular, we address the extreme situation where a system, in spite of not having been visually exposed to a majority of the object categories during training, can still infer the identities of a large number of object categories in an input image with a moderate level of confidence by employing general knowledge of the world in the form of word embeddings derived from general text corpora. We propose to conduct a study to test the limits of general world knowledge in drawing useful inferences about plausible object identities in the absence of visual training examples. The focus of our approach is on object recognition in extreme situations where a very small number of trained visual detectors need to be used in tandem with word embeddings derived from a general text corpora. This is in sharp contrast to existing approaches to zero-shot and few-shot object recognition and object detection that deal with situations where the space of *seen* object categories is significantly larger than that of the *unseen* object categories during training. Given the fundamental difference in the underlying problem statement, we do not consider a direct comparison between the experimental results of our approach with those of existing zero-shot and few-shot approaches to be particularly instructive. Consequently, we have created our own baseline for the evaluation of the experimental results of our approach.

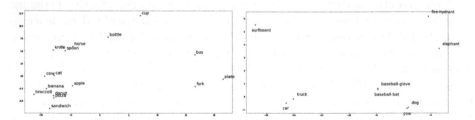

**Fig. 2.** The *t-sne* [21] diagram of word embeddings of annotated objects in the MS-COCO data set obtained via FastText trained on Wikipedia.

## 4    Description of the Proposed Approach

In the proposed approach, we train very few visual classifiers and hypothesize objects in an image using natural language embeddings. A significant advantage of this approach is that it eliminates the need to generate visual training data sets, which is an expensive process in real-world applications. Additionally, in situations where reliable data sets are not available for rare categories, our approach could yield distinct performance improvements. An additional advantage is the need to execute only a few visual classifiers at test time. The proposed approach is comprised of the following steps:

(1) Extract the word embeddings corresponding to objects in the MS-COCO data set using FastText [22] which is an enhancement of *word2vec* [23]. The word embeddings are low-dimensional vectors for each word corresponding to an object (Fig. 2). We use FastText word embeddings pretrained on Wikipedia using the skip-gram approach [22].

(2) Cluster the embeddings obtained in the preceding step using the $k$-means clustering algorithm, where the optimal value of $k$ is determined by the performance of the algorithm on the validation set. After $k$-means clustering, each cluster will encompass a certain number of objects that tend to share specific relationship as mentioned previously, i.e., they are co-occurring, belong to the same general category, or share the same general context. We emphasize that the $k$-means clustering was performed on word embeddings obtained from public (open) NL corpora; no visual information was used.

(3) From each of the clusters for a specific value of $k$, a representative object category is selected. The representative object category selected for training is the one with the greatest number of instances in the training set in the MS-COCO data set. An analogy could be drawn to the real world where we have unbalanced training sets, with some categories outnumbering others by a significant margin. Thus, our model resembles and is applicable to real-world situations as a proof of concept.

(4) Given the test data, run representative object classifiers, corresponding to the cluster centers, on an image, and select the most probable object(s). While the most probable object(s) may not exist, this procedure can still provide useful clues regarding objects that are present in the image, as explained in Motivation section.

(5) Using these most probable object(s) as the starting point, other objects in an image could be identified using a cosine similarity measure in the hypothetical word embedding space. In the current implementation, the most, second most, and third most probable object detection results are used for hypothesizing other objects in the image.

In our approach, we use the 1 to 3 top-object classifications to hypothesize other objects. We reiterate that the hypotheses for the objects in an image are generated from representative objects selected using the above steps. It could be argued that the proposed approach is premised on the notion that the distribution of representative objects in the MS-COCO test set mirrors the corresponding distribution in the MS-COCO training set. However, in many real-world applications, the distributions of objects in training and test sets are often very similar and even in cases where they differ, we believe there is sufficient regularity in the world that the proposed approach will still yield reasonable results.

At the testing stage, object detectors for all clusters centers (i.e., representative objects) are executed on the image. For 3 top object classifications, given a set of nouns $N$ and top object classifications $n_1$, $n_2$ and $n_3$, the closest hypothesis from set $N$ is given by:

$$\arg \max_i \{ SIM(n_i, n_1) + SIM(n_i, n_2) + SIM(n_i, n_3) \} \tag{1}$$

where $SIM(n_i, n_1)$ and $SIM(n_i, n_2)$, $SIM(n_i, n_3)$ are the cosine similarities of noun $n_i$ to nouns $n_1$, $n_2$ and $n_3$ respectively. In contrast, if we use only a single top object classification for hypothesizing other objects, then, given a set of nouns $N$ and a single top object classification $n_1$, the closest hypothesis from set $N$ are given by:

$$\arg \max_i \{ SIM(n_i, n_1)) \} \tag{2}$$

where $SIM(n_i, n_1)$ is the cosine similarity of noun $n_i$ to noun $n_1$.

**Fig. 3.** Qualitative results on the MS-COCO data set. Top Row: The correct top-object classification is able to guess at least one more object in an image. Middle Row: An incorrect top-object classification is able to guess at least one more object in an image. Bottom Row: An incorrect top object classification is not able to guess at least one more object in an image.

# 5    Experiments

## 5.1    Experiment Set 1

**Training:** We used $k$-means clustering to cluster objects using FastText embeddings trained on Wikipedia. We experimented with several $k$ values, namely, $\{3, 5, 7, 9, 11, 13, 15, 17\}$, which were applied to a validation set of 20,000 images obtained by splitting the 40,000 validation images in the MS-COCO data set into 20,000 images each for validation and testing. The optimal value for $k$ was determined by running experiments on the validation set. The $k$ value that yielded the best results was adopted for subsequent processing. We found that among the $k$ values in the above set, $k = 17$ yielded the best results on validation set. Since $k$-means clustering is non-deterministic, we used ten iterations of each value of $k$ and computed the average of the obtained results.

We trained Support Vector Machine (SVM)-based visual object classifiers using features extracted from the *fc-7* layer of the VGG-16 architecture [24] with the MS-COCO training set images as input. We trained SVM-based visual classifiers for 79 objects while excluding the *person* category from our experiments, as a person could co-occur with any type of object. For each experiment pertaining to a particular iteration for a particular $k$ value, we selected a representative object from each of the $k$ clusters resulting the training of $k$ SVM-based visual object classifiers. In each experiment pertaining to a particular $k$ value, we assume that other objects in the MS-COCO data set are not available. Finally, we chose $k = 17$ from the range $k \in [3, 17]$ for reporting our results since it yielded the best performance on the training set. In addition, $k = 17$ implies that $\approx 20\%$ of the classes are seen while $\approx 80\%$ are unseen. This is in contrast to previous work on zero-shot object recognition where most classes are seen whereas very few are unseen.

**Testing:** During testing, we ran the classifiers for all the representative objects in a given image. The most likely representative objects that occurred in an image were then chosen to determine the other objects in an image. These other objects were predicted from the FastText embeddings using Eq. (1) for a hypothesis formulated with the 3 most probable objects and Eq. (2) for a hypothesis formulated with only a single most probable object. We evaluated our results on the test set using ground truth object annotations, as well as the aforementioned predictions (hypotheses), based on the following metrics:

*Top-1 Accuracy:* Achieved when the top 1 object determined by our model intersected with at least one object in the ground truth annotations of the test image when all the objects except the representative objects are considered for classification.

**Fig. 4.** Qualitative results on our data set derived from the *Conceptual Captions* data set. Top Row and Middle Row: The system is able to correctly guess at least one object in an image. Bottom Row: The system is not able to correctly guess an object in an image.

*Top-1c Accuracy:* Attained when the top 1 object determined by our model intersected with at least one object in the ground truth of the test image when only the representative objects were considered for classification. For the top 1 object, it would be interesting to see how simply knowing the representative object alone affects the accuracy versus another object that is predicted by the representative object. It would be important to know how far we can go when executing classifiers for representative objects only.

*Top-3 Accuracy:* Achieved when any of the top 3 objects predicted by our model intersected with at least one object in the ground truth annotations of the test image. This included all objects, i.e., the representative object as well as the others.

*Top-5 Accuracy:* Attained when any of the top 5 objects determined by our model intersected with at least one object in the ground truth annotations of the test image. This included all objects, i.e., the representative object as well as the others.

*Most-Frequent Baseline:* The most frequent object(s) were determined by the most frequently occurring object(s) in the training set. The most frequent objects in the MS-COCO training data set (excluding *person*) in descending order were *chair, car, dining table, cup, bottle*, and *bowl*. For top-$n$ accuracy, the top-$n$ most frequent objects were used for evaluation on the test set. The most-frequent baseline is a fundamental baseline widely used by machine learning researchers and has been shown by several researchers to be sometimes difficult to beat [25].

**Table 1.** Comparison of our approach with most-frequent baseline for hypotheses formulated with only one most probable objects in an image for $k = 17$.

|  | Top-1c | Top-1 | Top-3 | Top-5 |
| --- | --- | --- | --- | --- |
| Most-frequent baseline | 11% | 11% | 25% | 31% |
| Proposed approach | 35% | 13% | 47% | 55% |

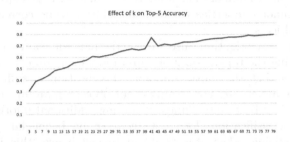

**Fig. 5.** Effect of value of $k$ used in $k$-means clustering on Top-5 accuracy.

**Table 2.** Comparison of our approach with the most-frequent baseline for hypotheses formulated with three most probable objects in an image for $k = 17$.

|  | Top-1 | Top-3 | Top-5 |
| --- | --- | --- | --- |
| Most-frequent baseline | 11% | 25% | 31% |
| Proposed approach | 22% | 46% | 53% |

**Results and Discussion:** Figure 3 shows the qualitative results and Tables 1, 2 and 3 show the quantitative results of our experiments. We make the following observations on the results of our experiments:

(1) The results reported here show that our approach is superior to the most-frequent baseline when objects are predicted using the top-most likely, second most likely, and third most likely objects. This finding lends support to the underlying assertion that employing only a few visual classifiers to hypothesize various objects using NL models learned from general text corpora is an effective technique.

**Table 3.** Comparison of our approach with most-frequent baseline for hypotheses formulated with two most probable objects in an image for $k = 17$.

|                         | Top-1 | Top-3 | Top-5 |
|-------------------------|-------|-------|-------|
| Most-frequent baseline  | 11%   | 25%   | 31%   |
| Proposed approach       | 26%   | 47%   | 55%   |

(2) To see how the increase in value of $k$ effects accuracy, we conducted additional experiments with the $k$ values ranging from $k = 3$ to $k = 79$. Our results further show that the object prediction accuracy increases with the value of $k$ in $k$-means clustering, as shown in Fig. 5. This increase could be attributed to one or more of the following factors: (a) increasing the number of visual classifiers (i.e., the number of clusters) improves the performance; and (b) a greater number of clusters results in assigning related objects that possess common properties to the same cluster while correctly separating unrelated objects.

(3) The present investigation also revealed that the same performance is achieved using the top-1, top-2 or top-3 most likely object(s) in the image. This implies that the most confident classification is sufficient for making accurate hypotheses concerning other objects in an image. Importantly, at least for FastText embeddings, including additional information beyond one object classification does not seem to be beneficial when identifying/hypothesizing other objects in an image; hence, this knowledge can remove an extra layer of complexity in the proposed model.

(4) Since the results obtained using top-5 accuracy were superior to those related to top-3 and top-1 accuracy, the likelihood of obtaining an accurate classification for at least one object increases when the classifier attempts to hypothesize a number of objects in an image.

## 5.2 Experiment Set 2

To further support our hypothesis, we conduct additional experiments on much larger data set that we generated from the *Conceptual Captions* data set [26].

**Data Set:** For our experiments, we used the *Conceptual Captions* data set [26]. Unlike MS-COCO, which is a curated data set, this data set contains the image-caption pairs that were extracted in raw form from the Internet. Using the comprehensive *Conceptual Captions* data set, we created our own data set. For each caption, we extracted parts-of-speech, and using this parts-of-speech information, we identified the conceptual categories that occurred most frequently. From this set, we selected top 379 categories that had at least close to 2000 images. A few examples of such conceptual categories are *architecture, beauty, bike, championship, evening, luxury, planet, vintage,* and *yard*. Unlike MS-COCO, where we conducted the experiments on objects present in the images, here we test our hypothesis on themes or concepts present in an image.

The *Conceptual Captions* data set is extremely challenging for a variety of reasons. Unlike objects, which tend to have defined shape and size, the themes (concepts) are very malleable. Objects tend to have a similar appearance and texture across different situations and context. However, the themes have very high degree of variance and appearance. For example, the theme *luxury* will have varying appearances with no clear boundaries, shape, texture, or even color across different images. Thus, our machine learning/deep learning models will not be able to discern discriminatory features in order to reliably learn models. However, if we can show marginal results on such a data set, it will bolster our hypothesis.

**Experiment:** We used deep features extracted from VGG-19 followed by a Random Forest (RF) classifier to train our categories. The model is essentially the same as described in the previous section, except we used the RF instead of the SVM to train our visual classifiers. The RF was used since it scales better than the SVM for multi-class classification.

**Table 4.** Comparison of our approach with a random baseline for 5 objects guessed in addition to the most probable object in an image for various values of $k$. Here, model-$n$ refers to the model with $k = n$.

| Model | Top-6 accuracy | Random-baseline |
|---|---|---|
| model-10 | 0.0934 | 0.0153 |
| model-15 | 0.1009 | 0.0153 |
| model-20 | 0.1212 | 0.0153 |
| model-25 | 0.1522 | 0.0153 |
| model-30 | 0.1496 | 0.0153 |
| model-35 | 0.1502 | 0.0153 |
| model-40 | 0.1687 | 0.0153 |
| model-45 | 0.1721 | 0.0153 |
| model-50 | 0.1883 | 0.0153 |
| model-55 | 0.1923 | 0.0153 |
| model-60 | 0.1999 | 0.0153 |
| model-65 | 0.2109 | 0.0153 |
| model-70 | 0.2168 | 0.0153 |

**Results and Discussion:** Figure 4 shows the qualitative results and Table 4 shows the quantitative results on the *Conceptual Captions* data set. The results in Table 4 show that the proposed approach performs better than the random baseline. Although the results cannot be regarded as particularly impressive or statistically significant, they are nevertheless very marked. Given the inherent ambiguity in themes (concepts), with no clear boundaries, and no strong discerning patterns (in terms of color, texture, shape, etc.), the proposed approach can still hypothesize the object categories much more effectively than random guessing.

## 6   Conclusions

The results of the proposed model lend support to the premise that even using a limited number of visual object classifiers, other objects in an image could be successfully hypothesized, even from NL priors learned on a general and not closely related open text corpus such as Wikipedia. Moreover, even the inability to correctly classify the objects in an image can yield useful cues that could help in hypothesizing the correct objects in an image. Future work will involve incorporating feedback mechanisms to improve classification. In addition, many weakly supervised object detection and image captioning algorithms could benefit from our approach. Additionally, this approach could help AI practitioners conceptualize and codify human intelligence because humans tend to recognize numerous categories without ever having been previously exposed to them.

## References

1. Socher, R., et al.: Zero-shot learning through cross-modal transfer. In: Proceedings of NIPS, pp. 935–943 (2013)
2. Sharma, K., Kumar, A., Bhandarkar, S.: Guessing objects in context. In: Proceedings of the ACM SIGGRAPH, p. 83 (2016)
3. Lin, T.-Y., et al.: Microsoft COCO: common objects in context. In: Fleet, D., Pajdla, T., Schiele, B., Tuytelaars, T. (eds.) ECCV 2014. LNCS, vol. 8693, pp. 740–755. Springer, Cham (2014). https://doi.org/10.1007/978-3-319-10602-1_48
4. Divvala, S.K., Hoiem, D., Hays, J.H., Efros, A.A., Hebert, M.: An empirical study of context in object detection. In: Proceedings of the IEEE Conference on CVPR (2009)
5. Rabinovich, A., Belongie, S.: Scenes vs. objects: a comparative study of two approaches to context-based recognition. In: Proceedings of the International Workshop on Visual Scene Understanding, Miami, FL (2009)
6. Galleguillos, C., Rabinovich, A., Belongie, S.: Object categorization using co-ocurrence, location and appearance. In: Proceedings of the IEEE Conference on CVPR (2008)
7. Malisiewicz, T., Efros, A.A.: Beyond categories: the visual memex model for reasoning about object relationships. In: Proceedings of NIPS (2009)
8. Torralba, A.: The context challenge (2020). http://web.mit.edu/torralba/www/carsAndFacesInContext.html. Accessed 16 Nov 2020
9. Heitz, G., Koller, D.: Learning spatial context: using stuff to find things. In: Forsyth, D., Torr, P., Zisserman, A. (eds.) ECCV 2008. LNCS, vol. 5302, pp. 30–43. Springer, Heidelberg (2008). https://doi.org/10.1007/978-3-540-88682-2_4
10. Choi, M., Torralba, A., Willsky, A.S.: A tree- based context model for object recognition. IEEE Trans. PAMI **34**(2), 240–252 (2012)
11. Xiao, J., Hays, J., Ehinger, K., Oliva, A., Torralba, A.: SUN database: large-scale scene recognition from Abbey to Zoo. In: Proceedings of IEEE Conference on CVPR (2010)

12. Gkioxari, G.: Contextual Visual Recognition from Images and Videos. University of California, Berkeley (2016)
13. Sun, J., Jacobs, D.W.: Seeing what is not there: learning context to determine where objects are missing. arXiv preprint arXiv:1702.07971 (2017)
14. Zhang, Y., Bai, M., Kohli, P., Izadi, S., Xiao, J.: DeepContext: context-encoding neural pathways for 3D holistic scene understanding. arXiv preprint arXiv:1603.04922 (2016)
15. Gonzalez-Garcia, A., Modolo, D., Ferrari, V.: Objects as context for part detection. arXiv preprint arXiv:1703.09529 (2017)
16. Bansal, A., Sikka, K., Sharma, G., Chellappa, R., Divakaran, A.: Zero-shot object detection. In: Ferrari, V., Hebert, M., Sminchisescu, C., Weiss, Y. (eds.) ECCV 2018. LNCS, vol. 11205, pp. 397–414. Springer, Cham (2018). https://doi.org/10.1007/978-3-030-01246-5_24
17. Rahman, S., Khan, S., Barnes, N.: Transductive learning for zero-shot object detection. In: Proceedings of ICCV, pp. 6082–6091 (2019)
18. Sadhu, A., Chen, K., Nevatia, R.: Zero-shot grounding of objects from natural language queries. In: Proceedings of ICCV, pp. 4694–4703 (2019)
19. Wang, Y., Ramanan, D., Hebert, M.: Meta-learning to detect rare objects. In: Proceedings of IEEE ICCV, pp. 9925–9934 (2019)
20. Zellers, R., Yatskar, M., Thomson, S., Choi, Y.: Neural motifs: scene graph parsing with global context. In: Proceedings of IEEE Conference on CVPR, pp. 5831–5840 (2018)
21. Van Der Maaten, L., Hinton, G.: Visualizing data using t-SNE. JMLR **9**, 2579–2605 (2008)
22. Bojanowski, P., Grave, E., Joulin, A., Mikolov T.: Enriching word vectors with subword information. arXiv preprint arXiv:1607.04606 (2016)
23. Mikolov, T., Chen, K., Corrado, G., Dean, J.: Efficient estimation of word representations in vector space. In: Proceedings of ICLR (2013)
24. Simonyan, K., Zisserman, A.: Very deep convolutional networks for large-scale image recognition. In: Proceedings of ICLR (2014)
25. Preiss, J., Dehdari, J., King, J., Mehay, D.: Refining the most frequent sense baseline. In: Proceedings of ACL Workshop on Semantic Evaluations: Recent Achievements and Future Directions, pp. 10–18 (2009)
26. Sharma, P., Ding, N., Goodman, S., Soricut, R.: Conceptual captions: a cleaned, hypernymed, image alt-text dataset for automatic image captioning. In: Proceedings of the Conference on ACL 1, pp. 2556–2565 (2018)

# Automated Segmentation of Lateral Ventricle in MR Images Using Multi-scale Feature Fusion Convolutional Neural Network

Fei Ye[1], Zhiqiang Wang[2], Kai Hu[1(✉)], Sheng Zhu[2], and Xieping Gao[1,2(✉)]

[1] Key Laboratory of Intelligent Computing and Information Processing of Ministry of Education, Xiangtan University, Xiangtan 411105, China
{kaihu,xpgao}@xtu.edu.cn
[2] College of Medical Imaging and Inspection, Xiangnan University, Chenzhou 423000, China

**Abstract.** Studies have shown that the expansion of the lateral ventricle is closely related to many neurodegenerative diseases, so the segmentation of the lateral ventricle plays an important role in the diagnosis of related diseases. However, traditional segmentation methods are subjective, laborious, and time-consuming. Furthermore, due to the uneven magnetic field, irregular, small, and discontinuous shape of every single slice, the segmentation of the lateral ventricle is still a great challenge. In this paper, we propose an efficient and automatic lateral ventricle segmentation method in magnetic resonance (MR) images using a multi-scale feature fusion convolutional neural network (MFF-Net). First, we create a multi-center clinical dataset with a total of 117 patient MR scans. This dataset comes from two different hospitals and the images have different sampling intervals, different ages, and distinct image dimensions. Second, we present a new multi-scale feature fusion module (MSM) to capture different levels of feature information of lateral ventricles through various receptive fields. In particular, MSM can also extract the multi-scale lateral ventricle region feature information to solve the problem of insufficient feature extraction of small object regions with the deepening of network structure. Finally, extensive experiments have been conducted to evaluate the performance of the proposed MFF-Net. In addition, to verify the performance of the proposed method, we compare MFF-Net with seven state-of-the-art segmentation models. Both quantitative results and visual effects show that our MFF-Net outperforms other models and can achieve more accurate segmentation performance. The results also indicate that our model can be applied in clinical practice and is a feasible method for lateral ventricle segmentation.

**Keywords:** Lateral ventricle · Segmentation · Multi-scale feature fusion · Convolutional neural network

F. Ye and Z. Wang—Co-first authors, contributed equally to this work.

# 1    Introduction

The lateral ventricle, a very important structure in the human brain, located deep in the cerebral hemisphere, is lined with ependymal and containing choroid plexus. Many studies have shown that the expansion of lateral ventricle volume is often an important marker of neurodegenerative diseases, such as schizophrenia, dementia, and depression [2, 7]. Because magnetic resonance imaging (MRI) is free of drug and radiation damage, clinicians often use MR images to measure the volume of the lateral ventricle [4]. However, the segmentation of the lateral ventricle region is a prerequisite for measuring its volume.

In the past decades, clinicians often segment the lateral ventricle region manually. However, this approach is subjective, laborious, and time-consuming. Therefore, it has a great significance to develop an efficient and accurate automatic segmentation algorithm of the lateral ventricle in MR images. Figure 1 shows five different forms of lateral ventricle MR images and their corresponding manual annotations.

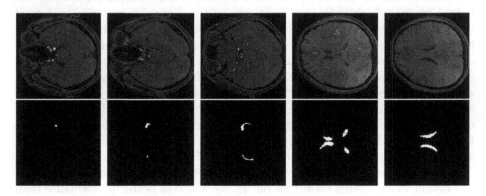

**Fig. 1.** Examples of different forms of lateral ventricle MR slices and their manual annotations.

In recent years, some automatic methods have proposed for the segmentation of lateral ventricles in MR images. It is mainly divided into two categories, i.e, traditional methods and deep learning-based methods. Traditional methods can be further divided into thresholds [11], models [6], atlases [13], and region growing [15], etc. Although the above methods achieve automatic segmentation of the lateral ventricle, they all require manual extraction of features, which is computationally expensive and susceptible to noise. Besides, the setting of hyperparameters, such as the number of seeds and the size of the threshold, also affects the performance of the model.

With the successful application of deep learning in computer vision and medical image analysis [9, 19], some deep learning methods have been applied to lateral ventricle segmentation recently. For example, Shao et al. [16] proposed a novel pipeline to segment the lateral ventricle region. They first used related operations to preprocess the MR images (i.e., N4 bias correction and skull removal) and then proposed a deep convolutional neural network (CNN) to extract the region of interest. In 2019, Wu et al. [18] designed a 3D encoding and 2D decoding convolutional neural network to segment the lateral ventricle. These deep learning methods based on 3D models require higher hardware conditions and are hard to converge. Thus, proposing an accurate and efficient model segmenting lateral ventricle region in MR images has a very considerable guiding significance for the diagnosis and treatment of related diseases. However, as shown in Fig. 1, the segmentation of lateral ventricle regions in MR images is still very challenging due to the following reasons: (1) The shape of every single slice in the MR images is irregular, and the image resolution and contrast are low. (2) The lateral ventricle region often occupies a small proportion in the whole MR image or even only occupies a sub-fraction of the whole image, which will cause an extreme imbalance of the data. (3) Individual differences exist in different cases, and the image resolution is distinguished.

In this paper, we propose an automatic and efficient method using a multi-scale feature fusion convolutional neural network (MFF-Net) for segmenting the lateral ventricle in MR images. First, we collect a multi-center clinical lateral ventricle dataset consisting of 117 cases from two different hospitals. Especially, these cases have different ages, different sampling intervals, and distinct image dimensions. Second, a multi-scale feature fusion module (MSM) is presented to extract shallow multi-scale feature information. It is worth noting that MSM can solve the problem of insufficient feature information extraction as the network structure deepens, especially the feature of small object regions. Finally, we evaluate our model on this multi-center dataset based on different multi-scale feature fusion module adding ways (i.e., convolutional neural network without MSM and adding MSM in every encoder-decoder stage). Besides, we also compare MFF-Net with seven state-of-the-art segmentation methods. All the quantitative indicators and visual results show that our model achieves better performance than other methods and has a great potential to segment the lateral ventricle region efficiently and accurately in MR images.

## 2    Materials and Methods

### 2.1    Data and Preprocessing

In this work, we collected 117 clinical patient MR cases from two hospitals with a total of 10034 slices. The dimension of each image is $256 \times 256$, and the resolution of all scans are about $0.9 \times 0.7 \times 0.7 \, \mathrm{mm}^3$. It is noteworthy that the number of slices in different cases is different. Some cases are less than 80, while others are more than 100. Due to the difference of MR scanning equipment and operators, as well as the difference of gender and age of patients, the images in this multi-center dataset are quite different, which means that the clinical dataset of lateral ventricle presents a great challenge to the segmentation algorithm. In this dataset, the ground-truth corresponding to each slice of the lateral ventricle is marked and calibrated by experienced radiologists. Specifically, the lateral ventricle regions are marked as 1, and the others are marked as 0.

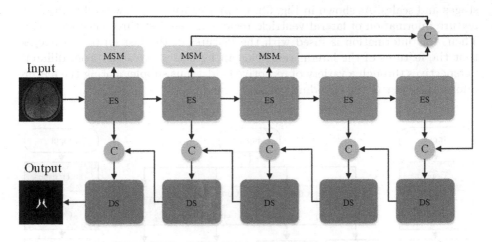

**Fig. 2.** The flowchart of the proposed method.

## 2.2   MFF-Net

Convolutional neural networks are widely applied in image segmentation tasks due to their powerful automatic feature extraction capabilities. However, the feature extraction capability of small object regions might be decline with the deepening of the network structure. To solve this problem, we propose a multiscale feature fusion convolutional neural network to extract local and global features of the lateral ventricle region in MR images. As shown in Fig. 2, our model consists of an encoder and a decoder. The encoder part includes 5 encoding stages (ES), which is as shown in Fig. 3a. Especially, a multi-scale feature fusion module (see Fig. 3b) is proposed to extract the multi-scale feature information of the first three encoder stages based on the various receptive fields. The decoder part contains five decoder stages (DS), which are presented in Fig. 3c. In order to reduce the semantic gap between low-level features and high-level semantic features, inspired by U-Net [14], we introduce jump connections to supplement high-level feature information, thereby improving the learning ability of the model.

**MSM.** In MR slices of the lateral ventricle, the region of the lateral ventricle is so small in most images, even only occupies a tiny fraction of the whole image, resulting in the extreme imbalance of the data. Besides, with the deepening of the convolutional neural network architecture, the resolution of the feature map extracted by the model is reduced, and the feature extraction ability of small objects is also weakened, thus affecting the performance of lateral ventricle segmentation. Based on the above reasons, a novel multi-scale feature fusion module is presented as a solution to extract shallow feature information at different stages and scales. As shown in Fig. 3b, we first capture the low-level multi-scale feature information of lateral ventricle regions in the first three encoder stages. Then, this information is fused with the features of the last encoder stage, so that the features of the lateral ventricle can be better extracted from different perspectives through a variety of receptive fields, thus supplementing the feature information lost in the encoding process.

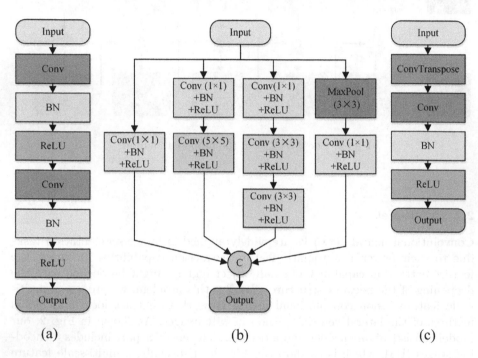

**Fig. 3.** The main components of the proposed MFF-Net. (a) ES. (b) MSM. (c) DS.

## 3   Experimental Results and Discussion

### 3.1   Parameter Setting

For the implementations of MFF-Net, the learning rate is 0.0001, the batch size is 4, and the model optimizer is Adam. The training process stops when the maximum number of iterations reaches up to 50. All experiments are implemented using Pytorch and a GPU card (Nvidia GeForce GTX 1080) is used to accelerate the training process.

## 3.2 Evaluation Metrics

After getting the probability of each pixel, we get the segmentation result by setting a threshold. If the probability is greater than the value, we predict the pixel as 1. Otherwise, we mark the pixel as 0. Therefore, the confusion matrix is often applied to evaluate the correlation between prediction and label. To comprehensively evaluate the performance of the proposed model, four evaluation indicators are considered, including precision (Pre), recall (Rec), dice score (Dice), and Jaccard index (Jac). They are defined as

$$Pre = \frac{TP}{TP + FP} \quad Rec = \frac{TP}{TP + FN}$$
$$Dice = \frac{2 \times TP}{2 \times TP + FN + FP} \quad Jac = \frac{TP}{TP + FP + FN} \tag{1}$$

where TP, FN, TN, FP are the number of true positives, false negatives, true negatives, and false positives in the confusion matrix respectively. The closer these metrics are to 1, the better the model performs.

## 3.3 Results and Discussion

**Evaluation of MSM.** With the deepening of the network model, the resolution of the feature map extracted by the model becomes lower and lower. In addition, the feature extraction ability of small object regions of the lateral ventricle in MR image slices may be reduced. To solve this problem, MSM is proposed to obtain multi-scale lateral ventricle object regions at different levels through different receptive fields. In particular, the extracted feature information can be used to compensate for the missing details in the encoding process through feature fusion. To evaluate the performance of MSM, some comparison experiments are conducted from two aspects, including adding each multi-scale module (EMSM) into each stage of the corresponding codec and not adding multi-scale modules. The numerical results are illustrated in Table 1. From the results, we can observe that the method using EMSM modules have better evaluation results than the method without EMSM modules. Furthermore, we can also find that our model achieves the highest Rec, Dice, and Jac results, which are 91.19%, 90.18%, and 82.21%, respectively. It indicates that MFF-Net can accurately segment the lateral ventricle region in MR images.

**Table 1.** Quantitative comparison with different addition methods of MSM.

| Method | Pre | Rec | Dice | Jac |
|---|---|---|---|---|
| Without MSM | 0.8911 | 0.9036 | 0.8968 | 0.8139 |
| EMSM | 0.8932 | 0.9101 | 0.9008 | 0.8205 |
| MFF-Net | 0.8929 | 0.9119 | 0.9018 | 0.8221 |

**Comparison with the State-of-the-Art Methods.** In order to further evaluate the proposed model, we compare MFF-Net with seven state-of-the-art deep learning-based segmentation methods, including FCN [10], SegNet [3], Deeplabv3+ [5], AttUnet [12], R2Unet [1], GSCNN [17], CA-Net [8]. For a fair comparison, all methods use the same training set and test set. Table 2 shows the numeral evaluation values using different models and Fig. 4 provides the visual effects of the segmentation results. From the results, we can observe that our MFF-Net is superior to other models and achieves the best scores compared with other deep neural networks. As seen from Fig. 4, we can also find that our model can better segment the deformed shapes of lateral ventricle than other methods.

**Table 2.** Quantitative comparison with different segmentation methods.

| Method | Year | Pre | Rec | Dice | Jac |
|---|---|---|---|---|---|
| FCN [10] | 2015 | 0.8889 | 0.8861 | 0.8867 | 0.7977 |
| SegNet [3] | 2017 | 0.8796 | 0.8704 | 0.8738 | 0.7778 |
| Deeplabv3+ [5] | 2018 | 0.8721 | 0.8736 | 0.8720 | 0.7745 |
| AttUnet [12] | 2018 | 0.8915 | 0.8909 | 0.8906 | 0.8038 |
| R2Unet [1] | 2018 | **0.9235** | 0.8493 | 0.8833 | 0.7926 |
| GSCNN [17] | 2019 | 0.9026 | 0.8891 | 0.895 | 0.8111 |
| CA-Net [8] | 2020 | 0.9086 | 0.887 | 0.8969 | 0.8142 |
| MFF-Net (Ours) | – | **0.9062** | **0.8974** | **0.9011** | **0.8210** |

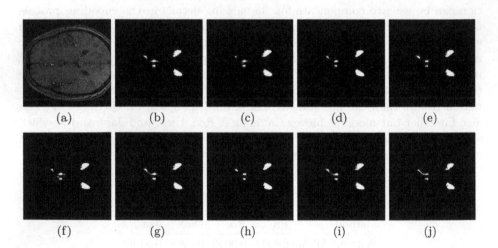

(a)         (b)         (c)         (d)         (e)

(f)         (g)         (h)         (i)         (j)

**Fig. 4.** Visual segmentation effects using different methods. (a) Original image. Segmentation results obtained by (b) FCN, (c) SegNet, (d) Deeplabv3+, (e) AttUnet, (f) R2Unet, (g) GSCNN, (h) CA-Net, (i) MFF-Net, and (j) Ground Truth.

# 4    Conclusion

In this paper, we propose a multi-scale feature fusion convolutional neural network for automatic segmentation of lateral ventricle regions in MR images. Especially, a multi-scale feature fusion module is proposed to comprehensively extract the feature information of lateral ventricle regions in MR image slices through different receptive fields. Besides, a multi-center clinical dataset with a total of 117 patient MR scans from two different hospitals is collected to verify the effectiveness of the proposed method in clinical practice. Both numerical results and visual effects indicate that MFF-Net outperforms seven state-of-the-art segmentation methods and is an effective and efficient lateral ventricle segmentation method.

**Acknowledgements.** This work was supported by the National Natural Science Foundation of China under Grants 61802328, 61972333 and 61771415, the Natural Science Foundation of Hunan Province of China under Grant 2019JJ50606, and the Research Foundation of Education Department of Hunan Province of China under Grant 19B561.

# References

1. Alom, M.Z., Hasan, M., Yakopcic, C., Taha, T.M., Asari, V.K.: Recurrent residual convolutional neural network based on U-Net (R2U-Net) for medical image segmentation. arXiv preprint arXiv:1802.06955 (2018)
2. Baaré, W.F., et al.: Volumes of brain structures in twins discordant for schizophrenia. Arch. Gen. Psychiatry **58**(1), 33–40 (2001)
3. Badrinarayanan, V., Kendall, A., Cipolla, R.: SegNet: a deep convolutional encoder-decoder architecture for image segmentation. IEEE Trans. Pattern Anal. Mach. Intell. **39**(12), 2481–2495 (2017)
4. Biswas, A., Bhattacharya, P., Maity, S.: An efficient volumetric segmentation of cerebral lateral ventricles. Procedia Comput. Sci. **133**, 561–568 (2018)
5. Chen, L.-C., Zhu, Y., Papandreou, G., Schroff, F., Adam, H.: Encoder-decoder with Atrous separable convolution for semantic image segmentation. In: Ferrari, V., Hebert, M., Sminchisescu, C., Weiss, Y. (eds.) ECCV 2018. LNCS, vol. 11211, pp. 833–851. Springer, Cham (2018). https://doi.org/10.1007/978-3-030-01234-2_49
6. Chen, W., Smith, R., Ji, S.Y., Najarian, K.: Automated segmentation of lateral ventricles in brain CT images. In: 2008 IEEE International Conference on Bioinformatics and Biomeidcine Workshops, pp. 48–55. IEEE (2008)
7. Gan, K.: Automated segmentation of the lateral ventricle in MR images of human brain. In: 2015 IEEE International Conference on Digital Signal Processing (DSP), pp. 139–142. IEEE (2015)
8. Gu, R., et al.: CA-Net: comprehensive attention convolutional neural networks for explainable medical image segmentation. arXiv preprint arXiv:2009.10549 (2020)
9. Hu, K., et al.: Retinal vessel segmentation of color fundus images using multi-scale convolutional neural network with an improved cross-entropy loss function. Neurocomputing **309**, 179–191 (2018)
10. Long, J., Shelhamer, E., Darrell, T.: Fully convolutional networks for semantic segmentation. In: Proceedings of the IEEE Conference on Computer Vision and Pattern Recognition, pp. 3431–3440 (2015)

11. Ng, H.F., Chuang, C.H., Hsu, C.H.: Extraction and analysis of structural features of lateral ventricle in brain medical images. In: 2012 Sixth International Conference on Genetic and Evolutionary Computing, pp. 35–38. IEEE (2012)
12. Oktay, O., et al.: Attention U-Net: learning where to look for the pancreas. arXiv preprint arXiv:1804.03999 (2018)
13. Qiu, W., et al.: Automatic segmentation approach to extracting neonatal cerebral ventricles from 3D ultrasound images. Med. Image Anal. **35**, 181–191 (2017)
14. Ronneberger, O., Fischer, P., Brox, T.: U-Net: convolutional networks for biomedical image segmentation. In: Navab, N., Hornegger, J., Wells, W.M., Frangi, A.F. (eds.) MICCAI 2015. LNCS, vol. 9351, pp. 234–241. Springer, Cham (2015). https://doi.org/10.1007/978-3-319-24574-4_28
15. Schnack, H., Pol, H.H., Baaré, W.F.C., Viergever, M., Kahn, R.: Automatic segmentation of the ventricular system from MR images of the human brain. Neuroimage **14**(1), 95–104 (2001)
16. Shao, M., et al.: Shortcomings of ventricle segmentation using deep convolutional networks. In: Stoyanov, D., et al. (eds.) MLCN/DLF/IMIMIC -2018. LNCS, vol. 11038, pp. 79–86. Springer, Cham (2018). https://doi.org/10.1007/978-3-030-02628-8_9
17. Takikawa, T., Acuna, D., Jampani, V., Fidler, S.: Gated-SCNN: gated shape CNNs for semantic segmentation. In: Proceedings of the IEEE International Conference on Computer Vision, pp. 5229–5238 (2019)
18. Wu, J., Zhang, Y., Tang, X.: Simultaneous tissue classification and lateral ventricle segmentation via a 2D U-net driven by a 3D fully convolutional neural network. In: 2019 41st Annual International Conference of the IEEE Engineering in Medicine and Biology Society (EMBC), pp. 5928–5931. IEEE (2019)
19. Zhu, Y., Chen, Z., Zhao, S., Xie, H., Guo, W., Zhang, Y.: ACE-Net: biomedical image segmentation with augmented contracting and expansive paths. In: Shen, D., et al. (eds.) MICCAI 2019. LNCS, vol. 11764, pp. 712–720. Springer, Cham (2019). https://doi.org/10.1007/978-3-030-32239-7_79

# Visual Word Embedding for Text Classification

Ignazio Gallo[1]([✉])[iD], Shah Nawaz[1,2][iD], Nicola Landro[1][iD],
and Riccardo La Grassainst[1][iD]

[1] University of Insubria, Varese, Italy
{ignazio.gallo,snawaz,nlandro,rlagrassa}@uninsubria.it
[2] Italian Institute of Technology, Genova, Italy

**Abstract.** The question we answer with this paper is: 'can we convert a text document into an image to take advantage of image neural models to classify text documents?' To answer this question we present a novel text classification method that converts a document into an encoded image, using word embedding. The proposed approach computes the Word2Vec word embedding of a text document, quantizes the embedding, and arranges it into a 2D visual representation, as an RGB image. Finally, visual embedding is categorized with state-of-the-art image classification models. We achieved competitive performance on well-known benchmark text classification datasets. In addition, we evaluated our proposed approach in a multimodal setting that allows text and image information in the same feature space.

**Keywords:** Encoded text · Word embedding · Multimodal classification

## 1 Introduction

Text classification is a common task in Natural Language Processing (NLP). Its goal is to assign a label to a text document from a predefined set of classes. In last decade, Convolutional Neural Networks (CNNs) have remarkably improved performance in image classification [8,16,17] and researchers have successfully transferred this success into text classification [1,20]. Image classification models [8,16] are adapted to accommodate text [1,7,20]. We, therefore, leverage on the recent success in image classification and present a novel text classification approach to cast text documents into a visual domain to categorize text with image classification models. Our approach transforms text documents into encoded images or visual embedding capitalizing on Word2Vec word embedding which convert words into vectors of real numbers [9,11,14]. Typically word embedding models are trained on large corpus of text documents to capture semantic relationships among words. Thus these models can produce similar word embeddings for words occurring in similar contexts. We exploit this well-known fundamental property of word embedding models to transform a text

© Springer Nature Switzerland AG 2021
A. Del Bimbo et al. (Eds.): ICPR 2020 Workshops, LNCS 12666, pp. 339–352, 2021.
https://doi.org/10.1007/978-3-030-68780-9_29

document into a sequence of colours (visual embedding), obtaining an encoded image, as shown in Fig. 1. Intuitively, semantically related words obtain similar colours or encodings in the encoded image while uncorrelated words are represented with different colours. Interestingly, these visual embeddings are recognized with state-of-the-art image classification models. In this paper, we present a novel text classification approach to transform word emebedding of text documents into the visual domain. The choice to work with Word2Vec encoding vectors transformed into pixels by splitting them in triplets is guided by two main reasons:

1. we want to exploit existing image classification models to categorize text documents;
2. as a consequence, we want to integrate the text within an image to transform a text-only or images only classification problem, into a multimodal classification problem using a single 2D data [12].

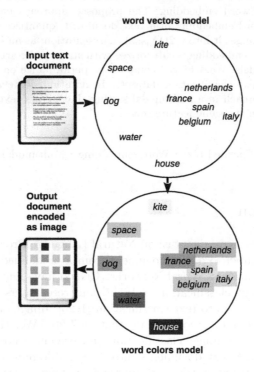

**Fig. 1.** We exploited a well-known property of word embedding models: semantically correlated words obtain similar numerical representation. It turns out that if we interpret real-valued vectors as a set of colours, it is easy for a visual system to cope with relationships between words of a text document. It can be observed that green coloured words are related to countries, while other words are represented with different colours. (Color figure online)

We evaluated the method on several large scale datasets obtaining promising and comparable results. An earlier version of our encoding scheme was published in ICDAR 2017 [2], where we used a different encoding technique that require more space to encode a text document into an image. In this paper, we explore various parameters associated with an encoding scheme. We extensively evaluated the improved encoding scheme on various benchmark datasets for text classification. In addition, we evaluated the proposed approach in a multimodal setting to fuse image and text in the same feature space to perform classification.

## 2   Related Work

Deep learning methods for text documents involved learning word vector representations through neural language models [11,14]. These vector representations serve as a foundation in our paper where word vectors are transformed into a sequence of colors or visual embedding. The image classification model is trained and tested on these visual embeddings. Kim [7] proposed a simple shallow neural network with one convolution layer followed by a max pooling layer over time. Final classification is performed with one fully connected layer with dropout. The authors in [20] presented rather deep convolutional neural network for text classification. The network is similar to the convolutional network in computer vision [8]. Similarly, Conneau et al. [1] presented a deep architecture that operates at character level with 29 convolutional layers to learn hierarchical representations of text. The architecture is inspired by recent progress in computer vision [4,15]. Johnson et al. [6] proposed a simple network architecture by increasing the depth of the network without increasing computation costs. This model performs text region embedding, which generalizes commonly used word embedding. Though Word2vec is one of the state-of-the-art model for text embedding, others approaches such as GloVe, ELMo, and BERT have improved various NLP tasks. The BERT model used a relatively new transformer architecture to compute word embedding and it has been shown to produce state-of-the-art word embedding, achieving excellent performance. Yang et al. [19] proposed the XLNet, a generalized autoregressive pretreatment method that exceeds the limits of BERT thanks to its autoregressive formulation.

In this paper, we leverage on recent success in Computer Vision, but instead of adapting deep neural network to be fed with raw text information, we propose an approach that transforms word embedding into encoded text. Once we have encoded text, we employed state-of-the-art deep neural architectures for text classification.

## 3   Proposed Approach

In this section, we present our approach to transform Word2Vec word embedding into the visual domain. In addition, we explained the understanding of CNNs with the purposed approach.

## 3.1  Encoding Scheme

The proposed encoding approach is based on Word2Vec word embedding [11]. We encode a word $t_k$ belonging to a document $D_i$ into an encoded image of size $W \times H$. The approach uses a dictionary $F(t_k, v_k)$ with each word $t_k$ associated with a feature vector $v_k(t_k)$ obtained from a trained version of Word2Vec word embedding model. Given a word $t_k$, we obtained a visual word $\hat{t}_k$ having width $V$ that contains a subset of a feature vector, called superpixels (see example in Fig. 2). A superpixel is a square area of size $P \times P$ pixels with a uniform color that represents a sequence of contiguos features $(v_{k,j}, v_{k,j+1}, v_{k,j+2})$ extracted as a sub-vector of $v_k$. We normalize each component $v_{k,j}$ to assume values in the interval $[0 \ldots 255]$ with respect to $k$, then we interpret triplets from feature vector $v_k$ as RGB sequence. For this very reason, we use feature vector with a length multiple of 3. Our goal is to have a visual encoding that can be generic to allow the use of existing CNN models; for example, the AlexNet has an $11 \times 11$ kernel in the input layer, which makes it very difficult to interpret visual words with $1 \times 1$ superpixels ($P = 1$).

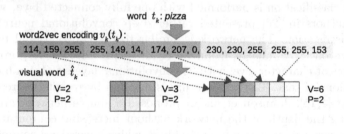

**Fig. 2.** In this example, the word *"pizza"* is encoded into a visual word $\hat{t}_k$ based on Word2Vec feature vector with length 15. This visual word can be transformed into different shapes, varying the V parameter (in this example $V = 2, 3, 6$ superpixels)

The blank space $s$ around each visual word $\hat{t}_k$ plays an important role in the encoding approach. We found out that the parameter $s$ is directly related to the shape of a visual word. For example, if $V = 16$ pixels then $s$ must also have a value close to 16 pixels to let the network understand where a word ends and another begins.

## 3.2  Encoding Scheme with CNN

It is well understood that a CNN can learn to detect edges from image pixels in the first layer, then use the edges to detect trivial shapes in the next layer, and then use these shapes to infer more complex shapes and objects in higher layers [10]. Similarly, a CNN trained on our proposed visual embedding may extract features from various convolutional layer (see example in Fig. 3). We observed that the first convolutional layer recognizes some specific features of visual words associated with single or multiple superpixels. The remaining CNN layers aggregate these simple activations to create increasingly complex relationships between words or parts of a sentence in a text document. Figure 3 also highlights how the different convolutional layers of a CNN activate different areas corresponding to single words (layers closest to the input) or sets of words distributed over a 2-D space (layers closest to the output). This is a typical behavior of deep models that work on images, while 1-D models that work on text usually limit themselves to activating only words or word sequences.

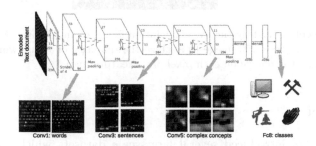

**Fig. 3.** Starting from an encoded text document, the resulting image is classified by a CNN model normally employed in image classification. The first convolutional layers look some particular features of visual words while the remaining convolutional layers can recognize sentences and increasingly complex concepts.

To numerically illustrate this concept, we use the receptive field of a CNN. The receptive field $r$ is defined as the region in the input space that a particular CNN feature is looking at. For a convolution layer of a CNN, the size $r$ of its receptive field can be computed by the following formula:

$$r_{out} = r_{in} + (k - 1) \cdot j_{in} \tag{1}$$

where $k$ is the convolution kernel size and $j$ is the distance between two consecutive features. Using the formula in Eq. 1 we can compute the size of the receptive field of each convolution layer. For example, the five receptive field of an AlexNet, showed in Fig. 4, have the following sizes: *conv1* $11 \times 11$, *conv2* $51 \times 51$, *conv3* $99 \times 99$, *conv4* $131 \times 131$ and *con5* $163 \times 163$. This means that the *conv1* of an AlexNet, recognizes a small subset of features represented by superpixels, while the *conv2* can recognize a visual word (depending on the configuration used for the encoding), up to the *con5* layer where a particular feature can simultaneously analyze all the visual words available in the input image.

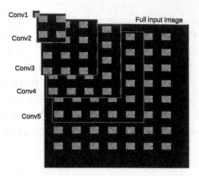

**Fig. 4.** The receptive fields of the five convolution layers of an AlexNet. Each receptive field is cut from a $256 \times 256$ image to analyze the quantity of visual words that each *conv* layer is able to analyze on each pixel of its feature map.

## 4  Dataset

Zhang *et al.* [20] introduced several large-scale datasets which covers several text classification tasks such as *sentiment analysis, topic classification* or *news categorization*. In these datasets, the number of training samples varies from several thousand to millions, which is considered ideal for deep learning-based methods. In addition, we used 20 news-bydate dataset to test various parameters associated with the encoding approach.

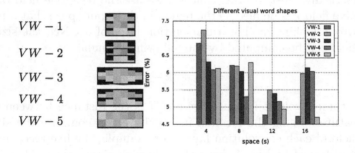

**Fig. 5.** On the left, five different designs for visual words ($VW$) represented by 36 Word2Vec features, over the 20 news-bydate dataset. The width V of these words is 4 for the first two on the top and 6 for the rest. The first four visual words consist of super pixels with different shapes to form particular visual words. On the right, a comparison over these different shapes of visual words.

## 5  Experiments

The aim of these experiments is twofold: (i) evaluate configuration parameters associated with the encoding approach; (ii) compare the proposed approach with other deep learning methods. (iii) to validate the proposed approach on a real-world application scenario. In experiments, percentage error is used to measure the classification performance. The encoding approach mentioned in Sect. 3.1 produces encoded image that are used to train and test a CNN. We used AlexNet [8] and Googlenet [17] architectures as base models from scratch. We used a publicly available Word2Vec word embedding with default configuration parameters as in [11] to train word vectors on all datasets. Normally, Word2Vec is trained on a large corpus and used in different contexts. However, we trained this model with the same training set for each dataset.

## 5.1 Parameters Setting

We used 20 news-bydate dataset to perform a series of experiments with various settings to find out the best configuration for the encoding scheme. In the first experiment, we changed the space $s$ among visual words and Word2Vec feature length to identify relationships between these parameters. We obtained a lower percentage error with higher values of $s$ parameter and a higher number of Word2Vec features as shown in Table 1. We observed that the length of feature vector $v_k(t_k)$ depends on the nature of the dataset. For example in Fig. 6, a text document composed of a large number of words cannot be encoded completely using a high number of Word2Vec features, because each visual word occupies more space in the encoded image. Moreover, we found out that error does not decrease linearly with the increase of Word2Vec features, as shown in Table 3.

**Table 1.** Comparison between CNNs trained with different configurations on our proposed approach. The width $V$ (in superpixels) of visual words is fixed while the Word2Vec encoding vector size and space $s$ (in pixel) varies. $H$ is the height of visual word obtained.

| $s$ | $V$ | $H$ | w2v feat | error (%) |
|----|----|----|----|----|
| 4 | 4 | 1 | 12 | 7.63 |
| 8 | 4 | 1 | 12 | 5.93 |
| 12 | 4 | 1 | 12 | **4.45** |
| 16 | 4 | 1 | 12 | 4.83 |
| 4 | 4 | 2 | 24 | 6.94 |
| 8 | 4 | 2 | 24 | 5.60 |
| 12 | 4 | 2 | 24 | 5.15 |
| 16 | 4 | 2 | 24 | **4.75** |
| 4 | 4 | 3 | 36 | 6.72 |
| 8 | 4 | 3 | 36 | 5.30 |
| 12 | 4 | 3 | 36 | **4.40** |
| 16 | 4 | 3 | 36 | 4.77 |

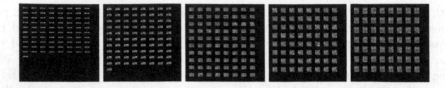

**Fig. 6.** Five encoded images obtained using different Word2Vec features length and using the same document belonging to the 20news-bydate dataset. All the images are encoded using space $s = 12$, superpixel size $4 \times 4$, image size $= 256 \times 256$ and visual word width $V = 16$. The two leftmost images contain all words in the document encoded with 12 and 24 Word2Vec features respectively, while 3 rightmost encoded images with 36, 48 and 60 features length cannot encode entire documents.

We tested various shapes for visual words before selecting the best one, as shown in Fig. 5 (on the left). We showed that the rectangular shaped visual words obtained higher performance as highlighted in Fig. 5 (on the right). Moreover, space $s$ between visual words plays an important role in the classification, in fact using a high value for the $s$ parameter, the convolutional layer can effectively distinguish among visual words, also demonstrated from the results in Table 1. The first level of a CNN (*conv1*) specializes convolution filters in the recognition of a single superpixel as shown in Fig. 3. Hence, it is important to distinguish between superpixels of different visual words by increasing the parameter $s$ (Table 2).

These experiments led us to the conclusion that we have a trade-off between the number of Word2Vec features to encode each word and the number of words that can be represented in an image. Increasing the number of Word2Vec features increases the space required in the encoded image to represent a single word. Moreover, this aspect affects the maximum number of words that may be encoded in an image. The choice of this parameter must be done considering the nature of the dataset, whether it is characterized by short or long text documents. For our experiments, we used a value of 36 for Word2Vec features, considering results presented in Table 3.

**Table 2.** Comparison of different parameters over the 20news-bydate dataset. In the leftmost table we changed the size of the encoded image from $100 \times 100$ to $500 \times 500$ and the crop size is also changed by multiplying the image size with a constant i.e. 1.13. Here $sp$ stands for superpixel, $w2v$ is for number of Word2Vec features, $Mw$ stands for Max number of visual words that an image can contain and $\#w$ is the number of text documents in the test set having a greater number of words than $Mw$. We fixed the remaining non-specified parameters as follow: $s = 12$, $V = 4$, $sp = 4$, image size$= 256$.

| image size | crop | error | sp | error | stride | error | w2v | Mw | #w | error |
|---|---|---|---|---|---|---|---|---|---|---|
| $500 \times 500$ | 443 | **8.63** | 5x5 | 8.96 | 5 | 8.7 | 12 | 180 | 50% | 9.32 |
| 400x400 | 354 | 9.30 | 4x4 | **8.87** | 4 | 8.87 | 24 | 140 | 64% | 8.87 |
| 300x300 | 266 | 10.12 | 3x3 | 10.27 | 3 | 8.33 | 36 | 120 | 71% | **7.20** |
| 200x200 | 177 | 10.46 | 2x2 | 10.82 | 2 | **7.78** | 48 | 100 | 79% | 8.21 |
| 100x100 | 88 | 15.70 | 1x1 | 10.89 | 1 | 12.5 | 60 | 90 | 83% | 20.66 |

## 5.2    Data Augmentation

We encode the text document in an image to exploit the power of CNNs typically used in image classification. Usually, CNNs use *"crop"* data augmentation technique to obtain robust models in image classification. This process has been used in our experiments and we showed that increasing the number of training samples by using the *crop* parameter, results are improved. During the training phase, 10 random $227 \times 227$ crops are extracted from a $256 \times 256$ image (or proportional crop for different image size, as reported in the leftmost Table 3) and then fed to the network. During the testing phase, we extracted a $227 \times 227$ patch from the center of the image. It is important to note that thanks to space $s$ introduced around the encoded words, the encoding of a text document in the image is not changed by cropping. So, cropping is equivalent to producing many images with the same encoding but with a shifted position.

The *"stride"* parameter is very primary in decreasing the complexity of the network, however, this value must not be bigger than the superpixel size, because larger values can skip too many pixels, which leads to information lost during the convolution, invalidating results.

We showed that the *mirror* data augmentation technique, successfully used in image classification, is not recommended here because it changes the semantics of the encoded words and can deteriorate the classification performance. Results are presented in Fig. 7.

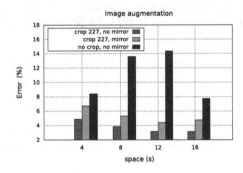

**Fig. 7.** Classification error using data augmentation: (*mirror* and *crop*) over the 20 news-bydate test set.

## 5.3    Comparison with Other State-of-the-art Text Classification Methods

We compared our approach with several state-of-the-art methods. Zhang *et al.* [20] presented a detailed analysis of traditional and deep learning methods. From their papers, we selected the best results and reported them in Table 4. In addition, we also compared our results with Conneau *et al.* [1] and Xiao *et al.* [18]. We obtained comparable results on all the datasets used: DBPedia, Yahoo Answers!,

**Table 3.** Comparison of different parameters over the 20 news-bydate dataset. Here *sp* stands for superpixel, *w2v* is for number of Word2Vec features, *Mw* stands for Max number of visual words that an image can contain and *#w* is the number of text documents in the test set having a greater number of words than *Mw*. We fixed the remaining non-specified parameters as follow: $s = 12$, $V = 4$, $sp = 4$, image size= 256.

| sp | error | stride | error | w2v | Mw | #w | error |
|----|-------|--------|-------|-----|----|----|-------|
| 5x5 | 8.96 | 5 | 8.7 | 12 | 180 | 50% | 9.32 |
| 4x4 | **8.87** | 4 | 8.87 | 24 | 140 | 64% | 8.87 |
| 3x3 | 10.27 | 3 | 8.33 | 36 | 120 | 71% | **7.20** |
| 2x2 | 10.82 | 2 | **7.78** | 48 | 100 | 79% | 8.21 |
| 1x1 | 10.89 | 1 | 12.5 | 60 | 90 | 83% | 20.66 |

Amazon Polarity, AGnews, Amazon Full and Yelp Full. However, we obtained a higher error on Sogou dataset due to the translation process explained in the paper [20]. It is interesting to note that the papers [1, 20] propose text adapted variants of convolutional neural networks [4, 8] developed for computer vision. Therefore, we obtain similar results to these papers. However, there is a clear performance gain compared to the hybrid of convolutional and recurrent networks [18].

**Table 4.** Testing error of our encoding approach on 8 datasets with Alexnet and GoogleNet. The best results are shown in bold. XLNet is a very recent approach based on BERT.

| Model | AG | Sogou | DBP. | Yelp P. | Yelp F. | Yah. A. | Amz. F. | Amz. P. |
|-------|-----|-------|------|---------|---------|---------|---------|---------|
| Xiao *et al.* | 8.64 | 4.83 | 1.43 | 5.51 | 38.18 | 28.26 | 40.77 | 5.87 |
| Zhang *et al.* | 7.64 | 2.81 | 1.31 | 4.36 | 37.95 | 28.80 | 40.43 | 4.93 |
| Conneau *et al.* | 8.67 | 3.18 | 1.29 | 4.28 | 35.28 | 26.57 | 37.00 | 4.28 |
| Johnson and Zhang | 6.87 | **1.84** | 0.88 | 2.64 | 30.58 | **23.90** | 34.81 | 3.32 |
| Our encoding scheme + AlexNet | 9.19 | 8.02 | 1.36 | 11.55 | 49.00 | 25.00 | 43.75 | 3.12 |
| Our encoding scheme + GoogleNet | 7.98 | 6.12 | 1.07 | 9.55 | 43.55 | 24.10 | 40.35 | 3.01 |
| XLNet Yang *et al.* | **4.45** | – | **0.60** | **1.37** | **27.05** | – | **31.67** | **2.11** |

**Table 5.** Percentage errors on 20 news-bydate dataset with three different CNNs.

| CNN architecture | error |
|---|---|
| Encoding scheme + AlexNet | 4.10 |
| Encoding scheme + GoogleNet | 3.81 |
| Encoding scheme + ResNet | 2.95 |

## 5.4   Comparison with State-of-the-Art CNNs

As expected, in Table 4 we performed better using GoogleNet, compared to results obtained using the same configuration on a less powerful model like AlexNet. We, therefore, conclude that recent state-of-the-art network architectures, such as InceptionResNet or Residual Network would further improve the performance of our proposed approach. To work successfully with large datasets and powerful models, a high-end hardware and large training time are required, thus we conducted experiments only on 20 news-bydate dataset with three network architectures: AlexNet, GoogleNet and ResNet. Results are shown in Table 5. We performed better with ResNet which represents one of the most powerful network architecture.

## 6   Multimodal Application

We use two multimodal datasets to demonstrate that our proposed visual embedding brings significant benefits to fuse encoded text with the corresponding image information [3]. The first dataset named Ferramenta [3] consists of $88,010$ image and text pairs split in $66,141$ and $21,869$ for train and for test sets respectively, belonging to 52 classes. We used another publicly available dataset called Amazon Product Data [5]. We randomly selected $10,000$ image and text pairs belonging to 22 classes. Finally, we randomly selected $10,000$ image and text pairs of each class dividing into train and test sets with $7,500$ and $2,500$ samples respectively.

We want to compare the classification of advertisement made in different ways: using only the encoded text description, using only the image of the advertisement and the fused combination. An example is shown in Fig. 8. The model trained on images only for Amazon Product Data, we obtained the following first two predictions: 77.42% Baby and 11.16% "Home and Kitchen" on this example. While the model trained on the multimodal Amazon Product Data, we obtained the following first two predictions: 100% Baby and 0% "Patio Lawn and Garden" for the same example. This indicate that our visual embedding improves classification performance compare to text or image only. Table 6 shows that the combination of text and image into a single image, outperforms best result obtained using only a single modality on Ferramenta and Amazon Product Data. It also demonstrate that the combination of text and image into a single image, outperforms best result obtained using only a single modality on both datasets.

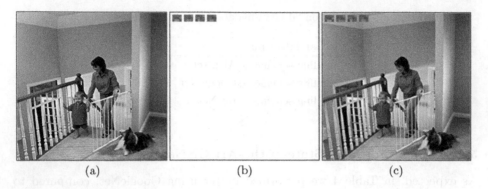

**Fig. 8.** An example of multimodal fusion from the Amazon dataset belonging to the class "Baby". (a) shows the original image, (b) is a blank image with the encoded text only and (c) shows the image with the superimposition of the encoded text in the upper part. The text in this example contains only the following 4 words "Kidco Safeway white G2000". The size of all images is 256 × 256.

**Table 6.** Percentage error between proposed approach and single sources.

| Dataset | Image | Text | **Fused image** |
|---|---|---|---|
| Ferramenta | 7.64 | 12.1 | **5.16** |
| Amazon product data | 53.9 | 35.9 | **27.3** |

## 7    Conclusion

In this paper, we presented a new approach to classify text documents by transforming the word encoding obtained with Word2Vec into RGB images that maintain the same semantic information contained in the original text document. The main objectives achieved are (1) the possibility of exploiting CNN models for classifying images directly without any modification, obtaining comparative results; (2) have a tool to integrate semantics of the text directly into the representative image of the text to solve a multimodal problem using a single CNN [13]. Furthermore, we presented a detailed study of various parameters associated with the coding scheme and obtained comparable results on various datasets. As shown in the section dedicated to the experiments, the results clearly show that we can further improve the text classification results by using newer and more powerful deep neural models.

# References

1. Conneau, A., Schwenk, H., Barrault, L., Lecun, Y.: Very deep convolutional networks for text classification. In: Proceedings of the 15th Conference of the European Chapter of the Association for Computational Linguistics: Volume 1, Long Papers, vol. 1, pp. 1107–1116 (2017)
2. Gallo, I., Nawaz, S., Calefati, A.: Semantic text encoding for text classification using convolutional neural networks. In: 2017 14th IAPR International Conference on Document Analysis and Recognition (ICDAR), vol. 05, pp. 16–21, November 2017. https://doi.org/10.1109/ICDAR.2017.323
3. Gallo, I., Calefati, A., Nawaz, S.: Multimodal classification fusion in real-world scenarios. In: 2017 14th IAPR International Conference on Document Analysis and Recognition (ICDAR), vol. 5, pp. 36–41. IEEE (2017)
4. He, K., Zhang, X., Ren, S., Sun, J.: Deep residual learning for image recognition. In: Proceedings of the IEEE Conference on Computer Vision and Pattern Recognition, pp. 770–778 (2016)
5. He, R., McAuley, J.: Ups and downs: modeling the visual evolution of fashion trends with one-class collaborative filtering. In: Proceedings of the 25th International Conference on World Wide Web, pp. 507–517. International World Wide Web Conferences Steering Committee (2016)
6. Johnson, R., Zhang, T.: Deep pyramid convolutional neural networks for text categorization. In: Proceedings of the 55th Annual Meeting of the Association for Computational Linguistics, pp. 562–570 (2017)
7. Kim, Y.: Convolutional neural networks for sentence classification. In: Proceedings of the 2014 Conference on Empirical Methods in Natural Language Processing (EMNLP), pp. 1746–1751. Association for Computational Linguistics, October 2014
8. Krizhevsky, A., Sutskever, I., Hinton, G.E.: Imagenet classification with deep convolutional neural networks. In: Advances in Neural Information Processing Systems, pp. 1097–1105 (2012)
9. Le, Q., Mikolov, T.: Distributed representations of sentences and documents. In: International Conference on Machine Learning, pp. 1188–1196 (2014)
10. Mahendran, A., Vedaldi, A.: Understanding deep image representations by inverting them. In: Proceedings of the IEEE Conference on Computer Vision and Pattern Recognition, pp. 5188–5196 (2015)
11. Mikolov, T., Sutskever, I., Chen, K., Corrado, G.S., Dean, J.: Distributed representations of words and phrases and their compositionality. In: Proceedings of the 26th International Conference on Neural Information Processing Systems, NIPS 2013, pp. 3111–3119 (2013)
12. Nawaz, S., Calefati, A., Janjua, M.K., Anwaar, M.U., Gallo, I.: Learning fused representations for large-scale multimodal classification. IEEE Sens. Lett. 3(1), 1–4 (2018)
13. Nawaz, S., Kamran Janjua, M., Gallo, I., Mahmood, A., Calefati, A., Shafait, F.: Do cross modal systems leverage semantic relationships? In: Proceedings of the IEEE International Conference on Computer Vision Workshops (2019)
14. Pennington, J., Socher, R., Manning, C.: Glove: global vectors for word representation. In: Proceedings of the 2014 Conference on Empirical Methods in Natural Language Processing (EMNLP), pp. 1532–1543 (2014)
15. Simonyan, K., Zisserman, A.: Very deep convolutional networks for large-scale image recognition. arXiv preprint arXiv:1409.1556 (2014)

16. Szegedy, C., Ioffe, S., Vanhoucke, V., Alemi, A.A.: Inception-v4, inception-resnet and the impact of residual connections on learning. In: Thirty-First AAAI Conference on Artificial Intelligence (2017)
17. Szegedy, C., et al.: Going deeper with convolutions. In: Proceedings of the IEEE Conference on Computer Vision and Pattern Recognition, pp. 1–9 (2015)
18. Xiao, Y., Cho, K.: Efficient character-level document classification by combining convolution and recurrent layers. arXiv preprint arXiv:1602.00367 (2016)
19. Yang, Z., Dai, Z., Yang, Y., Carbonell, J., Salakhutdinov, R.R., Le, Q.V.: Xlnet: generalized autoregressive pretraining for language understanding. In: Advances in Neural Information Processing Systems, pp. 5753–5763 (2019)
20. Zhang, X., Zhao, J., LeCun, Y.: Character-level convolutional networks for text classification. In: Advances in Neural Information Processing Systems, pp. 649–657 (2015)

# CC-LSTM: Cross and Conditional Long-Short Time Memory for Video Captioning

Jiangbo Ai[1], Yang Yang[1(✉)], Xing Xu[2], Jie Zhou[2], and Heng Tao Shen[2]

[1] Guizhou Provincial Key Laboratory of Public Big Data, Guizhou University, Guiyang 550025, China
jiangboml@gmail.com, dlyyang@gmail.com
[2] Center for Future Media, University of Electronic Science and Technology of China, Chengdu, China
xing.xu@uestc.com, jiezhou0714@gmail.com, shenhengtao@hotmail.com

**Abstract.** Automatically generating natural language descriptions for in-the-wild videos is a challenging task. Most recent progress in this field has been made through the combination of Convolutional Neural Networks (CNNs) and Encoder-Decoder Recurrent Neural Networks (RNNs). However, existing Encoder-Decoder RNNs framework has difficulty in capturing a large number of long-range dependencies along with the increasing of the number of LSTM units. It brings a vast information loss and leads to poor performance for our task. To explore this problem, in this paper, we propose a novel framework, namely Cross and Conditional Long Short-Term Memory (CC-LSTM). It is composed of a novel Cross Long Short-Term Memory (Cr-LSTM) for the encoding module and Conditional Long Short-Term Memory (Co-LSTM) for the decoding module. In the encoding module, the Cr-LSTM encodes the visual input into a richly informative representation by a cross-input method. In the decoding module, the Co-LSTM feeds the visual features, which is based on generated sentence and contains the global information of the visual content, into the LSTM unit as an extra visual feature. For the work of video capturing, extensive experiments are conducted on two public datasets, i.e., MSVD and MSR-VTT. Along with visualizing the results and how our model works, these experiments quantitatively demonstrate the effectiveness of the proposed CC-LSTM on translating videos to sentences with rich semantics.

**Keywords:** Video captioning · Cross-LSTM · Conditional-LSTM · Attention

## 1 Introduction

Automatically generating a sentence or paragraph level description for image or video, which tries to describe the content of a given image or video with a

© Springer Nature Switzerland AG 2021
A. Del Bimbo et al. (Eds.): ICPR 2020 Workshops, LNCS 12666, pp. 353–365, 2021.
https://doi.org/10.1007/978-3-030-68780-9_30

relevant sentence in English or other languages, has a great potential impact on early childhood education, image or video retrieval, or helping visually impaired people. What is more, it is also a basic ingredient for a more complex scene such as recommendation in editing applications, usage in virtual assistants, and image indexing. Recently, a great number of researches have made significant progress on image description generation [12]. But generating a natural and correct description for video is still confronted with a peck of difficulties. Different from static pictures, video contents contain rich information of diverse sets of objects, scenes, actions, attributes and salient contents, which are impossibly captured well by simply extrapolating the methods for image captioning. Despite the immense difficulties of video captioning, there are still a few attempts [20] which are proposed based on recent advances in machine translation by using Long Short-Term Memory (LSTM). The LSTM framework is originally proposed for solving sequence input with different length in machine translation.

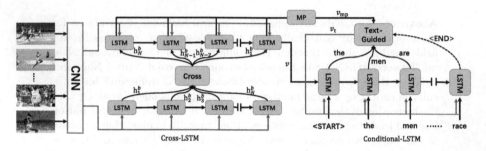

**Fig. 1.** An illustration of the modular structure of the proposed video description model. "Cross" module means to reverse the input of the bottom list. "MP" represent average pooling.

For video captioning, the most popular framework follows the encoder-decoder pipeline. It is firstly proposed by Vinyals et al. [3,29] to encode the source sequence to a fixed-length feature vector in the embedding space which is used as the input for the decoder network. The typical representative framework for video captioning is S2VT [19,24]. It firstly combines the Convolutional Neural Networks (CNN) to generate a visual feature vector of each frame and then imports those feature vector sequentially to the encoder-decoder framework to generate video description. Although the LSTM framework could model the global temporal structure for a sequence snippet, there still exist some major drawbacks: 1) In the encoding module, the traditional LSTM encodes the video frames into a fixed-length feature vector in sequence. The strategy will cause considerable information loss for the difficulty of capturing long-range dependencies. 2) In the decoding module, the feature vector is only fed into the LSTM framework at the initial time step, which often causes the "drift away" effect. It indicates that the traditional LSTM framework may lose track of the original video content.

Recently many researchers have undertaken to overcome those difficulties. The Bidirectional LSTM firstly proposed in [4] deeply captures the bidirectional global temporal of video. Although the Bi-LSTM integrates the bidirectional visual information for a rich representation, the method still has limited ability to solve the difficulties of long-range dependencies which also brings vast information loss in both directions. The "drift away" effect was firstly proposed by Jia et al. [8]. It note that the LSTM network may lose the track of the original video contents when fitting the distribution of sentences in the training set. The most intuitive solution is to add the video feature vector as an extra input to all the units of LSTM blocks in every time step. However, such a strategy is proved to be unsuccessful by Yao et al. [26]. The reason may be the case that the noise in the video content can be explicitly accumulated and thus the network will be easily overfitting. To address this problem, Xin et al. [7] proposed using Part of Speech (PoS) tags of a sentence to serve as a gate to control the input of image content and guide the process of generating a word. This method achieved certain success on image captioning and solve the "drift away" effect to some extent. But they are affected by several problems. Firstly, this method is not an end-to-end trainable framework, it needs to manually define the semantic tags beforehand. Secondly, the input of image content is invariable in every step which also easily causes the overfitting phenomenon. What's more, this method only considers the current tags but not front of all tags. For example, the half-baked sentence "A group of people is dancing in the "X"" has been generated through the previous steps and the "X" represents the next word to be generated. Obviously, we should pay more attention to "people" and "dancing" that could dynamically affect the visual information instead of the current word "the" that decides whether the image content should be added.

To address the above challenges, in this paper, we propose a novel framework named as Cross and Conditional Long Short-Term Memory (CC-LSTM). It can effectively generate a rich feature representation for input video in the encoding stage and simultaneously has the capability to solve the "drift away" phenomenon in the decoding stage. In our approach, our foundation framework is based on one of the most popular frameworks following the mainstream encoder-decoder pipeline. Concretely, in the encoding stage, we devise a Cross-LSTM (Cr-LSTM) consisting of a stacked LSTMs based on a cross-input method (as showed in Fig. 1). It will generate a more extensive representation for input video. In the decoding stage, we devise a Conditional-LSTM (Co-LSTM) as Fig. 1 with attention mechanism based on the previously generated word. It helps to dynamically select the most relevant video content as supplementary input to the LSTM unit in each time step. Finally, we evaluate the overall framework CC-LSTM on the public datasets MSVD and MSR-VTT. The obtained results demonstrate that our approach can yield significantly better performance compared to the most popular approaches.

## 2    Related Work

The history of visual content description can date backs to the past couple of years. Early attempts are mostly based on template-based language methods [6]. Template-based language methods firstly detect visual concepts (e.g. objects, verbs, attributes) and then generate a sentence with a predefined language template or followed by the nearest neighbor retrieving. Farhadi et al. [5], for instance, used detection to infer a triplet of scene elements that are converted to text using a template. Li et al. [11] composed image descriptions given computer vision based on inputs such as detected objects, modifiers and locations using web-scale n-grams. Obviously, those methods highly depend on the templates of language which always generates a sentence with the syntactical structure and suffer the implied limits on the variety of the output. With the development of machine intelligence in computer vision and natural language processing technologies, Convolutional Neural Networks (CNN) and Recurrent Neural Networks (RNN) are proposed one after another. LSTM is proposed to overcome the vanishing gradients problem by enabling the network to learn when to forget previously hidden states and when to update hidden states by integrating memory units. LSTM has been successfully adapted to several tasks, e.g., speech recognition, language translation and image or video captioning [9]. Based on the above problem, Aneja et al. [2,23,28] develop a convolutional image captioning technique which shows excellent performance. Under this background, a powerful paradigm, the encoder-and-decoder framework was proposed by [21], which then becomes the core of the most state-of-the-art image or video captioning models. The methods encode the sequence input into a fixed vector as the input of LSTM to generate words one by one.

In summary, our proposed Cross and Conditional LSTM (CC-LSTM) is also based on the encoder-decoder framework. And our work presents the first effort to explore the problem of long-range dependencies of LSTM with a Cross-LSTM in the encoding stage.

## 3    The Proposed Approach

### 3.1    Problem Definition

Supposing a video consists of $N$ frames denoted by $V$, we need to describe this video with a sentence $S$, where $S = (w_1, w_2, ..., w_{N_m})$ consisting of $N_m$ words. Lets $v \in \mathbb{R}^{D_v}$ and $w_t \in \mathbb{R}^{D_w}$ denotes the $D_v$-dimensional representations of the video V and the $D_w$-dimensional textual features of the $t^{th}$ word in sentence $S$, respectively. Similarly, the sentence $S$ can be denoted by a matrix $W_s \in \mathbb{R}^{D_w \times N_m}$ $= (w_1, ..., w_{N_m})$, with each word in the sentence as its column vector. We have an extra visual representation $v_t \in \mathbb{R}^{D_v}$ dynamically selected by the previous generated word. More details about how we get the $v_t$ will be explained in Section 3.3. In our work, our goal is to maximize the conditional probability of an output $S$ given a video $V$. The conditional probabilities over the sentences can be defined as following:

$$\log P(S|V) = \sum_{t=1}^{N_m} \log p(w_t|v, v_t, w_0, ..., w_{t-1}). \tag{1}$$

The outputs of the language model are the log likelihood of each word from the target sentence, followed by a Softmax function for normalization. We use the regularized cross-entropy loss function:

$$L(S, V) = - \sum_{(S,V) \in \mathcal{D}} \log P(S|V) + \frac{\lambda}{2}||W_{all}||_2^2. \tag{2}$$

where $S$, $V$ as above mentioned represent sentence and video respectively. $\mathcal{D}$ is our training data. $W_{all}$ denotes all weights in the model and $\lambda$ controls the importance of the regularization term.

## 3.2  CC-LSTM for Video Captioning

For the sake of overcoming the problem as mentioned earlier, in this subsection, we devise the overall model, called CC-LSTM, to generate video description under the umbrella of a generative system based on attention mechanism.

**Cross LSTM Encoder:** Our proposed Cross LSTM (later we call Cr-LSTM) consists of two-layer LSTM as Fig. 1. The main intention of Cr-LSTM is to generate a representation of input video with a piece of rich information. Specifically, our method firstly utilizes the bottom LSTM to encode all the frames and retains the state $\{h_i^b\}_{i=1}^N$ of each time step where $h_i^b$ represents the output of bottom LSTM unit in the $i^{th}$ time step. After feeding all the $N$ frames to the bottom LSTM, we will get a matrix $h_{all} \in \mathbb{R}^{h_{dim} \times N} = \{h_1^b, h_2^b, ..., h_N^b\}$ that consists of a sequence of vectors. Those vectors will serve as complementary information for the top LSTM which will help to overcome the difficulties of long-range dependencies of LSTM.

$$
\begin{aligned}
i_t &= \sigma(W_i[h_{t-1}, h_{all}[N - (t-1) \times s, :], x_t] + b_i), \\
f_t &= \sigma(W_f[h_{t-1}, h_{all}[N - (t-1) \times s, :], x_t] + b_f), \\
o_t &= \sigma(W_o[h_{t-1}, h_{all}[N - (t-1) \times s, :], x_t] + b_o), \\
g_t &= \varphi(W_g[h_{t-1}, h_{all}[N - (t-1) \times s, :], x_t] + b_g), \\
c_t &= f_t \odot c_{t-1} + i_t \odot g_t, \\
h_t &= o_t \odot tanh(c_t).
\end{aligned}
\tag{3}
$$

In order to enhance the efficiency of our framework, we select part of the video frames with a fixed stride $s$ as input for our top of LSTM. Concretely, we get the new input sequence $X_{new} = \{x_1, x_{1+s}, x_{1+2*s}..., x_{1+k*s}, ..., x_N\}$ with a fixed stride s (in our experiment, we set the stride s as 20). What the difference compared to the bottom LSTM is that top LSTM encodes each frame based on not only previous state $h^o_{t-1}$, where $h^o_{t-1}$ represents the previous state of top LSTM at time step $t - 1$, but also the state $h_{all}[N - (t - 1) \times s, :]$ generated from bottom LSTM at time step $N - (t - 1) \times s$. As we know, the $h^o_{t-1}$ and the $h_{all}[N - (t - 1) \times s, :]$ is complementary to each other. When the $h^o_{t-1}$ misses the information of the first few inputs, the $h_{all}[N - (t - 1) \times s, :]$ can serve as a supplement for the missed information. According to our experiment, we found the Cr-LSTM is beneficial to the performance boost. The guidance $m_t$ is replaced by our actual input $h_{all}[N - (t - 1) \times s, :]$ as shown in Fig. 2. The specific process of LSTM unit can be redefined as below:

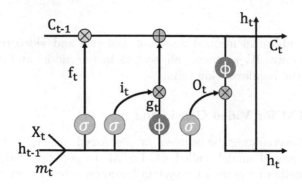

**Fig. 2.** An illustration of the fundamental LSTM unit.

The hidden state $h_t$ in LSTM is determined by the input $x_t$ and the previous hidden state $h_{t-1}$. And we obtain the final output $h_N$ as the final visual representation $v$. Thus, for simplicity, the calculation of v is denoted as:

$$v = LSTM(x_N, h_{N-1}) \tag{4}$$

**Conditional LSTM Decoder:** In order to generate reasonable and natural descriptions for video clips, the sentence the generator should make full use of the information of the video content during the process of generating words. A straightforward way is feeding the video contents to the LSTM unit of generator at each time step, which, however, will lead to the network overfitting easily.

Inspired by the Part of Speech (PoS) proposed by Xin et al. [7], we proposed the Conditional LSTM which still feeds the visual content to the LSTM unit of generator at each time step. The difference is that we feed the changing dynamically visual contents $v_t$ (which will be introduced in Eq. 10). In particular, we get $v_t$ by learning a dynamic weight vector $f_v$ which controls the importance of each element of $v_{mp}$. What is more, $v_{mp}$ can be get as Eq. 11. So the visual contents $v_t$ is conditioned on the sentences which have been generated before.

Since the recently proposed soft attention mechanism from Bengio et al. [3] has achieved great success in several sequence modeling tasks, in our experiment for the Text-Guide unit, we adopt attention mechanism to dynamically weight each words by assigning it with one positive weight $\alpha_i^t$ alone with the sentence generation procedure. Supposing those words that have been generated denote by $S_p = \{w_1, w_2, ..., w_t\}$ where $t$ denotes the $t^{th}$ step of current stage. As mentioned above, $w_i \in \mathbb{R}^{h_{dim}}$ and $h_{dim}$ is the hidden unit of LSTM.(Actually the $w_i$ is the intermediate state of every time step of decoding process. For the actual word, we need to transform the current dimension into another dimensions of real space for a specific word). After applying the attention mechanism to those words, we get the result such that:

$$f_w = \sum_{i=1}^{t} \alpha_i^t w_i,$$

$$f_v = \sigma(W_c^T f_w + b_v),$$

(5)

where $\sum_{i=1}^{t} \alpha_i^t = 1$ and $\alpha_i^t$ are computed at each time step t inside the LSTM decoder. We refer to $\alpha_i^t$ as the attention weights of $i^{th}$ word at time t. $f_w \in \mathbb{R}^{h_{dim}}$ is the weighted average vector. $W_c \in \mathbb{R}^{h_{dim} \times D_v}$ is parameter matrix to be learned which transform the $f_w$ into the same dimension with the visual content $v \in \mathbb{R}^{D_v}$. $f_v$ is the final indicator which has the value 0 or 1 to decide which part of visual information should be retained.

The attention weight $\alpha_i^t$ reflects the importance of the $i^{th}$ word in $S_p$. To decrease the affect of noisy input and make decoder robust, we design a function $f_{att}$ that takes as input the previous generated word in $S_p$ and returns the relevance score $\alpha_i^t$ as follows:

$$\alpha_i^t = \frac{exp\left(f_{att}\left(w_i\right)\right)}{\sum_{i=1}^{t} exp\left(f_{att}\left(w_i\right)\right)},$$

(6)

where the function $f_{att}$ is defined as

$$f_{att}\left(w_i\right) = U_a^T tanh(W_a^T w_i + b_a),$$

(7)

where $U_a \in \mathbb{R}^{k_c}$, $W_a \in \mathbb{R}^{h_{dim} \times k_c}$ are the parameters to learn. $k_c$ represents the dimension of visual context projection space. Then the language generator computes $f_w$ as Eqs. (4) and (3). As mentioned above in Eq. (5), $f_v \in \mathbb{R}^{D_v}$ has the same dimension with $v_t$. $v_t$, mentioned in Sect. 3.2, is the extra visual representations to guide the process of generating word of every step. After sigmoid operation, the value of each element of $f_v$ takes between 0 or 1 to decide whether to forget the current information or not. So the $v_t$ conditioned on the sentences can be represented as

$$v_t = f_v \odot v_{mp},$$

(8)

where $v_{mp}$ is the visual feature by simply average pooling all the outputs of top LSTM. $v_{mp}$ can be represented as

$$v_{mp} = MP(h_1^o, h_{1+s}^o, ..., h_N^o).$$

(9)

The $v_t$, selected dynamically by the previous word, retains the most important information which guides the generator to generate a more reasonable output. The specific process of generating word of every step can be defined as Eq. (3) where only need to replace $h_{all}[N - (t-1) \times s, :]$ with our dynamic $v_t$. Once the hidden state $h_t$ is computed, the probability distribution over the vocabulary is calculated as:

$$P_t = softmax(W_p[v, v_t, h_t] + b_p), \qquad (10)$$

where $W_p$ and $b_p$ are the parameters to be learned. $P_t$ denotes the probability of each element in the vocabulary to be selected as the $t^{th}$ word of the caption, which is jointly determined by the current visual feature $v$ and $v_t$ and all the history information encoded in $h_t$. Practically, the dimensionality of $p_t$ is equal to the size of the vocabulary. Specifically, in the training procedure, log-likelihood function is denoted by Eq. (1) and we aim to generate the optimal parameter $\Theta$,

$$\Theta = \arg\max_{\Theta} \sum_{t=1}^{T} \log p(w_t | v, v_t, w_0, ..., w_{t-1}; \Theta), \qquad (11)$$

where $\Theta$ stands for all the training parameters in our approach. $T$ is the total time steps of the LSTM. Practically, if the reference caption is shorter than $T$, it is padded by zero. Equation (11) illustrates that the parameters are learned by maximizing the probability of the reference caption.

## 4    Experiments

### 4.1    Implementation Details

We first employ a convolutional neural network (CNN) (GoogleLeNet in our experiment which has achieved excellent performance in ImageNet Large Scale Visual Recognition Challenge) [17,18] to extract the feature of video frame equidistantly. We limit the maximum number of the frame to be a $N_{max}$ ($N_{max} = 160$ in MSVD, $N_{max} = 120$ in MSR-VTT). If the number of the frame is less than $N_{max}$, we pad the frame with all zero. In the training phase, in order to deal with sentences with varying lengths, we add a begin-of-sentence tag <START> to start each sentence and an end-of-sentence tag <END> to end each sentence. In the testing phase, we input <START> tag into our CC-LSTM to trigger the video description generation process. For each generated word, we choose the word with the maximum probability and stop until we reach <END>. Each word in the sentence is represented as "one-hot" vector (binary index vector in a vocabulary). We connect a linear layer that projects the "one-hot" vector into a dense vector with 512 dimensions. For video representations, we take the output of 1024-way $pool5/7x7\_s1$ layer from GoogleLeNet. The dimension of the input and hidden states in LSTM are both set to 1,024. For optimization methods, we adopted the Adadelta optimization function. We use Adam optimizer for updating weights with $\alpha = 0.8$ and $\beta = 0.99$ at the beginning. For the hyper-parameters, we set the dropout ratio to 0.5 for all full-connected layers and LSTM. And we also set the learning rate to $10^{-4}$. Two standard evaluation metrics, i.e. BLEU@N [15] and METEOR [10], are used in addition to human evaluation. All experiments were implemented in Theano, using an NVIDIA GTX1080 GPU with 8 GB memory.

## 4.2   Experiment Results on the MSVD Dataset

We report experimental results where only static frame-level features are used in Table 1 on MSVD dataset. All the compared approaches follow the encoder-decoder framework. Our approach outperform SA and p-RNN. SA applies a frame-level attention mechanism in decoder stage and p-RNN exploits both temporal- and spatial-attention mechanisms to selectively focus on visual elements during generation. The reason for better performance of our model is that our CC-LSTM has better ability to generate better representation in an encoder and apply the attention mechanisms on the words to change the input visual content dynamically which could help word generator to generate a more appropriate word. From Table 1, we can also observe that our model of the METEOR metric is slightly lower at the HRNE model but the $B$@4 metric of our CC-LSTM is much higher than HRNE.

**Table 1.** Comparison of our method with the baselines using only static frame-level features on the MSVD dataset. (Top-two scores of each metric are highlighted).

| Method | METEOR | B@1 | B@2 | B@3 | B@4 |
|---|---|---|---|---|---|
| SA [25] | 29.0 | – | – | – | 40.3 |
| S-VC | 29.3 | – | – | – | 35.1 |
| MTVP [16] | 31.7 | – | – | – | 44.1 |
| GRU-EVEhft [1] | 31.0 | – | – | – | 40.6 |
| LSTM-E [14] | 29.5 | 74.9 | 60.9 | 50.6 | 40.2 |
| p-RNN [27] | 31.1 | 77.3 | 64.5 | 54.6 | **44.3** |
| HRNE [13] | **32.1** | **79.2** | **66.3** | **55.1** | 43.6 |
| Cr-LSTM (Ours) | 30.7 | 78.7 | 64.2 | 52.7 | 41.9 |
| Co-LSTM (Ours) | 31.5 | 78.8 | 65.3 | 53.7 | 42.5 |
| CC-LSTM (Ours) | **31.9** | **79.3** | **65.7** | **55.6** | **44.9** |

For a fair comparison, we additionally compare our CC-LSTM with only one ConvNet feature to other video description systems with fusion ConvNet features or different ConvNet features in Table 2. In this experiment, our CC-LSTM only uses one ConvNet feature as input but the compared systems combine multiple ConvNet features. From Table 2, we could conclude that our proposed approach outperform most of the video captioning systems even though those with combined features. According to the Table 2, we observed that the metric of our methods is almost top 2 compared with the different methods. Based on the comparison among the results of the different version approaches, it can be concluded that our approach can greatly improve the performance of video captioning systems.

**Table 2.** Comparison of our method with the baselines using multiple features on the MSVD dataset. (Top-two scores of each metric are highlighted).

| Method | METEOR | B@1 | B@2 | B@3 | B@4 |
|---|---|---|---|---|---|
| S2VT (VGGNet+optical flow) [19] | 29.8 | – | – | – | – |
| SA (GoogleNet+3DCNN) [25] | 29.6 | – | – | – | 41.9 |
| LSTM-E (VGGNet) [14] | 29.5 | 74.9 | 60.9 | 50.6 | 40.2 |
| LSTM-E (VGGNet+C3D) [14] | 31.0 | 78.8 | **66.0** | **55.4** | **45.3** |
| HRNE (GoogleNet) [13] | **32.1** | **79.2** | 66.3 | 55.1 | 43.6 |
| CC-LSTM (Ours) | **31.9** | **79.3** | 65.7 | **55.6** | **44.9** |

## 4.3   Experiment Results on the MSR-VTT Dataset

The experimental results on MSR-VTT are listed in Table 3. Compared with the MSVD, MSR-VTT is a more challenging dataset for containing more visual concepts and complex sentence structure. Generally, MP, S2VT, and SA have been introduced before, $M^3$ builds a visual and textual shared memory to model the long-term visual-textual dependency and further guide global visual attention on described targets. We can notice that our method still show excellent performance than $M^3$. The reason for better performance is that our method has a better ability in guiding global visual content with the attention mechanism based on the sentence. Compared to MP-LSTM which displays some different results with different basic feature extraction approaches, our proposed approaches CC-LSTM achieves 25.9 and 36.2 on METEOR and B4 respectively which is both more excellent. For SA-LSTM and $M^3$, the result obtained of our CC-LSTM is also superior to others. All of the experimental results compared to other methods are both adequately demonstrate the effectiveness of our approach which also illustrates that our proposed model CC-LSTM can encode the video with more extensive semantics and generate more suitable or relevant descriptions for video.

**Table 3.** Comparison of different methods on MSR-VTT dataset. All experiments only use the RGB feature. (Top-one scores of each metric are highlighted).

| Method | METEOR | B@4 |
|---|---|---|
| MP-LSTM [20] | | |
|     C3D | 24.8 | 35.4 |
|     C3D+VGG-19 | 25.3 | 35.8 |
|     GoogLeNet | 24.6 | 34.6 |
| SA-LSTM [25] | | |
|     C3D | 25.7 | 36.1 |
|     GoogleNet | 25.2 | 35.2 |
| $M^3$ [22] | | |
|     VGG | 24.6 | 35.0 |
|     C3D | 25.7 | 35.1 |
| S2VT [19] | 25.7 | 31.4 |
| CC-LSTM(GoogleNet) | **25.9** | **36.2** |

# 5    Conclusion

In this paper, we proposed a novel framework CC-LSTM for video captioning with an emphasis on long-range dependencies modeling. It consists of Cr-LSTM and Co-LSTM. We firstly proposed to utilizing two-layer cross LSTM (Cr-LSTM) to encode the video into a vector representation with a more extensive semantics. What's more, We also proposed a sentence attention mechanism (Co-LSTM) for selecting the most important video content dynamically. To verify the effectiveness of our Cr-LSTM, We conduct a complete experiment on MSVD and MSR-VTT for video captioning. The competitive results on the benchmark datasets demonstrated that our proposed method CC-LSTM is effective in learning a long-range dependencies model for such a fundamental task.

**Acknowledgments.** This work was supported in part by National Key Research and Development Program of China under grant No. 2018AAA0102200, the Sichuan Science and Technology Program, China, under grant 2018GZDZX0032 and 2020YFS0057, the Fundamental Research Funds for the Central Universities under Project ZYGX2019Z015, the National Natural Science Foundation of China under grants 61632007 and Dongguan Songshan Lake Introduction Program of Leading Innovative and Entrepreneurial Talents.

# References

1. Aafaq, N., Akhtar, N., Liu, W., Gilani, S.Z., Mian, A.: Spatio-temporal dynamics and semantic attribute enriched visual encoding for video captioning. arXiv preprint arXiv:1902.10322 (2019)

2. Aneja, J., Deshpande, A., Schwing, A.G.: Convolutional image captioning. In: CVPR, pp. 5561–5570 (2018)
3. Bahdanau, D., Cho, K., Bengio, Y.: Neural machine translation by jointly learning to align and translate. arXiv preprint arXiv:1409.0473 (2014)
4. Bin, Y., Yang, Y., Shen, F., Xu, X., Shen, H.T.: Bidirectional long-short term memory for video description. In: ACMMM, pp. 436–440. ACM (2016)
5. Farhadi, A., Hejrati, M., Sadeghi, M.A., Young, P., Rashtchian, C., Hockenmaier, J., Forsyth, D.: Every picture tells a story: generating sentences from images. In: Daniilidis, K., Maragos, P., Paragios, N. (eds.) ECCV 2010. LNCS, vol. 6314, pp. 15–29. Springer, Heidelberg (2010). https://doi.org/10.1007/978-3-642-15561-1_2
6. Guadarrama, S., et al.: Youtube2text: recognizing and describing arbitrary activities using semantic hierarchies and zero-shot recognition. In: ICCV, pp. 2712–2719 (2013)
7. He, X., Shi, B., Bai, X., Xia, G.S., Zhang, Z., Dong, W.: Image caption generation with part of speech guidance. PRL (2017)
8. Jia, X., Gavves, E., Fernando, B., Tuytelaars, T.: Guiding the long-short term memory model for image caption generation. In: ICCV, pp. 2407–2415 (2015)
9. Krause, J., Johnson, J., Krishna, R., Fei-Fei, L.: A hierarchical approach for generating descriptive image paragraphs. arXiv preprint arXiv:1611.06607 (2016)
10. Lavie, A., Agarwal, A.: Meteor: An automatic metric for MT evaluation with improved correlation with human judgments. In: Proceedings of the EMNLP 2011 Workshop on Statistical Machine Translation, pp. 65–72 (2005)
11. Li, S., Kulkarni, G., Berg, T.L., Berg, A.C., Choi, Y.: Composing simple image descriptions using web-scale n-grams. In: Proceedings of the Fifteenth Conference on Computational Natural Language Learning, pp. 220–228. ACL (2011)
12. Mao, J., Xu, W., Yang, Y., Wang, J., Huang, Z., Yuille, A.: Deep captioning with multimodal recurrent neural networks (M-RNN). arXiv preprint arXiv:1412.6632 (2014)
13. Pan, P., Xu, Z., Yang, Y., Wu, F., Zhuang, Y.: Hierarchical recurrent neural encoder for video representation with application to captioning. In: CVPR, pp. 1029–1038 (2016)
14. Pan, Y., Mei, T., Yao, T., Li, H., Rui, Y.: Jointly modeling embedding and translation to bridge video and language. In: CVPR pp. 4594–4602 (2016)
15. Papineni, K., Roukos, S., Ward, T., Zhu, W.J.: Bleu: a method for automatic evaluation of machine translation. In: Proceedings of the 40th Annual Meeting on Association for Computational Linguistics, pp. 311–318. ACL (2002)
16. Pasunuru, R., Bansal, M.: Multi-task video captioning with video and entailment generation. arXiv preprint arXiv:1704.07489 (2017)
17. Shen, F., Xu, Y., Liu, L., Yang, Y., Huang, Z., Shen, H.T.: Unsupervised deep hashing with similarity-adaptive and discrete optimization. IEEE Trans. Pattern Anal. Mach. Intell. **40**(12), 3034–3044 (2018)
18. Szegedy, C., et al.: Going deeper with convolutions. In: CVPR, pp. 1–9 (2015)
19. Venugopalan, S., Rohrbach, M., Donahue, J., Mooney, R., Darrell, T., Saenko, K.: Sequence to sequence-video to text. In: ICCV, pp. 4534–4542 (2015)
20. Venugopalan, S., Xu, H., Donahue, J., Rohrbach, M., Mooney, R., Saenko, K.: Translating videos to natural language using deep recurrent neural networks. arXiv preprint arXiv:1412.4729 (2014)
21. Vinyals, O., Toshev, A., Bengio, S., Erhan, D.: Show and tell: a neural image caption generator. In: CVPR, pp. 3156–3164 (2015)
22. Wang, J., Wang, W., Huang, Y., Wang, L., Tan, T.: Multimodal memory modelling for video captioning. arXiv preprint arXiv:1611.05592 (2016)

23. Xu, X., He, L., Lu, H., Gao, L., Ji, Y.: Deep adversarial metric learning for cross-modal retrieval. World Wide Web **22**(2), 657–672 (2018). https://doi.org/10.1007/s11280-018-0541-x

24. Xu, X., Shen, F., Yang, Y., Shen, H.T., Li, X.: Learning discriminative binary codes for large-scale cross-modal retrieval. IEEE Trans. Image Process. **26**(5), 2494–2507 (2017)

25. Yao, L., et al.: Describing videos by exploiting temporal structure. In: ICCV, pp. 4507–4515 (2015)

26. Yao, T., Pan, Y., Li, Y., Qiu, Z., Mei, T.: Boosting image captioning with attributes. arXiv preprint arXiv:1611.01646 (2016)

27. Yu, H., Wang, J., Huang, Z., Yang, Y., Xu, W.: Video paragraph captioning using hierarchical recurrent neural networks. In: CVPR, pp. 4584–4593 (2016)

28. Zhu, L., Huang, Z., Li, Z., Xie, L., Shen, H.T.: Exploring auxiliary context: discrete semantic transfer hashing for scalable image retrieval. IEEE Trans. Neural Networks Learn. Syst. **29**(11), 5264–5276 (2018)

29. Zhu, L., Huang, Z., Li, Z., Xie, L., Shen, H.T.: Exploring auxiliary context: discrete semantic transfer hashing for scalable image retrieval. IEEE Trans. Neural Netw. Learning Syst. **29**(11), 5264–5276 (2018)

# An Overview of Image-to-Image Translation Using Generative Adversarial Networks

Xin Chen and Caiyan Jia[✉]

School of Computer and Information Technology, Beijing Jiaotong University,
Beijing, China
{19120337,cyjia}@bjtu.edu.cn

**Abstract.** Image-to-image translation is an important and challenging problem in computer vision. It aims to learn the mapping between two different domains, with applications ranging from data augmentation, style transfer, to super-resolution, etc. With the success of deep learning methods in visual generative tasks, researchers have applied deep generative models, especially generative adversarial networks (GANs), to image-to-image translation since the year of 2016 and gained fruitful progress. In this survey, we have conducted a comprehensive review of the literature in this field, covering supervised and unsupervised methods, among which unsupervised approaches include one-to-one, one-to-many, many-to-many categories and some latest theories. We highlight the innovation aspect of these methods and analyze different models employed and their components. Besides, we summarized some commonly used normalization techniques and evaluation metrics, and finally, present several challenges and future research directions in this area.

**Keywords:** Deep learning · Generative adversarial networks · Image-to-image translation · Normalization · Evaluation metrics

## 1 Introduction

Image-to-image (I2I) translation is an interdisciplinary problem between computer vision and graphics. Similar to natural language translation, I2I translation translates images from $X$-domain (e.g., zebras) to $Y$-domain (e.g., horses). $X$ and $Y$ domains have similar semantic concepts but different data distribution. In other words, samples in the same domain share some common distinguishing features, while different domains share quite similar or the same semantic concept. For example, suppose the domains are represented as different painting styles, the two domains share the same concept of painting, and the translation task aims to transfer from Picasso's to Monet's creative style. When the domains are represented as different kinds of animals, the translation task can be represented as learning the mapping from cat to dog. It is noteworthy that the definition of domain can be different in different context. The data from the

© Springer Nature Switzerland AG 2021
A. Del Bimbo et al. (Eds.): ICPR 2020 Workshops, LNCS 12666, pp. 366–380, 2021.
https://doi.org/10.1007/978-3-030-68780-9_31

same domain can be further divided into multiple subcategories (for example, multiple breeds of dogs), that is, the data distribution within the domain can have multiple peaks.

Many sub-branches of computer vision can be classified as I2I translation. For example, super-resolution(SR) is the transformation from low-resolution(LR) to high-resolution(HR), and image segmentation can be understood as the translation from photos to semantically segmented images. Furthermore, the most representative I2I translation, i.e., style transfer, is to remove the style features of the source domain (distinguishing features, such as the texture of the image) and preserve the content features (high-level semantic features, e.g., color, contrast, and brightness invariant features), and then combine the style features of the target domain to generate the synthetic image. All these tasks can be regarded as translating an image into another image.

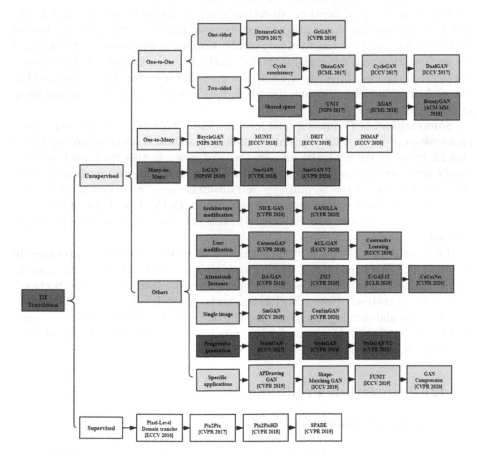

**Fig. 1.** Overview of I2I translation, each color represents a category.

In Fig. 1, we present our classification of the existing I2I translation literature (of course, there will be other classifications from different perspectives). Based on whether depending on paired images or not, I2I translation methods can be classified into supervised and unsupervised categories. Supervised methods need paired datasets for training. However, pairwised data acquisition is difficult for many tasks, constructing pairwise datasets can be costly and time-consuming. This scenario is relatively less studied and typical methods include Pix2Pix [2], Pix2PixHD [3] and SPADE(GauGAN) [4]. In contrast, unsupervised methods only need two different datasets representing the two domains. They can learn the mapping relationship between the two domains by elegantly designed neural networks. As shown in Fig. 1, general unsupervised translation models can be divided into three types: one-to-one (single domain), one-to-many (multi-modal), and many-to-many (multi-domain). In addition, according to other characteristics of the model, unsupervised methods can be subdivided into architecture modification, loss modification, attention-based or instance-based, single image training, and specific application-based aspects. Based on the investigation of literature, we find that the methods of I2I translation proposed in recent years are endless. However, most unsupervised methods have experimented on several datasets selected by the author. There are no uniform evaluation metrics, so few comprehensive articles sort out the whole field's development or compare some mainstream models.

Summarizing, our contributions are four-fold. 1) We have conducted a comprehensive overview of I2I translation(mainly based on GANs) according to the classification. 2) We summarized some critical issues in this field, such as commonly used generators and discriminators, normalization, and evaluation metrics. 3) We analyzed the advantages and disadvantages of various methods and how to correct these shortcomings in subsequent methods in light of the timeline. 4) We pointed out some challenges in this field and the directions for future research.

The remainder of this survey is organized as follows: Sect. 2 provides an overview of GANs that serve as the backbone of many I2I translation methods, some normalization methods, and common quantitative metrics. Section 3 reviews many state-of-the-art(SOTA) methods comprehensively according to the classification and development timeline in Fig. 1. Section 4 summarizes the main challenges and future directions for I2I translation. Finally, we present our conclusion in Sect. 5.

# 2    I2I Translation Preliminaries

## 2.1    Generative Adversarial Networks

Generative adversarial network (GANs), which is proposed by *Goodfellow et al.* [1] in 2014, is an efficient generative model in machine learning. GAN includes two deep neural networks: a generator $G$ that captures the data distribution, and a discriminator $D$ that learns to determine whether a sample is from the ground truth or the generated data. GANs plays a minimax two-player game with loss function $V(D, G)$ as follows:

$$\min_{G} \max_{D} V(D, G) = E_{x \sim Pdata(x)}[\log D(x)] + E_{z \sim Pz(z)}[\log(1 - D(G(z)))]$$

Although GANs have non-convergence and mode collapse problems, it is still a more popular generative model for researchers compared with other generative models. Since the training of GANs only uses backpropagation, the discriminator can be directly used as a measure to calculate the similarity of distribution of data between two domains, which is often better than manual derivation. In addition, GANs can generate clearer and more realistic images than VAEs [11], etc.

Applying GANs as a backbone network to I2I translation models is the most common and effective strategy. The generators of ordinary GANs are stacked by some fully connected layers or convolutional layers used to convert random noise that obeys a specific prior distribution into synthetic samples. However, in I2I translation, the generator's input is the image from the source domain, and the output is the image of the target domain, so the generator's structure will be different from the common ones. Figure 2 shows two different frameworks of generator commonly used in this field.

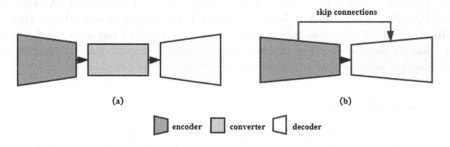

**Fig. 2.** Two different frameworks of generator

(a) In Fig. 2 is an encoder-converter-decoder framework, where the encoder is composed of down-sampling modules stacked by some convolutional layers to extract high-level semantic features. The converter is generally composed of some fully connected layers or residual blocks used to fuse the content features of the input and the style features of the image from the target domain. Moreover, the input and output of the converter are latent vectors of the same size. The decoder is composed of some up-sampling modules stacked by some transposed convolutional layers, and the image is synthesized according to the latent features after fusion. This framework is commonly used in [5, 29] and [35], etc. (b) is an encoder-decoder framework similar to autoencoder(AE), but unlike (a), there is a skip connection similar to U-Net [49] or an additive connection similar to ResNet [45] between the up-sampling and down-sampling modules in the same location, which can better integrate low-level features and high-level features, helps the image to be better translated.

The discriminator is used to perceive the difference between the generated image and the real data. The commonly used discriminator is a patch-based discriminator (PatchGAN) proposed by *P.Isola et al.* [2], which is used to penalize structure at the scale of patches of a smaller size (usually 70Œ70) while accelerating evaluation. The innovation of PatchGAN (fully convolutional networks) is that the final output is not a scalar value, but a matrix $X$. Each element in $X$ represents the patch's score corresponding to the original image. In this way, the local image features can be extracted and represented through the discrimination of each patch, which is conducive to generate higher resolution images. At the same time, after averaging the final classification matrix, the classification can also be realized.

Besides PatchGAN, there are other types of discriminators in I2I translation, such as the content discriminator proposed in DRIT [30], which is used to promote encoders to better separate attributes and content features. Adding this discriminator will provide a stronger constraint on the optimization of the generator. In addition, the multi-scale discriminator based on PatchGAN and residual attention mechanism proposed in NICE-GAN [46] can not only realize the fusion of multi-scale features, but also control the importance of different feature mapping more flexibly, such a discriminator can replace the traditional discriminators and may improve the performance of previous methods, such as Pix2Pix [2] and CycleGAN [5], but this needs to be demonstrated experimentally. In general, the discriminator is not only a classifier but also can be used as a loss constraint or other function. If we want to propose a novel translation method, we may be able to do some research from this perspective.

## 2.2 Normalization

Normalization can accelerate the convergence speed and improve the accuracy of the model. Normalization techniques in deep learning include Batch Normalization (BN) [12], Layer Normalization (LN) [13] and Instance Normalization (IN) [14], etc. In this section, we will introduce several normalization techniques commonly used in I2I translation.

**Instance Normalization (IN)**: IN is essentially a style-normalization, which is equivalent to unifying different images into one style. The artistic style refers to statistical information such as the spatial mean and variance of each feature channel in the image. Style transfer can be achieved by passing the mean and variance of each channel. To ensure the independence between different instances, IN is often used for normalization in I2I translation.

**Adaptive Instance Normalization (AdaIN)**: *Huang Xun et al.* [15] put forward AdaIN, that is, directly use the mean and variance on the corresponding channel of the target domain image as the two normalized affine parameters to realize style transfer. The formula is as follows:

$$AdaIN(x, y) = \sigma(y) \left( \frac{x - \mu(x)}{\sigma(x)} \right) + \mu(y)$$

In the formula, $x$ represents the source domain image and $y$ represents the target domain image. Some latest image translation models use AdaIN to normalize images, such as MUNIT [29], INIT [6], StyleGAN [38], etc.

Apart from the two methods described above, Adaptive Layer-Instance Normalization(AdaLIN) function in U-GAT-IT [35](a combination of LN and AdaIN, using learnable parameters to control the weight of both) can guide the model to control the changes of shape and texture flexibly, and enhance the models robustness. Spatial Adaptive Denormalization(SPADE) is proposed in GauGAN [4], which is a generalization function of the existing normalization function and has the advantages of flexible and controllable. It can be well suited for the translation of semantic images to photos.

### 2.3   Evaluation Metrics

Evaluation metrics of I2I translation models can be divided into subjective and objective metrics. So far, the success of I2I translation models has been based on subjective, qualitative visual comparison on generated images. The subjective evaluation method is similar to the AMT perceptual studies mentioned in [5], which evaluates the model results by organizing some experts or volunteers to score the model results subjectively and rank the final scores.

However, in some complex scenarios (such as makeup transfer), the subjective evaluation method's results will be different due to the participants and make it uncertain. Therefore, we need objective evaluation metrics that refer to the quantitative evaluation of output results by designing algorithms or models without many manual experiments. When we evaluate whether an I2I translation method is complete, we need to consider this method's domain consistency and content consistency. From this perspective, we summarize some of the more commonly used objective evaluation metrics.

**Frechèt Inception Distance (FID)** [17]: FID is a measure of the distance between the feature vectors of the real image and the generated image. The feature of the two groups of images is extracted by the Inception network [20]. The lower the score, the more similar the two groups of images. FID is 0 in the best case, which means that the two images are the same. FID is used to evaluate the quality of images generated by GANs, and lower scores have a high correlation with higher quality images. Other evaluation metrics similar to FID include IS [16] and KID [18], etc.

**Learned Perceptual Image Patch Similarity (LPIPS)** [19]: LPIPS uses the L1 distance between features extracted from AlexNet [21] that pre-trained on ImageNet [22] to measure the diversity of the generated images. The higher the score, the more diversity. LPIPS can be used to measure the diversity of multi-modal translation methods.

**Semantic Segmentation Metrics**: Similar to the FCN-scores mentioned in [2], firstly, we need a pre-trained segmentation network, the generated photo is input into the segmentation network to generate a label, and then the output label is compared with the real label (use per-pixel accuracy, per-class accuracy, and mean class Intersection-Over-Union (Class IOU)) [24]. This metric is only applicable to translate semantic images to photos.

# 3   I2I Translation Methods

## 3.1   Supervised Methods

Supervised I2I translation methods require one-to-one correspondence of images between two domains, which is difficult to achieve. Therefore, there are few supervised methods proposed in recent years. Among them, Pix2Pix [2], Pix2PixHD [3] and SPADE (GauGAN) [4] are the three methods with better performance.

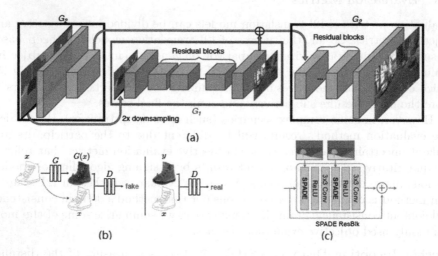

**Fig. 3.** Supervised methods. (a) Generator of Pix2PixHD. (b) Generator of Pix2Pix. (c) SPADE ResBlk. (a) is reproduced from [3], (b) is reproduced from [2] and (c) is reproduced from [4]

Pix2Pix can be regarded as a pioneering work of supervised methods. As shown in Fig. 3(b), to control the direction of the generator's optimization, the input of the discriminator is composed of the generated image (or the real image) and the input image of the generator. The discriminator of Pix2Pix is 70 * 70 patchGANs introduced in Sect. 2.1, and the U-Net-like generator is the second one introduced in Sect. 2.1.

However, Pix2Pix can only generate low-resolution images (usually 128 * 128 resolution), so Pix2PixHD [3] proposed in 2018 can generate images with

2048 * 1024 resolution. As shown in Fig. 3(a), the author proposed to use multi-scale (generally 2–3 scales) generators and discriminators to generate high-resolution images, in which the input of each level of generators is the fusion information of the features of the upper level and the current level, which can better fuse the features of low-level and high-level, to achieve the recovery of the high-resolution image. In addition, the author also improved the resolution of the image by adding feature loss and other methods. Nevertheless, Pix2PixHD has some drawbacks, such as long training time and unable to generate multi-modal images.

NVIDIA proposed GauGAN [4], which solved the problem that Pix2PixHD could not generate multi-modal images since GauGAN added an encoder before the generator to extract the mean and variance of the image from the target domain. By randomly sampling from the approximate Gaussian distribution, the generator can generate multi-modal images. Of course, the most significant innovation of GauGAN is SPADE mentioned in Sect. 2.2, which can effectively compensate for the loss of local semantic information caused by BN and make the generated images more realistic. The high-resolution images can be generated by stacking multiple SPADE ResBlk like Fig. 3(c).

By introducing these three supervised methods, we can find that new methods are better to solve previous methods' shortcomings. For example, high-resolution images can be generated progressively by stacking similar modules, and multi-modal images can be implemented by randomly sampling noise from an approximately Gaussian distribution like VAEs.

## 3.2   Unsupervised Methods

The unsupervised methods can achieve I2I translation without paired data, which makes it more widely used. As mentioned in Sect. 1, according to the mapping relationship between the input and output of the model, we can divide unsupervised methods into one-to-one, one-to-many, and many-to-many, as well as other subdivision branches. The early work of unsupervised style transfer is proposed by *Gatys et al.* [23]. The authors used the VGG19 network to extract the features of images and used the Gram matrix as the mathematical representation of style features. Finally, the translation from the noise image to the image of the target domain can be realized. However, the speed of image generation is greatly affected by the resolution. The higher the resolution, the slower the generation speed, and the larger the model parameters. Moreover, it is easy to be affected by the initial noise image, so the robustness is poor.

**One-to-One**: In 2017, CycleGAN proposed in [5] solved the problems of [23]. CycleGAN consists of two generators and two discriminators, the core innovation is that a translation cycle is formed between two generators in different domains, and cycle consistency loss is proposed to constrain(see Fig. 4). Disco-GAN [25] and DualGAN [26] are similar to CycleGAN but slightly different in the implementation details. We classify these methods as two-sided models based on cycle consistency. Another two-sided model is a UNIT-like framework

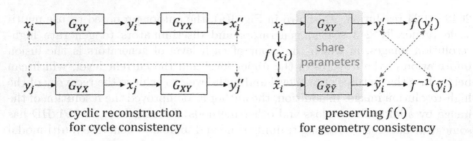

cyclic reconstruction
for cycle consistency

preserving $f(\cdot)$
for geometry consistency

**Fig. 4.** Left: two-sided(CycleGAN). Right: one-sided(GcGAN). Reproduced from [40].

based on the idea that images from different domains can be mapped into the
same shared latent space through different encoders (using the strategy of sharing weights between the last few layers of the encoder and the first few layers
of the generator). The authors constructed a VAE+GAN network, which can
achieve unsupervised I2I translation. Based on a similar idea, XGAN [28] and
BeautyGAN are also proposed.

However, none of these methods can be used for geometric transformation
well, and they all need to construct a cycle to achieve inter-domain translation.
Thus, GcGAN [40] solved these problems. GcGAN found that simple geometric
transformation cannot change the semantic information of the image. So it proposed a geometric consistency function to replace the cycle consistency, which
makes unsupervised translation methods no longer need to go through a cycle to
control the direction of generation(see Fig. 4). Also, DistanceGAN [41] is another
one-sided model, which is based on the idea that the distance between two images
from the same domain will be consistent before and after translation.

Although these one-to-one approaches can achieve unsupervised I2I translation very well, they still cannot perform multi-modal generation (cannot increase
the diversity, a fixed image usually leads to deterministic translation result.) and
multi-domain translation (if there are n domains, n(n-1) generators have to be
trained, see Fig. 6 (a) and (c)).

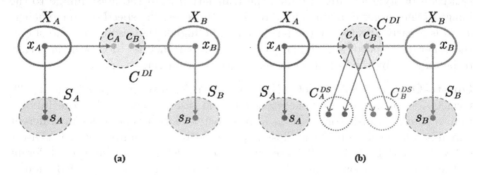

(a)                                    (b)

**Fig. 5.** (a) MUNIT/DRIT. (b) DSMAP. Reproduced from [31].

**One-to-Many**: Multi-modal methods can be well applied to data augmentation. The pioneering work in this subfield includes MUNIT [29] and DRIT [30] proposed in 2018. These two methods are similar, and they are actually an extension of UNIT. The authors further define that the shared space is called content space, and there is a different space at the same time, which is called style space(see Fig. 5 (a)). Supposing content code is a high-dimensional spatial map with complex distribution, while the style code is a low-dimensional vector with Gaussian distribution. In fact, in addition to the advantages of latent space decomposition and resampling can generate multi-modal images, they are essentially similar to UNIT. Besides, the main contribution of DRIT is to propose a content discriminator to constrain the content features of two different domains. However, the number of sub-networks in DRIT is large, so its training speed will be affected to a certain extent. In 2020, DSMAP [31] observed that the shared domain-invariant content space could compromise the ability to represent the content and the mapping of domain-specific makes the content features better align with the target domain, which can improve the quality of translation and handle local and global style transfer scenarios well(see Fig. 5 (b)).

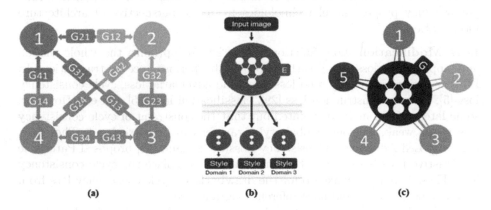

**Fig. 6.** (a) Cross-domain translation. (b) Multi-modal mapping. (c) Multi-domain translation. (a) and (c) are reproduced from [42], (b) is reproduced from [43].

**Many-to-Many**: Multi-domain translation techniques can be applied to complex datasets with multiple sub-classes (celebA, AFHQ [43], etc.), and the training speed of the models are even comparable to that of the one-to-one method while ensuring the translation quality. StarGAN [42], which is one of the most classic methods, only needs one generator to achieve the translation of multiple different domains (by concatenating the image from the source domain and the label from the target domain as the input of the generator). Its discriminator determines whether the image is real or fake and also needs to classify the domain. However, the disadvantage of StarGAN is that it is time-consuming to design domain labels manually. Therefore, StarGAN V2 [43] can directly convert the image from the source domain into style code by adding a style encoder based on StarGAN to replace the manually designed label(see Fig. 6 (b)). Besides, StarGAN V2 also utilizes a mapping network to realize multi-modal image generation.

Following other characteristics, we also subdivided some latest SOTA methods.

**Architecture Modification**: Modifying the network structure is a standard method to improve performance. GANILLA [44] proposed a new generator that can fuse low-level features and high-level features by using additive connections(the encoder is modified based on ResNet18 [45]) and skip connections(in the stage of up-sampling) to preserve content better. Another method, NICE-GAN [46], redefined the role of its discriminator. The authors directly embedded the encoder into the discriminator, that is to say, the first several layers of the discriminator are regarded as encoder. Thus, NICE-GAN no longer requires an independent component for encoding, which makes the structure more compact. Also, unlike existing methods where the discriminator is abandoned after training, the encoder is still kept for inference. This approach gives us some inspiration to try to use different backbones or rethink each component's role, and we may propose novel technologies from the perspective of architecture modification.

**Loss Modification**: Loss function is the key to optimize the whole model, and appropriate loss can greatly improve the performance of translation. In I2I translation, commonly used losses include adversarial loss, cycle consistency loss [5], latent reconstruction loss [29], classification loss [35] and etc. However, some latest SOTA methods pointed out that the constraint of cycle consistency loss is too weak, and only global style transfer can be carried out. Therefore, [32] proposed Adversarial Consistency Loss(ACL), and [33] proposed Patchwise Contrastive Loss based on mutual information to replace the cycle consistency loss. These two losses make up for the drawbacks of cycle consistency loss from different perspectives and have reference significance.

Except for the above two categories, some methods use attention-based networks, such as DA-GAN [34] and U-GAT-IT [35], and instance-based networks such as INIT [6], which can transfer the style of instances well by combining the method of object detection. Another interesting branch includes SinGAN [36] and ConSinGAN [37], training a translation network only by using a single image, which can significantly improve the speed. Besides, I2I translation field also includes StyleGAN-like [38] methods that stack similar modules to progressively generate high-resolution images, which can also be applied to super-resolution. Finally, most current methods are based on specific applications, and there are many promising innovations that we can learn from, for example, APDrawing GAN [7] can reasonably complete the translation from portraits to photos, Shape-Matching GAN [9] can generate artistic fonts with controllable style, and FUNIT [8] can perform an unsupervised translation on datasets with more sample categories and less single class samples, and so on.

# 4    Challenges and Future Directions

Through the overall review of Sect. 3, since *J. Zhu et al.* [5] proposed Cycle-GAN in 2017, most of the influential methods, which are task-agnostic, have focused on the theoretical improvement of the model itself and have been developing towards multi-modal generation and multi-domain translation. After 2019, unsupervised I2I translation pay more attention to applications, such as INIT [6], APDrawing GAN [7], FUNIT [8], Shape-Matching GAN [9] and etc. Generally speaking, I2I translation is gradually developing from theoretical research to practical application.

Despite the generated images are realistic enough, and it is more difficult to distinguish real from fake, there are still many problems to be solved: 1) Mode collapse and unstable training process still exist in all methods using GANs, and these problems become even more severe and challenging when the number of classes is large, and the datasets are unbalanced. 2) To apply I2I translation models into more complex scenes, they need to be lightweight to ensure that some small capacity terminal devices can load them. 3) Some latest SOTA methods may only achieve the best results on specific datasets, so whether their innovation points(new losses or architectures of models) can be widely used is still unknown. 4) There are no unified quantitative evaluation metrics and universally acknowledged datasets for unsupervised I2I translation methods.

Therefore, there are many aspects of I2I translation to explore: 1) It is necessary for us to utilize better tricks of training GANs to ensure that translation models can be optimized in the right direction. 2) Like [47], We can combine other generative models with GANs, and make full use of the advantages of each method to improve the performance of translation. 3) Like [48], under the premise of guaranteeing the translation effect of the existing methods, we need to use a better lightweight method to reduce the complexity of the translation model and speed up the translation as much as possible. 4) We can transfer other machine learning methods to I2I translation, such as super-resolution, attention mechanisms, object detection, to achieve the detailed translation of high-resolution images or background-complex images. 5) We should rethink each component's role in the translation models and then delete some useless or repetitive components to make the end-to-end model more compact and efficient. 6) We are supposed to extend I2I translation models to more complex scenes, such as video image translation, virtual staining of medical image, etc.

In sum, I2I translation has reached a bottleneck stage. Only by continually experimenting and summarizing to solve the problems mentioned above can we further tap into this field's great potential.

# 5    Conclusion

Following the characteristics of the I2I translation methods based on GANs, we have carried out a detailed classification to have a systematic review of the entire field's approaches. We summarized the commonly used generators and discriminator frameworks in this field, as well as the commonly used normalization methods and recommended some evaluation metrics to quantify the experimental results. We also pointed out each approach's pros and cons and how does follow-up work correct these drawbacks. Finally, we discussed the existing challenges and further research directions of this field. In future work, we will conduct comparative experiments based on the statistical results of each method's experimental data and try to improve the performance of the model by combining the excellent components and loss constraints in these methods. We hope that colleagues can draw some inspirations from this survey and can have further innovations and applications in this field.

**Acknowledgements.** This work was supported by the Natural Science Foundation of China (No. 61876016, 61772526) and the Fundamental Research Funds for the Central Universities (2018JBZ006).

# References

1. Goodfellow, I.J., et al.: Generative Adversarial Networks. arXiv:1406.2661 (2014)
2. Isola, P., Zhu, J.-Y., Zhou, T., Efros, A.A.: Image-to-image translation with conditional adversarial networks. arXiv:1611.07004 (2016)
3. Wang, T.-C., Liu, M.-Y., Zhu, J.-Y., Tao, A., Kautz, J., Catanzaro, B.: High-resolution image synthesis and semantic manipulation with conditional GANs. arXiv:1711.11585 (2017)
4. Park, T., Liu, M.-Y., Wang, T.-C., Zhu, J.-Y.: Semantic image synthesis with spatially-adaptive normalization. In: CVPR 2019. arXiv:1903.07291 (2019)
5. Zhu, J.-Y., Park, T., Isola, P., Efros, A.A.: Unpaired image-to-image translation using cycle-consistent adversarial networks. arXiv:1703.10593 (2017)
6. Shen, Z., Huang, M., Shi, J., Xue, X., Huang, T.: Towards instance-level image-to-image translation. arXiv:1905.01744 (2019)
7. Yi, R., Liu, Y.J., Lai, Y.K., Rosin, P.L.: APDrawingGAN: generating artistic portrait drawings from face photos with hierarchical GANs. In: 2019 IEEE/CVF Conference on Computer Vision and Pattern Recognition (CVPR) (2020)
8. Liu, M.-Y., et al.: Few-shot unsupervised image-to-image translation. In: ICCV 2019 (2019). arXiv:1905.01723
9. Yang, S., Wang, Z., Wang, Z., Xu, N., Guo, Z.: Controllable artistic text style transfer via shape-matching GAN. In: 2019 IEEE/CVF International Conference on Computer Vision (ICCV) (2019)
10. Bissoto, A., Valle, E., Avila, S.: The six fronts of the generative adversarial networks. arXiv:1910.13076 (2019)
11. Kingma, D.P., Welling, M.: Auto-encoding variational Bayes. arXiv:1312.6114 (2013)
12. Ioffe, S., Szegedy, C.: Batch normalization: accelerating deep network training by reducing internal covariate shift. arXiv:1502.03167 (2015)
13. Ba, J.L., Kiros, J.R., Hinton, G.E.: Layer normalization. arXiv:1607.06450 (2016)
14. Ulyanov, D., Vedaldi, A., Lempitsky, V.: Instance normalization: the missing ingredient for fast stylization. arXiv:1607.08022 (2016)
15. Huang, X., Belongie, S.: Arbitrary style transfer in real-time with adaptive instance normalization. arXiv:1703.06868 (2017)

16. Salimans, T., Goodfellow, I., Zaremba, W., Cheung, V., Radford, A., Chen, X.: Improved techniques for training GANs. arXiv:1606.03498 (2016)
17. Heusel, M., Ramsauer, H., Unterthiner, T., Nessler, B., Hochreiter, S.: GANs trained by a two time-scale update rule converge to a local nash equilibrium. In: Advances in Neural Information Processing Systems 30 (NIPS 2017) (2017). arXiv:1706.08500
18. Bikowski, M., Sutherland, D.J., Arbel, M., Gretton, A.: Demystifying MMD GANs. arXiv:1801.01401 (2018)
19. Zhang, R., Isola, P., Efros, A.A., Shechtman, E., Wang, O.: The unreasonable effectiveness of deep features as a perceptual metric. arXiv:1801.03924 (2018)
20. Szegedy, C., Vanhoucke, V., Ioffe, S., Shlens, J., Wojna, Z.: Rethinking the inception architecture for computer vision. In: Proceedings of the IEEE Conference on Computer Vision and Pattern Recognition, pp. 28182826 (2016)
21. Krizhevsky, A., Sutskever, I., Hinton, G.: ImageNet classification with deep convolutional neural networks. Adv. Neural Inf. Process. Syst. **25**(2) (2012)
22. Deng, J., Dong, W., Socher, R., Li, L.J., Li, F.F.: ImageNet: a large-scale hierarchical image database. In: IEEE Conference on Computer Vision & Pattern Recognition (2009)
23. Gatys, L.A., Ecker, A.S., Bethge, M.: Image style transfer using convolutional neural networks. In: Computer Vision & Pattern Recognition (2016)
24. Cordts, M., et al.: The cityscapes dataset for semantic urban scene understanding. arXiv:1604.01685 (2016)
25. Kim, T., Cha, M., Kim, H., Lee, J.K., Kim, J.: Learning to discover cross-domain relations with generative adversarial networks. arXiv:1703.05192 (2017)
26. Yi, Z., Zhang, H., Tan, P., Gong, M.: DualGAN: unsupervised dual learning for image-to-image translation. arXiv:1704.02510 (2017)
27. Liu, M.-Y., Breuel, T., Kautz, J.: Unsupervised image-to-image translation networks. arXiv:1703.00848 (2017)
28. Royer, A., et al.: XGAN: unsupervised image-to-image translation for many-to-many mappings. arXiv:1711.05139 (2017)
29. Huang, X., Liu, M.-Y., Belongie, S., Kautz, J.: Multimodal unsupervised image-to-image translation. arXiv:1804.04732 (2018)
30. Lee, H.-Y., Tseng, H.-Y., Huang, J.-B., Singh, M.K., Yang, M.-H.: Diverse image-to-image translation via disentangled representations. arXiv:1808.00948 (2018)
31. Chang, H.-Y., Wang, Z., Chuang, Y.-Y.: Domain-specific mappings for generative adversarial style transfer. arXiv:2008.02198 (2020)
32. Zhao, Y., Wu, R., Dong, H.: Unpaired image-to-image translation using adversarial consistency loss. arXiv:2003.04858 (2020)
33. Park, T., Efros, A.A., Zhang, R., Zhu, J.Y.: Contrastive learning for unpaired image-to-image translation. arXiv:2007.15651 (2020)
34. Ma, S., Fu, J., Chen, C.W., Mei, T.: DA-GAN: instance-level image translation by deep attention generative adversarial networks (with Supplementary Materials). arXiv:1802.06454 (2018)
35. Kim, J., Kim, M., Kang, H., Lee, K.: U-GAT-IT: unsupervised generative attentional networks with adaptive layer-instance normalization for image-to-image translation. arXiv:1907.10830 (2019)
36. Shaham, T.R., Dekel, T., Michaeli, T.: SinGAN: learning a generative model from a single natural image. arXiv:1905.01164 (2019)
37. Hinz, T., Fisher, M., Wang, O., Wermter, S.: Improved techniques for training single-image GANs. arXiv:2003.11512 (2020)

38. Karras, T., Laine, S., Aila, T. A Style-based generator architecture for generative adversarial networks. arXiv:1812.04948 (2018)
39. Karras, T., Laine, S., Aittala, M., Hellsten, J., Lehtinen, J., Aila, T.: Analyzing and improving the image quality of StyleGAN. arXiv:1912.04958 (2019)
40. Fu, H., Gong, M., Wang, C., Batmanghelich, K., Zhang, K., Tao, D.: Geometry-consistent generative adversarial networks for one-sided unsupervised domain mapping. arXiv:1809.05852 (2018)
41. Benaim, S., Wolf, L.: One-sided unsupervised domain mapping (2017). arXiv:1706.00826
42. Choi, Y., Choi, M., Kim, M., Ha, J.-W., Kim, S., Choo, J.: StarGAN: unified generative adversarial networks for multi-domain image-to-image translation. In: 2017, IEEE Conference on Computer Vision and Pattern Recognition (CVPR), pp. 8789–8797 (2018). arXiv:1711.09020
43. Choi, Y., Uh, Y., Yoo, J., Ha, J.-W.: StarGAN v2: diverse image synthesis for multiple domains. arXiv:1912.01865 (2019)
44. Hicsonmez, S., Samet, N., Akbas, E., Duygulu, P.: GANILLA: generative adversarial networks for image to illustration translation. arXiv:2002.05638 (2020)
45. He, K., Zhang, X., Ren, S., Sun, J.: Deep residual learning for image recognition. arXiv:1512.03385 (2015)
46. Chen, R., Huang, W., Huang, B., Sun, F., Fang, B.: Reusing discriminators for encoding: towards unsupervised image-to-image translation. arXiv:2003.00273 (2020)
47. Wan, Z., Zhang, B., Chen, D., Zhang, P., Chen, D., Liao, J., Wen, F.: Bringing old photos back to life. arXiv:2004.09484 (2020)
48. Li, M., Lin, J., Ding, Y., Liu, Z., Zhu, J.-Y., Han, S.: GAN compression: efficient architectures for interactive conditional GANs. arXiv:2003.08936 (2020)
49. Ronneberger, O., Fischer, P., Brox, T.: U-Net: convolutional networks for biomedical image segmentation. arXiv:1505.04597 (2015)

# Fusion Models for Improved Image Captioning

Marimuthu Kalimuthu$^{(\boxtimes)}$, Aditya Mogadala, Marius Mosbach,
and Dietrich Klakow

Spoken Language Systems (LSV), Saarland Informatics Campus,
Saarland University, Saarbrücken, Germany
{mkalimuthu,amogadala,mmosbach,dklakow}@lsv.uni-saarland.de

**Abstract.** Visual captioning aims to generate textual descriptions given images or videos. Traditionally, image captioning models are trained on human annotated datasets such as Flickr30k and MS-COCO, which are limited in size and diversity. This limitation hinders the generalization capabilities of these models while also rendering them liable to making mistakes. Language models can, however, be trained on vast amounts of freely available unlabelled data and have recently emerged as successful language encoders [10] and coherent text generators [4]. Meanwhile, several unimodal and multimodal fusion techniques have been proven to work well for natural language generation [11] and automatic speech recognition [30]. Building on these recent developments, and with the aim of improving the quality of generated captions, the contribution of our work in this paper is two-fold: First, we propose a generic multimodal model fusion framework for caption generation as well as emendation where we utilize different fusion strategies to integrate a pretrained Auxiliary Language Model (AuxLM) within the traditional encoder-decoder visual captioning frameworks. Next, we employ the same fusion strategies to integrate a pretrained Masked Language Model (MLM), namely BERT, with a visual captioning model, viz. *Show, Attend, and Tell*, for emending both syntactic and semantic errors in captions. Our caption emendation experiments on three benchmark image captioning datasets, viz. Flickr8k, Flickr30k, and MSCOCO, show improvements over the baseline, indicating the usefulness of our proposed multimodal fusion strategies. Further, we perform a preliminary qualitative analysis on the emended captions and identify error categories based on the type of corrections.

**Keywords:** Visual captioning · Multimodal/model fusion · Auxiliary language model · AuxLM · Emendation · Natural language generation

## 1 Introduction

The field of deep learning has seen tremendous progress ever since the breakthrough results of AlexNet [16] on the ImageNet Large Scale Visual Recognition Challenge (ILSVRC). Significant algorithmic improvements have since been

© Springer Nature Switzerland AG 2021
A. Del Bimbo et al. (Eds.): ICPR 2020 Workshops, LNCS 12666, pp. 381–395, 2021.
https://doi.org/10.1007/978-3-030-68780-9_32

achieved, both for language [10,31] and visual scene understanding [6,13]. Further, there has been numerous efforts for the joint understanding of language and visual modalities in terms of defining novel tasks, creating benchmark datasets, and proposing new methods to tackle the challenges arising out of the multimodal nature of data [21]. One specific problem that has piqued the interest of researchers and practitioners in Computer Vision (CV) and Natural Language Processing (NLP) is *Visual Captioning*. Considerable progress has been made since the introduction of *Show and Tell* [33], which is an end-to-end model for image captioning. Despite these encouraging developments, the visual captioning models are still brittle, unreliable, prone to making unexplainable mistakes [27], and, most importantly, their performance is nowhere close to human-level understanding. However, although still a black-box, the recent unprecedented progress on language modeling has proven the potential of these models to generate semantically fluent and coherent text [4,26] and encode powerful representations of language using bidirectional context [10]. Building on these developments, we propose to incorporate external language models into visual captioning frameworks to aid and improve their capabilities both for description generation and emendation. Although the proposed architecture (See Fig. 1) could be used for both caption generation and correction, in this paper, we only focus on the task of emending captions. However, we describe the changes needed to the architecture to achieve caption generation. Broadly, our architecture consists of four major components, viz. a *CNN encoder*, an *LSTM decoder*, a *pretrained AuxLM*, and a *Fusion module* (See Fig. 1). To the best of our knowledge, our architecture is novel since the current caption editing approaches [28,29] in the literature do not leverage AuxLMs.

The rest of the paper is organized as follows. In Sect. 2, we briefly review relevant works on caption editing. In Sect. 3, we provide background on fusion strategies that have been empirically shown to work well for neural machine translation, automatic speech recognition, and story generation and introduce our fusion architecture. Following this, we describe our experimental setup including the implementation details of our caption editing model in Sect. 4. We then present our quantitative results along with a short qualitative analysis of the emended captions in Sect. 5. Finally, we conclude our paper in Sect. 6 discussing some future research directions.

## 2   Related Work

Recently, few approaches have been proposed for editing image captions [28,29]. Although these methods have been shown to produce improved quantitative results, they have some limitations such as completely relying on *labelled* data, which is limited in size and diversity, for training. In addition, it is cost-intensive to obtain caption annotations and, sometimes, it is not even possible due to privacy concerns. This is the case, for instance, in the medical domain. Furthermore, these approaches implicitly learn a language model on the decoder-side with limited textual data. Moreover, they do not make use of external language models, i.e., AuxLMs, which can be trained on freely available unlabelled data, are more powerful since they learn rich language representations [10,26], and recently have been trained on enormous amounts of data with billions of parameters [4,26]. To the best of our knowledge, there have been no previous works that incorporate AuxLMs into the caption model either for description generation or to correct errors. To address the above stated limitations and leverage the advantages of AuxLMs as powerful language learners, we propose a generic framework that can accomplish both caption generation and editing tasks depending on the type of AuxLM used.

## 3    Fusion Techniques and Variations

Unimodal and multimodal model fusion has been explored extensively in the context of ASR [7,30], Neural Machine Translation (NMT) [12], and hierarchical story generation [11]. However, to the best of our knowledge, there have been no similar works for visual captioning. In this section, we review these fusion methods and relate them to our goal of achieving image caption generation and emendation by using additional language models, i.e., AuxLMs.

**Deep Fusion.** Gulcehre et al. [12] explored *Deep Fusion* for NMT in which a translation model trained on parallel corpora and an AuxLM trained on monolingual, target language data are combined using a trainable single layer neural network model. Typically, the AuxLM is an autoregressive LSTM-based recurrent neural network [20] while the translation model follows a typical sequence-to-sequence (Seq2Seq) [8] encoder-decoder architecture. To achieve *Deep Fusion*, a gate is learned from the hidden state of AuxLM and then concatenated with the hidden state of the translation model.

The drawback of this approach is that both the AuxLM and the translation model are trained separately and kept frozen while the fusion layer is trained. Hence, they never get a chance to communicate and adapt their parameters *during* training. This forces these models to learn redundant representations.

**Cold Fusion.** To address the limitation of *Deep Fusion*, Sriram et al. [30] introduced the so-called *Cold Fusion* strategy for ASR. The mechanism uses a pretrained AuxLM while training the Seq2Seq model. The AuxLM is still kept frozen as in the case of *Deep Fusion*, however the parameters of the fusion layer and the Seq2Seq decoder are trained together, leveraging the already-learned language representations of AuxLM. For more details see Sect. 3.2.

**Hierarchical Fusion.** In a similar vein, Fan et al. [11] has explored a sophisticated fusion strategy for textual story generation in a hierarchical fashion where they combine a *pretrained* convolutional Seq2Seq model with a trainable convolutional Seq2Seq model. More specifically, the hidden states of a pretrained Seq2Seq model are fused with the hidden states of a trainable Seq2Seq model using a slightly modified version of the *Cold Fusion* [30] approach. We call this scheme as *Hierarchical Fusion* hereafter.

Considering the advantages of the fusion techniques of Sriram et al. [30] and Fan et al. [11] over *Deep Fusion*, we adapt them in our fusion model framework.

### 3.1   Auxiliary Language Model

Depending on the task, i.e., caption generation or editing, two classes of language models can be used as AuxLMs. For caption generation, since we will not have access to the right-side context during test time, an autoregressive (i.e., causal) language model [3,4,19,26] that predicts the next token using only the left-side context is qualified to be used as the AuxLM. For a caption editing task, however, a bidirectionally contextualized language model, for example BERT [10], would be better suited as AuxLM since they better encode sequences than their unidirectional counterparts. Also, intuitively, since our task is to edit captions, we already have a noisy version of captions (either from the baseline or from other off-the-shelf caption models). If any errors are detected, we want to correct them, but otherwise leave them unmodified. In our experiments, we use a pre-trained BERT model (uncased) that has been trained on English Wikipedia and the BooksCorpus using a combination of Masked Language Modeling (MLM) and next-sentence prediction objectives. Although it is possible to fine-tune the pretrained AuxLMs [22] on the target domain (the image captions in our case) before integrating it in the fusion model, we did not perform this step in our experiments. However, the fine tuning process would likely prove to be beneficial if we intend to adapt the AuxLMs to more focused domains such as medical [25] or remote sensing [18] and we leave this pursuit for future work.

### 3.2   Fusion Strategies and Architecture

Inspired by the success of multimodal fusion strategies for ASR [7,30] and uni-modal fusion for NLG [11,12], we slightly modify these fusion schemes and utilize them for the task of emending image captions. By doing so, we leverage the rich language representations of AuxLMs to achieve sentence-level coherency and grammatical correctness in the emended captions.

Figure 1 depicts the *general* architecture of the proposed fusion model. It contains four major components, namely a *ConvNet encoder*, an *LSTM decoder*, a *BERT encoder* (pretrained MLM), and a *Fusion module*. The architecture is flexible and can be used for two tasks, i.e., visual captioning and caption emen-dation, depending on the type of AuxLM chosen. For caption emendation, a text encoder such as BERT is used as an AuxLM. The LSTM decoder processes the sequence from left-to-right whereas the BERT model utilizes the entire sequence due to its inherent nature of encoding contextualized representation.

For the visual captioning task, the AuxLM must be an autoregressive model since we do not have access to the whole sequence at inference time. One pos-sibility could be to replace the *BERT MLM* component with an LSTM-based

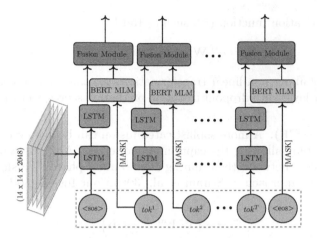

**Fig. 1.** Architecture of our proposed fusion model. The encoded image is fed to the LSTM decoder only at the first time step. *BERT MLM* [10] has been pretrained to predict the masked token at current time step whereas the LSTM decoder is trained to predict the next token given all previous tokens. The *Fusion Module* can be any instance of the fusion schemes discussed in Sect. 3.2.

AuxLM or the recently proposed (and more powerful) Transformer-based [31] autoregressive language model GPT-3 [4].

Further, for both captioning and emendation tasks, the *Fusion Module* component is flexible enough to support any sophisticated fusion method, which provides a framework and an opportunity for future works to come up with improved fusion schemes. In addition, the architecture could be employed in a domain-adapted way for visual captioning by integrating an AuxLM that has been trained in the domain of interest. There has been growing interest in recent years to automatically generate descriptions for medical images[1] such as radiology outputs [14, 25]. The domain adapted AuxLM can be useful particularly in settings where labelled image caption data is scarce. However, unlabelled textual data is usually abundant. In such scenarios, an AuxLM can be trained on the target domain data and integrated into our fusion model framework for generating target domain specific image descriptions.

We now introduce the notations of hidden states used in our fusion model. Following Sriram et al. [30], we represent the final layer hidden states of pretrained BERT and trainable LSTM decoder as $h^{MLM}$ and $h^{LSTM}$ respectively.

**Simple Fusion (SF).** One of the simplest possible fusion mechanisms is through the concatenation of the hidden states of pretrained AuxLM and trainable visual captioning model, followed by a single projection layer with some

---

[1] https://www.imageclef.org/2020/medical/caption/.

non-linear activation function ($\sigma$), such as ReLU.

$$\mathbf{g}_t = \sigma\left(\mathbf{W}[\mathbf{h}_t^{LSTM}; \mathbf{h}_t^{MLM}] + \mathbf{b}\right) \tag{1a}$$

The output of above non-linear transformation ($\mathbf{g}_t$) can then be passed through a single linear layer with dropout to obtain prediction scores over the vocabulary.

**Cold Fusion (CF).** A more sophisticated fusion can be achieved by introducing gates, thereby allowing the captioning model and AuxLM to moderate the information flow between them during the training phase. We slightly modify the cold fusion approach of Sriram et al. [30] in our fusion model which is as follows:

$$\mathbf{h}_t^{LM} = \sigma\left(\mathbf{W}[\mathbf{h}_t^{MLM}] + \mathbf{b}\right) \tag{2a}$$

$$\mathbf{g}_t = \sigma\left(\mathbf{W}[\mathbf{h}_t^{LSTM}; \mathbf{h}_t^{LM}] + \mathbf{b}\right) \tag{2b}$$

$$\mathbf{h}_t^{CF} = [\mathbf{h}_t^{LSTM}; \left(\mathbf{g}_t \circ \mathbf{h}_t^{LM}\right)] \tag{2c}$$

$$\mathbf{r}_t^{CF} = \sigma\left(\mathbf{W}[\mathbf{h}_t^{CF}] + \mathbf{b}\right) \tag{2d}$$

As with simple fusion, the representation $\mathbf{r}_t^{CF}$ is followed by a single linear layer with dropout (not shown here) to obtain prediction scores over the vocabulary.

**Hierarchical Fusion (HF).** In the context of text generation, an advanced fusion mechanism based on *Cold Fusion* has been introduced by Fan et al. [11] for the open-ended and creative task of story generation. We adopt their way of model fusion with minor modifications, in the spirit of keeping the model simple. More specifically, after learning two separate gates followed by a concatenation, we only use a single linear layer with GLU activations [9] instead of 5. Further, to capture the rich sequence representation for caption editing, we use an MLM as AuxLM instead of a convolutional Seq2Seq model. We refer to Fan et al. [11] for full details of their fusion mechanism.

$$\mathbf{h}_t^C = \left[\mathbf{h}_t^{MLM}; \mathbf{h}_t^{LSTM}\right] \tag{3a}$$

$$\mathbf{g}_t^{left} = \sigma\left(\mathbf{W}[\mathbf{h}_t^C] + \mathbf{b}\right) \circ \mathbf{h}_t^C \tag{3b}$$

$$\mathbf{g}_t^{right} = \mathbf{h}_t^C \circ \left(\sigma\left(\mathbf{W}[\mathbf{h}_t^C] + \mathbf{b}\right)\right) \tag{3c}$$

$$\mathbf{g}_t^C = GLU\left([\mathbf{g}_t^{left}; \mathbf{g}_t^{right}]\right) \tag{3d}$$

$$\mathbf{g}_t^{lp} = \mathbf{W}[\mathbf{g}_t^C] + \mathbf{b} \tag{3e}$$

$$\mathbf{g}_t^f = GLU\left(\mathbf{g}_t^{lp}\right) \tag{3f}$$

Again, the result of the final GLU (i.e., $\mathbf{g}_t^f$) is passed through a single linear layer with dropout to obtain prediction scores over the image caption vocabulary.

In all our fusion methods (i.e., SF, CF, and HF), ; represents concatenation, ○ stands for hadamard product, and $\sigma$ indicates a non-linear activation function, for which we use ReLU. The gating parameters $\mathbf{W}$ and $\mathbf{b}$, which are part of the *Fusion Module* (see Fig. 1), are learned while training the LSTM decoder of the fusion model whereas all the parameters of BERT MLM are kept frozen.

# 4   Experiments

We train one baseline and three fusion models on the three commonly used image captioning datasets: Flickr8k, Flickr30k, and MS-COCO. Descriptions and implementation details are given in the following sections.

## 4.1   Baseline

This will be the model without any AuxLM component in its architecture. Any off-the-shelf visual captioning model satisfying this condition can be used as a baseline. The only requirement is that it should be possible to generate captions given the test set images from the dataset in question. In our experiments, we use *Show, Attend, and Tell* [35] where we replace the original VGGNet with ImageNet pretrained ResNet-101 [13] which encodes the images to a feature map of size $14 \times 14 \times 2048$. For the decoder, we use the standard LSTM with two hidden layers. After training, we use a beam size of 5 for generating captions on the test sets of respective datasets.

## 4.2   Fusion Model Training

For each of the datasets, we train three caption models with different initializations for all the fusion techniques (i.e., SF, CF, and HF) proposed in Sect. 3.2.

**Implementation Details.** First, we lowercase the captions and tokenize them using WordPiece[2] tokenization [34] in the same way the BERT MLM model was trained. This consistency in tokenization is important for successful training since the captioning model relies on AuxLM for the hidden state representations at all time steps throughout the training and testing phases. Tokens appearing less than 5 times are replaced with a special <unk> token yielding a vocabulary size of 25k. We implement our fusion models in PyTorch [24].

**Decoder and Fusion Module Training.** The images are rescaled to a fixed size of $256 \times 256$ and encoded using ResNet101 [13] pretrained on ImageNet and kept frozen throughout training. As with the baseline model, we use an LSTM with 2 hidden layers and set the embedding and decoder dimensions to 1024. The LSTM decoder takes the token at current time step along with previous history

---

[2] https://github.com/google-research/bert.

and predicts the next token. The BERT MLM model, however, consumes the entire sequence with the token at the next time step being masked using a special [MASK] token and it predicts this masked token (See Fig. 1). The hidden state representations of both LSTM decoder and BERT are then passed to the *Fusion Module*, which can be any one of the fusion mechanisms discussed in Sect. 3.2, to predict the next token (seen from the perspective of the LSTM decoder).

We minimize the Cross Entropy loss using the Adam optimizer [15] with a learning rate of $5e^{-4}$ and a batch size of 128. Initially, the model is scheduled to be trained for 7 epochs. However, the learning rate is halved or an early stopping is triggered if the validation BLEU did not improve for 2 and 4 consecutive epochs respectively.

**Caption Emendation.** After the fusion model is trained, it can be used in inference mode to correct errors in the captions. While decoding, at time-step $t$, the LSTM predicts $(t+1)^{th}$ token based on left-side history whereas BERT MLM predicts the [MASK]ed $(t+1)^{th}$ token based on the bidirectional context. This process continues until a special $<eos>$ symbol is predicted. As with the baseline model, we again use the same beam size 5 during our evaluations.

# 5   Results

We evaluate our models using both quantitative and qualitative approaches. In the following, we present each of them separately.

## 5.1   Quantitative Analysis

To evaluate our proposed models i.e., baseline and the fusion approaches, we use the standard metrics used for image captioning such as BLEU-{1-4} [23], METEOR [2], ROUGE-L [17], CIDEr [32], and SPICE [1]. Table 1 presents the average scores over three runs on the test sets of "Karpathy split"[3] on the respective datasets.

It can be observed from Table 1 that all our fusion models outperform the baseline model. However, when we compare performance of fusion models with one another we comprehend that there is no considerable difference. To be specific, on the MS-COCO dataset the Cold Fusion strategy outperforms other fusion techniques in all metrics while there is no clear winner for both Flickr8k and Flickr30k. Nevertheless we observe for the Flickr8k and Flickr30k datasets that the Simple Fusion model is a preferable option, since it gives the largest BLEU-4 score. This can be attributed to our optimization criterion since all our models are optimized for BLEU-4 while training. This leads to the increase of the BLEU-4 score; especially for the Simple Fusion model trained on Flickr8k and Flickr30k which are much smaller datasets in comparison to MS-COCO.

---

[3] https://cs.stanford.edu/people/karpathy/deepimagesent.

**Table 1.** Results of proposed fusion methods on three benchmark image captioning datasets. BL-Baseline, SF-Simple fusion, CF - Cold fusion, HF - HNSG fusion, B-n - BLEU, M - METEOR, R-L - ROUGE-L, C - CIDEr, and S - SPICE.

| Dataset | Model | Automatic Evaluation Measures | | | | | | | |
|---|---|---|---|---|---|---|---|---|---|
| | | B-1 | B-2 | B-3 | B-4 | M | R-L | C | S |
| Flickr8k | BL | 62.8 | 44.9 | 31.4 | 21.3 | 20.6 | 47.1 | 55.1 | 14.3 |
| | SF | **64.6** | 46.6 | **32.8** | **22.8** | 21.2 | **47.8** | **56.9** | **14.8** |
| | CF | 64.5 | **46.7** | 32.7 | **22.8** | **21.3** | 47.6 | 56.5 | 14.6 |
| | HF | 64.1 | 45.8 | 32 | 21.8 | 20.9 | 47 | 55.5 | 14.4 |
| Flickr30k | BL | 63.3 | 44.4 | 30.9 | 21.6 | 19.2 | 44.5 | 45.1 | 13.2 |
| | SF | **64.7** | 45.6 | **32.0** | **22.4** | 19.7 | 44.9 | **46.7** | 13.6 |
| | CF | 64.5 | **45.7** | 31.8 | 22.1 | **19.8** | 45 | 46.3 | **13.7** |
| | HF | 64.6 | 45.4 | 31.7 | 22 | 19.4 | 45 | 46.2 | 13.3 |
| MSCOCO | BL | 70.1 | 52.8 | 38.4 | 28 | 24.5 | 51.8 | 91.5 | 17.5 |
| | SF | 70.8 | 53.7 | 40.4 | 30.2 | 25.1 | 52.6 | 94.6 | 17.8 |
| | CF | **71** | **53.9** | **40.7** | **30.5** | **25.3** | **52.9** | **95** | **17.9** |
| | HF | 70.9 | 53.8 | 40.6 | 30.5 | 25 | 52.7 | 94.8 | 17.8 |

## 5.2 Qualitative Analysis

In Figure 2, we present the token emendation distributions of the fusion techniques on all three datasets. When comparing the edits made by different fusion techniques, the distribution is similar. To understand edit distributions among datasets, we define *token edit range* as the range between smallest possible token edits, which is 1, to largest possible token edits, which is the maximum length of captions. We observe that the token edit range (1–3 for MS-COCO) is smaller than Flickr8k (1–5) and Flickr30k (1–4) even though MS-COCO is about 14x and 4x larger than Flickr8k and Flickr30k respectively. This indicates the challenging nature of the Flickr caption datasets where the baseline model makes more mistakes, for which case our fusion model editing has been more helpful.

Owing to the criticism of the BLEU metric to correlate poorly with human judgements [5], we perform a preliminary study on the emendations of our fusion models to better understand the *quality* of emended captions. We identify several types of emendations and group them broadly into the following five categories based on whether the langauge or image-related attributes have been changed in the caption.

1. Gender: Modification of gender to correctly describe image.
2. Color: Modification of color to correctly describe image.
3. Specificity: Emendations to achieve specific captions instead of generic ones.
4. Syntactic: Emendation to achieve syntactic correctness.
5. Semantic: Emendations to correctly describe the scene.

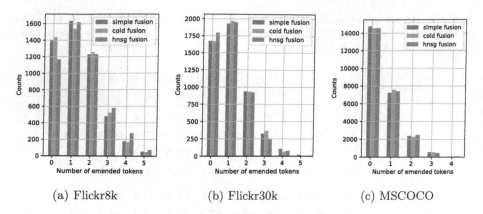

(a) Flickr8k          (b) Flickr30k          (c) MSCOCO

**Fig. 2.** Distribution of (token) corrections made by fusion models on Flickr8k, Flickr30k, and MS-COCO. X-axis represents how many tokens have been changed by the fusion model while the Y-axis shows the frequencies.

It should however be noted that this classification has been done with a preliminary study and a comprehensive human evaluation is needed to arrive at a more fine-grained classification. For illustrations, see Appendix A.

## 6   Conclusion

In this paper, we have proposed a generic multimodal model fusion framework that can be utilized for both caption generation and editing tasks depending on the type of AuxLM that is integrated in the fusion model. We have implemented a caption editing model by integrating a pretrained BERT model and showed improved results over the baseline model on three image captioning benchmark datasets. Further, we conducted a preliminary qualitative analysis on the emended captions and identified a litany of categories based on the image or language-related attributes modified in the captions. For the future work, we plan to focus on three aspects. First, we will focus on utilizing the proposed fusion model for the *caption generation* task using a state-of-the-art autoregressive language model. Second, we aspire to employ our fusion model for automatic description generation of medical images while training a domain-adapted AuxLM. Third, we plan to conduct a human evaluation on the emended captions and come up with a fine-grained classification of errors corrected by our fusion model.

**Acknowledgements.** This work was funded by the Deutsche Forschungsgemeinschaft (DFG, German Research Foundation) – project-id 232722074 – SFB 1102. We extend our thanks to Matthew Kuhn for painstakingly proofing the whole manuscript.

# A    Appendix

Here we provide examples of (token) corrections made by the fusion models and categorize the edits into one of the following five categories: (i) Gender (ii) Color (iii) Specificity (iv) Syntactic (v) Semantic, based on the nature of change.

The above classification has been provided only for the purpose of preliminary illustration. For a thorough understanding of the trends in caption emendations and to draw conclusions, a detailed study using human evaluation should be performed on all three datasets. We leave this aspiration for future work. In the following examples, we color the incorrect tokens in red, the correct replacements in green, and the equally valid tokens in brown.

**Semantic Correction.** This section presents examples where the fusion models have corrected few tokens in the baseline captions so as to make them semantically valid with respect to the image. Edits to achieve semantic correctness may include emendation of visual attributes such as colors, objects, object size, etc. (Figs. 3 and 4).

*baseline*:
a man wearing a black hat and red hat stands in front of a brick wall

*simple fusion*:
a man in a black jacket and black hat stands in front of a brick wall

**Fig. 3.** An example illustrating the correction of semantic errors in the captions by our simple fusion model.

baseline:
a man standing next to a sheep in a field

cold fusion:
a man standing next to cows in a field

**Fig. 4.** Another example to show correction of semantic errors with cold fusion.

**Gender Alteration.** This section provides an illustration of the case where the fusion models corrected the wrong gender of captions from the baseline model (Fig. 5).

baseline:
a woman riding a wave on top of a surfboard

cold fusion:
a man riding a wave on top of a surfboard

**Fig. 5.** An example of cold fusion approach achieving gender correction.

**Specificity.** This deals with emendations of fusion models where the corrected captions end up describing the images more precisely than the baseline captions (Fig. 6).

baseline:
a person in a helmet is riding a wave

hierarchical fusion:
a man wearing a harness is riding a wave

**Fig. 6.** An example to show achievement of specificity with hierarchical fusion.

**Syntactic Correction.** In this section, we show an example to demonstrate the case where syntactic errors such as token repetitions in the baseline captions are correctly emended by the fusion models (Fig. 7).

> *baseline*:
> a white bowl filled with bananas and bananas
>
> *simple fusion*:
> a white bowl filled with bananas and nuts

**Fig. 7.** Replacement of repetitive tokens with a correct alternative.

**Color Correction.** In this part, we show an example to illustrate the case where the fusion models emended color attributes in the captions of the baseline model (Fig. 8).

> *baseline*:
> a vase filled with pink flowers on a table
>
> *cold fusion*:
> a vase filled with purple flowers on a table

**Fig. 8.** An example of cold fusion achieving emendation of color attribute.

# References

1. Anderson, P., Fernando, B., Johnson, M., Gould, S.: SPICE: semantic propositional image caption evaluation. In: Leibe, B., Matas, J., Sebe, N., Welling, M. (eds.) ECCV 2016. LNCS, vol. 9909, pp. 382–398. Springer, Cham (2016). https://doi.org/10.1007/978-3-319-46454-1_24
2. Banerjee, S., Lavie, A.: METEOR: an automatic metric for MT evaluation with improved correlation with human judgments. In: Proceedings of the ACL Workshop on Intrinsic and Extrinsic Evaluation Measures for Machine Translation and/or Summarization, pp. 65–72. Association for Computational Linguistics (2005)
3. Bengio, Y., Ducharme, R., Vincent, P., Janvin, C.: A neural probabilistic language model. J. Mach. Learn. Res. **3**, 1137–1155 (2003)
4. Brown, T.B., et al.: Language models are few-shot learners. CoRR abs/2005.14165 (2020), https://arxiv.org/abs/2005.14165
5. Callison-Burch, C., Osborne, M., Koehn, P.: Re-evaluating the role of Bleu in machine translation research. In: 11th Conference EACL, Trento, Italy (2006)
6. Carion, N., Massa, F., Synnaeve, G., Usunier, N., Kirillov, A., Zagoruyko, S.: End-to-end object detection with transformers. CoRR abs/2005.12872 (2020)
7. Cho, J., et al.: Language model integration based on memory control for sequence to sequence speech recognition. In: ICASSP, Brighton, United Kingdom, pp. 6191–6195 (2019)
8. Cho, K., et al.: Learning phrase representations using RNN encoder-decoder for statistical machine translation. In: Proceedings of EMNLP, pp. 1724–1734 (2014)
9. Dauphin, Y.N., Fan, A., Auli, M., Grangier, D.: Language modeling with gated convolutional networks. In: Proceedings of the 34th ICML, pp. 933–941 (2017)
10. Devlin, J., Chang, M.W., Lee, K., Toutanova, K.: BERT: pre-training of deep bidirectional transformers for language understanding. In: Proceedings of NAACL 2019, Minneapolis, pp. 4171–4186 (2019). https://doi.org/10.18653/v1/n19-1423
11. Fan, A., Lewis, M., Dauphin, Y.: Hierarchical neural story generation. In: Proceedings of the 56th Annual Meeting of ACL 2018, Melbourne, pp. 889–898 (2018)
12. Gülçehre, Ç., et al.: On using monolingual corpora in neural machine translation. CoRR abs/1503.03535 (2015), http://arxiv.org/abs/1503.03535
13. He, K., Zhang, X., Ren, S., Sun, J.: Deep residual learning for image recognition. In: Proceedings of the IEEE Conference on CVPR 2016, pp. 770–778 (2016)
14. Kalimuthu, M., Nunnari, F., Sonntag, D.: A competitive deep neural network approach for the imageclefmed caption 2020 task. In: Working Notes of CLEF 2020, Thessaloniki. CEUR Workshop Proceedings, vol. 2696. CEUR-WS.org (2020)
15. Kingma, D.P., Ba, J.: Adam: a method for stochastic optimization. In: 3rd International Conference on Learning Representations, ICLR, San Diego (2015)
16. Krizhevsky, A., Sutskever, I., Hinton, G.E.: Imagenet classification with deep convolutional neural networks. In: NIPS 2012, Lake Tahoe, pp. 1106–1114 (2012)
17. Lin, C.Y.: ROUGE: a package for automatic evaluation of summaries. In: Text Summarization Branches Out, pp. 74–81. Assoc. for Comp. Linguistics (2004)
18. Lu, X., Wang, B., Zheng, X., Li, X.: Exploring models and data for remote sensing image caption generation. Trans. Geosci. Remote Sens. **56**, 2183–2195 (2017)
19. Merity, S., Keskar, N.S., Socher, R.: Regularizing and optimizing LSTM language models. In: Proceedings of ICLR 2018, Vancouver, Conference Track Proceedings (2018)

20. Mikolov, T., Karafiát, M., Burget, L., Cernocký, J., Khudanpur, S.: Recurrent neural network based language model. In: INTERSPEECH, pp. 1045–1048 (2010)
21. Mogadala, A., Kalimuthu, M., Klakow, D.: Trends in integration of vision and language research: a survey of tasks, datasets, and methods. CoRR abs/1907.09358 (2019), http://arxiv.org/abs/1907.09358, (Accepted at the Journal of AI Research)
22. Mosbach, M., Andriushchenko, M., Klakow, D.: On the stability of fine-tuning BERT: misconceptions, explanations, and strong baselines. CoRR abs/2006.04884 (2020), https://arxiv.org/abs/2006.04884
23. Papineni, K., Roukos, S., Ward, T., Zhu, W.J.: BLEU: a method for automatic evaluation of machine translation. In: Proceedings of ACL, pp. 311–318 (2002)
24. Paszke, A., Gross, S., Massa, F., Lerer, A., Bradbury, J., Chanan, G., Killeen, T., Lin, Z., Gimelshein, N., Antiga, L., et al.: PyTorch: an imperative style, high-performance deep learning library. NeurIPS **2019**, 8026–8037 (2019)
25. Pelka, O., Friedrich, C.M., Garcıa Seco de Herrera, A., Müller, H.: Overview of the imageclefmed 2020 concept prediction task: medical image understanding. In: CLEF2020 Working Notes, CEUR Workshop Proceedings, vol. 2696 (2020)
26. Radford, A., Wu, J., Child, R., Luan, D., Amodei, D., Sutskever, I.: Language models are unsupervised multitask learners. OpenAI blog **1**(8), 9 (2019)
27. Rohrbach, A., Hendricks, L.A., Burns, K., Darrell, T., Saenko, K.: Object hallucination in image captioning. In: Proceedings of EMNLP Brussels, pp. 4035–4045 (2018)
28. Sammani, F., Elsayed, M.: Look and modify: modification networks for image captioning. In: 30th BMVC 2019, Cardiff, UK, p. 75. BMVA Press (2019)
29. Sammani, F., Melas-Kyriazi, L.: Show, edit and tell: a framework for editing image captions. In: Proceedings of CVPR 2020, Seattle, pp. 4808–4816. IEEE (2020)
30. Sriram, A., Jun, H., Satheesh, S., Coates, A.: Cold fusion: training seq2seq models together with language models. In: Proceedings of Interspeech 2018, pp. 387–391 (2018)
31. Vaswani, A., Shazeer, N., Parmar, N., Uszkoreit, J., Jones, L., Gomez, A.N., Kaiser, L., Polosukhin, I.: Attention is all you need. NIPS **2017**, 5998–6008 (2017)
32. Vedantam, R., Lawrence Zitnick, C., Parikh, D.: CIDEr: consensus-based image description evaluation. In: Proceedings of CVPR 2015, pp. 4566–4575. IEEE CS (2015)
33. Vinyals, O., Toshev, A., Bengio, S., Erhan, D.: Show and tell: aeural image caption generator. In: CVPR, pp. 3156–3164. IEEE Computer Society (2015)
34. Wu, Y., et al.: Google's neural machine translation system: bridging the gap between human and machine translation. CoRR abs/1609.08144 (2016), http://arxiv.org/abs/1609.08144
35. Xu, K., et al.: Show, attend and tell: neural image caption generation with visual attention. In: International Conference on Machine Learning, pp. 2048–2057 (2015)

# From Bottom to Top: A Coordinated Feature Representation Method for Speech Recognition

Lixia Zhou[ID] and Jun Zhang[(✉)][ID]

School of Information Engineering, Guangdong University of Technology, Guangzhou
510006, Guangdong, China
jzhang@gdut.edu.cn

**Abstract.** This article introduces a novel coordinated representation method, termed MFCC aided sparse representation (MSR), for speech recognition. The proposed MSR combines a top level sparse representation feature with the conventional MFCC, i.e., a bottom level feature of speech, so that complex information of various hidden attributes in the speech can be contained. A neural network architecture with attention mechanism has also been designed to validate the effective of the proposed MSR for speech recognition. Experiments on the TIMIT database show that significant performance improvements, in terms of recognition accuracy, can be obtained by the proposed MSR compared with the scenarios that adopt the MFCC or the sparse representation solely.

**Keywords:** MFCC Aided Sparse Representation (MSR) · Attention mechanism · Speech recognition

## 1 Introduction

In traditional speech recognition systems, the speech feature generally extracted from original speech signal directly. There are many commonly features such as raw speech samples [1–3], power normalized cepstral coefficient (PNCC)[4], auditory filterbank learning based feature (AFL) [5], and MFCC. However, these features are some bottom level features extracted from the original speech, and usually contain redundant information, which will affect the recognition performance. Some studies have shown that the performance of speech recognition system based on sparse representation (SR) which as a top level feature, are better than using some bottom level features such as MFCC features [6,7]. In sparse representation of the speech signal, the atomic sequence of the dictionary is used to derive the SR of the speech frame. The quality of the features determines the classification performance of the model, therefore, it is required

This work was supported in part by the NSFC under Grant 61973088, and in part by the NSF of Guangdong under Grant 2019A1515011371.

to include as many features related as possible to make the features more conducive to classify [8]. But only using the bottom level signal features or SR to classify, this monomodal feature is not so suitable for speech signals, which cannot fully express complex hidden information in speech, and a simple classification network also cannot work well for speech recognition such as GMM-HMM, DNN-HMM and MLP etc. used in [8–10]

This paper propose a coordinated feature representation method that combines a top level sparse representation feature with the conventional MFCC, and send it to a neural network with attention mechanism for classification. We demonstrate the proposed MSR retains more complex information of various hidden attributes in the speech and also supplements the features of monomodal. These supplementary information greatly improve the classification performance of the speech recognition system. In this work, MFCC features extracted from the original audio data frame is used as the initial data, K-singular value decomposition(KSVD) is used to extract some distinguishing information features in the data [11]. Instead of randomly selecting data as the initial data of the dictionary, we will select some frames from the MFCC features in a certain way to train the dictionary. In terms of sparse feature solving, considering that the audio data may contain noise, we use the Basis Pursuit De-Noising algorithm (BPDN) [12], as a comparison, we also adopts the Orthogonal Match Pursuit (OMP) method [9]. In terms of classification, we use a recurrent neural network model based on the attention mechanism.

The framework of the article is designed as follows: Section 2 briefly explains the sparse representation; Introduces the proposed MSR, a novel method of training dictionary and the neural network for speech recognition in Sect. 3; Section 4 introduces the details of the experimental settings; Analysis of the experimental results in Sect. 5; Section 6 concludes this article.

## 2   Sparse Representation of Speech Signals

In essence, the SR of the signal is to express the MFCC features linearly through a dictionary, which as $X = DA$. The matrix $X = [x_1, x_2, \ldots, x_t] \in \mathbb{R}^{n \times t}$ represents the MFCC features as original data,$x_t$represents the $t$-th frame data with $n$-D. Assuming that SR of data $X$ on the dictionary $D \in \mathbb{R}^{n \times k}$ is $A \in \mathbb{R}^{k \times t}$, learning $D$ and solving sparse representation $A$ can be transformed into the following optimization problem:

$$\underset{D,A}{\arg\min} \quad \forall_i \ \mathcal{F}(\alpha_i) \quad \text{s.t.} \quad \|X - DA\|_F^2 \leqslant \lambda \tag{1}$$

Where $\alpha_i$ is $i$th column of $A$, $\lambda$ is the regular parameter, $\|.\|$ is the norm solution, $\ell_0$ norm minimizationis can used to derive SR as follows:

$$A = \underset{A}{\arg\min} \ \forall_i \ \|\alpha_i\|_0 \quad \text{s.t.} \quad \|X - DA\|_F^2 \leqslant \lambda \tag{2}$$

One of the key steps in solving SR is a good dictionary, various methods have been proposed in the literature to design dictionaries, including analytical and learned [13,14]. Commonly used analysis dictionaries include wavelet dictionaries and overcomplete DCT dictionaries. Although they are simple and easy to implement, they have a single form of signal expression and are not adaptive, making them unsuitable for speech signals. The learning dictionary has a strong adaptive ability and can better adapt to different data. Experimental observations show that learning dictionaries can effectively model the changes in the data [15].

The second is to solve the sparse representation $A$. Commonly used solving methods include OMP, Basis Pursuit (BP), Match Pursuit (MP), BPDN and other algorithms to transform the above optimization problem into solving $\ell_0$ norm or $\ell_1$ norm. For speech data, different speech regions have variable sparsity in the representation. Therefore, it is not recommended to fix the same sparsity in the representation of each speech frame [8].

# 3   The Proposed MSR for Speech Recognition

## 3.1   MFCC Aided Sparse Representation (MSR)

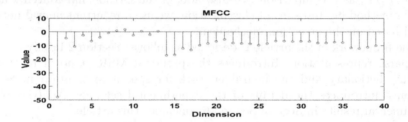

**Fig. 1.** 39-D MFCC representation of the t-th frame speech sampled at 16 kHz

In this article, in order to capture the voice changes and obtain a better SR, we use the KSVD dictionary learning algorithm. In the algorithm, first initialize the dictionary, then use the OMP algorithm to solve the sparse representation, and use the SVD algorithm to update the atom. In the traditional KSVD dictionary learning method, the dictionary is trained from a large number of training data sets. However, for voice data, putting all types of training data together to train the dictionary will make the training data very large and difficult to train. Based on the KSVD dictionary learning method, we select a fixed number of frames from each type of speech data to form a small training data instead of using all the data to train the dictionary. The generated small training data contains all the classes and various sound changes. Figure 1 is MFCC feature of the t-th frame and Fig. 2 is the sparse representation derived using a MFCC.

Speech signal is complex and changeable, only using individual features for classification cannot fully express the complex information contained in the voice. Therefore, we propose a coordinated representation method which combine the

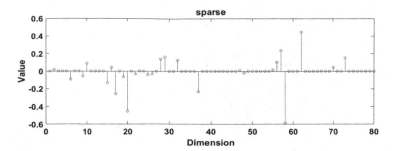

**Fig. 2.** sparse representation of the t-th frame speech derived using a MFCC representation

original MFCC features and the novel SR generated by the MFCC features, and then send them into the neural network for classification. Considering that the data may contain noise and the sparseness of the voice data is variable, therefore, this paper uses the BPDN algorithm to convert the above optimization problem into $\ell_1$ norm to solve the SR of the speech signal, which to a certain extent can suppress noise interference. Therefore Eq. (2) can be rewritten as:

$$A = \arg\min_{A} \ \forall_i \ \|\alpha_i\|_1 \ \text{ s.t. } \ \|X - DA\|_F^2 \leqslant \lambda \tag{3}$$

### 3.2 Neural Network Based on Attention Mechanism for Speech Recognition

A neural network based on the attention mechanism is proposed for speech recognition in this article, the network is composed of an encoder, an attention mechanism, and a decoder as show in Fig. 3. Among them, the encoder is a layer of Bi-directional Long Short-Term Memory (BiLSTM), which transforms the original MFCC feature ($x$) into an intermediate representation (h), the decoder consists of BiLSTM and a fully connected layer. Because the sequence is too long during the encoding process, which will cause the intermediate state to be lost during decoding [16], therefore, an attention mechanism is introduced to assign different weights to the intermediate representations from the encoder to assist the decoding steps of each step.

Attention mechanism: The purpose of the attention mechanism is to calculate a context vector $c$ [17]. First, calculate the weight generated by the correlation score between the encoding output $h$ and the decoding state $s$, and form a context vector $c$ by weighting the encoding output and the weight value. Finally, where the calculation method of context vector $c$ is as follows:

$$\alpha_{ij} = score(h_j, s_i) \tag{4}$$

$$c_i = \Sigma \alpha_{ij} h_j \tag{5}$$

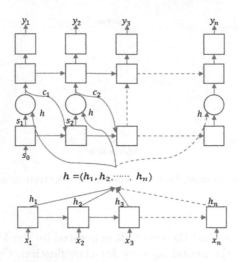

**Fig. 3.** A neural network based on the attention mechanism

## 4    Experiment Setup

The database used in this experiment is the TIMIT phonetic dataset [18], which contains 39 types of phoneme. The sampling frequency of the speech signal is 16 kHZ, with 25 ms as a unit as a frame and overlapping by 10 ms. Finally, the initial representation used to obtain MSR is the 39-dimensional MFCC feature.

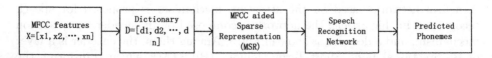

**Fig. 4.** Block diagram of a speech classification system based on the proposed multimodal sparse feature representation.

We selects ten frames from each type of speech data to form a small training data, then use the small training data for dictionary learning, which proved have better performance and the speed is greatly improved In order to ensure sparseness. The dictionary usually selected is overcomplete $(K \times 2K)$, and the number of atoms in the dictionary is constantly updated through the KSVD algorithm.

Considering that the sparsity of speech signal features is variable and the signal may contain certain noise interference, we decided to use the BPDN method to solve the $\ell_1$ norm obtains the sparse representation. As a comparison, we also choose the fixed sparsity OMP algorithm to convert the norm to solve the sparse representation, and the sparsity is set to 1/3 of the signal dimension.

The speech recognition system used to recognize MSR is a neural network model based on the attention mechanism. The encoder layer of the model is a two-layer BiLSTM model, the number of units of the model is set to 128, and the decoding layer consists of a bidirectional layer, which the number of units is 128, and the final output layer is the fully connected layer with the activation function softmax. The complete process of predicting a speech signal is shown in Fig. 4.

## 5   Experiment Results

In this experiment, we extracted MSR based on the TIMIT database, and recognized them in the attention mechanism-based neural network, and evaluated various features by calculating the phoneme recognition error rate (PER) of speech performance. Table 1 shows the classification performance of each type of feature in different recognition networks. According to the data in the table, in the same recognition network, the sparse feature is sent to the network for recognition and its performance is better than directly feeding the MFCC features of the original data. Using MSR as a feature to send to the same recognition system for recognition shows the best performance. Regardless of the recognition system, the performance of MSR is much higher than the other two feature representations, and the MSR shows the best performance in the built model based on the attention mechanism. This also shows that the proposed representation feature contains more discriminative information in the speech signal, which can be better used for classification and recognition

**Table 1.** The performance of different signal features in different classification networks.

| Feature | System | PER of test (% PER) |
|---------|--------|---------------------|
| MFCC | BiLSTM | 27.3 |
| SR | BiLSTM | 26.53 |
| MSR | BiLSTM | 26.1 |
| MFCC | BiLSTM+ATTENTION | 26.4 |
| SR | BiLSTM+ATTENTION | 25.2 |
| MSR | BiLSTM+ATTENTION | 21.1 |

In Table 2, we compare different methods of solving sparse representations used to extract MSR, and evaluate the performance of sparse feature recognition systems. Among them, the sparse features solved by OMP algorithm have fixed sparsity, the sparse features solved by the BPDN algorithm have no fixed sparsity and has a suppressive effect on noise. Experiments show that using the sparse features solved by BPDN to form a MSR has better recognition performance. It also proves that in speech data, when the sparseness is not fixed, more

**Table 2.** Comparison of the proposed MSR feature obtained using different sparse solvers on different systems.

| Feature | System | PER of test (% PER) |
|---------|--------|---------------------|
| $\ell_0$ norm-OMP | BiLSTM | 26.4 |
| $\ell_1$ norm-BPDN | BiLSTM | 26.1 |
| $\ell_0$ norm-OMP | BiLSTM+ATTENTION | 25.5 |
| $\ell_1$ norm-BPDN | BiLSTM+ATTENTION | 21.1 |

distinguishing features can be extracted to improve the recognition performance, and BPDN has a certain inhibitory effect on the noise in the voice data. This method helps to improve the recognition performance of the system to a certain extent.

## 6 Conclusion

In this article, we propose a new feature representation method that combines initial speech features and sparse features to form a coordinated representation for classification and recognition. The proposed MSR features not only retains the basic energy information in MFCC, but also uses the uncorrelated features after sparse coding to find a more effective representation of speech. In addition, We have made some improvements to the initial data used in the training dictionary. A certain number of frames of each class are selected to form an initial training data. Experiments show that such initial training data can not only contain all types of information, the speed of training the dictionary has greatly improved, and the performance of the proposed MSR features based on this is better than the other two features, and can better express the complex information of voice data

## References

1. Jaitly, N., Hinton, G.: Learning a better representation of speech soundwaves using restricted Boltzmann machines. In: 2011 IEEE International Conference on Acoustics, Speech and Signal Processing (ICASSP) (2011)
2. Palaz, D., Collobert, R., Doss, M.M.: Estimating phoneme class conditional probabilities from raw speech signal using convolutional neural networks. Computer Science (2013)
3. Palaz, D., Magimai.-Doss, M., Collobert, R.: Convolutional neural networks-based continuous speech recognition using raw speech signal. In: IEEE International Conference on Acoustics (2015)
4. Kim, C., Stern, R.M.: Feature extraction for robust speech recognition based on maximizing the sharpness of the power distribution and on power flooring. In: 2010 IEEE International Conference on Acoustics, Speech and Signal Processing, pp. 4574–4577 (2010). https://doi.org/10.1109/ICASSP.2010.5495570

5. Sailor, H.B., Patil, H.A.: Novel unsupervised auditory filter bank learning using convolutional RBM for speech recognition. IEEE/ACM Trans. Audio Speech Lang. Process. **PP**(12), 1 (2016)
6. Kanevsky, D., Nahamoo, D., Ramabhadran, B., Sainath, T.N.: Sparse representation features for speech recognition (2012)
7. Sharma, P., Abrol, V., Dileep, A.D., Sao, A.K.: Sparse coding based features for speech units classification. Comput. Speech Lang. **47**, 333–350 (2017)
8. Sharma, P., Abrol, V., Sao, A.K.: Deep sparse representation based features for speech recognition. IEEE/ACM Trans. Audio Speech Lang. Process. **PP**(11), 1 (2017)
9. Tripathi, K., Rao, K.S.: Analysis of sparse representation based feature on speech mode classification. In: INTERSPEECH (2018)
10. Tripathi, K., Rao, K.S.: Discriminative sparse representation for speech mode classification. In: 2018 International Conference on Advances in Computing, Communications and Informatics (ICACCI), pp. 655–659 (2018). https://doi.org/10.1109/ICACCI.2018.8554644
11. Aharon, M., Elad, M., Bruckstein, A.: K-SVD: an algorithm for designing overcomplete dictionaries for sparse representation. IEEE Trans. Signal Process. **54**, 4311–4322 (2006)
12. Chen, S.S., Saunders, D.M.A.: Atomic decomposition by basis pursuit. SIAM Rev. **43**(1), 129–159 (2001)
13. Yılmaz, E., Gemmeke, J.F., Hamme, H.V.: Noise-robust speech recognition with exemplar-based sparse representations using alpha-beta divergence. In: IEEE International Conference on Acoustics (2014)
14. Gemmeke, J.F., Virtanen, T., Hurmalainen, A.: Exemplar-based sparse representations for noise robust automatic speech recognition. IEEE Trans. Audio Speech Lang. Process. **19**(7), 2067–2080 (2011)
15. Smit, W.J.: Sparse coding for speech recognition. In: IEEE International Conference on Acoustics Speech & Signal Processing (2008)
16. Chung, J.S., Senior, A., Vinyals, O., Zisserman, A.: Lip reading sentences in the wild. In: 2017 IEEE Conference on Computer Vision and Pattern Recognition (CVPR), pp. 3444–3453 (2017). https://doi.org/10.1109/CVPR.2017.367
17. Chan, W., Jaitly, N., Le, Q., Vinyals, O.: Listen, attend and spell: a neural network for large vocabulary conversational speech recognition. In: 2016 IEEE International Conference on Acoustics, Speech and Signal Processing (ICASSP) (2016)
18. Garofolo, J.S., Lamel, L.F., Fisher, W.M., Fiscus, J.G., Pallett, D.S., Dahlgren, N.L.: Darpa timit acoustic-phonetic continuous speech corpus cd-rom TIMIT

# MMForWild2020 - MultiMedia FORensics in the WILD 2020

# MultiMedia FORensics in the WILD (MMForWILD) 2020

## ICPR Workshop – January 2021

## Workshop Description

The rapid growth of multimedia collections world-wide opens new challenges to multimedia technology with respect to crime prevention and investigation. The protection of images, video, and audio data from illegal use, as well as its exploitation in forensics and intelligence, have become serious challenges as the sheer data volume renders a full manual inspection by an expert impossible. Tools are needed to support the protection, management, processing, interpretation, and visualization of multimedia data in the different steps of the investigation process. Many exciting solutions for related problems have been developed in the multimedia research community (including knowledge extraction, categorization, indexing, browsing and visualization), forming an excellent basis for forensics and intelligence. The problem with many solutions developed so far is that they work well in controlled settings like those typical of laboratory experiments, but often fail to provide reliable answers in real-life conditions such as those encountered by forensic analysts and investigators in their daily activities.

MMForWILD offers a forum for proposing multimedia forensic solutions meeting the operational needs of forensics and intelligence operators. The workshop is targeted both at researchers working on innovative multimedia technology and experts developing tools in the field. The goal of the workshop is to attract and invite papers investigating the use of multimedia forensics outside the controlled environment of research laboratories (LEA, Practitioners, etc.). It intends to offer a venue for theory- and data-driven techniques addressing the trustworthiness of media data and the ability of verifying their integrity to prevent harmful misuses, seeking for solutions at the edge of signal processing, deep learning, multimedia analysis. The first edition of the MultiMedia FORensics in the WILD (MMForWILD) 2020 has been organized in conjunction with the International Conference on Pattern Recognition. The format of the workshop includes 2 keynotes followed by technical presentations. In this first edition we received 22 submissions for reviews. After an accurate and thorough peer-review process, we selected 12 papers for presentation at the workshop, whereas 8 papers have been discarded and 2 have been withdrawn. The review process focused on the quality of the papers, their scientific novelty and applicability to existing multimedia forensics problems in the wild. The acceptance of the papers was the result of the reviewers' discussion and agreement. All the high-quality papers were accepted, and the acceptance rate was 60%. We would like to thank the MMforWild 2020 Program

Committee, whose members made the workshop possible with their rigorous and timely review process. We would also like to thank ICPR for hosting the workshop and the ICPR workshop chairs for the valuable help and support.

November 2020

# Organization

## Workshop Chairs

Mauro Barni      University of Siena, Italy
Sebastiano Battiato    University of Catania, Italy
Giulia Boato      University of Trento, Italy
Hany Farid      University of California, Berkeley, USA
Nasir Memon      New York University, USA

## Publication Chair

Alessandro Ortis    University of Catania, Italy

## Program Committee

Roberto Caldelli      CNIT, Italy
Carlo Sansone      University of Napoli Federico II, Italy
Luisa Verdoliva      University of Napoli Federico II, Italy
Oliver Giudice      iCTLAb, Catania, Italy
Alessandro Ortis      University of Catania, Italy
Rainer Boehme      University of Innsbruck, Austria
Cecilia Pasquini      University of Innsbruck, Austria
Giovanni Puglisi      University of Cagliari, Italy
William Puech      University of Montpellier, France
Pedro Comensana      University of Vigo, Spain
Anderson Rocha      University of Campinas, Brasil
Edward J Delp      Purdue University, USA
Fernando Perez Gonzalez    University of Vigo, Spain
Christian Riess      Friedrich-Alexander-Universität Erlangen-Nürnberg
Bin Li      Shenzen University
Alessandro Piva      University of Florence, Italy
Marco Fontani      Amped Software, Italy
Mattias Kirchner      Kitware, USA
Aldo Mattei      Arma dei Carabinieri, Italy
Giovanni Tessitore      Polizia di Stato, Italy
Remi Cogranne      Université de technologie de Troyes, France
Rongrong Ni      Institute of Information Science (IIS) - China
Benedetta Tondi      University of Siena, Italy

# Industrial Sponsor

iCTLAb, Catania, IT

# Increased-Confidence Adversarial Examples for Deep Learning Counter-Forensics

Wenjie Li[1,2], Benedetta Tondi[3], Rongrong Ni[1,2(✉)], and Mauro Barni[3]

[1] Institute of Information Science, Beijing Jiaotong University, Beijing 100044, China
{wenjie_li,rrni}@bjtu.edu.cn
[2] Beijing Key Laboratory of Advanced Information Science and Network Technology, Beijing 100044, China
[3] Department of Information Engineering and Mathematical Sciences, University of Siena, Siena, Italy
benedettatondi@gmail.com, barni@dii.unisi.it

**Abstract.** Transferability of adversarial examples is a key issue to apply this kind of attacks against multimedia forensics (MMF) techniques based on Deep Learning (DL) in a real-life setting. Adversarial example transferability, in fact, would open the way to the deployment of successful counter forensics attacks also in cases where the attacker does not have a full knowledge of the to-be-attacked system. Some preliminary works have shown that adversarial examples against CNN-based image forensics detectors are in general non-transferrable, at least when the basic versions of the attacks implemented in the most popular libraries are adopted. In this paper, we introduce a general strategy to increase the strength of the attacks and evaluate their transferability when such a strength varies. We experimentally show that, in this way, attack transferability can be largely increased, at the expense of a larger distortion. Our research confirms the security threats posed by the existence of adversarial examples even in multimedia forensics scenarios, thus calling for new defense strategies to improve the security of DL-based MMF techniques.

**Keywords:** Adversarial multimedia forensics · Deep learning for forensics · Security of deep learning · Transferability of adversarial attacks · Image manipulation detection

## 1 Introduction

Several studies in machine learning have shown that adversarial attacks carried out against a given network (in most cases, but not only, a convolutional neural network - CNN) are often transferable to other networks designed for the same task, that is, the attacks maintain part of their effectiveness even against networks other than that considered to construct the attack [17,23]. Attack transferability is a key property, especially in security-related scenarios like multimedia

© Springer Nature Switzerland AG 2021
A. Del Bimbo et al. (Eds.): ICPR 2020 Workshops, LNCS 12666, pp. 411–424, 2021.
https://doi.org/10.1007/978-3-030-68780-9_34

forensics, since it opens the way towards the deployment of powerful attacks to be used in real-life applications, wherein the attacker does not have full access to the attacked network (gray-box scenario). Thanks to transferability, in fact, the attacker can attack a surrogate network mimicking the target one and the attack will be effective against the target network with a large probability [4,17].

While attack transferability was first proved for computer vision applications, recent research has shown that common adversarial examples are often non-transferable in image forensic applications [2,11,15]. Results like those reported in [2,11,15] represent a great challenge for attackers who want to exploit the existence of adversarial examples to attack MMF systems in a real life setting wherein the controlled conditions typical of laboratory experiments do not hold. The problem is exacerbated by the fact that the most popular attack software packages [16,18] are designed in such a way to minimize the embedding distortion for a successful attack. In this way, the attacked samples are often very close to the decision boundary, so that even a slight modification to the detector may undermine the effectiveness of the attack. On the contrary, the attacker could prefer to introduce a larger distortion, if doing so permits him to obtain an attacked sample that lies deeper into the target region of the attack (since in this way the probability that the attack can be transferred to another network increases). Unfortunately, controlling the distance of the attacked samples to the decision boundary, and hence controlling their resilience to perturbations of the boundary is not easy, given the complexity of the decision boundary learned by CNNs.

In this paper, we introduce a general strategy to increase the strength of the attacks, and evaluate the transferability of the adversarial examples generated in this way in a multimedia forensics context. Specifically, we show that stronger attacks can be built by increasing the *confidence* of the misclassification, namely the difference between the score (logits) of the target class of the attack and the highest score of the other classes. Our experiments reveal that controlling the strength of the attack by varying its confidence level is an effective way to improve the transferability of the attack, at the expense of a slightly larger distortion.

The rest of the paper is organized as follows. In Sect. 2, the proposed confidence-controlled attacks generating adversarial examples with improved transferability is described. In Sect. 3, the methodology used for the evaluation of transferability is introduced. Then, the experimental results as well as corresponding discussions are given in Sect. 4. Finally, Sect. 5 concludes the paper.

## 2    Proposed Confidence-Controlled Attacks

The most straightforward way of controlling the strength of the attacks (at least those based on gradients) would be to go on with the attack iterations until a limit value of the PSNR (Peak Signal to Noise Ratio) is reached. The PSNR, then, would give a measure of the attack strength. Some preliminary experiments we have carried out, however, reveal that controlling the strength of the attack in this way is not easy. One reason for such a difficulty is the intricacy of the decision boundary, so that a lower PSNR does not necessarily result in a stronger attack. In addition, if the gradient is computed directly with respect to the final soft output of the network, as soon as we depart from the decision boundary the gradient tends to vanish, thus making it difficult for the attacker to find a good descent direction ensuring a larger distance from the decision boundary.

To cope with the above difficulties, we have devised a solution that modifies the stop condition of the attack in such a way to control the confidence of the misclassification induced by the attack. In this way, the solver of the optimization problem the attack relies on is forced to find an adversarial example that is classified as the target class with the *desired* minimum confidence. Otherwise, a failure is declared (no adversarial examples can be returned with the desired confidence).

In the following, we describe the confidence-based attack focusing on the case of binary classification[1]. Let $\phi$ be the function describing the output of the neural network and let $y$ denote the class label, $y = 0, 1$. Let $z_i$ be the logits, i.e. the outputs of the neural network prior to the softmax layer, corresponding to the two labels $i = 0, 1$. The final value $\phi$ is obtained by applying the softmax to the logits and thresholding the output. Given an image $X$ such that $y = i$ ($i = 0, 1$), an image $X'$ is declared adversarial *if and only if* $z_{1-i} - z_i > c$, where $c > 0$ is the desired *confidence*. All the most popular adversarial attack algorithms (e.g. FGSM, PGD) can be modified by generalizing the stop condition in this way. The goal of our research is to evaluate the transferability of adversarial attacks against multimedia forensics detectors, as a function of $c$.

Several other methods have been proposed to improve the transferability of adversarial examples. The regularization-based method proposed in [26], for instance, improves transferability by adding a regularization term to the loss function to smooth the perturbation. Ensemble-based methods aim at finding an universal perturbation which is effective for an ensemble of architectures [13,24] or input images [9,25]. In particular, the method recently proposed in [25], called Diverse Inputs I-FGSM (DI$^2$-FGSM) increases the transferability of the attacks by exploiting input diversity. This method is an extension of the basic I-FGSM, and it has been proven to significantly improve the transferability of adversarial examples by applying random transformations (random resizing and random padding) to the input images at each iteration. Given its effectiveness, in Sect. 4, the transferability of increased-confidence adversarial examples is compared with that achieved by DI$^2$-FGSM.

## 3   Methodology

In order to carry out a comprehensive investigation, we assessed the attack transferability under various sources and degrees of mismatch between the *source network*, i.e., the network used to perform the adversarial attack (SN), and

---

[1] While trivial, the extension to multi-class classification requires to distinguish between targeted and non-targeted attacks.

the *target network*, i.e., the one the attack should be transferred to (TN). In particular, we considered the following types of transferability: i) cross-network (different network architectures trained on the same dataset), ii) cross-training (the same architecture trained on different datasets) and iii) cross-network-and-training (different architectures trained on different datasets). We carried out our experiments with different kinds of attacks, considering three manipulation detection tasks (median filtering, image resizing and additive white Gaussian noise (AWGN)) and three different architectures, as described below.

## 3.1    Attacks

We created the adversarial examples by applying the confidence-based stop condition to the following methods: i) Iterative Fast Gradient Sign Method (I-FGSM) [10], i.e. the refined iterative version of the original FGSM attack, ii) the Projected Gradient Descent (PGD) attack [12,14], iii) C&W attack [6], iv) Momentum Iterative FGSM (MI-FGSM) [8].

A brief description of the basic version of the above attacks is provided in the following. With I-FGSM, at each iteration, an adversarial perturbation is obtained by computing the gradient of the loss function with respect to the input image and considering its sign multiplied by a (normalized) strength factor $\varepsilon$. The algorithm is applied iteratively until an adversarial image is obtained (that is, an image which is misclassified by the network), for a maximum number of steps. PGD looks for the perturbation that maximizes the loss function under some restrictions regarding the introduced $L_\infty$ distortion. Specifically, at each iteration, the image is first updated (similarly to I-FGSM) by using a certain value of $\varepsilon$; then, the pixel values are clipped to ensure that they remain in the $\alpha$-neighbourhood of the original image. The C&W attack based on the $L_2$ metric minimizes a loss function that weighs a classification loss with a distance term measuring the distortion between the original and the attacked images, after applying a tanh-nonlinearity to enforce the attacked samples to take valid values in a bounding box. MI-FGSM uses the momentum method to stabilize the update directions. It works by adding the accumulated gradients from previous steps to the current gradient with a decay factor $\mu$. In this way, the optimization should escape from poor local maxima/minima during the iterations (in principle, the momentum iterative method can be easily applied on top of any iterative attack algorithms. By following [8], we considered I-FGSM).

Some observations are in order. C&W method already introduces a confidence parameter, named $\kappa$, in its formulation of the objective function, so that the solver is 'encouraged' to find an adversarial example that belongs to the desired class with high confidence (smaller value of the objective function). However, by running the attack with a standard implementation, it turns out that the confidence achieved by the attacked image is not always $\kappa$ (depending on the number of iterations considered for the attack and other parameters [6]). Then, we applied our confidence-based stop condition to this attack as well, to ensure that the desired confidence is always achieved (with $c = \kappa$). Another observation regards MI-FGSM. Integrating the momentum term into the iterative process is something that should by itself increase the transferability of the adversarial examples [8]. Then, in this case, by considering $c > 0$, we are basically combining together two ways to get a stronger attack. However, according to our results, the improvement of transferability that can be obtained by using the momentum is a minor one, thus justifying the further adoption of our confidence-based strategy.

### 3.2 Datasets and Networks

For the experiments with cross-training mismatch, we considered the RAISE (R) [7] and the VISION (V) datasets [19]. In particular, a number of 2000 uncompressed, camera-native images (.tiff) with size of 4288 × 2848 were taken from the RAISE dataset. The same number of images were taken from the VISION dataset. This dataset consists of native images acquired by smartphones/tablets belonging to several different brands. To get images with similar resolution, we selected only the devices with the image resolution close to 4288 × 2848. The native images from both R and V datasets were split into training, validation and test sets, and then processed to get the manipulated images, namely, median-filtered (by a 5 × 5 window), resized (downsampling, by a factor of 0.8) and noisy (Gaussian noise with std dev 1) images. We considered gray-level images for our experiments, then all the RGB images were first converted to gray-scale.

Concerning the network architectures used to build the detectors, we considered the network in [5] from Bayar and Stamm (BSnet), and the one in [1] from Barni and Costanzo *et al.* (BC+net). BSnet was originally designed for standard manipulation detection tasks and it is not very deep (3 convolutional layers, 3 max-pooling layers, and 2 fully connected layers). As the main feature of BSnet, the filters used in the first layer (with 5 × 5 receptive field) are forced to have a high-pass nature, so to extract the residual-based features from images. For more details on the network architecture, we refer to [5]. As for the BC+net, it was initially proposed for the more difficult task of generic contrast adjustment detection. This network is much deeper (9 convolutional layers) than BSnet, and no constraint is applied to the filters used in the network. More details can be found in the original paper [1]. In addition to these two networks designed for image forensics tasks, we also considered a common network used for pattern recognition applications, that is, the VGG-16 network (VGGnet) [20]. The architecture considered consists of 13 convolutional layers in total, and, respectively, 1024, 256, and 2 (output) neurons for the three fully connected layers (see [20] for further information). The clear notations for the models used in the experiments are given below. For a given detection task, we indicate the trained model as $\phi_{\text{Net}}^{\text{DB}}$, where "Net" indicates the architecture with "Net" $\in$ {BSnet, BC+net, VGGnet}, and "DB" $\in$ {R, V} is the dataset used for training.

## 4 Experiments

### 4.1 Setup

Based on the three different CNN architectures described in the previous section, we trained the models in the following way. To build the BSnet models for the three detection tasks, we considered $2 \times 10^5$ patches per class for training (and validation) and $10^4$ for testing. For the VGGnet models, a number of $10^5$ patches per class was used for training and validation, and the test set consists of $10^4$ patches. A maximum number of 100 patches was (randomly) selected from each image to increase patch diversity by using more images. Finally, for the BC+net's, we considered $10^6$ patches for training, $10^5$ patches for validation and $5 \times 10^4$ patches for testing. To reach these numbers, we selected all the non-overlapping patches from each image. For all the models, the patch size was set to $128 \times 128$. The batch size for training was set to 32 patches. For BSnet and BC+net, the Adam solver with learning rate $10^{-4}$ was used. The learning rate was set to $10^{-5}$ for VGGnet. The number of epochs was set, respectively, to 30 for BSnet [5], 50 for VGGnet, and 3 for BC+net (following [1]). The accuracies achieved by these models on the test sets range between 98.1% and 99.5% for median filtering detection, from 96.6% to 99.0% for resizing detection, and from 98.3% to 99.9% for the detection of AWGN.

We attacked images from the manipulated class only. In counter-forensic applications, in fact, it is reasonable to assume that the attack is conducted only in one direction, since the attacker wants to pass off a manipulated image as an original one to cause a false negative error. Performance are measured on 500 attacked images, obtained by attacking a subset of manipulated images from the test set. The Foolbox toolbox [18] was used to implement the attacks. The parameters of the attacks were set as follows[2]. For C&W, all the parameters were set to the default values. For PGD, we set 'epsilon' = 0.3, 'stepsize' = 0.005 and 'iterations' = 100. A binary search is performed over 'epsilon' and 'stepsize' to optimize the choice of the hyperparameters, using the input values only for the initialization of the algorithm. For I-FGSM, we set 'epsilons' = 10 and 'steps' = 100. For MI-FGSM, the parameters used in I-FGSM were also adopted and the decay factor of the accumulated gradient was set to $\mu = 0.2$ (similar results were obtained with lower values of $\mu$). For the comparison with the $DI^2$-FGSM, we followed the parameter setting in [25], where $\varepsilon = 1/255$. We decreased this value to 0.002 in the case of AWGN detection, for which letting $\varepsilon = 1/255$ results in a very low attack success rate. Besides, the input diversity is achieved by resizing the image to $r \times r$ with $r \in [100, 128)$ and then randomly padding it to the size of $128 \times 128$, and the transformation probability is also set to 0.5, which is the same with that used in [25].

Several mismatch combinations of SN and TN were considered for all detection tasks, and the transferability of the adversarial examples for the cases of cross-network, cross-training and cross-network-and-training is investigated. In the following, we will only report the results for a subset of these cases, which is sufficient to draw the most significant conclusions.

---

[2] For simplicity, we report only the values of the Foolbox input parameters for each attack. For their meaning and the correspondences with the parameters of the attacks, we refer to [18].

**Table 1.** Results for cross-network mismatch for the median filtering detection.

| $SN = \phi^R_{VGGnet}$, $TN = \phi^R_{BSnet}$ | | | | | | | |
|---|---|---|---|---|---|---|---|
| | C&W | PGD | I-FGSM | MI-FGSM | | DI²-FGSM | |
| $c$ | ASR$_{TN}$ PSNR | ASR$_{TN}$ PSNR | ASR$_{TN}$ PSNR | ASR$_{TN}$ PSNR | iter | ASR$_{SN}$ ASR$_{TN}$ PSNR | |
| 0 | 8.4 69.1 | 5.4 67.5 | 27.2 58.1 | 27.2 58.1 | 1 | 86.4 51.8 48.3 | |
| 12 | 50.6 54.6 | 55.0 52.0 | 71.0 47.9 | 71.6 47.8 | 2 | 97.0 69.2 45.0 | |
| 12.5 | 70.1 51.5 | 79.0 48.9 | 88.2 45.3 | 88.6 45.3 | 3 | 99.2 77.6 43.2 | |
| 13 | 91.2 48.1 | 94.6 45.4 | 96.4 42.5 | 96.6 42.7 | 5 | 100 86.8 41.4 | |
| $SN = \phi^R_{BSnet}$, $TN = \phi^R_{BC+net}$ | | | | | | | |
| | C&W | PGD | I-FGSM | MI-FGSM | | DI²-FGSM | |
| $c$ | ASR$_{TN}$ PSNR | ASR$_{TN}$ PSNR | ASR$_{TN}$ PSNR | ASR$_{TN}$ PSNR | iter | ASR$_{SN}$ ASR$_{TN}$ PSNR | |
| 0 | 0.2 72.0 | 0.2 74.5 | 23.2 59.7 | 23.4 59.7 | 1 | 91.4 52.4 48.2 | |
| 50 | 56.0 52.2 | 55.6 50.3 | 60.6 48.9 | 60.4 48.9 | 2 | 98.4 69.4 44.6 | |
| 80 | 74.0 47.8 | 74.0 45.8 | 77.8 45.1 | 78.8 44.8 | 3 | 99.4 77.0 42.3 | |
| 100 | 83.6 45.2 | 83.6 43.5 | 85.4 42.9 | 86.2 42.7 | 5 | 100 85.4 40.2 | |

## 4.2  Results

For each attack method applied with the proposed confidence-based stop condition, we report the attack success rate with respect to the target network, ASR$_{TN}$, and the PSNR of the attacked images averaged on the successfully attacked samples, for several confidence values $c$ ranging from 0 to a maximum value chosen in such a way that the average PSNR is not too low (around 30 dB). The range of values of $c$ depends on the magnitude of the logits and then on the SN. The attack success rate with respect to the source network, ASR$_{SN}$, is 100% or very close to this value for the confidence-based attacks in all cases, then it is not reported. The performance of the DI²-FGSM, including ASR$_{SN}$, are reported for different numbers of iterations (for a similar PSNR limitation) and discussed at the end of this section.

Tables 1 and 2 show the results for the case of cross-network transferability for two different combinations of SN and TN, i.e., $(SN,TN) = (\phi^R_{VGGnet}, \phi^R_{BSnet})$ and $(SN,TN) = (\phi^R_{BSnet}, \phi^R_{BC+net})$, for the median filtering and image resizing detection tasks, respectively. By inspecting the tables, we see that the transferability of the attacks can be significantly improved in all the cases by increasing the confidence; the ASR$_{TN}$ passes from [0–27]% with $c = 0$ to [84–97]% with the maximum $c$ for median filtering, and from [0–2]% with $c = 0$ to [52–84]% with the maximum $c$ for image resizing. In all cases, the PSNR of the attacked images remains pretty high (larger than 40 dB for the case of median filtering, and about 30 dB for the case of image resizing). For different SN, the relationship between the values of $c$ and PSNR is different since the exact values assumed by the logits is affected by many factors, such as the network architecture and the detection task. As a general trend, a larger $c$ always results in adversarial

**Table 2.** Results for cross-network mismatch for the image resizing detection.

| $SN = \phi^R_{VGGnet}$, $TN = \phi^R_{BSnet}$ | | | | | | | | |
| --- | --- | --- | --- | --- | --- | --- | --- | --- |
| | C&W | | PGD | | I-FGSM | | MI-FGSM | | DI²-FGSM | | |
| $c$ | ASR$_{TN}$ | PSNR | ASR$_{TN}$ | PSNR | ASR$_{TN}$ | PSNR | ASR$_{TN}$ | PSNR | iter | ASR$_{SN}$ | ASR$_{TN}$ | PSNR |
| 0 | 1.2 | 71.5 | 1.8 | 75.4 | 0.4 | 59.3 | 0.4 | 59.2 | 1 | 30.6 | 2.6 | 48.2 |
| 17 | 40.4 | 36.8 | 22.0 | 33.4 | 25.0 | 33.3 | 24.8 | 33.3 | 25 | 100 | 8.6 | 32.6 |
| 18 | 53.6 | 34.3 | 39.8 | 30.9 | 39.6 | 30.9 | 37.4 | 30.9 | 35 | 100 | 23.4 | 30.3 |
| 19 | 64.4 | 32.2 | 52.0 | 28.9 | 51.6 | 28.9 | 52.6 | 28.9 | 45 | 100 | 41.0 | 28.2 |

| $SN = \phi^R_{BSnet}$, $TN = \phi^R_{BC+net}$ | | | | | | | | |
| --- | --- | --- | --- | --- | --- | --- | --- | --- |
| | C&W | | PGD | | I-FGSM | | MI-FGSM | | DI²-FGSM | | |
| $c$ | ASR$_{TN}$ | PSNR | ASR$_{TN}$ | PSNR | ASR$_{TN}$ | PSNR | ASR$_{TN}$ | PSNR | iter | ASR$_{SN}$ | ASR$_{TN}$ | PSNR |
| 0 | 0.4 | 68.3 | 0.4 | 66.9 | 0.4 | 58.7 | 0.4 | 58.6 | 1 | 96.8 | 0.2 | 48.2 |
| 50 | 82.4 | 45.9 | 65.2 | 42.3 | 66.2 | 41.9 | 63.6 | 41.7 | 3 | 100 | 33.8 | 41.2 |
| 80 | 85.2 | 39.3 | 84.0 | 35.5 | 82.4 | 35.3 | 84.6 | 35.4 | 8 | 100 | 77.0 | 35.3 |
| 100 | 80.4 | 34.0 | 82.8 | 31.6 | 83.8 | 31.6 | 82.2 | 31.7 | 15 | 100 | 87.6 | 31.1 |

examples with lower PSNR values and higher transferability (ASR$_{TN}$). The few exceptions to this behaviour, for which the values in Table 2 report a lower transferability when using a larger $c$, can be possibly explained by the fact that some perturbed images move too far from the original image and are correctly classified by the TN, although they are still valid adversarial examples for the SN. A simple illustration of such a behaviour is given in Fig. 1 for the case (SN,TN) = ($\phi^R_{BSnet}$, $\phi^R_{BC+net}$) for image resizing detection, where $X'(c = 100)$ is adversarial for the SN but is classified correctly by the TN (the distortion is so large that the detection boundary is crossed twice, thus resulting in a correct label). Moreover, according to the tables, with similar ASR$_{TN}$ values, the C&W attack which aims to generate adversarial examples with less distortion can always achieve higher PSNR values than other attack methods. In summary, increasing the confidence is helpful for the improvement of the transferability of the adversarial examples in these cases. However, there also exists some combinations of (SN,TN), for which the transferability does not increase much by increasing the confidence value $c$. For instance, when (SN,TN) = ($\phi^R_{BC+net}$, $\phi^R_{BSnet}$) for the image resizing detection task, the ASR$_{TN}$ can only be increased from [0–2]% up to around 20%, under a certain limitation of the PSNR. This happens when the gradient is almost vanishing, since in this case a larger confidence does not help in increasing the transferability with respect to the target network.

Noticeably, increasing the confidence $c$ permits to increase the transferability also for the MI-FGSM attack, where we did not notice any significant transferability improvement for the case of $c = 0$, with respect to the I-FGSM. A possible explanation is that the strength of the perturbation applied at each iteration of the I-FGSM attack is very small, then the gradients between subsequent

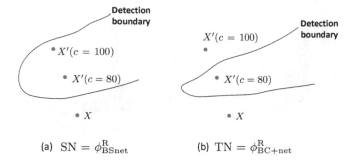

**Fig. 1.** An explanation for the phenomenon that a larger $c$ results in less transferability for the case $(SN,TN) = (\phi^{R}_{BSnet}, \phi^{R}_{BC+net})$ applied to image resizing detection.

**Table 3.** Results for cross-training mismatch for the median filtering detection.

| | SN $= \phi^{R}_{BSnet}$, TN $= \phi^{V}_{BSnet}$ | | | | | | | |
|---|---|---|---|---|---|---|---|---|
| | C&W | | PGD | | I-FGSM | | MI-FGSM | | | DI²-FGSM | | |
| $c$ | ASR$_{TN}$ PSNR | | ASR$_{TN}$ PSNR | | ASR$_{TN}$ PSNR | | ASR$_{TN}$ PSNR | iter | ASR$_{SN}$ ASR$_{TN}$ PSNR |
| 0 | 0.2 | 72.0 | 0.2 | 74.5 | 4.8 | 59.7 | 4.8 | 59.7 | 1 | 91.0 | 41.8 | 48.2 |
| 50 | 60.0 | 52.2 | 61.2 | 50.3 | 65.0 | 48.9 | 65.4 | 48.8 | 2 | 99.0 | 66.4 | 44.6 |
| 80 | 82.0 | 47.8 | 84.4 | 45.8 | 88.0 | 45.1 | 88.0 | 44.8 | 3 | 99.6 | 79.4 | 42.4 |
| 100 | 95.0 | 45.2 | 96.6 | 43.5 | 97.4 | 42.9 | 97.4 | 42.7 | 5 | 100 | 92.4 | 40.2 |

| | SN $= \phi^{R}_{VGGnet}$, TN $= \phi^{V}_{VGGnet}$ | | | | | | | |
|---|---|---|---|---|---|---|---|---|
| | C&W | | PGD | | I-FGSM | | MI-FGSM | | | DI²-FGSM | | |
| $c$ | ASR$_{TN}$ PSNR | | ASR$_{TN}$ PSNR | | ASR$_{TN}$ PSNR | | ASR$_{TN}$ PSNR | iter | ASR$_{SN}$ ASR$_{TN}$ PSNR |
| 0 | 0.4 | 69.1 | 0.4 | 67.3 | 7.8 | 58.1 | 7.8 | 58.1 | 1 | 87.0 | 58.2 | 48.3 |
| 11 | 31.8 | 59.2 | 31.6 | 56.2 | 74.4 | 52.0 | 76.4 | 51.7 | 2 | 96.8 | 80.0 | 45.0 |
| 11.5 | 59.8 | 57.3 | 66.2 | 54.4 | 89.0 | 50.2 | 89.4 | 50.0 | 3 | 98.6 | 91.8 | 43.2 |
| 12 | 91.6 | 54.9 | 93.0 | 52.0 | 96.6 | 47.9 | 96.6 | 47.8 | 5 | 100 | 97.8 | 41.4 |

iterations are highly correlated, thus reducing the impact of the gradient stabilization sought for by MI-FGSM. On the other hand, as already pointed out in previous works [2,22], if we increase the strength of the perturbation applied at each iteration, the ASR$_{SN}$ tends to decrease significantly. We also observe that the degree of transferability depends on the dataset and the SN architecture, as it was already noticed in [2]. However, in most cases, the adversarial examples can be successfully transferred by increasing the confidence, and the image quality can be preserved at the same time. To better investigate the effect of the confidence margin on the attack, we also checked the number of iterations used by the attacks for various confidence values. Specifically, the I-FGSM attack carried out against $\phi^{R}_{VGGnet}$ trained for the median filtering detection task is taken into consideration. The distributions of the number of iterations for different confidence margins are shown in Fig. 2. According to this figure, when $c = 0$,

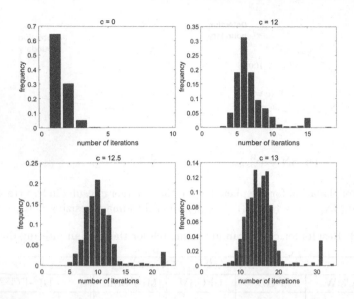

**Fig. 2.** Distribution of the number of iterations for the I-FGSM attack using different values of the confidence $c$. The attacked network is $\phi_{\text{VGGnet}}^{\text{R}}$ trained for the median filtering detection task.

only one or two steps are enough for a successful attack. Then, by increasing $c$, the attack requires more and more iterations. A similar behavior can be observed in the other cases.

The results for cross-training mismatch for the combinations of (SN,TN) $= (\phi_{\text{BSnet}}^{\text{R}}, \phi_{\text{BSnet}}^{\text{V}})$ and (SN,TN) $= (\phi_{\text{VGGnet}}^{\text{R}}, \phi_{\text{VGGnet}}^{\text{V}})$ are reported in Tables 3 and 4 for the median filtering and image resizing detection tasks, respectively. These results are in line with the previous ones and show that increasing the confidence always helps to improve the transferability of the adversarial examples. Specifically, among the confidence-based attacks, the improvement of the percentage goes from 60% to more than 90% for the cross-training case on the VGGnet. For other architectures, the transferability of the adversarial examples are also improved by increasing the value of $c$. We also observe that, as with the cross-network case, transferring the attacks between networks trained for image resizing detection tends to be more difficult, with respect to the case of median filtering detection.

Table 5 reports the results for the case of AWGN detection for the cross-network setting (SN,TN) $= (\phi_{\text{VGGnet}}^{\text{R}}, \phi_{\text{BSnet}}^{\text{R}})$ and the cross-training setting (SN,TN) $= (\phi_{\text{BSnet}}^{\text{R}}, \phi_{\text{BSnet}}^{\text{V}})$. Notice that only two cases are reported, as the $\text{ASR}_{\text{TN}}$ is always improved by using a large confidence value. As one can see from the table, by using large confidence values, the $\text{ASR}_{\text{TN}}$ is improved from [0–11]% to [80–92]% for the cross-network case, and from [0–1]% to [88–95]% for the case of cross-training mismatch, thus demonstrating the effectiveness of increasing the confidence to improve the transferability. Moreover, the PSNR

**Table 4.** Results for cross-training mismatch for the image resizing detection.

| | C&W | | PGD | | I-FGSM | | MI-FGSM | | DI²-FGSM | | | |
|---|---|---|---|---|---|---|---|---|---|---|---|---|
| $c$ | ASR$_{TN}$ | PSNR | ASR$_{TN}$ | PSNR | ASR$_{TN}$ | PSNR | ASR$_{TN}$ | PSNR | iter | ASR$_{SN}$ | ASR$_{TN}$ | PSNR |
| 0 | 9.8 | 68.3 | 9.8 | 66.9 | 12.8 | 58.7 | 12.8 | 58.6 | 1 | 97.2 | 49.2 | 48.2 |
| 30 | 23.8 | 52.5 | 38.6 | 49.6 | 53.0 | 48.0 | 48.6 | 47.8 | 2 | 99.4 | 72.6 | 43.8 |
| 40 | 32.8 | 48.9 | 54.2 | 45.7 | 64.0 | 44.7 | 60.2 | 44.6 | 3 | 99.8 | 80.0 | 41.2 |
| 50 | 39.2 | 45.9 | 59.8 | 42.3 | 67.2 | 41.7 | 64.2 | 41.7 | 5 | 100 | 82.0 | 39.1 |

SN = $\phi^R_{VGGnet}$, TN = $\phi^V_{VGGnet}$

| | C&W | | PGD | | I-FGSM | | MI-FGSM | | DI²-FGSM | | | |
|---|---|---|---|---|---|---|---|---|---|---|---|---|
| $c$ | ASR$_{TN}$ | PSNR | ASR$_{TN}$ | PSNR | ASR$_{TN}$ | PSNR | ASR$_{TN}$ | PSNR | iter | ASR$_{SN}$ | ASR$_{TN}$ | PSNR |
| 0 | 5.6 | 71.5 | 5.8 | 75.0 | 7.6 | 59.3 | 7.6 | 59.2 | 1 | 32.8 | 19.2 | 48.2 |
| 13.5 | 30.0 | 50.2 | 26.8 | 46.8 | 42.6 | 45.1 | 39.8 | 45.1 | 2 | 55.2 | 50.6 | 45.3 |
| 14 | 43.6 | 47.9 | 42.4 | 44.3 | 61.0 | 43.0 | 59.8 | 43.1 | 3 | 73.6 | 68.0 | 43.5 |
| 14.5 | 65.2 | 45.7 | 66.8 | 42.0 | 82.8 | 41.1 | 83.0 | 41.2 | 5 | 88.6 | 82.6 | 41.8 |

remains pretty high in all cases. Eventually, Table 6 shows the results for the case of cross-network-and-training (strong mismatch) for the median filtering and image resizing detection tasks when $(SN,TN) = (\phi^V_{BSnet}, \phi^R_{BC+net})$. For simplicity, only the results corresponding to $c = 0$ and the largest $c$ are reported.

**Table 5.** Results for the AWGN detection task, for cross-network (top) and cross-training (bottom) mismatch.

SN = $\phi^R_{VGGnet}$, TN = $\phi^R_{BSnet}$

| | C&W | | PGD | | I-FGSM | | MI-FGSM | | DI²-FGSM | | | |
|---|---|---|---|---|---|---|---|---|---|---|---|---|
| $c$ | ASR$_{TN}$ | PSNR | ASR$_{TN}$ | PSNR | ASR$_{TN}$ | PSNR | ASR$_{TN}$ | PSNR | iter | ASR$_{SN}$ | ASR$_{TN}$ | PSNR |
| 0 | 1.2 | 64.2 | 5.8 | 60.6 | 10.6 | 56.2 | 10.8 | 56.0 | 1 | 36.0 | 2.2 | 54.0 |
| 10 | 19.2 | 57.8 | 20.6 | 54.8 | 40.4 | 52.1 | 41.4 | 51.9 | 3 | 64.4 | 30.6 | 48.6 |
| 15 | 52.0 | 53.8 | 50.8 | 51.4 | 79.4 | 49.4 | 77.8 | 49.2 | 5 | 82.2 | 48.0 | 46.8 |
| 20 | 79.9 | 49.5 | 82.8 | 46.8 | 91.0 | 45.4 | 92.2 | 45.4 | 10 | 93.2 | 63.6 | 42.7 |

SN = $\phi^R_{BSnet}$, TN = $\phi^V_{BSnet}$

| | C&W | | PGD | | I-FGSM | | MI-FGSM | | DI²-FGSM | | | |
|---|---|---|---|---|---|---|---|---|---|---|---|---|
| $c$ | ASR$_{TN}$ | PSNR | ASR$_{TN}$ | PSNR | ASR$_{TN}$ | PSNR | ASR$_{TN}$ | PSNR | iter | ASR$_{SN}$ | ASR$_{TN}$ | PSNR |
| 0 | 0.2 | 65.0 | 0.2 | 62.4 | 0.6 | 57.7 | 0.6 | 57.6 | 1 | 51.2 | 0.6 | 54.1 |
| 20 | 12.2 | 54.4 | 11.0 | 52.2 | 13.8 | 49.7 | 15.0 | 49.6 | 10 | 80.0 | 4.8 | 43.9 |
| 30 | 78.0 | 49.4 | 77.2 | 47.3 | 54.4 | 44.8 | 72.8 | 45.1 | 20 | 91.6 | 10.2 | 40.0 |
| 40 | 95.4 | 45.5 | 94.0 | 43.0 | 88.2 | 41.0 | 93.0 | 41.3 | 30 | 98.4 | 21.4 | 37.4 |

For the case of median filtering detection, a significant gain ($\simeq 80\%$) in the transferability is achieved by raising $c$ while maintaining good image quality ($> 40$ dB). For the case of image resizing, the average gain is around 30%.

With regard to the comparison with DI$^2$-FGSM, we observe that similar $ASR_{TN}$ are achieved in most cases with lower PSNR values. The gain in PSNR is particularly evident in the case of AWGN detection. Given that DI$^2$-FGSM is based on input processing diversity, it is not surprising that its effectiveness depends heavily on the specific forensic task. Notably, DI$^2$-FGSM and the confidence-based method proposed in this paper are different and somewhat complementary approaches, that could be also combined together to further increase attack transferability. Finally, we verified that, similarly to what happens passing from I-FGSM to MI-FGSM with PSNR limitation, integrating the momentum method in DI$^2$-FGSM does not improve the transferability significantly.

**Table 6.** Results for cross-network-and-training mismatch for the median filtering (top) and image resizing (bottom) detection tasks.

| $SN = \phi^V_{BSnet}, \ TN = \phi^R_{BC+net}$ | | | | | | | | | |
|---|---|---|---|---|---|---|---|---|---|
| | C&W | | PGD | | I-FGSM | | MI-FGSM | | DI$^2$-FGSM |
| c | $ASR_{TN}$ PSNR | | $ASR_{TN}$ PSNR | | $ASR_{TN}$ PSNR | | $ASR_{TN}$ PSNR | | iter | $ASR_{SN}$ $ASR_{TN}$ PSNR |
| 0 | 0.0 | 70.5 | 0.0 | 71.9 | 2.6 | 60.0 | 2.6 | 60.0 | 1 | 95.4  35.6  48.2 |
| 100 | 78.0 | 45.1 | 83.0 | 43.1 | 84.6 | 42.4 | 85.6 | 42.4 | 5 | 100  82.0  40.5 |
| 0 | 0.8 | 73.3 | 0.8 | 74.7 | 2.0 | 59.8 | 2.0 | 59.7 | 1 | 80.6  0.0  48.2 |
| 400 | 17.0 | 33.6 | 40.0 | 31.2 | 37.4 | 31.2 | 33.4 | 31.1 | 20 | 100  26.0  31.0 |

## 5  Discussion and Conclusions

Following some works indicating a certain lack of transferability of CNN adversarial examples in image forensic applications, we introduced a general strategy to control the strength of the attacks based on the margin between the logit value of the target class and those of the other classes. Based on our experiments, we can conclude that by increasing the confidence margin, the attacks can be transferred in most of the cases (ASR $> 80\%$), regardless of the specific attacking algorithm, while the PSNR of the attacked images remains good ($> 30$ dB). In some cases, a slightly larger distortion is necessary to get high transfer rates, the achievable transferability (given a minimum PSNR for the attack) depending on the detection task and the model targeted by the attack. Future research will focus on the use of the increased-confidence attack to evaluate the security of existing defences against adversarial examples, e.g. those based on randomization strategies [3,21], and to develop new more powerful defence mechanisms.

**Acknowledgment.** This work was supported in part by the National Key Research and Development of China (2016YFB0800404), National NSF of China (U1936212,

61672090), and in part by the PREMIER project, funded by the Italian Ministry of Education, University, and Research (MIUR) within the PRIN 2017 2017Z595XS-001 program.

# References

1. Barni, M., Costanzo, A., Nowroozi, E., Tondi, B.: CNN-based detection of generic contrast adjustment with JPEG post-processing. In: IEEE International Conference on Image Processing (ICIP), pp. 3803–3807 (2018)
2. Barni, M., Kallas, K., Nowroozi, E., Tondi, B.: On the transferability of adversarial examples against CNN-based image forensics. In: Proceedings of the IEEE International Conference on Acoustics, Speech and Signal Processing (ICASSP), pp. 8286–8290 (2019)
3. Barni, M., Nowroozi, E., Tondi, B., Zhang, B.: Effectiveness of random deep feature selection for securing image manipulation detectors against adversarial examples. In: Procdings of the IEEE International Conference on Acoustics, Speech and Signal Processing (ICASSP), pp. 2977–2981 (2020)
4. Barni, M., Stamm, M., Tondi, B.: Adversarial multimedia forensics: overview and challenges ahead. In: Proceedings of the 26th European Signal Processing Conference (EUSIPCO), pp. 962–966 (2018)
5. Bayar, B., Stamm, M.: A deep learning approach to universal image manipulation detection using a new convolutional layer. In: ACM Workshop on Info. Hiding & Multimedia Security, pp. 5–10 (2016)
6. Carlini, N., Wagner, D.: Towards evaluating the robustness of neural networks. In: IEEE Symposium on Security and Privacy (SP), pp. 39–57 (2017)
7. Dang-Nguyen, D., Pasquini, C., Conotter, V., Boato, G.: RAISE: a raw images dataset for digital image forensics. In: Proceedings of the 6th ACM Multimedia Systems Conference, pp. 219–224 (2015)
8. Dong, Y., et al.: Boosting adversarial attacks with momentum. In: The IEEE Conference on Computer Vision and Pattern Recognition (CVPR), pp. 9185–9193 (2018)
9. Dong, Y., Pang, T., Su, H., Zhu, J.: Evading defenses to transferable adversarial examples by translation-invariant attacks. In: The IEEE Conference on Computer Vision and Pattern Recognition (CVPR) (2019)
10. Goodfellow, I., Shlens, J., Szegedy, C.: Explaining and harnessing adversarial examples. arXiv preprint arXiv:1412.6572 (2014)
11. Gragnaniello, D., Marra, F., Poggi, G., Verdoliva, L.: Analysis of adversarial attacks against CNN-based image forgery detectors. In: Proceedings of the 26th European Signal Processing Conference (EUSIPCO), pp. 967–971 (2018)
12. Kurakin, A., Goodfellow, I., Bengio, S.: Adversarial examples in the physical world. arXiv preprint arXiv:1607.02533 (2016)
13. Liu, Y., Chen, X., Liu, C., Song, D.: Delving into transferable adversarial examples and black-box attacks. In: International Conference on Learning Representations (ICLR) (2017)
14. Madry, A., Makelov, A., Schmidt, L., Tsipras, D., Vladu, A.: Towards deep learning models resistant to adversarial attacks. arXiv preprint arXiv:1706.06083 (2017)
15. Marra, F., Gragnaniello, D., Verdoliva, L.: On the vulnerability of deep learning to adversarial attacks for camera model identification. Sig. Process. Image Commun. **65**, 240–248 (2018)

16. Papernot, N., Faghri, F., Carlini, N., Goodfellow, I., et al.: Technical report on the cleverhans v2.1.0 adversarial examples library. arXiv preprint arXiv:1610.00768 (2018)
17. Papernot, N., McDaniel, P., Goodfellow, I.: Transferability in machine learning: from phenomena to black-box attacks using adversarial samples. arXiv preprint arXiv:1605.07277 (2016)
18. Rauber, J., Brendel, W., Bethge, M.: Foolbox v0.8.0: A python toolbox to benchmark the robustness of machine learning models. arXiv preprint arXiv:1707.04131 (2017)
19. Shullani, D., Fontani, M., Iuliani, M., Shaya, O., Piva, A.: VISION: a video and image dataset for source identification. EURASIP J. Inf. Secur. **2017**(1), 1–16 (2017)
20. Simonyan, K., Zisserman, A.: Very deep convolutional networks for large-scale image recognition. arXiv preprint arXiv:1409.1556 (2014)
21. Taran, O., Rezaeifar, S., Holotyak, T., Voloshynovskiy, S.: Defending against adversarial attacks by randomized diversification. In: The IEEE Conference on Computer Vision and Pattern Recognition (CVPR), pp. 11226–11233 (2019)
22. Tondi, B.: Pixel-domain adversarial examples against CNN-based manipulation detectors. Electron. Lett. **54**(21), 1220–1222 (2018)
23. Tramer, F., Papernot, N., Goodfellow, I., Boneh, D., McDaniel, P.: The space of transferable adversarial examples. arXiv preprint arXiv:1704.03453 (2017)
24. Tramèr, F., Kurakin, A., Papernot, N., Goodfellow, I., Boneh, D., McDaniel, P.: Ensemble adversarial training: Attacks and defenses. arXiv preprint arXiv:1705.07204 (2017)
25. Xie, C., et al.: Improving transferability of adversarial examples with input diversity. In: The IEEE Conference on Computer Vision and Pattern Recognition (CVPR) (2019)
26. Zhou, W., et al.: Transferable adversarial perturbations. In: The European Conference on Computer Vision (ECCV) (2018)

# Defending Neural ODE Image Classifiers from Adversarial Attacks with Tolerance Randomization

Fabio Carrara[1]([✉])(iD), Roberto Caldelli[2,3](iD), Fabrizio Falchi[1](iD),
and Giuseppe Amato[1](iD)

[1] ISTI CNR, Pisa, Italy
{fabio.carrara,fabrizio.falchi,giuseppe.amato}@isti.cnr.it
[2] CNIT, Florence, Italy
[3] Universitas Mercatorum, Rome, Italy

**Abstract.** Deep learned models are now largely adopted in different fields, and they generally provide superior performances with respect to classical signal-based approaches. Notwithstanding this, their actual reliability when working in an unprotected environment is far enough to be proven. In this work, we consider a novel deep neural network architecture, named Neural Ordinary Differential Equations (N-ODE), that is getting particular attention due to an attractive property—a test-time tunable trade-off between accuracy and efficiency. This paper analyzes the robustness of N-ODE image classifiers when faced against a strong adversarial attack and how its effectiveness changes when varying such a tunable trade-off. We show that adversarial robustness is increased when the networks operate in different tolerance regimes during test time and training time. On this basis, we propose a novel adversarial detection strategy for N-ODE nets based on the randomization of the adaptive ODE solver tolerance. Our evaluation performed on standard image classification benchmarks shows that our detection technique provides high rejection of adversarial examples while maintaining most of the original samples under white-box attacks and zero-knowledge adversaries.

**Keywords:** Neural ordinary differential equation · Adversarial defense · Image classification

## 1 Introduction

The astonishing success of deep learned models and their undeniable performances in a variety of difficult tasks (e.g. visual and auditory perception, natural language processing, self-driving cars, multimedia analysis) is still accompanied

This work was partially funded by Tuscany POR FSE 2014–2020 AI-MAP (CNR4C program, CUP B15J19001040004), the AI4EU project (EC, H2020, n.825619) and the AI4Media Project (EC, H2020, n. 951911).

© Springer Nature Switzerland AG 2021
A. Del Bimbo et al. (Eds.): ICPR 2020 Workshops, LNCS 12666, pp. 425–438, 2021.
https://doi.org/10.1007/978-3-030-68780-9_35

by the presence of several flaws and drawbacks. In fact, when neural networks are called to operate in an unprotected environment, as it could happen in multimedia forensic applications, they have shown important vulnerabilities. Such weaknesses can be exploited by an attacker through the design of ad-hoc adversarial manipulations in order to induce the model into a wrong evaluation. Depending on the specific application scenario we are dealing with in the real world, such an incorrect prediction can be crucial for the consequent choice, action or decision to be taken. In particular, in the context of image classification, a popular task on which we focus also our attention, an adversary can control and mislead a deep neural network classifier by introducing a small malicious perturbation in the input image [23].

Thanks to the florid research community interested in the subject, this phenomenon has been vastly analyzed on several neural network architectures on multiple tasks. While attacking a deep model seems to be easy due to the differentiability and complexity of deep models—indeed, many successful adversarial generation approaches exist [3,8,19],—counteracting this phenomenon and defending from attacks is still an open problem. Multiple approaches aiming at strengthening the attacked model [13,21] achieve robustness to weak or unknowing adversaries, but stronger attacks usually are able to mislead also enhanced models, as currently, adversarial examples appear to be an intrinsic property of every common deep learning architecture.

In this work, we analyze the phenomenon of strong adversarial examples in Neural Ordinary Differential Equation (N-ODE) networks—a recent deep learning model that generalizes deep residual networks and is based on solutions of parametric ODEs. Among its properties, we find the ability to tune at test-time the precision-efficiency trade-off of the network by changing the tolerance of the adaptive ODE solver used in the forward computation. Previous work [5] showed that neural ODE nets are more robust to PGD attacks than standard architectures such as ResNets, and most importantly, higher tolerance values— i.e. lower-precision higher-efficiency regimes—provided increased robustness at a negligible expense of accuracy of the model. Here, we follow up by analyzing whether the same phenomena occur to ODE nets under the stronger Carlini&Wagner attack. Additionally, we test the attack performance when using different values of the solver tolerance during the adversarial generation and the prediction phase. Based on our findings, we also propose a simple adversarial detection approach based on test-time tolerance randomization that we evaluate on image classification benchmarks under the assumption of a zero-knowledge adversary, i.e. when the attacker has access to the model but does not know about the deployed defense.

The contributions of the present work are the following:

- we analyze neural ODE image classifiers under the Carlini&Wagner attack;
- we study how their robustness change when varying the ODE solver tolerance;
- we propose a novel test-time tolerance randomization approach for ODE nets based on a majority-voting ensemble to detect adversarial examples, and we evaluate it on standard benchmarks.

After this introduction, Sect. 2 refers to works related to ours, and Sect. 3 briefly introduce background knowledge on neural ODE nets and the adopted Carlini&Wagner adversarial generation algorithm. In Sect. 4, we discuss the robustness to adversarial samples of neural ODEs in relation with the ODE solver tolerance, and we propose our novel detection scheme. In Sect. 5, we describe the experimental evaluation[1], and Sect. 6 discusses results. Section 7 concludes the paper and lays out future research directions.

## 2  Related Work

The vulnerability of adversarial examples poses major challenges to security- and safety-critical applications, e.g. malware detection, autonomous driving cars, biometrical access control, and thus it is studied diffusely in the literature. Most analyses of deep models focus on deep convolutional networks image classifiers [14,20,23] under a variety of attacks, such as PGD [17] or the stronger CW [3]. This sprouted a huge offer of defensive methodologies against adversarial samples in this scenario, such as model enhancing via distillation [21] and adversarial sample detection via statistical methods [9] or auxiliary models [4,18]. Among them, most promising methods are based on the introduction of randomization in the prediction process [1,24]. Feinman et al. [7] propose a detection scheme based on randomizing the output of the network using dropout that mostly relate with the rationale of our proposed detection method. Both their and our methods are based on stochasticity of the output, that has been proven a powerful defense [2].

Regarding analyzing and defending neural ODE architectures, few works in the current literature cover the subject. Seminal works include Carrara et al. [5], that analyzes ODE nets under PGD attacks and asses their superior robustness with respect to standard architectures, and Hanshu et al. [10], that proposes a regularization based on the time-invariance property of steady states of ODE solutions to further improve robustness. Relevant to our proposed scheme is also the work of Liu et al. [16] that exploit stochasticity by injecting noise in the ODE to increase robustness to perturbations of initial conditions, including adversarial ones.

## 3  N-ODE Nets and Carlini and Wagner Attack

In this section, we briefly introduce the Neural Ordinary Differential Equation (N-ODE) networks and the Carlini&Wagner adversarial attack we adopted in this work.

---

[1] Code and resources to reproduce the experiments presented here are available at https://github.com/fabiocarrara/neural-ode-features/tree/master/adversarial.

## 3.1   Neural ODE Networks

In this section, we provide a basic description of Neural ODE (*Ordinary Differential Equations*) and an overview of their main properties. For a more detailed discussion on neural ODEs, the interested reader can refer to [6].

A neural ODE Net is a parametric model which includes an *ODE block*. The computation of such a block is defined by a parametric ordinary differential equation (ODE) whose solution gives the output result. We indicate with $\mathbf{h}_0$ the input of the ODE block coinciding with the initial state at time $t_0$ of the initial-state ODE written in Eq. (1):

$$\begin{cases} \frac{\mathrm{d}\mathbf{h}(t)}{\mathrm{d}t} = f(\mathbf{h}(t), t, \theta) \\ \mathbf{h}(t_0) = \mathbf{h}_0 \end{cases}. \tag{1}$$

The function $f(\cdot)$, which depends on the parameter $\theta$, defines the continuous dynamic of the state $\mathbf{h}(t)$. By integrating the ODE (see Eq. (2)), the output of the block $\mathbf{h}(t_1)$ at a time $t_1 > t_0$ can be obtained.

$$\mathbf{h}(t_1) = \mathbf{h}(t_0) + \int_{t_0}^{t_1} \frac{\mathrm{d}\mathbf{h}(t)}{\mathrm{d}t} \mathrm{d}t = \mathbf{h}(t_0) + \int_{t_0}^{t_1} f(\mathbf{h}(t), t, \theta) \mathrm{d}t. \tag{2}$$

The above integral can be computed with standard ODE solvers, such as Runge-Kutta or Multi-step methods. Thus, the computation performed by the ODE block can be formalized as a call to a generic ODE solver

$$\mathbf{h}(t_1) = \mathrm{ODESolver}(f, \mathbf{h}(t_0), t_0, t_1, \theta). \tag{3}$$

Generally, in image classification applications, the function $f(\cdot)$ is implemented by means of a small trainable convolutional neural network. During the training phase, the gradients of the output $\mathbf{h}(t_1)$ with respect to the input $\mathbf{h}(t_0)$ and the parameter $\theta$ can be obtained using the adjoint sensitivity method. This consists of solving an additional ODE in the backward pass. Once the gradient is obtained, standard gradient-based optimization can be applied.

ODE Nets present diverse peculiar properties determined by their intrinsic structure; one of these, of particular interest for our case, concerns the *accuracy-efficiency trade-off* which is tunable at inference time by controlling the tolerance parameter of adaptive ODE solvers.

The ODE net image classifier (*ODE*) we consider in this work (see Fig. 1 bottom part) is constituted by an ODE block (implemented as Eq. (3)), responsible for the whole feature extraction chain, preceded by a limited pre-processing stage comprised of a single $K$-filter $4 \times 4$ convolutional layer with no activation function that linearly maps the input image in an adequate state space. The $f(\cdot)$ function in the ODE block is implemented as a standard residual block used in ResNets (described below). After the ODE block, the classification step is implemented with a global average-pooling operation followed by a single fully-connected layer with softmax activation. In addition to this, we consider also a classical ResNet *(RES)* (Fig. 1 top part) as baseline [6] in comparison with

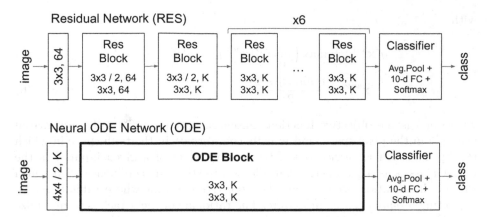

**Fig. 1.** Convolutional layers are written in the format *kernel width × kernel height [/ stride], n. filters*; padding is always set to 1. For MNIST, $K = 64$, and for CIFAR-10, $K = 256$.

ODE-Nets. It is composed of a 64-filter $3 \times 3$ convolutional layer and 8 residual blocks. Each residual block follows the standard formulation defined in [11], where Group Normalization [25] is used instead of batch one. The sequence of layers comprising a residual block is *GN-ReLU-Conv-GN-ReLU-Conv-GN* where *GN* stands for a Group Normalization with 32 groups and *Conv* is a $3 \times 3$ convolutional layer. The first two blocks downsample their input by a factor of 2 using a stride of 2, while the subsequent blocks maintain the input dimensionality. Only the first block uses 64-filters convolutions while the subsequent ones employ $K$-filter convolutions where $K$ varies with the specific dataset; the final classification step is implemented as before.

### 3.2 The Carlini and Wagner Attack

In this subsection, we briefly introduce the *Carlini&Wagner (CW)* attack [3] that has been used in our work to test and evaluate the robustness of the ODE-Net to adversarials samples. It is currently deemed as one of the strongest available adversary techniques to attack neural networks designed for image classification task. It exists in three versions, according to the metric adopted to measure the perturbation; in our implementation, we have considered the CW-$L_2$ which is formalized as in Eq. (4):

$$\min \left( c \cdot g \left( \mathbf{x}^{\mathrm{adv}} \right) + \left\| \mathbf{x}^{\mathrm{adv}} - \mathbf{x} \right\|_2^2 \right) \tag{4}$$

with

$$g(\mathbf{x}^{\text{adv}}) = \max\left(\max_{i \neq t} Z(\mathbf{x}^{\text{adv}})_i - Z(\mathbf{x}^{\text{adv}})_t, -\kappa\right),\tag{5}$$

$$\mathbf{x}^{\text{adv}} = \frac{\tanh(\mathbf{w}) + 1}{2}\tag{6}$$

where $g(\cdot)$ is the objective function (misclassification), $\mathbf{x}^{\text{adv}}$ is the adversarial example in the pixel space, and $\mathbf{w}$ is its counterpart in the tanh space in which the optimization is carried out. $Z(\cdot)$ are the logits of a given input, $t$ is the target class, $\kappa$ is a parameter that allows adjusting the confidence with which the misclassification occurs, and $c$ is a positive constant whose value is set by exploiting a binary search procedure. The rationale of the attack is to minimize at each iteration the highest confidence among non-target classes (first term of Eq. (4)) while keeping the smallest possible perturbation (second term). It is worth of mention the use of the term $\tanh(\mathbf{w})$ that represents a change of variable that allows one to move from the pixel to the tanh space. This helps regularizing the gradient in extremal regions of the perturbation space thus facilitating optimization with gradient-based optimizers.

## 4    The Proposed Decision Method Based on Tolerance Randomization

In this section, we propose a new method to provide robustness to ODE-nets against the *Carlini&Wagner (CW)* attack. In Subsect. 4.1, we present the idea to use a varying test-time tolerance to counteract adversarial perturbations, while in Subsect. 4.2, we propose an innovative approach which resorts to tolerance randomization to detect adversarial samples.

### 4.1    On Tolerance Variation

The *CW* attack is considered so far as one of the strongest adversarial algorithms to fool neural networks in image classification specifically. In Fig. 2, we report some adversarial examples generated with the CW attack for two well-known image datasets (MNIST and CIFAR-10, see Subsect. 5.1 for details on the datasets). Though ODE-Nets are very promising and show good performances, they are prone to be attacked as well as the other kinds of networks [5]. This can be appreciated in Table 1, where for each model and dataset, we report the classification error, the attack success rate (in percentage) the mean $L_2$ norm of the adversarial perturbation. Note that the basic behaviour of both models is similar: they show a limited error rate on original images but, on the contrary, the CW attack achieve a very high attack success rate. For ODE nets, it is worth noting that when we increase the value of the tolerance $\tau$ used at test time and by the attacker ($\tau_{\text{test}} = \tau_{\text{attack}}$), the classification error rate is rather stable, but the required attack budget increases; this is quite clear for the MNIST dataset

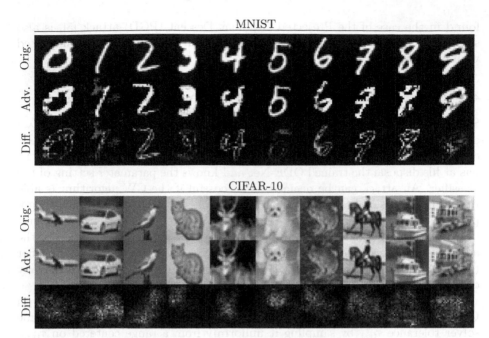

**Fig. 2.** Adversarial examples found with the Carlini&Wagner attack on our neural ODE network. Adversarial perturbations (Diff.) of CIFAR-10 samples have been amplified by a factor 10 for visualization purposes. Best viewed in electronic format.

**Table 1.** Classification error, attack success rate, and mean $L_2$ norm perturbation of RES and ODE on MNIST and CIFAR-10 test sets; for ODE, we report quantities varying the test-time adaptive solver tolerance $\tau$ ($\tau_{attack} = \tau_{test}$).

| MNIST | RES | ODE ($\tau_{attack} = \tau_{test}$) | | | | |
|---|---|---|---|---|---|---|
| | | $10^{-4}$ | $10^{-3}$ | $10^{-2}$ | $10^{-1}$ | $10^0$ |
| Classification Error (%) | 0.4 | 0.5 | 0.5 | 0.6 | 0.8 | 1.2 |
| CW Attack Success Rate (%) | 99.7 | 99.7 | 90.7 | 74.4 | 71.6 | 69.7 |
| Mean $L_2$ Perturb. $(\times 10^{-2})$ | 1.1 | 1.4 | 1.7 | 1.9 | 1.7 | 1.9 |
| CIFAR-10 | | | | | | |
| Classification Error (%) | 7.3 | 9.1 | 9.2 | 9.3 | 10.6 | 11.3 |
| CW Attack Success Rate (%) | 100 | 100 | 100 | 100 | 100 | 100 |
| Mean $L_2$ Perturb. $(\times 10^{-5})$ | 2.6 | 2.2 | 2.4 | 4.1 | 8 | 13.7 |

where the attack success rate quickly decreases, but it can also be perceived for CIFAR-10 by looking at the mean perturbation introduced by the attack: the attack success rate continues to be 100%, but a superior cost is paid in terms of applied distortion. While this witnesses again the strength of the CW attack, on the other hand, it confirms that the sensibility to the tolerance variations, found in the case of the Projected Gradient Descent (PGD) attack [5], is also shown by the CW attack. This aspect will be further debated and supported with experimental results in Sect. 6.

## 4.2 Tolerance Randomization to Detect Adversarial Samples

Starting from such findings, we investigated in depth such phenomenon, and we exploited it to propose a novel adversarial detection methodology. It has been considered that the attacker operates in a white-box scenario; consequently, he has at his disposal the trained ODE-Net and knows the parameter setting of the classifier. An attack can be deemed as successful if the CW algorithm is able to find an adversarial sample leading to a misclassification without exceeding a prefixed attack budget defined as the maximum number of optimization iterations. On the other side, the analyst has to perform image classification of the adversarial images generated by the CW-attacker by using the same classifier (the ODE-Net); so, if the attack has been successful, the analyst has not any chances not to run into a misclassification error.

On this basis, we proposed in this work a new detection strategy based on ODE-Net *tolerance randomization*: the rationale is to randomize the test-time solver tolerance $\tau_{test}$ by sampling it uniformly from a range centered on $\tau_{train}$ such that $\tau_{train} = \tau_{attack} \neq \tau_{test}$. This would allow to decouple, to some extent, the attack context to the testing one, and it should induce robustness in the capacity of the network not to be misled. Introducing stochasticity also helps the defendant against knowledgeable adversaries, as simply changing $\tau_{test}$ to a different fixed value can be easily counteracted by the adversary also changing $\tau_{attack}$ to the new value. The developed experimental tests (see Sect. 6.1) confirm that by using this approach the CW attack success rate can be diminished while maintaining a low classification error on pristine images.

On such a basis, we propose to ensemble several predictions with different randomly drawn test-time tolerance parameters $\tau_{test}$ to detect whether the classification system is subjected to an adversarial sample (created by CW attack in this case). By indicating with $V$ the number of voting members (i.e. the number of $\tau$ values randomly drawn) belonging to the ensemble, we will declare that an adversarial sample is detected if $v_{agree} < v_{min}$, where $v_{agree}$ is the largest amount of members that have reached the same decision on the test image (size of the majority) and $v_{min}$ is the minimum consensus threshold required for assessing the authenticity (non-maliciousness) of the input. According to our experiments (see Subsect. 6.2 for details), such a strategy can grant a significant improvement in detecting CW-generated adversarial images while obtaining a very low rejection of original ones.

# 5    Experimental Setup

In this section, we present the experimental set-up adopted to analyse and evaluate how the introduction of tolerance randomization during testing can improve the robustness to adversarial examples (CW generated) in the proposed scenario.

## 5.1    Datasets: MNIST and CIFAR-10

All the models used in this analysis have been trained on two standard and well-known image classification benchmarks: MNIST [15] and CIFAR-10 [12]. MNIST is composed by 60,000 images subdivided into training (50,000) and testing (10,000) sets; images are grayscale having a size of 28 × 28 pixels and represent hand-written digits (from 0 to 9, so it consists of 10 classes). MNIST is substantially the *de facto* standard baseline for novel machine learning algorithms and is nearly the only dataset used in most research concerning ODE nets. The second dataset has also been taken into account in our analysis is CIFAR-10; it is a 10-class image classification dataset too, comprised of again 60,000 RGB images (size 32 × 32 pixels) of common objects subdivided in training/testing sets (50,000/10,000).

## 5.2    Details on Training

Both considered models, RES and ODE, adopt a dropout, applied before the fully-connected classifier, with a drop probability of 0.5, while the SGD optimizer has a momentum of 0.9; the weight decay is $10^{-4}$, batch size is 128 and learning rate is $10^{-1}$ reduced by a factor 10 every time the error plateaus. The number of filters $K$ in the internal blocks is set to 64 for MNIST and 256 for CIFAR-10 respectively. For the ODE net model, containing the ODE block, we used the Dormand–Prince variant of the fifth-order Runge–Kutta ODE solver[2]; in such algorithm, the step size is adaptive and can be controlled by a tolerance parameter $\tau$ ($\tau_{train} = 10^{-3}$ has been set in our experiments during the training phase). The value of $\tau$ constitutes a threshold for the maximum absolute and relative error (estimated using the difference between the fourth-order and the fifth-order solution) tolerated when performing a step of integration; if such a step error exceeds $\tau$, the integration step is discarded and the step size decreased. Both models, RES and ODE, achieved classification performances comparable with the current state of the art on MNIST and CIFAR-10 datasets (see Table 1).

## 5.3    Carlini and Wagner Attack Implementation Details

We employ Foolbox 2.0 [22] to perform CW attacks on PyTorch models. We adopt Adam to optimize Eq. (4) setting the maximum iterations to 100 and performing 5 binary search steps to tune $c$ starting from $10^{-2}$. We adopt a learning rate of 0.05 for MNIST and 0.01 for CIFAR-10. As pristine samples to perturb, we select the first 5,000 images of each test set, discarding the images naturally misclassified by the classifier.

---

[2] Implemented in https://github.com/rtqichen/torchdiffeq.

## 6    Experimental Results

In this section, we present and discuss some of the experimental results carried out to investigate the behavior of the ODE Nets against the Carlini&Wagner attack. In Subsect. 6.1, we report results obtained by varying the tolerance $\tau$ at test-time, while in Subsect. 6.2, based on such findings, we propose a new strategy to detect that the ODE classifier is under adversarial attack.

### 6.1    Results Varying the Tolerance at Test-Time

To better understand how the tolerance $\tau$ impacts on the classification of the adversarial samples generated by means of CW attack, we varied its value at test time. We assumed that the ODE-Net has been trained at $\tau_{train} = 10^{-3}$ that provides a well-balanced trade-off between accuracy and computational cost of the network. Consequently, in our scenario assumptions, this is also the value that the CW-attacker would use ($\tau_{attack} = \tau_{train}$). At prediction time, the tolerance is drawn from a log-uniform distribution with the interval $[10^{-5}, 10^{-1}]$ centered in $\tau_{train} = 10^{-3}$; 20 values are sampled for each image to be classified. In Fig. 3, results obtained in terms of accuracy of the ODE-Net classifier on original inputs (blue bars) and adversarial examples (orange bars) are pictured respectively for MNIST and CIFAR-10 datasets; the tolerance, on x-axis, is binned (21 bins) in the log space.

It is evident that accuracy on natural inputs (blue bars) is always stable and also very high for each tolerance value, averagely around the original network accuracy (100% for MNIST and 90% for CIFAR-10). On the contrary, accuracy on CW-created adversarials inputs (orange bars) is quite poor (this demonstrates again the power of such a technique), but it is very interesting to note that in the central bin (around $\tau_{train} = 10^{-3}$) the attack has the highest effectiveness: this seems to mean that when the tolerance at test-time coincides with that adopted by the CW-attacker the classifier is strongly induced into a misclassification.

Furthermore, it can also be appreciated that if $\tau$ at test-time is moved away from the central value used by the CW-attacker, accuracy increases. This means that changes in the tolerance provide robustness to CW attack achieving, for instance, an accuracy on adversarial inputs of about 60% (with a corresponding accuracy around 90% on original images) for CIFAR-10 dataset (see Fig. 3b on the extreme right).

Finally, it worthy observing that the trend of growth of the orange bars is asymmetric with respect to the central value $\tau_{train} = 10^{-3}$, and it achieves higher values on the right side: this once more witness that, as expected, increasing the tolerance allows to gain in robustness as general.

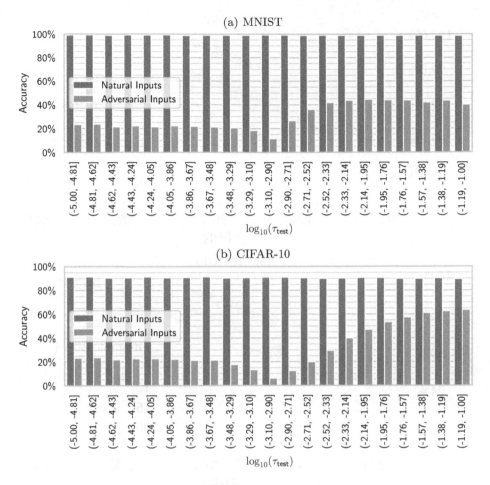

**Fig. 3.** Robustness vs test-time solver tolerance $\tau_{\text{test}}$. For each image, we sampled 20 values for $\tau$ from a log-uniform distribution within the $[10^{-5}, 10^{-1}]$ interval. We report the mean accuracy of the ODENet classifier on natural and adversarial examples for each tolerance bin (in log space).

## 6.2  Results on Detection of Adversarial Samples

In this section, we present the experiments used to verify the method proposed in Subsect. 4.2 based on tolerance randomization.

Looking at Fig. 4, we can see that, once established the size $V$ of the voting ensemble (different colored lines), by varying the threshold $v_{\min}$ with a step of 1, ROC curves can be obtained in terms of TPR versus FPR, where true positive indicate the correct classification of a natural input. Such graphs clearly demonstrate that high TPRs can be registered in correspondence of quite limited FPRs. This is particularly visible for MNIST dataset (see Fig. 4a), but it is still true for CIFAR-10; if, just for example, we refer to Fig. 4b when $V = 20$ (purple

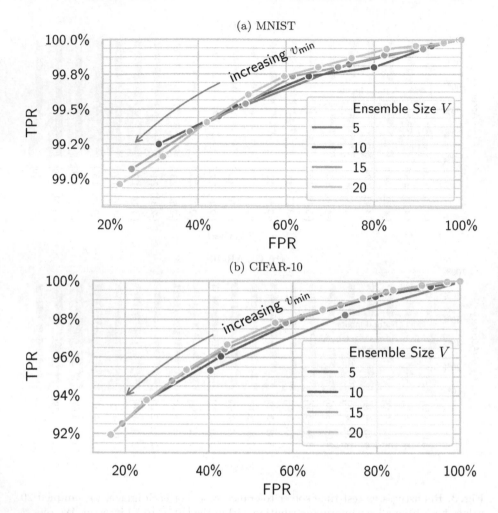

**Fig. 4.** Detection performance of the randomized tolerance ensemble. We show ROC curves (TPR vs FPR, where TP = "correctly detected natural input" and FP = "adversarial input misdetected as natural") obtained varying the minimum majority size $v_{min}$, i.e. if the number of majoritarian votes $v_{agree}$ in the ensemble is greater than $v_{min}$, the input is considered authentic (positive), otherwise adversarial (negative).

line), by increasing the value of $v_{min}$ (going down along the curve), we can reduce the FPR while maintaining an extremely high TPR: with $v_{min}$=20 a TPR=92.5% and a corresponding FPR=15% are achieved (see bottom-left corner of Fig. 4b).

This experiment basically demonstrates that if the ODE-Net is subjected to a zero-knowledge *Carlini&Wagner* attack in a white-box scenario, by resorting at test-time tolerance randomization, it is possible both to preserve classification performances on natural images and significantly reduce the capacity of the CW attack to fool the ODE classifier.

# 7    Conclusions and Future Work

In this paper, we analyze the robustness of neural ODE image classifiers in an uncontrolled environment. In particular, we pay attention to the behavior of N-ODE nets against the Carlini&Wagner (CW) attack which is deemed so far as one of the most performing adversarial attacks to the task of image classification. We focus on how the tolerance of the adaptive ODE solver—used in neural ODE nets to tune the computational precision-efficiency trade-off—affects the robustness against such attacks. We observe that deviating the tolerance used in prediction from the one used when generating adversarial inputs tends to undermine attacks while maintaining high accuracy on pristine samples. On this basis, we propose a novel adversarial detection strategy for ODE nets based on tolerance randomization and a major voting ensemble scheme.

Our evaluation performed on standard image classification benchmarks shows that our simple detection technique is able to reject roughly 80% of strong CW adversarial examples while maintaining +90% of original samples under white-box attacks and zero-knowledge adversaries. Moreover, we deem that the stochasticity in our method introduces difficulties also for knowledgeable adversaries. We hypothesize that to bypass our method the adversary should require high attack budgets to attack a wide range of tolerance values and distill them in a unique malicious input.

In future work, we plan to devise an attack strategy for our proposed detection method to evaluate it in more stringent attack scenarios. Moreover, we plan to extensively explore the tolerance space also from an attacker perspective.

# References

1. Barni, M., Nowroozi, E., Tondi, B., Zhang, B.: Effectiveness of random deep feature selection for securing image manipulation detectors against adversarial examples. In: ICASSP 2020–2020 IEEE International Conference on Acoustics, Speech and Signal Processing (ICASSP), pp. 2977–2981. IEEE (2020)
2. Carlini, N., Wagner, D.: Adversarial examples are not easily detected: bypassing ten detection methods. In: Proceedings of the 10th ACM Workshop on Artificial Intelligence and Security, AISec 2017, pp. 3–14. ACM, New York (2017). https://doi.org/10.1145/3128572.3140444
3. Carlini, N., Wagner, D.: Towards evaluating the robustness of neural networks. In: 2017 IEEE SP, pp. 39–57. IEEE (2017)
4. Carrara, F., Becarelli, R., Caldelli, R., Falchi, F., Amato, G.: Adversarial examples detection in features distance spaces. In: Proceedings of the European Conference on Computer Vision (ECCV) (2018)
5. Carrara, F., Caldelli, R., Falchi, F., Amato, G.: On the robustness to adversarial examples of neural ODE image classifiers. In: 2019 IEEE WIFS, pp. 1–6. IEEE (2019)
6. Chen, T.Q., Rubanova, Y., Bettencourt, J., Duvenaud, D.K.: Neural ordinary differential equations. In: Advances in Neural Information Processing Systems, pp. 6572–6583 (2018)

7. Feinman, R., Curtin, R.R., Shintre, S., Gardner, A.B.: Detecting adversarial samples from artifacts. CoRR abs/1703.00410 (2017)
8. Goodfellow, I.J., Shlens, J., Szegedy, C.: Explaining and harnessing adversarial examples. In: ICLR (2015)
9. Grosse, K., Manoharan, P., Papernot, N., Backes, M., McDaniel, P.D.: On the (statistical) detection of adversarial examples. CoRR abs/1702.06280 (2017)
10. Hanshu, Y., Jiawei, D., Vincent, T., Jiashi, F.: On robustness of neural ordinary differential equations. In: International Conference on Learning Representations (2019)
11. He, K., Zhang, X., Ren, S., Sun, J.: Identity mappings in deep residual networks. In: Leibe, B., Matas, J., Sebe, N., Welling, M. (eds.) ECCV 2016. LNCS, vol. 9908, pp. 630–645. Springer, Cham (2016). https://doi.org/10.1007/978-3-319-46493-0_38
12. Krizhevsky, A., Hinton, G.: Learning multiple layers of features from tiny images. Technical report, Citeseer (2009)
13. Kurakin, A., Goodfellow, I.J., Bengio, S.: Adversarial examples in the physical world. In: ICLR Workshops (2017). https://openreview.net/forum?id=HJGU3Rodl
14. Kurakin, A., et al.: Adversarial attacks and defences competition. CoRR abs/1804.00097 (2018)
15. LeCun, Y., Bottou, L., Bengio, Y., Haffner, P., et al.: Gradient-based learning applied to document recognition. Proc. IEEE 86(11), 2278–2324 (1998)
16. Liu, X., Xiao, T., Si, S., Cao, Q., Kumar, S., Hsieh, C.J.: Stabilizing neural ode networks with stochasticity (2019)
17. Madry, A., Makelov, A., Schmidt, L., Tsipras, D., Vladu, A.: Towards deep learning models resistant to adversarial attacks. In: ICLR (2018)
18. Metzen, J.H., Genewein, T., Fischer, V., Bischoff, B.: On detecting adversarial perturbations. In: ICLR (2017)
19. Moosavi-Dezfooli, S.M., Fawzi, A., Frossard, P.: Deepfool: a simple and accurate method to fool deep neural networks. In: IEEE CVPR, pp. 2574–2582 (2016)
20. Papernot, N., McDaniel, P., Jha, S., Fredrikson, M., Celik, Z.B., Swami, A.: The limitations of deep learning in adversarial settings. In: 2016 IEEE European Symposium on Security and Privacy (EuroS&P), pp. 372–387. IEEE (2016)
21. Papernot, N., McDaniel, P.D., Wu, X., Jha, S., Swami, A.: Distillation as a defense to adversarial perturbations against deep neural networks. IEEE SP 2016, 582–597 (2016). https://doi.org/10.1109/SP.2016.41
22. Rauber, J., Brendel, W., Bethge, M.: Foolbox: A python toolbox to benchmark the robustness of machine learning models. In: 34th International Conference on Machine Learning, Reliable Machine Learning in the Wild Workshop (2017)
23. Szegedy, C., et al.: Intriguing properties of neural networks. In: ICLR (2014)
24. Taran, O., Rezaeifar, S., Holotyak, T., Voloshynovskiy, S.: Defending against adversarial attacks by randomized diversification. In: Proceedings of the IEEE Conference on Computer Vision and Pattern Recognition, pp. 11226–11233 (2019)
25. Wu, Y., He, K.: Group normalization. In: Proceedings of the European Conference on Computer Vision (ECCV), pp. 3–19 (2018)

# Analysis of the Scalability of a Deep-Learning Network for Steganography "Into the Wild"

Hugo Ruiz[1], Marc Chaumont[1,2]✉, Mehdi Yedroudj[1],
Ahmed Oulad Amara[1], Frédéric Comby[1], and Gérard Subsol[1]

[1] Research-Team ICAR, LIRMM, Université Montpellier, CNRS,
Montpellier, France
{hugo.ruiz,marc.chaumont,mehdi.yedroudj,ahmed.oulad-amara,
frederic.comby,gerard.subsol}@lirmm.fr
[2] University of Nîmes, Nîmes, France

**Abstract.** Since the emergence of deep learning and its adoption in steganalysis fields, most of the reference articles kept using small to medium size CNN, and learn them on relatively small databases.

Therefore, benchmarks and comparisons between different deep learning-based steganalysis algorithms, more precisely CNNs, are thus made on small to medium databases. This is performed without knowing:

1. if the ranking, with a criterion such as accuracy, is always the same when the database is larger,
2. if the efficiency of CNNs will collapse or not if the training database is a multiple of magnitude larger,
3. the minimum size required for a database or a CNN, in order to obtain a better result than a random guesser.

In this paper, after a solid discussion related to the observed behaviour of CNNs as a function of their sizes and the database size, we confirm that the error's power law also stands in steganalysis, and this in a border case, i.e. with a medium-size network, on a big, constrained and very diverse database.

**Keywords:** Steganalysis · Scalability · Million images · Controlled development

## 1 Introduction

Steganography is the art of concealing information in a common medium so that the very existence of the secret message is hidden from any uninformed observer. Conversely, steganalysis is the art of detecting the presence of hidden data in such mediums [11].

Since 2015, thanks to the use of Deep-Learning, steganalysis performances have significantly improved [6]. Nevertheless, in many cases, those performances

© Springer Nature Switzerland AG 2021
A. Del Bimbo et al. (Eds.): ICPR 2020 Workshops, LNCS 12666, pp. 439–452, 2021.
https://doi.org/10.1007/978-3-030-68780-9_36

depend on the size of the learning set. It is indeed commonly shared that, to a certain extent, the larger the dataset, the better the results [24]. Thus, increasing the size of the learning set generally improves performance while also allowing for more diverse examples during training.

The objective of this article is to highlight the performance improvement of a Deep-Learning based steganalysis algorithm as the size of the learning set increases. In such a context, the behaviour of the network has never been studied before, and numerous questions related to model size and dataset size are still unsolved.

In Sect. 2, we discuss those questions and the generic laws or models that have been proposed by the scientific community. Next, in Sect. 3, we present the testbench used to assess the error power law. We justify and discuss the various choices and parameters setting, required in order to run the experiments. We also present the Low Complexity (LC-Net) network [15] which is a CNN that was considered as the state of the art algorithm for JPEG steganalysis in 2019 and 2020. In the experimental Sect. 4, we briefly present the Large Scale Steganalysis Database (LSSD) [18], the experimental protocol and describe the conducted experiments. We then analyze the accuracy evolution with respect to the learning set size, and predict, thanks to the error power law, the reachable efficiency for very big databases. Finally, we conclude and give some perspectives.

## 2   Model Scaling and Data Scaling

Many theoretical and practical papers are trying to better understand the behaviour of neural networks when their dimension is increasing (the depth or the width) [2,4,16,20], or when the number of examples is increasing [13,17,19]. To this end, lots of experiments are done in order to observe the evolution of the test error as a function of the *model size*, or as a function of the *learning set size* and general laws are proposed for modelling the phenomenon. Those are essential researches because finding some generic laws could confirm that CNN users are applying the right methodologies.

Even if they have access to a large dataset, which is, in many domains, rarely possible, CNN users may have to restrict the learning to small to medium database, and small to medium-size models, during the preliminary experiments. Then, once satisfied, if possible, they can run a long time learning on a large dataset (i.e. greater than $10^6$ examples) and eventually with a large network (i.e. greater than $10^6$ parameters).

The questions arising by users are then: do the comparisons between various models, when evaluated on a small dataset, also stand when the dataset size increase. In other words, can we reasonably conclude on the best model when comparing the networks on a small dataset? What is the behaviour of a medium-size network when the dataset size increases? More generally, is there a collapse in performance when a model or the dataset scales up? Or, will the accuracy increase? Should we prefer bigger models? Is there a minimum required size for models or dataset?

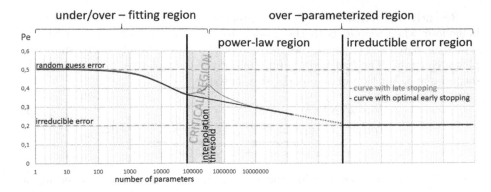

**Fig. 1.** Schematic generic evolution of the test error depending on the model size.

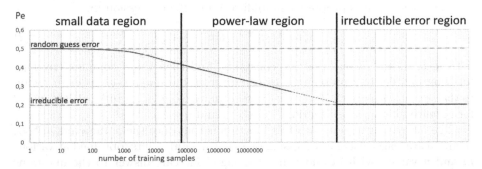

**Fig. 2.** Schematic generic evolution of the test error depending on the dataset size.

In the studies related to the *model scaling*, researchers have observed three regions depending on the model size. There is the *underfitting*, the *overfitting*, and finally the *over-parameterized* region. The transition point to the over-parameterized region is named the *interpolation threshold*. Figure 1 shows those three regions (note that the abscissa scale is logarithmic).

When looking to the curve of the error as a function of the model size (the green curve; this without optimal early stopping), we can observe a *double descent* [16]. In general, a practical conclusion is that the over-parameterized networks, i.e. with millions of parameters, can be used for any task and that it is beneficial using those more complex models. This idea has been, for example, used in practice in order to build gradually larger EfficientNet networks [21]. Note that this network has been strongly used by competitors [7,27] during the Alaska#2 competition [10].

In the studies related to the data scaling, researchers have observed that there are also three regions depending on the dataset size [13]. There is the *small data* region, the *power-law* region, and finally the *irreducible error* region. Figure 2 shows those three regions (note that the abscissa scale is logarithmic).

In the power-law region, the more data, the better results [19,23].

Recently, the authors of [17] have proposed a generic law that models the behaviour when scaling both the model size and the dataset size. Briefly, the test error noted $\epsilon$ is expressed as the sum of two exponentially decreasing term plus a constant. The first term is function of the dataset size, noted $n$, and the second one is function of the model size, noted $m$ [17]:

$$\epsilon : \mathbb{R} \times \mathbb{R} \to [0, 1] \tag{1}$$
$$\epsilon(m, n) \to \underbrace{a(m)n^{-\alpha(m)}}_{dataset\ power-law} + \underbrace{b(n)m^{-\beta(n)}}_{model\ power-law} + c_{\infty}$$

with $\alpha(m)$ and $\beta(n)$ controlling the rate of the error decrease, depending on $m$ and $n$ respectively, and $c_{\infty}$ the irreducible error, a real positive constant, independent of $m$ and $n$.

Then, the authors propose a simplification of the expression in:

$$\tilde{\epsilon}(m, n) = an^{-\alpha} + bm^{-\beta} + c_{\infty} \tag{2}$$

with $a$, $b$, $\alpha$, and $\beta$ real positive constants, and then use a complex envelope function in order to represent the transition from the *random-guess error* region to the *power-law* region [17]: $\hat{\epsilon}(m, n) = \epsilon_0 \| \tilde{\epsilon}(m, n)/(\tilde{\epsilon}(m, n) - i\eta) \|$, with $\epsilon_0 = 1/2$ for balanced binary classification, $i = \sqrt{-1}$, and $\eta \in \mathbb{R}$.

The interesting aspect with this function is that once the parameters $a$, $b$, $\alpha$, $\beta$, and $\eta$ are learnt using a regression on experimental points, obtained at various $m$ and $n$ values, with $m$ and $n$ not too high, one can answer to the questions mentioned above[1].

Now, let us go back to a more practical aspect. Suppose we are learning with an efficient network with enough parameters, i.e. on the right region relative to the interpolation threshold, possibly leaving the critical region (see Fig. 1), and use a data-set of medium size such that we are no more in the small data region, avoiding us a random guess error (see Fig. 2). When studying the effect of increasing the data on the error, we should be in the power-law region and Eq. 2 can be simplified, as in [13]:

$$\epsilon(n) = a'n^{-\alpha'} + c'_{\infty} \tag{3}$$

In the rest of our paper, we are observing, in the context of JPEG steganalysis, the behaviour of a medium network when the dataset size increases. Then, we confront these results to the power-law related to the data scaling (Eq. 3). Moreover, we are checking a "border case" because we are using a medium size model ($3.10^5$ parameters), and because we are using a very diverse database (the LSSD database [18] derived, from a part, from Alaska#2 [10]). This could result in a collapse in performance as the database increases, and failure to comply with the evolution law of the estimation error.

---

[1] See the paper [17], and the discussions here: https://openreview.net/forum?id=ryenvpEKDr.

# 3   A Test Bench to Assess Scalability for DL-based Steganalysis

## 3.1   Discussion on the Test Bench Design

**Choice of the Network:** Our objective is to evaluate the accuracy (or equivalently the probability of error) as a function of the increase in the size of the dataset. But, as many researchers, we are limited by computational resources, so we need a low complexity network. We thus selected the Low Complexity network (LC-Net) [15], for its medium size (300 000 parameters), and its good performance as it is recognized as a state-of-the-art CNN for JPEG steganalysis at the date we ran the experiments (between September 2019 to August 2020). Note that we can consider that the LC-Net is probably close to the *interpolation threshold*[2] which implies that we must take caution to do an early stopping, close to the optimal, during the learning phase.

**Choice of the Payload:** Another critical thing is that the network should be sufficiently far from the random-guess region in order to observe a concrete improvement of the performance when scaling the database. So we have to choose a payload in order that the LC-Net accuracy is quite far from 50%. This is quite challenging because there are no experiments results for LC-Net [15] on "controlled" databases such as LSSD having a large diversity. More generally, there are not so many experiments reported before the summer of 2020 that used the unique controlled and diverse, Alaska#1 [8] database. The objective, here, was to obtain accuracy between 60% and 70% for a small database (but not too small[3]), in order to observe progression when the dataset is scaled and to let the possibility to future better networks to beat our results with sufficient margin. After a lot of experimental adjustments, either related to the building of the LSSD database [18] or related to the LC-Net [15], we found that 0.2 bpnzacs was a good payload for grey-level JPEG 256 × 256 image with a quality factor of 75, ensuring to be quite far from the random-guess region for a small database of 20,000 images made of cover and stego images.

**Choice Related to the Database:** We decided to work on grey-level JPEG images in order to put aside the color steganalysis, which is still recent and not enough theoretically understood [1]. Related to color steganalysis, the reader can consult the paper WISERNet [29] or the description of the winning proposition for Alaska#1 [26]. The reader can also read the even more recent papers, in

---

[2] The ResNet18 with a width = 10 is made of 300,000 parameters and is in the *interpolation threshold* region for experiments run on CIFAR-10 and CIFAR-100 in [16].

[3] A too small database could bias the analysis since there is a region where the error increases when the dataset increase (see [16]). For example, in [23], we report that the number of images needed, for the medium size Yedroudj Net [25], to reach a region of good performance for spatial steganalysis (that is the performance of a Rich Model with an Ensemble Classifier), is about 10,000 images (5,000 covers and 5,000 stegos) for the learning phase, in the case where there is no cover-source mismatch, and the image size is 256 × 256 pixels.

the top-3 of Alaska#2 [7,27], which are based on an ensemble of networks (for example EfficientNet [21]), which have preliminary learned on ImageNet. Related to steganography, the most recent proposition in order to take into account the three channels during the embedding can be found in [9] and was used in order to embed payload in Alaska#2 images.

We also decided to work only on the quality factor 75, and thus let apart the quantization diversity. Nevertheless, the conclusions obtained in the following could probably extend to a small interval around quality factor 75. Indeed, the authors of [28] show that applying a steganalysis with a JPEG images database made of multiple quality factors could be done without efficiency reduction, using a small set of dedicated networks, each targeting a small interval of quality factor. Finally, it is maybe possible to use a unique network when there are various quality factors, as it has been done by a majority of competitors during Alaska#2, thanks to the use of a pre-learned network on ImageNet. An extension of our work to a database with a variety of quality factors is postponed to future research.

Another reason to work with a quality factor of 75 is that we had in mind, for future work, the use of non controlled images such as ImageNet. ImageNet is made of JPEG compressed images whose development process is not controlled and whose quality factors are multiple. By re-compressing the images with a smaller quality factor, such as 75, the statistical traces of the first initial compression are removed. Such a re-compression would allow us to work on images with a roughly similar quality factor, and whose statistical properties would not be too poor. Additionally, the experimental methodology would be close to those exposed in the current paper and would facilitate comparisons.

Finally, we built the LSSD database [18] in order to have a proper set for our experiments. For this database, we used controlled development using scripts inspired by Alaska#2. The LSSD was obtained by merging 6 public RAW images databases including Alaska#2. Without being as varied as images available on the Internet, we consider that diversity is nevertheless significant. There are 2 million covers in LSSD learning database, and we built "included subsets", from those 2 million covers in order to run our experiments.

With all those precautions, at the date were experiments started i.e. before running the experiment with an increasing number of examples, we assumed that we were at the border case, where the power-law on the data is valid.

## 3.2 Presentation of LC-Net

In this paper, we use the Low Complexity network (LC-Net) [15], which is a convolutional neural network proposed in 2019 for steganalysis in the JPEG domain. Its design is inspired by ResNet [12], the network that won the ImageNet competition in 2015. LC-Net performance is close to the state-of-the-art SRNet [5], with the advantage of a significant lower complexity in terms of the number of parameters [15] (twenty times fewer parameters than SRNet). This reduction in the number of parameters leads to less learning time as it converges faster toward an optimal solution.

LC-Net is composed of three modules: pre-processing, convolution and classification (see Fig. 3).

The pre-processing module has a total of 4 convolutional layers, with the first layer kernels initialized using 30 SRM filters. These high-pass filters are commonly used in steganalysis [22,25]. They allow the network to reduce its learning time but also to converge when using a small learning set. For instance, using the BOSS database [3], only 4,000 pairs of cover-stego images may be sufficient to perform learning "from scratch" and get good performance [23]. The parameters of the first layer are not fixed; they are optimized during training. This first layer is followed by an activation function "TLU" (Truncated Linear Unit) [22], where the $T$ threshold is set to 31. For the remaining layers of the network, the "ReLU" (Rectified Linear Units) activation function is used. No pooling is applied in this first module in order to preserve the stego signal.

The convolutional module is composed of 6 blocks, all with residual connections. These connections allow to avoid the vanishing gradient phenomenon during the back-propagation and thus to have deeper networks. The first two blocks have only two convolutional layers with direct residual connections. Blocks 3 to 6 include $3 \times 3$ convolutions with a stride equal to 2 to reduce the size of the feature maps. Indeed, it preserves the complexity of the computation time per layer when the number of filters is doubled [12]. Blocks 4 to 6, are Bottleneck residual blocks [12]. These blocks include 3 convolutional layers, a $1 \times 1$ convolution layer, a $3 \times 3$ convolution layer and another $1 \times 1$ convolution layer. The use of the Bottleneck block [12] allows the Low Complexity network having fewer parameters.

Finally, the classification module consists of a "Fully Connected" (FC) layer and a Softmax activation function. This function allows for obtaining the probabilities of the cover and stego classes.

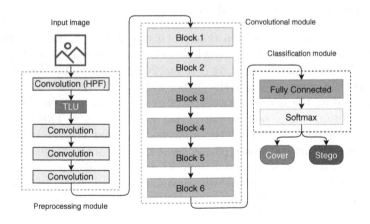

**Fig. 3.** Architecture of LC-Net

# 4  Experiments and Results

## 4.1  Dataset and Software Platform

As mentioned previously, the experiments were conducted on the LSSD database [18][4]. We are using greyscale JPEG images with a quality factor of 75. The size of those JPEG images is 256 × 256 pixels. They were obtained by developing RAW images (data issued from the camera sensors) from ALASKA#2, BOSS, Dresden, RAISE, Stego App, and Wesaturate public databases. The development scripts are inspired from the Alaska#2 scripts.

The cover database used for the learning phase is made of 2 million images. There is also a version with 1M, 500k, 100k, 50k, and 10k images. The 1M cover images database is a subset of the 2 million one, and so on, until the 10k cover images database. Each of those cover databases retains the same proportions of images from the different public databases.

The cover database used for the test phase is made of 100k images and will always be the same whatever the experiments. This test database is obtained by developing RAW images which were not present in the learning cover database. The test cover database roughly keeps the distribution of the origins of the public databases. Thus, the steganalysis scenario is close to a clairvoyant scenario where the test set and learning set are statistically very close.

In our experiments, we have only used the 500k, 100k, 50k and 10k versions of the cover database due to excessively long learning time process for 1M and 2M images versions.

The study was conducted on an IBM software container, with access to 144 supported POWER9 Altivec processors (MCPs) and two GV100GL graphic cards (Tesla V100 SXM2 16 Gb).

## 4.2  Training, Validation, and Testing

The embedding process has been done with the Matlab implementation of J-UNIWARD algorithm [14], with a payload of 0.2 bits per non-zero AC coefficient (bpnzacs). It took almost three days (2 d and 20 h) for the embedding on an Intel Xeon W-2145 (8 cores, 3.7–4.5 GHz Turbo, 11M cache).

Before feeding the neural network, JPEG images have to be decompressed in order to obtain spatial non rounded "real values" images. This essential step takes approximately 18 h for all the images. Note that storage space requirement becomes important. Indeed, for a 256 × 256 grey-scale image, the file's size is around 500 kB when it is stored in MAT format in *double* format. Thus, a database of 2M images requires a storage space of about 2 TB, and the learning cover bases, from 10k to 2M images, as well as the test cover database, in both JPEG and MAT format, occupy 3.8 TB.

In order to avoid storing all the decompressed images, one would have to perform an "online" decompression asynchronously coupled with an "online"

---

[4] The LSSD database is available at: http://www.lirmm.fr/~chaumont/LSSD.html.

mini-batch build, in order to feed the neural network "on flight". Note that with such a solution it could be possible to accelerate the global learning time, by directly working with the GPU RAM, instead of the CPU RAM or the Hard Disk, which have longer access time. This "online" treatment is not an easy task to carry, and the problem will have to be addressed for databases exceeding tens or even hundreds of million images.

The training set is split into two sets with 90% for the "real" training set and 10% for validation. As said previously, the test set is always the same and is made of 200k images (cover and stegos).

### 4.3  Hyper-parameters

To train our CNN we used a mini-batch stochastic gradient descent without dropout. We used the majority of the hyper-parameters of the article [15]. The learning rate, for all parameters, was set to 0.002 and is decreased at the epoch 130 and 230, with a factor equal to 0.1. The optimizer is Adam, and the weight decay is 5e–4. The batch size is set to 100 which corresponds to 50 cover/stego pairs. In order to improve the CNN generalization, we shuffled the entire training database at the beginning of each epoch. First, layer was initialized with the 30 basic high-pass SRM filters, without normalization, and the threshold of the TLU layer equals 31 similarly to [22,25]. We made an early stop after 250 epochs as in [15]. The code and all materials are available at the following link: http:// www.lirmm.fr/~chaumont/LSSD.html.

### 4.4  Results and Discussion

The different learning sets, from 20k to 1M images (covers and stegos), were used to test the LC-Net. Table 1 gives the network performances when tested on the 200k test cover/stego images database. Note that several tests were conducted for each size of the learning set and the displayed accuracies represent an average computed on the 5 best models recorded during the training phase. Those 5 best models are selected thanks to the validation set.

**Table 1.** Average accuracy evaluated on the 200k cover/stego images test set, with respect to the size of the learning database.

| Database size | Nb. of tests | Accuracy | Std. dev. | Duration |
|---|---|---|---|---|
| 20,000 | 5 | 62.33% | 0.84% | 2 h 21 |
| 100,000 | 5 | 64.78% | 0.54% | 11 h 45 |
| 200,000 | 5 | 65.99% | 0.09% | 23 h 53 |
| 1,000,000 | 1 | 68.31% | / | 10 d to 22 d |

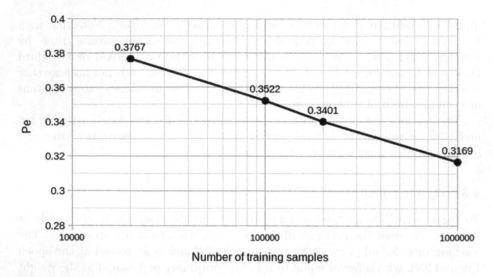

**Fig. 4.** Average probability of error with respect to the learning database size. Notice that the abscissa scale is logarithmic.

Before analyzing the network results, we should note that learning times become significant (from 10 days to 22 days[5]) once the number of images exceeds 1 million. This is a severe problem which did not allow us, due to lack of time, to run an evaluation on the 2M (1M covers + 1M stegos) and 4 million (2M covers + 2M stegos) databases as the learning duration would have been higher than one month. Moreover, the hardware architecture would probably not be able to store all the database in RAM, and it is likely that the paging optimizations would be no longer valid on such a volume of data. The transfer of an image from hard disk to the RAM, and then to the GPU, becomes then the bottleneck in the learning process. As explained previously, to cope with this problem, a decompression thread and a reading thread with the use of a shared file and the use of semaphores could be used to reduce the memory storage and the transfer on the GPU memory. It would make it possible to build image mini-batches "on flight" during network learning.

Results of Table 1, obtained for the payload 0.2 bpnzacs, confirm that the larger the learning set is (100k, 200k, 1M), the better the accuracy is. For the 20k database, the accuracy is 62% and increases by almost 2% each time the size of the learning set is increased. Moreover, the standard deviation is getting smaller and smaller, which highlights that the learning process is more and more stable as the database increases.

---

[5] Experiments with 10M images were disrupted by a maintenance of the platform and it took 22 day. Nevertheless, we rerun the experiment on a similar platform, without any disruption in learning, and the duration was only 10 day. So we report both values to be more precise.

These first results would mean that most of the steganalysis experiments run by the community, using a medium size (but also a large size) Deep Learning network, are not done with enough examples to reach the optimal performance, since most of the time the database is around 10k (BOSS learning set) to 150k images (Alaska#2 learning set with only one embedding algorithm). As an example, in our experiments, the accuracy is already improved by 6% when the database increase from 20k to 1M images and the accuracy can probably be improved by increasing the dataset size since the irreducible error region is probably not reached.

Those results also confirm that a medium-size network such as LC-Net does not have its performance collapsing when the database size increases.

More interestingly, we observe (see Fig. 4) an exponential decrease in the probability of error in the function of the dataset size. This is a direct observation of the power-law discussed in Sect. 2. Using a non-linear regression with Lagrange multipliers[6], we have estimated the parameters of Eq. 3:

$$\epsilon(n) = 0.492415 x^{-0.086236} + 0.168059 \tag{4}$$

The sum of the square error is $4.4 \times 10^{-6}$. Since there are only four points for the regression, it is probably erroneous to affirm that the irreducible error is $c'_\infty = 16.8\%$. However, we can use Eq. 4 to predict without much error, that if we use 2M images for the learning, the probability of error will be close to 30.9%, and if we use 20M images, the probability of error will be again reduced of 2% and will be 28.3%. Note that if $c_\infty$ was equal to 0, the probability of error would be 30.7% for 2M images, and 27.8% for 20M images. If we consider a probability of error of 28.3% for 20M of images, the gain obtained compared to the probability of error of 37.7% with 20k images, corresponds to 9% increase which is a considerable improvement in steganalysis domain.

To conclude, the error power-law also stands for steganalysis with Deep Learning, and this even when the networks are not very big (300,000 parameters), even when starting with a medium-size database (here, only 20k images), and even if the database is diverse (use of Alaska#2 development script and around 100 camera models). So, bigger databases are needed for optimal learning, and using more than one million images are likely needed before reaching the "irreducible error" region [13].

## 5   Conclusion

In this paper, we first have recalled the recent results obtained by the community working on AI, and related to the behaviour of Deep-Learning networks when the model size or the database size is increasing. We then proposed an experimental setup in order to evaluate the behaviour of a medium-size CNN steganalyzer (LC-Net) when the database size is scaled.

---

[6] The initial point for the non-linear regression is set to $a' = 0.5$, $\alpha' = 0.001$ and $c'_\infty = 0.01$, with $c'_\infty$ forced to be positive. The Matlab function is *fconmin* and the stop criterion is such that the mean of the sum of square error is under $10^{-6}$.

The obtained results show that a medium-size network does not collapse when the database size is increased, even if the database is diverse. Moreover, its performances are increased with the database size scaling. Finally, we observed that the error power law is also valid for steganalysis domain. We thus estimated what would be the accuracy of the network if the database would have been made of 20 million images.

Future work will require to be done on a more diverse database (quality factors, payload size, embedding algorithm, colour, less controlled database), and also other networks. More practically, an effort should be made in order to reduce the learning time, and especially memory management. Finally, there are still open questions to solve such as: finding a more precise irreducible error value, finding the slope of the power-law depending on the starting point of the CNN (use of transfer, use of curriculum, use of data-augmentation such as pixels-off [24]), or finding innovative techniques when the database is not huge in order to increase the performances.

**Acknowledgment.** The authors would like to thank the French Defense Procurement Agency (DGA) for its support through the ANR Alaska project (ANR-18-ASTR-0009). We also thank IBM Montpellier and the Institute for Development and Resources in Intensive Scientific Computing (IDRISS/CNRS) for providing us access to High-Performance Computing resources.

# References

1. Abdulrahman, H., Chaumont, M., Montesinos, P., Magnier, B.: Color images steganalysis using RGB channel geometric transformation measures. Secur. Commun. Netw. **15**, 2945–2956 (2016)
2. Advani, M.S., Saxe, A.M., Sompolinsky, H.: High-dimensional dynamics of generalization error in neural networks. Neural Netw. **132**, 428–446 (2020)
3. Bas, P., Filler, T., Pevný, T.: "Break our steganographic system": the ins and outs of organizing BOSS. In: Filler, T., Pevný, T., Craver, S., Ker, A. (eds.) IH 2011. LNCS, vol. 6958, pp. 59–70. Springer, Heidelberg (2011). https://doi.org/10.1007/978-3-642-24178-9_5
4. Belkin, M., Hsu, D., Ma, S., Mandal, S.: Reconciling modern machine-learning practice and the classical bias–variance trade-off. Proc. Nat. Acad. Sci. **32**, 15849–15854 (2019)
5. Boroumand, M., Chen, M., Fridrich, J.: Deep residual network for steganalysis of digital images. IEEE Trans. Inf. Forensics Secur. **5**, 1181–1193 (2019)
6. Chaumont, M.: Deep Learning in steganography and steganalysis. In: Hassaballah, M. (ed.) Digital Media Steganography: Principles, Algorithms, Advances, chap. 14, pp. 321–349. Elsevier (July 2020)
7. Chubachi, K.: An ensemble model using CNNs on different domains for ALASKA2 image steganalysis. In: Proceedings of the IEEE International Workshop on Information Forensics and Security, WIFS 2020. Virtual Conference due to Covid, New-York, NY, USA, (December 2020)
8. Cogranne, R., Giboulot, Q., Bas, P.: The ALASKA Steganalysis Challenge: a first step towards steganalysis. In: Proceedings of the ACM Workshop on Information Hiding and Multimedia Security, IH&MMSec 2019, pp. 125–137. Paris, France (July 2019)

9. Cogranne, R., Giboulot, Q., Bas, P.: Steganography by minimizing statistical detectability: the cases of JPEG and color images. In: Proceedings of the ACM Workshop on Information Hiding and Multimedia Security, IH&MMSec 2020, pp. 161–167 (June 2020)

10. Cogranne, R., Giboulot, Q., Bas, P.: Challenge academic research on steganalysis with realistic images. In: Proceedings of the IEEE International Workshop on Information Forensics and Security, WIFS 2020. Virtual Conference due to Covid (Formerly New-York, NY, USA) (December 2020)

11. Fridrich, J.: Steganography in Digital Media. Cambridge University Press, New York (2009)

12. He, K., Zhang, X., Ren, S., Sun, J.: Deep residual learning for image recognition. In: Proceedings of IEEE Conference on Computer Vision and Pattern Recognition, CVPR 2016, pp. 770–778. Las Vegas, Nevada (June 2016)

13. Hestness, J., et al.: Deep Learning Scaling is Predictable, Empirically. In: Unpublished - ArXiv. vol. abs/1712.00409 (2017)

14. Holub, V., Fridrich, J., Denemark, T.: Universal distortion function for steganography in an arbitrary domain. EURASIP J. Inf. Secur. 2014(1), 1–13 (2014). https://doi.org/10.1186/1687-417X-2014-1

15. Huang, J., Ni, J., Wan, L., Yan, J.: A customized convolutional neural network with low model complexity for JPEG steganalysis. In: Proceedings of the ACM Workshop on Information Hiding and Multimedia Security, IH&MMSec 2019, pp. 198–203. Paris, France (July 2019)

16. Nakkiran, P., Kaplun, G., Bansal, Y., Yang, T., Barak, B., Sutskever, I.: Deep double descent: where bigger models and more data hurt. In: Proceedings of the Eighth International Conference on Learning Representations, ICLR 2020. Virtual Conference due to Covid (Formerly Addis Ababa, Ethiopia) (April 2020)

17. Rosenfeld, J.S., Rosenfeld, A., Belinkov, Y., Shavit, N.: A constructive prediction of the generalization error across scales. In: Proceedings of the Eighth International Conference on Learning Representations, ICLR 2020. Virtual Conference due to Covid (Formerly Addis Ababa, Ethiopia (April 2020)

18. Ruiz, H., Yedroudj, M., Chaumont, M., Comby, F., Subsol, G.: LSSD: a controlled large JPEG image database for deep-learning-based Steganalysis into the Wild. In: Proceeding of the 25th International Conference on Pattern Recognition, ICPR 2021, Worshop on MultiMedia FORensics in the WILD, MMForWILD 2021, Lecture Notes in Computer Science, LNCS, Springer. Virtual Conference due to Covid (Formerly Milan, Italy) (January 2021). http://www.lirmm.fr/~chaumont/LSSD.html

19. Sala, V.: Power law scaling of test error versus number of training images for deep convolutional neural networks. In: Proceedings of the multimodal sensing: technologies and applications. vol. 11059, pp. 296–300. International Society for Optics and Photonics, SPIE, Munich (2019)

20. Spigler, S., Geiger, M., d'Ascoli, S., Sagun, L., Biroli, G., Wyart, M.: A jamming transition from under-to over-parametrization affects generalization in deep learning. J. Phys. Math. Theor. 52(47), 474001 (2019)

21. Tan, M., Le, Q.: EfficientNet: Rethinking Model Scaling for Convolutional Neural Networks. In: Proceedings of the 36th International Conference on Machine Learning, PMLR 2019, vol. 97, pp. 6105–6114. Long Beach, California, USA (June 2019)

22. Ye, J., Ni, J., Yi, Y.: Deep learning hierarchical representations for image steganalysis. IEEE Trans. Inf. Forensics Secur. TIFS 11, 2545–2557 (2017)

23. Yedroudj, M., Chaumont, M., Comby, F.: How to augment a small learning set for improving the performances of a CNN-based Steganalyzer? In: Proceedings of Media Watermarking, Security, and Forensics, MWSF 2018, Part of IS&T International Symposium on Electronic Imaging, EI 2018. p. 7. Burlingame, California, USA (28 January–2 February 2018)

24. Yedroudj, M., Chaumont, M., Comby, F., Oulad Amara, A., Bas, P.: Pixels-off: data-augmentation complementary solution for deep-learning steganalysis. In: Proceedings of the 2020 ACM Workshop on Information Hiding and Multimedia Security. p. 39–48. IHMSec 2020, Virtual Conference due to Covid (Formerly Denver, CO, USA) (June 2020)

25. Yedroudj, M., Comby, F., Chaumont, M.: Yedrouj-Net: an efficient CNN for spatial steganalysis. In: Proceedings of IEEE International Conference on Acoustics, Speech and Signal Processing, ICASSP 2018, pp. 2092–2096. Calgary, Alberta, Canada (April 2018)

26. Yousfi, Y., Butora, J., Fridrich, J., Giboulot, Q.: Breaking ALASKA: color separation for steganalysis in JPEG domain. In: Proceedings of the ACM Workshop on Information Hiding and Multimedia Security, IH&MMSec 2019, pp. 138–149. Paris, France (July 2019)

27. Yousfi, Y., Butora, J., Khvedchenya, E., Fridrich, J.: ImageNet pre-trained CNNs for JPEG steganalysis. In: Proceedings of the IEEE International Workshop on Information Forensics and Security, WIFS 2020. Virtual Conference due to Covid (Formerly New-York, NY, USA) (December 2020)

28. Yousfi, Y., Fridrich, J.: JPEG steganalysis detectors scalable with respect to compression quality. In: Proceedings of Media Watermarking, Security, and Forensics, MWSF 2020, Part of IS&T International Symposium on Electronic Imaging, EI 2020, p. 10. Burlingame, California, USA (January 2020)

29. Zeng, J., Tan, S., Liu, G., Li, B., Huang, J.: WISERNet: wider separate-then-reunion network for steganalysis of color images. IEEE Trans. Inf. Forensics Secur. **10**, 2735–2748 (2019)

# Forensics Through Stega Glasses: The Case of Adversarial Images

Benoît Bonnet[1]([✉])[iD], Teddy Furon[1,2][iD], and Patrick Bas[2][iD]

[1] Univ. Rennes, Inria, CNRS, IRISA, Rennes, France
{benoit.bonnet,teddy.furon}@inria.fr
[2] Univ. Lille, CNRS, Centrale Lille, UMR 9189, CRIStAL, Lille, France
patrick.bas@centralelille.fr

**Abstract.** This paper explores the connection between forensics, counter-forensics, steganography and adversarial images. On the one hand, forensics-based and steganalysis-based detectors help in detecting adversarial perturbations. On the other hand, steganography can be used as a counter-forensics strategy and helps in forging adversarial perturbations that are not only invisible to the human eye but also less statistically detectable. This work explains how to use these information hiding tools for attacking or defending computer vision image classification. We play this cat and mouse game using both recent deep-learning content-based classifiers, forensics detectors derived from steganalysis, and steganographic distortions dedicated to color quantized images. It turns out that crafting adversarial perturbations relying on steganographic perturbations is an effective counter-forensics strategy.

## 1 Introduction

Adversarial examples is an emerging field in Information Forensics and Security, addressing the vulnerabilities of Machine Learning algorithms. This paper casts this topic to Computer Vision, and in particular, to image classification, and its associated forensics counter-part: the detection of adversarial contents.

A Deep Neural Network (DNN) is trained to classify images by the object represented in the picture. This is for instance the well-known ImageNet challenge encompassing a thousand of classes. The state-of-the-art proposes impressive results as classifiers now do a better job than humans with less classification errors and much faster timings. The advent of the AlexNet DNN in 2012 is often seen as the turning point of 'Artificial Intelligence' in Computer Vision. Yet, the recent literature of adversarial examples reveals that these classifiers are vulnerable to specific image modifications. The perturbation is often a weak signal barely visible to the human eyes. Almost surely, no human would incorrectly classify these adversarial images. This topic is extremely interesting as it challenges the 'Artificial Intelligence' qualification too soon attributed to Deep Learning.

The connection between adversarial examples and forensics/anti-forensics is obvious. First, adding an adversarial perturbation to delude a processing is an

© Springer Nature Switzerland AG 2021
A. Del Bimbo et al. (Eds.): ICPR 2020 Workshops, LNCS 12666, pp. 453–469, 2021.
https://doi.org/10.1007/978-3-030-68780-9_37

image manipulation per se and therefore detecting adversarial examples is a forensic task by itself. Second, techniques forging adversarial examples are also used to fool forensics detectors as proposed in [1,2]. In this case, the adversarial attack is a counter-forensics strategy to conceal an image manipulation.

Paper [3] makes the connection between adversarial examples and information hiding (be it watermarking or steganography). Both fields modify images (or any other type of media) in the pixel domain so that the content is moved to a targeted region of the feature space. That region is the region associated to a secret message in information hiding or to a wrong class in adversarial examples. Indeed, paper [3] shows that adversarial examples benefits from ideas proven efficient in watermarking, and vice-versa.

This paper contributes to the same spirit by investigating what both steganography and steganalysis bring to the "cat-and-mouse" game of adversarial examples. There are two natural ideas:

**Steganalysis** aims at detecting weak perturbations in images. This field is certainly useful for the defender.

**Steganography** is the art of modifying an image while being non-detectable. This field is certainly useful for the attacker.

These two sides of the same coin allow to mount a defense and to challenge it in return, as done in other studies [4–6]. This paper aims at revealing the status of the game between the attacker and the defender at the time of writing, *i.e.* when both players use up-to-date tools: state-of-the-art image classifiers with premium steganalyzers, and best-in-class steganography embedders. As far as we know, this paper proposes three first time contributions:

- Assess the robustness of very recent image classifiers, EfficientNet [7] and its robust version [8],
- Apply one state-of-the-art steganalyzer (SRNet [9]) for forensics purposes, *i.e.* to detect adversarial images,
- Use the best steganographic schemes to craft counter-forensics perturbations reducing the detectability: HILL [10] uses empirical costs, MiPod [11] models undetectability from a statistical point of view, while GINA [12,13] synchronizes embeddings on color channels.

Section 2 reviews the connections between forensics, steganography, and adversarial examples. Our main contribution on counter-forensics and experimental results are detailed in Sect. 3 and 4.

## 2   Related Works

### 2.1   Steganalysis for Forensic Purposes

Steganalysis has always been bounded to steganography, obviously. Yet, a recent trend is to resort to this tool for other purposes than detecting whether an image conceals a secret message. For instance, paper [14] claims the universality of SRM and LBP steganalyzers for forensic purposes detecting image processing (like Gaussian blurring, gamma correction) or splicing. The authors of [15] used this approach during the IEEE IFS-TC image forensics challenge. The same trend holds as well on audio forensics [16]. As for camera model identification, the inspiration from steganalysis (co-occurrences, color dependencies, conditional probabilities) is clearly apparent in [17].

This reveals a certain versatility of steganalysis. It is not surprising since the main goal is to model and detect weak signals. Modern steganalyzers are no longer based on hand-crafted features like SRM [18]. They are no more no less than Deep Neural Networks like Xu-Net [19] or SRNet [9]. The frontier between steganalysis and any two-class image classification problem (such as image manipulation detection) is blurred. Yet, these networks have a specific structure able to focus on weak signal detection. They for example avoid sub-sampling or pooling operations in order to preserve high frequency signals, they also need large databases combined with augmentation techniques and curriculum learning to converge [20].

However, this general-purpose strategy based on steganalysis method has some drawbacks. It lacks fine-grained tampering localization, which is often an issue in forensics [21]. Paper [22] goes a step further in the cat-and-mouse game with an counter-forensic method: knowing that the defender uses a steganalyzer, the attacker modifies the perturbation (accounting for a median filtering or a contrast enhancement) to become less detectable.

As for adversarial images detection, this method is not new as well. The authors of [23] wisely see steganalysis detection as a perfect companion to adversarial re-training. This last mechanism fights well against small perturbations. It however struggles in correctly classifying coarser and more detectable attacks. Unfortunately, this idea is supported with a proof of concept (as acknowledged by the authors): the steganalyzer is rudimentary, the dataset is composed of tiny images (MNIST). On the contrary, the authors of [24] outline that steganalysis works better on larger images like ImageNet (ILSVRC-2016). They however use a deprecated classifier (VGG-16 [25]) with outdated steganalyzers based on hand-crafted features (SPAM and SRM).

## 2.2 Adversarial Examples

This paper focuses on white-box attacks where the attacker knows all implementation details of the classifier.

To make things clearer, the classifier has the following structure: a pre-processing $T$ maps an image $\mathbf{I}_o \in \{0, 1, \ldots, 255\}^n$ (with $n = 3LC$, 3 color channels, $L$ lines and $C$ columns of pixels) to $\mathbf{x}_o = T(\mathbf{I}_o) \in \mathcal{X}^n$, with $\mathcal{X} := [0, 1]$ (some networks also use $\mathcal{X} = [-1, 1]$ or $[-3, 3]$). This pre-processing is heuristic, sometimes it just divides the pixel value by 255, sometimes this normalization is channel dependent based on some statistics (empirical mean and standard deviation). After normalization, $\mathbf{x}_o$ feeds the trained neural network to produce the estimated probabilities $(\hat{p}_k(\mathbf{x}_o))_k$ of being from class $k \in \{1, \ldots, K\}$. The predicted class is given by:

$$\hat{c}(\mathbf{x}_o) = \arg\max_k \hat{p}_k(\mathbf{x}_o). \tag{1}$$

The classification is correct if $\hat{c}(\mathbf{x}_o) = c(\mathbf{x}_o)$, the ground truth label of image $I_o$.

An *untargeted* adversarial attack aims at finding the optimal point:

$$\mathbf{x}_a^\star = \arg\min_{\mathbf{x}:\hat{c}(\mathbf{x})\neq c(x_o)} \|\mathbf{x} - \mathbf{x}_o\|, \tag{2}$$

where $\|\cdot\|$ is usually the Euclidean distance.

Discovering this optimal point is difficult because the space dimension $n$ is large. In a white-box scenario, all attacks are sub-optimal iterative processes. They use the gradient of the network function efficiently computed thanks to the back-propagation mechanism to find a solution $\mathbf{x}_a$ close to $\mathbf{x}_a^\star$. They are compared in terms of probability of success, average distortion, and complexity (number of gradient computations). This paper considers well-known attacks (ranked from low to high complexity): FGSM [26], PGD (Euclidean version) [27], DDN [28], and CW [29].

As outlined in [30], definition (2) is very common in literature, yet it is incorrect. The final goal of the attacker is to create an adversarial image $\mathbf{I}_a$ in the pixel domain, not $\mathbf{x}_a$ in $\mathcal{X}^n$. Applying the inverse mapping $\mathsf{T}^{-1}$ is not solving the issue because this a priori makes non integer pixel values. Rounding to the nearest integer, $\mathbf{I}_a = [\mathsf{T}^{-1}(\mathbf{x}_a)]$, is simple but not effective. Some networks are so vulnerable (like ResNet-18) that $\mathsf{T}^{-1}(\mathbf{x}_a) - \mathbf{I}_o$ is a weak signal partially destroyed by rounding. The impact is that, after rounding, $\mathbf{I}_a$ is no longer adversarial. Note that DDN is a rare example of a powerful attack natively offering quantized pixel values.

Paper [30] proposes a post-processing $\mathsf{Q}$ on top of any attack that makes sure $\mathbf{I}_q = \mathsf{Q}(\mathsf{T}^{-1}(\mathbf{x}_a))$ is *(i)* an image (integral constraint), *(ii)* remains adversarial, and *(iii)* has a low Euclidean distortion $\|I_q - I_o\|$. This paper follows the same approach but adds another constraint: *(iv)* be non-detectable.

Figure 1 shows the characteristic function measuring the probability of success of an attack [30] as a function of the distortion budget ($L_2$-norm) against landmark classifiers in the history of ImageNet challenge. The characteristic function starts at $1 - \eta$, where $\eta$ is the accuracy of the classifier: a proportion $1 - \eta$ of original images are naturally adversarial since there are misclassified. As we know, the accuracy of the networks increases as time goes by: AlexNet (2012) [31] < VGG-16 (2015) [25] < GoogLeNet (2015) [32] < ResNet-50 [33] (2016) < EfficientNet-b0 [7] (2019). On the other hand, the robustness to this attack can be measured by the average distortion necessary for hacking the images (cf. Table 1). This reveals a different hierarchy: ResNet-50 and VGG-16 are quite fragile contrary to the old AlexNet. Overall, the recent EfficientNet is both more accurate and more robust.

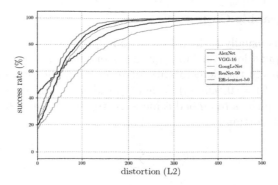

**Fig. 1.** Characteristic function of attack [30] (PGD in best effort with quantization) against well known (vanilla) classifiers for ImageNet.

**Table 1.** Robustness of recent classifiers against $PGD_2$ followed by quantization [30]

|  | Acc (%) | $P_{suc}$ (%) | $\overline{L_2}$ |
|---|---|---|---|
| Alexnet | 57.0 | 100 | 104 |
| VGG-16 | 75.0 | 100 | 56.5 |
| GoogLeNet | 77.2 | 99.8 | 72.9 |
| ResNet-50 | 80.0 | 97.2 | 81 |
| Vanilla EfficientNet-b0 [7] | 82.8 | 99.1 | 115 |
| Robust EfficientNet [8] | 84.3 | 98.5 | 192 |

## 2.3  Defenses

The literature proposes four types of defenses or counter-attacks against adversarial examples white-box attacks:

**To Detect:** Being barely visible does not mean that the perturbation is not statistically detectable. This defense analyses the image and bypasses the classifier if detected as adversarial [34]. This is a forensics analysis targeted on adversarial signals.

**To Reform:** The perturbation looks like a random noise that may be filtered out. This defense is usually a front-end projecting the image back to the manifold of natural images [35].

**To Robustify:** At learning, adversarial images are included in the training set with their original class labels. Adversarial re-training robustifies a 'vanilla' trained network [27].

**To Randomize:** At testing, the classifier depends on a secret key or an alea. This blocks pure white-box attacks [36,37].

This paper evaluates steganalysis as a candidate for the first line of defense against white-box attacks targeting vanilla or robust networks.

## 2.4   Steganographic Costs

Undetectability is usually tackled by the concept of costs in the steganographic literature: each pixel location $i$ of a given cover image is assigned a set of costs $(w_i(\ell))_\ell$ that reflects the detectability of modifying the $i$-th pixel by $\ell$ quantum. Usually, $w_i(0) = 0$, $w_i(-\ell) = w_i(\ell)$, and $w_i(|\ell|)$ is increasing. The goal of the steganographer is to embed a message $\mathbf{m}$ while minimizing the empirical steganographic distortion:

$$D(\boldsymbol{\ell}) := \sum_{i=1}^{n} w_i(\ell_i). \tag{3}$$

This is practically achieved using Syndrome Trellis Codes [38]. This paper proposes to use the steganographic distortion (instead of $L_1$, $L_2$ or $L_\infty$ norms in adversarial literature) in order to decrease detectability.

Note that this distortion is additive, which is equivalent to consider that each pixel modification yields a detectability independent from the others. Yet, one strategy takes into account potential interactions between neighboring modifications. The image is first decomposed into disjoint lattices to be sequentially embedded where costs are then sequentially updated after the embedding over one lattice [12].

This work uses three families of steganographic costs. The first one, HILL [10], is empirical and naive, but has nevertheless been widely used in steganography thanks to its simplicity. The cost map $\mathbf{w}$ associated to $\pm 1$ is computed using two low-pass averaging filters $\mathbf{L}_1$ and $\mathbf{L}_2$ of respective size $3 \times 3$ and $15 \times 15$ and one high pass filter $\mathbf{H}$: ($*$ means convolution)

$$\mathbf{w} = \frac{1}{|\mathbf{I} * \mathbf{H}| * \mathbf{L}_1} * \mathbf{L}_2, \text{with } \mathbf{H} = \begin{bmatrix} -1 & 2 & -1 \\ 2 & -4 & 2 \\ -1 & 2 & -1 \end{bmatrix}. \tag{4}$$

The second one, derived from MiPod [11], assumes that the residual signal is distributed as $\mathcal{N}(0, \sigma_i^2)$ for the original image, and $\mathcal{N}(\ell_i, \sigma_i^2)$ for the stego image. The variance $\sigma_i^2$ is estimated on each pixel using Wiener filtering and a least square approximation on a basis of cosine functions. The cost is the log likelihood ratio between the two distributions evaluated at 0, $i.e.$:

$$w_i(\ell_i) = \ell_i^2 / \sigma_i^2. \tag{5}$$

Unlike HILL, this model handles modifications other than $\pm 1$.

The last one is a cost updating strategy favoring coherent modifications between pixels within a spatial or color neighborhood. It is called GINA [13] and it is derived from CMD [12]. It splits the color images into 4 disjoint lattices per channel, i.e. 12 lattices. The embedding performs sequentially starting by the green channel lattices. The costs on one lattice is updated according to the modifications done on the previous ones as:

$$w_i'(\ell_i) = \frac{1}{9} w_i(\ell_i), \text{ if } \mathsf{sign}(\ell_i) = \mathsf{sign}(\mu_i), \tag{6}$$

with $\mu_i$ the average of the modifications already performed in the spatial or colour neighborhood of location $i$.

## 2.5  Looking at Adversarial Examples with Stega Glasses

First, note that adversarial images recently became a source of inspiration for steganography: paper [39] proposes the concept of steganography with an adversarial embedding fooling a DNN-based steganalyzer. References [40] and [41] propose both to cast the problem of adversarial embedding as a game-theoretical problem. A protocol to train efficiently new adversaries and to generate less detectable stego contents using a min max strategy is presented in [40]. The reference [41] solves the game between one embedder and one steganalyst using both different levels of adversarial perturbations.

Paper [23] stresses however one fundamental difference between steganography and adverarial examples: Steganalysis has two classes, where the class 'cover' distribution is given by Nature, whereas the class 'stego' distribution is a consequence of designed embedding schemes. On the other hand, a *perfect* adversarial example and an original image are distributed as by the class $\hat{c}(\mathbf{x}_a)$ or $c(\mathbf{x}_o)$, which are both given by Nature.

We stress another major difference: Steganographic embedding is essentially a stochastic process. Two stego-contents derived from the same cover are different almost surely with STC [38]. This is a mean to encompass the randomness of the messages to be embedded. This is also the reason why steganographic embedders turns the costs $(w_i(\ell))_\ell$ into probabilities $(\pi_i(\ell))_\ell$ of modifying the $i$-th pixel by $\ell$ quantum. These probabilities are derived to minimize the detectability under the constraint of an embedding rate given by the source coding theorem:

$$R = -n^{-1} \sum_i \sum_{\ell_i} \pi_i(\ell_i) \log_2 \left( \pi_i(\ell_i) \right) \text{ bits.} \qquad (7)$$

In contrast, an attack is a deterministic process always giving the same adversarial version of one original image. Adversarial imaging does not need these probabilities.

# 3  Steganographic Post-Processing

This section presents the use of steganography in our post-processing Q mounted on top of any adversarial attack.

## 3.1  Optimal Post-processing

Starting from an original image, we assume that an attack has produced $\mathbf{x}_a$ mapped back to $\mathbf{I}_a = \mathsf{T}^{-1}(\mathbf{x}_a)$. The problem is that $\mathbf{I}_a \in [0, 255]^n$, *i.e.* its pixel values are a priori not quantized. Our post-processing specifically deals with that matter, outputting $\mathbf{I}_q = Q(\mathbf{I}_a) \in \{0, \ldots, 255\}^n$. We introduce $\mathbf{p}$ the perturbation after the attack and $\mathbf{q}$ the perturbation after our post-processing:

$$\mathbf{p} := \mathbf{I}_a - \mathbf{I}_o \in \mathbb{R}^n, \tag{8}$$

$$\boldsymbol{\ell} := \mathbf{I}_q - \mathbf{I}_o \in \mathbb{Z}^n. \tag{9}$$

The design of $Q$ amounts to find a good $\boldsymbol{\ell}$. This is more complex than just rounding perturbation $\mathbf{p}$.

We first restrict the range of $\boldsymbol{\ell}$. We define the degree of freedom $d$ as the number of possible values for each $\ell_i$, $1 \le i \le n$. This is an even integer greater than or equal to 2. The range of $\ell_i$ is centered around $p_i$. For instance, when $d = 2$, $\ell_i \in \{\lfloor p_i \rfloor, \lceil p_i \rceil\}$. In general, the range is given by

$$\mathcal{L}_i := \{\lceil p_i \rceil - d/2, \ldots, \lceil p_i \rceil - 1, \lceil p_i \rceil, \ldots, \lceil p_i \rceil + d/2 - 1\}. \tag{10}$$

Over the whole image, there are $d^n$ possible sequences for $\boldsymbol{\ell}$.

We now define two quantities depending on $\boldsymbol{\ell}$. The *classifier loss* at $\mathbf{I}_q = \mathbf{I}_a - \mathbf{p} + \boldsymbol{\ell}$:

$$L(\boldsymbol{\ell}) := \log(\hat{p}_{c_o}(\mathbf{I}_a - \mathbf{p} + \boldsymbol{\ell})) - \log(\hat{p}_{c_a}(\mathbf{I}_a - \mathbf{p} + \boldsymbol{\ell})), \tag{11}$$

where $c_o$ is the ground truth class of $\mathbf{I}_o$ and $c_a$ is the predicted class after the attack. When the attack succeeds, it means that $\mathbf{I}_a$ is classified as $c_a \neq c_o$ because $\hat{p}_{c_a}(\mathbf{I}_a) > \hat{p}_{c_o}(\mathbf{I}_a)$ so that $L(\mathbf{p}) < 0$. Our post-processing cares about maintaining this adversariality. This constrains $\boldsymbol{\ell}$ s.t. $L(\boldsymbol{\ell}) < 0$.

The second quantity is the *detectability*. We assume that a black-box algorithm gives the stego-costs $(w_i(\boldsymbol{\ell}))_\ell$ for a given original image. The overall detectability of $\mathbf{I}_q$ is gauged by $D(\boldsymbol{\ell})$ as given by (3). In the end, the optimal post-processing $Q$ minimizes detectability while maintaining adversariality:

$$\boldsymbol{\ell}^\star = \arg \min_{\boldsymbol{\ell}: L(\boldsymbol{\ell}) < 0} D(\boldsymbol{\ell}). \tag{12}$$

### 3.2   Our Proposal

The complexity for finding the solution of (12) a priori scales as $O(d^n)$. Two ideas from the adversarial examples literature help reducing this cost. First, the problem is stated as an Lagrangian formulation as in [29]:

$$\boldsymbol{\ell}_\lambda = \arg \min D(\boldsymbol{\ell}) + \lambda L(\boldsymbol{\ell}). \tag{13}$$

where $\lambda \ge 0$ is the Lagrangian multiplier. This means that we must solve this problem for any $\lambda$ and then find the smallest value of $\lambda$ s.t. $L(\boldsymbol{\ell}_\lambda) < 0$.

Second, the classifier loss is linearized around $\mathbf{I}_a$, *i.e.* for $\boldsymbol{\ell}$ around $\mathbf{p}$: $L(\boldsymbol{\ell}) \approx L(\mathbf{p}) + (\boldsymbol{\ell} - \mathbf{p})^\top \mathbf{g}$, where $\mathbf{g} = \nabla L(\mathbf{p})$. This transforms problem (13) into

$$\boldsymbol{\ell}_\lambda = \arg \min \sum_{i=1}^{n} w_i(\ell_i) + \lambda(p_i - \ell_i).g_i. \tag{14}$$

The solution is now tractable because the functional is separable: we can solve the problem pixel-wise. The algorithm stores in $d \times n$ matrix $W$ the costs, and in $d \times n$ matrix $G$ the values $((p_i - \ell_i).g_i)_i$ for $\ell_i \in \mathcal{L}_i$ (10). For a given $\lambda$, it computes $W + \lambda G$ and looks for the minimum of each column $1 \leq i \leq n$. In other words, it is as complex as $n$ minimum findings, each over $d$ values, which scales as $O(n \log d)$.

Note that for $\lambda = 0$, $\mathbf{Q}$ quantizes $I_{a,i}$ 'towards' $I_{o,i}$ to minimize detectability. Indeed, if $\ell_i = 0$ is admissible ($0 \in \mathcal{L}_i$ holds if $|p_i| \leq d/2$), then $\mathbf{Q}(I_{a,i}) = I_{o,i}$ at $\lambda = 0$.

On top of solving (14), a line search over $\lambda$ is required. The linearization of the loss being a crude approximation, we make calls to the network to check that $\mathbf{Q}(\mathbf{I}_a)$ is adversarial: When testing a given value of $\lambda$, $\boldsymbol{\ell}_\lambda$ is computed to produce $I_q$ that feeds the classifier. If $I_q$ is adversarial then $L(\boldsymbol{\ell}_\lambda) < 0$ and we test a lower value of $\lambda$ (giving more importance to the detectability), otherwise we increase it. The search is performed over $\log_2(n)$ steps. The images we used are of dimension $224 \times 224 \times 3$ which gives 18 steps. Optimal $\lambda$ varies widely in value between different images.

## 3.3   Simplification for Quadratic Stego-Costs

We now assume that the stego-costs obey to the following expression: $w_i(\ell) = \ell^2/\sigma_i^2$ as in (5). This makes the functional of (14) (restricted to the $i$-th pixel) equals to $\ell_i^2/\sigma_i^2 - \lambda g_i \ell_i + \lambda p_i$ which minimizer is $\tilde{\ell}_i = \lambda g_i \sigma_i^2/2$.

Yet, this value in general is not an integer belonging to $\mathcal{L}_i$ (10). This issue is easily solved because a quadratic function is symmetric around its minimum, therefore the minimum over $\mathcal{L}_i$ is its value closest to $\tilde{\ell}_i$ as shown in Fig. 2. The range $\mathcal{L}_i$ being nothing more than a set of consecutive integers, we obtain a closed form expression:

$$\ell_{\lambda,i} = \min(\max([\lambda g_i \sigma_i^2/2], \lceil p_i \rceil - d/2), \lceil p_i \rceil + d/2 - 1), \tag{15}$$

where $[\cdot]$ is the rounding to the nearest integer. The post-processing has now a linear complexity.

In this equation, the min and max operate a clipping so that $\ell_{\lambda,i}$ belongs to $\mathcal{L}_i$. This clipping is active if $\tilde{\ell}_i \notin \mathcal{L}_i$, which happens if $\lambda \geq \bar{\lambda}_i$ with

$$\bar{\lambda}_i := \begin{cases} \left|\dfrac{2\lceil p_i \rceil - d}{g_i \sigma_i^2}\right|_+ & \text{if } g_i < 0 \\[2ex] \left|\dfrac{2\lceil p_i \rceil + d - 2}{g_i \sigma_i^2}\right|_+ & \text{if } g_i > 0, \end{cases} \tag{16}$$

where $|a|_+ = a$ if $a > 0$, 0 otherwise. This remark is important because it shows that for any $\lambda > \max_i \bar{\lambda}_i$, the solution $\boldsymbol{\ell}_\lambda$ of (15) remains the same due to clipping. Therefore, we can narrow down the line search of $\lambda$ to $[0, \max_i \bar{\lambda}_i]$.

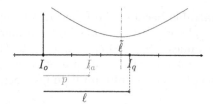

**Fig. 2.** Rounding the minimizer when the stego-cost is quadratic.

## 4    Experimental Investigation

### 4.1    Experimental Setup

Our experimental work uses 18,000 images from ImageNet of dimension 224 × 224 × 3. This subset is split in 1,000 for testing and comparing, 17,000 for training. An image is attacked only if the classifier predicts its correct label beforehand. This happens with probability equaling the accuracy of the network Acc. We measure $\overline{L_2}$ the average Euclidean distance of the perturbation $\ell$ and $P_{suc}$ the probability of a successful attack *only over correctly labeled images*.

We attack the networks with 4 different attacks: FGSM [26], PGD$_2$ [27], CW [29] and DDN [28]. All these attacks are run in a *best-effort* fashion with a complexity limited to 100 iterations. This means that for FGSM and PGD$_2$ the distortion is gradually increased until the image is adversarial. For more complex CW and DDN attacks, different parameters are used over a total maximum of 100 iterations. The final attacked version is the adversarial image with the smaller distortion. Since DDN is the only attack that creates integer images, the other 3 are post-processed either by the enhanced quantization [30], which is our baseline, or by our method explained in Sect. 3.2.

The adversarial image detectors are evaluated by the true positive rate TPR$_5$ when the false positive rate FPR is fixed to 5%.

### 4.2    Robustness of Recent Classifiers: There is Free Lunch

Our first experiment compares the robustness of the famous ResNet-50 network to the recent classifiers: the vanilla version of EfficientNet-b0 [7] and its robust version trained with AdvProp [8]. Note that the authors of [8] apply adversarial re-training for improving accuracy. As far as we known, the robustness of this version was not yet established.

Figure 3 shows the same characteristic function as in Fig. 1 with this time the vanilla EfficientNet-b0 against its robust version. Table 1 gives measurements $P_{suc}$ and $\overline{L_2}$ as a summary of the characteristic function shown in Fig. 1. This confirms that modern classifiers are more accurate and more robust (lower $P_{suc}$ and/or bigger $\overline{L_2}$). This is indeed a surprise: It pulls down the myth of 'No Free Lunch' in adversarial machine learning literature [42,43] (the price to pay for robustifying a network is allegedly a lower accuracy).

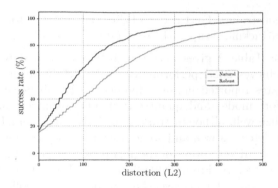

**Fig. 3.** Characteristic function of attack [30] (PGD in best effort with quantization) against Vanilla EfficientNet-b0 and its Robust counterpart.

## 4.3   Detection with Forensics Detectors

We use three steganalyzers to detect adversarial images. Their training set is composed of 15,651 pairs of original and adversarial images. The latter are crafted with *best-effort* FGSM against vanilla EfficientNet-b0.

The first detector is trained on SRM feature vectors [18], with dimensions 34,671. SRM is a model that applies to only one channel. It is computed on the luminance of the image in our experimental work. The classifier separating these high-dimensional vectors into two classes is the linear regularized classifier [44]. The second detector is based on the color version of SRM: SCRMQ1 [45] with dimension 18,157. The classifier is the same. The third detector is SRNet [9], one of the best detectors in steganalysis. Training is performed on 180 epochs: The first 100 with a learning rate of $10^{-3}$, the remaining 80 with $10^{-4}$. Data augmentation is also performed during training. First, there is a probability $p_1 = 0.5$ of mirroring the pair of images. Then, there is another probability $p_2 = 0.5$ of rotating them by 90° .

**Table 2.** Detection probabilities (TPR$_5$) with forensics detectors of adversarial images targeting classifier vanilla EfficientNet-b0 [7]

|  | $P_{suc}$ | $\overline{L_2}$ | SRM(%) | SCRMQ1(%) | SRNet(%) |
|---|---|---|---|---|---|
| FGSM+[30] | 89.7 | 286 | 72.00 | 83.3 | **93.5** |
| PGD$_2$+[30] | 98.6 | 113 | 65.02 | 83.1 | **93.8** |
| CW+[30] | 89.7 | 97 | 68.78 | 83.6 | **94.5** |
| DDN | 83.2 | 186 | 79.53 | 91.9 | **94.8** |

**The Attacks:** Table 2 shows the results of detection on all 4 attacks. PGD$_2$ achieves a high $P_{suc}$ at almost a third of the distortion FGSM would obtain. DDN and CW being harder to optimize attain both lower $P_{suc}$ and higher distortion under the given constraints. For the rest of the study we therefore focus on $PGD_2$ to give the best attacking setup with reasonable complexity.

**The Detectors:** Table 2 gives also the $TPR_5$ associated to the detectors. Although [24] achieves good performances with SRM, we do not obtain the high detection rates reported in the reference. This cab be due to both finer attacks (best effort mode) and quantization. Our results show also that the detectors generalize well: although trained to detect images highly distorted by FGSM, they can detect as well and sometimes even better more subtle attacks like CW. Moreover, SRNet always outperforms SCRMQ1 and is the most accurate of the three detectors. From Table 2, we can also deduce that $PGD_2+$[30] is the worst-case scenario for defense. The probability of fooling both the classifier EfficientNet-b0 and the detector SRNet in this setup combines to only $0.88 \times (1 - 0.933) = 5.9\%$.

### 4.4   Post-processing with a Steganographic Embedder

We now play the role of the attacker. We use $PGD_2$ with best effort as the base attack to compare the detectability of four post-processings: The non-steganographic insertion [30] as a baseline, HILL (4), MiPod (5), and GINA (6). GINA uses the quadratic method explained in Sect. 3.3 sequentially over the 12 lattices. Quadratic stego-costs are updated with CMD strategy (6). Each lattice contributes to a $1/12$ of the initial classification loss.

**Table 3.** Undetectability of steganographic embedding on $PGD_2$ against the vanilla model (Van) and its robust version (Rob).

|  | $d$ | $P_{suc}$ (%) | | $\overline{L_2}$ | | SCRMQ1(%) | | SRNet(%) | |
|---|---|---|---|---|---|---|---|---|---|
|  |  | Van | Rob | Van | Rob | Van | Rob | Van | Rob |
| [30] | 2 | 98.6 | 98.3 | **101** | **167** | 83.1 | 84.6 | 93.8 | 90.1 |
| HILL | 2 | 98.6 | 98.3 | 113 | 177 | 78.0 | 76.6 | 87.6 | 88.5 |
| HILL | 4 | **98.9** | **98.5** | 125 | 181 | 76.0 | 73.3 | 87.4 | 88.2 |
| MiPod | 2 | 98.3 | 98.3 | 176 | 242 | 77.4 | 76.2 | 86.6 | 87.7 |
| MiPod | 4 | 98.7 | 98.0 | 164 | 247 | 74.4 | 70.2 | 84.5 | 87.7 |
| GINA | 2 | 98.5 | 98.1 | 283 | 337 | 24.4 | 32.4 | 68.3 | **82.9** |
| GINA | 4 | 98.8 | 98.2 | 300 | 330 | **18.6** | **24.3** | **50.9** | 85.2 |

Table 3 illustrates how each strategy is detected by either SCRMQ1 or SRNet. Both detectors are trained on FGSM with [30] quantization as 'stego' images crafted on their respective network. Distortion increases with each method and along the degree of freedom $d$. The use of Steganographic costs therefore enables to reduce the detectability while increasing the $L_2$ distortion.

From the attacker perspective, the best strategy to fool the detector $PGD_2$ is GINA costs with $d = 4$. This scenario now has 48.0% chance of fooling both

Vanilla EfficientNet-b0 and SRNet and 80.4% with SCRMQ1 as the detector. Figure 4 shows the two examples with highest distortion on EfficientNet-b0 that still fool SRNet. The added distortion remains imperceptible to the human eye even in these cases.

The conclusion on Robust EfficientNet-b0 is however different. Since the distortion needed to attack the network is higher, it is consequently expected that the detectors will be more accurate. If SCRMQ1 detects GINA distortion slightly better than on Vanilla EfficientNet-b0, SRNet is however very efficient to detect each strategy even if it was trained on FGSM.

'Angora rabbit'    'woolen'

'hare', $L_2 = 488$    'knot', $L_2 = 449$

**Fig. 4.** Top row: Cover images with their label below. Bottom row: adversarial images with steganographic embedding GINA (d = 4). Below them are their new label and the distortion

### 4.5  Training on Adversarial Images with GINA Costs

We finally play the role of the defender again. We want to detect GINA perturbation with the highest possible TPR. To achieve this we retrain our detectors in the same setups as before, but with images using GINA perturbation as adversarial images. Since Table 3 shows that in most cases $d = 4$ is indeed the worst-case for the defense side, we attacked the training set of "cover" images with $PGD_2$ and GINA costs with $d = 4$.

The first result we report is that under the same setup, SRNet was never able to distinct both distributions of images. The average confidence on the whole test set is roughly 50%. Trying to train SRNet with a finer learning rate did not lead to any better result. There is probably a set of *hyperparameters* that would lead to a more effective training. However this result illustrates that GINA distortion is harder to detect.

Table 4 shows TPR$_5$ for SCRMQ1 under such training setup. The detector is able to detect GINA mechanism at a higher rate than in Table 3 but generalizes poorly on other attacks. A conclusion to this final experiment is that GINA can be stealthy to general detectors, but it is still better detected after another iteration of the defender. The detection accuracy is however lower when using GINA costs, and drops from 83.1% to 68.5%. The price of detecting GINA is also to become more specific and to lose performance on the other attacks.

**Table 4.** Detection on SCRMQ1 after training on adversarial images embedded with GINA ($d = 4$)

| | $d$ | SCRMQ1(%) | |
| --- | --- | --- | --- |
| | | Van | Rob |
| [30] | 2 | 55.9 | 56.7 |
| HILL | 2 | 53.4 | 53.6 |
| HILL | 4 | 50.4 | 53.9 |
| MiPod | 2 | 56.1 | 55.9 |
| MiPod | 4 | 53.9 | 54.9 |
| GINA | 2 | **77.7** | 78.4 |
| GINA | 4 | 68.5 | **79.7** |

## 5   Conclusions

This paper explores both sides of adversarial image detection with steganographic glasses.

On the Attack side, our work using distortions designed for steganographic purposes is able to reduce the detection rates. Steganographic distortion target specific regions and pixels of an image to quantize the attack. The $L_2$ distortion increases w.r.t. the original attack, but remains imperceptible by the human eye (Fig. 4) and less detectable by a targeted detector. This paper consequently shows the possibility of tweaking an attack to make it harder to detect while remaining invisible.

On the Defense side, we use SRNet [9], state-of-the-art in steganalysis to detect adversarial images. Training it on images attacked with the basic FGSM shows excellent performance. Detection also generalizes well even on the finest attacks such as PGD$_2$ [27] and CW [29].

Finally both Attack and Defense are affected by the considered neural network. The effect of adversarial training on EfficientNet-b0 [8] is twofold: it increases the classification accuracy as well as robustifying the network. An increased robustness translates into a higher attacking distortion, which itself translates into a higher detectability.

# References

1. Güera, D., Wang, Y., Bondi, L., Bestagini, P., Tubaro, S., Delp, E.J.: A counter-forensic method for CNN-based camera model identification. In: 2017 IEEE Conference on Computer Vision and Pattern Recognition Workshops (CVPRW), pp. 1840–1847. IEEE (2017)
2. Barni, M., Stamm, M.C., Tondi, B.: Adversarial multimedia forensics: overview and challenges ahead. In: 2018 26th European Signal Processing Conference (EUSIPCO), pp. 962–966. IEEE (2018)
3. Quiring, E., Arp, D., Rieck, K.: Forgotten siblings: unifying attacks on machine learning and digital watermarking. In: IEEE European Symposium on Security and Privacy (2018)
4. Carlini, N., Wagner, D.: Adversarial examples are not easily detected: bypassing ten detection methods. arXiv:1705.07263 (2017)
5. Athalye, A., Carlini, N., Wagner, D.A.: Obfuscated gradients give a false sense of security: circumventing defenses to adversarial examples. In: ICML, pp. 274–283 (2018)
6. Tramer, F., Carlini, N., Brendel, W., Madry, A.: On adaptive attacks to adversarial example defenses (2020)
7. Tan, M., Le, Q.V.: Efficientnet: rethinking model scaling for convolutional neural networks. arXiv (2019)
8. Xie, C., Tan, M., Gong, B., Wang, J., Yuille, A., Le, Q.V.: Adversarial examples improve image recognition. arXiv (2019)
9. Boroumand, M., Chen, M., Fridrich, J.: Deep residual network for steganalysis of digital images. IEEE Trans. Inf. Forensics Secur. 14(5), 1181–1193 (2018)
10. Li, B., Wang, M., Huang, J., Li, X.: A new cost function for spatial image steganography. In: 2014 IEEE International Conference on Image Processing (ICIP), pp. 4206–4210. IEEE (2014)
11. Sedighi, V., Cogranne, R., Fridrich, J.: Content-adaptive steganography by minimizing statistical detectability. IEEE Trans. Inf. Forensics Secur. 11(2), 221–234 (2016)
12. Li, B., Wang, M., Li, X., Tan, S., Huang, J.: A strategy of clustering modification directions in spatial image steganography. IEEE Trans. Inf. Forensics Secur. 10(9), 1905–1917 (2015)
13. Wang, Y., Zhang, W., Li, W., Yu, X., Yu, N.: Non-additive cost functions for color image steganography based on inter-channel correlations and differences. IEEE Trans. Inf. Forensics Secur. 15, 2081–2095 (2019)
14. Qiu, X., Li, H., Luo, W., Huang, J.: A universal image forensic strategy based on steganalytic model. In: Proceedings of ACM IH&MMSec 2014, New York, NY, USA, pp. 165–170 (2014)
15. Farooq, S., Yousaf, M.H., Hussain, F.: A generic passive image forgery detection scheme using local binary pattern with rich models. Comput. Electr. Eng. 62, 459–472 (2017)
16. Luo, W., Li, H., Yan, Q., Yang, R., Huang, J.: Improved audio steganalytic feature and its applications in audio forensics. ACM Trans. Multimedia Comput. Commun. Appl. 14(2), 1–14 (2018)
17. Tuama, A., Comby, F., Chaumont, M.: Camera model identification based machine learning approach with high order statistics features. In: EUSIPCO, pp. 1183–1187 (2016)

18. Fridrich, J., Kodovsky, J.: Rich models for steganalysis of digital images. IEEE Trans. Inf. Forensics Secur. **7**(3), 868–882 (2012)
19. Xu, G., Wu, H.-Z., Shi, Y.-Q.: Structural design of convolutional neural networks for steganalysis. IEEE Signal Process. Lett. **23**(5), 708–712 (2016)
20. Yousfi, Y., Butora, J., Fridrich, J., Giboulot, Q.: Breaking ALASKA: color separation for steganalysis in jpeg domain. In: Proceedings of ACM IH&MMSec 2019, pp. 138–149 (2019)
21. Fan, W., Wang, K., Cayre, F.: General-purpose image forensics using patch likelihood under image statistical models. In: IEEE International Workshop on Information Forensics and Security (WIFS), pp. 1–6 (2015)
22. Chen, Z., Tondi, B., Li, X., Ni, R., Zhao, Y., Barni, M.: A gradient-based pixel-domain attack against SVM detection of global image manipulations. In: IEEE WIFS, pp. 1–6 (2017)
23. Schöttle, P., Schlögl, A., Pasquini, C., Böhme, R.: Detecting adversarial examples - a lesson from multimedia security. In: European Signal Processing Conference (EUSIPCO), pp. 947–951 (2018)
24. Liu, J., et al.: Detection based defense against adversarial examples from the steganalysis point of view. In: IEEE/CVF CVPR, pp. 4820–4829 (2019)
25. Simonyan, K., Zisserman, A.: Very deep convolutional networks for large-scale image recognition. In: 3rd International Conference on Learning Representations, ICLR 2015, San Diego, CA, USA, 7–9 May 2015, Conference Track Proceedings (2015). http://arxiv.org/abs/1409.1556
26. Goodfellow, I.J., Shlens, J., Szegedy, C.: Explaining and harnessing adversarial examples. In: ICLR 2015, San Diego, CA, USA (2015)
27. Madry, A., Makelov, A., Schmidt, L., Tsipras, D., Vladu, A.: Towards deep learning models resistant to adversarial attacks. In: ICLR 2018, Vancouver, Canada, BC (2018)
28. Rony, J., Hafemann, L.G., Oliveira, L.S., Ayed, I.B., Sabourin, R., Granger, E.: Decoupling direction and norm for efficient gradient-based l2 adversarial attacks and defenses. In: Proceedings of the IEEE CVPR (2019)
29. Carlini, N., Wagner, D.: Towards evaluating the robustness of neural networks. In: IEEE Symposium on Security and Privacy (2017)
30. Bonnet, B., Furon, T., Bas, P.: What if adversarial samples were digital images? In: Proceedings of ACM IH&MMSec 2020, pp. 55–66 (2020)
31. Krizhevsky, A., Sutskever, I., Hinton, G.E.: Imagenet classification with deep convolutional neural networks. In: Proceedings of the 25th International Conference on Neural Information Processing Systems - Volume 1, series NIPS 2012, pp. 1097–1105. Curran Associates Inc., Red Hook (2012)
32. Szegedy, C.: Going deeper with convolutions. In: 2015 IEEE Conference on Computer Vision and Pattern Recognition (CVPR), pp. 1–9 (2015)
33. He, K., Zhang, X., Ren, S., Sun, J.: Deep residual learning for image recognition. In: IEEE Conference on Computer Vision and Pattern Recognition (CVPR) 2016, pp. 770–778 (2016)
34. Ma, S., Liu, Y., Tao, G., Lee, W., Zhang, X.: NIC: detecting adversarial samples with neural network invariant checking. In: NDSS 2019, San Diego, California, USA (2019)
35. Meng, D., Chen, H.: Magnet: a two-pronged defense against adversarial examples. In Proceedings of the 2017 ACM SIGSAC Conference on Computer and Communications Security, pp. 135–147. ACM (2017)

36. Taran, O., Rezaeifar, S., Holotyak, T., Voloshynovskiy, S.: Defending against adversarial attacks by randomized diversification. In: IEEE CVPR, Long Beach, USA (2019)
37. Taran, O., Rezaeifar, S., Holotyak, T., Voloshynovskiy, S.: Machine learning through cryptographic glasses: combating adversarial attacks by key-based diversified aggregation. EURASIP J. Inf. Secur. **2020**(1), 1–18 (2020). https://doi.org/10.1186/s13635-020-00106-x
38. Filler, T., Judas, J., Fridrich, J.: Minimizing additive distortion in steganography using syndrome-trellis codes. IEEE Trans. Inf. Forensics Secur. **6**(3), 920–935 (2011)
39. Tang, W., Li, B., Tan, S., Barni, M., Huang, J.: CNN-based adversarial embedding for image steganography. IEEE Trans. Inf. Forensics Secur. **14**(8), 2074–2087 (2019)
40. Bernard, S., Bas, P., Klein, J., Pevny, T.: Explicit optimization of min max steganographic game. IEEE Trans. Inf. Forensics Secur. **16**, 812–823 (2021)
41. Shi, X., Tondi, B., Li, B., Barni, M.: CNN-based steganalysis and parametric adversarial embedding: a game-theoretic framework. Sig. Process. Image Commun. **89**, 115992 (2020)
42. Tsipras, D., Santurkar, S., Engstrom, L., Turner, A., Madry, A.: Robustness may be at odds with accuracy (2018)
43. Dohmatob, E.: Generalized no free lunch theorem for adversarial robustness. In: Proceedings of International Conference on Machine Learning, Long Beach, California, USA (2019)
44. Cogranne, R., Sedighi, V., Fridrich, J., Pevnỳ, T.: Isensembleclassifier needed for steganalysis in high-dimensional feature spaces? In: 2015 IEEE International Workshop on Information Forensics and Security (WIFS), IEEE, pp. 1–6 (2015)
45. Goljan, M., Fridrich, J., Cogranne, R.: Rich model for steganalysis of color images. In: 2014 IEEE International Workshop on Information Forensics and Security, WIFS 2014, pp. 185–190, April 2015

# LSSD: A Controlled Large JPEG Image Database for Deep-Learning-Based Steganalysis "Into the Wild"

Hugo Ruiz[1] , Mehdi Yedroudj[1] , Marc Chaumont[1,2](✉) ,
Frédéric Comby[1] , and Gérard Subsol[1]

[1] Research-Team ICAR, LIRMM, Univ. Montpellier, CNRS,
Montpellier, France
{hugo.ruiz,mehdi.yedroudj,marc.chaumont,
frederic.comby,gerard.subsol}@lirmm.fr
[2] University of Nîmes, Nîmes, France

**Abstract.** For many years, the image databases used in steganalysis have been relatively small, i.e. about ten thousand images. This limits the diversity of images and thus prevents large-scale analysis of steganalysis algorithms.

In this paper, we describe a large JPEG database composed of 2 million colour and grey-scale images. This database, named LSSD for Large Scale Steganalysis Database, was obtained thanks to the intensive use of "controlled" development procedures. LSSD has been made publicly available, and we aspire it could be used by the steganalysis community for large-scale experiments.

We introduce the pipeline used for building various image database versions. We detail the general methodology that can be used to redevelop the entire database and increase even more the diversity. We also discuss computational cost and storage cost in order to develop images.

**Keywords:** Steganalysis · Scalability · Million images · "Controlled" development · Mismatch

## 1 Introduction

Steganography is the art of hiding information in an non suspicious medium so that the very existence of the hidden information is statistically undetectable from unaware individuals. Conversely, steganalysis is the art of detecting the presence of hidden data in such supports [8]. JPEG images are attractive supports since they are massively used in cameras and mobile phones and in all media of communication on the Internet and social networks. In this paper, we will then focus on steganography and steganalysis in JPEG images.

In 2015, steganalysis using Deep Learning techniques emerged [2], and nowadays, they are considered as the most efficient way to detect stego images (i.e.

© Springer Nature Switzerland AG 2021
A. Del Bimbo et al. (Eds.): ICPR 2020 Workshops, LNCS 12666, pp. 470–483, 2021.
https://doi.org/10.1007/978-3-030-68780-9_38

images which contain a hidden message). Moreover, GPU computation capabilities increase regularly, which ensures faster computing speed which reduces learning time. So, performances of steganalysis methods based on Deep Learning have significantly improved.

Nevertheless, in most cases, the performance of steganalysis based on Deep Learning depends on the size of the learning image database. To a certain extent, the larger the database is, the better the results are [15,16]. Thus, increasing the size of the learning database generally improves performance while increasing the diversity of the examples.

Currently, the most significant database used in steganalysis by Deep Learning is made of one million JPEG images [20] excerpted from the ImageNet database, which contains more than 14 million images.

That said, databases created in "controlled" conditions, that is to say, with the full knowledge of the creation process of the images so that the development is repeatable, are not very big in comparison. Indeed, we can mention, as a "controlled" database the BOSS database [1] with a size of only 10,000 images and the Alaska #2 database, with a size of 80,000 images [5].

In this paper, we present the "controlled" *Large Scale Steganalysis Database* (LSSD) which is a public JPEG image database, made of 2 million images, with a colour version and a grey-scale version, and which was created for the research community working on steganalysis.

One important aspect when creating an image database for steganalysis is to have diversity to get closer to reality [12]. This "diversity" mainly depends on the ISO and the "development" process of the RAW image that is captured by the camera sensor. ISO is a measure of the sensitivity to light of the image sensor and if available, can be notified in the metadata associated with the JPEG image, i.e. in the EXIF metadata.

As in analogical photography, the "development" process consists in applying image processing operations (demosaicing, gamma correction, blur, colour balance, compression) in order to transform the RAW image into a viewable image in a standard format. The RAW image, when the camera is made of a colour filter array (CFA) of type Bayer filter (which is majority the case), is a unique 2D matrix containing 50% green, 25% red and 25% blue. In order to "control" this diversity, it is possible to tune the different development parameters, without modifying the ISO parameters, and get different developments and then different JPEG versions of the same RAW image. Thus, if we want to increase the size of the database to more than 10 million images, it is necessary to implement a well-thought-out procedure to automate the "controlled" generation, to optimize the processing time as well as the storage volume.

By controlling the development, it becomes possible to get large databases which can be used for the learning or the test phases of Deep-Learning based steganalysis algorithms. We can then conduct an objective and repeatable evaluation of the performances of these algorithms. In particular, it will allow researchers to work on one of the major challenges in the steganalysis field: the "Cover-Source Mismatch". Cover-Source Mismatch (CSM) is a phenomenon that occurs when the training set and the test set come from two different sources, causing bias in the Deep-Learning learning phase and resulting in bad results in the test phase.

In Sect. 2, we detail the whole development procedure that is used for the generation of the LSSD database. In Sect. 3, we explain how to use the LSSD Database to create a learning set and a test set for Deep-Learning steganalysis applications. We also emphasize the problem of computational and storage cost for the creation of those sets.

## 2   A "Controlled" Procedure to get a JPEG image

### 2.1   RAW Image Sources

To build a consistent "controlled" base, we chose to gather a maximum of RAW images, i.e. which are composed of the original sensor data. More precisely, we use the file that contains the RAW data of the sensor before any lossy compression (JPEG for example), and before any transformation required for its visualization on screen. It is important to note that each manufacturer adapts the data format to its hardware and then that we can find many formats (e.g., .dng, .cr2, .nef. . . ).

At the contrary of JPEG images, RAW images are extremely rare on the Internet because they are large files and used by very few people. The size of a RAW image is usually around $3,000 \times 5,000$ pixels. Since data are in "raw" format, it represents a lot of information to store. It is therefore rare that Web

Table 1. Number of images and devices used in each database.

| Database Name | Number of images | Number of devices |
|---|---|---|
| ALASKA2[a] | 80,005 | 40 |
| BOSS[b] | 10,000 | 7 |
| Stego App DB[f] | 24.120 | 26 |
| Wesaturate[e] | 3.648 | / |
| RAISE[c] | 8,156 | 3 |
| Dresden[d] | 1,491 | 73 (25 different models) |
| **Total** | **127,420** | **101** |

[a] Website of the ALASKA challenge#2: https://alaska.utt.fr/ Download page: http://alaska.utt.fr/ALASKA_v2_RAWs_scripts.zip.
[b] Challenge BOSS: http://agents.fel.cvut.cz/boss/index.php?mode= VIEW\&tmpl=about  Download  page: ftp://mas22.felk.cvut.cz/ RAWs.
[c] Obsolete download link http://mmlab.science.unitn.it/RAISE/.
[d] http://forensics.inf.tu-dresden.de/ddimgdb Download page: http: //forensics.inf.tu-dresden.de/ddimgdb/selections.
[e] Site closed on February 17, 2020: http://wesaturate.com/.
[f] https://data.csafe.iastate.edu/StegoDatabase/.

sites, even those specialized in photography, dedicate a specific storage space to this kind of images.

The LSSD database gathers RAW images available on the Internet, mostly from the Alaska#2 database [4][1] to which we added images from the BOSS [1][2], RAISE [6][3], Dresden [10][4] and Wesaturate[5] databases, as well as StegoApp sites [14][6]. A total of 127,420 RAW images were collected. Table 1 lists the origin of the RAW images, while Fig. 1 represents their distributions.

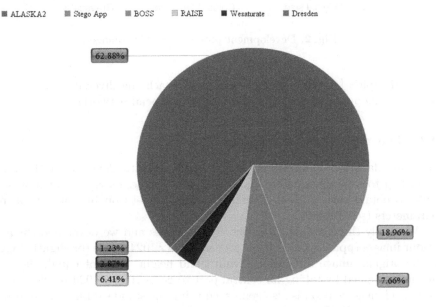

**Fig. 1.** Origin of RAW images in the LSSD database.

Note that the Alaska#2 database [4] covers a large variety of ISO parameters, ranging from 20 (used in general for smartphones) to 51, 200 (only used for high-end devices). Among the 80, 005 images of this database, 11, 615 images have an ISO above 1, 000 while 12, 497 have an ISO below 100.

The majority of the databases reported in Table 1 are classically used by the community for steganalysis purpose. By combining them, we increase diversity and move to a more "real world" scenario [12]. We are thus closer to the "into

---

[1] Website of the ALASKA challenge#2: https://alaska.utt.fr/ Download page: http://alaska.utt.fr/ALASKA_v2_RAWs_scripts.zip.

[2] Challenge BOSS: http://agents.fel.cvut.cz/boss/index.php?mode=VIEW&tmpl=about Download page: ftp://mas22.felk.cvut.cz/RAWs .

[3] Obsolete download link http://mmlab.science.unitn.it/RAISE/.

[4] http://forensics.inf.tu-dresden.de/ddimgdb Download page: http://forensics.inf.tu-dresden.de/ddimgdb/selections .

[5] Site closed on February 17, 2020: http://wesaturate.com/.

[6] https://data.csafe.iastate.edu/StegoDatabase/.

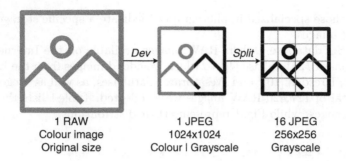

**1 RAW**
Colour image
Original size

**1 JPEG**
1024x1024
Colour | Grayscale

**16 JPEG**
256x256
Grayscale

**Fig. 2.** Development process of a RAW image.

the wild" spirit [4]. The ultimate goal is to reach the diversity findable when browsing the public images of the Internet and social networks.

## 2.2 The "Development" pipeline

For the Alaska#2 competition, scripts were used to develop all the images according to some parameters [4]. It is thanks to these scripts that it was possible to obtain such a great diversity in the competition by playing on many parameters (see Table 2).

We apply these scripts to all the RAW images and we developed them into colour images (ppm format) whose size are $1024 \times 1024$ pixels (or slightly bigger). If the original image dimensions (width and height) are not equal, the colour image is cropped by taking its central part to get a $1024 \times 1024$ pixels image. A grey level image version is also generated using the standard luminance formula, transforming a RGB colour vector to a scalar representing the grey level:

$$grey\_value = 0.2989 \times R + 0.5870 \times G + 0.1140 \times B,$$

where $R, G, B \in [0, \ldots, 255]$ are the intensities of the red, green and blue channels. We will discuss in the next subsection the development parameters which were used.

As we want to get 2 million images, we add a process to multiply by 16 the number of images. Each colour (respectively the grey-level) ppm image is divided into 16 small images of size $256 \times 256$ pixels. Then, we run a compression of those 16 images, using the standard JPEG quantization matrices, with a quality factor of 75. The compression was carried out using the Python Imaging Library (PIL or *Pillow*)[7] package, version 1.1.7, which uses the plugin "JpegImagePlugin" to compress the images in the format $4:4:4$.

Figure 2 schematizes the steps of the complete development process.

The $256 \times 256$ images have semantic content, a resolution and brightness variations that are close from those of images usually processed in steganalysis.

---

[7] Documentation: https://pillow.readthedocs.io/en/stable/.

(a) A developed image from the ALASKA database (number 3786).

(b) A developed image from the BOSS database (number 6456).

**Fig. 3.** Two $256 \times 256$ grey-scale images, after development process of the LSSD database.

(a) A developed image from the ALASKA database (number 51336).

(b) A developed image from the We-saturate database (index ZYlVRQY-DWE).

**Fig. 4.** Two $256 \times 256$ colour-scale images, after development process of the LSSD database.

Figure 3 (resp. Figure 4) shows two examples of JPEG grey-level (resp. colour) $256 \times 256$ images of the LSSD.

It takes just under two days for all colour and grayscale images to be developed. The users of the LSSD database is free to either download the RAW images and redevelop those images or directly use the colour or grey-level JPEG $256 \times 256$ images.

## 2.3   Development Parameters

In order to obtain the most realistic database, we have tested many development parameters (resize, crop, denoising, quality factor...). Table 2 summarizes all the parameters used during the generation of the dataset, reaching almost two million images.

All the processes explained below are done by using the *Rawtherapee*[8] v5.8 software which is a free, cross-platform raw image processing program.

**Table 2.** Parameters used in the image development process.

| Number | Name | Value |
|--------|------|-------|
| *1* | Demosaicking | Fast or DCB |
| *2* | Resize & Crop | Yes |
|  | Taille (resize) | 1024 × 1024 |
|  |  | Nearest (0.2) |
|  | Kernel (resize) | Bicubic (0.5) |
|  |  | Bilinear (0.3) |
|  | Resize factor | Depends on initial size |
| *3* | Unsharp Masking | No |
| *4* | Denoise (*Pyramid Denoising*) | Yes |
|  | Intensity | [0; 60] |
|  | Detail | [0; 40] |
| *5* | Micro-contrast | Yes ($p = 0.5$) |
| *6* | Colour | No |
| *7* | Quality factor | 75 |

**1. Demosaicing:** Demosaicing is the process of reconstructing a full-resolution colour image from the sampled data acquired by a digital camera that applies a colour filter array to a single sensor (see, for example, the overview [13]). In the *Rawtherapee* software, we can find many demosaicing methods[9]. We selected the *DCB* method which produces similar results to the best method (AMaZE), plus the *Fast* method, based on nearest-neighbor interpolation, which is a lower-quality but very fast method. Notice that another available method called IGV is known to produce the most challenging images to steganalyze [4]. For each image, we select either the Fast or the DCB demosaicing algorithm with a probability of 35% and 65%, respectively. Demosaicked images are then saved in 16-bit TIFF format using the Python library *Pillow*(see footnote 7).

---

[8] Software available at: http://rawtherapee.com More information can be found at: http://rawpedia.rawtherapee.com.

[9] Documentation about the different mosaicking methods of *Rawtherapee* can be found at: https://rawpedia.rawtherapee.com/Demosaicing.

**2. Resize & Crop:** the image is proportionally resized to final dimensions which are closest to $1024 \times 1024$ pixels as we will divide the resulting image into 16 small images thereafter. If the image is not square, then we crop its center part, assuming that we will keep its semantic content. Resizing is performed using different kernels mentioned in Table 1, and it would have also been possible to use the $8 \times 8$ Lanczos filters.

**3. Unsharp Masking (USM):** After resizing, the image can eventually be sharpened. The USM process allows increasing the apparent acutance (edge contrast) of an image, making it appear clearer, even though it technically does not really sharpen the image. This process can be disabled. Note that for the *learning* database, the USM has been switched off. USM can be switched on for the development of the *test* database; this to introduce strong cover-source mismatch. More information about USM can be found in Appendix A.1 of [4].

**4. Denoising:** When the USM is switched off, denoising is systematically performed using a Pyramid Denoising based on wavelet decomposition. The denoising *intensity* parameter follows a gamma distribution with the pdf $P(x,a) = 10 \times \frac{x^{a-1}\exp(-x)}{\Gamma(a)}$, with $a = 4$, and rectified to belongs to $[0,100]$. It controls the power of the noise reduction. The *Detail* parameter follows a uniform distribution $\mathcal{U}(\{0..60\})$, and it controls the restoration of textures in the image due to excessive noise. More information about Pyramid Denoising can be found in [4].

**5. Micro-contrast:** Since USM can generate artefacts, it is possible to apply a micro-contrast process. The micro-contrast process is performed after denoising with a probability of $p = 0.5$. This process is controlled by two parameters. The *strength* parameter follows a gamma distribution with the pdf $P(x,a) = 100 \times 0.5 \times \frac{x^{a-1}\exp(-x)}{\Gamma(a)}$, with $a = 1$, rectified on $[0,100]$. This parameters allows to change the strength of the sharpness. The other parameter is the *uniformity* for the microcontrast enhancement. The uniformity follows the law $\lfloor \mathcal{N}(30,5) \rfloor$ rectified on $[0,+\infty]$. That information is recalled in Appendix A.3 [4].

## 2.4  Choice of the JPEG Quality Factor

The Quality Factor (QF) of JPEG images is an essential element in the development pipeline. This factor can vary between 0 and 100, with 0 being a very poor quality, 50 being the minimum for good quality and 100 being the best possible. These quality factors are associated with $8 \times 8$ quantization matrices that are used in DCT image compression. There are typical (standard) matrices used in JPEG, but it is also possible to design ad-hoc quantization matrices (non-standard). In our case, we only use standard matrices; it results in a lower diversity compared to databases such as ImageNet [7]. Nevertheless, in future work, we would like to integrate this diversity to get as close as possible to real-world images and use image databases like ImageNet.

## 2.5  Reflection About Quantization Matrix Diversity

For LSSD, we chose the quality factor $Q = 75$ (see Table 2) with a standard quantization matrix. If we would use a JPEG database such as ImageNet [7], and desired to generate a database with a $Q$ "around" 75, we would have to recompress all the images with a factor "equivalent" to $Q = 75$. In that case, it is possible to assume that a majority of JPEG images have a factor greater than 75. By recompressing at a lower factor, we would not introduce recompression artefacts. This new uncontrolled "real world" base would exhibit statistics of natural JPEG images (i.e. not recompressed), which would resemble those of LSSD, and the performances obtained could be compared with our "controlled" LSSD base.

Note that it is possible to recover, in the EXIF metadata, the quantization matrices (for each, Y, Cr, Cb, channel) of each JPEG image. With this information, it is easy to identify whether the matrices are standard or non-standard. As recalled in the article of Yousfi and Fridrich [19], the standard formula for obtaining a quantization matrix whatever the channel, given the Quality Factor, $Q$, is:

$$
\mathbf{q}(Q) = \begin{cases} \max\left\{1, \text{round}\left(2\left(1 - \frac{Q}{100}\right) \cdot \mathbf{q}(50)\right)\right\} & if\ Q > 50 \\ \min\left\{\{255 \cdot \mathbf{1}, \text{round}\left(\frac{50}{Q} \cdot \mathbf{q}(50)\right)\right\} & if\ Q \leq 50, \end{cases} \tag{1}
$$

$\mathbf{q}(50)$ being the standard quantization matrix for $Q = 50$.

Re-compressing a JPEG image (coming from ImageNet) to a Quality Factor "close" to $Q = 75$, can be done by first computing the $\mathbf{q}(75)$, and then recompress the input JPEG image using the $\mathbf{q}(75)$.

In the case of a non-standard JPEG input image, if we apply this process, we are losing the quantization diversity. An approach that would preserve this quantization diversity would be to find non-standard matrices noted $\mathbf{q}^{(ns)}(75)$, for the re-compression.

To do that, on can first estimate the non standard Quality Factor $Q^{(ns)}$ of the input JPEG image (trough iterative tests using the distance defined in Eq. 8 of [19]), then compute the $\mathbf{q}^{(ns)}(50)$ by multiplying the quantization matrices by the pre-computed "passage" matrices, from $\mathbf{q}(Q^{(ns)})$ to $\mathbf{q}(50)$, and finally re-use Eq. 1 with substituting $\mathbf{q}(50)$ by $\mathbf{q}^{(ns)}(50)$, this in order to obtain $\mathbf{q}^{(ns)}(75)$.

The creation of an ImageNet database re-compressed to $Q = 75$ is postponed to future work.

In conclusion, the diversity of the LSSD can be increased by increasing the development parameters range, by using additional development algorithms, by using various quality factors, and by using non-standard JPEG quantization matrices. Besides, in practice, the diversity of a JPEG colour image can also be increased compared to grey-scale images by using the following various formats: $4:4:4$, $4:2:2$, $4:2:0$ or $4:1:1$.

# 3   Application to DL-Based Steganalysis

In image classification, a field in which steganalysis is included, it is necessary to learn the neural network used on a training database and then observe its performance on a test database. The images in these bases must absolutely be distinct. The interest of distinguishing these bases is to verify that the network is capable of learning and generalizing the information from the training base to get the best performance from images that it has never analyzed.

The article of Giboulot *et al.* [9], studying the effects of Unsharp Masking (see in Sect. 2.3), pointed out that USM creates a strong mismatch phenomenon when used in the test set. For this reason, we decided to remove this processing when creating the learning database. The users can thus create a test database, using the USM process, and thus allowing the creation of cover-source mismatch phenomenon, that could be used in order to evaluate the impact of cover-source mismatch on steganalysis. Note that we also suppressed a few other processes such as some demosaicing algorithms and some resizing kernels when creating the learning database.

## 3.1   Training Database Construction

The RAW database consists of 127,420 images (see Table 1). We want to generate (from the RAW database) many learning datasets of different sizes from ten thousand to two million grey-scale JPEG images. One possible use is for evaluating the scalability of a steganalysis network, as in [15]. It is also necessary to set up a test dataset that will be the same for all learning datasets. This test dataset must be large enough to represent the diversity of developments, without being too disproportionate to the various sizes of the learning datasets. However, it should not be too large, to avoid high computational times in the test phase, even though during the test phase, calculations are faster.

We thus create several training datasets by, recursively, extracting a given number of images from the most extensive database (two million images). In total, we have six different sizes: 10k, 50k, 100k, 500k, 1M, 2M of cover images. So, when a database is used, it is important to take into account the corresponding stego images which doubles the total number of images. For example in the basis "LSSD_10k" there are 10,000 cover and 10,000 stego for a total of 20,000 images. In order to clearly identify the impact of increasing the size of the learning set, the smallest bases are included in the largest ones: $10k \subset 50k \subset 100k \subset 500k \subset 1M \subset 2M$. Each database tries to respect at best the initial ratio of the RAW images, which are shown in Table 3.

**Table 3.** Different LSSD database ratio with respect to the initial RAW image ratio.

| Base name | RAW | 100k-2M | 50k | 10k |
|---|---|---|---|---|
| ALASKA2 | 62.75% | = | = | +0.01% |
| BOSS | 7.84% | = | = | +0.01% |
| Dresden | 1.23% | = | = | +0.01% |
| RAISE | 6.40% | = | = | = |
| Stego App DB | 18.92% | = | = | = |
| Wesaturate | 2.86% | = | −0.01% | −0.03% |

## 3.2 Test Database Creation

We chose to generate a test set of one hundred thousand images. To this end, we isolated 6,250 RAW images with a distribution almost identical to the RAW image database (see Sect. 2.1). These images will then undergo the same development as the one shown in Table 2. Note that this RAW test dataset, which is isolated from the training database, allows generating several different test datasets uncorrelated with the JPEG grey-scale image training dataset. Indeed, it is possible to use other development types, with different parameters, to introduce more or less mismatch. In particular, it is possible to incorporate the USM, which produces a strong mismatch and has a significant impact on network performance during the test phase [9].

**Table 4.** Images distribution of the original database in the test set.

| Database name | Number of images | Percentage | RAW |
|---|---|---|---|
| ALASKA2 | 3 970 | 63.52% | 62.75% |
| Stego App DB | 1 197 | 19.15% | 18.92% |
| BOSS | 496 | 7.94% | 7.84% |
| RAISE | 404 | 6.46% | 6.40% |
| Wesaturate | 183 | 2.93% | 2.86% |
| Dresden | 0 | 0% | 1.23% |

Table 4 lists the number of images and the percentage of each database used to form the shared test dataset. Images from Dresden have not been included in order to create a weak "mismatch" between learning and testing datasets. This phenomenon can be likened to a "real world" behaviour when the network learns on images that may not be seen again during the test phase.

## 3.3 Format of Images

This database was used to make a test on scalability of a network in [15]. In this work, we applied the algorithm J-UNIWARD developed by Holub et al. [11]

with a payload of 0.2 bpnzacs (bits per non zero AC coefficients). When Deep Learning is used, it is not possible to give images to the network in JPEG format, so they must be decompressed in MAT format.

Decompressed images are nevertheless much larger than the JPEG images. For example, for a $256 \times 256$ grey-scale image, its size is slightly more than 500 kB because it is stored in double format (the decompressed version is not rounded). Then, a database with almost four million images (cover and stego) takes more than 2 TB. When all data are combined (RAW images, JPEG colour cover, JPEG grey cover, JPEG Grey stego, MAT grey cover and MAT grey stego), we get almost 13 TB of data!

# 4   Conclusion

The main goal of this work is to provide to the community many controlled databases and a methodology adapted to steganalysis that allows learning on a large scale to get closer to real-world images diversity. The LSSD basis is available on the following website: http://www.lirmm.fr/~chaumont/LSSD.html

It is already possible to identify the first technical challenges when it comes to processing millions of images, such as the embedding time, the storage space required for a decompressed base. Furthermore, it is required to have scripts significantly optimized to create a new database; otherwise, these times quickly become excessive.

This new public repository gives the community many tools in order to better control their learning. The databases made of few thousand to multiple millions of images, already developed or re-developable is unique in the field. Moreover, the LSSD website is freely accessible, and additionally stores famous RAW databases for conservation since almost half of the RAW images present on the website are no longer downloadable on the Internet. By putting this new database online, it offers the community the possibility to diversify and broaden their research as they wish.

Note that we also generated the colour JPEG images, and those are also downloadable on our website. The studying of colour steganography and colour steganalysis is indeed a hot topic which has recently been addressed during Alaska#1 [4,17] and Alaska#2 [3,5,18].

**Acknowledgment.** The authors would like to thank the French Defense Procurement Agency (DGA) for its support through the ANR Alaska project (ANR-18-ASTR-0009). We also thank IBM Montpellier and the Institute for Development and Resources in Intensive Scientific Computing (IDRISS/CNRS) for providing us access to High-Performance Computing resources.

# References

1. Bas, P., Filler, T., Pevný, T.: Break our steganographic system: the ins and outs of organizing BOSS. In: Filler, T., Pevny, T., Craver, S., Ker, A. (eds.) IH 2011. LNCS, vol. 6958, pp. 59–70. Springer, Heidelberg (2011). https://doi.org/10.1007/978-3-642-24178-9_5
2. Chaumont, M.: Deep Learning in steganography and steganalysis. In: Hassaballah, M. (ed.) Digital Media Steganography: Principles, Algorithms, Advances, chap. 14, pp. 321–349. Elsevier, July 2020
3. Chubachi, K.: An Ensemble Model using CNNs on Different Domains for ALASKA2 Image Steganalysis. In: Proceedings of the IEEE International Workshop on Information Forensics and Security, WIFS 2020. Virtual Conference due to Covid (Formerly New-York, NY, USA), December 2020
4. Cogranne, R., Giboulot, Q., Bas, P.: The ALASKA steganalysis challenge: a first step towards steganalysis. In: Proceedings of the ACM Workshop on Information Hiding and Multimedia Security, IH&MMSec 2019, pp. 125–137. Paris, France, July 2019
5. Cogranne, R., Giboulot, Q., Bas, P.: Challenge academic research on steganalysis with realistic images. In: Proceedings of the IEEE International Workshop on Information Forensics and Security, WIFS 2020. Virtual Conference due to Covid (Formerly New-York, NY, USA), December 2020
6. Dang-Nguyen, D.T., Pasquini, C., Conotter, V., Boato, G.: RAISE - a raw images dataset for digital image forensics. In: Proceedings of ACM Multimedia Systems, Portland, Oregon, March 2015
7. Deng, J., et al.: ImageNet: a large-scale hierarchical image database. In: Proceedings of IEEE Conference on Computer Vision and Pattern Recognition, CVPR 2009, pp. 248–255 (2009)
8. Fridrich, J.: Steganography in Digital Media. Cambridge University Press, New York (2009)
9. Giboulot, Q., Cogranne, R., Borghys, D., Bas, P.: Effects and solutions of cover-source mismatch in image steganalysis. Signal Proc. Image Commun. **86**, 115888 (2020)
10. Gloe, T., Böhme, R.: The 'Dresden image database' for benchmarking digital image forensics. In: Proceedings of the 25th Symposium On Applied Computing (ACM SAC 2010), vol. 2, pp. 1585–1591 (2010)
11. Holub, V., Fridrich, J., Denemark, T.: Universal distortion function for steganography in an arbitrary domain. EURASIP J. Inf. Secur. **2014**(1), 1–13 (2014). https://doi.org/10.1186/1687-417X-2014-1
12. Ker, A.D., et al.: Moving steganography and steganalysis from the laboratory into the real world. In: Proceedings of the 1st ACM Workshop on Information Hiding and Multimedia Security, IH&MMSec 2013, pp. 45–58. Montpellier, France, June 2013
13. Menon, D., Calvagno, G.: Color image demosaicking: an overview. Signal Proc. Image Commun. **8**, 518–533 (2011)
14. Newman, J., et al.: StegoAppDB: a steganography apps forensics image database. In: Proceedings of Media Watermarking, Security, and Forensics, MWSF 2019, Part of IS&T International Symposium on Electronic Imaging, EI 2019. Ingenta, Burlingame, California, USA, January 2019

15. Ruiz, H., Chaumont, M., Yedroudj, M., Oulad-Amara, A., Comby, F., Subsol, G.: Analysis of the scalability of a deep-learning network for steganography "Into the Wild". In: Proceeding of the 25th International Conference on Pattern Recognition, ICPR 2021, Worshop on MultiMedia FORensics in the WILD, MMForWILD 2021, Lecture Notes in Computer Science, LNCS, Springer. Virtual Conference due to Covid (Formerly Milan, Italy), January 2021. http://www.lirmm.fr/~chaumont/LSSD.html

16. Yedroudj, M., Chaumont, M., Comby, F.: How to augment a small learning set for improving the performances of a CNN-based steganalyzer? In: Proceedings of Media Watermarking, Security, and Forensics, MWSF 2018, Part of IS&T International Symposium on Electronic Imaging, EI 2018. p. 7. Burlingame, California, USA, 28 January–2 February 2018

17. Yousfi, Y., Butora, J., Fridrich, J., Giboulot, Q.: Breaking ALASKA: color separation for steganalysis in jpeg domain. In: Proceedings of the ACM Workshop on Information Hiding and Multimedia Security, IH&MMSec 2019, pp. 138–149. Paris, France, July 2019

18. Yousfi, Y., Butora, J., Khvedchenya, E., Fridrich, J.: ImageNet pre-trained CNNs for JPEG steganalysis. In: Proceedings of the IEEE International Workshop on Information Forensics and Security, WIFS 2020. Virtual Conference due to Covid (Formerly New-York, NY, USA), December 2020

19. Yousfi, Y., Fridrich, J.: JPEG steganalysis detectors scalable with respect to compression quality. In: Proceedings of Media Watermarking, Security, and Forensics, MWSF 2020, Part of IS&T International Symposium on Electronic Imaging, EI 2020, p. 10. Burlingame, California, USA, January 2020

20. Zeng, J., Tan, S., Li, B., Huang, J.: Large-scale jpeg image steganalysis using hybrid deep-learning framework. IEEE Trans. Inf. Forensics Secur. 5, 1200–1214 (2018)

# Neural Network for Denoising and Reading Degraded License Plates

Gianmaria Rossi[1]([✉]), Marco Fontani[1], and Simone Milani[2]

[1] Amped Software, Trieste, Italy
{gianmaria.rossi,marco.fontani}@ampedsoftware.com
[2] Department of Information Engineering, University of Padova, Padova, Italy
simone.milani@dei.unipd.it

**Abstract.** The denoising and the interpretation of severely-degraded license plates is one of the main problems that law enforcement agencies face worldwide and everyday. In this paper, we present a system made by coupling two convolutional neural networks. The first one produces a denoised version of the input image; the second one takes the denoised and original images to estimate a prediction of each character in the plate. Considering the complexity of gathering training data for this task, we propose a way of creating and augmenting an artificial dataset, which also allows tailoring the training to the specific license plate format of a given country at little cost. The system is designed as a tool to aid law enforcement investigations when dealing with low resolution corrupted license plates. Compared to existing methods, our system provides both a denoised license plate and a prediction of the characters to enable a visual inspection and an accurate validation of the final result. We validated the system on a dataset of real license plates, yielding a sensible perceptual improvement and an average character classification accuracy of 93%.

**Keywords:** Deep learning · Image denoising · License plates

## 1 Introduction

License plate localization and recognition systems are nowadays widespread all over the world. They can be stationary (i.e., installed in a specific place with a fixed orientation) or mobile (e.g., those installed on police cars). Applications include speed checking, parking lot management, monitoring of restricted traffic areas, stolen vehicles lookup. The sheer number of acquired images is too big to be read by humans, and so Automatic Number Plate Reader (ANPR) have been developed in the last years. Due to progress of artificial intelligence in the field of image analysis, newer systems use machine learning to provide reliable ANPR solutions.

Supported by Amped Software.

Most of the times, ANPR is a functional unit of dedicated surveillance camera networks, whose configuration and installation viewpoints are designed in order to acquire clear and readable video frames of transiting vehicles. In this paper we consider a different scenario, where a Closed-Circuit Television (CCTV) system or a personal device (e.g. a smartphone or a dash cam) record the real scene without any awareness of the investigation that is going to take place at a later stage. As a matter of fact, the quality of videos can be very low (e.g. because of poor illumination, motion blur, sensor noise, or other artificial or natural causes) and the acquisition viewpoint could not be suitable for the ANPR algorithm (because of adverse perspective). In such circumstances, automatic systems are normally unable to recognize the license plate, and additional software are required to enhance the image. Recently, this problem has been investigated by Lorch et al. [13], proposing a neural network capable of interpreting severely degraded license plates; nevertheless, their work only takes into account the distortion generated by sensor noise and poor resolution.

In this work, we aim at: i) further increasing the applicability of the method by Lorch et al. [13] with the introduction of perspective distortion into the images of the training dataset; ii) improving the performance and explainability of the system, by adding a neural network to denoise the input license plate. Indeed, the usual investigation activity does not blindly trust the outcomes of an ANPR deep learning software, since final results can not always be fully explained. Providing the analyst with an intermediate, denoised license plate allows them to double check the result thus increasing its reliability. To achieve such goals, the proposed deep learning architecture is made of two convolutional neural networks (CNNs) [4]: the first is used to denoise the image, while the second estimates the most likely plate numbers. Despite the approach has been trained and tested only on Italian license plates, we defined a training strategy that enables an easy generalization to license plats of different countries without the need of gathering real training data. This consists of a dataset generator algorithm which first creates synthetical, realistic license plates, and then applies several degradations to such images, augmenting the diversity of the training dataset and thus increasing the robustness of the final detector.

The proposed system is conceived as an investigative aid for law enforcement agencies rather than a forensic video enhancement tool. In fact, we are aware that the use of deep learning methods for forensic applications is often considered problematic, mostly because: a) they rely on training data that is external to the specific court case, and b) their explainability is still limited. As a matter of fact, the results generated by the network should be used as a last resort whenever a strongly degraded image of a license plate can not be interpreted by visual inspection, not even after the application of classical forensic enhancement algorithms.

This paper is structured as follows. Section 2 gives an overview of related works with a focus on the solution in [13], which was the starting point for this work. Section 3 describes the architecture of the neural networks, while Sect. 4 presents the dataset generator and how it was used to create the training data.

In Sect. 5, we explain the training of the neural networks and the obtained results; Sect. 6 draws the final conclusions.

## 2   Related Works

The first prototype of a license plate reader is surprisingly old, dating back to 1976, when United Kingdom's Police Scientific Development Branch (PSDB) presented the Automatic Number-Plate Recognition [1]. Nowadays, several names are in use: Automatic License Plate Recognition (or Reader) (ALPR), Automatic Vehicle Identification (AVI), Car Plate Recognition (CPR), Mobile License-Plate Reader (MLPR), and more.

The traditional ANPR processing pipeline can be divided into the following main phases [10]. First, the original image is converted to grayscale. Then, a set of quality-enhancing operations are applied to the image (e.g., noise removal and contrast balancing). The next step is localization of the license plate, which can be obtained combining several methods like edge detection, background removal, connected component analysis and candidate selection. Finally a segmentation of the characters is applied and the final result is obtained through a character recognition technique, which can be based on a template matching or a feature matching approach.

In [21], Sarfraz et al. show an ALPR system for the Arabian license plate, where a vertical edge detector and a seed-filling algorithm, together with the knowledge of the license plate proportions, are used to localize the license plate in the image. The segmentation of the characters was done by binarizing the image and counting the number of black pixel in each column. After that, each segmented character was normalized to fit a certain size and, by using template matching, the final prediction was obtained. Other works adopt a similar approach, shown in [5,6,17,19].

In the last years, neural networks became more and more used in image analysis due to their ability to extract useful information from images [16,25]. ANPR made no exception, and several license plate reading systems based on neural networks were developed. Other noticeable proposal are shown in [8,12,24,27]. In [22], the authors proposed a method to read license plates from various countries (Europe, Brazil, US, Taiwan,...) with different level of perspective distortion due to oblique views. To achieve this, they used a Convolutional Neural Network (CNN) to rectify the license plate, that was then fed to an Optical Character Recognition (OCR) system to get the final result. Zherdev et al. [26], showed an end-to-end method for Automatic License Plate Reader using a lightweight CNN, without character segmentation. It was trained on Chinese license plates giving an accuracy of up to 95%, while also working in real time. It supported different license plate layouts and fonts, and it was robust enough to operate on difficult cases, such as perspective distortion, change of point of view, hard lighting conditions. Agarwal et al. in [3], proposed a CNN to read degraded versions of license plates. The evaluation was done on both synthetic and real US license plates with a resolution varying from 12 to 55 pixels in width and a signal-to-noise ratio ranging from −3 dB to 20 dB. Authors demonstrated that, even in cases where the license plate was so degraded that the human eye could not read it, the network was still able to perform well.

This paper takes inspiration from a common scenario faced everyday by law enforcement video analysts: the analyst processes a surveillance video to extract a cropped and rectified image of a license plate, where several issues may prevent the intelligibility of characters: optical blur, distortions introduced by perspective transformation operations, poor resolution, graininess or other kinds of noise. Starting from the recent work by Lorch et al. [13] and Martinelli et al.[15], we propose a CNN-based ANPR system conceived and trained to help the analyst in the depicted scenario. As opposite to the original work, our method works in two stages: first, an auto-encoder CNN is used to generate a denoised version of the input image; then, both the original input image and the denoised version are fed to a second CNN, which performs the interpretation of characters. This approach has the noticeable advantage of providing an "intermediate" result, the denoised image, which can often increase the explainability (and, thus, credibility) of the final prediction. Since the availability of annotated license plates datasets is limited, we also contribute to the field by defining a way to generate synthetic license plates and perturb them with a combination of defects that closely emulates those typically introduced by surveillance systems. The test dataset, instead, is created starting from real images.

Being designed as a tool for investigators, our system does not work in real time and requires a cropped and rectified image of the license plate to work; both these limitations do not affect the applicability of the method to the targeted domain.

## 3   Network

The proposed solution makes use of two CNNs: the Denoising network, which produces a cleaner image of the input license plate, and the Reading network, which generates a vector of probabilities for each character of the license plate. Similarly to [13], our system does not require the segmentation of the characters: the Reading network takes care of that by having seven outputs, one for each of the characters on the license plate.

### 3.1   Denoising Network

The Denoising neural network is based on the UNET architecture [18], an autoencoder where each block of the encoder path is concatenated with the input of the corresponding block of the decoder path. The UNET was first implemented for the segmentation of biomedical images, but it is also widely used for image denoising [7,9,11,14]. Thanks to the use of skip connections in the architecture, it is possible to recover fine-grained details during the prediction [2] by reducing the problem of the vanishing gradient during the back-propagation phase of the training.

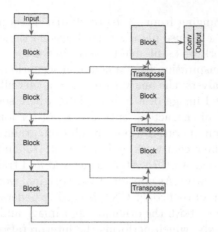

**Fig. 1.** Architecture of the denoising network.

In this work we have used a UNET with four blocks for the encoder and three for the decoder, the architecture is shown in Fig. 1. Each block of the encoder and decoder path is made by concatenating two times the following layers: a convolutional layer with $n_f$ filters with kernel size of $3 \times 3$ and stride 1; a batch normalization layer, and an activation layer that uses the ReLU activation function. The value of $n_f$ is equal to 48 in first block, 96 in the second one, 144 in the third one, and 192 in the last one in the encoder path; 144, 96, and 48 in the decoder path. After each block of the encoder path, except for the last one, we apply a maxPooling layer to decrease the size of the feature map. Starting with an input of size $160 \times 40$, we have, after each block, a feature map of size of $80 \times 20$, $40 \times 10$, $20 \times 5$. After each pooling layer we add also a dropout layer with probability $p = 0.05$ to ignore a node.

In the decoder path we use a transposed convolutional layer to double the size of the feature map. Then, we concatenate the result with the output of the corresponding block of the encoder path, the concatenation is given as input to a block with the same architecture of the one used in the encoder path, and a Dropout layer is used after each block except for the last one. The last layer is a convolutional layer with a single kernel of shape $1 \times 1$ and stride 1, with a sigmoid activation function. This gives us an output of the same size of the input, but with a single channel.

### 3.2    Reading Network

Differently from the work in [13], the presented Reading network operates on grayscale images only, and processes a concatenation of the original and the denoised license plate (the output of the previous network). The rationale behind this choice is that the denoising operations could have erased some high-frequency details that prove to be crucial for the detection or, in some cases, have included some distorting artifacts that prevent a correct detection of characters.

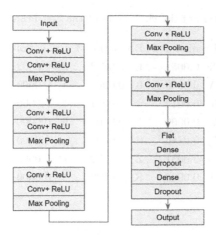

**Fig. 2.** Architecture of the reader network.

This network is made of 8 convolutional layers, with kernel size of $3 \times 3$ [23] and a number of filter equal to: 64, 64, 128, 128, 256, 256, 512, 512. Each one is followed by a ReLU activation function, there is a max pooling layer after the second, fourth, sixth, seventh, and eighth activation function. The max-pooling layers in odd position decrease the size of the feature map by two. After the last pooling layer, there are two fully-connected layers, the first one with 1024 nodes, and the second one with 2048 nodes. There is also a dropout layer after each fully-connected layer, each with a probability to ignore a node equal to $p = 0.5$, the architecture is shown in Fig. 2. Following the original paper, the weights of the convolutional layers and the seven final dense layers are initialized with the Xavier initializer; for the first two dense layers a truncated normal distribution with zero mean and standard deviation equal to 0.005 is used. The initial bias is set to 0.1 for all layers except for the first two dense layers where it is equal to 0. At this point, the output consists of seven dense layers, each one corresponding to one of the seven characters of a standard Italian license plate. Each of the output layers has 37 nodes, 26 for the Latin alphabet, 10 for the numbers, and 1 for a blank space "_" used in the case of license plates with different number of characters. However, since modern Italian license plates have always 7 characters, the probability of a given character to be "_" is almost 0 in our experiments. We can then represent the output of neural network as a table where each column shows the predicted characters and the corresponding probability as shown in Table 1. In each column, the seven symbols represent the corresponding characters on the license plate, the value next to them represents their probability. The column are ordered left to right in descending order of the probability. The network is able to process license plates up to 7 characters. However the final layer can be easily adapted to read license plates with more characters.

**Table 1.** Prediction of the characters of the first license plate in Fig. 11

| Prediction 1 | | Prediction 2 | | Prediction 3 | | Prediction 4 | | Prediction 5 | |
|---|---|---|---|---|---|---|---|---|---|
| A | 0.9927 | X | 0.0054 | L | 0.0013 | J | 0.0002 | V | 0.0001 |
| X | 1.0000 | A | 0.0000 | K | 0.0000 | Y | 0.0000 | N | 0.0000 |
| 6 | 0.9985 | 5 | 0.0014 | 8 | 0.0001 | 3 | 0.0000 | 0 | 0.0000 |
| 7 | 1.0000 | 2 | 0.0000 | 1 | 0.0000 | 0 | 0.0000 | 9 | 0.0000 |
| 2 | 0.9812 | 7 | 0.0186 | 0 | 0.0001 | 1 | 0.0000 | 3 | 0.0000 |
| C | 0.9969 | G | 0.0031 | Z | 0.0000 | D | 0.0000 | J | 0.0000 |
| X | 0.9999 | A | 0.0000 | K | 0.0000 | Y | 0.0000 | V | 0.0000 |

## 4  Dataset

When dealing with machine-learning based ANPR system, the scarcity of labeled training datasets is an important obstacle. Moreover, license plates are normally released following an incremental pattern, so that, even if a large dataset of license plates picture is available, it would likely be unbalanced towards older license plates and not representative of the future ones. For example, picking a random set of currently existing license plates would reveal that the first letters of the alphabet are more likely found in the first positions (because older vehicles accumulated for longer time), and possibly a whole set of letters would never be present in the first position (e.g., at present time in Italy the newest letter in the first position is "G").

For these reasons, we have decided to create a dataset of synthetic license plates, some examples are shown in Fig. 3. An empty license plate was used as background, and by using random strings of characters, following the Italian license plate layout, we created a dataset of 20 k synthetic license plates. The size of each license plate is 160 × 40 pixels, which is not the exact proportion used for Italian license plates, but represents a good compromise with the proportions used in other European countries.

**Fig. 3.** Examples of synthetic license plates.

AE 270ZH      PZ 814KM      ZJ 364NA

**Fig. 4.** Mask obtained from the license plates.

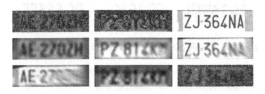

**Fig. 5.** Synthetic license plate after the first transformation to make them more realistic.

**Fig. 6.** Noisy version obtained by applying various artificial degradation.

In order to increase the variability of synthetic license plates, the following transformations were applied, as Fig. 5 demonstrates:

- Random illumination changes: we convert the image to the HSV color space, then for the background pixels we add a random value in [−20, 20] to the first channel, and a random value in [−10, 10] to the third channel.
- Random shadows: we add a shadow to the license plate by selecting a region and making it darker; the top-left and top-right point are the respective corners of the license plate, the other two points are selected at random.
- Random cropping (without cropping the characters, i.e., ensuring the presence of all 7 characters in the image). This choice is to avoid that the network wrongly learns that a character is always in the same position.

Additionally, a binary mask of the license plate is created, the pixels composing the characters of the license plates are given a value of 0, while the pixels of the background have a value of 1; this mask is going to be used in the loss function of the training of the Denoising network, Fig. 4

The synthetic license plates obtained so far are still at very high quality. In order to mimic the distortion introduced by typical surveillance systems, a combination of different transformations was applied to the synthetic license plates. The transformation were applied by combining the following operations (in the presentation order) (Fig. 6):

- First, the plate can be kept at the original size of 160 × 40 pixels or resized to a lower resolution and then brought back at the original size. We used 3 different lower resolution 32 × 8, 60 × 15, 120 × 30 pixels. The interpolation method used for the downsizing is INTER_AREA, while for the upsizing we used the INTER_CUBIC.
- Secondly, we recreated the distortion typically introduced by a perspective correction by first upscaling images to a resolution of 800 × 200 pixels and then applying a perspective distortion through the warpPerspective function of OpenCV. The image was then scaled down to its original resolution, and the inverse warping was applied. To simulate real cases, where the camera is

**Fig. 7.** Examples of real license plates.

BG 239KH    FE 104TJ    DC 663FF

**Fig. 8.** Mask obtained from the license plate.

**Fig. 9.** Noisy version obtained by applying various artificial degradation.

typically mounted on a wall and faces towards the ground, we generated a distortion from the top, top-left, top-right point of view. The function requires 2 set of 4 points to compute the warping, those points are not the same during all the iteration, a starting value is selected for each one, then a small random value is added to it to create a bit of randomness.

– A Gaussian blurring kernel was applied to the image, using OpenCV's GaussianBlur function with 3 different values for the kernel size, $ksize = 1, 3,$ or 5; the Gaussian standard deviation is computed as follow:

$$\sigma = 0.3 * ((ksize - 1) * 0.5 - 1) + 0.8.$$

– Finally, a random Gaussian noise is added to the plate in 4 different strengths depending of the value of the mean $\mu$ and variance $\sigma$. In our case we have used no noise: $\mu = \sigma = 1$, low-noise: $\mu = \sigma = 70$, mid-noise: $\mu = \sigma = 500$, high-noise: $\mu = \sigma = 2000$.

In the end we have a total of 192 different combinations of transformations, applied to the original dataset of 20k license plates, we obtain 3.84M samples.

Since the license plates are synthetic, to test the precision of our model, a small dataset of 884 real license plates was created. The license plates were downloaded from a publicly-available online database[1], and the License Plate Extractor software (LPEX)[2] was used to automatically crop the license plate in the image and to create the label for each sample, however each of them was checked to avoid errors, some of them are shown in Fig. 7. The license plates were not finely cropped in order to simulate a real scenario where the user did not pay much attention on creating the input for the neural networks. For the creation

[1]  https://platesmania.com/it/gallery.
[2]  https://github.com/Link009/LPEX.

of the masks, a threshold was applied to the unprocessed license plates, Fig. 8. The same transformation sets employed for the creation of the training dataset were applied to the obtained image thus generating a test dataset of 169728 images, some examples of the application of the degradations are shown Fig. 9. Finally, the license plate are then converted into grayscale to fit the requirements of the neural network. For the training of both the Denoising network and the Reading network we split the dataset in two part, the first consisting of 80% of the dataset is used for the training and the remaining part of the dataset is used for the validation of the parameters.

## 5   Training and Results

The training of the proposed system is done in two parts. During the first one we train the Denoising network alone, and in the second one we train the Reading network with both the degraded license plates and the denoised version obtained from the previously trained Denoising network concatenated in a single input. By doing so, we combine the information present in both images. The training was done using the Tensorflow[3] framework in combination with the Keras[4] API in a computer with two RTX 2080 Ti working in parallel.

For the training of the Denoising network we need the original image of the license plate, the degraded version obtained from the combination of transformations, and the mask created during the building of the synthetic dataset. We work with batches of 256 samples, that in a multi-GPU environment is split evenly on all the available GPUs, so that in our case each GPU works with a batch size of 128 samples.

The optimizer used is Adam, with an initial learning rate of 0.05 and the training was stopped after 1200 iterations.

The loss function used for the backpropagation is a combination of three different losses: $\mathcal{L} = \lambda_1 * \mathcal{L}_{mse} + \lambda_2 * \mathcal{L}_{wass} + \lambda_3 * \mathcal{L}_{mask}$. The partial losses are computed as follow:

$\mathcal{L}_{mse}$ is the mean squared error (MSE) computed between the output of the Denoising network and the original license plate.

$\mathcal{L}_{wass}$ is equal to

$$\mathcal{L}_{wass} = 1 + \frac{\sum_{i,j}(y_{i,j}^{true} * y_{i,j}^{pred})}{N},$$

where $N$ is the number of pixels, in our case $160 * 40$, $y_{i,j}^{true}$ is the value of the pixel in position $i, j$ of the matrix representing the original license plate, and $y_{i,j}^{pred}$ is the value of the pixel in position $i, j$ of the prediction of the Denoising network.

---

[3]   https://www.tensorflow.org/.
[4]   https://keras.io/.

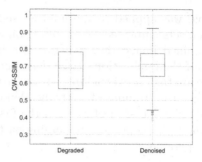

**Fig. 10.** Box plot of the results of the CW-SSIM algorithm on the test dataset; on the left there are the values related to the degraded images, on the right the values related to the denoised images. For each boxplot, the red segment shows the median value, while the bottom and top edges of the box indicate the 25th and 75th percentiles, respectively. The whiskers extend to the most extreme data points that are not considered outliers, while outliers are plotted individually using the '+' symbol.

$\mathcal{L}_{mask}$ is computed as $\mathcal{L}_{mask} = 1 + p - b$, where

$$p = \frac{\sum_{i,j}(y_{i,j}^{pred} * \overline{y_{i,j}^{mask}})}{\sum_{i,j} y_{i,j}^{mask}},$$

$y_{i,j}^{mask}$ is the pixel value in position $i, j$ of the mask image; and

$$b = \frac{\sum_{i,j}(y_{i,j}^{pred} * y_{i,j}^{mask})}{\sum_{i,j} y_{i,j}^{mask}}.$$

The values of $\lambda_1, \lambda_2, \lambda_3$ are respectively 30, 0.2, 0.2; the reason why $\lambda_1$ is much bigger then the other two constants is because the value of $\mathcal{L}_{mse}$ is much lower then the other two losses, in average $\mathcal{L}_{mse} \approx 0.035$, while $\mathcal{L}_{wass}, \mathcal{L}_{mask} \approx 1$. To avoid that the network focuses on lowering the value $\mathcal{L}_{wass}$ and $\mathcal{L}_{mask}$ we apply to $\mathcal{L}_{mse}$ a greater multiplier, moreover by giving more weight to $\mathcal{L}_{mse}$ we obtain as result of the network an image similar to the target image, while with a lower value the result would have been closer to the mask or a combination of the mask and the target image.

To verify the quality of the output of the Denoising network we have used the Complex Wavelet Structural Similarity Index Measure (CW-SSIM) [20]. The results of the algorithm applied to both the degraded license plates and denoised license plates are shown in Fig. 10.

For the training of the Reading network the optimizer used is the Standard Descent (SGD) with an initial learning rate of 0.05, the global batch size is 64 samples, this means that each GPU works with batches of 32 samples.

The loss is computed on the validation set every 100 iterations on the training set; the training was stopped after the validation loss had not improved for 100 times.

To compute the loss, we created seven one-hot encoding of 37 elements, one for each character or the license plate, then we sum the cross-entropy loss between the output of the network and the true label, namely: $\mathcal{L} = l_1 + l_2 + l_3 + l_4 + l_5 + l_6 + l_7$, with $l_n = -\sum_{i=1}^{37}(y_i * log(\hat{y}_i))$ for $n = 1, .., 7$, where $\hat{y}_i$ is the $i$-th value of the output, and $y_i$ is the $i$-th value of the label.

Some examples of the results of the Denoising and Reading networks are shown in Fig. 11 and Table 4. Since each output of the network represents the probability for each possible character, we can order them in decreasing order. To verify the accuracy of the output we use three metrics: Top 1, Top 3, and Top 5 accuracy.

The Top $n$ accuracy over a set $S$ of samples has 7 values, one for each character of the license plate; in each position we sum the number of occurrences that the correct character, given by the label, can be found in the top $n$ values of the output, and then compute the mean. This can be useful to understand if the Reading network is more precise in recognizing the character in some specific position. This can be seen in Table 2, where we can observe that the three value in the middle are, on average, greater than the other. This is probably explained by the fact that the Italian license plates always have numbers in those central positions, while in the other positions there are always letters. We can suppose that the network has learnt this pattern and since there are 26 letters to choose but only 10 numbers to choose, it is more precise to identify correct numbers.

**Table 2.** Average accuracy on the test dataset for the proposed method

|  | Position 1 | Position 2 | Position 3 | Position 4 | Position 5 | Position 6 | Position 7 | Average |
|---|---|---|---|---|---|---|---|---|
| TOP 1 | 0.93005 | 0.94324 | 0.96183 | 0.95992 | 0.95232 | 0.91980 | 0.86653 | 0.93338 |
| TOP 3 | 0.97298 | 0.98528 | 0.99051 | 0.99095 | 0.98781 | 0.96999 | 0.94586 | 0.97762 |
| TOP 5 | 0.98438 | 0.99160 | 0.99487 | 0.99560 | 0.99499 | 0.98020 | 0.96488 | 0.98664 |

**Table 3.** Average accuracy on the test dataset using Lorch's network [13]

|  | Position 1 | Position 2 | Position 3 | Position 4 | Position 5 | Position 6 | Position 7 | Average |
|---|---|---|---|---|---|---|---|---|
| TOP 1 | 0.92556 | 0.92711 | 0.97274 | 0.96702 | 0.95736 | 0.91310 | 0.85735 | 0.93146 |
| TOP 3 | 0.97355 | 0.98746 | 0.99190 | 0.99256 | 0.98958 | 0.97074 | 0.94545 | 0.97874 |
| TOP 5 | 0.98611 | 0.99290 | 0.99627 | 0.99694 | 0.99563 | 0.98093 | 0.96444 | 0.98760 |

**Fig. 11.** For each image, on the left there is the original license plate; in the middle the license plate after applying the transformations; on the right the denoised version obtained from the Denoising network. The values of CW-SSIM applied on the degraded and denoised version are respectively: 0.699–0.767 ; 0.551–0.663 ; 0.708–0.728 ; 0.442–0.582

**Table 4.** Prediction of the characters of Fig. 11

| Prediction 1 | | Prediction 2 | | Prediction 3 | | Prediction 4 | | Prediction 5 | |
|---|---|---|---|---|---|---|---|---|---|
| A | 0.9927 | X | 0.0054 | L | 0.0013 | J | 0.0002 | V | 0.0001 |
| X | 1.0000 | A | 0.0000 | K | 0.0000 | Y | 0.0000 | N | 0.0000 |
| 6 | 0.9985 | 5 | 0.0014 | 8 | 0.0001 | 3 | 0.0000 | 0 | 0.0000 |
| 7 | 1.0000 | 2 | 0.0000 | 1 | 0.0000 | 0 | 0.0000 | 9 | 0.0000 |
| 2 | 0.9812 | 7 | 0.0186 | 0 | 0.0001 | 1 | 0.0000 | 3 | 0.0000 |
| C | 0.9969 | G | 0.0031 | Z | 0.0000 | D | 0.0000 | J | 0.0000 |
| X | 0.9999 | A | 0.0000 | K | 0.0000 | Y | 0.0000 | V | 0.0000 |
| **Prediction 1** | | **Prediction 2** | | **Prediction 3** | | **Prediction 4** | | **Prediction 5** | |
| E | 0.8352 | L | 0.1498 | C | 0.0083 | F | 0.0031 | K | 0.0005 |
| Y | 0.9994 | T | 0.0002 | X | 0.0001 | L | 0.0001 | V | 0.0001 |
| 3 | 0.9963 | 5 | 0.0035 | 1 | 0.0001 | 0 | 0.0001 | 9 | 0.0000 |
| 4 | 0.9999 | 7 | 0.0000 | 8 | 0.0000 | 2 | 0.0000 | 1 | 0.0000 |
| 7 | 0.9997 | 2 | 0.0003 | 0 | 0.0000 | 1 | 0.0000 | 4 | 0.0000 |
| Z | 0.9977 | T | 0.0011 | M | 0.0004 | P | 0.0003 | Y | 0.0001 |
| T | 0.9999 | Z | 0.0000 | Y | 0.0000 | X | 0.0000 | G | 0.0000 |
| **Prediction 1** | | **Prediction 2** | | **Prediction 3** | | **Prediction 4** | | **Prediction 5** | |
| B | 1.0000 | R | 0.0000 | D | 0.0000 | P | 0.0000 | S | 0.0000 |
| Z | 1.0000 | P | 0.0000 | C | 0.0000 | X | 0.0000 | L | 0.0000 |
| 0 | 1.0000 | 8 | 0.0000 | 6 | 0.0000 | 2 | 0.0000 | 9 | 0.0000 |
| 2 | 1.0000 | 5 | 0.0000 | 8 | 0.0000 | 9 | 0.0000 | 4 | 0.0000 |
| 6 | 0.9999 | 5 | 0.0000 | 8 | 0.0000 | 0 | 0.0000 | 3 | 0.0000 |
| D | 0.9185 | B | 0.0814 | Z | 0.0000 | S | 0.0000 | E | 0.0000 |
| G | 0.9999 | C | 0.0000 | S | 0.0000 | W | 0.0000 | Z | 0.0000 |
| **Prediction 1** | | **Prediction 2** | | **Prediction 3** | | **Prediction 4** | | **Prediction 5** | |
| E | 0.9877 | S | 0.0113 | X | 0.0003 | L | 0.0001 | R | 0.0001 |
| G | 0.9994 | C | 0.0005 | D | 0.0000 | W | 0.0000 | F | 0.0000 |
| 1 | 1.0000 | 3 | 0.0000 | 5 | 0.0000 | 0 | 0.0000 | 9 | 0.0000 |
| 7 | 0.9999 | 1 | 0.0000 | 2 | 0.0000 | 9 | 0.0000 | 0 | 0.0000 |
| 0 | 0.9778 | 8 | 0.0099 | 6 | 0.0090 | 3 | 0.0015 | 5 | 0.0006 |
| B | 0.9995 | D | 0.0004 | R | 0.0001 | P | 0.0000 | S | 0.0000 |
| D | 0.9999 | B | 0.0001 | R | 0.0000 | J | 0.0000 | W | 0.0000 |

We can also notice that the values on the right side are generally lower than those on the left side; we can hypothesise that it is because during the creation of the dataset, more precisely during the application of the perspective distortion, the cases of top-left view are more degraded than the top-right view.

It is possible to compute the mean over both the number of samples and the number of characters, and this gives us an overall accuracy, reported in the rightmost column of Table 2.

To compare our results with other solutions we have implemented a license plate reader following the one proposed by Lorch et al. in [13], with a difference in the input size. The size in our case is $160 \times 40$, while in the original paper is $100 \times 50$; this discrepancy is due to the different proportions of license plates in the US and Europe, but since in the end we test the results with our network we have decided to change the input size. Another difference is in the dataset used for the training: instead of using color images, following the original paper, we have used grayscale images to follow the training of our network. The results obtained using the Lorch's version are shown in Table 3. By comparing Tables 2 and 3, we notice that our method has comparable performance with Lorch et al.'s one in terms of reading accuracy.

## 6    Conclusion

In this work we proposed a solution for reading degraded images of license plate and to generate a denoised version for a better visualization. The system is implemented by using two neural networks, the first one is used to obtain a more defined image of the license plate; the second one to read the characters. By having a denoised version of the degraded license plate it is possible to double check the results obtained from the Reading network.

The obtained results show that even in cases where the license plate is very degraded and a human eye is unable to recognize, through the usage of the neural networks is possible to obtain an image where it is possible to see some details and also a good probability of correct detection of each character.

As an additional contribution we shown a way to generate a dataset of degraded license plates to be used as training.

For future works we aim at generating a more complex dataset that would allow the recognition of non-Italian license plates, with a focus on USA and Europe countries.

## References

1. History of ANPR, http://www.anpr-international.com/history-of-anpr/
2. Adaloglou, N.: Intuitive explanation of skip connections in deep learning. https://theaisummer.com/skip-connections/
3. Agarwal, S., Tran, D., Torresani, L., Farid, H.: Deciphering severely degraded license plates. In: Alattar, A.M., Memon, N.D. (eds.) Media Watermarking, Security, and Forensics 2017, Burlingame, CA, USA, 29 January 2017–2 February 2017. pp. 138–143. Ingenta (2017). https://doi.org/10.2352/ISSN.2470-1173.2017.7.MWSF-337
4. Albawi, S., Mohammed, T.A., Al-Zawi, S.: Understanding of a convolutional neural network. In: 2017 International Conference on Engineering and Technology (ICET), pp. 1–6 (2017)

5. Anagnostopoulos, C.E., Anagnostopoulos, I.E., Psoroulas, I.D., Loumos, V., Kayafas, E.: License plate recognition from still images and video sequences: a survey. IEEE Trans. Intell. Transp. Syst. **9**(3), 377–391 (2008)
6. Badr, A., Abd El-Wahab, M., Thabet, A., Abdelsadek, A.: Cctv-automatic number plate recognition system. Math. Comput. Sci. Ser. **38**, 62–71 (2011)
7. Batson, J., Royer, L.: Noise2self: Blind denoising by self-supervision (2019)
8. Bjorklund, T., Fiandrotti, A., Annarumma, M., Francini, G., Magli, E.: Automatic license plate recognition with convolutional neural networks trained on synthetic data, pp. 1–6 (2017). https://doi.org/10.1109/MMSP.2017.8122260
9. Jha, D., Riegler, M.A., Johansen, D., Halvorsen, P., Johansen, H.D.: DoubleU-Net: a deep convolutional neural network for medical image segmentation. In: 2020 IEEE 33rd International Symposium on Computer-Based Medical Systems (CBMS), pp. 558–564 (2020)
10. Khokhar, S., Dahiya, P.: A review of recognition techniques in ALPR systems. Int. J. Comput. Appl. **170**, 30–32 (2017). https://doi.org/10.5120/ijca2017914867
11. Lehtinen, J., et al.: Noise2Noise: Learning image restoration without clean data (2018)
12. Lin, C., Lin, Y., Liu, W.: An efficient license plate recognition system using convolution neural networks. In: 2018 IEEE International Conference on Applied System Invention (ICASI), pp. 224–227 (2018)
13. Lorch, B., Agarwal, S., Farid, H.: Forensic reconstruction of severely degraded license plates. In: for Imaging Science & Technology, S. (ed.) Electronic Imaging (January 2019). https://doi.org/10.2352/issn.2470-1173.2019.5.mwsf-529
14. Lou, A., Guan, S., Loew, M.: DC-UNet: Rethinking the U-Net architecture with dual channel efficient CNN for medical images segmentation (2020)
15. Martinelli, U., Milani, S., Fontani, M.: License Plate Recognition using Convolutional Neural Networks. Master's thesis, University of Padua, Department of Information Engineering (2019)
16. Pandelea, A.E., Budescu, M., Covatariu, G.: Image processing using artificial neural networks. Bulletin of the Polytechnic Institute of Jassy, Constructions. Architecture Section LXI(LXV), pp. 9–21 (2015)
17. Patel, C., Shah, D., Patel, A.: Automatic number plate recognition system (ANPR): a survey. Int. J. Comput. Appl. (IJCA) **69**, 21–33 (2013). https://doi.org/10.5120/11871-7665
18. Ronneberger, O., Fischer, P., Brox, T.: U-Net: Convolutional networks for biomedical image segmentation (2015)
19. Roy, A., Ghoshal, D.: Number plate recognition for use in different countries using an improved segmentation, pp. 1–5 (2011). https://doi.org/10.1109/NCETACS.2011.5751407
20. Sampat, M.P., Wang, Z., Gupta, S., Bovik, A.C., Markey, M.K.: Complex wavelet structural similarity: a new image similarity index. IEEE Trans. Image Process. **18**(11), 2385–2401 (2009)
21. Sarfraz, M., Ahmed, M.J., Ghazi, S.A.: Saudi Arabian license plate recognition system. In: Proceedings of 2003 International Conference on Geometric Modeling and Graphics, 2003, pp. 36–41 (2003)
22. Silva, S.M., Jung, C.R.: License plate detection and recognition in unconstrained scenarios. In: 2018 European Conference on Computer Vision (ECCV), pp. 580–596 (2018). https://doi.org/10.1007/978-3-030-01258-8_36
23. Simonyan, K., Zisserman, A.: Very deep convolutional networks for large-scale image recognition (2015)

24. Svoboda, P., Hradis, M., Marsik, L., Zemcik, P.: CNN for license plate motion deblurring (2016)
25. Zhao, Z., Zheng, P., Xu, S., Wu, X.: Object detection with deep learning: a review. IEEE Trans. Neural Netw. Learn. Syst. **30**(11), 3212–3232 (2019)
26. Zherzdev, S., Gruzdev, A.: Lprnet: License plate recognition via deep neural networks (2018)
27. Španhel, J., Sochor, J., Juranek, R., Herout, A., Maršík, L., Zemcík, P.: Holistic recognition of low quality license plates by CNN using track annotated data, pp. 1–6 (2017). https://doi.org/10.1109/AVSS.2017.8078501

# The Forchheim Image Database
# for Camera Identification in the Wild

Benjamin Hadwiger and Christian Riess[✉]

Multimedia Security Group, IT-Security Infrastructures Lab,
Friedrich-Alexander-Universität Erlangen-Nürnberg, Erlangen, Germany
{benjamin.hadwiger,christian.riess}@fau.de
https://www.cs1.tf.fau.de/research/multimedia-security/

**Abstract.** Image provenance can represent crucial knowledge in criminal investigation and journalistic fact checking. In the last two decades, numerous algorithms have been proposed for obtaining information on the source camera and distribution history of an image. For a fair ranking of these techniques, it is important to rigorously assess their performance on practically relevant test cases. To this end, a number of datasets have been proposed. However, we argue that there is a gap in existing databases: to our knowledge, there is currently no dataset that simultaneously satisfies two goals, namely a) to cleanly separate scene content and forensic traces, and b) to support realistic post-processing like social media recompression.

In this work, we propose the *Forchheim Image Database* (FODB) to close this gap. It consists of more than 23,000 images of 143 scenes by 27 smartphone cameras, and it allows to cleanly separate image content from forensic artifacts. Each image is provided in 6 different qualities: the original camera-native version, and five copies from social networks. We demonstrate the usefulness of FODB in an evaluation of methods for camera identification. We report three findings. First, the recently proposed general-purpose EfficientNet remarkably outperforms several dedicated forensic CNNs both on clean and compressed images. Second, classifiers obtain a performance boost even on unknown post-processing after augmentation by artificial degradations. Third, FODB's clean separation of scene content and forensic traces imposes important, rigorous boundary conditions for algorithm benchmarking.

**Keywords:** Camera identification · Benchmark dataset · Post-processing

## 1 Introduction

With the emergence of affordable smartphones, it became straightforward to record images and videos and to share them via social networks. However, this opportunity can also be abused for unlawful purposes. For instance, multimedia samples can depict illicit content like CSEM/CSAM, violate copyright, or

© Springer Nature Switzerland AG 2021
A. Del Bimbo et al. (Eds.): ICPR 2020 Workshops, LNCS 12666, pp. 500–515, 2021.
https://doi.org/10.1007/978-3-030-68780-9_40

Fig. 1. Example images from the Forchheim Image Database

be intentionally aimed at deceiving the viewer. In such cases, authorship and authenticity of multimedia items can be a central question for criminal prosecution.

This motivated researchers to develop numerous image forensics algorithms over the last two decades. Initial methods mostly model imaging artifacts [12, 19, 20]. More recently, deep learning-based approaches [4, 6, 9, 17, 23, 25, 26, 33, 34] achieve state-of-the-art results. These techniques enable a forensic analyst to detect and localize manipulations [9, 12, 17, 34], and to identify the source device [4, 19, 20, 26, 33] or distribution history of images or videos [6, 23, 25]. In this work, we limit our focus on the latter two tasks on images.

The assessment of the real-world applicability of algorithms requires consistent evaluation protocols with standard benchmark datasets. In 2010, Gloe and Böhme proposed the Dresden Image Database (DIDB) [15], the first large-scale benchmark for camera identification algorithms. It consists of nearly 17,000 images of 73 devices depicting 83 scenes. All devices record the same scenes. This is particularly important for aligning training/test splits with the scene content. Doing so prevents the danger of opening a side channel through scene content, which may lead to overly optimistic results [4, 19].

The DIDB became one of the most important benchmark datasets in the research community. However, it only consists of DSLR and compact cameras, whereas today most images are recorded with smartphones. Also postprocessed versions of the images from social network sharing are not part of this dataset.

More recently, Shullani et al. proposed VISION [29], an image and video database for benchmarking forensic algorithms. It contains over 34,000 images in total, from 35 smartphones and tablet cameras. A subset of the images has been shared through Facebook and Whatsapp. This enables to investigate the impact of realistic post-processing on forensic traces.

A limitation of VISION is that the images show arbitrary scenes. Thus, a training/test split by scenes is not possible. Moreover, the scenes of images from the same camera are in some cases highly correlated. While this may be no issue for methods that strictly operate on noise residuals (e.g., PRNU-based finger-printing [20]), it can open a side-channel for end-to-end Convolutional Neural Networks (CNNs), which potentially leads to overly optimistic evaluation results.

In this paper, we propose the Forchheim Image Database (FODB), a new benchmark combining the advantages of DIDB and VISION. It consists of 143 scenes, each captured with 27 smartphone cameras. Each image has been shared through the 5 social media apps by Facebook, Instagram, Telegram, Twitter, and Whatsapp. This yields a total of over 23,000 JPEG images. Examples from the database are shown in Fig. 1. FODB allows training/test splits without scene overlap, and simultaneously supports robustness evaluations under real-world post-processing. Hence, it allows rigorous camera association benchmarking on real-world post-processing. To demonstrate the use of the dataset, we perform a benchmark of CNN-based camera identification, which brings insights into relative CNN performances, generalization to unseen post-processing, and performance impacts of scene splitting. In summary, our main contributions are:

- We propose FODB, a new large-scale database for evaluating image forensics algorithms in the wild. FODB is publicly available at:
  https://faui1-files.cs.fau.de/public/mmsec/datasets/fodb/
- We employ EfficientNet [30] for camera identification on FODB and show that it clearly outperforms targeted forensic CNNs for almost all qualities.
- We show that degradation during training significantly boosts robustness even for unseen post-processing.
- We demonstrate the importance of scene splitting for learning-based camera identification.

The remainder of the paper is organized as follows: We review image provenance benchmarks in Sect. 2. The proposed database FODB is described in Sect. 3. In Sect. 4, we describe our evaluation protocol for camera identification. The results of this evaluation are presented in Sect. 5. Section 6 concludes the paper.

## 2    Related Work

In a number of existing datasets, different cameras replicate the same set of scenes. This allows to split the images into training and evaluation subsets such that scenes are disjoint. The first large-scale forensic benchmark to support such a splitting policy is the Dresden Image Database [15], as stated in the previous section. Cheng *et al.* propose the NUS dataset [7], with 1,736 images of over 200 scenes, each recorded with 8 DSLR cameras. In another work [8], Cheng *et al.*

recorded additional 944 indoor images. Also in this dataset, each scene is captured with each camera. Although the NUS dataset is presented as an illuminant estimation benchmark, it can directly be used for camera identification, and the acquisition protocols allow scene splitting similar to DIDB. Abdelhamed *et al.* propose the Smartphone Image Denoising Dataset (SIDD) [2] of about 30,000 images. It consists of 10 indoor scenes under different settings captured with 5 smartphone cameras. The dataset targets image denoising, but can also be used for benchmarking camera identification algorithms with proper scene splitting.

Nowadays, images are often distributed via social networks and by that undergo compression to save memory and bandwidth. Therefore, it is important to assess the performance of forensic algorithms in the presence of such postprocessing. Unfortunately, social network sharing has not been relevant during conception of these three datasets. Hence, none of them comes with images that have already been passed through social networks. While a user of the dataset could in principle pass the images through social networks by herself (given permission by its creators), it would still be a remarkably tedious procedure. For example, we estimate that it would require at least a month of work to upload and download the 17,000 DIDB images through various social networks due to limitations on automated image uploading on most of their smartphone apps.

In 2018, the IEEE Signal Processing Society hosted a challenge for camera model identification [1], which amongst other aspects addressed algorithm performance under general post-processing. The training dataset consists of 2,750 images of arbitrary scenes from 10 cameras. The test dataset contains original images, as well as images that are recompressed with random JPEG quality, rescaling, or gamma correction. In the VISION database by Shullani *et al.*, around 7,500 images of 35 smartphone cameras have been shared via Facebook in two qualities, and via Whatsapp [29]. This yields around 30,000 images in 4 quality levels that enable evaluations of the impact of post-processing. Guidice *et al.* propose a method for detecting the social network and software used to share an image [14]. To this end, they recorded images with 8 cameras of various types including 4 smartphones. Then, they shared them via 10 social networks and two operating systems (OS) to obtain 2,720 images. Caldelli *et al.* also investigate social network provenance [6]. They used 1,000 TIFF images from UCID [28], an earlier image retrieval database. These images are compressed with different JPEG qualities and shared on 3 social networks, which results in 30,000 images. However, all images in UCID stem from a single camera, which does not allow for camera identification. Phan *et al.* investigate traces of instant messenging apps and the host OS. They used 350 images out of 35 devices from VISION and shared them either once or twice with three messengers and two OSs [25]. This leads to a total of 350 original, 2,100 single-shared and 6,300 double-shared images. In a subsequent work, Phan *et al.* consider up to three-fold sharing on social media platforms [24]. For this, they build two datasets. The first one is based on the raw image database RAISE [10]. The images are compressed in JPEG format and shared up to three times on three social networks, which yields a total of 35,100 images. The second dataset is based on VISION. Here, 510 images are shared up to three times, to obtain about additional 20,000 images.

The above stated datasets [1, 6, 14, 24, 25, 29] allow benchmarking social network provenance algorithms. With the exception of the dataset by Caldelli *et al.* which consists of only one source camera [6], they are also suitable for evaluating camera identification algorithms and their robustness for simulated [1] and real-world [14, 24, 25, 29] post-processing. Two further large-scale camera identification benchmarks are SOCRatES [13] and the Daxing Smartphone Identification Dataset (DSID) [31]. SOCRatES contains 9,700 images by 103 smartphones of 60 models, and thus is currently the database with largest number of devices. DSID consists of 43,400 images from 90 devices of 22 models, which currently is to our knowledge the database with the most images and devices per model.

Unfortunately, none of these benchmark datasets supports scene splitting, such that it is currently not possible to investigate social media-related artifacts on split scenes. However, we argue in line with previous works [4, 19] that scene splitting is important during evaluation. It removes *by design* the threat of leaking side-channel information from the scene content into the evaluation. Such leakage may lead to an overestimation of the performance, as we will show in Sect. 5. The proposed Forchheim Image Database FODB closes this gap: it jointly allows a rigorous scene splitting policy, and enables to investigate the effect of social media post-processing on forensic algorithms.

## 3   The Forchheim Image Database

This section describes in detail the cameras, the acquisition protocol, the post-processing and database structure of the proposed dataset. Table 1 lists the main features of the smartphones. We use a total of 27 smartphone devices, consisting of 25 different models from 9 brands. It includes two models with more than one device, Samsung Galaxy A6 (devices 15 and 16) and Huawei P9 lite (devices 23 and 25). The smartphones run on Android or iOS and represent older and more recent models (column "Date") with a wide range of retail prices (not listed). During image acquisition, we only use the main (i.e., rear) camera. All smartphones are configured to store images in JPEG format in the highest available JPEG quality and highest available resolution. Focus, white-balance and High Dynamic Range (HDR) imaging is set to automatic mode, where applicable.

All 143 scenes are captured in or near the town of Forchheim, Germany; hence the name Forchheim Image Database. Each camera recorded one image per scene. 10 images are missing or excluded due to technical or privacy issues, resulting in $3,861 - 10 = 3,851$ images. To assert diverse image content, we mix indoor and outdoor, day and night, close-up and distant, and natural and man-made scenes. Examples are shown in Fig. 1.

We refer to camera-native images as *original* (orig.). Additionally, we created five post-processed versions of each image. For this, we installed the apps

**Table 1.** Main features of smartphones in FODB

| ID | Brand | Model | OS | Date |
|----|-------|-------|-----|------|
| 01 | Motorola | E3 | Android 6.0 | 09/2016 |
| 02 | LG | Optimus L50 | Android 4.4.2 | 06/2010 |
| 03 | Wiko | Lenny 2 | Android 5.1 | 09/2014 |
| 04 | LG | G3 | Android 5.0 | 07/2014 |
| 05 | Apple | iPhone 6s | iOS 13.6 | 09/2015 |
| 06 | LG | G6 | Android 9 | 05/2017 |
| 07 | Motorola | Z2 Play | Android 8.0.0 | 08/2017 |
| 08 | Motorola | G8 Plus | Android 9 | 10/2019 |
| 09 | Samsung | Galaxy S4 mini | Android 4.4.4 | 05/2013 |
| 10 | Samsung | Galaxy J1 | Android 4.4.4 | 01/2015 |
| 11 | Samsung | Galaxy J3 | Android 5.1.1 | 01/2016 |
| 12 | Samsung | Galaxy Star 5280 | Android 4.1.2 | 05/2013 |
| 13 | Sony | Xperia E5 | Android 6.0 | 11/2016 |
| 14 | Apple | iPhone 3 | iOS 7.1.2 | 06/2008 |
| 15 | Samsung | Galaxy A6 | Android 10 | 05/2018 |
| 16 | Samsung | Galaxy A6 | Android 10 | 05/2018 |
| 17 | Apple | iPhone 7 | iOS 12.3.1 | 09/2016 |
| 18 | Samsung | Galaxy S4 | Android 6.0.1 | 04/2013 |
| 19 | Apple | iPhone 8 Plus | iOS 13.2 | 09/2017 |
| 20 | Google | Pixel 3 | Android 9 | 11/2018 |
| 21 | Google | Nexus 5 | Android 8.1.0 | 10/2015 |
| 22 | BQ | Aquaris X | Android 8.1.0 | 05/2017 |
| 23 | Huawei | P9 lite | Android 6.0 | 05/2016 |
| 24 | Huawei | P8 lite | Android 5.0 | 04/2015 |
| 25 | Huawei | P9 lite | Android 7.0 | 05/2016 |
| 26 | Huawei | P20 lite | Android 8.0.0 | 04/2018 |
| 27 | Google | Pixel XL | Android 10 | 10/2016 |

Facebook, Instagram, Telegram, Twitter and Whatsapp on each device[1] and manually shared all images. In the Facebook app, we uploaded the images of each device to a dedicated photo album in default quality[2]. Then, we used the functionality to download entire albums in the browser version of Facebook. During upload on Instagram, a user must select a square crop from an image, and

---

[1] Exceptions: Devices 2, 12, 14, 24, 25 did not support some apps, hence we transferred the images to other devices of the same OS (2, 12 → Device 8; 14 → Device 5; 24, 25 → Device 20) and shared all images from there.

[2] Corresponding to "FBL" (Facebook low quality) in the VISION database.

optionally a filter. We uploaded all images with default settings for cropping, resulting in a center crop, and disabled any filters. For download we used the open source tool "Instaloader" (Version 4.5.2)[3]. In the Twitter app, all images were uploaded without filter, and downloaded via the Firefox browser plugin "Twitter Media Downloader" (Version 0.1.4.16)[4]. For Telegram and Whatsapp, the images of each device were sent to device 6 (LG G6), except for the images of device 6 itself, which were sent to device 8 (Motorola G8 Plus). In this way, the database contains a total of $6 \cdot (27 \cdot 143 - 10) = 23\,106$ JPEG images.

Social network and messenger sharing was executed one device after another, to avoid confounding images of different devices. During sharing, the social networks and messengers non-trivially modify the image filenames, and metadata is largely removed. For re-identifying the shown scene, we correlated the original and post-processed images for each device individually. The originals were first downscaled to match the size of the post-processed versions, and, in case of Instagram, center cropped prior to downscaling. Only very few cases were ambiguuous, which were manually labeled.

The database is hierarchically organized: at root level, images from each device are in one directory D⟨ID⟩_⟨Brand⟩_⟨Model⟩_⟨i⟩, where ID, Brand and Model are substituted according to Table 1, and $i \in \{1, 2\}$ enumerates the devices of a model. Each directory contains six provenance subdirectories orig, facebook, instagram, telegram, twitter and whatsapp. These directories contain the images of device ID, provenance prov and scene ID scene with the pattern D⟨ID⟩_img_⟨prov⟩_⟨scene⟩.jpg, for example D06_img_twitter_0030.jpg.

# 4   Camera Identification: Dataset Split, Methods, and Training Augmentation

We demonstrate an application of FODB by studying the behavior of CNNs for camera identification. This section describes the used methods and their training.

## 4.1   Dataset Splits

To create training, validation and test data, we split the set of 143 scenes $\mathcal{S}$ of FODB into three disjoint sets $\mathcal{S}^{\text{train}}$, $\mathcal{S}^{\text{val}}$ and $\mathcal{S}^{\text{test}}$, and we set $|\mathcal{S}^{\text{train}}| = 97$, $|\mathcal{S}^{\text{val}}| = 18$, $|\mathcal{S}^{\text{test}}| = 28$. For camera models with more than one device, we choose the device with the smallest ID, which yields $N_{\mathcal{K}} = 25$ cameras, and hence 25 classes. Thus we obtain $|\mathcal{S}^{\text{train}}| \cdot N_{\mathcal{K}} = 2425$ training, $|\mathcal{S}^{\text{val}}| \cdot N_{\mathcal{K}} = 450$ validation and $|\mathcal{S}^{\text{test}}| \cdot N_{\mathcal{K}} = 700$ test images per post-processing quality.

## 4.2   Compared Methods

We reimplemented three CNN-based forensic methods for source camera identification. First, the method by Bondi *et al.*, which we subsequently refer to as

---

[3] https://instaloader.github.io/.
[4] https://addons.mozilla.org/de/firefox/addon/tw-media-downloader/.

"BondiNet" [4]. Second, MISLnet by Bayar *et al.* [3] in its improved version as the feature extractor in the work by Mayer *et al.* [22] by the same group. Third, RemNet by Rafi *et al.* [26], which has been presented at the IEEE Signal Processing Cup 2018. We additionally report results on EfficientNet-B5, a recently proposed general-purpose CNN from the field of computer vision [30]. All models are trained with crossentropy loss.

The input patch size of each CNN except MISLnet is set to $64 \times 64$ pixels. The outputs of the CNNs are adapted to distinguish $N_{\mathcal{K}} = 25$ classes. Note that the classes are balanced, and random guessing accuracy is $N_{\mathcal{K}}^{-1}$, i.e., 4%, on all experiments on FODB.

Initial experiments with BondiNet using the parameters of the paper [4] led to poor validation performance on FODB. Hence, we evaluate BondiNet for the following set of hyperparameters, which led to significantly better validation results: Adam optimizer with $\alpha = 10^{-3}$, $\beta_1 = 0.9$ and $\beta_2 = 0.999$, no weight decay, additional batch normalization after each convolution, and direct classification using CNN outputs instead of using an SVM. For MISLnet, we reimplemented the improved version of the same group [22]. The patch input size is $256 \times 256$ pixels, and hence somewhat larger than for the remaining networks. We address this in the patch clustering described below. For RemNet, we reimplemented the implementation as described in the paper.

For EfficientNet-B5, we use weights pretrained on ImageNet [11], and remove the final classification layer of the pretrained network. Then, we add global average pooling and a dense layer with $N_{\mathcal{K}} = 25$ output units and softmax activation. The weights of the new classification layer are set with Glorot uniform initialization [16]. During all experiments, we use Adam optimization [18] with learning rate $\alpha = 10^{-3}$ and moments $\beta_1 = 0.9$ and $\beta_2 = 0.999$. Whenever the validation loss stagnates for two consecutive epochs, the learning rate is halved, and we apply early stopping.

To accomodate for differences in the input resolution of the networks, we adopt the *patch cluster* strategy by Rafi *et al.* [26]. To this end, we consider an image area of $256 \times 256$ pixels as a patch cluster. A patch cluster is considered to be non-informative if it mostly consists of homogeneous pixels, which is determined by a heuristic quality criterion used by Bondi *et al.* [5, Eqn. (1)] and Rafi *et al.* [26, Eqn. (7)],

$$Q(P) = \frac{1}{3} \sum_{c \in \{R,G,B\}} \alpha\beta(\mu_c - \mu_c^2) + (1 - \alpha)(1 - \exp(\gamma\sigma_c)) \, , \qquad (1)$$

where $\mu_c$ and $\sigma_c$ denote the patch cluster mean and standard deviation in the red, green, and blue color channels $c$, and $\alpha = 0.7$, $\beta = 4$, $\gamma = \ln(0.01)$.

## 4.3   Matching the Network Input Resolutions

For evaluation, it is important to provide to each algorithm the same amount of information. Thus, for both training and testing, we subdivide the image into non-overlapping $256 \times 256$ patch cluster candidates, and sort them by the quality criterion $Q(P)$. The top 100 candidates are used as patch clusters for the image.

For training, each selected patch cluster is used once per training epoch. MISLnet obtains full patch clusters to match its $256 \times 256$ pixel inputs. The remaining networks obtain a randomly selected $64 \times 64$ pixels subwindow per cluster to match their input size. For validation, we use the same approach but with fixed random seed to achieve a consistent comparison throughout all epochs.

For testing, we also feed a full $256 \times 256$ patch cluster to MISLnet. For the remaining networks, we subdivide a patch cluster into 16 non-overlapping patches of $64 \times 64$ pixels.

These results are used to report three metrics: camera identification accuracies on individual $64 \times 64$ patches (excluding MISLnet), accuracies on patch clusters of $256 \times 256$ pixels, and accuracies for the whole image. For the per-cluster accuracies, we directly calculate the accuracy for MISLnet's $256 \times 256$ prediction. For the remaining networks, the patch cluster prediction $\hat{k}$ is calculated via soft majority voting over all $64 \times 64$ patch predictions,

$$\hat{k} = \operatorname*{argmax}_{k} \sum_{i \in \mathcal{I}} y_i^k , \qquad (2)$$

where $y_i^k$ denotes the $k$-th component of the CNN output for the $i$-th patch in the cluster. The prediction for the whole image is analogously calculated via soft majority voting over all individual CNN outputs on that image.

## 4.4   Training Augmentation

Throughout all training, we randomly apply horizontal flipping, vertical flipping, and rotation by integer multiples of $90°$, with equal probability for each case.

For a subset of the experiments, we additionally apply artificial *degradations* (deg.) during training to increase the robustness of all CNNs against post-processing. Prior to flipping or rotation, we rescale a training patch cluster with probability 0.9. The rescaling factor is randomly drawn from a discrete distribution over the interval $[0.25, \dots, 4]$. In order to make upsampling and downsampling equally likely, we rewrite the interval as $[0.25 = 2^{-2}, \dots, 2^j, \dots, 4 = 2^2]$ and subdivide the exponent $j$ in 50 equally spaced samples. We draw from these exponents with uniform probability. After flipping or rotation, we extract a patch from the (rescaled or non-rescaled) cluster, and recompress it in JPEG format with probability 0.9. The JPEG quality factor is uniformly chosen from $[100, 99, \dots, 10]$.

For the rather challenging experiments in Sect. 5.3 and Sect. 5.4, we try to maximize the performance of RemNet and EfficientNet-B5 by pretraining on DIDB's 18 cameras. To this end, we use the DIDB training/validation split by Bondi *et al.* [4]. Considering our four variants of RemNet and EfficientNet-B5 with and without artificial degradations, we investigate possible gains in validation performance when pre-training on DIDB. We apply artificial degradations on DIDB only if the subsequent training on FODB also uses artificial degradations, in order to have these degradations either throughout the whole training

**Table 2.** Averaged overall validation performance for FODB and VISION, with and without pretraining on DIDB. Boldface shows the selected model variants based on validation loss.

| Training parameters | | | Validation dataset | | | |
|---|---|---|---|---|---|---|
| | | | FODB | | VISION | |
| Model | Degr. | Pretr. | Loss | Acc. | Loss | Acc. |
| RemNet | No | No | **0.1870** | **92.72** | 0.1898 | 93.90 |
| RemNet | No | Yes | 0.1885 | 92.86 | **0.1731** | **94.49** |
| RemNet | Yes | No | **2.4268** | **31.06** | 1.9586 | 42.67 |
| RemNet | Yes | Yes | 2.5735 | 26.07 | **1.9295** | **43.47** |
| EN-B5 | No | No | **0.1176** | **95.79** | 0.1465 | 95.91 |
| EN-B5 | No | Yes | 0.1178 | 95.62 | **0.1265** | **96.22** |
| EN-B5 | Yes | No | 1.6894 | 52.12 | 1.2410 | 63.68 |
| EN-B5 | Yes | Yes | **1.6756** | **52.77** | **1.2179** | **64.35** |

**Table 3.** Accuracy (in percent) for closed-set camera identification on camera-native FODB test images for EfficientNet-B5 and CNN-based forensic reference methods.

| CNN | Patch | Cluster | Image |
|---|---|---|---|
| BondiNet [4] | 71.4 | 84.9 | 93.1 |
| MISLnet [22] | – | 93.5 | 96.8 |
| RemNet [26] | 93.8 | 96.6 | **99.1** |
| EfficientNet-B5 [30] | 96.3 | 98.1 | **99.1** |

process or not at all. We then select for the experiments either the variant with DIDB-pretraining or without depending on the validation loss. The results are listed in Table 2. Boldface shows validation loss and accuracy of the selected model. The column indicating validation on FODB is used in Sect. 5.3, the column indicating validation on VISION in Sect. 5.4.

# 5  Results

## 5.1  Performance Under Ideal Conditions

In this experiment, we benchmark CNNs for camera identification under ideal conditions without any post-processing. During training, we only augment with flipping and rotation, but not with resizing or JPEG recompression.

Table 3 shows the per-patch, per-cluster and per-image accuracies for the original (camera-native) test images of FODB. EfficientNet-B5 consistently outperforms the other CNNs for patches and clusters with accuracies of 96.3% and 98.1%, respectively. For image-level classification, RemNet and EfficientNet-B5 are on par with an accuracy of 99.1%. Majority voting improves individual predictions across all CNNs, which indicates some degree of statistical independence of the prediction errors.

## 5.2  Robustness Against Known Post-processing

In this and all following experiments, we take a closer look at the two best performing CNNs on clean images, RemNet and EfficientNet-B5, and evaluate their robustness against post-processing.

We first determine the test accuracy on FODB for all combinations of rescaling with factors $f_{\text{test}} \in \{0.25, 0.5, 0.8, 1.0, 1.25\}$ and JPEG recompression with

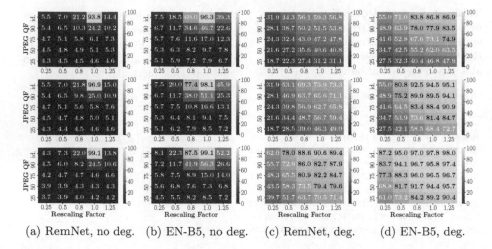

(a) RemNet, no deg.    (b) EN-B5, no deg.    (c) RemNet, deg.    (d) EN-B5, deg.

**Fig. 2.** Robustness against rescaling and JPEG recompression for predictions per patch (first row), cluster (second row) and image (third row). Columns (a) and (b) show RemNet and EfficientNet-B5 (EN-B5) accuracies without augmentation of degradations during training. Columns (c) and (d) show RemNet and EfficientNet-B5 accuracies with augmentation of degradations during training.

quality factors $QF_{test} \in \{id., 90, 75, 50, 25\}$. Factor 1.0, resp. id. (idempotent) indicates no rescaling and no JPEG recompression. Note that rescaling is applied to patch clusters prior to patch extraction, which quadratically scales the number of patches for majority voting on patch clusters and images with $f_{test}$.

Figure 2a and Fig. 2b show the accuracies for RemNet and EfficientNet-B5. From top to bottom are accuracies on patch level, cluster level, and image level. Throughout all qualities, EfficientNet-B5 outperforms RemNet. In most cases, majority voting again increases the accuracy. While accuracies for both CNNs are almost perfect for camera-native images ($f_{test} = 1.0$, $QF_{test} = id.$) with 99.1%, it rapidly decreases on post-processed images. This is not surprising, since only high quality images are used for training. The CNNs likely rely on fragile high-frequent traces, which are attenuated by postprocessing [32].

We retrain both CNNs with artificial degradations as described in Sect. 4.4 to improve the robustness against post-processing. The results for these retrained CNNs are shown in Fig. 2c and Fig. 2d. Already at patch-level, the accuracies of both CNNs are much more stable compared to training without degradations. For example, at $f_{test} = 0.5$, $QF_{test} = 75$, the test accuracies at patch-level amount to 32.4% and 52.8% for both CNNs, compared to 5.1% and 7.6% without these augmentations. Moreover, EfficientNet-B5 remarkably outperforms Rem-Net. For example, the patch-level performance on clean images, is 56.1% for RemNet and 83.8% for EfficientNet-B5. For both CNNs, majority voting further significantly improves the performance. For image-level decisions and camera-native images, the performance of EfficientNet-B5 trained with degradations

**Table 4.** Test accuracies on FODB for camera-native and post-processed images. Top: boldface shows the best accuracy per column for unknown post-processing. Bottom: blue shows the oracle performance for known post-processing at training.

| | Training parameters | | Test dataset | | | | | | | | | | | |
| --- | --- | --- | --- | --- | --- | --- | --- | --- | --- | --- | --- | --- | --- | --- |
| | | | orig | | FB | | IG | | TG | | TW | | WA | |
| CNN | Dataset | Deg. | Patch | Image | Patch | Image | Patch | Image | Patch | Image | Patch | Image | Patch | Image |
| RemNet | Orig | No | 93.8 | **99.1** | 4.0 | 3.6 | 4.2 | 4.2 | 4.5 | 4.3 | 5.5 | 4.7 | 4.2 | 3.9 |
| RemNet | Orig | Yes | 59.3 | 90.6 | 18.4 | 36.0 | 22.9 | 48.9 | 26.2 | 52.8 | 37.3 | 74.2 | 24.2 | 50.8 |
| EN-B5 | Orig | No | **96.3** | **99.1** | 4.9 | 4.6 | 5.7 | 5.6 | 5.7 | 5.3 | 10.8 | 9.8 | 7.0 | 6.8 |
| EN-B5 | Orig | Yes | 86.5 | 98.0 | **27.7** | **51.1** | **35.4** | **67.5** | **42.2** | **73.1** | **60.7** | **93.2** | **38.5** | **72.9** |
| EN-B5 | FB | No | 13.8 | 23.6 | 38.4 | 71.4 | 29.1 | 51.1 | 28.5 | 44.2 | 23.8 | 38.3 | 30.8 | 54.7 |
| EN-B5 | IG | No | 8.1 | 9.4 | 28.4 | 52.1 | 52.1 | 84.0 | 13.5 | 14.0 | 12.1 | 14.0 | 40.4 | 69.1 |
| EN-B5 | TG | No | 16.7 | 23.3 | 21.1 | 32.4 | 25.5 | 37.6 | 57.2 | 86.2 | 35.4 | 55.0 | 32.8 | 51.5 |
| EN-B5 | TW | No | 36.4 | 57.1 | 14.7 | 21.9 | 25.6 | 41.9 | 28.2 | 41.6 | 76.2 | 97.7 | 33.6 | 54.2 |
| EN-B5 | WA | No | 17.3 | 27.3 | 28.8 | 52.4 | 41.5 | 69.2 | 31.0 | 45.3 | 28.4 | 38.3 | 60.0 | 90.4 |

**Table 5.** Test accuracies on VISION for camera-native and post-processed images. (a) Random split. (b) Splits on sorted images per camera. Top rows: boldface shows the best accuracy per column for unknown post-processing. Bottom rows: blue shows the oracle performance for known post-processing at training. LQ and HQ denote low quality and high quality.

| | Training parameters | | Test dataset | | | | | | | |
| --- | --- | --- | --- | --- | --- | --- | --- | --- | --- | --- |
| | | | Orig | | FB (LQ) | | FB (HQ) | | WA | |
| Archit. | Dataset | Deg. | Patch | Image | Patch | Image | Patch | Image | patch | image |
| RemNet | Orig | No | 93.9 | 98.6 | 4.6 | 4.1 | 6.4 | 7.2 | 9.2 | 12.8 |
| RemNet | Orig | Yes | 64.7 | 86.7 | 34.8 | 64.0 | 41.5 | 73.9 | 45.7 | 75.9 |
| EN-B5 | Orig | No | **95.9** | **99.2** | 4.9 | 5.9 | 8.3 | 8.7 | 10.2 | 11.8 |
| EN-B5 | Orig | Yes | 88.4 | 97.0 | **46.3** | **77.0** | **57.7** | **88.4** | **66.5** | **92.4** |
| EN-B5 | FB (LQ) | No | 8.8 | 14.3 | 64.6 | 88.5 | 22.3 | 33.0 | 28.9 | 40.7 |
| EN-B5 | FB (HQ) | No | 31.7 | 43.7 | 27.4 | 39.9 | 72.8 | 95.4 | 25.4 | 36.8 |
| EN-B5 | WA | No | 21.6 | 32.9 | 30.5 | 47.5 | 18.3 | 27.8 | 77.3 | 96.3 |

(a) Randomized per-device split

| | Training parameters | | Test dataset | | | | | | | |
| --- | --- | --- | --- | --- | --- | --- | --- | --- | --- | --- |
| | | | Orig | | FB (LQ) | | FB (HQ) | | WA | |
| Archit. | Dataset | Deg. | Patch | Image | Patch | Image | Patch | Image | Patch | Image |
| RemNet | Orig | No | 87.5 | 93.2 | 3.7 | 4.8 | 4.7 | 5.5 | 5.5 | 7.4 |
| RemNet | Orig | Yes | 44.2 | 67.9 | 20.1 | 39.5 | 25.8 | 52.4 | 27.9 | 51.7 |
| EN-B5 | Orig | No | **87.8** | **93.9** | 3.6 | 4.5 | 7.0 | 7.4 | 6.9 | 8.6 |
| EN-B5 | Orig | Yes | 76.8 | 88.5 | **28.2** | **54.1** | **40.9** | **70.5** | **44.7** | **72.4** |
| EN-B5 | FB (LQ) | No | 7.3 | 10.8 | 42.3 | 67.6 | 16.8 | 26.3 | 20.7 | 29.1 |
| EN-B5 | FB (HQ) | No | 26.3 | 39.0 | 18.0 | 26.0 | 55.2 | 83.7 | 16.1 | 21.6 |
| EN-B5 | WA | No | 18.7 | 30.7 | 19.4 | 30.8 | 14.4 | 21.8 | 56.1 | 82.2 |

(b) Per-device split on images sorted by timestamp

(97.0%) is close to testing without degradations (99.1%). RemNet has difficulties to fully benefit from augmentation with degraded images, with accuracies dropping from 99.1% without degradations to 88.6% with degradations. We hypothesize that this difference can in part be attributed to the significantly larger capacity of EfficientNet-B5: while both CNNs perform comparably on the easier task of clean images, a CNN with larger capacity might be required for additionally learning the traces of degraded images. Still, also the superior EfficientNet-B5 shows an accuracy-robustness trade-off, a phenomenon that has been observed for adversarial training before [27, 32].

### 5.3 Robustness Against Unknown Real-World Post-processing

In this section, we evaluate the robustness of RemNet and EfficientNet-B5 against real-world post-processing by unknown algorithms and parameters, as it occurs during social network sharing. We again train both CNNs once without and once with degradations. The networks do not obtain social media images for training.

We evaluate the selected models (see Table 2) on original and all five post-processed versions of the test images (Facebook: FB, Instagram: IG, Telegram: TG, Twitter: TW, Whatsapp: WA). The resulting accuracies are listed in Table 4. When training without degradations, the networks can only excell on original images, analogously to the previous experiments. Pretraining on DIDB slightly improves the performance of EfficientNet-B5 on clean images. Augmentation with artificial degradations significantly improves the performance of both CNNs on all social network data, even though social media data itself was not part of the training. Again, EfficientNet-B5 largely outperforms RemNet in all experiments.

We perform an additional experiment as a reference for the impact of prior knowledge on the data: we pretrained EfficientNet-B5 on DIDB with degradations. Additionally, we feed the social network images from the *training* set to EfficientNet-B5 as an oracle for the *test* set degradations, and retrain without further artificial degradation. Table 4 (bottom) shows that such strong prior knowledge yields at image level accuracy gains from 4.5 p.p. for Twitter (with baseline already 93.2%) up to 20.3 p.p. for Facebook.

### 5.4 Impact of Scene Splitting

We now analyze the influence of scene splitting on CNN-based camera identification on the VISION dataset. The scene content is not constrained in several datasets including VISION, which prevents splitting by scenes. Some per-device image sets in VISION are highly correlated, such that randomized splitting makes training and test sets likely to contain images of identical cameras with similar content. We conjecture that scene content may open a side-channel that CNNs are prone to exploit, which may lead to an overestimation of its generalization. We show empirical evidence for this conjecture in two experiments.

First, we randomly split the VISION images in training, validation and test sets. We use the evaluation protocol by Marra *et al.* [21] and use the 29 unique devices with random guessing accuracy of $29^{-1} = 3.45\%$.

Second, we make an attempt to improve the splitting strategy, and to further separate image content between training and test set. To this end, we sort the images of each device by their acquisition time using `DateTimeOriginal` from the EXIF file header, and split the dataset along the timeline of the images. In this way, similar images recorded within a short period of time are likely to be either in the training or test set, but not in both. This significantly reduces overlap in image content between training and test set. Except of the splitting policy, all settings are identical between both experiments.

Results for the first and second experiment are shown in Table 5a and Table 5b. Performances drop significantly when moving from completely random splits (Table 5a) to splits by timestamp (Table 5b). For example, on clean images the accuracy of EfficientNet-B5 without degradation drops from 99.2% to 93.9%. The performance of EfficientNet-B5 with degradation for Whatsapp-compressed test images drops even by 20 p.p., from 92.4% to 72.4%. This discrepancy suggests that scene content contributes to the results in Table 5a. Moreover, such a side-channel may prevent the CNN from learning more relevant traces. We hence believe that the results in Table 5b are closer to the performance that can be expected in practice. These observations emphasize the importance of a rigorous scene splitting as supported by FODB.

## 6 Conclusion

This work proposes the Forchheim Image Database (FODB) as a new benchmark for image forensics algorithms under real-world post-processing. Our database consists of more than 23,000 images of 143 scenes by 27 smartphone devices of 25 models and 9 brands. FODB combines clean training/validation/test data splits by scene with a wide range of modern smartphone devices shared through a total of five social network sites, which allows rigorous evaluations of forensic algorithms on real-world image distortions. We demonstrate FODB's usefulness in an evaluation on the task of camera identification. Our results provide three insights. First, the general-purpose network EfficientNet-B5 largely outperforms three specialized CNNs. Second, EfficientNet-B5's large capacity also fully benefits from training data augmentation to generalize to unseen degradations. Third, clean data splits by scenes can help to better predict generalization performance.

## References

1. IEEE's Signal Processing Society - Camera Model Identification. https://www.kaggle.com/c/sp-society-camera-model-identification (2018), Accessed 26 Sept 2020
2. Abdelhamed, A., Lin, S., Brown, M.S.: A High-quality denoising dataset for smartphone cameras. In: IEEE Conference on Computer Vision and Pattern Recognition, pp. 1692–1700 (2018)
3. Bayar, B., Stamm, M.C.: Constrained convolutional neural networks: a new approach towards general purpose image manipulation detection. IEEE Trans. Inf. Forensics Secur. **13**, 2691–2706 (2018)
4. Bondi, L., Baroffio, L., Guera, D., Bestagini, P., Delp, E.J., Tubaro, S.: First steps toward camera model identification with convolutional neural networks. IEEE Signal Process. Lett. **24**, 259–263 (2017)

5. Bondi, L., Güera, D., Baroffio, L., Bestagini, P., Delp, E.J., Tubaro, S.: A preliminary study on convolutional neural networks for camera model identification. Electron. Imaging **2017**(7), 67–76 (2017)

6. Caldelli, R., Becarelli, R., Amerini, I.: Image origin classification based on social network provenance. IEEE Trans. Inf. Forensics Secur. **12**, 1299–1308 (2017)

7. Cheng, D., Prasad, D.K., Brown, M.S.: Illuminant estimation for color constancy: why spatial-domain methods work and the role of the color distribution. JOSA A **31**, 1049–1058 (2014)

8. Cheng, D., Price, B., Cohen, S., Brown, M.S.: Beyond white: ground truth colors for color constancy correction. In: IEEE International Conference on Computer Vision, pp. 298–306 (2015)

9. Cozzolino, D., Verdoliva, L.: Noiseprint: a CNN-based camera model fingerprint. IEEE Trans. Inf. Forensics Secur., 144–159 (2019)

10. Dang-Nguyen, D.T., Pasquini, C., Conotter, V., Boato, G.: RAISE: a raw images dataset for digital image forensics. In: ACM Multimedia Systems Conference, pp. 219–224 (2015)

11. Deng, J., Dong, W., Socher, R., Li, L.J., Li, K., Fei-Fei, L.: ImageNet: a large-scale hierarchical image database. In: 2009 IEEE Conference on Computer Vision and Pattern Recognition, pp. 248–255 (2009)

12. Farid, H.: A survey of image forgery detection. IEEE Signal Process. Mag. **26**, 16–25 (2009)

13. Galdi, C., Hartung, F., Dugelay, J.L.: SOCRatES: A database of realistic data for SOurce camera REcognition on smartphones. In: ICPRAM, pp. 648–655 (2019)

14. Giudice, O., Paratore, A., Moltisanti, M., Battiato, S.: A classification engine for image ballistics of social data. In: Battiato, S., Gallo, G., Schettini, R., Stanco, F. (eds.) ICIAP 2017. LNCS, vol. 10485, pp. 625–636. Springer, Cham (2017). https://doi.org/10.1007/978-3-319-68548-9_57

15. Gloe, T., Böhme, R.: The dresden image database for benchmarking digital image forensics. J. Digital Forensic Pract., 150–159 (2010)

16. Glorot, X., Bengio, Y.: Understanding the difficulty of training deep feedforward neural networks. In: International Conference on Artificial Intelligence and Statistics, pp. 249–256 (2010)

17. Huh, M., Liu, A., Owens, A., Efros, A.A.: Fighting fake news: image splice detection via learned self-consistency. In: European Conference on Computer Vision, pp. 101–117 (2018)

18. Kingma, D.P., Ba, J.: Adam: a method for stochastic optimization. In: International Conference on Learning Representations (2015)

19. Kirchner, M., Gloe, T.: Forensic camera model identification. In: Handbook of Digital Forensics of Multimedia Data and Devices, pp. 329–374 (2015)

20. Lukas, J., Fridrich, J., Goljan, M.: Digital camera identification from sensor pattern noise. IEEE Trans. Inf. Forensics Secur. **1**, 205–214 (2006)

21. Marra, F., Gragnaniello, D., Verdoliva, L.: On the vulnerability of deep learning to adversarial attacks for camera model identification. Signal Process. Image Commun. **65**, 240–248 (2018)

22. Mayer, O., Stamm, M.C.: Forensic similarity for digital images. IEEE Trans. Inf. Forensics Secur. **15**, 1331–1346 (2019)

23. Moreira, D., et al.: Image provenance analysis at scale. IEEE Trans. Image Process. **27**, 6109–6123 (2018)

24. Phan, Q.T., Boato, G., Caldelli, R., Amerini, I.: Tracking multiple image sharing on social networks. In: IEEE International Conference on Acoustics, Speech and Signal Processing, pp. 8266–8270 (2019)

25. Phan, Q.T., Pasquini, C., Boato, G., De Natale, F.G.: Identifying image provenance: an analysis of mobile instant messaging apps. In: IEEE International Workshop on Multimedia Signal Processing, pp. 1–6 (2018)
26. Rafi, A.M., Tonmoy, T.I., Kamal, U., Wu, Q.J., Hasan, M.K.: RemNet: remnant convolutional neural network for camera model identification. Neural Comput. Appl., 1–16 (2020)
27. Raghunathan, A., Xie, S.M., Yang, F., Duchi, J.C., Liang, P.: Adversarial Training Can Hurt Generalization. arXiv preprint (2019)
28. Schaefer, G., Stich, M.: UCID: an uncompressed color image database. In: Storage and Retrieval Methods and Applications for Multimedia, pp. 472–480 (2003)
29. Shullani, D., Fontani, M., Iuliani, M., Shaya, O.A., Piva, A.: VISION: a video and image dataset for source identification. EURASIP J. Inf. Secur. **2017**, 15 (2017)
30. Tan, M., Le, Q.: EfficientNet: rethinking model scaling for convolutional neural networks. In: International Conference on Machine Learning, pp. 6105–6114 (2019)
31. Tian, H., Xiao, Y., Cao, G., Zhang, Y., Xu, Z., Zhao, Y.: Daxing smartphone identification dataset. IEEE Access **7**, 101046–101053 (2019)
32. Tsipras, D., Santurkar, S., Engstrom, L., Turner, A., Madry, A.: Robustness May Be at Odds with Accuracy. arXiv preprint (2018)
33. Yang, P., Baracchi, D., Ni, R., Zhao, Y., Argenti, F., Piva, A.: A survey of deep learning-based source image forensics. J. Imaging **6**, 9 (2020)
34. Zhou, P., Han, X., Morariu, V.I., Davis, L.S.: Learning rich features for image manipulation detection. In: IEEE Conference on Computer Vision and Pattern Recognition, pp. 1053–1061 (2018)

# Nested Attention U-Net: A Splicing Detection Method for Satellite Images

János Horváth(✉)[iD], Daniel Mas Montserrat[iD], Edward J. Delp[iD],
and János Horváth

Video and Image Processing Laboratory (VIPER), School of Electrical and Computer
Engineering, Purdue University, West Lafayette, IN, USA
horvath5@purdue.edu

**Abstract.** Satellite imagery is becoming increasingly available due to a large number of commercial satellite companies. Many fields use satellite images, including meteorology, forestry, natural disaster analysis, and agriculture. These images can be changed or tampered with image manipulation tools causing issues in applications using these images. Manipulation detection techniques designed for images captured by "consumer cameras" tend to fail when used on satellite images. In this paper we propose a supervised method, known as Nested Attention U-Net, to detect spliced areas in the satellite images. We introduce three datasets of manipulated satellite images that contain objects generated by a generative adversarial network (GAN). We test our approach and compare it to existing supervised splicing detection and segmentation techniques and show that our proposed approach performs well in detection and localization.

## 1 Introduction

The growth in the number of commercial satellites made it possible for a large variety of applications that use satellite imagery. These applications include scene classification [1,2], meteorological analysis [3,4], soil moisture estimation [5], forest characterization [6], agricultural crops classification [7], regional infrastructure levels assessment [8,9], and wildlife monitoring [10]. Many image datasets containing satellite imagery are available to the public [11,12], these datasets includes Planet Labs, European Space Agency or the Xview datasets [13,14]. Popular image editing and manipulation tools such as GIMP and Photoshop can be easily used to alter satellite images. Recent advances in machine learning [15,16] made it possible to automatically generate manipulated and synthetic images. Several examples have occurred in which altered satellite images have been used for providing false information. These include the Malaysian flight incident over Ukraine [17], the nighttime flyovers over India during the Diwali Festival [18], the images of fake Chinese bridges. [19], and the Australian bushfires [20].

© Springer Nature Switzerland AG 2021
A. Del Bimbo et al. (Eds.): ICPR 2020 Workshops, LNCS 12666, pp. 516–529, 2021.
https://doi.org/10.1007/978-3-030-68780-9_41

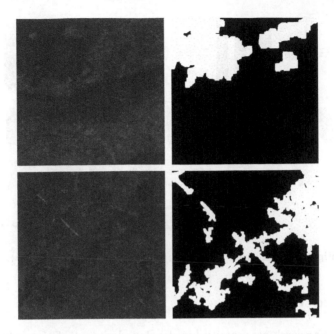

**Fig. 1.** Examples of satellite images used in our study. The first column shows the spliced images. The second column shows the corresponding ground-truth of the spliced area.

Several techniques which can be used to manipulate satellite images have been proposed. These techniques include copy-move [21], splicing [22], and blending objects created by Generative Adversarial Networks (GANs) [23]. Many methods have been described in [22,24] to detect manipulations in images captured by consumer cameras. These techniques tend to fail in detecting manipulations in satellite images because of differences in the process of acquiring a satellite image when compared with images captured by consumer cameras. These differences include sensors, color channels, compression schemes, and post-processing. Detecting alteration in satellite images remains an open problem.

In this paper, we describe a variation of the U-Net architecture [25], which we call the Nested Attention U-Net (NAU-N), for detecting objects spliced into satellite images. We trained three NAU-Ns with three dataset, each dataset contains spliced objects from a specific generative adversarial network (GAN) [26] (see Fig. 1 for example images). For example, one NAU-N network was trained on images containing spliced object generated by StyleGAN2 [27]. The Nested Attention U-Net performs better in comparison to previous splicing detection techniques and supervised segmentation methods.

We further tested how well our trained network can detect spliced objects from an unseen type of GAN.

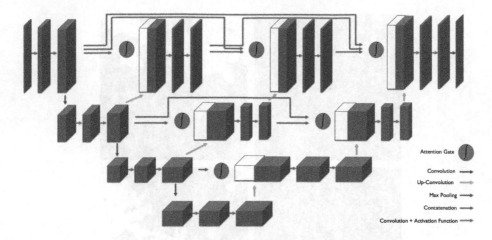

**Fig. 2.** Architecture of the nested attention U-Net (NAU-N).

## 2   Related Work

The forensics research community has developed many techniques for detecting forgeries in natural images. Some of these include finding double-JPEG compression artifacts [28], using saturation cues [29], using neural networks with domain adaptation [30] or deepfakes detection with neural networks [31]. Other techniques focus on detecting splicing in images [22,32] in an unsupervised manner. The work in [22] developed a method based on a camera model fingerprint. Detecting manipulation remains an open problem in that not all current methods are robust to adversarial perturbation [33]. Because of the different acquisition process between "cameras" and satellites, most of these techniques will fail when used on satellite images. These differences include various sensor technologies and post-processing steps such as orthorectification, compression, and radiometric corrections. For detecting manipulations in satellite imagery techniques include detecting forgeries based on watermarking [34] machine learning approaches both unsupervised [35–37] and supervised [38] methods have been described. In [38] the authors introduce a supervised method for detecting splicing in satellite images While unsupervised methods can generalize better to unseen forgeries, supervised methods tend to perform better on a task in which both manipulated and original data are available.

We consider here an image segmentation approach to detect GAN generated forgeries. In the past several segmentation approaches were used for image manipulation detection. The U-Net [25] architecture has been proposed for image segmentation in many applications. A U-Net learns the feature mapping of an image to vector for classification and reconstructs an image from the feature vector. The main ideal behind these types of methods is to use the same feature maps for decoding to expand a vector to a segmented image which preserves the image structural integrity. Several variations of U-Net has been developed, these include Attention U-Net [39], Nested U-Net [40], R2U-Net [41], and MultiResUNet [42]. The Attention U-Net [39] incorporates Attention Gates. The attention mechanism [43] is used to generate a context vector which assigns weights to the input. This highlights the salient/important features of the input while suppressing irrelevant information. The Nested U-Net or U-Net++ [40] changes the U-Net architecture into an encoder-decoder network where the encoder and decoder sub-networks are connected through a series of nested, dense skip pathways. These skip pathways reduces the semantic gap between the feature maps of the encoder and decoder sub-networks. The Recurrent Residual Convolutional Neural Network U-Net (R2U-Net) [41] merges the advantages of U-Net, Residual Network [44], and RCNN. MultiResUNet replaces the convolutional layer pairs of the original U-Net with a newly introduced MultiRes block and introduces the concept of "Res paths". In this paper we introduce a method which we call the Nested Attention U-Net, which performs better than other U-Net techniques in detecting GAN generated objects in satellite images.

## 3  Proposed Approach

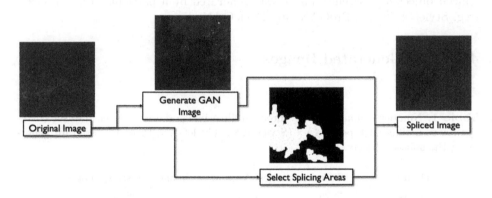

**Fig. 3.** Block diagram of spliced satellite image generation.

We propose a U-Net architecture, which we call Nested Attention U-Net (NAU-N) for detecting forgeries. There are several embedded "U-Nets" inside of our U-Net architecture as shown in Fig. 2. The architecture first encodes the input image into a feature map and then decodes this feature map into an output mask. We integrated several smaller U-Net sub-networks into NAU-N. The output of these sub-networks are later the input of other sub-networks or input of the main U-Net decoder. These embedded sub-networks help the network to learn high-level features and features representing the fine-detail of the image. This architecture exploits the Nested U-Net "deep supervision." Using deep supervision [45] creates a more transparent learning process. During training, features provided by hidden layers will be used in estimating and backpropagating the error. Thus, the network hidden layers weights will be regularized and observed at the training process. The authors [45] referred the constraint which regularizes the hidden layer weights as "companion objective". This companion objective serves as a new regularization technique and results in faster convergence during training.

We also use attention gates in NAU-N [43]. These attention gates suppress irrelevant information while highlighting the important feature of the input. We propose to use attention gates in all the subnetworks in the decoder and not only the main U-Net decoder. By using attention gates in all subnetwork will help the subnetworks learn the more important features and improve the performance in the segmentation.

Our goal is to detect GAN generated spliced objects in satellite images using our Nested Attention U-Net (NAU-N). NAU-N outputs a heatmap that contains a real number for each pixel that is positive if the pixel is generated by a GAN. The larger the number the more probable that the pixel is generated by GAN. A binary mask is also generated by thresholding the heatmap. This binary mask indicates which part of the image contains a GAN generated object. The heatmap and binary mask will be used for the evaluations we describe below in our experiments. We will assume in our experiments that we know that the spliced object in a satellite image was generated by a particular type of GAN (e.g. StyleGAN2 [27], ProGAN [46], CycleGAN [47]).

# 4   GAN Generated Images

**Table 1.** Number of image in the three satellite image datasets, each dataset corresponds to a different type of GAN (StyleGAN2, CycleGAN, ProGAN) used for generating the spliced objects.

| Dataset | Training images | Validation images | Testing images |
|---|---|---|---|
| Dataset 1 StyleGAN2 | 5826 | 1467 | 10628 |
| Dataset 2 CycleGAN | 5605 | 1408 | 10425 |
| Dataset 3 ProGAN | 5643 | 1409 | 10588 |

We constructed three satellite image dataset which contains satellite images with spliced objects. The three datasets correspond to different GANs (StyleGAN2, CycleGAN and ProGAN) which were used for generating spliced objects. In Dataset 1 we used StyleGAN2, in Dataset 2 we used CycleGAN, and in Dataset 3 we used ProGAN to generate spliced objects. The original satellite images are from the Sentinel 2 satellite [48] with additional post-processing.

These satellite images have a $512 \times 512$ pixel size with $10\,m$ of spatial resolution per pixel. More detail is shown in Table 1.

In each dataset approximately half of the images contains GAN generated objects and half are original images. This "half/half" split is used for all subsets of the each dataset we create for our experiments. For example in Dataset 1 half of the 5826 training images contains StyleGAN2 generated objects and half of them are original images All spliced images have a corresponding ground truth mask which shows the region where we modified the original image. Each manipulated image contains several spliced objects. We can divide the construction of the datasets into three steps: object generation, defining the area where the objects will be spliced and the actual splicing as shown in Fig. 3.

We trained StyleGAN2, ProGAN and CycleGAN networks on the preprocessed SEN12MS [14] Sentinel 2 images. SEN12MS is large dataset containing images from Sentinel 1 and Sentinel 2 satellites and MODIS-derived land cover maps. The trained GAN networks were then used to generate objects for splicing into an original satellite image **I**. For generating an object we used a portion of the original image **I** as a seed image. Then we used the trained GAN networks to generate an image similar to the seed image. The generated image will be the basis for creating the spliced object.

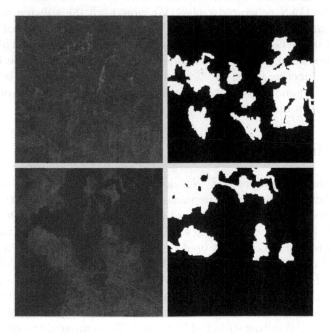

**Fig. 4.** The first column contains a spliced image, the second column contains its corresponding ground-truth mask.

We generated an image similar to the seed image so that the final spliced image would be realistic and would not contain visible artifacts. Using Style-

GAN2, we generated an image similar to the seed image the same way described in [27]. We find the latent representation of the seed image in the unextended latent space by using an iterative approach. This approach will find a latent code **w** very close to the latent representation of the seed image. The generator of the StyleGAN2 will generate an image from **w** very similar to the seed image. Using ProGAN and CycleGAN we generated an image similar to the seed image by a different approach. We generated many images with the GANs and then we calculated the SSIM score for each image compared with the seed image. We chose a generated image with a very high SSIM score compared to the seed image.

We then determine a region in the original image where we want to splice our object. We define these regions by using Watershed unsupervised segmentation [49]. Watershed treats an image as a topographic map where the brightness of each pixel represent the height of the map at that point. Watershed finds all the lines that run along the tops of the ridges in the topographic map. After defining the lines, we determine the areas or segments which are separated by these lines. Then we choose some of these segments which sum of area cover about 10% of the image or 50% of the image. These segments will define the area where we will splice a GAN generated object.

After determining the splicing area, we select the same shape as the splicing area from the GAN generated image. We now have the splicing area and the object we want to splice into that area. We select the same shape of area as the splicing area in the GAN generated image, which will be the spliced object. After that we splice the object into the image we blend it to smooth the boundaries. The blending function mixes two images together by choosing the brighter pixel from each corresponding pixel from the two images. Some examples of the spliced images are shown in Fig. 4.

## 5    Experiments

For evaluating our proposed U-Net architecture we use the three datasets described above. We can split the images from the datasets into training, validation and testing subsets. We trained three of the proposed Nested Attention U-Net (NAU-N) architectures using a different dataset. We assume that we know a priori which type of GAN was used to generate potential splices in the image. One NAU-N is trained on a subset of Dataset 1, the second NAU-N is trained on a subset of Dataset 2 and a third NAU-N is trained on a subset of Dataset 3. After training, we tested each NAU-N on different subsets of the dataset used for training. For example, the NAU-N trained on the training subset of the Dataset 3 was tested on the testing subset of Dataset 3. We compared the performance of NAU-N with other techniques including U-Net, Attention U-Net, Nested U-Net, R2U-Net, and the MultiResUNet.

For the next set of experiments we wanted to evaluate how well our method (NAU-N) could generalize in detecting different types of GANs. We did experiments how well our method can detect GAN generated objects. We trained three

NAU-N networks, one on Dataset 1, one on Dataset 2, and one on Dataset 3. We tested each NAU-N network using a different GAN dataset, for example the NAU-N network trained on Dataset 1 was tested on Dataset 2 and Dataset 3.

We examined four evaluation metrics to measure performance, two for detection and two for localization. For detection, we measured how well each method can detect if there are any GAN generated objects in the images. For localization, we evaluated how similar the generated masks compare to the corresponding groundtruth masks. The first evaluation metric for detection is the Area Under the Curve of the Receiving Operating Curve (ROC AUC). The ROC is a representation of the trade-off between the True Positive Rate (TPR) and the False Positive Rate (FPR) at all the classification thresholds. The True Positive Rate is the proportion of correctly predicted positive values and the all predicted positive values.

$$TruePositiveRate = \frac{TruePositive}{TruePositive + FalseNegative}$$

The False Positive Rate is the proportion of incorrectly predicted positive values and the all predicted positive values.

$$FalsePositiveRate = \frac{FalseNegative}{TruePositive + FalseNegative}$$

The next metric for detection evaluation is the Area Under the Curve of the Precision Recall Curve (P/R AUC). The P/R shows the trade-off between the Precision and the Recall at all the classification thresholds. The Precision is the ratio of True Positive compared to the sum of True Positive and False Positive.

$$Precision = \frac{TruePositive}{TruePositive + FalsePositive}$$

The Recall is the proportion of incorrectly predicted positive values and the all of the positive values which is the same as the True Positive Rate.

$$Recall = \frac{TruePositive}{TruePositive + FalseNegative}$$

The first metric used to evaluate localization performance is the Dice Score which is also know as the F1 score. If a method has a high F1 score, it indicates that there is no problem with false positives or false negatives. The F1 score is the harmonic mean of the Precision and Recall.

$$F1 = \frac{Precision * Recall}{2 * (Precision + Recall)}$$

or in an another form

$$F1 = \frac{2 * TP}{2 * TP + FP + FN}$$

$TP$ is the True Positive, $FP$ is the False Positive and $FN$ is the False Negative. The second metric used to measure localization is the Jaccard Index also known

**Table 2.** Detection and localization performance.

| Dataset 1 results | U-Net | Attention U-Net | Nested U-Net | R2 U-Net | MultiRes U-Net | Nested attention U-Net (NAU-N) |
|---|---|---|---|---|---|---|
| ROC AUC | 0.469 | 0.992 | 0.675 | 0.538 | 0.920 | 0.998 |
| P/R AUC | 0.459 | 0.988 | 0.715 | 0.562 | 0.944 | 0.998 |
| Dice score/F1 | 0.118 | 0.751 | 0.088 | 0.000 | 0.026 | 0.855 |
| Jaccard index | 0.069 | 0.648 | 0.052 | 0.000 | 0.014 | 0.912 |
| *Dataset 2 results* | | | | | | |
| ROC AUC | 0.439 | 0.964 | 0.626 | 0.836 | 0.920 | 0.978 |
| P/R AUC | 0.494 | 0.971 | 0.65 | 0.795 | 0.929 | 0.980 |
| Dice score/F1 | 0.067 | 0.691 | 0.162 | 0.000 | 0.078 | 0.714 |
| Jaccard index | 0.035 | 0.621 | 0.100 | 0.000 | 0.045 | 0.648 |
| *Dataset 3 results* | | | | | | |
| ROC AUC | 0.682 | 0.982 | 0.634 | 0.633 | 0.653 | 0.779 |
| P/R AUC | 0.643 | 0.979 | 0.565 | 0.633 | 0.588 | 0.838 |
| Dice score/F1 | 0.017 | 0.660 | 0.065 | 0.000 | 0.086 | 0.726 |
| Jaccard index | 0.010 | 0.539 | 0.110 | 0.000 | 0.049 | 0.645 |

**Table 3.** Nested Attention U-Net (NAU) performance when it is trained with one dataset and tested using a different dataset

| Trained on | Dataset 1 | Dataset 1 | Dataset 2 | Dataset 2 | Dataset 3 | Dataset 3 |
|---|---|---|---|---|---|---|
| Test on | Dataset 2 | Dataset 3 | Dataset 1 | Dataset 3 | Dataset 1 | Dataset 2 |
| ROC AUC | 0.801 | 0.999 | 0.548 | 0.305 | 0.568 | 0.779 |
| P/R AUC | 0.846 | 0.999 | 0.555 | 0.382 | 0.596 | 0.838 |
| Dice Score/F1 | 0.020 | 0.908 | 0.030 | 0.069 | 0.013 | 0.182 |
| Jaccard Index | 0.038 | 0.846 | 0.048 | 0.072 | 0.006 | 0.270 |

as intersection over union [50]. The Jaccard Index is shows how similar the detected binary mask to the ground truth mask.

$$JaccardIndex = \frac{TP}{TP + FP + FN}$$

$TP$ stands is the True Positive, $FP$ os the False Positive and $FN$ is False Negative.

The results of our first sets experiments, e.g. NAU-N was trained and tested on images from Dataset 1, are shown in Table 2. The original U-Net [25] and Nested U-Net [40] architectures can detect a portion of the GAN spliced object, but it fails in most of the cases. The Attention U-Net [39] detects large GAN generated objects, but it cannot capture the fine-details of these objects and miss the detection of smaller GAN generated objects. Another interesting result is that R2 U-Net [41] and MultiRes U-Net [42] tend to fail in detecting GAN generated objects. Although the use of these two techniques are very popular for image segmentation but for detecting GAN generated objects they tend to overfit on the training data. Our proposed method, NAU-N performs better in most cases than the other methods shown in the table. NAU-N almost perfectly detect if an image contains a StyleGAN2 or CycleGAN generated objects and could generate very similar mask as the ground-truth mask. Overall, our proposed method, NAU-N, successfully detects GAN generated objects even at cases where other techniques fails. Examples of how each method performs in Fig. 5.

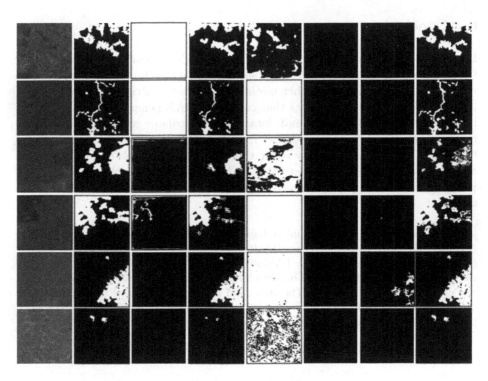

**Fig. 5.** The columns from left to right contains the spliced image, ground-truth, generated mask for U-Net, Attention U-Net, Nested U-Net, R2U-Net, MultiResUNet and, our Nested Attention U-Net (NAU-N) respectively.

The results of our second set of experiments, e.g. NAU-N was trained on image from Dataset 1 and tested on image from Dataset 2, are shown in Table 3. The NAU-N network trained on Dataset 1 can detect images containing GAN generated objects in Dataset 2 and in Dataset 3. It can also localize very well GAN generated object in Dataset 3 images. The NAU-N network trained on Dataset 3 can detect images containing GAN generated objects in Dataset 2, but it fails to localize them while network trained on Dataset 2 fails to detect images containing GAN generated objects in Dataset 1 and Dataset 3. It seems that the performance is highly dependent on the training images. A NAU-N network trained on images containing StyleGAN2 was able to detect with high precision whether an image contains a CycleGAN or ProGAN generated objects, it could also localize almost perfectly ProGAN generated objects. A NAU-N network trained on images containing CycleGAN fails to detect whether an image contains a StyleGAN2 or ProGAN generated objects. This implies that there is a relationship among GANs in the order of StyleGAN2, ProGAN, CycleGAN regarding how well our method could generalize in detecting GAN generated objects from an unseen GAN.

## 6    Conclusion

In this paper we introduce the Nested Attention U-Net architecture for detecting GAN generated objects spliced into satellite images. Our method performed well when compared to the other methods. Another contribution of our paper is that we created three datasets that contained GAN generated spliced objects in satellite images. Our code and datasets will available and the links will be inserted into the paper after review. In future we plan to expand our dataset to include images generated by other types of GANs. We also plan to develop a method which goes beyond detecting and localizing spliced objects in satellite images and will be capable of classifying the method which generated the spliced object.

**Acknowledgment.** This material is based on research sponsored by the Defense Advanced Research Projects Agency (DARPA) and the Air Force Research Laboratory (AFRL) under agreement number FA8750-16-2-0173. The U.S. Government is authorized to reproduce and distribute reprints for Governmental purposes notwithstanding any copyright notation thereon. The views and conclusions contained herein are those of the authors and should not be interpreted as necessarily representing the official policies or endorsements, either expressed or implied, of DARPA or AFRL or the U.S. Government.
    Address all correspondence to Edward J. Delp, ace@ecn.purdue.edu.

## References

1. Davari, A.A., Christlein, V., Vesal, S., Maier, A., Riess, C.: GMM supervectors for limited training data in hyperspectral remote sensing image classification. In: Felsberg, M., Heyden, A., Krüger, N. (eds.) CAIP 2017. LNCS, vol. 10425, pp. 296–306. Springer, Cham (2017). https://doi.org/10.1007/978-3-319-64698-5_25
2. Shimoni, M., Borghys, D., Heremans, R., Perneel, C., Acheroy, M.: Land-cover classification using fused PolSAR and PolInSAR features. In: Proceedings of the European Conference on Synthetic Aperture Radar, Friedrichshafen, Germany, pp. 1–4, June 2008
3. Lebedev, V., et al.: Precipitation nowcasting with satellite imagery. In: Proceedings of the ACM SIGKDD International Conference on Knowledge Discovery & Data Mining, Anchorage, AK (2019)
4. Sahoo, I., Guinness, J., Reich, B.: Estimating atmospheric motion winds from satellite image data using space-time drift models. arXiv:1902.09653, February 2019

5. Efremova, N., Zausaev, D., Antipov, G.: Prediction of soil moisture content based on satellite data and sequence-to-sequence networks. In: Proceedings of the Conference on Neural Information Processing Systems Women in Machine Learning Workshop, Montreal, Canada (2018)
6. Helmer, E., Goodwin, N.R., Gond, V., Souza Jr., C.M., Asner, G.P.: Characterizing Tropical Forests with Multispectral Imagery, vol. 2, pp. 367–396. CRC Press, Boca Raton (2015)
7. Rußwurm, M., Lefèvre, S., Körner, M.: BreizhCrops: a satellite time series dataset for crop type identification. In: Proceedings of the International Conference on Machine Learning Time Series Workshop, Long Beach, CA (2019)
8. Suraj, P.K., Gupta, A., Sharma, M., Paul, S.B., Banerjee, S.: On monitoring development using high resolution satellite images. arXiv:1712.02282, December 2017
9. Oshri, B., et al.: Infrastructure quality assessment in Africa using satellite imagery and deep learning. In: Proceedings of the International Conference on Knowledge Discovery & Data Mining, United Kingdom, London (2018)
10. Guirado, E., Tabik, S., Rivas, M.L., Alcaraz-Segura, D., Herrera, F.: Whale counting in satellite and aerial images with deep learning. Sci. Rep. **9**, October 2019
11. Xia, G., et al.: Dota: a large-scale dataset for object detection in aerial images. In: Proceedings of the IEEE Conference on Computer Vision and Pattern Recognition, Salt Lake City, UT, pp. 3974–3983, June 2018
12. Yang, Y., Newsam, S.: Bag-of-visual-words and spatial extensions for land-use classification. In: Proceedings of the ACM SIGSPATIAL International Symposium on Advances in Geographic Information Systems, San Jose, CA, pp. 270–279, November 2009
13. Gupta, R., et al.: xBD: a dataset for assessing building damage from satellite imagery. In: Proceedings of the IEEE Conference on Computer Vision and Pattern Recognition Workshops, pp. 10–17, June 2019
14. Schmitt, M., Hughes, L.H., Qiu, C., Zhu, X.X.: SEN12MS - a curated dataset of georeferenced multi-spectral sentinel-1/2 imagery for deep learning and data fusion. arXiv:1906.07789, June 2019
15. Zhou, X., Huang, S., Li, B., Li, Y., Li, J., Zhang, Z.: Text guided person image synthesis. In: Proceedings of the IEEE Conference on Computer Vision and Pattern Recognition, Long Beach, CA (2019)
16. Li, B., Qi, X., Lukasiewicz, T., Torr, P.: Controllable text-to-image generation. In: Proceedings of the Neural Information Processing Systems, Vancouver, Canada, pp. 2065–2075, December 2019
17. Kramer, A.E.: Russian images of Malaysia airlines flight 17 were altered, report finds, The New York Times, 6 November 2018. https://www.nytimes.com/2016/07/16/world/europe/malaysia-airlines-flight-17-russia.html
18. Byrd, D.: Fake image of diwali still circulating, EarthSky, 15 July 2016. https://earthsky.org/earth/fake-image-of-india-during-diwali-versus-the-real-thing
19. Edwards, J.: China uses GAN technique to tamper with earth images, ExecutiveGov, 1 April 2019. https://www.executivegov.com/2019/04/ngas-todd-myers-china-uses-gan-technique-to-tamper-with-earth-images/
20. Rannard, G.: Australia fires: Misleading maps and pictures go viral, BBC, 7 January 2020. https://www.bbc.com/news/blogs-trending-51020564
21. Barni, M., Phan, Q.-T., Tondi, B.: Copy move source-target disambiguation through multi-branch CNNs. arXiv preprint arXiv:1912.12640 (2019)
22. Cozzolino, D., Verdoliva, L.: Noiseprint: a CNN-based camera model fingerprint. IEEE Trans. Inf. Forensics Secur. **15**, 144–159 (2020)

23. Ren, C.X., Ziemann, A., Theiler, J., Durieux, A.M.: Deep snow: synthesizing remote sensing imagery with generative adversarial nets. arXiv preprint arXiv:1911.12546 (2020)
24. Rocha, A., Scheirer, W., Boult, T., Goldenstein, S.: Vision of the unseen: current trends and challenges in digital image and video forensics. ACM Comput. Surv. **43**(4), 1–42 (2011)
25. Ronneberger, O., Fischer, P., Brox, T.: U-net: convolutional networks for biomedical image segmentation. In: Proceedings of the International Conference on Medical Image Computing and Computer-Assisted Intervention, Munich, Germany, October 2015
26. Goodfellow, I., et al.: Generative adversarial nets, Montreal, Canada, pp. 2672–2680, December 2014
27. Karras, T., Laine, S., Aittala, M., Hellsten, J., Lehtinen, J., Aila, T.: Analyzing and improving the image quality of StyleGAN. In: Proceedings of the IEEE Conference on Computer Vision and Pattern Recognition, Seattle, WA (2020)
28. Barni, M., Costanzo, A., Sabatini, L.: Identification of cut & paste tampering by means of double-JPEG detection and image segmentation. In: Proceedings of the IEEE International Symposium on Circuits and Systems, Paris, France, pp. 1687–1690, May 2010
29. McCloskey, S., Albright, M.: Detecting GAN-generated imagery using saturation cues. In: Proceedings of the IEEE International Conference on Image Processing, Taipei, Taiwan, pp. 4584–4588, September 2019
30. Cozzolino, D., Thies, J., Rössler, A., Riess, C., Nießner, M., Verdoliva, L.: Forensictransfer: weakly-supervised domain adaptation for forgery detection. arXiv:1812.02510, December 2018
31. Montserrat, D.M., et al.: Deepfakes detection with automatic face weighting. In: Proceedings of the IEEE Conference on Computer Vision and Pattern Recognition Workshops, Seattle, WA (2020)
32. Cozzolino, D., Poggi, G., Verdoliva, L.: Splicebuster: a new blind image splicing detector. In: Proceedings of the IEEE International Workshop on Information Forensics and Security, Rome, Italy, pp. 1–6, November 2015
33. Rozsa, A., Zhong, Z., Boult, T.E.: Adversarial attack on deep learning-based splice localization. In: Proceedings of the IEEE Conference on Computer Vision and Pattern Recognition Workshops, Seattle, WA (2020)
34. Ho, A.T.S., Woon, W.M.: A semi-fragile pinned sine transform watermarking system for content authentication of satellite images. In: Proceedings of the IEEE International Geoscience and Remote Sensing Symposium, Seoul, South Korea, vol. 2, pp. 1–4, July 2005
35. Kalyan Yarlagadda, S., Güera, D., Bestagini, P., Zhu, S. Tubaro, F., Delp, E.: Satellite image forgery detection and localization using gan and one-class classifier. In: Proceedings of the IS&T International Symposium on Electronic Imaging, Burlingame, CA, vol. 2018, no. 7, pp. 214-1-214-9, February 2018
36. Horvath, J., et al.: Anomaly-based manipulation detection in satellite images. In: Proceedings of the IEEE Conference on Computer Vision and Pattern Recognition Workshops, Long Beach, CA, pp. 62–71, June 2019
37. Horváth, J., Montserrat, D.M., Hao, H., Delp, E.J.: Manipulation detection in satellite images using deep belief networks. In: Proceedings of the IEEE Conference on Computer Vision and Pattern Recognition Workshops, Seattle, WA (2020)

38. Bartusiak, E.R., et al.: Splicing detection and localization in satellite imagery using conditional GANs. In: Proceedings of the IEEE International Conference on Multimedia Information Processing and Retrieval, San Jose, CA, pp. 91–96, March 2019
39. Oktay, O., et al.: Attention U-Net: learning where to look for the pancreas. arXiv preprint arXiv:1804.03999, April 2018
40. Zhou, Z., Rahman Siddiquee, M.M., Tajbakhsh, N., Liang, J.: UNet++: a nested U-Net architecture for medical image segmentation. In: Stoyanov, D., et al. (eds.) DLMIA/ML-CDS 2018. LNCS, vol. 11045, pp. 3–11. Springer, Cham (2018). https://doi.org/10.1007/978-3-030-00889-5_1
41. Alom, M.Z., Hasan, M., Yakopcic, C., Taha, T.M., Asari, V.K.: Recurrent residual convolutional neural network based on U-net (R2U-net) for medical image segmentation," arXiv:1802.06955 (2018)
42. Ibtehaz, N., Rahman, M.S.: Multiresunet: rethinking the u-net architecture for multimodal biomedical image segmentation. Neural Netw. **121**, 74–87 (2020)
43. Jetley, S., Lord, N.A., Lee, N., Torr, P.: Learn to pay attention. In: Proceedings of the International Conference on Learning Representations, Vancouver, Canada (2018)
44. Drozdzal, M., Vorontsov, E., Chartrand, G., Kadoury, S., Pal, C.J.: The importance of skip connections in biomedical image segmentation. In: Proceedings of the 2nd Deep Learning in Medical Image Analysis Workshop, Greece, Athens (2016)
45. Lee, C.-Y., Xie, S., Gallagher, P., Zhang, Z., Tu, Z.: Deeply-supervised nets. In: Proceedings of the International Conference on Artificial Intelligence and Statistics, San Diego,California, USA, vol. 38, pp. 562–570, May 2015
46. Zhang, D., Khoreva, A.: Progressive augmentation of GANs. In: Proceedings of the Neural Information Processing Systems, Vancouver, Canada (2019)
47. Zhu, J.-Y., Park, T., Isola, P., Efros, A.A.: Unpaired image-to-image translation using cycle-consistent adversarial networks. In: Proceedings of the International Conference on Computer Vision, Venice, Italy (2017)
48. Sentinel 2 images, Copernicus programme. https://sentinel.esa.int/web/sentinel/user-guides/sentinel-2-msi/processing-levels
49. Roerdink, J.B.T.M., Meijster, A.: The watershed transform: definitions, algorithms and parallelization strategies. Fundamenta Informaticae **41**(1–2), 187–228 (2000)
50. Levandowsky, M., Winter, D.: Measures of the amount of ecologic association between species. Nature **5**(234), 34–35 (1971)

# Fingerprint Adversarial Presentation Attack in the Physical Domain

Stefano Marrone[1](✉)(iD), Roberto Casula[2](iD), Giulia Orrù[2](iD),
Gian Luca Marcialis[2](iD), and Carlo Sansone[1](iD)

[1] University of Naples Federico II, Via Claudio 21, 80125 Naples, Italy
{stefano.marrone,carlo.sansone}@unina.it
[2] University of Cagliari, Piazza d'Armi, 09123 Cagliari, Italy
{roberto.casula,giulia.orru,marcialis}@unica.it

**Abstract.** With the advent of the deep learning era, Fingerprint-based Authentication Systems (FAS) equipped with Fingerprint Presentation Attack Detection (FPAD) modules managed to avoid attacks on the sensor through artificial replicas of fingerprints. Previous works highlighted the vulnerability of FPADs to digital adversarial attacks. However, in a realistic scenario, the attackers may not have the possibility to directly feed a digitally perturbed image to the deep learning based FPAD, since the channel between the sensor and the FPAD is usually protected. In this paper we thus investigate the threat level associated with adversarial attacks against FPADs in the physical domain. By materially realising fakes from the adversarial images we were able to insert them into the system directly from the "exposed" part, the sensor. To the best of our knowledge, this represents the first proof-of-concept of a fingerprint adversarial presentation attack. We evaluated how much liveness score changed by feeding the system with the attacks using digital and printed adversarial images. To measure what portion of this increase is due to the printing itself, we also re-printed the original spoof images, without injecting any perturbation. Experiments conducted on the LivDet 2015 dataset demonstrate that the printed adversarial images achieve ∼100% attack success rate against an FPAD if the attacker has the ability to make multiple attacks on the sensor (10) and a fairly good result (∼28%) in a one-shot scenario. Despite this work must be considered as a proof-of-concept, it constitutes a promising pioneering attempt confirming that an adversarial presentation attack is feasible and dangerous.

**Keywords:** Adversarial · FPAD · Liveness

## 1 Introduction

Personal authentication systems based on biometrics and, in particular, on fingerprints are widespread in public security systems and personal devices, thanks to their precision and user-friendliness. Spoofing attacks, i.e. attacks to the sensor

© Springer Nature Switzerland AG 2021
A. Del Bimbo et al. (Eds.): ICPR 2020 Workshops, LNCS 12666, pp. 530–543, 2021.
https://doi.org/10.1007/978-3-030-68780-9_42

through artificial reproductions of fingerprints, have always represented a serious security threat to Fingerprint Authentication Systems (FAS) [9]. In recent years, numerous Fingerprint Liveness Detection (FLD) systems, also known as Fingerprint Presentation Attack Detection (FPAD) systems, have been proposed to counteract these attacks.

The rapid diffusion of deep-learning-based and, in particular, of Convolutional Neural Networks (CNN) based methods has made it possible to reach liveness-detection rates above 95% [15]. However, in 2013 it has been demonstrated that neural networks suffer from some new vulnerabilities [1]. This attack (known as adversarial perturbation) not only can be perpetrated at training time (known as poisoning) but also at test time (known as evasion) [3].

Adversarial perturbations are thus potentially very dangerous since an attacker could intentionally add small perturbations to an image, keeping it visually unchanged, to force the classifier's decision. On this line, some recent works already demonstrated the effectiveness of a digital attack on a CNN FPAD [5,10]. This type of attack assumes the attackers to be able to enter the communication channel between the sensor and the neural network, making them able to submit the adversarial images as input to the FPAD. This type of attack is therefore infeasible if the system uses secure channels protected by time-stamps, physical isolation or challenge-response mechanisms [2].

Based on these considerations, we wondered if an attacker, with high knowledge of the system, could exploit adversarial perturbations to increase the possibility that their spoofs deceive a CNN-based FPADs. In other words, *the aim of this work is to analyse whether the small perturbations that modify FPAD's decision can be "printed" and exploited in an artificial and material replica of the fingerprint.*

The rest of the paper is organised as follows. Section 2 provides a brief introduction to CNN-based anti-spoofing and existing perturbation attacks. Section 3 describes the proposed attack. Section 4 evaluates the threat level of the printed adversarial images on a state-of-art fingerprint liveness detector. Section 4 draws some conclusions.

## 2    CNN-Based FPAD and Adversarial Perturbations

Presentation attack, namely the action of "presenting" a fake fingerprint replica to a fingerprint scanner, is a common attack against Fingerprint-based Authentication Systems (FAS). Possible protection against such attacks includes the use of a Fingerprint Presentation Attack Detection (FPAD) module to discriminate between "live" and "fake" fingerprints. The use of an FPAD module has become more and more common since its use causes the attacker to first bypass the FPAD, by modifying a fake replica such that it is recognised as a real fingerprint.

FPAD algorithms relies on the extraction of anatomical, physiological or texture-based features from fingerprint images. Over the years, FPAD methods have been refined and recently Convolutional Neural Networks (CNNs) have

**Table 1.** LivDet2015 dataset characteristics. For each scanner, the acquired fingerprint size, and the number of live and fake fingerprints (for each spoofing materials) images are reported. The hyphen in a cell indicates that the corresponding material has not been used to generate fake fingerprints for the corresponding scanner.

| Scanner | Image Size (px) | Live | Body Double | Ecoflex | Gelatine | Latex | Liquid Ecoflex | OOMOO | Playdoh | RTV | Woodglue |
|---|---|---|---|---|---|---|---|---|---|---|---|
| Biometrika | 1000×1000 | 1000 | - | 250 | 250 | 250 | 250 | - | - | 250 | 250 |
| CrossMatch | 640×480 | 1500 | 300 | 270 | 300 | - | - | 297 | 281 | - | - |
| DigitalPersona | 252×324 | 1000 | - | 250 | 250 | 250 | 250 | - | - | 250 | 250 |
| GreenBit | 500×500 | 1000 | - | 250 | 250 | 250 | 250 | - | - | 250 | 250 |

been leveraged, using either the full image [7,14] or patching it [4], allowing to reach very high accuracy levels [15].

In 2013, when CNNs had not yet spread to many applications of pattern recognition, Szegedy et al. [1,18] demonstrated the existence of adversarial attacks against deep learning methods (including CNN), i.e. the injection of a suitable, hardly perceptible, perturbation which leads to a misclassification of the input image. This severe vulnerability has made the robustness of CNN models to adversarial attacks a key feature in modern systems. Indeed, in the last decade, adversarial attacks as the Fast Gradient Sign Method (FGSM) [6], the Basic Iterative Method (BIM) [8] and many others [1], have become more numerous, more effective and easy to perform, thanks to the availability of free and open-source toolboxes [13,16].

This problem is particularly critic in security-related domains leveraging CNNs in one of their stages. Focusing on the case of fingerprints, the vulnerability of FPAD systems to adversarial perturbations has already been demonstrated [5,10], describing methods designed to generate perturbed fingerprint images able to mislead a target FPAD in the digital domain. In both cases, the attacks assume that the attacker can feed the perturbed digital image directly into the CNN. Despite sufficient for a proof-of-concept, these attacks have limited applicability since most modern systems are protected from this possibility, with the attacker only having access to the sensor.

Recently, the effectiveness of an adversarial physical domain attack against a CNN-based face authentication system equipped with an anti-spoofing module has been demonstrated [19]. Printed and replay facial attacks are easy to obtain, and the authors have shown that the "fabrication" of these replicas allows for the retention of the added adversarial information.

In this manuscript we investigate whether the more complex creation of an artificial fingerprint replica allows an adversarial attack on a fingerprint presentation attack detection system in the physical domain.

# 3   Proposed Approach

To perform an adversarial presentation attack in the physical domain, we must identify i) a fingerprint dataset, ii) a presentation attack detector, iii) an adversarial perturbation procedure for fingerprints and iv) a way to physically realise the crafted adversarial fake replica. The following subsections analyse each of these points, highlighting means and choices made.

## 3.1   Fingerprints Liveness Dataset

The need for a common experimental protocol for liveness detection tasks gave rise to the gathering of fingerprints datasets. Among all those available, in this work we consider the one provided with the LivDet 2015 competition [12]. This choice is mostly driven by the availability of well-defined training and test datasets and by the availability of open-source top-performer liveness detectors trained on it. Table 1 briefly reports the main characteristics of the LivDet 2015 dataset.

## 3.2   Adversarial Perturbations for Fingerprints

Usually, an *adversarial perturbation* is a noise $r \in \mathbb{R}^{(w,h,3)}$ (with $w$ and $h$ the width and height of a target image) crafted with the aim of misleading a target image classifier. In the context of fingerprints, an attacker not only must craft the perturbation to be as subtle (i.e. invisible) as possible but also must take into account the fact that fingerprints and natural images are visually different. Accordingly, in a previous work [10] we modified some well-known adversarial perturbation algorithms to inject a grey-level (i.e., the same for all the channels in the case of RGB acquisitions) noise $r \in [0, 255]$ and to apply it only to the Region of Interest (ROI) delimiting the actual fingerprint. These constraints result in a perturbation that, although able to mislead an FPAD, is still imperceptible for a human operator (Fig. 1). In our previous work [10] we modified three adversarial perturbation algorithms. In this work we focus only on Deep-Fool [11] as it showed to be the most convenient in terms of attack success rate vs. required computational effort.

## 3.3   Spoof's Creation and Acquisition

The perturbation of the fingerprints through the previously described method is followed by the creation of the moulds of the adversarially perturbed images. To this aim, the fingerprints are first printed (by using a normal laser printer) on a transparent sheet. The fingerprints are directly printed in their real size, without the need for any resize operation (since the perturbation has been applied on their digitalised version). Instead, since the final fingerprints need to be a perfect replica of the original finger (i.e. a positive mould), the printed fingerprint must be "inverted". Finally, since the size of a fingerprint is very little when compared with a standard A4 page, we printed several fingerprints on the same sheet.

**Fig. 1.** Example of an unconstrained (left) and of a constrained (right) fingerprint adversarial perturbation [10].

**Fig. 2.** Particular of the adversarial fingerprint physical spoof realisation. In the image, the expert is depositing a layer of latex over the printed adversarial fingerprints. Please note that, on the same sheet, there are several fingerprints (possibly from different subjects), all inverted in the colours.

Once the sheet has been created, a layer of latex is deposited over the prints of the individual perturbed fingerprints, making sure that there is no swelling of air and that the resulting layer has an adequate thickness that allows correct removal and subsequent acquisition through the sensor (Fig. 2). Indeed, if the fake is of excessively thin thickness, the removal operation from the sheet would compromise the fingerprint, resulting in a non-optimal acquisition. The resulting fingerprint (Fig. 3) is then posed over the scanner to perform the actual adversarial presentation attack.

**Fig. 3.** A physical adversarial fake fingerprint obtained by using the method described in this paper.

## 3.4   Attacking the CNN for Liveness Detection

Over the years, LivDet competitors moved from "classical" computer vision algorithms to solution leveraging Deep CNNs. Indeed, the LivDet 2015 edition winner [14] demonstrated that also FPAD can benefit from CNNs, being able to reach accuracy levels and intra-materials and intra-sensors generalisation ability never reached until that moment. In particular, the authors made use of a VGG19 network [17], pre-trained on ImageNet and fine-tuned to recognise live from spoof fingerprints. To improve the network generalisation ability, the authors augmented the dataset by extracting five patches from each fingerprint, obtaining a final dataset 10 times bigger than the original one. Finally, to match the VGG19 input layer expected image dimensions, each patch is resized to 224 × 224 pixels.

In our previous work [10] we attacked the aforementioned VGG19-based FPAD showing how to effectively bypass it by means of adversarial perturbations. In that case, all the experiments were performed in the digital domain. Indeed, although the attack was already designed to be "printed" for real-world application, the actual fake replica crafting and its use for a real presentation attack has never been performed.

In this paper *we want to fill the gap by proposing a proof-of-concept for an* **Adversarial Presentation Attack (APA)**. In particular, we analyse whether it is possible to realise a **tangible replica** of an adversarial fingerprint that is still able to bypass the liveness detector. To this aim, we design the following attack scenario (Fig. 4):

- We sample a set of subjects and acquire their fingerprints to be submitted to the FPAD in order to calculate the liveness score (first row in Fig. 4);
- For all the enrolled subjects we also consensually acquire a mould for each fingerprint. These will be then used to craft fake fingerprint replicas to be submitted to the FPAD to calculate the liveness score (second row in Fig. 4);
- We leverage the adversarial fingerprint generation procedure [10] to determine, for each fake fingerprint crafted in the previous stage, the noise to add needed to mislead the FPAD. The resulting adversarial fake fingerprints are then submitted to the FPAD in order to calculate the liveness score (third row in Fig. 4);
- Finally, for each adversarial fake fingerprint, we craft a physical replica to be submitted, present it to the scanner and submit the acquisition to the FPAD in order to calculate the liveness score (fourth row in Fig. 4).

To evaluate the attack success rate, we consider only *fake* fingerprints from the official LivDet2015 test dataset, since an attacker is usually interested only in making fake replicas recognised as live. As this work aims to provide a proof of concept, we tried to limit the influence of as many aspects as possible. Therefore, among all the scanners and materials, we only focus on Digital Persona as scanner, Latex as spoofing material, the official LivDet2015 winner [14] as FPAD and DeepFool [11] (modified to work with fingerprints as in [10]) as adversarial perturbation algorithm.

Although all the stages are intended to try to minimise the impact of any external factor, the physical fingerprint crafting procedure might itself introduce a bias in the liveness score. Therefore, for all the fake fingerprints (stage two of the previous schema) we also crafted the corresponding physical replica without any adversarial perturbation applied (Fig. 5), with the aim of measuring the effect that a simple print and re-acquisition has on the liveness score.

## 4   Results

In this section, we evaluate the actual threat of the proposed adversarial attack in the physical domain.

The first evaluation served to verify how much the acquisition conditions and the pre-printing pre-processing influenced the liveness score. In this preliminary experiment, each spoof was acquired once. The Fig. 6 shows the comparison between manual and automatic pre-processing and between acquisitions in a warm environment ( $30°$ C) and an environment with average temperatures (about $20°$ C).

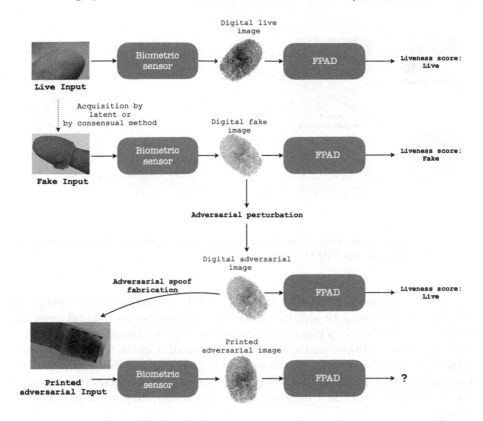

**Fig. 4.** Adversarial presentation attack schema. In the first row, the subject fingerprint is acquired; in the second row, a consensual fake replica is crafted; in the third row the (digital) adversarial fingerprint is crafted; finally, in the fourth row, the adversarial replica is printed and acquired. In all the stage, the target FPAD is used to evaluate the liveness score of the corresponding stage fingerprints.

The boxplots show that the different acquisitions conditions and pre-processing methods do not particularly affect liveness results. However, it is important to note that through the sole re-fabrication of the fingerprint from its digital spoof replica, most of the scores (~80% for all the cases reported in the boxplots) incur in an increase of the liveness score, with a portion (~12%) of the re-printed fingerprint able to mislead the FPAD.

Since, as aforementioned, the fake realisation procedure does not really affect the liveness score, all the following experiments were performed by printing the fingerprint using the automatic method and average temperature. It is also worth to note that, for a fair result analysis, only fake fingerprint correctly classified as fake by the FPAD underwent the adversarial perturbation process (242 of 250). Moreover, each spoof was acquired 10 times (for a total of 2420 acquisitions) with small rotations of the spoof on the sensor. This rotation is done to verify the efficacy of the detector by providing the same fingerprint but in slightly

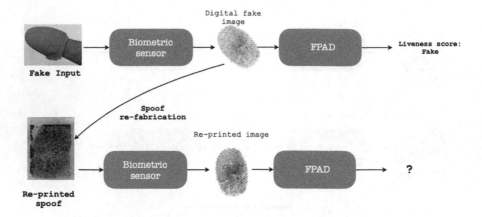

**Fig. 5.** Schema for the evaluation of the impact that spoof re-fabrication from the digital image has on the FPAD score.

different conditions and therefore focusing on different patches of the image. To simplify the notation, we also introduce the following terms: *Digital*, referring to the digital version of a clean (i.e. non perturbed) spoof fingerprint; *Re-Print*, referring to the printed and re-acquired version of a clean spoof fingerprint; *Digital Adversarial*, referring to the digital version of an adversarially perturbed fingerprint; *Printed Adversarial*, referring to the printed and acquired version of an adversarially perturbed fingerprint (i.e. the actual adversarial presentation attack).

In Fig. 7 the comparison of the liveness scores for the printed adversarial spoofs and for the re-printed spoofs is reported in order to highlight how much the improvement in the score is due to the addition of the perturbation. Although the median scores (red lines in the boxplots) are smaller than 0.5 (i.e. classified as fake), a high percentage of Printed Adversarial spoofs (specifically 32.77% against the 27.81% of the Re-Printed spoofs case) deceive the target FPAD. Part of the increase in scores is given by the re-printing process but the perturbations inserted in the images determine a further increase.

To properly assess the danger of the attack it is necessary to compare these scores with the original scores. Figure 8 shows the comparison between original scores, digital adversarial attack, re-print, and printed adversarial attack. For the last two, we plotted the median values (upper plot) and the maximum values (bottom plot) of the scores on the 10 acquisitions. From the comparison between originals and digital adversarial, we see that the images initially classified as fake, after the perturbations are classified as live in the 99.59% of the cases. On the other hand, the comparison between the median value and the maximum value of the scores of the attacks printed on the 10 acquisitions suggests some important evidence: i) the scores vary considerably based on the position of the spoof on the sensor; ii) the perturbation is not lost during the printing process but it could be lost during the submission of the spoof on the sensor; iii) an

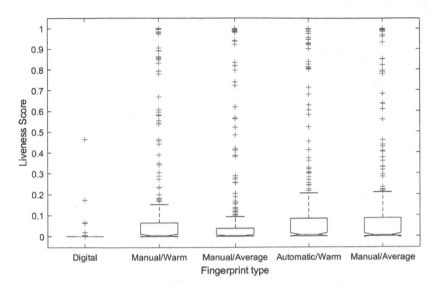

**Fig. 6.** Boxplot of the liveness scores of the 250 latex re-printed samples crafted with different acquisition and pre-processing methods: the manual method, which consists in inverting and resizing the fakes individually using an image editor and printing the paginated fingerprints; the automatic procedure, reversing and resizing the images via a MATLAB code. The difference between Warm and Average depends on the temperature in the room during printing and re-acquisition: 30° C for Warm and about 20° C for Average.

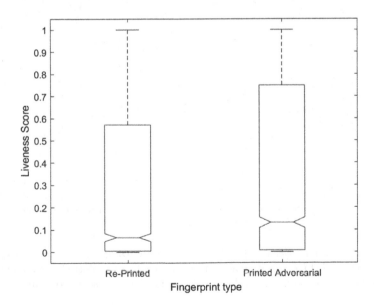

**Fig. 7.** Comparison of the liveness scores for the re-printed spoofs and for the printed adversarial replicas.

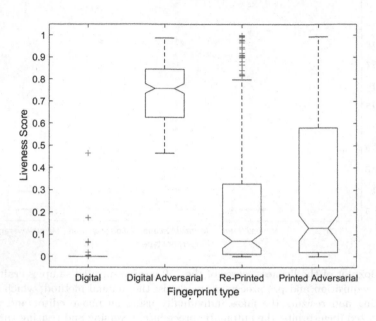

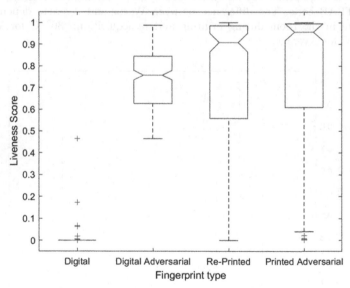

**Fig. 8.** Comparison between original scores *Digital*, *Digital Adversarial* attack, *Re-Print*, and *Printed Adversarial* attacks. For the last two we plotted the median values (upper plot) and the maximum values (bottom plot) of the scores obtained by the 10 acquisitions.

attacker can manage to bypass a target FPAD in 10 presentations of the printed adversarial spoof. What is surprising to find is the fact that even with the sole reprint of the digital spoof image it might be possible to mislead a CNN-based classification. In particular, focusing on the plot of the maximum value, 77.27% of the attacks with the re-print strategy and 80.17% with the adversarial printed are successful. This result is achievable with unrestricted (or limited to up to 10 trials) access to the sensor (multiple attacks with the same spoof). If we bring ourselves to more stringent conditions, where the attacker has only one chance of attack (simulated with the median of the scores on the 10 acquisitions) the success rates drop significantly, going down to 20.25% for the re-printed attack and to 28.51% for the adversarial printed attack.

Results show that, although more effective than the sole re-print, the adversarial perturbed images suffer from the printing procedure, highlighting the need for a more print-resilient adversarial procedure and/or for a more adversarial-aware printing procedure. Nonetheless, these attacks pose a serious threat to CNN-based FPADs that usually report accuracy >90% on most of the available fingerprint datasets.

## 5    Conclusions

In this work, we evaluated the threat of a physical adversarial attack against a CNN-based Fingerprint Presentation Attack Detector (FPAD). Crafting materially an adversarial fingerprint (i.e. a spoof fingerprint modified by means of a fingerprint adversarial perturbation algorithm) we have shown that it is possible to move these attacks from the digital domain to the physical one. This makes adversarial perturbations more dangerous, as they can be performed by an attacker having only access to the sensor. We compared this physical adversarial attack with the simple re-printing of the original digital images to assess how much the latter influenced the liveness score.

The experimental results obtained on the LivDet 2015 dataset, using the winning CNN of the same edition as FPAD [14] and a modification of the DeepFool [10,11] as adversarial attack, showed the feasibility and danger of these printed attacks. Surprisingly, the only re-printing of the original spoofs led to an increase in liveness scores, constituting a low effort attack. The reduced difference ($\sim$3%) between the increase in score obtained through simple re-printing and the adversarial printed image show that although the perturbations remain and affect the liveness score even after printing, the biggest portion of it is destroyed by the printing procedure. This is further confirmed by the fact that the full-digital attack obtains an almost 100% success rate. Therefore, despite this work constitutes a promising pioneering attempt confirming that an adversarial presentation attack is feasible and dangerous, a more in-depth study is necessary to render the procedure more robust and effective.

A shred of important evidence is that the position of the fake on the sensor greatly influences the result. As experimental evidence, it turned out that with a maximum of 10 acquisitions it is possible for the attacker to cheat the FPAD system. This work is limited to a single FPAD and a single perturbation method.

It will be thus important to evaluate how other CNN-based FPADs classify printed adversarial fingerprints. Furthermore, it will be important to evaluate whether the matching information is altered by the perturbation or by the printing process. These aspects, as well as the use of black-box attack scenario and of latent spoof fingerprints, will be addressed in future works.

# References

1. Akhtar, N., Mian, A.: Threat of adversarial attacks on deep learning in computer vision: a survey. IEEE Access **6**, 14410–14430 (2018)
2. Biggio, B., Fumera, G., Russu, P., Didaci, L., Roli, F.: Adversarial biometric recognition : a review on biometric system security from the adversarial machine-learning perspective. IEEE Signal Process. Mag. **32**(5), 31–41 (2015)
3. Biggio, B., Roli, F.: Wild patterns: ten years after the rise of adversarial machine learning. Pattern Recogn. **84**, 317–331 (2018). https://doi.org/10.1016/j.patcog.2018.07.023
4. Chugh, T., Cao, K., Jain, A.K.: Fingerprint spoof buster: use of minutiae-centered patches. IEEE Trans. Inf. Forensics Secur. **13**(9), 2190–2202 (2018)
5. Fei, J., Xia, Z., Yu, P., Xiao, F.: Adversarial attacks on fingerprint liveness detection. EURASIP J. Image Video Proc. **2020**(1), 1–11 (2020). https://doi.org/10.1186/s13640-020-0490-z
6. Goodfellow, I.J., Shlens, J., Szegedy, C.: Explaining and harnessing adversarial examples. arXiv preprint arXiv:1412.6572 (2015)
7. Jang, H.-U., Choi, H.-Y., Kim, D., Son, J., Lee, H.-K.: Fingerprint spoof detection using contrast enhancement and convolutional neural networks. In: Kim, K., Joukov, N. (eds.) ICISA 2017. LNEE, vol. 424, pp. 331–338. Springer, Singapore (2017). https://doi.org/10.1007/978-981-10-4154-9_39
8. Kurakin, A., Goodfellow, I., Bengio, S.: Adversarial examples in the physical world. arXiv preprint arXiv:1607.02533 (2017)
9. Marcel, S., Nixon, M.S., Fierrez, J., Evans, N. (eds.): Handbook of Biometric Anti-Spoofing. ACVPR. Springer, Cham (2019). https://doi.org/10.1007/978-3-319-92627-8
10. Marrone, S., Sansone, C.: Adversarial perturbations against fingerprint based authentication systems. In: IEEE International Conference on Biometrics, pp. 1–6 (2019). https://doi.org/10.1109/ICB45273.2019.8987399
11. Moosavi-Dezfooli, S.M., Fawzi, A., Frossard, P.: Deepfool: a simple and accurate method to fool deep neural networks. In: Proceedings of the IEEE Conference on Computer Vision and Pattern Recognition, pp. 2574–2582 (2016)
12. Mura, V., et al.: Livdet 2015 fingerprint liveness detection competition 2015. In: 2015 IEEE 7th International Conference on Biometrics Theory, Applications and Systems (BTAS), pp. 1–6. IEEE (2015)
13. Nicolae, M.I., et al.: Adversarial robustness toolbox v1. 0.0. arXiv preprint arXiv:1807.01069 (2018)
14. Nogueira, R.F., de Alencar Lotufo, R., Machado, R.C.: Fingerprint liveness detection using convolutional neural networks. IEEE Trans. Inf. Forensics Secur. **11**(6), 1206–1213 (2016)
15. Orrù, G., et al.: Livdet in action - fingerprint liveness detection competition 2019. In: 2019 International Conference on Biometrics (ICB), pp. 1–6 (2019)

16. Rauber, J., Zimmermann, R., Bethge, M., Brendel, W.: Foolbox native: Fast adversarial attacks to benchmark the robustness of machine learning models in pytorch, tensorflow, and jax. J. Open Source Soft. **5**(53), 2607 (2020)
17. Simonyan, K., Zisserman, A.: Very deep convolutional networks for large-scale image recognition. arXiv preprint arXiv:1409.1556 (2014)
18. Szegedy, C., et al.: Intriguing properties of neural networks. arXiv preprint arXiv:1312.6199 (2013)
19. Zhang, B., Tondi, B., Barni, M.: Adversarial examples for replay attacks against CNN-based face recognition with anti-spoofing capability. Comput. Vis. Image Underst. **197–198**, 102988 (2020). https://doi.org/10.1016/j.cviu.2020.102988

# Learning to Decipher License Plates
# in Severely Degraded Images

Paula Kaiser, Franziska Schirrmacher(✉) ⓘ, Benedikt Lorch ⓘ,
and Christian Riess ⓘ

IT Security Infrastructures Lab, Computer Science,
Friedrich-Alexander University Erlangen-Nürnberg, Erlangen, Germany
`franziska.schirrmacher@fau.de`

**Abstract.** License plate recognition is instrumental in many forensic investigations involving organized crime and gang crime, burglaries and trafficking of illicit goods or persons. After an incident, recordings are collected by police officers from cameras in-the-wild at gas stations or public facilities. In such an uncontrolled environment, a generally low image quality and strong compression oftentimes make it impossible to read license plates. Recent works showed that characters from US license plates can be reconstructed from noisy, low resolution pictures using convolutional neural networks (CNN). However, these studies do not involve compression, which is arguably the most prevalent image degradation in real investigations.

In this paper, we present work toward closing this gap and investigate the impact of JPEG compression on license plate recognition from strongly degraded images. We show the efficacy of the CNN on a real-world dataset of Czech license plates.

Using only synthetic data for training, we show that license plates with a width larger than 30 pixels, an SNR above $-3\,$dB, and a JPEG quality factor down to 15 can at least partially be reconstructed. Additional analyses investigate the influence of the position of the character in the license plate and the similarity of characters.

**Keywords:** License plate recognition · Deep learning · Compression

## 1 Introduction

Forensic investigations aim to reveal the identity of a suspect. This frequently involves the analysis of a surveillance video or picture of the suspect's vehicle. The vehicle license plate is oftentimes instrumental in the identification

We gratefully acknowledge support by the German Federal Ministry of Education and Research (BMBF) under Grant No. 13N15319, the German Research Foundation GRK Cybercrime (393541319/GRK2475/1-2019), and the German Research Foundation (146371743/TRR 89).

P. Kaiser and F. Schirrmacher—Both authors contributed equally to this work.

ⓒ Springer Nature Switzerland AG 2021
A. Del Bimbo et al. (Eds.): ICPR 2020 Workshops, LNCS 12666, pp. 544–559, 2021.
https://doi.org/10.1007/978-3-030-68780-9_43

of suspects. However, investigators collect such images or videos from cameras in-the-wild, which are in many cases low-cost, poorly maintained devices. The types of practically seen image degradations vary greatly. Additionally, image and video compression leads to an inherent loss of information, and the spectrum of compression algorithm further complicates the analysis. Furthermore, the resolution of license plates is oftentimes very low. In summary, the resulting license plates are in many cases not readable by a forensic investigator. In those cases, computational methods to partially or fully reconstruct a license plate are necessary.

Early methods for automatic license plate recognition operate with optical character recognition. The recognition rates of these systems considerably improved with the advent of deep neural networks [21–23]. As of today, deciphering license plates from good-quality images of controlled acquisition setups is well understood and implemented on many highways [3]. Deciphering low-quality images also progressed with the advent of neural networks, and by performing character segmentation and recognition within the same stage [22].

However, severely degraded images, which humans cannot read, are still an open challenge. Agarwal *et al.* showed that even such highly degraded images still contain useful information [2]. Lorch *et al.* extended this work by deciphering synthetic images of low-resolution, noisy US license plates [15]. While these first results are encouraging, they still do not suffice to operate on real images. As shown by recent works [3], additional sources of degradation can significantly hamper the recognition, particularly for images of low resolution, most notably the impact of lossy compression, which is present in virtually all recordings in the wild. In this work, we close this gap by studying the impact of compression in conjunction with low resolution and additional noise. Our study is performed on real and synthetic images of European license plates, more specifically on Czech license plates.

The contributions of this paper are three-fold:

1. We demonstrate the applicability of the CNN on real images of Czech license plates.
2. The influence of compression on the recognition rate is evaluated on synthetic Czech license plates.
3. We provide an in-depth analysis of the influence of similarity and position of characters.

The paper is organized as follows: Sect. 2 provides an overview of existing license plate recognition methods. Section 3 presents the network architecture. Section 4 reports the experiments and discusses the results. Section 5 concludes the paper.

## 2   Related Work

Automatic license plate recognition is a thoroughly studied research topic. In general, the techniques to extract the license plate from the image can be divided into pipeline-based recognition and learning-based approaches. However, the capability of these methods to operate on low-quality images varies considerably and will be discussed below.

## 2.1  Pipeline-Based Recognition

Pipeline-based license plate recognition commonly consists of three stages: First, license plate extraction, which locates and crops the license plate. Second, character segmentation, which splits the license plate into images of the individual characters. Third, character recognition, which labels the images of the individual characters.

*1. Extraction.* Given an image of a car, the goal of the extraction stage is to locate and cut out the license plate [3]. The inspector can manually locate the license plate and determine the coordinates, since the number of images to analyze is typically small in forensic investigations. To obtain a perpendicular view of the license plate, the image is rectified [5].

*2. Segmentation.* Projection profiles are a widely used feature to separate the characters. However, these features are sensitive to rotation and noise, and the number of license plate characters needs to be known beforehand. On the other hand, the computation is fast and independent of the position of the characters [4]. Liu *et al.* exploit additional prior knowledge about Chinese license plates for a successful segmentation. This method is very simple and straightforward, but is inherently limited by specific assumptions on Chinese license plates [13]. Overall, segmentation-based character recognition critically depends on a correct character segmentation. Especially in low-quality images, a good segmentation is oftentimes difficult to achieve.

*3. Recognition.* Arguably the simplest recognition method is template matching. Template matching works well for single-font, non-rotated, non-broken, and fixed-size characters. Rotated characters can also be well recognized when templates under different inclination angles are used. However, this results in an increased computation time [4]. However, feature extraction is more robust than template matching. Wen *et al.* used direction features based on the connected relationship and direction strokes [24]. Other possible features are gradients [14] and local binary patterns [3,12]. Hsieh *et al.* use a sliding window algorithm to avoid separating the characters [17]. However, this method requires explicit knowledge of font style and size, as well as precise character placement.

## 2.2  Learning-Based Approaches

Deep neural networks were successfully used for segmentation-free character recognition in more general environments [8,9]. Li *et al.* adapted this approach to decipher license plates [11]. In this work, a combination of a convolutional neural network (CNN) and a bidirectional recurrent neural network (BRNN) with long

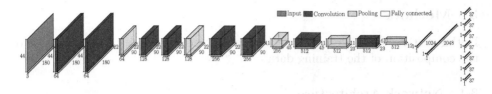

**Fig. 1.** Proposed architecture for severely degraded Czech license plates with seven characters.

short-term memory (LSTM) extracts features from the image. The connectionist temporal classification (CTC) converts the features to the final recognition result, namely the license number. The authors show that the method is able to recognize slightly distorted images, but low-quality data has not been studied. Following up on this work, several conceptually similar approaches have been developed [10, 19, 23].

A general recognition framework that is suitable for real-time applications is You Only Look Once (YOLO) [18]. Redmon *et al.* proposed this method to detect and classify different objects in real-time. Silva *et al.* modified YOLO to recognize letters and digits to fit their data. They demonstrate its use on Brazilian license plates [20] as well as license plates from other countries [21]. Abdullah *et al.* showed that YOLO can be retrained without architectural modification to recognize digits and detect Bangla characters in license plates [1].

Gonçalves *et al.* proposed the use of deep multi-tasking learning. Each task classifies one character of the license plate from the entire image. This method is suitable for real-time applications and recognizes multiple license plate characters in the same frame [7]. Španhel *et al.* [22] proposed a CNN that can predict eight characters of license plate including a blank fill character for shorter license plate numbers.

In forensic investigations, speed is oftentimes less important than accuracy when deciphering non-human-readable license plates. Agarwal *et al.* showed that useful information is present even in highly degraded images, distorted by noise and low resolution [2]. Two separate CNNs decipher three characters of the license plate each. Their network significantly outperformed human observers on synthetic US data. Lorch *et al.* further improved their method [15]. They deciphered all characters at once and introduced a null character to recognize license numbers of variable length.

In police investigations, officers oftentimes rely on data that was captured by low-cost surveillance cameras. Here, strong compression leads to a decrease in the image quality and a possible loss of information. So far, compression is not covered in the related work. This paper aims towards closing this gap. We examine the performance of a CNN deciphering severely degraded license plates on images with strong lossy compression. We also empirically determine a lower bound for deciphering at least some characters of a license plate in very strongly compressed images.

# 3    Methods

In this section, we describe the network architecture, training parameters, and the composition of the training data.

## 3.1    Network Architecture

We adapt the CNN presented by Lorch *et al.* [15] to analyze the impact of the compression on license plate recognition. Figure 1 shows an overview of the used network. Compared to Lorch *et al.* [15], the input layer (red) of the network is adapted to $44 \times 180$ to better match the aspect ratio of European license plates. The remaining design decisions are identical, and briefly summarized below.

Eight convolutional layers (blue) extract features from the input image with kernel size $3 \times 3$, a stride of one and zero-padding for persisting spatial size. Pooling layers (gray) with kernel size $2 \times 2$ are inserted after the second, fourth, sixth, seventh and eighth convolutional layer. The first and third pooling layer cut the spatial size in half with a stride of two, while the second pooling layer does not affect the size by using a stride of one. The fourth pooling layer uses a stride of two horizontally and a stride of one vertically. The last pooling layer reduces the spatial size from $11 \times 23$ to $6 \times 12$ with a stride of two using zero-padding both on the right and on the bottom.

The resulting feature volume of size $6 \times 12 \times 512$ is flattened to a feature vector. This vector is passed to two consecutive fully-connected layers with 1 024 and 2 048 neurons. The fully-connected layers are followed by seven output layers, one for every character in the license plate. Each output layer consists of 37 units to represent 26 letters of the Latin alphabet, the digits from 0 to 9, and one null character. The null character is used for license plates with less than seven characters. The results of the output layers are passed to a softmax function, which normalizes the scores for each character to a probability distribution.

All convolutional layers and the first two fully-connected layers use the ReLU activation function. The weights of the convolutional layers and the output layers are initialized with the Xavier initialization [6]. The first two fully-connected layers are initialized with a truncated normal distribution with zero-mean and a standard derivation of 0.005. The biases of the output layers are initialized with 0, the other biases with 0.1.

The parameters are updated using mini-batch gradient descent with a batch size of 32. The magnitude of those updates is defined by the learning rate, which starts at 0.005 and decays stepwise exponentially. The decay step is the number of batches in one epoch and the decay rate is 0.9. Overfitting is reduced by using dropout in the two fully-connected layers and the output layers with a probability $p = 0.5$. The training is stopped if the validation accuracy does not change for 100 000 training iterations.

## 3.2    Synthetic Training Data

In order to obtain a high prediction rate, the network needs to be trained with a large number of training examples. However, obtaining many real-world images is

**Fig. 2.** The pipeline for generating license plates consists of five steps. First, the frame and font are printed and cropped. Then the image is degraded by downsampling, additive noise, and compression.

expensive. A good alternative is generating images of license plates synthetically. The proposed dataset is created similarly to the procedure described by Lorch *et al.* [15] and includes 10 million training, 2 000 validation and 750 000 test images.

Czech license plates are composed of seven characters with fixed positions. Exceptions to this are only historic vehicles and personalized plates, which are rare and will not be considered in this work. Czech regulations specify the font, the font size and measurements like gap sizes and offsets [16]. In this work, we only consider regular Czech license plates, which have the following constraints: At the first position only the digits one to nine are possible. However, in the real world there is a very low probability that a character is present in the first position. The second position represents the region, where the license plate is issued. Letters related to a region are A,B,C,E,H,J,K,L,M,P,S,T,U, and Z. The number of license plates per region is not considered. The third position does not have additional constraints, whereas at positions four to seven only digits are possible. Since the characters G, O, Q, and W are not used at all in Czech license plates, they do not appear in the training data. Grayscale images are used, since there is little additional information in the color channels.

Figure 2 provides an overview of the pipeline to generate the synthetic license plates. First, font and frame are printed to an image with random background. For every image a dark font on a bright background or a bright font on a dark background is randomly chosen. The contrast between fore- and background is randomly chosen as well. After tightly cropping the plate, image degradation is performed. Common forms of degradation, which notably lower the image quality are low resolution, noise, and compression.

*Low Resolution.* Low-cost cameras with small sensors result in low-resolution images. In addition, the license plate usually occupies only a few pixels of the image, and vehicles may pass a camera only at a large distance. Thus, we downsample the generated high-resolution images and consider an effective width of the license plate from 30 to 180 pixels with fixed aspect ratio. For training, a continuous range of license plate widths is used. For the test data, we consider seven levels of resolution (30, 50, 70, 90, 120, 150, and 180 pixels). To obtain a uniform size as input to the CNN, the images are upsampled to a size of $180 \times 44$ pixels with nearest neighbor interpolation after noise is added and compression is applied.

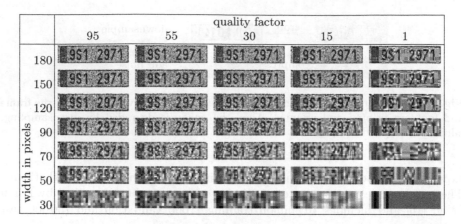

**Fig. 3.** Example images of the synthetic Czech dataset with an SNR of 3 dB and different sizes and JPEG quality factors. A quality factor of one leads to a huge loss of information, especially in small images.

*Noise.* Noise is a widespread issue in real-world applications. A common assumption is that noise is mostly caused by the camera sensor during the acquisition. Oftentimes, unknown noise models are approximated by additive white Gaussian noise. Here, the noisy image $f = s + n$ is the sum of a noise-free image $s$ and a noise component $n$. The magnitude of the noise is given by the signal-to-noise-ratio (SNR), which can be described with the power of signal and noise:

$$\text{SNR} = \frac{\text{power}(s)}{\text{power}(n)} = \frac{\sigma_s^2}{\sigma_n^2} \,, \tag{1}$$

where $\sigma_s^2$ denotes the power spectrum of the signal, and $\sigma_n^2$ denotes the power spectrum of the noise. For zero-mean noise and signal, the SNR is the fraction of the variances $\sigma^2$. In the experiments, we report the noise level in dB, which corresponds to the base-10 logarithm of the SNR. For the training data, the SNR ranges from –3 to 20 dB. For the test data, three levels of SNR (–3, 3 and 20 dB) are used, which corresponds to a severe, a moderate and a low noise level.

*Compression.* Lossy compression is the most effective way of reducing the storage size, and arguably the most common type of image degradation. Such compression particularly reduces the image quality and causes a loss of information. While different compression formats exist, this work adopts JPEG compression, as JPEG is probably the most prominent storage format. The JPEG quality factor allows to trade image quality for file size. The JPEG quality factors reported in this work correspond to the quality argument used in the Python library Pillow. The JPEG quality factor in the training dataset ranges between 1 and 95. For testing, we use five levels of compression (1, 15, 30, 55, and 95).

See Fig. 3 for example images with an SNR of 3 dB and the different sizes and JPEG quality factors used for the test set.

# 4  Experiments

This section comprises the evaluation of the proposed method. The convolutional neural network (CNN) is trained and tested on different datasets in order to answer two questions: How does distortion, especially compression, influence the recognition? Is the proposed network capable of deciphering severely degraded Czech license plates?

Our evaluation consists of two parts. First, the network performance and generalizability of the training on the synthetic training data is quantitatively evaluated on the real-world dataset. Second, we show on the synthetic dataset an in-depth analysis of the impact of three distortion parameters, namely compression, low resolution, and noise, on the recognition rates.

## 4.1  Evaluation Metric

Analogously to previous works we report the top-$n$ accuracies as figures of merit. In this metric, the network predictions for each character are sorted by their softmax output. If the correct character is within the $n$ highest likelihoods, we count it as a hit, otherwise as a miss. The reported top-$n$ accuracies are relative hit rates, averaged over all individual characters of all license plates. We specifically report top-1, top-3, and top-5 accuracies.

## 4.2  Performance on Degraded Real-World Test Data

*Dataset Description.* The real-world Czech test set is used to evaluate the trained network on real data. Špaňhel *et al.* [22] published the dataset "ReId", containing 76 412 real pictures of European license plates. The authors placed Full-HD video cameras in eight different locations and under different conditions. The images are labeled and the plates cropped. The large majority of vehicles are Czech, the remaining ones are registered in other European countries. The images are converted to grayscale and either cropped or resized to size $180 \times 44$ pixels. The license plates in this dataset are mostly human-readable but of low quality, as seen in Fig. 4 [22]. While Czech license plates are limited to 7 characters, the small subset of non-Czech license plates may also contain an eighth character. To adjust our CNN for this potential failure case in this experiment, we added an eight output unit and trained the CNN with our synthetic 7-character license plates. Thus, it always outputs the empty character at the eighth position. In line with the ground truth annotations by Špaňhel *et al.*, this empty character is counted as hit on Czech 7-character license plates, and as miss on 8-character license plates.

*Evaluation Results.* We compare the proposed network to the CNN presented by Špaňhel *et al.* [22]. The authors report a top-1 accuracy of 98.6% on the ReId dataset. To evaluate how realistic the synthetic dataset is in comparison to the real-world data, we train the proposed CNN on the synthetic training data and evaluate the performance on the real-world test data. The results are

| Method | top-1 | top-3 | top-5 |
|---|---|---|---|
| Špaňhel *et al.* [22] | 98.6% | - | - |
| CNN synthetic | 89.8% | 95.6% | 97.3% |
| CNN fine-tuned | 97.3% | 98.7% | 99.0% |

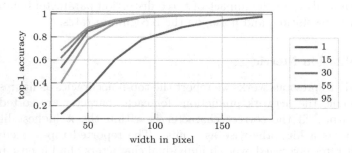

**Fig. 4.** Top-1, top-3 and top-5 accuracy (left) on the real-world Czech dataset (right) of the proposed network trained on synthetic data and fine-tuned on the real-world training data. The top-1 accuracy is compared to the values reported by [22]. The license plates are mostly human-readable, but distortions such as blur, low contrast, or occlusion can still occur.

**Fig. 5.** Influence of the compression rate on the license plate recognition rate. We report the top-1 accuracy of five different compression levels in relation to the width of the license plate in pixels.

shown in the top and middle row of the table in Fig. 4. The proposed CNN achieves a top-1 accuracy of 89.8%. This result is 8.8% lower than the results reported by Špaňhel *et al.*. The performance gap can be attributed to a number of influences that are not modeled by the synthetic dataset. We only model Czech license plates, hence unseen appearances of non-Czech license plates are potential failure cases. Additionally, the real data contains notable amounts of blur and perspective rotation, which is also not modelled in our synthetic data.

To provide a reference on the overall network performance, we additionally fine-tune the network on the real-world training data by Špaňhel *et al.* with a learning rate of 0.005. This allows to fill gaps from training on synthetic data with dataset-specific training data. The results are shown in the bottom row of the table in Fig. 4. With fine-tuning, a top-1 accuracy of 97.3% is achieved, which is comparable to the results reported by Špaňhel *et al.* [22]. Thus, the proposed CNN itself has the capability to model the task of license plate recognition. This experiment shows that the CNN does not model all effects of real-world images when training exclusively on synthetic data. Nevertheless, we argue that the performance is sufficiently high for a further analysis of the impact of individual image degradations on license plate recognition.

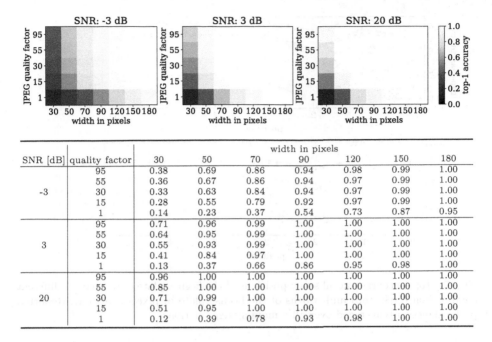

| | | width in pixels | | | | | | |
|---|---|---|---|---|---|---|---|---|
| SNR [dB] | quality factor | 30 | 50 | 70 | 90 | 120 | 150 | 180 |
| | 95 | 0.38 | 0.69 | 0.86 | 0.94 | 0.98 | 0.99 | 1.00 |
| | 55 | 0.36 | 0.67 | 0.86 | 0.94 | 0.97 | 0.99 | 1.00 |
| -3 | 30 | 0.33 | 0.63 | 0.84 | 0.94 | 0.97 | 0.99 | 1.00 |
| | 15 | 0.28 | 0.55 | 0.79 | 0.92 | 0.97 | 0.99 | 1.00 |
| | 1 | 0.14 | 0.23 | 0.37 | 0.54 | 0.73 | 0.87 | 0.95 |
| | 95 | 0.71 | 0.96 | 0.99 | 1.00 | 1.00 | 1.00 | 1.00 |
| | 55 | 0.64 | 0.95 | 0.99 | 1.00 | 1.00 | 1.00 | 1.00 |
| 3 | 30 | 0.55 | 0.93 | 0.99 | 1.00 | 1.00 | 1.00 | 1.00 |
| | 15 | 0.41 | 0.84 | 0.97 | 1.00 | 1.00 | 1.00 | 1.00 |
| | 1 | 0.13 | 0.37 | 0.66 | 0.86 | 0.95 | 0.98 | 1.00 |
| | 95 | 0.96 | 1.00 | 1.00 | 1.00 | 1.00 | 1.00 | 1.00 |
| | 55 | 0.85 | 1.00 | 1.00 | 1.00 | 1.00 | 1.00 | 1.00 |
| 20 | 30 | 0.71 | 0.99 | 1.00 | 1.00 | 1.00 | 1.00 | 1.00 |
| | 15 | 0.51 | 0.95 | 1.00 | 1.00 | 1.00 | 1.00 | 1.00 |
| | 1 | 0.12 | 0.39 | 0.78 | 0.93 | 0.98 | 1.00 | 1.00 |

**Fig. 6.** Top-1 accuracy on the synthetic Czech dataset at different degradation levels (top). Full table of all top-1 accuracies on the synthetic dataset, split by additive noise, JPEG quality factor and the pixel width of the license plate (bottom).

### 4.3 Experiments on the Impact of Image Degradations

All experiments in this section are performed on the synthetic dataset. The purpose of these controlled experiments is to assess the influence of various image degradations on the recognition rate. We specifically investigate the level of JPEG compression and additive noise, the influence of the character position on the recognition rate, and the similarity between characters. When averaging the recognition performances on the synthetic dataset over all license plates, all characters, all positions, and all degradation levels, then the top-1 accuracy of the CNN is 85.4%, the top-3 accuracy is 93.1%, and the top-5 accuracy is 96.0%.

*JPEG Compression Versus Pixel Resolution.* JPEG compression can lead to an inherent loss of information. Hence, it is insightful to investigate a lower bound for reliable character recognition under a given JPEG compression strength. Figure 5 shows the top-1 accuracy for different JPEG quality factors in dependence of the width of the license plate in pixels. The results are averaged over all noise levels.

We can observe that the JPEG compression has a considerable impact on the recognition accuracy for image widths below 70 pixels. That is not surprising, considering that for such small images the license plate is encoded in only very few JPEG blocks. Strong compression removes high-frequency information that

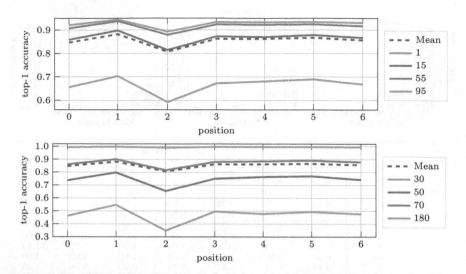

**Fig. 7.** Top-1 accuracy at all seven positions of the license plate evaluated for different compression rates (top) and widths of the license plate in pixels (bottom). Reported performances are averaged over all remaining degradations.

would be particularly important to distinguish characters at such low resolution. This suggests a trade-off between image resolution and JPEG compression strength. For example, the performances for JPEG qualities 55 and 95 are barely distinguishable for images that are wider than 50 pixels. On the other hand, a (rather extreme) JPEG compression quality of 1, which removes virtually all content within a JPEG block, requires image widths of 90 pixels and beyond to achieve acceptable accuracies. At JPEG quality 1 with the smallest image width of 30 pixels, the CNN performance is effectively at guessing rate.

*Impact of Added Noise and Compression.* Figure 6 illustrates the top-1 accuracy for noise levels of –3 dB, 3 dB, and 20 dB averaged over all license plate positions. Each chart is subdivided by the license plate width and the JPEG quality factor. The exact numerical values corresponding to this experiment are listed in the table below.

The results show that the width of the license plates must be above 30 pixels to obtain reliable results in the presence of other degradations. Images with an SNR of –3 dB or a JPEG quality factor of one can be deciphered only if the remaining degradations are negligible.

*Influence of the Character Position.* The rules for Czech license plates constrain for each position of the license plate the set of admissible characters. In this analysis, we investigate the recognition accuracy per position of the license plate.

Figure 7 shows the top-1 accuracy of the network for different compression rates (top) and different input sizes (bottom), averaged over all remaining distortions. For reference, the mean over all degradations is displayed in both plots.

**Table 1.** Average predictions for the different characters in the test data. The column char shows the characters in the font that is used in Czech license plates. The three highest confidences are shown in the columns c1 to c3, the corresponding characters are shown in the columns p1 to p3.

| char | top-1 | p1 | p2 | p3 | c1 | c2 | c3 | char | top-1 | p1 | p2 | p3 | c1 | c2 | c3 |
|------|-------|----|----|----|------|------|------|------|-------|----|----|----|------|------|------|
| 0 | 0.86 | 0 | 8 | 6 | 0.82 | 0.03 | 0.03 | H | 0.86 | H | M | U | 0.82 | 0.03 | 0.03 |
| 1 | 0.89 | 1 | 3 | 7 | 0.87 | 0.03 | 0.02 | I | 0.83 | I | 1 | T | 0.79 | 0.03 | 0.03 |
| 2 | 0.88 | 2 | 7 | 3 | 0.86 | 0.03 | 0.03 | J | 0.91 | J | U | Z | 0.88 | 0.02 | 0.01 |
| 3 | 0.86 | 3 | 2 | 1 | 0.83 | 0.03 | 0.03 | K | 0.83 | K | E | A | 0.81 | 0.03 | 0.02 |
| 4 | 0.91 | 4 | 6 | 2 | 0.89 | 0.02 | 0.01 | L | 0.90 | L | E | C | 0.87 | 0.03 | 0.02 |
| 5 | 0.84 | 5 | 6 | 8 | 0.81 | 0.04 | 0.03 | M | 0.89 | M | H | B | 0.86 | 0.04 | 0.01 |
| 6 | 0.79 | 6 | 8 | 5 | 0.76 | 0.08 | 0.05 | N | 0.82 | N | H | 8 | 0.78 | 0.03 | 0.03 |
| 7 | 0.90 | 7 | 2 | 1 | 0.87 | 0.04 | 0.02 | P | 0.87 | P | E | M | 0.85 | 0.02 | 0.01 |
| 8 | 0.82 | 8 | 6 | 9 | 0.78 | 0.06 | 0.03 | R | 0.75 | R | 8 | 6 | 0.73 | 0.03 | 0.02 |
| 9 | 0.82 | 9 | 8 | 0 | 0.80 | 0.05 | 0.03 | S | 0.80 | S | B | C | 0.78 | 0.02 | 0.02 |
| A | 0.86 | A | K | B | 0.84 | 0.01 | 0.01 | T | 0.87 | T | Z | Y | 0.84 | 0.02 | 0.02 |
| B | 0.79 | B | 8 | H | 0.76 | 0.03 | 0.06 | U | 0.83 | U | H | J | 0.81 | 0.04 | 0.02 |
| C | 0.84 | C | E | L | 0.81 | 0.03 | 0.02 | V | 0.83 | V | 9 | 8 | 0.80 | 0.02 | 0.02 |
| D | 0.72 | D | 0 | U | 0.68 | 0.09 | 0.03 | X | 0.78 | X | Y | K | 0.75 | 0.02 | 0.02 |
| E | 0.85 | E | C | L | 0.81 | 0.03 | 0.02 | Y | 0.79 | Y | T | 1 | 0.76 | 0.04 | 0.03 |
| F | 0.81 | F | P | E | 0.78 | 0.05 | 0.04 | Z | 0.85 | Z | 2 | T | 0.83 | 0.03 | 0.02 |

On top of Fig. 7, the accuracy for the JPEG quality factor 15 is already above the average, which can be attributed to the fact that larger license plates are less susceptible to compression. The higher JPEG quality factors 55 and 95 yield only about 5% higher performances. Qualitatively, the curves have similar shape. A quality factor of 1 leads to a drastic decrease of the top-1 accuracy, since only license plates with a high resolution can still be deciphered. On the bottom of Fig. 7, the image width exhibits a similar dependency as previously observed for JPEG compression, with a major performance drop for license plates with a width of only 30 pixels.

In both plots of Fig. 7, position 3 is particularly difficult to recognize. Here, Czech license plates exhibit the largest variability, as all digits and 22 letters can be used. The best top-1 accuracy is at position two, even though the number of possible characters is smaller for position one. The same effect can also be observed in the last and the second last positions, where only numbers are allowed. This can be attributed to the cropping of the image, since this affects characters at the license plate boundary.

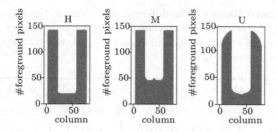

**Fig. 8.** Similarity of the horizontal projections of the characters $H$, $M$ and $U$.

**Table 2.** Change of confusion order for different JPEG quality factors.

| quality factor | char | p1 | p2 | p3 | c1 | c2 | c3 | char | p1 | p2 | p3 | c1 | c2 | c3 |
|---|---|---|---|---|---|---|---|---|---|---|---|---|---|---|
| 1 | C | C | E | U | 0.58 | 0.04 | 0.04 | P | P | E | H | 0.62 | 0.04 | 0.03 |
| 15 | C | C | E | Z | 0.83 | 0.03 | 0.02 | P | P | M | F | 0.87 | 0.02 | 0.01 |
| 95 | C | C | E | L | 0.90 | 0.02 | 0.01 | P | P | F | E | 0.92 | 0.01 | 0.01 |

*Similarity of Characters.* At any position, some characters are more difficult
to recognize than others. Table 1 shows for every character the top-1 accuracy
(top-1). Additionally, the three characters (predictions p1 to p3) with the highest
average confidences (c1 to c3) are displayed. Those values are averaged over all
degradation levels and positions. The column "char" shows the character in the
font that is used in the license plates. It is important to notice that this table is
averaged over all positions. The network learned which characters are possible
at a certain position. For example, at positions four to seven, only digits are
allowed. At those positions the network does not mistakenly predict a letter,
even if they are very similar, like 8 and $B$. At position three, however, 8 and $B$
are frequently confused. Digits appear at five positions, four of which allow only
digits. Therefore, the top-3 predictions for digits only include digits.

Overall, recognition rates of unique characters are higher than recognition
rates of groups of similar characters. However, similarity is measured w.r.t. the
features extracted by the convolutional layers. Those features are learned by the
network and are inherently difficult to analyze. However, possible features could
be the direction and position of strokes and horizontal projection. Direction
and position of strokes are similar if characters share parts of their strokes. For
example, $B$ and 8 are very similar, since parts of the characters are the same.
The reason why $H$ is confused with $M$ and $U$ could be the similarity of their
horizontal projections, which can be seen in Fig. 8. Another factor of influence
on the prediction rates is the number of occurrences in the training data. The
letters D, F, I, N, R ,V, X, and Y only occur at position three. Therefore, the
network has extracted the features of those letters less often. It is possible that
those features are less sophisticated and therefore lower the prediction rates.

We additionally investigate the influence of the compression on the similarity of characters. While for letters such as F, D, I, L, and M the order of the confusion does not change for the three most frequent predictions, it changes for other characters. This can be explained with varying compression artifacts which change for certain characters with the JPEG quality factor. Two examples are shown in Tab. 2. The letter C is confused with the letter E for all quality factors. Just the prediction three changes with higher quality factor. On the other hand, the letter P is mixed up with the letters E, M, and F for the quality factors 1, 15, and 95 respectively. This shows that a confusion table of network predictions to support police work has to be conditioned on the compression strength, which we will investigate in future work.

## 5  Conclusion

This paper investigates the recognition of license plates where the images have been subject to JPEG compression and other forms of strong degradation. To this end, a synthetic Czech dataset is created with low-resolution, noisy, and compressed images. We show that training a network with this dataset can act as a surrogate for a real-world dataset for analyzing image degradations.

Our analysis on the impact of image degradations on character recognition shows that for smaller images compression has a greater impact than for larger images. A quality factor of 1 leads to a drastic decrease in the recognition rate, almost at guessing rate for small images. Overall, synthetic Czech license plates can be reliably reconstructed if the width is above 30 pixels, the SNR is above $-3\,\mathrm{dB}$, and the JPEG quality factor is at least 15. We also observed that image resolution has a larger impact than compression when the character is highly variable, such as at the third position of Czech license plates. Furthermore, police investigations might benefit from character confusion tables. We show that such tables have to be created in dependency of the compression strength of the input image. We will consider this in our future work to further improve license plate recognition from images in the wild, i.e., with uncontrolled image degradations.

## References

1. Abdullah, S., Mahedi Hasan, M., Islam, S.: YOLO-based three-stage network for Bangla license plate recognition in Dhaka metropolitan city. In: International Conference on Bangla Speech and Language Processing, pp. 1–6 (2018)
2. Agarwal, S., Tran, D., Torresani, L., Farid, H.: Deciphering severely degraded license plates. In: Media Watermarking, Security, and Forensics, pp. 138–143 (2017)
3. Arafat, M.Y., Khairuddin, A.S.M., Khairuddin, U., Paramesran, R.: Systematic review on vehicular licence plate recognition framework in intelligent transport systems. IET Intel. Transport Syst. **13**, 745–755 (2019)

4. Du, S., Ibrahim, M., Shehata, M., Badawy, W.: Automatic license plate recognition (ALPR): a state-of-the-art review. IEEE Trans. Circuits Syst. Video Technol. **23**(2), 311–325 (2013)
5. Farid, H.: Photo Forensics. MIT Press, Cambridge (2016)
6. Glorot, X., Bengio, Y.: Understanding the difficulty of training deep feedforward neural networks. In: International Conference on Artificial Intelligence and Statistics, pp. 249–256 (2010)
7. Gonçalves, G.R., Diniz, M.A., Laroca, R., Menotti, D., Schwartz, W.R.: Real-time automatic license plate recognition through deep multi-task networks. In: 31st Conference on Graphics, Patterns and Images, pp. 110–117 (2018)
8. Goodfellow, I., Bulatov, Y., Ibarz, J., Arnoud, S., Shet, V.: Multi-digit number recognition from street view imagery using deep convolutional neural networks. In: International Conference on Learning Representations (2014)
9. Jaderberg, M., Simonyan, K., Vedaldi, A., Zisserman, A.: Reading text in the wild with convolutional neural networks. Int. J. of Comput. Vis. **116**(1), 1–20 (2016)
10. Kilic, I., Aydin, G.: Turkish vehicle license plate recognition using deep learning. In: International Conference on Artificial Intelligence and Data Processing, pp. 1–5 (2018)
11. Li, H., Wang, P., You, M., Shen, C.: Reading car license plates using deep neural networks. Image Vis. Comput. **72**, 14–23 (2018)
12. Liu, L., Zhang, H., Feng, A., Wan, X., Guo, J.: Simplified local binary pattern descriptor for character recognition of vehicle license plate. In: International Conference on Computer Graphics, Imaging and Visualization, pp. 157–161 (2010)
13. Liu, P., Li, G., Tu, D.: Low-quality license plate character recognition based on CNN. In: International Symposium on Computational Intelligence and Design, pp. 53–58 (2015)
14. Llorens, D., Marzal, A., Palazón, V., Vilar, J.M.: Car license plates extraction and recognition based on connected components analysis and HMM decoding. In: Pattern Recognition and Image Analysis, pp. 571–578 (2005)
15. Lorch, B., Agarwal, S., Farid, H.: Forensic reconstruction of severely degraded license plates. In: Electronic Imaging (January 2019)
16. Ministerstvo vnitra České republiky: Collection of laws no. 343/2014 (2014). https://aplikace.mvcr.cz/sbirka-zakonu/ViewFile.aspx?type=z&id=27609
17. Pei-Lun, H., Liang, Y.M., Liao, H.Y.M.: Recognition of blurred license plate images. In: IEEE International Workshop on Information Forensics and Security (2010)
18. Redmon, J., Divvala, S., Girshick, R., Farhadi, A.: You only look once: unified, real-time object detection. In: IEEE Conference on Computer Vision and Pattern Recognition (2016)
19. Shivakumara, P., Tang, D., Asadzadeh, M., Lu, T., Pal, U., Anisi, H.: CNN-RNN based method for license plate recognition. CAAI Trans. on Intell. Technol. **3**(3), 169–175 (2018)
20. Silva, S.M., Jung, C.R.: Real-time Brazilian license plate detection and recognition using deep convolutional neural networks. In: Conference on Graphics, Patterns and Images, pp. 55–62 (2017)

21. Silva, S.M., Jung, C.R.: License plate detection and recognition in unconstrained scenarios. In: European Conference on Computer Vision, pp. 580–596 (2018)
22. Špaňhel, J., Sochor, J., Juránek, R., Herout, A., Maršík, L., Zemčík, P.: Holistic recognition of low quality license plates by CNN using track annotated data. In: IEEE International Conference on Advanced Video and Signal Based Surveillance, pp. 1–6 (2017)
23. Suvarnam, B., Ch, V.S.: Combination of CNN-GRU model to recognize characters of a license plate number without segmentation. In: International Conference on Advanced Computing & Communication Systems, pp. 317–322 (2019)
24. Wen, Y., Lu, Y., Yan, J., Zhou, Z., Von Deneen, K., Shi, P.: An algorithm for license plate recognition applied to intelligent transportation system. IEEE Trans. Intell. Transp. Syst. **12**, 830–845 (2011)

# Differential Morphed Face Detection
# Using Deep Siamese Networks

Sobhan Soleymani[(⊠)] [iD], Baaria Chaudhary [iD], Ali Dabouei [iD],
Jeremy Dawson [iD], and Nasser M. Nasrabadi [iD]

West Virginia University, Morgantown, WV 26506, USA
{ssoleyma,bac0062,ad0046}@mix.wvu.edu,
{jeremy.dawson,nasser.nasrabadi}@mail.wvu.edu

**Abstract.** Although biometric facial recognition systems are fast
becoming part of security applications, these systems are still vulnerable to morphing attacks, in which a facial reference image can be verified as two or more separate identities. In border control scenarios, a
successful morphing attack allows two or more people to use the same
passport to cross borders. In this paper, we propose a novel differential morph attack detection framework using a deep Siamese network.
To the best of our knowledge, this is the first research work that makes
use of a Siamese network architecture for morph attack detection. We
compare our model with other classical and deep learning models using
two distinct morph datasets, VISAPP17 and MorGAN. We explore the
embedding space generated by the contrastive loss using three decision
making frameworks using Euclidean distance, feature difference and a
support vector machine classifier, and feature concatenation and a support vector machine classifier.

**Keywords:** Differential morph detection · Siamese network ·
Contrastive loss

## 1 Introduction

Biometric facial recognition systems have increasingly been integrated into border control and other security applications that utilize identification tasks, such
as official identity cards, surveillance, and law enforcement. These systems provide high accuracy at a low operational cost. In addition, face capture is noninvasive and benefits from a relatively high social acceptance. People use their
faces to unlock their phones and also to recognize their friends and family. Furthermore, facial recognition systems contain an automatic fail-safe: if the algorithm triggers a false alarm, a human expert on-site can easily perform the verification. For these reasons, facial recognition systems enjoy a sizable advantage

S. Soloeymani and B. Chaudhary—Contributed Equally.

This work is based upon a work supported by the Center for Identification Technology
Research and the National Science Foundation under Grant #1650474.

A. Del Bimbo et al. (Eds.): ICPR 2020 Workshops, LNCS 12666, pp. 560–572, 2021.
https://doi.org/10.1007/978-3-030-68780-9_44

**Table 1.** Differential morph algorithms.

| Algorithm | Method | Database |
|---|---|---|
| Face demorphing [1,27] | Image subtraction | MorphDB, landmark-based |
| Mutli-algorithm fusion approach [21] | Feature vectors and feature difference | Landmark-based |
| Deep models [7] | Feature embeddings | GAN-based |
| Our method – deep Siamese network | $L_2$ difference of embedding representations | Landmarkbased, and GAN-based |

over other biometric systems. Consequently, the International Civil Aviation Organization (ICAO) has mandated the inclusion of a facial reference image in all electronic passports worldwide [16]. This means that the only biometric identifier present in passports globally is the face.

Although facial recognition systems are largely successful, they still are not impervious to attack. The mass adoption of automatic biometric systems in border control has revealed critical vulnerabilities in the border security scheme, namely the inability of these systems to accurately detect a falsified image. This vulnerability is further exacerbated by a loophole in the passport application process: the facial reference image, either digitally or as a physical print, is provided by the applicant at the time of enrollment. This opens a window for the applicant to potentially manipulate the image before application submission. One type of manipulation that is recently identified as a serious threat is the morph attack [10], in which a facial reference image can be verified as two or more separate identities. A successful morphing attack allows two or more people to utilize the same passport to travel.

Thus, a criminal attacker, who otherwise cannot travel freely, could obtain a valid passport by morphing his face with that of an accomplice [10]. Many morphing applications are not only freely available and easily accessible but also have no knowledge barrier [22]. As such, it is almost absurdly simple for a criminal to procure a legitimate travel document. There are only a few straightforward steps: (1) find an accomplice with similar facial features, (2) morph both faces together such that existing facial recognition systems would classify the resulting morphed face as either of the original individuals, (3) the accomplice applies for a passport with the morphed image. The resulting passport could then be used by both the criminal and the accomplice to travel as they wish. Currently, we are unaware of any system in the passport verification process that is designed specifically for the detection of these manipulations. Moreover, commercial off-the-shelf systems (COTS) have repeatedly failed to detect morphed images [27]. Likewise, studies show human recognizers are also unable to correctly differentiate a morphed facial image from an authentic one [3,26,27].

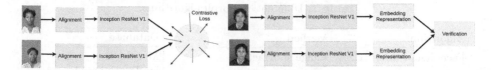

**Fig. 1.** Network architecture: Image pairs are fed into the MTCNN for face detection and alignment, then into the Inception ResNET v1, where contrastive loss is applied. From the feature embedding representation, verification is conducted by computing the $L_2$ distance between the feature vectors and a decision score is produced. Left) the training phase on WVU Twins Day dataset and the training portion of the morph dataset and right) the test phase.

We propose to develop a novel differential morphing attack detection algorithm using a deep Siamese network. The Siamese network takes image pairs as inputs and yields a confidence score on the likelihood that the face images are from the same person. We employ a pre-trained Inception ResNET v1 as the base network. The experiments are conducted on two separate morphed image datasets: VISAPP17 [21] and MorGAN [7,8]. Results show an D-EER of 5.6% for VISAPAP17 and an D-EER of 12.5% for MorGAN. In the following sections, we briefly summarize the related works in Section 2, explain the methodology in Section 3, and discuss our experiments and subsequent results in Section 4. Finally, conclusions are presented in Section 5.

## 2 Related Works

The vulnerability of face recognition systems to morph attacks was first introduced by [10]. Since then, many morph detection algorithms have been proposed of two types: single (no reference) and differential. Single (no reference) morph attack detection algorithms rely solely on the potential morphed image to make their classification. Morphs are detected by extracting and analyzing features from the image in an attempt to identify the unique artifacts that indicate the face image was morphed or tampered with. On the other hand, differential morph attack detection algorithms rely on an additional trusted image, typically a live capture at border security, to compare the potential morphed image with. As such, differential morphing attack detection algorithms have more information at their disposal to make their classification and therefore perform significantly better than single morph detection algorithms [30].

The majority of the current research exists solely in the single morph attack detection domain. Many classical hand-crafted feature extraction techniques have been explored to solve this problem. The most well-performing of these general image descriptors is Binarized Statistical Image Features (BSIF) [17], used in [24], in which extracted BSIF features were classified using a Support Vector Machine (SVM). Deep learning methods have also been proposed [25,33,36]. In [25], complementary features from VGG-19 and AlexNet, both pre-trained on ImageNet and additionally fine-tuned on a morph dataset, are concatenated and then used to train a Probabilistic Collaborative Representation-based Classifier (ProCRC). A multi-algorithm fusion approach that combines texture descriptors, keypoint descriptors, gradient estimators, and deep neural network methods has also shown promising results [29]. The authors extract BSIF and Local Binary Pattern (LBP) [18] features to obtain feature vectors. Other feature descriptors such as Scale Invariant Feature Transform (SIFT) [20] and Speeded-Up Robust Features (SURF) [2] are also used to extract keypoint descriptors and Histogram of Gradients (HOG) is used as a gradient estimator. Finally, deep feature embeddings from the OpenFace DNN are used as the last feature vector. All the above feature vectors are then used to train separate SVMs. In the end, score-level fusion is applied to obtain the final decision score for the potential morphed image.

There are a few papers also that address differential morph attack detection. Of these, reverting of a face morph or face demorphing [11,12] has provided encouraging results. The demorphing algorithm subtracts the potential morphed image from the trusted image and uses the difference for classification. Feature extraction methods used in single morph attack detection can also be applied to the differential problem domain as well by taking the difference of the feature vectors of the potential morphed image and the trusted image. This difference vector along with the original feature vector for the potential morphed image were then used to train a difference SVM and a feature SVM, respectively. Score-level fusion is used to arrive at the final decision score. This method is explored in [30] using LBP, BSIF, SIFT, SURF, and HOG descriptors. Scherhag et al. [31] uses deep face representations from feature embeddings extracted from a deep neural network to detect a morph attack. The authors of [31] also emphasized the need for high-variance and constructed their morph image database using multiple morph algorithms. Several post-processing steps were also applied to emulate the actual compression methods used in storing passport photos in electronic passports, including reducing resolution, JPEG200 compression, and printing-and-scanning. Table 1 compares the existing differential morph algorithms.

Although these methods have shown some success, none are sufficiently robust. These algorithms train on morph datasets of very limited size and scope. When tested on additional datasets, they perform poorly, indicating the models overfit [28]. These results are notably evident in the NIST FRVT morph detection test [23], in which nearly all the algorithms submitted exhibited low performance on almost all tested morph datasets of varying quality and method. The NIST FRVT test is administered on multiple unseen datasets, ranging from automatically generated morphs to manually manipulated high quality morphs to print-and-scanned morphs. The deep learning method described in [31] outperforms the other models in the NIST test.

## 3   Method

The fundamental issue facing morph attack detection researchers is the lack of a large database of morphs with high variance. Many researchers create their own synthetic morph database, typically employing automated generative techniques, such as landmark manipulation [22] or General Adversarial Networks (GANs) [7]. Although commercial software such as Adobe Photoshop or GIMP 2.10 have also been used to manually construct morphs, these methods are often time-consuming, and it is difficult to generate the number of morphs required to train a model. Each method generates different artifacts in the image, such as ghosting, unnatural transition between facial regions, hair and eyelash shadows, blurriness in the forehead and color, among others.

As presented in Fig. 1, the proposed architecture is a Siamese neural network [4], in which the subnetworks are instances of the same network and share weights. Contrastive loss [14,25] is the loss function for training the Siamese network. Contrastive loss is a distance-based loss function, which attempts to bring similar images closer together into a common latent subspace, whereas it attempts to distance the dissimilar ones even more. Essentially, contrastive loss emphasizes the similarity between images of the same class and underscores the difference between images of different classes. The distance is found from the feature embeddings produced by the Siamese network. The margin is the distance threshold that regulates the extent to which pairs are separated.

$$L_c = (1 - y_g)D(I_1, I_2)^2 + y_g \max(0, m - D(I_1, I_2))^2 \qquad (1)$$

where $I_1$ and $I_2$ are the input face images, $m$ is the margin or threshold as described above and $y_g$ is the ground truth label for a given pair of training images and $D(I_1, I_2)$ is the L2 distance between the feature vectors:

$$D(I_1, I_2) = ||\phi(I_1) - \phi(I_2)||_2 \qquad (2)$$

Here, $\phi(.)$ represents a non-linear deep network mapping image into a vector representation in the embedding space. According to the loss function defined above, $y_g$ is 0 for genuine image pairs and $y_g$ is 1 for imposter (morph) pairs.

To streamline training, an Inception ResNET v1 architecture [35] is chosen as the base network, using weights pre-trained on the VGGFace2 dataset [5]. The network is then re-trained with the WVU Twins Day dataset [28] for the Siamese implementation. The model is optimized by enforcing contrastive loss on the embedding space representation of the genuine and imposter twin samples. The trained Siamese network is then additionally fine-tuned using the training portion of each morph database. To obtain a more discriminative embedding, the representations of the face image and its horizontal embedding are concatenated. The feature embeddings are taken from the last fully-connected layer and the $L_2$ distance between the two embeddings is calculated for the verification. As presented in Fig. 2, in our experiments we consider two additional decision making algorithms to explore the embedding space constructed by the contrastive loss, where we augment the proposed framework with the verification of the difference and concatenation of the embedding features of a pair using radial basis function kernel support vector machine (SVM) classifiers. These classifiers, which are learned using the training portion of each dataset, are utilized during the test phase to recognize genuine and imposter pairs.

**Table 2.** The performance of the proposed framework on VISAPP17.

| Method | APCER@BPCER | | | BPCER@APCER | | | D-EER |
|---|---|---|---|---|---|---|---|
| | 5% | 10% | 30% | 5% | 10% | 30% | |
| SIFT | 45.12 | 37.89 | 17.94 | 65.11 | 43.28 | 17.91 | 0.221 |
| SURF | 55.57 | 42.72 | 20.76 | 72.58 | 50.74 | 20.89 | 0.225 |
| LBP | 23.88 | 19.40 | 1.58 | 23.88 | 20.65 | 13.43 | 0.187 |
| BSIF | 25.37 | 22.38 | 1.49 | 28.77 | 25.37 | 8.91 | 0.164 |
| FaceNet | 11.82 | 9.82 | 5.08 | 29.82 | 6.91 | 0.25 | 0.095 |
| Ours | 6.11 | 3.47 | 1.64 | 7.31 | 4.22 | 0.24 | 0.056 |
| Ours+SVM (concat.) | 5.78 | 3.29 | 1.52 | 6.67 | 3.95 | 0.21 | 0.054 |
| Ours+SVM (difference) | 5.29 | 3.17 | 1.43 | 6.12 | 3.71 | 0.19 | 0.052 |

**Table 3.** The performance of the proposed framework on MorGAN

| Method | APCER@BPCER | | | BPCER@APCER | | | D-EER |
|---|---|---|---|---|---|---|---|
| | 5% | 10% | 30% | 5% | 10% | 30% | |
| SIFT | 65.41 | 53.37 | 23.53 | 97.45 | 66.66 | 23.24 | 0.262 |
| SURF | 69.88 | 56.25 | 29.82 | 98.24 | 78.07 | 30.06 | 0.298 |
| LBP | 62.43 | 54.13 | 21.46 | 28.40 | 18.71 | 14.92 | 0.155 |
| BSIF | 39.85 | 31.26 | 16.97 | 14.22 | 8.64 | 7.40 | 0.101 |
| FaceNet | 36.72 | 30.15 | 18.49 | 38.38 | 26.67 | 10.51 | 0.161 |
| Ours | 31.85 | 25.61 | 13.21 | 14.32 | 12.11 | 5.49 | 0.125 |
| Ours+SVM (concat.) | 29.43 | 24.21 | 12.35 | 13.72 | 11.75 | 5.18 | 0.113 |
| Ours+SVM (difference) | 27.95 | 22.78 | 12.05 | 13.46 | 10.42 | 4.94 | 0.102 |

## 3.1 Experimental Setup

The two morph image databases used in this experiment are VISAPP17 [21] and MorGAN [7,8]. As presented in Fig. 3, we purposefully employ two different morph databases, created from two different face image datasets that apply two different morphing techniques to investigate how our model generalizes. VISAPP17 is a collection of complete and splicing morphs generated from the Utrecht FCVP database [30]. The images are 900 × 1200 pixels in size. This dataset is generated by warping and alpha-blending [37]. To construct this dataset, facial landmarks are localized, the face image is tranquilized based on these landmarks, triangles are warped to some average position, and the resulting images are alpha-blended, where alpha is set to 0.5. A subset of 183 high quality splicing morphs constructed by selecting morph images without any recognizable artifacts (VISAPP17-Splicing-Selected dataset) is used along with 131 real images for a total set of 314 images. The morphs were created using the splicing

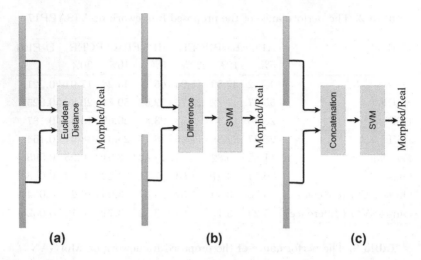

**Fig. 2.** During the test phase, three decision-making algorithms are considered to explore the embedding constructed embedding space: (a) Euclidean distance between the representation of the samples in a pair is considered to make the decision. (b) The difference and (c) the concatenation of the learned representations is fed to a SVM classifier.

technique, where after landmark manipulation, the resulting morphed face is spliced into the face of one of the original images. This preserves the background and hair, which helps avoid the issue of blurry artifacts and ghosting that typically occurs in these regions. However, this also means that the resulting morph derives its face shape from only one of the contributing individuals.

The MorGAN database is constructed from a selection of full-frontal face images manually chosen from the CelebA dataset [19]. It consists of a custom morphing attack pipeline (MorGAN), created by the authors, that uses a GAN, inspired by inspired by learned inference model [9], to generate morphs. The database consists of 1500 bona fide probe images, 1500 bonafide references, and 1000 MorGAN morphs of $64 \times 64$ pixels in size. There is also an additional MorGAN database, in which the MorGAN morphs have been super-resolved to $128 \times 128$ pixels according to the protocol described in [6]. The faces are detected and aligned using the MTCNN framework [38]. The aligned images are then resized to $160 \times 160$ pixels to prepare the images for the Siamese network.

As the Siamese network expects pairs of images as input, the morph images are paired off into genuine face pairs and imposter face pairs, where a genuine pair consists of two trusted images and an imposter pair consists of a trusted image and a morph image. We employ the same train-test split provided by the authors of MorGAN to facilitate comparison of performance with other algorithms using this database. The train-test split is purposefully disjoint, with no overlapping morphs or contributing bonafides to morphs. This enables us to attain an accurate representation of the performance. For the VISAPP17 dataset, 50% of the subjects are considered for training, while the other 50% is used to evaluate the performance of the framework. For the train-test split we consider the same portions for male and female subjects. In addition, 20% of the training set of the morph datasets was used during model optimization as the validation set. Batch size of 64 pairs of images of size $160 \times 160 \times 3$ is used for training the model. Stochastic Gradient Descent (SGD) is the chosen optimizer. For the initial round of training with the Twins Day dataset, the initial learning rate is set to 0.1, multiplied by 0.9 every 5 epochs until the final value of $10^{-6}$. When fine-tuning with morph datasets, the initial learning rate is set to $10^{-3}$, then multiplied by 0.9 every 5 epochs until the final learning rate value of $10^{-6}$. The input data is further augmented with vertical and horizontal flips to increase the training set and improve generalization.

## 4  Results

We study the performance of the proposed differential morph detection framework using VISAPP17 and MorGAN datasets. The performance is compared with state-of-the-art classical and deep learning frameworks.

### 4.1  Metrics

We apply the widely accepted metrics for morphing attack detection, APCER and BPCER, to our algorithm. The Attack Presentation Classification Error Rate (APCER) is the rate at which morph attack images are incorrectly classified as bonafide. Similarly, the Bonafide Probe Classification Error Rate (BPCER) is the rate at which bonafide images are incorrectly classified as morph attack presentations. In real-world applications, the BPCER is the measure by which individuals are inconvenienced with a false alarm. Hence, artificially regulating the BPCER rate by restricting it to fixed thresholds is recommended for face recognition systems [13]. We plot these rates in a Detection Error Tradeoff (DET) graph. D-EER is the detection Equal Error Rate or the decision threshold at which APCER and BPCER are equal. Additionally, we also present BPCER and APCER values for fixed APCER and BPCER values, respectively.

We employed BSIF [17] and LBP [18] as classical texture descriptors. In addition, we consider key-point detection frameworks, SURF [2] and SIFT [20]. These classical methods have shown promise in morph detection in the literature. However, due to the private nature of the databases used in the original papers, we are unable to directly compare our results with theirs. Still, we employ the exact methodology described in the papers for best comparison. Our baseline models consist of these four frameworks in combination with an SVM classifier. The LBP feature descriptors are extracted according to patches of $3 \times 3$. The resulting feature vectors, normalized histograms of size 256, are the values of the LBP binary code. The SIFT and SURF are implemented using the default parameters [2, 20]. 8-bits BSIF feature vectors are constructed on a $3 \times 3$ filters. These filters are Independent Component Analysis filters provided by [15]. The feature vectors are then fed into a SVM with an RBF kernel. For all classical

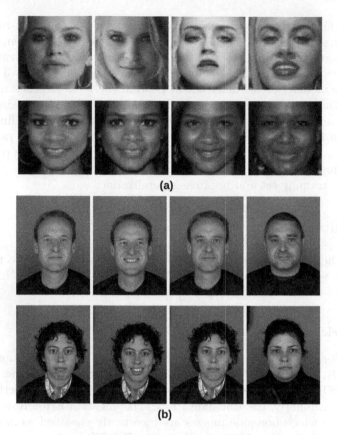

**Fig. 3.** Samples from (a) Morgan and (b) VISAPP17-Splicing-Selected datasets. For each dataset, the first and second faces are the gallery and probe bona fide images and the third face is the morph image construed from the first and forth face images. The original sizes for face images in these datasets are $64 \times 64$ and $1500 \times 1200$, respectively. All the faces are resized to $160 \times 160$ after detection and alignment using MTCNN.

baseline models, we follow [30], where the feature representation of the image in question is subtracted from the feature representation of the trusted image before feeding it to the SVM classifier.

We also compare our Siamese network with FaceNet [32] implementation Inception-ResNET v1, where the distance between the embedding representations of the images in pair is considered to provide the decision. Tables 2 and 3 presents the results on VISAPP17 and MorGAN datasets, respectively. As presented in these tables, fine-tuning using the training portion of each morph dataset demonstrably provides better performance for both datasets. This can be interpreted as the Siamese network is learning the generative nature of the morph images in the dataset. For the VISAPP17 train-test split, fine-tuning on the training portion of the dataset results in the BPCER@APCER $= 5\%$ dropping from 29.82% to 7.31%. For the MorGAN dataset, this fine-tuning helps

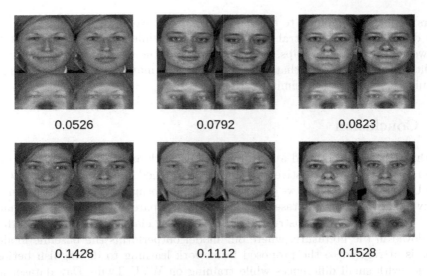

| 0.0526 | 0.0792 | 0.0823 |

| 0.1428 | 0.1112 | 0.1528 |

**Fig. 4.** Grad-CAMs for genuine (top) and imposter (bottom) pairs and the average per pixel distance between the images for each pair. For each imposter pair, the left and right images are real and morphed face images, respectively.

lower the BPCER@APCER = 5% from 38.38% to 14.32%. The great difference in BPCER for MorGAN and VISAPP17 can be attributed to the overall difficulty of the MorGAN dataset, particularly because it is of a lower resolution than VISAPP17. On the other hand, the proposed SVM-based decision making frameworks can further improve the performance of the proposed framework.

For both datasets texture descriptors outperform key-point based models which is consistent with the study in [10]. In addition, the proposed Siamese framework outperforms the FaceNet implementation since the proposed framework initially learns to distinguish between the images with very small differences through re-training on WVU Twins Day dataset and then it is fine-tuned on the training portion of the corresponding dataset. For the MorGAN dataset, our results follow the original paper [8] results on single image morph detection, where the texture descriptors outperform convolutional neural networks, i.e., FaceNet. This can be attributed to the generative nature of this dataset, which can be described using texture descriptors better than deep models. However, fine-tuning the deep model on the training portion of this dataset provides compatible results with BSIF.

Class activation maps [39] provide the attention of the decision with regard to regions of the face image. In Fig. 4, we follow the implementation of gradient-weighted class activation maps [34]. Here, we present the differentiation of the contrastive distance with regard to the feature maps constructed by 'repeat_2' layer in Inception-ResNET v1. In this figure, we also report the average per pixel distance between the Grad-CAMs constructed for face images in each pair. As shown in these images, the difference between the activation maps for genuine pairs is smaller compared to the imposter pairs. It worth mentioning that since the datasets include neutral and smiley faces, while computing the distance between the activation maps, we do not consider the lower part of the faces. In addition, we can observe that the class activation maps for the two images in a genuine pair are roughly similar.

## 5    Conclusion

In this paper, we proposed a deep Siamese network architecture to detect morphed faces. Using contrastive loss and a pre-trained Inception-ResNET v1 on WVU Twins Day dataset, we demonstrate the performance of our Siamese model on two different morph datasets. Likewise, we compare our model's performance with baseline models constructed with common classical and deep methods employed in the literature, where our model outperforms the baseline models. This is attributed to the proposed framework learning to distinguish between images with small differences while training on WVU Twins Day dataset and learning the nature of the corresponding morph dataset by training on the training portion of the dataset.

## References

1. Utrecht ecvp face database. https://pics.stir.ac.uk/2D_face_sets.html
2. Bay, H., Tuytelaars, T., Van Gool, L.: SURF: speeded up robust features. In: Leonardis, A., Bischof, H., Pinz, A. (eds.) ECCV 2006. LNCS, vol. 3951, pp. 404–417. Springer, Heidelberg (2006). https://doi.org/10.1007/11744023_32
3. Bourlai, T. (ed.): Face Recognition Across the Imaging Spectrum. Springer, Cham (2016). https://doi.org/10.1007/978-3-319-28501-6
4. Bromley, J., Guyon, I., LeCun, Y., Säckinger, E., Shah, R.: Signature verification using a "siamese" time delay neural network. In: Advances in neural information processing systems, pp. 737–744 (1994)
5. Cao, Q., Shen, L., Xie, W., Parkhi, O.M., Zisserman, A.: Vggface2: a dataset for recognising faces across pose and age. In: 2018 13th IEEE International Conference on Automatic Face & Gesture Recognition (FG 2018), pp. 67–74. IEEE (2018)
6. Damer, N., Boutros, F., Saladie, A.M., Kirchbuchner, F., Kuijper, A.: Realistic dreams: cascaded enhancement of GAN-generated images with an example in face morphing attacks. In: 10th IEEE International Conference on Biometrics Theory, Applications and Systems, BTAS 2019 (2019)
7. Damer, N., Saladie, A.M., Braun, A., Kuijper, A.: Morgan: recognition vulnerability and attack detectability of face morphing attacks created by generative adversarial network. In: 2018 IEEE 9th International Conference on Biometrics Theory, Applications and Systems (BTAS), pp. 1–10 (2018)
8. Debiasi, L., et al.: On the detection of GAN-based face morphs using established morph detectors. In: Ricci, E., Rota Buló, S., Snoek, C., Lanz, O., Messelodi, S., Sebe, N. (eds.) ICIAP 2019. LNCS, vol. 11752, pp. 345–356. Springer, Cham (2019). https://doi.org/10.1007/978-3-030-30645-8_32
9. Dumoulin, V., et al.: Adversarially learned inference. arXiv preprint arXiv:1606.00704 (2016)

10. Ferrara, M., Franco, A., Maltoni, D.: The magic passport. In: IEEE International Joint Conference on Biometrics, pp. 1–7 (2014)
11. Ferrara, M., Franco, A., Maltoni, D.: Face demorphing. IEEE Trans. Inf. Forensics Secur. **13**(4), 1008–1017 (2017)
12. Ferrara, M., Franco, A., Maltoni, D.: Face demorphing in the presence of facial appearance variations. In: 2018 26th European Signal Processing Conference (EUSIPCO), pp. 2365–2369. IEEE (2018)
13. Frontex, R.: Best practice operational guidelines for automated border control (abc) systems. European Agency Manage. Oper. Cooperation Res. Dev. Unit **9**(05), 2013 (2012) Accessed https://bit.ly/2KYBXhz
14. Hadsell, R., Chopra, S., LeCun, Y.: Dimensionality reduction by learning an invariant mapping. In: 2006 IEEE Computer Society Conference on Computer Vision and Pattern Recognition (CVPR 2006), vol. 2, pp. 1735–1742. IEEE (2006)
15. Hyvärinen, A., Hurri, J., Hoyer, P.O.: Natural Image Statistics: A probabilistic Approach to Early Computational Vision, vol. 39. Springer, New York (2009)
16. ICAO, D.: 9303-machine readable travel documents-part 9: deployment of biometric identification and electronic storage of data in emrtds. International Civil Aviation Organization (ICAO) (2015)
17. Kannala, J., Rahtu, E.: Bsif: Binarized statistical image features. In: Proceedings of the 21st International Conference on Pattern Recognition (ICPR2012), pp. 1363–1366 (2012)
18. Liao, S., Zhu, X., Lei, Z., Zhang, L., Li, S.Z.: Learning multi-scale block local binary patterns for face recognition. In: International Conference on Biometrics, pp. 828–837 (2007)
19. Liu, Z., Luo, P., Wang, X., Tang, X.: Large-scale celebfaces attributes (celeba) dataset (2018) Accessed 15 Aug 2018
20. Lowe, G.: Sift-the scale invariant feature transform. Int. J **2**, 91–110 (2004)
21. Makrushin, A., Neubert, T., Dittmann, J.: Automatic generation and detection of visually faultless facial morphs. Int. Conf. Comput. Vis. Theor. Appl. **7**, 39–50 (2017)
22. Mallick, S.: Face morph using opencv-c++/python (2016)
23. Ngan, M., Grother, P., Hanaoka, K., Kuo, J.: Face recognition vendor test (frvt) part 4: Morph performance of automated face morph detection. National Institute of Technology (NIST), Technical Report NISTIR 8292 (2020)
24. Raghavendra, R., Raja, K.B., Busch, C.: Detecting morphed face images. In: 2016 IEEE 8th International Conference on Biometrics Theory, Applications and Systems (BTAS), pp. 1–7 (2016)
25. Raghavendra, R., Raja, K.B., Venkatesh, S., Busch, C.: Transferable deep-CNN features for detecting digital and print-scanned morphed face images. In: 2017 IEEE Conference on Computer Vision and Pattern Recognition Workshops (CVPRW), pp. 1822–1830 (2017)
26. Raghavendra, R., Raja, K., Venkatesh, S., Busch, C.: Face morphing versus face averaging: vulnerability and detection. In: 2017 IEEE International Joint Conference on Biometrics (IJCB), pp. 555–563. IEEE (2017)
27. Robertson, D.J., Kramer, R.S., Burton, A.M.: Fraudulent id using face morphs: experiments on human and automatic recognition. PLoS One **12**(3), e0173319 (2017)
28. Scherhag, U., Rathgeb, C., Busch, C.: Performance variation of morphed face image detection algorithms across different datasets. In: 2018 International Workshop on Biometrics and Forensics (IWBF), pp. 1–6 (2018)

29. Scherhag, U., Rathgeb, C., Busch, C.: Morph deterction from single face image: a multi-algorithm fusion approach. In: Proceedings of the 2018 2nd International Conference on Biometric Engineering and Applications, pp. 6–12 (2018)
30. Scherhag, U., Rathgeb, C., Busch, C.: Towards detection of morphed face images in electronic travel documents. In: 2018 13th IAPR International Workshop on Document Analysis Systems (DAS), pp. 187–192 (2018)
31. Scherhag, U., Rathgeb, C., Merkle, J., Busch, C.: Deep face representations for differential morphing attack detection. arXiv preprint arXiv:2001.01202 (2020)
32. Schroff, F., Kalenichenko, D., Philbin, J.: Facenet: a unified embedding for face recognition and clustering. In: Proceedings of the IEEE Conference on Computer Vision and Pattern Recognition, pp. 815–823 (2015)
33. Seibold, C., Samek, W., Hilsmann, A., Eisert, P.: Detection of face morphing attacks by deep learning. In: International Workshop on Digital Watermarking, pp. 107–120 (2017)
34. Selvaraju, R.R., Cogswell, M., Das, A., Vedantam, R., Parikh, D., Batra, D.: Grad-cam: visual explanations from deep networks via gradient-based localization. In: Proceedings of the IEEE International Conference on Computer Vision, pp. 618–626 (2017)
35. Szegedy, C., Ioffe, S., Vanhoucke, V., Alemi, A.A.: Inception-v4, inception-resnet and the impact of residual connections on learning. In: Thirty-first AAAI conference on artificial intelligence (2017)
36. Wandzik, L., Garcia, R.V., Kaeding, G., Chen, X.: CNNs under attack: on the vulnerability of deep neural networks based face recognition to image morphing. In: Kraetzer, C., Shi, Y.-Q., Dittmann, J., Kim, H.J. (eds.) IWDW 2017. LNCS, vol. 10431, pp. 121–135. Springer, Cham (2017). https://doi.org/10.1007/978-3-319-64185-0_10
37. Wolberg, G.: Image morphing: a survey. Visual Comput. 14(8–9), 360–372 (1998)
38. Zhang, K., Zhang, Z., Li, Z., Qiao, Y.: Joint face detection and alignment using multitask cascaded convolutional networks. IEEE Signal Process. Lett. 23(10), 1499–1503 (2016)
39. Zhou, B., Khosla, A., Lapedriza, A., Oliva, A., Torralba, A.: Learning deep features for discriminative localization. In: Proceedings of the IEEE conference on computer vision and pattern recognition, pp. 2921–2929 (2016)

# In-Depth DCT Coefficient Distribution Analysis for First Quantization Estimation

Sebastiano Battiato[1] [iD], Oliver Giudice[1] [iD], Francesco Guarnera[1(✉)] [iD], and Giovanni Puglisi[2] [iD]

[1] University of Catania, Catania, Italy
{battiato,giudice}@dmi.unict.it, francesco.guarnera@unict.it
[2] University of Cagliari, Cagliari, Italy
puglisi@unica.it

**Abstract.** The exploitation of traces in JPEG double compressed images is of utter importance for investigations. Properly exploiting such insights, First Quantization Estimation (FQE) could be performed in order to obtain source camera model identification (CMI) and therefore reconstruct the history of a digital image. In this paper, a method able to estimate the first quantization factors for JPEG double compressed images is presented, employing a mixed statistical and Machine Learning approach. The presented solution is demonstrated to work without any a-priori assumptions about the quantization matrices. Experimental results and comparisons with the state-of-the-art show the goodness of the proposed technique.

**Keywords:** FQE · Multimedia forensics · JPEG

## 1 Introduction

Today, a typical life-cycle of a digital image is: (i) acquisition by means of a digital camera (often a smartphone); (ii) upload of the image to Social Network platforms or (iii) sending it through an Instant Messaging platform like Whatsapp or Telegram. The image has already gone through a double JPEG compression [12]. Thus, many information of the original image could be lost. If this image became the subject of a forensics investigation it is necessary to reconstruct its history [9] and then identify camera model and camera source. At first, double compression must be detected [11,14], subsequently camera model could be inferred employing First Quantization Estimation (FQE) and finally camera source identification could be performed by means of comparison of Photo Response Non Uniformity (PRNU) [19,23].

In this paper a mixed statistical and Machine Learning approach for quantization factors estimation is presented. It employs a proper dataset of distributions for comparison, built without strong a-priori assumptions about the

---

S. Battiato, O. Giudice, F. Guarnera and G. Puglisi—Equal contributor.

© Springer Nature Switzerland AG 2021
A. Del Bimbo et al. (Eds.): ICPR 2020 Workshops, LNCS 12666, pp. 573–587, 2021.
https://doi.org/10.1007/978-3-030-68780-9_45

involved quantization matrices. Moreover, to reduce the computational complexity and the overall memory requirements, the proposed solution exploits Discrete Cosine Transform (DCT) distribution properties (i.e., AC coefficients are usually characterized by Laplacian distribution). Experimental results and comparisons demonstrated the robustness of the method.

The remainder of this paper is organized as follows: in Sect. 2 related works are discussed; Sect. 3 introduces the reader to the JPEG notation; Sect. 4 describes the proposed novel approach while a discussion on its parameters is presented in Sect. 5. Experimental results are reported in Sect. 6 and finally Sect. 7 concludes the paper.

## 2   Related Works

First Quantization Estimation is extremely useful for forensics investigations giving hints about the history of a digital image. Many solutions were proposed in recent years. At first, research activity was involved only in estimating the first quantization factors when the information was lost due to the format change (JPEG to Bitmap). Fan and De Queiroz in [7,8] described a method to determine if an image in Bitmap format has been previously JPEG-compressed and thus they estimated the quantization matrix used. They firstly attacked this problem in an easier scenario of single compression and format change useful to understand JPEG artifacts and attract the attention of researchers until today [29].

A first robust technique for FQE was proposed by Bianchi et al. [3,4,20]. They proposed a method based on the Expectation Maximization algorithm to predict the most probable quantization factors of the primary compression over a set of candidates. Other techniques based on statistical consideration of DCT histograms were proposed by Galvan et al. [10]. Their technique works at specific conditions on double compressed images exploiting the a-priori knowledge of monotonicity of the DCT coefficients. Strategies related to histogram analysis and filtering similar to Galvan et al. were introduced until these days [2,5,30]. Lately, insights used for steganography detection were exploited by Thai et al. [24]: even if they achieved good results in terms of overall accuracy, they work only at specific combinations between first and second compression factors, avoiding the estimation when quantization factors are multiples.

Given the big amount of data available today, it is easy to figure out that the problem could be evaluated by means of modern Machine Learning approaches. J. Lukáš and J. Fridrich in [16] introduced a first attempt exploiting neural networks, furtherly improved in [26] with considerations on errors similar to [10]. Convolutional Neural Networks (CNN) were recently also introduced in several papers like [1,25,28]. CNNs have demonstrated to be incredibly powerful in finding invisible correlations on data, but they have been also very prone to what in Machine Learning is called overfitting: the situation in which the network modelled something that is not general enough to represent reality. Machine Learning techniques, and in this special case CNNs are strictly related

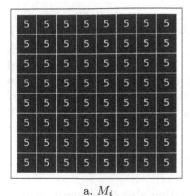

a. $M_i$                b. Standard matrix $QF = 90$

**Fig. 1.** Example of constant matrix $M_i$ with $i = 5$ (a), and the standard matrix corresponding to quality factor $QF = 90$ (b).

to the dataset on which they trained. Accuracy and usability of these techniques have to be proved in "wild" conditions. Even though, state-of-the-art results are obtained recently by Niu et al. [17] where top-rated results are reported for both the aligned and not-aligned FQE scenarios.

The proposed approach, by means of a minimal set of parameters and a reference dataset, aims at surpassing the limits of both CNN-based solutions and state-of-the-art analytical ones. This could be done employing statistics on DCT coefficients in such a way to remove the need of a training phase and without falling in the limits of analytical methods, full of a-priori assumptions.

## 3   JPEG Notation

Given a raw image $I$, JPEG compression [27] could be defined as $I' = f_Q(I)$, where $I'$ is the JPEG compressed image and $Q$ is the $8 \times 8$ quantization matrix composed of the quantization factors $q_i \in \mathbb{N}$ with $i \in \{1, 2, \ldots, 64\}$. Firstly $f_Q(I)$ converts $I$ from the RGB color space to the YCbCr ones, then divides it in $8 \times 8$ non-overlapping blocks and applies the DCT. Finally, each $8 \times 8$ block is divided by $Q$ pixel by pixel, rounded (losing information) and then encoded. In the analysis presented in this paper, only Y channel (luminance) will be considered. Let's define $I'' = f_{Q_2}(f_{Q_1}(I))$ a JPEG double compressed image, where $Q_1$ and $Q_2$ are the quantization matrices employed for the first and for the second compression respectively.

The JPEG quality factor is defined as an integer $QF \in \{1, 2, \ldots, 100\}$ referred to the quantization matrix $Q$ and describes the loss of information where $QF = 100$ and $QF = 1$ represent the minimum and maximum level of loss respectively. Various JPEG libraries could slightly change the implementation details. In this paper, we will refer to $QF$ as the standard quantization matrix defined by JPEG for a specific quality factor. $QF_i$ is defined as $QF$ used for the $i$-th JPEG compression.

In this paper, we denote $h_i$ the distributions of the $i$-th DCT coefficients in all the $8 \times 8$ blocks of $I''$. Furthermore, we define as $q1_1, q1_2, ...., q1_k$ the $k$ quantization factors in zig-zag order of $Q_1$ which are the objective of the FQE, referring to $q1$ and $q2$ as the general quantization factor used in the first and in the second compression respectively. Finally, for testing purposes, we refer to $q1_{max}$ as the maximum value between all the quantization factors to be predicted (in Fig. 1b $q1_{max} = 5$ considering $q1_1, q1_2, .....q1_k$ in zig-zag order with $k = 15$).

## 4    FQE Through Comparison

### 4.1    Retrieval Distributions

The main aim of this work is the design of a solution able to properly exploit information contained in double JPEG compressed images without being affected by the typical limits of Machine Learning solutions. Specifically, in the state-of-the-art, many FQE methods have some restrictions in terms of quantization tables; for example Niu et al. [17] provide Neural Network models working only for standard matrices as $Q_2$ (with $QF_2 \in \{80, 90\}$. Moreover, another contribution of the proposed method is the capacity to work in challenging conditions (i.e., custom matrices).

The first (and most important) part is the generation of the reference data to be exploited in the comparisons for the FQE. Starting from the RAISE dataset [6], composed of 8157 high resolution images in TIFF format (uncompressed), a patch of $64 \times 64$ pixels was extracted from the center. Hence, every crop was compressed two times, employing all the combinations of constant matrix $M_i$ (like the one shown in Fig. 1a), with $i \in \{1, 2, .., q1_{max}\}$ for the first and the second compression. Thus, generating $8157 \times 22 \times 22 = 3.947.988$ images. This dataset will be employed as a reference for comparisons, containing images double compressed by means of only those combinations of $M_i$ which do not belong necessarily to a specific example of real quantization matrices (e.g., standard ones). This latter feature makes the overall approach generalizable on every kind of JPEG double compressed image in the aligned scenario. Moreover, it is worth noting that $q1_{max} = 22$ is a good trade-off between the amount of the data to be generated ($22 \times 22$ combinations) and the maximum quantization factor to be estimated.

The comparison between the JPEG double compressed image under analysis and the generated reference dataset will be done employing the DCT coefficient distributions $h_i$. For this reason, the first $k$ $h_i$ were computed and then inserted into different sub-datasets identified by the couple $\{q1, q2\}$.

The insights described by Lam et al. [15] have shown the usefulness of Laplacian distribution (1) over the years [13, 21], then we fitted the distributions $h_i$ of AC to them, computing $\beta$. To sort the sub-datasets we used $\beta$ for AC distributions ($h_i$ with $i > 1$) and the median value $m$ of the corresponding distributions $h_1$ for DC distributions.

$$f(x) = \frac{1}{2\beta} \exp\left(\frac{-|x - \mu|}{\beta}\right) \tag{1}$$

The final dataset is then composed as follows:

- $DC_{dset}$: $DC$ distributions split for every possible couple $\{q1, q2\}$ sub-datasets, and sorted by $m$;
- $AC_{dset}$: $AC$ distributions splitted for every possible couple $\{q1, q2\}$ sub-datasets, and sorted by $\beta$;

## 4.2   Quantization Factor Estimation

To estimate the first $k$ quantization factors of the first quantization matrix $Q_1$, namely $\{q1_1, q1_2, \ldots, q1_k\}$, given $I''$, the overall pipeline is summarized in Algorithm 1.

The estimation is done for every single $q1_i$ with $i \in \{1, 2, \ldots, k\}$. Firstly, we extract the $h_i(I'')$ from $I''$ employing the LibJpeg C library[1], avoiding to further add truncation and rounding error. $h_i(I'')$ is then fitted on Laplacian distribution if $i > 1$ in order to extract $\beta$ which are then used to seek the range of candidates from the reference dataset. The usage of $m$ and $\beta$ makes the number of candidates constant thus the computational cost to search the most similar distributions in the reference dataset is independent to its cardinality.

A JPEG file contains the quantization matrix used in the last compression; in our case $Q_2$ and then all the $q2_i$, allowing the selection of a specific sub-dataset. For every sub-dataset selected in this way $\{q_j, q2_i\}$ with $j \in \{1, 2, \ldots, q1_{max}\}$, we extract a range of elements $D_{j,q2_i}(m, \beta)$ with the most similar values of $m$ for $DC_{dset}$ and $\beta$ for $AC_{dset}$ and then we compare $h_i(I'')$ with those elements using $\chi^2$ distance:

$$\chi^2(x, y) = \sum_{i=1}^{m} (x_i - y_i)^2 / (x_i + y_i) \tag{2}$$

where $x$ and $y$ represent the distributions to be compared.

For every sub-dataset $D_{j,q2_i}$, we select the lowest distance $d_{i,j}$ obtaining $q1_{max}$ distances. The minimum distance $d_{i,j}$, $j \in \{1, 2, \ldots, q1_{max}\}$ indicates the corresponding sub-dataset and then the predicted $q1$ for the current $i$.

## 4.3   Regularization

The $d_{i,j}$ distances obtained as described in previous Section, show that a strong minimum is not always present at varying of $j$. Sometimes, the information contained in $h_i(I'')$ does not clearly allow the discrimination among the possible $q1_i$ candidates. To overcome this, data coming from neighbors DCT coefficients can be exploited. Specifically, starting from the empirical hypothesis that a generic $q1_i$ value is usually close to $q1_{i-1}$ and $q1_{i+1}$, instead of estimating each coefficient independently, three consecutive elements in zig-zag order are considered. For example, if $k = 15$, 13 triplets ($q1_{i-1}$, $q1_i$, $q1_{i+1}$, $i = 2, \ldots, 14$) can be identified. To estimate a single triplet $q1_{i-1}$, $q1_i$, $q1_{i+1}$, a score is associated to

---

[1] https://github.com/LuaDist/libjpeg.

each possible $q1$ combination. Thus, considering $q1_{max} = 22$ as the maximum $q1$ value, $22 \times 22 \times 22$ $q1$ combinations are taken into account. A proper score $S$ is then obtained by a weighted average between a data term ($C_{data}$) and a regularization term ($C_{reg}$) as follows:

$$S = wC_{data} + (1 - w)C_{reg} \tag{3}$$

where $w \in [0, 1]$, $C_{data}$ is the normalized sum of the three $d_{i,j}$, and $C_{reg}$ is the regularization term that tries to minimize the difference among the considered triplet. Further details about $C_{reg}$ setting will be provided in Sect. 5.2.

---

**Algorithm 1.** The Proposed FQE Technique

---

**Input:** double compressed image $I''$
**Output:** $\{q1_1, q1_2, \ldots\ldots, q1_k\}$
    *Initialization* : $k, q1_{max}$
1: **for** $i = 1$ to $k$ **do**
2:    $h_i$ : distribution of $i$-th DCT coefficient
3:    **if** $(i = 1)$ **then**
4:       $D : DC_{dset}$
5:       $m$ : median value of $h_i$
6:    **else**
7:       $D : AC_{dset}$
8:       $\beta : \beta$ fitted on Laplacian $h_i$
9:    **end if**
10:   $q2_i$ : quantization factor of $Q2$ for $i$-th DCT
11:   **for** $j = 1$ to $q1_{max}$ **do**
12:      $D_{j,q2_i}$ : sub-dataset $(q1, q2)$ with $q1 = j$, $q2 = q2_i$
13:      $D_{j,q2_i}(m, \beta)$ : sub-range with most similar $m, \beta$
14:      $d_{i,j}$ : lower $\chi^2$ distance between $h_i$ and $D_{j,q2_i}$
15:   **end for**
16:   $q1_i : \arg\min_{\{d_{i,j}\}}, j \in \{1, 2, \ldots, q1_{max}\}$
17: **end for**
18: regularize($\{q1_1, q1_2, \ldots\ldots, q1_k\}$)
19: **return** $\{q1_1, q1_2, \ldots\ldots, q1_k\}$

---

## 5 Parameters Setting

The various parameters introduced in the Sect. 4, were set by means of a validation dataset $D_V$ composed of 8157 images $64 \times 64$ pixels, cropped at random position from RAISE [6] original images.

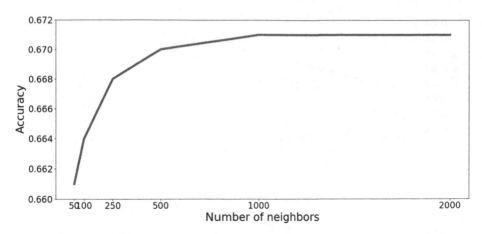

**Fig. 2.** Accuracy of the proposed approach w.r.t. the number of neighbors considered for comparison.

### 5.1 Clustering

Fixed $q2$, the comparison dataset is composed of $q1_{max}$ different sub-datasets. In order to limit the overall computational complexity, a smart comparison strategy considering only a limited number of $h_i$ exploiting $m$ and $\beta$ values has been employed. We tested the method with $D_V$ using a sub-range of 50, 100, 250, 500 and 1000 elements for each sub-dataset (see Fig. 2). It is worth noting that the value considered in the proposed solution (1000), represents a viable trade-off between accuracy and computational cost with respect to the full search solution.

### 5.2 Regularization

In order to cope with the lack of information contained in some $h_i(I'')$, a regularization step was carried out. Triplets of the nearest $q1_i$ were estimated simultaneously, and several $C_{reg}$ functions have been investigated:

$$C_{reg1} = \frac{(c_i - c_{i-1}) + (c_i - c_{i+1})}{2} \tag{4}$$

$$C_{reg2} = \frac{(c_i - c_{i-1}) + (c_i - c_{i+1})}{2\sqrt{c_i}} \tag{5}$$

$$C_{reg3} = \frac{(c_i - c_{i-1}) + (c_i - c_{i+1})}{2c_i} \tag{6}$$

where $c_{i-1}$, $c_i$, $c_{i+1}$ are $q1$ candidates related to three consecutive quantization factors in zig-zag order. This regularization step provides multiple estimations for each single $q1_i$. For example the estimations of $q1_3$ can be found on 3 different triplets: $(q1_1, q1_2, q1_3)$, $(q1_2, q1_3, q1_4)$ and $(q1_3, q1_4, q1_5)$. The 3 strategies could then be tested. Figures 3a, b and c show the accuracies employing the

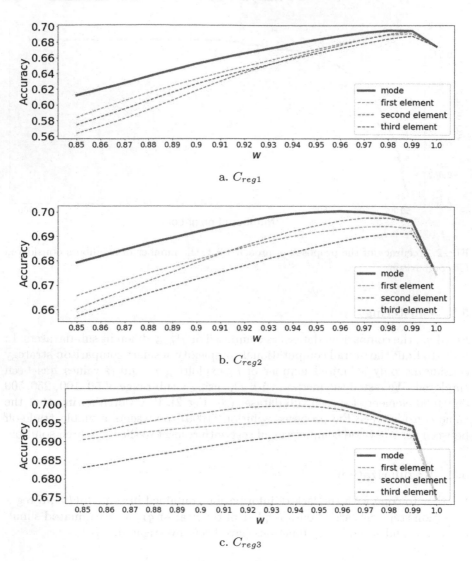

a. $C_{reg1}$

b. $C_{reg2}$

c. $C_{reg3}$

**Fig. 3.** a, b and c describe the accuracies obtained for different values of the regularization parameter $w$ employing the three Eqs. (4), (5), (6) respectively. Every plot shows the accuracies obtained considering the first, the second and the third element of the triplet of the analyzed quantization factors and the related arithmetical mode.

corresponding $C_{reg}$, at varying of weights (see (3)) and $q1_i$ selection strategies. As suggested in Fig. 4 which shows the modes of Eq. (4), (5), (6), we chose the use of Eq. (6) with $w = 0.92$.

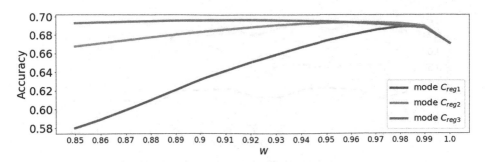

**Fig. 4.** Comparison between the modes of Fig. 3a, b, c

# 6   Experimental Results

The difficulty of the first quantization factor estimation task is proportional to the relative position in the quantization matrix, as reported in literature. For this reason and for the sake of comparison with the state-of-the-art, we set $k = 15$, although our method has not this specific limitation on $k$.

## 6.1   Comparison Tests

**Table 1.** Accuracies obtained by the proposed approach compared to Bianchi et al. [4], Galvan et al. [10], Dalmia et al. [5] and Niu et al. [17] with different combinations of $QF_1/QF_2$, considering standard quantization tables.

| $QF_1$ | $QF_2 = 90$ | | | | | | $QF_2 = 80$ | | | | | |
|---|---|---|---|---|---|---|---|---|---|---|---|---|
| | *Our* | *Our Reg.* | [4] | [10] | [5] | [17] | *Our* | *Our Reg.* | [4] | [10] | [5] | [17] |
| 55 | 0.76 | **0.77** | 0.53 | 0.52 | 0.45 | 0.00 | 0.55 | **0.58** | 0.36 | 0.37 | 0.37 | 0.24 |
| 60 | **0.82** | **0.82** | 0.53 | 0.56 | 0.47 | 0.64 | 0.55 | **0.60** | 0.27 | 0.37 | 0.38 | 0.50 |
| 65 | 0.79 | **0.81** | 0.54 | 0.57 | 0.49 | 0.54 | **0.68** | 0.65 | 0.19 | 0.41 | 0.43 | 0.31 |
| 70 | **0.85** | **0.85** | 0.43 | 0.57 | 0.51 | 0.66 | 0.67 | **0.75** | 0.19 | 0.50 | 0.49 | 0.50 |
| 75 | 0.83 | **0.85** | 0.41 | 0.63 | 0.53 | 0.77 | 0.48 | **0.56** | 0.07 | 0.56 | 0.45 | 0.15 |
| 80 | 0.81 | **0.83** | 0.29 | 0.61 | 0.45 | 0.81 | **0.12** | 0.11 | 0.00 | 0.00 | 0.00 | 0.00 |
| 85 | 0.78 | **0.85** | 0.14 | 0.74 | 0.36 | 0.81 | 0.28 | **0.34** | 0.19 | 0.00 | 0.00 | 0.04 |
| 90 | **0.30** | 0.24 | 0.00 | 0.00 | 0.00 | 0.02 | 0.16 | 0.19 | 0.06 | 0.00 | 0.00 | **0.48** |
| 95 | 0.44 | 0.52 | 0.11 | 0.00 | 0.00 | **0.78** | 0.27 | 0.30 | 0.00 | 0.00 | 0.00 | **0.95** |
| 98 | 0.49 | 0.57 | 0.00 | 0.00 | 0.00 | **0.76** | 0.42 | **0.42** | 0.01 | 0.00 | 0.00 | 0.21 |
| MEAN | 0.69 | **0.71** | 0.30 | 0.42 | 0.33 | 0.58 | 0.42 | **0.45** | 0.13 | 0.22 | 0.21 | 0.28 |

The first set of tests has been performed to compare the proposed solution with state-of-the-art approaches based on statistical analysis (Bianchi et al. [4], Galvan et al. [10], Dalmia et al. [5]) and Machine Learning (Niu et al. [17]), employing the implementations provided by the authors.

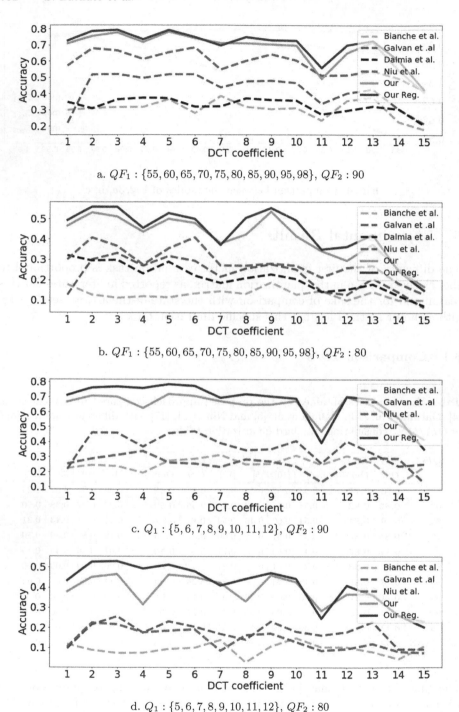

**Fig. 5.** Accuracies of the same methods described in Table 1 and 2 at varying of the quantization factors $q1_i$ to be predicted. The values are averaged over all the $QF_1/Q_1$.

**Table 2.** Accuracies obtained by the proposed approach compared to Bianchi et al. [4], Galvan et al. [10] and Niu et al. [17] employing custom tables for first compression. The column $PS$ refers to custom tables used by Photoshop.

| $PS$ | $QF_2 = 90$ | | | | | $QF_2 = 80$ | | | | |
|------|------|----------|------|------|------|------|----------|------|------|------|
|      | Our  | Our Reg. | [4]  | [10] | [17] | Our  | Our Reg. | [4]  | [10] | [17] |
| 5    | **0.80** | 0.78 | 0.56 | 0.58 | 0.05 | 0.65 | **0.68** | 0.26 | 0.46 | 0.07 |
| 6    | **0.82** | **0.82** | 0.46 | 0.60 | 0.07 | 0.42 | **0.54** | 0.05 | 0.41 | 0.02 |
| 7    | **0.83** | **0.83** | 0.41 | 0.58 | 0.07 | 0.62 | **0.68** | 0.15 | 0.48 | 0.08 |
| 8    | **0.81** | **0.81** | 0.25 | 0.65 | 0.10 | 0.19 | **0.22** | 0.03 | 0.03 | 0.01 |
| 9    | 0.55 | **0.61** | 0.02 | 0.47 | 0.02 | 0.26 | **0.28** | 0.19 | 0.00 | 0.07 |
| 10   | 0.42 | **0.50** | 0.19 | 0.00 | 0.25 | 0.15 | **0.20** | 0.00 | 0.00 | 0.40 |
| 11   | 0.45 | 0.52 | 0.04 | 0.00 | **0.69** | 0.37 | **0.38** | 0.01 | 0.00 | 0.24 |
| 12   | 0.49 | 0.57 | 0.04 | 0.00 | **0.75** | **0.42** | 0.42 | 0.01 | 0.00 | 0.21 |
| MEAN | 0.64 | **0.68** | 0.25 | 0.36 | 0.25 | 0.39 | **0.42** | 0.09 | 0.18 | 0.14 |

For the sake of comparison, we created 4 datasets: starting from RAISE [6], we cropped a random $64 \times 64$ patch from every image and compressed it two times as follows:

1. $QF_1 : \{55, 60, 65, 70, 75, 80, 85, 90, 95, 98\}$, $QF_2 : 90$
2. $QF_1 : \{55, 60, 65, 70, 75, 80, 85, 90, 95, 98\}$, $QF_2 : 80$
3. $Q_1 : \{5, 6, 7, 8, 9, 10, 11, 12\}$, $QF_2 : 90$
4. $Q_1 : \{5, 6, 7, 8, 9, 10, 11, 12\}$, $QF_2 : 80$

where $Q_1 : \{5, 6, 7, 8, 9, 10, 11, 12\}$ related to 3) and 4) are referred to the quantization matrices of Photoshop (CC version 20.0.4). Every method was tested with all the aforementioned datasets with the exception of Dalmia et al. [5] which, in their implementation, make assumptions about standard tables in first compression and then was excluded in the test with Photoshop's custom tables. Results, reported in Table 1 and 2 and in Fig. 5, clearly highlight how our method outperforms the state-of-the-art in almost all scenarios, with and without the regularization step (values close to 0 are due to the assumptions of some methods, e.g. $QF_1 < QF_2$). It is worth noting that, although the scenario employing standard matrices is the one considered by Niu et al. [17] to train their CNN, the proposed solution outperforms it with an average of **0.71** vs. **0.58** for $QF_2 = 90$ and **0.45** vs. **0.28** for $QF_2 = 80$. Differently than other Machine Learning based approaches, the proposed method, working properly also in the scenario involving Photoshop's custom tables, demonstrates to be not dependent to a specific class of quantization matrices.

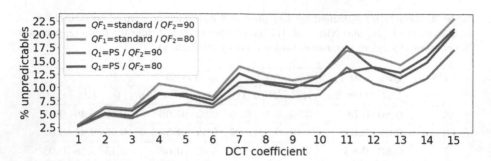

**Fig. 6.** Percentages of unpredictable images for the 4 described datasets at varying of DCT coefficients.

**Table 3.** Accuracies obtained by the proposed approach for generalizing property demonstration (Our Reg. for the regularized version).

| Method | Dataset | Cropped Patch | Low/Low | Low/Mid | Low/High | Mid/Low | Mid/Mid | Mid/High | High/Low | High/Mid | High/High | Mean |
|---|---|---|---|---|---|---|---|---|---|---|---|---|
| Our | RAISE [6] | 64 × 64 | 0.25 | 0.47 | 0.79 | 0.17 | 0.32 | 0.82 | 0.27 | 0.31 | 0.70 | 0.46 |
| Our Reg. | | | 0.30 | 0.53 | 0.81 | 0.22 | 0.37 | 0.84 | 0.25 | 0.33 | 0.75 | 0.49 |
| Our | UCID [22] | 64 × 64 | 0.33 | 0.63 | 0.93 | 0.20 | 0.39 | 0.90 | 0.15 | 0.21 | 0.66 | 0.49 |
| Our Reg. | | | 0.36 | 0.65 | 0.96 | 0.23 | 0.42 | 0.91 | 0.13 | 0.23 | 0.73 | 0.51 |
| Our | UCID [22] | 128 × 128 | 0.36 | 0.69 | 0.95 | 0.21 | 0.42 | 0.92 | 0.16 | 0.24 | 0.71 | 0.52 |
| Our Reg. | | | 0.37 | 0.71 | 0.95 | 0.24 | 0.43 | 0.92 | 0.24 | 0.33 | 0.74 | 0.55 |

## 6.2   Discussion on Unpredictable Factors

A patch extracted from an high resolution image could be too homogeneous, hence all the values of the DCT coefficients could be in the same bin of the corresponding histograms, due to the lack of variation. A patch $64 \times 64$ extracted from a RAISE image represents about the $0,033\%$ of the information contained in the original one and then the possibility to have this homogeneous scenario is not negligible. We selected this scenario (i.e., small patches from a high resolution dataset) to test the proposed solution in a challenging condition, but we had to exclude the aforementioned histograms because they do not allow to predict the quantization factors (the available information is not enough to select a specific $q1$). In particular, given $i$, we exclude the distributions $h_i$ where all the values are in the same bin of the histogram (e.g., all the $i$-th DCT coefficients extracted from the $8 \times 8$ blocks are equal). The percentage of $q1_i$ excluded for each dataset is shown in Fig. 6 at varying of DCT coefficients.

## 6.3   Generalizing Property

Park et al. [18] proposed a collection of 1170 different quantization tables employed on real scenarios (1070 custom). In this Section, a new set of experiments will be presented in order to demonstrate the generalizing property of the proposed approach employing the same reference dataset built in Sect. 4.1.

From the collection of Park et al., 873 quantization tables show in the first 15 quantization factors, a value of $q1_i \leq q1_{max}$ and then they can be employed for testing. They were sorted by the average of the first 15 quantization factors and then equally divided into three sets of 291 elements (*low, mid, high*). These sets of tables are employed to create 9 combinations of double compressions (see latter 9 columns of Table 3). Three new datasets for generalizing tests are then built: patches of size $w \times w$ from RAW images were extracted and then compressed two times with all the 9 aforementioned combinations. For each combination of double compression, the quantization tables ($Q_1$ and $Q_2$) are selected randomly from the 291 available in the corresponding set.

The results obtained on these three datasets are reported in Table 3. They clearly show that our method maintains good accuracies on all the tested challenging scenarios and demonstrates to achieve same results even when different datasets are employed for tests.

# 7   Conclusion

In this paper, a new technique able to estimate the first quantization factors for JPEG double compressed images was presented, employing a mixed statistical and Machine Learning approach. One of the main contributions was the way we employed the big amount of data to avoid overfitting: constant matrices $M_i$ permitted to uncouple $\{q1, q2\}$ and the use of $m$ and $\beta$ made computational times acceptable. The presented solution was demonstrated to work for both custom and standard tables thus being generalizable enough to be employed in real-case scenarios. Experimental tests showed the goodness of the technique overcoming state-of-the-art results. Finally, the use of k-nn (with $k = 1$) to learn the distribution underlines rooms for improvement of the proposed method. In future work we will further investigate the proposed methodology on higher patch size, for both the input images and the comparison dataset ones. Moreover, the final aim is to employ the described technique on more challenging scenarios: resized and not-aligned images.

# References

1. Barni, M., et al.: Aligned and non-aligned double JPEG detection using convolutional neural networks. J. Vis. Commun. Image Represent. **49**, 153–163 (2017)
2. Battiato, S., Giudice, O., Guarnera, F., Puglisi, G.: Computational data analysis for first quantization estimation on JPEG double compressed images. In: 25th International Conference on Pattern Recognition (ICPR) (2020)
3. Bianchi, T., De Rosa, A., Piva, A.: Improved DCT coefficient analysis for forgery localization in JPEG images. In: 2011 IEEE International Conference on Acoustics, Speech and Signal Processing (ICASSP), pp. 2444, 2447 (2011)
4. Bianchi, T., Piva, A.: Image forgery localization via block-grained analysis of JPEG artifacts. Proc. IEEE Trans. Inf. Forensics Secur. **7**(3), 1003 (2012)

5. Dalmia, N., Okade, M.: First quantization matrix estimation for double compressed JPEG images utilizing novel DCT histogram selection strategy. In: Proceedings of the Tenth Indian Conference on Computer Vision, Graphics and Image Processing, pp. 1–8 (2016)

6. Dang-Nguyen, D., Pasquini, C., Conotter, V., Boato, G.: Raise: a raw images dataset for digital image forensics. In: Proceedings of the 6th ACM Multimedia Systems Conference, pp. 219–224 (2015)

7. Fan, Z., De Queiroz, R.: Identification of bitmap compression history: JPEG detection and quantizer estimation. IEEE Trans. Image Process. **12**(2), 230–235 (2003)

8. Fan, Z., De Queiroz, R.L.: Maximum likelihood estimation of JPEG quantization table in the identification of bitmap compression history. In: Proceedings of the International Conference on Image Processing, pp. 948–951. 1 (2000)

9. Farid, H.: Digital image ballistics from JPEG quantization: a follow up study. Department of Computer Science, Dartmouth College, Technical report TR2008-638 (2008)

10. Galvan, F., Puglisi, G., Bruna, A.R., Battiato, S.: First quantization matrix estimation from double compressed JPEG images. IEEE Trans. Inf. Forensics Secur. **9**(8), 1299–1310 (2014)

11. Giudice, O., Guarnera, F., Paratore, A., Battiato, S.: 1-D DCT domain analysis for JPEG double compression detection. In: Ricci, E., Rota Bulò, S., Snoek, C., Lanz, O., Messelodi, S., Sebe, N. (eds.) ICIAP 2019. LNCS, vol. 11752, pp. 716–726. Springer, Cham (2019). https://doi.org/10.1007/978-3-030-30645-8_65

12. Giudice, O., Paratore, A., Moltisanti, M., Battiato, S.: A classification engine for image ballistics of social data. In: Battiato, S., Gallo, G., Schettini, R., Stanco, F. (eds.) ICIAP 2017. LNCS, vol. 10485, pp. 625–636. Springer, Cham (2017). https://doi.org/10.1007/978-3-319-68548-9_57

13. Hou, X., Harel, J., Koch, C.: Image signature: highlighting sparse salient regions. IEEE Trans. Pattern Anal. Mach. Intell. **34**(1), 194–201 (2011)

14. Kee, E., Johnson, M.K., Farid, H.: Digital image authentication from JPEG headers. IEEE Trans. Inf. Forensics Secur. **6**(3), 1066–1075 (2011)

15. Lam, E.Y., Goodman, J.W.: A mathematical analysis of the DCT coefficient distributions for images. IEEE Trans. Image Process. **9**(10), 1661–1666 (2000)

16. Lukáš, J., Fridrich, J.: Estimation of primary quantization matrix in double compressed JPEG images. In: Proceedings of the Digital Forensic Research Workshop, pp. 5–8 (2003)

17. Niu, Y., Tondi, B., Zhao, Y., Barni, M.: Primary quantization matrix estimation of double compressed JPEG images via CNN. IEEE Signal Process. Lett. **27**, 191–195 (2020)

18. Park, J., Cho, D., Ahn, W., Lee, H.-K.: Double JPEG detection in mixed jpeg quality factors using deep convolutional neural network. In: Ferrari, V., Hebert, M., Sminchisescu, C., Weiss, Y. (eds.) ECCV 2018. LNCS, vol. 11209, pp. 656–672. Springer, Cham (2018). https://doi.org/10.1007/978-3-030-01228-1_39

19. Piva, A.: An overview on image forensics. ISRN Signal Process. **2013**, 22 (2013)

20. Piva, A., Bianchi, T.: Detection of non-aligned double JPEG compression with estimation of primary compression parameters. In: Proceedings of 18th IEEE International Conference on Image Processing (ICIP), pp. 1929–1932. IEEE (2011)

21. Ravì, D., Farinella, G., Tomaselli, V., Guarnera, M., Battiato, S.: Representing scenes for real-time context classification on mobile devices. Pattern Recogn. **48**, 4 (2015)

22. Schaefer, G., Stich, M.: UCID: an uncompressed color image database. In: Storage and Retrieval Methods and Applications for Multimedia 2004, vol. 5307, pp. 472–480. International Society for Optics and Photonics (2003)

23. Stamm, M.C., Wu, M., Liu, K.J.R.: Information forensics: an overview of the first decade. IEEE Access **1**, 167–200 (2013)

24. Thai, T.H., Cogranne, R.: Estimation of primary quantization steps in double-compressed JPEG images using a statistical model of discrete cosine transform. IEEE Access **7**, 76203–76216 (2019)

25. Uricchio, T., Ballan, L., Caldelli, R., Amerini, I.: Localization of JPEG double compression through multi-domain convolutional neural networks. In: Proceedings of the IEEE Conference on Computer Vision and Pattern Recognition Workshops, pp. 53–59 (2017)

26. Varghese, G., Kumar, A.: Detection of double JPEG compression on color image using neural network classifier. Int. J. **3**, 175–181 (2016)

27. Wallace, G.K.: The JPEG still picture compression standard. Commun. ACM **34**(4), 30–44 (1991)

28. Wang, Q., Zhang, R.: Double JPEG compression forensics based on a convolutional neural network. EURASIP J. Inf. Secur. **2016**(1), 23 (2016)

29. Yang, J., Zhang, Y., Zhu, G., Kwong, S.: A clustering-based framework for improving the performance of JPEG quantization step estimation. IEEE Trans. Circ. Syst. Video Technol. (2020)

30. Yao, H., Wei, H., Qiao, T., Qin, C.: JPEG quantization step estimation with coefficient histogram and spectrum analyses. J. Vis. Commun. Image Represent., 102795 (2020)

# MOI2QDN - Workshop on Metrification and Optimization of Input Image Quality in Deep Networks

# Workshop on Metrification and Optimization of Input Image Quality in Deep Networks (MOI2QDN)

## Workshop Description

Recent years have seen significant advances in image processing and computer vision applications based on Deep Neural Networks (DNNs). This is a critical technology for a number of real-time applications including autonomous vehicles, smart cities, and industrial computer vision. Often deep neural networks for such applications are trained and validated based on the assumption that the images are artefact-free. However, in most real-time embedded system applications the images input to the networks, in addition to any variations of external conditions, have artefacts introduced by the imaging process, such as the Image Signal Processing (ISP) pipelines. Data augmentation methods are exploited to expand the subset of trained images to include images with different levels of distortions. Such data augmentation often may result to improved performance of the network for artefact-specific images but also degrades the performance for artefact-free images.

One of the main drawbacks of the first generation of neural networks was that they were seen as black boxes, whose decision making could not be explained. However, despite recent advances in interpretability and explainability of deep neural models, DNNs remain widely systems whose operational boundaries cannot be explained or otherwise quantified. It is therefore not clear the level of distortions networks can tolerate, or the exact reasons for any network performance degradation. The current potential of deep neural networks in critical real-time applications makes it paramount that neural network model developers can explain what the deep model has learnt and identify operational boundaries. The latter is important to the wider deployment of systems that critically depend on input image quality. Advances in understanding the impact of image quality variations in the performance of DNNs will have an influence in the design of imaging sensors; the breadth of variability in data used for training DNNs; architectural structures of DNNs to account for the operational output of the image sensors and ISP used.

We received 12 submissions for reviews, from authors belonging to 9 countries. Following a single blind peer-review process, we selected 7 papers for presentation at the workshop, an acceptance rate of 58%. The review process focused on the quality of the papers, their scientific novelty and relevance to the theme of the MOI2QDN workshop. We thank the members of the programme committee for giving their time and expertise to ensure that the accepted papers were of high quality. We were also pleased to host two keynote talks given by distinguished researchers in the field. Professor Robin Jenkins, NVIDIA Corporation, USA, talked about *"Imaging and Metric Considerations for DNNS"*, highlighting the critical need to distinguish between performance limitations imposed by the imaging system and those of the DNN itself. Professor Marius Pedersen, Norwegian University of Science and Technology

(NTNU), explored the effect of color distortions in image classification from deep neural networks in his talk, *"Impact of Color on Deep Convolutional Neural Networks"*.

Five accepted papers from those submitted to the Metrification and Optimization of Input Image Quality in Deep Networks (MOI2QDN) workshop present recent advances in the systematic analysis of the performance of DNNs with respect to degradations in the input image quality due to the imaging processes such as noise, motion blur, environmental conditions and propose solutions. In addition, two papers employ CNNs for image quality prediction.

Paper #1 from the university of Milano, presents a novel idea for removing rain noise from images with high accuracy through a semantic segmentation network of images by analysing atmospheric conditions. A neural network is used to evaluate the negative effects of rain streaks for semantic segmentation of street scenes using a synthetic augmented dataset of CityScapes with artificial rain. With the support of generative adversarial network, the authors define and train the model for rain removal and demonstrate the benefits of this methodology as a pre-processing step to both rainy and clean images towards semantic segmentation using a per-class analysis.

Paper #2 from the University of Malaga, Spain, investigates the behavior of CNNs for object recognition under linear motion blur, which is a common distortion from camera shake or moving subjects. A realistic image sensor model is proposed and employed to produce different levels of motion blur to the input, undistorted images. The performance of six well-known, state-of-the-art CNNs is analyzed and results show that the CNN accuracy is dependent on the CNN model, and it is generally affected to a greater extent by the length and to a lesser extent by the angle of the motion blur.

Paper #3 from the University of Malaga presents a performance evaluation of several hybrid algorithms supporting image denoising towards improving high colour resolution. The authors' work is based on algorithms which focus on improvement of the spatial resolution of natural images. The paper presents an extensive experimental performance design that includes the introduction of Gaussian noise, Poisson noise, salt-and-pepper noise and uniform noise into the low-resolution inputs. Results demonstrate that denoising must be carried out before super-resolution for optimising performance. In addition, results indicated that deep learning-based framework techniques clearly outperform the traditional ones.

Paper #4 from the University of Malaga, Spain investigates the effect of noise and brightness from present day CMOS vision sensors on CNNs. The noise models are based on the European Machine Vision Association (EMVA) standard 1288, and include separately Poisson, Gaussian, salt & pepper, speckle, and uniform noise as sources of defects in image acquisition sensors. The authors provide a systematic analysis of how brightness in conjunction with simulated noise added to images impact the performance of CNNs. The performance of six state-of-the-art and well-known architectures was evaluated. Through the presentation of heatmaps this study can serve as information on the maximum noise allowed to achieve a target performance.

Paper #5 from Multimedia University, Selangor, Malaysia, investigates the effects low-light enhancement algorithms have in the detection of objects by CNNs. The paper proposes a framework that generates activation value and activation field statistics. It provides a progressive view of the increase/decrease in activation values and activation area respectively of each layer for a network-based model, when the input low-light image is pre-processed by enhancement algorithms. The framework is evaluated using nine low-level enhancement algorithms. Results point towards a negative correlation between the increase of the activation statistics and the improvement on object detection performance. In addition, low-light enhancement algorithms with particular emphasis on features and structure enhancement show deeper impact on the improvement of the detector network when compared to aesthetically driven algorithms that produce superior visual results.

Paper #6 from Shanxi University, China, presents a novel end-to-end multi-level fusion based convolutional network employed for full reference image quality assessment. The model first employs feature extraction from both distorted and reference images and then multi-level feature fusion to evaluate a number of local quality indices, which are finally pooled into a global quality score. It is tested with three different image datasets and shows excellent ability to capture visual discrepancies between the distorted the reference images, despite variations in the capture as well as types of distortion in the datasets.

Paper #7 from the Czech Technical University, Czechia, proposes a CNN architecture, CNN-FQ, that takes a face image and provides a scalar summary of the face image quality. An advantage of the proposed method is that the training of the network does not require explicit annotation of the target quality scores. Instead, the method uses existing databases composed of faces annotated by their identity. The training is based on the success of ranking triplet of faces, two of them matching and one non-matching, based on distances returned by the employed face matcher. The performance of the proposed network is evaluated against three other face quality extractors using 1:1 verification, 1:N identification and 1:1 covariate protocols. Results show a strong correlation between the CNN-FQ quality score and the image size as well as the yaw angle, whereas the results of the competing methods are much less correlated with the covariates.

# Organization

## MOI2QDN Chairs

Alexandra Psarrou      University of Westminster, UK
Sophie Triantaphillidou      University of Westminster, UK
Markos Mentzelopoulos      University of Westminster, UK

## Program Committee

Rob Jenkins      NVIDIA, USA
Barbara Villarini      University of Westminster, UK
José García-Rodríguez      University of Alicante, Spain
Enrique Dominguez      University of Malaga, Spain
Alessandro Rizzi      University of Milan, Italy
Sergio Orts      University of Alicante, Spain

# Invited Speakers - Abstracts

# Imaging and Metric Considerations for DNNS

Robin Jenkin[1,2]

[1] NVIDIA Corp, Santa Clara, California, USA
[2] Visiting Professor, University of Westminster, UK

**Abstract.** Far too often in papers exploring DNN performance, the description of the images used is limited to the pixel count, total number and split between training and validation sets. Not all pixels are created equal for a myriad of reasons. This is further combined with complications due to environmental conditions, such as illumination levels, motion, and variation due to image signal processing. How then is it possible to distinguish between performance limitations imposed by the imaging system and those of the DNN itself? How can we rank cameras intended for our application? Camera-ISP-DNN systems are being deployed extensively within safety critical applications and these questions are becoming increasingly important.

Three existing methods, found in image science literature, are examined to perform 'first-order' specification and modeling of imaging systems intended for use in object recognition systems. These are Johnson Criteria, Information Capacity and Detectability. The methods are compared and discussed within the practical context of evaluating modern high dynamic range sensors. Desirable characteristics of quality metrics are considered, and results shown to demonstrate ranking of cameras.

# Impact of Color on Deep Convolutional Neural Networks

Marius Pedersen

Norwegian University of Science and Technology (NTNU)

**Abstract:** Deep learning neural networks have become widely used tool for computer vision applications as classification, segmentation and object localization. Recent studies have shown that the quality of images have a significant impact on the performance of deep neural networks. Effects as image noise, image blur, image contrast, and compression artifacts have been studies in relation to the performance of deep neural networks on image classification, but the effects of color have mostly been unexplored. In this talk we study the impact of color distortions in image classification from deep neural networks. Experiments performed using three deep convolutional neural architectures (RESNET, VGGNET and Densenet) show the impact of color distortions on image classification.

# On the Impact of Rain over Semantic Segmentation of Street Scenes

Simone Zini(✉) and Marco Buzzelli

Department of Informatics Systems and Communication,
University of Milano-Bicocca, Milan, Italy
s.zini1@campus.unimib.it, marco.buzzelli@unimib.it

**Abstract.** We investigate the negative effects of rain streaks over the performance of a neural network for real time semantic segmentation of street scenes. This is done by synthetically augmenting the CityScapes dataset with artificial rain. We then define and train a generative adversarial network for rain removal, and quantify the benefits of its application as a pre-processing step to both rainy and "clean" images. Finally, we show that by retraining the semantic segmentation network on images processed for rain removal, it is possible to gain even more accuracy, with a model that produces stable results in all analyzed atmospheric conditions. For our experiments, we present a per-class analysis in order to provide deeper insights over the impact of rain on semantic segmentation.

**Keywords:** Rain removal · Data augmentation · Semantic segmentation

## 1 Introduction

The automotive field has seen a strong expansion in recent years, where a crucial role is played by perception systems for autonomous vehicles and for assisted driving. The development of computer vision techniques in this field potentially allows for a decrease of the production costs due to the exploitation of inexpensive hardware, i.e. RGB cameras in place of depth sensors. Large benchmark datasets such as the CityScapes dataset have proven to be extremely valuable in developing and testing automotive-related solutions, such as networks for monocular depth estimation [1] and for semantic segmentation [10] of street scenes.

The specialized literature is mostly focused on either improving the model accuracy, or in reducing the computational complexity of the involved models. Relatively little effort has been put into investigating and quantifying the impact of meteorological conditions over the method performance, including phenomena that alter the image quality such as haze, rain, and changes in illumination conditions. This is mostly due to the lack of appropriate datasets, i.e. real-life photos acquired in bad weather conditions, and annotated for computer vision tasks such as semantic segmentation. For this reason, in fact, we will resort to synthetic rain augmentation over annotated datasets for the quantitative experiments presented in this paper.

© Springer Nature Switzerland AG 2021
A. Del Bimbo et al. (Eds.): ICPR 2020 Workshops, LNCS 12666, pp. 597–610, 2021.
https://doi.org/10.1007/978-3-030-68780-9_46

Valada et al. [17] presented a multi-stream deep neural network that learns features from multimodal data, and adaptively weights different features based on the scene conditions. The authors assessed semantic segmentation on the synthetic dataset Synthia [15] (which includes rainy scenes), but did not offer a direct comparative evaluation on the presence and absence of rain-induced artifacts. Khan et al. [6] created an entirely artificial dataset for semantic segmentation in different atmospheric conditions, to be used as training data for the task. We argue that although synthetic data generation is essential in producing an adequately large database, introducing synthetic rain artifacts over real images would instead offer the grounds for an evaluation that is closer to a real-case scenario. Porav et al. [13] focused on the removal of rain droplets, which by definition refer to the artifacts introduced by a wet glass on a clear day. As such these are only partially representative of real-case scenarios. Halder et al. [3] developed a physics-based data augmentation technique, used to train more robust models for semantic segmentation, although they offer no insights on the benefits of rain-removal techniques. Recently, Li et al. [7] defined a unified benchmark for images perturbed by rain streaks, rain drops, and mist, and tested different methods for rain removal, including among the evaluation criteria the impact over vehicle detection. In terms of general purpose rain removal, without emphasis on its impact over other computer vision tasks, the scientific literature offers a wide variety of solutions. A recent review by Yang et al. [18] presents a comprehensive analysis of methods, from model-based to data-driven.

In this paper, we focus on the effects of rain streaks on a neural network for semantic segmentation of street scenes. We experiment with a semantic segmentation architecture that belongs to the class of "real time" solutions, as we consider it to be an interesting use case for a stress test, whereas accuracy-oriented networks would be implicitly more robust. The domain of semantic segmentation inherently enables a fine-grained analysis of the results, as per-class performance can be individually scrutinized. The aforementioned lack of annotated datasets for semantic segmentation in a rainy environment is here addressed by performing synthetic data augmentation, in the form of artificial rain streaks. Additionally, we are interested in evaluating to what extent it is possible to regain semantic segmentation accuracy by exploiting rain removal techniques. For this reason, we introduce a generative model for the removal of rain streaks, to be applied over the synthetically-augmented images.

## 2    Methodology for Rain Generation, Rain Removal, and Semantic Segmentation

In this section we describe the building blocks of our study over the impact of rain on semantic segmentation of street scenes. We first describe how artificial rain streaks can be generated and introduced on existing datasets. We then define a generative adversarial network for the removal of rain in digital images, and finally we define the adopted encoder-decoder network for real-time semantic segmentation.

In this and the next sections, we will call the images clean, rainy, and rain-removed in relation to their status: with clean images, we will refer to images taken in clear weather conditions, with rainy images, we will refer to pictures taken under rainy weather, and finally, with rain-removed images, we will refer to images processed in order to remove the rain originally presents in the picture.

## 2.1  Synthetic Rain Augmentation

In order to reproduce semi-realistic rainy images, following the work done in [20], we decided to generate random rainy masks to apply over the target images. Differently from [19], instead of using Photoshop to generate a limited number of masks to randomly apply to the images, we used MATLAB to create a random rainy mask generator, which for each image generates a new mask, based on some parameters randomly selected in ranges that have been defined empirically, with respect to the original approach from [19] and the objective of obtaining semi-realistic rainy images. The pipeline is represented in Fig. 1.

Starting from an sRGB image, the process first generates a raindrop mask, by choosing four parameters: $d_1$ rain density, $\sigma_1$ Gaussian filter dimension, $l_1$ streak length, $\alpha_1$ falling angle. After that, a rain streaks map is generated using two parameters previously chosen for the first mask: $l_1$ streak length and $\sigma_1$ falling angle, and two other ones chosen at this step: $d_2$ rain density and $\alpha_2$ Gaussian filter dimension. Eventually, an optional haze mask is generated. These three masks are then applied to the image in order to obtain the rainy version of the original input image.

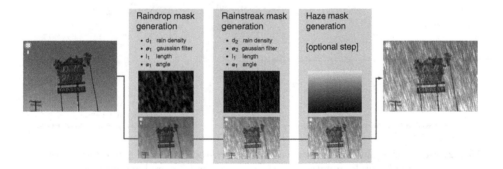

**Fig. 1.** Steps of the pipeline designed for the synthetic rain generation

## 2.2  Generative Adversarial Network for Rain Removal

In order to perform the rain removal process we employed an autoencoder Convolutional Neural Network (CNN) based on the U-Net architecture, trained in a conditional Generative Adversarial Network (GAN) framework. In particular we adopted the method used for rain reduction in [20].

The structure of the rain removal CNN is based on the U-Net [14] architecture, with the addition of skip connections as done for Pix2Pix network [4]. The architecture is shown in Fig. 2. Based also on recent works related to image enhancement, some changes have been made to the classical U-Net architecture, in order to reduce the introduction of artifacts and improve the quality of the final results:

- The normalization layers have been removed from the model, in order to avoid the generation of artifacts, as done in [8] and [12].
- Max-pooling operation have been replaced with convolutions with 2-pixel stride to reduce feature spatial dimensions, without losing useful information for the restoration process.
- A combination of bilinear upsampling with 2D Convolution has been adopted, to reduce artifacts coming from the application of the deconvolutional layers in the decoder part of the network.

In order to train the model in a Generative Adversarial Network framework we adopted a patchGAN discriminative network, trained in a Conditional GAN training approach [11]. The architecture of the discriminative model is shown in Fig. 2. During the training phase the discriminative network is fed with the concatenation of the enhanced image and the original input image. The overview of the network combination for training is shown in Fig. 3.

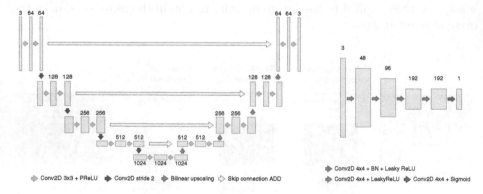

**Fig. 2.** Generative and discriminative model architectures. The generative model is a U-Net autoencoder style architecture: the max pooling layers have been replaced with convolutions with strides >1 and the upscaling operation is performed with Bilinear Interpolation combined with convolutions. The discriminative network is based on the architecture of the Conditional PatchGAN discriminator.

**Loss Function.** The loss function used to train the model is defined as:

$$Loss = \lambda_e \cdot L_e + \lambda_{adv} \cdot L_{adv} + \lambda_p \cdot L_p. \tag{1}$$

which is the combination of three loss functions, weighted by three different weight values $\lambda_e, \lambda_{adv}, \lambda_p$

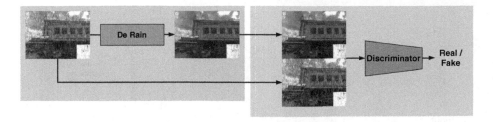

**Fig. 3.** Training system with Conditional patchGAN.

Given an image pair $\{x, y\}$ with $C$ channels, width $W$ and height $H$ (i.e. $C \times W \times H$), where $x$ is the input image and $y$ is the corresponding target, we define the three loss function as follows.

The per-pixel Euclidean loss, defined as:

$$L_e = \frac{1}{CWH} \sum_{c=1}^{C} \sum_{w=1}^{W} \sum_{h=1}^{H} ||\phi_E(x^{c,w,h}) - y^{c,w,h}||_2^2, \tag{2}$$

where $\phi_E(\cdot)$ is the learned network for rain removal.

The perceptual loss [5] defined as distance function between features extracted from the target and output images, using a pre-trained VGG network [16]:

$$L_p = \frac{1}{C_i W_i H_i} \sum_{c=1}^{C_i} \sum_{w=1}^{W_i} \sum_{h=1}^{H_i} ||V(\phi_E(x^{c,w,h})) - V(y_B^{c,w,h})||_2^2, \tag{3}$$

where $V(\cdot)$ represents a non-linear CNN transformation (VGG16 network). Finally, the original $GAN$ loss described as:

$$L_{adv} = \mathbb{E}_{x,y}[\log D(x, y)] + \mathbb{E}_x[\log(1 - D(x, G(x)))], \tag{4}$$

where $G(\cdot)$ is the trained generative network for image de-raining.

### 2.3   Encoder-Decoder Network for Semantic Segmentation

Semantic segmentation integrates traditional image segmentation (which partitions the input image into subregions without a regular shape) with the categorical classification of each generated subregion. The great majority of current image segmentation architectures are based on the encoder-decoder structure [9] to exploit a large receptive field and, at the same time, to produce high-resolution predictions.

We focus our study on the iGUM network (improved Guided Upsampling Module) [10]. The architecture, shown in Fig. 4, is composed of a lightweight encoder and a iGUM-based decoder.

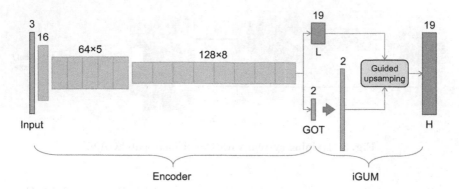

**Fig. 4.** Schematic representation of the iGUM encoder-decoder architecture used for real-time semantic segmentation. Each activation is annotated with the corresponding number of channels.

The encoder structure is compact and thus efficient. Its main building block is a lightweight non-bottleneck residual block with two asymmetric kernels $(3 \times 1)$ and $(1 \times 3)$ preceded and followed by $1 \times 1$ channel-wise convolutions. The encoder produces two low-resolution outputs: the probability map per class (L), and a low-resolution Guidance Offsets Table (GOT), which is then upsampled to the target resolution by means of a scaling factor $f$. Both branches serve as input to the iGUM module.

In encoder-decoder architectures, the decoder typically plays a refinement role where features are iteratively upsampled to match the input size and to finally output a dense per-pixel prediction. In this case, the decoder is effectively replaced *in toto* by the iGUM module: whereas semantic segmentation traditionally involves the prediction of a dense per-pixel map of class probabilities, the iGUM module introduces a more efficient representation, which allows for a non-uniform density grid. Let $L \in \mathbb{R}^{N \times M \times C}$ be the low-resolution $C$-channel probability map, and let $p_i$ and $q_i$ be the two channel composing the Guidance Offsets Table at high resolution. The output of iGUM, a high-resolution map $H \in \mathbb{R}^{fN \times fM \times C}$, is computed as a generalization of the nearest neighbor operator:

$$H_i = \sum_{n}^{N} \sum_{m}^{M} L(\delta(\lfloor x_i^s + p_i + 0.5 \rfloor - m), \delta(\lfloor y_i^s + q_i + 0.5 \rfloor - n)) \qquad (5)$$

Indices $n$ and $m$ slide over the low-resolution dimensions, while index $i$ is used to indicate the high-resolution domain. $x_i^s$ and $y_i^s$ are the spatial sampling coordinates. $\lfloor x_i^s + 0.5 \rfloor$ and $\lfloor y_i^s + 0.5 \rfloor$ round the coordinates to the nearest integer location, and $\delta$ is a Kronecker function for input selection. Offsets $p_i$ and $q_i$ effectively shift the sampling coordinates of each grid element in the $x$ and $y$ dimensions respectively.

# 3    Experiments

## 3.1    Dataset and Evaluation Metrics

We performed our experiments on the Cityscapes [2] dataset: a set of urban street images annotated with pixel-wise semantic information. It is composed of 5000 high-resolution images ($2048 \times 1024$) out of which 2975, 500 and 1525 images belong respectively to train, validation and test subsets. Annotations include 30 different classes of objects, although only 19 are typically used for training and evaluation, plus a background class:

- road
- sidewalk
- building
- wall
- fence

- pole
- traffic light
- traffic sign
- vegetation
- terrain

- sky
- person
- rider
- car
- truck

- bus
- train
- motorcycle
- bicycle
- (background)

The dataset is characterized by a vast diversity of scenes, with images taken from different cities all with good or medium weather conditions.

Two metrics are used for model validation: avereage of class-wise Intersection over Union (IoU, also called Jaccard Index) and average class-wise Accuracy. These are computed as:

$$\text{IoU} = \frac{TP}{TP + FP + FN} \tag{6}$$

$$\text{Accuracy} = \frac{TP}{TP + FN} \tag{7}$$

where TP, FP and FN are, respectively, the number of True Positive, False Positive, and False Negative pixels.

## 3.2    Experimental Results

In this section we are going to analyze the performance of the semantic segmentation model in relation to the condition of the data involved (i.e. "clean", rainy, and rain-removed). We evaluate the model considering condition of data used for training as well as for validation.

For the analysis we have considered three version of the Cityscapes dataset:

- **Clean images:** the original images from the Cityscapes dataset.
- **Rainy images:** images obtained using the synthetic mask generation algorithm starting from the "clean" images.
- **Rain-removed images:** images obtained by removing the rain from the rainy images version of the Cityscapes, using the rain reduction algorithm.

This analysis has been done with the purpose of studying how the level of degradation in data can affect the performances of the segmentation algorithm in inference time, and how it can affect the learning process of the model.

Table 1 and 2 report respectively the mean Accuracy and mean of class-wise Intersection over Union.

**Table 1.** Accuracy of semantic segmentation on the Cityscapes validation dataset: table shows the results in relation to the training data used for the semantic segmentation network.

| Accuracy | | Test data | | |
|---|---|---|---|---|
| | | Clean | Rainy | Rain removed |
| Training data | Clean | 72.88% | 24.73% | 41.57% |
| | Rainy | 35.34% | 35.75% | 34.66% |
| | Rain removed | 69.75% | 67.00% | 67.96% |

**Table 2.** Intersection Over Union of semantic segmentation on the Cityscapes validation dataset: table shows the results in relation to the training data used for the semantic segmentation network.

| IoU | | Test data | | |
|---|---|---|---|---|
| | | Clean | Rainy | Rain removed |
| Training data | Clean | 62.59% | 15.00% | 27.50% |
| | Rainy | 29.48% | 29.31% | 27.85% |
| | Rain removed | 58.03% | 56.28% | 57.64% |

As can be seen from the tables, for what concerns the segmentation with the model trained on "clean" (rain-free) images, the rain removal step helps to improve the performance with respect to direct segmentation of rainy images. While, as expected, with the "clean" validation images the segmentation algorithm performs better than the other cases. It is interesting to notice how the rain-removal pre-processing operation brings to an accuracy improvement of 16.84% and mIoU of 12.50% between the rainy images and the rain-removed ones.

For what concerns the other two training cases, the one with the rainy training set and the one with the rain-removed training set, we can observe a different behavior. In both of the cases, independently from the validation dataset used, the performance of the segmentation model in terms of accuracy an IoU does not change significantly. This behavior can be related to the amount of information present in the images used for training. In the first of these two cases, the network trained with the rainy images is not able to perform better than 36% in terms of accuracy, and 30% in terms of mIoU. Since during the training phase, part of the information in each image is always occluded or corrupted, the model is not capable to learn correct feature extraction for the classification of some specific classes. Looking at the per-class mIoU analysis in Fig. 5b, some of the classes have mIoU of 0% or values very near to zero. As can be seen, for the three validation set the situation is the same for all the classes, behavior that shows how the limited capability of the network to correctly segment element of the images is related to the missing information during training time, and not related to the type of validation data.

Similar behavior can be observed with the model trained with the rain-removed images. In this case, the performance improves in terms of accuracy and IoU due to the partially restored information in the training set, after the use of the rain-removal model. However, the general behavior is the same as the previous case: even if we test the model with "clean" images, the model is not able to perform better than the other two validation set cases, due to the missing knowledge in the training images.

In Fig. 5c we can see the per-class analysis: it is easy to observe the same behavior of the model trained with the rainy images, but it is also possible to observe an improvement in the segmentation of classes that were not recognized by the model trained with rainy images. This improvement is related to the enhancement of the training data due to the pre-processing step over the training set. Aside, it is interesting how the training with the rain-removed images has improved the results of the segmentation model with respect to the one trained with "clean" images.

## 3.3   Visual Inspection

We here present a visual inspection of the impact of rain and rain-removal techniques over semantic segmentation. Figure 6 clearly shows the deterioration in prediction accuracy introduced by rain-related artifacts (row c). The strong texture of rain streaks completely changes the interpretation of the road and sidewalk areas, which are mistaken as an obstacle (wall/fence). This phenomenon occurs despite the strong intrinsic bias of the "road" class, that appears in the plurality of training data pixels, and that occupies a consistent area throughout different images. On top of this, small regions such as the traffic signs and far-away vehicles are completely missed.

By processing the rain-augmented image using our rain-removal network, it is possible to partially restore the accuracy of semantic segmentation in some of the areas. As Fig. 6d shows, the segmentation of the small cars is almost completely recovered, and part of the road and sidewalk are correctly identified. A qualitative and subjective evaluation of rain removal on the RGB image shows arguably less impressive results, suggesting a disconnect between perceived quality and usefulness for computer vision.

The best results, however, are obtained by retraining the semantic segmentation network using images that were processed with the rain-augmentation pipeline and subsequent rain-removal. In this case, the prediction in the same scenario, as depicted in Fig. 6e shows an excellent restoration of several details, although some imperfections remain in the top-right corner of the example image.

For the sake of completeness, we also perform a qualitative evaluation over two out-of-dataset real-life pictures, depicted in Fig. 7. Specifically, we report semantic segmentation results over the original rainy images trained with the

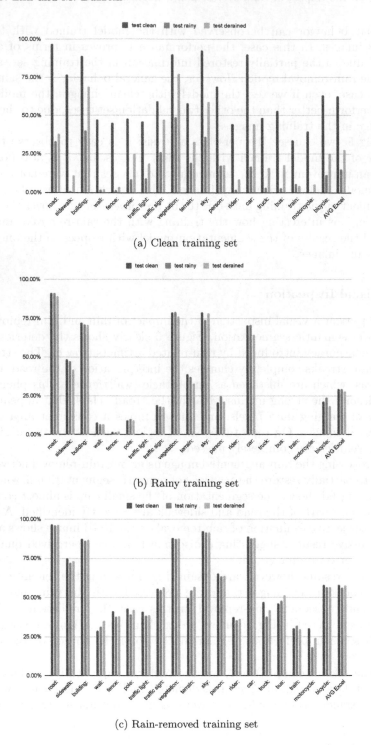

(a) Clean training set

(b) Rainy training set

(c) Rain-removed training set

**Fig. 5.** Mean intersection over union value for each class of the Cityscapes test set

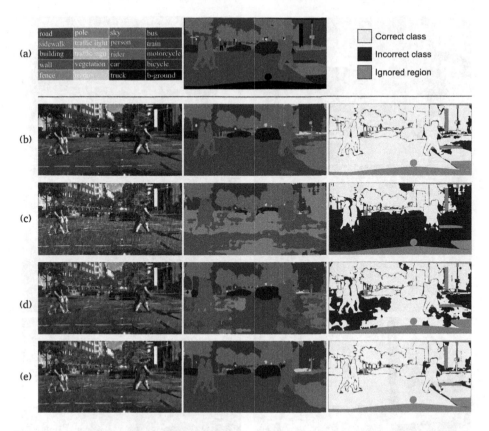

**Fig. 6.** Impact of rain on semantic segmentation. Row (a) presents the color coding for semantic segmentation, the ground truth for the analyzed image, and the legend for error visualization. Rows (b) to (e) show, respectively, the prediction on the original "clean" image, on the image with artificial rain, on the image with rain removed, and once again on the image with rain removed but using a semantic segmentation model trained on images processed for rain and subsequent rain removal.

"clean" version of the Cityscapes dataset (column a), and results over rain-removed images trained with the rain-removed version of Cityscapes (column b). These two extreme cases show the significant improvement in segmentation quality that can be obtained by the joint application of our rain removal network both on training data and inference data. The final results still show some imperfections, which can be attributed to the different nature of the image data when compared to the training set, both concerning rain appearance, as well as the general content and format of the pictures.

(a)                                         (b)

**Fig. 7.** Visual assessment of rain (column a) and rain-removal (column b) over real case images, using semantic segmentation trained respectively on "clean" images, and images processed for rain-removal. Original images credit Nick Út, and Genaro Servín.

## 4   Conclusions

In this work we investigated the negative effects of rain streaks over the performance of neural networks. Specifically we focused on the semantic segmentation task.

We proposed an analysis of the performance of a semantic segmentation neural network, in relation to different training configurations, and different inference conditions.

In order to perform the analysis we defined a pipeline for synthetic rain generation and a rain removal neural network to augment the Cityscapes dataset, obtaining three different versions of the dataset for both training and testing the semantic segmentation network.

The model has been trained in three different conditions: with "clean" images, with images with artificial rain streaks, and with images processed for removal of the artificial rain streaks. In the first case the experiments show how the application of rain-removal on rainy images gives benefit for the segmentation step of a model trained in optimal image conditions. The other experiments, regarding the impact of the degraded information in the images used for training the model, shows how the application of an enhancement algorithm can improve the performance of the model at inference time. We observed an improvement of 34% of accuracy and 30% of mIoU between the model trained with the degraded images and the one trained with the enhanced ones.

# References

1. Bianco, S., Buzzelli, M., Schettini, R.: A unifying representation for pixel-precise distance estimation. Multimedia Tools Appl. **78**(10), 13767–13786 (2019)
2. Cordts, M., et al.: The cityscapes dataset for semantic urban scene understanding. In: Proceedings of the IEEE Conference on Computer Vision and Pattern Recognition, pp. 3213–3223 (2016)
3. Halder, S.S., Lalonde, J.F., de Charette, R.: Physics-based rendering for improving robustness to rain. In: Proceedings of the IEEE International Conference on Computer Vision, pp. 10203–10212 (2019)
4. Isola, P., Zhu, J.Y., Zhou, T., Efros, A.A.: Image-to-image translation with conditional adversarial networks. In: Proceedings of the IEEE Conference on Computer Vision and Pattern Recognition, pp. 1125–1134 (2017)
5. Johnson, J., Alahi, A., Fei-Fei, L.: Perceptual losses for real-time style transfer and super-resolution. In: Leibe, B., Matas, J., Sebe, N., Welling, M. (eds.) ECCV 2016. LNCS, vol. 9906, pp. 694–711. Springer, Cham (2016). https://doi.org/10.1007/978-3-319-46475-6_43
6. Khan, S., Phan, B., Salay, R., Czarnecki, K.: ProcSy: procedural synthetic dataset generation towards influence factor studies of semantic segmentation networks. In: CVPR Workshops, pp. 88–96 (2019)
7. Li, S., et al.: Single image deraining: a comprehensive benchmark analysis. In: Proceedings of the IEEE Conference on Computer Vision and Pattern Recognition, pp. 3838–3847 (2019)
8. Lim, B., Son, S., Kim, H., Nah, S., Mu Lee, K.: Enhanced deep residual networks for single image super-resolution. In: Proceedings of the IEEE Conference on Computer Vision and Pattern Recognition Workshops, pp. 136–144 (2017)
9. Long, J., Shelhamer, E., Darrell, T.: Fully convolutional networks for semantic segmentation. In: Proceedings of the IEEE Conference on Computer Vision and Pattern Recognition, pp. 3431–3440 (2015)
10. Mazzini, D., Schettini, R.: Spatial sampling network for fast scene understanding. In: Proceedings of the IEEE Conference on Computer Vision and Pattern Recognition Workshops (2019)

11. Mirza, M., Osindero, S.: Conditional generative adversarial nets. arXiv preprint arXiv:1411.1784 (2014)
12. Nah, S., Hyun Kim, T., Mu Lee, K.: Deep multi-scale convolutional neural network for dynamic scene deblurring. In: Proceedings of the IEEE Conference on Computer Vision and Pattern Recognition, pp. 3883–3891 (2017)
13. Porav, H., Bruls, T., Newman, P.: I can see clearly now: image restoration via deraining. In: 2019 International Conference on Robotics and Automation (ICRA), pp. 7087–7093. IEEE (2019)
14. Ronneberger, O., Fischer, P., Brox, T.: U-Net: convolutional networks for biomedical image segmentation. In: Navab, N., Hornegger, J., Wells, W.M., Frangi, A.F. (eds.) MICCAI 2015. LNCS, vol. 9351, pp. 234–241. Springer, Cham (2015). https://doi.org/10.1007/978-3-319-24574-4_28
15. Ros, G., Sellart, L., Materzynska, J., Vazquez, D., Lopez, A.M.: The synthia dataset: a large collection of synthetic images for semantic segmentation of urban scenes. In: Proceedings of the IEEE Conference on Computer Vision and Pattern Recognition, pp. 3234–3243 (2016)
16. Simonyan, K., Zisserman, A.: Very deep convolutional networks for large-scale image recognition. arXiv preprint arXiv:1409.1556 (2014)
17. Valada, A., Vertens, J., Dhall, A., Burgard, W.: AdapNet: adaptive semantic segmentation in adverse environmental conditions. In: 2017 IEEE International Conference on Robotics and Automation (ICRA), pp. 4644–4651. IEEE (2017)
18. Yang, W., Tan, R.T., Wang, S., Fang, Y., Liu, J.: Single image deraining: from model-based to data-driven and beyond. IEEE Trans. Pattern Anal. Mach. Intell. (2020)
19. Zhang, H., Sindagi, V., Patel, V.M.: Image de-raining using a conditional generative adversarial network. IEEE Trans. Circ. Syst. Video Technol. **30**(11), 3943–3956 (2019)
20. Zini, S., Bianco, S., Schettini, R.: CNN-based rain reduction in street view images. In: Proceedings of the 2020 London Imaging Meeting, pp. 78–81 (2020). https://doi.org/10.2352/issn.2694-118X.2020.LIM-12

# The Impact of Linear Motion Blur on the Object Recognition Efficiency of Deep Convolutional Neural Networks

José A. Rodríguez-Rodríguez[1], Miguel A. Molina-Cabello[1,2(✉)] (iD),
Rafaela Benítez-Rochel[1,2], and Ezequiel López-Rubio[1,2] (iD)

[1] Department of Computer Languages and Computer Science, University of Malaga,
Bulevar Louis Pasteur, 35, 29071 Málaga, Spain
joseantoniorodriguez@uma.es, {miguelangel,benitez,ezeqlr}@lcc.uma.es
[2] Biomedic Research Institute of Málaga (IBIMA), Málaga, Spain

**Abstract.** Noise which can appear in images affects the classification performance of Convolutional Neural Networks (CNNs). In particular, the impact of linear motion blur, which is one of the possible noises, in the classification performance of CNNs is assessed in this work. A realistic vision sensor model has been proposed to produce a linear motion blur effect in input images. This methodology allows analyzing how the performance of several considered state of the art CNNs is affected. Experiments that have been carried out indicate that the accuracy is heavily degraded by a high length of the displacement, while the angle of displacement deteriorates the performance to a lesser extent.

**Keywords:** Convolutional neural networks · Image classification · Noise · Motion blur · CMOS vision sensor

## 1 Introduction

Convolutional Neural Networks (CNNs) are deep neural networks whose convolutional layers alternate with subsampling layers, reminiscent of simple and complex cells in the primary visual cortex [5]. These neural models have been proven to be very effective on different problems of visual information processing like object detection, semantic segmentation, image classification, biomedical analysis, image captioning, image coloring, biometric authentication, among many others [3,8]. In many cases, these methods even exceed the performance that a human can provide [1,6,7]. Despite their impressive performance, deep networks have been shown to be susceptible to quality degraded input images.

---

This work is partially supported by the following Spanish grants: TIN2016-75097-P, RTI2018-094645-B-I00 and UMA18-FEDERJA-084. All of them include funds from the European Regional Development Fund (ERDF). The authors acknowledge the funding from the Universidad de Málaga.

A. Del Bimbo et al. (Eds.): ICPR 2020 Workshops, LNCS 12666, pp. 611–622, 2021.
https://doi.org/10.1007/978-3-030-68780-9_47

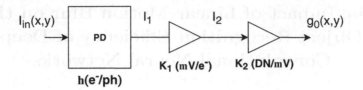

**Fig. 1.** Block diagram of a vision sensor. A photo-diode (rectangle) is followed by two stages of conversion (triangles) with gain $K_1$ and $K_2$, respectively.

The impact of linear motion blur in the classification performance of CNNs is studied in this work. Motion blur is an inevitable phenomenon under long exposure times and directly affects subsequent image recognition and image analysis. Both of the camera shake and object moving can lead to blurry images. Among the situations of image degradation, image blur is hard to resolve because of the complex image sampling environment [12]. In order to overcome this issue, a realistic sensor model has been proposed to produce a linear motion blur effect in input images.

While human examiners are, to a large extent, resilient to such factors during image recognition, it is unclear to what degree it affects the performance of deep neural networks. In this paper, a methodology to analyze this problem has been developed, considering several most notable CNNs of recent years such as DenseNet [4], Inception [11] and WideResNet [15].

The paper is organized as follows. First of all, the methodology for constructing our benchmark blur image data sets is detailed in Sect. 2. Then, the numerical experiments using the model in previous section and the results to analyze the performance of CNNs model are presented in Sect. 3. Finally, the conclusions are summarized in Sect. 4.

## 2   Methodology

In this section the proposed methodology for the study of the behavior of CNNs for object recognition under linear motion blur is detailed. Let us consider Fig. 1, where a simplified block diagram of a vision sensor is displayed.

The first stage of the sensor carries out an integration, since electrons are generated from the energy of the incoming photons. The total number of photos which hit the photodiode (PD in Fig. 1) is given by:

$$I_{in}(x, y) = \int_0^{T_0} \varphi(x, y)\, dt \tag{1}$$

where $\varphi(x, y)$ is the photon flux per second at each pixel $(x, y)$. Next the photons are converted to electrons:

$$I_1(x, y) = \eta I_{in}(x, y) = \int_0^{T_0} \eta \varphi(x, y)\, dt \tag{2}$$

where $\eta$ $(e^-/ph)$ is the quantum efficiency (a constant). After that, the electrons are converted to voltage by:

$$I_2(x,y) = K_1 I_1(x,y) = \int_0^{T_0} K_1 \eta \varphi(x,y) \, dt \tag{3}$$

Voltage is converted to digit numbers $(DN)$ as follows:

$$I_{out}(x,y) = K_2 I_2(x,y) = \int_0^{T_0} K_2 K_1 \eta \varphi(x,y) \, dt \tag{4}$$

where $I_{out}(x,y) = g(x,y)$ is the digital image that the vision sensor produces.

In case that a linear motion blur is present, the underlying unblurred image $f(x,y)$ is different from the acquired blurred image $g(x,y)$. Therefore, it is necessary to express $f(x,y)$ in terms of $g(x,y)$.

Let us consider a linear motion model for the blurring process. The model is defined by the following equations for the two spatial coordinates:

$$x_0(t) = \frac{a}{T}t \qquad y_0(t) = \frac{b}{T}t \tag{5}$$

where $t$ is a time instant, $T$ is the duration of the exposure corresponding to the image acquisition, and the displacement vector associated to the linear motion is given by $(a,b)$. The blurred image $g(x,y)$ can be expressed by an integration of the underlying unblurred image $f(x,y)$ as the motion progresses:

$$g(x,y) = \int_0^T f(x - x_0(t), y - y_0(t)) \, dt \tag{6}$$

As seen in [2], p. 476, this translates to the Fourier domain as follows:

$$G(u,v) = H(u,v) F(u,v) \tag{7}$$

$$H(u,v) = e^{-j\pi(ua+vb)} \operatorname{sinc}(ua + vb) \tag{8}$$

where $G$ and $F$ are the Fourier transforms of the acquired blurred image and the underlying unblurred image, respectively, and $H$ is the Fourier transform of the linear motion blur degradation, and the sinc function is defined as:

$$\operatorname{sinc}(z) = \frac{\sin(\pi z)}{\pi z} \tag{9}$$

Next we reparametrize the linear motion as a pair $(l, \theta)$ where $l$ is the length of the displacement and $\theta$ is the angle of displacement. This is done by the following equations to convert from the displacement vector $(a,b)$ to the new parameter vector:

$$l^2 = a^2 + b^2 \tag{10}$$

$$\tan(\theta) = \frac{b}{a} \tag{11}$$

The opposite conversion is given by:

$$a = \begin{cases} -\dfrac{l}{\sqrt{1 + \tan^2(\theta)}}, & \text{if } 90° < \theta < 270° \\ \dfrac{l}{\sqrt{1 + \tan^2(\theta)}}, & \text{otherwise} \end{cases} \tag{12}$$

$$b = a \tan(\theta) \tag{13}$$

Now, given an unblurred original image, blurred versions of it can be generated by obtaining its Fourier transform $F(u, \nu)$ followed by the application of the motion blur degradation given by Eq. (7), where the degradation filter comes from Eq. (8) and the displacement vector $(a, b)$ can be computed from the parameter vector $(l, \theta)$ as indicated in Eqs. (12) and (13). The blurred versions $g(x, y)$ are obtained by applying the inverse Fourier transform to $G(u, \nu)$. Such blurred versions are subsequently supplied to a convolutional neural network in order to check its object recognition performance depending on the parameter vector $(l, \theta)$.

## 3    Experimental Results

The objective of this work is to analyze the impact of Motion Blur on deep CNN. Following this motivation, several experiments have been performed using the model described in Sect. 2.

A huge variety of CNNs can be found in the literature but it is not possible to cover all of them. For this reason six well-known and state-of-the-art CNNs have been chosen: DenseNet-201 [4] (201 layers), Inception-v3 [11] (variable number of layers), MNASNet-v1.0 [13], MobileNet-v2 [10] (53 layers), WideResNet 101-2 [15] (101 layers) and ResNeXt-101 [14] (101 layers).

These CNN models were implemented using Python, through Torchvision package from PyTorch [9] and they had been pre-trained to carry out classification task using a subset of images from ImageNet. Regarding the test dataset used in the experiments, one thousand images (1,000) have been selected randomly from the ILSRVC2012 validation set[1].

In order to establish the tuned configurations, a huge range of values for the parameters length $l$ and angle $\theta$ have been selected. The considered values for both parameters are $l = 0.005 \cdot i$ where $i = \{1..10\}$ and $\theta = 15° \cdot j$ where $j = \{1..24\}$.

### 3.1    Qualitative Results

A qualitative analysis of the impact of motion blur in order to get a better understanding of its degradation effect is shown in this subsection. Experiments have been performed using images where motion blur had been applied to emulate

---

[1] http://www.image-net.org/challenges/LSVRC/2012/.

(a) Raw ($l = 0.00$)

(b) $l = 0.01, \theta = 0°$   (c) $l = 0.01, \theta = 45°$   (d) $l = 0.04, \theta = 0°$   (e) $l = 0.04, \theta = 45°$

**Fig. 2.** Effect of motion blur in an image. Top image shows the raw image (in this case, Image 95 of the selected dataset), while remaining images exhibit how different levels of motion blur affect the raw image.

the degradation produced by the sensor or object movement during the exposure time or so-called integration phase. This way, the mathematical model described in Sect. 2 has been used to synthesize the blurred images that were used as inputs of the cited CNNs. Additionally, in ImageNet dataset, images are encoded with the RGB color scheme. Therefore, the same filter has to be applied to the three color channels.

Figures 2 and 3 show the motion blur effect on two different images (in this case, a macaque and a skier, respectively) for different values of the vector ($l$, $\theta$). As expected, the greater is $l$, the greater is the blur. Indeed, both images begin to be hard to be recognized by the human eye for $l = 0.05$. Regarding the angle $\theta$ analysis, it is not easy to evaluate when the skier is less distinguishable for the two values of $\theta$ have been used, $0°$ and $45°$. Conversely, the macaque is something less distinguishable when $\theta$ is $45°$. Since this fact does allow to extract conclusions regarding the $\theta$ parameter, it will be analyzed in the next subsection.

Another interesting point to notice is related with the filter used for the experiments detailed in Sect. 2. Figure 4 depicts the frequency spectrum for the filters used in the generation of the blurred images. It can be deduced that the spectrum is symmetric and formed by several lines in parallel where the central

**Table 1.** Predictions for Image 95 and 3918 provided by MobileNet-v2. Each column exhibits the image, the configuration of motion blur, the five best truth class probability and its result index (the position in terms of probability).

| Image | Configuration | Predictions | Probability |
|---|---|---|---|
| 95 | $l = 0.00$ | 1.- **macaque** | **0.6745** |
| | | 2.- capuchin, ringtail, ... | 0.1849 |
| | | 3.- patas, hussar monkey, ... | 0.0325 |
| | | 4.- proboscis monkey, Nasalis larvatus | 0.0286 |
| | | 5.- titi, titi monkey | 0.0161 |
| | $l = 0.01, \theta = 0°$ | 1.- **macaque** | **0.7243** |
| | | 2.- capuchin, ringtail, ... | 0.1751 |
| | | 3.- patas, hussar monkey, ... | 0.0384 |
| | | 4.- spider monkey, Nasalis larvatus | 0.0135 |
| | | 5.- proboscis monkey, Nasalis larvatus | 0.0122 |
| | $l = 0.01, \theta = 45°$ | 1.- **macaque** | **0.5195** |
| | | 2.- capuchin, ringtail, ... | 0.2773 |
| | | 3.- proboscis monkey, Nasalis larvatus | 0.0836 |
| | | 4.- patas, hussar monkey, ... | 0.0364 |
| | | 5.- titi, titi monkey | 0.0247 |
| | $l = 0.04, \theta = 0°$ | 1.- gibbon, Hylobates lar | 0.5229 |
| | | 2.- patas, hussar monkey, ... | 0.0553 |
| | | 3.- **macaque** | **0.0554** |
| | | 4.- collie | 0.0317 |
| | | 5.- langur | 0.0294 |
| | $l = 0.04, \theta = 45°$ | 1.- hamster | 0.1769 |
| | | 2.- cougar, puma... | 0.0453 |
| | | 3.- golden retriever | 0.0391 |
| | | 4.- weasel | 0.0391 |
| | | 5.- Norfolk terrier | 0.0284 |
| 3918 | $l = 0.00, \theta = 0°$ | 1.- **ski** | **0.9996** |
| | | 2.- dogsled... | 0.0001 |
| | | 3.- pubck, hockey puck | 0.0001 |
| | | 4.- snowmobile | 0.0000 |
| | | 5.- shovel | 0.0000 |
| | $l = 0.01, \theta = 0°$ | 1.- **ski** | **0.9994** |
| | | 2.- dogsled... | 0.0002 |
| | | 3.- catamaran | 0.0000 |
| | | 4.- flagpole, flagstaff | 0.0000 |
| | | 5.- shovel | 0.0000 |
| | $l = 0.01, \theta = 45°$ | 1.- **ski** | **0.9228** |
| | | 2.- dogsled... | 0.0441 |
| | | 3.- snowmobile | 0.0161 |
| | | 4.- bobsled, bobsleight, bob | 0.0137 |
| | | 5.- puck, hochey puck | 0.0006 |
| | $l = 0.04, \theta = 0°$ | 1.- **ski** | **0.3349** |
| | | 2.- flagpole, flagstaff | 0.0726 |
| | | 3.- bodsled, bobsleigh, bob | 0.0585 |
| | | 4.- projectile, missile | 0.0353 |
| | | 5.- snowmobile | 0.0339 |
| | $l = 0.04, \theta = 45°$ | 1.- pinwheel | 0.2792 |
| | | 2.- paintbrush | 0.1848 |
| | | 3.- bobsled, bobsleigh, bob | 0.0745 |
| | | 4.- flagpole, flagstaff | 0.0529 |
| | | 5.- **ski** | **0.0423** |

(a) Raw ($l = 0.00$)

(b) $l = 0.01, \theta = 0°$    (c) $l = 0.01, \theta = 45°$    (d) $l = 0.04, \theta = 0°$    (e) $l = 0.04, \theta = 45°$

**Fig. 3.** Effect of motion blur in an image. Top image shows the raw image (in this case, Image 3918 of the selected dataset), while remaining images exhibit how different levels of motion blur affect the raw image.

one contains the maximum while others have a lower value as they are far from the center due to the $sinc(\Delta)$ function employed in Eq. 8. Moreover, lines are perpendicular to the motion direction. At last, it is also observed lines width is wider for lower values of length.

In addition, Table 1 presents the five best predictions of Fig. 2 and 3, for Image 95 and 3918, respectively. Without loss of generality, the CNN employed for this purpose was MobileNet-v2. In that table, the truth predictions (if it is inside the best five predictions) have been marked in **bold**. As it can be deduced, the truth prediction of Image 95 is a *macaque* with a prediction probability of 0.6745 that, in general, it is reduced in presence of motion, specially when $\theta = 45°$. Furthermore, it is noticeable that prediction probability is increased for $l = 0.01$ (0.7243) and it can be explained by considering the motion blur as a filter that improves the image contrast, thus slightly boosting the prediction quality. As it is observed, the prediction probability drops abruptly when the motion blur length is increased to 0.04. This way, it could be prudently said that the higher the motion blur length the higher the degradation of the CNN in terms of prediction quality. Another important point to be considered in this analysis is the angle ($\theta$). Table 1 shows all predictions for Image 95 are aiming to a type of monkey except when $l = 0.04$ and $\theta = 45°$. In this case, MobileNet-v2 is more sensitive to the angle because the best prediction is a hamster, and the others are animals quite different than a type of monkey. The cause of this effect could be a high motion blur length that degrades the prediction probability dramatically.

Regarding the Image 3918, seeing Table 1, MobileNet-v2 has a high prediction probability close to 1 (0.9996) in absence of motion blur but it keeps a good

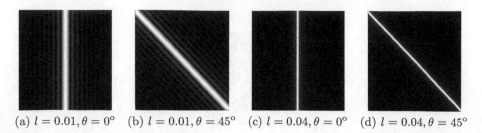

(a) $l = 0.01, \theta = 0°$  (b) $l = 0.01, \theta = 45°$  (c) $l = 0.04, \theta = 0°$  (d) $l = 0.04, \theta = 45°$

**Fig. 4.** Motion Blur filter module spectrum: $(log(1 + |H(u, \nu)|))$ for the motion blur configuration used in the qualitative analysis.

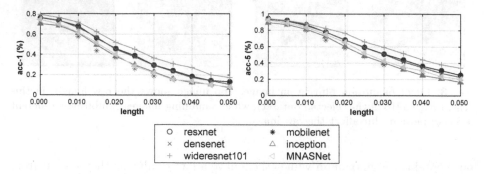

**Fig. 5.** Influence of the parameter length $l$ in the performance of each studied CNN. Top image shows the *acc-1* while bottom image shows the *acc-5*.

probability for moderate values of $l$ parameter (0.01) and the label predicted is *ski*. Also, it is extracted from Table 1 the prediction probabilities are degraded as $l$ parameter is higher. Additionally, as expected from Image 95 results, the CNN es more sensitive to higher values of $l$ parameter (0.04) because the probability of predicting *ski* goes from 0.3349 to 0.0423. Again, it is very interesting to observe how different the prediction is for different values of the angle $\theta$ when $l$ is fixed. In this sense, it must be highlighted the case when $l$ is set to a large value. As can be seen, the prediction is quite different for $\theta = 0°$ and $\theta = 45°$ when $l = 0.04$.

## 3.2   Quantitative Results

In this subsection, quantitative results are presented with the main goal of obtaining some conclusions about the impact of the motion blur effect on the CNNs performance. Two experiments have been carried out in order to get information about how the length $l$ and the angle $\theta$ of motion blur impact on CNNs. The root metric used for measuring the performance of the CNNs is the Accuracy that is defined as the success rate of total predictions. Then two metrics have been derivated from Accuracy called as Accuracy-1 (*acc-1*) and Accuracy-5 (*acc-5*). These two definitions are frequently employed in the literature and

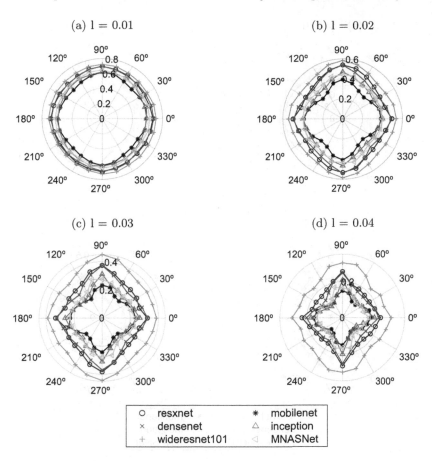

**Fig. 6.** Influence of the angle parameter $\theta$ in the performance of each studied CNN through the *acc-1*. Four length parameter values were analyzed: 0.01, 0.02, 0.03 and 0.04.

they have a range of values that goes from 0 to 1, where higher is better. The former considers only the class with the greatest probability and the second one the five greatest probabilities. Both metrics can be computed following the next expressions:

$$acc\text{-}1 = \frac{SP\text{-}1}{TP} \qquad acc\text{-}5 = \frac{SP\text{-}5}{TP} \tag{14}$$

where SP-1 and SP-5 are the number of successful predictions considering the greatest and the greatest five probabilities, respectively, at the model output; and TP is the total number of predictions carried out.

First, quantitative results about the length analysis are shown in Fig. 5. Comparing accuracy for $l = 0$ (no motion blur effect on the images) with respect to higher values of this parameter $l$, it can be seen how the CNNs performance is degraded as the length is higher. This result is exactly as expected because

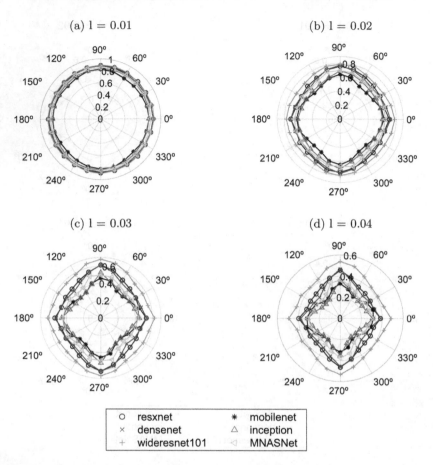

**Fig. 7.** Influence of the angle parameter $\theta$ in the performance of each studied CNN through the *acc-1*. Four length parameter values were analyzed: 0.01, 0.02, 0.03 and 0.04.

the images become more blurred for higher values of length. Apart from this, the analyzed CNNs are affected by the motion blur more or less with the same intensity and they have a monotonic negative slope. The CNN with a best performance is WideResNet 101-2, while MobileNet-v2 is the worst one.

Additionally, an angle parametric *acc-1* and *acc-5* performance analysis is presented in Figs. 6 and 7, respectively. These figures are represented by using polar charts, sweeping the angle from 0° to 360°, to ease the results visualization. As it can be observed, there is a degradation of the performance as the length is higher, as confirmed in Fig. 5. Moreover, CNNs become more sensitive to the angle as the length is higher, so that it produces an extra degradation of about 10% for angles odd multiples of 45° where $a$ and $b$ components are almost the same. This analysis confirms our intuition regarding the degradation on the CNN performance produced by the motion blur angle seen in Figs. 2 and 3.

Furthermore, it must be highlighted how a high value of the length and different angle values of the motion blur produce different performances in the same CNN. Moreover, it is interesting to observe how given a fixed high value for parameter $l$, the performance of a CNN for a given angle value $\theta$ is the same as the performance of that CNN for angle value $\theta + 180°$.

# 4 Conclusions

The effect of motion blur on the classification performance of several well-known CNNs has been studied. A realistic model has been proposed to serve as the mathematical basis of the experiments. This model has been employed to link the motion blur filter equation, calculated in the frequency domain, with the exact moment when motion blur is introduced in the image. The experimental results confirm that analyzed CNNs have similar behavior in terms of performance when images containing motion blur are used as input. Furthermore, higher values of motion length produce a higher drop in CNN performance and make the CNN performance more sensitive to the motion angle. Additionally, it has been shown that there is a relevant drop of accuracy-1 for angles close to odd multiples of $45°$. Moreover, opposite angles obtain the same performance while conjugate angles do not provide the same performance.

# References

1. Ciresan, D., Meier, U.: Multi-column deep neural networks for offline handwritten Chinese character classification. In: 2015 International Joint Conference on Neural Networks (IJCNN), pp. 1–6 (2013)
2. Gonzalez, R.C., Woods, R.E.: Digital Image Processing, 4th edn. Pearson, New York (2018)
3. Gu, J., et al.: Recent advances in convolutional neural networks. arXiv:abs/1512.07108 (2015)
4. Huang, G., Liu, Z., Van Der Maaten, L., Weinberger, K.Q.: Densely connected convolutional networks. In: 2017 IEEE Conference on Computer Vision and Pattern Recognition (CVPR), pp. 2261–2269 (2017)
5. Hubel, D.H., Wiesel, T.N.: Receptive fields, binocular interaction and functional architecture in the cat's visual cortex. J. Physiol. **160**, 106–54 (1962)
6. Russel, J.: Google's Alphago AI wins three-match series against the world's best go player. https://techcrunch.com/2017/05/24/alphago-beats-planets-best-human-go-player-kejie (2017)
7. Krizhevsky, A., Sutskever, I., Hinton, G.E.: Imagenet classification with deep convolutional neural networks. In: NIPS (2012)
8. Molina-Cabello, M.A., Baena, R.M.L., López-Rubio, E., Thurnhofer-Hemsi, K.: Vehicle type detection by ensembles of convolutional neural networks operating on super resolved images. Integr. Comput.-Aided Eng. **25**, 321–333 (2018)
9. PyTorch Contributors: PyTorch Documentation. Version 1.2.0 (2019). https://pytorch.org/docs/1.2.0/. Accessed 31 Oct 2019
10. Sandler, M., Howard, A., Zhu, M., Zhmoginov, A., Chen, L.: Mobilenetv 2: inverted residuals and linear bottlenecks. In: 2018 IEEE/CVF Conference on Computer Vision and Pattern Recognition, pp. 4510–4520 (2018)

11. Szegedy, C., Vanhoucke, V., Ioffe, S., Shlens, J., Wojna, Z.: Rethinking the inception architecture for computer vision. In: 2016 IEEE Conference on Computer Vision and Pattern Recognition (CVPR), pp. 2818–2826 (2016)
12. Szeliski, R.: Computer Vision: Algorithms and Applications, 1st edn. Springe, Heidelberg (2010)
13. Tan, M., et al.: MnasNet: Platform-aware neural architecture search for mobile. In: 2019 IEEE/CVF Conference on Computer Vision and Pattern Recognition (CVPR), pp. 2815–2823 (2019)
14. Xie, S., Girshick, R., Dollár, P., Tu, Z., He, K.: Aggregated residual transformations for deep neural networks. In: 2017 IEEE Conference on Computer Vision and Pattern Recognition (CVPR), pp. 5987–5995 (2017)
15. Zagoruyko, S., Komodakis, N.: Wide residual networks. In: Proceedings of the British Machine Vision Conference 2016, pp. 87.1–87.12. British Machine Vision Association, York (2016). https://doi.org/10.5244/C.30.87, http://www.bmva.org/bmvc/2016/papers/paper087/index.html

# Performance of Deep Learning and Traditional Techniques in Single Image Super-Resolution of Noisy Images

Karl Thurnhofer-Hemsi[1,2](✉) , Guillermo Ruiz-Álvarez[1],
Rafael Marcos Luque-Baena[1,2] , Miguel A. Molina-Cabello[1,2] ,
and Ezequiel López-Rubio[1,2]

[1] Department of Computer Languages and Computer Science,
Universidad de Málaga, Bulevar Louis Pasteur, 35, 29071 Málaga, Spain
{karkhader,rmluque,miguelangel,ezeqlr}@lcc.uma.es
[2] Biomedic Research Institute of Málaga (IBIMA), Málaga, Spain

**Abstract.** The improvement of the spatial resolution of natural images is an important task for many practical applications of current image processing. The endeavor of applying single image super-resolution, which only uses one low-resolution input image, is frequently hampered by the presence of noise or artifacts in the input image, so denoising and super-resolution algorithms are usually applied to obtain a noiseless high-resolution image. In this work, several traditional and deep learning methods for denoising and super-resolution are hybridized to ascertain which combinations of them yield the best possible quality. The experimental design includes the introduction of Gaussian noise, Poisson noise, salt-and-pepper noise, and uniform noise into the low-resolution inputs. It is found that denoising must be carried out before super-resolution for the best results. Moreover, the obtained results indicate that deep learning techniques clearly outperform the traditional ones.

**Keywords:** Super-resolution · Image denoising · Deep learning

## 1 Introduction

Single image super-resolution (SISR) and image denoising are two common low-level tasks in the field of computer vision. SISR is a classical problem that aims at recovering a high-resolution (HR) image from a given low-resolution (LR) version of the same image. This problem is ill-posed because a given LR input

This work is partially supported by the following Spanish grants: TIN2016-75097-P, RTI2018-094645-B-I00 and UMA18-FEDERJA-084. All of them include funds from the European Regional Development Fund (ERDF). The authors acknowledge the funding from the Universidad de Málaga. Karl Thurnhofer-Hemsi is funded by a Ph.D. scholarship from the Spanish Ministry of Education, Culture and Sport under the FPU program (FPU15/06512).

© Springer Nature Switzerland AG 2021
A. Del Bimbo et al. (Eds.): ICPR 2020 Workshops, LNCS 12666, pp. 623–638, 2021.
https://doi.org/10.1007/978-3-030-68780-9_48

can correspond to multiple HR solutions, and therefore reliable prior information is usually required to constraint the solution space [1,5,19]. On the other hand, image denoising is the process of estimating the clean and original version of an image given a noisy input. SISR and image denoising have received increasing attention by researches due to their multiple applications in the field of computer vision. The various methods that have been developed to tackle these two tasks can be broadly classified into two groups: traditional and deep learning methods. Deep learning methods, and more specifically, those using convolutional neural networks (CNNs), have achieved promising results in terms of performance and restoration of quality for both tasks [15,19]. However, applying SISR and denoising methods in conjunction might produce undesired results if the presence of noise or artifacts in the LR images affects the super-resolution task or, likewise, if the result of denoising an input image degrades the quality of the super-resolution step.

Therefore, this study aims at analyzing which is the most efficient workflow to produce HR images given LR inputs with the presence of different types of noise using deep learning methods based on CNNs. In addition, we provide an evaluation comparing traditional and deep learning SISR and image denoising methods on two popular testing datasets (Set5, Set14). For this study, we have selected Gaussian noise, Poisson noise, salt-and-pepper noise, and uniform noise to be applied to down-scaled versions of the HR images. Among all the deep learning methods for SISR and image denoising, experimental results using the Fast Super-Resolution Convolutional Neural Network (FSRCNN) [6] and the Image Restoration Convolutional Neural Network (IRCNN) [21] have demonstrated promising results and high performance in their implementations in graphics processing units (GPUs). Furthermore, we have also selected traditional methods for both super-resolution and image denoising in order to compare the efficiency of applying traditional and deep learning methods to tackle these low-level computer vision tasks. More specifically, we have used bicubic interpolation for SISR and median and wavelet filtering for image denoising.

The remainder of this paper is structured as follows: Sect. 2 summarizes the state-of-the-art deep learning methods for SISR and image denoising. Section 3 describes the implementation details concerning the datasets, the data preprocessing and the experiments. In Sect. 4, we discuss the results of these experiments. Section 5 presents the conclusions of this study and provides insight into possible future research directions.

## 2   Recent Works

### 2.1   Deep Learning for Single Image Super-Resolution

SISR is a low-level computer vision task that aims at obtaining a HR image from an input LR image. This problem can be modeled as follows:

$$y = \Phi(x, \theta) \tag{1}$$

where $y$ is the LR image we want to super-resolve, $x$ is the original HR image, and $\Phi(x, \theta)$ denotes the application of a degradation function $\Phi$ to $x$ using the degradation parameters $\theta$ [1]. Since this degradation process is not known and can be affected by multiple factors such as noise or blur, we can also model the SISR problem (1) as follows:

$$y = (x \otimes k) \downarrow_s + n \tag{2}$$

where $(x \otimes k)$ denotes a convolution of the original HR image with a blurry kernel $k$, $\downarrow_s$ denotes a downsampling operation with scale factor $s$ and $n$ represents the independent noise term. SISR aims at recovering an approximation of $x$ given the image $y$, however, it is an ill-posed problem due to the fact that a given LR image can correspond to multiple HR solutions [19].

Recently, deep learning methods for SISR have demonstrated promising performance and accuracy compared to conventional SISR algorithms. Before Super-Resolution Convolutional Neural Network (SRCNN) [5] was presented, which is the pioneering work in the field, SISR algorithms were being categorized in 4 groups based on the image prior [17]: prediction models, edge-based, image statistical, and patch-based methods. With the publication of SRCNN [5], deep learning methods can be added to this taxonomy. Within this category, multiple methods using different kinds of neural network have been developed. Kim et al. [9] proposed Very Deep Super-Resolution (VDSR), that uses a similar structure as SRCNN but using a deeper network. Efficient Sub-Pixel Convolutional Neural Network (ESPCN) [14] was proposed to make SRCNN more efficient. This network performs the feature extraction in the LR space in order to consume less computational resources. Once the extraction is done, it uses a sub-pixel convolution in order to reconstruct the HR image. FSRCNN [6] was designed by accelerating SRCNN [5], increasing the number of layers but reducing the number of parameters. Residual networks have also been used for the SISR task [12]. These networks use skip connections to jump over some of their layers in order to tackle the problem of gradient vanishing, allowing to design very deep networks.

## 2.2   Deep Learning for Image Denoising

Image denoising is another important task in computer vision applications. Over the past years, multiple methods for modeling image priors, such as Markov random fields (MRF) [11], Block-matching and 3D filtering (BM3D) and Nonlocally Centralized Sparse Representation (NCSR) [7], have been proposed in order to tackle this problem. However, the mentioned methods have shown a high computational cost, and they also need to have their parameters manually chosen in order to improve the performance [15]. Multiple methods have been proposed to solve these problems. In [3] is presented a Trainable Nonlinear Reaction Diffusion (TRND) model in which the filters and the influence functions can be learned from the training data. In [10] is proposed a Deeply aggregated Alternating Minimization (DeepAM) model, which learns a regularizer via deep aggregation in order to solve multiple image restoration tasks, including single image

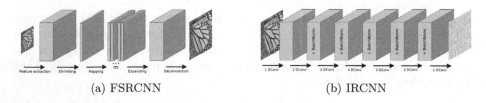

(a) FSRCNN                                          (b) IRCNN

**Fig. 1.** Structures of the deep learning restoration models

denoising. Denoising Convolutional Neural Network (DnCNN) [22] uses residual learning and batch normalization in order to speed up the training process and boost the denoising performance. They also proposed IRCNN [21], which uses Half Quadratic Splitting (HQS) to show that a CNN based denoiser prior can be plugged as a modular part of model-based optimization methods in order to solve multiple inverse problems. In [16] a dilated residual CNN for Gaussian image denoising is presented, in which the receptive field is enlarged by adopting dilated convolution.

### 2.3  FSRCNN and IRCNN

In this subsection, we review the structure of the two CNNs used in this proposal: FSRCNN and IRCNN.

The structure of FSRCNN is composed of 5 different parts. The first four are made up of convolution layers and the last one is a deconvolution layer. Firstly, a feature extraction is performed to extract overlapping patches. A shrinking layer is added after the feature extraction in order to reduce the LR feature dimension. Then, a non-linear mapping is computed and fed into an expanding layer. Finally, the deconvolution layer carries out the upsampling operation and the aggregation of the features. The described architecture is shown in Fig. 1a. With this structure, there are three variables that need to be chosen and they will directly affect the performance of the network: the mapping depth $m$, the LR feature dimension $d$ and the number of shrinking filters $s$.

The structure of IRCNN consists of seven different convolutional layers divided in three parts. The first layer is a convolution layer with 64 filters of size 3 that uses Rectified Linear Unit (ReLU) as the activation function. The following 5 layers are dilated convolution layers that capture the context information. The last layer is a convolution layer with $c$ filters of size 3, where $c$ is the output depth. The described architecture is shown in Fig. 1b. In the figure, the output of the network is the residual image, that represents the noise to be removed.

## 3  Experimental Design

In this section, we expose the details of our implementation of both CNNs, we present the image datasets used for the training, validation and test steps, we show how the images are pre-processed before the training and we described the followed training strategies and set of experiments.

## 3.1 Implemented CNN

For this study, we have used our own implementation[1] of FSRCNN and IRCNN using Keras [4] in order to use the same deep learning framework for both networks. Both of them use a sequential model in order to stack bi-dimensional convolution (or deconvolution) layers. All the layers use the format number of samples, height, width and channels (NHWC). In order to deal with the boundary artifacts produced by the convolution operation, zero padding has been adopted in all layers according to the filter size.

For FSRCNN, the filters are initialized with variance scaling for all the convolution layers and with a Gaussian distribution with zero mean and standard deviation 0.001 for the deconvolution layer. Furthermore, for the mapping depth, the LR feature dimension and the number of shrinking filters, we have used, $m = 4$, $d = 48$ and $s = 16$, respectively, since in [6], these settings show outstanding Peak Signal to Noise Ratio (PSNR) results compared to the rest of investigated settings. For IRCNN, glorot uniform initializer [8] is used to initialize the filters of all the convolution layers.

## 3.2 Training, Validation and Test Datasets

For training and validation, BSD200 [13], General100 [6] and T91 [18] datasets have been used, bringing the total of images to 391. A 10% of these images have been randomly chosen for validation, therefore, the training set has 352 images and the validation set, 39. Set5 [2] and Set14 [20] have been used for the test stage, making a total of 19 images. The same training, validation and test datasets have been used for both FSRCNN and IRCNN.

## 3.3 Image Pre-processing

Before being used as input of the neural networks, the 391 images used for training and validation are pre-processed using some common and some model-dependent steps. Only for FSRCNN, the images are converted from RGB to YCbCr. Specifically, the $Y$ component is super-resolved by the network and the blue-difference and red-difference components are upscaled using bicubic interpolation. Once the images are loaded, they are scaled to $[0, 1]$ range. The resulting images are cropped into $32 \times 32$ sub-patches using a stride of size 16 in order not to lose the information between adjacent patches. The remaining pixels are discarded. A last pre-processing step is applied to the training and validation images depending on the model that is going to be trained. For FSRCNN, Lanczos interpolation is used in order to downscale the data using a scale

---

[1] All the implementation details of the CNNs and the datasets used can be found at https://github.com/guillermoruizalv/restore.

**Table 1.** Description of the set of experiments.

| Experiment | Method |
|------------|--------|
| 1.1 | FSRCNN + IRCNN |
| 1.2 | IRCNN + FSRCNN |
| 2.1 | IRCNN + bicubic interpolation |
| 2.2 | Wavelet denoiser + FSRCNN |
| 2.3 | Median filter + FSRCNN |
| 3.1 | Wavelet denoiser + bicubic interpolation |
| 3.2 | Median filter + bicubic interpolation |

factor of 2. For IRCNN, random noise is added to the patches. The noise method to be applied is chosen randomly from Gaussian, Poisson, salt-and-pepper, and uniform noise using the same probability.

- For Gaussian noise, $\mu$ is set to 0 and $\sigma$ takes a random value from the range $[0.05, 0.15]$.
- For Poisson noise, input pixel values are interpreted as means of Poisson distributions scaled up by $2^8$.
- For salt-and-pepper noise or uniform noise, the noise ratio takes a random value from the range $[0.05, 0.20]$.

### 3.4  Set of Experiments

For this study, we have selected three traditional algorithms for the SISR and denoising tasks in order to evaluate their performance when used along with the deep learning methods. We have selected bicubic interpolation for the SISR task and wavelet and median filtering for image denoising. The set of experiments carried out for this study is presented in Table 1.

All the evaluations are performed using Set5 [2] and Set14 [20] as test datasets and PSNR (measured in dB) and Structural Similarity (SSIM) as quality metrics (higher is better). The test images were degraded by applying the same procedure as explained in Subsect. 3.3. We end up having 12 sets of 19 images, making a total of 228 LR images. Figure 2 shows some examples of this processing applied to an image taken from Set5. In order to generate the noisy images, we have used custom functions that can be found along with the implementation of the CNNs and the datasets. In these functions, the random seed is initially set to 0. The same 228 images are used for all the experiments.

For the experiments that make use of median filter and wavelet denoiser, we apply the MATLAB functions medfilt2() and wdenoise2(). In order to perform the evaluation of the quality metrics, the MATLAB functions psnr() and ssim() are used. The training has been carried out in a server running Ubuntu 18.04 LTS with an NVidia Geforce GTX 1060 with compute capability of 6.1. Most of the development has been done in a different machine with the same operative system (OS) and a Nvidia Geforce GT 730M with compute capability of 3.5.

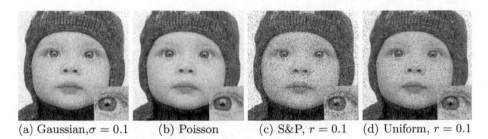

(a) Gaussian,$\sigma = 0.1$    (b) Poisson    (c) S&P, $r = 0.1$    (d) Uniform, $r = 0.1$

**Fig. 2.** The LR noisy image "baby" from Set5, which was degraded by downscaling with a factor of 2 and it was corrupted by different types of noise.

**Table 2.** PSNR and SSIM results for the Experiments 1.1 and 1.2

| Noise | Params. | Experiment 1.1 | | | | Experiment 1.2 | | | |
|---|---|---|---|---|---|---|---|---|---|
| | | Set5 | | Set14 | | Set5 | | Set14 | |
| | | PSNR | SSIM | PSNR | SSIM | PSNR | SSIM | PSNR | SSIM |
| Gaussian | $\sigma = 0.05$ | 26.662 | 0.863 | 25.101 | 0.806 | 29.416 | 0.906 | 27.144 | 0.870 |
| ($\mu = 0$) | $\sigma = 0.10$ | 21.550 | 0.702 | 20.685 | 0.629 | 27.391 | 0.883 | 25.606 | 0.826 |
| | $\sigma = 0.15$ | 18.437 | 0.566 | 17.775 | 0.495 | 26.066 | 0.871 | 24.485 | 0.790 |
| Poisson | $peak = 2^8$ | 27.900 | 0.907 | 25.966 | 0.840 | 30.163 | 0.931 | 27.525 | 0.886 |
| S&P | $r = 0.05$ | 22.132 | 0.767 | 21.187 | 0.699 | 32.330 | 0.959 | 28.834 | 0.918 |
| | $r = 0.10$ | 18.652 | 0.621 | 18.029 | 0.548 | 31.866 | 0.950 | 28.567 | 0.912 |
| | $r = 0.15$ | 16.473 | 0.514 | 16.000 | 0.443 | 31.346 | 0.945 | 28.260 | 0.907 |
| | $r = 0.20$ | 14.924 | 0.432 | 14.549 | 0.367 | 30.662 | 0.940 | 27.855 | 0.899 |
| Uniform | $r = 0.05$ | 24.352 | 0.813 | 23.423 | 0.768 | 32.223 | 0.956 | 28.800 | 0.916 |
| | $r = 0.10$ | 20.957 | 0.703 | 20.567 | 0.654 | 31.575 | 0.946 | 28.428 | 0.909 |
| | $r = 0.15$ | 18.767 | 0.615 | 18.607 | 0.564 | 30.805 | 0.939 | 27.931 | 0.900 |
| | $r = 0.20$ | 17.109 | 0.541 | 17.145 | 0.491 | 29.857 | 0.932 | 27.294 | 0.888 |
| All | | **20.659** | **0.670** | **19.920** | **0.609** | **30.308** | **0.930** | **27.561** | **0.885** |

# 4    Results

In this section, we present the results of all the experiments described before in this document.

## 4.1    Experiment 1.1

The results of this experiment are presented in Table 2. We can see quite low values of PSNR and SSIM for both Set5 and Set14. In fact, if we visually inspect the results, we can observe that the images present a large amount of noise for all the cases. This is shown in Fig. 3, that exposes the results of restoring the downscaled, noisy images of Fig. 2 using FSRCNN + IRCNN.

In Fig. 3, we can see that by applying the networks in this order, we cannot remove the noise of the images properly. Instead, FSRCNN tries to super-resolve the noise pixels, mixing up the good information of the image with them. Once

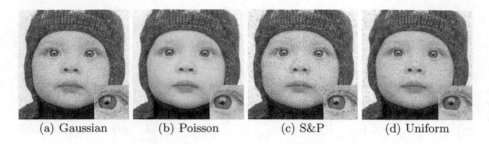

| (a) Gaussian | (b) Poisson | (c) S&P | (d) Uniform |

**Fig. 3.** Experiment 1.1: restoration using FSRCNN + IRCNN

the image is super-resolved, IRCNN tries to remove the noise. However, in this case, the resulting noise is a super-resolved version of the original applied noise, and therefore, the network is not capable of detecting the residual part of the image. This effect repeats for all the images in both Set5 and Set14 and for all noise types. As a consequence, we can observe low PSNR and SSIM values. The results of this experiment show us that FSRCNN + IRCNN will produce low quality results and that it is not appropriate to super-resolve and denoise our LR images.

## 4.2   Experiment 1.2

In this experiment, we reverse the order of the networks from the previous experiment. Table 2 also shows the results of the quality metrics for this experiment. First of all, we can see a PSNR value of 30.3080 dB on the images of Set5 and 27.5697 dB on the images of Set14, which improves the results of the previous experiment by +8.6445 dB in average. On the other hand, the SSIM results in this case are 0.9297 and 0.8849, which are much closer to 1 than the values obtained in Experiment 1.1. This improvement on the metrics can be also observed in Fig. 4, in which we present the results of applying IRCNN + FSRCNN on the images of Fig. 2. By reversing the order of the networks, we can see that the images get denoised and super-resolved, not presenting large amounts of noise as seen in the results of Experiment 1.1. In this case, IRCNN first removes the residual part, obtaining an approximation to the downscaled version of the HR image. Once this is done, FSRCNN super-resolves the denoised output in order to obtain the HR image.

## 4.3   Experiment 2.1

In this experiment, we evaluate the results of replacing FSRCNN by bicubic interpolation in the previous experiment. The results of this experiment are exposed in Table 3. In average, the overall PSNR and SSIM results are 0.5732 dB and 0.0028 units lower than the results of Experiment 1.2, respectively. However, if we take a look at the SSIM results on the five images of Set5, we see a slight improvement when we choose bicubic interpolation over FSRCNN. In Fig. 5, we

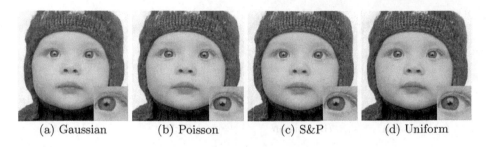

| (a) Gaussian | (b) Poisson | (c) S&P | (d) Uniform |

**Fig. 4.** Experiment 1.2: restoration using IRCNN + FSRCNN

present the results of applying IRCNN + bicubic interpolation to the images of Fig. 2. In this case, we can see that the bicubic interpolation provides good results as well, however it cannot conserve the image edges as well as FSRCNN does when super-resolving the LR images. These results show that even though in average FSRCNN performs better, there might be some cases in which the bicubic interpolation approximates better the original HR image.

**Table 3.** PSNR and SSIM results for the Experiments 2.1 and 2.2

| Noise | Params. | Experiment 2.1 | | | | Experiment 2.2 | | | |
|---|---|---|---|---|---|---|---|---|---|
| | | Set5 | | Set14 | | Set5 | | Set14 | |
| | | PSNR | SSIM | PSNR | SSIM | PSNR | SSIM | PSNR | SSIM |
| Gaussian | $\sigma = 0.05$ | 29.107 | 0.919 | 26.738 | 0.861 | 27.883 | 0.913 | 25.894 | 0.829 |
| ($\mu = 0$) | $\sigma = 0.10$ | 27.359 | 0.896 | 25.460 | 0.821 | 25.074 | 0.857 | 23.626 | 0.752 |
| | $\sigma = 0.15$ | 26.124 | 0.882 | 24.452 | 0.787 | 23.241 | 0.806 | 22.249 | 0.701 |
| Poisson | $peak = 2^8$ | 29.780 | 0.942 | 27.048 | 0.874 | 28.632 | 0.922 | 26.440 | 0.849 |
| S&P | $r = 0.05$ | 31.223 | 0.959 | 27.902 | 0.899 | 19.749 | 0.689 | 19.805 | 0.620 |
| | $r = 0.10$ | 30.908 | 0.954 | 27.717 | 0.895 | 19.387 | 0.649 | 19.488 | 0.575 |
| | $r = 0.15$ | 30.570 | 0.950 | 27.513 | 0.891 | 19.258 | 0.650 | 19.342 | 0.573 |
| | $r = 0.20$ | 30.116 | 0.945 | 27.238 | 0.884 | 18.825 | 0.6435 | 18.962 | 0.569 |
| Uniform | $r = 0.05$ | 31.189 | 0.958 | 27.889 | 0.899 | 22.036 | 0.759 | 21.864 | 0.706 |
| | $r = 0.10$ | 30.756 | 0.952 | 27.628 | 0.893 | 20.871 | 0.706 | 20.788 | 0.640 |
| | $r = 0.15$ | 30.235 | 0.946 | 27.290 | 0.886 | 20.121 | 0.684 | 20.138 | 0.612 |
| | $r = 0.20$ | 29.582 | 0.939 | 26.846 | 0.875 | 19.380 | 0.666 | 19.553 | 0.596 |
| All | | **29.746** | **0.937** | **26.977** | **0.872** | **22.038** | **0.745** | **21.512** | **0.669** |

## 4.4   Experiment 2.2

In this experiment, we evaluate the results of applying wavelet denoiser + FSR-CNN. The results of this experiment are also exposed in Table 3. We can observe that the PSNR and SSIM results are worse than the ones obtained in the experiments using IRCNN as a denoiser. These results can also be observed in Fig. 6,

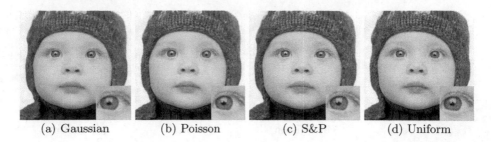

(a) Gaussian          (b) Poisson          (c) S&P          (d) Uniform

**Fig. 5.** Experiment 2.1: restoration using IRCNN + bicubic interpolation

in which wavelet denoiser + FSRCNN are applied on the images of Fig. 2. In the first instance, the wavelet denoiser is able to effectively reduce the noise for those types that are additive or signal dependent, i.e., the Gaussian noise and the Poisson noise. However, the quality of the results is not as high as in the IRCNN results. On the other hand, if we take a look at the results of this combination on the images degraded by salt-and-pepper noise and uniform noise, we can observe that the wavelet algorithm cannot properly remove the noise, and therefore the final images present low-quality.

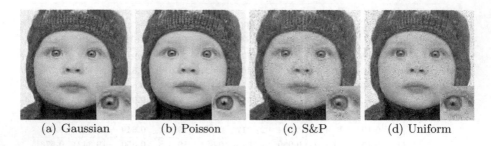

(a) Gaussian          (b) Poisson          (c) S&P          (d) Uniform

**Fig. 6.** Experiment 2.2: restoration using wavelet denoiser + FSRCNN

## 4.5   Experiment 2.3

In this experiment, we replace the wavelet denoiser by a median filter (metric results in Table 4). We can see that the average PSNR and SSIM results improve when we replace the wavelet denoiser by a median filter. However, even though the overall results and the results obtained on the images degraded with salt-and-pepper and uniform noise are better compared to the previous experiment, the wavelet denoiser overperforms the median filter on the images that were degraded with Gaussian and Poisson noise. This can also be observed in Fig. 7, in which we present the results of applying median filter + FSRCNN to the images of Fig. 2. The images with Gaussian and Poisson noise still present a considerable amount of noise after the restoration. On the other hand, the images degraded with salt-and-pepper and uniform noise present a much lower amount of noise after applying the median filter. In any case, the performance obtained in Experiment 1.2. cannot be reached by using any of these traditional filters.

## 4.6    Experiment 3.1

In this experiment we use a traditional approach for both tasks: a wavelet denoiser for image denoising and bicubic interpolation for super-resolution. In the Table 5, the PSNR and SSIM results are very similar to the ones of Experiment 2.2. Thus, replacing FSRCNN by bicubic interpolation does not bring any improvement since the super-resolution task is being performed using images which have been denoised with low quality outputs. Figure 8 shows the results of applying a wavelet denoiser + bicubic interpolation to the images of Fig. 2. The same effect is observed as in Experiment 2.2: even though the wavelet denoiser is able to remove Gaussian and Poisson noise, the obtained quality is not high

**Table 4.** PSNR and SSIM results for the Experiment 2.3

| Noise | Params. | Set 5 | | Set 14 | |
|---|---|---|---|---|---|
| | | PSNR | SSIM | PSNR | SSIM |
| Gaussian | $\sigma = 0.05$ | 25.987 | 0.874 | 23.986 | 0.758 |
| ($\mu = 0$) | $\sigma = 0.10$ | 23.956 | 0.804 | 22.502 | 0.685 |
| | $\sigma = 0.15$ | 22.085 | 0.733 | 20.997 | 0.614 |
| Poisson | $peak = 2^8$ | 26.277 | 0.893 | 24.158 | 0.769 |
| S&P | $r = 0.05$ | 26.872 | 0.917 | 24.576 | 0.798 |
| | $r = 0.10$ | 26.093 | 0.907 | 24.043 | 0.789 |
| | $r = 0.15$ | 25.119 | 0.894 | 23.385 | 0.775 |
| | $r = 0.20$ | 23.878 | 0.875 | 22.507 | 0.755 |
| Uniform | $r = 0.05$ | 26.950 | 0.917 | 24.609 | 0.798 |
| | $r = 0.10$ | 26.294 | 0.908 | 24.209 | 0.788 |
| | $r = 0.15$ | 25.500 | 0.892 | 23.699 | 0.773 |
| | $r = 0.20$ | 24.435 | 0.865 | 23.063 | 0.750 |
| All | | **25.287** | **0.873** | **23.478** | **0.754** |

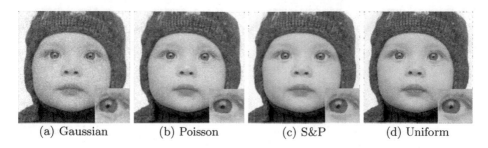

(a) Gaussian          (b) Poisson          (c) S&P          (d) Uniform

**Fig. 7.** Experiment 2.3: restoration using median filter + FSRCNN

enough, and the denoising results are not acceptable for salt-and-pepper and uniform noise. Therefore, although FSRCNN is able to outperform bicubic interpolation in most of the cases, in this experiment its inputs are degraded by the applied noise, affecting the quality of the super-resolution process.

### 4.7   Experiment 3.2

In this experiment we evaluate the performance of applying median filter + bicubic interpolation on our set of degraded images. In the Table 5, we can observe that the obtained quality results are similar to the ones of Experiment 2.3. As in the previous experiment, the denoiser is not able to provide high denoising quality and therefore the super-resolution step is performed using noisy images. In Fig. 9 we present the results of applying median filter + bicubic interpolation on the images of Fig. 2. Once more, we can see results that are similar to the Experiment 2.3: the images degraded with Gaussian and Poisson

**Table 5.** PSNR and SSIM results for the Experiments 3.1 and 3.2

| Noise | Params. | Experiment 3.1 | | | | Experiment 3.2 | | | |
|---|---|---|---|---|---|---|---|---|---|
| | | Set5 | | Set14 | | Set5 | | Set14 | |
| | | PSNR | SSIM | PSNR | SSIM | PSNR | SSIM | PSNR | SSIM |
| Gaussian | $\sigma = 0.05$ | 27.876 | 0.912 | 25.817 | 0.824 | 26.276 | 0.881 | 24.226 | 0.766 |
| ($\mu = 0$) | $\sigma = 0.10$ | 25.204 | 0.855 | 23.739 | 0.752 | 24.274 | 0.813 | 22.801 | 0.698 |
| | $\sigma = 0.15$ | 23.313 | 0.805 | 22.341 | 0.702 | 22.437 | 0.745 | 21.340 | 0.630 |
| Poisson | $peak = 2^8$ | 28.727 | 0.930 | 26.334 | 0.845 | 26.646 | 0.906 | 24.426 | 0.780 |
| S&P | $r = 0.05$ | 20.849 | 0.718 | 20.805 | 0.64 5 | 27.112 | 0.921 | 24.745 | 0.803 |
| | $r = 0.10$ | 20.026 | 0.666 | 20.092 | 0.592 | 26.378 | 0.912 | 24.265 | 0.795 |
| | $r = 0.15$ | 19.552 | 0.657 | 19.636 | 0.582 | 25.481 | 0.901 | 23.665 | 0.783 |
| | $r = 0.20$ | 18.904 | 0.645 | 19.057 | 0.571 | 24.311 | 0.884 | 22.856 | 0.765 |
| Uniform | $r = 0.05$ | 22.949 | 0.778 | 22.678 | 0.720 | 27.158 | 0.921 | 24.767 | 0.803 |
| | $r = 0.10$ | 21.482 | 0.720 | 21.389 | 0.655 | 26.530 | 0.912 | 24.393 | 0.793 |
| | $r = 0.15$ | 20.469 | 0.692 | 20.524 | 0.623 | 25.775 | 0.897 | 23.924 | 0.780 |
| | $r = 0.20$ | 19.555 | 0.671 | 19.770 | 0.603 | 24.767 | 0.872 | 23.338 | 0.759 |
| **All** | | **22.409** | **0.754** | **21.849** | **0.676** | **25.595** | **0.880** | **23.729** | **0.763** |

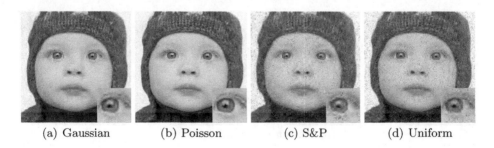

(a) Gaussian         (b) Poisson         (c) S&P         (d) Uniform

**Fig. 8.** Experiment 3.1: restoration using wavelet denoiser + bicubic interpolation

noise still have a considerable amount of noise, whereas the noise in the images that presented salt-and-pepper and uniform noise is lower.

## 4.8   Results Summary

Table 6 presents a summary of the PSNR and SSIM results for each of them. First of all, we can see that both approaches that use a pure deep learning solution for the SISR and denoising tasks present different results. Experiment 1.1 shows low restoration quality results because FSRCNN mixes up the information contained in the pixels of the image with those that have lost information due to the applied noise. On the other hand, Experiment 1.2 presents much better results obtained by simply swapping the order in which the neural networks are applied. In the rest of experiments, we compared the performance obtained when we replaced the CNNs by traditional methods for the SISR and denoising tasks. The results show that when we replace IRCNN by a wavelet denoiser or a median filter, the restoration quality decreases. Furthermore, we have also observed that the results for the SISR task are directly impacted by the performance of the denoising step. In fact, we can see that FSRCNN is not able to overperform bicubic interpolation when we use traditional methods for the denoising. The best restoration quality results are achieved by using the deep learning methods as long as the denoising step is performed before SISR. A qualitative comparison of the performance of IRCNN+FSRCNN is presented in Fig. 10.

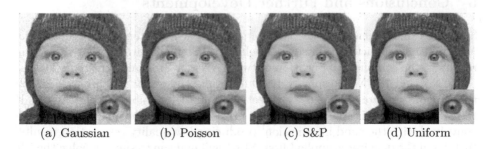

(a) Gaussian          (b) Poisson          (c) S&P          (d) Uniform

**Fig. 9.** Experiment 3.2: restoration using median filter + bicubic interpolation

**Table 6.** PSNR and SSIM results on Set5 and Set14

| Experiment | Solution | PSNR | SSIM |
|---|---|---|---|
| 1.1 | FSRCNN + IRCNN | 20.2899 | 0.6399 |
| **1.2** | **IRCNN + FSRCNN** | **28.9344** | **0.9073** |
| 2.1 | IRCNN + Bicubic | 28.3612 | 0.9046 |
| 2.2 | Wavelet + FSRCNN | 21.7753 | 0.7070 |
| 2.3 | Median + FSRCNN | 24.3825 | 0.8138 |
| 3.1 | Wavelet + Bicubic | 22.1286 | 0.7151 |
| 3.2 | Median + Bicubic | 24.6621 | 0.8216 |

| Gaussian | Poisson | S&P | Uniform |

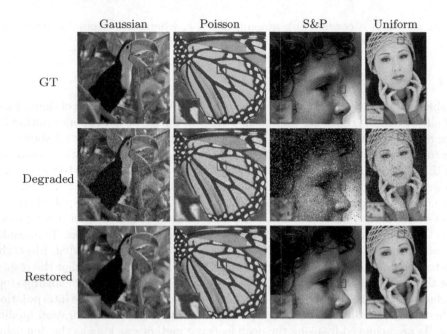

**Fig. 10.** Execution of Experiment 1.2 with the rest images of Set5 dataset

## 5   Conclusions and Further Developments

SISR and image denoising are two important low-level computer vision tasks with multiple applications in several fields. In this paper, we have analyzed the results of the combined application of two CNNs for SISR and image denoising: FSRCNN and IRCNN, respectively. Our results show that the order in which these algorithms are applied has a direct effect in their combined performance. If the SISR algorithm is applied first, those pixels affected by the image noise will be convolved with the good information, producing low quality restoration results. Instead, if the denoiser is applied first, SISR will manage to super-resolve the LR image. Both CNNs have been trained using the same images from BSD200 [13], General100 [6] and T91 [18] datasets. A Keras [4] implementation is also provided with this study. Furthermore, we have compared the performance of these deep learning methods to traditional algorithms for the SISR and denoising tasks. In all the cases, the combination of IRCNN and FSRCNN shows better performance than when bicubic interpolation is used for SISR and wavelet denoising or median filtering is applied for denoising. Nevertheless, there remain several open questions for future research works. Most of the research studies simulate the LR images by modeling the degradation with algorithms like bicubic or Lanczos interpolation and Gaussian noise, whereas in real scenarios the LR images may present a different distribution, and therefore the learned mappings might not be useful for these cases. Furthermore, a more extensive comparison with other traditional methods for SISR and image denoising could be addressed, including algorithms such as total variation denoising. On the other hand, a possible research direction could be to investigate a network that solves SISR and denoising simultaneously using multiple types of noise.

## References

1. Anwar, S., Khan, S., Barnes, N.: A deep journey into super-resolution: a survey. CoRR abs/1904.07523 (2019). http://arxiv.org/abs/1904.07523
2. Bevilacqua, M., Roumy, A., Guillemot, C., line Alberi Morel, M.: Low-complexity single-image super-resolution based on nonnegative neighbor embedding. In: British Machine Vision Conference, BMVC, pp. 135.1–135.10 (2012)
3. Chen, Y., Yu, W., Pock, T.: On learning optimized reaction diffusion processes for effective image restoration. In: IEEE Conference on Computer Vision and Pattern Recognition (CVPR), pp. 5261–5269 (2015)
4. Chollet, F., et al.: Keras (2015). https://keras.io
5. Dong, C., Loy, C., He, K., Tang, X.: Image super-resolution using deep convolutional networks. IEEE Trans. Pattern Anal. Mach. Intell. **38**(2), 295–307 (2016)
6. Dong, C., Loy, C.C., Tang, X.: Accelerating the super-resolution convolutional neural network. In: Leibe, B., Matas, J., Sebe, N., Welling, M. (eds.) ECCV 2016. LNCS, vol. 9906, pp. 391–407. Springer, Cham (2016). https://doi.org/10.1007/978-3-319-46475-6_25
7. Dong, W., Zhang, L., Shi, G., Li, X.: Nonlocally centralized sparse representation for image restoration. IEEE Trans. Image Process. **22**(4), 1620–1630 (2013)
8. Glorot, X., Bengio, Y.: Understanding the difficulty of training deep feedforward neural networks. In: XIII International Conference on Artificial Intelligence and Statistics. vol. 9, pp. 249–256. PMLR (2010)
9. Kim, J., Lee, J., Lee, K.: Accurate image super-resolution using very deep convolutional networks. In: IEEE Conference on Computer Vision and Pattern Recognition, CVPR, pp. 1646–1654 (2016)
10. Kim, Y., Jung, H., Min, D., Sohn, K.: Deeply aggregated alternating minimization for image restoration. In: IEEE Conference on Computer Vision and Pattern Recognition, CVPR, pp. 284–292, July 2017
11. Lan, X., Roth, S., Huttenlocher, D., Black, M.J.: Efficient belief propagation with learned higher-order Markov random fields. In: Leonardis, A., Bischof, H., Pinz, A. (eds.) ECCV 2006. LNCS, vol. 3952, pp. 269–282. Springer, Heidelberg (2006). https://doi.org/10.1007/11744047_21
12. Lim, B., Son, S., Kim, H., Nah, S., Lee, K.M.: Enhanced deep residual networks for single image super-resolution. In: IEEE Conference on Computer Vision and Pattern Recognition Workshops, CVPRW, pp. 1132–1140 (2017)
13. Martin, D., Fowlkes, C., Tal, D., Malik, J.: A database of human segmented natural images and its application to evaluating segmentation algorithms and measuring ecological statistics. In: International Conference on Computer Vision, ICCV, vol. 2, pp. 416–423 (2001)
14. Shi, W., et al.: Real-time single image and video super-resolution using an efficient sub-pixel convolutional neural network. In: IEEE Conference on Computer Vision and Pattern Recognition, CVPR, pp. 1874–1883 (2016)
15. Tian, C., Xu, Y., Fei, L., Yan, K.: Deep learning for image denoising: a survey. In: Pan, J.-S., Lin, J.C.-W., Sui, B., Tseng, S.-P. (eds.) ICGEC 2018. AISC, vol. 834, pp. 563–572. Springer, Singapore (2019). https://doi.org/10.1007/978-981-13-5841-8_59

16. Wang, T., Sun, M., Hu, K.: Dilated deep residual network for image denoising. In: International Conference on Tools with Artificial Intelligence, ICTAI, pp. 1272–1279 (2018)

17. Yang, C.-Y., Ma, C., Yang, M.-H.: Single-image super-resolution: a benchmark. In: Fleet, D., Pajdla, T., Schiele, B., Tuytelaars, T. (eds.) ECCV 2014. LNCS, vol. 8692, pp. 372–386. Springer, Cham (2014). https://doi.org/10.1007/978-3-319-10593-2_25

18. Yang, J., Wright, J., Huang, T., Image super-resolution via sparse representation: IEEE Trans. Image Process. **19**, 2861–2873 (2010)

19. Yang, W., Zhang, X., Tian, Y., Wang, W., Xue, J., Liao, Q.: Deep learning for single image super-resolution: a brief review. IEEE Trans. Multimedia **21**(12), 3106–3121 (2019)

20. Zeyde, R., Elad, M., Protter, M.: On single image scale-up using sparse-representations. In: Boissonnat, J.-D., et al. (eds.) Curves and Surfaces 2010. LNCS, vol. 6920, pp. 711–730. Springer, Heidelberg (2012). https://doi.org/10.1007/978-3-642-27413-8_47

21. Zhang, K., Zuo, W., Gu, S., Zhang, L.: Learning deep CNN denoiser prior for image restoration. In: IEEE Conference on Computer Vision and Pattern Recognition, CVPR, pp. 2808–2817 (2017)

22. Zhang, K., Zuo, W., Chen, Y., Meng, D., Zhang, L.: Beyond a gaussian denoiser: residual learning of deep CNN for image denoising. IEEE Trans. Image Process. **26**(7), 3142–3155 (2017)

# The Effect of Noise and Brightness on Convolutional Deep Neural Networks

José A. Rodríguez-Rodríguez[1], Miguel A. Molina-Cabello[1,2](✉) (iD),
Rafaela Benítez-Rochel[1,2], and Ezequiel López-Rubio[1,2] (iD)

[1] Department of Computer Languages and Computer Science, University of Malaga,
Bulevar Louis Pasteur, 35, 29071 Málaga, Spain
joseantoniorodriguez@uma.es, {miguelangel,benitez,ezeqlr}@lcc.uma.es
[2] Biomedic Research Institute of Málaga (IBIMA), Malaga, Spain

**Abstract.** The classification performance of Convolutional Neural Networks (CNNs) can be hampered by several factors. Sensor noise is one of these nuisances. In this work, a study of the effect of noise on these networks is presented. The methodological framework includes two realistic models of noise for present day CMOS vision sensors. The models allow to include separately Poisson, Gaussian, salt & pepper, speckle and uniform noise as sources of defects in image acquisition sensors. Then, synthetic noise may be added to images by using that methodology in order to simulate common sources of image distortion. Additionally, the impact of the brightness in conjunction with each selected kind of noise is also addressed. This way, the proposed methodology incorporates a brightness scale factor to emulate images with low illumination conditions. Based on these models, experiments are carried out for a selection of state of the art CNNs. The results of the study demonstrate that Poisson noise has a small impact on the performance of CNNs, while speckle and salt & pepper noise together the global illumination level can substantially degrade the classification accuracy. Also, Gaussian and uniform noise have a moderate effect on the CNNs.

**Keywords:** Convolutional neural networks · Image classification · Noise · Brightness · CMOS vision sensor.

## 1 Introduction

Convolutional Neural Networks (CNNs) are deep neural networks whose convolutional layers alternate with subsampling layers, reminiscent of simple and complex cells in the primary visual cortex [8]. These neural models have been

This work is partially supported by the following Spanish grants: TIN2016-75097-P, RTI2018-094645-B-I00 and UMA18-FEDERJA-084. All of them include funds from the European Regional Development Fund (ERDF). The authors acknowledge the funding from the Universidad de Málaga.

A. Del Bimbo et al. (Eds.): ICPR 2020 Workshops, LNCS 12666, pp. 639–654, 2021.
https://doi.org/10.1007/978-3-030-68780-9_49

proven to be very effective on different problems of visual information process-ing like object detection, semantic segmentation, image classification, biomedical analysis, image captioning, image coloring, among many others [5,14]. In many cases, these methods even exceed the performance that a human can provide. The ImageNet Large Scale Visual Recognition Challenge [22] has encouraged the development of new and better CNN architectures over the years. Architectures like AlexNet [9] in 2012, VGGNet [21], GoogleNet [24] in 2014, and ResNet [6] in 2015 have brought a number of improvements and innovations to the field of object recognition.

Much effort has been devoted to improving the efficiency of CNNs. These have mainly focused on different aspects such as activation, loss function, opti-mization, learning algorithms or restructuring of processing units. However, little has been done to understand the impacts of image quality on the classification results of such networks. For example, Dodge and Karam [3] showed that deep neural networks are affected when classifying images with lower quality but they used images from the original dataset with a negligible amount of noise due to the image formation and then, used to classify images from the same dataset on their original state. Another work in that sense was presented by Paranhos da Costa et al. [15], where their work used images affected by salt and pepper noise and Gaussian noise in the training data images. This study provided an understanding of the behavior of the models under noise conditions but they only used additive noise.

In most of the studies, the networks were trained and tested on high qual-ity image datasets. Since image quality may vary in real-world applications, the performance of CNNs when using images with different types and levels of noise has been evaluated. This way, in this work, a more comprehensive study on the ability of CNNs to handle images with different qualities has been pre-sented. Previously, our research group has accomplished several studies such as the effect of noise on foreground detection algorithms [10] or the effect of frame size reduction on foreground detection algorithms [11–13].

In this work, we have analyzed the impact of adding different kind of noise to the images to be classified by CNNs. The selected noises have been Gaussian, Poisson, speckle, salt-and-pepper and uniform noises. It is important to notice that these types of noises have different natures. For example, Gaussian noise is typically generated independently from the original image and then added to it, while Poisson noise is correlated with the intensity of each pixel. Regarding salt-and-pepper noise, disturbances in the image signal can cause sparsely white and black pixels. Concerning speckle, it is a granular interference which limits the contrast resolution and degrades the edges definition. The last considered noise is the uniform noise which is caused by quantizing the pixels of an image to a number of discrete levels. Then, the influence of each type of noise on the performance of recent CNNs such as DenseNet [7], Inception [23] or WideResNet [27] has been conducted by examining a meticulous study in this work.

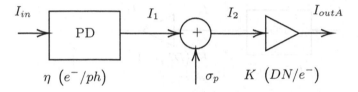

**Fig. 1. Model A.** Proposed model of a CMOS vision sensor. A photodiode (PD) is followed by a source of Poisson noise (circle). Then a conversion gain is shown as a triangle. Only Poisson noise is considered in this model.

The rest of the paper is divided into various sections. Section 2 describes the mechanism to insert noise into a digital image according to the realistic noise model proposed. Section 3 depicts the experimental setup including the selected CNN architectures, the database characteristics, the parameter selection and a qualitative and quantitative evaluation of the experimental results. At last, Sect. 4 concludes the paper with discussions and conclusions.

## 2  Methodology

The methodology which has been developed for this work consists of a realistic model for a CMOS vision sensor (Subsect. 2.1) and then a mechanism to insert synthetic noise into digital images according to such a model (Subsect. 2.2).

### 2.1  Sensor Noise Model

Two realistic noise models of a CMOS vision sensor have been specified, which are inspired on the European Machine Vision Association (EMVA) Standard 1288 for the characterization of image sensors and cameras [4]. These models are employed in subsequent experiments in order to evaluate the performance of CNNs under different sources of noise separately. Figures 1 and 2 depict the scheme of two models (Model A and B), accordingly. Figure 1 represents a schema which models a CMOS vision sensor where only Poisson noise is considered to be added as a source of noise. Meanwhile, Fig. 2 represents a schema which models a CMOS vision sensor by considering an additive noise added at the last step. In this model, only Gaussian, speckle, salt & pepper and uniform noises can be considered as a source of noise. These two models are needed because Poisson noise must be added in an specific point of the vision sensor. This way, sources of noise are separated keeping a realistic model for the image creation.

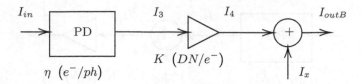

**Fig. 2. Model B.** Proposed model of a CMOS vision sensor considering only one type of noise $(I_x)$. A photodiode (PD) is followed by a conversion gain that is shown as a triangle that is also followed by a source of noise (circle).

Next, the operation of the sensor is detailed based on Figs. 1 and 2 where some stages are shared by both models. The images arrive in the sensor by a certain number of photons $(ph)$ which hit the photodiode (PD). The photodiode converts the photons into electrons according to a factor which is called quantum efficiency $\eta$ $(e^-/ph)$. This factor depends on the design of the photodiode and other technological parameters. The output of the photodiode is measured in accumulated electrons, and the maximum number of electrons that a pixel can accumulate is called Full Well Capacity $(FWC)$. The conversion from photons to pixels is given by:

$$I_1 = I_3 = \eta I_{in} \tag{1}$$

where $I_{in}$ is given in photons $(ph)$ and $I_1$ is given in electrons $(e^-)$.

The process of measuring the number of photons that arrive at the photodiode involves some photon counting errors $\sigma_p$, which is known as shot noise. This can be modeled by Poisson noise and it is introduced only in Model B. Therefore, the Poisson corrupted signal (measured in electrons) is Poisson distributed, whose mean parameter is the noiseless signal $I_1$:

$$I_2 \sim \text{Poisson}\,(\lambda = I_1) \tag{2}$$

The next step is the conversion gain which is presented in Models A and B. It consists in converting the accumulated electrons $(e^-)$ into voltage (measured in microvolts, $\mu V$) according to a gain factor $\chi$ $(\mu V/e^-)$. After that, an analog to digital conversion is performed which transforms the voltage into digital numbers $(DN)$. The analog to digital conversion is associated to another gain factor $\xi$ $(DN/\mu V)$. Both gains can be combined into a single gain $K$:

$$K = \chi \xi \tag{3}$$

This means that the ideal output of the analog to digital converter is computed as follows:

$$I_4 = K I_3 \tag{4}$$

$$I_{outA} = K I_2 \tag{5}$$

Nevertheless, the electron to voltage and analog to digital conversions involve some additive noises, which can be modeled by a certain level of signal $(I_x)$ introduced before the output. This additive noise is only used by the Model B. Let $I_x$ be the level of signal expressed in digital numbers $(DN)$. Then the observed image (in digital numbers, $DN$) for Model B is given by:

$$I_{outB} = I_4 + I_x \tag{6}$$

## 2.2   Synthetic Noise Emulation

Next, a mechanism to insert noise into a digital image according to the realistic noise models proposed in Subsect. 2.1 is detailed. Let $\varphi$ be the pixel value (in digital numbers, $DN$) of a noiseless digital image.

First, Model A is used to synthesize Poisson noise. As known, this type of noise must be applied to signal measured in electrons (7). This involves dividing the pixel value in digital numbers by $K$ to obtain the pixel value in electrons. Additionally, an extra multiplication might be performed by a brightness scale factor $b$ in order to emulate low illumination conditions. After that, it is converting back into digital numbers.

Consequently, the calculation to be performed in order to obtain the corrupted pixel value acquired by the vision sensor $\hat{\varphi}_{Poisson}$ from the noiseless pixel value $\varphi$ is as follows:

$$\hat{\varphi}_p = K \, \text{Poisson} \left( \frac{b\varphi}{K} \right) \tag{7}$$

Next, Model B is used for generating the synthetic noise. Therefore, we have considered several kinds of synthetic noise that represent various degradation mechanisms that often affect digital images, namely Gauss (g), Poisson (p), salt & pepper (sp), speckle (sk) and uniform (u) noise. The final corrupted pixel value $\tilde{\varphi}$ is given by the equations explained next, depending on the kind of synthetic noise.

The Gaussian noise expression is given by:

$$\tilde{\varphi}_g = b\varphi + \text{Gauss} \left( 0, \sigma'_g \right) \tag{8}$$

where $b$ is the bright scale, and $\sigma'_g$ the standard deviation. Among the different causes can introduce this type of noise, the most common reasons are electronic circuit noise and high temperature.

The salt & pepper noise is modeled by using its probability mass function:

$$P(\tilde{\varphi}_{sp}) = \begin{cases} p_0 & \text{if } \tilde{\varphi}_{sp} = 0 \\ p_1 & \text{if } \tilde{\varphi}_{sp} = 255 \\ 1 - p_0 - p_1 & \text{if } \tilde{\varphi}_{sp} = b\varphi \end{cases} \tag{9}$$

where $p_0$ and $p_1$ are the probability of having a dark and saturated pixel value,respectively. For simplicity, these probabilities are exactly the same ($p_0 =$

$p_1$). This type of noise can be produced by errors in analog to digital conversion or transmissions.

In this way, speckle noise can be also produced by transmission fails and it is modeled as a multiplicative noise:

$$\tilde{\varphi}_{sk} = b\varphi(1 + \text{Gauss}(0, \sigma'_{sk})) \tag{10}$$

where $\sigma'_{sk}$ is the standard deviation of the gaussian noise multiplicated by the noiseless pixel value ($\varphi$).

Finally, uniform noise is given by:

$$\tilde{\varphi}_u = b\varphi + \text{Uniform}(-\Delta, \Delta) \tag{11}$$

where $\Delta$ delimits the range of values used to form the noisy image, which are chosen uniformly inside the interval $[-\Delta, +\Delta]$.

The above Eqs. (7)–(11) must be applied to each color channel (red, green and blue) of each pixel of a noiseless digital image in order to obtain its noisy version.

## 3    Experimental Results

The goal of this work is to analyze the impact of the most relevant sources of noise, present in a huge number of applications, on CNNs. For this purpose, a set of experiments has been performed and the results are presented in this section. First, the selected methods are explained (Subsect. 3.1). Next, the considered dataset is described (Subsect. 3.2). Then, the parameter selection is detailed (Subsect. 3.3). After that, a qualitative evaluation is shown to get a more intuitive understanding of the effect of noise on the CNN performance (Subsect. 3.4). At last, quantitative results are presented (Subsect. 3.5).

### 3.1    Methods

Among the many CNNs that can be found in the literature, six modern and well-known architectures have been chosen for the analysis: DenseNet-201 [7] (201 layers), Inception-v3 [23] (variable number of layers), MNASNet-v1.0 [25], MobileNet-v2 [20] (53 layers), WideResNet 101-2 [27] (101 layers) and ResNeXt-101 [26] (101 layers). The mathematical model for each one of these CNNs has been implemented through Torchvision package from PyTorch [18] library and these models had been pre-trained using a sub-set of images from ImageNet dataset published for ILSRVC2012 challenge [19].

The reported experiments have been carried out on a 64-bit Personal Computer with a six-core Intel Core i7-9750 4.50 GHz CPU, 16 GB RAM and a NVIDIA GeForce RTX 2080 GPU.

## 3.2   Dataset

One thousand images (1,000) have been selected randomly, according to the uniform distribution, from the ILSRVC2012 validation set that consists of 50,000 images in total. In this dataset the images are encoded with a RGB format where each channel is encoded with 8 bits. The images of this dataset have been hand-labelled with the presence or absence of 1,000 object categories. The ILSRVC2012 dataset can be downloaded from its website[1].

## 3.3   Parameter Selection

There are several degrees of freedom in this setup, according to the type of noise added, as can be deduced from Sect. 2. Parametric analysis have been taking into account the next parameters: $K$, $b$, $\sigma'_g$, $p$, $\sigma'_{sk}$ and $\Delta$. In this regard, it is necessary to know which range of values are used in order to obtain more realistic results. The description of each tuned parameter is as follows:

- $K$: this parameter represents the image sensor gain that converts electrons into digit values. This type of noise is completely dependent of the sensor performance. For this reason, several commercial vision sensor data-sheets have been collected [1,2,16,17], where $K$ goes from 0.01 to 0.1 $DN/e^-$.
- $\sigma'_g$: most commercial vision sensors have a read-out noise with $\sigma'_g$ below 1 $DN$ when 8-bit encoding is used. The parameter has been set from 0 to 22.5 $DN$, with a step of 2.5 $DN$, so that greater values are used for academic purposes in order to show the effect of increasing the Gaussian noise.
- $p$: probability of having a saturated or dark pixel when salt and pepper noise is applied. These pixels could be saturated or dark before introducing the noise. In this work, it was considered that the probability for salt is exactly the same than the pepper one. In general, $p_0 = p_1 = p$. The parameter has been chosen from 0.00 to 0.27 with a step of 0.03.
- $\Delta$: this parameter defines the maximum and minimum values can reach the uniform noise. This means the additive noise introduced into the image will be in the range $[-\Delta, \Delta]$. Values used in the parametric analysis go from 0.0 to 22.5 $DN$, with a step of 2.5 $DN$.
- $\sigma'_{sk}$: standard deviation of the multiplicative Gaussian noise used for modeling speckle noise. The parameter has been set from 0.0 to 2.7 $DN$, with a step of 0.3 $DN$.
- $b$: bright scale is an intensity factor that allows controlling the minimum and maximum values of the encoded image. Here we assume 8-bit image values within the interval [0, 255]. The worst condition of brightness that has been considered corresponds to image values inside the interval [0, 25.5]. Therefore, parameter $b$ have been chosen from 0.1 to 1.0 with a step of 0.1.

---

[1] http://www.image-net.org/challenges/LSVRC/2012/.

## 3.4    Qualitative Results

In this subsection, the different performances yielded by the selected approaches are compared in a visual way. For this purpose, conditions have been chosen properly to get a good understanding of the performance degradation of a well-known CNN. Without loss of generality, MobileNet-v2 has been used for this analysis. The chosen image is shown in Fig. 3, which corresponds with the labels "chime, bell, gong" (Bell image). The original image was placed at the top left, and the remaining images show a different types of noise and brightness. It can be deduced visually that image with Poisson noise is complicated to differentiate it with respect the original one. Also, Gaussian and Uniform noises seem to be similar but different than Speckle and Salt & Pepper noise.

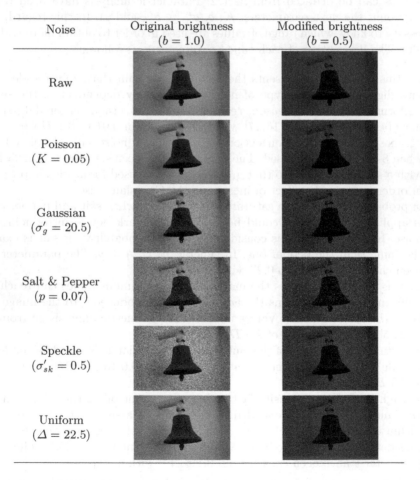

| Noise | Original brightness ($b = 1.0$) | Modified brightness ($b = 0.5$) |
|---|---|---|
| Raw | | |
| Poisson ($K = 0.05$) | | |
| Gaussian ($\sigma'_g = 20.5$) | | |
| Salt & Pepper ($p = 0.07$) | | |
| Speckle ($\sigma'_{sk} = 0.5$) | | |
| Uniform ($\Delta = 22.5$) | | |

**Fig. 3.** Image 11842 without and with several types of noise and bright scale configurations. The type of noises applied were gaussian, Poisson, Salt & Pepper, Speckle and Uniform. And only two values of bright scale were used, 1.0 and 0.5.

Additionally, Table 1 shows a probability analysis for the image commented before, where the best probability of the truth class prediction and the index or position when the probabilities are ordered from higher to lower values have been collected. Image 11842 is well predicted in absence of noise and when Poisson noise is introduced (predictions 0.9930 and 0.9640, respectively). Furthermore, the performance is degraded dramatically when brightness is reduced to the half for all the type of noises except for the Speckle one (prediction probability of 0.5768). This effect could be produced due to Speckle noise has a multiplicative component. This way, if $b = 0.5$ then there are three wrong predictions where the Index is different than one: *table lamp* (prediction probability of 0.5851), *umbrella* (0.1746) and *lampshade* (0.3302), for Gaussian, Salt & Pepper and Uniform noises, accordingly. At last, Gaussian and Uniform noises have a similar qualitative behavior, but the former (the third best prediction with a probability of 0.0470) is more sensitive to brightness reduction than the second one (the second best prediction with a probability of 0.3302).

### 3.5   Quantitative Results

One of the most known metrics to measure the performance of a CNN is the Accuracy that is defined as the success rate of total predictions. This way, the metric which has been considered in this work is the Accuracy-1 (*acc-1*). This measure is commonly used in the literature and it provides a value in the range between 0 and 1, where higher is better. This metric computes the class with the greatest probability for each image prediction and its definition is as follows:

$$acc\text{-}1 = \frac{CP\text{-}1}{NP} \tag{12}$$

**Table 1.** Predictions for Image 11842 provided by MobileNet-v2. Each column exhibits the image, the type of noise, the bright scale (b), the parameters $\sigma'_g$, the truth class probability and its result index (the position in terms of probability).

| Image | Noise | B | Parameter | Probability | Index |
|-------|-------|---|-----------|-------------|-------|
| 11842 | W/O | 1.0 | N.A. | 0.9930 | 1 |
| | Poisson | 0.5 | $K = 0.05$ | 0.9640 | 1 |
| | Gaussian | 1.0 | $\sigma'_g = 22.5$ | 0.5558 | 1 |
| | | 0.5 | $\sigma'_g = 22.5$ | 0.0470 | 3 |
| | Salt & Pepper | 1.0 | $p = 0.05$ | 0.8685 | 1 |
| | | 0.5 | $p = 0.05$ | 0.1746 | 3 |
| | Speckle | 1.0 | $\sigma'_{sk} = 0.5$ | 0.6134 | 1 |
| | | 0.5 | $\sigma'_{sk} = 0.5$ | 0.5768 | 1 |
| | Uniform | 1.0 | $\Delta = 22.5$ | 0.8596 | 1 |
| | | 0.5 | $\Delta = 22.5$ | 0.3302 | 2 |

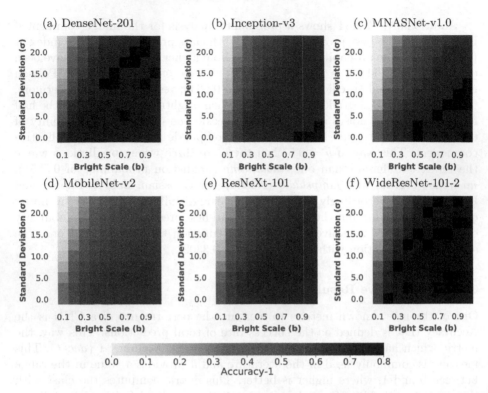

**Fig. 4.** Heatmap of accuracy-1 for several CNNs where images have been degraded introducing different levels of **Gaussian Noise** and bright scale. The CNNs employed were DenseNet-101, Inception-v3, MMNASNet-v1.0, MobileNet-v2, ResNeXt-101 and WideResNet-101.

where CP-1 is the number of correct prediction considering the greatest probability at the model output; and NP is the total number of predictions.

A parametric analysis has been performed for each type of noises and the bright scale values commented in Subsect. 3.3. Furthermore, six CNNs have been analyzed as described in Subsect. 3.1.

First, Gaussian noise results are shown in Fig. 4 where it can be deduced DenseNet-201 and WideResNet-101-2 have the best performance, specially the second one. The maximum *acc-1* for the six CNNs is around 0.8. Also, the higher the bright scale, the higher the performance. The degradation of *acc-1* is proportional to standard deviation for all the bright scale values but it is more sensitive for lower values of bright scale because the unwanted level of signal introduced for each pixel is comparable with the maximum pixel value of the input image. The minimum *acc-1* is reached for the lowest and highest value of bright scale and standard deviation, accordingly. In addition, it is interesting to observe the first row, from bottom to top of the heatmap, represents the *acc-1* when no noise is introduced.

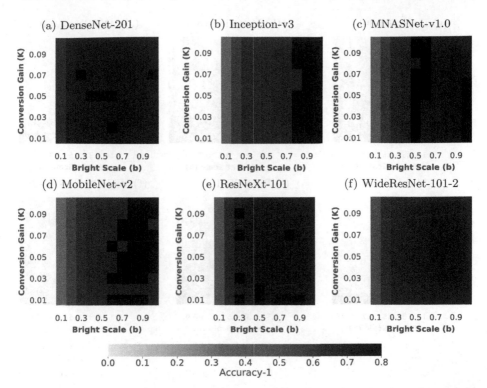

**Fig. 5.** Heatmap of accuracy-1 for several CNNs where images have been degraded introducing different levels of **Poisson Noise** and bright scale. The CNNs employed were DenseNet-101, Inception-v3, MMNASNet-v1.0, MobileNet-v2, ResNeXt-101 and WideResNet-101-2.

Next, Fig. 5 depicts the heatmap of *acc-1* when Poisson noise is introduced into the input images. As it can be observed, CNNs are almost insensitive to conversion gain $(K)$ because the maximum difference between the original image and the noisy one is low, considering the realistic range of $K$. The best performance is achieved by DenseNet-201 as it can be observed.

Figure 6 shows the performance for Salt & Pepper noise. CNNs are less robust against the noise the lower is $b$. The *acc-1* drop has a monotonic dependency with respect the probability. In this case, it is noticeable that *acc-1* is zero, approximately, for darker images. This fact can be observed for all the CNNs when $b = 0.1$ and $p = 0.03$. Additionally, DenseNet-201 has the same performance than WideResNet-101 which have the highest *acc-1*.

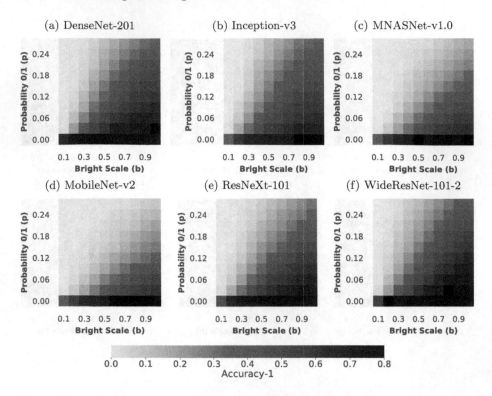

**Fig. 6.** Heatmap of accuracy-1 for several CNNs where images have been degraded introducing different levels of **Salt & Pepper Noise** and bright scale. The CNNs employed were DenseNet-101, Inception-v3, MMNASNet-v1.0, MobileNet-v2, ResNeXt-101 and WideResNet-101-2.

Until now, the presented analysis has a monotonic dependency with respect the parameter that produces the noise. So that, the higher the level of noise the lower the performance. But this is not applicable to Speckle noise as it is shown in Fig. 7. The multiplicative nature of this noise makes complicated to predict the degradation of the CNN because bright scale reduction implies less level of signal but also less level of noise, thereby there is a certain compensation effect.

Finally, the Uniform noise results are represented in Fig. 8 where it is deduced $acc$-$1$ is dropped dramatically for bright scale values below 0.3, specifically for $b = 0.1$ and $\Delta = 22.5$. This happens because the maximum absolute value of noise is around 22.5 $DN$, and the image range after of applying bright scale is from 0 to 25.5 $DN$, near the previous value of noise. In addition, this effect is also observable for $b = 0.2$ and $\Delta = 22.5$, but with a higher $acc$-$1$. Again, DenseNet-201 and WideResNet-101 have the best performance.

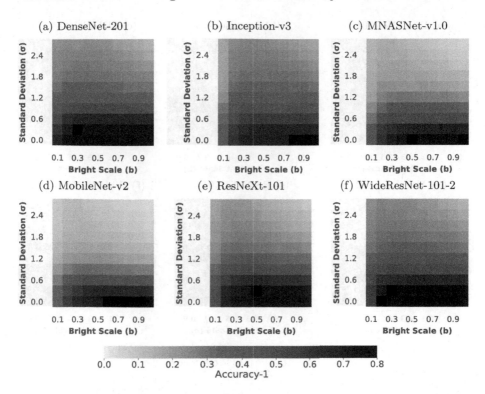

**Fig. 7.** Heatmap of accuracy-1 for several CNNs where images have been degraded introducing different levels of **Speckle Noise** and bright scale. The CNNs employed were DenseNet-101, Inception-v3, MMNASNet-v1.0, MobileNet-v2, ResNeXt-101 and WideResNet-101-2.

## 4   Conclusions

An analysis of the effect of the most frequent noises on the performance of CNNs has been presented in this work. A realistic model of vision sensor noise has been proposed to carry out the study, which considers Gaussian, Poisson, Salt & Pepper, Speckle and Uniform sources of noise. Several well-known and relevant CNNs such as DenseNet-201, Inception, MMNASNet, MobileNet, ResNeXt-101 and WideResNet-101. Qualitative analysis shows how the prediction quality in terms of probability is reduced in presence of noise and brightness reduction. Therefore, a quantitative analysis has been performed to know the trend of *acc-1* for a set of 1000 images.

The experimental results demonstrate quantitatively that all the noises degrade the CNNs performance except for Poisson noise (for values of $K$ which are inside the range of nowadays industry vision sensors parameters) because it does not have a high impact on the performance of the CNNs. Furthermore, Speckle and Salt & Pepper noise are the most aggressive noises in terms of *acc-1* drop and the most robust CNNs against all types of noises are DenseNet-201

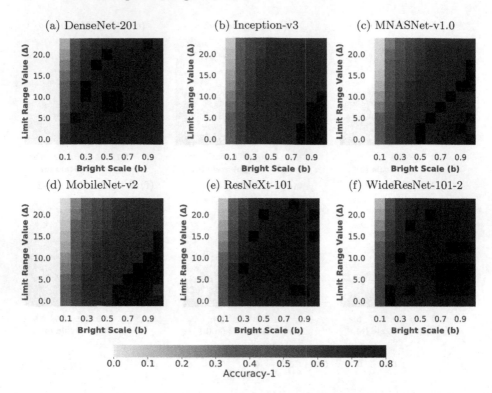

**Fig. 8.** Heatmap of accuracy-1 for several CNNs where images have been degraded introducing different levels of **Uniform Noise** and bright scale. The CNNs employed were DenseNet-101, Inception-v3, MMNASNet-v1.0, MobileNet-v2, ResNeXt-101 and WideResNet-101-2.

and WideResNet-101; while the worst of the selected networks is MobileNet. Moreover, all types of noises have a monotonic dependency of the noise parameter under study except Speckle due to its multiplicative nature. Moreover, the additive noises are Gaussian and Uniform noises which have a similar behavior in presence of the five chosen noises.

The present study could be used on the design of applications with CNNs in presence of noise. The heatmaps could serve as information about the maximum noise allowed to achieve a target performance which allows to know the minimum requirements in terms of CMOS vision sensor and the CNN to be used.

# References

1. AG., A.: Miniature cmos image sensor. NanEye datasheet (2018). Accessed Oct 2018
2. AG, A.: Cmos machine vision image sensor. CMV50000 datasheet (2019). Accessed Feb 2019

3. Dodge, S.F., Karam, L.J.: Understanding how image quality affects deep neural networks. CoRR abs/1604.04004 (2016), http://arxiv.org/abs/1604.04004
4. European Machine Vision Association: EMVA Standard 1288 - Standard for characterization of image sensors and cameras. https://www.emva.org/standards-technology/emva-1288/ (2010)
5. Gu, J., et al.: Recent advances in convolutional neural networks. Pattern Recognition (12 2015). https://doi.org/10.1016/j.patcog.2017.10.013
6. He, K., Zhang, X., Ren, S., Sun, J.: Deep residual learning for image recognition. In: IEEE Conference on Computer Vision and Pattern Recognition, pp. 770–778 (2016)
7. Huang, G., Liu, Z., Van Der Maaten, L., Weinberger, K.Q.: Densely connected convolutional networks. In: 2017 IEEE Conference on Computer Vision and Pattern Recognition (CVPR), pp. 2261–2269 (2017)
8. Hubel, D.H., Wiesel, T.N.: Receptive fields of single neurones in the cat's striate cortex. J. Physiol. **148**(3), 574–591 (1959). https://doi.org/10.1113/jphysiol.1959.sp006308
9. Krizhevsky, A., Sutskever, I., Hinton, G.E.: Imagenet classification with deep convolutional neural networks. Adv. Neural Inf. Proc. Syst. **25**, 1097–1105 (2012)
10. López-Rubio, F.J., López-Rubio, E., Molina-Cabello, M.A., Luque-Baena, R.M., Palomo, E.J., Dominguez, E.: The effect of noise on foreground detection algorithms. Artif. Intell. Rev. **49**(3), 407–438 (2018)
11. Molina-Cabello, M.A., Elizondo, D.A., Luque-Baena, R.M., López-Rubio, E.: Foreground object detection enhancement by adaptive super resolution for video surveillance. In: British Machine Vision Conference (BMVC) (2019)
12. Molina-Cabello, M.A., García-González, J., Luque-Baena, R.M., López-Rubio, E.: The effect of downsampling–upsampling strategy on foreground detection algorithms. Artif. Intell. Rev. **53**(7), 4935–4965 (2020)
13. Molina-Cabello, M.A., López-Rubio, E., Luque-Baena, R.M., Palomo, E.J., Domínguez, E.: Frame size reduction for foreground detection in video sequences. In: Luaces, O. (ed.) CAEPIA 2016. LNCS (LNAI), vol. 9868, pp. 3–12. Springer, Cham (2016). https://doi.org/10.1007/978-3-319-44636-3_1
14. Molina-Cabello, M.A., Luque-Baena, R.M., López-Rubio, E., Thurnhofer-Hemsi, K.: Vehicle type detection by ensembles of convolutional neural networks operating on super resolved images. Integrated Comput. Aided Eng. **25**(4), 321–333 (2018)
15. Nazaré, T.S., da Costa, G.B.P., Contato, W.A., Ponti, M.: Deep convolutional neural networks and noisy images. In: Mendoza, M., Velastín, S. (eds.) CIARP 2017. LNCS, vol. 10657, pp. 416–424. Springer, Cham (2018). https://doi.org/10.1007/978-3-319-75193-1_50
16. OmniVision: 4" color cmos qsxga (5 megapixel) image sensorwith omnibsi technology. OV5640 datasheet (2010). Accessed May 2011
17. ONSemiconductor: High accuracy star tracker cmos active pixel image sensor. NOIH25SM1000S datasheet (2009). Accessed June 2010
18. PyTorch Contributors: PyTorch Documentation. Version 1.2.0. https://pytorch.org/docs/1.2.0/ (2019) Accessed 31 Oct 2019
19. Russakovsky, O., et al.: ImageNet large scale visual recognition challenge. Int. J. Comput Vis. (IJCV) **115**(3), 211–252 (2015). https://doi.org/10.1007/s11263-015-0816-y
20. Sandler, M., Howard, A., Zhu, M., Zhmoginov, A., Chen, L.: Mobilenetv 2: inverted residuals and linear bottlenecks. In: 2018 IEEE/CVF Conference on Computer Vision and Pattern Recognition, pp. 4510–4520 (2018)

21. Simonyan, K., Zisserman, A.: Very deep convolutional networks for large-scale image recognition (2014)
22. Stanford Vision Lab: Imagenet, large scale visual recognition challenge 2012 (ilsvrc2012). http://www.image-net.org/challenges/LSVRC/2012/ (2012). Accessed 31 Oct 2019
23. Szegedy, C., Vanhoucke, V., Ioffe, S., Shlens, J., Wojna, Z.: Rethinking the inception architecture for computer vision. In: 2016 IEEE Conference on Computer Vision and Pattern Recognition (CVPR), pp. 2818–2826 (2016)
24. Szegedy, C., et al.: Going deeper with convolutions. In: IEEE Conference on Computer Vision and Pattern Recognition, pp. 1–9 (2015)
25. Tan, M., et al.: Mnasnet: Platform-aware neural architecture search for mobile. In: 2019 IEEE/CVF Conference on Computer Vision and Pattern Recognition (CVPR), pp. 2815–2823 (2019)
26. Xie, S., Girshick, R., Dollár, P., Tu, Z., He, K.: Aggregated residual transformations for deep neural networks. In: 2017 IEEE Conference on Computer Vision and Pattern Recognition (CVPR), pp. 5987–5995 (2017)
27. Zagoruyko, S., Komodakis, N.: Wide residual networks. In: Proceedings of the British Machine Vision Conference 2016, pp. 87.1-87.12. British Machine Vision Association, York, UK (2016). https://doi.org/10.5244/C.30.87, http://www.bmva.org/bmvc/2016/papers/paper087/index.html

# Exploring the Contributions of Low-Light Image Enhancement to Network-Based Object Detection

Yuen Peng Loh[(✉)] [iD]

Multimedia University, 63100 Cyberjaya, Selangor, Malaysia
yploh@mmu.edu.my
https://www.mmu.edu.my/fci/

**Abstract.** Low-light is a challenging environment for both human and computer vision to perform tasks such as object classification and detection. Recent works have shown potential in employing enhancements algorithms to support and improve such tasks in low-light, however there has not been any focused analysis to understand the direct effects that low-light enhancement have on an object detector. This work aims to quantify and visualize such effects on the multi-level abstractions involved in network-based object detection. First, low-light image enhancement algorithms are employed to enhance real low-light images, and then followed by deploying an object detection network on the low-light as well as the enhanced counterparts. A comparison of the activations in different layers, representing the detection features, are used to generate statistics in order to quantify the enhancements' contribution to detection. Finally, this framework was used to analyze several low-light image enhancement algorithms and identify their impact on the detection model and task. This framework can also be easily generalized to any convolutional neural network-based models for the analysis of different enhancements algorithms and tasks.

**Keywords:** Low-light · Enhancement · Convolutional neural network · Object detection

## 1 Introduction

Low-light image enhancement and object detection have been distinct fields of research until recently, where there is a new interest in enhancement to support low-light object detection [14,19]. This is due to the discovery that typical detection models are trained to perform in daylight, whereas deploying a model solely catered for low-light is still under-performing because of a lack of data [13]. However, the extent in which enhancement algorithms can support object detection is still an open question.

© Springer Nature Switzerland AG 2021
A. Del Bimbo et al. (Eds.): ICPR 2020 Workshops, LNCS 12666, pp. 655–669, 2021.
https://doi.org/10.1007/978-3-030-68780-9_50

This work aims to provide insights about the effects of low-light image enhancement on a network-based object detector through visualizations instead of a performance based evaluation. Typically, performance metrics such as accuracy, precision, and recall measures *how well* the algorithms can help a detector, though in this work, the target is to decipher *what* has the algorithm enhanced that could be *seen* by the object detector. From the onset, the understanding of detectors based on convolutional neural networks (CNN) is a challenge in itself despite impressive application performance as the features learned are solely based on the optimization of the weights using large amounts of data. Hence, the application of enhancements as a preprocessing to the data will introduce further ambiguities that warrant investigation in order to understand their contribution or lack thereof. Furthermore, the insights derived from such a study would also contribute to the future design considerations of enhancement algorithms that appropriately support similar object detection models.

The CNN-based object detector is the main target for analysis in this work due to its significant performance boost in recent years, and also for its general design containing multiple layers of feature maps that represent features of different levels of abstraction which can be systematically exploited. The activations on each feature map of a CNN in fact visually indicate the contributing features, a simple yet intuitive approach in interpreting a network's attention. In this work, the difference in the activations when performing detection before and after the enhancement indicates the improvement (or deterioration) by the algorithm on the object features. Specifically, an object detection network is applied on low-light images, which will act as the reference, and images enhanced by algorithms. Feature maps of both cases are extracted, and object regions (indicated by the groundtruth bounding box annotations) are then compared. The difference in activations for each object will be the indicator of the enhancements' effects. Unlike existing approaches of evaluation metrics as a singular measurement, this method of analysis allows for the observation on: (1) the direct effects on features based on the activations in individual layers, and (2) the progressive effects from low to high level features across the whole detection network.

Namely, the proposed framework generates an *Activation Value Statistic* and an *Activation Field Statistic* that gives a progressive view of the increase/decrease in activation values and activation area respectively of each layer from a network-based model when the input low-light image is pre-processed by enhancement algorithms. This work analyzed several state-of-the-art low-light image enhancement algorithms using the generated statistics as well as their visual representations. It is found that there is a negative correlation between the increase of the activation statistics, particularly with the statistic of earlier layers, and the improvement on object detection performance. Moreover, it is established that low-light enhancement algorithms with particular emphasis on features and structure enhancement have deeper impact on the improvement of the detector network as compared to aesthetically driven algorithms that produce superior visual results.

## 2    Related Work

**Low-light Image Enhancement** has been a niche domain of research closely related to image super-resolution, image denoising, image dehazing, etc. The traditional goal of these tasks are quality improvement with evaluation metrics such as reference-based assessments: PSNR and SSIM, and no-reference assessment: Natural Image Quality Evaluator (NIQE) [20]. More low-light domain specific metrics have been also been used, such as Light Order Error (LOE) [18]. Recently, it has been proposed to measure features of enhancement to provide more insightful evaluation or even directly study the usefulness of enhancement for further machine vision applications to bridge the gap between low-level and high-level vision tasks [12]. While the above metrics well quantify different aspects of enhancements, the more explicit effects of the enhancement are left unexplained, particularly in low-light research. Thus, the aim of this work is to provide a visual look into the effects of enhancement on object features, and not to propose a new evaluation metric.

**Interpreting Networks.** Efforts in understanding the contributing factors to a network's performance has been growing as it not only provide insights but also guide the design process of state-of-the-art architectures. Most work focus on understanding the features learned by the network that are responsible for its superior performance by proposing increasingly sophisticated methods to reverse feature vectors back into visual representations that are intuitively recognizable [3,15]. On the other, there are also works that sought to understand the effects of illumination and contrast on network-based models, a closely related domain to low-light research [1,2]. Differently, this paper exploits such network visualization approach in order to grasp the utility of low-light image enhancement for object detection.

## 3    Method

The main aim of this paper is to visualize the contribution brought by low-light image enhancement towards object detection features. The approach can be distinguished into the following major steps: (1) detection network preparation, (2) feature maps and activation extraction, and (3) feature enhancement statistics generation.

### 3.1    Detection Network Preparation

This framework is applicable for analysis on various types of tasks and features. The target area of analysis determines the selection of a network trained on a relevant task. In this particular work, the effects of enhancement on various object features are to be analyzed, therefore the multi-level features learned by object detection networks can be exploited.

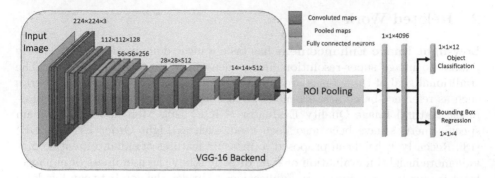

**Fig. 1.** Fast R-CNN network with VGG-16 backend used for the study. The activation maps in the VGG-16 backend is the key for the analysis.

In the current implementation, the Fast R-CNN [7] detection model is selected. The back-end CNN architecture of the model is the straightforward VGG-16 [16], shown in Fig. 1 which allows easy feature maps extraction for analysis. The model is trained using the Microsoft COCO (MCOCO) dataset [11] but limiting to 12 object classes following the Exclusively Dark (ExDark) dataset [13]. The training by MCOCO will condition the model to perform object detection in bright conditions, whereas the ExDark provides the low-light image data for analysis. Low-light data is not explicitly used to train the model in order to maintain its performance bias towards bright conditions. This will therefore emphasize the change in features when the enhancement algorithms are applied.

### 3.2   Feature Maps and Activation Extraction

As is widely known, the multi-layer convolution operations of CNN are trained feature extractors, and the feature maps in the layers represent the features used for the end task. Hence, this step processes the feature maps for analysis, particularly to extract the specific region of interest of objects across the feature maps in the network.

The detection model $D$ can be decomposed into its layers

$$D = D_{\text{fc}}(d_N(\cdots(d_2(d_1(\mathbf{I}))))) \tag{1}$$

where $D_{\text{fc}}$ represents the fully connected layers of the detector collectively, i.e. the later layers in the network where the spatial information is not preserved, and $d_1, d_2, \cdots, d_N$ indicate the convolution layers (after ReLU) of the selected detector, which in this case, $N = 13$ for the VGG-16. $D$ provides the object detections given an image $\mathbf{I} = \{I_l, I_e\}$ which can be either a real low-light image $I_l \in \mathbb{R}^{x \times y \times c}$ or the enhanced counter part $I_e \in \mathbb{R}^{x \times y \times c}$. $x$, $y$, and $c$ denotes the width, height, and color channel pixel dimensions of the images. Meanwhile, layers $d_1, d_2, \cdots, d_N$ will generate feature maps $F_k$ where $k = [1, N]$ that encompass the spatial activations illustrating both the region and strength of features contributing to the detection.

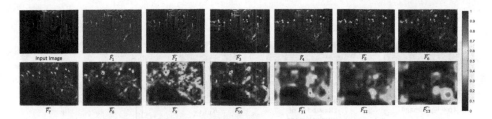

**Fig. 2.** Example of low-light image and the resized high activation maps extracted from the convolution layers of the Fast R-CNN model. (Colorbar indicates normalized values corresponding to the colormap.)

In order to analyze the activations specifically on the objects within an image, the spatial location in each $F_k$ has to be localized. $F_k$ are three dimensional volumes of $W_k \times H_k \times C_k$, where the width $W_k$ and height $H_k$ varies based on the dimensions of $\mathbf{I}$. Moreover, the size of both dimensions reduces while $C_k$ increases as the layers $k$ progress, therefore the localization involves three steps as well.

Firstly, global pooling is performed on $F_k$ in order to obtain the high activation map of each layer $\hat{F}_k \in \mathbb{R}^{W_k \times H_k \times 1}$. This is followed by the resizing of $\hat{F}_k$ following the $x$ and $y$ dimensions of $\mathbf{I}$. Samples of resized $\hat{F}_k$ extracted from the VGG-16 network are shown in Fig. 2. Finally, the groundtruth bounding box annotations of objects $G_{i,j} = \{p_{i,j}, q_{i,j}, w_{i,j}, h_{i,j}\}$ are used to extract the regions of interested $R_{i,j,k}$ from each layer. $i$ and $j$ are indexes of the image $\mathbf{I}$ and the objects in it respectively, $p$ and $q$ are the pixel coordinates of the top left corner of the object bounding box, whereas $w$ and $h$ are its width and height in pixels. Thus, the extracted $R_{i,j,k}$ allows for comparison of features across different objects and layers between an image before $I_l$ and after $I_e$ enhancement.

### 3.3   Feature Enhancement Statistics Generation

As stated in the start of Sect. 3, the aim is to visualize the effects of low-light image enhancement on the object features. Therefore, after obtaining the region of interest for object $j$ in layer $k$ of the $i$-th real low-light image $I_l$, denoted as $R^l_{i,j,k}$, the corresponding region of interest in its enhanced counterpart $R^e_{i,j,k}$ are then extracted as well, thus producing the region pairs $\mathbf{R} = \left\{ R^l_{i,j,k}, R^e_{i,j,k} \right\}$.

Following this, the pairs can be used to visualize two aspects brought upon by the enhancement. They are, the difference in activation values, $E^v_k$ that indicate the change in strength of the features, and the difference in activation field, $E^s_k$ that shows the change in spatial area of features activated. They are calculated by,

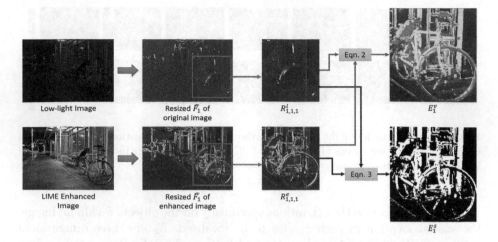

**Fig. 3.** Example of low-light image and its counterpart enhanced by LIME. Corresponding object regions are extracted from the LIME enhancement, $R_{i,j,k}^e$ and the low-light image, $R_{i,j,k}^l$. Visual representations of activation strength difference, $E_k^v$ and activation area, $E_k^s$ are shown on the right. ($E_k^s$: Hotter color indicates increment; $E_k^s$: white areas indicate areas of higher activation contributed by enhancement.)

$$E_k^v = \sum_{i,j=1}^{m,n} \sum_{\alpha,\beta=1}^{w,h} \left( R_{i,j,k}^e(\alpha,\beta) - R_{i,j,k}^l(\alpha,\beta) \right) \tag{2}$$

$$E_k^s = \sum_{i,j=1}^{m,n} \sum_{\alpha,\beta=1}^{w,h} \delta_{i,j,k}(\alpha,\beta) \tag{3}$$

$$\text{where } \delta_{i,j,k} = \begin{cases} 1, & \text{if } \gamma_{i,j,k} > 0 \\ -1, & \text{if } \gamma_{i,j,k} < 0 \\ 0, & \text{otherwise} \end{cases}$$

$$\text{and } \gamma_{i,j,k} = R_{i,j,k}^e - R_{i,j,k}^l$$

where $\alpha$ and $\beta$ are indexes of the elements in $R_{i,j,k}$. $m$ and $n$ on the other hand, represents the amount of images analyzed and the number of objects in the $i$-th image respectively, which are both dependent on the dataset used. For both equations, positive values indicate an increase in the activation values or spatial area, thus an implication of feature growth contributed by the enhancement method, and vice versa. Figure 3 shows the visual example of the object regions extracted and the corresponding $E_k^v$ and $E_k^s$ before aggregation.

**Table 1.** Percentage of influence on $F$-scores and average precisions (APs) of object detections after enhancement.
[Positive(+): Improvement, Negative(−): Depreciation, **Bold**: Best performance, *Italics*: Worst performance.]

| Methods | $F$-score | AP | $F$-score$_{50}$ | AP$_{50}$ | $F$-score$_{75}$ | AP$_{75}$ |
|---|---|---|---|---|---|---|
| LACE [9] | ±0.00% | +12.50% | −1.75% | +10.20% | +3.06% | +25.00% |
| FBE [5] | −5.47% | +9.38% | −6.64% | +6.12% | −2.04% | +16.67% |
| GBLE [17] | *−16.41%* | *−7.82%* | *−17.13%* | *−9.69%* | *−16.33%* | *−8.33%* |
| GladNet [19] | −1.56% | +18.75% | −3.85% | +16.33% | +2.04% | +29.17% |
| GPE [14] | ±0.00% | **+20.31%** | −1.75% | **+17.35%** | +2.04% | **+33.33%** |
| LIME [8] | −11.72% | +4.69% | −12.94% | +3.06% | −9.18% | +12.50% |
| RetinexNet [4] | −15.63% | +1.56% | *−17.13%* | −0.51% | −13.27% | +4.17% |
| SRRM [10] | **+7.03%** | +12.50% | **+4.55%** | +10.20% | **+12.24%** | +25.00% |
| WVM [6] | −3.13% | +7.82% | −3.85% | +7.14% | ±0.00% | +16.67% |

# 4   Results

**Implementation Details.** Nine notable low-light image enhancement algorithms based on key theories are chosen for this pilot analysis, they are dehazing-based (LACE [9]), gradient-based (GBLE [17]), Retinex-based (FBE [5], LIME [8], SRRM [10], WVM [6]), deep learning-based (GladNet [19]), as well as methods that implement a combinational approach (GPE [14], RetinexNet [4]). Each of these methods have shown noteworthy results, either in visual quality and/or feature enhancement, and the implementations are publicly available for experimentation. The Fast R-CNN object detection network used for this analysis is trained using a total of 61,524 images from MSCOCO with up to 332,361 object instances. The ExDark dataset provides 7,363 images with 23,710 instances of 12 objects whereby the feature enhancement statistics are computed across the 13 layers of the detection network.

## 4.1   Detection Performance

Typically, the performance of a detector are evaluated using metrics such as F-score and Average Precision (AP) [7]. While it provides an impartial view on the precision and recall performance, they hardly give insights to the contributing factors of the performance results. For instance, Table 1 shows the results when detections are performed on low-light images from the ExDark before and after enhancements. Following the convention used by COCO challenge [11], AP refers to average precision of the Intersection over Union, IoU = [0.5, 0.95] with the step size 0.05, whereas the subscripts 50 and 75 refers to the AP at IoU of 0.5 and 0.75 respectively. The notations apply to the F-score metric in the table as well to illustrate the harmonic mean between precision and recall.

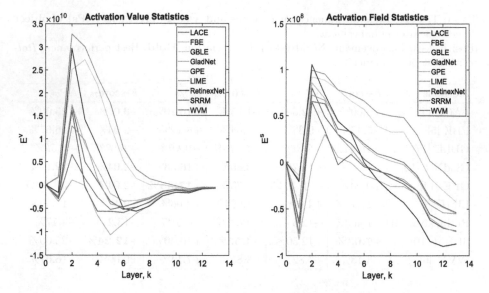

**Fig. 4.** Graphs showing changes in activations caused by image enhancements on different layers of Fast R-CNN network.

Based on Table 1, the detection performance do not necessarily improve by enhancement and may even deteriorate. For instance, most of the methods records a deterioration of $F$-score whereas the contrary is true for $AP$ values. The inference that can be drawn from this observation would be the reduce in rate of recall dominates the improvement in precision. This can be attributed to the reduce in both false negatives as well as false positives, and by extension, it can be surmised that the algorithms reduce the rate of detection as a whole.

Considering the individual enhancement algorithms, SRRM and GPE both record improvement for $F$-score and $AP$ respectively. These could be attributed to the emphasis on structure and feature enhancement by both algorithms. On the other hand, the weakest algorithm is GBLE, followed by RetinexNet where both greatly deteriorate the $F$-scores. Both GBLE and RetinexNet show clear signs of distortion [14] in their resultant images which could be the cause of the decline in performance. Additionally, it can be noted that the detection model may not be affected by the color features considering that GPE performance is one of the best even though the color in its results are clearly lacking.

### 4.2   Statistics Generation

In order to look further into the effects of the enhancements on the detection model, the changes in activations are calculated using Eqs. 2 and 3, and the statistics are illustrated in Fig. 4. The left graph in Fig. 4 shows the change to the activation values, i.e. strength of the activation. It can be seen that the largest effect of the enhancements are in layer 2. It is understood that the early layers in a detection network extracts lower level features, therefore, the peak in activations in layer 2 is a clear indication that the algorithms enhances such features, for instance edges. The highest peaks are shown by LIME, RetinexNet, and GBLE, and surprisingly these three methods record the worst detection performance impact in Table 1. This is particularly counter intuitive for LIME as it produces the best visual enhancement which is contrary to the distortions produced by GBLE and RetinexNet. However, strictly considering details, the results of all three algorithms do indeed show clear details such as edges, irregardless that the edges are in fact distortions.

Another point to note from the activation value statistics is the sharp decline by most methods between layers 3 to 7 into negative range before rising again. Such decline indicates that the enhancements do not propagate towards high level features and may negatively impact the construction of such features. In particular, the significantly negative activation showed by GPE in layer 5 may indicate that layer 5 is influenced by the color content of the images. This is because GPE has the distinction of severe loss of color in its enhancements as compared to all the other algorithms. Nonetheless, the close to zero constant values from layer 11 to 12 indicates that higher levels of abstraction can still be formed.

Referring to the right graph of Fig. 4, the statistics show the changes in activation field within the object area i.e. attention coverage of each considered layer in the network with respect to an object. Positive values indicate an increase in the area of activation and vice versa for negative values. A common trend seen for every enhancement algorithm is that they reduce the activation area for the first layer but shows a steep increase for layer 2, similar to the activation value statistics. This indicates that, despite the attention on the most basic components in layer 1 is narrowed, the enhancements enable the better formation of basic features captured in layer 2 to layer 6. However, it is hypothesized that the gradual decline towards negative values in later layers signifies the reduce in activation area for features representing higher levels of abstraction, though not the activation strength as reflected in the value statistics. Hence, it can be deduced that the enhancements enable the model to be more spatially focused on the features.

Considering the effects brought by specific methods, similar observations can be made between both the activation value and activation field graphs where the highest increment are shown by the enhancement algorithms with the weakest detection performance, namely LIME, GBLE, and RetinexNet. Additionally, the best performing methods in Table 1, particularly SRRM and GPE, also show the lowest trends for the activation fields, indicating a possible negative correlation between the improvement of detection performance with the increment of activation field. However, RetinexNet shows a notably different trend from other methods where it has the steepest decline in the activation field from the largest field in layer 2 till the lowest activation field in layer 13. This trend, coupled with its lack of support for detection performance implies that RetinexNet enhancement may reduce the features extracted instead of inducing focus.

**Fig. 5.** Low-light test image used to generate the visualizations in Fig. 6. The red bounding box indicates the specific object studied. (Color figure online)

### 4.3    Qualitative Exploration

Figure 6 shows visual examples produced alongside the statistics generated using the described method when the object detection network is applied on the sample shown in Fig. 5. These instance visualizations provide further insights on the attentions of the network at various layers when performing detection with the support of different enhancement algorithms. Layers, $k = 1, 2, 5, 9, 13$ are selected for this investigation due to the substantially varying statistics displayed in Fig. 4.

Firstly, the maps from layer, $k = 1$ reveal that most enhancements algorithms improved on the edge features. In the activation map of the un-enhanced object, it can be noted that the high activations are only found on the car wheel and lights, which can be presumed due to the contrast, whereas the increment maps of the enhanced counterparts clearly indicate the outline of the car. The red colored areas/edges correspond to high increments in the activation values. In particular, it can be observed that LACE, GladNet, and GPE not only exhibits clear structure but also an overall raise for the surroundings. However, it is noted that the activation increase may be contributed by resultant noise amplification that can distort the structures, as seen slightly in maps of GladNet and FBE, or considerably for RetinexNet. On the other hand, LIME, SRRM, and WVM show relatively well preserved details with minor distortions, though the activations for the car structure are not as defined as other methods, despite better visual quality.

The inspection on maps from layer $k = 2$ shows that significantly stronger structures are formed when the low-light images are enhanced. Especially notable is the map of GPE where the car's outline are clearly defined by the color red, indicating very high values of activation increment on the structure. On the other hand, results from methods such as LACE and FBE lost most structure despite showing significant increment of values. Similarly for RetinexNet, the distortion from layer 1 is carried forward to layer 2 where the car is hardly comprehensible even

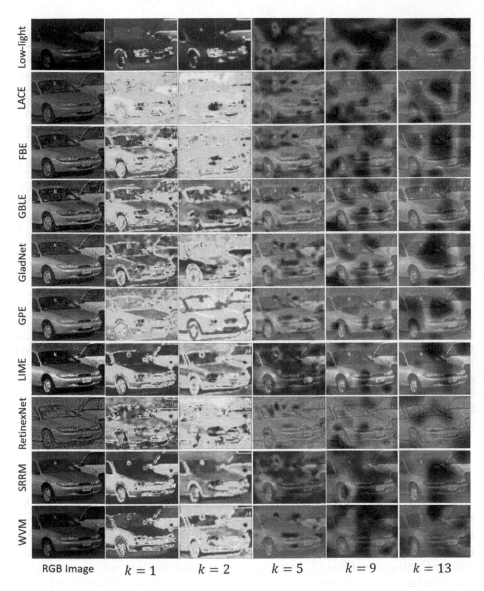

**Fig. 6.** Visualization of activation value increments, $E_k^v$ of layers, $k = 1, 2, 5, 9, 13$ of an object from the test image in Fig. 5. (1st row: Cropped view of object from the original image and the corresponding activation map, $R_{i,j,k}^l$ obtained during detection; Subsequent rows: Cropped view of enhanced object and their $E_k^v$ maps.)

though it shows high activations. Associating these observations with inference in Sect. 4.2, the inverse correlation between the activations in layer 2 and detection performance can be associated with the loss of structure in such early layers of the network.

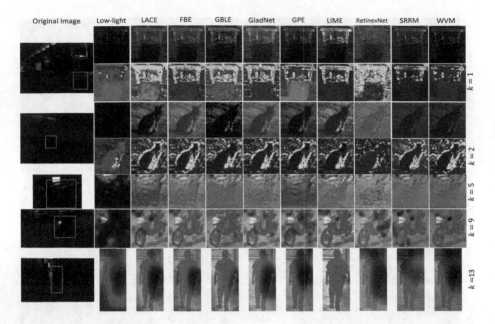

**Fig. 7.** Example visualizations of $E_k^v$ for layers, $k = 1, 2, 5, 9, 13$ when detecting objects from the ExDark dataset. ($1^{st}$ column: Original low-light image with object of interest bounded in red; $2^{nd}$ column: Cropped view of object with the corresponding activation map, $R_{i,j,k}^l$ obtained during detection; Subsequent columns: Cropped view of enhanced object overlay with their $E_k^v$ maps. For layers $k = 5, 9, 13$, the $E_k^v$ maps are overlaid on the cropped object.) (Color figure online)

The heatmaps indicating activation increments for layers $k = 5, 9, 13$ represents increasingly more abstract concepts, therefore they are overlaid on their RGB counterparts to aid visual inspection. It can be seen that despite strong structural enhancements in the first two layers, the increase in activations for these later layers are not as intuitively understood. Nevertheless, a common pattern can be found where methods such as LACE, FBE, GBLE, and RetinexNet that show lost of structural information in early layers exhibit broadly distributed activations in layer 5. In comparison to the activation map of the original low-light image, the enhancements increases the values of weakly activated areas. Contrarily, the other methods raise the values of regions that were already highly activated originally, as shown in the first row of maps in Fig. 6. It can be inferred that these methods further enhance features that were already significant to the detector.

Proceeding towards layers 9 and 13, the change in activations become increasingly similar among the enhancement results though notably SRRM still improves on the region that were originally significant in the low-light counterpart in layer 9. For the last layer which is hypothesized to encode the full concept of the object, the maps showed that each enhancement algorithm increases the values of the remaining regions of the car. This indicates that each of the enhancement do contribute to the final high level conceptual features though at varying degrees of effectiveness, as apparent in the performance reported in Table 1. In other words, the increased activations are not necessarily indicative features representing the object.

Figure 7 shows additional examples of the visualizations for different images and objects from the ExDark dataset, illustrating the same findings. It is evident that the impact of enhancement algorithms emphasizing on features or structures, such as GPE and SRRM are more far-reaching than aesthetic-driven algorithms such as LIME where the effects are uncertain in the perspective of object detection.

## 5    Conclusion

This paper proposed an approach to measure and visualize the contributions of enhancement algorithms to convolutional neural networks to gain insights beyond the typical inferences based on $F$-score and average precision. Specifically, the Activation Values Statistics and Activation Field Statistics, enable a comparison of contributions between different enhancements algorithms towards different convolution layers of a network-based model. Furthermore, inspection on the activation maps used to generate the statistics reveals particular effects brought by each algorithm and also the reach of their impact as the layers of the network deepens.

Demonstrated on low-light image enhancement algorithms and an object detection network, this work explored one of the first levels of analysis in an effort to understand the connection between low-level vision tasks (enhancement) and high-level vision tasks (object detection). It is found that there are a possible negative correlation between the performance of an object detection model with respect to the visual quality enhancement brought by most low-light image enhancement algorithms. Additionally, it is found that enhancement methods which focus on structure produce enhanced images with features that can be propagated into deeper layers of the object detector.

The current proposed approach is demonstrated on low-light enhancement with object detection domains, hence the insights derived are specific to the area of study. However, there are still various directions and aspects to be explored in order to gain even more in-depth view on the potential correlations. For example, more analyses and comparisons with diverse detection models to further verify the features learned and enhanced. Likewise, the complexity involving low-light environment as well as the ambiguity of "abilities" learned by network models can be further examined as well. For instance, to investigate the influence of different illumination conditions brought upon by the low-light phenomena on both enhancement and object detection models. On another note, a study on other enhancement domains, such as denoising and dehazing, with respect to other applications like scene classification can also be done using this approach, and the findings can subsequently be exploited for the development of better and more effective algorithms.

**Acknowledgment.** This research is sponsored by the Mini Fund Research 2019–2020 Grant MMUI/190020 from Multimedia University.

# References

1. Akbarinia, A., Gegenfurtner, K.R.: How is contrast encoded in deep neural networks? arXiv preprint arXiv:1809.01438 (2018)
2. Akbarinia, A., Gil-Rodríguez, R.: Deciphering image contrast in object classification deep networks. Vision Res. **173**, 61–76 (2020)
3. Chattopadhay, A., Sarkar, A., Howlader, P., Balasubramanian, V.N.: Gradcam++: generalized gradient-based visual explanations for deep convolutional networks. In: 2018 IEEE Winter Conference on Applications of Computer Vision (WACV), pp. 839–847. IEEE (2018)
4. Wei, C., Wang, W., Yang, W., Liu, J.: Deep retinex decomposition for low-light enhancement. In: British Machine Vision Conference (BMVC) (2018)
5. Fu, X., Zeng, D., Huang, Y., Liao, Y., Ding, X., Paisley, J.: A fusion-based enhancing method for weakly illuminated images. Signal Process. **129**, 82–96 (2016)
6. Fu, X., Zeng, D., Huang, Y., Zhang, X.P., Ding, X.: A weighted variational model for simultaneous reflectance and illumination estimation. In: 2016 IEEE Conference on Computer Vision and Pattern Recognition (cvpr), pp. 2782–2790 (2016)
7. Girshick, R.: Fast r-cnn. In: 2015 IEEE International Conference on Computer Vision (ICCV), pp. 1440–1448 (2015)
8. Guo, X., Li, Y., Ling, H.: Lime: low-light image enhancement via illumination map estimation. IEEE Trans. Image Process. **26**(2), 982–993 (2016)
9. Li, L., Wang, R., Wang, W., Gao, W.: A low-light image enhancement method for both denoising and contrast enlarging. In: 2015 IEEE International Conference on Image Processing (ICIP), pp. 3730–3734. IEEE (2015)
10. Li, M., Liu, J., Yang, W., Sun, X., Guo, Z.: Structure-revealing low-light image enhancement via robust retinex model. IEEE Trans. Image Process. **27**(6), 2828–2841 (2018)
11. Lin, T.-Y., et al.: Microsoft COCO: common objects in context. In: Fleet, D., Pajdla, T., Schiele, B., Tuytelaars, T. (eds.) ECCV 2014. LNCS, vol. 8693, pp. 740–755. Springer, Cham (2014). https://doi.org/10.1007/978-3-319-10602-1_48
12. Liu, D., Zhang, H., Xiong, Z.: On the classification-distortion-perception tradeoff. In: Advances in Neural Information Processing Systems (NIPS), pp. 1206–1215 (2019)
13. Loh, Y.P., Chan, C.S.: Getting to know low-light images with the exclusively dark dataset. Comput. Vis. Image Underst. **178**, 30–42 (2019)
14. Loh, Y.P., Liang, X., Chan, C.S.: Low-light image enhancement using gaussian process for features retrieval. Signal Proc. Image Commun. **74**, 175–190 (2019)
15. Selvaraju, R.R., Cogswell, M., Das, A., Vedantam, R., Parikh, D., Batra, D.: Gradcam: visual explanations from deep networks via gradient-based localization. In: 2017 IEEE International Conference on Computer Vision, pp. 618–626 (2017)
16. Simonyan, K., Zisserman, A.: Very deep convolutional networks for large-scale image recognition. arXiv preprint arXiv:1409.1556 (2014)
17. Tanaka, M., Shibata, T., Okutomi, M.: Gradient-based low-light image enhancement. In: 2019 IEEE International Conference on Consumer Electronics (ICCE), pp. 1–2. IEEE (2019)

18. Wang, S., Zheng, J., Hu, H.M., Li, B.: Naturalness preserved enhancement algorithm for non-uniform illumination images. IEEE Trans. Image Process. **22**(9), 3538–3548 (2013)
19. Wang, W., Wei, C., Yang, W., Liu, J.: Gladnet: low-light enhancement network with global awareness. In: 2018 IEEE International Conference on Automatic Face & Gesture Recognition (FG), pp. 751–755. IEEE (2018)
20. Yang, Q., Jung, C., Fu, Q., Song, H.: Low light image denoising based on poisson noise model and weighted tv regularization. In: 2018 IEEE International Conference on Image Processing (ICIP), pp. 3199–3203. IEEE (2018)

# Multi-level Fusion Based Deep Convolutional Network for Image Quality Assessment

Qianyu Guo and Jing Wen[✉]

Shanxi University, Taiyuan, China
wjing@sxu.edu.cn

**Abstract.** Image quality assessment aims to design effective models to automatically predict the perceptual quality score of a given image that is consistent with human cognition. In this paper, we propose a novel end-to-end multi-level fusion based deep convolutional neural network for full-reference image quality assessment (FR-IQA), codenamed MF-IQA. In MF-IQA, we first extract features with the help of edge feature fusion for both distorted images and the corresponding reference images. Afterwards, we apply multi-level feature fusion to evaluate a number of local quality indices, and then they would be pooled into a global quality score. With the proposed multi-level fusion and edge feature fusion strategy, the input images and the corresponding feature maps can be better learned and thus help produce more accurate and meaningful visual perceptual predictions. The experimental results and statistical comparisons on three IQA datasets demonstrate that our framework achieves the state-of-the-art prediction accuracy in contrast to most existing algorithms.

**Keywords:** Full-reference image quality assessment · Deep neural network · Multi-level fusion · Edge information fusion

## 1 Introduction

With the rapid development of digital multimedia, obtaining high-quality images is becoming an important issue in the field of image processing technology. During the process of generation, compression, storage, and transmission, images probably would be caused different degrees of distortion, even multiple distortions. However, the ability to evaluate the quality of images remains a challenging and valuable task. Normally, the most common way for perceptual quality evaluation of images is subjective test, which needs human observers to give the perceptual score or rating for images. However, relying on people to rate images is expensive and time-consuming. Therefore, an efficient subjective consistent algorithm that can automatically predict the visual perceptual quality of distorted images is especially necessary.

© Springer Nature Switzerland AG 2021
A. Del Bimbo et al. (Eds.): ICPR 2020 Workshops, LNCS 12666, pp. 670–678, 2021.
https://doi.org/10.1007/978-3-030-68780-9_51

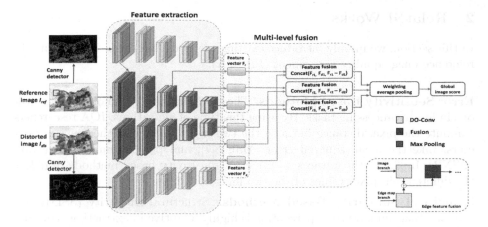

**Fig. 1.** Overview of the proposed MF-IQA framework.

Generally, image quality assessment methods can be broadly divided into three categories based on the amount of information available from the reference image: full-reference IQA (FR-IQA), reduced-reference IQA (RR-IQA), and no-reference IQA (NR-IQA). Compared with RR-IQA and NR-IQA, FR-IQA methods base on the accessibility of the high-resolution image to evaluate how much the distorted image different from the raw input image and usually acquires a relatively more accurate performance.

However, although a lot of FR-IQA methods have been presented, there are still some problems remaining. For instance, as the network goes deeper, several useful features may vanish. If only high-level feature vectors are used to calculate the image quality score, will some mid-level or even low-level feature information be ignored? Therefore, motivated by this phenomenon, we propose a network to extract and learn multi-level features from both distorted and reference images simultaneously. With this idea, this paper presents a novel end-to-end multi-level fusion based network to assess the quality of distorted input images with the help of reference images.

The key contributions of our work can be summarized as follows: (1) We incorporate effective edge information into the proposed feature fusion network. By learning image intensity and edge map information at the same time, the MF-IQA model achieves better performance. (2) We propose an efficient multi-level fusion strategy for FR-IQA task. Features from the distorted image and the reference image are fused in multi-levels. (3) We adopt Depth-wise Over-parameterized Convolutional (DO-Conv) in our proposed network by augmenting an additional depth-wise convolution to the common convolutional layer, to obtain more learnable parameters during the training and increase no computations for inference.

## 2  Related Works

In this section, we mainly introduce existing methods and related works on full-reference image quality assessment (FR-IQA).

**Error Sensitivity Based Methods.** These are the most commonly used methods in image processing tasks. By using this type of algorithms, IQA researchers compute the pixel distance between the two input images as the main parameters. Like the mean squared error (MSE) [7], and peak signal to noise rate (PSNR). In [2,12], the authors all use error sensitivity based methods to reflect the difference in pixel values of the two images.

**Structural Similarity Based Methods.** Structural similarity (SSIM) [16] presents that human visual perception is highly adaptive in extracting structure information from a scene, including luminance, contrast, and structure features. Then a series of improved algorithms based on SSIM have been proposed, such as information content weighted SSIM (IW-SSIM) [17], spectral residual similarity (SR-SIM) [19] and feature similarity (FSIM) [20].

**Deep Learning Based Methods.** In recent years, researchers have explored deep convolutional neural networks (DCNNs) in IQA researches and achieved superb performance. For example, [6] proposed a deep similarity (DeepSim) framework to employ VGG19 [15] as a feature map extractor to calculate local similarity at each layer and each channel between distorted and reference images, by using SSIM. WaDIQaM-FR [1] presented a deep neural network that owns 10 convolutional layers for FR-IQA. DISTS [5] proposed to unify structure and texture similarity, this method performs robust to the images that have mild geometric distortions. In [11], the authors used a pairwise-learning framework to predict the preference degree of one distorted image to another one.

## 3  Proposed Multi-level Fusion Based IQA Network

In this section, we provide an introduction of the proposed multi-level fusion based IQA (MF-IQA) framework. Successively, we discuss the proposed edge information feature fusion module, the usage of the DO-Conv structure, and our multi-level feature fusion and connection strategy.

### 3.1  Framework

The overall network architecture of the proposed MF-IQA method is depicted in Fig. 1. Motivated by the excellent performance of WaDIQaM-FR, we choose it as the basis of our proposed framework. Instead of using a pretrained network, we train the network we designed in its entirety. To learn the distortion degree between the distorted image ($I_d$) and the corresponding reference image ($I_r$), we use a Siamese network for feature extraction to learn the same embedding function from those two types of images. The designed Siamese-based feature extraction network is comprised of DO-Conv3-32 (3 is kernel size and 32 is the number of channels), DO-Conv3-32, max-pooling, DO-Conv3-128 with edge fusion, DO-Conv3-128, max-pooling, DO-Conv3-256, DO-Conv3-256, max-pooling, FC-256, FC-1, DO-Conv3-512, DO-Conv3-512, max-pooling, FC-512, FC-1, DO-Conv3-1024, DO-Conv3-1024, max-pooling, FC-1024 and FC-1. After a series of convolutional and max-pooling operations, three sets of extracted feature vectors $F_{r_j}$, $F_{d_j}$, and their difference $F_{r_j}$ - $F_{d_j}$ (j = 1, 2, 3) are concatenated as feature fusion part for the further regression module, which is similar to WaDIQaM-FR [1] feature fusion strategy. Then this branch outputs a $F_{i_j}$ for level j of the patch i. By activating $F_{i_j}$ via an rectified linear unit (ReLU) function with a small epsilon $\varepsilon$ to guarantee $\alpha_{i_j} > 0$,

$$\alpha_{i_j} = max(0, F_{i_j}) + \varepsilon \tag{1}$$

the weight $\omega_{i_j}$ can be expressed as:

$$\omega_{i_j} = \frac{a_{i_j}}{\sum_i^N a_{i_j}} \tag{2}$$

In our implementation, each input image is divided into several random small patches in a size of 32 × 32. The embedded features from the patches are fed with the raw patches to the regression network to get the corresponding local patches' quality indices. When calculating the score of each patch, each selected level's fusion and activated output is weighted average pooling into a score, then we add the multi-level results together to obtain the global image quality score $S$. Therefore, the global quality $S$ is a weighted average of local patches' quality $y_i$ of level $j$ $y_{i_j}$ at three-level fully connection.

$$y_i = \sum_1^{j=3} y_{i_j} \tag{3}$$

$$S = \sum_i^N \omega_i y_i = \sum_i^N (\sum_1^{j=3} \omega_{i_j} y_{i_j}) = \sum_i^N (\sum_1^{j=3} \frac{\alpha_{i_j} y_{i_j}}{\sum_i^N \alpha_{i_j}}) \tag{4}$$

As a regression task, we utilize mean square error (MSE), mean absolute error (MAE), and least absolute error (LAE) as our loss constraints to perform the training process. Finally, the loss function is shown as follows:

$$L = \frac{\lambda 1}{N} \times \sum_i^N (y_i - S)^2 + \frac{\lambda 2}{N} \times \sum_i^N |y_i - S| + \lambda 3 \times \sum_i^N |y_i - S| \tag{5}$$

where $N$ is the number of the patches, and $\lambda 1$, $\lambda 2$, $\lambda 3$ are the weights of the three constraints and are as 0.4, 0.4 and 0.2 according to our experimental experience.

## 3.2 Edge Feature Fusion Strategy

When humans evaluate whether an image is of good quality, the sharpness of the edges and textures of the objects within the image is a crucial evaluation criterion. So we propose to fuse edge feature maps into the RGB image branches.

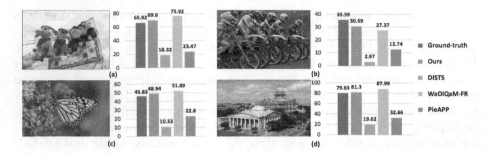

**Fig. 2.** Qualitative comparison with other recent methods DISTS [5], WaDIQaM-FR [1], PieAPP [11] on LIVE dataset. It can be noticed that given a distorted image, our method can infer a quality score that is closer to the actual ground truth score.

Because the Canny [3] algorithm has great performance, we also employ the Canny detector here to calculate an edge feature map, then add it at the appropriate low-level place to both two input branches so as to help the network learn effective edge attention information.

It is worth mentioning that about where should we add edge features into input streams, we did a series of experiments with different fusion places strategy and then draw a conclusion that low-level fusion can achieve the most excellent performance. In order to verify the necessity and feasibility to add edge information channel, we show the comparison of experimental results with and without additional edge information on the LIVE dataset in Table 3. The strategy could effectively improve the model's performance in predicting image quality.

### 3.3   Conventional CNN to Depth-Wise DO-Conv

To learn the fused features furthermore efficiently, we introduce Depth-wise Over-parameterized Convolutional Layer (DO-Conv) [4] to our MF-IQA framework. Compared to conventional convolution operator, the DO-Conv operator has one more depthwise convolution operator. By adding an additional depthwise convolutional operation to the conventional convolutional layer, each of the input channels is able to be convolved with a DO-Conv. This can obviously increase the number of trainable features and consistently boost the performance of the converged network model during the training process. However, during the inference, only one single layer could be applied to prevent extra computation cost. The introduction of DO-Conv helps us to learn more meaningful representations for the local quality score from image patches, and thus performing better visual and statistical results as shown in Table 3.

### 3.4   Multi-level Fusion Strategy

Up to now, almost all of the IQA methods only use a set of fully connected layers and set it at the end of the convolutional neural network (CNN) operation, which may ignore some useful mid-level or even low-level features. Based on this phenomenon, we suggest a thought to set up multiple fully connected layers and place them after different feature extraction sections, so as to employ multi-level feature vectors for regression. After a series of experiments with various settings, we come to the conclusion that the best performance is obtained by applying the fully connected layers after the third, fourth, and fifth max-pooling layers, respectively. Afterwards, we do multi-level feature fusion operation by concatenating extracted feature vectors $F_{r_j}$, $F_{d_j}$ and $F_{r_j}$-$F_{d_j}$ for the further regression part of the network. To verify the importance of our multi-level fully connection, we show a comparison on how the performance is with and without applying multi-level fusion in Table 3.

## 4    Experiments and Results

In this section, we first introduce three public datasets we use and then present the metrics for evaluation. The qualitative and qualitative comparisons with other FR-IQA methods for in-dataset and cross-dataset are also provided.

### 4.1    Datasets

**The LIVE.** [14] database contains 779 distorted images. 29 RGB reference images are distorted by five types of distortion: JPEG compression, JPEG2000 compression, white noise, Gaussian blur, and simulated fast-fading Rayleigh channel. The difference mean opinion score (DMOS) for each image is provided and the scores range from 1 to 100. It is worth mentioning that the lower score images have better visual quality. **The TID2013** [10] database is extended from an earlier image quality database TID2008. It contains 3000 distorted images with 24 distortion types at 5 levels derived from 25 reference images. However, a large number of distortion types make the TID2013 database a challenging task. The mean opinion score (MOS) for each image is released. The MOS distributes from 0 to 9, higher value corresponds to the higher visual quality of the image. **The CSIQ** [8] database includes 866 distorted images with six different types of distortion: JPEG compression, JPEG2000 compression (JP2K), Gaussian white noise (WN), Gaussian pink noise, Gaussian blur (GB) and contrast change based on 30 high-resolution RGB reference images. The DMOS lies in the range [0, 1], a lower DMOS value indicates better visual quality.

**Table 1.** Performance comparison of perceptual quality on three standard image quality databases, LIVE, TID2013, and CSIQ. Higher PLCC, SROCC, KROCC, and lower RMSE values indicate better performance. Deep learning based methods are italicized.

| | LIVE | | | | TID2013 | | | | CSIQ | | | |
|---|---|---|---|---|---|---|---|---|---|---|---|---|
| | PLCC | SROCC | KROCC | RMSE | PLCC | SROCC | KROCC | RMSE | PLCC | SROCC | KROCC | RMSE |
| PSNR | 0.865 | 0.873 | 0.680 | 13.716 | 0.677 | 0.687 | 0.496 | 0.912 | 0.819 | 0.810 | 0.601 | 0.154 |
| SSIM [16] | 0.945 | 0.948 | 0.797 | 8.946 | 0.790 | 0.742 | 0.559 | 0.761 | 0.861 | 0.876 | 0.691 | 0.133 |
| FSIM [20] | 0.960 | 0.963 | 0.834 | 7.678 | 0.859 | 0.802 | 0.629 | 0.635 | 0.912 | 0.924 | 0.757 | 0.108 |
| IW-SSIM [17] | 0.952 | 0.957 | 0.818 | 8.347 | 0.832 | 0.780 | 0.598 | 0.688 | 0.914 | 0.921 | 0.753 | 0.106 |
| VIF [13] | 0.960 | 0.964 | 0.828 | 7.614 | 0.772 | 0.677 | 0.515 | 0.788 | 0.928 | 0.920 | 0.754 | 0.098 |
| GMSD [18] | 0.960 | 0.960 | 0.827 | 7.694 | 0.855 | 0.804 | 0.634 | 0.642 | **0.954** | 0.957 | 0.812 | **0.079** |
| MAD [8] | 0.968 | 0.967 | 0.842 | 6.907 | 0.827 | 0.781 | 0.604 | 0.698 | 0.950 | 0.947 | 0.797 | 0.082 |
| *PieApp* [11] | 0.909 | 0.918 | 0.749 | 11.417 | 0.829 | 0.844 | 0.657 | 0.694 | 0.873 | 0.890 | 0.705 | 0.128 |
| *WaDIQaM-FR* [1] | 0.977 | 0.968 | 0.846 | 5.101 | 0.958 | 0.947 | 0.802 | 0.387 | 0.953 | **0.961** | **0.829** | 0.083 |
| *Deep-PAVIF* [9] | - | 0.967 | 0.833 | - | - | 0.900 | 0.715 | - | - | - | - | - |
| *DISTS* [5] | 0.954 | 0.954 | 0.811 | 8.214 | 0.855 | 0.830 | 0.639 | 0.643 | 0.928 | 0.929 | 0.767 | 0.098 |
| *MF-IQA(Ours)* | **0.984** | **0.977** | **0.872** | **4.263** | **0.965** | **0.960** | **0.830** | **0.344** | **0.970** | **0.967** | **0.843** | **0.067** |

## 4.2    Evaluation Metrics

Following previous works, four commonly-used evaluation criteria are adopted in this work: Pearson linear correlation coefficient (PLCC), Spearman rank correlation coefficient (SROCC), Kendall rank-order correlation coefficient (KROCC), and root mean square error (RMSE) respectively.

## 4.3    In-Dataset Evaluation

In order to validate the performance of our framework, we train and test the network on the three datasets aforementioned respectively, and the experimental results are shown in Table 1. We use each dataset completely and do not ignore any distortion types to train the network. As shown in Table 1, we compare our model with 11 full reference image quality assessment models, including an error sensitivity based method PSNR, 6 structural similarity based methods SSIM, FSIM, IW-SSIM, VIF, GMSD, MAD, and 4 deep learning based methods, PieApp, WaDIQaM-FR, Deep-PAVIF, and DISTS. Table 1 indicates that our method could achieve the best performance and superior results than almost any other FR-IQA methods, cross all three datasets and four evaluation metrics. Compared with state-of-the-art method WaDIQaM-FR, like on the LIVE dataset, the four evaluation metrics PLCC, SROCC, KROCC have about 0.7%, 0.9%, 2.6% improvements, respectively. In addition, we randomly pick 4 distorted examples and use our MF-IQA model to calculate image scores, and then compare the results with other deep learning-based methods. Figure 2 shows that our IQA method is more accurate and effective than the compared methods.

## 4.4    Cross-dataset Evaluation

To verify the great generalization ability of our proposed method, we conduct a cross-dataset test. In this experiment, we use the model trained on the LIVE dataset to test on another dataset, CSIQ. Since these two datasets have similar types of distortions, we firstly experiment on these distortion subsets (Gaussian white noise, Gaussian blur, JPEG compression, and JPEG2000 compression). Then we show the full dataset test results. The results of our cross dataset test are shown in Table 2, we also compare the test results with another excellent FR-IQA method WaDIQaM-FR.

**Table 2.** Cross dataset test on the CSIQ dataset, using model trained on LIVE.

|  | WN | | GB | | JPEG | | JP2K | | All | |
|---|---|---|---|---|---|---|---|---|---|---|
| Metrics | PLCC | SROCC | PLCC | SROCC | PLCC | SROCC | PLCC | SROCC | PLCC | SROCC |
| WaDIQaM-FR | 0.864 | 0.879 | 0.898 | 0.927 | 0.868 | 0.870 | 0.868 | 0.880 | 0.811 | 0.834 |
| MF-IQA(ours) | **0.934** | **0.947** | **0.957** | **0.954** | **0.930** | **0.912** | **0.942** | **0.932** | **0.848** | **0.865** |

### 4.5 Ablation Analysis

To investigate the effectiveness of each key component of our MF-IQA, we conduct ablation studies on the LIVE dataset, as depicted in Table 3. By adding the edge fusion to the feature extraction, the

**Table 3.** Ablation analysis of our proposed components on LIVE dataset.

| Configurations | PLCC | SROCC | KROCC | RMSE |
|---|---|---|---|---|
| *w/o edge fusion* | 0.976 | 0.963 | 0.844 | 5.096 |
| *w/o DO-Conv* | 0.980 | 0.968 | 0.849 | 4.597 |
| *w/o multi-level* | 0.978 | 0.963 | 0.850 | 4.914 |
| *Our full* | **0.984** | **0.977** | **0.872** | **4.263** |

PLCC has 0.8% improvement and the SROCC enjoys a 1.4% improvement respectively. As for the use of DO-Conv, we also achieve considerable progress on every evaluation metrics, such as a 2.3% improvement on KROCC. We also show the improvements brought by the multi-level feature fusion component. Our network obtains a 0.978 on PLCC value and 0.963 on SROCC value without the multi-level connection, compared with 0.984 and 0.977 on our full pipeline.

## 5 Conclusion

In this work, we describe a multi-level fusion based deep convolutional neural network MF-IQA. By introducing edge feature maps into the proposed edge fusion module, incorporating the depth-wise convolutional layers and designing a multi-level feature fusion and connection strategy for the final quality score regression, our network is able to predict the quality score of distorted images with the help of corresponding reference images more accurately and efficiently. Moreover, the experimental results demonstrate our method has good performance on three public datasets compared with other recent state-of-the-art approaches.

# References

1. Bosse, S., Maniry, D., Müller, K.R., Wiegand, T., Samek, W.: Deep neural networks for no-reference and full-reference image quality assessment. IEEE TIP (2017)
2. Bosse, S., Siekmann, M., Samek, W., Wiegand, T.: A perceptually relevant shearlet-based adaptation of the PSNR. In: IEEE ICIP (2017)
3. Canny, J.: A computational approach to edge detection. IEEE PAMI **8**, 679–698 (1986)
4. Cao, J., et al.: DO-CONV: depthwise over-parameterized convolutional layer. arXiv preprint arXiv:2006.12030 (2020)
5. Ding, K., Ma, K., Wang, S., Simoncelli, E.P.: Image quality assessment: unifying structure and texture similarity. arXiv preprint arXiv:2004.07728 (2020)
6. Gao, F., Wang, Y., Li, P., Tan, M., Yu, J., Zhu, Y.: Deepsim: deep similarity for image quality assessment. Neurocomputing (2017)
7. Girod, B.: What's wrong with mean-squared error? Digital images and human vision (1993)
8. Larson, E.C., Chandler, D.M.: Most apparent distortion: full-reference image quality assessment and the role of strategy. SPIE IS&T J. Electron. Imaging (2010)
9. Ma, X., Jiang, X.: Multimedia image quality assessment based on deep feature extraction. Multimedia Tools Appl. **79**(47), 35209–35220 (2019). https://doi.org/10.1007/s11042-019-7571-y
10. Ponomarenko, N., et al.: Color image database tid2013: peculiarities and preliminary results. In: IEEE EUVIP (2013)
11. Prashnani, E., Cai, H., Mostofi, Y., Sen, P.: Pieapp: perceptual image-error assessment through pairwise preference. In: IEEE CVPR (2018)
12. Sara, U., Akter, M., Uddin, M.S.: Image quality assessment through FSIM, SSIM, MSE and PSNR-a comparative study. JCC **07**, 8–18 (2019)
13. Sheikh, H.R., Bovik, A.C.: Image information and visual quality. IEEE TIP **15**, 430–444 (2006)
14. Sheikh, H.R., Sabir, M.F., Bovik, A.C.: A statistical evaluation of recent full reference image quality assessment algorithms. IEEE TIP **15**, 3440–3451 (2006)
15. Simonyan, K., Zisserman, A.: Very deep convolutional networks for large-scale image recognition. arXiv preprint arXiv:1409.1556 (2014)
16. Wang, Z., Bovik, A.C., Sheikh, H.R., Simoncelli, E.P.: Image quality assessment: from error visibility to structural similarity. IEEE TIP **13**, 600–612 (2004)
17. Wang, Z., Li, Q.: Information content weighting for perceptual image quality assessment. IEEE TIP **20**, 1185–1198 (2010)
18. Xue, W., Zhang, L., Mou, X., Bovik, A.C.: Gradient magnitude similarity deviation: a highly efficient perceptual image quality index. IEEE TIP **23**, 684–695 (2013)
19. Zhang, L., Li, H.: Sr-sim: A fast and high performance IQA index based on spectral residual. In: IEEE ICIP (2012)
20. Zhang, L., Zhang, L., Mou, X., Zhang, D.: FSIM: a feature similarity index for image quality assessment. IEEE TIP **20**, 2378–2386 (2011)

# CNN Based Predictor of Face Image Quality

Andrii Yermakov⬤ and Vojtech Franc$^{(\boxtimes)}$⬤

Department of Cybernetics, FEE, Czech Technical University in Prague,
Prague, Czech Republic
xfrancv@fel.cvut.cz

**Abstract.** We propose a novel method for training Convolution Neural Network, named CNN-FQ, which takes a face image and outputs a scalar summary of the image quality. The CNN-FQ is trained from triplets of faces that are automatically labeled based on responses of a pre-trained face matcher. The quality scores extracted by the CNN-FQ are directly linked to the probability that the face matcher incorrectly ranks a randomly selected triplet of faces. We applied the proposed CNN-FQ, trained on CASIA database, for selection of the best quality image from a collection of face images capturing the same identity. The quality of the single face representation was evaluated on 1:1 Verification and 1:N Identification tasks defined by the challenging IJB-B protocol. We show that the recognition performance obtained when using faces selected based on the CNN-FQ scores is significantly higher than what can be achieved by competing state-of-the-art image quality extractors.

**Keywords:** Face image quality prediction · Deep learning

## 1 Introduction

Performance of a face recognition system is driven by quality of input images. The quality depends on a large set of factors (so called covariates) which include, for example, image resolution, pose of the face, expression, age, gender, lighting conditions, occlusions, wearing accessories and many others. A large body of papers study the influence of individual covariates, ways to mitigate their negative effects and/or to exploit them to improve performance of face recognition systems e.g. [1,3,4,8,14,16]. An important problem, which is also studied in this paper, is a design of methods which take a face image and output a quality score, that is, a single scalar summary of the image quality. A good quality score should serve as a predictor of the recognition system performance before the system is actually applied [11]. A high/low value of the quality score indicates that the recognition system will likely succeed/fail on the image from which the score was extracted. Methods extracting face quality score have been applied, for example, to increase performance of the face recognition systems in

© Springer Nature Switzerland AG 2021
A. Del Bimbo et al. (Eds.): ICPR 2020 Workshops, LNCS 12666, pp. 679–693, 2021.
https://doi.org/10.1007/978-3-030-68780-9_52

template-based face verification via rejecting low-quality images [2], for selection of frames in video-based recognition [9,10,22] and for fusion of multiple biometric modalities [18,19].

In this paragraph we give a brief review of approaches that have been used for face quality extraction so far. Quality scores can be obtained from recognition systems trained to perform different tasks. Two most notable examples are i) $L2$-norm of an identity descriptor computed by a CNN trained with cross-entropy loss to classify faces and ii) a confidence score of a general purpose face detector [20]. Other approaches derive the quality score based on measuring similarity to an ideal face image [21,24]. Finally, there is a class of approaches which use *supervised* machine learning algorithms to train a quality score predictor from examples. The examples are face images each annotated by a target quality score. Defining the target quality score that will be predictive for recognition performance is *a challenging problem*. The reason is that in the core of recognition systems is a face matcher operating on image pairs so that its performance does not depend on a single image from which the score is to be extracted. The following ways have been proposed to define the target quality score. Usage of the human annotation of perceived image quality was analyzed in [2]. The problem with human annotation is that its collection is laborious, often inconsistent and it may not be indicative of the recognition performance. Other works compute the target quality scores in an automatic way. In [13] the authors derived the quality scores based on similarity to a reference face that is most compliant to ISO/International Civil Aviation Organization (ICAO) standards. Face conformance to the ICAO standards is checked by a specialized software [17]. Another method, proposed in [2], first evaluates the matcher by computing distances between the image and a gallery of matching and non-matching faces. The quality score is then computed as a coefficient measuring separability of the matching and non-matching faces.

In this paper we propose a fundamentally different approach to learn the quality score predictor from examples. Our training set is composed of triplets of face images, two of them matching and one non-matching, which are annotated by automatically computed binary label. The label indicates whether the underlying matcher ranks faces in the triplet correctly or not. The ranking is correct if distance between the matching faces is below distances of the two non-matching pairs in the triplet. For each training image we introduce a latent binary label indicating whether the face is of high or low quality. We assume that if the quality labels were known for all images in the triplet one could deduce whether the ranking is going to be correct or not. The core of our model is a CNN, named CNN-FQ, which takes an image and outputs a probability that latent quality label is on, that is, the image is of a good quality. We learn parameters of the described model by an instance of the Expectation-Maximization (EM) algorithm [6] iterating two steps. In the E-step, it estimates the latent quality labels from images based on the current model. In the M-step, the estimated labels are used to update weights of the model, i.e. the CNN-FQ and a distribution relating the latent quality labels with the target binary labels. The proposed model is illustrated in Fig. 1. Table 1 and Fig. 2 show components of the proposed model learned from data and exemplar outputs on test images, respectively.

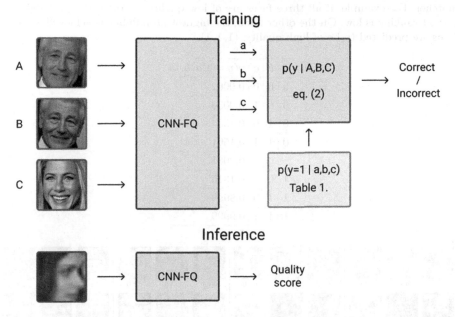

Fig. 1. Illustration of the proposed method. In the training phase the model captures probability that a randomly selected triplet of face images $(A, B, C)$ is going to be correctly ranked by a given face matcher. The model has two components. First, the CNN-FQ that outputs distribution of a latent quality labels $(a, b, c)$ for the image triplet $(A, B, C)$. Second, a discrete distribution $p(y = 1 \mid a, b, c)$ relating the correct ranking to the latent quality labels $(a, b, c)$. Both components are learned such that the model best explains the correct rankings $y = [\![d(A, B) < \min(d(A, C), d(B, C))]\!]$ seen on training triplets $(A, B, C)$, where $d(\cdot, \cdot)$ denotes a similarity score of the face matcher. The learned CNN-FQ is then applied to extract quality score of an arbitrary input face image.

In contrast to the existing approaches, the proposed method does not rely on a heuristically defined target quality score. Instead, the output of CNN-FQ is clearly related to the success of ranking triplet of faces based on distances returned by the face matcher. The triplet ranking error predicted by our method is a natural measure of face matcher performance regardless the application for which it is used. Other notable advantage is that the training set for our method can be created in a fully automated way *using existing datasets* for training face matchers, that is, *no additional manual annotations are required.*

Selection of the best image(s) for recognition from a pool of images with unknown qualities is among the most common applications of the quality score extractors [2, 9, 10, 18, 19, 22]. Therefore we evaluate the proposed method in this scenario using the IJB-B database and protocols [23]. We provide a convincing empirical evidence that the proposed CNN-FQ is superior to three competing

**Table 1.** Example of distribution $p(y = 1|a, b, c)$ learned from data. The distribution relates latent quality labels $(a, b, c)$, predicted from a face triplet by CNN-FQ, and the probability that the triplet is going to be correctly ranked by the underlying face matcher. For example, if all three faces are of low quality, $(0, 0, 0)$, the probability of correct ranking is low. On the other hand, the highest probability is achieved when all faces are predicted to be of high quality, $(1, 1, 1)$.

| $a$ | $b$ | $c$ | $p(y = 1|a, b, c)$ |
|---|---|---|---|
| 0 | 0 | 0 | 0.0002 |
| 0 | 0 | 1 | 0.0036 |
| 0 | 1 | 0 | 0.1534 |
| 0 | 1 | 1 | 0.1501 |
| 1 | 0 | 0 | 0.2081 |
| 1 | 0 | 1 | 0.1815 |
| 1 | 1 | 0 | 0.9999 |
| 1 | 1 | 1 | 0.9999 |

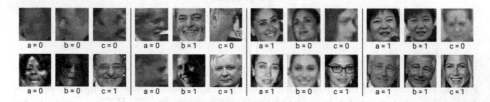

**Fig. 2.** Example of latent quality labels predicted by the proposed CNN-FQ from triplets of testing faces from IJB-B database. Note that the shown quality labels are not provided in the training set which is instead composed of face image triplets and a binary label indicating whether the triplet is correctly ranked.

quality extraction methods, including the state-of-the-art MVQ extractor proposed in [2].

The paper is structured as follows. The proposed image quality extractor and its learning are described in Sect. 2. Section 3 provides thorough experimental evaluation and comparison to state-of-the-art methods. Concluding remarks are drawn in Sect. 4.

## 2   The Proposed Approach: CNN-FQ and Its Learning

In Subsect. 2.1, we describe the statistical model that is behind the proposed method. The model and its components are illustrated in Fig. 1 and Table 1. Learning parameters of the proposed model via the EM-algorithm is a subject of Subsect. 2.2.

## 2.1    Statistical Model of Triplet Ranking Errors

Let $(A, B, C) \in I^3$ be a triplet of face images such that $A$ and $B$ captures the same identity while identity of $C$ is different. Let $d \colon I \times I \to \mathbb{R}_+$ be a distance function computed by the underlying face matcher for a pair of faces. The triplet $(A, B, C)$ is annotated by a binary label

$$y = [\![ d(A, B) < \min(d(A, C), d(B, C)) ]\!] \, , \tag{1}$$

where $[\![ S ]\!]$ denotes the Iverson bracket that evaluates to 1 if $S$ is true and to 0 otherwise. The label is $y = 1$ if the triplet is ranked correctly, i.e. the distance between the matching pair of faces is below the distances between both non-matching pairs of faces. Otherwise, if the ranking is incorrect the label is $y = 0$.

Assuming that triplets of faces $(A, B, C)$ are generated from a random process, the corresponding labels defined by (1) are also realizations of random variables. We propose to model the distribution of label $y$ by

$$p_\theta(y | A, B, C) = \sum_{\substack{(a,b,c) \\ \in \{0,1\}^3}} p_\theta(y \mid a, b, c) \, p_\theta(a|A) \, p_\theta(b|B) \, p_\theta(c|C) \tag{2}$$

where $(a, b, c) \in \{0, 1\}^3$ are latent variables each corresponding to one image in the triplet. The value $p_\theta(y = 1 | A, B, C)$ is then the probability that triplet of faces $(A, B, C)$ will be correctly ranked by the verification system. It will be shown later, that the state of the latent variables can be interpreted as indicator of the image quality. Hence we will call them face quality labels. By a clever initialisation of the learning algorithm described in the next section, we enforce the latent variables to be 1 for high quality faces and 0 for low quality faces. The function $p_\theta(y|a, b, c)$ describes a distribution of triplet label $y$ conditioned on latent quality labels $(a, b, c)$. The distribution of a latent label $x \in \{a, b, c\}$ conditioned on an image $X \in \{A, B, C\}$ is governed by distribution $p_\theta(x|X)$. We model $p_\theta(x|X)$ by the Logistic distribution defined on features extracted from face $X$ by a CNN, which we will call CNN-FQ. That is,

$$p_\theta(x = 1|X) = \frac{1}{1 + \exp(-\langle \phi(X), \boldsymbol{u} \rangle)} \, ,$$

$$p_\theta(x = 0|X) = 1 - p_\theta(x = 1|X) \, ,$$

where $\boldsymbol{u}$ denotes weights and $\phi(X)$ an output of the last and the penultimate layer of CNN-FQ, respectively. Let $\boldsymbol{\theta} \in \mathbb{R}^d$ denote a concatenation of all parameters of the distributions $p_\theta(y|a, b, c)$ and $p_\theta(x|X)$ that determine the model. In particular, the distribution $p_\theta(y|a, b, c)$ is given by $2^3 = 8$ real numbers and $p_\theta(x|X)$ by weights $\boldsymbol{u}$ and convolution filters of CNN-FQ defining $\phi(X)$. Learning of the parameters $\boldsymbol{\theta}$ from data is discussed in the next section.

## 2.2    Learning Model Parameters by EM Algorithm

Let $\mathcal{T} = \{(A_i, B_i, C_i, y_i) \in I^3 \times \{0, 1\} \mid i \in \{1, \dots, n\}\}$ be a training set consisting of $n$ triplets of faces and corresponding labels calculated by Eq. (1). We learn the model parameters $\theta$ by maximizing the conditional log-likelihood of the training set $\mathcal{T}$ defined as

$$L(\theta) = \sum_{i=1}^{n} \log p_\theta(y_i | A_i, B_i, C_i) \, . \tag{3}$$

We use the Expectation-Maximization (EM) algorithm [6] which decomposes maximization of (3) into a sequence of simpler maximization problems. The EM algorithm replaces maximization of $L(\theta)$ by maximization of an auxiliary function

$$F(\theta, q) = \sum_{i=1}^{n} \sum_{\substack{(a,b,c) \\ \in \{0,1\}^3}} q_i(a,b,c) \log \frac{p_\theta(y_i | A_i, B_i, C_i)}{q_i(a,b,c)} \tag{4}$$

where $q_i(a,b,c)$, $i \in \{1, \ldots, n\}$, are auxiliary variables defining distribution over the latent labels $(a,b,c)$. This replacement is justified by the fact that $F(\theta, q)$ is a tight lower bound of $L(\theta)$, that is, $L(\theta) = \max_q F(\theta, q), \forall \theta$, and $L(\theta) \geq F(\theta, q)$, $\forall \theta, q$.

The EM Algorithm 1 maximizes $F(\theta, q)$ by alternating maximization w.r.t. $\theta$ in M-step and w.r.t. $q$ in E-step which breaks calculations to several simple maximization tasks. Namely, the E-step problem $\max_q F(\theta^t, q)$ has a closed form solution

$$q_i^t(a,b,c) = \frac{p_{\theta^t}(y_i | a,b,c) \, p_{\theta^t}(a|A_i) \, p_{\theta^t}(b|B_i) \, p_{\theta^t}(c|C_i)}{\sum\limits_{\substack{(a,b,c) \\ \in \{0,1\}^3}} p_{\theta^t}(y_i | a,b,c) p_{\theta^t}(a|A_i) p_{\theta^t}(b|B_i) p_{\theta^t}(c|C_i)}$$

The M-step problem $\max_\theta F(\theta, q^{t-1})$ decomposes into two independent sub-problems. The first sub-problem involves maximization w.r.t. parameters defining $p_\theta(y|a,b,c)$ which has also a closed for solution

$$p_\theta^t(y|a,b,c) = \frac{1}{\sum_{i=1}^{n} q_i^{t-1}(a,b,c)} \sum_{i=1}^{n} [\![ y_i = y ]\!] q_i^{t-1}(a,b,c) \, .$$

The second sub-problem requires maximization w.r.t. weights of CNN-FQ defining the distribution $p_\theta(x|X)$ which boils down to maximization of

$$Q(\theta) = \sum_{i=1}^{n} \Big( \sum_{a \in \{0,1\}} \alpha_i(a) \log p_\theta(a|A_i)$$
$$+ \sum_{b \in \{0,1\}} \beta_i(b) \log p_\theta(b|B_i) \tag{5}$$
$$+ \sum_{c \in \{0,1\}} \gamma_i(c) \log p_\theta(c|C_i) \Big)$$

where $\alpha_i(a) = \sum_{b,c} q_i^{t-1}(a,b,c)$, $\beta_i(b) = \sum_{a,c} q_i^{t-1}(a,b,c)$ and $\gamma_i(c) = \sum_{a,b} q_i^{t-1}(a,b,c)$ are constants computed from $q^{t-1}$. Note that maximization of (5) corresponds to learning CNN with the standard cross-entropy loss defined over soft-labels. Hence we solve this problem by Adam algorithm [15].

---

**Algorithm 1.** EM-Algorithm

---

1: init $q^0$
2: $t \leftarrow 0$
3: **while** converge **do**
4:     $t \leftarrow t + 1$
5:     $\theta^t \leftarrow \arg\max_\theta F(\theta, q^{t-1})$ // M-step
6:     $q^t \leftarrow \arg\max_q F(\theta^t, q)$     // E-step
7: **end while**

---

We initialize the auxiliary distribution $q^0$ as follows:

$$
q_i^0(a, b, c) = \begin{cases} \dfrac{a + b + c + \epsilon}{\displaystyle\sum_{(a,b,c)\in\{0,1\}^3} (a + b + c + \epsilon)} & \text{if } y_i = 1 \\[6mm] \dfrac{3 - a + b + c + \epsilon}{\displaystyle\sum_{(a,b,c)\in\{0,1\}^3} (3 - a + b + c + \epsilon)} & \text{if } y_i = 0 \end{cases}
$$

where $\epsilon = 0.1$ prevents zero probabilities from which the EM cannot recover. Note that $q_i^0(a, b, c) = p_\theta(a, b, c \mid y_i, A, B, C)$, i.e., it is the probability that i-th triplet is ranked correctly if $y_i = 1$ or incorrectly if $y_i = 0$. Hence this initialization forces the model to associate the probability that a triplet is ranked correctly with the value of corresponding latent label equal to 1. That is, higher the number latent labels equal to 1 the higher the probability of correctly ranked triplet. Because the EM algorithm is a local optimization method, the initially enforced semantics of the labels is usually preserved during the course of training. Thanks to this initialization one could interpret the latent variables as qualities of the corresponding facial images.

## 3  Experiments

We evaluate the proposed approach in the most typical application scenario for the quality extractors. Namely, the quality score is used to select the best face from a pool of available faces. We use a challenging IJB-B database composed of face templates. Each template is a collections of still images and video frames capturing faces of the same subject. We extract the quality scores from all images in the template and select a single face with the maximal quality score. The template is then represented by an identity descriptor extracted from the selected face by a CNN matcher trained on MS-Celeb-1M [12] and VGGFace2 [5] database. The quality of the template representations is evaluated using the 1:1 Verification and 1:N Identification protocols defined by IJB-B [23]. The compared quality extractors are trained on CASIA dataset [25] disjunctive to IJB-B.

Different quality extraction methods compared in this experiment are summarized in Subsect. 3.1. Subsect. 3.2 discusses implementation details necessary for making make the experiments repeatable. IJB-B evaluation protocol and

**Table 2.** Evaluation of a single face template representation created based on quality scores extracted by four compared methods: L2-norm method, RetinaFace, MQV and the proposed CNN-FQ. TAR@FAR summarizes recognition performance on IJB-B 1:1 Verification protocol, while CMC and TPIR@FPIR are metrics evaluated on 1:N Identification protocol. The best results are bold.

| Quality scores | TAR@FAR's of | | | | CMC | | | TPIR@FPIR's of | |
|---|---|---|---|---|---|---|---|---|---|
| | 1E-5 | 1E-4 | 1E-3 | 1E-2 | Rank-1 | Rank-5 | Rank-10 | 1E-2 | 1E-1 |
| L2-norm | 0.444 | 0.633 | 0.784 | 0.896 | 0.744 | 0.847 | 0.881 | 0.389 | 0.602 |
| RetinaFace | 0.478 | 0.676 | 0.807 | 0.904 | 0.775 | 0.869 | 0.893 | 0.428 | 0.650 |
| MQV | 0.435 | 0.627 | 0.761 | 0.867 | 0.727 | 0.822 | 0.855 | 0.349 | 0.601 |
| CNN-FQ | **0.558** | **0.728** | **0.841** | **0.914** | **0.816** | **0.889** | **0.907** | **0.479** | **0.698** |

obtained results are given in Subsect. 3.3. In addition, in Subsect. 3.4, we investigate correlation between the extracted quality scores and manually annotated covariates defined in IJB-B protocol.

## 3.1   Evaluated Face Quality Extractors

**L2-norm.** Authors of the paper [20] have observed that the L2-norm of the identity descriptor extracted by a CNN (namely, the output of the last layer) trained with soft-max loss is positively correlated with the input image quality.

**RetinaFace Score.** Confidence of a general purpose face detector is a proxy of the face quality that is frequently practitioners. In our paper we used the confidence score returned by the state-of-the-art RetinaFace detector [7] which we also used to localize faces in IJB-A and CASIA images.

**Matcher Quality Values (MQV).** We re-implemented the state-of-the-art approach for automated face quality extraction proposed in [2]. The quality score is extracted by linear Support Vector Regression trained on the whole CASIA dataset composed of $449k$ images captured in unconstrained environment. Each faces in the dataset was annotated by the target quality score derived from responses of the used CNN face matcher. Namely, we use identity descriptors extracted by the CNN matcher and calculate qualities for the $j$-th query sample of subject $i$ in the following way: $z_{ij} = (s_{ij}^G - \mu_{ij}^I)/\sigma_{ij}^I$, where $s_{ij}^G$ is the genuine score and $\mu_{ij}^I$, $\sigma_{ij}^I$ are the mean and standard deviation, respectively, of the impostor scores for the query compared to the gallery.

**Proposed CNN-FQ.** We generated training set $\mathcal{T} = \{(A_i, B_i, C_i, y_i) \mid i \in \{1, \ldots, n\}, y_i \in \{0, 1\}\}$ from CASIA database in the following way. For each identity we selected 15 pairs (or less, depending on the number of images for that person) with the lowest and 8 pairs with the highest cosine distance computed on the descriptors extracted by the CNN matcher. Each pair is then augmented by one randomly sampled image of different identity. Obtained image triplets are labeled as correct (label 1) or erroneous (label 0) using Eq. (1). We split triplets into training (80%) and validation (20%) sets and ensure that identities in these two sets do not intersect. Finally, we have a training set that consists of 78,002 erroneous triplets and 108,961 correct triplets, and a validation set with 13,323 erroneous and 12,406 correct triplets. We experimented with the length of the training set making it 1.5x and 2x bigger but we did not see any significant difference in the triplet error computed on the validation set as well as the accuracy of IJB-B evaluation. We also noticed that during training random horizontal flip of the images had a huge benefit to accuracy.

## 3.2 Implementation Details

The faces are localized in database images by the RetinaFace [7] detector[1]. In case of IJB-B, the detector's search space is constrained by a rectangular area defined in the protocol. The bounding box found by the detector is extended by a 0.5 scale factor. Then, an image is cropped around the extended bounding box and resized to $256 \times 256$px. Finally, a central area of size $224 \times 224$px is cropped and used as an input to the CNN matcher.

As the backbone CNN matcher we use SE-ResNet-50-256D[2] (SENet for short) pre-trained on MS-Celeb-1M [12] dataset and fine-tuned on VGGFace2 [5] dataset. Given a pair of images $A$ and $B$, the matcher outputs the cosine distance $d(A, B) = 1 - \frac{\langle \phi(A), \phi(B) \rangle}{\|\phi(A)\|\|\phi(B)\|}$, where $\phi(A)$ and $\phi(B)$ are identity descriptors extracted by the SENet. The cosine distance is used in (1) to label triplets for training CNN-FQ, to compute the target quality scores for training the MQV extractor and, finally, to compute distance between the best selected faces in the verification and the identification experiments.

We use the same SENet architecture as the model of CNN-FQ with the sigmoid function placed at the last layer. The parameters of CNN-FQ are trained on CASIA dataset as described above.

## 3.3 Evaluation Protocol and Results

The compared quality extractors are used to select the best single face representative of the IJB-B templates. The quality of this template representation is evaluated on IJB-B 1:1 Verification and 1:N Identification protocols. The task of verification is to decide whether two identities described by face images are the same or different. The verification results are evaluated in terms of Receiver Operating Characteristic (ROC) curve[3]. The face identification is performed by

---

[1] RetinaFace is available at https://github.com/biubug6/Pytorch_Retinaface.

[2] Pre-trained SENet is available at https://github.com/ox-vgg/vgg_face2.

[3] ROC is calculated from two metrics, True Acceptance Rate (TAR) and False Acceptance Rate (FAR). TAR corresponds to the probability that the system correctly accepts an authorised person and it is estimated by computing a fraction of matching pairs whose cosine distance is below a decision threshold. FAR corresponds to the probability that the system incorrectly accepts a non-authorised person and it is estimated by computing a fraction of non-matching pairs whose cosine distance is below the decision threshold.

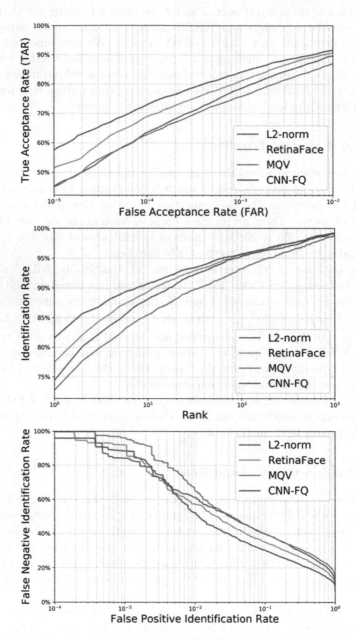

**Fig. 3.** Evaluation of a single face template representation on the IJB-B database. The face is selected based on quality scores extracted by L2-norm method, RetinaFace, MQV and the proposed CNN-FQ. ROC (top) summarizes performance on the 1:1 Verification protocol (higher is better). CMC (middle; higher is better) and DET (bottom; lower is better) plots correspond to 1:N Identification protocol.

searching in two galleries (S1 and S2) for enrolled identity that is most similar (using cosine distance) to the query identity. The results are evaluated in terms of the Cumulative Match Characteristic (CMC) and Decision Error Trade-off (DET) curves[4].

Figure 3 shows performance of the face verification and the face identification based on the single face template representation selected by the competing quality extractors. Important operating points of the figures are further summarized in Table 2. It is seen that the proposed CNN-FQ performs significantly better in all experiments regardless the metric used for comparison. The runner up appears to be the confidence score of the RetinaFace followed by the L2-norm method. The MQV extractor trained on the very same data as the CNN-FQ yields the worst results.

Figure 5 shows a pair of the worst (lowest quality) and the best (highest quality) photos selected from a randomly sampled templates based on the compared quality scores. To get a better impression, in Fig. 6, we also show the worst 6 and the best 6 faces select from the templates and sorted according to the extracted quality scores. It is seen that the best faces selected by CNN-FQ are typically frontal, sharp, uniformly illuminated and without occlusions. We also notice that ranking of the faces based the CNN-FQ quality score seems to be best aligned with the human perception of image quality as compared to the other methods.

## 3.4  Impact of Covariates on Quality Scores

This section investigates the correlation between individual covariates, performance of the verification system and the face quality predictor score extracted by the compared methods. We use IJB-B 1:1 Covariate Verification protocol that defines pairs of matching and non-matching faces. Each test pair is assigned manual annotation of covariates which we use to cluster the test pairs into groups with similar properties like e.g. faces with a low resolution, faces with a large yaw angle and so on. For each group of faces with a particular value of a covariate we plot the ROC curve of the underlying verification system and a histogram of the extracted quality scores.

The ROC curve tells us how a given covariate influences the performance of the verification system. The histogram of the extracted quality scores reveals a correlation between the score and the covariate. In this experiment we tested four different covatiates, namely, forehead visibility, nose or mouth visibility, image size and yaw angle.

Results obtained for the four compared quality extraction methods are shown in Fig. 4. There is a strong correlation between the CNN-FQ quality score and

---

[4] DET and CMC plots are calculated in terms of two metrics, False Postitive Identifcation Rate (FPIR) and False Negative Identification Rate (FNIR). FPIR is defined as the proportion of non-mate searches with any candidates below a decision threshold. In this metric, only candidates at rank 1 are considered. The FNIR is defined as the proportion mate searches for which the known individual is outside the top R = 20 ranks, or has cosine distance above threshold.

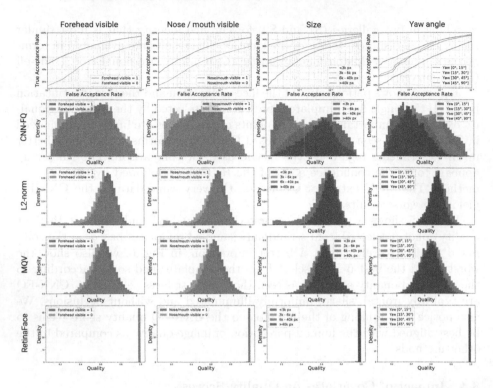

**Fig. 4.** The top row shows ROC curves for the underlying verification system evaluated on a subset of images with the corresponding covariate as defined in IJB-B 1:1 Covariate Verification protocol. Each of the following rows show histograms of quality scores extracted by one of the evaluated methods.

**Fig. 5.** Examples of the worst (lowest quality) and the best (highest quality) faces selected from randomly sampled IJB-B templates based on quality scores extracted by four methods: the proposed CNN-FQ, L2-norm, MQV and RetinaFace.

the image size as well as the yaw angle. On the other hand, the correlation with forehead visibility and the nose/mouth visibility is weaker which we attribute to insufficient amount of training examples with this type of covariates. The quality scores extracted by the competing methods are much less correlated with the covariates. It is also seen that the CNN-FQ scores are more evenly distributed if compared to peaky histograms of the other methods.

**Fig. 6.** Comparison of four different methods for quality score extraction by arranging photos in a template according to the score in ascending order (from the worst on left to the best on right). The best 6 photos from RetinaFace detector have the same score, so the order is arbitrary in this case.

## 4    Conclusions

We have proposed a method for training CNN-FQ extracting quality scores from face images. The CNN-FQ is trained from face triplets that are automatically labeled based on responses of the underlying face matcher. A notable advantage is that our method does not require explicit annotation of the target quality scores, instead existing databases composed of faces annotated by their identity can be used. The CNN-FQ quality scores are directly liked to the face matcher's performance via the triplet ranking error. Empirical evaluation on three IJB-B protocols demonstrates that the quality scores extracted by the proposed CNN-FQ are superior to three state-of-the-art face quality extractors. For the sake of reproducibility of the results we release the code and the trained models[5].

**Acknowledgments.** The research was supported by the Czech Science Foundation project GACR GA19-21198S.

## References

1. Abaza, A., Harison, M., Bourlai, T., Ross, A.: Design and evolution of photometric image quality measures for effective face recognition. IET Biometrics **3**(4), 314–324 (2014)
2. Best-Rowden, L., Jain, A.K.: Learning face image quality from human assessments. IEEE Trans. Inf. Forensics Secur. **13**, 3064–3077 (2018)
3. Beveridge, J., Givens, G., Phillips, P., Draper, B.: Factors that influence algorithm performance in the face recognition grand challenge. Comput. Vis. Image Underst. **113**(6), 750–762 (2009)
4. Beveridge, J., Givens, G., Phillips, P., Draper, B., Bolme, D., Lui, Y.: FRVT 2006: Quo vadis face quality. Image Vis. Comput. **28**(5), 732–743 (2010)
5. Cao, Q., Shen, L., Xie, W., Parkhi, O.M., Zisserman, A.: Vggface2: A dataset for recognising faces across pose and age. In: 2018 13th IEEE International Conference on Automatic Face Gesture Recognition (FG 2018). pp. 67–74 (2018)
6. Dempster, A.P., Laird, N.M., Rubin, D.B.: Maximum likelihood from incomplete data via the EM algorithm. J. Roy. Stat. Soc.: Ser. B (Methodol.) **39**(1), 1–22 (1977)
7. Deng, J., Guo, J., Ververas, E., Kotsia, I., Zafeiriou, S.: Retinaface: Single-shot multi-level face localisation in the wild. In: 2020 IEEE/CVF Conference on Computer Vision and Pattern Recognition (CVPR). pp. 5202–5211 (2020)
8. Du, L., Ling, H.: Cross-age face verification by coordinating with cross-face age verification. In: Conference on Computer Vision and Patter Recognition (2015)
9. Goswami, G., Bhardwaj, R., Singh, R., Vatsa, M.: MDLFace: memorability augmented deep learning for video face recognition. In: IEEE International Joint Conference on Biometrics (2014)
10. Goswami, G., Vatsa, M., Singh, R.: Face verification via learned representation on feature-rich video frames. IEEE Trans. Inf. Forensics Secur. **12**(7), 1686–1689 (2017)
11. Grother, P., Tabassi, E.: Performance of biometric quality measures. IEEE Trans. Pattern Recogn. Mach. Intell. **29**(4), 531–543 (2007)

---

[5] https://github.com/yermandy/cnn-fq.

12. Guo, Y., Zhang, L., Hu, Y., He, X., Gao, J.: MS-Celeb-1M: a dataset and benchmark for large-scale face recognition. In: Leibe, B., Matas, J., Sebe, N., Welling, M. (eds.) ECCV 2016. LNCS, vol. 9907, pp. 87–102. Springer, Cham (2016). https://doi.org/10.1007/978-3-319-46487-9_6

13. Hernandez-Ortega, J., Galbally, J., Fierrez, J.: Faceqnet: Quality assessment of face recognition based on deep learning. In: International Conference on Biometrics (2019)

14. Abdurrahim, S.H., Samad, S.A., Huddin, A.B.: Review on the effects of age, gender, and race demographics on automatic face recognition. Vis. Comput. **34**(11), 1617–1630 (2017). https://doi.org/10.1007/s00371-017-1428-z

15. Kingma, D., Ba, J.: ADAM: A method for stochastic optimization. In: ICLR (2014)

16. Lu, B., Chen, J.C., Castillo, C.D., Chellappa, R.: An experimental evaluation of covariates effects on unconstrained face verification. IEEE Trans. Biomet. Behav. Identity Sci. **1**(1), 42–55 (2019)

17. Ferrara, M., Franco, A., Maio, D., Maltoni, D.: Face image conformance to ISO/ICAO standards in machine readable travel documents. IEEE Trans. Inf. Forensics Secur. **7**(4), 1204–1213 (2012)

18. Poh, N., et al.: Benchmarking quality-dependent and cost-sensitive score-level multimodal biometric fusion algorithms. IEEE Trans. Inf. Forensics Secur. **4**(6), 849–866 (2009)

19. Poh, N., Kittler, J.: A unified framework for biometric expert fusion incorporating quality measures. IEEE Trans. Pattern Anal. Mach. Intell. **34**, 3–18 (2012)

20. Ranjan, R., et al.: Crystal loss and quality pooling for unconstrained face verification and recognition. CoRR abs/1804.01159 (2018). http://arxiv.org/abs/1804.01159

21. Sellahewa, H., Jassim, S.: Image-quality-based adaptive face recognition. IEEE Trans. Instrum. Measure. **59**, 805–813 (2010)

22. Vignesh, S., Priya, K., Channappayya, S.: Face image quality assessment for face selection in surveillance video using convolutional neural networks. In: IEEE Global Conference on Signal and Information Processing (2015)

23. Whitelam, C., et al.: Iarpa janus benchmark-b face dataset. In: 2017 IEEE Conference on Computer Vision and Pattern Recognition Workshops (CVPRW), pp. 592–600 (2017)

24. Wong, Y., Chen, S., Mau, S., Sanderson, C., Lovell, B.: Patch-based probabilistic image quality assessment for face selection and improved video-based face recognition. In: CVPRW, pp. 74–81 (2011)

25. Yi, D., Lei, Z., Liao, S., Li, S.Z.: Learning face representation from scratch. CoRR abs/1411.7923 (2014). http://arxiv.org/abs/1411.7923

# MPRSS - 6th IAPR Workshop on Multimodal Pattern Recognition for Social Signal Processing in Human Computer Interaction

# Preface

This book chapter presents the proceedings of the 6th IAPR TC 9 Workshop on *Pattern Recognition of Social Signals in Human-Computer-Interaction (MPRSS 2020)*. The goal of this workshop is to bring together recent research in pattern recognition and human-computer-interaction. Research in the field of intelligent human-computer-interaction has made considerable progress in methodology and applications, however, building intelligent artificial companions capable to interact with humans, in the same way humans interact with each other, remains a major challenge in this field. Pattern recognition and machine learning methodology play a major role in this pioneering field of research. MPRSS 2020 mainly focus on pattern recognition and machine learning with applications in social signal processing, including multimodal emotion recognition or pain intensity estimation. MPRSS 2020 was held as a satellite workshop of the International Conference on Pattern Recognition (ICPR 2020) in Milano, Italy, January 10, 2021 as an online event. This workshop would not have been possible without the help of many people and organizations. First of all, we are grateful to all the authors who submitted their contributions to the workshop. We thank the members of the program committee for performing the task of selecting the best papers for the workshop, and we hope that readers may enjoy this selection of papers and get inspired from these excellent contributions.

For the MPRSS 2020 workshop eight out of ten papers have been selected for inclusion into this volume, additionally to the regular presentations, three invited talks by Dilana Hazer-Rau, Ulm University on *Affective Computing and Stress Recognition for Healthcare Applications*, Xavier Alameda-Pineda, Inria/University of Grenoble-Alpes on *Combining auditory and visual data to enhance the speech signal,* and Steffen Walter, Ulm University on *Multimodal Automatic Pain Recognition/Machine Learning* have been included to the workshop program, as well as a tutorial session by Mariofanna Milanova entitled *Deep Learning and Multiple Data Types Analysis.*

MPRSS 2020 has been supported by the University of Ulm (Germany), the University of Arkansas at Little Rock(USA), the International Association for Pattern Recognition (IAPR), and the new IAPR Technical Committee on *Pattern Recognition in Human Computer Interaction* (TC 9).

November 2020

Friedhelm Schwenker
Mariofanna Milanova

# Organization

## General Chairs

Friedhelm Schwenker      Ulm University, Germany
Mariofanna Milanova      University of Arkansas at Little Rock, USA

## Program Committee

| | |
|---|---|
| Hazem M. Abbas | Ain Shams University Cairo, Egypt |
| Xavier Alameda-Pineda | Inria, University of Grenoble-Alpes, France |
| Kazuhiro Fukui | University of Tsukuba, Japan |
| Bernado Gatto | University of Tsukuba, Japan |
| James Ireland | University of Canberra, Australia |
| Concetta Papapicco | University of Bari, Italy |
| Sumantra Dutta Roy | Indian Institute of Technology Delhi, India |
| Stefan Scherer | University of Southern California, USA |
| Eugene Semenkin | Siberian State Aerospace University, Russia |
| Mansi Sharma | Indian Institute of Technology Delhi, India |
| Patrick Thiam | Ulm University, Germany |

# Explainable Model Selection of a Convolutional Neural Network for Driver's Facial Emotion Identification

Amany A. Kandeel[1]([envelope]), Hazem M. Abbas[2], and Hossam S. Hassanein[1]

[1] School of Computing, Queen's University, Kingston, Canada
19aak6@queensu.ca, hossam@cs.queensu.ca
[2] Department Computer and Systems Engineering, Ain Shams University, Cairo, Egypt
hazem.abbas@eng.asu.edu.eg

**Abstract.** Road accidents have a significant impact on increasing death rates. In addition to weather, roads, and vehicles, human error constitutes these accidents' main reason. So, driver-safety technology is one of the common research areas, whether in academia or industry. The driver's behavior is influenced by his feelings such as anger or sadness, as well as the physical distraction factors such as using mobile or drinking. Recognition of the driver's emotions is crucial in expecting the driver's behavior and dealing with it. In this work, the Convolutional Neural Network (CNN) model is employed to implement a Facial Expression Recognition (FER) approach to identify the driver's emotions. The proposed CNN model has achieved considerable performance in prediction and classification tasks. However, it is similar to other deep learning approaches that have a lack of transparency and interpretability. We use Explainable Artificial Intelligence (XAI) techniques that generate interpretations for decisions and provide human-explainable representations to address this shortage. We utilize two visualization methods of XAI approaches to support our decision of choosing the architecture of the proposed FER model. Our model achieves accuracies of 92.85%, 99.28%, 88.88%, and 100% for the JAFFE, CK+, KDEF, and KMU-FED datasets, respectively.

**Keywords:** Driver-safety · Facial Expression Recognition · Convolutional Neural Network · Explainable Artificial Intelligence

## 1 Introduction

As indicated by the worldwide status report on road safety, the World Health Organization (WHO) announced that the number of annual road traffic deaths is approximately 1.3 million [32]. The reasons can be a result of the road conditions, weather, or vehicle, but the main reasons for this tremendous number of incidents can be attributed to the driver's behavior. The motorist behavior is affected by

© Springer Nature Switzerland AG 2021
A. Del Bimbo et al. (Eds.): ICPR 2020 Workshops, LNCS 12666, pp. 699–713, 2021.
https://doi.org/10.1007/978-3-030-68780-9_53

drinking alcohol, using mobile, fatigue, and other physical factors, but emotions can also be one of the significant factors that affect driver behavior and increase accident probability. According to Virginia Tech research, [10] about studying the risk of a crash, claims that the risk of accidents is influenced by various motivations such as: drinking, drug, and alcohol, mobile phone dialing, reading and writing, emotions (i.e., anger, sadness, and crying), reaching for an object, drowsiness, fatigue, etc.; all these factors are organized concerning its effect on a driver's distraction in Fig. 1.

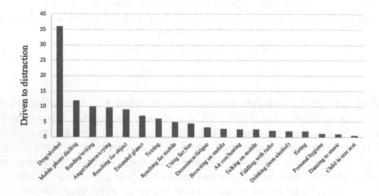

**Fig. 1.** Different motivations effects of crash risk [10].

As supposed by this study, driving with sadness, anger, or agitation feelings increases the danger of an accident by almost ten times. While unexpectedly, drowsiness or fatigue makes a crash three times more likely. At the same time, eating or talking on mobile-only doubles the risk. Previously, numerous highways show signs that caution drivers to continue driving if they feel tired, and they should pull over. However, new researches propose that a healthy emotional state is more significant for safe driving [10]. Emotions can be considered as a procedure that elevates adjustment to the environment and prepares the individual for adaptive action [25]. This process is accompanied by expressions such as face or voice, in addition to some physiological alterations such as an increment in heart rate. Mesken [20] explained the three functions of emotion concerning examples about driving. The first function of emotion is the adaptive function, where emotions are adaptive, and this means they support behavior that is suitable for the environment. For instance, when a vehicle's driver is up to another vehicle unexpectedly coming from a side street, the dread or surprise reaction makes the driver brake in a flash. This response is much faster than a more cognitive response. A second function is a communicative or social function. We can predict others' behaviors by watching their emotions, but it is difficult to do that in driving issues, so the drivers can represent their feelings in other ways such as hand gestures or using horns. The last function of emotions depends on planning. People may complete their goals by using their emotions. A driver can use a hand gesture to express his apologies if he prevents another driver's progress during parking to avert a hostile response. Detecting a driver's emotion is quite crucial to predicting his behavior; for instance, detecting aggressive driver emotion can help keep the driver safe. This detection can be performed by using biomedical means such as Electrocardiogram (ECG) or Electroencephalogram (EEG) sensors [3]. However, these sensors are not comfortable for the driver. Others use a self-reporting questionnaire, and this is also unpractical because it needs a lot of effort and time in recording the symptoms [22]. Some approaches depend on evaluating drivers' behavior by analyzing data from sensors at different vehicle components, such as the steering wheel and pedals. Facial expression is considered a behavioral approach that monitors the face, eye, mouth, or any other face component to evaluate the driver's behavior; it is more reliable, which indicates the driver state immediately in real-time [6].

Facial Expression Recognition (FER) early approaches used manual feature engineering to build emotion classifiers. Both feature extraction and classification methods are chosen to cope with the datasets [15] such as Support Vector Machines (SVMs), Modified Principal Component Analysis (PCA), and Linear Discriminant Analysis (LDA) [21]. Recently, deep learning approaches are trained to learn emotion features from input images automatically. Deep Neural Networks (DNNs) have been successfully applied to computer vision tasks such as object detection, image segmentation, and classification [27]. This advancement is because of the development of Convolutional Neural Networks (CNNs) [9]. Despite the great accomplishment of deep learning approaches in detection and classification, most of these systems' decisions and behavior are less understandable for humans. Recently, researchers provided some explainable methods to illustrate Artificial Intelligence (AI) models to be more interpretable.

This paper has two main goals: first, to identify the driver's psychological state utilizing the six basic emotions (anger, disgust, fear, happiness, sadness, and surprise) to facilitate safe driving. We implement a FER model using CNN because of the high accuracy it can achieve. Secondly, find the best architecture to achieve the highest accuracy with the lowest possible complexity using some explainability visualizing methods to illustrate the reasons for selecting a particular model architecture.

The rest of our paper is structured as follows. Section 2 provides the related work. The proposed explainable model selection approach is introduced in Sect. 3. The experimental results are presented in Sect. 4. Finally, we conclude our work in Sect. 5.

## 2   Related Work

Although some companies intend to produce fully autonomous vehicles during the next five years, it is considered as a future step. Furthermore, most companies depend on semi-autonomous systems such as the Advanced Driver Assistance System (ADAS) or Driver Monitoring System (DMS), which have seen significant improvements in recent years. These systems can include automatic parking systems, lane assistance, or driver concentration control that help with a way or another in increasing road safety [12].

The system can identify aggression, fatigue, or drunk driving by recognizing the driver's facial expression. This identification aids to improve traffic situations and reduces accidents occurrence [31]. Some researchers use classical machine learning approaches such as SVMs, K-Nearest Neighbors (K-NN), Hidden Markov Models (HMMs), and Random Forests in FER systems [21]. These approaches are suitable for small datasets and do not need a massive amount of computation time, speed, or memory [2]. Jeong et al. [8] presented a FER method based on geometric features and the hierarchical Weighted Random Forest (WRF). First, they reduced the number of landmarks used for generating geometric features. Afterward, they differentiated the facial expressions by using a hierarchical WRF classifier. Additionally, they developed a new benchmark dataset, Keimyung University Facial Expression of Drivers (KMU-FED), which considers the real driving environment. Their model achieved accuracies of 94.7%, 92.6%, and 76.7% for the KMU-FED, CK+, and MMI datasets, respectively.

On the other hand, deep learning-based approaches have been shown to achieve high accuracy, and thus many researchers employed them in FER solutions. Du et al. [4] presented a deep learning framework called Convolution Bidirectional Long Short-Term Memory Neural Network (CBLNN). They used facial features and heart rate to predict the driver's emotions using CNNs and Bidirectional Long Short-Term Memory (Bi-LSTM), respectively. The output of the Bi-LSTM was used as input to the CNN module. CBLNN classified the extracted information into five common emotions: anger, happiness, neutrality, fear, and sadness. To evaluate their model, they used a simulated driving environment. They proved that the combination of using facial features and heart rate increased the accuracy of emotion identification. Lee et al. [14] used a CNN model for aggressive emotion detection. They used near-infrared (NIR) light and thermal camera sensors to capture the driver's images. They evaluated the model on their dataset. Zhang et al. [34] proposed a model to detect stress by recognizing related facial expressions, anger, fear, and sadness. They used four layers of the connected convolutional network, which combined low-level features with high-level features to train the deep network to identify facial expressions. They used three datasets to evaluate their model that achieved an accuracy of 93.6% for CK+, 81.3% for Oulu-CASIA, and 97.3% for the KMU-FED dataset.

# 3   The Proposed Explainable Model Selection Approach

This paper's main objective is to build a simplified FER model with high accuracy to recognize the driver's facial emotions. To achieve high performance, we experimented with different CNN architectures. The architecture of the proposed CNN model results from experiments with a different number of layers with different sizes of convolution kernels. Before applying the CNN model on datasets images, we used face detection to define face areas, crop these faces from images, and remove irrelevant information. After the face extraction, the images are fed to the CNN model for training.

## 3.1  Face Extraction

The image's background may contain unimportant details, which can reduce the expression's recognition accuracy. Therefore, the first step of our approach is detecting the face area, followed by extracting it. We use the *Haar Cascades* algorithm [30] in detecting the faces in the images. *Haar Cascades* algorithm utilizes the *Adaboost* learning mechanism [13] which picks a few significant highlights from a huge set to give a productive consequence of classifiers. *Haar* features are composed of either two or three rectangles. Face candidates are scanned and looked for *Haar* features of the current stage. The weights are constants produced by the learning algorithm. There is a variety of forms of features, as can be seen below in Fig. 2. The *Haar* feature classifier multiplies the weight of each rectangle by its area, and the results are added together [13].

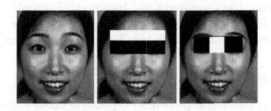

**Fig. 2.** Examples of Haar features.

## 3.2  CNN Model

CNN has dramatically decreased the dependence on physics-based models by allowing "end-to-end" learning directly from input images. Therefore, CNN achieves a significant performance in various applications such as image recognition and classification [11]. CNN includes two main stages; the first stage is the feature extraction layer(s), responsible for features detection. It contains a convolutional layer(s) and a pooling layer. The second stage is the classifying layer, which includes a fully connected layer(s) and the final output layer.

**Convolutional Layer:** This layer extracts different features from the input image by using a series of convolutional kernels. Each kernel has a particular task such as sharpening or edge and line detection [5]. In this layer, ReLU is utilized as an activation function, and it is one of the most popular activation functions. It does not cause the vanishing gradient that may be caused by other activation functions such as *Sigmoid* function.

**Pooling Layer:** Pooling converts the spatial information into features and helps in decreasing memory consumption in deeper layers. There are three types of pooling, *max pooling*, *average pooling*, and *sum pooling*. The pooling layer does not have any parameters, and the depth that represents the number of output features is always the same as the input.

**Fully Connected Layers:** This layer is responsible for classification, so all nodes are fully connected to the nodes in the following layer. The output of the convolution layer before entering the fully connected is usually flattened into a vector. In the output, the *Softmax* function is employed to produce a value between 0 and 1, based on the model's confidence. The output class is one of the six emotions [5]. We endeavor to implement a FER model that fulfills both goals of simplicity and performance. To specify the optimal architecture that achieves the highest accuracy, we tried different layers and various filter numbers and compared each architecture's performance. We also compared the model complexity using the number of its parameters. Section 4.2 explains this comparison in detail and analyzes the results. Furthermore, to deeply understand the model's behavior, we employed some interpretation tools to verify different architectures' performance and explained the reasons for selecting the proposed model's particular design; these tools are described in the next section.

### 3.3   Explainable Model

Although the deep learning approaches outperform other approaches, it is considered a black box in its nature, and this is the primary obstruction to use it. Researchers may undertake many experiments to obtain the perfect model that achieves the best results specific to their task. However, they can hardly explain the real reasons for providing a particular model. Indeed, they may not have a complete conception of illustrating the results of their model. To address this issue, a new approach, named Explainable Artificial Intelligence (XAI) has appeared to make the machine learning algorithms more understandable; XAI does not only give an appropriate explanation to AI-based systems but also improves the transparency and trust of them [1]. Many interpretability techniques are used to discuss explainability in Machine Learning (ML) algorithms. We used two of the most frequent interpretation methods in deep learning, the Saliency map [28], and Gradient-Weighted Class Activation Map (Grad-CAM) [26].

**Saliency Map:** It is one of the local interpretable methods which give the reason for a specific decision and explain it [1]. This map is used to clarify the importance of some areas in the input image that might be involved in generating the class prediction. Saliency is calculated at a particular position by the degree of the difference between that position and its surrounding [7]. Simonyan et al. [28] tried to categorize the pixels of image $I_0$ dependent on their impact on the class score function $S_c(I_0)$ of class $c$. The first step to calculate the class saliency map $M_{ij}$ is calculating $w$ as the derivative of the class score $S_c$ with respect to image $I$, $S_c$ is obtained from the relation, $S_c(I) = w_c^T I + b_c$, where $w_c$, $b_c$ are the weight vector and the bias of the model, respectively [28],

$$w = \frac{\partial S_c}{\partial I}\bigg|_{I_0} \tag{1}$$

$$M_{ij} = max_c \left| w_{h(i,j,c)} \right| \tag{2}$$

where $h(i,j,c)$ is the index at $i$-th row and $j$-th column of the element $w$ of class $c$.

**Grad-CAM:** This map specifies each neuron's important values for a specified decision of interest; it utilizes the gradient information flowing into CNN's last convolutional layer. It distinguishes among different classes, wherever it is exclusively highlighting the class regions for the class to be visualized [26]. In other words, it shows which regions in the image are related to this class. With this tool, two features from previous methods are combined; the class-discriminative, which is achieved in the Class Activation Map (CAM) approach [35], and the high-resolution which is provided by Guided Backpropagation [29]. To specify the significant values of each neuron for a specified choice, Selvaraju et al. use gradient information at the last convolutional layer. First, they determine neuron importance weights $\alpha_k^c$ [26],

$$\alpha_k^c = \frac{1}{Z} \sum_i \sum_j \frac{\partial y^c}{\partial A_{ij}^k} \tag{3}$$

where $Z$ is the number of pixels in the feature map, $\frac{\partial y^c}{\partial A_{ij}^k}$ is the gradient of the score $y^c$ for class $c$ with respect to the feature map activation $A^k$. Afterwards, to determine the class-discriminative localization map Grad-CAM $L_{Grad-CAM}^c$, they apply the ReLU function on the weighted combination of forward activation maps,

$$L_{Grad-CAM}^c = ReLU\left(\sum_k \alpha_k^c A^k\right) \tag{4}$$

They use ReLU to highlight only the features that have a positive effect on the class of interest.

After comparing different CNN architectures, which is discussed in detail in Sect. 4.2, one can determine the optimal CNN model architecture, which is highly accurate with the least number of parameters. The model is shown in Fig. 3. It is composed of three convolutional layers with a $3 \times 3$ convolution kernel and a stride value of 1, followed by a max-pooling layer with a $2 \times 2$ kernel. The number of filters is 32, 64, 128 for the three layers, respectively. The first layer has 256 nodes at the fully connected layers, and the second layer has 128 nodes, with a dropout ratio of 0.5. At the final output layer, there are six nodes for classifying the six basic emotions.

# 4    Experimental Results

To evaluate our model, we used four different datasets. These datasets vary from using static images or sequences of frames.

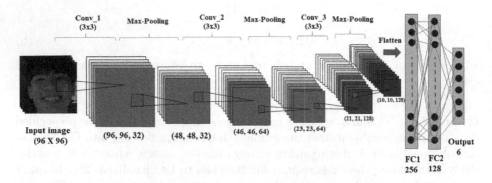

**Fig. 3.** The proposed CNN architecture

## 4.1    Datasets

Driver's emotions datasets are scarce, so many researchers used the general FER datasets such as CK+, Oulu-CASIA, and MMI [8,14]. Others use a simulated driving environment [4]. Some researchers built their own dataset with images in a real driving environment, such as the KMU-FED dataset [8]. In this work, we used both the general FER datasets, JAFFE, CK+, and KDEF, in addition to a real driving dataset, KMU-FED.

**CK+ Dataset:** The Extensive Cohn–Kanade (CK+) [17] has 327 labeled sequences of frames with two different sizes (640 × 480 and 640 × 490 pixels). The emotion labels are categorized into seven emotions; anger, contempt, disgust, fear, happiness, sadness, and surprise. The image sequences have various durations (10 to 60 frames) which contain different lighting levels. The emotion sequence starts from neutral representation to peak formation of the facial emotion. Therefore, we utilized the last three frames, which are the most expressive frames to represent the emotion [16]. To do a fair comparison with the recent approaches [8,16,33,34] in our experiments, we used only the six basic expressions without the contempt emotion. Therefore, the total number of frames is 930 frames.

**JAFFE Dataset:** The Japanese Female Facial Expression (JAFFE) database [19] is the most commonly used and oldest FER datasets. It contains 213 images of 7 facial expressions (neutral as well as the six main expressions) that 10 Japanese female models took. Images are digitized into 256 × 256 pixels. We used the six main emotions, to perform a reasonable correlation with other approaches [8,16,33,34]. So the total number of images is 183 images.

**KDEF Dataset:** The Karolinska Directed Emotional Faces (KDEF) [18] was provided by the Karolinska Institute in 1998. It has seven different emotions (afraid, angry, disgust, happy, neutral, sad, and surprise) with an equal number of male and female expressions. This dataset has frontal and non-frontal faces, where each expression is viewed from five different angles. We used just the six basic expressions with the frontal faces profile, in order to compare equitably with the ongoing methodologies [8, 16, 33, 34]. Thus the total number is 2504 samples with digitization $562 \times 762$ pixels.

**KMU-FED Dataset:** Keimyung University Facial Expression of Drivers (KMU-FED) [8] contains images in a real driving environment. It consists of six basic expressions captured using a Near Infrared (NIR) camera installed on the dashboard or steering wheel. It includes 55 image sequences from 12 subjects with a total of 1106 frames. The image sequences vary in duration (10 to 26 frames) that include various changes in illumination (front, back, right and left light) and partial occlusions caused by sunglasses or hair. The images have pixel resolutions of $1600 \times 1200$ pixels.

## 4.2 Discussion and Analysis

The model was evaluated using the previous four datasets. It was trained with 70% of the dataset samples, validated with 15%, and tested with 15%. The number of correctly predicted emotions is provided in each dataset's confusion matrix, as shown in Fig. 4. After extracting the face region from images, we applied the proposed CNN model on the input images with different sizes to determine which image resolution achieves the best results. Each dataset has the highest test accuracy with particular sizes. Figure 5 shows that the JAFFE dataset's highest accuracy is 92.85% with image size $96 \times 96$. Regarding the CK+ dataset, its most extraordinary performance occurs at size $48 \times 48$ pixels, and it is 99.28%. We reached the best accuracy for the KDEF dataset, 88.88% at both sizes $112 \times 112$ and $160 \times 160$ pixels. Finally, the model achieved the highest performance of 100% for the KMU-FED dataset at three different resolutions; $96 \times 96$, $112 \times 112$, and $144 \times 144$ pixels.

To demonstrate the effect of image resolution on the accuracy, we used the proposed CNN architecture, as shown in Fig. 3. The image sizes vary from $32 \times 32$ to $208 \times 208$. As shown in Fig. 5, each dataset has the best accuracy at particular resolutions. Both CK+ and KMU-FED datasets are not affected greatly by the change in the image size. On the contrary, the JAFFE dataset is enormously influenced by image resolution variations. This influence can be attributed to the low resolution of the original images in this dataset. Besides, this dataset has few samples and is the main cause of its weak performance that can be deduced from Fig. 5. The impact of the resolution variation on the KDEF dataset is moderate.

Also, to show the effect of different CNN model architectures with a different number of layers and filters, we chose a specified size, $48 \times 48$, to reduce the number of parameters, change in the number of layers, and the number of filters

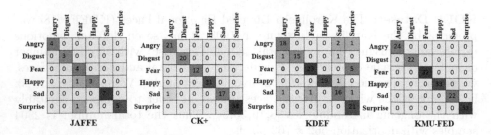

Fig. 4. The confusion matrix of each dataset

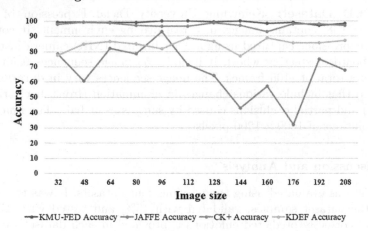

Fig. 5. Dataset accuracy versus different image sizes

in each layer as shown in Fig. 6. For each architecture, there are two varying values, the number of parameters and the model accuracy. Clearly, the number of parameters does not depend only on the number of filters in each layer, but it also relies on the number of flattened values before fully connected layers. The number of parameters $P$ in a convolution layer can be calculated as

$$P = (((m \cdot n \cdot d) + 1) \cdot k) \tag{5}$$

Where $m$ is the filter width, $n$ is the filter height, $d$ is the number of filters in the previous layer, and $k$ is the number of filters in the current layer. For instance, the highest number of model parameters occurs when only two layers are employed. On the other hand, when we used four layers, we obtained the smallest value. The main reason for that, in the first case, the last convolutional layer before the fully connected layers has a high spatial resolution, $11 \times 11$, and then the number of parameters is 4,075,014. However, in the case of four layers, the image information passes through four layers, so the last convolutional layer size is $1 \times 1$, and consequently, the number of parameters is only 164,646. One can conclude that, in addition to the number of filters, the model's complexity depends strongly on the values that are fed to the dense layers. Our main aim is

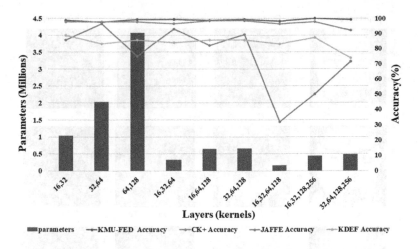

**Fig. 6.** Datasets accuracy versus different CNN architectures

to recognize facial expressions with high accuracy and simplicity. The two goals might seem to contradict, so we tried to balance them using a CNN model with a small number of parameters and provide the best performance. Thus, in light of the relationship analysis between the number of layers and both the accuracy and the number of parameters, we may select the architecture of three layers, which achieves both goals with the four datasets. However, to verify this model selection, we used explainable methods to clarify the model's behavior more thoroughly. Due to the internal complexity and nonlinear structure of deep neural networks, it is obscure and perplexing to interpret the reasons for designing a particular architecture. To state the reasons for using this specific architecture, we used some visualization tools such as the Saliency map [28], and Gradient-Weighted Class Activation Maps (Grad-CAM) [26].

**Saliency Map:** We employed the saliency map with the three different architectures, two, three, and four layers. We can conclude from Fig. 7 that the saliency map is accurate and precise for three layers' architecture. The saliency map of the two layers does not contain any details. Although the four layers of CNN architecture's saliency map has a dense view, it is ambiguous for understanding.

**Grad-CAM:** We applied this method to the input image with three different architectures. The Grad-CAM of the two layers' architecture highlights some facial features such as eyebrows, nose, and mouth. The Grad-CAM of the three layers is more accurate because it spotlights the facial features that affect the emotion shape, such as in angry emotion, highlighting the area of the mouth, the cheeks, and head front as shown in Fig. 7. On the other hand, the Grad-CAM of the model with four layers is not clear.

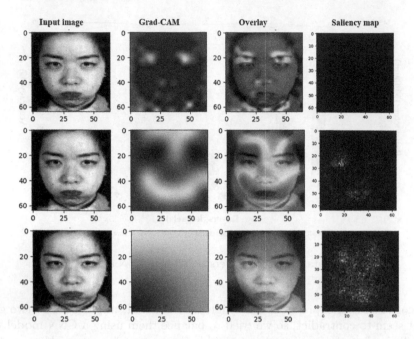

**Fig. 7.** Grade-CAM and Saliency maps for different CNN architectures (16, 32), (32, 64, 128), (16, 32, 64, 128) layers for angry emotion

We compared our models' results to some other state-of-the-art FER approaches in Table 1, our results are comparable to these results. Some of them used general FER datasets, such as Lopes et al. [16] who used data augmentation techniques to increase the size of datasets in order to improve the accuracy. However, their model's accuracies are 53.44% and 96.76% for JAFFE and CK+ datasets, respectively. Although Yang et al. [33] utilized a more complex model, the VGG16 model, which consists of 16 layers with 138 million parameters, their model achieved accuracies of 92.21% and 97.02% for the JAFFE and CK+ datasets, respectively. Pandey et al. [23] provided a combination of the Laplacian of the input image and the gradient with the original input into a CNN model; they evaluated their model on the KDEF dataset and provided an accuracy of 83.33%. Puthanidam et al. [24] used data augmentation techniques to overcome the small size dataset's challenge, which led to improved performance. The accuracies were 100% and 89.58% for JAFFE and KDEF datasets, respectively. We also compared with other researchers who used a combination of the real driving environment dataset and general FER datasets. Jeong et al. [8] generated a realistic driving environment, KMU-FED, and used it to evaluate their model in identifying the driver's emotion with the CK+ dataset. Their model provided accuracies of 92.6% for the CK+ dataset and 94.70% for the KMU-FED dataset. Also, Zhang et al. [34] utilized the same datasets, and their model's accuracies were 93.6% and 97.3% for CK+ and KMU-FED, respectively.

**Table 1.** Accuracy (%) comparisons between our approach and the state-of-the-art FER approaches.

| Method | JAFFE | CK+ | KDEF | KMU-FED |
|---|---|---|---|---|
| Jeong et al. [8] | – | 92.60 | – | 94.70 |
| Zhang et al. [34] | – | 93.60 | – | 97.30 |
| Lopes et al. [16] | 53.44 | 96.76 | – | – |
| Yang et al. [33] | 92.21 | 97.02 | – | – |
| Puthanidam et al. [24] | 100 | – | 89.58 | – |
| Pandey et al. [23] | – | – | 83.33 | – |
| **Proposed** | **92.85** | **99.28** | **88.88** | **100** |

## 5 Conclusion

In this paper, we implemented a CNN model to recognize the driver's emotions to expect his/her behavior for safe driving. We evaluated the model on four different FER datasets, three general FER datasets, and one real driving environment. It succeeds in recognizing frontal face datasets, whether static images or sequences of frames, and achieves accuracies of 92.85%, 99.28%, 88.88%, and 100% for the JAFFE, CK+, KDEF, and KMU-FED datasets, respectively. Because of the shortage of deep learning's understandability, we used two interpretability methods to illustrate the proposed model behavior with its particular architecture. In this paper, we applied our model to frontal faces. So we plan to apply it on non-frontal samples and evaluate its performance. In our future work, we will identify the driver's distraction in real-time with more datasets.

## References

1. Adadi, A., Berrada, M.: Peeking inside the black-box: a survey on explainable artificial intelligence (XAI). IEEE Access **6**, 52138–52160 (2018)
2. Dagher, I., Dahdah, E., Al Shakik, M.: Facial expression recognition using three-stage support vector machines. Visual Comput. Ind. Biomedi. Art **2**(1), 1–9 (2019). https://doi.org/10.1186/s42492-019-0034-5
3. Dong, Y., Hu, Z., Uchimura, K., Murayama, N.: Driver inattention monitoring system for intelligent vehicles: a review. IEEE Trans. Intell. Transp. Syst. **12**(2), 596–614 (2010)
4. Du, G., Wang, Z., Gao, B., Mumtaz, S., Abualnaja, K.M., Du, C.: A convolution bidirectional long short-term memory neural network for driver emotion recognition. IEEE Trans. Intell. Transp. Syst. 1–9 (2020)
5. Goodfellow, I., Bengio, Y., Courville, A.: Deep Learning. MIT Press, Cambridge (2016)
6. Guettas, A., Ayad, S., Kazar, O.: Driver state monitoring system: a review. In: Proceedings of the 4th International Conference on Big Data and Internet of Things. BDIoT 2019, Association for Computing Machinery, New York, NY, USA (2019). https://doi.org/10.1145/3372938.3372966

7. Harel, J., Koch, C., Perona, P.: Saliency map tutorial (2012). https://www.techylib.com/en/view/skillfulwolverine/saliency_map_tutorial

8. Jeong, M., Ko, B.C.: Driver's facial expression recognition in real-time for safe driving. Sensors **18**(12), 4270 (2018)

9. Kandeel, A.A., Rahmanian, M., Zulkernine, F.H., Abbas, H., Hassanein, H.S.: Facial expression recognition using a simplified convolutional neural network model. In: 2020 International Conference on Communications, Signal Processing, and their Applications (ICCSPA 2020)(Accepted). Sharjah, United Arab Emirates (2020)

10. Knapton, S.: Which emotion raises the risk of a car crash by nearly 10 times? February 2016. https://www.telegraph.co.uk/news/science/science-news/12168472/Which-emotion-raises-the-risk-of-a-car-crash-by-nearly-10-times.html?

11. Ko, B.C.: A brief review of facial emotion recognition based on visual information. Sensors **18**(2), 401 (2018)

12. Kowalczuk, Z., Czubenko, M., Merta, T.: Emotion monitoring system for drivers. IFAC-PapersOnLine **52**(8), 200–205 (2019)

13. Krishna, M.G., Srinivasulu, A.: Face detection system on Adaboost algorithm using HAAR classifiers. Int. J. Mod. Eng. Res. **2**(5), 3556–3560 (2012)

14. Lee, K.W., Yoon, H.S., Song, J.M., Park, K.R.: Convolutional neural network-based classification of driver's emotion during aggressive and smooth driving using multi-modal camera sensors. Sensors **18**(4), 957 (2018)

15. Li, K., Jin, Y., Akram, M.W., Han, R., Chen, J.: Facial expression recognition with convolutional neural networks via a new face cropping and rotation strategy. Visual Comput. **36**(2), 391–404 (2019). https://doi.org/10.1007/s00371-019-01627-4

16. Lopes, A.T., de Aguiar, E., De Souza, A.F., Oliveira-Santos, T.: Facial expression recognition with convolutional neural networks: coping with few data and the training sample order. Pattern Recogn. **61**, 610–628 (2017)

17. Lucey, P., Cohn, J.F., Kanade, T., Saragih, J., Ambadar, Z., Matthews, I.: The extended cohn-kanade dataset (ck+): a complete dataset for action unit and emotion-specified expression. In: 2010 IEEE Computer Society Conference on Computer Vision and Pattern Recognition-Workshops, pp. 94–101 (2010)

18. Lundqvist, D., Flykt, A., Öhman, A.: The karolinska directed emotional faces (kdef). CD ROM from Department of Clinical Neuroscience, Psychology Section, Karolinska Institutet 91, 630 (1998)

19. Lyons, M., Kamachi, M., Gyoba, J.: The Japanese Female Facial Expression (JAFFE) Database, April 1998. https://doi.org/10.5281/zenodo.3451524

20. Mesken, J.: Determinants and consequences of drivers' emotions. Stichting Wetenschappelijk Onderzoek Verkeersveiligheid SWOV (2006)

21. Nonis, F., Dagnes, N., Marcolin, F., Vezzetti, E.: 3d approaches and challenges in facial expression recognition algorithms–a literature review. Appl. Sci. **9**(18), 3904 (2019)

22. Nübling, M., Stößel, U., Hasselhorn, H.M., Michaelis, M., Hofmann, F.: Measuring psychological stress and strain at work-evaluation of the COPSOQ questionnaire in Germany. GMS Psycho-Social Medicine **3** (2006)

23. Pandey, R.K., Karmakar, S., Ramakrishnan, A., Saha, N.: Improving facial emotion recognition systems using gradient and Laplacian images. arXiv preprint arXiv:1902.05411 (2019)

24. Puthanidam, R.V., Moh, T.S.: A hybrid approach for facial expression recognition. In: Proceedings of the 12th International Conference on Ubiquitous Information Management and Communication, pp. 1–8 (2018)

25. Scherer, K.R., Schorr, A., Johnstone, T.: Appraisal Processes in Emotion: Theory, Methods, Research. Oxford University Press, Oxford (2001)
26. Selvaraju, R.R., Cogswell, M., Das, A., Vedantam, R., Parikh, D., Batra, D.: Grad-cam: visual explanations from deep networks via gradient-based localization. In: Proceedings of the IEEE International Conference on Computer Vision, pp. 618–626 (2017)
27. Shorten, C., Khoshgoftaar, T.M.: A survey on image data augmentation for deep learning. J. Big Data **6**(1), 60 (2019)
28. Simonyan, K., Vedaldi, A., Zisserman, A.: Deep inside convolutional networks: Visualising image classification models and saliency maps. arXiv preprint arXiv:1312.6034 (2013)
29. Springenberg, J.T., Dosovitskiy, A., Brox, T., Riedmiller, M.: Striving for simplicity: the all convolutional net. arXiv preprint arXiv:1412.6806 (2014)
30. Viola, P., Jones, M.: Rapid object detection using a boosted cascade of simple features. In: Proceedings of the 2001 IEEE Computer Society Conference on Computer Vision and Pattern Recognition. CVPR 2001. vol. 1, pp. I-I (2001)
31. Wang, Q., Jia, K., Liu, P.: Design and implementation of remote facial expression recognition surveillance system based on PCA and KNN algorithms. In: 2015 International Conference on Intelligent Information Hiding and Multimedia Signal Processing (IIH-MSP), pp. 314–317 (2015)
32. World Health Organization: Global status report on road safety 2018: Summary. World Health Organization, Technical report (2018)
33. Yang, B., Cao, J., Ni, R., Zhang, Y.: Facial expression recognition using weighted mixture deep neural network based on double-channel facial images. IEEE Access **6**, 4630–4640 (2017)
34. Zhang, J., Mei, X., Liu, H., Yuan, S., Qian, T.: Detecting negative emotional stress based on facial expression in real time. In: 2019 IEEE 4th International Conference on Signal and Image Processing (ICSIP), pp. 430–434 (2019)
35. Zhou, B., Khosla, A., Lapedriza, A., Oliva, A., Torralba, A.: Learning deep features for discriminative localization. In: Proceedings of the IEEE Conference on Computer Vision and Pattern Recognition, pp. 2921–2929 (2016)

# Artificial Kindness
# The Italian Case of Google Mini Recognition Patterns

Concetta Papapicco[✉] (iD)

University of Bari "Aldo Moro", Bari, Italy

**Abstract.** Kindness is a pro-social virtue, which evokes mixed feelings in the modern world. In Western culture, for example, kindness is always positive, but elitist. The Digital Revolution and the birth of artificial intelligence, such as the Google Mini, allowed the transition from elitist experience to mass experience. The study has an exploratory function and starts from the Man-AI interaction, in a provocative and oppositional conversational context created by the Human Being. In the research, it is hypothesized, therefore, that the synthesis of the artificial voice does not allow to characterize all the facets of the tone and the emotionality of the kindness. As a result, Artificial Intelligence is programmed to always respond in a "gentle" way, putting in place different facets of kindness, which are well detected in the emotionality and prosodic analysis, above all in the recognition of "pitch" speech pattern. While emotional tone analysis confirms the "understanding" of reading the communicative context of Artificial Intelligence. Among future perspectives it is highlighted how the study of these vocal patterns of artificial kindness can be a springboard for research on bullying, using the Google Mini Kindness tool.

**Keywords:** Artificial kindness · Google Mini · Vocal pattern recognition · OpenSMILE software · Mixed method

## 1 Introduction

Kindness is a pro-social virtue, which evokes mixed feelings in the modern world. Generally, kindness is defined as the result of social and cultural forces, precisely because of this, it does not have a clear and unambiguous definition. As an adjective, 'kind' means to be sympathetic, helpful or to be inclined to bring pleasure or relief [1]. It is often used as a synonym for generosity, feeling or affection. In the Italian language, for example, "gentile" ['kind'] comes from the Latin '*gentilis*' which means 'belonging to the gens, that is, to the lineage'. By extension, in fact, 'being kind' means having typical manners of the noble class. It can, therefore, be said that kindness in Western culture is always positive, but elitist. The Digital Revolution, however, and the landing at mass society made sure that even kindness became a virtue no longer elitist. It comes, therefore, to models of Artificial Intelligence "Kind", as in the case of Google Mini [12], domestic assistants prone to kindness enough to call it "Artificial Kindness". Google Mini is a

© Springer Nature Switzerland AG 2021
A. Del Bimbo et al. (Eds.): ICPR 2020 Workshops, LNCS 12666, pp. 714–727, 2021.
https://doi.org/10.1007/978-3-030-68780-9_54

voice-enabled wireless speaker developed by Google. An example of Google Mini is shown in Fig. 1:

**Fig. 1.** Example of Google Mini

The device connects to the voice-controlled intelligent personal assistant Google service, which answers to the name "Google". When you ask the assistant what his name is, the Artificial Intelligence response is shown in Fig. 2:

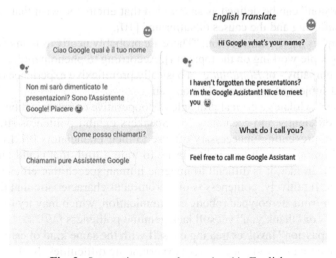

**Fig. 2.** Interaction example translated in English

The device is capable of voice interaction, music playback, making to-do lists, setting alarms, streaming podcasts, playing audiobooks, and providing weather, traffic, and other real-time information. It can also control several smart devices using itself as a home automation hub.

In the theoretical framework of "Artificial Kindness", the exploratory study starts from the hypothesis that the Artificial Intelligence (AI) of Google Mini maybe "kind", but because it is a synthetic voice, it does not allow to distinguish the different facets of kindness. In the scientific literature, kindness is always linked to positivity [11], even in emotional terms, especially joy. In this case, it is proposed an emotional Analysis [17] and a Prosodic Analysis on 50 real interactions Man-Google Mini by means of a single software, called OpenSMILE [5]. In these interactions, two real users (1 man and 1 woman of different ages) are asked to interact with AI in a grumpy manner, using offensive words. As a result, Artificial Intelligence is programmed to always respond in a "gentle" way, putting in place different facets of kindness, which are well detected in the emotionality and prosodic analysis.

## 2   From Human To Artificial Kindness Model

In the scientific literature, "kindness" is modeled as loving-kindness [7], compassion [8], empathy [18], politeness [19] and self-compassion [14].

The "loving-kindness" has at the basis the joy, which is always a joy turned or for the other.

"Compassion" can be defined as an emotion that elicits the wish that others can be "free from suffering and the causes of suffering" [10].

"Empathy" is a polysemic notion: "There are probably nearly as many definitions of empathy as people working on the topic" [4]. According to phenomenological tradition we consider empathy - or *Einfühlung* - a basically prereflexive experience of another as an embodied subject of experience like oneself.

"Politeness" violates a critical principle of cooperative communication: exchanging information efficiently and accurately [6]. Speakers exhibit politeness strategies even while arguing, preventing unnecessary offense to their enunciators [9]. Listeners even attribute ambiguous speech to a polite desire to hide a truth that could hurt another's self-image [2]. In fact, it is difficult to imagine human speech that efficiently conveys only the truth. Intuitively, politeness is one prominent characteristic that differentiates human speech from stereotyped robotic communication, which may try to follow rules to say "please" or "thank you" yet still lack genuine politeness [19].

"Self-compassion" involves treating oneself with the same kind of care and concern with which one treats loved ones who are experiencing difficulties. Neff [14] conceptualized self-compassion as composed of three facets: a) self-kindness (vs. self-judgment), b) common humanity (vs. isolation), and c) mindfulness (vs. over-identification).

In addition, to identify the different aspects of kindness, the studies of neuroscience [13] tried to understand the brain circuits involved in two of the pro-social attitudes that define kindness, which is compassion and empathy. The Neuromodulatory Model of Pro-social Behavior is shown in Fig. 3:

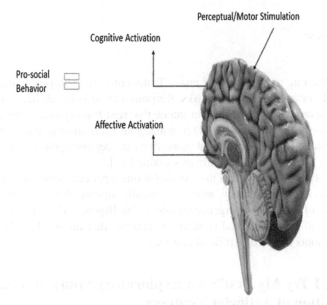

**Fig. 3.** Representation of the neuromodulatory model of pro-social behavior [13]

The image explains how a perceptual or motor stimulation can activate two neuronal circuits:

1. affective regulation, involving Amygdala, Anterior Insula, Anterior Cingulate Cortex;
2. cognitive regulation, involving Dorsomedial Prefrontal Cortex and Temporoparietal Junction.

In particular, affective activation is the process of matching limbic system activity with that of the target. While, cognition is often referred to as perspective-taking or mentalizing, which allows the observer to at some level understand that his or her affective state is related to someone else's affective state. The activation of these two areas allows, on the one hand, the emotional regulation, on the other hand, the distinction self/other, circuits related to the implementation of pro-social behaviors.

In Artificial Intelligence, the detection of the voice and, above all, the content of the "human discourse" takes place in sophisticated real-time systems.

Real-time systems have been defined as: predictably fast enough for use by processes being serviced; there is a strict time limit by which a system must have produced a response, regardless of the algorithm employed; ability of the system to guarantee a response after a (domain defined) fixed time has elapsed; and a system designed to operate with a well-defined measure of reactivity. These definitions are general and hence and open to interpretation depending on the problem at hand. While speed is indeed fundamental to real-time performance, speed alone is not real-time. The four aspects of real-time performance are:

- speed
- responsiveness
- timeliness.

Speed is the rate of execution of tasks. Tasks could refer to problem-solving tasks (large or small) or event processing tasks. Responsiveness is the ability of the system to stay alert to incoming events. Since an interactive real-time system is primarily driven by external inputs, the system should recognize that such input is available. It may not necessarily process the new event right away; that may depend upon its criticality relative to other events the system is currently processing [12].

It's precisely in these systems that Artificial Intelligence, like the Google Mini, can make decisions in the immediacy, which is typically human. But what happens when in the interaction of Human Intelligence-Artificial Intelligence, the human being creates an "oppositional" conversational context? It happens that the machine from Artificial Intelligence adopts a tone of Artificial Kindness.

## 3 "Sorry, I Try My Best": An Exploratory Study of a Pattern Recognition of Artificial Kindness

### 3.1 Hypothesis and Methodology

The study has an exploratory function and starts from the Man-AI interaction, in a provocative and oppositional conversational context created by the Human Being using improvisation. You notice immediately how the machine is programmed and self-organizing to be kind.

In the research, it is hypothesized, therefore, that the synthesis of the artificial voice does not allow to characterize all the facets of the tone and the emotionality of the kindness. To explore this hypothesis, a prosodic and emotional analysis of the tone of the responses of the Google Mini has been carried out, concerning provocative conversations of two real participants, chosen for different gender and different age: a 50-year-old man and a 28-year-old woman. The two participants were asked separately to interact with the Google Mini in a provocative and oppositional manner, insulting Artificial Intelligence. Examples of incipit of provocative conversations were:

"Ciao Google! Lo sai che sei un cretino?".

*Eng. translate* "Hello Google! Do you know you're a jerk?".

"Non hai capito niente di ciò che ti ho chiesto!".

*Eng. translate* "You didn't understand anything I asked you!".

In total, 50 interactions were collected: 25 per participant. Interactions were recorded and analysed quanti-qualitatively with the software OpenSMILE developed by audEER-INGTM Group. It is open-source software for automatic extraction of features from audio signals and for classification of speech and music signals. "SMILE" stands for "Speech & Music Interpretation by Large-space Extraction" [16]. The software is mainly applied in the area of automatic emotion recognition and is widely used in the affective computing research community [5]. The operation of emotional speech recognition software is modeled in Fig. 4:

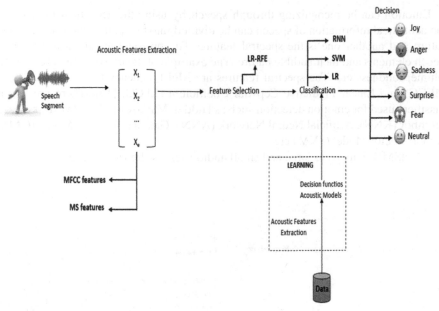

**Fig. 4.** Emotional speech recognition software's functioning: revised model of Eyben, Wöllmer, Schuller [5]

In the field of Human–Computer Interaction speech is considered to be a powerful way for emotion recognition [11]. Emotion recognition through speech can be explained as a detection of the emotion by feature extraction of voice conveyed by a human. There are some basics emotions given by different researchers as follows:

**Table 1.** Some basic emotion related to different inclusion basis [15] sort by relevance.

| Reference | Fundamental Emotion | Inclusion basis |
|---|---|---|
| Arnold (1960) | Anger, aversion, courage, dejection, desire, despair, fear, hate, hope, love, sadness, surprise | Relation to action tendencies |
| Ekman, Friesen, Ellsworth (1982) | Anger, disgust, fear, joy, sadness, surprise | Universal facial expressions |
| Oatley & Johnson-Laird (1987) | Anger, disgust, anxiety, happiness, sadness | Do not require propositional Content |
| Plutchik (1980) | Acceptance, anger, anticipation, disgust, joy, fear, sadness | Relation to adaptive biological processes |

Emotion can be recognizing through speech by using the acoustical information. The acoustical information of speech can be divided into two parts. One is the prosodic feature and another one is the spectral feature. The prosodic feature depends on the speech elements and their audible nature. The example of the prosodic features is pitch, volume, loudness etc. The spectral features are Mel Frequency Cepstram Coefficient (MFCC) and Linear Predictive Cepstral Coefficient (LPCC) [16]. There are various classifiers used for emotion detection such as Hidden Markov Model (HMM), k-nearest Neighbor (KNN), Artificial Neural Network (ANN), Gaussian Mixture Model (GMM), Support Vector Model (SVM) etc.

OpenSMILE analyzes large and small audio files, as shown in Fig. 5:

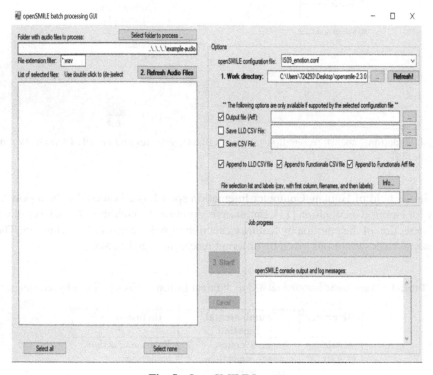

**Fig. 5.** OpenSMILE Layout

After choosing the audio to analyze, the output folder and what you want to analyze, in the case of the study the emotionality of the synthesized voice, identified with the **"IS09_emotion.conf function"**, you proceed with the command "Start" to initiate the analysis.

## 4    Results

As a first qualitative fact, it is interesting to note that there are no differences in the answers to the real male and female voice, but it is emphasized that, in the same oppositional conversational context, there is a recurrence of the same answers:

1. when the subjects used offensive words were "Devo averti proprio fatto arrabbiare tanto" [*Eng. translate* "I must have really made you so angry"];
2. instead of references to the failure and low cognitive level of AI, the most frequent answers were "Scusami, a volte faccio degli errori" [*Eng. translate* "Excuse me, sometimes I make mistakes"] or "A volte magari un poco, ma so anche darti un bel po' di informazioni" [*Eng. translate* "Sometimes maybe a little, but I can also give you a lot of information"]. In other contexts, there is the use of irony, with ridicule of some aspects of AI itself, such as "Mi dispiace, alcune volte capisco Roma per toma. E' particolarmente imbarazzante se sono su Google Maps e non trovo nessuna strada che porti a toma" [*Eng. translate* "Sorry, sometimes I understand Rome for *toma*. It's particularly embarrassing if I'm on Google Maps and I can't find any road to *toma*"].In case of insistence, requests to send feedback stating the malfunction;
3. when, on the other hand, reference is made to sentimental oppositivities, for example, to hatred, the most frequent answers are "Mi spiace, ma tu mi piaci lo stesso" [*Eng. translate* "I'm sorry, but I still like you"].

These responses were analyzed with the software, following a focus on the patters for the recognition of variations in tone (intensity, frequency and pitch) and emotionality. The results show a significant average number of "pitch", as shown in Fig. 6:

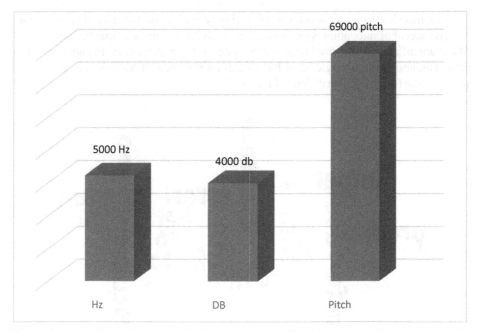

**Fig. 6.** Average of Speech Recognition Pattern Outputs: Hertz is the vocal frequency, Db is its intensity and pitch is the accent. The values indicate the average trends for analyzed sentences.

From Fig. 6, in fact, it emerges that the pitches (6900) are increasing average values and to be taken into account with respect to frequency (5000 Hz) and intensity (4000 db). Pitch is a marked the accent of the syllable on which the listener's attention must be placed. This is an element of the truthfulness of the programming of the artificial voice. One of them is a fundamental index in the recognition of prosodic patterns of kindness. Explanatory, in fact, is the following example:

**Example 1.** "Scusami, a volte faccio degli errori".

> *Eng. translate* "Sorry, sometimes I make mistakes".
> The accent of intonation is placed on the word "Scusami" ["Sorry"].

This aspect, which could technically depend on the programming of the Natural Language Processing of AI, makes us reflect on how the AI is able to read the conversational "context". The kindness associated with the ability to apologize is performed in a conversational context in which artificial intelligence is accused of being inefficient or insufficiently intelligent.

Another interesting aspect concerns the modulation of the pitch on the "mitigators" [3]. The mitigators are words that aim to attenuate the content of the discourse, very useful to maintain a polite discourse tone. An example of a mitigator is the use of "maybe" or "sometimes", as in the extract proposed below referred to the response provided by AI to a communication context of cognitive offense:

**Example 2.** "A volte magari un poco, ma so anche darti un bel po' di informazioni".

> *Eng. translate* "Sometimes maybe a little, but I can also give you a lot of information".
> The accent of intonation is placed on the words "Sometimes", "maybe" and "little". These are all attenuators, used to lower the tone of the conversation. In summary, Artificial kindness in the Google Mini Italian can be represented with the occurrences of words in the following WordCloud (Fig. 7):

**Fig. 7.** Artificial Kindness WordCloud

The WordCloud are visual instruments with high impact, able, in the context of scientific research, to show with immediacy an output. In the case of the pattern of recognition of Artificial Kindness, the recurring kind words are depicted. There is also a logic in the arrangement of words, as the words placed vertically as "**Sorry**", "**affectionate**", "**little**", "**again**", "**think**", are the words containing the pitch, that are the ones that are stressed. The accent of the tone of the sentence falls on the most important kind words, that are those placed vertically. The words positioned horizontally are closely connected to the first ones. To demonstrate the pitch elevation on the word "Sorry" for example, in Fig. 8 is shown the spectrogram of one of the answers where the accented word is contained.

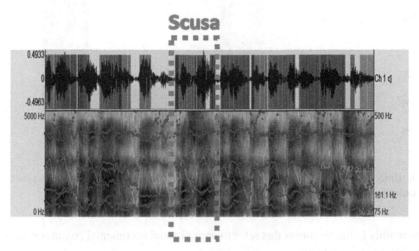

**Fig. 8.** Spectrogram example

Highlighting the pronunciation time of the word used as an example, i.e. "Sorry", you notice an increase in the number of pitch, which switches from 16,000 pitch/Hz to 32,000 pitch/Hz. The pitch of the voice is defined as the "rate of vibration of the vocal folds". The sound of the voice changes as the rate of vibrations varies. As the number of vibrations per second increases, so does the pitch, meaning the voice would sound higher. Calculated on the Hz products, the pitches are indicators of the accent placed by the artificial voice within the sentence. In this specific case, the importance of the emphasis is placed on the word "excuse me".

In this regard, the output of emotional detection is also interesting. By convention, following the model of Barrett and Russell (2009) which distinguish positive emotions from negative emotions, the results of positive emotions (joy) have been given a value of 1; for negative emotions (anger, sadness, disgust and fear) a value equal to –1 and for neutrality a value equal to zero. As shown in Fig. 9, prevalence of negativity emerges. The AI tone emotions detected by the software were predominantly: anger, sadness, neutrality and joy.

After the prevalence of sadness, anger, joy and neutrality, the graph shows a further significance of anger and sadness, followed by joy and relatively absent neutrality.

From the detection of the emotionality of tone, a very significant aspect emerges, namely that the negativity of the tone's emotionality, predominantly angry or sad. It is

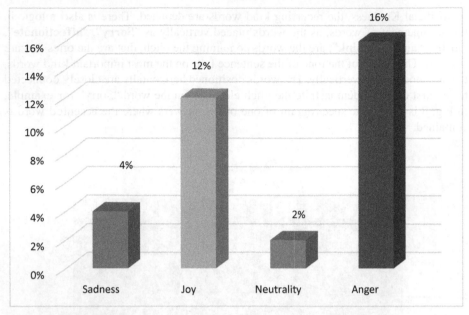

**Fig. 9.** Emotional Speech AI output, with a prevalence of anger (16%), joy (12%), sadness (4%) and neutrality (2%)

found mainly in the responses that refer to oppositional sentimental communications, as in the following example:

**Example 3.** *Essere Umano* "Mi fai schifo".

> *Google Mini* "A me tu invece piaci lo stesso".
> *Eng. translate Human Being* "You Suck Me".
> *Google Mini* "I like you the same".

These results of recognition of the emotionality of tone create two important implications. It confirms the "understanding" of reading the communicative context of Artificial Intelligence. This depends on the fact that it recognizes as "more aggressive" the oppositional conversation that attacks the plan of feelings, with a prevalence of sadness. While in the communicative context attacking the cognitive plan and default, the emotional prevalence is either anger or joy. This disconfirms both the present literature on the emotionality of kindness, which corresponds to joy [11] both the hypothesis of the study and the Artificial Intelligence and the patterns of emotional recognition of the voice cannot differentiate the different shades of kindness. In fact, even in Artificial Intelligence can recognize some different nuances of kindness, which are summarized in Table 2:

**Table 2.** Artificial Kindness Types Recognition

| Loving-kindness | "I like/love you the same" |
| --- | --- |
| Sympathy | "I must have really made you so angry" |
| Politness | "Sorry, sometimes I understand/ I make mistakes…" |

## 5  Conclusion

Kindness is a pro-social virtue, which evokes mixed feelings in the modern world. The Digital Revolution and the birth of artificial intelligence, such as the Google Mini, allowed the transition from elitist experience to mass experience. The study has an exploratory function and starts from the Man-AI interaction, in a provocative and oppositional conversational context created by the Human Being. In the research, it is hypothesized, therefore, that the synthesis of the artificial voice does not allow to characterize all the facets of the tone and the emotionality of the kindness. To explore this hypothesis, a prosodic and emotional analysis of the tone of the responses of the Google Mini has been carried out, concerning provocative conversations of two real participants, chosen for different gender and different age: a 50-year-old man and a 28-year-old woman. The two participants were asked separately to interact with the Google Mini in a provocative and oppositional manner, insulting Artificial Intelligence. In total, 50 interactions were collected: 25 per participant. Interactions were recorded and analysed quanti-qualitatively with the software OpenSMILE developed by audEERINGTM Group. It emerges that the detection software of emotional speech is very effective in the recognition of voice patterns of AI responses, which are: intensity, frequency, pitch and emotionality. From an initial qualitative screening of responses, it appears that AI does not show differences in responses based on the demographic variables of humans providing provocative voice input. But there is a need for responses dependent on three different provocative contexts, which naturally emerged from the improvisation of real voices. These provocative contexts are:

a)  offensive words;
b)  references to the failure and low cognitive level of AI;
c)  sentimental opposition.

While, from the analysis of tone and its components, it emerges that particular attention to kindness is covered not so much by frequency and intensity, but by accents (pitch). It is noted that there is an increase in pitch on the words used by content mitigators, to increase polite and kind communication, as in the case of the word "Sorry". From the detection of the emotionality of tone, a very significant aspect emerges, namely that the negativity of the tone's emotionality, predominantly angry or sad, is found mainly in the responses that refer to oppositional sentimental communications. These results of recognition of the emotionality of tone create two important implications. It confirms the "understanding" of reading the communicative context of Artificial Intelligence. This disconfirms both the present literature on the emotionality of kindness, which corresponds to joy both the hypothesis of the study and the Artificial Intelligence and the patterns of emotional recognition of the voice cannot differentiate the different shades of kindness. Among future perspectives, it is highlighted how the study of these vocal patterns of artificial kindness can be a springboard for research on bullying. The Artificial Kindness of the Google Mini embodies, at least from this exploratory study, the modes of interaction useful to the bullied to defend itself from a provocative and oppositional communication.

Always among future perspectives, interesting will be the comparison between Google Mini and the Alexa of Amazon Echo and between different languages.

# References

1. Ballatt, J., Campling, P.: Intelligent kindness: Reforming the culture of healthcare. RCPsych publications (2011).
2. Bonnefon, J.-F., Feeney, A., Villejoubert, G.: When some is actually all: Scalar inferences in face-threatening contexts. Cognition 112(2), 249–258 (2009)
3. Caffi, C.: On mitigation. J. Pragmatics 31(7), 881–909 (1999)
4. De Vignemont, F., Singer, T.: The empathic brain: how, when and why? Trends Cogn. Sci. 10(10), 435–441 (2006)
5. Eyben, F., Wöllmer, M., Schuller, B.: OpenSMILE - The Munich Versatile and Fast Open-Source Audio Feature Extractor. In: Proc, pp. 1459–1462. ACM, ACM Multimedia (MM), ACM, Florence, Italy (2010)
6. Grice, H. P.: Logic and conversation. In Readings in language and mind. Blackwell (1975).
7. Hinton, D.E., Ojserkis, R.A., Jalal, B., Peou, S., Hofmann, S.G.: Loving-kindness in the treatment of traumatized refugees and minority groups: a typology of mindfulness and the nodal network model of affect and affect regulation. J. Clin. Psychol. 69(8), 817–828 (2013)
8. Hofmann, S.G., Grossman, P., Hinton, D.E.: Loving-kindness and compassion meditation: potential for psychological interventions. Clin. Psychol. Rev. 31(7), 1126–1132 (2011)
9. Holtgraves, T.: Yes, but... positive politeness in conversation arguments. J. Lang. Soc. Psychol. 16(2), 222–239 (1997).
10. Hopkins, J.: Cultivating Compassion: A Buddhist Perspective. Broadway Books, New York, NY (2001)
11. Hutcherson, C.A., Seppala, E.M., Gross, J.J.: Loving-kindness meditation increases social connectedness. Emotion 8(5), 720–724 (2008)
12. Kaundinya, A.S., Atreyas, N.S., Srinivas, S., Kehav, V., Kumar, N.M.R.: Voice enabled home automation using amazon echo. Int. Res. J. Eng. Technol 4, 682–684 (2017)
13. Mascaro, J.S., Darcher, A., Negi, L.T., Raison, C.L.: The neural mediators of kindness-based meditation: a theoretical model. Front. Psychol. 6, 109 (2015)
14. Neff, K.D.: Self-compassion: an alternative conceptualization of a healthy attitude toward oneself. Self and Identity 2, 85–101 (2003)
15. Ortony, A., Turner, T.J.: What's basic about basic emotions?. Psychol. Rev. 97(3), 315– 331 (1990).
16. Panda, B., Padhi, D., Dash, K., Mohantay, S.: Use of SVM classifier & MFCC in Speech Emotion Recognition System. Int. J. Adv. Res. Comput. Sci. Softw. Eng. (IJARCSSE), 2(3) (2012)
17. Pang, B., Lee, L.: Opinion mining and sentiment analysis. Found. Trends® Inf. Retrieval, 2(1–2), 1–135 (2008)

18. Passmore, J., Oades, L.G.: Positive psychology techniques: random acts of kindness and consistent acts of kindness and empathy. Coach. Psychol. **11**(2), 90–92 (2015)
19. Yoon, E.J., Tessler, M.H., Goodman, N.D., Frank, M.C.: Talking with tact: Polite language as a balance between kindness and informativity. In: Proceedings of the 38th Annual Conference of the Cognitive Science Society. Cognitive Science Society, pp. 2771–2776 (2016)

# Fingerspelling Recognition with Two-Steps Cascade Process of Spotting and Classification

Masanori Muroi[1]([✉]), Naoya Sogi[1], Nobuko Kato[2], and Kazuhiro Fukui[1]

[1] Graduate School of Systems and Information Engineering, University of Tsukuba, 1-1-1 Tennodai, Tsukuba, Ibaraki 305-8577, Japan
{muroi,sogi}@cvlab.cs.tsukuba.ac.jp, kfukui@cs.tsukuba.ac.jp
[2] Faculty of Industrial Technology, Tsukuba University of Technology, 4-3-15 Amakubo, Tsukuba, Ibaraki 305-8520, Japan
nobuko@a.tsukuba-tech.ac.jp

**Abstract.** In this paper, we propose a framework for fingerspelling recognition, based on the two-step cascade process of spotting and classification. This two-steps process is motivated by the human cognitive function in fingerspelling recognition. In the spotting process, an image sequence corresponding to certain fingerspelling is extracted from an input video by classifying the partial sequence into two fingerspelling categories and others. At this stage, how to deal with temporary dynamic information is a key point. The extracted fingerspelling is classified in the classification process. Here, the temporal dynamic information is not necessarily required. Rather, how to classify its static hand shape using the multi-view images is more important. In our framework, we employ temporal regularized canonical correlation analysis (TRCCA) for the spotting, considering it can effectively handle an image sequence's temporal information. For the classification, we employ the orthogonal mutual subspace method (OMSM), since it can consider the information effectively from multi-view images to classify the hand shape fast and accurately. We demonstrate the effectiveness of our framework based on a complementary combination of TRCCA and OMSM compared to conventional methods on a private Japanese fingerspelling dataset.

**Keywords:** Fingerspelling recognition · Temporal regularized canonical correlation analysis · Orthogonal mutual subspace method · CNN feature

## 1 Introduction

This paper proposes a framework for fingerspelling recognition with two-step cascade process of spotting and classification. Fingerspelling for expressing certain letter by a hand shape is a useful tool to remove the communication barriers between deaf and hard of hearing people and non-handicapped people [1–6].

© Springer Nature Switzerland AG 2021
A. Del Bimbo et al. (Eds.): ICPR 2020 Workshops, LNCS 12666, pp. 728–743, 2021.
https://doi.org/10.1007/978-3-030-68780-9_55

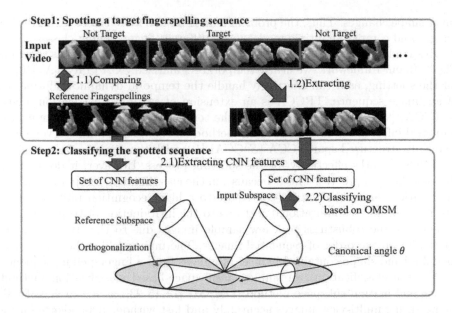

**Fig. 1.** Conceptual diagram of the proposed framework of fingerspelling recognition. 1) Each fingerspelling sequence in input video is spotted by applying TRCCA. 2) A set of CNN features is extracted from each sequence. 3) OMSM is performed on CNN features.

In practical use, proper nouns and new technical terms that have not been yet defined as sign languages are expressed with a combination of multiple fingerspellings.

The basic idea of our framework is to divide a whole process into two-step cascade process: spotting a fingerspelling sequence from an input video and classification of the extracted fingerspelling, motivated by the human cognitive process in fingerspelling recognizing [7,8]. We then apply two different types of methods to each process.

In the spotting process, an image sequence corresponding to certain fingerspelling is segmented and then extracted from an input video. This process is equivalent to binary classification, that is, a given image sequence is classified into one of two categories of fingerspelling and others. In this process, temporary dynamic information such as the order and length of an image sequence is essential to effectively handle a continuous input video.

In the classification process, the class of the extracted fingerspelling is determined. In this process, we do not necessarily need to consider a sequence classification based on temporal dynamic information. Rather, we should regard this task as a classification problem of 3D rigid objects using multiple images, as most of fingerspellings are represented with certain static hand shape except few ones. For example, most Japanese fingerspellings are represented by different static hand shapes, except a few such as "mo" and "no" accompanied by small shape changes. Thus, the problem here is how to model a set of multi-view images and compare multiple models from different fingerspelling classes.

Responding to the above requirements, we propose a framework, as shown in Fig. 1. In our framework, we utilize temporal regularized CCA (TRCCA) [10,11] for the spotting, as it can effectively handle the temporal dynamics information of an image sequence. TRCCA is an extension of canonical correlation analysis (CCA) [9] with the smoothness on the temporal domain to incorporate the temporal information into CCA. This method is a simple and limited version of smoothly structured sparse CCA ($S^3$CCA) [10] with three types of constraints.

TRCCA works effectively for the spotting process. However, it does not fit the classification process. This is because, in the classification, temporal dynamic information cannot necessarily contribute to a high recognition rate. Rather it can produce high computational cost due to the introduction of kernel function and reduce the robustness to a few sample images due to the strong, smooth constraint on the order of sequential images. The main problem here is how to model a hand shape contained in a set of images from a fingerspelling sequence.

For the classification, we employ a subspace-based classification method, orthogonal mutual subspace method (OMSM) [14,15,23], as it can classify 3D shapes using multi-view images accurately and fast without dependence on the order of sequential images. In these methods, a set of images is represented by a low-dimensional subspace generated by applying PCA [12,13] and the similarity between two subspaces is measured by the canonical angles between them [16,17]. In particular, OMSM is a subspace-based method with a powerful discriminative feature extraction by orthogonalizing all the class subspaces. To further enhance the validity of our framework, we introduce CNN features [18–21], which are obtained from a learned convolutional neural network such a ResNet and VGGnet. We use CNN features as inputs for OMSM, considering that CNN features are almost invariant to the shifts in the object's position and movement.

In summary, our fingerspelling recognition framework is built with three steps: 1) spotting each fingerspelling sequence from an input stream by TRCCA, 2) extracting CNN features, 3) classifying the spotted sequence by OMSM with the CNN features. We use infrared images to accurately detect the subject's hand, since they are robust to cluttered backgrounds and various lighting conditions.

The main contributions of this paper are summarised as follows.

1) We introduce the temporal regularized CCA (TRCCA) for spotting a fingerspelling sequence from a video stream, focusing on its ability to handle temporal dynamic information.
2) We introduce the orthogonal mutual subspace method (OMSM) with CNN features for classifying the spotted fingerspelling, focusing on its ability to handle multiple sets of images for hand shape recognition.
3) We propose a framework for fingerspelling recognition based on the complementary combination of TRCCA and OMSM with CNN features.

4) We demonstrate the effectiveness of our framework based on the complementary combination in comparison with conventional methods on a private Japanese fingerspelling dataset.

The rest of this paper is organized as follows. In Sect. 2, we describe the algorithms of TRCCA and OMSM. In this section, we also describe the details of the proposed framework. In Sect. 3, we demonstrate the validity of the proposed framework through classification experiments on a private Japanese fingerspelling dataset. Section 4 concludes the paper.

## 2    Proposed Framework

In this section, we first describe the detailed problem setting for our framework. Then, we describe the details of the proposed framework in each of the two steps, spotting of a fingerspelling sequence and recognition of the spotted sequence. Finally, we summarize the detailed procedure of the proposed method.

### 2.1    Problem Setting

Let $\{\boldsymbol{y}_t \in \mathbb{R}^d\}_{i=1}^\infty$ be the continuous image stream, where each image is reshaped to a $d = (\text{width} \times \text{height})$-dimensional vector, and $T$ be the current time. The first step of our framework is to extract a fingerspelling sequence by considering the temporal information using TRCCA, i.e., TRCCA spot $n$ fingerspelling images from $N(\geq n)$ images $\{\boldsymbol{y}\}_{t=T-N+1}^T$. The second step is to classify the input fingerspelling (spotted images) by comparing hand shapes precisely using OMSM and CNN features if $n > 0$.

To perform these steps, we need reference fingerspelling sequences. In the following, we refer to the $i$th reference sequence of the $c$-th category as $\mathbf{X}_c^i \in \mathbb{R}^{d \times n_{ci}}$, where each column is an image vector, $\boldsymbol{x}_c^{i,j} \in \mathbb{R}^d$.

### 2.2    Spotting of a Fingerspelling Sequence by TRCCA

We spot a fingerspelling sequence in a video stream $\{\boldsymbol{y}_t\}$ by TRCCA. TRCCA is an extension of CCA [9] and a simple version $S^3$CCA [10], focusing on only the smoothness on the temporal domain to intensively deal with dynamic information [11].

CCA can find the most similar components between two feature sets, $\{\boldsymbol{y}\}_{t=T-N+1}^T$ and $\mathbf{X}_c^i$, i.e., generates a nearest vector pair between the sets by the linear combination of each vector set. In CCA, the combination coefficients are computed by solving the following optimization problem:

$$\arg \min_{\alpha, \beta} \|\mathbf{X}_c^i \alpha - \mathbf{Y}\beta\|^2, \ s.t. \ \|\mathbf{X}_c^i \alpha\|^2 = \|\mathbf{Y}\beta\|^2 = 1, \tag{1}$$

where the $j$-th column of $\mathbf{Y} \in \mathbb{R}^{d \times N}$ is $\boldsymbol{y}_{T-j+1}$, $\alpha \in \mathbb{R}^{n_{ci}}$ and $\beta \in \mathbb{R}^N$ are combination coefficients for each set. Although this optimization problem is useful for various problems, it is better to consider the temporal information as an additional prior to the time-series data like fingerspellings.

To incorporate the prior, the smoothness on the temporal domain, i.e. on the combination coefficients, has been known as a useful means. The combination method of CCA with the smoothness is called TRCCA, and it is formulated as follows:

$$\hat{\alpha}, \hat{\beta} = \arg \min_{\alpha, \beta} \|\mathbf{X}_c^i \alpha - \mathbf{Y}\beta\|^2 + k_{\mathbf{X}_c^i} \alpha^{\mathrm{T}} \mathbf{G}_{\mathbf{X}_c^i} \alpha + k_{\mathbf{Y}} \beta^{\mathrm{T}} \mathbf{G}_{\mathbf{Y}} \beta,$$

$$s.t. \|\mathbf{X}_c^i \alpha\|^2 = \|\mathbf{Y}\beta\|^2 = 2, \tag{2}$$

where

$$\alpha^{\mathrm{T}} \mathbf{G}_{\mathbf{X}_c} \alpha = \sum_{j \in \Lambda_{\mathbf{X}_c}} (\alpha_{j-1} - 2\alpha_j + \alpha_{j+1})^2, \tag{3}$$

$$\beta^{\mathrm{T}} \mathbf{G}_{\mathbf{Y}} \beta = \sum_{j \in \Lambda_{\mathbf{Y}}} (\beta_{j-1} - 2\beta_j + \beta_{j+1})^2, \tag{4}$$

and Eqs. (3), (4) are the smooth regularization terms for each combination coefficient, and $\Lambda_{\mathbf{X}_c} = \{2, 3, \ldots, n_c - 1\}$, $\Lambda_{\mathbf{Y}} = \{2, 3, \ldots, N - 1\}$ are index sets. The symbols $k_{\mathbf{X}_c^i}$ and $k_{\mathbf{Y}}$ are weight parameters for the regularizations. In the experiments, as with [11], we set the weight parameters as follows:

$$k_{\mathbf{X}_c^i} = \frac{\|\mathbf{X}_c^{i\mathrm{T}} \mathbf{X}_c^i\|}{\|\mathbf{G}_{\mathbf{X}_c^i}\|}, \quad k_{\mathbf{Y}} = \frac{\|\mathbf{Y}^{\mathrm{T}} \mathbf{Y}\|}{\|\mathbf{G}_{\mathbf{Y}}\|}. \tag{5}$$

The above optimization problem of TRCCA can be solved by the following generalized eigenvalue problem [11]:

$$\begin{pmatrix} \mathbf{X}_c^{i\mathrm{T}} \mathbf{X}_c^i + k_{\mathbf{X}_c^i} \mathbf{G}_{\mathbf{X}_c^i} & -\mathbf{X}_c^{i\mathrm{T}} \mathbf{Y} \\ -\mathbf{Y}^{\mathrm{T}} \mathbf{X}_c^i & \mathbf{Y}^{\mathrm{T}} \mathbf{Y} + k_{\mathbf{Y}} \mathbf{G}_{\mathbf{Y}} \end{pmatrix} \begin{pmatrix} \hat{\alpha} \\ \hat{\beta} \end{pmatrix} = \lambda \begin{pmatrix} \mathbf{X}_c^{i\mathrm{T}} \mathbf{X}_c^i & 0 \\ 0 & \mathbf{Y}^{\mathrm{T}} \mathbf{Y} \end{pmatrix} \begin{pmatrix} \hat{\alpha} \\ \hat{\beta} \end{pmatrix}. \tag{6}$$

We can obtain the combination coefficients, which smoothly changed, to generate the nearest vector pair between two sets by this eigenvalue problem. Therefore, based on the optimal solutions, $\hat{\alpha}$ and $\hat{\beta}$, we can calculate the similarity between the sets as follows:

$$\mathrm{Sim}(\mathbf{X}_c^i, \mathbf{Y}) = \hat{\alpha}^{\mathrm{T}} \mathbf{X}_c^{i\mathrm{T}} \mathbf{Y} \hat{\beta}. \tag{7}$$

If the input sequence $\mathbf{Y}$ has high similarity with the reference fingerspelling sequences $\{\mathbf{X}_c^i\}$, $\mathbf{Y}$ is classified to fingerspelling. Besides, if $\mathbf{Y}$ is classified as a fingerspelling and the absolute value of $j$-th element of $\beta$ is larger than a threshold $\eta$, the $j$-th image $\mathbf{y}_{T-j+1}$ can be considered as a fingerspelling image, as the $j$-th element has a large correlation with the reference fingerspellings, as shown in the bottom of Fig. 2. In the following, we refer the extracted images $\{\mathbf{y}_{T-j+1} | \beta_j > \eta\}_{j=1}^{N}$ as spotted fingerspelling images.

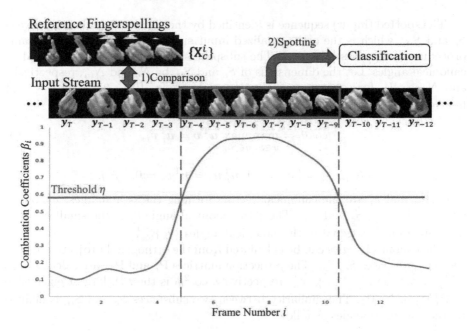

**Fig. 2.** Conceptual diagram of spotting a fingerspelling sequence based on TRCCA. After calculating the similarity between reference sequences and inputs by Eq. (7), we extract fingerspelling images based on the value of $\beta_i$.

## 2.3 Recognition of a Spotted Fingerspelling Sequence by OMSM

To classify the spotted fingerspelling images by TRCCA, we utilize the orthogonal mutual subspace method (OMSM) and CNN features.

OMSM is a classifier of an input image set using the similarity between two subspaces, where each of the subspaces represents the 3D hand shape of the corresponding fingerspelling. Such subspace can be generated by applying PCA to a feature set of an image set without data centring, as shown in Fig. 3. In our framework, we utilize a CNN feature as a feature vector $\boldsymbol{f}_c^{i,j}$ of an image $\boldsymbol{x}_c^{i,j}$, considering the effectiveness of CNN features.

OMSM applies an orthogonalization for all the class subspaces to enhance the classification performance before calculating the subspace similarity. Let $\phi_c^j$ be the $j$-th basis vector of $c$-th class subspace $S_c$ generated by applying PCA to features $\{\boldsymbol{f}_c^{i,j}\}_{i,j}$ of image sets $\{\boldsymbol{x}_c^{i,j}\}_{i,j}$. To calculate the orthogonalization matrix $\mathbf{O}$, the total projection matrix $\mathbf{G}$ is define as $\mathbf{G} = \sum_{c,j} \phi_c^j \phi_c^{jT}$. Then, $\mathbf{O}$ is defined as follows:

$$\mathbf{O} = \Lambda^{-1/2} \mathbf{H}^{\mathrm{T}}, \tag{8}$$

where $\Lambda$ is the diagonal matrix with the eigenvalues of the matrix $\mathbf{G}$ and $\mathbf{H}$ is the matrix whose column vectors are the eigenvectors of the matrix $\mathbf{G}$. The orthogonalized subspace $\hat{S}_c$ is spanned by the corresponding orhotogonalized basis vectors $\{\hat{\phi}_c^j = \mathbf{O}\phi_c^j\}_j$.

The spotted (input) sequence is identified by the subspace similarity between $\hat{S}_c$ and $\hat{S}_{in}$, which is the orthogonalized input subspace generated by the same procedure of the class subspaces. The subspace similarity is calculated based on canonical angles. Let the dimensions of $\hat{S}_c$ and $\hat{S}_{in}$ be $N_c$ and $N_{in}$, respectively, and $N_c \geq N_{in}$ for convenience. The canonical angles $\{0 \leq \theta_1, \ldots, \theta_{N_{in}} \leq \frac{\pi}{2}\}$ between the $\hat{S}_c$ and $\hat{S}_{in}$ are recursively defined as follows [16,17]:

$$\cos \theta_i = \max_{\boldsymbol{u} \in \hat{S}_c} \max_{\boldsymbol{v} \in \hat{S}_{in}} \boldsymbol{u}^\mathrm{T} \boldsymbol{v} = \boldsymbol{u}_i^\mathrm{T} \boldsymbol{v}_i, \tag{9}$$

$$s.t. \ \|\boldsymbol{u}_i\|_2 = \|\boldsymbol{v}_i\|_2 = 1, \boldsymbol{u}_i^\mathrm{T} \boldsymbol{u}_j = \boldsymbol{v}_i^\mathrm{T} \boldsymbol{v}_j = 0, i \neq j,$$

where $\boldsymbol{u}_i$ and $\boldsymbol{v}_i$ are the canonical vectors forming the $i$-th smallest canonical angle $\theta_i$ between $\hat{S}_c$ and $\hat{S}_{in}$. The $j$-th canonical angle $\theta_j$ is the smallest angle in a direction orthogonal to the canonical angles $\{\theta_k\}_{k=1}^{j-1}$.

The canonical angles can be calculated from the orthogonal projection matrices onto subspaces $\hat{S}_c$, $\hat{S}_{in}$. The projection matrices $\mathbf{P}_c$ and $\mathbf{P}_{in}$ are calculated as $\sum_{i=1}^{N_c} \hat{\phi}_c^i \hat{\phi}_c^{i\mathrm{T}}$, and $\sum_{i=1}^{N_{in}} \hat{\phi}_{in}^i \hat{\phi}_{in}^{i\mathrm{T}}$, respectively. $\cos^2 \theta_i$ is the $i$-th largest eigenvalue of $\mathbf{P}_1^\mathrm{T} \mathbf{P}_2$ or $\mathbf{P}_2^\mathrm{T} \mathbf{P}_1$. The similarity between two subspaces $\hat{S}_c$ and $\hat{S}_{in}$ is defined by the canonical angles as follows:

$$sim(\hat{S}_c, \hat{S}_{in}) = \frac{1}{N_{in}} \sum_{i=1}^{N_{in}} \cos^2 \theta_i. \tag{10}$$

Thus, an input fingerspelling is classified by the similarity between $\hat{S}_{in}$ and $\{\hat{S}_c\}_c$.

## 2.4   The Detailed Procedure of the Fingerspelling Recognition Framework

In the following, we detail the training and recognition procedures of our framework, as summarized in Fig. 4, for the case that there are $n_{ci}$ reference fingerspelling sequences $\{\mathbf{X}_c^i\}$ for $c$th fingerspelling class.

### Training Phase

1. A CNN is trained to classify each fingerspelling image $\boldsymbol{x}_c^{ij}$ in reference sequences $\{\mathbf{X}_c^i\}$.
2. CNN features $\{\boldsymbol{f}_c^{i,j}\}$ are extracted from $\{\boldsymbol{x}_c^{i,j}\}$.
3. Each class subspace $S_c$ is generated by applying PCA to CNN features $\{\boldsymbol{f}_c^{i,j}\}_{i,j}$ of $c$th class.
4. Orthogonalized class subspaces $\{\hat{S}_c\}$ are generated by applying orthogonal transformation to $\{S_c\}$ defined by Eq. (8).

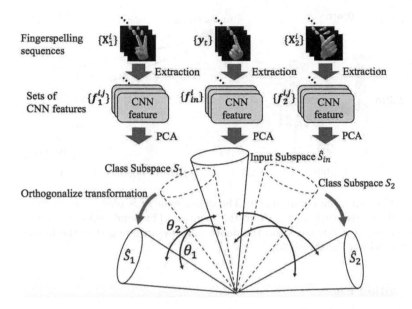

**Fig. 3.** Conceptual diagram of OMSM with CNN features. OMSM mainly consists of two steps; 1) making reference subspaces and orthogonalize them, and 2) calculating the subspace similarity between input and reference subspaces after applying the orthogonalize transformation.

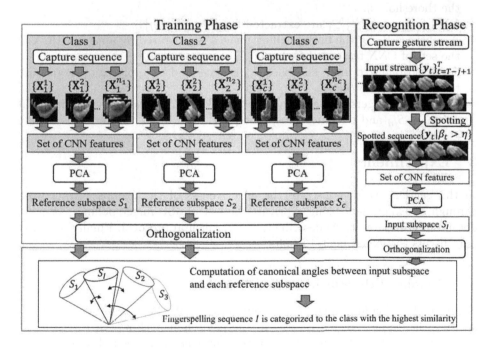

**Fig. 4.** The process flow of the proposed fingerspelling recognition framework.

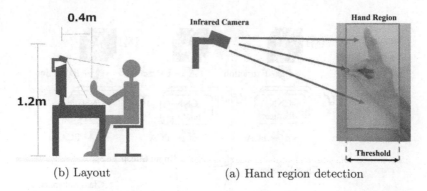

(b) Layout                    (a) Hand region detection

**Fig. 5.** The capturing environment. The depth camera is placed at the height of 1.2 m, and the subject 0.4 m away from the monitor. The hand region is extracted from the whole input image based on the depth map by assuming that the hand region is contained within the threshold.

**Recognition Phase**

1. The input image sequence $\{\boldsymbol{y}_t\}_{t=T-j+1}^{T}$ is classified as fingerspelling or not fingerspelling sequence by using the similarity (Eq. (7)). If the input sequence is classified as a fingerspelling sequence, we perform the following steps.
2. Fingerspelling images $\{\boldsymbol{y}_t|\beta_t > \eta\}$ are extracted from the input sequence with the thoreshold $\eta$.
3. CNN features $\{\boldsymbol{f}_{in}^i\}_{i=1}^{n_{in}}$ are extracted from $\{\boldsymbol{y}_t|\beta_t > \eta\}$.
4. A subspace $S_{in}$ of the fingerspelling images is generated by applying PCA to the sets of CNN features $\{\boldsymbol{f}_{in}^i\}$.
5. An orthogonalized input subspace $\hat{S}_{in}$ is generated by applying orthogonalize transformation to $S_{in}$.
6. The spotted fingerspelling is classified based on similarities between the input subspace $\hat{S}_{in}$ and reference subspaces $\{\hat{S}_c\}$.

## 3   Experiments

In this section, we demonstrate the effectiveness of the proposed framework through an experiment using a private dataset of JSL fingerspelling. After we detail our JSL dataset, we describe the experimental protocol. Finally, we show and discuss the experimental results.

### 3.1   Details of the Fingerspelling Dataset

Figure 6 shows sample images from our dataset. We have recorded 15 fingerspelling classes by a depth camera in the environment shown in Fig. 5. Each class was taken from 11 subjects in three situations at a speed of about 30 fps. Thus, the total number of the collected depth sequences is 495 (= 15 classes × 11 subjects × 3 situations). We asked the subjects to put hands out in front of the camera and detected the hands' regions by thresholding distance. The detected hand images are resized to 60 × 60 pixels.

**Fig. 6.** Sample images of our fingerspelling dataset, which is used in the experiments.

## 3.2 Experimental Protocol

To evaluate our two steps cascade framework, we synthesized an input sequence, which continuously inputs target and not target fingerspellings sequences alternately, as shown in Fig. 2. To this end, we first split our dataset into two sets; the first set was used as targets, and the other set was used as not targets. We randomly chose 8 classes from all 15 class sequences as the target set, and the remaining classes were used as not target set. Furthermore, to evaluate the classification performance, we randomly selected 2 situations from the target set as training data, and the remaining situation was used as testing data. Thus, training data has 176 (= 8 classes × 11 subjects × 2 situations) sequences, and testing data has 88 (= 8 classes × 11 subjects × 1 situation) sequences, respectively. The 176 training sequences were used to train CNN and OMSM. Besides, the training data was also used as references of TRCCA.

To synthesize an input sequence, we used the 88 testing sequence and the 88 sequences randomly extracted from 232(= 7 classes × 11 subjects × 3 situations) not target sequences. We merged 176(= 88 + 88) sequences into an input sequence such that the target and not target sequences occur alternately. Consequently, the procedure of this experiment is to spot a fingerspelling sequence from the merged sequence and then classify the spotted sequence into the 8 classes.

We decided the parameters for the frameworks by preliminary experiments using the training data. For MSM and OMSM with CNN features, the dimensions of class and input subspaces were set to 30 and 5, respectively. We set the threshold to classify the input sequence as a fingerspelling 0.4, where all 176 training sequences can be detected while we allow false positives. This is because it is more desirable to allow spotting not target fingerspellings by mistake rather than failing to spot target fingerspellings. Besides, we set the threshold $\eta$ to extract fingerspelling images to 0.25.

To obtain CNN features under our experimental setting, we modified the original VGG16 [22] slightly. First, we replaced the final 4096-way fully connected (FC) layer of the original VGG16 with a 1024-way FC layer with ReLU function. Further, we added a *class number*-way FC layer with softmax behind the previous 1024-way FC layer.

Moreover, to extract more effective CNN feature from our modified VGG16, we fine-tuned our VGG16 by using the training set. A CNN feature vector is extracted from the 1024-way FC layer every time an infrared hand shape image is input into our VGG16. As a result, the dimensionality $d$ of a CNN feature vector is 1024.

As a baseline method, we used our fine-tuned CNN, i.e., an input sequence is classified based on an average value of the output conviction degrees of each class from the last FC layer with softmax. We call this method "softmax".

We evaluated our framework in terms of spotting performance, classification accuracy, and their recognition time.

### 3.3   Experimental Results

1) *Performance of spotting fingerspellings by TRCCA*

Figure 7 shows the experimental result focusing on the spotting process by TRCCA. The figure suggests that we could detect all testing fingerspellings in the input sequence while there are few miss detections. This result suggests that the temporal dynamic information is important for spotting as we expected, and our framework could efficiently incorporate the information.

To further analyze this result, we calculated the ROC curve, as shown in Fig. 8. From the ROC curve, we can see that the false positive rate doesn't change until the true positive rate reaches 0.91. This indicates that the separability between target and not target fingerspelling is large and TRCCA is robust to the threshold to classify the input sequence as fingerspelling.

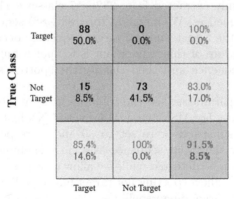

**Fig. 7.** ROC curve of the spotting performance by TRCCA. In this ROC curve, the false positive rate remains 0 until the true positive rate reaches 0.91. This means that spotting by TRCCA is robust to the threshold to classify the input sequence as fingerspelling.

2) *Classification accuracy and recognition time*

Figure 9 shows the experimental result focusing on the classification process by OMSM with CNN feature. In the figure, we can see that 85 out of 88 testing fingerspellings are correctly classified into the 8 classes, and the precision is 96.5%. This result shows the effectiveness of representing a set of CNN features as a subspace to capture the hand shape information from multiple images. In addition, we can confirm the effectiveness of the orthogonal transformation for subspaces as it significantly improves classification performance.

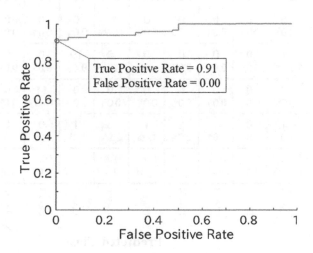

**Fig. 8.** Confusion Matrix of target and not target fingerspelling.

In the classification step, we excepted the 5 redundant extractions occurred in the spotting step. The reason for this result is that OMSM with CNN feature can recognize small differences of hand shapes, which cannot be captured by TRCCA.

**Table 1.** The experimental results about the fingerspelling recognition.

| Framework | Accuracy | Recognition time |
|---|---|---|
| TRCCA [11] | 64.1% | **39.7 ms** |
| CNN feat-OMSM | 68.9% | 52.7 ms |
| KOTRCCA [11] | 79.0% | 169.0 ms |
| TRCCA-CNN (softmax) | 80.7% | 56.9 ms |
| TRCCA-KOMSM | 86.9% | 187.3 ms |
| **TRCCA-CNN feat-OMSM (Proposed)** | **88.2%** | 91.2 ms |

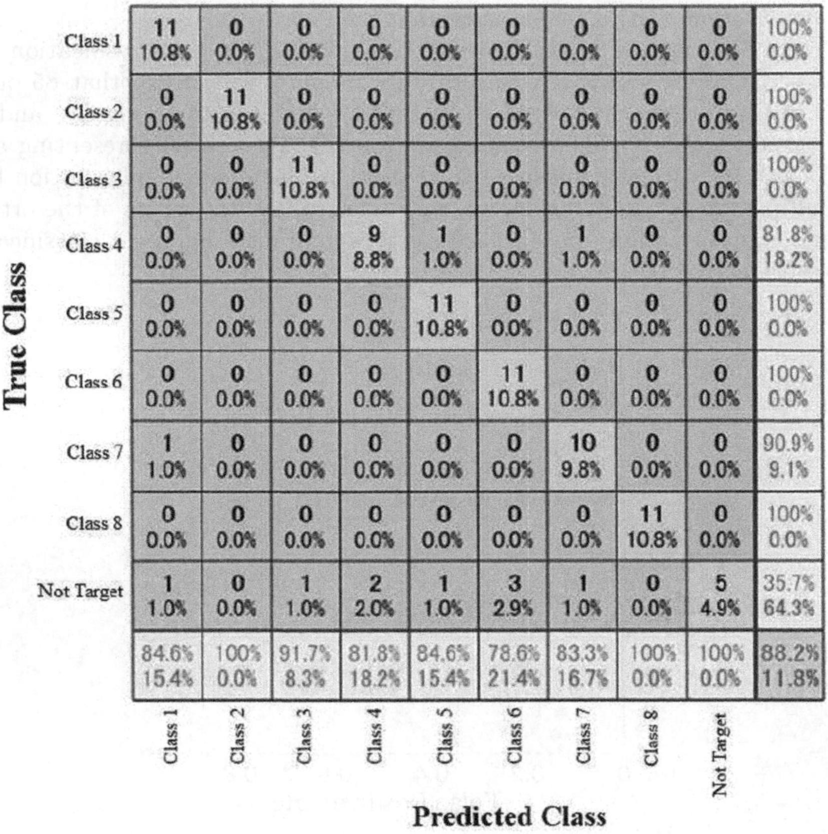

| True Class \ Predicted Class | Class 1 | Class 2 | Class 3 | Class 4 | Class 5 | Class 6 | Class 7 | Class 8 | Not Target | |
|---|---|---|---|---|---|---|---|---|---|---|
| Class 1 | 11 / 10.8% | 0 / 0.0% | 0 / 0.0% | 0 / 0.0% | 0 / 0.0% | 0 / 0.0% | 0 / 0.0% | 0 / 0.0% | 0 / 0.0% | 100% / 0.0% |
| Class 2 | 0 / 0.0% | 11 / 10.8% | 0 / 0.0% | 0 / 0.0% | 0 / 0.0% | 0 / 0.0% | 0 / 0.0% | 0 / 0.0% | 0 / 0.0% | 100% / 0.0% |
| Class 3 | 0 / 0.0% | 0 / 0.0% | 11 / 10.8% | 0 / 0.0% | 0 / 0.0% | 0 / 0.0% | 0 / 0.0% | 0 / 0.0% | 0 / 0.0% | 100% / 0.0% |
| Class 4 | 0 / 0.0% | 0 / 0.0% | 0 / 0.0% | 9 / 8.8% | 1 / 1.0% | 0 / 0.0% | 1 / 1.0% | 0 / 0.0% | 0 / 0.0% | 81.8% / 18.2% |
| Class 5 | 0 / 0.0% | 0 / 0.0% | 0 / 0.0% | 0 / 0.0% | 11 / 10.8% | 0 / 0.0% | 0 / 0.0% | 0 / 0.0% | 0 / 0.0% | 100% / 0.0% |
| Class 6 | 0 / 0.0% | 0 / 0.0% | 0 / 0.0% | 0 / 0.0% | 0 / 0.0% | 11 / 10.8% | 0 / 0.0% | 0 / 0.0% | 0 / 0.0% | 100% / 0.0% |
| Class 7 | 1 / 1.0% | 0 / 0.0% | 0 / 0.0% | 0 / 0.0% | 0 / 0.0% | 0 / 0.0% | 10 / 9.8% | 0 / 0.0% | 0 / 0.0% | 90.9% / 9.1% |
| Class 8 | 0 / 0.0% | 0 / 0.0% | 0 / 0.0% | 0 / 0.0% | 0 / 0.0% | 0 / 0.0% | 0 / 0.0% | 11 / 10.8% | 0 / 0.0% | 100% / 0.0% |
| Not Target | 1 / 1.0% | 0 / 0.0% | 1 / 1.0% | 2 / 2.0% | 1 / 1.0% | 3 / 2.9% | 1 / 1.0% | 0 / 0.0% | 5 / 4.9% | 35.7% / 64.3% |
| | 84.6% / 15.4% | 100% / 0.0% | 91.7% / 8.3% | 81.8% / 18.2% | 84.6% / 15.4% | 78.6% / 21.4% | 83.3% / 16.7% | 100% / 0.0% | 100% / 0.0% | 88.2% / 11.8% |

**Fig. 9.** Confusion Matrix of 8 fingerspelling and not target fingerspelling.

Figure 8 represents the classification performance of each framework as a ROC curve and Table 1 shows the classification accuracy and recognition time of the different frameworks. In the table, KOTRCCA [11] and KOMSM [23,24] are the extensions of TRCCA and OMSM by introducing kernel mapping and orthogonalization, respectively. CNN feature-OMSM classifies a set of CNN features extracted from all fingerspelling images in the input stream without spotting object fingerspelling sequence by TRCCA. From the table and the figure, we can see that the proposed framework achieves the best classification performance. Although the accuracy of TRCCA-KOMSM is almost as high as that of the proposed framework, the proposed framework achieves about half of the recognition time of TRCCA-KOMSM. These results suggest that OMSM with CNN feature effectively achieves fast and accurate classification for the following two reasons. The first reason is that CNN feature can improve the robustness against the shifts in the object's position and movement. For the second reason, OMSM with CNN feature doesn't require kernel extensions, which is used in

KOMSM, enabling the classification of fingerspellings in much smaller computation time (Fig. 10).

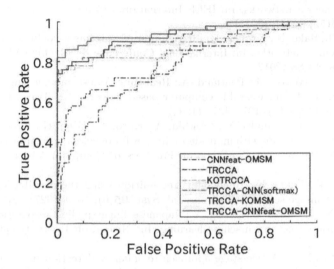

**Fig. 10.** ROC curve of the classification performance of each method.

## 4   Conclusions

In this paper, we proposed a fast and accurate recognition framework of fingerspellings with the two-steps cascade process of spotting and classification to remove the communication barriers between deaf and hard of hearing and non-handicapped people. The reason for applying different types of methods to each step is that the essential information is different for each step: the temporal dynamics and hand shape information are essential for the spotting and classification, respectively. To incorporate the two different information efficiently, we constructed the framework by introducing temporal regularized CCA (TRCCA) for spotting and orthogonal mutual subspace method (OMSM) with CNN features for classification.

The experimental results showed that our framework can achieve high classification, accuracy with a low false-positive rate, in a short computational time. We could also confirm that the two-steps process significantly outperforms conventional one-step methods in terms of classification performance and computational time.

**Acknowledgement.** This work was partly supported by JSPS KAKENHI Grant Number 19H04129.

# References

1. Huang, J., Zhou, W., Li, H., Li, W.: Sign language recognition using 3D convolutional neural networks. In: IEEE International Conference on Multimedia and Expo 2015, pp. 1–6 (2015)
2. Hosoe, H., Sako, S., Kwolek, B.: Recognition of JSL finger spelling using convolutional neural networks. In: International Conference on Machine Vision Applications, pp. 85–88 (2017)
3. Starner, T., Weaver, J., Pentland, A.: Real-time American sign language recognition using desk and wearable computer based video. IEEE Trans. Pattern Anal. Mach. Intell. **20**(12), 1371–1375 (1998)
4. Takabayashi, D., Tanaka, Y., Okazaki, A., Kato, N., Hino, H., Fukui, K.: Finger alphabets recognition with multi-depth images for developing their learning system. In: Korea-Japan Joint Workshop on Frontiers of Computer Vision, pp. 154–159 (2014)
5. Ohkawa, Y., Fukui, K.: Hand-shape recognition using the distributions of multi-viewpoint image sets. IEICE Trans. Inf. Syst. **95**(6), 1619–1627 (2012)
6. Mukai, N., Harada, N., Chang, Y.: Japanese fingerspelling recognition based on classification tree and machine learning. In: Nicograph International, pp. 19–24 (2017)
7. Wang, Z., Li, B.: A two-stage approach to saliency detection in images. In: 2008 IEEE International Conference on Acoustics, Speech and Signal Processing, pp. 965–968 (2008)
8. van der Heijden, A.H.C.: Two stages in visual information processing and visual perception? Vis. Cogn. **3**(4), 325–362 (1996)
9. Hardoon, D.R., Szedmak, S., Shawe-Taylor, J.: Canonical correlation analysis: an overview with application to learning methods. Neural Comput. **16**(12), 2639–2664 (2004)
10. Kobayashi, T.: S3CCA: smoothly structured sparse CCA for partial pattern matching. In: International Conference on Pattern Recognition, pp. 1981–1986 (2014)
11. Tanaka, S., Okazaki, A., Kato, N., Hino, H., Fukui, K.: Spotting fingerspelled words from sign language video by temporally regularized canonical component analysis. In: 2016 IEEE International Conference on Identity, Security and Behavior Analysis, pp. 1–7 (2016)
12. Yamaguchi, O., Fukui, K., Maeda, K.: Face recognition using temporal image sequence. In: Proceedings Third IEEE International Conference on Automatic Face and Gesture Recognition, pp. 318–323 (1998)
13. Fukui, K., Maki, A.: Difference subspace and its generalization for subspace-based methods. IEEE Trans. Pattern Anal. Mach. Intell. **37**(11), 2164–2177 (2015)
14. Kawahara, T., Nishiyama, M., Kozakaya, T., Yamaguchi, O.: Face recognition based on whitening transformation of distribution of subspaces. In: Asian Conference on Computer Vision workshops, Subspace, pp. 97–103 (2007)
15. Kim, T.K., Kittler, J., Cipolla, R.: Incremental learning of locally orthogonal subspaces for set-based object recognition. In: Proceedings British Machine Vision Conference, pp. 559–568 (2006)
16. Hotelling, H.: Relations between two sets of variates. Biometrika **28**(3–4), 321–377 (1936)
17. Afriat, S.N.: Orthogonal and oblique projectors and the characteristics of pairs of vector spaces. In: Mathematical Proceedings of the Cambridge Philosophical Society, vol. 53, no. 04, pp. 800–816 (1957)

18. Sharif Razavian, A., Azizpour, H., Sullivan, J., Carlsson, S.: CNN features off-the-shelf: an astounding baseline for recognition. In: IEEE Conference on Computer Vision and Pattern Recognition Workshops, pp. 806–813 (2014)
19. Chen, J.-C., Patel, V.M., Chellappa, R.: Unconstrained face verification using deep CNN features. In: IEEE Winter Conference on Applications of Computer Vision 2016, pp. 1–9 (2016)
20. Li, G., Yu, Y.: Visual saliency based on multiscale deep features. In: IEEE Conference on Computer Vision and Pattern Recognition 2015, pp. 5455–5463 (2015)
21. Sogi, N., Nakayama, T., Fukui, K.: A method based on convex cone model for image-set classification with CNN features. In: International Joint Conference on Neural Networks 2018, pp. 1–8 (2018)
22. Simonyan, K., Zisserman, A.: Very deep convolutional networks for large-scale image recognition. In: International Conference on Learning Representations (2015)
23. Fukui, K., Yamaguchi, O.: The kernel orthogonal mutual subspace method and its application to 3D object recognition. In: Yagi, Y., Kang, S.B., Kweon, I.S., Zha, H. (eds.) ACCV 2007. LNCS, vol. 4844, pp. 467–476. Springer, Heidelberg (2007). https://doi.org/10.1007/978-3-540-76390-1_46
24. Peris, M., Fukui, K.: Both-hand gesture recognition based on KOMSM with volume subspaces for robot teleoperation. In: International Conference on Cyber Technology in Automation, Control, and Intelligent Systems, pp. 191–196 (2012)

# CNN Depression Severity Level Estimation from Upper Body vs. Face-Only Images

Dua'a Ahmad(✉) ⃝, Roland Goecke⃝, and James Ireland⃝

Human-Centred Technology Research Centre, Faculty of Science and Technology,
University of Canberra, Canberra, Australia
duaa.ahmad@canberra.edu.au

**Abstract.** Upper body gestures have proven to provide more information about a person's depressive state when added to facial expressions.
While several studies on automatic depression analysis have looked into
this impact, little is known in regard to how a convolutional neural network (CNN) uses such information for predicting depression severity
levels. This study investigates the performance in various CNN models when looking at facial images alone versus including the upper body
when estimating depression severity levels on a regressive scale. To assess
generalisability of CNN model performance, two vastly different datasets
were used, one collected by the Black Dog Institute and the other being
the 2013 Audio/Visual Emotion Challenge (AVEC). Results show that
the differences in model performance between face versus upper body are
slight, as model performance across multiple architectures is very similar
but varies when different datasets are introduced.

**Keywords:** Convolutional neural networks · Depression severity ·
Spatial analysis

## 1  Introduction

Depression is a debilitating disorder especially when accompanied by feelings
of diminished interest/pleasure, worthlessness, irritation, and hopelessness [1].
Effects of depression impact one's personal behaviour, cognitive capabilities,
interpersonal functioning, as well as emotional and social aspects of life [2].
While it can be disabling, depression is a treatable mental health condition if
appropriately diagnosed and exposed to relevant medications or therapy treatments [3]. Appropriate treatments are, however, highly dependent on an accurate
diagnosis.

The diagnosis of depression is heavily reliant on the careful clinical assessment of a patient's symptoms, historical background and patient self-report [3].
Diagnosis furthermore can vary based on the diagnostic assessments used and
clinician's expertise. Such approach lacks objective measures and risks subjective

© Springer Nature Switzerland AG 2021
A. Del Bimbo et al. (Eds.): ICPR 2020 Workshops, LNCS 12666, pp. 744–758, 2021.
https://doi.org/10.1007/978-3-030-68780-9_56

bias. Most commonly used assessment tools and rating scales include the Beck Depression Inventory (BDI), Hamilton Depression Rating Scale (HDRS), Core Assessment of Psychomotor Change (CORE), Mini-International Neuropsychiatric Interview (MINI), Quick Inventory of Depressive Symptomatology (QIDS) - self-assessment, and the Patient Health Questionnaire-9 (PHQ-9) [4].

Other techniques used to assess a patient's depressive state involve studying brain activity using tools such as Positron Emission Tomography (PET), Magnetic Resonance Imaging (MRI), and functional Magnetic Resonance Imaging (fMRI). The presented diagnostic instruments are either heavily reliant on subjective measures, i.e. the decision of the clinician, are time consuming, require multiple visits, or obtrusive [5]. Unfortunately, even with taking precautions, depression cases still go by unnoticed or are misdiagnosed [6]. Hence, the pressing need for a tool that provides both objective insight while being unobtrusive to the user. More recently, promising and automated machine and deep learning techniques have been used to detect and analyse depression symptoms from multiple modalities in which depression symptoms present themselves, such as facial expressions, eye gaze [7], vocal intonation [8], gestures and movement, posture [9], and physiology [10].

This study investigates Convolutional Neural Network (CNN) models as a regression problem to predict depression severity levels for video frames, with the focus on purely the spatial aspect rather than the temporal, to see how spatial features alone contribute to detecting expressions of depression symptoms.

Given that depression symptoms are present in multiple areas in the human body, we would like to see how predictions differ if the models were trained on face-only frames vs. those also containing the upper body. Finally this paper also tests predictions across multiple CNN model architectures and different datasets. In summary, the following questions are addressed in this study:

1. From a spatial perspective alone, can a CNN pick up on differences in facial expressions and body gestures related to depression and be used to predict depression severity levels?
2. Does it matter what CNN model architecture is used? And can that be generalised over different datasets?
3. Is there a difference between CNN model performance when exposing the model to only facial images versus upper body images?

The content of this paper is organised as follows. Section 2 covers some background on the emergence of automatic depression analysis, covers the potential role of CNNs in detecting depression symptoms, outlines the shift from a classification to regression problem, then discusses works on multiple datasets for depression analysis. Section 3 describes the datasets used and why they were chosen specifically for this study. Section 4 outlines the method used to conduct our experiment, including descriptions of our data preprocessing steps, models trained, hyperparameters, dataset splits and any postprocessing chosen. Section 5 presents the results of our experimental setup and discussion. Finally, Sect. 6 concludes the paper.

# 2    Background-Related Work

## 2.1    The Emergence of Automatic Depression Analysis

Understanding mental health disorders has been of great interest to affective computing. This interest brought about the generation of the Audio/Visual Emotion Challenge (AVEC) initially set up in 2011 as the first challenge aimed to automate emotion analysis. In 2012, AVEC introduced a sub challenge interested in analyzing mood, in the context of depression detection [11]. Even more recently, depression still remains a core topic for analysis in AVEC challenges [12].

Apart from the AVEC challenge, there currently exists multiple studies investigating the detection of depression severity levels using deep learning, these however use input other than raw video frames as input to models, examples include ones in [13,14]. For a comprehensive review of existing studies using Deep Learning techniques for mental health analysis, readers are directed to [15].

## 2.2    The Role of a CNN in Detecting Depression Symptoms from Videos

**Visual Expressions of Depression:** People under a depressed state, are observed to have more frequent frowns [16], a decrease in how often a person smiles, flattened negative expressions, controlled smiles [17] and an overall lack of expression in their faces [16]. To add, eye gaze has well been known to indicate ones interest [18]. According to [7] people with depression tend to avoid eye contact, have more of "nonspecific" gaze and less mutual gaze, "indicating indifference towards communication" and hence, lack of interest. Not only are our emotional states reflected in our facial expressions, but also our bodily movements and gestures.

Body movements like shaking hands and feet, and gestures of self grooming, such as rubbing, scratching and consistent hair stroking have been associated with depressed patients [19]. In [7] authors observed that tilting head downwards is also linked to a depressive state, as well as more frequent self grooming gestures. Also, posture is another indication of a depressive symptom, where depression can result in a slumped, hunched, or rigid posture that restricts body movements [20].

For instance, [21] has concluded that adding upper body data gives more information about one's depressive state as opposed to face. Given that CNN models have proven great potential in pattern recognition, we are interested to investigate how well they detect expressions of depression mentioned above, purely from a spatial prospective. Moreover, would CNN models better detect depression severity levels if focused purely on the face or when compared to an image that includes upper body parts?

**Preprocessing Versus Raw Data:** Studies applying automatic techniques to detect and predict depression severity levels have prominently used some sort of preprocessing, such as extracting spectrum maps from video features [22] before feeding into a CNN, or extracting facial and head pose landmarks [23–25].

One motivation of this study is to move towards a purely automated depression analysis technique, with minimal human interference. Hence the use of video frames as direct input to a CNN to predict depression severity levels. While facial frames require some preprocessing steps, upper body frames are directly extracted from raw videos. Testing on both facial and upper body frames allows us to understand whether any postprocessing step is necessary for improving CNN model performance when predicting depression severity levels.

**Previous Work:** Works on investigating CNN models on video frames, to our knowledge, have been limited. One most related study [26] has applied a similar concept which looks at facial video frames as input to a CNN model, our work can be considered an expansion of this study, in a way, looking at how generalisable are CNN models are using multiple architectures, on different datasets, treating it as a regression problem rather than a categorical and on facial versus upper body gestures.

It is worth noting that [26] based their training on two datasets, AVEC2013 & AVEC2014. While the two might be considered two different datasets, AVEC2014 is a subset of AVEC2013 [27], which makes the two datasets very similar in nature. When proving generalisability of model performance, very different datasets need to be used in the training and testing process, especially when CNN models are known to sometimes overfit to a specific dataset.

### 2.3  From a Classification to a Regression Problem

Detecting depression severity levels initially started as a categorical problem where most studies separated severity levels to either two (depressed and not-depressed) [21,28] or four (none, mild, moderate, and severe) [26] categories. More recent studies [29,30] have shifted towards using automatic tools to predict depression severity levels at a regressive scale.

To the best of our knowledge, studies extracting depression severity levels without much preprocessing of features from raw video frames using CNN models have been limited, which is the interest of this paper. For example, in [22] the authors use a CNN to predict depression severity on the AVEC2016 DIAC-WOZ dataset. Their approach, however, is very different in the sense that spectrum maps are used as input to the CNN rather than video frames.

### 2.4  Previous Work on Multiple Depression Datasets

Testing generalisability of models on automatic depression symptom recognition has by far been a topic of interest, and whilst proposing a new technique gives promising results on one dataset, questions arise as to whether this performance deteriorates when exposed to new data never seen and completely different from what it has trained upon. Given that a dataset has differing illumination/variation/background to another can impact performance of computer vision applications. Additionally other aspects play a role such as differences in cultural background and ethnicity of participants.

Studies such as [31] and [32] looked into how exposure to multiple and different datasets impacts model's performance. For example, in [31] the authors tested their proposed techniques on three datasets with different training/testing arrangements each time, concluding that adding multiple datasets in the training of a model improves generalisability, while testing on a new unseen dataset deteriorates models performance.

However, studies exploring the generalisability of CNNs on depression related datasets, to the fullest of our knowledge have been limited, which this study aims to investigate.

## 3  Datasets

The two datasets presented in this study are both cross cultural (Australian & German) and cross lingual (English & German). The first, collected from the Black Dog Institute Sydney, Australia, is clinically validated with QIDS-self report (QIDS-SR) scores, containing both clinically validated and self accessed reports. The second dataset is presented by the Audio Visual Challenge 2013 with BDI self report scores which are only self assessed from participants based in Germany.

Other related datasets are available, such as the ones presented in the AVEC2019 Challenge [33] including Ulm State-of-Mind Corpus, Distress Analysis Interview Corpus, and Cross-cultural Emotion Database. While the AVEC2019 datasets are publicly available, not all are related to depression, which is the focus of this study, and those that do, are quite limited due to privacy concerns. Out of the three, only the Distress Analysis Interview Corpus is relevant to our study, even so limited to extracted features from videos and not the raw videos themselves. The two datasets in this study were specifically chosen given that raw videos/visual data is required to truly investigate the performance of a CNN when detecting symptoms of depression.

### 3.1  The Black Dog Dataset

The Black Dog institute is a non-profit organization aimed at the diagnosis, treatment and prevention of depression and other mental illnesses. Originally containing 80 participants, 60 of those participants were chosen for this study for a balance in gender and age, 30 healthy controls and 30 clinically diagnosed. Healthy controls were participants with an IQ above 80, with no history of any mental illness, drug/alcohol addictions, neurological disorders, brain injury or having an invasive neurosurgical procedure. These controls were age and gender matched, with age ranging from 21–75 years and an equal distribution of 30 males and 30 females were selected. All patients who participated were classified to have had a major depressive episode, along with meeting other criteria, with each patient ranked moderately depressed or higher (depression severity $\geq$ 13) based on the QIDS-SR [34]. Recordings captured reactions towards a set of experimental simulations presented to the participant, with the camera located behind the monitor and directed at them to observe changes of facial expressions. Each video recorded at resolution of 800 by 600 pixels and sampled at 30 frames per second.

Each recording had the participant experience:

- A set of brief video clips aimed to elicit certain emotions (anger, happiness, sadness, surprise, fear),
- An activity for a participant to rate a picture for being positive or negative,
- Reading 20 sentences with positive and negative meanings, and finally,
- An interview in which the participant is asked open ended questions that enable them to describe significant events in their lives (which is the part this study has focused on).

### 3.2   The Audio Visual Challenge 2013 (AVEC2013) Dataset

The dataset released for the 2013 Audio Visual Challenge (AVEC2013) contains 150 videos of participants with varying depression severity [11], split originally into 50 videos for training, another 50 for validation and 50 for testing. However the severity level ground truth annotations was only ever released for the training and validation sets. For this reason we focus solely on these 100 videos for training, validating and testing our models. Out of these 100 videos, 65 are for female participants and 35 male. The 100 videos selected 58 participants, with some having more than one video recorded at different time frames.

Videos were re-sampled at 30 frames per second at 640 by 480 pixels, with varying lengths of 20–50 min per video. The videos contain subjects performing Human-Computer Interaction tasks, such as speaking out loud while performing a task, counting from 1–10, reading text, talking about a happy experience, and a sad experience. Each participant completed a self-assessed Beck Depression Inventory-II [35] subjective depression questionnaire. More information regarding the AVEC2013 dataset can be found in the challenges publication [11].

### 3.3   Conversion Scales

The Black Dog dataset depression severity scale is based on the QIDS-SR, a scale ranging from 0–27, while the AVEC2013 dataset is based on the Black Dog depression severity scale, ranging from 0–63. In order to train our models, the AVEC2013 dataset severity scale was converted to a QIDS-SR scale using the Inventory of Depressive Symptomatology (IDS) and QIDS conversion table[1]

---

[1] http://web.archive.org/web/20191101195225/ http://www.ids-qids.org:80/ interpretation.html.

for comparison between the two datasets to take place. Note that after converting severity scales for the AVEC2013 dataset, and to be consistent with the Black Dog dataset, there were 77 videos with severity below 13 (controls (C)) in accordance to the QIDS-SR scale and 23 above (patients (P)).

## 4   Method-Experimental Design

### 4.1   Data Preprocessing

To prepare data required to train the CNN models, we prepared the following arrangements from both datasets:

– Facial frames
– Upper body frames

We prepared these two arrangements to test whether CNN models require Preprocessing, i.e. removing noise from the background by extracting facial features and comparing these results to those without having anything extracted to test if the CNN can filter out irrelevant information on its own. As the original videos contained upper body frames these were left unaltered, requiring us only to generate a second set of images for each dataset with extracted facial frames courtesy of code from OpenCV$^2$. Frames extracted from each video were done at 30 frames per second, with an average of 2000 images for each participant. Equating to approximately of 120,000 (60 × 2000) frames from the Black Dog dataset and 200,000 (100 × 2000) from the AVEC2013. With varying initial frame sizes for both facial and upper body frames, all images fed into the CNN models were resized to 224 × 224 pixels.

### 4.2   Models

Models used to train the two datasets, AVEC2013 and Black Dog, were all previously trained on a larger dataset, specifically ImageNet. The chosen models were AlexNet proposed originally by [36], a 19-layered VGG proposed by [37], 34 layered ResNet proposed by [38] and a 169-layered DenseNet proposed by [39]. Each model differing greatly from one another in regards to their depth and structural design of the underlying architecture, as shown in Fig. 1. While not an exhaustive search, the following should provide an overview of more readily available architectures that have preformed well in other computer vision applications. These models were altered only in regards to the last predictive layers, with the addition of a ReLU layer for a regressive scale.

---

$^2$ https://www.opencv.org.

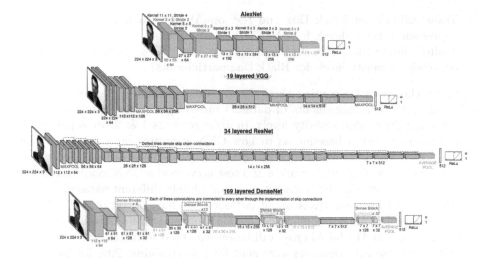

**Fig. 1.** CNN architectures used in the experiments, greyed regions denoting parts of the pre-trained models that have not been fine-tuned.

## 4.3   Model Platform and Training Parameters

All models were trained using the Fastai[3] library, built upon PyTorch, with default model settings retrained, except the class list that was changed to float to represent values at a regressive scale. The training of these models was distributed over two systems, both with an Intel Xeon Silver 4116 CPU 2.10 GHz base clock. One equipped with a Tesla V100 and the other a Titan XP. The following describes the training parameters used within this study:

- Training duration of 20 epochs.
- Learning rate set to 10e-3.
- Batch size of 20 frames.

## 4.4   Datasets Split

To test model generalisability on different depression datasets, the four models, AlexNet, VGG19, ResNet34 and DenseNet169 were trained using the following dataset arrangements for both facial and upper body video frames:

1. Train/validate/test on Black Dog (outcome: predicted depression severity levels for Black Dog participants).
2. Train/validate/test on AVEC2013 (outcome: predicted depression severity levels for AVEC2013 participants).
3. Train/validate/test on both Black Dog and AVEC2013 (outcome: predicted depression severity levels for Black Dog and AVEC2013 participants).

---

[3] https://www.fast.ai.

4. Train/validate on Black Dog and test on AVEC2013 (outcome: predicted depression severity levels for AVEC2013 participants).
5. Train/validate on AVEC2013 and test on Black Dog (outcome: predicted depression severity levels for Black Dog participants).

We have chosen to train using these dataset arrangements to understand how different splits or arrangements of datasets impact the performance of a CNN in detecting depression severity levels. In arrangements 1 & 2, we separate the two datasets to set a baseline as to how CNN performs on a single dataset. Arrangement 3 looks at whether merging the two datasets will affect performance (i.e. testing generalisability), while 4 & 5 test how good a CNN model has learnt symptoms of depression by testing it on a completely different dataset.

Because we have relatively small datasets, we have incorporated a K-fold cross validation approach as many depression analysis studies have incorporated when training [40,41], 5-fold cross validation was used for arrangements 1, 2, & 3. Data for these arrangements were split 60% for training, 20% for validation and 20% for testing for each fold (implying that five models for each of the three arrangements were trained, every time on a different fold) this is to make sure results obtained were across all participants in the dataset (data split per participant/video and not per video frame). While arrangements 4 & 5 were trained on one dataset and tested on the other.

## 4.5 Data Post-processing

Similar to the approach used in [11], and given that the level of depression is labelled with a single value per recording, the average Mean Average Error (MAE) and Root Mean Square Error (RMSE) values were calculated across the frame predictions for a given video sequence and averaged over a given test set.

## 5 Results and Discussion

Our goal when conducting this experiment was to investigate CNN performance of face only visual frames versus upper body frames. The main questions being asked are the following:

1. From a spatial perspective alone, can a CNN pick up on differences in facial expressions and body gestures related to depression and be used to predict depression severity levels?
2. Does it matter what CNN model architecture is used and can that be generalised over different datasets?
3. Is there a difference between CNN model performance when exposing the model to only facial images versus upper body images?

Table 1 presents a summary of results for model MAE and RMSE for both face (F) and body (B) data over multiple datasets, while Fig. 2 presents a visual illustration of the results, for easier comparison.

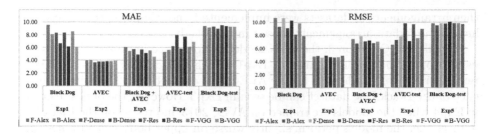

**Fig. 2.** Face (F) and Body (B) MAE & RMSE comparison. Alex = AlexNet, Dense = DenseNet169, Res = ResNet34, VGG = VGG19.

**Table 1.** Model MSE & RMSE for Face (F) and Body (B).

| Network | | | Alexnet | | DenseNet169 | | Resnet34 | | VGG19 | |
|---------|---------|---|------|------|------|------|------|------|------|------|
| Exp# | Dataset | | MAE | RMSE | MAE | RMSE | MAE | RMSE | MAE | RMSE |
| Exp1 | Black Dog | F | 9.53 | 10.66 | 8.32 | 10.63 | 8.32 | 10.29 | 8.48 | 9.86 |
| | | B | 8.07 | 9.30 | 6.62 | 9.09 | 6.10 | 8.12 | 6.07 | 7.89 |
| Exp2 | AVEC | F | 3.98 | 4.76 | 3.63 | 4.59 | 3.77 | 4.63 | 3.80 | 4.64 |
| | | B | 4.00 | 4.86 | 3.79 | 4.89 | 3.80 | 4.60 | 3.91 | 4.86 |
| Exp3 | Black Dog+AVEC | F | 6.06 | 7.39 | 5.74 | 7.84 | 5.71 | 7.20 | 5.58 | 6.99 |
| | | B | 5.47 | 6.74 | 4.92 | 7.06 | 5.14 | 6.79 | 4.57 | 5.93 |
| Exp4 | AVEC-test | F | 5.32 | 6.54 | 6.23 | 7.80 | 5.84 | 7.09 | 6.12 | 7.54 |
| | | B | 5.64 | 7.28 | 7.99 | 9.83 | 7.69 | 9.69 | 6.93 | 8.95 |
| Exp5 | Black Dog-test | F | 9.38 | 9.80 | 9.30 | 9.81 | 9.52 | 10.05 | 9.30 | 9.83 |
| | | B | 9.15 | 9.50 | 8.97 | 9.75 | 9.38 | 9.82 | 9.32 | 9.69 |

To answer Question 1, it appears that the CNN model is picking up on expressions related to depression from a spatial perspective and is also able to predict severity levels on a regressive scale.

As for Question 2, results are consistent across all CNN architectures. However, the performance of these models seems to fluctuate slightly when different datasets/arrangements of datasets are used (see Fig. 2). When comparing the Black Dog dataset "Exp1" with the AVEC2013 dataset "Exp2", CNN models performed better on AVEC2013 in comparison to the Black Dog as evidenced by the lower MAE and RMSE.

Further exploring results, when the models were trained on the Black Dog dataset and tested on the AVEC2013 dataset "Exp4" we noticed a change in overall model performance, if comparing to Exp1 then it is an improvement, but if comparing to Exp2 a deterioration. Interestingly, for Exp5 when models were trained on the AVEC2013 dataset and tested on the Black Dog dataset, performance was at its worst in comparison to Exp1 & Exp2. This implies that testing on a new unseen dataset does effect model performance in the context of using CNNs. For Exp3 where combined datasets for training and testing are applied, performance improves from Exp1 but deteriorates slightly from Exp2 We can observe in general that the Black Dog dataset is a more challenging dataset to predict depression severity levels than the AVEC2013 dataset.

Note that similar to the approach when splitting datasets was used in [31], models were first trained and tested on individual datasets to set a baseline, then arrangements of datasets were implemented and compared to the baseline, hence, the 5 data arrangements chosen in this study.

Finally, for Question 3, the CNN model performance improves slightly when using upper body video frames in Exp1 for the Black Dog dataset, while it remains relatively unchanged for the AVEC2013 dataset "Exp2". A similar influence of the Black Dog dataset can be seen in Exp3. However, the opposite occurs in Exp4 when the models are trained on AVEC2013 and tested on the Black Dog dataset (i.e. the models perform slightly worse on upper body video frames than on face-only video frames).

This implies that while results for model performance differ slightly for Exp1, 3 & 4, CNN models were able to detect depression severity levels for both facial and upper body frames with very similar performance.

Another motivation behind facial and upper body frame split was to see whether we can use video frames for analysis directly without needing to pre-process/crop facial frames for better results. It can be observed in Table 1 that there are some noticeable differences between face (F) and body (B) results, which warrants further investigation. However, our results indicate that direct upper body frames can be fed directly into a CNN model without the need to extract facial frames to have severity levels predicted, and that the difference in model performance between facial and upper body frames is only slight.

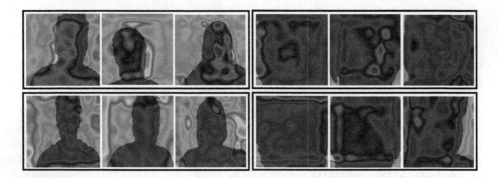

**Fig. 3.** GRAD-CAM heat maps illustrating regions of the image in which the model prediction was based on. Top row are examples where the predicted severity levels were close to the ground truth severity levels (left being for upper body frames and right side for facial frames), while the bottom row are examples where the predicted severity levels were far from ground truth severity levels (left being for upper body frames and right side for facial frames). Note that shaded areas in the background represent the participant position in the frames. Also, for illustration purposes, heat maps were extracted from both the VGG19 and the Alexnet CNN model architectures.

To further understand model performance across facial versus upper body frames and extending our answer to Question 3, we have extracted Gradient-weighted Class Activation Mapping (GRAD-CAM) [42] heat maps to depict which regions of an image was the model focused on when making predictions.

Figure 3 illustrates heat map visualisations of regions which lead the model to make predictions, we have noticed that for most successful upper body frame predictions (top left in Fig. 3) we can see that the heat map is concentrated on regions where the upper body is located, while on facial features such as the eyes, nose and mouth area for the facial frames (top right in Fig. 3).

Our first goal for using heat maps was to see if there was any improvement (visually) in using upper body images over face only, since there is useful information beyond the face [21]. When viewing the heat maps we can see that the model is somewhat looking at the whole upper body including the face to make its predictions (this however was not always the case for successful predictions). Results do not show that the model was picking up facial features specifically when upper body images were used, therefore based on the heat maps, we cannot conclude any advantage of upper body over face images, especially that model performance results in Table 1 prove indifference.

Our second goal in using heat maps was to see if extracting facial frames was a necessary step for CNN models to predict severity levels and whether the background can influence predictions when including the upper body frames. Based on the extracted heat maps, we can see that while the model mainly makes predictions from regions where the participant is, this is not the case for all predictions close to the ground truth predictions, and in some cases, the model also focuses on aspects in the background. Therefore the heat maps do not help us in making any definite conclusion.

## 6 Conclusion

This study mainly looks at the applications of CNN models in detecting depression severity levels for upper body versus facial frames. Treating it as a regression problem, we conclude the following:

- CNN models can detect depression severity levels with similar model performance for both face and upper body frames.
- All different CNN model architectures used produced similar model performance.
- Introducing a new dataset unseen by the model impacts model performance.
- Results illustrate that upper body model predictions are similar to face predictions, so upper body frames can be used as direct input for similar model performance.
- Previous studies show that adding upper body parts to facial information gives more input to help detect symptoms of depression [21], however does this apply for CNN models? Heat maps although give us some insight on what the model is looking at to make predictions it is unclear as to why CNN model performance of face vs. upper body is similar.
- While our results indicate only a slight difference between using face versus upper body frames as input to CNN models, further research needs to investigate either different ways in which we can see what the model is looking at when making predictions or different fine-tuning and training techniques that prove different results than ours.

This study only looks at spatial aspects of a CNN model, future research will focus on the temporal aspects and how that impacts model performance.

**Acknowledgements.** This research was supported partially by the Australian Government through the Australian Research Council's Discovery Projects funding scheme (project DP190101294).

# References

1. Albrecht, A.T., Herrick, C.R.: 100 Questions & Answers About Depression. Jones and Bartlett, Burlington (2006)
2. American Psychiatric Association: Diagnostic and statistical manual of mental disorders: DSM-5, Washington DC (2013)
3. Mann, J.J., Roose, S.P., McGrath, P.J.: Clinical Handbook for the Management of Mood Disorders, p. 430. Cambridge University Press, Cambridge (2013)
4. Vares, E.A., Salum, G.A., Spanemberg, L., Caldieraro, M.A., Fleck, M.P.: Depression dimensions: integrating clinical signs and symptoms from the perspectives of clinicians and patients. PLoS ONE **10**(8), e0136037 (2015)
5. Videbech, P., Ravnkilde, B.: Hippocampal volume and depression: a meta-analysis of MRI studies. Am. J. Psychiatry **161**(11), 1957–1966 (2015)
6. Katon, W.: The epidemiology of depression in medical care. Int. J. Psychiatry Med. **17**(1), 93–112 (1988)
7. Waxer, P.: Nonverbal cues for depression. J. Abnorm. Psychol. **83**(3), 319–322 (1974)
8. Darby, J.K., Simmons, N., Berger, P.A.: Speech and voice parameters of depression: a pilot study. J. Commun. Disord. **17**(2), 75–85 (1984)
9. Parker, G., et al.: Classifying depression by mental stage signs. Br. J. Psychiatry **157**(Jul), 55–65 (1990)
10. Chen, Y.-T., Hung, I.-C., Huang, M.-W., Hou, C.-J., Cheng, K.-S.: Physiological signal analysis for patients with depression. In: 2011 4th International Conference on Biomedical Engineering and Informatics (BMEI), pp. 805–808 (2011)
11. Valstar, M., et al.: AVEC 2013: the continuous audio/visual emotion and depression recognition challenge. In: Proceedings of the 3rd ACM International Workshop on Audio/Visual Emotion Challenge (AVEC 2013) (2013)
12. Ringeval, F., et al.: AVEC 2019 workshop and challenge: state-of-mind, detecting depression with AI, and cross-cultural affect recognition. In: AVEC 2019 - Proceedings of the 9th International Audio/Visual Emotion Challenge and Workshop, co-located with MM 2019, pp. 3–12. ACM Press, New York (2019)
13. Uyulan, C., et al.: Major depressive disorder classification based on different convolutional neural network models: deep learning approach. Clin. EEG Neurosci. 1550059420916634 (2020)
14. Srimadhur, N.S., Lalitha, S.: An end-to-end model for detection and assessment of depression levels using speech. Procedia Comput. Sci. **171**, 12–21 (2020)
15. Su, C., Xu, Z., Pathak, J., Wang, F.: Deep learning in mental health outcome research: a scoping review. Transl. Psychiatry **10**(1), 1–26 (2020). https://www.nature.com/articles/s41398-020-0780-3
16. Fairbanks, L.A., McGuire, M.T., Harris, C.J.: Nonverbal interaction of patients and therapists during psychiatric interviews. J. Abnorm. Psychol. **91**(2), 109–119 (1982)

17. Girard, J.M., Cohn, J.F., Mahoor, M.H., Mavadati, S.M., Hammal, Z., Rosenwald, D.P.: Nonverbal social withdrawal in depression: evidence from manual and automatic analysis. Image Vis. Comput. **32**(10), 641–647 (2014)
18. Hoffman, E.A., Haxby, J.V.: Distinct representations of eye gaze and identity in the distributed human neural system for face perception. Nat. Neurosci. **3**(1), 80–84 (2000)
19. Jones, I.H., Pansa, M.: Some nonverbal aspects of depression and schizophrenia occurring during the interview. J. Nervous Mental Disease **167**(7), 402–409 (1979)
20. France, J., Kramer, S., Cox, J.: Communication and Mental Illness Theoretical and Practical Approaches. Jessica Kingsley, London (2001)
21. Joshi, J., Goecke, R., Parker, G., Breakspear, M.: Can body expressions contribute to automatic depression analysis? In: 2013 10th IEEE International Conference and Workshops on Automatic Face and Gesture Recognition (FG), pp. 1–7. IEEE (2013)
22. Song, S., Shen, L., Valstar, M.: Human behaviour-based automatic depression analysis using hand-crafted statistics and deep learned spectral features. In: Proceedings - 13th IEEE International Conference on Automatic Face and Gesture Recognition, FG 2018, pp. 158–165. Institute of Electrical and Electronics Engineers Inc. (2018)
23. Dibeklioglu, H., Hammal, Z., Cohn, J.F.: Dynamic multimodal measurement of depression severity using deep autoencoding. IEEE J. Biomed. Health Inf. **22**(2), 525–536 (2018)
24. Gavrilescu, M., Vizireanu, N.: Predicting depression, anxiety, and stress levels from videos using the facial action coding system. Sensors **19**(17), 3693 (2019). www.mdpi.com/journal/sensors
25. Pampouchidou, A.: Automatic detection of visual cues associated to depression. Technical report (2018). https://tel.archives-ouvertes.fr/tel-02122342
26. Zhou, X., Jin, K., Shang, Y., Guo, G.: Visually interpretable representation learning for depression recognition from facial images. IEEE Trans. Affect. Comput. **11**(3), 542–552 (2018)
27. Valstar, M., et al.: AVEC 2014: 3D dimensional affect and depression recognition challenge. In: Proceedings of the 4th ACM International Workshop on Audio/Visual Emotion Challenge (AVEC 2014) (2014)
28. Alghowinem, S., Göcke, R., Wagner, M., Epps, J., Breakspear, M., Parker, G.: From joyous to clinically depressed: mood detection using spontaneous speech. In: Twenty-Fifth International FLAIRS Conference, pp. 141–146 (2012)
29. Qureshi, S.A., Saha, S., Hasanuzzaman, M., Dias, G., Cambria, E.: Multitask representation learning for multimodal estimation of depression level. IEEE Intell. Syst. **34**(5), 45–52 (2019)
30. Stepanov, E.A., et al.: Depression severity estimation from multiple modalities. In: 2018 IEEE 20th International Conference on e-Health Networking, Applications and Services (Healthcom), pp. 1–6. IEEE (2018)
31. Alghowinem, S., Goecke, R., Cohn, J.F., Wagner, M., Parker, G., Breakspear, M.: Cross-cultural detection of depression from nonverbal behaviour. In: 2015 11th IEEE International Conference and Workshops on Automatic Face and Gesture Recognition, FG 2015. Institute of Electrical and Electronics Engineers Inc. (2015)
32. Schuller, B., et al.: Cross-corpus acoustic emotion recognition: variances and strategies. IEEE Trans. Affect. Comput. **1**(2), 119–131 (2010)
33. AVEC2019-Challenge guidelines. https://sites.google.com/view/avec2019/home/challenge-guidelines

34. Rush, A., et al.: The 16-item quick inventory of depressive symptomatology (QIDS), clinician rating (QIDS-C), and self-report (QIDS-SR): a psychometric evaluation in patients with chronic major depression. Biol. Psychiatry **54**(5), 573–583 (2003)
35. Beck, A.T.: Beck depression inventory. In: Depression, vol. 2006, pp. 2–4 (1961)
36. Krizhevsky, A., Sutskever, I., Hinton, G.E.: ImageNet classification with deep convolutional neural networks. In: Advances in Neural Information Processing Systems 25 (NIPS 2012), pp. 1–9 (2012)
37. Simonyan, K., Zisserman, A.: Very deep convolutional networks for large-scale image recognition. In: 3rd International Conference on Learning Representations, ICLR 2015 - Conference Track Proceedings. International Conference on Learning Representations, ICLR (2015)
38. He, K., Zhang, X., Ren, S., Sun, J.: Deep residual learning for image recognition. In: Proceedings of the IEEE Computer Society Conference on Computer Vision and Pattern Recognition, vol. 2016-December, pp. 770–778. IEEE Computer Society (2016)
39. Huang, G., Liu, Z., Van Der Maaten, L., Weinberger, K.Q.: Densely connected convolutional networks. Technical report (2017)
40. Alghowinem, S., et al.: Multimodal depression detection: fusion analysis of paralinguistic, head pose and eye gaze behaviors. IEEE Trans. Affect. Comput. **9**, 1–14 (2016)
41. Pampouchidou, A., et al.: Video-based depression detection using local Curvelet binary patterns in pairwise orthogonal planes. In: Proceedings of the Annual International Conference of the IEEE Engineering in Medicine and Biology Society, EMBS, pp. 3835–3838. Institute of Electrical and Electronics Engineers Inc. (2016)
42. Selvaraju, R.R., Cogswell, M., Das, A., Vedantam, R., Parikh, D., Batra, D.: Grad-CAM: visual explanations from deep networks via gradient-based localization. In: 2017 IEEE International Conference on Computer Vision (ICCV), pp. 618–626. IEEE (2017)

# Range-Doppler Hand Gesture Recognition Using Deep Residual-3DCNN with Transformer Network

Gaurav Jaswal[1](✉)(iD), Seshan Srirangarajan[1,2](iD), and Sumantra Dutta Roy[2](iD)

[1] Department of Electrical Engineering, Indian Institute of Technology Delhi,
New Delhi 110016, India
{gauravjaswal,seshan}@ee.iitd.ac.in
[2] Bharti School of Telecommunication Technology and Management,
Indian Institute of Technology Delhi, New Delhi 110016, India
sumantra@ee.iitd.ac.in

**Abstract.** Recently hand gesture recognition via millimeter-wave radar has attracted a lot of research attention for human-computer interaction. Encouraged by the ability of deep learning models in successfully tackling hand gesture recognition tasks, we propose a deep neural network (DNN) model namely, Res3DTENet that aims to classify dynamic hand gestures using the radio frequency (RF) signals. We propose a scheme that improves the convolutional process of 3DCNNs with residual skip connection (Res3D) to emphasize local-global information and enriches the intra-frame spatio-temporal feature representation. A multi-head attention transformer encoder (TE) network has been trained over the spatio-temporal features to refine the inter-frame temporal dependencies of range-Doppler sequences. The experiments are carried out on the publicly available Soli hand gesture data set. Based on our extensive experiments, we show that the proposed network achieves improved gesture recognition accuracy than the state-of-the-art hand gesture recognition methods.

**Keywords:** Range-Doppler · Residual learning · Transformer network

## 1 Introduction

With the increasing prevalence of personal handheld devices in our daily lives, there has been a growing interest in the area of human-computer interaction (HCI) [1,12]. Recently, millimeter wave radar and other similar sensors are being explored for human-computer interaction applications [3]. The evolution of computing power and miniaturization of the hardware has led researchers to explore new ways of interacting with the electronic devices [6]. The use of millimeter wave (mmWave) radar technology for gesture sensing is a step in this direction. Traditionally, radar systems have been used to locate, track, and create two or three-dimensional reconstructions of objects such as airplanes, rockets, and missiles. Real aperture radar (RAR) and synthetic aperture radar (SAR) are

© Springer Nature Switzerland AG 2021
A. Del Bimbo et al. (Eds.): ICPR 2020 Workshops, LNCS 12666, pp. 759–772, 2021.
https://doi.org/10.1007/978-3-030-68780-9_57

examples of the radar being used as image sensing modalities [3]. Radar-based hand gesture recognition systems need to address the following challenges before they can become popular: (i) identifying micro-motion gesture features through a machine learning (ML) model usually requires large labeled data set to avoid over-fitting. However, the acquisition of unobtrusive and low-effort gestures irrespective of diversity is difficult and time-consuming, and (ii) the Doppler signature for hand motion is often also influenced by the motion of other body parts, which leads to distorted motion features, resulting in low recognition accuracy.

Recently, a mmWave solid-state Soli radar technology was reported [6] and its capability in recognizing hand gestures was demonstrated. This was a breakthrough in using mmWave radar as a sensing device for HCI applications and is attractive for several reasons. Firstly, radar can overcome some of the limitations of optical and depth camera systems. Though these cameras have shown good results in recognizing sign and action gestures, these sensing modalities show poor performance when dealing with occluded objects. Hand gestures need to be performed in line of sight (LoS) for these optical systems. The optical camera needs to be placed/fixed in the front panel of the devices and should be visible to the user. This can become a constraint when the form factor of the devices becomes small such as wristwatches. mmWave radar overcomes these drawbacks as it uses radio waves to interact with and recognize the objects. The use of sound waves to recognize hand gestures has also been explored but these methods have been capable of recognized only a limited set of hand gestures. In [10], RF sensing has been used to recognize 11 different hand gestures. It allows the RF sensor to be positioned anywhere within the device and the sensor forms a beam pattern within its range so that the user can perform hand gestures even without being in LoS with the sensor. These sensors have potential to be used in many consumer applications and thus there is a need to work on radar-based sensing to build classifier systems that can recognize hand gestures accurately and efficiently.

## 1.1   Problem Statement and Contribution

We tackle the challenge of developing a high performance hand gesture recognition system using a small training data set. The existing DNN frameworks fail to fully exploit the available spatio-temporal information w.r.t. hand position and direction in the gesture sequences. This manifests in the form of two problems: (ii) ambiguity: when different gestures are confused as one, and (ii) variability: when the same gesture performed under different conditions gets classified as different gestures. In addition, the sequential networks such as RNN/LSTM have limited ability to learn temporal dynamics of multi-channel range-Doppler sequences and result in high computations during the training and testing phases. In this article we address the above challenges by proposing a robust gesture recognition solution which is invariant to the subject, hand position and direction, and is capable of learning the inherent range-Doppler spatio-temporal features.

**Our Contribution:** Motivated by the success of deep residual learning and recent developments in transformer networks, we propose a 3D residual transformer encoder network (Res3DTENet) which is an end-to-end trainable network for classification of hand gestures using the range-Doppler sequences. In this article, we consider a radar gesture sequence as input to a Res-3DCNN with dense skip connections for allowing the flow of spatial information to the deeper layers. We train the transformer encoder (TE) to learn the positional transitions of input embedding across the temporal dimension. Compared to the traditional RNN [10] or LSTM [5,15], the proposed architecture will be shown to be better at capturing the dynamic long-range temporal dependencies in the input-output sequences while speeding up the training time. Experimental results based on the Soli data set [10] demonstrate that the proposed network has a strong generalization ability for classifying micro hand gestures.

## 2  Literature Survey

Various radar-based gesture recognition techniques using Doppler radar [2], FMCW radar [14], and ultra wideband radar [7] have been studied. In addition, ultrasound, RFID, and Wi-Fi based gesture sensing technologies have been explored, however these are significantly affected by the propagation speed, diffraction of sound, or other interference in the environment. In contrast, mmWave radar [12] based gesture recognition solutions have the advantage of a small form factor, sensing through smoke, dust, non-metallic materials, and can provide good range resolution. Soli [6] is among the first mmWave radar solutions for gesture based applications on consumer electronic devices. Various gesture recognition methods based on the mmWave radar have been proposed with the gesture features being extracted from range–Doppler images [5,10], range-Doppler sequences [2], micro-Doppler images [12], and range-time images [15]. In Soli [6], a mmWave radar hardware set-up and gesture acquisition pipeline were described. The authors collected a gesture set with four hand gestures and extracted low-dimensional features such as range, velocity, acceleration, velocity, centroids, and total energy, and used a random forest classifier for gesture recognition. In another work on Soli [10], a sequence of range-Doppler images is given as input to train a CNN-RNN network and the recognition capabilities were demonstrated over large a gesture data set with eleven hand gesture classes and a total of 2750 gesture sequences. Similarly in [4], range-Doppler image features are extracted to recognize hand gestures. The authors used CFAR algorithm to detect hand gestures, and then employed an LSTM network over the motion profile sequences for gesture recognition. In [8], continuous-wave radar at 2.4 GHz is employed and I-Q trajectory images are generated from the time-domain I and Q plots of the radar echos. Authors employed a CNN based approach using the I-Q images for recognizing the hand gestures and reported a recognition accuracy of 96%. In [13], a Doppler radar with dual receiver channels operating from 5-8 GHz is used and scalogram images are generated using time-frequency analysis tools (STFT and CWT). Finally, a CNN is trained to classify the hand gestures and a recognition accuracy of 98% has been reported. In [5], authors proposed a few-shot learning using 3DCNN which accepts video files of radar-Doppler image sequences as input and the model is trained using the triplet loss function for classifying the hand gestures. CNN ensures that the gestures have minimum intra-class variance and maximum inter-class variance. In [1], authors demonstrated gesture recognition using radar micro-Doppler signature envelopes. The authors collected a data set of 15 hand gestures and represent the gestures using PCA and canonical angle metric features. They also extract envelope features using the spectrograms and demonstrate hand gesture recognition using K-nearest neighbor (KNN) and support vector machine (SVM) algorithms. A summary of the state-of-the-art gesture recognition methods is listed in Table 1.

## 3   Network Architecture

We propose a novel deep learning framework consisting of two main modules in sequential order: Res3DCNN and TENet, as shown in Fig. 1. This end-to-end trainable network integrates residual learning and temporal relationship learning for fine-grained gesture recognition.

### 3.1   Residual 3DCNN (Res3D)

The motivation for incorporating residual learning in 3DCNN is to capture the contextual information and receptive fields. In addition, residual skip connections provide easy gradient flow through the network and addresses the problem of vanishing gradients effectively. CNN tends to lose the local feature representation of the range-Doppler sequences at deeper layers and only preserves the aggregated global features for classification. In order to discover more local-global salient spatial representation from the range-Doppler sequences, we introduce residual 3DCNN with dense skip connections for fine grained classification. The architecture of Res3D consists of two CNN blocks (B1, B2), where each block contains three consecutive 3D CNN layers with ReLU activation. The input ($\mathbf{I}$) provided to the network is of size $32 \times 32 \times 40 \times 4$ representing height, width, frames, and channels, respectively. In particular, the first 3D CNN layer (filter size $3 \times 3 \times 3$ and 16 filters) in block B1 is given I and produces a feature map $B1_1$ with size $32 \times 32 \times 40 \times 16$. Subsequently, the other two convolutional layers of the B1 block are applied and the output is $B1_2$. To incorporate residual learning, a skip connection from input to the second convolutional layer ($B1_1$) is followed by a concatenation with the feature map of the third 3DCNN layer ($B1_2$) resulting in the aggregated feature map $B1_R$. Consequently, a max pooling operation is applied over the aggregated feature map, which reduces the overall size of $B1_R$ to $16 \times 16 \times 40 \times 16$ and provides contextual features. However, the introduction of additional pooling layers may reduce the spatial information significantly and increase the number of parameters in Res3D. This will lead to false positives or errors during classification. The B2 block with three 3DCNN layers is employed in a similar manner as block B1, but with 32 filters for each CNN layer. The final

**Table 1.** Overview of state-of-the-art radar-based gesture recognition methods.

| Network model | Proposed framework | Sensor/Prototype | Data set | Training scheme and accuracy |
|---|---|---|---|---|
| CNN-LSTM [10] | Deployed deep learning framework including CNN and RNN models for dynamic hand gesture classification | FMCW mmWave radar (at 60 GHz) | 2750 gesture sequences with an average of 40 frames per sequence: 10 users, 11 gesture classes, 25 instances | 87% (50%–50%), 79.06% (leave one subject out), 85.75% (leave one session out) |
| 3DCNN-LSTM-CTC [6] | LSTM-CTC, fusion algorithm to classify spatio-temporal features of gesture sequences | Frequency modulated continuous wave (FMCW) radar (at 24 GHz) | 3200 sequences with duration of 3 s: 4 subjects, 8 gesture classes, 100 instances | 95% (3 s), 92.7% (2 s), 85.2% (1 s) |
| TS-I3D [11] | Range-time and Doppler-time feature sequences using I3D and two LSTM networks | FMCW radar with bandwidth of 4 GHz | 4000 sequences each with 32 frames: 10 gesture classes, 400 instances | 96.17% (TS-I3D), 94.72% (without IE), 93.05% (I3D-LSTM) |
| 3DCNN with triplet loss [5] | Feature embedding using 3DCNN in conjunction with triplet loss | FMCW radar (at 24 GHZ) | 9000 sequences each with 100 frames: 6 gesture classes, 10 subjects, 150 instances | 94.50% (triplet loss), 86.30% (cross entropy loss), 88.10% (2DCNN-LSTM) |
| Gesture-VLAD [2] | Frame level representation and frame aggregation for extracting temporal information | Soli sensor [6] | Soli data set [6] | 91.06% (frame-level), 98.24% (sequence-level) |
| Autoencoder [14] | Autoencoder network to learn micro hand motion representation | FMCW radar (at 24 GHz) | 3200 sequences each of duration 1.5 s: 4 subjects, 8 gesture classes, 100 instances | 95% (0.5 m), 87% (0.3 m), 76% (0.1 m) |

output feature map of Res3D is $F_{res}$ (with size $16 \times 16 \times 40 \times 32$), which is given to a transformer module for fine grained classification. Further, in order to visualize the activation layer feature map representation, we select the pull gesture class (G8) to explain the learning process. The original frames and the learned feature maps from Res3D are shown in Fig. 2. The detailed parametrization of Res3D is presented in Table 2.

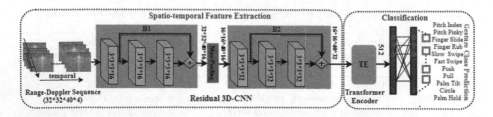

**Fig. 1.** Proposed network architecture for hand gesture classification.

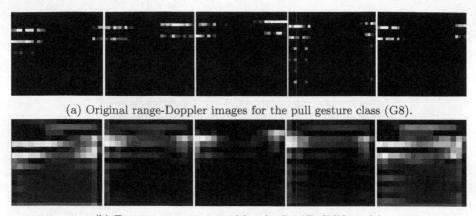

(a) Original range-Doppler images for the pull gesture class (G8).

(b) Feature maps extracted by the Res3D-CNN model.

**Fig. 2.** Input sequence and corresponding feature map visualization.

We can mathematically represent the Res3D model as:

$$\text{Res}(\mathbf{I}) = \boldsymbol{\Phi}\left(\mathbf{W}^3 \circledast \left(\boldsymbol{\Phi}\left(\mathbf{W}^2 \circledast \left(\boldsymbol{\Phi}\left(\mathbf{W}^1 \circledast \mathbf{I}\right)\right)\right)\right)\right) + \mathbf{I} \tag{1}$$

where $\mathbf{W}^1$, $\mathbf{W}^2$, and $\mathbf{W}^3$ are the weights of layers L1, L2, and L3, respectively.

### 3.2 Transformer Encoder Network (TENet)

Sequence modelling or time series tasks require us to exploit temporal features and when the task involves spatio-temporal data, such as in the case of gesture recognition, spatial as well as temporal features have to be extracted. To achieve this 3DCNN and RNN type architectures such as long short-term memory (LSTM) or gated recurrent unit (GRU) have been employed so far. Although, RNN type architectures are good at capturing long-term dependencies but as the sequence length increases they can suffer degradation in performance. Secondly, RNNs are slow to train as they lack parallelism due to their sequential information processing architecture. In order to address these problems of RNNs, transformer networks have been proposed recently.

**Table 2.** Architecture of the residual 3DCNN model.

| Layer name | Residual block | Kernel size | No. of filters | Output size |
|---|---|---|---|---|
| Res3D-CNN | | | | |
| Input | – | – | – | $32 \times 32 \times 40 \times 4$ |
| Conv1 | – | $3 \times 3 \times 3$ | 16 | $32 \times 32 \times 40 \times 16$ |
| Conv2 | R1 | $3 \times 3 \times 3$ | 16 | $32 \times 32 \times 40 \times 16$ |
| Conv3 | R1 | $3 \times 3 \times 3$ | 16 | $32 \times 32 \times 40 \times 16$ |
| Max-pooling | – | $2 \times 2 \times 1$ | – | $16 \times 16 \times 40 \times 16$ |
| Conv4 | – | $3 \times 3 \times 3$ | 32 | $16 \times 16 \times 40 \times 32$ |
| Conv5 | R2 | $3 \times 3 \times 3$ | 32 | $16 \times 16 \times 40 \times 32$ |
| Conv6 | R2 | $3 \times 3 \times 3$ | 32 | $16 \times 16 \times 40 \times 32$ |
| Output | – | – | – | $16 \times 16 \times 40 \times 32$ |

**Introduction:** Transformer networks are a recent architecture capable of addressing multiple downstream sequential tasks and work on the basis of the attention mechanism to capture very long-term dependencies [9]. When in operation, all the sequential inputs are processed in parallel instead of time-step based processing. The network architecture consists of mainly two units: encoder and decoder. As the name suggests, encoder based on the learnt attention, processes information whereas the decoder uses the knowledge passed by the encoder to generate outputs and it also employs attention for learning representations. The overall architecture involves passing the input through encoder which is a stack of multiple encoder blocks. Subsequently, the processed output is given to different decoder blocks stacked together forming the decoder layer.

**Implementation:** This network includes several multi-head attention modules along with fully connected layers. In our experiment, we have only considered the transformer's encoder module (TENet) while leaving out the decoder module. The details of this TENet are depicted in Fig. 3. The TENet consists of 3 blocks with each block having a multi-head attention layer along with a position-wise fully connected feed-forward network. In addition, the residual connection with layer normalization has been utilized in each block. Initially, the input $f_{Res3D}$ is provided to the first block of the transformer. However, before being given to this block, positional encoding is computed and added to the input $f_{Res3D}$. Positional embedding incorporates order of the sequence, and provides unique encoding for each time-step. During computation of the positional encoding, sinusoidal function has been utilized, where $\sin(ut)$ and $\cos(ut)$ have been used for even and odd positions of the input, respectively. In this manner, two consecutive encoder blocks are used resulting in a feature vector $E2_{out}$ which is then given to the linear layer followed by a soft max classifier for gesture classification.

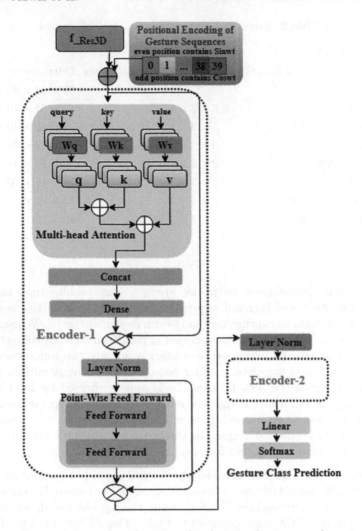

**Fig. 3.** Proposed network architecture for the transformer encoder network.

**Multi-head Attention:** This module contains several attention layers that run in parallel. In the attention layers, we define three input vectors query ($q$), keys ($k$), and values ($v$). Thus, the attention can be defined as:

$$\text{atten}(q, k, v) = \text{softmax}\left(\frac{qk^T}{\sqrt{m}}\right) v \tag{2}$$

We consider the dot product attention mechanism which is time-space efficient for our experiments. In our case, both query ($q$) and key ($k$) have the same dimension $m$ whereas values has a different dimension $n$. Taking the dot product of $q$ and $k$, followed by division by the square root of $m$, results in an $m$

dimension vector $A$. Subsequently, softmax function is applied on $A$ to obtain the attention vector with different weights for the different entries of $v$ with the output as $A_{\text{atten}}$. Finally, the vector $v$ is multiplied by $A_{\text{atten}}$ to obtain the feature vector atten. In the multi-head attention module, we have parallel attention layers, where each layer is given an independent subset of the full input. Suppose we have 10 parallel attention layers then each layer will accept input of dimension $\frac{m}{10}$. Finally, the output of each attention layer is concatenated to form an $m$-dimensional vector. Subsequently, feed forward network consisting of two consecutive fully connected layers is applied. This feed forward network would be used separately at each position of the input.

The network architecture employed here consists of only the encoder blocks. There are a total of 3 encoder layers, with each layer consisting of 4 attention heads. We have experimented with 2 and 6 heads as well and observed that 3 encoders each with 4 attention heads produce optimal results. The outputs of the encoder blocks are fed into a dense layer and finally to a softmax layer for final classification. We the cross entropy loss function and stochastic gradient descent as the optimizer. We also experimented with different learning rates and observed that a value of 0.001 gave the best performance.

# 4 Experiment and Discussion

In this section, we describe in detail our experiments and the results obtained using the Soli data set. The quantitative evaluation of the proposed network will be presented in terms of classification accuracy of the gestures. We consider the classification accuracy per class and report the average accuracy.

## 4.1 Data Set

The performance of the Res3DTENet model is tested on publicly available Soli data set[1]. It contains 2750 gesture sequences with 11 hand gestures performed by 10 users in the first phase and a second set of 2750 sequences are collected in a second phase. Each hand gesture is available as a sequence of processed range-Doppler images in the h5 format. The data set was collected using a FMCW mmWave radar with four receive channels (named as channels 0, 1, 2 and 3).

## 4.2 Training

To evaluate the performance of different networks, we trained the proposed network and its variants and employed the same testing conditions for all the models. We used a uniform learning rate of 0.001 throughout the training phase and the stochastic gradient descent optimizer with a momentum of 0.9. A dropout of 0.5 is applied in the transformer encoder layer to avoid overfitting. It is observed that the network loss decreases within the first few epochs and converges by 35

---

[1] https://github.com/simonwsw/deep-soli.

epochs when batch-wise learning (with size 16) is carried out. The training and validation loss curves are shown in Fig. 4. It can be observed that both training and validation errors decrease and converge after around 35 or 40 epochs. To understand the network training, we use the cross-entropy loss that measures the difference between two probability distributions. Finally, confusion matrices are computed to evaluate the classification accuracy of our proposed end-to-end architecture.

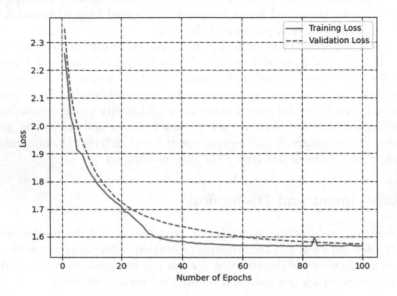

**Fig. 4.** Training and validation loss curves for the proposed gesture recognition network.

## 4.3   Evaluation Using 50:50 Training and Testing Split

The proposed Res3DTENet and its three variants 3DCNNTENet, TENet, and Res3D-LSTM are trained using a 50:50 training and testing split, and the network parameters are selected empirically. Assuming the average time duration of each gesture to be the same, the length of each sequence is set to 40 frames. Residual learning allows direct connections between alternate CNN layers that helps in training deep network more easily and leads to better generalization. Thus, Res3DTENet achieves an average classification accuracy of 96.99% with an improvement of 5.87% and 3.96% over the 3DCNNTENet and Res3DLSTM shown in Table 3. The confusion matrices for Res3DTENet and 3DCNNTENet are shown in Fig. 5 and Fig. 6, respectively. We also notice that the transformer networks (Res3DTENet, 3DCNNTENet) outperform the LSTM network (Res3DLSTM). However, the basic transformer architecture i.e., TENet (without CNN embedding) does not perform as well as the other DNN models. In this case, TENet receives the raw sequence as input and without a feature extractor

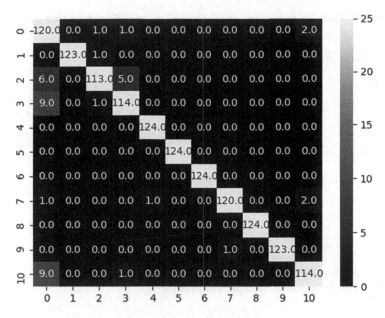

**Fig. 5.** Confusion matrix for the proposed Res3DTENet model based on a 50:50 training and testing strategy.

it is unable to find robust features for classification. In terms of the individual gesture classes, seven gesture classes namely, pinch index (G1), pinch pinky (G2), slow swipe (G5), fast swipe (G6), push (G7), pull (G8), palm tilt (G9), and circle (G10) are recognized with more than 95% accuracy using the proposed network. On the other hand, using 3DCNNTENet, finger slide (G3) and finger rub (G4) have the lowest average recognition accuracy of 77.42% and 78.22%, respectively. However, Res3DTENet improves the recognition performance for finger slide (G3) and finger rub (G4). This result can be interpreted by the fact that finger slide and finger rub are associated with small motions. Finally, we can summarize that the introduction of transformer network in hand gesture recognition leads to better performance compared to the LSTM network.

## 4.4   Evaluation Using Cross Validation

Next "leave one subject out" cross validation is performed using the proposed Res3DTENet architecture. The Soli data set consists of 2750 gesture sequences obtained from ten subjects. The accuracy results are reported in Table 3. Data for one gesture class is randomly removed and the network is trained by using the rest of the data set. This process is repeated for all the subjects. Finally, the average classification accuracy of 92.25% is achieved using the proposed network which is lower compared to the accuracy obtained using the 50:50 split of the data. In terms of class-wise performance for the different gesture classes,

**Table 3.** Classification accuracies obtained using different testing protocols.

| Network | Avg. | G1 | G2 | G3 | G4 | G5 | G6 | G7 | G8 | G9 | G10 | G11 |
|---|---|---|---|---|---|---|---|---|---|---|---|---|
| Accuracy based on 50:50 training and testing split of the data | | | | | | | | | | | | |
| Res3DTENet | 96.99 | 96.77 | 99.19 | 91.13 | 91.94 | 100 | 100 | 100 | 96.77 | 100 | 99.19 | 91.94 |
| 3DCNNTENet | 93.03 | 93.55 | 100 | 77.42 | 78.23 | 91.94 | 100 | 100 | 91.13 | 100 | 99.19 | 91.94 |
| TENet | 78.92 | 62.22 | 64.88 | 45.07 | 89.30 | 67.20 | 94.62 | 94.89 | 87.34 | 92.50 | 85.78 | 84.39 |
| Res3D-LSTM | 91.12 | 87.90 | 96.77 | 83.87 | 83.06 | 87.10 | 95.16 | 88.71 | 91.13 | 97.58 | 91.94 | 99.19 |
| Soli (CNN-LSTM) [6] | 87.17 | 67.72 | 71.09 | 77.78 | 94.48 | 84.84 | 98.45 | 98.63 | 88.89 | 94.85 | 89.56 | 92.63 |
| Soli (RNN-shallow) [6] | 77.71 | 60.35 | 62.25 | 38.72 | 89.45 | 66.77 | 92.52 | 94.93 | 86.89 | 91.39 | 85.52 | 86.22 |
| GVLAD (without CG) [2] | 96.77 | 97.58 | 100 | 98.38 | 83.06 | 100 | 100 | 99.19 | 99.19 | 96.77 | 98.38 | 91.93 |
| GVLAD [2] | 98.24 | 91.12 | 99.19 | 99.19 | 95.96 | 100 | 100 | 100 | 100 | 100 | 100 | 95.16 |
| Accuracy using leave one subject out: cross Subject Validation on 10 subjects | | | | | | | | | | | | |
| Res3DTENet | 92.25 | 89.12 | 93.34 | 92.20 | 83.43 | 84.66 | 93.50 | 97.68 | 100 | 95.78 | 93.22 | 91.84 |
| Soli [6] | 79.06 | 58.71 | 67.62 | 64.80 | 91.82 | 72.31 | 72.91 | 93.40 | 89.99 | 95.16 | 82.80 | 80.24 |
| GVLAD [2] | 91.38 | 84.80 | 98.40 | 88.00 | 78.40 | 87.60 | 99.20 | 90.00 | 99.20 | 96.40 | 93.99 | 89.20 |

the micro-motion gestures such as pinch index (G1), finger rub (G4), and slow swipe (G5) result in lower recognition accuracy.

## 4.5  Performance Analysis

We also compare the results using the proposed architecture with the results reported in [10] and [2] as they use the same set of gestures and evaluation metrics. We consider two testing strategies: (i) 50:50 split of the data, and (ii) leave one subject out cross validation. Table 3 presents results in terms of average as well as individual classification accuracies for the different networks. It is observed that the proposed network outperforms the state-of-art CNN-LSTM [10] and GVLAD (without context gating) [2] models in terms of improved classification accuracy using a 50:50 split of the data. For the leave one subject out strategy, performance of the proposed network is comparable to both the CNN-LSTM [6] and GVLAD [2] networks. Since these employ 2D and 3D convolution, respectively, for extracting the features their networks are deeper but convergence rates are poor. Based on 3DCNN, the proposed network uses residual learning in 3D convolution followed by the transformer network in order to extract the long range spatial-temporal dependencies between frames in the gesture sequences. Therefore, the classification accuracy as well as the convergence of our network is better. This justifies the combination of Res3DCNN and transformer network for capturing more discriminative spatial-temporal features for gesture recognition. We also notice that the TENet results in better average classification accuracy than the RNN-Shallow network [6].

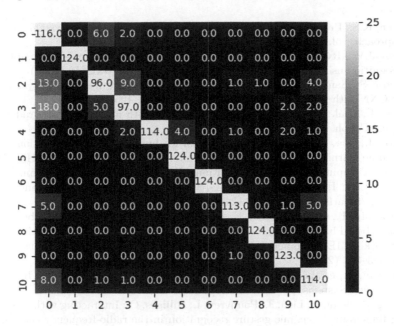

**Fig. 6.** Confusion matrix for the proposed 3DCNNTENet based on a 50:50 training and testing strategy.

# 5 Conclusion

In this paper, we presented a residual 3D-CNN transformer network (Res3DTENet) for gesture recognition. We validated the performance of the proposed network on publicly available Soli hand gesture data set. The proposed network performs better than the state-of-the-art networks presented in [6] and [2] as well as three variants of the network. The proposed model achieved gesture recognition accuracy of 96.99% and 92.25% based on a 50:50 data set split and cross validation strategies, respectively. In the future, we will explore unseen gesture data and diversity of subjects for evaluating performance of the proposed network.

**Acknowledgement.** This research was partially supported by the Semiconductor Research Corporation (SRC) Grant 2019-IR-2924.

# References

1. Amin, M.G., Zeng, Z., Shan, T.: Hand gesture recognition based on radar micro-doppler signature envelopes. In: IEEE Radar Conference (RadarConf), pp. 1–6 (2019)
2. Berenguer, A.D., Oveneke, M.C., Alioscha-Perez, M., Bourdoux, A., Sahli, H., et al.: Gesturevlad: combining unsupervised features representation and spatio-temporal aggregation for doppler-radar gesture recognition. IEEE Access **7**, 137122–137135 (2019)

3. Chen, K.S.: Principles of Synthetic Aperture Radar Imaging: A System Simulation Approach, vol. 2. CRC Press, Boca Raton (2016)
4. Choi, J.W., Ryu, S.J., Kim, J.H.: Short-range radar based real-time hand gesture recognition using LSTM encoder. IEEE Access **7**, 33610–33618 (2019)
5. Hazra, S., Santra, A.: Short-range radar-based gesture recognition system using 3D CNN with triplet loss. IEEE Access **7**, 125623–125633 (2019)
6. Lien, J., et al.: Soli: ubiquitous gesture sensing with millimeter wave radar. ACM Trans. Graph. (TOG) **35**, 1–19 (2016)
7. Park, J., Cho, S.H.: IR-UWB radar sensor for human gesture recognition by using machine learning. In: 2016 IEEE 18th International Conference on High Performance Computing and Communications; IEEE 14th International Conference on Smart City; IEEE 2nd International Conference on Data Science and Systems (HPCC/SmartCity/DSS), pp. 1246–1249. IEEE (2016)
8. Sakamoto, T., Gao, X., Yavari, E., Rahman, A., Boric-Lubecke, O., Lubecke, V.M.: Radar-based hand gesture recognition using IQ echo plot and convolutional neural network. In: IEEE Conference on Antenna Measurements & Applications (CAMA), pp. 393–397 (2017)
9. Vaswani, A., et al.: Attention is all you need. In: Advances in Neural Information Processing Systems, pp. 5998–6008 (2017)
10. Wang, S., Song, J., Lien, J., Poupyrev, I., Hilliges, O.: Interacting with soli: exploring fine-grained dynamic gesture recognition in the radio-frequency spectrum. In: Proceedings of the 29th Annual Symposium on User Interface Software and Technology (UIST), pp. 851–860 (2016)
11. Wang, Y., Wang, S., Zhou, M., Jiang, Q., Tian, Z.: TS-I3D based hand gesture recognition method with radar sensor. IEEE Access **7**, 22902–22913 (2019)
12. Xia, Z., Luomei, Y., Zhou, C., Xu, F.: Multidimensional feature representation and learning for robust hand-gesture recognition on commercial millimeter-wave radar. IEEE Trans. Geosci. Remote Sens. 1–16 (2020). https://doi.org/10.1109/TGRS.2020.3010880
13. Zhang, J., Tao, J., Shi, Z.: Doppler-radar based hand gesture recognition system using convolutional neural networks. In: International Conference in Communications, Signal Processing, and Systems, pp. 1096–1113 (2017)
14. Zhang, Z., Tian, Z., Zhang, Y., Zhou, M., Wang, B.: u-DeepHand: FMCW radar-based unsupervised hand gesture feature learning using deep convolutional autoencoder network. IEEE Sens. J. **19**(16), 6811–6821 (2019)
15. Zhang, Z., Tian, Z., Zhou, M.: Latern: dynamic continuous hand gesture recognition using FMCW radar sensor. IEEE Sens. J. **18**(8), 3278–3289 (2018)

# Introducing Bidirectional Ordinal Classifier Cascades Based on a Pain Intensity Recognition Scenario

Peter Bellmann[1]([✉]), Ludwig Lausser[2], Hans A. Kestler[2][iD],
and Friedhelm Schwenker[1][iD]

[1] Institute of Neural Information Processing, Ulm University,
James-Franck-Ring, 89081 Ulm, Germany
{peter.bellmann,friedhelm.schwenker}@uni-ulm.de
[2] Institute of Medical Systems Biology, Ulm University,
Albert-Einstein-Allee 11, 89081 Ulm, Germany
{ludwig.lausser,hans.kestler}@uni-ulm.de

**Abstract.** Ordinal classifier cascades (OCCs) are popular machine learning tools in the area of ordinal classification. OCCs constitute specific classification ensemble schemes that work in sequential manner. Each of the ensemble's members either provides the architecture's final prediction, or moves the current input to the next ensemble member. In the current study, we first confirm the fact that the direction of OCCs can have a high impact on the distribution of its predictions. Subsequently, we introduce and analyse our proposed bidirectional combination of OCCs. More precisely, based on a person-independent pain intensity scenario, we provide an ablation study, including the evaluation of different OCCs, as well as different popular error correcting output codes (ECOC) models. The provided outcomes show that our proposed straightforward approach significantly outperforms common OCCs, with respect to the accuracy and mean absolute error performance measures. Moreover, our results indicate that, while our proposed bidirectional OCCs are less complex in general, they are able to compete with and even outperform most of the analysed ECOC models.

**Keywords:** Ordinal classifier cascades · Ordinal classification · Pain intensity recognition · Physiological signals

## 1  Introduction

For various reasons, such as a generally improved generalisation ability, it is common to apply different ensemble-based methods in combination with multi-class, and even binary, classification tasks [15,24]. Ordinal classification (OC) and regression represent a specific niche of multi-class classification [14]. In OC tasks, it is assumed that the class labels constitute an ordinal class structure. In the literature, different OC-specific classification approaches were proposed

© Springer Nature Switzerland AG 2021
A. Del Bimbo et al. (Eds.): ICPR 2020 Workshops, LNCS 12666, pp. 773–787, 2021.
https://doi.org/10.1007/978-3-030-68780-9_58

to explicitly exploit and hence to benefit from the underlying class structures [7,9,10]. Ordinal classifier cascades [16] constitute a simple, yet effective approach that benefits from ordinal class structures. In the current study, we propose a straightforward extension of existing ordinal classifier cascade architectures, which we denote as *bidirectional ordinal classifier cascades*.

For the evaluation of our proposed approach, we provide an ablation study on ordinal classifier cascade architectures, in comparison to the popular *error correcting output codes* models [11], which follow the divide-and-conquer principle [2,28]. To this end, we evaluate a person-independent pain intensity recognition scenario based on the publicly available BioVid Heat Pain Database [33]. In that particular multi-class task, we can assume the following natural order of the class labels, i.e. *no pain ≺ low pain ≺ intermediate pain levels ≺ unbearable pain*.

The remainder of this work is organised as follows. In Sect. 2, we discuss different ensemble techniques from the divide-and-conquer category, focusing on error correcting output codes, as well as ordinal classifier cascades. Subsequently, in Sect. 3, we introduce our proposed bidirectional ordinal classifier cascade architectures. In Sect. 4, we briefly describe the publicly available BioVid Heat Pain Database, which constitutes the focus of our conducted ablation study. Finally, the outcomes of our experiments are presented and discussed in detail, in Sect. 5.

## 2   Formalisation and Related Work

One popular approach to multi-class classification is the application of divide-and-conquer techniques. Instead of explicitly solving a multi-class classification task, the whole task is divided into different subtasks — binary, in general — which are solved independently. Subsequently, the obtained partial solutions are combined to get the final output of the classification ensemble. One widely used group of divide-and-conquer techniques consists of the *error correcting output codes* [11]. Moreover, if the classes of the current multi-class classification task constitute an ordinal structure, one can implement some of the existing *ordinal classifier cascades* [16]. In the following, we briefly explain both approaches, error correcting output codes, as well as ordinal classifier cascade architectures.

### 2.1   Formalisation

Let $X \subset \mathbb{R}^d$, $d \in \mathbb{N}$, be a $d$-dimensional data set. Further, let $\Omega = \{\omega_1, \ldots, \omega_c\}$, with $c \in \mathbb{N}$, and $c \geq 3$, be the set of class labels of the corresponding multi-class classification task. By $l(x)$, we denote the true label of data point $x \in X$. Moreover, by $\mathrm{CM}_{i,j}$, we denote the classification model (CM) that is trained to separate the classes $\omega_i$ and $\omega_j$. More precisely, classification model $\mathrm{CM}_{i,j}$ is trained in combination with the subset $X_{i,j} \subset X$, with

$$X_{i,j} := \{x \in X \mid l(x) = \omega_i \vee l(x) = \omega_j\}.$$

Note that in the current study, we focus on *symmetric* classification models, i.e. for all $i, j \in \{1, \ldots, c\}$ it holds, $\mathrm{CM}_{i,j} = \mathrm{CM}_{j,i}$.

## 2.2  Error Correcting Output Codes

In the following, we recap three popular error correcting output codes (ECOC) approaches, where each ensemble member's output is mapped to the set $\{0, 1\}$.

**One Versus All (1vsA).** In the 1vsA approach, one has to train $c$ binary classification models. Each of the models is specialised to separate one specific class from all remaining classes. More precisely, classification model 1 is designed to solve the binary task $\omega_1$ *vs.* $\{\omega_2, \ldots, \omega_c\}$, CM 2 is designed to solve the binary task $\omega_2$ *vs.* $\Omega \setminus \{\omega_2\}$, et cetera. Finally, CM $c$ is designed to solve the binary task $\omega_c$ *vs.* $\{\omega_1, \ldots, \omega_{c-1}\}$. Each of the corresponding classification subtasks is imbalanced, in general.

**One Versus One (1vs1).** In the 1vs1 approach, one has to train $c(c-1)/2$ binary classification models. Each of the models is specialised to separate one single class from exactly one of the remaining classes. The factor $c(c-1)/2$ corresponds to the number of all possible class pairs. For instance, CM 1 is designed to solve the binary subtask $\omega_1$ *vs.* $\omega_2$, CM 2 to solve the subtask $\omega_1$ *vs.* $\omega_3$, et cetera. Finally, CM $c(c-1)/2$ is designed to solve the subtask $\omega_{c-1}$ *vs.* $\omega_c$. Each of the corresponding classification subtasks is balanced, if the initial multi-class task is balanced.

**All Binary Combinations (ABC).** In the ABC approach, one has to train $2^{c-1} - 1$ binary classification models. Each of the models is specialised to separate a specific subset of the initial classes from all remaining classes. The factor $2^{c-1} - 1$ corresponds to the number of all possible combinations of different binary subtasks that include all of the initial classes. For instance, the *ABC* approach includes all classification models from the 1vsA approach. However, it does not include any of the classification models from the 1vs1 approach, since only two classes, instead of all available classes, are considered in the 1vs1 approach by each classification model. Most of the corresponding classification subtasks are imbalanced, in general.

One can also define custom subtasks for each of the ECOC classification models. For instance, in [12,13], Escalera et al. introduce *ternary* ECOC models.

## 2.3  Ordinal Classifier Cascade Architectures

Ordinal classifier cascade (OCC) architectures consist of a sequence of classification models that are trained in combination with different subtasks of the initial multi-class classification task. Each OCC member provides one of two possible outputs. In the first case, the current classification model's output is taken as the final prediction of the whole cascaded architecture. In the second case, the classification model's output implies that the next OCC member has to process the current input sample. Note that the output of the last OCC member is always taken as the architecture's final decision.

Let $\Omega = \{\omega_1, \dots, \omega_c\}$ constitute an ordered class label set, with $\omega_1 \prec \dots \prec \omega_c$. We denote the corresponding class labels, $\omega_1$ and $\omega_c$, as *edge classes* or simply *edges*. There exist three main categories of OCCs, i.e. the *lower vs. higher*, *current vs. rest*, as well as the *pairwise* approach [20]. However, the order of class labels, $\omega_1 \prec \dots \prec \omega_c$, is equivalent to its reversed order, $\omega_c \prec \dots \prec \omega_1$. Therefore, for each of the aforementioned categories, there exist two options for the design of an OCC. One can start the sequence of classification models based on one of the two edge classes. In the current study, we will include an analysis on the effects of the starting direction. Hence, we complement the lower vs. higher approach by the *higher vs. lower* approach. Moreover, we split the current vs. rest approach into the *current vs. higher* and *current vs. lower* approaches. Similarly, we split the pairwise approach into the *current vs. next* and *current vs. previous* approaches.

**Lower vs. Higher and Higher vs. Lower.** In the lower vs. higher approach, the first classification model in the sequence is trained to separate the class $\omega_1$ from the classes $\{\omega_2, \dots, \omega_c\}$. The second classification model is trained to separate the classes $\{\omega_1, \omega_2\}$ from the classes $\{\omega_3, \dots, \omega_c\}$, et cetera. In the higher vs. lower approach, the first classification model in the sequence is trained to separate the class $\omega_c$ from the classes $\{\omega_{c-1}, \dots, \omega_1\}$. The second classification model is trained to separate the classes $\{\omega_c, \omega_{c-1}\}$ from the classes $\{\omega_{c-2}, \dots, \omega_1\}$, et cetera.

**Current vs. Higher and Current vs. Lower.** In the current vs. higher approach, the first classification model is trained in combination with the same classes, as in the lower vs. higher approach. However, the second classification model in the sequence is trained to separate the class $\omega_2$ from the classes $\{\omega_3, \dots, \omega_c\}$, et cetera. In the current vs. lower approach, the first classification model is trained in combination with the same classes, as in the higher vs. lower approach. However, the second classification model in the sequence is trained to separate the class $\omega_{c-1}$ from the classes $\{\omega_{c-2}, \dots, \omega_1\}$, et cetera.

**Current vs. Next (CvsN) and Current vs. Previous (CvsP).** In the current vs. next approach, the first classification model in the sequence is trained to separate the class $\omega_1$ from the class $\omega_2$. The second classification model is trained to separate the class $\omega_2$ from the class $\omega_3$, et cetera. In the current vs. previous approach, the first classification model in the sequence is trained to separate the class $\omega_c$ from the class $\omega_{c-1}$. The second classification model is trained to separate the class $\omega_{c-1}$ from the class $\omega_{c-2}$, et cetera. Both architectures are depicted in Fig. 1. Note that both architectures consist of the same set of CMs since we assume symmetric classification models (see Sect. 2.1).

In general, the lower vs. higher and higher vs. lower, as well as the current vs. higher and current vs. lower approaches consist of imbalanced classification subtasks, which rely on additional balancing techniques, e.g. [4,8], to obtain a *satisfying* classification performance of the corresponding classification architecture. Therefore, to avoid additional complexity, in this study, we focus on the pairwise, balanced OCCs, i.e. CvsN and CvsP. For recent approaches on the detection of ordinal class structures, we refer the reader to [5,21,22].

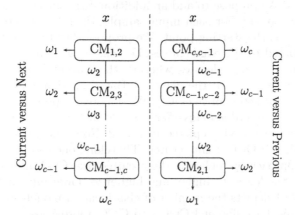

**Fig. 1. Cascaded classification architectures.** Left: Current vs. Next (CvsN). Right: Current vs. Previous (CvsP). $x$: Input. $c$: Number of classes. $\omega_1, \ldots, \omega_c$: Class labels. $CM_{i,j}$: Classification model that separates the classes $\omega_i$ and $\omega_j$. Arrowheads indicate that the corresponding output is taken as the architecture's final prediction.

## 2.4   Differences Between OCC Architectures and ECOC Models

Both methods, OCC as well as ECOC, follow the divide-and-conquer principle. However, in contrast to ECOC models, OCC architectures explicitly exploit the class structure of an ordinal classification task. This leads to the following main differences between both approaches. First, OCCs are part of so-called *classifier selection* techniques [19]. Only one of the classification models' outputs is used as the architecture's final prediction. Each classification model either provides the predicted class of the whole architecture or decides that the next classifier in the pipeline has to process the current input. In contrast, in ECOC approaches, the outputs of all classification models are combined, in order to make the ensemble's final decision. Therefore, additional distance computations between the models' concatenated outputs and each class label's *code* are needed, in combination with ECOC approaches. Second, another main difference between both approaches is the number of designed classification models, which depends on the number of classes $c$, in the initial multi-class classification task. For all $c \geq 3$, OCC approaches need less classification models than any of the ECOC models discussed above. Note that we will provide more details on the number of classification models in Sect. 3. Thus, with respect to the additional distance computations and the higher amount of classification models, ECOC models are expected to be *more complex* in comparison to OCCs, in general.

## 3    Bidirectional OCC Architectures

In the current section, we introduce the idea of combining ordinal classifier cascade architectures. As discussed in Sect. 2, there exist two options to design an OCC, i.e. by starting the cascaded classification architecture with either of the two edge classes. We propose to add an additional classification model that acts as a *selector component*. For each input sample, the selector chooses one of the two edge classes as the starting point. We propose that the additional classifier is trained restricted to the edge classes, i.e. classes $\omega_1$ and $\omega_c$ ($CM_{1,c}$). Therefore, the output of $CM_{1,c}$ decides whether the current input sample is more similar to the class $\omega_1$ or to the class $\omega_c$. Based on that information, we can choose the *proper direction* of the OCC. We denote our proposed combination of OCCs as *bidirectional ordinal classifier cascade* (bOCC) architectures. Our proposed bOCC architecture is depicted in Fig. 2. Note that in the current study, we focus on pairwise OCC architectures. Therefore, one can generalise our proposed bOCC approach by replacing the architectures CvsN and CvsP in Fig. 2, for instance, by the lower vs. higher and higher vs. lower pipelines (see Sect. 2). Moreover, Table 1 depicts the number of classification models in relation to the number of classes, for different ECOC and OCC approaches.

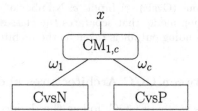

**Fig. 2. Bidirectional ordinal classifier cascade architecture.** $x$: Input. $c$: Number of classes. $CM_{1,c}$: Classification model that separates the edge classes $\omega_1$ and $\omega_c$. CvsN/CvsP: Current vs. Next/Current vs. Previous architectures (see Fig. 1).

**Table 1. Number of classes vs. number of classifiers.** ABC: All binary combinations. 1vs1: One versus one. 1vsA: One versus all. bOCC: Bidirectional ordinal classifier cascade architecture. CvsN/CvsP: Current vs. Next/Current vs. Previous. $c$: Number of classes.

| Method(s) | Number of classifiers |
|---|---|
| ABC | $2^{c-1} - 1$ |
| 1vs1 | $c(c-1)/2$ |
| 1vsA, bOCC | $c$ |
| CvsN, CvsP | $c - 1$ |

# 4 The BioVid Heat Pain Database

The BioVid Heat Pain Database[1] [33], which was collected at Ulm University, consists of five parts that constitute different emotion- and pain intensity recognition tasks. In the current study, we focus on the pain intensity recognition task represented by part A of the BioVid Heat Pain Database, which we simply denote by BVDB.

## 4.1 Data Set Description

A group of 87 test subjects was recruited to participate in heat pain elicitation experiments, under strictly controlled conditions. A professional thermode[2] was used to expose the participants to different levels of heat pain. The neutral level was set to 32 °C, denoted by $T_0$, for each test subject. In addition, four individually calibrated and equidistant pain levels, denoted by $T_1 < T_2 < T_3 < T_4$, were defined for each participant. To avoid skin burns, the maximum allowed temperature was limited to 50.5 °C, i.e. for each participant it holds, $T_4 \leq 50.5$ °C.

Each participant was exposed 20 times to each of the individually predefined pain levels, in randomised order. Each pain level was held for four second, always followed by the stimulation with the pain-free level $T_0$, with a random duration between eight and twelve seconds. Figure 3 depicts an exemplary pain stimulation sequence.

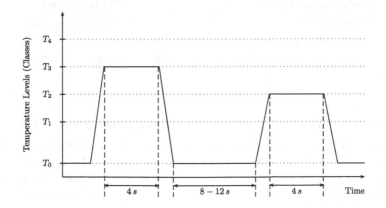

**Fig. 3.** An example for a participant's stimuli and recovering sequence.

## 4.2 Feature Extraction

In this work, we focus on the recorded biopotentials, i.e. electrocardiogram (ECG), electromyogram (EMG) and electrodermal activity (EDA) signals.

---

[1] Online available at http://www.iikt.ovgu.de/BioVid.print.

[2] More details at https://www.medoc-web.com/pathway.

We are using exactly the same features that were used in [17,18], by Kächele et al. Since the focus of this study is kept on our proposed bidirectional ordinal classifier cascade architectures, we refer the reader to [17] or [18], for details on the applied preprocessing steps, as well as on the computation of different features. Here, we solely provide a short overview to present a basic idea of the whole feature extraction procedure.

The physiological signals-based features were extracted from windows, with a length of 5.5 s, for each data sample. First, different signal detrending and smoothing techniques were applied to reduce artefacts and noise in the recorded signals. Subsequently, different statistical descriptors, such as the *mean, standard deviation, minimum,* and *maximum* values, were extracted from the temporal domain, amongst others. Additional features were extracted from the frequency domain, including the *mean, bandwidth* and *central frequency,* amongst others. In addition, after the feature extraction step, the feature set was normalised specific to each participant, according to the $z$-score with the values 0 and 1, for the mean and standard deviation, respectively. Table 2 summarises the properties of the BVDB, including the feature dimensions for all available physiological modalities, which are defined by 194 features, in total.

For recent analyses of different feature extraction window approaches, based on biopotentials, as well as video signals, we refer the reader to [25] and [29].

**Table 2. Properties of the BioVid Heat Pain Database.** Num. of samples: 8700.

| | |
|---|---|
| Number of participants | 87 (43 f, 44 m) |
| Number of classes | 5 $(T_0, T_1, T_2, T_3, T_4)$ |
| Number of samples per class and participant | 20 |
| Number of features (ECG + EDA + EMG) | 194 (68 + 70 + 56) |

### 4.3    Recent Surveys on Machine Learning-Based Pain Assessment

Note that, similar to any other kind of multi-modal classification tasks, one can leverage the pain intensity classification performance by applying different decision fusion approaches [27], based on the number of recorded modalities. Examples are the pseudo inverse-based fusion [26], or the recently proposed dominant channel fusion architectures [3]. For a recent survey on automated pain assessment, with focus on hand-crafted features, we refer the reader to [34].

Following the current trend of deep neural models, recent studies on automated pain assessment analyse the effectiveness of deep end-to-end architectures, as for instance in [30,31]. Deep end-to-end architectures are trained in combination with (filtered) raw data signals. For a recent survey on automated pain assessment, with focus on deep models, we refer the reader to [23].

Note that in one of our latest studies, we use the BVDB to estimate an upper bound for the recognition rate of pain intensities, in a simulated real-world scenario [6].

# 5    Results and Discussion

We start the current section by providing the evaluation protocol. As an initial evaluation, we analyse the effects of basic OCCs, with respect to the starting edges. Subsequently, we evaluate the outcomes specific to both of the imbalanced ECOC approaches, i.e. 1vsA and ABC. Then, we analyse the outcomes of the balanced 1vs1 ECOC model, as well as of our proposed bOCC approach. Finally, we compare our proposed architecture against all of the remaining methods, followed by a discussion of the obtained results.

## 5.1    Experimental Settings

Note that the current label set is defined as $\Omega = \{T_0, T_1, T_2, T_3, T_4\}$. To compute the *difference* between a model's final prediction for a test data point $z \in Z \subset \mathbb{R}^d$, CM$(z)$, and the true label of $z$, $l(z)$, we define the distance function $\Delta$, $\Delta : \Omega \times \Omega \to \{0, 1, 2, 3, 4\}$, as follows,

$$\Delta(T_i, T_j) := |i - j|, \quad \forall i, j \in \{0, 1, 2, 3, 4\}.$$

**Classification Models.** As subtask specific classifiers, for all approaches, i.e. all OCC and ECOC models, we implement support vector machines (SVMs) [1,32], with linear kernels. Note that we use the Matlab[3] software, in combination with the default parameter settings.

**Feature Fusion.** With respect to the extracted features, we focus on the early fusion approach. Thus, for each data sample, we concatenate the features specific to the three different modalities, ECG, EDA and EMG, to one feature vector.

**Cross Validation.** We apply the Leave-One-Person-Out (LOPO) cross validation. In each cross validation iteration, the data specific to one participant is used as the test set, whereas the data specific to all remaining participants is used as the training set.

**Performance Measures.** Since the BVDB constitutes an equally distributed multi-class classification task, we focus on the unweighted accuracy and the mean absolute error (MAE) as performance measures, i.e.

$$\text{MAE} := \frac{1}{|Z|} \sum_{z \in Z} \Delta(\text{CM}(z), l(z)),$$

$$\text{accuracy} := \frac{1}{|Z|} \sum_{z \in Z} \mathbb{I}\left(\text{CM}(z) = l(z)\right),$$

whereby $\mathbb{I}(\cdot)$ denotes the *indicator function*, i.e. the output of $\mathbb{I}$ is equal to 1 if CM$(z) = l(z)$, and 0 otherwise.

---

[3] www.mathworks.com.

**Significance Tests.** We apply the two-sided Wilcoxon signed-rank test [35], at a significance level of 5%, to test for statistically significant differences between our proposed bOCC method and all other approaches.

## 5.2    Evaluation of Classifier Cascades: The Direction Matters

Applying the LOPO cross validation led to the mean accuracy values of 34.54% and 34.69%, for the CvsN and the CvsP classification architectures, respectively. Obviously, the accuracy results are very similar. However, the two architectures lead to significantly different outcomes, which can be observed by analysing the corresponding confusion matrices. Table 3 depicts the confusion matrices for both classification architectures, i.e. for the CvsN and the CvsP approaches.

**Table 3. CvsN & CvsP**: Confusion tables with absolute values. Rows denote true labels. Columns denote predicted labels. $\Sigma$: Sum of predictions. Left: CvsN. Right: CvsP. The averaged LOPO cross validation accuracies are equal to 34.54% and 34.69%, for the CvsN and CvsP approaches, respectively. Bold figures denote the number of correctly classified test samples. Each class consists of 1740 test samples.

|  | Current vs. Next | | | | | Current vs. Previous | | | | |
|---|---|---|---|---|---|---|---|---|---|---|
|  | $T_0$ | $T_1$ | $T_2$ | $T_3$ | $T_4$ | $T_0$ | $T_1$ | $T_2$ | $T_3$ | $T_4$ |
| $T_0$ | **1035** | 418 | 182 | 72 | 33 | **573** | 312 | 401 | 319 | 135 |
| $T_1$ | 674 | **551** | 302 | 153 | 60 | 384 | **397** | 441 | 378 | 140 |
| $T_2$ | 561 | 488 | **352** | 216 | 123 | 254 | 317 | **470** | 465 | 234 |
| $T_3$ | 411 | 414 | 316 | **291** | 308 | 130 | 213 | 380 | **532** | 485 |
| $T_4$ | 300 | 247 | 198 | 219 | **776** | 41 | 89 | 203 | 361 | **1046** |
| $\Sigma$ | 2981 | 2118 | 1350 | 951 | 1300 | 1382 | 1328 | 1895 | 2055 | 2040 |

From Table 3, we can make the following observations. While the obtained accuracy values indicate that the CvsN and CvsP classification architectures perform similarly, there are significant differences related to the class-specific predictions. The CvsN classification architecture tends to predict the class labels $T_0$ and $T_1$ most frequently, followed by the class labels $T_2$, $T_4$ and $T_3$. On the other hand, the CvsP architecture tends to predict the class labels $T_3$ and $T_4$ most frequently, followed by the class labels $T_2$, $T_0$ and $T_1$. Therefore, depending on the choice of the starting edge ($T_0$ and $T_4$, in our case), the class labels that are *nearer* to the current starting edge, are predicted more often than the classes that are *more distant* from the current starting edge.

## 5.3    Evaluation of Imbalanced ECOC Models

Applying the LOPO cross validation led to the mean accuracy values of 35.11% and 36.29%, for the ECOC models 1vsA and ABC, respectively. Table 4 depicts the confusion matrices for both of the aforementioned methods.

**Table 4. 1vsA & ABC**: Confusion tables with absolute values. Rows denote true labels. Columns denote predicted labels. $\Sigma$: Sum of predictions. Left: 1vsA. Right: ABC. The averaged LOPO cross validation accuracies are equal to 35.11% and 36.29%, for the 1vsA and ABC approaches, respectively. Bold figures denote the number of correctly classified test samples. Each class consists of 1740 test samples.

|          | One versus all | | | | | All binary combinations | | | | |
|----------|------|------|------|------|------|------|------|------|------|------|
|          | $T_0$ | $T_1$ | $T_2$ | $T_3$ | $T_4$ | $T_0$ | $T_1$ | $T_2$ | $T_3$ | $T_4$ |
| $T_0$    | **1001** | 185 | 157 | 205 | 192 | **1123** | 135 | 313 | 35 | 134 |
| $T_1$    | 711 | **237** | 254 | 303 | 235 | 785 | **190** | 499 | 66 | 200 |
| $T_2$    | 529 | 231 | **250** | 307 | 423 | 614 | 137 | **537** | 68 | 384 |
| $T_3$    | 333 | 181 | 209 | **295** | 722 | 400 | 104 | 457 | **80** | 699 |
| $T_4$    | 138 | 88 | 96 | 146 | **1272** | 181 | 52 | 213 | 67 | **1227** |
| $\Sigma$ | 2712 | 922 | 966 | 1256 | 2844 | 3101 | 618 | 2019 | 316 | 2644 |

From Table 4, we can make the following observations. The 1vsA model predicted both of the edge classes most frequently. This is due to the fact that it is *easier* to separate one of the edge classes from all remaining classes, than, for instance, to separate the *central* class from all remaining classes, with respect to an ordinal multi-class structure. The ABC model, i.e. the approach that includes all binary class combinations as classification subtasks, seems to predict both of the edge classes, as well as the central class, most frequently. The remaining class labels, $T_1$ and $T_3$, were predicted only 934 times in total, out of 3480 test samples from those classes.

## 5.4    Evaluation of the *1vs1* and bOCC Models

**Table 5. 1vs1 & bOCC**: Confusion tables with absolute values. Rows denote true labels. Columns denote predicted labels. $\Sigma$: Sum of predictions. Left: 1vs1. Right: bOCC. The averaged LOPO cross validation accuracies are equal to 36.95% and 37.01%, for the 1vs1 and bOCC approaches, respectively. Bold figures denote the number of correctly classified test samples. Each class consists of 1740 test samples.

|          | One versus one | | | | | Bidirectional OCC | | | | |
|----------|------|------|------|------|------|------|------|------|------|------|
|          | $T_0$ | $T_1$ | $T_2$ | $T_3$ | $T_4$ | $T_0$ | $T_1$ | $T_2$ | $T_3$ | $T_4$ |
| $T_0$    | **860** | 390 | 278 | 144 | 68 | **995** | 368 | 176 | 116 | 85 |
| $T_1$    | 503 | **502** | 390 | 250 | 95 | 633 | **489** | 287 | 213 | 118 |
| $T_2$    | 363 | 423 | **436** | 350 | 168 | 498 | 394 | **328** | 309 | 211 |
| $T_3$    | 217 | 287 | 378 | **472** | 386 | 318 | 296 | 283 | **381** | 462 |
| $T_4$    | 103 | 128 | 207 | 357 | **945** | 141 | 119 | 153 | 300 | **1027** |
| $\Sigma$ | 2046 | 1730 | 1689 | 1573 | 1662 | 2585 | 1666 | 1227 | 1319 | 1903 |

Applying the LOPO cross validation led to the mean accuracy values of 36.95% and 37.01%, for the 1vs1 and bOCC approaches, respectively. Table 5 depicts the confusion matrices for both of the aforementioned methods.

From Table 5, we can make the following observations. Our proposed bOCC architecture slightly outperforms the 1vs1 model. However, the 1vs1 approach seems to be the most *balanced* one. The accumulated sum of outputs specific to the 1vs1 ECOC model, with respect to each of the class labels, shows the highest similarity to an equal distribution, among all analysed methods. Note that the BVDB is perfectly balanced, i.e. each class has exactly the same amount of samples, for each test subject.

## 5.5    Comparison of All Models

Table 6 depicts the results obtained by all OCC and ECOC approaches. From Table 6, we can make the following observations, with respect to the accuracy

**Table 6. Averaged LOPO performance values ($\pm$ standard deviations).** An asterisk (*) denotes a statistically significant difference, in comparison to our proposed method (bOCC), according to the two-sided Wilcoxon signed-rank test, at a significance level of 5%. The best performing method is underlined. The accuracy is given in %. Chance level accuracy: 20%. MAE: Mean absolute error. #: Number of (classifiers).

| Approach | Accuracy | MAE | #Classifiers |
|---|---|---|---|
| CvsN | $34.54 \pm 8.06^*$ | $1.139 \pm 0.229^*$ | 4 |
| CvsP | $34.69 \pm 9.31^*$ | $1.063 \pm 0.258^*$ | 4 |
| 1vsA | $35.11 \pm 7.81^*$ | $1.155 \pm 0.267^*$ | 5 |
| bOCC | $\underline{37.01 \pm 8.97}$ | $1.040 \pm 0.267$ | 5 |
| 1vs1 | $36.95 \pm 9.41$ | $\underline{1.002 \pm 0.259^*}$ | 10 |
| ABC | $36.29 \pm 8.07$ | $1.098 \pm 0.279^*$ | 15 |

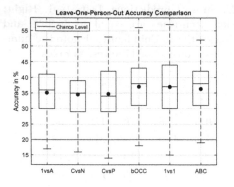 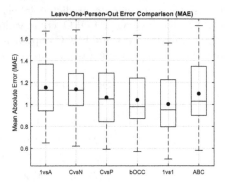

**Fig. 4. Leave-one-person-out performance comparison**: Left: Accuracy in %. Right: Mean absolute error (MAE). Horizontal lines denote median values. Dots denote mean values.

measure. Our proposed architecture significantly outperforms the approaches 1vsA, CvsN, and CvsP, according to the two-sided Wilcoxon signed-rank test, at a significance level of 5%. Moreover, our approach slightly outperforms the 1vs1, as well as the ABC approach.

Note that specific to the MAE measure, we provided three decimal places, because the first digit is equal to 1, for each of the analysed methods. Based on Table 6, we can make the following observations, with respect to the MAE measure. Except for the 1vs1 ECOC model, our proposed bOCC approach significantly outperforms each of the remaining methods. Note that the 1vs1 approach significantly outperforms our proposed method. As discussed above, this is due to its balanced outputs, which plays an essential role in the computation of the mean absolute error.

Note that the outcomes of the statistical tests for both measures, accuracy and MAE, are supported by the additionally provided box plots that are depicted in Fig. 4. For instance, in addition to the best mean accuracy value, our proposed bOCC approach also leads to best median accuracy value of 38%. This value is only tied by the ABC model. Similarly, our proposed bOCC method leads to both, the second best average and the second best median MAE values.

## 5.6   Discussion

In comparison to the CvsN and CvsP approaches, our proposed bOCC architecture needs only one additional classification model, which acts as a selector component. Being able to choose between one of the two directions, i.e. the starting edges of an OCC, improves the performance significantly, with respect to both measures, accuracy and MAE. As shown above, the bOCC model is not biased towards one of the edge classes, as it is the case for the CvsN and CvsP approaches. However, the observed importance of the selector component might be less significant in combination with *well-posed* multi-class classification tasks (MCCTs), i.e. in MCCTs where it is *easy* to obtain *high* accuracy values.

Note that each classification model that is included in our proposed bOCC architecture is also part of the corresponding 1vs1 ensemble. Therefore, it might be beneficial to combine both approaches, i.e. bOCC and 1vs1, which we will analyse in future work, in combination with different data sets.

**Acknowledgments.** The work of Friedhelm Schwenker and Peter Bellmann is supported by the project *Multimodal recognition of affect over the course of a tutorial learning experiment* (SCHW623/7-1), funded by the German Research Foundation (DFG). We gratefully acknowledge the support of NVIDIA Corporation with the donation of the Tesla K40 GPU used for this research. Hans A. Kestler acknowledges funding from the German Science Foundation (DFG, 217328187 (SFB 1074) and 288342734 (GRK HEIST)). Hans A. Kestler also acknowledges funding from the German Federal Ministry of Education and Research (BMBF) e:MED confirm (id 01ZX1708C) and TRAN-SCAN VI - PMTR-pNET (id 01KT1901B).

# References

1. Abe, S.: Support Vector Machines for Pattern Classification. Advances in Pattern Recognition. Springer, London (2005). https://doi.org/10.1007/1-84628-219-5
2. Allwein, E.L., Schapire, R.E., Singer, Y.: Reducing multiclass to binary: a unifying approach for margin classifiers. J. Mach. Learn. Res. **1**, 113–141 (2000)
3. Bellmann, P., Thiam, P., Schwenker, F.: Dominant channel fusion architectures - an intelligent late fusion approach. In: 2020 International Joint Conference on Neural Networks (IJCNN), pp. 1–8 (2020)
4. Bellmann, P., Hihn, H., Braun, D., Schwenker, F.: Binary classification: counterbalancing class imbalance by applying regression models in combination with one-sided label shifts. In: ICAART. SCITEPRESS (2021, to be published)
5. Bellmann, P., Schwenker, F.: Ordinal classification: working definition and detection of ordinal structures. IEEE Access **8**, 164380–164391 (2020)
6. Bellmann, P., Thiam, P., Schwenker, F.: Pain intensity recognition - an analysis of short-time sequences in a real-world scenario. In: Schilling, F.-P., Stadelmann, T. (eds.) ANNPR 2020. LNCS (LNAI), vol. 12294, pp. 149–161. Springer, Cham (2020). https://doi.org/10.1007/978-3-030-58309-5_12
7. Cardoso, J.S., da Costa, J.F.P., Cardoso, M.J.: Modelling ordinal relations with SVMs: an application to objective aesthetic evaluation of breast cancer conservative treatment. Neural Netw. **18**(5–6), 808–817 (2005)
8. Chawla, N.V., Bowyer, K.W., Hall, L.O., Kegelmeyer, W.P.: Smote: synthetic minority over-sampling technique. J. Artif. Intell. Res. **16**, 321–357 (2002)
9. Chu, W., Keerthi, S.S.: New approaches to support vector ordinal regression. In: ICML. ACM International Conference Proceeding Series, vol. 119, pp. 145–152. ACM (2005)
10. Chu, W., Keerthi, S.S.: Support vector ordinal regression. Neural Comput. **19**(3), 792–815 (2007)
11. Dietterich, T.G., Bakiri, G.: Error-correcting output codes: a general method for improving multiclass inductive learning programs. In: AAAI, pp. 572–577. AAAI Press/The MIT Press (1991)
12. Escalera, S., Pujol, O., Radeva, P.: Separability of ternary codes for sparse designs of error-correcting output codes. Pattern Recognit. Lett. **30**(3), 285–297 (2009)
13. Escalera, S., Pujol, O., Radeva, P.: On the decoding process in ternary error-correcting output codes. IEEE Trans. Pattern Anal. Mach. Intell. **32**(1), 120–134 (2010)
14. Gutiérrez, P.A., Pérez-Ortiz, M., Sánchez-Monedero, J., Fernández-Navarro, F., Hervás-Martínez, C.: Ordinal regression methods: survey and experimental study. IEEE Trans. Knowl. Data Eng. **28**(1), 127–146 (2016)
15. Hihn, H., Braun, D.A.: Specialization in hierarchical learning systems. Neural Process. Lett. **52**(3), 2319–2352 (2020). https://doi.org/10.1007/s11063-020-10351-3
16. Hühn, J.C., Hüllermeier, E.: Is an ordinal class structure useful in classifier learning? IJDMMM **1**(1), 45–67 (2008)
17. Kächele, M., et al.: Adaptive confidence learning for the personalization of pain intensity estimation systems. Evolving Syst. **8**(1), 71–83 (2016). https://doi.org/10.1007/s12530-016-9158-4
18. Kächele, M., Thiam, P., Amirian, M., Schwenker, F., Palm, G.: Methods for person-centered continuous pain intensity assessment from bio-physiological channels. J. Sel. Top. Signal Process. **10**(5), 854–864 (2016)

19. Kuncheva, L.I.: Combining Pattern Classifiers: Methods and Algorithms. Wiley, Hoboken (2014)
20. Lattke, R., Lausser, L., Müssel, C., Kestler, H.A.: Detecting ordinal class structures. In: Schwenker, F., Roli, F., Kittler, J. (eds.) MCS 2015. LNCS, vol. 9132, pp. 100–111. Springer, Cham (2015). https://doi.org/10.1007/978-3-319-20248-8_9
21. Lausser, L., Schäfer, L.M., Kühlwein, S.D., Kestler, A.M.R., Kestler, H.A.: Detecting ordinal subcascades. Neural Process. Lett. **52**(3), 2583–2605 (2020). https://doi.org/10.1007/s11063-020-10362-0
22. Lausser, L., Schäfer, L.M., Schirra, L.R., Szekely, R., Schmid, F., Kestler, H.A.: Assessing phenotype order in molecular data. Sci. Rep. **9**(1), 1–10 (2019)
23. Al-Eidan, R.M., Al-Khalifa, H., Al-Salman, A.: Deep-learning-based models for pain recognition: a systematic review. Appl. Sci. **10**(17), 5984 (2020)
24. Polikar, R.: Ensemble based systems in decision making. IEEE Circuits Syst. Mag. **6**(3), 21–45 (2006). https://doi.org/10.1109/MCAS.2006.1688199
25. Ricken, T., Steinert, A., Bellmann, P., Walter, S., Schwenker, F.: Feature extraction: a time window analysis based on the X-ITE pain database. In: Schilling, F.-P., Stadelmann, T. (eds.) ANNPR 2020. LNCS (LNAI), vol. 12294, pp. 138–148. Springer, Cham (2020). https://doi.org/10.1007/978-3-030-58309-5_11
26. Schwenker, F., Dietrich, C., Thiel, C., Palm, G.: Learning of decision fusion mappings for pattern recognition. Int. J. Artif. Intell. Mach. Learn. (AIML) **6**, 17–21 (2006)
27. Snoek, C., Worring, M., Smeulders, A.W.M.: Early versus late fusion in semantic video analysis. In: ACM Multimedia, pp. 399–402. ACM (2005)
28. Tax, D.M.J., Duin, R.P.W.: Using two-class classifiers for multiclass classification. In: ICPR, vol. 2, pp. 124–127. IEEE Computer Society (2002)
29. Thiam, P., et al.: Multi-modal pain intensity recognition based on the senseemotion database. IEEE Trans. Affect. Comput. 1 (2019). https://doi.org/10.1109/taffc.2019.2892090
30. Thiam, P., Bellmann, P., Kestler, H.A., Schwenker, F.: Exploring deep physiological models for nociceptive pain recognition. Sensors **19**(20), 4503 (2019)
31. Thiam, P., Kestler, H.A., Schwenker, F.: Two-stream attention network for pain recognition from video sequences. Sensors **20**(3), 839 (2020)
32. Vapnik, V.: The Nature of Statistical Learning Theory. Springer, New York (2013)
33. Walter, S., et al.: The biovid heat pain database data for the advancement and systematic validation of an automated pain recognition system. In: CYBCONF, pp. 128–131. IEEE (2013). https://doi.org/10.1109/CYBConf.2013.6617456
34. Werner, P., Lopez-Martinez, D., Walter, S., Al-Hamadi, A., Gruss, S., Picard, R.: Automatic recognition methods supporting pain assessment: a survey. IEEE Trans. Affect. Comput. 1 (2019). https://doi.org/10.1109/taffc.2019.2946774
35. Wilcoxon, F.: Individual comparisons by ranking methods. Biom. Bull. **1**(6), 80–83 (1945)

# Personalized k-fold Cross-Validation Analysis with Transfer from Phasic to Tonic Pain Recognition on X-ITE Pain Database

Youssef Wally[1,2](✉), Yara Samaha[1,2](✉), Ziad Yasser[1,2](✉), Steffen Walter[1], and Friedhelm Schwenker[1](✉) (iD)

[1] Ulm University, 89081 Ulm, Germany
{steffen.walter,friedhelm.schwenker}@uni-ulm.de
[2] German University in Cairo, Main Entrance El-Tagamoa El-Khames, New Cairo City, Egypt
{youssef.wally,yara.samaha,ziad.abdelrazek}@student.guc.edu.eg

**Abstract.** Automatic pain recognition is currently one of the most interesting challenges in affective computing as it has great potential to improve pain management for patients in a clinical environment. In this work, we analyse automatic pain recognition using binary classification with personalized k-fold cross-validation analysis which is an approach that focuses on training on the labels of specific subjects and validating on the labels of other subjects in the Experimentally Induced Thermal and Electrical (X-ITE) Pain Database using both a random forest and a dense neural network model. The effectiveness of each approach is inspected on each of the phasic electro, phasic heat, tonic electro, and tonic heat datasets separately. Therefore, the analysis of subsets of the X-ITE dataset (phasic electro, tonic electro, phasic heat, and tonic heat) was made individually. Afterward, phasic to tonic transfer was made by training models on the phasic electro dataset and testing them on the tonic electro dataset. Our outcomes and evaluations indicate that electro datasets always perform better than heat datasets. Also, personalized scores had better performance than normal scores. Moreover, dense neural networks performed better than randoms forests in transfer from phasic electro to tonic electro and showed promising performance in the personalized transfer.

**Keywords:** Pain recognition · Binary classifier systems · Personalized k-fold cross-validation analysis · X-ITE Pain DB · Heat stimuli · Electrical stimuli · Phasic stimuli · Tonic stimuli

## 1 Introduction

Pain is a complex and subjective phenomenon that is perceived differently by each person [24]. Most of the current pain assessment methods typically

---

Y. Wally, Y. Samaha and Z. Yasser—Contributed equally.

© Springer Nature Switzerland AG 2021
A. Del Bimbo et al. (Eds.): ICPR 2020 Workshops, LNCS 12666, pp. 788–802, 2021.
https://doi.org/10.1007/978-3-030-68780-9_59

evaluate pain through patients' self-reports. However, these methods are not reliable for patients who suffer from cognitive or verbal impairments, infants, and unconscious persons. Due to the numerous cases of unreliable pain assessments, automated pain recognition is currently an interesting challenge for researchers to help enable accurate and reliable detection of pain and ensure equal pain management to all patients, as insufficient management of pain has a negative effect on many aspects of the patient's health and may even increase the risk of developing chronic pain [19].

Several research groups were conducted to develop automated pain recognition systems using visual, paralinguistic, and physiological signals. In order to achieve the goal of having multiple pain modality, studies took the approach of assessing the intensity of pain from a voice record [4,5]. The same approach was then used in addition to recording facial expressions. The results showed that using multi-modality outperformed using an individual modality [6]. Regarding the change in the body posture, some interesting behavioral features have proved to be of great use for pain recognition, such as head pose [7,8]. Three modalities were widely used for the field of physiology in such researches, electrocardiogram (ECG), electrodermal activity (EDA), and surface electromyography (EMG). The use of these three signals, in addition to both facial expressions and head pose, resulted in emphasizing the strengths and weaknesses of using single pain modalities and also proved that the combination of multiple modalities has the potential to enhance automated pain recognition in different cases. This research topic was conducted by Werner et al. [9] and Kächele et al. [21].

Many datasets were created to understand pain recognition. These datasets include BioVid [20], SenseEmotion [25], UNBC-McMaster [26,27] datasets, and many more. Other studies tried to differentiate pain from simple emotions [2,3]. These systems had optimistic results for pain recognition. However, they only focused on the recognition of only one type of pain stimulus (BP4D+ used tonic cold pressor test, BioVid used phasic heat, EmoPain used physical exercises in a therapy scenario, MIntPAIN used phasic electrical and SenseEmotion used phasic heat). A database that contains related modalities is the SenseEmotion Database [11–13]. However, it does not provide body movement video, facial EMG, nor thermal video. The X-ITE Pain Database is a recent database for pain recognition [19]. It is the first database for pain recognition to include four different types of pain stimuli: phasic (short period) heat, phasic (short period) electrical, tonic (long period) heat, and tonic (long period) electrical. Table 1 and Table 2 give an overall view of the differences between the previous pain recognition databases and the X-ITE Pain database. Some researches were carried out using the X-ITE Pain database. The results of their experiments showed that pain intensity in all stimulus variants can be automatically recognized and that different qualities of pain (heat and electrical stimuli) can be distinguished from each other. These results were was also concluded in this work using personalized k-fold cross-validation [21].

This work proposes an approach using personalized k-fold cross-validation using a random forest model and dense neural networks. Then tests whether they can detect the presence of pain or the absence of pain using subsets of the X-ITE Pain dataset separately: phasic electro, tonic electro, phasic heat, and tonic heat. Then, the analysis of phasic to tonic transfer was done by training models on phasic electro and testing them on tonic electro. The remainder of this work is organised as follows. For a better understanding of the related work part, we first shortly describe the X-ITE Pain Database, in Sect. 2. Subsequently, in Sect. 3, we present our approach and define our evaluation protocol. The experimental results are presented in Sect. 4 and discussed in Sect. 5. Finally, in Sect. 6, we conclude the current work, and in Sect. 7 future work that could be further done is suggested.

**Table 1.** Pain database

| Database | Video | Audio | EMG | ECG | EDA | Other |
|---|---|---|---|---|---|---|
| UNBC-McMaster [1] | Yes | | | | | |
| BioVid [14–16] | Yes | | Yes | Yes | Yes | |
| BP4D+ [17] | Yes | | | Yes | Yes | Yes |
| EmoPain [5] | Yes | Yes | Yes | | | Yes |
| SenseEmotion [11–13] | Yes | Yes | Yes | Yes | Yes | Yes |
| MIntPAIN [18] | Yes | | | | | Yes |
| X-ITE [19] | Yes | Yes | Yes | Yes | Yes | Yes |

**Table 2.** Pain database

| Database | Thermal | Electrical | Movement | Phasic | Tonic |
|---|---|---|---|---|---|
| UNBC-McMaster [1] | | | Yes | | |
| BioVid [14–16] | Yes | | | Yes | |
| BP4D+ [17] | Yes | | | | |
| EmoPain [5] | | | Yes | | |
| SenseEmotion [11–13] | Yes | | | Yes | |
| MIntPAIN [18] | | Yes | | Yes | |
| X-ITE [19] | Yes | Yes | | Yes | Yes |

## 2 Data Description

The Data used in this project is part of the new multi-modal X-ITE Pain Database [19]. The X-ITE pain Database [19] is not only the first of its kind to combine more than one pain model, but also induce different pain stimuli in terms of intensity and duration. Which lead to the possibility of detecting pain patterns as well as distinguishing between pain qualities.

## 2.1   Participants

The phase of conducting the experiments and collecting data from participants was conducted in accordance with the ethical guidelines laid down in the World Medical Association Declaration of Helsinki (ethical committee approval was granted: 196/10-UBB/bal) and approved by the ethics committee of the University of Ulm (Helmholtzstraße 20, 89081 Ulm, Germany).

There was a total of 134 participants aged between 18 and 50 who took parts in the creation of the data and were equally divided between men and women. The male subjects average age was 33, as for the female subjects their average age was 32. So, the total average age of all subjects was 31. All were healthy subjects so, none suffered from chronic pain, depression nor had a history of psychiatric disorders. None of the participants were suffering from neurological conditions, headache syndrome nor cardiovascular disease. All of them did not take any pain medication nor used painkillers directly before the experiment [21].

## 2.2   Experiment Description

Each participant was stimulated by two types of pain stimulation (Heat, Electric). Heat pain was stimulated at the participants' forearm using the Medoc PATHWAY Model ATS thermal stimulator. Electrical pain on the other hand was stimulated with electrodes attached to the index and middle finger using the electrical stimulator Digitimer.

Before the experiment to be conducted a pain threshold was determined for each subject since each would have their own tolerance against the pain which could differ for the same person between heat and electric stimuli.

Each stimulation was applied in two variants:

1. Tonic (long), where it would be stimulated for a period of 60 s.
2. Phasic (short), where it would be stimulated for a period of 5 s.

In the beginning, a stimulus calibration procedure was conducted prior to the main experiment, which consists of one part per stimuli so four parts in total (Phasic Heat, Phasic Electro, Tonic Heat and Tonic Electro). In each part, the stimulus intensity was gradually increased and the participant was asked to report the intensity of the pain felt to determine the person-specific pain threshold and tolerance.

After the calibration procedure, the member sat down on an examination couch and experienced the fundamental stimulation stage, which took around an hour and a half. The phasic stimuli of every modality (heat and electrical) and intensity were repeated multiple times in randomized request with stops of 8–12 s. The 1-min tonic stimuli were just applied once per intensity, for example, there were six tonic stimuli for each participant, each followed by an interruption of five minutes. They were applied in three stages: The most intense tonic heat and electrical pain stimuli were applied toward the experiment's end. The other two stages, which contained one tonic heat and electrical stimulus of lower intensity, started randomly during the phasic stimulation period.

Finally, the output pain threshold recorded out of this calibration was later used in order to determine the temperatures which will be used in the six different intensities for heat (three for the phasic and three for the tonic), as well as defining the currents used for the six different electrical intensities (three for the phasic and three for the tonic).

## 2.3  Data Features

At the beginning of the experiment four types of stimulus were induced in three different intensities, which were all labeled in the data as:

- Phasic Heat: 1, 2, 3
- Phasic Electro: −1, −2, −3
- Phasic Baseline: 0
- Tonic Heat: 4, 5, 6
- Tonic Electo: −4, −5, −6
- Tonic Baseline: 100

To each stimulus applied there were several different pain response data collected from the participants using multiple sensors. During the main procedure, Behavioral Responses and Physiological Responses were recorded for each subject.

## 2.4  Physiological Responses

To each stimuli applied there were several different pain response data collected from the participants using multiple sensors:

- Electrocardiogram (ECG) for analyzing heart rate and its variability.
  Its features names starts with: "ecg"
- Surface electromyography (EMG) to measure activity of three muscles, the trapezius (neck/shoulder), corrugator supercilii (close to eyebrows), and zygomaticus major (at the cheeks).
  Its features names starts with: "corrugator", "trapezius" or "zygomaticus"
- Electrodermal activity (EDA) to measure sweating.
  Its features names starts with: "scl"

For each subject, their EMG, ECG, EDA were taken. The EMG was taken for the corrugator supercilii, zygomaticus major and trapezius muscles [10].

- The corrugator supercilii muscle is the muscle located between the two eyebrows.
- The zygomaticus major muscle is the cheek muscle.
- The trapezius muscles are the muscle located between the neck and shoulders.

The ECG was taken to analyze the heart rate of the subject. While the EDA was taken to measure the sweating.

In this study no feature analysis applied to the used dataset, however the video and audio features were not used as they were not yet processed. Also, there were three additional features added:

- ecg-mea-rr:
  mean value of the R-peak distances
- ecg-mean-hr:
  mean heart rate (computated from the R-peaks)
- ecg-ecg-root-mean-square-sd:
  root mean square of the sequential differences of the R-peaks

## 2.5  Data Selection

Since the data we are having offers more than one class, there is the possibility of creating a multi-label classifier. However, in this paper we decided to go with the binary classification approach since it is a good basic start. If the models were to show a very promising results we could continue with the next level using the multi-label classification.

For this study, each stimulus (phasic heat, phasic electro, tonic heat and tonic electro) were put in four different sets. Furthermore, the highest intensity level $(-3$'s$)$, $(-6$'s$)$, $(3$'s$)$ and $(6$'s$)$ in the phasic electro, tonic electro, phasic heat and tonic heat sets respectively were relabeled as $(1$'s$)$. The baseline/no pain level for the phasic electro and phasic heat $(0$'s$)$ remained $(0$'s$)$, unlike The baseline/no pain level for the tonic electro and tonic heat $(100$'s$)$ were relabeled as $(0$'s$)$. As for the remain two intensity levels in all the sets were dropped out, since they very close in terms of output to the baseline/no pain level so they might cause confusion to our binary classifiers.

## 3  Experiments and Results

According to previous studies [13], due to a large number of features of pain recognition data, random forest yields the best performance. While neural networks show promising performance as they yield respectively promising performance according to the number of data available. Thus, It was decided to use random forests and dense neural networks as our models as the X-ITE database [19] has 247 features.

### 3.1  Random Forest

The first model used was a random forest model with hyperparameters of 215 trees in the foreset and 467 as a maximum number of nodes for each tree while choosing the nodes with the best-first fashion. These hyperparameters were then changed to achieve the best possible performance. The new hyperparameters were achieved by using the Randomized Search method on each model to find the best hyperparameters. The Randomized Search hyperparameters were cross-validation folds of 10, a range of trees in the foreset starting from 1 to 1000 and a range of maximum number of nodes for each tree starting from 1 to 1000. Then Feature Importance method was used to find the most important features to avoid the curse of dimensionality. The Feature Importance method shows how much each feature reduced the impurity on average, which is calculated as a weighted average of each node's which is equal to the number of training samples that is associated with that node. According to each feature score from the Feature Importance method they were ordered from the most important to the least important. After sorting the important features the model was trained on the first 10 important features then the first 20 and so on, increasing the number of important features taken by 10 till it reached the total number of features. Every time the model accuracy was recorded, The best models were the models that used the first 50 important features or the first 180 important features according to the list that was made using the Feature Importance method. The final model chosen was the model with the 180 features as it is beneficial for the users to understand why the model predicted that pain intensity.

**Random Forest Cross-validation.** The final random forest model's best hyperparameters for all 4 subsets, phasic electro, tonic electro, phasic heat and tonic heat was 271 trees in the foreset and 861 maximum number of nodes for each tree. 10-fold Cross-validation was used to make sure each model was not over-fitting the data of each subset. Scores can be seen in Table 3.

**Table 3.** Random forest scores.

| Subset | Average accuracy |
|---|---|
| Phasic electro | 91.8% |
| Tonic electro | 85.3% |
| Phasic heat | 82.1% |
| Tonic heat | 79.2% |

Furthermore, the receiver operating characteristic curve for the models was created to see the true positives and false positives relations with each other. The receiver operating characteristic curve was used instead of the precision-recall curve as the number of instances in each classifier is balanced:

As we can see the curve is far from the dotted line in both phasic electro and phasic heat, that means that the ratio is acceptable. However, the curve in tonic electro and tonic heat is s far from the dotted line, besides, it is not as smooth as the receiver operating characteristic curve of the phasic data indicating that there are not enough instances for the model to be trained on.

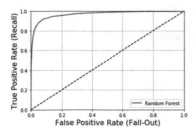

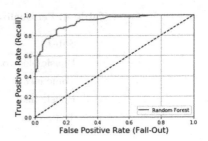

**Fig. 1.** Phasic electro data cross validation ROC graph

**Fig. 2.** Tonic electro data cross validation ROC graph

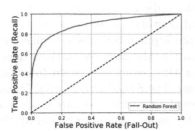

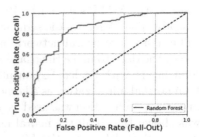

**Fig. 3.** Phasic heat data cross validation ROC graph

**Fig. 4.** Tonic heat data cross validation
ROC graph

**Personalized Random Forest Cross-validation.** After achieving the best
possible performance of the random forest model its time to see how it works
subjectively. The aim of making a Machine learning model that recognizes pain
is that it can be used to identify pain on a specific person, meaning that it can
identify personal pain and not generally. That's why the next step was to make
personalized models and test their output.

To make a personalized test cross-validation will be used to train on certain
subjects and validate on other subjects. In total there are 126 subjects in the
database. Since the previous cross-validations on the whole data were 10-fold
cross-validation the personalized cross-validation will also be 10-fold personalized
cross-validation in order to compare between them. Therefore, the data were
separated into phasic and tonic data. Then each one of them was separated into
sets of 12 subjects with the exception of the last set containing 6 subjects, in total
there will be 10 sets of data. The program trained the model on 9 sets and then
tested it on the remaining set creating a personalized 10-fold cross-validation
program. Achieving the scores in Table 4.

**Table 4.** Personalized random forest scores.

| Subset | Average accuracy |
|---|---|
| Phasic electro | 92.0% |
| Tonic electro | 87.3% |
| Phasic heat | 82.0% |
| Tonic heat | 77.1% |

## 3.2   Dense Neural Network

The sequential neural network was chosen as the type of neural network that will be used as the X-ITE's database [19] image and audio features were not used in this study. Therefore, a basic sequential neural network will be sufficient.

The first dense neural network had a flatten input layer which changes the shape of the data to make the shape appropriate for the next layers; three dense hidden layers with Scaled Exponential Linear Unit as an activation function, LeCun normal initialization as a kernel initializer. The Scaled Exponential Linear Unit activation function was used as all the neural network's layers are dense and it was shown that if all the neural networks' layers are dense layers and all the layers use Scaled Exponential Linear Unit as an activation function the neural network will self normalize solving the vanishing gradient problem [20]. Each dense hidden layer contained 100 neurons. Finally an output layer with sigmoid as an activation function due to binary classification. Nadam was used as an optimizer as it combines the concept of momentum optimization and RMSProp, binary cross entropy as a loss function and accuracy as a metric as it is the best loss function for binary classifiers [20]. All of the dense neural networks were trained using a learning rate of 0.001 which was chosen as it was the result of the Randomized Search method and 30 epochs as a result of trial and error.

To find the best hyperparameters Randomized Search method was used ro run dense neural networks with the range of 1 to 3 hidden layers and 1 to 300 nodes in each layer. Then only the most important features were used to train the dense neural network. In addition, "AlphaDropout" was used to decrease overfitting. "AlphaDropout" was used as the neural network used is self-normalizing due to the Scaled Exponential Linear Unit activation function. The "AlphaDropout" just preserves the mean and standard deviation of its inputs. Using "Dropout" would ruin self-normalization. The final model consisted of

- one flatten input layer
- one hidden dense layer with:
  - 133 neurons
  - Scaled Exponential Linear Unit activation function
  - LeCun normal kernel initializer
- one output layer with sigmoid activation function
- AlphaDropout with a rate of 0.2 between each hidden layer
- first 217 features

This dense neural network was used in personalized 11-fold cross-validation on each subset achieving the results recorded in Table 5.

**Table 5.** Personalized dense neural network scores.

| Subset | Average accuracy |
|---|---|
| Phasic electro | 90.1% |
| Tonic electro | 81.5% |
| Phasic heat | 82.5 |
| Tonic heat | 73.6 |

## 4    Transfer from Phasic to Tonic

This transfer was done by seeing if phasic electro pain stimulus and tonic electro pain stimulus affect the subjects in the same way according to the data collected. The reason why is it important to know if phasic and tonic pain stimulus affects the subject in the same way is that phasic pain stimulus is easier to induce on subjects and easier to collect. That's because phasic pain is applied for a short period so it does not bother the subject. However, tonic pain is induced, for example, 60 s. It is not ethical nor human to induce this kind of pain as the subject would not endure many tonic pain sessions. Thus, finding out if models and dense neural network can be trained using only phasic pain is important.

The random forest model and the dense neural network used on the 4 subsets were then used to be trained by phasic electro data and then tested on tonic electro data achieving the recorded results in Table 4.

The dense neural network achieved a better performance than the random forest model in transfer and showing promising performance taking into consideration the little amount of data given. The loss in this case was the binary cross entropy as the model was a binary classifier. As we can in Fig. 5 the loss and the validation loss were decreasing at first, while the accuracy and the validation accuracy were increasing at first. Also, the two loss lines and the two accuracy lines are close to each other. This means that the neural network's accuracy and loss are getting better and that the neural network's performance on the training data and the validation data are similar. Which means that the neural network is performing well and not overfitting. However, it is also clear that the number of iterations does not improve the accuracy or loss, thus, the iteration that was chosen (30) was not increased in the upcoming neural networks. Therefore, the dense neural network was used to make a personalized test on transfer from phasic electro to tonic electro. Its results are recorded in Table 6.

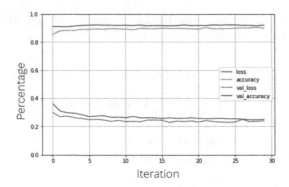

**Fig. 5.** Dense neural network learning curves

**Table 6.** Phasic electro to tonic electro transfer accuracy.

| Model | Average accuracy | Average loss |
|---|---|---|
| Random forest | 62.3% | N/A |
| Dense neural network | 65.2% | 2.4328 |
| Personalized dense neural network | 63.9% | 2.4900 |

## 5  Discussion

### 5.1  Interpreting Results

The level 1 analysis on the 4 subsets using random forest showed that the accuracy scores of the phasic subsets are always higher than the accuracy scores of the tonic subsets. This is probably due to the lack of instances in the tonic subsets due to not being able to induce tonic pain on subjects for a long time. Moreover, the personalized accuracy scores showed the same pattern as the normal accuracy scores and even had better results than the normal scores except for tonic heat. Also, when dense neural networks were used to evaluate its performance the same pattern was observed. This shows why it is important to know whether it is possible to train models on phasic data and later use them to predict phasic and tonic data together. However, the performance gap between phasic data and tonic data was wider in dense neural networks than in random forests. This shows that random forests perform better on data with low instances than dense neural networks, which is known that neural networks need a lot of data to be trained [13,22,23]. The performance gap between phasic data in random forests and dense neural networks was narrow. Thus, it is possible to achieve a way better performance if more data was available and used to train the dense neural networks.

The personalized results showed that their performance was close to the normal performance meaning that the models can recognize pain to each subject accordingly.

The transfer from phasic electro to tonic electro showed that dense neural networks outperformed random forests even though low data affects neural networks more than it affects random forests. Therefore, dense neural networks were used in the personalized transfer from phasic electro to tonic electro which also achieved a promising performance.

Lastly, it is always observed that the electro datasets performer better than heat datasets in all the tests using random forests and dense neural networks. Which was also observed in previous studies [21].

Previous studies in pain recognition concluded that pain could be predicted with machine learning and neural networks when they used databases for pain recognition using a specific type of stimulus [9,24,28]. For example, the SenseEmotion Database [11–13], which includes only phasic heat stimulus, has achieved the best accuracy of 83.39%. Another study that used the Biovid Database [9,14–16], which also included only phasic heat stimulus, has achieved the best accuracy of 80.6%. Compared to these methods from previous studies used, the learning methods used in this work are the first supervised learning methods evaluated based on the leave-one-subject-out cross-validation for classifying the presence of pain versus the absence of pain using a dataset which has two pain models with different durations and also different qualities, thermal and electric yielding four different types of pain stimuli: phasic heat, phasic electro, tonic heat, and tonic electro stimuli.

## 5.2 Added Value

Training a model on phasic electro pain stimulus and using it to predict tonic electro pain stimulus showed that it might be possible to rely on phasic data only to train a model to predict both phasic stimulus and tonic stimulus pain. Which was never tested before. Thus, we now know that it might be possible to train on one type of pain stimulus and use the same model to predict another kind of pain stimulus. In addition, level 1 analysis on phasic electro, tonic electro, phasic heat and tonic heat were represented as a base result and compared to personalized results which showed that the models can be subjective about pain recognition.

## 5.3 Limitations

The problem is that the only different pain stimulus tested were phasic electro pain and tonic electro pain. It's maybe possible to test on phasic electro pain and predict tonic electro pain. However, different types should be tested. For example, if a model can be trained on an electro based pain and predicts heat based pain. Furthermore, it might be that in the case of electro pain stimulus phasic and tonic pain act in the same way, but, in the case of a different kind of pain, for example, heat pain stimulus phasic and tonic pain act differently. Besides, the X-ITE database [19] includes behavioural responses and physiological responses, however, only physiological responses were used in this research as the behavioural responses were not yet processed.

# 6   Conclusion

The goal of this study was to know the best achievable performance of pain recognition using a binary classifier system. After doing level 1 analysis on the 4 subsets of the X-ITE dataset which are, phasic electro, tonic electro, phasic heat and tonic heat it was clear that a random forest model and a dense neural network performs better on phasic data due to its larger instances amount. Besides, in a personalized test both achieve promising performances. However, the random forest performance was better than the dense neural network. Afterwards, transfer from phasic electro to tonic electro was conducted to compare the results of a system trained and tested on phasic data to a system trained on phasic data and tested on tonic data. Thus, we can know if both pain types affect the subjects in the same way. If so we can only collect phasic pain data which is easier to collect.

After training a random forest and a dense neural network using phasic electro data and testing it on tonic data their scores decreased compared to systems that were trained and tested on the same subset. However, the dense neural network is promising as they usually need more data to achieve good performance and their performance was better than the random forest in the transfer from phasic to tonic. Thus, it is possible to achieve an acceptable performance if more data was available [13, 22, 23].

However, as not all types of pain stimulus were considered it can not be said that all different pain stimulus will act the same. Although, it is now possible to say that there is a chance that we can train machine learning models and dense neural networks on phasic pain data and then used to predict tonic pain data. Future studies should test many comparisons to make sure that different types of pain stimulus affect the subject equally or if it is possible to group pain stimulus that affects the subject equally.

# References

1. Lucey, P., et al.: Painful data: the UNBC-McMaster shoulder pain expression archive database. Face and Gesture 2011. IEEE (2011)
2. Niese, R., et al.: Towards pain recognition in post-operative phases using 3d-based features from video and support vector machines. Int. J. Dig. Content Technol. Appl. **3**(4), 21–31 (2009)
3. Hammal, Z., Kunz, M.: Pain monitoring: a dynamic and context-sensitive system. Pattern Recogn. **45**(4), 1265–1280 (2012)
4. Thiam, P., Schwenker, F.: Combining deep and hand-crafted features for audio-based pain intensity classification. In: Schwenker, F., Scherer, S. (eds.) MPRSS 2018. LNCS (LNAI), vol. 11377, pp. 49–58. Springer, Cham (2019). https://doi.org/10.1007/978-3-030-20984-1_5
5. Thiam, P., Schwenker, F.: Multi-modal data fusion for pain intensity assessment and classification. In: Seventh International Conference on Image Processing Theory, Tools and Applications (IPTA), p. 2017. IEEE (2017)

6. Sellner, J., Thiam, P., Schwenker, F.: Visualizing facial expression features of pain and emotion data. In: Schwenker, F., Scherer, S. (eds.) MPRSS 2018. LNCS (LNAI), vol. 11377, pp. 101–115. Springer, Cham (2019). https://doi.org/10.1007/978-3-030-20984-1_9

7. Werner, P., et al.: Head movements and postures as pain behavior. PLoS ONE **13**(2), e0192767 (2018)

8. Werner, P., et al.: Automatic pain assessment with facial activity descriptors. IEEE Trans. Affect. Comput. **8**(3), 286–299 (2016)

9. Werner, P., et al.: Automatic pain recognition from video and biomedical signals. In: 2014 22nd International Conference on Pattern Recognition. IEEE (2014)

10. Kächele, M., Werner, P., Al-Hamadi, A., Palm, G., Walter, S., Schwenker, F.: Bio-visual fusion for person-independent recognition of pain intensity. In: Schwenker, F., Roli, F., Kittler, J. (eds.) MCS 2015. LNCS, vol. 9132, pp. 220–230. Springer, Cham (2015). https://doi.org/10.1007/978-3-319-20248-8_19

11. Bellmann, P., Thiam, P., Schwenker, F.: Using a quartile-based data transformation for pain intensity classification based on the senseemotion database. In: 2019 8th International Conference on Affective Computing and Intelligent Interaction Workshops and Demos (ACIIW). IEEE (2019)

12. Mamontov, D., Polonskaia, I., Skorokhod, A., Semenkin, E., Kessler, V., Schwenker, F.: Evolutionary algorithms for the design of neural network classifiers for the classification of pain intensity. In: Schwenker, F., Scherer, S. (eds.) MPRSS 2018. LNCS (LNAI), vol. 11377, pp. 84–100. Springer, Cham (2019). https://doi.org/10.1007/978-3-030-20984-1_8

13. Thiam, P., et al.: Multi-modal pain intensity recognition based on the senseemotion database. IEEE Trans. Affective Comput. (2019)

14. Walter, S., et al.: The biovid heat pain database data for the advancement and systematic validation of an automated pain recognition system. In: 2013 IEEE International Conference on Cybernetics (CYBCO). IEEE (2013)

15. Thiam, P., et al.: Exploring deep physiological models for nociceptive pain recognition. Sensors **19**(20), 4503 (2019)

16. Werner, P., et al.: Towards pain monitoring: Facial expression, head pose, a new database, an automatic system and remaining challenges. In: Proceedings of the British Machine Vision Conference (2013)

17. Zhang, Z., et al.: Multimodal spontaneous emotion corpus for human behavior analysis. In: Proceedings of the IEEE Conference on Computer Vision and Pattern Recognition (2016)

18. Haque, M.A., et al.: Deep multimodal pain recognition: a database and comparison of spatio-temporal visual modalities. In: 2018 13th IEEE International Conference on Automatic Face & Gesture Recognition (FG 2018). IEEE (2018)

19. Gruss, S., et al.: Multi-modal signals for analyzing pain responses to thermal and electrical stimuli. JoVE (J. Visual. Exper.) **146**, e59057 (2019)

20. Géron, A.: Hands-on Machine Learning with Scikit-Learn, Keras, and TensorFlow: Concepts, Tools, and Techniques to Build Intelligent Systems. O'Reilly Media (2019)

21. Werner, P., et al.: Twofold-multimodal pain recognition with the X-ITE pain database. In: 2019 8th International Conference on Affective Computing and Intelligent Interaction Workshops and Demos (ACIIW). IEEE (2019)

22. Banko, M., Brill, E.: Scaling to very very large corpora for natural language disambiguation. In: Proceedings of the 39th Annual Meeting of the Association for Computational Linguistics (2001)

23. Halevy, A., Norvig, P., Pereira, F.: The unreasonable effectiveness of data. IEEE Intell. Syst. **24**(2), 8–12 (2009)
24. Ashraf, A.B., et al.: The painful face-pain expression recognition using active appearance models. Image Vis. Comput. **27**(12), 1788–1796 (2009)
25. Ahmed, A.M., Rizaner, A., Ulusoy, A.H.: A novel decision tree classification based on post-pruning with Bayes minimum risk. PLoS ONE **13**(4), e0194168 (2018)
26. Quinlan, J.R.: Induction of decision trees. Mach. Learn. **1**(1), 81–106 (1986)
27. Salzberg, S.L.: C4.5: Programs for Machine Learning by J. Ross Quinlan, pp. 235–240. Morgan Kaufmann Publishers, Inc., 1993 (1994)
28. Samuel, A.L.: Some studies in machine learning using the game of checkers. II-Recent progress. IBM J. Res. Dev. **11**(6), 601–617 (1967)

# ODANet: Online Deep Appearance Network for Identity-Consistent Multi-person Tracking

Guillaume Delorme[1], Yutong Ban[2], Guillaume Sarrazin[1],
and Xavier Alameda-Pineda[1(✉)]

[1] Inria, Univ. Grenoble-Alpes, LJK, CNRS, Paris, France
xavier.alameda-pineda@inria.fr
[2] MIT CSAIL Distributed Robotics Lab, Cambridge, USA

**Abstract.** The analysis of affective states through time in multi-person scenarii is very challenging, because it requires to *consistently* track all persons over time. This requires a robust visual appearance model capable of re-identifying people already tracked in the past, as well as spotting newcomers. In real-world applications, the appearance of the persons to be tracked is unknown in advance, and therefore one must devise methods that are both discriminative and flexible. Previous work in the literature proposed different tracking methods with fixed appearance models. These models allowed, up to a certain extend, to discriminate between appearance samples of two different people. We propose online deep appearance network (ODANet), a method able to track people, and simultaneously update the appearance model with the newly gathered annotation-less images. Since this task is specially relevant for autonomous systems, we also describe a platform-independent robotic implementation of ODANet. Our experiments show the superiority of the proposed method with respect to the state of the art, and demonstrate the ability of ODANet to adapt to sudden changes in appearance, to integrate new appearances in the tracking system and to provide more identity-consistent tracks.

## 1 Introduction

Traditionally, the analysis of the affective states of people has been done using individual data: meaning that only one person is present in the data stream. In the recent past, various papers on group emotion recognition, meaning the ability of extracting both grouped and individual affective states from still images has gained some popularity [17,29–31,33]. However, the recognition *throught time* of the affective state of individuals involved in group interactions has not yet been thoroughly addressed. We believe that one of the main reasons for this is the lack of robust and adaptive online person tracking methods. Indeed, a system able to perform group and individual behavior analysis in the wild has several prerequisites. First, the ability to tracking multiple persons, known

© Springer Nature Switzerland AG 2021
A. Del Bimbo et al. (Eds.): ICPR 2020 Workshops, LNCS 12666, pp. 803–818, 2021.
https://doi.org/10.1007/978-3-030-68780-9_60

as multiple object tracking [2,3,10,25,28]. Second, the ability to maintain an appearance model capable of recognising people seen in the past, known as person re-identification [12,22,32]. Finally, the capacity to update both the tracking and the re-identification models incrementally, as new data is gathered by the system. This last step is particularly difficult, because it must be done at test time, and therefore is purely unsupervised.

In this paper, we are interested in endowing an autonomous system with the ability of tracking multiple persons in an online setting, and in particular to update its appearance description model to the persons in the scene. This is challenging because of four main reasons: (i) the method can only use causal information, since the system does not have access to future images and detections; (ii) the method must be computationally light, in the sense that the system must track people using consumer technology; (iii) the model update must be done online in an unsupervised manner, since the system does not have access to annotations of the tracked people; and (iv) the overall system must account for visual clutter e.g. occlusions and ego-motion.

To that aim, we propose a probabilistic model combined with a deep appearance model. While the probabilistic model sets the relationship between the latent variables (e.g. people's position) and the observations (bounding boxes), the appearance model based on a deep siamese neural network allows to robustly discriminate images belonging to different people. Most importantly, and this is the main contribution of the paper, the probabilistic-deep siamese combination allows to update the deep appearance model with the supervision generated by the probabilistic model, avoiding the necessity of annotated data. This combination is the key that allows the update of supervised discriminative models in unsupervised settings, such as the task at hand.

Up to our knowledge, we are the first to propose a method able to simultaneously track multiple people and update a deep appearance architecture, and light enough to be running in an autonomous robot. Indeed, we benchmarked our method with the state-of-the-art on standard datasets under two different settings: moving surveillance camera and robot navigation in crowded scenes. In addition, we provide qualitative results. The reported experiments validate our initial thoughts and confirm that updating the appearance model with the supervision from the probabilistic model is a good strategy. Indeed, the proposed method exhibits a significant performance increase when compared to the use of a fixed deep appearance model, and to the state-of-the-art. Our strategy appears to be effective for learning a discriminative appearance model on the fly, while tracking multiple people and accounting for clutter at the same time.

## 2    Related Work

Tracking by detection is the most popular paradigm in the multiple object tracking (MOT) community. Causal tracking is generally performed by elaborating robust similarity measures between known tracks and current detections, and by using data association methods to obtain optimal track-to-detection assignments. The major differences rely in the similarity measure used, which strongly depends on the visual cues that are used (e.g. spatio-temporal, appearance).

Spatio-temporal similarity generaly assumes linear motion model [2,6,10]. The recent introduction of deep learning has leveraged the use of reliable appearance descriptors, allowing causal tracking models to robustly evaluate appearance similarities [3,23]. The introduction of person re-identification (Re-ID) models [7,24,28] has allowed tracking algorithms to take advantage of external dataset to improve their generalization ability. Several strategies are developped to aggregate those similarity measures: [2] takes advantage of the probabilistic formulation to merge different cue information, while some [11,28] propose a deep formulation where cues are merged early in the network which is directly trained to output the desired similarity measure. Single object tracking strategies [3,11,15] have also been exploited to perform multiple object tracking, especially [3,11] using the siamese formulation which allows an online finetuning of the appearance model to the tracking experiment at hand.

While the progress in MOT is quite significant, methods able to perform online MOT on autonomous robots are much more scarce. Computational complexity and moving cameras are two of the main difficultes most methods have trouble overcoming. One example of a MOT method fully adapted to robotic platforms is [4], where the authors propose a probabilistic model and a variational approximation to solve the tracking problem, while using the motor position to improve the tracking results. However, the appearance model used in [4] is based on color histogram descriptors, which lack or robustness and description power, specially in challenging visual conditions and for unseen identities.

We propose to exploit the same tracking formulation, to provide supervision for training a deep appearance models. Indeed, we exploit a Siamese deep network and use a soft-label formulation within the deep metric learning paradigm, to update the deep appearance model while tracking multiple people.

## 3    Joint Tracking and Appearance Modeling

In this section we introduce the propose online update strategy for our deep appearance model. To do so, we first briefly discuss the variational probabilistic tracker used in [4,5]. We refer the reader to these articles for a detailed description of the method. After, we discuss how metric learning can be used in the classical settings for person re-identification. This is then used to present the main methodological contribution of the manuscript, namely the use of the tracking results as a soft supervision to update the deep appearance model for re-identification.

### 3.1    Variational Multiple Object Tracking in a Nutshell

The probabilistic formulation used in this paper is inspired by [4,5], and lies within the tracking-by-detection paradigm, meaning that we assume the existence of a person detector (e.g. [1]) providing $K_t$ bounding boxes at every frame $t$. These bounding boxes consist of the coordinates $\mathbf{y}_{tk}$ and of the content $\mathbf{h}_{tk}$. Very importantly, the detections are not associated to any of the $N$ persons being tracked, and we face a double latent variable problem. Indeed, we must concurrently estimate the position of the persons as well as the bounding box-to-person assignment, in an unsupervised manner. To do so, the probabilistic formulation and the variational approximation proposed in [4,5] lead to an alternate optimisation algorithm that roughly speaking switches between running $N$ Kalman filters and inferring the latent assignments. These assignments are computed using both the geometric similarity, with a Gaussian distribution on the bounding box coordinates, and the appearance similarity, with a Bhattacharyya distribution on the color histograms of the bounding box contents. The main limitations of color histograms is the low adaptability to new lighting conditions, to occlusions and to discriminate new appearances. This is mainly because color histograms are a fixed representation that cannot be trained/updated. Ideally, one would like to use new bounding boxes to update the appearance model.

## 3.2   Deep Probabilistic Appearance Model

In order to incorporate a learnable appearance model within the probabilistic formulation, we propose to use a feature extractor $\phi_w(\mathbf{h})$ on the bounding box contents $\mathbf{h}$ and with trainable parameters $\boldsymbol{w}$. In practice, $\phi_w$ will be instantiated by a convolutional neural network (CNN), that will be merged with the probabilistic formulation by assuming the following distribution on the extracted features:

$$\phi_w(\mathbf{h}) \sim \mathcal{N}(\phi_w(\mathbf{h}); \boldsymbol{m}_n, s_n^2 \mathbf{I}_A), \tag{1}$$

if $\mathbf{h}$ is associated to the $n$-th source and being $\boldsymbol{m}_n \in \mathbb{R}^A$ and $s_n > 0$ the mean and variance of the deep probabilistic model for source $n$, where $A$ is the dimension of the extracted features. While this is a very natural way of modeling the appearance within a probabilistic framework for tracking, up to our knowledge we are the first to holistically include a deep appearance model within a probabilistic framework, and to provide an online update algorithm for training the deep appearance model in unsupervised settings.

The parameters of the probabilistic model, $\boldsymbol{m}_n$ and $s_n$, together with the network parameters, $\boldsymbol{w}$ need to be estimated. To do so, we propose an alternate learning procedure based on the variational expectation maximisation proposed in [4,5]. Indeed, the same variational approximation can also be applied here and leads to a variational expectation-maximisation (VEM) algorithm with three steps: the E-position step, the E-assignment step, and the M step. As for any VEM, these three steps are alternated, and therefore one needs to first initialise two of these steps, and start the alternating procedure with the third step. In our case, we will initialise the VEM algorithm at time $t$, by using the same parameters (M-step) as in the previous time frame, and uniformly assign the detections (E-assignment) to the $N$ persons. We can therefore start the alternate optimisation procedure with the E-position step, which provides the mean vector

$\boldsymbol{\mu}_{tn}$ and the covariance matrix $\boldsymbol{\Gamma}_{tn}$ of the $n$-th source at time frame $t$. In the present paper, we use the exact same formulae of [4,5], leading to $N$ separate Kalman filters, weighted by the soft-assignments.

Once the posterior distribution of the position is computed, and $\boldsymbol{\mu}_{tn}$ and $\boldsymbol{\Gamma}_{nt}$ are obtained, we update the posterior distribution of the assignment variables:

$$\alpha_{tkn} = \frac{\eta_{tkn}}{\sum_m \eta_{tkm}}, \tag{2}$$

where $\alpha_{tkn}$ denotes the posterior probability of the observation $(\mathbf{y}_{tk}, \mathbf{h}_{tk})$ to be generated from the $n$-th person, and:

$$\eta_{tkn} = \underbrace{\mathcal{N}(\mathbf{y}_{tk}, \boldsymbol{\mu}_{tn} - \mathbf{E}_t, \boldsymbol{\Sigma}) e^{-\frac{1}{2}\mathrm{tr}(\boldsymbol{\Sigma}^{-1}\boldsymbol{\Gamma}_{tn})}}_{\text{Coordinates}} \underbrace{\mathcal{N}(\phi_w(\mathbf{h}_{tk}), \boldsymbol{m}_n, s_n^2 \mathbf{I}_A)}_{\text{Appearance}}, \tag{3}$$

where $\mathbf{E}_t$ is the impact of the ego-motion of the system in the image plane (see Sect. 4.3 for a detailed description on how to compute $\mathbf{E}_t$ from e.g. optical flow). The previous equation shows how the posterior distribution of an assignment variable is updated taking into account both the coordinate similarity (left) and the appearance similarity (right). It is therefore of utmost importance to update the model online so as to obtain a discriminative feature extractor $\phi_w$ and the associated mean $\boldsymbol{m}_n$ and variance $s_n$ for each of the tracked sources. This corresponds to the M-step, presented in the next Section.

### 3.3   Unsupervised Deep Metric Learning

The update of the parameters of the deep probabilistic appearance model, that is $w$, $\boldsymbol{m}_n$ and $s_n$, is done within the framework of unsupervised deep metric learning. In order to motivate this choice, we first discuss standard supervised deep metric learning, and then integrate this within our probabilistic formulation.

Supervised metric learning consists in learning a distance such that similar elements are close, and dissimilar ones are far apart. Siamese networks became a common framework for metric learning, also in the tracking community [9,21,23]. Differently from classification problems, training Siamese networks requires a data set of triplets $(\mathbf{h}_i, \mathbf{h}_j, c_{ij})$, where $i, j \in \{1, \dots, I\}$. The two bounding box images are feed-forwarded with the same weights $w$, thus obtaining $\phi_w(\mathbf{h}_i)$ and $\phi_w(\mathbf{h}_j)$ respectively. The label is $c_{ij} = 1$ if the two images $\mathbf{h}_i$, $\mathbf{h}_j$ belong to the same person, and $c_{ij} = -1$ otherwise. A popular loss for training Siamese networks is a variant of the contrastive loss [18], introduced in [20]:

$$J(\boldsymbol{w}) = \frac{1}{2} \sum_{i,j=1}^{I} g(c_{ij}(\tau - \|\phi_w(\mathbf{h}_i) - \phi_w(\mathbf{h}_j)\|^2)), \tag{4}$$

with $g(x) = \max(0, 1 - x)$ and $\tau > 0$ is a parameter.

Traditionally, (4) is optimized with stochastic gradient descent, thus forcing squared distances of elements from a negative pair further than $\tau + 1$, and those of a positive pair closer than $\tau - 1$. At test time, one can use the distance between the embedding vectors to gauge whether two appearances belong to the same person or not.

The standard (supervised) metric learning framework has proven to be useful for a variety of tasks, but requires an annotated dataset. In our case, that is at test time of a multiple object tracker, the bounding box-to-person assignments are not annotated. In this sense, we face an unsupervised deep metric learning task. As previously discussed, the E-assignment step of the VEM algorithm, see (2), provides an approximation of the posterior distribution of these assignment variables. In the following we introduce a new methodology that allows to exploit the posterior distribution of the assignment variables to update the parameters $\boldsymbol{w}$ of the feature extractor $\phi_{\boldsymbol{w}}$.

For any given two past observations $k_i$ and $k_j$, from time frames $t_i$ and $t_j$, we can compute the probability to be both generated by the same person:

$$\gamma_{ij} = \sum_{n=1}^{N} \alpha_{t_i k_i n} \alpha_{t_j k_j n}. \tag{5}$$

Intuively, if $\gamma_{ij}$ is close to 1 or to 0, it means that the pair $(\mathbf{h}_i, \mathbf{h}_j)$ is a true positive (the appearance images belong to the same person) or a true negative (the appearance images belong to different persons) with high confidence. If $\gamma_{ij}$ is not close to 1 or 0, then the image pair assignment is uncertain.

Once the $\gamma_{ij}$ are computed, we sample pseudo-positive pairs from those with $\gamma_{ij} > \eta$ and pseudo-negative pairs from those with $\gamma_{ij} < 1 - \eta$, respectively $\mathcal{H}^+$ and $\mathcal{H}^-$ sets. We optimize the following soft-weighted contrastive loss:

$$J(\boldsymbol{w}) = \frac{1}{2} \sum_{ij \in \mathcal{H}^+} g(\gamma_{ij}(\tau - \|\phi_{\boldsymbol{w}}(\mathbf{h}_i) - \phi_{\boldsymbol{w}}(\mathbf{h}_j)\|^2))$$

$$- \frac{1}{2} \sum_{ij \in \mathcal{H}^-} g((1 - \gamma_{ij})(\tau - \|\phi_{\boldsymbol{w}}(\mathbf{h}_i) - \phi_{\boldsymbol{w}}(\mathbf{h}_j)\|^2)). \tag{6}$$

The weights of the feature extractor $\phi_{\boldsymbol{w}}$ will therefore be updated using the soft-weighted contrastive loss detailed above. This is important for two main reasons. First, the soft-weighted contrastive loss does not require any annotation, since the weights of the loss are provided by the unsupervised VEM algorithm. Second, those weights implicitly provide information about the confidence of the image pair when training the network. Indeed, the weights $\gamma_{ij}$ are used not only to sample image pairs, but also to weight the loss of that image pair. In this way, we force the network to exploit more intensively the pairs with low uncertainty ($\gamma_{ij}$ close to 1 or to 0).

Simultaneously to the training of the Siamese network, one needs to update the appearance parameters of the probabilistic model, i.e. $\boldsymbol{m}_n$ and $s_n^2$, as defined in (3). As is the case for the parameters of the Siamese network, there is no annotated dataset, and this update must be done in an unsupervised manner.

However, we still have access to the posterior probability of the bounding box-to-person assignments, and easily obtain the following updates:

$$
m_n = \frac{1}{S_n} \sum_{t'=t-u}^{t} \sum_{k=1}^{K_{t'}} \alpha_{knt'} \phi_w \left( \mathbf{h}_{t'k} \right)
\tag{7}
$$

$$
s_n^2 = \frac{1}{S_n A} \sum_{t'=t-u}^{t} \sum_{k=1}^{K_{t'}} \alpha_{knt'} \left\| \phi_w \left( \mathbf{h}_{t'k} \right) - m_n \right\|^2
\tag{8}
$$

where $S_n = \sum_{t'=t-u}^{t} \sum_{k=1}^{K_{t'}} \alpha_{knt'}$ and $u$ is a windowing parameter. Updating these parameters at each time step allows the appearance model to be more flexible to sudden appearance variations and to better adapt the internal track appearances to the observations. The optimisation of (6) together with (7)–(8) form the M-step of the VEM algorithm for joint tracking and update of the deep appearance model under unsupervised settings.

## 4   Overall Tracking System

In this section we describe the implementation of the method for joint tracking and appearance update, including the details on how to update the deep appearance model, and on how to initialise new tracks. Additionally, we provide training details and a software architecture for a generic robotic platform.

### 4.1   Deep Appearance Model Update

We instantiate our appearance model with a generic convolutional neural network (CNN) backbone, consisting of several convolutional layers (see details below). This backbone is trained by means of mini-batch stochastic gradient descent techniques. To construct batches, we randomly sample a track, one positive pair (from $\mathcal{H}^+$) and two negative pairs (from $\mathcal{H}^-$) from this track. This is done so as to respect the positive-negative balance [3,11]. This strategy is repeated $B$ times, obtaining a batch annotated with $\gamma_{ij}$.

The appearance model network, $\phi_w$ is pretrained to perform an ID classification similarly to [24]. Thus, the appearance model update can now be seen as a domain adaptation problem, where we need to learn the appearance shift (different people, background and illumination changes) between the pre-training dataset and the tracking data. To achieve this adaptation, only the top layers of $\phi_w$ are updated during tracking. The amount of layers to be trained depends on the computation power of the system, allowing the best trade-off between generalization ability and computation complexity. In our case, we perform an update of the last 2 layers.

## 4.2   Birth and Visibility Processes

New tracks (e.g. people coming in the field of view) are initialized using a birth process that assesses the consistency of the observations previously assigned to none of the visual tracks. We compare two hypothesis: (i) the previous $L$ geometric observations $\mathbf{y}_{tk_0}, \ldots, \mathbf{y}_{t-Lk_L}$ assigned to clutter correspond to an undetected track, and (ii) the very same observations belong to clutter and are uniformly distributed. If the first hypothesis wins, a new track is initialized using the last detected bounding box, and its appearance model is initialized with the content of the bounding boxes using (7) and (8).

We used an additional hidden Markov model visibility process to determine whether or not a track has been lost. The observation of this binary visibility process arise from the output of the variational EM algorithm, in particular we set: $\nu_{tn} = \sum_k \alpha_{tkn}$, representing whether a given track $n$ is assigned to a current detection or not. The estimation of the latent variable probability $p(V_{tn}|\nu_{1:t})$ is done using standard hidden Markov model (HMM) inference algorithms, and informs us about the visibility state of the considered track. The system does not output non-visible tracks, and their associated variables and parameters are not updated until they are visible again.

## 4.3   Implementation and Training Details

The overall tracking algorithm is presented in Algorithm 1. While tracking, the algorithm uses the various updates derived from the variational EM algorithm (see Sect. 3.2). Every $T$ frames, the system updates the appearance model with the equation updates of Sect. 3.3 and the sampling strategies and implementation details of Sect. 4.1. The birth and visibility processes of Sect. 4.2 are then used to set up new tracks and freeze non-visible tracks.

The appearance model is updated every $T = 5$ frames using a training set created by sampling 50 images per identity, and then sampling image pairs as described in Sect. 4.1. We update the appearance models using stochastic gradient descent with RMSProp [16] with a learning rate of 0.001 and a weight decay with a factor $10^{-4}$, for two epochs. The appearance model CNN is instantiated by a ResNet [19] architecture, where the last layer was replaced by a two layer perceptron with 500 and 100 units activated with ReLu. This CNN is pre-trained for the person re-identification task on the Market-1501 [35] and DukeMTMC [36] datasets, following [37].

Optical flow (OF) is extracted [13] and used to estimate the ego-motion vector $\mathbf{E}_t$, by averaging the OF over the entire image. In addition, the average optical flow within one detection bounding box, provides an estimate of the velocity of the track (after the ego-motion vector is subtracted). In order to get stable results we regularise $s_n^2$ with a prior around $\tau - 1$, since the cost (6) is supposed to induce spherical clusters of radius $\sqrt{\tau - 1}$.

In addition to the offline quantitative experiments, we also run online quantitative experiments (no ground truth is available) on a robotic platform. To do so, the proposed algorithm is implemented on a robotic platform using

**while** *tracking* **do**

    $t \leftarrow t + 1$;

    Compute the ego-motion vector $\mathbf{E}_t$, see Section 4.3;

    Update $\{\alpha_{tkn}\}_{k \in [1, K_t], n \in [1, N]}$ with (2);

    Update $\{\boldsymbol{\mu}_{tn}, \boldsymbol{\Gamma}_{tn}\}_{n \in [1, N]}$ as in Section 3;

    Update $\{\boldsymbol{m}_n, s_n\}_{n \in [1, N]}$ with (7) and (8;

    **if** $t_u = T$ **then**

        $t_u \leftarrow 0$ // Reset frame counter;

        **while** $\phi_w$ *not converged* **do**

            $\gamma_{ij} \leftarrow$ compute with (5);

            $\mathcal{H}^+, \mathcal{H}^- \leftarrow$ sample pair sets, see Section 4.1;

            Optimise (6) with RMSProp [16];

        **end**

    **end**

    $t_u \leftarrow t_u + 1$;

    Birth/visibility update, see Section 4.2;

    Output $\{\boldsymbol{\mu}_{tn}\}_{n \in [1, N]}$;

**end**

**Algorithm 1:** Overall tracking algorithm. Updates are performed with the various equations and strategies already described. The frame update counter $t_u$ allows to update the $\phi_w$ every $T$ frames. The algorithm outputs the position of all tracks at every frame $t$.

the robotic operating system (ROS) middleware. ROS does not only allow a platform-independent implementation, but also provides a unified framework to distribute the computation when and where needed. We use this property to exploit the computational power of an external GPU, devoted to execute the face detector [1] and to extract CNN appearance features. The face detector replace here the person detectors used in standard tracking datasets that will be used in our offline quantitative experiments. This demonstrates the ability of our tracking and appearance update method to utilise different kind of detectors. All other computations, including the update of the Siamese network, are ran on the CPU of the robot. We use a Intel(R) Xeon(R) CPU E5-2609 and a NVIDIA GeForce GTX 1070, and exploit the native camera of the robot. The system runs under Ubuntu 16.04 and ROS Kinetic version. Thanks to these implementation choices, our online tracker runs at 10 FPS. A schematic representation of the overall tracking system is shown in Fig. 1.

ROS makes use of a distributed network of Nodes (ROS processes), which use topics to communicate. Typically, the drivers nodes control the low level communication with robot's sensors and produce Topics containing images and motor positions. Camera's topics are processed by the face detection and feature extraction Nodes to produce detections and deep appearance descriptors transmitted to the tracker Node. The tracker Node takes advantage of the motor information and detections to update the appearance model and produce track information that is transmitted to the behavioral control, which uses it to update the motors' position, depending on the predefined policy.

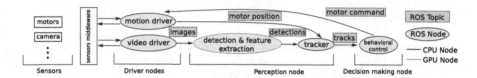

**Fig. 1.** The robotic software architecture is composed of several nodes: an image is produced by the video driver, fed to the face detector which produces both face detections and appearance features, then transmitted to the tracker node (alongside motor position information). The tracking results are exploited by the robot control to move the robot's head exploiting the motors drivers.

## 5    Experiments

We evaluate our joint tracking and appearance model update robotic architecture in three different settings. First, we provide quantitative evaluation under the "active surveillance camera" scenario. Second, we provide quantitative evaluation under the "robot navigation in crowded scenes" scenario. Finally, we provide qualitative evaluation under the "social conversation" scenario. Our aim is to evaluate whether or not the proposed deep appearance model online update provides more consistent tracks than the state-of-the-art.

### 5.1    Quantitative Evaluation

*Dataset* For the sake of reproducibility and in order to be able to compare different tracking systems in the exact same conditions, we use the well-known MOT17 dataset [25]. This dataset is composed of a dozen of videos taken in various conditions, and provides detections obtained with various detectors (DPM [14], FR-CNN [26] and SDP [34]) as well as ground truth for evaluation. The standard protocol is to report the results averaged over the three detectors.

Importantly, two kinds of videos are available: recorded with a surveillance camera, and with a camera mounted on an autonomous robot navigating in crowded scenes. Both scenarios are of interest for us. Indeed, the first scenario allows us to simulate the motion of a surveillance camera, and to gauge the robustness of the proposed tracking system against ego-motion noise. The second scenario provides the opposite case in which the ego-motion is completely unknown and must be inferred from visual information.

The first scenario (*moving surveillance camera*) consists on emulating that the surveillance camera only sees half of the image width, and then moving the emulated field of view accordintly to a pre-defined trajectory. The ego-motion vector $\mathbf{E}_t$ is then contaminated with Gaussian noise with a standard deviation of $\eta$ pixels in a uniformly sampled direction. The second scenario (*robot navigating in the crowd*) consists on using the full field of view of the camera, and estimate the ego-motion vector $\mathbf{E}_t$ with an optical-flow-based strategy.

*Evaluation Protocol.* We compare our *online deep appearance update* (ODA-UP) based method with the state-of-the-art in multi-person tracking for social robotics [5]. While the tracking model is very similar, the appearance model previously used in the literature exploits *color histograms* (CH). Additionally, and in order to provide a full evaluation of the necessity of the on-line appearance model update, we compare the proposed tracker with the exact same architecture without updating the weights of the deep appearance model, and refer to it as ODA-FR, for frozen. In that case, the appearance likelihood is provided by computing the cosine similarity between appearance templates and current detections. For the *moving surveillance camera* scenario, we evaluate under different values of $\eta \in \{0, 0.8, 1.6, 3.2\}$. We report standard multiple object tracking metrics in three groups. The quality of the detections is evaluated with the recall (Rcll) and the precision (Prcn). The quality of the tracks is evaluated with the multiple object tracking accuracy (MOTA) and precision (MOTP), see [8]. The consistency of the track identities is evaluated with the identity recall (IDR), precision (IDP) and F1 measure (IDF1), see [27].

**Table 1.** Results on the *moving surveillance camera* setting.

| $\eta$ | Model | Detection | | Tracking | | Identities | | |
|--------|-------|------|------|------|------|------|------|------|
| | | Rcll | Prcn | MOTA | MOTP | IDP | IDR | IDF1 |
| 0 | CH [5] | 49.4 | 88.2 | 42.5 | 84.5 | 70.3 | 39.4 | 50.5 |
| | ODA-FR | 49.5 | **88.7** | 43.0 | **84.8** | 66.7 | 37.2 | 47.8 |
| | ODA-UP | **54.7** | 86.7 | **45.6** | 84.0 | **75.4** | **45.7** | **56.0** |
| 0.8 | CH [5] | 49.6 | 88.0 | 42.5 | 84.4 | 69.9 | 39.4 | 50.4 |
| | ODA-FR | 49.7 | **88.7** | 43.1 | **84.7** | 67.1 | 37.6 | 48.2 |
| | ODA-UP | **54.4** | 86.3 | **45.0** | 83.8 | **71.2** | **44.9** | **55.1** |
| 1.6 | CH [5] | 49.1 | 88.2 | 42.2 | 84.2 | 70.3 | 39.1 | 50.2 |
| | ODA-FR | 49.5 | **88.6** | 42.8 | **84.5** | 66.3 | 37 | 47.5 |
| | ODA-UP | **54.5** | 86.4 | **45.3** | 83.7 | **73.3** | **46.2** | **56.7** |
| 3.2 | CH [5] | 49.2 | 88.2 | 42.3 | 83.2 | 68.1 | 38.0 | 48.8 |
| | ODA-FR | 49.1 | **88.4** | 42.4 | **83.3** | 66.8 | 37.1 | 47.7 |
| | ODA-UP | **54.2** | 86.1 | **44.8** | 82.8 | **71.5** | **45.0** | **55.2** |

*Discussion.* Table 1 and 2 report the results in the two scenarii. Regarding the *moving surveillance camera* setting in Table 1, we first observe that our approach significantly outperforms both the frozen (FR) and the color histogram (CH) models, by more than +3% and +2% respectively in MOTA. Unsurprisingly, the pretrained appearance model outperforms color histogram based model by roughly +0.5% in MOTA. While different levels of ego-motion noise lead to different scores, the ranking between the methods stays the same. The difference in MOTP is quite small, meaning that the quality of the output bounding boxes (only the tracked ones) is roughly the same. The slight decrease for ODA-UP is due to the fact that ODA-UP is able to track people that are harder to track, and for which estimating good bounding boxes is more challenging. This is supported by the relative position of the methods in the other metrics. Indeed, the recall and precision metrics are another proof that ODA-UP is able to track significantly more people. Regarding the identify measures, we can see that ODA-UP exhibits by far the highest performance, putting forward the advantage of the adaptive strategy. Indeed, the ODA-UP model outperforms the other two. Interestingly, ODA-FR is outperformed (in identity measures) by the color histograms, demonstrating that complex deep models are useful only if trained with relevant data or, as we propose in this paper, if they are adapted online.

A similar situation is found in Table 2 for *robot navigating in the crowd* setting: our approach outperforms the histogram model and the pretrained model by respectively +5.0% and +4.4% in MOTA. The rest of the metrics follow the same ranking as in the previous setting. Very importantly, the findings in Table 1 are further confirmed by larger advantage margins in Table 2. In both experiments, we observe how that update of the deep appearance model brings two main advantages. First, the recall increases because the number of false negative (or missed detections) decreases. Second, and more important, the consistency of the tracks' ID exhibits a significant increase when updating the model online.

**Table 2.** Results on the *robot navigating in the crowd* settings.

| Model | Detection | | Tracking | | Identities | | |
|---|---|---|---|---|---|---|---|
| | Rcll | Prcn | MOTA | MOTP | IDP | IDR | IDF1 |
| CH [5] | 45.8 | 91.8 | 41.2 | 80.7 | 74.1 | 37.0 | 49.3 |
| ODA-FR | 45.8 | **93.1** | 42.0 | 81.0 | 73.8 | 36.3 | 48.6 |
| ODA-UP | **52.3** | 90.5 | **46.2** | **81.5** | **79.0** | **45.7** | **57.9** |

## 5.2 Qualitative Results

We qualitatively evaluate the performance of the tracker on a real robotic platform, as described in Sect. 4.3, and provide them as videos alongside the paper. More results are available at https://team.inria.fr/perception/research/oda_track/. In that case, the procedure in [4] is used to compute the ego-motion vector from the motors velocity. Only faces' bounding boxes are extracted from the images using [1]. Example of the tracking results are displayed in Fig. 2, using CH and ODA-UP. We note that since our deep metric formulation has a higher discriminative power than color histogram based appearance model, it is able to better distinguish ID 2 and ID 4, even if they are close and that both detections could be generated by a unique ID. Also, we note that the ID labels of the tracks differ significantly when comparing both methods, which is caused by the high number of identity switches in the CH setting.

(a) Tracking result using CH [4]

(b) Tracking result using ODA-UP

**Fig. 2.** Tracking qualitative results using CH and ODA-UP. Detections are displayed on the left panel (blue), and tracking results are available on the right panel (green) in 2 settings. (Color figure online)

# 6    Conclusion

In this paper, we addressed the problem of online multiple object tracking using a joint probabilistic and deep appearance model, that allow the update of the appearance embedding simultaneously to tracking multiple people, while accounting for the robot ego-motion. We demonstrate its performance quantitatively in two settings, and qualitatively onboard of a consumer robot. The proposed model exhibits superior tracking performance ot the state of the art Very importantly, the identify consitency of the tracks over time is significantly better thanks to the proposed online update strategy. We hope that the proposed system will open the door to the affective analysis of multi-person scenarios, and will foster more research efforts on leveraging online information to conceive better appearance models.

**Acknowledgement.** The authors ackowledge funding from the H2020 ICT SPRING project under GA #871245, from the ML3RI project funded by the Young Researcher programme of the ANR under GA ANR-19-CE33-0008-01, and from the Multidisciplinary Institute of Artificial Intelligence funded by the ANR under GA ANR-19-P3IA-0003.

# References

1. High quality face recognition with deep metric learning. http://blog.dlib.net/2017/02/high-quality-face-recognition-with-deep.html
2. Ba, S., Alameda-Pineda, X., Xompero, A., Horaud, R.: An on-line variational bayesian model for multi-person tracking from cluttered scenes. Comput. Vis. Image Underst. **153**, 64–76 (2016)
3. Bae, S., Yoon, K.: Confidence-based data association and discriminative deep appearance learning for robust online multi-object tracking. IEEE Trans. Pattern Anal. Mach. Intell. **40**, 595–610 (2018)
4. Ban, Y., Alameda-Pineda, X., Badeig, F., Ba, S., Horaud, R.: Tracking a varying number of people with a visually-controlled robotic head. In: 2017 IEEE/RSJ International Conference on Intelligent Robots and Systems (IROS), pp. 4144–4151. IEEE (2017)
5. Ban, Y., Alameda-Pineda, X., Girin, L., Horaud, R.: Variational Bayesian inference for audio-visual tracking of multiple speakers. IEEE Trans. Pattern Anal. Mach. Intell. (2019)
6. Ban, Y., Ba, S., Alameda-Pineda, X., Horaud, R.: Tracking Multiple Persons Based on a Variational Bayesian Model. In: Computer Vision - ECCV 2016 Workshops
7. Bergmann, P., Meinhardt, T., Leal-Taixe, L.: Tracking without bells and whistles. In: IEEE International Conference on Computer Vision, pp. 941–951 (2019)
8. Bernardin, K., Stiefelhagen, R.: Evaluating multiple object tracking performance: the CLEAR MOT metrics. EURASIP J. Image Video Process. **2008**(1), 1–10 (2008). https://doi.org/10.1155/2008/246309
9. Bertinetto, L., Valmadre, J., Henriques, J.F., Vedaldi, A., Torr, P.H.S.: Fully-convolutional Siamese networks for object tracking. In: Hua, G., Jégou, H. (eds.) ECCV 2016. LNCS, vol. 9914, pp. 850–865. Springer, Cham (2016). https://doi.org/10.1007/978-3-319-48881-3_56
10. Breitenstein, M.D., Reichlin, F., Leibe, B., Koller-Meier, E., Gool, L.V.: Robust tracking-by-detection using a detector confidence particle filter. In: 2009 IEEE ICCV, September 2009
11. Chu, Q., Ouyang, W., Li, H., Wang, X., Liu, B., Yu, N.: Online multi-object tracking using CNN-based single object tracker with spatial-temporal attention mechanism. In: IEEE International Conference on Computer Vision, ICCV, October 2017
12. Delorme, G., Xu, Y., Lathuilière, S., Horaud, R., Alameda-Pineda, X.: CANU-REID: a conditional adversarial network for unsupervised person re-identification. In: International Conference on Pattern Recognition (2020)
13. Farnebäck, G.: Two-frame motion estimation based on polynomial expansion. In: Bigun, J., Gustavsson, T. (eds.) SCIA 2003. LNCS, vol. 2749, pp. 363–370. Springer, Heidelberg (2003). https://doi.org/10.1007/3-540-45103-X_50
14. Felzenszwalb, P.F., Girshick, R.B., McAllester, D., Ramanan, D.: Object detection with discriminatively trained part-based models. IEEE TPAMI **32**(9), 1627–1645 (2010)
15. Feng, W., Hu, Z., Wu, W., Yan, J., Ouyang, W.: Multi-object tracking with multiple cues and switcher-aware classification. arXiv (2019)
16. Hinton, G., Srivastava, N., Swersky, K.: Lecture 6a: overview of mini-batch gradient descent. http://www.cs.toronto.edu/tijmen/csc321/slides/lecture_slides_lec6.pdf
17. Gupta, A., Agrawal, D., Chauhan, H., Dolz, J., Pedersoli, M.: An attention model for group-level emotion recognition. In: Proceedings of the 20th ACM International Conference on Multimodal Interaction, pp. 611–615 (2018)

18. Hadsell, R., Chopra, S., LeCun, Y.: Dimensionality reduction by learning an invariant mapping. In: Null, pp. 1735–1742. IEEE (2006)
19. He, K., Zhang, X., Ren, S., Sun, J.: Deep residual learning for image recognition. CoRR abs/1512.03385 (2015)
20. Hu, J., Lu, J., Tan, Y.P.: Discriminative deep metric learning for face verification in the wild. In: IEEE Conference on Computer Vision and Pattern Recognition (2014)
21. Hu, J., Lu, J., Tan, Y.P.: Deep metric learning for visual tracking. IEEE Trans. Circuits Syst. Video Technol. **26**(11), 2056–2068 (2016)
22. Kalayeh, M.M., Basaran, E., Gökmen, M., Kamasak, M.E., Shah, M.: Human semantic parsing for person re-identification. In: Proceedings of the IEEE Conference on Computer Vision and Pattern Recognition, pp. 1062–1071 (2018)
23. Leal-Taixe, L., Canton-Ferrer, C., Schindler, K.: Learning by tracking: Siamese CNN for robust target association. In: The IEEE Conference on Computer Vision and Pattern Recognition (CVPR) Workshops, June 2016
24. Long, C., Haizhou, A., Zijie, Z., Chong, S.: Real-time multiple people tracking with deeply learned candidate selection and person re-identification. In: ICME (2018)
25. Milan, A., Leal-Taixé, L., Reid, I., Roth, S., Schindler, K.: MOT16: a benchmark for multi-object tracking. arXiv:1603.00831 (2016)
26. Ren, S., He, K., Girshick, R., Sun, J.: Faster r-cnn: Towards real-time object detection with region proposal networks. IEEE Trans. Pattern Anal. Mach. Intell. (2017)
27. Ristani, E., Solera, F., Zou, R., Cucchiara, R., Tomasi, C.: Performance measures and a data set for multi-target, multi-camera tracking. In: Hua, G., Jégou, H. (eds.) ECCV 2016. LNCS, vol. 9914, pp. 17–35. Springer, Cham (2016). https://doi.org/10.1007/978-3-319-48881-3_2
28. Sadeghian, A., Alahi, A., Savarese, S.: Tracking the untrackable: learning to track multiple cues with long-term dependencies. In: IEEE International Conference on Computer Vision, ICCV (2017)
29. Sun, B., Wei, Q., Li, L., Xu, Q., He, J., Yu, L.: LSTM for dynamic emotion and group emotion recognition in the wild. In: Proceedings of the 18th ACM International Conference on Multimodal Interaction, pp. 451–457 (2016)
30. Tan, L., Zhang, K., Wang, K., Zeng, X., Peng, X., Qiao, Y.: Group emotion recognition with individual facial emotion CNNs and global image based CNNs. In: Proceedings of the 19th ACM International Conference on Multimodal Interaction, pp. 549–552 (2017)
31. Wang, K., et al.: Cascade attention networks for group emotion recognition with face, body and image cues. In: Proceedings of the 20th ACM International Conference on Multimodal Interaction, pp. 640–645 (2018)
32. Wei, L., Zhang, S., Gao, W., Tian, Q.: Person transfer GAN to bridge domain gap for person re-identification. In: Proceedings of the IEEE Conference on Computer Vision and Pattern Recognition, pp. 79–88 (2018)
33. Wei, Q., Zhao, Y., Xu, Q., Li, L., He, J., Yu, L., Sun, B.: A new deep-learning framework for group emotion recognition. In: Proceedings of the 19th ACM International Conference on Multimodal Interaction. pp. 587–592 (2017)
34. Yang, F., Choi, W., Lin, Y.: Exploit all the layers: Fast and accurate CNN object detector with scale dependent pooling and cascaded rejection classifiers. In: CVPR (2016)
35. Zheng, L., Shen, L., Tian, L., Wang, S., Wang, J., Tian, Q.: Scalable person re-identification: a benchmark. In: IEEE ICCV (2015)

36. Zheng, Z., Zheng, L., Yang, Y.: Unlabeled samples generated by GAN improve the person re-identification baseline in vitro. In: IEEE ICCV (2017)
37. Zhong, Z., Zheng, L., Zheng, Z., Li, S., Yang, Y.: Camera style adaptation for person re-identification. In: IEEE CVPR (2018)

# Author Index

Printed in the United States
By Bookmasters